ARNHEM

ARNHEM

THE COMPLETE STORY OF OPERATION MARKET GARDEN

17–25 SEPTEMBER 1944

WILLIAM F. BUCKINGHAM

AMBERLEY

As ever, for those who were there and especially those who did not come back

First published 2019

Amberley Publishing
The Hill, Stroud
Gloucestershire, GL5 4EP

www.amberley-books.com

British Library Cataloguing in Publication Data.
A catalogue record for this book is available from the British Library.

ISBN 978 1 8486 8109 5 (print)
ISBN 978 1 4456 3716 7 (ebook)

Origination by Amberley Publishing.
Printed in the UK.

Contents

Foreword

On Sunday 17 September 1944, two thousand and twenty-three transport aircraft and four hundred and seventy-eight gliders lifted off from airfields across southern and eastern England carrying troops from the US 82nd and 101st Airborne Divisions and the British 1st Airborne Division. They were the first lift of the largest Airborne operation in history, Operation MARKET, which was intended to open a sixty-mile corridor across five major water obstacles for Allied ground forces, codenamed GARDEN, running from the Belgian border to the Dutch city of Arnhem on the Lower Rhine. The equivalent of a Battalion managed to secure the north end of the road bridge in Arnhem, where they were cut off and overrun after fighting for three days and four nights against overwhelming odds; the remainder of the 1st Airborne Division was all but destroyed in futile attempts to reach them and then holding on for nine days at Oosterbeek. The GARDEN ground force took six days rather than the scheduled forty-eight hours to reach the south bank of the Lower Rhine west of Arnhem and after a token attempt at reinforcement assisted in evacuating approximately 2,500 of the 1st Airborne Division's survivors across the river on the night of 25-26 September 1944. They left behind well over a thousand Airborne dead and over six thousand wounded and Prisoners of War in addition to the similar numbers of dead and wounded sustained by the 82nd and 101st Airborne Divisions in forcing the Airborne Corridor and keeping it open.

The deserved elevation of the Battle of Arnhem to legendary status began virtually as soon as 1st Airborne Division's survivors had been evacuated across the Lower Rhine. Within two years the feature film **Theirs is the Glory** had been shot in the ruins of Oosterbeek starring men who had participated in the battle, and in the seventy-two years since then another Hollywood feature film, dozens of books and several television documentaries dealing with the battle have appeared; viewing **A Bridge Too Far** during a family holiday on the Isle of Wight in the year it was released was the present author's introduction to the Battle of Arnhem. As one would expect with this degree of coverage, the course of events that led up to MARKET GARDEN and during the fighting at Arnhem and Oosterbeek have been largely established, and most of the factors that contributed to the failure of MARKET GARDEN have been at least identified, along with a few canards and red herrings; the latter include the enduring myth that the 1st Airborne Division descended upon two fully equipped and functioning *SS Panzer Divisions*, for example. The present author was still working on his PhD on the establishment and initial development of British Airborne Forces when invited to write his first book on Arnhem in 2000, but research soon revealed clear similarities between the two, insofar as popular perceptions were somewhat at variance with the verifiable reality. Thus while the spectacular bare bones of what happened in Holland in September 1944 had been fairly clearly established, a great deal more was missing or had gone unremarked. As with any undertaking on the scale of MARKET GARDEN there were a myriad of factors that contributed to failure but while most have been acknowledged, in some instances they have been slanted subtly for camouflage and in others simply hidden in plain sight. It is popularly assumed the 1st Airborne Division failed to reach its objectives because of enemy action for example, whereas the root of the problem was actually poor leadership and planning at the Division and Brigade level; similarly the tardiness of 30 Corps' advance, and specifically that of the Guards Armoured Division, is routinely excused on the grounds of enemy resistance and poor terrain, but were actually proven to be due to lack of application, rigid and inappropriate operating procedures and contradictory operational instructions from Corps level. All this was apparent from a relatively superficial analysis of official accounts and secondary sources, but subsequent in-depth research in primary source material and especially the operational records across the last nine years not only conclusively proved this was the case, but also revealed that the litany of poor planning, leadership and decision making was actually much worse than suspected.

This work therefore builds upon the foundation of the present author's 2001 work on the Battle of Arnhem by providing a more in-depth account of not just the nine days of the battle but of the events and strategic developments that led to Operation MARKET GARDEN, and the planning and other decisions that resulted in it being executed in the way it was. In addition, the extensive use of primary source material, specifically unit War Diaries, permits the construction of a much more detailed narrative from Platoon to Corps level than has been provided hitherto, leavened with participant accounts for additional detail. This in turn permits focussed analysis that explains why events unfolded as they did, and in the process reveals who and what was responsible for key decisions and the ramifications thereof and not just to allow the superficial assigning of responsibility; this also reveals a host of extraordinary men at all levels doing extraordinary things as if they were merely routine, many of them at the cost of their lives. In addition, the narrative is augmented with material from the German side for clarity and balance along with detailed examination of the activities of the two US Airborne Divisions up to the point where they put the GARDEN force across the River Waal at Nijmegen. Although the US contribution was absolutely vital in both the front-line fighting and the transport spheres, it does not always receive the acclaim it merits from the British perspective; while the 1st Airborne Division was tasked to secure two permanent crossings over a single watercourse, its US equivalents were tasked to secure twelve crossings over seven watercourses and succeeded in securing and holding the majority of them, for example. In short, the aim is to show what happened, when it happened and why it happened as it did.

In closing I should like to thank Mr Henk Capelle from Oosterbeek for providing me with a copy of his wartime memoir, other local material and correcting some of my misunderstandings; Richard Anderson of the TankNet Internet Military Forum for providing the US Army Advanced Officer Course monographs; George F. Cholewczynski for kindly providing me with a copy of his work and permission to quote therefrom; Stephen King for the always stimulating discussion on the Arnhem landing zones and providing me with numerous items of material; Mr William J. Stone, formerly of the 321st Glider Field Artillery Battalion 101st Airborne Division, for providing me with a copy of his unpublished memoir; William McVean for keeping me informed of matters connected to the 23rd Field Company RCE and Russell Kennedy for kindly providing me with a copy of his work on that unit; Jonathan Reeve and his successors at Amberley for their forbearance with my somewhat elastic approach to deadlines; and last but not least my wife Aileen once again for her patience, forbearance in putting up with it all and her toleration of research diversions whilst supposedly on holiday. Finally, all opinions, conclusions, errors, misconceptions and mistakes are entirely my own.

William F. Buckingham
Hamilton, South Lanarkshire

Introduction

The patrol left friendly lines near the Dutch village of Zetten before midnight on the night of Sunday 22 October 1944. Shiny surfaces had been dulled, anything that might rattle or make noise had been taped down or discarded, and the men were carrying only weapons and ammunition. The patrol was drawn from Company E, 2nd Battalion 506th Parachute Infantry Regiment and was led by the Company commander, 1st Lieutenant Frederick Heyliger. Other members included 2nd Lieutenants Harry Welsh and Edward Shames, Corporals Walter Gordon and Francis Mellett, and Private Ralph Stafford.[1] The file of men moved stealthily through the murky, drizzle-filled darkness following a strip of white engineer tape leading to the south bank of the Lower Rhine, where a number of British wood and canvas assault boats had been cached among a stand of trees the previous night. There they settled down to wait for the signal to cross to the German-held side of the river. Company E had parachuted onto Drop Zone C north-west of Son with the rest of the 2nd Battalion in the afternoon of Sunday 17 September 1944. The drop was part of Operation MARKET GARDEN, which was intended to sidestep the fixed defences along the German border and open the way into northern Germany. MARKET involved securing a series of water crossings along a line of advance that projected sixty miles into enemy-held territory. The 101st Airborne Division was to secure the city of Eindhoven and bridges over the Wilhelmina and Zuid Willems Canal and rivers Aa and Dommel to the north of the city; the 82nd Airborne Division was tasked to seize crossings over the rivers Maas and Waal and canal linking the two in and near Nijmegen; and most northerly of all the British 1st Airborne Division was to secure a series of bridges across the Lower Rhine in the vicinity of Arnhem. GARDEN referred to the ground aspect of the plan, which was for the British 30 Corps to advance north from an existing bridgehead over the Meuse-Escaut Canal at Neerpelt and relieve each airborne formation in turn within forty-eight hours.

In the event, matters did not unfold as planned. The ground advance was delayed by a destroyed bridge at Son, and dogged German resistance at Nijmegen held the ground advance up until an assault river crossing could be arranged. Things went most awry at Arnhem. Only a relatively small party succeeded in securing the northern end of one bridge, where they held on for over three days until overwhelmed. After battling unsuccessfully to reach the bridge, the remainder of the 1st Airborne Division formed a defensive perimeter in the nearby town of Oosterbeek, which it defended doggedly until the survivors were finally evacuated to the Allied-held south bank of the Lower Rhine on the night of 25-26 September. Easy Company spent that period battling numerous German attempts to cut the airborne corridor near Eindhoven, before moving up to take over its positions on the south bank of the Lower Rhine from the British 43rd Division on 2 October 1944.

Lieutenant Heyliger's patrol was prompted by the arrival of Lieutenant-Colonel David Dobie on the Allied-held bank of the Lower Rhine a week or so previously.[2] Dobie had commanded the British 1st Parachute Battalion during MARKET and was wounded and captured when his Battalion fought itself to destruction in the western suburbs of Arnhem in an abortive attempt to reach the British force holding the north end of the Arnhem road bridge on Tuesday 19 September.[3] After escaping from the Dutch hospital where he was to undergo treatment for grenade shrapnel wounds in his head, eye and arm later in the day, he made contact with the Dutch Resistance which eventually ended up sheltering several hundred British and other personnel, including several senior Airborne officers; Dobie was therefore despatched across the river to organise arrangements for their evacuation to friendly territory. The chosen concentration site for the evaders was the village of Renkum, adjacent to the drop and landing zones employed by the British 1st Airborne Division on 17 September. As the village was opposite the section of the Lower Rhine covered by the 506th Parachute Infantry Regiment, its commander, Lieutenant-Colonel Robert F. Sink, was asked to assist with what became codenamed Operation PEGASUS, to be carried out on the night of 23-24 October 1944; he duly delegated the task to Lieutenant Heyliger and Company E.

The American paratroopers obtained canvas assault boats from British 30 Corps, which were stealthily cached in readiness near the crossing point. An artillery box barrage was registered to seal off the relevant sector of the German-held bank, machine-guns and mortars were sighted on likely German positions on the north bank and a US anti-aircraft unit was tasked to provide a visual navigation marker for the rescue party by firing red tracer from its Bofors guns along a fixed line; in an effort to allay German suspicion the Bofors fired on the same line for several nights preceding Operation PEGASUS.[4] Lieutenant-Colonel Dobie co-ordinated arrangements with the Dutch Resistance via the local civilian telephone system which was still functioning and, surprisingly, free from German monitoring. The operation was brought forward twenty-four hours when the Resistance used the increased road traffic generated by the forced evacuation of Bennekom, a village near Renkum, as cover to concentrate the evaders. By the afternoon of Sunday 22 October between 138 and 150 men were gathered in woods north-west of Bennekom, where they changed back into uniform and were issued weapons. At least 120 were personnel from the 1st Airborne Division, including Brigadier Gerald Lathbury, Major Digby Tatham-Warter and Major Anthony Deane-Drummond, commanders of the 1st Parachute Brigade, A Company 2nd Parachute Battalion and second in command of 1st Airborne Divisional Signals respectively. The remainder included ten Dutch volunteers for Allied service, several aircrew including four USAAF personnel, two escaped Soviet prisoners of war and a solitary soldier from the US 82nd Airborne Division.[5]

The evaders moved off from their hiding place for the bank of the Lower Rhine at approximately 23:00 on 22 October. Despite the circumstances, their passage was by no means silent; Major Tatham-Warter likened it to a herd of elephants thundering through the woods.[6] Despite this they managed to reach the riverbank undetected and flashed a red V for Victory signal. It is unclear if this was the signal for the Bofors to begin firing the red tracer, or whether the latter was already firing on a pre-arranged schedule. Whichever, one or the other was the signal for Heyliger's party to carry the assault boats the last few yards to the river and begin paddling across to the north bank. On arrival 2nd Lieutenant Welsh secured the boats for the return journey, Corporals Gordon and Mellett set up .30 Browning machine-guns up to cover either flank and Private Stafford took point on the advance to the rendezvous point, backed by Heyliger. Contact was made despite a startling encounter with a roosting bird and Heyliger was soon shaking hands with and receiving thanks from Brigadier Lathbury. The trip back to the boats was made similarly unscathed, although not apparently without more needless noise; according to one account the Easy Company men and Lieutenant Welsh in particular became increasingly exasperated by loudly expressed good wishes from their Allies as the latter climbed aboard the boats.[7]

The precise time the patrol began is unclear, with different sources citing midnight or 01:00 but both rescuers and rescued appear to have been safely back at Zetten drinking coffee by 02:00, before the latter were evacuated back to Nijmegen.[8] There were no casualties and the only German reaction was a sprinkling of artillery fire on US positions, some of which fell close to Lieutenant-Colonel Sink's command post.[9] A second large-scale operation on the night of 18-19 November 1944, codenamed Operation PEGASUS II, did not fare so well. One party making for the rendezvous ran into a German patrol, and Major John Coke from the 7th Battalion King's Own Scots Borderers was killed in the ensuing firefight along with an unnamed Airborne soldier and a Dutch guide; the Germans were apparently on alert due to unsanctioned press publicity for the first Operation PEGASUS. Be that as it may, all the parties were obliged to scatter and only seven men made it across the river to safety. Thereafter such evacuations were carried out on a small group or individual basis, with preference given to doctors, glider pilots, soldiers and airmen in that order.[10] Operation PEGASUS thus arguably marked the end of Operation MARKET GARDEN, which had in turn been the largest and most sophisticated Airborne operation ever attempted. Before moving on to analyse the planning and execution of MARKET GARDEN, it may therefore be illuminating to examine the development of airborne warfare, beginning with the evolution of the technical means.

The Means and a Template for Imitation:

Early Developments and German Airborne Operations in Scandinavia and the Low Countries to 1940

Deploying troops from the air is currently a routine and commonplace military technique and has been so for the better part of a century, but the notion preceded the means by a considerable period. The idea of a man-carrying parachute dates back to at least the 1480s, when the Florentine artist and inventor Leonardo da Vinci sketched a design consisting of four equilateral triangles formed into a pyramid-shaped canopy supported by a wooden frame. Da Vinci does not appear to have carried out any full-scale tests of his design, but its basic soundness has been proven in more recent trials. On 18 June 2001 British skydiver Adrian Nicholas used a precise, seven-metre-tall replica of da Vinci's design constructed using contemporary tools, materials and techniques to carry out a balloon jump at Mpumalanga in South Africa. The design worked perfectly in a descent from 10,000 feet, although Mr Nicholas cut himself free at 2,000 feet and completed the descent with a regular parachute; the separation was prompted by fears that the 187-pound bulk of the da Vinci replica would cause injury on landing.[1] The effectiveness of da Vinci's pyramidal canopy was reinforced eight years later when Swiss base-jumper Olivier Vietti Teppa successfully landed using a version that dispensed with the wooden frame and was manufactured with modern lightweight material. The modern version also performed perfectly in a 2,130-foot jump from a helicopter at Payerne military airfield near Geneva on 28 April 2008, with a lack of steering ability being the only reported drawback.[2]

Although he also drew up designs for armed chariots and a tank-like vehicle da Vinci does not appear to have considered the military possibilities of his parachute. It took a further three centuries for the idea of applying the basic concept to purely military ends to occur, and then using hot air balloons rather than parachutes. On 19 October 1783 three Frenchmen took to the air in Paris to become the first human passengers in a tethered hot air balloon, and a free flight with two passengers was carried out a month later on 21 November. On the latter occasion the balloon was launched from a royal hunting lodge in the Bois de Boulogne on the outskirts of Paris and attained a height of 500 feet, crossing the River Seine before landing safely within the city after covering around five miles. US Ambassador, scientist and Founding Father Benjamin Franklin was among the worthies in attendance and he was so impressed that he wrote a detailed and glowing description of the balloon for the President of the Royal Society in London, urged the inventors to develop a method of steering the craft once aloft, and also hypothesised on the military potential of what he had seen:

> Five thousand balloons, capable of raising two men each, could not cost more than five ships of the line…And where is the Prince who can afford so to cover his country with troops for its defence, as that ten thousand men descending from the clouds might not in many places do an infinite deal of mischief before a force could be brought together to repel them?[3]

Given the novelty of what he has witnessed, Franklin can be forgiven for failing to fully appreciate the practical drawbacks of his hypothesising. Given the total vulnerability of balloons to the vagaries of wind and weather, there was no guarantee that the troop-bearing balloons would arrive safely in the selected prince's territory. It was also highly likely that any that did so would be widely scattered and thus unlikely to be capable of generating more than negligible amounts of mischief at best. Nonetheless, Franklin was thinking along the right lines and he also inadvertently touched upon another factor, that of cost in both fiscal and manpower terms; writing just over two centuries after Franklin on the British airborne debacle at Arnhem, John Terraine criticised the '…sheer wastefulness of the airborne style of war', the waste of elite troops and drain on other resources.[4]

Those points are arguable, but while balloons were of limited utility from a military perspective they did provide the means to advance development of the parachute for over a hundred years. Two years after the Bois de Boulogne demonstration witnessed by Benjamin Franklin a French balloonist named Jeanne Pierre Blanchard used a dog to test a small parachute based on da Vinci's design. The animal landed safely but, apparently unimpressed by the experience, fled the landing site and was not seen again; according to some reports Blanchard went on to make a jump himself in 1793, which resulted in a broken leg after an excessively rapid descent. The first successful human descent appears to have been carried out by another Frenchman, André-Jacques Garnerin, on 22 October 1797. Garnerin attached his silk parachute, of the rigid type which used umbrella-like spokes to support the canopy, to a balloon for the ascent over the *Parc Monceau* in Paris, and landed safely after jettisoning the balloon at a height of 3,000 feet. He repeated his feat in London in September 1802, using a twenty-three-foot-diameter canopy made of canvas and this time descending from a reported 8,000 feet. The descent took over ten minutes and was marked by oscillations so severe that eyewitnesses claimed the passenger basket swung up level with the canopy on several occasions. Despite a heavy landing behind St. Pancras church, Garnerin was unscathed apart from cuts, bruises and nausea.

A subsequent effort by a British inventor named Robert Cocking was not so fortunate. Cocking was convinced that a canopy with the open side up would cure the oscillation problem and he therefore constructed a convex framework of hoops formed from tin tubing connected with timber stringers to support the canopy; the latter was constructed from panels of Irish linen and the whole apparatus weighed in at just under 400 pounds including the passenger basket and Cocking himself. It took two years to develop a balloon capable of lifting such a payload, and Cocking finally took to the air to demonstrate his invention to a large crowd amid much fanfare over Vauxhall Park in London just before sunset on 24 July 1837. Cocking cast off from the balloon at a height of approximately 4,000 feet and initially the parachute remained stable as advertised, but then a section of the tubular frame buckled, tearing the canopy and precipitating a total collapse that sent the unfortunate Cocking plummeting to his death. His spectacular public demise not only earned Cocking the dubious honour of being the first recorded parachute fatality, but also prompted a typically British knee-jerk reaction from Parliament, which passed legislation banning British subjects from parachuting. Foreigners, however, were still permitted to perform parachute jumps in Britain for entertainment purposes.[5] Parachute research and experimentation thus continued on the Continent and the United States where governments were less restrictive, and the latter hosted three successive developments that saw the parachute develop virtually into its current form. The first was the invention of the 'limp' parachute canopy that dispensed with the supporting framework used hitherto, by trapeze artist brothers Samuel and Thomas Baldwin. The brother's aim was to develop a parachute for demonstration and emergency use from balloons, which they realised by using a limp canopy to reduce bulk and save weight; this permitted the parachute to be stowed aboard the balloon in a container until required. After experiments with scale models and a full-size canopy weighted with sandbags over a period of years, Thomas Baldwin successfully tested the concept using an oversized canopy dubbed 'Eclipse' on 30 January 1887, jumping from a balloon tethered at

5,000 feet in front of a large crowd in Golden Gate Park in San Francisco. Such jumps became a popular feature of travelling carnivals thereafter, and there matters essentially remained for a quarter of century, until powered flight overtook balloons as a method of delivery.

The second development came from another carnival parachutist named Leo Stevens, who designed and fabricated a cone-shaped metal container for mounting a parachute on an aircraft for emergency use by the pilot. Stevens' device was successfully if somewhat precariously tested by Captain Albert Berry on 28 February 1912. Flying as a passenger in a Benoit pusher biplane piloted by Anthony Jannus, Berry had to climb down onto the axle of the machine's landing gear and unship the parachute container before making his jump from an altitude of 1,000 feet. He landed safely inside the perimeter of Jefferson Barracks, Missouri but not on the drill field as planned, alighting instead behind the mess hall. He was carried back to the field by a crowd of enthusiastic soldier onlookers, some of whom set off in pursuit of his abandoned parachute, and thus became the first man to carry out a parachute descent from a powered aircraft. The third development came from yet another American carnival parachutist named Charles Broadwick who had turned his hand to designing parachutes and balloons. Also seeking to perfect the parachute as an emergency item for pilots like Stevens, Broadwick turned his attention to securing the parachute to the body. Early pioneers like Garnerin and Cocking had attached their parachute canopies to baskets of the type used by balloonists, Thomas Baldwin had improvised a harness from knotted rope and Berry was apparently not attached to his parachute at all; according to one account he actually descended on a trapeze bar attached to the parachute rigging lines.

Broadwick addressed this with his 'parachute coat', which mounted the parachute canopy in a pouch stitched to the back of a sleeveless jerkin. The apex of the canopy was attached to the inside of the pouch flap with a break cord, and a length of rope with a hook was attached to the outside of the flap. The hook was to be attached to a strongpoint on the balloon or aircraft before the jump, and the weight of the parachutist's body would then pull the flap open and allow the canopy to deploy from the pouch without any input from the jumper. Broadwick had thus not only invented a practical means for the parachute to be worn on the body, but also the static-line method of canopy extraction and opening that remains the standard method for military parachuting to this day. The parachute coat was demonstrated to a delegation from the US Army Signal Corps at the US Army Flying School at San Diego in April 1914. As an additional bit of salesmanship the demonstration was carried out by Broadwick's twenty-two-year-old daughter Tiny, jumping from a Curtiss biplane piloted by one of the school's civilian instructors. Ms Broadwick was herself a seasoned carnival parachutist who had been jumping from the age of fifteen, and she made a perfect landing in front of the suitably impressed General Scriven, head of the Signal Corps delegation. Despite Scriven's presumably positive report the Broadwick parachute was not adopted by the fledgling US Army Air Service.[6]

Thus by the outbreak of the First World War the parachute was a practical proposition, although it did not fully resemble the modern item with a backpack mounted on a harness of webbing straps until American entrepreneur Leslie Irvin came up with the competition-winning model formally adopted by the US Army following a demonstration at McCook Field near Dayton, Ohio on 19 April 1919. The major omission in 1914 was therefore aircraft, for with the isolated exception of Igor Sikorski's giant four-engine *Ilya Muromets* that flew that summer, there were no machines of sufficient size or payload to carry parachutists.[7] The more standard service machines were too small and/or underpowered to carry parachutes for the emergency use envisioned by Stevens and Broadwick; some models tested by the British Air Board in January 1917 weighed up to 40 pounds for example.[8] As a result the carriage of parachutes did not become a viable option for the pilots of powered aircraft until the latter stage of the conflict when the machines had become more developed, and even then only the Germans appear to have used them operationally; the *Luftsreitkräfte* issued powered-aircraft crewmen with a static-line parachute designed by Otto Henecke from May 1918.[9] Henecke's parachute pack was stowed as the airman's seat cushion, with the rigging lines attached to a harness via two D-rings; in an emergency the parachute container was jettisoned prior to baling out and the weight of the airman's body pulled the canopy free.[10] Despite its rather cumbersome-sounding nature, the system appears to have worked well. Fighter ace Ernst Udet used the system twice in the last six months of the conflict, for example, and US fighter ace Eddie Rickenbacker recorded witnessing an opponent using a parachute to escape from his burning machine in his memoir.[11]

Parachutes were more widely employed as an emergency device by the crews of observation balloons which, with the onset of trench warfare, rapidly became a primary means for both sides to monitor enemy activity and provide data for their artillery. The highly flammable hydrogen gas with which they were filled made manning such craft a fairly risky business at best, and the hazard increased significantly when they became priority targets for enemy aircraft, which were frequently equipped with special incendiary ammunition. All sides thus began to issue parachutes to their balloon crewmen in 1915. The British Army adopted inventor and railway engineer Everard Calthrop's 'Guardian Angel' parachute and possibly another model produced by the balloon manufacturer C. G. Spencer & Sons, while their opponents used a model designed and produced by the German female parachute pioneer Käthe Paulus.[12] All appear to have been static-line operated and were stowed on the balloon rather than the crewman, who wore a harness that was attached to the parachute rigging lines before the ascent. The major difference appears to have been the location of the parachute pack on the balloon: the British stowed the container on the outside of the passenger basket, while the Germans preferred to locate it out of the way above the basket on the rigging. Like Broadwick's model, the Guardian Angel and Paulus parachutes had been originally designed for use by powered-aircraft pilots, but were rejected by their respective officialdoms. Parachutes were also employed during the conflict for more offensive tasks. In the man-carrying role they are reported to have been used to insert small sabotage and intelligence carrying parties behind enemy lines,[13] although it is unclear what aircraft were employed to carry them. The British used them to deliver individual agents and their equipment including carrier pigeons on the Western and Italian fronts.[14] Perhaps more pertinently for future developments, they were also employed by the British for dropping supplies to conventional ground forces.

In May 1915 an Anglo-Indian force built around the Indian Army's 6th Poona Division commanded by Major-General Charles Townshend began an advance up the River Tigris in Mesopotamia, with the intent of securing Baghdad. The town of Amara was captured on 3 June, followed by Kut-al-Amara and Aziziya on 28 September and 5 October 1915 respectively. Progress was slowed by unexpectedly severe climatic conditions, a concomitant shortage of medical personnel and supplies, and logistic difficulties; large numbers of native rivercraft, nicknamed 'Townshend's Regatta', were pressed into service in an effort to relieve the latter. The advance stalled at Aziziya for over a month due to high-level political wrangling, and was reversed after an inconclusive battle with Turkish forces at Ctesiphon, twenty-five miles short of Baghdad, between 22 and 25 November. Having suffered over 4,000 casualties, Townshend withdrew to Kut-al-Amara where his 8,500-strong force was invested from 7 December 1915. The resulting siege saw the first large-scale attempt to supply a ground force from the air. Beginning in March 1916, parachutes were used to deliver a 70-pound millstone and a host of other items including medical supplies, mail and newspapers, parts for the garrison's motor launch engine and wireless components. Some items were free-dropped. In mid-April Townshend requested a minimum daily supply of 5,000 pounds, made up of chocolate, flour, salt and ghee cooking oil. A total of 3,350 pounds was delivered on 15 April and over the next fourteen days leading up to Townshend's surrender to the Turks on 29 April 1916, 140 separate flights had delivered a total of 19,000 pounds of supplies, all but 2,200 pounds of which reached the Kut garrison.[15]

The effort at Kut might have been abortive but the idea of supply by air caught on in the Middle East; in September 1918 the single Handley Page 0/400 bomber stationed there was pressed into service to deliver a ton of assorted supplies and other items to an isolated RAF detachment. Perhaps more pertinently, the technique was also employed on the Western Front to keep front-line units supplied in the closing stages of the conflict. On 4 July 1918 No.9 Squadron RAF used twelve specially modified RE8 aircraft to deliver over 100,000 rounds of small-arms ammunition to elements of the 4th Australian Division. A signalling system using large cloth letters allowed the ground units to specify clipped rifle or belted machine-gun ammunition, which was delivered via forty-eight sorties over a six-hour period for the loss of two aircraft. Further drops that included added signal flares and rolls of barbed wire along with ammunition were carried out on 21-22 August and 1-2 October, and food was subsequently added to the list. RAF Nos. 82 and 218 Squadrons dropped a total of thirteen tons of individual rations to isolated Belgian and French units on 2 and 3 October and on 13 October No.35 Squadron flew seventeen sorties to deliver two tons of food to the starving population of Le Cateau.[16]

The advent of large multi-engine bomber aircraft like the Handley Page 0/400 during the First World War meant that, in conjunction with the pre-war development of the limp backpack parachute, the tools necessary for airborne warfare were in existence by 1918. The conflict also saw at least two examples of theorising on the matter. In October 1917 Winston Churchill published a paper covering a number of air-related matters, positing 'flying columns' of air-transported troops for deployment behind enemy lines.[17] The second appeared a year later, when Colonel William Mitchell, a staff officer serving with the US 1st Army, came up with a novel concept for capturing the city of Metz. His scheme involved using Handley Page 0/400 bombers belonging to the British Independent Air Force to parachute 12,000 men from the US 1st Infantry Division behind German lines in ten-man increments. Mitchell's proposal is routinely hailed as a 'milestone in airborne history',[18] but such plaudits do not really stand up to scrutiny. It is unlikely that 12,000 parachutes were available or indeed even in existence at that time, while providing even basic parachute training for the troops and aircrew involved would have been a formidable and time-consuming task in itself. In addition, it is highly unlikely that the RAF would have been willing to risk its fledgling strategic bomber force in such a fanciful scheme for the British Army, never mind a foreign one. Given all this it would perhaps be more accurate to regard Mitchell's idea, like Churchill's, as a piece of pro-airpower hypothetical propaganda than a practical and implementable plan for an airborne operation.

Be that as it may, Churchill and Mitchell's theorising did accurately predict the pattern of future airborne development, for although aircraft with sufficient payload were available by 1918 and the backpack parachute was refined into a reliable, mass-produced item by American entrepreneur Leslie Irvin the following year, the two pieces of technology were not immediately linked. In fact, airborne development followed two parallel tracks through the interwar period and beyond: the delivery of troops *from* the air and transporting troops *by* air, with the latter coming first. During the 2nd Nicaraguan War of 1925-29 for example, the United States Marine Corp moved a total of 21,148 men in and out of isolated outposts by air, and routinely used aircraft for supply and casualty evacuation. This lead was followed by the US Army, which moved field artillery units across the Panama Canal Zone by air in the early 1930s, and air-landed a small infantry force during manoeuvres in Delaware in 1932.[19] The Soviets were carrying out similar experiments at the same time, beginning with a reinforced-company size exercise in 1929. A similar-sized 'motorised landing detachment' formed in the Leningrad Military District in March 1931 was expanded to brigade size in December 1932, and additional units of varying size were established in other Military Districts from March 1933.[20] The Germans also got in on the act; between July and September 1936 the *Luftwaffe* airlifted 9,000 Nationalist troops from Morocco to the Spanish mainland with all their equipment, heavy weapons, ammunition and other supplies.[21]

The pioneers in this area were the British, however, who rapidly adopted the technique during operations in the Empire. On 21 September 1920 two Handley Page 0/400s lifted a dismantled mountain gun, its crew and ammunition from Heliopolis to Almaza in Egypt and the crew brought the gun into action within seven minutes of the aircraft touching down. The entry of the specially designed Vickers Vernon into service at the end of the following year permitted complete units to be moved in a single lift. Two companies of Sikh troops were carried from Kingerban to Kirkuk in Iraq to quell civil disorder in February 1923, followed by a company from the Inniskilling Fusiliers in response to a renewed outbreak in May 1924. Such lifts became a regular feature of British imperial policing thereafter for emergency and more routine deployments, and not just in Iraq. In India, the idea of using aircraft to carry out the Chitral Relief, a six-monthly exchange of garrisons on the North-West Frontier that usually involved over a month of marching for the units involved, was first raised in 1927; by 1938 the shuttling of complete infantry companies was commonplace and the 1940 Relief was carried out entirely by air. In the Middle East a detachment from the South Wales Borderers was lifted from Egypt to Jerusalem in August 1929, and a company from the King's Regiment became the first troops to be airlifted across the open sea after being despatched to Cyprus from Palestine, again in response to an outbreak of civil disorder. The largest single British airlift of the interwar period commenced in 1932 when twenty-five Vickers Victorias carried the 526-strong 1st Battalion Northamptonshire Regiment over 800 miles from Egypt to Iraq. The lift took thirty-six separate sorties spaced over the six-day period between 22 and 27 June, and was repeated more leisurely in reverse between 18 July and 12 August. By the end of the 1930s large-scale operations were being orchestrated and supplied by air as a matter of routine. During the Waziristan Campaign, for example, a total of 5,700 troops and 400 tons of supplies were moved by air in the seven-month period between November 1936 and May 1938.[22]

The British also made extensive use of aircraft for tasks other than troop movement in the Empire. Parachutes were routinely employed for supply drops from at least as early as 1923, when items including 1,000 pairs of boots and 3,000 pairs of socks were dropped to troops operating in Kurdistan.[23] However, while it was undeniably useful, the process could also be both wasteful and hazardous for the recipients. An eyewitness to one drop reported that items were scattered haphazardly across the area, with an unfortunate mule being felled and a tent demolished by a sack of horseshoes; the drop was cancelled when a group of officers narrowly missed being flattened like the mule.[24] Despite such hiccups the technique became increasingly common. The 1930 Chitral Relief was supplied solely by air for two days, with rations and forage for 1,400 men and their animals totalling six tons being dropped at pre-arranged points, and troops operating in the Khaisora Valley in Waziristan were supplied exclusively by air between October 1936 and January 1937 after heavy rains made road transport impossible.[25]

Aircraft were also used to evacuate battle casualties and victims of accidents and disease. The RAF contribution to the Somaliland campaign in January 1920 included a DH9 light bomber modified as an air ambulance and somewhat worryingly nicknamed 'The Hearse' due to the shape of its modified fuselage. In the early 1920s the Air Ministry procured three Vickers Vimy Commercial transports specially modified with loading doors in the nose and stretcher rails; the first example, which was written off in an accident before becoming operational, was also equipped with a toilet, oxygen equipment, cooling fans and even an electric kettle.[26] These appear to have been employed alongside standard Vickers Vernon transports to lift 255 casualties over 200 miles from Girde Telleh in Kurdistan to Baghdad via Kirkuk in May 1923 following an outbreak of dysentery, saving the sick a six-day journey by mule.[27] In April 1929 a regular medical air shuttle to Port Said was set up for serious cases requiring sea evacuation to Britain, a service later extended to include the port of Jaffa. Across the Middle East an average of 120 casualties a year were airlifted to hospitals in Egypt, Iraq and Palestine in the decade after 1925. The service was extended to India in May 1935 in the wake of the Quetta earthquake. RAF aircraft evacuated 136 casualties to Karachi, Lahore and Risalpur for treatment, and delivered an Army medical unit, 12,750 pounds of medical supplies and food and 4,300 pounds of clothing into the earthquake zone over a twenty-one-day period. By the end of the 1930s India had overtaken the Middle East in the medical evacuation stakes and 2,600 patients had been carried a total of 320,000 miles. In an allied task, aircraft were also involved in the evacuation of government officials and civilians from threatened areas. Sixty-seven evacuees were lifted from Sulaimaniya in Iraq in September 1922, and an uprising in the Afghan capital Kabul in November 1928 prompted the evacuation of the British and other legations; 586 civilians and 24,000 pounds of luggage were flown to safety in India over an eight-week period leading up to February 1929 in the face of severe winter conditions.[28]

The use of aircraft in a variety of transport roles was thus a regular and routine feature of British imperial policing up to the late 1930s and beyond. Despite this, the British did not take what appears to be the next logical step and create a parachute-deployable force, and there were a number of perfectly valid reasons for the omission. Not least of these was that funding was barely sufficient to maintain existing commitments for much of the interwar period as the government sought to limit military expenditure to the bare minimum necessary for national safety from before the end of hostilities in 1918; the Army, for example, had its budget cut every year between 1919 and 1932.[29] Inter-service rivalry was inevitably sharpened by the resultant struggle for resources, and this in turn militated against the co-operation between the Air Ministry and War Office necessary to set up a parachute force. Neither organisation was willing to cede control over any contribution to such a project, not least because it risked provoking additional funding cuts on the grounds of supposed duplication, and the effects of this were exacerbated by the Air Ministry's desire to safeguard its newly won independent status. The RAF had only become an independent service in April 1918 via the amalgamation of the Royal Flying Corps and Royal Naval Air Service, and tended to regard both the War Office and Admiralty as 'wicked uncles' just waiting for an opportunity to reclaim their lost assets.[30] Over and above all this however, there was a more straightforward explanation, which was that there was no place for parachute delivery of troops within the framework of British imperial policing as practised in the interwar period. Insertion by parachute would have been an inappropriate method for urban insurrection, and the relatively low numbers of troops and aircraft available made the technique of limited utility in the wider Empire. In short, the British did not establish a parachute force before 1940 because there was no perceived need and the technique offered no real advantage over conventional airlift.

Be that as it may, the necessary equipment was available had the British decided to form such a force. Even biplane transport aircraft like the Vickers Victoria, Vernon and Valentia were perfectly capable of dropping parachute troops, and later models such as the Bristol Bombay and Handley Page Harrow compared favourably with the machines employed for the task by other nations in the 1940s. Indeed, they were far better suited than the obsolete Armstrong Whitworth Whitley and Albemarle that the Air Ministry succeeded in saddling British Airborne Forces with after 1940.[31] Suitable parachutes were also available, albeit off the shelf from a foreign supplier. In April 1919 Major E. L. Hoffman of the US Air Service invited parachute designers and manufacturers to demonstrate their wares at McCook Field in Ohio, with the aim of selecting a standard model for use by the US military aviators. Among the attendees was a former film stuntman and parachute manufacturer from Buffalo, New York named Leslie 'Sky High' Irvin; the nickname referred to his experience as a parachutist, which went back to his early teenage years before the First World War. Irvin had developed Charles Broadwick's idea by attaching the parachute pack to the back of a webbing harness rather than a jacket. He had also modified the opening mechanism by adding a small, spring-activated pilot parachute to the main canopy, and had discarded the static line in favour of a chest-mounted ripcord to initiate the opening sequence; this allowed the parachutist to choose when to open the canopy. The demonstration jump Irvin made at McCook Field on 28 April 1919 was thus the first free-fall parachute descent in history, and he made the most of the occasion by not deploying his canopy until the last moment. Major Hoffman and the assembled military board members were suitably impressed. Irvin left Ohio a few days later bearing a US Government contract for 300,000 parachutes, and the parachute as it is generally known today had arrived.[32]

The first to exploit this new technology for deploying troops were the Italians, presumably as part of the Fascist preoccupation with modernity and harnessing cutting-edge technology. In

1927 they set up the world's first formal military parachute training course at Cinisello airfield near Milan, catering for 250 students, and on 6 November that year nine course graduates carried out the world's first collective military parachute drop, complete with weapons and equipment. Matters slowed somewhat thereafter, possibly due to death of the commander of the new force, a *Generale* Guidoni, in a parachuting accident the following year, although the Italians did form a number of parachute units by the end of the 1930s, some of which were deployed to the Italian colonies in North Africa.[33] However, the real parachute pioneers in the interwar period were the Soviets. Like the British, the latter also employed aircraft in the imperial policing role, primarily against Moslem *Basmachi* tribesmen in the remote reaches of their Central Asian territories.[34] The Soviets went further by adding a tactical combat role to their activities, which required the aircrew to land and engage the enemy, using automatic weapons to offset their lack of numbers. This practice went back to at least May 1928, when the 8th Independent Reconnaissance Aviation Detachment conducted an 'air-landing assault' in the Turkestan Military District, one of three such operations carried out that year.[35] A similar operation was credited with breaking a *Basmachi* siege on the town of Garm in Tadzhikistan in 1929.[36]

The Soviets were quick to appreciate the advantages that the parachute might offer for such operations. Tests were carried out in 1930, with experimental drops to identify ways of minimising dispersal and speeding up post-jump re-organisation at Voronezh in August, followed by a successful raid on a divisional headquarters by a small parachute detachment during exercises in September. This success led to further experiments in the Leningrad Military District in 1931, and the creation of a forty-six-strong 'parachute echelon' to spearhead the 'motorised landing detachment' stationed near Leningrad from March 1931. The parachute echelon was expanded to battalion size when the landing detachment was enlarged to a brigade in December 1932 and within two years or so had attained brigade if not divisional status in its own right. Practical developments were paralleled by theoretical work on the employment of the new force, starting with a paper on the initial development in the Leningrad Military District in the late 1920s collated by future Marshal of the Soviet Union Mikhail Tukhachevsky, who had overseen the tests and may have been inspired by the operations against the *Basmachi*.

Tukhachevsky's lead was taken up by the Chief of Staff of the Red Army's aviation wing, General A. N. Lapchinsky, and Chief of Airborne Service of the Red Army Air Force staff, I. E. Tatarchenko. By 1932 a properly formulated set of guidelines for the employment of parachute- and air-landed troops had been drawn up, entitled 'Technical, Organisational, and Operational Questions of Air Assault Forces'. This recommended employing airborne units to threaten enemy flanks, disrupt their communications and seize key terrain features in support of conventional ground forces. Multiple and widely spaced landings, possibly using darkness and/or poor weather to enhance surprise, were recommended, spearheaded by small parties of parachutists tasked to locate suitable landing sites. These pathfinders would then call in larger parachute units to secure the landing sites and protect them from enemy interference while the main body was air-landed with its vehicles and heavy weapons. Once everything was on the ground the whole force would then co-ordinate its activities with friendly mechanised forces. These guidelines were incorporated into the Soviet's new doctrine of Deep Battle, as laid out in the Red Army's 1936 Field Service Regulations; Article 7 of the latter defined parachute troops as an 'effective means [of] disorganizing the command and rear services of the enemy. In coordination with forces attacking along the front, parachute landing units can go a long way toward producing a complete rout of the enemy on a given axis'.[37]

The influence of this doctrine was clear in the large-scale manoeuvres held by the Soviets in front of assorted foreign observers in the mid-1930s. The 1935 manoeuvres in the Kiev Military District featured a mechanised corps attack spearheaded by a simultaneous drop by 1,188 paratroops to secure crossing over the River Dnieper and landing areas beyond the river. A further 1,765 troops were then flown in, along with artillery and armoured vehicles including light tanks, followed by a further 2,500 men within a forty-minute period. The manoeuvres held in the Moscow Military District in September the following year had an even larger airborne component. 2,200 paratroops were dropped to secure river crossings and disrupt the 'enemy' rear areas. An hour later a further 3,000 parachute troops seized an airfield twenty-five miles away, which was then used to ferry in an entire infantry division.[38] Thereafter, the technique was employed operationally. The Soviet force deployed to repel the Imperial Japanese Army from Mongolian territory along the Khalkin Gol in the summer of 1939 included the 212th Airborne Brigade and all the requisite ancillary units and equipment, although the speed of the Japanese collapse rendered airborne operations superfluous and the Brigade fought in the ground role instead. In June the following year the 201st, 204th and 214th Airborne Brigades spearheaded the Soviet invasion of Bessarabia, carrying out a number of jumps including two full brigade drops and securing the cities of Bolgrad, Izmael and Kagul in advance of ground forces.[39]

Although there were shortages of equipment and aircraft, by June 1941 the Red Army's Airborne Force had been expanded to five complete corps, an independent brigade and a host of smaller units, whose role was laid out in Article 28 of the 1941 Field Service Regulations. Basic parachute training was not a problem, owing to State-sponsored civilian sport parachuting under the auspices of the *Komsomol* and *Osoaviakhim*,[40] which provided training towers and other facilities in every major town in the Soviet Union.[41] The scale and success of this initiative was considerable; according to one contemporary source 2,000,000 individuals had undergone parachute training of some kind by 1939.[42] In the event, many parachute units were thrown into the fight against the German invasion in the ground role, although a number of small-scale diversionary parachute operations were carried out, beginning with a company-size attack on German motor transport near Gorki on 14 July 1941. Several parachute brigades were involved in drops to screen Moscow in the period December 1941-January 1942, and large-scale operations in support of ground offensives were carried out in the regions of Viaz'ma in January and February 1942, near Demiansk between February and April in 1942, and in the crossing of the Dnieper in September 1943. Although little known in the West, these were comparable in size and scope with Western airborne operations.

The Soviets made no secret of their airborne activities during the 1930s, quite the contrary. They invited numerous foreign military observers to attend their exercises, and a film of the 1935 manoeuvres in the Kiev Military District was screened at the Soviet Embassy in London before a specially invited audience at the beginning of 1936; similar footage was subsequently included in newsreels shown in cinemas worldwide.[43] This may have prompted the French to form two parachute companies and a squadron of troop-carrying aircraft in 1936, which carried out experimental work before being disbanded in 1939.[44] More directly, the Soviets set up and staffed a parachute training school at La Rosas for use by Spanish Republican forces during the Spanish Civil War. Personnel trained at the school planned an attack on the German Condor Legion base at Barbastro in April 1938, but a shortage of suitable aircraft led to the scheme being abandoned.[45]

The Poles also emulated the Soviet model independently and quite closely, despite their general antipathy to all things Russian. The LOPP mirrored the functions of the *Komsomol* and *Osoaviakhim* by promoting both sport parachuting and gliding and providing the necessary public facilities.[46] Seventeen public parachuting towers had been erected across the country by 1939, beginning with one in Warsaw in 1936, and Polish Boy Scouts used the expertise they had gained to carry out a demonstration jump at the 5th International Scouting Jamboree at Bloemendaal in the Netherlands in August 1937.[47] Military parachuting towers were erected at the officer cadet schools at Bydgoscz and Legionovo and the infantry school at Komorovo, and initially parachute training was used as a semi-official character-building exercise for officers, with volunteers undergoing a four-week course that included ground training, parachute packing and up to three jumps from a captive balloon and three more from an aircraft.[48] A dedicated parachute diversion and sabotage force was established in September 1937, and the facility at Bydgoscz was expended into a central Military Parachuting Centre in May 1939, tasked to carry out research and development work and to provide training for military volunteers from all branches of the army. The centre's first course graduated in June 1939 but the German invasion in September cut the second short; the centre was destroyed in the subsequent fighting and the staff, trainees and graduates dispersed.[49] Some of these men escaped to Britain, taking with them techniques and operational procedures that played an important role in the establishment and development of the British and Polish Airborne units that carried out Operation MARKET GARDEN.

While the Soviets undoubtedly invented the concept, the first operational exponents of airborne warfare were the Germans. Like the Poles, the latter's initial inspiration also appears to have also been the Soviets, and probably during the co-operation between the *Reichswehr* and Red Army under the provisions of the 1922 Rapallo Treaty before Hitler ordered contact severed in 1933. Future *Generalfeldmarschall* Erich von Manstein attended a parachute exercise in the Trans-Caucasian Military District in September 1932 for example,[50] and Hermann Göring and *Major* Kurt Student, future heads of the *Luftwaffe* and the German Airborne Force respectively, are also alleged to have attended another Soviet parachute demonstration the previous year.[51] Von Manstein's presence is fully in line with his service at that time as a *Major* on the *Reichswehr's* General Staff department tasked to gather information on foreign militaries, but Student and Göring's involvement is less certain. The latter was not a serving officer at that time and it is therefore unclear in what capacity he might have been involved in the highly secret Rapallo exchanges, and the former had been involved in co-operating with the Soviets but was posted to an infantry unit in East Prussia in December 1928 to enhance his command skills.[52]

Be that as it may, Göring was responsible for the creation of the first German parachute unit. The process began in East Prussia in February 1933 with the formation of a para-military police unit named *Polizeiabteilung* 'Wecke', later redesignated *Landespolizeigruppe* Wecke, which contained a small parachute-trained section dubbed the *Luftaufsicht*. With the creation of the *Luftwaffe* in February 1935, the *Landespolizeigruppe* was integrated into the newly formed *Hermann Göring Regiment*, and later in the year the decision was taken to turn one of the Regiment's battalions into a parachute unit under the commander of the *Regiment's Bataillon 1*, *Major* Bruno Bräuer. The entire Regiment was paraded at Jüterborg airfield in northern Germany on 1 October 1935 for a less than inspiring parachute demonstration that ended with the demonstrator unconscious and injured, presumably after a bad landing. Six hundred volunteers nonetheless came forward the following day. This cadre was expanded into a fully autonomous airborne arm via a *Luftwaffe* Order of the Day issued on 29 January 1936 calling for more volunteers to undergo training at the new parachute school at Stendhal near Berlin. Training began on 11 May 1936 and within five months a platoon of *Fallschirmjäger* had taken part in exercises in Saxony followed by a larger parachute demonstration in front of Hitler in the spring of 1937. At the same time the *Oberkommando der Heer* (*OKH*) also decided to get in on the act, contributing an infantry regiment for training in the air-landing role and forming its own parachute company. The latter was expanded to a battalion, commanded by *Major* Richard Heidrich, in June 1938. Parachute training was carried out at Stendal as the *Heer* lacked the necessary facilities.

The various components of the new arm received their first clear mission on 1 June 1938, when Göring placed them under Student's overall command; the latter had transferred to the Luftwaffe from the army and Göring assigned him the task of eliminating Czechoslovakian border fortifications near Freundenthal to clear the way for the German invasion; all planning and preparation were to be complete by 15 September. The following month *Oberkommando der Luftwaffe* (*OKL*) created *7 Flieger Division* as an umbrella headquarters to oversee the operation, and Student reported his new command combat-ready on 1 September 1938. The latter declaration was somewhat optimistic however, for the single regiment of air-landing troops provided by the *Heer* was insufficient for the projected tasks and *OKH* simply refused to supply any more troops for what it perhaps understandably regarded as fanciful experiments; Göring's public boasting of the prowess of the *Luftwaffe* component may also have played a part in *Heer* intransigence. Whether or not, the latter obliged Student to draft in largely untrained personnel from the *Feldherrnhalle Regiment*, a ceremonial *Sturmabteilung* (*SA*) unit as an emergency stopgap, leavened with a hasty injection of experienced officers. It was thus perhaps fortunate that the Munich Agreement at the end of September 1938 rendered the operation unnecessary, although the cancellation added to Student's woes as *OKH* promptly removed *Major* Heidrich's parachute battalion and the air-landing regiment from *7 Flieger Division* control.

The inter-service wrangling and bloody-mindedness between the *Heer* and *Luftwaffe* masked genuine differences over the best way to employ the new arm. The *Luftwaffe* concept envisaged using small groups of parachute troops as a sabotage and demolition force to strike targets that could not be reached by bomber aircraft, whereas the *Heer* were looking to employ parachute troops as a spearhead for air-landing operations in the Soviet mould, and thus as an operational level adjunct to assist ground operations. A third, more radical alternative was put forward by Student himself. This proposed the creation of a self-contained airborne force complete with its own parachute and air-landing troops, air-portable artillery and transport and close-support aircraft that would operate under a doctrine dubbed the 'drops of oil' technique. This involved the simultaneous seizure of multiple landing sites well behind enemy lines in order to dilute the enemy response, which would be maintained and reinforced by air. The pockets would then expand, link up and eventually be joined by advancing friendly ground forces. Whilst radical, Student's doctrine was hardly as original as it is sometimes hailed. The oil drop analogy harked back to a French colonial technique employed by *Marshal* Hubert Lyautey in Morocco in the first quarter of the twentieth century, and the airborne portion was basically a reiteration of Tartarchenko's 1932 paper on the 'Technical, Organisational, and Operational Questions of Air Assault Forces'. Original or not, the result was a compromise imposed by *Oberkommando der Wehrmacht* (*OKW*) that incorporated facets of all three approaches.

Although he failed to sell his airborne doctrine in its entirety, Student did retain his position at the head of the new arm. When the Germans moved into the Sudetenland in October 1938, Göring ordered Student to go ahead with the air-landing operation at Freundenthal as a propaganda showcase for his *Luftwaffe*. Student began by drafting in the population of Freundenthal to clear a suitable landing area, readying his fleet of 242 assorted transport aircraft and adapting the planning work produced for the original landing operation by his divisional staff under *Hauptmann* Heinz Trettner. He then put on a carefully choreographed exercise in front of Göring, the head of the *SA* Viktor Lutze and a retinue of staff officers, accompanied by music from at least one military band. The landing went like clockwork, marred only by two aircraft suffering undercarriage failure, which did not appear to have injured any of the passengers.

Not everyone present was convinced by the display. *Major* Helmut Groscurth from the *Heer's* intelligence arm, the *Abwehr*, dismissed the exercise as a theatrical performance.[53] However, it was Göring's opinion that counted and he was visibly impressed, to the extent that he remarked that the new arm had a great future. With his support the fledgling German airborne force was pulled back from the brink of extinction and Student's career was in the ascendant. On 1 January 1939 he was appointed Inspector General of Airborne Forces and his new command had been expanded to include more than the existing *7 Flieger Division*. After some political infighting *Major* Heidrich's *Heer* parachute battalion had been transferred to the *Luftwaffe*, and Student also had operational control of another *Heer* formation, 22 *Luftlande Division*, a specially trained and equipped air-landing unit. As an additional sign of the favour Student and the Airborne arm now enjoyed with the Nazi hierarchy, a battalion of *Fallschirmjäger* was invited to participate in the parade to mark Hitler's birthday in April 1939, now led by *Oberstleutnant* Bräuer.

By that time *7 Flieger Division* boasted a fully manned *Pionier Kompanie* and reconnaissance, anti-tank, artillery, signal and medical divisional units were being formed. The Division's cutting edge was its parachute infantry, the three-*bataillon Fallschirmjäger Regiment 1* commanded by *Oberstleutnant* Bräuer, and the two-*bataillon Fallschirmjäger Regiment 2* commanded by the recently promoted *Oberstleutnant* Heidrich. These units were manned by volunteers with an average age of eighteen, selected after a rigorous process designed to weed out all but the mentally and physically toughest and most aggressive. Successful candidates were then put through an intensive twelve-week course that covered infantry tactics, demolition, parachute packing, ground training and landing techniques. The latter were particularly important for two reasons. First, the low and narrow passenger door on the standard *Luftwaffe* transport aircraft, the tri-motor Junkers 52, made exiting the aircraft cleanly an awkward manoeuvre for the parachutist. Second, the risers on the standard *Luftwaffe* Z1 parachute canopy were attached to the parachute harness in the middle of the wearer's back; this meant that the parachute could not be steered in any meaningful way and as the parachutist was left dangling at a slight forward angle, landings had to be made on all fours. This took considerable practice even in ideal conditions, and *Fallschirmjäger* were issued thickly padded gloves and knee pads in an attempt to minimise landing injuries.

Those who passed the first phase were then despatched to Stendal for a sixteen-day parachute course that included tower jumps and six descents from an aircraft, the final one a mass drop from 400 feet under battle conditions. Individuals who completed the course were then awarded the distinctive *Luftwaffe* metal parachute qualification badge, which depicted a diving eagle in a wreath of laurel leaves. Receiving the award was no mean feat, given that only one candidate in four passed the course. Perhaps inevitably, given the times and National Socialist leanings of the *Luftwaffe*, ideology also played a part in shaping the troop's attitudes. The result was an extremely fit, highly trained, motivated, resourceful and aggressive soldier who, to an extent, reflected the nihilistic, pseudo-Nietzschean attitudes displayed by storm-troops during the First World War. This would certainly appear to be how they were viewed by the upper echelons of the Nazi regime. Hitler himself drew up 'Ten Commandments' for Student's men that urged the *Fallschirmjäger* to consider battle as a personal fulfilment, to die rather than surrender and to be '...as agile as a greyhound, as tough as leather, as hard as Krupp steel...and [thus] be the German warrior incarnate'.[54] Similarly, Josef Goebbels ensured that his view of the *Fallschirmjäger* as an icon of the new National Socialist Germany was amply reflected in the propaganda output of his Ministry, and encouraged members of his staff to volunteer for Airborne service when called up.[55] This ideological edge clearly present in the official *Fallschirmjäger* song, which mirrored the urgings of Hitler's Commandments, and Student's men appear to have carried it onto the battlefield, in spite of the widespread popular British perception of them as a hard-fighting but chivalrous foe.[56]

Student also added an additional and novel element to his Airborne force. The *Reichswehr* had sponsored public sport gliding in much the same way as the *Komsomol*, *Osoaviakhim* and LOPP had sponsored civilian sport parachuting, in this instance as a means of circumventing Versailles Treaty restrictions on training military pilots. Student was involved in this work and, quickly appreciating the potential of the glider for more aggressive military purposes, he commissioned the German Research Institute for Gliding to produce a design for a troop-carrying machine. After Student had personally test-flown the prototype, the machine was accepted for service as the DFS 230. With a crew of two in tandem seats and of high-wing, tubular metal and fabric construction, the DFS 230 was thirty-seven feet long with a wingspan of around seventy-two feet, and was capable of being towed with a ton payload at speeds up to 100 miles per hour. It could carry eight fully equipped troops seated astride a central bench, who exited via two small side doors; the pilot and co-pilot exited the cockpit by jettisoning the Perspex canopy and, as a *Luftwaffe* warplane, the DFS 230 also sported a roof hatch mounting an *MG15* machine-gun.[57]

Student viewed the glider not as a subsidiary to the parachute, but as a superior method for delivering troops cohesively onto specific targets with pinpoint accuracy. To that end he authorised the formation of an experimental glider unit in November 1939 codenamed Test Section Friedrichshafen, made up of *Hauptmann* Walther Koch's company from *I Bataillon, Fallschirmjäger Regiment 1*, augmented with the *Pionier Kompanie* from *II Bataillon, Fallschirmjäger Regiment 1* commanded by *Oberleutnant* Rudolf Witzig. The Section was tasked to test the glider's utility as transport for assault engineers attacking fixed defences, in line with the original *Luftwaffe* concept of airborne troops as a means of striking targets too difficult for bomber aircraft. When the trials proved the viability of the concept, the Test Section was formally established as *Sturmabteilung* Koch, named for its commander and intended to be the elite of the German Airborne arm.[58] Unlike Student's doctrinal theorising, this development appears to have been original and it was taken up by the Soviets, who began to add glider units to their airborne units from 1940.[59] The idea of using gliders was also taken up by the British and US armies when they followed the German airborne lead in 1940, although they tended toward the opposite tack and employed the glider in a secondary role to the parachute. The British, especially, employed larger machines to carry infantry or vehicles, guns and heavy equipment, with the very occasional exception. These included the ill-fated attempt to attack the German heavy water plant at Vermork in Norway in November 1942, and the spectacularly successful seizure of the Orne Canal and River bridges at Bénouville in Normandy on the eve of the Allied landings in June 1944.[60]

Hitler earmarked his new and as yet untried airborne force to play a leading role in his attack into the Low Countries, which he revealed to Student on 27 October 1939. The bulk of *7 Flieger* and *22 Luftlande Divisions*, augmented with troops from the *Bataillon* Brandenburg Special Forces unit, were tasked to assist the advance of *Generaloberst* Fedor von Bock's *Heeresgruppe* B into and across Holland by seizing river crossings and vertically outflanking the Dutch defences. The first, vital step in this process was the neutralisation of the Belgian fortress at Eben Emael, which controlled the Albert Canal bridges that were to carry the German ground invasion. The mission was allotted to *Sturmabteilung* Koch, and may have been the catalyst for the formation of Test Section Friedrichshafen. Whether or not, Koch's men embarked on an intensive training regime from December 1939, which included full-scale assaults on recently vacated Czechoslovak border fortifications that closely replicated the Belgian defences at Eben Emael. These practice assaults were made with live ammunition and explosives, and led to the design and fabrication of shaped charges especially configured to penetrate thickly armoured turret cupolas.[61]

However, events intervened and the first operational employment of the German airborne force was actually carried out by four *kompanien* of *Fallschirmjäger* from *I Bataillon, Fallschirmjäger Regiment 1*. Hitler had ordered *OKW* to prepare plans for an invasion of Scandinavia on 21 February 1940, in order to secure Germany's northern flank and supplies of Swedish iron ore. Operation *Weserübung* began at 04:15 on 9 April 1940, when German ground forces crossed the Danish border. *Hauptmann* Walther Gericke's *4 Kompanie* was to drop in platoon increments ahead of the ground advance to secure two airfields at Aalborg, and the 3,000-metre Stoerstrom bridge linking the Gedser ferry terminal and Copenhagen. Fog delayed take-off and the drop did not go in until 07:00, but both airfields surrendered to the attackers without a fight. One party under *Hauptmann* Gericke rapidly secured the approach to the ferry terminal and another used commandeered civilian bicycles to overtake and disarm a Danish guard detachment en route to its duty station. Another group tasked to neutralise a Danish coastal defence fort moved off from the drop zone without pausing to recover their weapon containers, opting instead to overrun the stunned Danish garrison armed only with their side arms. The small dimensions of the Junkers 52 exit door cited above prevented *Fallschirmjäger* jumping with anything larger than a pistol for personal protection, and rifles, machine pistols and machine-guns had to be dropped separately in containers slung beneath the aircraft. This was a significant tactical flaw that was to have serious repercussions, but in this instance it was concealed by the overall success of the Danish phase of *Weserübung*. Overawed by the speed and novelty of the German assault and faced with imminent attack on civilian areas by circling *Luftwaffe* bombers, the Danish government surrendered at 09:20 on 9 April 1940.[62]

Matters did not proceed so smoothly for the two *kompanien* of *Fallschirmjäger* tasked to secure the Norwegian airfields at Fornebu near Oslo and at Sola, farther west near Stavanger. The fog that had delayed the attack on Aalborg and Copenhagen extended up to 2,000 feet over the Skaggerrak Strait separating Denmark and Norway and reduced visibility to less than thirty yards. These were extremely hazardous conditions for large formations of transport aircraft, and the first wave of Junkers 52 carrying *Major* Erich Walther, the commander of *I Bataillon, Fallschirmjäger Regiment 1*, his HQ element and 2 *Kompanie* were obliged to turn back at 08:20. Two aircraft failed to return, having either collided or crashed into the sea in the murk; the approach flight appears to have been made at low level to escape detection.

The second wave, carrying elements of *193 Infanterie Division*, pressed on, apparently unaware that their parachute spearhead had aborted its mission, and arrived at Fornebu in clear visibility to find six of the eight assigned Messerschmitt 110 heavy fighters strafing the unsuppressed Norwegian anti-aircraft defences. The two missing Messerschmitts had been shot down earlier in a dogfight with Norwegian Gloster Gladiator fighters, and the remainder were not only running low on fuel and ammunition but three had also lost engines. The precise detail of what happened next is unclear. According to one account, one of the damaged Messerschmitts, flown by a *Leutnant* Lent, was ordered to attempt a landing by his commander *Oberleutnant* Hansen and the Junkers 52 transports followed him down.[63] Another refers to a single transport carrying a *Fallschirmjäger* signal section settling down to land as soon as it arrived over the airfield despite the anti-aircraft fire, and almost colliding with *Leutnant* Lent's machine as they landed on convergent runways. Whichever, the remaining Messerschmitts landed and provided covering fire for the *Fallschirmjäger* signallers with the last of their ammunition, and *Oberleutnant* Hansen took personal command of events after landing, directing *Heer* troops from subsequent transports that began to arrive at 09:15 to clear the Norwegian defenders from their positions. He later signalled the operation HQ in Hamburg that his fighter squadron was responsible for securing the airfield.[64]

The transports carrying *Leutnant Freiherr* von Brandis' 3 *Kompanie* carried on through the fog and after spending thirty minutes re-establishing formation made a low-level approach to Sola, rising to 400 feet, just long enough to drop their hundred *Fallschirmjäger*. As the latter drifted down along the edge of the airfield they began to take fire from the Norwegian defenders, but six Messerschmitt 110s appeared in the nick of time and began strafing the defender's positions. Within thirty minutes von Brandis' men had finished the job and Sola joined Fornebu in German hands. 1 *Kompanie*, commanded by *Leutnant* Herbert Schmidt, had been held in reserve but was subsequently tasked to prevent newly arrived British forces linking up with the Norwegians in the Gudbrandsal Valley north of Oslo. To this end, Schmidt and his men dropped near Dombas, ninety miles north of Oslo, at twilight on 14 April 1940. The operation did not begin well. Accurate ground fire brought down one Junkers 52 and caused a number of casualties during the jump including *Leutnant* Schmidt, who was wounded in the hip and stomach. Only sixty-one men rallied at the assembly area, but this little band nonetheless managed to establish a blocking position on a nearby major road. They held out there for four days until their ammunition was exhausted, at which point they were obliged to surrender. By that time Schmidt had only thirty-four men left alive; he was subsequently awarded the Knight's Cross for continuing to exercise command despite his wounds.[65]

The attack on the Low Countries, part of operation *Fall Gelb*, was launched on 10 May 1940. At 04:30 the first of forty-one Junkers 52 transports, each towing a DFS 230 glider, began to take off into the pre-dawn blackness at thirty-second intervals from Butzweilerhof and Ostheim airfields near Cologne. The gliders were the sum total available in the *Luftwaffe* inventory, and contained the 363 men of *Sturmabteilung* Koch, who had lived and trained for their mission in almost total isolation at an airfield at Hildesheim from November 1939.[66] Once airborne, the glider combinations headed for the Dutch border in the vicinity of Aachen, guided by a chain of searchlights. Koch's force was divided into four sections, each with a specific objective. The primary mission of neutralising the Eben Emael fortress was allotted to *Oberleutnant* Witzig's *Sturmgruppe* Granit (Granite), made up of eleven gliders and eighty-five men. Once again, the mission did not begin well. Two gliders, one of them Witzig's, became separated from their tugs not long after take-off. Both landed unscathed but the attack force had lost its leader before leaving German airspace, and command devolved to *Oberfeldwebel* Wenzel. The remaining nine gliders cast off from their tugs at 05:00, five minutes ahead of schedule owing to an unexpected tailwind. At 05:32 all touched down on the 1,000-by-1,750-yard plateau atop the Eben Emael fortress, which was actually an underground complex burrowed into a steep bluff overlooking the Albert Canal and River Meuse.

The long months of intensive training paid off. Within minutes, Witzig's men had placed their explosive charges on armoured cupolas and gun barrels and disabled the seven artillery casemates covering the Albert Canal; Wenzel radioed a success signal to *Hauptmann* Koch at 05:40. However, the fort proper remained in Belgian hands, and *Sturmgruppe* Granit was effectively marooned atop an enemy force that outnumbered it by over ten to one. At 08:30 some small reinforcement arrived in the shape of a DFS 230 carrying *Oberleutnant* Witzig, who had arranged for a replacement tug to lift his glider and fellow passengers from the field where they had force-landed; he immediately took command of the effort to keep the Belgian garrison bottled up. The *Heer* relief force was delayed because Dutch troops had demolished bridges further north at Maastricht, but despite this, counter-attacks by the garrison and enemy artillery fire, they succeeded in holding out through the night of 10-11 May. By the time reinforcements from *Pionier Bataillon 51* finally arrived at around 0700 hours on 11 May the men from Granite were all but out of ammunition, but a hastily prepared final effort later in the morning finally persuaded the garrison commander, a Major Jottrand, that the game was up. The Eben Emael fortress and its garrison of around 1,200 men surrendered at 13:15 on 11 May 1940, having lost twenty dead and an undetermined number of wounded. The thirty-six-hour fight cost Witzig's little band six dead and twenty wounded.[67]

The remainder of *Sturmabteilung* Koch had been tasked to seize three bridges across the Albert Canal covered by the Eben Emael fortress to assist the German ground advance, all of which were thought to be rigged with demolition charges. *Oberleutnant* Gustav Altmann's ninety-two-strong *Sturmgruppe* Stahl (Steel) was to seize the steel-frame bridge at Veldwezelt, just under four miles north of Eben Emael; *Sturmgruppe* Beton (Concrete), commanded by *Leutnant* Gerhard Schacht with ninety-six men, was assigned the modern concrete bridge at Vroenhoven; and the bridge nearest Eben Emael at Canne was to be secured by *Sturmgruppe* Eisen's (Iron's) ninety men commanded by *Leutnant* Martin Schächter. The gliders carrying *Sturmgruppen* Concrete and Steel touched down alongside their targets at 05:15 and 05:20 respectively; the time difference was presumably due to the unexpected tailwind. Both objectives were secured in the face of heavy Belgian fire, and Altmann's men discovered that the demolition charges had been fortuitously removed from the Veldwezelt bridge; both parties were relieved by *Heer* troops at around 21:30 after a day beating off numerous Belgian counter-attacks. *Sturmgruppe* Iron was less fortunate. The Belgian troops guarding the bridge at Canne were alerted by a German motorised column advancing prematurely and detonated their demolition charges as the gliders began their landing run. The latter were badly shot up and the attackers suffered a number of casualties including *Leutnant* Schächter, who was killed. Command thus devolved to *Leutnant* Joachim Meissner, who rallied the survivors and repulsed two Belgian attacks before finally being relieved at 23:30.

While *Sturmabteilung* Koch was busying itself atop Eben Emael and the nearby bridges, the remainder of Student's airborne force was pursuing its own objectives deeper inside Holland. *Gruppe Süd*, consisting of the bulk of *7 Flieger Division* and some attached elements from *22 Luftlande Division*, was tasked to secure a series of road and rail bridges at Dordrecht,

Moerdijk and Rotterdam. The objective was to open an avenue into western Belgium and the Channel ports, while striking at the heart of so-called 'Fortress Holland' to deny the RAF use of airfields to strike at Germany, and to vertically outflank the Dutch 'Grebbe' and 'New Water' defence lines.[68] Along with the water crossings, an airfield at Waalhaven, south-east of Rotterdam, was to be seized in order to fly in reinforcements and heavy weapons. The *Fallschirmjäger* of *Gruppe Süd* began to drop at around 06:00 on 10 May, thirty minutes after the attack on Eben Emael commenced. The bridges at Rotterdam were seized via an imaginative *coup-de-main* operation that utilised twelve Heinkel He 59 seaplanes; these landed on the river and taxied up to the objective, allowing their passengers from 22 *Luftlande Division* to disembark directly onto it.[69] The bridges at Dordrecht and Moerdijk were captured intact by *Major* Walther's I *Bataillon*, *Fallschirmjäger Regiment 1* and *Hauptmann* Fritz Prager's II *Bataillon, Fallschirmjäger Regiment 2* respectively, with simultaneous drops at the north and south ends.

The seizure of Waalhaven airfield began with III *Bataillon Fallschirmjäger Regiment 1* commanded by *Hauptmann* Karl-Lothar Schulze, dropping along the edges of the field to distract the defenders while other Junkers 52s landed to deliver their troops from II *Bataillon Fallschirmjäger Regiment 2* directly onto the target. At least one Dutch anti-aircraft position was still in operation when the transports began to land and damaged several aircraft, but the attackers rapidly overran the airfield, interrupting a party for the Dutch commandant's fortieth year of service in the process. With the airfield secured more transports began to shuttle in reinforcements despite Dutch artillery fire and attacks by RAF bombers, including an anti-tank unit and Student himself with his forward HQ element. Linking up with the troops holding the bridges went less smoothly, and the relieving forces became embroiled in fierce street-fighting as the Dutch mounted a stubborn resistance that included repeated counter-attacks against the German troops holding the various bridges. The troops holding the north end of the Rotterdam bridges were cut off for the better part of two days, and the Dutch also succeeded in driving *Major* Walther's *Fallschirmjäger* off the bridge at Dordrecht for a time, obliging Student to despatch the force earmarked to protect Waalhaven airfield to recapture it. The fighting continued until 9 *Panzer Division*, the spearhead of *Heeresgruppe* B, arrived in the area on 13 May 1940.[70] The dead included *Leutnant Freiherr* von Brandis, who had led the jump onto Sola airfield in Norway only a month earlier.

The second strand of the German airborne attack on Holland was entrusted to *Gruppe Nord*, consisting of the bulk of 22 *Luftlande Division* with a parachute spearhead. Their mission was to decapitate the Dutch state politically and militarily by seizing the Dutch Royal family, government and military leadership located in the Dutch capital, Den Haag. To this end six companies of *Fallschirmjäger*, drawn from I *Bataillon, Fallschirmjäger Regiment 2* and *Infanterie Regiment 47* were to secure three airfields at Ockenburg, Valkenburg and Ypenburg. These airfields would then be used as an airhead to fly in additional units for a speedy advance on Den Haag. The *Fallschirmjäger* spearhead succeeded in securing Valkenburg, but the grass field was too soft to carry the weight of a fully laden Junkers 52 and the field quickly became jammed with bogged machines; the final wave had to be diverted to Waalhaven. Matters went even more awry at Ockenburg and Ypenburg. The parachute drops there was scattered and the *Fallschirmjäger* were unable to recover their weapon containers before the first wave of Junker 52s arrived and tried to land. The fully alert Dutch defenders, who had scattered obstacles across the landing area and were standing by their anti-aircraft guns, were quick to take advantage of a succession of virtually sitting ducks. Eleven of the thirteen Junkers in the first wave at Ypenburg were either shot down or severely damaged, with many catching fire. The remainder diverted to Ockenburg only to find the same process underway; the casualties sustained there included the machine carrying the commander of 22 *Luftlande Division, Generalmajor* Hans *Graf* von Sponeck, which crash-landed after being badly shot up. Unable to alight at the airfields, some pilots attempted to set down anywhere they could – in fields, on the Den Haag-Amsterdam motorway and even on nearby beaches. The confusion and casualties were so great that the attack on Den Haag had to be abandoned, and a wounded von Sponeck led the survivors to link up with *Gruppe Süd*, arriving at Rotterdam on the night of 13-14 May.[71]

There was another, little-known German airborne operation on 10 May 1940 in addition to the spectacular events at Eben Emael and in Holland. *Fall Gelb* had originally been the main German effort in the West, but that changed on 9 January 1940 when a *Luftwaffe* liaison aircraft carrying an officer with a copy of the plan landed in error at the Belgian airfield at Mechelen. The German plan was thus modified with an additional predominantly armoured thrust by *Generaloberst* Gerd von Rundstedt's *Heeresgruppe* A, codenamed *Unternehmen Sichelschnitt*, which envisaged a rapid advance through northern Luxemburg, the Ardennes and across the River Meuse into France at Sedan. *Fall Gelb* thus became the anvil, and *Sichelschnitt* the hammer swing that would crush the Allied defence against it. As *7 Flieger* and *22 Luftlande Divisions* and the whole of the *Luftwaffe* transport and glider fleet were fully committed to *Fall Gelb* there were no Airborne assets available to deploy in support of the *Sichelschnitt* advance. However, Göring himself came up with the novel idea of using 100 of the *Luftwaffe's* fleet of Fieseler *Storch* co-operation aircraft as *ad hoc* transports. The *Storch* was a single-engine, high-wing monoplane with a forty-six-foot wingspan and a top speed of 109 miles per hour, and had a very good short take-off and landing performance. The machine's nickname was inspired by its long, shock-absorber-cushioned undercarriage legs. The major problem was that the *Storch* was only capable of lifting two fully equipped infantrymen in addition to its crew, and moving the proposed force would therefore take two full lifts. The troops were drawn from *10* and *11 Kompanien, 3 Bataillon, Infanterie* Regiment *Grossdeutschland* commanded by *Oberstleutnant* Eugen Garski and *Hauptmann* W. Krüger respectively.

The operation was codenamed *Unternehmen NiWi* after the two proposed landing areas at Nives and Witry in the Belgian Ardennes on the line of advance of *1* and *2 Panzer Divisions* respectively, the former assigned to *10 Kompanie* and the latter to *11 Kompanie*. Their collective mission was to cut Belgian communications along the roads linking Neufchâteau, Bastogne and Martelange, threaten the Belgian border fortifications from the rear and block any Belgian advance from Neufchâteau; *10 Kompanie* was also tasked to push on toward Bodange to ease the way for *1 Panzer Division*. The first lift took off from airfields around Bitburg at 05:20 on 10 May 1940, crossed the Luxemburg border at low level at 05:35 and flew into Belgian airspace near Martelange at approximately 05:50. It was then that the plan began to unravel. All but five of the Fieselers carrying *Oberstleutnant* Garski's *10 Kompanie* became separated in fog or low cloud and inadvertently re-formated with *Hauptman* Krüger's group heading for Nives. This error was compounded when the lead pilot in Krüger group became disoriented while avoiding ground fire and began to fly in the wrong direction. As a result, *Oberstleutnant* Garski landed as planned near Witry at precisely 06:00 to find himself accompanied by only five aircraft, while the bulk of his men landed with *Hauptmann* Krüger's group near Léglise, approximately ten miles from their designated landing zone. A number of aircraft were damaged on landing, some so seriously that they caught fire and the arrival of Belgian troops supported by armoured cars prompted Krüger to withdraw north toward Witry, where he linked up with Garski at around 13:00.

Fortunately for Garski, the second lift into Witry had arrived intact and on time at 08:00, and the reinforcement permitted him to rebuff a Belgian probe before moving off toward Bodange as planned in the late afternoon; contact was established with the lead elements of *1 Panzer Division* near Fauvillers at 17:30. Back at Nives the second wave also arrived accurately and intact at 08:05 and command of this part of the operation devolved to a *Leutnant* Obermeier, who established a blocking position astride the road between Bastogne and Neufchâteau and held it through the day against numerous attacks by Belgian troops and elements of a French formation, *5ᵉᵐᵉ Division de Cavalerie Légère*. An armoured attack by the latter in the early evening finally obliged *Leutnant* Obermeier to withdraw, but the French were disinclined to pursue them in the gathering darkness and they withdrew in turn, leaving the way clear for

2 *Panzer Division* the following day.[72] By 14 May the *Panzers* were across the River Meuse at Sedan and by 23 May had the bulk of the British Expeditionary Force (BEF) and a large number of French troops penned into a coastal pocket around the French port of Dunkirk. Belgium surrendered on 28 May, a day after the British began an evacuation of Dunkirk, codenamed Operation DYNAMO. By 4 June 338,226 men had been lifted to safety, and by 20 June the remainder of the BEF and a large number of Allied military and civilian personnel had been removed from ports along the north and western French seaboard.[73] It left behind 68,111 men dead, missing or prisoners of war, 2,472 assorted artillery pieces, 63,879 vehicles, 76,697 tons of ammunition, 415,940 tons of stores and 164,929 tons of fuel.[74]

Collectively the German airborne operations launched on 10 May 1940 played a significant role in all this, but individually the picture was less rosy. On the one hand *Sturmabteilung* Koch's spectacular success at Eben Emael undeniably opened the way for *Heeresgruppe* B to penetrate into eastern Holland, and *Gruppe Süd* provided an equally vital conduit for the latter to access northern Belgium and the Channel ports, thus paving the way for the encirclement of the bulk of the BEF at Dunkirk. On the other hand, *Gruppe Nord* totally failed in its attempt militarily and politically to decapitate the Dutch state, and *Unternehmen NiWi* did little to aid the advance of *Heeresgruppe* A either, apart from possibly alerting the Belgians and French to the German line of advance through the Ardennes. Successful or otherwise, the cost was close to the edge of being prohibitive, if not over it. Two-thirds of the 430 Junkers 52 transports engaged in *Fall Gelb* as a whole were destroyed or so badly damaged that they had to be written off, while the transport unit assigned to *Gruppe Nord* suffered a ninety per cent loss rate.[75] The human toll was also heavy. According to one source many of the aircrew manning the transports were instructors drafted in from training establishments, and the losses they incurred had an adverse effect on subsequent aircrew recruitment and training.[76] Of the ground troops, 22 *Luftlande Division* lost forty per cent of its officers and twenty-eight per cent of its rank and file killed or missing; 1,600 of the latter were captured, most of whom were evacuated to Britain for incarceration.[77] It is also important to note that a good deal of this was not due solely to enemy action, but to flawed operating procedures; these included launching operations with faulty or insufficient intelligence, dropping *Fallschirmjäger* separate from their weapons, and attempting air-landings in the face of unsuppressed enemy defences. Neither did Student or his staff learn the requisite lessons from all this, and the process was repeated at even greater cost at Maleme airfield and other locations on the Greek island of Crete in the latter half of May 1941.

Even allowing for all that, however, the German airborne operations in the Low Countries proved spectacularly that airborne warfare was effective in a battlefield context. More importantly, it also supplied the catalyst for their current and future enemies to emulate the concept by forming Airborne Forces of their own, which were to carry out Operation MARKET GARDEN.

Framing the Battlefield and Marshalling the Players:

II SS *Panzerkorps*, 30 Corps and the 1st Allied Airborne Army 16 August – 8 September 1944

Although it was not immediately apparent, the chain of events that led to Arnhem began almost exactly a month before Operation MARKET GARDEN was launched. With the initial invasion force safely ashore along a sixty-mile stretch of the Normandy coastline stretching from Ouistreham to St. Mère Église by 9 June 1944, the Allies then spent almost two months consolidating their beachhead. To the west, US forces concentrated on clearing the Cotentin Peninsula to access the port of Cherbourg after linking the OMAHA and UTAH landing areas at Carentan> To the east British and Commonwealth forces slowly advanced inland in the face of fierce German resistance toward the city of Caen, a rather optimistic D-Day objective and ostensibly key to the local communication network. The breakout began on 25 July with Operation COBRA, an attack south from St. Lô by the US VII and VIII Corps. The US advance pushed south before swinging east in a sweeping pincer movement that pressed the Germans back against British and Canadian units advancing south from Caen, which had been secured on 8 July. By 16 August approximately 100,000 German troops from *7 Armee* and *Panzergruppe* Eberbach with all their vehicles, livestock and equipment had been hemmed into an area sixty miles deep and thirty-five miles wide running west from Chambois, which was dubbed the Falaise Pocket. Within two days remorseless Allied pressure had compressed that area by half, and the capture of St. Lambert by the 4th Canadian Armoured Division on 18 August brought them within a couple of miles of the US 90th Infantry Division pushing up to Chambois from the south.

Elements of General Stanislaw Maczek's 1st Polish Armoured Division made contact with the US 359th Infantry Regiment in Chambois in the early evening of Saturday 19 August, but with insufficient strength to block the exit from the Pocket. Two battlegroups totalling approximately 1,500 men supported by eighty tanks and representing half the Division's combat strength thus moved five miles or so to the east and occupied the commanding height of Mont Ormel, also known as Hill 262 after its spot height. The Poles codenamed their new position *Maczuga* (Mace) and spent the night of 19-20 August digging in. This was a wise precaution, for Hill 262 provided panoramic views of the surrounding area for artillery observervation and lay squarely in the centre of the exit from the Falaise Pocket. Despite being cut off, the Poles held out against increasingly desperate attacks from elements of five *Waffen SS* and two *Heer* Panzer divisions in some of the most ferocious and intense fighting of the war. By the evening of Sunday 20 August, for example, one of the two Polish battlegroups on Mont Ormel had been reduced to 110 men and their supporting tanks were down to five rounds of main gun ammunition apiece. The situation was sufficiently serious that the battlegroup commander, Lieutenant-Colonel Antoni Stefanowicz of the 1st Polish Armoured Regiment, made a fatalistic farewell speech to his men pointing out the futility of surrendering to the _SS_ and urging them to die for Poland and civilisation by fighting to the last man.[1] Relief finally arrived in the afternoon of Monday 21 August in the shape of the 22nd Canadian Armoured Regiment, after the Poles had expended virtually all their remaining ammunition rebuffing a last ditch attack by elements of _2 SS Panzer Division_. In all, the two Polish battlegroups suffered 352 killed, 1,002 wounded and 114 missing during the two-day battle for Mount Ormel, a casualty rate of roughly seventy-five per cent.[2] German losses included 2,000 dead, fifty-five tanks and 152 assorted armoured vehicles.[3]

The Falaise Pocket was finally sealed in the evening of 21 August, and by the following day the only German troops west of Mont Ormel were either dead or prisoners. The bulk of _Heeresgruppe B's_ combat strength had been destroyed with the loss of some 10,000 dead, 50,000 prisoners and almost all their transport and heavy equipment; Allied post-battle surveys counted 304 armoured vehicles, 3,178 assorted soft-skin vehicles and 166 assorted artillery pieces destroyed or abandoned within the Pocket.[4] However, the tenacity of the Poles was matched by some German units battling to force open escape routes to the east, and their efforts permitted around 20,000 men to evade the Allied trap.[5] Many were individuals and small groups intent only on escape on foot or by vehicle, but there were also larger, more organised and disciplined groupings. The latter included _Obergruppenführer_ Wilhelm Bittrich's _II SS Panzerkorps_, which was to play a key role in the German response to the British advance into Holland in mid-September. Bittrich's formation consisted of two divisions: _9 SS Panzer Division_ 'Hohenstaufen', commanded by _Standartenführer_ Friedrich Wilhelm Bock; and _Brigadeführer_ Heinz Harmel's _10 SS Panzer Division_ 'Frundsberg'. _II SS Panzerkorps_ had arrived in Normandy from the Eastern Front toward the end of June 1944 and was immediately plunged into some of the most intense fighting of the campaign, blocking British attacks at the eastern end of the invasion area including Operations EPSOM, CHARNWOOD, GOODWOOD and BLUECOAT. By mid-August, _10 SS Panzer Division_ was making a fighting withdrawal along the shrinking southern perimeter of the Falaise Pocket following the abortive German counter-attack at Mortain, and after regrouping near Villedieu-les-Bailleul broke out of the trap and linked up with _II SS Panzerkorps HQ_ east of the River Dives during the night of 20 August. _9 SS Panzer Division_ had been withdrawn from the Vire area on the British front south-west of Caen on 13 August and after regrouping near Argentan was ordered out of the still-forming trap to Vimoutiers, from where it launched an abortive attack on elements of the 4th Canadian Armoured Division holding the north shoulder of the Falaise Gap in the early hours of 20 August.

The sealing of the Falaise Pocket on 21 August obliged _II SS Panzerkorps_ HQ and the surviving combat elements of the _Hohenstaufen_ and _Frundsberg Divisions_ to embark on the odyssey that would ultimately carry them to Arnhem. The move began in the wake of their service and support elements, which had begun to withdraw across the River Seine on 17 August. The most direct route was to the east, but that was blocked by US forces who had by-passed the fighting to close the Gap and pushed east for over sixty miles to reach the Seine near Mantes on 19 August. The _SS_ units therefore moved north-east toward Rouen, where the only crossings over the Seine remaining in German hands were located. Elements of both Divisions fought a blocking action against Canadian troops in the vicinity of Bernay and Orbec, roughly midway between Vimoutiers and Rouen, on 23-24 August. This action was instrumental in buying time for an estimated 150,000 German troops and 25,000 assorted vehicles to escape across the Seine to safety. The remainder of _9_ and _10 SS Panzer Divisions_ continued their journey north-east while these rearguard actions were underway, regrouping in the vicinity of Bourgtheroulde, east of Rouen, while some elements pushed on to organise matters at their designated crossing points from 24 August. The _Hohenstaufen_ was directed to a crossing over the Seine ten miles north of Rouen in the vicinity of Duclair, where the _Kriegsmarine_ were operating a 100-ton-capacity steam-powered ferry. The engineers of _SS Panzer Pionier Abteilung 9_ augmented this with a motley collection of pontoon ferries, inflatable rafts and assault boats, with which the bulk of the division were ferried to relative safety by dusk on 29 August. The remainder crossed the following day, with elements of _SS Artillerie Regiment 9_ led by a _Hauptsturmführer_ Nickmann making the final crossing using rafts improvised from timber and fuel cans. The *Frundsberg* was ordered to cross the Seine three miles or so upstream from Rouen, using the damaged Oissel railway bridge. This was fortuitously supplemented with a nearby emergency bridge discovered by *SS Panzer Aufklärungs Abteilung 10*, and the bulk of the *Frundsberg* was safely across the river by the evening of 27 August. This was achieved by restricting access, at gunpoint, to the emergency bridge solely to *Frundsberg* units and personnel, a rather drastic measure prompted by the sheer volume of traffic trying to cross the Seine; one eyewitness estimate reported up to 7,000 vehicles jammed three abreast and nose to tail along every approach road to Oissel.[6]

The German retreat across the Seine thus had the potential to become another Falaise, and disaster was only averted, at least in part, by the weather. The latter broke on or around 25 August, and the subsequent rain and low cloud prevented fighter-bombers from the RAF's 2ⁿᵈ Tactical Air Force and the US IX Tactical Air Command from taking full advantage of the situation.[7] Even so, Allied airpower did interfere significantly with German cross-river traffic. In the seven-day period leading up to 23 August 300 barges were sunk, and on 24 August Allied aircraft destroyed a bridge at Elbeuf and damaged others at Oissel and Rouen proper. USAAF P-47 Thunderbolts also attacked the Duclair ferry in the afternoon of 24 August, killing the commander of *SS Panzer Regiment 9*, *Obersturmbannführer* Otto Meyer, and an *Untersturmführer* Suhrkämpfer from SS *Panzer Pionier Abteilung 9*.[8] However, the main factor that saved the Germans was that Allied ground units needed time to mop up the Falaise Pocket and reorganise, as well as untangle and reorient formation and Army group boundaries and lines of advance. The latter process presented a considerable staff and logistic challenge, even for units that had not been involved in the Falaise fighting. It was at this point that the British formations that were to be tasked with carrying out the ground advance to Arnhem came into the picture, and they provide a good example of these problems. Lieutenant-General Brian Horrocks' 30 Corps was released from the British 2ⁿᵈ Army reserve on 20 August to spearhead the advance to the Seine and beyond, and getting the lead 43ʳᵈ Division forward to its designated crossing point entailed moving 4,400 vehicles and a bridging train seventy miles from the vicinity of Chambois. The process took five days, with the Division divided into three increments because the move coincided with the reorientation of the US 19ᵗʰ Corps across the same local road net. As a result the 43ʳᵈ Division was only permitted access to a maximum of two routes for periods of four to six hours at a time; this remained the case until the last elements of the US formation finally cleared the 21ˢᵗ Army Group boundary in the early hours of 28 August.[9]

Not all the formations to be involved in Holland were moving with such urgency and purpose. The Guards Armoured Division, which was to play a leading role in the pursuit from the Seine and spearhead 30 Corps' subsequent advance into Holland, went into British 2ⁿᵈ Army reserve on 16 August in the vicinity of Condé-sur-Noireau. There it remained while the Falaise Pocket was closed and the pursuit eastward began, resting, reorganising and absorbing replacements for the 249 dead, 975 wounded and 176 missing the Division had sustained since 31 July.[10] ENSA concerts were provided for entertainment,[11] while the upper echelons of the Division did some entertaining of their own. On 16 August the Division was visited by General Sir Bernard Law Montgomery accompanied by Secretary of State for War Sir Anthony Eden. The latter made a second visit to Division HQ four days later, which also played host to the Major-General Commanding the Brigade of Guards on 23 August.[12] One infantry platoon commander from the 3ʳᵈ Battalion Irish Guards, Lieutenant Brian Wilson, referred to the period as 'an idle life' and recalled an inter-brigade boxing tournament between the Irish and Welsh Guards that jammed approach roads with vehicles in a manner reminiscent of the German withdrawal across the Seine at Oissel, and to his Battalion organising a party for local French children.[13] There were a hundred children for whom the Battalion Quartermaster, a Lieutenant R. Hastings, managed to provide food while they were entertained by the Battalion pipers and motorcyclists performing riding tricks.[14] Lieutenant Robert Boscawen, a Troop Commander with the 1ˢᵗ (Armoured) Battalion, Coldstream Guards, appears to have been typical in spending much of the time dining with acquaintances in other units in the Division, sightseeing as far afield as Mont St. Michel on the US side of the invasion area and a period at a rest camp on the coast at St. Aubin-sur-Mer inland from the JUNO landing beaches.[15] The sojourn ended in the last days of August when the Division was assigned to Horrocks' 30 Corps for the breakout across northern France, starting with a Movement Order on 27 August for a move to the area of L'Aigle-Verneuil-La Ventreuse, sixty miles to the east and halfway to the River Seine.[16]

Despite the traffic problems encountered en route, the 43rd Division was in place on the south bank of the River Seine by Friday 25 August, the same day US troops liberated Paris. The town of Vernon, located approximately forty miles north-west of Paris and which boasted a road and a rail bridge, was selected as the crossing point, although the road bridge was badly damaged and the rail bridge had been partially demolished. The attackers therefore employed wooden storm boats capable of carrying twenty troops, and the crossing commenced in the early evening of 25 August under cover of smoke after a fifteen-minute artillery barrage. The assault wave suffered a number of casualties from enemy fire after some craft became grounded on submerged islands, and subsequent waves were thus delayed until after dark; by dawn on 26 August more than a battalion of infantry had established a foothold on the north bank. In the course of the day, high ground overlooking the crossing site was secured despite several German counter-attacks, while engineers constructed a bridge capable of carrying light armoured vehicles; a number of tanks were ferried across the river early the next morning. By 28 August the whole of the 43rd Division was firmly ensconced on the east bank of the Seine, having expanded the bridgehead to a depth of four miles at a cost of 550 casualties. The Vernon crossing was quickly followed by additional bridgeheads downstream at Louviers and Elbeuf on 27 and 28 August respectively.[17]

The tentative German plan had been to hold on the Seine for around seven days, while a coherent defence line was organised further east, but this was overtaken by US forces crossing the Seine at a number of points to the south-east of Vernon. *Generalfeldmarschall* Walther Model, the commander of *Heeresgruppe* B, consequently ordered a sixty-mile withdrawal to the River Somme on Friday 25 August. *II SS Panzerkorps* was allotted the task of protecting the withdrawal, and *Obergruppenführer* Bittrich issued the necessary orders two days later, while his constituent formations were still withdrawing across the Seine at Duclair and Oissel. Both Divisions were to despatch all rear echelon elements and vehicles eastward and amalgamate their combat elements into *kampgruppen* (battlegroups) to cover the withdrawal to the new line. *Brigadeführer* Harmel's *Frundsberg* appears to have moved off first, arriving at Beauvais as ordered on 29 August while the 3,500 strong *Hohenstaufen Kampfgruppe*, commanded by *Obersturmbannführer* Walther Harzer, moved off for Amiens via Neufchâtel the same day. Harzer appears to have succeeded *Standartenführer* Bock as division commander on 29 August, which is presumably why the latter had been specifically ordered to accompany the division's rear echelon elements directly to the Dutch border.[18]

However, events had once again overtaken German intentions. After crossing the Seine via a newly constructed Class 9 pontoon bridge, the 11th Armoured Division led a breakout from the Vernon bridgehead at 06:00 on Monday 28 August directly along *II SS Panzerkorps'* line of withdrawal to Amiens and Beauvais.[19] The *Hohenstaufen Kampfgruppe* was thus ordered out of Amiens in the afternoon of Wednesday 30 August to establish a blocking position north-west of Laon. The move came in the nick of time, for elements of the 11th Armoured Division entered Amiens early the next morning after a night march in heavy rain. One Troop from the 23rd Hussars took the opportunity to refuel their Shermans at a civilian filling station in the town centre, and reconnaissance troops from the 2nd Fife and Forfar Yeomanry captured the commander of *7 Armee*, *General der Panzertruppe* Heinrich Eberbach, who was trying to establish contact with his units accompanied by *Oberstgruppenführer* Sepp Dietrich, commander of *5 Panzer Armee*, who managed to escape. According to one source, a Corporal Byrne took Eberbach prisoner while the latter was eating his breakfast,[20] but an intelligence summary issued by the British 2nd Army HQ clearly stated that *General* Eberbach was captured travelling in a

Volkswagen after his staff car had been shot up, presumably by Allied aircraft.[21] Whatever the truth of the matter, the two main bridges over the River Somme in the centre of Amiens were secured by late morning and by evening 11th Armoured Division had handed over to the 50th Division in preparation to continue the advance.[22]

Harmel had meanwhile been ordered to pull the *Frundsberg* back from Beauvais to the River Somme. There he subdivided his force into two parts commanded by *Standartenführer* Otto Paetsch and *Obersturmbannführer* Schultze. *Kampfgruppe* Paetsch was despatched to defend Bray and *Kampfgruppe* Schultze to defend Peronne – the latter unwittingly drew the short straw in the process. The fall of Amiens obliged Schultze to withdraw to Albert to avoid being cut off, and his arrival coincided with another general withdrawal order from *Heeresgruppe B*, this time all the way to a line running from Antwerp to Maastricht on the Belgian-Dutch border. Schultze was ordered to hold Albert 'to the last man' in order to cover this withdrawal, which he did, firstly against reconnaissance troops from B Squadron, 2nd Household Cavalry and then Grenadier Guards tanks and infantry from the 5th Guards Armoured Brigade. The SS rebuffed attempts to break into the town, knocking out several tanks in the process, after which the Guards maintained a screen around the town until relieved by elements of the 50th Division, possibly 231 Infantry Brigade.[23] The latter then attacked and cleared *Kampfgruppe* Schultze from Albert in a house-to-house battle that went on throughout Friday 1 September and into the night, during which *Obersturmbannführer* Schultze was killed; a handful of SS survivors managed to break contact in the early hours of Saturday 2 September. *Kampfgruppe* Paetsch was more fortunate, holding its position in Bray until dark on 1 September before withdrawing to Cambrai where it made passing contact with the *Hohenstaufen Kampfgruppe*.[24] It then continued moving north-east, fighting a sharp action against elements of the 2nd Irish Guards holding Douai, twelve miles north of Cambrai, in the process.[25] Meanwhile the *Hohenstaufen Kampfgruppe* had abandoned its ordered move to Laon to avoid being cut off by armoured columns from the US 19th Corps, and instead withdrew north-east to Cambrai. There, like Schultze, Harzer was ordered to support the general withdrawal to the Antwerp-Maastricht line, in this instance by denying the Allies access to Cambrai and thus the routes running into Belgium until nightfall on 2 September. To this end, Harzer therefore deployed *SS Flak Abteilung 9's* eighteen 88-mm anti-aircraft guns in the anti-tank role covering the roads from Arras and Bapaume, set *SS Panzer Pionier Abteilung 9* to demolishing nearby canal bridges and tasked the survivors of *SS Panzergrenadier Regiments 19* and *20* to protect the *flak* guns. Preparations were complete by 09:00 on 2 September. According to Harzer, his position was then attacked by a force of 200 US tanks whose advance was only stymied by the Escaut Canal, despite losing forty tanks to the *Hohenstaufen's* guns by 15:00.[26] Interestingly, the US official history does not mention any such epic battle at Cambrai, and the sole reference to the town is connected to it being a stop-line for the US 5th Armored Division running to Cambrai from Landrecies, a few miles to the east. Most US units reportedly ran out of fuel in the region of Landrecies on 2 September before reaching the stop-line, and by the afternoon of 3 September the '...only resistance, encountered near Landrecies, had been overcome without difficulty. Relatively few prisoners were taken'.[27]

Be that as it may, according to Harzer *SS Flak Abteilung 9* had somehow lost most of its guns by the time the *Hohenstaufen Kampfgruppe* withdrew after dark on 2 September toward Mons, thirty-eight miles to the north-east. In the process the fifteen vehicles carrying Harzer and his command group became separated from the main body. After spending daylight on 3 September hiding around the Canadian First World War memorial in Bourlon Wood just outside Cambrai, they made their way to safety by travelling under cover of darkness over successive nights, inadvertently but fortuitously following the boundary between the British 2nd and US 1st Armies; according to Harzer the journey also involved disguising his own vehicles with Allied recognition panels, brazenly looting unattended Allied vehicles, and using his *SS Feldgendarmerie* to halt Allied columns and allow progress where necessary.[28] Meanwhile, the bulk of the *Kampfgruppe* paused for several hours en route to allow the command group to catch up, possibly at Valenciennes where one of *SS Flak Abteilung 9*'s batteries were obliged to abandon a number of their seriously wounded to become POWs under the care of a medical orderly named Gottschalk after their vehicle broke down.[29] The withdrawal to Mons was resumed when Harzer's party failed to appear. There the *Kampfgruppe* was joined by *Hauptsturmführer* Klaus von Allwörden and *SS Panzerjäger Abteilung 9*, which had recently arrived by rail from East Prussia with twenty-one *Panzerjäger* IV tank destroyers. Some of these were damaged by Allied fighter bombers while being unloaded and others were lost in hasty rearguard actions, probably against the US 1st Infantry and 3rd Armored Divisions. The latter occupied Mons on 3 September after performing a spectacular ninety-degree shift in its line of advance to block the German line of retreat to the north-east, while elements of the US 5th and 19th Corps pressed in from the south and west respectively.[30] The *Hohenstaufen Kampfgruppe* evaded the trap at Mons and reached the *II SS Panzerkorps* assembly point at Hasselt in eastern Belgium on 5 September, where it was reunited with Harzer and his command group. After a day's respite, what remained of 9 and 10 SS *Panzer Divisions* moved again, following two routes north into Holland via Eindhoven and Venlo to their final assembly area near Arnhem, where they arrived on 7 and 8 September 1944 respectively.[31]

Although they had no way of knowing, the *Frundsberg* and *Hohenstaufen Kampfgruppen* had only been a step ahead of 30 Corps and the Guards Armoured Division during their retreat, and sometimes not even that. The Guards Armoured Division began its move to the front on 28 August, with three RASC companies carrying the tanks on transporters while the infantry elements moved in their own troop-carrying vehicles.[32] In the event the move did not stop at L'Aigle but transformed into a tactical advance to the River Seine and beyond in the wake of the 11th Armoured Division. The Grenadier Guards Group led 5th Guards Armoured Brigade across the Seine at Vernon on 29 August with Division HQ following the next day, and on 31 August launched Operation SUPERCHARGE II; by nightfall the Division's lead elements had advanced some eighty-five miles, receiving the first of many triumphal greetings from French civilians at Beauvais in the process.[33] The following day the Coldstream Guards Group and the 2nd Welsh Guards liberated Arras,[34] while the 2nd Household Cavalry and the Grenadier Guards Group clashed with and then masked *Kampfgruppe* Schultze at Albert. With Arras secured the 2nd (Armoured) Battalion Irish Guards was brought up from reserve at 17:30 on 1 September, reinforced with a company from 5th Battalion Coldstream Guards, and ordered to move immediately on Douai fifteen miles further east. The move was carried out without incident, apart from running across a mob of French civilians intent on lynching a 'disagreeable' German officer with a car packed with looted brandy. On arrival, the Battalion commander disposed Nos. 1, 2 and 3 Squadrons to cover the roads to Arras, Lille and Cambrai respectively before meeting with the mayor of Douai and after a round of speeches and toasts ascertained that the Germans were in fact retiring from Lille by persuading the mayor to telephone his counterpart there. At 21:30 No. 3 Squadron's roadblock was attacked by *Kampfgruppe* Paetsch as it retired from Cambrai. In the ensuing fight Troop commander Lieutenant John Swann was killed and the crew of another tank led by a Sergeant Mews were taken prisoner but escaped later. Six German vehicles were set ablaze and the SS broke contact and bypassed the roadblock, leaving approximately a dozen dead behind.[35]

After pausing for forty-eight hours at Douai, the Guards Armoured Division resumed the advance on 3 September, moving north-east along two parallel tracks toward the Belgian border. The Grenadier Guards Group on the left covered only fourteen miles before becoming embroiled in a three-hour battle with the German defenders of Pont á Marq that cost them twenty-two dead and thirty-one wounded; German losses totalled 125 dead and the same number of prisoners.[36] Nonetheless, the Division's lead elements crossed the Belgian border at 13:30 and orders were issued to continue the advance to Brussels during the afternoon. Just over eight hours after crossing the border a scout car from A Squadron, 2nd Household Cavalry was in the centre of Brussels, closely followed by a Welsh Guards tank commanded by Lieutenant J. A. W. Dent. The reaction of the civilian population was ecstatic, to the extent that the Guards had great difficulty in moving through the celebrating crowds to their assigned locations. This was especially problematic as there were still many Germans in Brussels. Lieutenant Dent had shot up a German bus and knocked out a tank on his move into the city for example, and the tanks accompanying Lieutenant Brian Wilson of the 3rd Irish Guards fought a brief action against a German anti-tank gun en route to establishing a roadblock at the Forêt de la Soigne on the south-east edge of the city. Wilson's men subsequently shot up several German vehicles that tried to force the roadblock in the course of the night, and were in turn subjected to an ineffectual machine-gunning by some retreating German tanks after first light.[37]

By 4 September the situation in Brussels had stabilised sufficiently for the Guards Armoured Division commander, Major-General Allan Adair, to make an official entry into Brussels at 14:00, having spent the previous night with his HQ on the city's outskirts.[38] The Division as a whole remained in the Belgian capital for a further forty-eight hours, which was spent in reorganisation and maintenance by many units. Although there is no mention in the official and unit histories, a participant account claims that the pause at Brussels was also necessary to allow supplies, and especially fuel, to catch up with 30 Corps' rapid advance.[39] However, this is not fully borne out by the Division War Diary daily fuel stock entries, which records higher fuel stocks on the day of the Division's arrival in Brussels than it possessed on arrival at Arras and Albert, and approximately the same stocks between leaving Douai, arriving in Brussels and pushing on from the latter.[40] Neither does the Guards Armoured Division appear to have been short of organic logistic support in spite of being transferred to 30 Corps at short notice and then being pitched into an open-ended advance across northern France and Belgium virtually straight from the approach march. The Division's logistic tail, dubbed the Administrative Group, was engaged on tasks for British 8th Corps and 2nd Army when Guards Armoured was ordered to move up, prompting Lieutenant-Colonel W. M. Sale from the Division's Quarter Master General section to raise the matter with Lieutenant-General Horrocks in person. The latter appears to have permitted additional time for the Administrative Group to concentrate and reorganise.[41]

Not all the Guards Armoured Division's formations spent the pause in Brussels resting or carrying out maintenance. At 13:00 on 4 September No. 3 Squadron, 2nd Irish Guards were ordered south to Waterloo to assist the Belgian resistance deal with a reported force of 200 Germans supported by three tanks. The Belgian estimate was treated with some scepticism until Lieutenant W. C. T. McFetridge's Sherman was knocked out by a Panther and the Battalion commander, Lieutenant-Colonel John Vandeleur, lost his scout car to enemy fire. A *Panzer* IV was knocked out in return before the Guards withdrew, with Lieutenant McFetridge and his crew swimming a nearby river to rejoin the Battalion; as the Battalion War Diary drily observed, 'The second battle of Waterloo was not as successful as the first.'[42] While all this was going on D Squadron, 2nd Household Cavalry and the Grenadier Guards Group had been despatched to secure the university town of Louvain, eighteen miles east of Brussels. On arrival a Household Cavalry Troop commanded by Lieutenant T. F. J. Hanbury seized an intact bridge over the River Dyle in the town centre and held out against determined German counter-attacks until relieved by the Grenadiers. The arrival of the latter effectively ended German resistance and prompted another celebratory outburst by the local civilian population, after which the Guards established a perimeter and spent the subsequent twenty-four hours patrolling and rounding up German stragglers.[43]

Major-General Adair issued orders for a continuation of the advance across the Belgian border into Holland during a conference on 5 September, following a route through Eindhoven, Grave and Nijmegen to Arnhem; it is unclear if Adair was informed at this time but the British 1st Airborne Division and attached 1st Polish Independent Parachute Brigade were slated to support the advance by seizing water crossings ahead of the advance, codenamed Operation COMET.[44] The first stage was an advance up to and across the Albert Canal, and the Division began to move out of Brussels at first light the following day. The advance was again a two-pronged affair screened by the Household Cavalry, with the Grenadier Guards Group leading the 5th Guards Armoured Brigade toward a bridge over the Canal near Oosthem. The Welsh Guards tanks and 32nd Guards Brigade headed for Beeringen, five miles to the south-east, and only ten miles from *II SS Panzerkorps'* assembly point at Hasselt. The survivors of the *Hohenstaufen* and *Frundsberg Divisions* appear to have departed for Arnhem as the Guards Armoured Division commenced its advance from Brussels. In the event, the advance on Oosthem was halted when 2nd Household Cavalry patrols reported that the bridge there had been destroyed, and the 5th Guards Armoured Brigade was instructed to use the crossing at Beeringen, where the Welsh Guards had discovered the bridge to be only partially demolished. On being informed by a Belgian civilian that the Germans were withdrawing, the 1st Welsh Guards moved quickly and pushed Lieutenant J. F. R. Burchell's Carrier Platoon across the damaged structure, closely followed by the Battalion's rifle companies. While they established a defensive perimeter, men from the Division's RE contingent set about assembling a temporary bridge for light traffic from barges and repairing the bridge proper, which, despite heavy rain and German shelling, was declared fit for heavy vehicles in the early hours of 7 September. The 2nd Welsh Guards' tanks, which had been employed in patrolling out to the flanks, then crossed to link up with their infantry brethren from the 1st Welsh Guards and prepared advance to the Meuse-Escaut Canal, fifteen miles or so to the north.[45]

It was at this point that Guards Armoured ran into the first properly organised German resistance encountered by 30 Corps since crossing the River Seine, and began paying the price for the enforced two-day halt at Brussels. As we have seen, *Generalfeldmarschall* Model at *Heeresgruppe B* had ordered a general withdrawal to a line running from Antwerp to Maastricht on 1 September, but this was undermined by the 11th Armoured Division's liberation of Antwerp on 4 September. This not only disjointed German defensive plans but also cut off *General* Gustav von Zangen's *15 Armee* which had been withdrawing along the French and Belgian coast, leaving it with a single line of retreat across the Scheldt estuary into Holland. The loss of Antwerp also prompted the German high command to step in over *Heeresgruppe B*, with *Generaloberst* Alfred Jodl, chief of staff at *OKW*, ordering the creation of a new front along the line of the Albert Canal. The defence was entrusted to *Generaloberst* Kurt Student, head of German Airborne Forces, who was placed in command of the newly created 1 *Fallschirmjäger Armee* which was to be formed from units scattered across northern Germany including *176 Infanterie Division* and a *kranken* (ill) formation made up of men with medical and physical disabilities stationed near Aachen. Units from these formations began to arrive on the new line from 6 September.

In the meantime the *Wehrmachtbefehlshaber Niederlande, General der Flieger* Friedrich Christiansen, was ordered to plug the gap with whatever troops he had to hand. At the time the Guards Armoured Division was paused at Brussels these amounted to a handful of Dutch *SS* internal security units, some *Luftwaffe* and *Kriegsmarine* training units and *Generalleutnant* Karl Sievers' *719 Infanterie Division*. The latter was a *festung* (fortress) unit made up mainly of overage personnel, which had been deployed on the Dutch coast since 1940. It was ordered to move south and dig in along the northern bank of the Albert Canal on 4 September, where Sievers was fortuitously assisted by the unilateral actions of *Generalleutnant* Kurt Chill. The latter had arrived at his designated assembly point at Turnhout near the Belgian-Dutch border on 4 September with the remnants of his *85 Infanterie Division* on 4 September, accompanied by elements of *84* and *89 Infanterie Divisions* gathered up during the retreat from France. Although he had been ordered to take his Division back to Germany to rest and refit, on hearing of the fall of Brussels and Antwerp Chill instead moved south and deployed his formation along the stretch of the Albert Canal backed by the Meuse-Escaut Canal, which was coincidentally directly astride 30 Corps' line of advance. Reception posts were organised on crossings over the Albert Canal to redirect troops from the flood of personnel moving east to safety; the flow appears to have peaked on 5 September, the day dubbed *Gekke Dinsdag* (Mad Tuesday) by Dutch civilians who witnessed it. Chill reported his dispositions and battle readiness to the local *Korps* commander, *General der Infanterie* Hans Reinhard, the same day and was promptly reinforced with a regiment from *719 Infanterie Division* and had his polyglot command renamed *Kampfgruppe* Chill; he may also have been responsible for the destruction of the Albert Canal crossings.[46]

The Welsh Guards Group appears to have run into elements of *Kampfgruppe* Chill on the morning of 7 September. The Beeringen perimeter was left in the hands of a company from the Scots Guards, reinforced later by the 2nd and 3rd Irish Guards while the Welsh Guards Group advanced east toward Helchteren on the main road running north over the Meuse Escaut Canal to Eindhoven. Before moving, the Welsh Guards battalions broke up into their constituent units and paired each tank squadron with an infantry company, which formed the basic tactical unit thereafter. This pairing by cap badge appears to have been an exclusively idiosyncratic Guards Armoured Division practice that dated back to the July fighting in Normandy, when armoured and motorised infantry battalions were permanently grouped by regimental cap badge across the formal brigade structure; this differed from the standard British armoured division way of doing things, where tank and infantry units remained under the control of their respective brigade structures and were only teamed up on a temporary basis for specific tasks. The Guards practice was good from a tribal regimental affiliation perspective, but even one of the Divisional histories admitted that treating armoured reconnaissance and motorised infantry battalions like their standard tank and infantry equivalents nullified their special training and superior cross-country vehicle and communications equipment. More importantly, it also involved '…sacrificing some of the flexibility innate in the organisation of an Armoured Division'.[47] As we shall see, it was also to prove a serious hindrance when the Guards Armoured Division was tasked to carry out Operation GARDEN.

Nevertheless, the Welsh Guards groupings made good progress at first, capturing Helchteren and overrunning a German battalion drawn up for a parade of some kind on the road in the process, killing many and taking 150 prisoners. Resistance stiffened thereafter however, and especially after the advance was reoriented north toward the crossroads village of Hechtel, where newly arrived troops from Student's 1 *Fallschirmjäger Armee* fought the British advance to a standstill on the evening of 7 September, despite the 2nd Welsh Guards' tanks inflicting heavy casualties.[48] A second attack the following day secured a lodgement on the edge of the village but another on 9 September failed to make any headway, and the Germans responded with a determined counter-attack in the evening that cut off a Scots Guards company operating with the Welsh Guards Group. Hechtel was finally taken on Tuesday 12 September after two days of house-to-house fighting. At least 150 *Fallschirmjäger* were killed in the course of the five-day battle and a further 720 were captured, including over 200 wounded. Three tanks, thirteen guns and numerous machine-guns and mortars were also recovered.[49] The check at Hechtel on 7 September raised the risk of the Welsh Guards spearhead being cut off by German forces located west of the axis of advance, and especially those holding Bourg Leopold and Heppen on the ten miles of road running west from Hechtel to the northward loop of the Albert Canal. This was underscored by a strong German counter-attack against the Beeringen bridgehead after the Welsh Guards Group had passed through en route to Helchteren. The Coldstream Guards Group was thus ordered forward in the early hours of 8 September to secure Bourg Leopold, five miles west of Hechtel. The initial attack was rebuffed with the loss of several tanks, apparently due in part to a lack of artillery support, but a subsequent flanking attack by an infantry company commanded by Major J. Chandos-Pole cleared the town in a close-quarter, house-to-house fight.[50] Opposition at Heppen was equally determined, and this appears to have been exacerbated by demands for haste. Ordered to secure the village before dark, infantry from the lead Squadron/Company team penetrated as far as the railway station but were unable to dislodge the defenders, and three of their supporting tanks were knocked out by German self-propelled guns and at least one Panther. More self-propelled gunfire disjointed a flanking move around the west of the village, separating tanks and infantry, and the tanks were obliged to withdraw after the lead vehicle was knocked out after being mistakenly informed that the Germans had been cleared from that sector of the village.[51] Infantry losses had also been severe. Several officers including Major Chandos-Pole had become casualties, and one rifle company was cut off for a time.[52]

The attack was thus suspended until the morning of 9 September, when it was resumed with substantial artillery support, and Heppen was cleared after a short but intense fight, and at heavy cost to the Guards. No. 3 Company, 5th Coldstream Guards lost all its officers killed or wounded in the renewed attack and command devolved to Company Sergeant Major James Cowley, who rallied the Company, established communications with the accompanying tanks and consolidated his men on the objective; he was awarded the Distinguished Conduct Medal for his efforts on 1 March 1945.[53] With Heppen secured, the Coldstream Group handed over to the 15th/19th Hussars on the evening of 9 September, and withdrew to south of the Albert Canal to regroup and reorganise. The two-day fight for Bourg Leopold and Heppen cost the 1st Coldstream Guards nine dead and seventeen wounded including four officers, while the 5th Coldstream Guards lost four officers and twenty two men killed and six officers and sixty-three men wounded; the Divisional War Diary records a total of twelve tank casualties for the day, although some of these appear to have been lost in the fighting at nearby Hechtel.[54] The fight at Heppen was also the Coldstream Guards' first contact with the 88mm armed *Jagdpanther*, one of which knocked out at least one of the 1st Coldstream Guards' Shermans at point-blank range, the armour-piercing shell amputating one of the commander's legs and killing two of the crew in the process. It was knocked out later in Hechtel, and appears to have ended up on display in the Imperial War Museum in London.[55]

Nor was the fighting restricted to the troops pushing forward into German-held territory. As we have seen, the Germans launched a strong counter-attack against the Beeringen perimeter just after the Welsh Guards Group had passed through en route to Helchteren, followed by heavy and accurate mortar and artillery fire directed from observation posts located in the mining spoil heaps that overlooked the bridgehead. The 3rd Irish Guards therefore launched a company attack to clear the spoil heaps in the evening of 6 September, supported by the 2nd Irish Guards tanks and fire support from an attached Royal Northumberland Fusiliers' machine-gun company and 55 Field Regiment RA. Although soft ground hindered the movement of the supporting tanks, the attack succeeded in expanding the perimeter and clearing the spoil heaps but at the cost of nine dead and nineteen wounded. This resulted in a marked diminution in the accuracy of the German mortar and artillery fire, although it remained a constant menace; four Irish Guards officers were wounded by mortar bombs, possibly at a conference of some kind, early in the morning of 8 September, for example. The Guards' role in protecting Beeringen ended later the same day when they were relieved by the Dutch *Prinses Irene* Brigade. Perhaps predictably, the latter's arrival was soon greeted by yet another German counter-attack.[56]

***

While 30 Corps was pursuing *II SS Panzerkorps* across northern France, Belgium and into Holland, the upper echelons of the Allied airborne force in the UK had been adapting to a modified command structure designed to streamline and regularise co-ordination between its British and US elements. By 1944 the former comprised the 1st and 6th Airborne Divisions, grouped into 1 Airborne Corps commanded by Lieutenant-General Frederick Browning from his HQ at Moor Park, just north of London, which also had responsibility for the 1st Polish Independent Parachute Brigade and 1st Special Air Service Brigade. These formations were joined in the summer by the 52nd (Lowland) Division, an Airportable formation that had originally been configured for mountain warfare. The US contingent consisted of the 82nd and 101st Airborne Divisions, which returned to the UK in mid-July 1944 after spearheading the Normandy invasion. Both formations came under the command of Major-General Matthew B. Ridgway's newly created US 18th Airborne Corps from 25 August 1944; Ridgway's command was expanded within twenty-four hours by the arrival of the US 17th Airborne Division from the continental US. The idea of bringing all Allied airborne formations and air transport units under a single unified command was raised by Allied supreme commander General Dwight D. Eisenhower in May 1944. The intention appears to have been to rationalise administration and planning and to enhance and regularise co-operation between the British and US forces, which was already occurring in an *ad hoc*, piecemeal manner. By mid-1944 US Pathfinders were equipped with the British Eureka/Rebecca radar homing device for guiding aircraft onto drop zones for example, and US units were also adopting the British practice of equipping paratroopers with leg-mounted kit bags for weapons and extraneous kit.[57]

Perhaps most importantly, a merged overall command would have permitted a more efficient allocation of air transport assets. This was a matter of some urgency, given that the British were becoming increasingly reliant upon USAAF resources owing to the ongoing failure of the Air Ministry to supply sufficient aircraft and personnel to lift more than a fraction of the British Airborne force. SHAEF had already made some effort in this direction by issuing a set of guidelines entitled 'Standard Operating Procedure for Airborne and Troop Carrier Units' in March 1944, although this does not appear to have improved matters much, at least in the short term. At the end of the following month the commander of the 4ᵗʰ Parachute Brigade, Brigadier John Hackett, compiled a list of complaints from his battalion commanders following Exercise DOROTHY, a two-day affair that began on 8 April with a jump from USAAF C-47s. The complaints ranged from insufficient sheltered accommodation, inadequate canteen provision and poor latrine arrangements to poor ground liaison, late aircrew and ignorance of British 'Standing Orders for Parachuting' and drop cancellation signals.[58] To be fair, some of this may have stemmed from differing operational practices rather than incompetence, as US parachute units trained and provided their own jumpmasters while their British counterparts relied on RAF aircrew, but even then, misunderstandings over such basic matters during training did not augur well for combat operations.

This and similar incidents likely underlay Eisenhower's suggestion for a combined Allied Airborne HQ, and SHAEF issued a proposal to that effect on 2 June 1944. The idea was endorsed by Eisenhower's superior, General George C. Marshall, and the head of the USAAF Major-General Henry 'Hap' Arnold on the US side, and on the British by Montgomery and presumably, given that he was looking to be appointed head of the new command, Browning. Enthusiasm was not universal on the US side, however. Lieutenant-General Omar Bradley, commander of the US 1ˢᵗ Army, Ridgway and the commander of the 82ⁿᵈ Airborne Division considered the proposed new command level an unnecessary bureaucratic burden, and were also in favour of deploying the US Airborne force in support of US ground operations, as it had been hitherto in Sicily and Normandy. They were concerned that any joint command structure would be dominated by the British and more specifically, that it might place the US airborne divisions under Browning's command, a worry born from first-hand experience of his high-handed behaviour and empire-building tendencies. Ridgway had commanded the 82ⁿᵈ Airborne Division throughout its deployment to the Mediterranean theatre, and during preparations for the invasion of Sicily Browning had turned up unannounced at his HQ at Oujda. Browning had installed himself as Eisenhower's adviser on airborne matters despite having little practical and no operational experience. He had no official authority and both men were nominally equal in rank. Nonetheless, Browning proceeded to lay out his own scheme for the operation that made it clear he would be in charge before unsuccessfully demanding to see Ridgway's plans, at which point the meeting ended on a 'testy note'. Within days Browning had reinforced Ridgway's suspicion that he viewed the US Airborne force as part of his personal fiefdom by carrying out an inspection of the US 509ᵗʰ Parachute Infantry Battalion and then attempting to make the US unit an honorary member of British Airborne Forces complete with maroon berets, all without any reference whatever to the US chain of command.[59] Undoubtedly, part of the problem was a clash of personalities, for Browning's immaculate Guards turnout and bearing presented a privileged stereotype guaranteed to upset the egalitarian sensibilities of even the most Anglophile American, while Ridgway was a rather pompous individual convinced of his destined greatness. Nonetheless, Ridgway was not alone in his suspicions, even allowing for personal enmity, which was amply reciprocated by Browning as then Colonel and later Major-General James M. Gavin was to discover.

In November 1943 Colonel Gavin was posted temporarily as an airborne adviser to the Staff Supreme Allied Command (COSSAC) staff in London. At a final pre-departure briefing Ridgway warned Gavin to beware of Browning's 'machinations and scheming', and in the event he received a graphic demonstration almost immediately on arrival. Gavin was greeted by COSSAC British Chief of Staff, Lieutenant-General Frederick Morgan, in the latter's office in St. James's Square. While the niceties were underway they were joined by Browning, who interjected a snide and unwarranted remark into the conversation, criticising Ridgway for not jumping into Sicily with his unit the previous July. Gavin tactfully expressed the opinion that Ridgway had handled his command well in the circumstances and that his commander's responsibilities extended further than just the initial parachute assault. Although his account is quite matter-of-fact, the incident appears to have made an impression on Gavin, given that he specifically mentioned it shortly afterward to his new superior, Major-General Raymond Barker. The latter responded with the telling remark 'Ah yes, he is an empire builder.'[60] At best, Browning's remark was crass and ill mannered, especially for a supposed military diplomat. At worst, it was simply hypocritical given that Browning lacked any operational Airborne experience whatsoever, or indeed formal parachute qualification. Ridgway had carried out a successful voluntary parachute jump at Fort Benning in mid-August 1942, even though as a divisional staff officer he was not required to do so and despite him suffering the long-term consequences of a serious back injury sustained in a riding accident at West Point. Neither did Ridgway's lack of formal parachute training prevent him making a fully equipped combat jump into Normandy with his Division on D-Day.[61] For his part, Browning made only two training jumps and injured himself both times, and while he did subsequently qualify as a glider pilot, this was flying the General Aircraft Hotspur which, as little more than a militarised sport glider, was nothing like as demanding as the heavier Horsa and Hamilcar types flown operationally by the Glider Pilot Regiment.[62] Their respective qualifications aside, Browning's comment to Gavin inadvertently revealed the underlying reason for his antipathy toward Ridgway. Browning had originally been appointed to an Airborne command for administrative rather than operational reasons, but had nonetheless turned British Airborne Forces into his personal fiefdom.[63] However, from 1943 onward the number of demonstrably able and operationally experienced officers coming through the system increased as the Allied Airborne establishment and deployments expanded, to the point where political connections and acumen were no longer sufficient for maintaining position or securing advancement. Consequently, from Browning's perspective Ridgway posed an intolerable threat to his ambition of becoming head of a unified Allied airborne structure, because the American was simply better qualified in virtually all areas.

In the event Browning did beat Ridgway in securing the highest Army Airborne appointment although concern over the insecurity of his position was to play a crucial and seriously deleterious role in shaping subsequent Allied airborne operations. The SHAEF proposal was approved by Eisenhower on 20 June 1944 and the 1st Allied Airborne Army was formally created on 2 August, with a HQ at Sunninghill Park, Ascot, and an Advanced HQ at Maison Lafitte near Paris. It was commanded by USAAF Lieutenant-General Lewis H. Brereton, formerly the head of the US 9th Air Force, with Browning appointed as his deputy commander.[64] The establishment of the new command was the result of a series of compromises that actually created more conflict than convergence. Placing an airman in charge of the Airborne arm was met with disquiet by many Army officers. The commander of the Allied Expeditionary Air Force, Air Chief Marshal Sir Trafford Leigh-Mallory, was unhappy at relinquishing control of the US 9th Troop Carrier Command while the Air Ministry were similarly unhappy at potentially losing control of the RAF's two transport formations, Nos. 38 and 46 Groups. As a leading and long-standing advocate of air power, Brereton himself considered his appointment a demotion; indeed, he confided in his diary that he 'took a dim view' of his appointment.[65] For his part, Browning was resentful at not attaining the senior post for himself and being obliged to serve under what he viewed as an Airborne parvenu who was four months his inferior by date of rank;

to complicate things yet further the two men did not get on personally either.[66] This antipathy soon developed into a serious clash in early September 1944 over resources and priorities for a provisional operation that led to Browning tendering his resignation in writing after Brereton not only refused to heed his advice, but placed Ridgway on standby to replace him. In the event, the matter was conveniently resolved when Eisenhower cancelled the operation.[67]

The only at least partially satisfied parties in the affair would therefore appear to have been Eisenhower as the author of the idea and who thus presumably saw it as a validation of his conciliatory command style, and the faction led by Bradley who succeeded in preventing the top command appointment going to a British officer and thus placing them in a position to dominate proceedings. Bradley was unhappy with Brereton's performance as head of the US 9th Air Force, holding him personally responsible for the badly scattered delivery of the two US Airborne Divisions into the Cotentin Peninsula on the eve of the Normandy invasion, and for failing to provide adequate air support for Bradley's US 1st Army thereafter. Bradley thus appears to have played a behind-the-scenes role in Brereton's appointment, and reportedly remarked 'Thank goodness' on being informed of the latter's removal from command of the 9th Air Force.[68] The upshot was therefore a largely unwanted and arguably unnecessary new command level headed by two disgruntled and antipathetic senior officers with little if any operational airborne experience. This was arguably the worst of all possible worlds, but was nonetheless the arrangement under which the Allied Airborne force was to fight for the remainder of the war in Europe.

While the upper echelons of the Allied Airborne force were getting to grips with their bureaucratic infighting, the 1st Allied Airborne Army's constituent formations were gearing up for operations. As we have seen, the British 1st Airborne Division, in some instances along with the 52nd (Lowland) Division and smaller units including 1st Polish Independent Parachute Brigade, 1st Special Air Service Regiment and US 504th Parachute Infantry Regiment had spent the period from June to August preparing to varying degrees for eight aborted operations. In order to rationalise the demands upon the airborne force, one of Browning's first acts on assuming deputy command of the 1st Allied Airborne Army was to draw up a schedule of what formations and units could be deployed with what period of notice.[69] By the beginning of August 1944 the US 82nd and 101st Airborne Divisions were also back on the operationally available list. The former had been withdrawn from Normandy on 8 July after losing a total of 5,245 men, 1,282 of whom had been killed. The latter, which had suffered 4,670 casualties and included the highest ranking airborne officer killed in Normandy, Brigadier-General Donald Pratt, left two days later; in both instances the casualty rate equated to around half of both formations' pre-battle strength.[70]

Thus in early August 1944 the 101st Airborne Division was slated alongside the 1st Airborne Division, the 52nd (Lowland) Division and 1st Polish Independent Parachute Brigade to carry out Operation TRANSFIGURATION.[71] The Operation was originally intended to support a US armoured break-out from Normandy, and a warning order on 4 August saw the Pathfinders of the 21st Independent Parachute Company move to RAF Broadwell in preparation to mark drop zones for the 1st Parachute Brigade. The Company was stood down on 6 August when the plan was reconfigured, and interestingly does not appear to have been involved in the Operation thereafter; while the 1st Parachute Brigade's constituent units received their first warning order for TRANSFIGURATION on or around 10 August, the 21st Independent were busy with Exercise STOPGAP, a joint scheme with the US Pathfinder School at North Witham.[72] The Operation was rescheduled for 16 August, with the participating units moving to their marshalling areas, drawing kit and fitting parachutes from 15 August. The Airborne units slated for TRANSFIGURATION also despatched a large sea tail to France, made up of transport and other administrative elements from the Division's constituent units. The 1st Parachute Battalion's Motor Transport section left the Battalion billets at Grimsthorpe Castle in newly issued, factory-fresh Bedford trucks at 20:00 on 12 August, for example. Similarly, the 2nd Parachute Battalion's section left Grantham on the same day and embarked on the SS *Sammesse* at London's West India Docks on 14 August,[73] while the 101st Airborne Division's seaborne element left the Divisional concentration area around Newbury the same day.[74] In the event, TRANSFIGURATION was cancelled on 18 August after a twenty-four-hour postponement because the ground advance had rendered it superfluous; as we have seen, US troops reached the River Seine near Mantes the following day. The fact that SHAEF had directed Allied air transport resources to ferrying supplies for the US 3rd Army might also have had some bearing on the cancellation.[75] Whatever the reason, by the time of cancellation the British sea tail was in France and the fact that it included virtually all the constituent unit's organic transport loaded with the airborne component's spare clothing and kit caused problems until both groupings were reunited at Nijmegen over a month later.[76]

TRANSFIGURATION was joined and then succeeded on 17 August by Operation BOXER, the primary objective of which was the capture of the French port of Boulogne, using the same forces. According to the British official history they remained on standby in their marshalling areas, but the operational records suggest that they returned to their billets before BOXER was officially cancelled on 26 August. The 1st Parachute Battalion, for example, returned to Grimsthorpe Castle on 22 August, assisted RE troops in erecting Nissen huts after carrying out a fifteen-mile forced march on 24 August, and despatched a third of the Battalion on thirty-six hours leave the same day BOXER was cancelled.[77] Interestingly, the 1st Parachute Battalion War Diary makes no mention of that operation, and neither do the 2nd Parachute Battalion or 21st Independent Parachute Company War Diaries. Operation LINNET is the next operation specifically cited after BOXER in all three.[78] BOXER may therefore have been one of the provisional operations that did not move beyond Corps or Divisional planning staffs before being cancelled. Whatever the reason, the cancellation also marked a change in the focus and source of provisional Allied airborne operations. Up to and including BOXER, they had originated with SHAEF, and been focussed upon reinforcing and/or enlarging the beachhead area, or securing dock facilities to assist in supplying the invasion force. Once 1st Allied Airborne Army HQ became active on 2 August however, it assumed responsibility for framing missions, and focussed upon support for the break-out from Normandy.

Thus the next projected mission, codenamed AXEHEAD and scheduled for 25 August, envisaged the 1st Airborne Division and 1st Polish Independent Parachute Brigade securing crossing points over the River Seine; like TRANSFIGURATION it was rendered superfluous by the rapid advance of Allied ground forces detailed above. AXEHEAD was superseded by Operation LINNET, which involved deploying all three of 1st Allied Airborne Army's divisions in the area of Lille on or after 3 September 1944, in order to block the German line of retreat eastward and seize a foothold on the east bank of the River Escaut. LINNET was the reason for the Guards Armored Division's forty-eight-hour pause at Douai from 1 September, and it is unclear from British accounts whether it was cancelled because the Guards Armoured Division resumed the advance toward the Belgian border on 3 September, or whether the latter moved on because LINNET had been cancelled. However, one US participant account refers to the Operation being cancelled on 3 September because Lieutenant-General Courtney H. Hodges' US 1st Army had already reached the objective,[79] which is backed up by another US account that refers to Montgomery ordering Brereton to implement the cancellation at 22:24 on 2 September, after Hodges' troops reached Tournai, just east of Lille.[80] The same account also refers to Bradley unsuccessfully arguing with Eisenhower against LINNET, because it meant diverting airlift from supplying the ground advance, and to Bradley claiming that LINNET cost the latter a minimum of 5,000 tons of supplies.[81]

Either way, the Airborne units again went through the entire sequence of preparation. The 21st Independent Parachute Company again moved to Broadwell on 29 August, and prepared to drop in and mark seven landing areas at first light, twenty minutes ahead of the main force.[82] The 1st Parachute Brigade began to move to their marshalling area after receiving a warning order the same day, while their counterparts from the 101st Airborne Division began the same process two days later.[83] All three divisions remained on stand-by in their respective marshalling areas while

LINNET morphed into LINNET II, which proposed shifting the location of the operation east to the area of Maastricht on the German border. The intention was to exploit the US 1st Army's momentum and assist it in crossing the *Westwall* defences and push into Germany near Aachen, and possibly on up to the River Rhine. The scheme sparked a fierce dispute between Eisenhower, Bradley and Montgomery over the allocation of resources, and the underlying motivations for the resultant dispute between Brereton and Browning vary according to the source. One British source, for example, claims that Browning was motivated by concerns over the haste with which LINNET II was being launched, in particular a lack of maps for junior commanders, and because he was unwilling '...to see his troops thrown carelessly into battle',[84] while a US source suggests that Browning's resignation was a ploy to corner Allied resources for Montgomery's 21st Army Group.[85] The latter would appear to rely largely on the still-popular US view that the British were more interested in exercising their Machiavellian tendencies to gain control over US assets than in fighting the Germans. Browning's conduct and demeanour did little to allay such concerns, and his behaviour hitherto does not really suggest a man overly concerned with the well-being of his subordinates either, quite the contrary. He blatantly interfered with and potentially compromised Frost's plan for the Bruneval raid in February 1942 for example, and he did nothing to rein in Hopkinson's virtually criminal mishandling of the 1st Airlanding Brigade in the invasion of Sicily in July the following year. This tendency was to become even more noticeable during the 1st Allied Airborne Army's deployment into Holland.

LINNET II was cancelled on 5 September, and the cancellation coincided with another shift in the 1st Allied Airborne Army's operational focus, from supporting the Normandy breakout to extending post-break-out exploitation. To this end, the formation was placed at the direct disposal of 21st Army Group, primarily to assist in 30 Corps' advance over the Albert Canal and on into Holland that began the same day. However, one other Airborne operation under the 1st Allied Airborne Army's earlier mandate was briefly considered before attention turned to the new brief. Operation INFATUATE was intended to secure the fortified island of Walcheren in the mouth of the Scheldt Estuary, in order to clear the way for supplies to be run into the port of Antwerp. Walcheren was too small to make a parachute assault a viable option, and the fact that virtually the entire island apart from the perimeter dyke was below sea level, dotted with flooded areas and criss-crossed with dykes effectively ruled out a glider landing. As a result, planning for INFATUATE did not progress beyond the feasibility study stage before it was abandoned.

LINNET II and INFATUATE were succeeded by Operation COMET, scheduled for 8 September and tailored specifically to spearhead 30 Corps' advance into southern Holland. According to Major-General Stanislaw Sosabowski, commanding the 1st Polish Independent Parachute Brigade, COMET was originally dubbed FIFTEEN, being renamed on 5 September; this is supported by the 1st Parachute Brigade and 156 Parachute Battalion War Diaries which both refer to 'Operation Fifteen' on 5 and 7 September respectively.[86] Warning Orders and briefings for the Operation appear to have begun to circulate from as early as 1 September, when the 11th Parachute Battalion was confined to barracks in preparation for the Operation.[87] Sosabowski refers to learning of it on 2 September, but most units received word on or around 6 September, the day the commander of the 1st Airborne Division, Major-General Robert Urquhart, gave a detailed briefing at RAF Cottesmore. The 3rd Parachute Battalion, for example, received the warning order on 4 September and immediately authorised local leave for the troops, before holding a Battalion Orders (O) Group at 17:30 on 6 September.[88] The 1st Parachute Battalion only appears to have received the order on or around 6 September, given that the Battalion War Diary refers to an O Group for COMET being held on the following day.[89]

The COMET plan envisaged the 1st Airborne Division, reinforced with the 1st Polish Independent Parachute Brigade, seizing crossings over the Rivers Maas, Waal and Lower Rhine ahead of 30 Corps' advance. In essence the plan was a slightly modified repeat of the 6th Airborne Division's assault into Normandy the previous June, with an insertion just after first light rather than at night; the original plan appears to have been for the latter, but was possibly altered due to the bad scattering suffered by the 6th Airborne's parachute elements on D-Day. The crossings at Grave were to be seized by the 4th Parachute Brigade, those at Nijmegen by the 1st Airlanding Brigade and 1st Polish Independent, and the 1st Parachute Brigade were responsible for the road and pontoon bridges at Arnhem. The latter, codenamed WATERLOO and PUTNEY respectively, were to be seized in a *coup-de-main* glider attack by a company from the 2nd Battalion South Staffordshire Regiment at 04:30 on D-Day. Two hours and fifteen minutes later, around or just after first light, the 21st Independent Parachute Company was to jump in and mark the main drop and landing zones west of Arnhem proper. They were to be followed at 07:33 by three Hamilcar gliders carrying 1st Parachute Brigade HQ element, followed three minutes later by gliders carrying the 1st Airlanding Anti-Tank Battery. The final glider increment, twenty-five Horsas carrying the 1st Parachute Brigade's vehicles and heavy equipment, was scheduled to arrive fourteen minutes later, at 07:54. The main parachute insertion was to commence at 08:00, spearheaded by the 2nd Parachute Battalion accompanied by a parachute-trained Dutch liaison officer and a party from the Royal Army Service Corps (RASC); the latter was tasked to commandeer vehicles for use by the Airborne force. They were to be followed by the 1st and 3rd Parachute Battalions at five-minute intervals. After reorganising, the force was to move along two parallel routes into Arnhem to relieve the South Staffords holding the bridges: TIGER, running along the Heelsum to Arnhem road through Oosterbeek and LEOPARD, which ran along the northern edge of the latter. The second lift, consisting of twenty Horsas carrying the remainder of the Brigade's non-parachute elements, was scheduled to arrive just before dusk, at 18:41.[90]

The COMET plan was not greeted with unalloyed enthusiasm when Urquhart unveiled it at Cottesmore on Wednesday 6 September, and there were two interlinked matters of concern. These were that the selected drop and landing zones were around seven miles from the objective and that the plan took no account of possible German reaction to the landing, relying on intelligence reports that there were no German forces in the Arnhem area. What appears to have been the general reaction was succinctly summarised by the commander of the 4th Parachute Brigade, Brigadier John Hackett. In common with some of the earlier aborted missions, he condemned COMET as a potential disaster, and laid the blame firmly upon the RAF planners for drawing up plans without regard to anything outside the narrow technical parameters of their craft and with no regard whatsoever for the tactical and operational realities facing the troops they were delivering.[91] Hackett's appreciation was correct with regard to the RAF planner's priorities, which were a matter of deliberate institutional policy rather than merely bureaucratic indifference, the roots of which lay in the inter-service horse trading between the Air Ministry and War Office when the British Airborne force had been established in 1940. On the other hand, Hackett does not appear to have acknowledged the fact that the designated landing zones were the only option available, as there was no suitable terrain closer to Arnhem. Hackett's comments appear to have come after the event, but Sosabowski made his opinion absolutely clear at the time, interrupting Urquhart's briefing several times before uttering his much-quoted query, 'But the Germans, General, the Germans!'[92] Sosabowski's reservations were so strong that he asked Urquhart to confirm his orders in writing on 8 September, the day COMET was to have been launched. As a result, when the Operation was postponed for twenty-four hours due to bad weather and German resistance to 30 Corps' advance over the Albert Canal, Urquhart flew him to Browning's 1 Airborne Corps HQ at Moor Park to explain his case. After trying and failing to brush the matter aside via small talk and flattery, Browning asked Sosabowski for his solution; the Polish commander responded by pointing out that the three individual COMET missions required a division apiece rather than a reinforced brigade.

It is unclear whether or not Sosabowski got his orders in writing, but the matter swiftly became moot. Operation COMET was cancelled at 14:00 on Sunday 10 September, just four hours short of take-off. Unlike the previous fifteen or more cancelled missions, however, that was not to be the end of it, for COMET was not simply abandoned after cancellation. It formed the basis for an expanded mission with the same objectives codenamed MARKET GARDEN.

COMET to MARKET: The Evolution of Operation MARKET

10 September – 11 September 1944

On the surface, the reason for the cancellation of Operation COMET was the resistance presented to the Guards Armoured Division's push across the Albert Canal by *Kampfgruppe* Chill and *1 Fallschirmjäger Armee*. Whilst this was a key factor, the reasons also ran wider and deeper than the immediate tactical situation on the Belgian-Dutch border, and arose from the way in which the pursuit phase of the Falaise breakout across northern France and Belgium had taken on a life of its own. The Supreme Commander of the Allied Expeditionary Force, General Dwight D. Eisenhower, had envisaged a measured and systematic advance on a broad front with a pause to regroup on the River Seine. However, by the beginning of September the Allied advance east from Normandy had not only exceeded expectations in geographic terms but had also split into two divergent axes running north and south of the rugged Ardennes region. As we have seen, in the north Montgomery's 21st Army Group was on the Dutch border, while to the south Patton's 3rd Army had penetrated deep into the French province of Lorraine. This divergence was not a problem in itself, for Eisenhower had anticipated precisely such a development least a month before the invasion was launched; a planning paper from May 1944 explicitly referred to the two axes of advance, with priority being given to the northerly advance into the Ruhr.[1] The problem lay in the speed with which the divergent axes of advance had developed, and more specifically the impact this had upon Allied logistical planning and resources.

This impact was considerable, for it totally derailed Allied logistical arrangements, which were already under considerable strain before Falaise. The Germans had expected the Allies to launch their invasion with the seizure of a major port and had thus expended a great deal of effort and resources to counter such a move. In order to avoid tackling the resulting formidable defences head on, the Allies therefore planned to supply the invasion force over the beach initially via two specially designed and prefabricated harbours codenamed MULBERRY. These were towed across the Channel and assembled in place, MULBERRY A off the OMAHA landing area in the US sector, and MULBERRY B off the GOLD landing area at Arromanches. Both were complete and functioning by 9 June 1944, just three days after the invasion commenced. In the event, MULBERRY A was destroyed by a storm ten days later, on 19 June. Had matters run according to plan this would not have been so serious a setback, for US forces were scheduled to capture the port of Cherbourg on the tip of the Cotentin Peninsula by 21 June, thereby opening an additional, high-capacity supply conduit. However, Cherbourg was not fully secured until 29 June, when the last German defensive fortification surrendered, and as expected the defenders had made the most of the opportunity for demolition.[2] All the cranes and other equipment for servicing the port's deep water quays had been blown into the water with the quays themselves demolished atop them, while the harbour area had been extensively blocked with sunken ships and sown with mines, many of which had also been modified with anti-sweep devices and booby-traps to prevent handling by divers. Clearing the latter cost three minesweepers and seven other vessels, but the outer harbour was able to accept its first deep draught ship on 16 July, although the need to unload vessels via DUKW amphibious trucks restricted the flow of supplies to little more than a relative trickle for a considerable period.[3]

Virtually the entire burden of supplying the Allied invasion lodgement therefore fell upon MULBERRY B. The Falaise breakout morphed the requirement into maintaining a high-speed mechanised advance in excess of 300 miles into eastern France, and efforts to alleviate the situation met with limited success at best. The British 11th Armoured Division had secured the Belgian port of Antwerp, the largest facility of its kind in Europe, on 4 September for example, but the Germans held not only the banks of the River Scheldt leading to the port but also the island of Walcheren in the mouth of the river estuary; as a result, Allied supply vessels were unable to access Antwerp until Walcheren had been secured via an amphibious assault on 8 November 1944. Similarly, the British 49th (West Riding) and 51st (Highland) Divisions, supported by two tank brigades and specialised armour from the 79th Armoured Division, mounted a full-scale assault on the port of Le Havre beginning on 10 September. The port was secured after a two-day battle but as at Cherbourg, the port facilities were so badly damaged that it took until 9 October to make them workable.[4] In the meantime, the lack of Allied access to a major port resulted in a shortage of supplies, especially fuel. This was on occasion alleviated to an extent by utilising captured German stocks, including a warehouse full of salt liberated in Belgium, but fuel was more urgently required and the problem increased with every mile the Allied spearheads moved away from Normandy. By 20 August, for example, the US advance alone was consuming well over 800,000 gallons of fuel per day, and before the end of the month the supply trucks ferrying the fuel up to the front were consuming an additional 300,000 gallons daily.[5]

The supply shortage sparked an intense bout of competition between British and US commanders for what resources were available, which in turn exacerbated already fraught Anglo-American relations. Montgomery had formulated a scheme for a narrow thrust operation through Holland and into the Ruhr and possibly the North German Plain while commanding the Allied invasion lodgement as Commander-in-Chief Allied Ground Forces. The scheme was revealed to Bradley on 17 August in order to elicit support, and then to Lieutenant-Generals Courtney Hodges, Henry Crerar and Sir Miles Dempsey, commanding the US 1st, Canadian 1st and British 2nd Armies respectively, at a specially convened meeting two days later. Montgomery then tried to sell the idea to Eisenhower during a meeting on 23 August, just prior to the latter taking over command of the invasion force in his capacity as Supreme Commander Allied Expeditionary Force on 1 September. The pitch proved to be only a partial success, for Eisenhower refused to allocate all available resources to 21st Army Group and maintained his preference for a broad front advance. He did, however, subsequently agree to give priority to Montgomery's northern thrust and to that end assigned Hodges' US 1st Army to protect the British right flank and allocated control of SHAEF's sole strategic reserve, the 1st Allied Airborne Army, to 21st Army Group control following a subsequent meeting on 4 September. This was done with the caveat that British forces secure the port of Antwerp before the thrust commenced and Montgomery was officially informed of the decision via signal the following day.[6] However, the prospect of being side-lined into a subsidiary role did not go down well with Eisenhower's senior US commanders. By 23 August Bradley appears to have decided to discard his tacit agreement with Montgomery's scheme in favour of a push along the southern Allied axis by the US 12th Army Group towards the Saar industrial region on the Franco-German border. The idea appears to have been to persuade Eisenhower to reverse his decision to give supply priority to Montgomery's 21st Army Group by presenting him with a US *fait accompli*, and to this end Bradley issued a directive to his 12th Army Group on 10 September ordering the US 1st and 3rd

Armies to secure bridgeheads across the River Rhine in the areas of Bonn-Cologne-Koblenz and Mainz-Mannheim respectively.[7] Bradley's thinking was greeted with enthusiasm by Patton, who was convinced that his 3rd Army could advance eastward with impunity because there was nothing between it and the unmanned *Westwall* defences protecting the German border. Patton therefore persuaded Bradley to maintain the 3rd Army advance into Lorraine toward the French garrison city of Metz, which he (Patton) achieved by the simple expedient of intercepting and redirecting ammunition and fuel supplies intended for Hodges' US 1st Army; Patton himself labelled his behaviour the 'stone soup method', analogous to strangers or a tramp wheedling the ingredients for proper soup from unwitting householders.[8] As the 1st Army's supply receipts were running at over a third below minimum at 1,500 tons per day, the impact of Patton's depredations was exacerbated sharply, and drew vociferous complaints from Montgomery when he learned of them.[9]

In the event all this availed Patton little, for the US 3rd Army still literally ran out of fuel on the approaches to Metz, and he was subsequently disabused of the notion that the Germans posed no real obstacle to the advance of his Army. By the end of August 1944 *OKW* had begun implementing measures to seal the approaches to the German frontier, which included bringing in reinforcements from as far afield as Italy; this went some way to explaining the stiff resistance Patton's men encountered in their various pushes across the River Moselle.[10] Furthermore, attempts to force the old fixed defences protecting Metz by attacking Fort Driant from 27 September presented the US Army with its first serious check since the breakout at St. Lô on 25 July and the attempt was finally called off on the night of 12-13 October after bitter fighting; the defences were not finally dealt with until the following month, and then only after a thorough tactical rethink.[11] As the US official History points out, the idea that a chance to win the war in short order was lost by failing to provide the US advance and Patton in particular with the supplies he requested, whilst popular at the time and since, was a chimera. The US advance would have run into resistance stiff enough to bring it to a halt on the Rhine, if not the Moselle, and quite possibly with more severe consequences given the inescapable logistical constraints.[12]

Bradley relayed the content of his 10 September directive to 12th Army Group to Eisenhower on 12 September but he was forty-eight hours too late, for by that time the Supreme Commander had decided to back Montgomery's scheme for a narrow thrust through Holland and into Germany.[13]

Montgomery received a further opportunity to sell an updated version of his scheme employing the entire 1st Allied Airborne Army to Eisenhower on Sunday 10 September, with Deputy Supreme Commander Air Chief Marshal Sir Arthur Tedder in attendance.[14] The meeting took place at Brussels and was held in Eisenhower's aircraft, as he had been rendered almost immobile by a knee injury. The location was also dictated by inadequate communication links with SHAEF Forward HQ, which had relocated from Portsmouth to Granville at the western base of the Cotentin Peninsula on 7 August 1944.[15] The French seaside town was off the beaten track by any measure, and the rapid Allied advance post-Falaise placed it over 400 miles from the scene of the action virtually at a stroke. This was compounded by an inexplicable failure to provide the Forward HQ with anything like adequate communications facilities, to the extent that there were no direct links to SHAEF's subordinate Army Groups, with all the potentially detrimental repercussions that entailed. During the airborne operations in Holland in the latter half of September for example, SHAEF's Air Commander-in-Chief, Air Chief Marshal Sir Trafford Leigh-Mallory, was obliged to plead for information via private telephone calls to members of 21st Army Group staff. Similarly, Eisenhower's 5 September signal allocating supply priority and command of the US 1st Army and 1st Allied Airborne Army to 21st Army Group was not actually despatched in its entirety for several days, with the first half being transmitted 09:00 on 7 September and the remainder at 10:15 two days later.[16] The situation was alleviated somewhat when SHAEF HQ relocated to the Trianon Palace Hotel at Versailles on the outskirts of Paris at the end of September 1944.[17]

There does not appear to be any official record of what took place at the 10 September meeting, and accounts therefore rely on references to it in subsequent meetings, signals and diary entries. All the signs are that it did not begin well, however. Montgomery was still smarting from being superseded as Commander-in-Chief Allied Ground Forces despite the move being a long-standing arrangement, and he appears to have taken the opportunity to vent his spleen over perceived shortcomings in Eisenhower's performance as Supreme Commander until the latter diplomatically pointed out the inappropriateness of his subordinate's behaviour by patting him on the knee and remarking 'Steady Monty. You can't speak to me like that. I'm your boss.'[18] Montgomery then apologised and matters appear to have proceeded on more amicable lines. The scheme Montgomery laid out was essentially a revised version of Operation COMET, rejigged to employ three Airborne divisions rather than one to secure water crossings for a ground advance over the sixty miles between Eindhoven and Arnhem. The operation was codenamed MARKET GARDEN, with the former referring to the Airborne insertion and the latter to the ground relief element. Eisenhower approved the scheme with some enthusiasm, as is apparent from his somewhat verbose comment to Montgomery in a letter the following day: 'I must say that it [MARKET GARDEN] is not only designed to carry out most effectively my basic conception with respect to this campaign but it is in exact concordance with all the understandings that we now have'.[19]

Eisenhower's comment, and particularly the ending, suggests that he considered agreement to have been reached across the board. This view was shared to an extent by Tedder, who commented that the meeting had 'cleared the air' when relaying details of it to the Chief of the Air Staff, Air Chief Marshal Sir Charles Portal. However, Tedder also referred to Montgomery '...making great play over the word "priority"...[and insisting that in]...his interpretation the word implies absolute priority, to the exclusion of all other operations if necessary.' He also pointed out that Montgomery would 'dislike not getting a blank cheque'.[20] The latter observation was forensically accurate, for Montgomery began badgering Eisenhower about his dissatisfaction with the supply priorities the day after the meeting, claiming that under existing arrangements MARKET GARDEN could not be launched until at least 23 and probably 26 September, and that the delay would permit the Germans to organise and implement defensive measures. Eisenhower responded on 12 September by despatching his Chief-of-Staff, Lieutenant-General Walter Bedell Smith, to Brussels to clarify 21st Army Group's supply requirements and on 13 September pointed out to Montgomery via telegram that his demands for a daily delivery of 1,000 tons by air to the Brussels area were unrealistic and could only be achieved by diverting aircraft from Operation MARKET. He did, however agree to divert US road transport temporarily to delivering materiel to 21st Army Group at the rate of 500 tons per day as a temporary emergency measure, even though it meant diverting virtually all US transport assets and thus immobilising US divisions and other tactical units until 1 October; Montgomery was to expedite the remainder of the supply effort via emergency measures of his own.[21] Eisenhower's decision was both fair-minded and courageous, given that he was already fighting the perception among US commanders in Europe and the US public alike that he was overly sympathetic to British interests.[22] Although the evidence shows that Eisenhower still intended to maintain his broad front strategy and permit US forces to continue the advance into the Saar region as soon as the supply situation permitted,[23] Montgomery appears to have decided that Eisenhower's compromise equated to capitulation to his narrow northern thrust strategy. This is clear from a subsequent communication to the Vice Chief of the Imperial General Staff Lieutenant-General Sir Archibald Nye, in which Montgomery claimed to have personally ensured the advance into the Saar had been permanently curtailed, set a firm date for launching his narrow front attack and explicitly referred to gaining approval for his scheme as 'a great victory'.[24] On that basis he also issued a Directive to the British 2nd Army on 14 September instructing it to begin planning for an immediate post-MARKET GARDEN advance east into Germany to secure Hamm as a springboard to isolate and capture the Ruhr, even though Eisenhower had authorised no such future operations.[25]

Montgomery's self-serving interpretations aside, the key point here is that Eisenhower had approved MARKET GARDEN, and D-Day had been set for Sunday 17 September 1944. However, before moving on to examine the airborne planning and preparation for the Operation, it might be illuminating to clarify the thinking behind Montgomery's choice of Holland as a venue for his narrow-thrust strategy. Montgomery was criticised in a television interview decades after the event for not moving north-east to cross the Rhine at Wesel instead, by then Brigadier R. F. K. Belchem, who served as Brigadier General Staff (Operations) at 21st Army Group HQ in 1944-45; Belchem appears to have based his appreciation on post-war discussion with former *Heer* officers who claimed that the Germans would have been unable to oppose such an attack.[26] Following such a course would certainly have been beneficial, as it would have improved contact between the divergent British and US lines of advance. However, it was simply not feasible to execute a large-scale Airborne operation in the area of Wesel in September 1944 because doing so would have exposed the transport aircraft and gliders to the Ruhr's formidable, and at that point undisrupted, anti-aircraft defences with the very real prospect of losing a significant proportion of the Airborne troops before they even reached the ground. In addition, the ground route to Wesel involved forcing a crossing of the River Maas and then fighting through the twenty-mile-deep *Reichswald* section of the *Westwall* defence line in the region of Cleve, Goch and Xanten. That process took 21st Army Group just over a month in early 1945 with a significant amount of preparation and while the same could be said of the Germans on that occasion, the speed with which the German defences crystallised from scratch in the face of the Guards Armoured Division's advance across the Albert Canal on 7 September 1944 strongly suggests that the extravagant claims of Belchem's German confidants should be treated with utmost caution. It can therefore be argued that given the prevailing operational situation, there was no practical alternative to a northward attack into Holland toward Arnhem for 21st Army Group. The idea did have some merit in its own right. Securing Arnhem and the corridor leading to it would not only provide a springboard for a subsequent attack toward the Ruhr, it would also provide a means of bypassing the German *Westwall* border defences, which ended in the *Reichswald* forest just east of Nijmegen, and thus open the way for a thrust into the North German Plain toward Berlin. Indeed, this was the precise slant put on Montgomery's gaining approval for MARKET GARDEN by Lieutenant-General Nye when he passed on the news to his superior, Chief of the Imperial General Staff Field-Marshal Sir Alan Brooke. The CIGS was accompanying Churchill at the OCTAGON Conference in Quebec, and Nye's communication specifically referred to the area of Münster as the ultimate objective of the thrust into Holland, in preparation for a further advance on Berlin.[27]

The rationale behind Montgomery's choice of line of advance is clear, but the same cannot be said of the thought process that underlay it. This is an important point, not least because it has become fashionable to place all responsibility for the failure of MARKET GARDEN squarely upon Montgomery's shoulders,[28] a process facilitated greatly by his reticence; unlike the other battles he fought, Montgomery refrained from commenting about MARKET GARDEN after the event.[29] Montgomery's battlefield reputation was based on meticulous preparation and methodical execution of carefully prepared plans, the object of which was to minimise friendly casualties. This was a legacy of his service on the Western Front during the First World War, and is clearly discernible in virtually every action he fought from El Alamein in October-November 1942 through the various actions he commanded in Sicily, on the eastern flank of the Normandy invasion area and onto the operations to clear the *Reichswald* and force a crossing of the River Rhine in February-March 1945. Indeed, Montgomery's reputation for tactical prudence was well known to foe as well as friend; the commander of the reconstituted *Heeresgruppe B* in Holland, *Generalfeldmarschall* Walther Model and his chief-of-staff *General* Hans Krebs discounted the possibility of an Allied airborne operation in Holland precisely because Montgomery was in charge.[30] Embarking on a risky venture like MARKET GARDEN was thus demonstrably out of character for Montgomery, and none of the background factors really provide a satisfactory explanation for his abandonment of past practice. The fact that he had to persuade Eisenhower to accept his scheme for an advance toward Arnhem rules out imposition from above, and the precarious supply situation was an argument against launching such a potentially risky venture, not in favour of it. Perhaps the most obvious factor would have been a desire to capitalise upon German disorganisation and weakness resulting from their flight across France and Belgium following Falaise. However, as mentioned earlier, this peaked in Holland on 5 September, which the locals who witnessed the chaos and confusion of the German retreat dubbed 'Mad Tuesday',[31] the same time briefings for Operation COMET and preparatory supporting ground actions were being prepared or delivered. Thus that particular window of opportunity had closed by the time Montgomery finally succeeded in obtaining permission from Eisenhower to proceed with his scheme on 10 September, and it is highly unlikely Montgomery was unaware of the fact, given the degree of resistance encountered by the Guards Armoured Division in its push across the Albert Canal at Beeringen between 6 and 9 September. Another possible driver was political pressure, but this does not appear to have been the case either. Admittedly, Montgomery did show Eisenhower a British government communication on 10 September urging haste in securing western Holland in order to neutralise launch sites for German V2 missiles, the first of which had hit London two days previously. However, Montgomery's behaviour during the meeting strongly suggests that the communication was merely introduced as an additional means of exerting pressure on the Supreme Commander rather than a significant factor in its own right. Even if that were the case, it is doubtful whether this equated to the kind of political pressure Montgomery was exposed to during his stint in North Africa, or indeed during his repeated and unsuccessful attempts to break through the German lines near Caen after the Normandy landings. On those occasions he refused to be diverted from his methodical approach, and he continued to do so at the beginning of the Falaise breakout when the justification for changing tack was arguably greater. Although the 43rd Division was across the River Seine at Vernon by dawn on 26 August, Montgomery imposed a two-day pause to allow the British 2nd Army to regroup and reorient before loosing the 11th Armoured Division across northern France toward the Belgian border at dawn on 28 August.

There is, however, another factor to consider when attempting to analyse Montgomery's thinking in the immediate run-up to MARKET GARDEN. That factor is the role played by the Deputy Commander of the 1st Allied Airborne Army, Lieutenant-General Frederick Browning. Browning was present at 21st Army Group HQ on 10 September, and the popular view is of him waiting dutifully for Montgomery to return from his meeting with Eisenhower, receiving instructions and then racing back by air to report to his superior Lieutenant-General Lewis H. Brereton at 1st Allied Airborne Army HQ, before briefing the senior Air and Airborne commanders.[32] According to one account, Browning also asserted that the British 1st Airborne Division would be capable of holding the Arnhem bridges for a maximum of four days, to which Montgomery responded by insisting only two days would be necessary. This is then alleged to have prompted Browning's oft-quoted comment that MARKET GARDEN might be 'going a bridge too far'.[33] This version of events accords with the recent tendency to saddle Montgomery with the blame for subsequent events in Holland, but there is a bit more to it. According to the commander of the 1st Airborne Division, Major-General Robert Urquhart, the meeting between Browning and Montgomery actually took place on Saturday 9 September, the day *before* Montgomery's meeting with Eisenhower, and in Montgomery's caravan at 21st Army HQ.[34] This also accords with the fact that Browning appears to have received the go ahead for MARKET on 10 September from the commander of the British 2nd Army, Lieutenant-General Sir Miles Dempsey, rather than Montgomery.[35] This version of events makes much more sense and is a much better fit for the timeline, given that Browning was back at British 1st Airborne Corps HQ at Moor Park by 14:30 on 10 September and was presenting a detailed briefing on MARKET to the assembled Air and Airborne commanders and their staffs there at 18:00.[36] According to one account, Browning was summoned to Belgium on 10 September on Montgomery's orders, and with no prior notice of the purpose of the summons.[37] This, however, seems unlikely. Had Browning met with Montgomery on 9 September as Urquhart claims, then he would have had a pretty fair idea of the reason for his summons. Furthermore, it is inconceivable that Montgomery would have tried to sell his scheme to Eisenhower on 10 September without a detailed plan for MARKET and all the relevant Airborne facts and figures at his fingertips, and as his interaction with, and thus knowledge of, Airborne matters was limited, he had little option but to seek advice. Given that he had prior contact with Browning, going back at least as far as his machinations for the elevation of his protégé Urquhart to command the 1st Airborne Division at the beginning of 1944, through the string of aborted missions slated after 6 June 1944 – to say nothing of the fact that he held the penultimate Allied Airborne command – it therefore made perfect sense for Montgomery to make Browning his primary source of Airborne information and advice for Operation MARKET. This also fitted with the tendency for the upper echelons of the British Army establishment to behave as if they were members of a close-knit club rather than a military organisation.

This leads to the question of what exactly passed between Browning and Montgomery on Saturday 9 September 1944, and there are two problems with the received version of the event. First, there does not appear to be any official record or verifiable eyewitness accounts to the exchange, and only two subsequent accounts refer to it explicitly as an important meeting in its own right. The first passing mention appears in Urquhart's 1958 account but with no citation, and he cannot have heard it first-hand because he was in the UK at the time. Cornelius Ryan's account, which takes Browning's alleged comment as its title, appeared sixteen years later and cites the whole conversation in quote marks but again with no reference, and claims it took place *after* the meeting with Eisenhower to boot. It is of course possible that a third party recorded the conversation, but given its prophetic nature it is curious that they have never come forward or been named. There is also the fact that the precise wording of Browning's caveat varies between sources. According to Ryan for example, Browning said 'I think we might be going a bridge too far,'[38] whereas Harvey's more recent work renders the sentence as 'I think we might be going one bridge too far.'[39] Given this, it is legitimate to question whether or not Browning actually said anything of the kind, a point raised by both Harvey's and Urquhart's biographer, who suggested that the observation might well have actually come from Montgomery.[40] Whatever the truth of the matter, the key point is that Browning was fully aware that failure to seize any one crossing rendered the whole of MARKET GARDEN redundant and pointless. Consequently, if he really did believe the Operation was going a bridge too far, he should have been arguing strenuously against launching it at all, rather than making platitudinous excuses for future mitigation.

Second, received wisdom and virtually all accounts invariably present Browning as the dutiful and compliant subordinate, standing by to carry out the wishes of his superiors without question. However, this view is somewhat at variance with the reality of Browning as a ruthless, ambitious and manipulative empire-building bureaucrat *par excellence*, and it is also important to acknowledge that he also had a vested interest in MARKET going ahead. Despite being appointed to fight the Airborne bureaucratic corner at Whitehall, Browning had adroitly expanded his role to encompass the operational aspect too, turning British Airborne Forces into his personal barony in the process and using it as a platform to attain the second highest operational post in the Allied Airborne establishment. The problem was that by September 1944 political acumen and connections were no longer sufficient to sustain such a key appointment because there was no shortage of airborne officers with operational combat experience. Browning's arch rival and commander of the US 18th Airborne Corps, Major-General Matthew B. Ridgway, comes immediately to mind, but he was by no means alone. Major-General Richard Gale MC, who had been instrumental in the conversion and expansion of the British Airborne Force from a small-scale raiding force and who had commanded the 6th Airborne Division in the Normandy invasion was also a strong candidate. In short, Browning urgently needed to address his total lack of operational experience in order to justify his position, and personally commanding the largest Allied airborne operation of the war would bolster his position in the Allied Airborne hierarchy, and by extension, his position in the post-war British Army.

Browning was fully aware of the precariousness of his position, not least from having it pointed out in no uncertain terms by his immediate superior Brereton during the preparations for Operation LINNET II. As we have seen, this envisaged dropping the 1st Allied Airborne Army in the region of Maastricht on the Dutch-German border and resulted in a dispute of uncertain provenance between Browning and Brereton; British accounts claim Browning was concerned over a lack of maps for the troops, whereas at least one US commentator claims Browning was really acting in support of Montgomery's effort to secure additional resources for his northern axis of advance. Whatever the truth of the matter, when Brereton overruled his objections Browning threatened to resign and put his intentions formally in writing, to which Brereton responded by placing Ridgway on stand-by to assume Browning's post. The cancellation of LINNET II on 5 September removed the immediate source of friction, but the episode left Browning in no doubt of the shakiness of his position on the Allied airborne ladder, or of his expendability.[41] From Browning's perspective it was therefore vital that MARKET went ahead, and viewing matters with this in mind casts things in a different light. Given that he was Montgomery's chief and presumably only adviser on Airborne matters, Browning was in a prime position to forward his own interests by subtly weaving them into the larger scheme of things. It thus takes no great effort of imagination to see him putting the best interpretation on things to Montgomery, playing up the benefits and minimising the risks inherent in laying an Airborne carpet across sixty miles of German-held territory, especially given Montgomery's general lack of familiarity with the technicalities and realities of Airborne operations. This scenario certainly provides a plausible explanation for Montgomery's otherwise inexplicable and short-lived embrace of high risk, and also for his reticence after the fact. On the surface it seems perhaps a little far-fetched to extrapolate so much from a couple of unminuted meetings and some contradiction and/or confusion over dates and places in secondary accounts. However, as we shall see, Browning went on to make a series of decisions in the run-up to the launch of MARKET for which there is no real explanation apart from a determination that the Operation should go ahead at all costs.

Events moved quickly in the Airborne camp once Dempsey relayed Montgomery's authorisation for MARKET on 10 September. Browning's aircraft landed on the golf course at Moor Park, his British 1st Airborne Corps HQ, at 14:30. From there he travelled to 1st Allied Airborne Army HQ at Sunninghill Park, Ascot, where he reported the go-ahead for MARKET and presented an outline plan drawn up by either Montgomery or Dempsey to the Army commander, Lieutenant-General Lewis H. Brereton.[42] Brereton then handed formal control of the airborne side of MARKET to Browning, and placed the US 82nd and 101st Airborne Divisions under his command for the Operation. Browning then issued summonses to the Divisional commanders involved, along with other staff and commanders, to attend a formal preliminary briefing for Operation MARKET at Sunninghill Park at 18:00; this was to be followed by a conference to sort out the airlift details at US 9th Troop Carrier Command at Grantham the following day, Monday 11 September, and another conference for the divisional commanders to brief back their plans at Moor Park on Thursday 14 September. The audience for the initial MARKET briefing on 10 September numbered thirty-four and included the commander of the British 1st Airborne Division, Major-General Robert Urquhart and that of the attached 1st Polish Independent Parachute Brigade, Major-General Stanislaw Sosabowski; Brigadier-General James M. Gavin and Major-General Maxwell D. Taylor commanding the US 82nd and 101st Airborne Divisions respectively, the former having been promoted to his command on 16 August;

Major-General Paul L. Williams, commanding the US 9th Troop Carrier Command; and the commanders of RAF Nos. 38 and 46 Groups, Air Vice-Marshal Leslie Hollinghurst DFC and Air Commodore Lawrence Darvall respectively. Browning opened the briefing by presenting the undated outline plan he had brought back from Brussels which divided the sixty-mile airborne corridor into three sections, each of which was allocated to a specific Airborne division. The first twenty miles or so was assigned to the 101st Airborne Division, which was to secure a total of six bridgesL two bridges over the Wilhelmina Canal just north of Eindhoven, another over the River Dommel at St. Oedenrode, two more across the Willems Canal near Veghel and another over the River Aa in Veghel proper. Next, the 82nd Airborne Division was tasked to seize the road and rail bridges over the River Maas near Grave and Mook respectively, four crossings over the Maas-Waal Canal and the major road and rail bridges across the River Waal in Nijmegen. The most northerly objectives, the road, rail and pontoon bridges over the Lower Rhine at Arnhem, were allotted to the 1st Airborne Division, also given the subsidiary mission of securing an airfield north of the city at Deelen to permit the British 52nd (Lowland) Division to be flown in as reinforcements.

The plan, while ambitious, was therefore relatively straightforward apart from the allocation of divisional tasks, which gave the least experienced and arguably least battleworthy formation the key and most remote objective. It may have been because on paper at least the 1st Airborne Division was fresh, whereas its two US counterparts had suffered heavy casualties in Normandy. It may also have been intended to give the least experienced formation the least complicated mission; the three objective bridges at Arnhem were in close proximity on a single watercourse, whereas the US Divisions' objectives were spread over several watercourses and a considerable distance in relative terms. The precise reason for the MARKET prioritisation is unclear however, even among the senior commanders at the time. According to Urquhart the rationale was political, and was intended to offset the repercussions of a British ground force failing to relieve an embattled US Airborne formation in what was essentially a British operation.[43] While feasible, this explanation seems rather heavily coloured with hindsight, and the fact that both US Airborne formations were misused as conventional infantry under British command for a considerable period after the failure of MARKET suggests that concern for US casualties or sensibilities did not figure highly in Montgomery or Browning's calculations. Gavin's explanation was more pragmatic, and assumed that the divisional tasks were linked to their base locations in the UK relative to the objectives in Holland.[44] Again, this makes a certain amount of sense, but overlooks that the key factor was the location of the airfields from which MARKET was launched, rather than the areas in which the individual formations were billeted. While the 1st Airborne Division's parachute units launched from airfields near the Divisional billets in the English East Midlands for example, the Division's glider element was lifted from airfields the farthest away from Arnhem, fifty miles or more west of London.

According to one account the divisional tasks were actually allotted by Dempsey when drawing up the outline plan, but it is doubtful he had the necessary authority as an Army-level commander to dictate such matters to an equivalent level of command.[45] Any such decisions must therefore have been Montgomery's, and as he had neither the experience nor detailed knowledge of the formations it is perfectly possible that Browning was in fact responsible and had recommended the allocations to Montgomery during their meeting on 9 September. Given the tribal nature of the British Army it is also possible Browning was seeking to give his former command the bulk of the kudos for MARKET; placing a formation commanded by one of Montgomery's protégés in the forefront of the action would do nothing to harm his post-war prospects with the British Army's most senior soldier either. Furthermore, having British troops on the ground at the tip of the springboard for further exploitation was in Montgomery's best interests, and given the trouble he took to secure Urquhart command of the 1st Airborne Division there was again the seasoning of advancing a protégés' career in the process. Whatever the reasoning for the divisional tasking, after presenting the outline plan, Browning handed over to Brereton, who insisted that all seventeen bridges had to be seized 'with thunderclap surprise' and stressed that time constraints meant any arrangements agreed at this stage had to be binding, before promptly imposing a series of conditions and constraints that tended to run counter to those aims.[46] He began the latter by announcing that MARKET was to be launched in four days' time on Thursday 14 September, an extremely short and unrealistic lead time that possibly betrays Brereton's lack of Airborne experience. While the 1st Airborne and Polish Independent Brigade had at least some preparation in hand from the aborted Operation COMET, there was still an immense amount of work to be done and the US divisions were approaching MARKET from scratch. Consequently, and unsurprisingly, Brereton's announcement drew vociferous opposition from the assembled Airborne commanders, to the extent that he relented and put the launch date back three days, to Sunday 17 September. This decision created additional problems however, for while 14 September fell in a period of waning moon, pushing the launch date back to 17 September put MARKET into a no-moon period. This meant that the initial MARKET insertion had to be made in daylight, because large-scale Airborne landing were simply not viable in moonless conditions. Both parachutists and glider pilots required a degree of natural illumination in order to judge height, orientation and rate of descent, and landings without at least some moonlight virtually guaranteed a large proportion of landing accidents with the attendant injuries, lost or damaged equipment and probably fatalities.

This basic truth is frequently overlooked in criticism of the MARKET plan, which often assumes that a night landing was a simple panacea for other flaws in the scheme. It also overlooks the fact that night insertion had not been the Allied norm hitherto because it was a superior method in its own right. Rather, it had been a pragmatic response to the *Luftwaffe* threat during the formative period of the Allied Airborne operations or, as with the D-Day landings, a necessity dictated by other operational factors. Whatever the underlying reasons, large-scale night landings had not proved to be a success. The various Allied landings on Sicily in 1943 were badly scattered, as were those in Normandy, where an unexpected cloudbank disrupted the inbound US transport formations so badly that few US paratroops or gliders were actually delivered to the correct landing zones; some were dropped up to twenty miles astray and a few may have landed in the English Channel.[47] The British 6th Airborne Division suffered similarly, with some sticks being dropped over ten miles or more from their assigned landing zone.[48] One Horsa glider was released over the Pas de Calais rather than Normandy, a navigation error of fifty miles east in a notional fifty-mile flight.[49] In the event, the daylight landing on 17 September proved to be one of the least costly and problematic aspects of MARKET; Gavin later commented that the drop was 'better than had ever been experienced'.[50]

It is unclear whether it was dealt with during the initial 10 September briefing or at the conference at 9th Troop Carrier Command HQ the next day, but Brereton's next point concerned the MARKET air plan and aircraft allocations, and had far more wide-reaching implications and repercussions. Fifty-eight squadrons of transport aircraft were available for MARKET, forty-three from 9th Troop Carrier Command, nine from No. 38 Group and six from No. 46 Group, approximately 1,575 aircraft in all.[51] Of the RAF contribution, only No. 46 Group's six squadrons were equipped with purpose-built Douglas C-47 transports, dubbed the Dakota in British service. No. 38 Group's squadrons employed obsolete Armstrong Whitworth Albemarle, Handley Page Halifax or Short Stirling bombers pressed into service as glider tugs or makeshift parachute transports.[52] In the event, the RAF contribution was insufficient to carry even the 1st Airborne Division's first lift and an additional 130 C-47s from the US 61st and 314th Troop Carrier Groups had to be drafted in to deliver the 1st Parachute Brigade.[53] That aside, the crux of the problem was that there were simply not enough aircraft to lift three Airborne divisions simultaneously and Brereton therefore prioritised the first lift allocation from south to north. This was both logical and sensible, for prompt relief of the formations holding the central and northern portions of the Airborne Corridor was reliant on the first, vital link in the chain.

Neither was the disparity in allocation especially marked, with the 101st Airborne Division being allotted 550 aircraft, the 82nd Airborne Division 515, and 1st Airborne Division 480.[54]

The real problem was not so much the divisional aircraft allocations but Brereton's subsequent decree that there would be only a single lift per day for the entirety of Operation MARKET.[55] Brereton made this decision on the advice of his senior air commander, Major-General Paul L. Williams, who had commanded the US 9th Troop Carrier Command from February 1944 and thus during Airborne operations in support of the Normandy landings. Williams had hitherto been known for his willingness to accommodate the needs of the Airborne soldiers, but on this occasion he expressed serious concerns over the number of aircraft held by his units, which had recently doubled with no concomitant increase in groundcrew; shortage of the latter was an ongoing concern dating back to before the Normandy invasion.[56] He therefore advised Brereton against carrying out more than a single lift on the first day of MARKET, citing concerns over aircrew fatigue and, more importantly, because he did not think his undermanned groundcrews would be able to refuel, carry out routine maintenance and repair battle damage with sufficient speed to make multiple lifts per day a practical proposition. Brereton's decision to act on Williams' reservations was not greeted with enthusiasm by his audience and especially Urquhart, whose formation had already drawn the short straw with regard to aircraft allocation. The single lift per day edict compounded the latter deficiency by spreading the delivery of 1st Airborne Division over three consecutive days. As MARKET GARDEN was predicated on a forty-eight-hour timetable assuming everything ran to schedule, this meant the final increment of the Division would not land in Holland until the day *after* the ground relief force had reached Arnhem. The combination of smaller aircraft allocation and single lift per day thus significantly reduced Urquhart's flexibility in executing his mission, and to an arguably greater degree than the other MARKET formations. Brereton's edict was not accepted without comment. Air-Vice Marshal Hollinghurst, who was in charge of air-ground co-ordination of the Arnhem portion of MARKET as well as exercising overall command of the RAF contingent, told Urquhart that Nos. 38 and 46 Groups were capable of carrying out two lifts on the first day with a pre-dawn take-off. Despite this, Brereton still turned down Urquhart's subsequent request for his formation to be permitted two lifts on the first day. The problem here was that because the two RAF Groups were unable to muster sufficient machines on their own, the 1st Airborne Division's first lift was dependent upon US resources for over a quarter of its aircraft, a fact which presumably influenced Brereton's reaction. A subsequent attempt by Montgomery to sway Brereton met with a similar lack of success, although it is unclear exactly when and how Montgomery became aware of the single-lift edict. According to one source Montgomery spotted the 'disastrous flaw' himself on receiving a copy of the MARKET plan, but given the latter had not yet been drawn up at this time and his lack of Airborne expertise it is more likely he was alerted to and drawn into the argument by Browning in support of his determination that MARKET went ahead at all costs. However he learned of it, Montgomery despatched Brigadier Belchem, who was apparently serving as his temporary chief-of-staff at the time, to plead Urquhart's case. Brereton again refused to be swayed, this time justifying his position by citing his original insistence that initial decisions had to be binding, and because there was insufficient time for the disruption such a revision of the plan would entail.[57]

As a result of these edicts, Brereton is widely considered to have compromised MARKET, both at the time and since. Air-Vice Marshal James Scarlett-Streatfield, Hollinghurst's successor as head of No. 38 Group, made this point explicitly in the RAF post-operation report.[58] Similar criticisms, especially regarding the delivery of the 1st Airborne Division in three increments, are a recurring theme in more recent works on MARKET GARDEN,[59] with some also suggesting that Brereton's support for Williams was influenced, unconsciously or deliberately, by his background as an airman rather than a soldier.[60] However, as with the daylight insertion, the criticism fails to address whether Brereton's edicts were indeed avoidable and objective analysis of the evidence suggests they were not. In addition to his paucity of groundcrew, Williams was also grappling with a shortage of experienced or even fully trained aircrew, which again pre-dated the Normandy invasion. Although the 52nd Troop Carrier Wing had been drafted in from the Mediterranean for that operation, only one of its three constituent Groups had any combat experience and the other two required intensive navigation, night flying and formation flying training; this was also the case with the 50th and 53rd Wings, which had come directly from the US. The shortage of navigators was so acute that only four out of every ten C-47 crews employed on the D-Day drop included one, usually flying at the head of a serial.[61] The situation is unlikely to have improved by September 1944, especially given Williams' reference to the doubling of his units' aircraft holdings. While possibly not so critical to formations taking off before dawn, the shortage of navigators would have been more problematic for aircraft returning in darkness, as would have been the case with a second lift in the shortening September days.

In fact, the key issue was the lack of natural illumination. The Allied Airborne landings in Sicily and Normandy may have been carried out at night, but the aircraft had taken off before twilight because merely assembling the large numbers involved into formation was a major operation in its own right. The US first lift into Normandy, for example, involved marshalling almost 900 C-47s and gliders into a block of sky 300 miles long and 1,000 feet wide, and MARKET envisaged doing the same with around 1,600 aircraft taking off from airfields spread across the length and breadth of southern and central England. With fully trained and experienced aircrew, carrying out such an undertaking in moonlight would have been dangerous in the extreme; with inexperienced and partially trained aircrew in the total darkness of a no-moon period it would have been little short of suicidal. Hollinghurst was presumably willing to carry out a pre-dawn take-off because his RAF and Commonwealth aircrew were trained and practised in night-flying techniques; No. 38 Group had reportedly carried out conventional night bombing missions in the run-up to D-Day, for example.[62] However, it is difficult to see how even this would permit the RAF contingent to form up and maintain formation in total darkness, and particularly as most of the RAF machines were slated as glider tugs. It is also significant that the acknowledged experts on night flying, RAF Bomber Command, did not countenance formation flying, preferring to allow aircraft to proceed independently after well-spaced take-offs to avoid collisions. This was obviously not an option for serials carrying troops or towing gliders for a division-sized Airborne landing. Williams' insistence on a single lift per day and Brereton's acceptance of it may therefore have been less than ideal, but it was the only realistic option in the prevailing circumstances, hindsight-based criticism notwithstanding.

The next bone of contention to arise on 11 September was connected to the MARKET drop and landing zones. The ones attached to the outline plan were the same zones selected by the RAF planners for Operation COMET, and the reaction of the US division commanders to their work was mixed. Gavin was concerned at his 82nd Airborne Division being dispersed across four widely dispersed drop zones spread over an area of roughly twenty-five miles. Two of these zones lay either side of the River Maas near Grave, with a large combined drop and landing zone five miles to the east between Mook and Groesbeek and another regiment-sized drop zone just to the north-east of that between Groesbeek and Wyler. Such dispersal flew in the face of past experience on Sicily, which indicated that it was wiser to land on or close to the objective, even at the cost of casualties, than landing safely at a distance and then being obliged to fight through to the objective. However, after examining the intelligence gathered at British 1st Airborne Corps at Moor Park and given the equally dispersed nature of his objectives, Gavin appears to have concluded that there was no practical alternative under the circumstances and accepted the drop zones as proposed.[63]

Major-General Taylor's reaction was somewhat different and justifiably so, for the 101st Airborne Division had been allocated a string of individual battalion drop zones running north from Eindhoven through Son, St. Oedenrode and Veghel. Taylor consequently wasted no time in voicing his objections to Browning at having his Division scattered in highly vulnerable increments across southern Holland. According to the 101st Airborne Division's semi-official history, Browning responded by inviting Taylor to travel to British 2nd Army HQ in Belgium to explain his objections to Lieutenant-General Dempsey in person. When the latter accepted Taylor's objections, Browning in turn persuaded Brereton to permit the 101st Airborne Division to modify its landing zones.[64] Once again, it is unclear precisely what authority or expertise permitted Dempsey to adjudicate on such matters, although it is possible that his involvement was the result of political manoeuvring by Browning, aimed at offsetting his reduced personal stock with Brereton following their disagreement over LINNET II. Brereton's acquiescence may also have been due in part to the intervention of Brigadier-General Stuart Cutler, the 1st Allied Airborne Army's Deputy Chief-of-Staff, who sparked an acrimonious exchange by pointing out that as presented, the 101st Airborne Division's landing plan was counter to official US War Department Airborne doctrine. Brereton bridled at the suggestion but relented after Gavin and Taylor were brought in and supported Cutler.[65] Whatever the precise details, the important point was that Taylor's objections were taken on board and the 101st Airborne Division ended up landing in just three locations; two small drop zones located either side of the Willems Canal near Veghel, and a large combined drop and landing zone seven miles or so to the south-west, between the Wilhelmina Canal and River Dommel located within a few hundred yards of the Division's objectives at Son, Best and St. Oedenrode.

The allocation of landing areas once again impacted most severely on Urquhart's 1st Airborne Division, which was assigned the same landing area as that for Operation COMET. This consisted of a drop zone and two landing zones astride the Arnhem–Ede railway line near Wolfheze, seven miles west of the Division's primary objective, the Arnhem road bridge. The only significant difference was that the MARKET plan dispensed with the pre-dawn glider *coup-de-main* landings to seize the pontoon, railway and road bridges in Arnhem proper. Urquhart's first reaction was to try and switch to new landing zones on both sides of the Lower Rhine closer to his objectives. When that failed he tried to get the glider *coup-de-main* reinstated but that too was unsuccessful, despite his enlisting the support of Colonel George Chatterton, commander of the Glider Pilot Regiment. Chatterton's intervention was rebuffed on the grounds that any revision was impossible because it would add additional complication to an already complex air plan. The primary obstacle to Urquhart's suggested revisions to the air plan was Hollinghurst, who came up with a number of seemingly plausible reasons for vetoing the soldier's requests. The RAF planners had forecast losses of up to forty per cent for the Arnhem portion of the MARKET plan as originally formulated, and approaching close to Arnhem at all was thus deemed too dangerous for transport aircraft, tugs and gliders alike. This was justified by referencing reports from RAF reconnaissance flights that claimed there were forty-four heavy guns and almost three times as many light pieces emplaced in Arnhem and its immediate vicinity. In addition, moving the landing zones east and closer to the 1st Airborne Division's objectives was not considered an option because it would oblige the transport aircraft to overfly the German-held airfield at Deelen, seven miles north of Arnhem, and thus expose themselves to its allegedly extensive *flak* defences. Breaking east was not an option due to the Ruhr *flak* defences, and breaking west would risk entanglement with the transports delivering the US divisions further down the airborne corridor. Finally, it was claimed the polder land south of the Arnhem road bridge was too riven with ditches and embankments for parachute landings, and too soft and boggy for glider landings or general troop movement.

There was little to support most of these claims. In the event, the projected forty per cent aircraft loss figure proved wildly inaccurate, for not one of the aircraft assigned to the first lift into Arnhem was lost. No verifiable evidence for the *flak* gun numbers Hollinghurst claimed has been uncovered, although unverified information from the Dutch resistance is sometimes cited as the source,[66] and his claim appears to have been based upon unverified reports from RAF bomber crews flying over the area en route to their targets in Germany, which was a tenuous source at best. Significantly, no such concerns had been raised during the preparations for COMET only days previously, when intelligence disseminated by No. 38 Group to its aircrew referred only to heavy anti-aircraft guns at Nijmegen and Deelen airfield and the possible presence of mobile *flak* guns in the general area.[67] There was some evidence with regard to Deelen airfield, although it ran counter to Hollinghurst's claims as the airfield had been heavily bombed by the RAF on 3 September, presumably as part of the preparations for COMET. Subsequent reconnaissance by RAF No. 541 Squadron showed that the airfield been rendered at least temporarily unusable and all the surviving *flak* guns had been removed.[68] It is unclear if Hollinghurst was privy to this information on 11 September and if not why that was so, but by that time the German presence at Deelen airfield appears to have consisted of a single *Kompanie* from *Nachrichten Regiment 213*, a *Luftwaffe* signals unit commanded by *Hauptmann* Willi Weber.[69] On the other hand, Hollinghurst's claims that the polder south of Arnhem was unsuitable for airborne landing was arguably correct at least as far as gliders were concerned, as the area was soft and criss-crossed with drainage ditches. It was not correct with regard to parachute landings however, as Hollinghurst must have known given that the final MARKET plan designated that very area as DZ K and allotted it to the 1st Polish Independent Parachute Brigade for the third lift; in the event the Poles landed on 21 September on near-identical terrain 3,000 yards to the west.[70]

All this raises the suspicion that these objections were deployed primarily to avoid the bother of adapting the air plan rather than concern over the threat posed by German deployments, a view expressed at the time. Urquhart, for example, was of the opinion that having compromised over the daylight landing the RAF planners were unwilling to make further concessions in the air plan.[71] Either way, the crucial point here is that Hollinghurst was able unilaterally to stymie attempts to modify or indeed shape the air plan to the needs of the ground component of the operation, and the reason he was able to do so goes back to the very beginnings of the British Airborne Force. At that time the Air Ministry, while covertly attempting to strangle the project at birth by starving it of resources, nonetheless ensured that it maintained sole control over the planning of Airborne operations. As an Air Ministry policy document from December 1940 put it, '…for economy of resources, the staging and conduct of airborne operations should be a Royal Air Force responsibility planned to meet Army requirements.'[72] This, incidentally, explains why Hollinghurst had been appointed to oversee air-ground co-ordination of the Arnhem portion of MARKET while there does not appear to have been any equivalent arrangement on the US side. In practical terms this arrangement gave the RAF planners total and undisputed control over Airborne operations up to the point the landing force was on the ground and while the soldiers were at liberty to provide input, the planners were not in any way obliged to heed it. Most crucial of all, there was no machinery to compel them to do so. The arrangement endured, arguably more by luck than judgement, until the advent of Operation MARKET brought the differing Army and RAF approaches to operational matters into direct conflict. The priority of the former, as a manpower-centred force, was to achieve its assigned mission at whatever cost; the guiding priority of the latter, as a technologically centred force, was to preserve its *raison d'etre*, its aircraft. This was a fundamental mismatch, and thanks to the untrammelled autonomy of the RAF planners, the result was an air plan precisely tailored to meet RAF priorities and preferences despite running counter to all Airborne experience to date, and indeed basic tactical and operational common sense. As such, it provides a textbook example of placing the institutional cart before the operational horse and the heinous consequences thereof.

The War Office accepted RAF primacy over airborne planning presumably because it had little option due to the RAF's independent status and all that entailed, and because it conveniently obviated the need to expend its own resources. Nonetheless, the War Office is culpable up to a point for failing to address the RAF planning monopoly before it became a crucial issue, although the principle of air forces being responsible for planning was widely accepted as the Airborne norm, even though the formal arrangement between the RAF and Army was a purely

British idiosyncrasy.[73] The arrangement did not pass totally without comment at the time. Urquhart, for example, complained about RAF intransigence, albeit resignedly, while Brigadier John Hackett likened the RAF planners to naïve cooks blithely putting together technically marvellous plans that paid no heed whatsoever to the subsequent realities faced by those they were transporting to battle.[74] This was reinforced by Major Anthony Deane Drummond from 1st Airborne Division Signals, who expressed the opinion that the RAF planners selected the MARKET landing area purely because it fitted their preconceptions of what a landing zone should look like.[75]

Hollinghurst's veto was not accepted without complaint. When the latter turned down Urquhart's plea for the reinstatement of the glider *coup-de-main*, Chatterton, possibly influenced by Taylor's refusal to accept the 101st Airborne Division's landing areas as allotted, took the matter further up the chain of command to Browning; who finally brought the matter to a close by repeating the RAF objections, announcing that the matter was out of the Army's hands and pointing out that in any case it was now too late because everything had been decided.[76] The irony here is that while the RAF planners can be considered culpable for refusing to tailor the air plan to meet the Army's tactical requirements, they had no control over the decision to deliver the 1st Airborne Division in three lifts and, more importantly, neither did they have any real choice with regard to the landing areas. It was arguably feasible to secure the Arnhem bridges via glider *coup-de-main* and to deliver parachute units to the area just south of Arnhem, but there was no option but to use the glider landing zones selected in the vicinity of Renkum and Wolfheze because they were the only certifiably suitable terrain within striking distance of the 1st Airborne Division's objectives, as an examination of contemporary maps clearly shows. Browning's decision therefore cast the die as far as the 1st Airborne Division's air plan went, and Urquhart withdrew with his staff to his HQ at Cottesmore to prepare his detailed plans, which were to be presented to another conference on Thursday 14 September.

Although it suited his intention to see MARKET go ahead at all costs, Browning was therefore largely blameless in this particular instance. While he does not appear to have challenged Hollinghurst and his planners directly he did, to his credit, seek an independent second opinion on the matter from Major-General Richard Gale, arguably the only man in the British Army with sufficient operational experience to proffer a valid judgement. Gale, it will be recalled, had been instrumental in converting the original British airborne cadre from a small group of raiders into a conventional parachute brigade, and had planned and led the British 6th Airborne Division's vital spearhead landing for the Normandy invasion. However, if Browning was seeking reassurance he was sorely disappointed, for Gale endorsed Urquhart's objections and his insistence that the best option for securing the Arnhem road bridge was a glider landing on the objective followed by a brigade-strength landing in the immediate vicinity. Perhaps unsurprisingly, Browning requested Gale not to mention the matter or his appreciation to Urquhart, ostensibly to avoid damaging the latter's confidence. Gale appears to have held his peace until the 1970s, when he told Major G. G. Norton, then curator of the Airborne Forces Museum, in confidence that he would have resigned his command rather than execute MARKET as it was foisted upon Urquhart.[77] It is unclear if Gale made his views clear to Browning at the time, and it is also interesting to speculate how matters might have developed had they become more widely known at the time.

Browning's motive in concealing Gale's appreciation of the Arnhem portion of MARKET may indeed have been to avoid undermining Urquhart's confidence, but the fact remains that it also accorded equally well with promoting the go-ahead for MARKET at all costs. While this may sound circumstantial or indeed far-fetched, another incident at this time provides much clearer and unambiguous evidence of Browning's duplicity. On 10 September the Senior Intelligence Officer at British 1st Airborne Corps HQ, Major Brian Urquhart, received an Intelligence Summary from 21st Army Group.[78] The summary referred to the presence of 9 and 10 SS Panzer Divisions in the area of Arnhem. Understandably alarmed owing to the 1st Airborne Division's imminent departure for that locale, Major Urquhart brought the report to the attention of the Corps Operations Officer, Lieutenant-Colonel Charles Mackenzie, Deputy Corps Commander Brigadier Gordon Walch and finally, to Browning himself over the following few days. When all three made light of his concerns Urquhart ordered an aerial reconnaissance to take oblique photographs of wooded areas in the vicinity of Arnhem on his own authority. The results of the reconnaissance flight arrived on Friday 15 September, just forty-eight hours before MARKET was scheduled to commence, and the photographs appeared to confirm the 21st Army Group Summary; according to Urquhart's subsequent account the photographs showed *Panzer* III and IV tanks close to Arnhem. Major Urquhart understandably wasted no time presenting this latest evidence to Browning. The latter responded by ordering 1st Airborne Corps' Senior Medical Officer, Colonel Austin Eagger, to diagnose Major Urquhart as suffering from nervous strain and exhaustion and to send him on sick leave with immediate effect. Eagger complied, albeit with personal reservations, and Urquhart was presented with the choice of accepting the medical diagnosis or facing a court martial.[79] He left Moor Park and the preparations for Operation MARKET shortly thereafter, and the intelligence on *9 and 10 SS Panzer Divisions* and German armour being located near Arnhem went with him, for there was no mention of it in subsequent intelligence summaries passed down to the 1st Airborne Division.[80] In fact, the intelligence was suppressed so effectively that the Official History of British Airborne Forces published in 1951 specifically stated that 'there was no previous knowledge of the presence of II SS Panzer Corps, consisting of 9 and 10 SS Panzer Division, which were refitting in the neighbourhood.'[81] The Official Campaign History which appeared in 1968 followed largely the same line, referring to *II SS Panzerkorps* and to its constituent divisions arriving in the area of Arnhem earlier in September with the inference that the information came from prisoners taken by 1st Airborne Division in the early stages of MARKET.[82]

Much is made of Major Urquhart's intelligence, which appears to be largely responsible for the enduring but erroneous myth that the 1st Airborne Division landed on top of two fully functioning *SS Panzer Divisions*. However, in the event his concern was, at least to an extent, misplaced. As we shall see, there were no German troops from *II SS Panzerkorps* or any other significant unit at all between the 1st Airborne Division's landing area and Arnhem when MARKET commenced, and only one *ad hoc* unit was in a position to respond to the landings in a timely manner. The only unit equipped with a significant number of tanks was a *bataillon* from *SS Panzer Regiment 10* billeted at Vorden, twenty miles north-east of Arnhem. It played no part in the fight against the British Airborne formation, being despatched south to block the Allied advance from Nijmegen on the night of 19-20 September. Incidentally, all the tank units employed against the 1st Airborne Division after the landings on 17 September were brought in from outside the Arnhem area, some from as far afield as Germany. The nearest unit to the landing area equipped with armoured vehicles was *SS Panzer Aufklärungs Abteilung 9*, located at Hoenderloo just over ten miles north of Arnhem and equipped with a total of ten eight-wheel armoured cars, thirty assorted armoured half-tracks and a number of trucks armoured with sand-filled oil drums. Elements of this unit harassed the 1st Parachute Battalion in its vain attempt to secure high ground to the north of Arnhem in the late afternoon and night of 17-18 September, while a larger increment led by the *Abteilung* commander moved south over the Arnhem road bridge at dusk to block any Allied ground advance from the south; it was destroyed trying to re-cross the bridge during the morning of 18 September by the British Airborne force then holding the north end of the structure. Major Urquhart's aerial reconnaissance might also have seen armoured vehicles belonging to *II SS Panzerkorps* that were despatched south to reinforce the front at Neerpelt on or around 13 September, although the transfer did not include any tanks, consisting as it did of armoured half-tracks, ten self-propelled artillery pieces and up to twice that number of *Jagdpanzer* IV tank destroyers.[83]

All that lay in the future, however, and the crucial point here is that Browning deliberately withheld potentially vital intelligence from the 1st Airborne Division, for he had no way of knowing that Major Urquhart's concern was misplaced at that time. In addition, he may therefore also have been responsible for the mysterious disappearance of similar information on German strength and capabilities in the Arnhem area that had been included in the intelligence summaries for COMET but which also did not appear in those for MARKET.[84] This suppression is not a new revelation. Middlebrook, for example, suggests that Browning's action was prompted by fear for the morale of the 1st Airborne Division, and the potential political repercussions of a British general jeopardising the success of the greatest and largely US airborne operation of the war. Powell, on the other hand, admits to finding Browning's behaviour inexplicable, while insisting there was no evidence to question his integrity and that it was inconceivable that he would not put the interests of his soldiers first.[85] Of the two, Middlebrook's reference to political factors is nearer the mark, albeit for different reasons, if only because Powell's characterisation is somewhat at odds with Browning's proven Machiavellian tendencies; it is difficult to reconcile the requirements of operational efficiency or the best interests of the soldiers with the installation of an inexperienced Montgomery protégé as commander of the 1st Airborne Division, for example. In any event, none of the existing explanations mooted satisfactorily explain Browning's actions on an individual basis, or in their entirety. The only factor that explains and links them is Browning's personal ambition and consequent need for MARKET to go ahead at all costs, and suppressing Gale's appreciation and Major Urquhart's intelligence was not to be his final act in this regard.

4

Up to the Brink: II SS *Panzerkorps*, 30 Corps and the 1ˢᵗ Allied Airborne Army

11 September – 16 September 1944

While the 1ˢᵗ Allied Airborne Army's senior commanders were arguing over resources and plans, their opposite numbers were settling into billets near Arnhem. The remnants of *II SS Panzerkorps* had regrouped at a rendezvous point at Hasselt after their odyssey across northern France and Belgium, with *Brigadeführer* Heinz Harmel's *10 SS Panzer Division* arriving first at some point between 1 and 3 September, having helped themselves to vehicles, weapons and equipment from abandoned German supply depots en route. The booty included up to twenty self-propelled artillery pieces 'liberated' from an unguarded train during an air raid alert.[1] On 4 September Harmel was ordered to establish a defensive pocket on the west bank of the Maas-Albert Canal fifteen miles or so east of Hasselt, but the order was countermanded during the night of 5 September and he was directed to a new assembly area to refit and receive replacements near Arnhem, seventy miles to the north; the move took two days. The bulk of *Obersturmbannführer* Walther Harzer's *9 SS Panzer Division* arrived at Hasselt slightly later, on or around 5 September, having also commandeered supplies from depots en route. After linking up with Harzer's command group, which had become separated during the withdrawal from Cambrai on the night of 2-3 September, the reunited formation also began to move to Arnhem on Thursday 7 September, using two routes running through Eindhoven and Venlo respectively. It arrived in the Arnhem area the following day.[2]

The assembly area was actually in the area north and east of Arnhem, with *Obergruppenführer* Wilhelm Bittrich's *II SS Panzerkorps* HQ located at Doetinchen, around seventeen miles east of the city. Harzer established his Division HQ around sixteen miles north of Arnhem at Apeldoorn while Harmel set up his HQ at Ruurlo, to the north-east of and twenty-five miles from Arnhem. In part this dispersal was to avoid the attentions of Allied air power, but billeting units away from major urban areas was also intended to avoid exposing them to attack by Resistance fighters, which became a regular occurrence in France and Belgium after the Normandy invasion. *9 SS Panzer Division's* units were thus spread amongst the villages and small towns along the roads leading north from Arnhem to Apeldoorn, and north-east to Zutphen, while those of *10 SS Panzer Division* were located to the north and east in or around Deventer, Ruurlo and Vorden. On arrival, the combined strength of *II SS Panzerkorps* may already have been as low as 6,000 to 7,000 men, with approximately half that total being service and supply personnel rather than combat troops.[3] The latter were also badly under-armed and equipped. *SS Panzer Regiment 9* consisted of a composite infantry battalion formed from dismounted tank crew, fitters and logistic personnel reinforced with a draft of *Kriegsmarine* personnel, for example, while *SS Panzerjäger Abteilung 9* was able to muster just two *Panzerjäger* IV self-propelled guns and a handful of towed 75mm *PaK* 40 pieces.[4] *II SS Panzerkorps* was thus able to muster half a division in manpower and much less in materiel, and its combat power was soon further reduced. Harmel had been warned that his Division might be required to detach elements to shore up the front on 6 September, and on 10 September *10 SS Panzer Division* was duly ordered to form an all-arms group to support 1 *Fallschirmjäger Armee* in its fight against the British on the Meuse-Escaut Canal at Neerpelt. Dubbed *Kampfgruppe* Heinke after its commander *Sturmbannführer* Heinke, the force was built around two *Panzergrenadier bataillonen*, one drawn from *SS Panzergrenadier Regiment 21* commanded by *Hauptsturmführer* Walther Krause and the other from *Hauptsturmführer* Dr Karl Segler's *SS Panzergrenadier Regiment 19* from the *Hohenstauffen*. These units were supported by *Hauptsturmführer* Franz Roestel's *SS Panzerjäger Abteilung 10* equipped with between fifteen and twenty-one *Jagdpanzer* IVs and up to a dozen *PaK* 40 towed pieces; the latter had been despatched to the front while the Division was at Hasselt. Additional support was provided by elements of *SS Panzer Aufklärungs Abteilung 10*, *SS Panzer Pionier Abteilung 10*, and a battery of ten self-propelled 105mm guns from *SS Panzer Artillerie Regiment 10*.[5] The *Kampfgruppe* appears to have been ordered south to Neerpelt on 13 September and spearheaded a counter-attack against the Guards Armoured Division bridgehead there shortly thereafter, although *Hauptsturmführer* Krause's unit may also have been despatched earlier; according to one source it had been in the Neerpelt area for a week before 13 September.[6]

This was a significant reduction in *II SS Panzerkorps'* strength, which was subsequently compounded by instructions from *OKW* for *10 SS Panzer Division* to refit in place while *9 SS Panzer Division* was withdrawn to Siegen in Germany to receive new equipment and replacement personnel. Advance parties drawn from the *Hohenstaufen's* support echelon began to depart on 12 September.[7] In the meantime, Harzer's units were ordered to turn over their serviceable weapons, heavy equipment and vehicles to *10 SS Panzer Division* and the denuded *Hohenstaufen* units were then temporarily designated *Warnungs Kompanien* (Alarm Companies) while awaiting their transport to Germany. There was not a great deal to transfer, but Harzer's men appear to have been loath to part with the vehicles that had borne them from Normandy across northern France and into Holland. This attitude appears to have emanated from the top, given that Bittrich did not conceal his opposition to the order when passing it on to Harmel and Harzer, and the latter had no intention of parting with his equipment as he distrusted the supply system to provide replacements.[8] The *Hohenstaufen's* units therefore resorted to some administrative sleight of hand to avoid handing over their vehicles by simply removing and concealing key components and then declaring them unserviceable. In most instances this involved just a handful of vehicles. *SS Pionier Abteilung 9* hung onto two half-track personnel carriers for example, while *SS FlaK Abteilung 9* managed to keep back one 88mm gun and one half-track-mounted 20mm piece and *SS Panzerjäger Abteilung 9* retained two *Jagdpanzer* IVs. *SS Panzer Regiment 9* took things further by retaining three *Panzer* III command tanks, four *Panzer* IVs, eight *Sturmgeschütz* (*StuG*) assault guns and possibly five Panthers.[9] The most prolific practitioners were *Hauptsturmführer* Viktor Gräbner and his men from *SS Panzer Aufklärungs Abteilung 9*, who removed weapons, optical equipment, wheels and tracks from thirty armoured half-tracks of various types and ten eight-wheeled armoured cars.[10] Most if not all of these vehicles had likely been despatched to Germany by 17 September, and Gräbner's small fleet had been loaded onto railway flatcars to follow them, in line with Harzer's personal decision to entrain his best units last; as six trains per day had been made available to move 9 SS *Panzer* the move was also five days ahead of schedule.[11]

This clearly shows that German strength in the Arnhem area was far less than is frequently assumed, and nowhere near the level of a fully equipped and functioning *Panzer* division. According to one source, by the time MARKET commenced on 17 September both the *Hohenstaufen* and *Frundsberg* were equivalent to weak brigades, with a maximum strength of 2,500 to 3,000 men apiece. However, this was still potentially a formidable foe for a lightly armed Airborne force to face. This was perhaps most relevant with regard to *SS Panzer Aufklärungs*

Abteilung 9, given its proximity to Arnhem, for even a modicum of armour plating offered infinitely more protection than a Denison smock. The important point is therefore whether any of 9 *SS Panzer Division's* sub-units were in a position to interfere with the 1ˢᵗ Airborne Division's designated landing area at Wolfheze or subsequent movement to its objectives in and around Arnhem during or immediately after the landings. Interfering in the initial phase of the operation was key because the most effective way of derailing an Airborne operation was to prevent the attackers from reaching and securing their objectives in the first place; once the Airborne troops were ensconced on their objective tackling them became a much more challenging prospect. Arguably the most compelling evidence for this truism lies in the fact that it took the Germans three days to recapture the north end of the Arnhem road bridge from a scratch force hastily assembled around an understrength Parachute Battalion, despite outnumbering the defenders and deploying tanks and self-propelled artillery against them.

In all, 9 *SS Panzer Division* was divided into nineteen *Warnungs Kompanien*, spread across twelve separate locations and totalling approximately 2,500 men.[12] Of these, only two were within reasonable proximity to Wolfheze. The nearest was *Obersturmführer* Harder's battalion group, made up of dismounted tank crew, fitters and logistic troops from *SS Panzer Regiment 9*, augmented with a draft of *Kriegsmarine* personnel; according to one source Harder may also have retained three Panther tanks, which were presumably immobilised in some way to avoid handing them over to 10 *SS Panzer Division*.[13] Located approximately six miles north of Arnhem on the road to Apeldoorn, Harder's unit was nine miles from the Wolfheze landing area in a straight line. The other unit was *Hauptsturmführer* Gräbner's *SS Panzer Aufklärungs Abteilung* 9, located at Hoenderloo, roughly ten miles north of Arnhem and around twelve miles from Wolfheze. 9 *SS Panzer Division's* HQ and logistic elements, located six miles further north at Apeldoorn with *SS Panzerjäger Abteilung* 9, commanded by *Hauptsturmführer* Klaus von Allwörden, were too far north to interfere in the initial stages of an Airborne landing at Wolfheze. This was even more the case with the remainder of the *Hohenstaufen's* units which were located east and north of Arnhem along the eighteen miles leading to Zutphen, and thus on the wrong side of the city. *SS Panzergrenadier Regiment 20* was camped on a former Dutch military training area near Rheden six miles east of Arnhem and thus closer to the Arnhem road bridge than 1ˢᵗ Airborne Division's landing area, but by 17 September the unit had handed in all personal weapons and combat equipment in readiness for rail transport to Germany and was thus unarmed.[14] The remainder, *SS Panzer Artillerie Regiment* 9, a detachment of SS anti-aircraft gunners under *Obersturmführer* Heinz Gropp and an *SS Panzergrenadier bataillon* commanded by *Hauptsturmführer* Karl-Heinz Euling billeted in and around Dieren eleven miles from Arnhem, *Hauptsturmführer* Hans Möller's *SS Panzer Pionier Abteilung* 9 at Brummen and *SS Panzergrenadier Regiment 19* in Zutphen, were also all too far away to intervene at Wolfheze in the short term.

Despite being the closest to Wolfheze, Harder's *bataillon* group was also incapable of interfering with a landing or advance eastward in the immediate aftermath without the aid of motor transport, which was in extremely short supply. Moving on foot would have taken at least two hours if not more, by which time any Airborne force ought to have been reorganised and well on the way to its objective.[15] Furthermore, even had they been capable of doing so it is doubtful that a collection of dismounted tank crew, technical and support personnel and land-bound sailors would have been able to do much more than harass a properly functioning British Parachute Brigade. Much is sometimes made of a month-long anti-airborne training cycle carried out by the *Hohenstaufen* in September 1943, but the practical value of this a year later and after the Division's losses in Normandy is arguable at best.[16] Be that as it may, Gräbner's *SS Panzer Aufklärungs Abteilung* 9 was not able to interfere immediately either, partly because it had deliberately rendered itself immobile, and partly because by 17 September its vehicles had been loaded onto railway flatcars for transport to Siegen. In fact, there was only one German unit definitely capable of interfering with a British landing and advance from Wolfheze within the necessary time frame, and it was not part of the *Hohenstaufen*. This was *Hauptsturmführer* Sepp Krafft's *SS Panzergrenadier Ausbildungs und Ersatz Bataillon 16*, sometimes referred to as *Bataillon* Krafft, a replacement training unit billeted near Oosterbeek, three-and-a-half miles east of Wolfheze and thus midway between the 1ˢᵗ Airborne Division's landing area and Arnhem proper. With between 306 and 435 men organised into two infantry and one heavy weapons *kompanien*, Krafft's command appears fairly formidable on paper but almost half its personnel were officially classified as not yet combat ready.[17] Whatever its level of training, such a relatively lightly armed unit was again only capable of harassing a multi-brigade Airborne landing at best, and dealing with it should have been well within the capabilities of a properly functioning Parachute Brigade. In addition, the German policy of not billeting troops in large urban areas meant that once Krafft's unit had been side-lined or destroyed there was nothing standing between the 1ˢᵗ Airborne Division and Arnhem proper, which at least partially nullified the handicap of distance between landing area and objective. However, success still depended on the Airborne interlopers making the absolute maximum of the element of surprise, by moving from the landing area with sufficient speed, urgency and aggression to reach and secure their objectives before the Germans could react and formulate counter-measures.

There was at least one other German presence in Oosterbeek besides Krafft's training and replacement unit, somewhat smaller but more illustrious. The creation of a new front in Holland to counter the British advance toward the Meuse-Escaut Canal was only part of a reorganisation of German forces in Holland under a reconstituted *Heeresgruppe B*, still commanded by *Generalfeldmarschall* Walther Model. By 13 September the area between the Meuse-Escaut Canal and the River Waal had been designated the Forward Combat Zone, manned by 1 *Fallschirmjäger Armee*, *Kampfgruppe* Chill and *176* and *719 Infanterie Divisions* which were tasked to prevent any further Allied advance. The area north of the Waal, dubbed the Rear Combat Zone, was configured to support operations to the south. This involved setting up reception centres to screen and redirect retreating troops, and preparing positions and covering detachments to guard crossing points over various rivers and canals that criss-crossed the area. To this end an eleven-strong demolition party was stationed at the south end of the Arnhem railway bridge, and the nearby road bridge was protected by a twenty-five-strong detachment, for example; both locations were also equipped with a handful of light *flak* guns. All depot, internal security and replacement training units from all branches within the Rear Combat Zone were considered first-line reinforcements for the Forward Zone, which in the Arnhem area amounted to Krafft's unit and *SS Wacht Bataillon 3*, a largely Dutch internal security unit based twelve miles west of Arnhem at Ede. All this was controlled by *Heeresgruppe B* HQ, which by 13 September was housed in the Hotel Tafelberg in southern Oosterbeek. *Generalfeldmarschall* Model had thus inadvertently placed his HQ just three miles or so from the 1ˢᵗ Airborne Division's designated landing area, and directly in its line of advance to Arnhem.

***

While all this was going on around Arnhem, the Guards Armoured Division was continuing to press forward sixty miles to the south. Having pushed across the Albert Canal at Beeringen on 7 September, it took the Guards a further five days to clear the villages of Bourg Leopold, Heppen and Hechtel, roughly seven miles short of the next water obstacle, the Meuse-Escaut Canal. The Grenadier Guards Group resumed the advance north on Saturday 9 September, while the fight for Hechtel was still in progress but ran into determined German resistance that inflicted a number of casualties, including twenty-one-year-old Lieutenant Sir Howard Frederick Frank, Second Baronet of Withyham, who was mortally wounded when his tank was hit.[18] The advance also involved the Irish Guards Group. After handing over the Beeringen bridgehead to elements of the 11ᵗʰ Armoured Division at 17:30 on Friday 8 September, the 3ʳᵈ Irish Guards made a dusk move to Helchteren and spent the night laagered short of the town with tanks from the Regiment's 2nd Battalion.[19] The halt highlighted that there was more to tank-infantry co-operation than merely pairing up units according to cap badge, and that the Guards Armoured Division was deficient in such expertise, despite its experience in Normandy. Even though at least one of the 3rd Irish Guards companies was deployed in front of the 2nd Irish Guards tanks, the latter adhered to their apparently standard practice of spraying fire from their .30 machine-guns at any sound or movement in the darkness to their front; as a result one infantry company HQ was pinned down in the farmhouse it had occupied, and one of its platoon commanders was obliged to run the gauntlet of 'friendly' fire in order to obtain tank support against a German probe.[20] The 3rd Irish Guards lost a total of nine killed and eighteen wounded over the period 8-9 September. Three of the dead were officers killed in the morning at Beeringen; whether any of the remainder resulted from the Irish Guards tanks is unclear.[21]

This lack of training or practical co-operation was further highlighted the following day. At 14:00 the 3rd Irish Guards was ordered to move forward to the village of Exel, two or three miles north-east of Hechtel, riding the 2nd Battalion's tanks rather than using its own troop-carrying vehicles. As Lieutenant Brian Wilson, a platoon commander in the 3rd Battalion's 2nd Company, commented:

> For most of us it was our first close-up view of a tank. On reflection, it seems surprising that, for infantry in an armoured division, training in Britain did not include any exercises in company with tanks. We had to be told on that particular day that, if an infantryman needed to speak to a tank crew, he should do so by means of the telephone set on the back of the tank. Otherwise, engine noise would make ordinary conversation inaudible. It did on the telephone, too.[22]

The move appears to have gone uneventfully and Exel was reached at approximately 18:00, although there were ample signs of recent German occupation of the area, including knocked-out vehicles, groups of prisoners guarded by Grenadier Guardsmen, German military road signs and large pits for concealing tanks and other large vehicles. However, fresh orders obliged another move as the infantry were deploying to night defensive positions. A patrol from the 2nd Household Cavalry commanded by Lieutenant J. N. Creswell had located an intact bridge across the Meuse-Escaut Canal seven miles or so to the north, and the Irish Guards Group was thus tasked to move immediately to secure it, following a route marked by other Household Cavalry vehicles covering side roads.

It is uncertain when the Irish Guards Group reached the de Groot Bridge, located just west of Neerpelt, but it was secured in a hasty attack by Captain J.A.H. Hendry's No. 2 Company supported by a troop of Shermans commanded by Lieutenant D. Lampard.[23] The rapid British advance appears to have come as a total surprise to the German troops tasked to defend the bridge. Two prisoners taken in the process claimed to have only recently arrived from garrison duty in Denmark, and that they and their comrades had mistaken the Irish Guards' tanks for friendly vehicles. With the bridge secured, a Captain Hutton RE moved in to make safe and remove a number of demolition charges; according to Lieutenant Wilson, who met him near the bridge, Hutton was assisted by four Irish Guardsmen 'volunteered' for the task by their RSM. Whatever the truth of that, Hutton was subsequently awarded the Military Cross for his part in the affair.[24] In all, the action cost the Irish Guards one dead and five wounded, although the fatality and two of the wounded may have been suffered earlier.[25] Immediate German reactions were muted, but began in earnest at around 09:00 the following day, with an infantry counter-attack supported by a single armoured vehicle variously reported as a self-propelled gun or a Tiger tank. The attack was driven off but not before the armoured vehicle had closed to within a hundred yards of the 3rd Irish Guards' HQ. It is unclear whether it was knocked out but the Battalion MT officer, Captain Edward Rawlence, was killed while stalking it with a PIAT. The RSM appears to have suffered blast and burn injuries to the eyes and face in the same incident. The day's action cost the Irish Guards three more killed and ten wounded, some of the latter apparently hit by German mortar and artillery fire that also wrecked a number of vehicles, including a staff car belonging to the Battalion commander, Lieutenant-Colonel John O. E. Vandeleur. The captured bridge was christened 'Joe's Bridge' the following day as some kind of compensation.[26]

In the meantime the Germans were forming a new unit to block and repel the British penetration across the Meuse-Escaut Canal. Named after the *Fallschirmjäger Oberst* who commanded it, *Kampfgruppe* Walther was ordered into existence on 12 September and initially comprised a handful of *Luftwaffe* units. These included *Oberstleutnant* Friedrich von der Heydte's *Fallschirmjäger Regiment 6*, *Fallschirmjäger Ausbildungs Regiment* Hoffmann, a replacement training unit commanded by an *Oberstleutnant* Helmuth von Hoffmann and *Luftwaffe Strafbataillon 6*, a penal unit drafted in from Italy still wearing tropical uniform. Despite their *Fallschirmjäger* titles the former two formations contained large numbers of partially or totally untrained *Luftwaffe* ground personnel, reportedly up to ninety per cent in the case of von Hoffmann's unit, and the penal unit proved to be marginally effective at best.[27] They were therefore augmented with *Sturmbannführer* Heinke's *Kampfgruppe* from 10 SS *Panzer Division*, which arrived in the area from Arnhem on 12 or 13 September. *Oberst* Walther himself reportedly arrived at Valkenswaard, seven miles north of Neerpelt, in the early hours of Wednesday 13 September. After taking charge of his new command from *Oberstleutnant* von Hoffmann, Walther immediately issued orders for a co-ordinated attack to be mounted against the Neerpelt bridgehead the following day.[28] Although cloudy weather protected preparations from air attack, vigilant British artillery observers brought down heavy fire on any detected activity, and the HQ of von Hoffmann's *I Bataillon* located at Luyksgestel, three miles north-west of the bridge, suffered this unwelcome attention on several occasions. A comment by *Leutnant* Heinz Volz, the *Bataillon* adjutant, illustrates the deleterious effects:

> Lieutenant Hansbach was killed on 13 or 14 September by a direct artillery strike on his trench. A member of the staff was torn to pieces as a shell splinter set off the hand grenades he was carrying. At the same time a *Feldwebel* fell before the door of the command post, killed by a mortar burst. Another of these persistent strikes…landed when Lieutenant-Colonel von der Heydte happened to be present. With an elegant leap he disappeared through the ground floor window. I – with splinters flying all at around, covered in plaster and dust – got further under the table.

A ringing field telephone had to be left unattended during the shelling; when a lull finally permitted Volz to answer it he received a dressing down from a *Major* Schacht at *1 Fallschirmjäger Armee* HQ who touchily reminded Volz that keeping a superior waiting on the telephone was a breach of military protocol.[29] On the British side the point of the bridgehead, just a mile or so short of the Dutch border, was taken over by the 5th Coldstream Guards on 12 September. The 2nd Irish Guards' tanks were withdrawn across the Albert Canal, while the 3rd Irish Guards took over a sector of pine forest on the left of the perimeter. Lieutenant Wilson's 2nd Company was designated to provide close protection for Battalion HQ, although enthusiasm for what appeared to be a cushy task waned when it became apparent that it included digging slit trenches for the HQ personnel in addition to their own. Matters were enlivened by sporadic German shelling, and a nuisance night bombing attack by an unidentified light aircraft.[30]

Kampfgruppe Walther's attack was to be spearheaded by *Fallschirmjäger Regiment 6* attacking the western sector of the bridgehead, by securing the hamlet of La Colonie and moving across Heunel Heath to the bridge. *Fallschirmjäger Ausbildungs Regiment* Hoffman and *Hauptsturmführer* Dr Segler's battalion from *SS Panzergrenadier Regiment 19* were to mount diversionary attacks astride and east of the Hasselt-Eindhoven highway, supported by a number of *Jagdpanzer* IVs from *Hauptsturmführer* Roestel's *SS Panzerjäger Abteilung 10*. The attack was launched at 08:00 on 14 September in light drizzle and under low cloud that kept Allied fighter-bombers at bay, although some elements may have moved in before daylight; at least one British unit reported activity by infiltrators armed with machine-guns and *Panzerfausts*.[31] Von der Heydte's men overran some outlying positions on the approach to La Colonie but then ran into defensive artillery fire called down by the British at 08:30 and the advance subsequently became bogged down in the village. To the east the supporting attacks did little to alleviate the pressure, for the *Jagdpanzers'* narrow tracks had difficulty coping with the boggy conditions off-road, and their presence also appears to have prompted counter-attack by British armour. Up to three of Roestel's vehicles may have been knocked out in the course of the day's action.[32] The German attack may have been rebuffed, but it did put the 3rd Irish Guards under heavy pressure, and especially No. 3 Company defending the edge of the wood occupied by the Battalion. The thickness of the forest made it difficult to prevent German infiltration, and Lieutenant Humphrey Kennard's platoon became the focus of determined German attack. This grew so intense that Lieutenant Wilson's platoon, which was still providing close protection for Battalion HQ, was ordered to detach a Rifle Section as reinforcement. The section, led by a Sergeant Sullivan, ran into a German assault and was overrun with at least one man being killed and the remainder taken prisoner.[33] The attack finally ceased at nightfall when the Germans broke contact under cover of an intense artillery and mortar barrage, while the Guards took advantage of the lull to reorganise into a tighter perimeter. The days fighting cost the 3rd Battalion seven dead including Lieutenant Kennard, twenty-three wounded and five missing; the latter appear to have been Sergeant Sullivan's ill-fated section.[34] Darkness did not mean a lull for everyone, however. Lieutenant Wilson was detailed to carry out a reconnaissance patrol to determine whether the Germans remained in front of No. 3 Company's original positions, and if so in what strength. Accompanied by two volunteers, he initially lost his bearings but after gingerly skirting a pair of burning farms that had not featured in his pre-patrol appraisal, he eventually ascertained that the woods 600 yards to the Battalion's front were occupied by von der Heydte's *Fallschirmjäger*. The patrol regained the safety of the Battalion perimeter after two hours or so, and only a few yards from the start point.[35]

The Guards Armoured Division was relieved by elements of the 50th (Northumbrian) Division on 15 September, with the 3rd Irish Guards' positions being taken over by the 1st Hampshires from 231 Infantry Brigade.[36] Lieutenant Wilson witnessed the arrival of the Hampshire advance party while breakfasting on bully beef and 'liberated' German champagne; the cold breakfast was apparently due to the 2nd Company's cook truck being damaged by German shellfire the previous day.[37] The handover occurred around midday, with the Guards marching back to meet their motor transport at an abandoned factory just south of Joe's Bridge, which then carried them to billets farther south. In all, the Guards Armoured Division had suffered a total of 113 killed, 405 wounded and 80 missing in the eleven days between liberating Brussels and its withdrawal from the bridgehead, with the burden falling mainly upon the 1st Welsh, 3rd Irish and 5th Coldstream Guards.[38] The 3rd Irish Guards may have been especially badly affected by this, given that officer losses from 8 September obliged the Battalion to reorganise eight days later.[39] Nonetheless, the general attitude appears to have been a desire to get on with the job and puzzlement that things were not being pressed with greater urgency. As Lieutenant Wilson put it:

> It was now 15 September, four whole days after the capture of Joe's Bridge. Everyone was perturbed by the delay in the advance and could not understand it…every day of inaction would probably result in greater opposition ahead. This became only too apparent in days to come [and] subsequent events showed that the risk in continuing the advance at once might have been justified.[40]

Having sustained considerable losses in the 14 September attack, *Kampfgruppe* Walther reverted to containing the British incursion, but there was at least one attempt to deal with Joe's Bridge using a more unconventional method. During the afternoon of Friday 15 September a party of *Kriegsmarine* combat swimmers appeared unannounced at the HQ of *SS Panzergrenadier Regiment 21* on the eastern extremity of the perimeter; the Regiment's original commander, *Hauptsturmführer* Krause, appears to have been succeeded by *Hauptsturmführer* Friedrich Richter by this time. Having checked their credentials from *OKW* and ascertained their mission was to destroy the bridge utilising a 500-kg sea mine, Richter passed his visitors along to the company adjacent to the Meuse-Escaut Canal escorted by his adjutant, *Obersturmführer* Heinz Damaske. A truck was used to move the team and its equipment to a farm close to the front line after dark, but thereafter matters unfolded in a less than satisfactory manner. The only manpower available to assist was a handful of signal personnel from the company HQ, which proved insufficient to move the mine silently in the darkness, and this was compounded by a ten-foot drop to the water of the canal. The result was predictable, and the British troops on the opposite bank, alerted by the scuffling, muffled conversation and splashing, opened fire on the source of the noise with machine-guns and mortars.[41] As *Obersturmführer* Damaske drily noted later: 'It did not bear thinking what would happen should it [the mine] be struck by a mortar round. This is precisely what occurred to the naval team as well. Their task they decided was impossible under these prevailing conditions, and they left us alone with their "package."'[42]

With that, attempts to demolish the bridge appear to have come to an end, and the units encircling the bridgehead were obliged to restrict their activities to monitoring British activity. Richter's men reported hearing heavy vehicles moving on the Hechtel-Valkenswaard road to the south, along with vehicle lights, as did other *Kampfgruppe* Walther men and other units. *719 Infanterie Division* reported continuous vehicle movement on the roads behind the Albert Canal throughout the night of 15-16 September, and *Kampfgruppe* Chill prophesied a major attack once the British had finished concentrating additional armour within the bridgehead.[43] Whatever else it might have been, Operation GARDEN was clearly not going to be a surprise for the German troops immediately facing it.

***

Meanwhile the senior commanders from the Guards Armoured, 43rd and 50th Divisions and attached units and formations were being introduced to their roles in Operation GARDEN via a large-scale briefing at 11:00 on Saturday 16 September held in the cinema at Bourg Leopold. The gathering appears to have resembled a fancy-dress party owing to the wide variety of non-issue garb on display: 'The variety of headgear was striking…The Royal Armoured Corps affected brightly coloured slacks or corduroys. The Gunners still clung for the most part to riding breeches or even jodhpurs. Few had retained their ties, but wore in their place scarves of various colours, dotted with white spots. Sniper's smocks, parachutist's jackets, jeep coats, all contributed to the amazing variety of costume.'[44] The briefing was delivered in person by the commander of 30 Corps, Lieutenant-General Brian Horrocks. After striding theatrically down the aisle and mounting the stage, he opened proceedings with the oft-quoted line 'This is a tale you will tell your grandchildren….and mighty bored they'll be!'

Horrocks then outlined the concept of MARKET GARDEN with the aid of a large map board with the airborne objectives at Eindhoven, Nijmegen and Arnhem marked with violet tape. 30 Corps' role in the operation marked on the map with black arrows running between the airborne objectives. The Guards Armoured Division, led by the Irish Guards Group, was to spearhead the breakout from the Neerpelt bridgehead and lead the advance north. The 43rd Division was to trail the Guards, along with the equipment necessary to span the broad Dutch rivers and canals and 9,000 engineers to erect it. This included not only assets belonging to 30 Corps and its three subordinate Divisions but also 21st Army Group's Bridge Column and an additional 2,000 truckloads of equipment gathered from across the theatre. All this was sufficient to bridge the Wilhelmina Canal, the Maas-Waal Canal and Rivers Waal and Lower

Rhine, while the additional truckloads provided sufficient equipment to totally resupply the formation and division-level bridging units and to put pontoon bridges across all the major water obstacles too.[45] If any of the major bridges were destroyed before the airborne troops could secure them, the Guards Armoured Division was to peel away to the flanks and permit the 43rd Division to move up and cover the engineers while they went about their work. Once the Lower Rhine had been crossed the 43rd Division was to take over the point of the advance, pushing on from Arnhem across the River Ijssel and on to Deventer and Zutphen, while the 50th Division followed on as the Corps' reserve.[46] Horrocks stressed that speed was vital, reiterating Montgomery's priority expressed at their meeting on 12 September, and specified that Arnhem had to be reached within forty-eight hours if possible. This was a tight schedule by any standard, for to meet it the ground advance would have to reach Eindhoven by approximately 17:00 on Sunday 17 September, Veghel by midnight, Grave by midday Monday 18 September, Nijmegen by 18:00 and finally Arnhem by 15:00 on Tuesday 19 September.

While this timetable was not issued as an explicit operational requirement, the idea of a forty-eight-hour deadline appears to have originated at the meeting between Montgomery and Browning in the former's caravan at 21st Army Group HQ on 9 September; Montgomery allegedly announced that the operation should be achievable within two days, while Browning allegedly suggested that the airborne force could hold on for four.[47] More pertinently, a primary source simultaneously explains why no specific timetable has been found and indicates the likely source of the forty-eight-hour deadline: '...in a discussion before the operation, General Dempsey said that he expected to reach Arnhem by D+2...No latest date was fixed for a junction between 30 Corps and 1 Airborne Div and dates were not discussed with General Horrocks.'[48] This also accords with Browning receiving his orders to proceed with MARKET from Dempsey, rather than Montgomery, as popularly but erroneously assumed.[49] Horrocks may not have been privy to these discussions but he nonetheless specifically stated that his intent was to reach Arnhem 'if possible in forty-eight hours' during the Bourg Leopold briefing.[50] The timings necessary to achieve this deadline also permeated down the chain at least as far as the 5th Guards Armoured Brigade. Its commanding officer personally signed a declaration of future operations on 15 September which read 'Intention: To reach the area north of Eindhoven 4321 before dark on 17th September in preparation for advance at first light on the following day, 18th September'. This intention was repeated and signed again the following day.[51] Thus while it is true that the forty-eight-hour relief deadline was not issued explicitly, it is clear that it emanated from the top and more importantly, was disseminated to and accepted by virtually all parties and command levels involved in MARKET GARDEN.

It is unclear how long the Bourg Leopold briefing took; according to Lieutenant-Colonel Curtis D. Renfro, a liaison officer from the 101st Airborne Division, Horrocks talked for an hour.[52] Details may also have been disseminated to subordinate formations and units beforehand, given that Lieutenant Wilson and the 3rd Irish Guards appear to have been briefed on their part in Operation GARDEN while the Bourg Leopold briefing was still underway. The briefing placed the Irish Guards Group at the very forefront of the attack, a rather curious choice given that the infantry component had only been out of the line for less than forty-eight hours, and was presumably due to the atypical Guards habit of permanently grouping tank and infantry units by regimental affiliation. The reaction of the 3rd Irish Guards to being assigned the spearhead of the new advance was not recorded.[53] Interestingly and perhaps significantly, the presence of Allied airborne troops along the GARDEN route only appears to have been seen as an incidental factor in either briefing as related, which concentrated on simply reaching the assigned crossing points. It is also curious that Horrocks waited four days to reveal GARDEN officially to his subordinate commanders, although the details may have been disseminated twenty-four hours earlier via 30 Corps' Operation Instructions No. 24, issued on 15 September.[54] Horrocks may therefore have been waiting for Montgomery's official authorisation for the Operation, which did not appear until 14 September as part of a wide-ranging directive.[55]

Horrocks' reticence nonetheless remains curious because the prevailing circumstances and sheer scale of GARDEN required every possible minute of preparation time; the initial attack involved gathering and marshalling in the region of 20,000 assorted vehicles, for example.[56] Furthermore, future events strongly suggest that 30 Corps was not fully ready to launch GARDEN on 17 September, and while this would appear to have been largely due to the fight across the Albert and Maas-Escaut Canals, Horrocks' tardiness may nonetheless have also sacrificed valuable preparation time. The root of the problem was likely Horrocks' physical condition; some observers at the Bourg Leopold briefing noted that he looked unwell, which was indeed the case. Horrocks had been seriously wounded in a *Luftwaffe* strafing attack near Bizerte in Tunisia on 24 June 1943, and his wounds required multiple operations and over a year of recuperation.[57] At that point in his rehabilitation Horrocks approached Field Marshal Sir Alan Brooke, the Chief of Imperial General Staff, in person and requested another corps level command.[58] His case was doubtless assisted by his status as a long-standing Montgomery protégé, having commanded a battalion and then a brigade in the latter's 3rd Division in the retreat to Dunkirk in 1940. Whatever the rationale, Horrocks was given command of 30 Corps at the beginning of August 1944, although his recovery does not appear to have been complete given that he was suffering 'periodic bouts of high temperature and sickness' that incapacitated him for several days at the end of August 1944.[59] This would certainly explain why Horrocks' approach to the preparations for Operation GARDEN appears to be somewhat casual, and indeed his subsequent behaviour.

***

While all this was going on in Holland, the airborne troops tasked to carry out Operation MARKET were busy recovering from the cancellation of Operation COMET on 10 September. Unit responses varied. The 1st Parachute Battalion, based at Grimsthorpe Castle and Bourne in Lincolnshire, remained on 'instant standby' until 14 September when all ranks were granted thirty-six hours' leave.[60] Fourteen miles to the east at Spalding, the 3rd Parachute Battalion were released on thirty-six hours' leave on the day the cancellation was announced, and then spent the period 12 to 15 September assisting local farmers, presumably with harvesting.[61] The 11th Parachute Battalion, based forty miles to the north-west at Melton Mowbray in Leicestershire, were allowed out of camp on Tuesday 12 September, and then despatched on forty-eight hours' leave the following day. It is unclear whether its running mate, 156 Parachute Battalion, also billeted at Melton Mowbray, was allowed leave after being stood down from COMET on 10 September.[62] The pattern was similar in the US formations. According to Sergeant George Kosimaki, a radio operator with the 101st Airborne Divisions HQ, twenty-four-hour passes were cancelled on 11 September, and the rank and file were aware that an operation was in the offing as the Divisional 'War Room' was placed under strict guard. Leave appears to have been granted the following day, and football practice with newly arrived equipment was arranged for the day after that, Wednesday 13 September.[63]

Meanwhile the Airborne Division commanders, accompanied by key staff members, reconvened at Browning's 1st British Airborne Corps HQ at Moor Park on the morning of Thursday 14 September. All three commanders had spent the days after the conferences on 10 and 11 September drawing up their detailed operational plans and conferring with staff and subordinate commanders, and they now presented their work to Browning and their opposite numbers. Major-General Maxwell D. Taylor, the 101st Airborne Division's commander, began the briefback. The most northerly of the Division's objectives, the four road and rail bridges across the Willems Canal and River Aa at Veghel, were assigned to Colonel Howard R. Johnson's 501st Parachute Infantry Regiment and utilised two drop zones (DZs). The larger, dubbed DZ A, was located just over two miles south-west of Veghel and was initially intended to house the entire Regiment. This was amended after Lieutenant-Colonel Harry W. O. Kinnard suggested inserting part of the landing force closer to the bridges over the River Aa in order to sidestep possible resistance on the western edge of Veghel. Kinnard's 1st Battalion was thus assigned its own DZ dubbed A-1 between the Aa and Willems Canal, adjacent to the railway line running a mile or so north of Veghel. The 501st Regiment's 3rd Battalion, commanded by Lieutenant-Colonel Julian Ewell, was tasked to secure the town of Eerde just west of DZ A, and to block the Veghel-St. Oedenrode road just to the east while Lieutenant-Colonel Robert A. Ballard's 2nd Battalion moved straight for the two bridges over the Willems Canal in the western outskirts of Veghel.

The remainder of the 101st Airborne Division was to land on a large combined drop and landing zone seven miles south-west of Veghel. The southern third of the area, codenamed DZ C, was assigned to Colonel Robert F. Sink's 506th Parachute Infantry Regiment. The latter's mission was to secure the three bridges over the Wilhelmina Canal just south of Son before moving on to secure Eindhoven. To this end Major James L. La Prade's 1st Battalion was tasked to move rapidly through the Zonsche Forest that bordered the landing area, along the north bank of the Wilhelmina Canal and to seize the three bridges. Lieutenant-Colonel Robert L. Strayer's 2nd Battalion was tasked to advance through Son and approach the bridges from the north, while Lieutenant-Colonel Oliver M. Horton's 3rd Battalion brought up the rear as Regimental reserve. DZ B, the northern third of the landing area, was assigned to Colonel John H. Michaelis' 502nd Parachute Infantry Regiment. His 1st Battalion, commanded by Lieutenant-Colonel Patrick C. Cassidy, was tasked to move north-east and secure the four bridges across the River Dommel in St. Oedenrode while the 2nd and 3rd Battalions, commanded by Lieutenant-Colonels Steve A. Chappuis and Robert G. Cole respectively, protected the landing area and acted as Division reserve. The exception was Captain Robert E. Jones' Company H from the 3rd Battalion, which was tasked to move south-west and secure the road and rail bridges across the Wilhelmina Canal just south of Best, reinforced with a platoon drawn from Company C and a detachment from the 326th Airborne Engineer Battalion. The Best bridges were added to the 101st Airborne's list of objectives by Major-General Taylor despite British lack of interest, and it is unclear whether the initiative figured in the 14 September briefback or whether 30 Corps were informed.[64] The central third of the landing area, designated Landing Zone (LZ) W, was reserved for seventy Waco CG4 gliders carrying elements of Lieutenant-Colonel Harry W. Elkins' 377th Parachute Field Artillery Battalion. The glider lift was scheduled to arrive an hour after the parachute landing.

Brigadier-General James Gavin's plan for the 82nd Airborne Division ended up being a little more complicated. The task of securing the Division's most westerly objective, the nine-span 1,800-foot bridge across the River Maas in Grave, appears to have been allocated to the 2nd and 3rd Battalion of Colonel Reuben H. Tucker's 504th Parachute Infantry Regiment, commanded by Majors Edward M. Wellems and Julian A. Cook respectively. In order to seize both ends of the bridge simultaneously, the 2nd Battalion's Company E was to be delivered to a small DZ on the western bank of the River Maas, while the remainder of the two Battalions used the large Regimental DZ O between the Maas and the Maas-Waal Canal to the north-east of Grave. Tucker's 1st Battalion, commanded by Major Willard E. Harrison, was to secure crossings over the Maas-Waal Canal, just east of DZ O. These were located, running south to north, near Molenhoek, Malden and Hatert.[65] A fourth crossing farther north at Honinghutie, a substantial combined road and rail structure, was not included in the 82nd Airborne Division's list of objectives; Gavin listed it as a provisional additional objective to be secured jointly by the 504th and Colonel Roy E. Lindquist's 508th Parachute Infantry Regiments to deal with, dependent upon 'the development of the fight once the landings were accomplished.'[66] Gavin's decision was presumably based on a desire to avoid stretching his units too thinly, and justified by the fact that the MARKET mission orders only specified seizure of 'at least one' of the four crossings.[67] The 82nd Airborne Division's other primary mission was the seizure of the major road and rail bridges that spanned the River Waal in the northern outskirts of Nijmegen.

Accomplishing the latter mission was complicated by Browning directly interfering in Gavin's planning. In his Operation Instruction No. 1 dated Wednesday 13 September, Browning stated that securing the Groesbeek Heights, a wooded plateau south and east of Nijmegen, was of equal importance to securing the Nijmegen and Grave bridges. He went further at the 14 September briefing. After Gavin had finished outlining his Divisional plan, Browning specifically forbade him from moving on the Nijmegen bridges until the whole of the Groesbeek Heights had been secured.[68] Browning's edict raises two points. First, it presents the interesting spectacle of an officer with no operational airborne experience whatsoever and whose sole combat experience was restricted to a brief period of platoon-level command on the Western Front during the First World War, telling arguably the most competent and combat-experienced Allied Airborne commander of the war how to go about his business. Second, it shows that despite being the titular head of British Airborne Forces for three years, Browning had failed to grasp the basic principles of Airborne operations and, more importantly, the capabilities of the formations created to fulfil them. Browning's concern stemmed from the fact that the western end of the Groesbeek Heights overlooked the roads into Nijmegen and the city itself, and presented a potential conduit for German counter-attacks from the nearby *Reichswald* Forest, which lay just inside the nearby German border; according to Gavin, the British were convinced that German armoured units were stationed inside the *Reichswald*.[69]

Interestingly, Gavin shared Browning's concern regarding the ridge overlooking Nijmegen and the approaches to the city, rather than the Heights in their entirety. Even allowing for this, however, the Groesbeek Heights were still a secondary priority and one that could and should have been left largely to the relieving ground forces, not least because the lightly armed Airborne troops lacked the means to withstand armoured attack. Browning ought therefore to have been concentrating upon securing the road and rail bridges over the River Waal, without which the advance north to Arnhem and beyond simply could not take place. In the event, Browning's edict forced Gavin to deploy his three lightly armed Regiments around a perimeter twenty-five miles in circumference, which left him no option but to spread his men wide and thin across key terrain features and road and track junctions. Browning therefore elicited precisely the opposite result to that intended, insofar as his injunction undermined the 82nd Airborne Division's collective ability to defend against serious attack from the *Reichswald* or anywhere else. It was also arguably unnecessary, given that the Nijmegen bridges were not actually visible from the Groesbeek Heights as claimed, and it would have been perfectly feasible to establish a much tighter perimeter running through the more defensible urban terrain in the outskirts of Nijmegen.[70] In short, possession of the Nijmegen bridges was absolutely crucial for a successful execution of MARKET GARDEN while possession of the Groesbeek Heights was not, and seizing the bridges should therefore have been the first priority. By ordering otherwise, Browning had clearly failed to identify the primary aim and was seemingly oblivious to the crucial need to concentrate upon it rather than peripheral issues. As we shall see, the 82nd Airborne Division was to pay a high price for Browning's fixation with the Groesbeek Heights, and neither was this to be his sole deleterious intervention in the MARKET planning phase.

Gavin's memoir gives no hint that he was anything other than in full accord with Browning's concerns and instructions over the Groesbeek Heights, while the US official history based on his post-war testimony only mentions Browning in passing and gives the impression that Gavin decided to prioritise the Heights over the Nijmegen bridge on his own initiative.[71] However, this is undoubtedly due to Gavin's scrupulously neutral and unfailingly courteous attitude to superiors and subordinates alike, which characterises his writings even when he would have been more than justified in complaining or criticising. Furthermore, despite claiming to fully concur with Browning's edict, Gavin nonetheless admitted to being 'deeply troubled by the prospect of failing to accomplish some of my objectives'. Even more pertinently, in the run-up to MARKET Gavin held regular discussions on the matter with Colonel Roy E. Lindquist, whose Regiment was tasked to secure the north end of the Heights and was thus nearest the Nijmegen bridges. These discussions culminated in Gavin verbally ordering Lindquist to '…commit his first battalion against the Nijmegen bridge without delay after landing but to keep a very close eye on it in the event he needed it to protect himself against the *Reichswald*.[72] Gavin went so far as to work out and provide a circuitous route to the road bridge intended to avoid becoming disoriented in Nijmegen's streets. With hindsight, it is clear that Gavin was trying to subtly encourage Lindquist to circumvent Browning's order, but subsequent events would show that Lindquist did not fully grasp Gavin's intent; the latter later admitted to being 'a bit ambiguous' and that Colonel Tucker's 504th Parachute Infantry Regiment would have been better placed to go for the Nijmegen bridges, and Tucker presumably more perceptive to subtle hinting as well.[73]

Be that as it may, Gavin was obliged to re-jig his plan to conform to Browning's wishes, and the 82nd Airborne Division's two remaining Regiments thus utilised two separate DZs selected to permit a rapid seizure of the Groesbeek Heights. Colonel William E. Ekman's 505th Parachute Infantry Regiment was to drop onto DZ N, five miles east of the 504th Regiment's main landing area, at the southern edge of the Heights. The DZ, which was also to be used by Gavin's Division HQ and Lieutenant-Colonel Wilbur Griffiths' 376th Parachute Artillery Battalion, was midway between the *Reichswald* to the south-east and the village of Groesbeek to the north-east. Ekman was therefore tasked to secure Groesbeek village, establish a perimeter along the southern edge of the Heights, and establish contact with the 504th Regiment to the west across the Maas-Waal Canal. Colonel Lindquist and the 508th Parachute Infantry Regiment's DZ T was located roughly two miles to the north-east, between Groesbeek and the village of Wyler, which lay just inside the German border. Lindquist was tasked to secure the Heights, establish a perimeter along their eastern and northern edges, and to protect the landing area for Colonel George Billingslea's 325th Glider Infantry Regiment which was scheduled to arrive with the second lift on 18 September; two adjacent glider LZs had been selected just east of Groesbeek, in the area separating the parachute DZs. Occupying the whole of the Groesbeek Heights created a perimeter of around twenty-five miles, which was a tall order even for a formation as experienced and professional as Gavin's, and he was therefore obliged to spread his units wide and thin as a result. As Powell points out, occupying a smaller perimeter extending three miles of so from the centre of Nijmegen would have denied the Germans access and observation over the city and approach roads, but that would not have complied with Browning's insistence on occupying the Groesbeek Heights in their entirety.[74]

The third and final contributor to the 14 September briefback was Major-General Robert Urquhart, commanding the 1st Airborne Division. Urquhart's plan was essentially COMET minus the glider *coup-de-main* landing to seize the Arnhem road bridge. As we have seen, the RAF planners had elected to put the 1st Airborne Division down on an area of heath and farmland approximately seven miles west of Arnhem. The first lift employed two landing areas, a combined drop and landing area south-west of Wolfheze and a smaller landing area just north of the town. The former extended north from Heelsum to the Arnhem-Ede railway line just west of Wolfheze, and was divided almost equally down the middle by a convenient belt of trees. The western half, dubbed DZ X, was assigned to Brigadier Gerald Lathbury's 1st Parachute Brigade, the 1st Parachute Squadron RE and the 16th Parachute Field Ambulance. The adjacent LZ Z was allotted to Lathbury's glider-borne elements, Major C.F.H. 'Freddie' Gough's 1st Airborne Reconnaissance Squadron, the 1st Airlanding Anti-Tank Battery RA, the 1st Airlanding Light Regiment RA, 9th Field Company RE and the 181st Airlanding Field Ambulance. Urquhart's Tactical HQ and Brigadier Philip Hicks' 1st Airlanding Brigade was assigned LZ S, the smaller landing area north of the railway line. Another parachute landing area two miles or so west of Wolfheze, codenamed DZ Y, was earmarked for use by the 4th Parachute Brigade for the second lift on Monday 18 September while the remainder of the 1st Airlanding Brigade were to be delivered onto LZ S and a redesignated LZ X. The third lift, scheduled for Tuesday 19 September, envisaged putting the 1st Polish Independent Parachute Brigade onto DZ K, on the polder land just south of the Arnhem road bridge, while the Poles' transport and heavy equipment were put down on LZ L, two miles east of Wolfheze, along with the 878th US Airborne Engineer Battalion.[75]

Urquhart's plan once on the ground was relatively straightforward. Hicks' 1st Airlanding Brigade was tasked to protect the landing area for the second lift on Monday 18 September, along with Urquhart's Tactical HQ and all the Divisional units brought in on the first lift. Major Gough's 1st Airborne Reconnaissance Squadron was to speed off from the landing area in its armed Jeeps, trailed by Brigadier Lathbury's 1st Parachute Brigade. Gough's men were to seize the Division's primary objective, the Arnhem road bridge, and hold on until Lathbury's men arrived to erect a properly defensible perimeter around it. Once the second lift, consisting mainly of Brigadier John Hackett's 4th Parachute Brigade, was down on the second day, it and the 1st Airlanding Brigade were to expand the Division perimeter in Arnhem to the north, picking up the Polish and other glider-borne elements from LZ L en route. The arrival of the 1st Polish Independent Parachute Brigade near the Arnhem road bridge on the third lift was thus somewhat superfluous, and the Poles were tasked to cross the bridge and set up defensive positions in Arnhem's eastern suburbs.[76] The intent may have been to employ the Poles in the subsequent advance to the Zuider Zee or east across the River Ijssel to Deventer or Zutphen; according to one participant from the 44th Royal Tank Regiment (RTR), his unit was briefed to support a Polish parachute drop near the Zuider Zee.[77]

Urquhart was soon to join Gavin in suffering the interference of Browning. On Friday 15 September Urquhart had somehow managed to find time amidst the preparations for MARKET for a round of golf on the course adjacent to the Moor Park HQ. While playing he was approached by his Operations Officer, Lieutenant-Colonel Charles Mackenzie, who informed him that 'a few' gliders were being trimmed from 1st Airborne Division's first lift; Urquhart acquiesced without objection, apart from instructing Mackenzie to ensure that the reduction did not impinge on delivery of the guns of the 1st Airlanding Anti-Tank Battery RA.[78] Urquhart's reaction was rather surprising, not least because the 1st Airborne Division was already short of airlift. The 'few' gliders actually numbered thirty-eight, thirty-two of which were Horsas, sufficient to lift two-thirds of an Airlanding infantry battalion; the remaining six were Waco CG4s of unknown provenance.[79] Even more surprising, given that Urquhart's first lift was light on infantry, the gliders appear to have been trimmed from the 2nd South Staffords, allotted only twenty-two of the fifty-six machines necessary to move the Battalion in its entirety in the first lift, with the remaining thirty-four Horsa loads being bumped over to the second lift.[80]

Urquhart's lack of reaction may well have been due to the reason for the glider trimming. The thirty-eight machines had been earmarked to carry Browning and his Advanced 1st Airborne Corps HQ into the 505th Parachute Infantry Regiment's landing area south of Groesbeek.[81] This was the means by which Browning had chosen to remedy his total lack of Airborne operational experience, and thus shore up his claim to the top Allied Airborne post. He intended to do it in some style. According to Colonel George Chatterton, who flew Browning's Horsa, Browning was accompanied by an entourage that included his batman, Corps Medical Officer, personal cook, tent and Jeep.[82] There was no practical or operational justification for Browning's inclusion in the first lift or indeed for being in Holland at all, as there was nothing he could do there that could not be done from his 1st Airborne Corps HQ at Moor Park. His presence in Holland was therefore superfluous and nothing more than an exercise in self-promotion at the expense of the men under his command, as subsequent events were to show.

All that, however, lay in the future. Although it does not appear to have been generally expressed overtly, Urquhart's plan was not especially well received by the more experienced Airborne officers present on 14 September. In his memoir Gavin admitted to not believing his ears when Urquhart unveiled his plan and at the time remarked to his Operations Officer, Colonel John Norton, 'My God, he can't mean it.' The latter responded, 'He does, and he is going to try to do it.'[83] Although he astutely noted that it was beyond Urquhart's control, Gavin's comment was initially directed at the seven-mile distance between the 1st Airborne Division's landing area and its primary objective, although it should be noted that the nearest of the 82nd Airborne Division's DZs was five miles from the Nijmegen bridges, and on the wrong side of the Groesbeek Heights to boot. However, Gavin's appreciation ran deeper, as his subsequent comment that Urquhart's plan 'seemed more like a peacetime exercise than war' clearly shows.[84] The options available to Urquhart's first lift were externally dictated and thus arguably acceptable, although that is a matter to which we shall return, but the same cannot be said of the plan for the second lift. While risky, assuming that the 1st Airborne Reconnaissance Squadron and the 1st Parachute Brigade would be capable of pushing through to the Arnhem road bridge was nonetheless reasonable, given that they had the element of surprise and providing they moved with sufficient speed. To expect the 1st Airlanding and 4th Parachute Brigades to repeat the feat after giving the Germans up to twenty-four hours' notice of their intent was anything but reasonable, especially as they would also be saddled with the task of shepherding the Divisional units as well. It is therefore difficult to view Urquhart's assumption that they could do so as anything other than a combination of overconfidence and naivety, arguably to the point of stupidity. It was likely this factor that moved Major-General Sosabowski to reprise his vocal objection to the COMET plan by rising from his seat behind Gavin and calling out 'But the Germans, how about the Germans, what about *them*?'[85]

The underlying problem here was Urquhart's lack of airborne experience, which is evident in almost every facet of his plan. Bitter experience had taught both Gavin and Taylor the crucial importance of starting with the maximum number of fighting troops to hand; consequently the 82nd and 101st Airborne Division's first lift included all three of their organic parachute infantry Regiments, each equivalent to a British brigade, augmented with a few engineer and artillery elements. In contrast, Urquhart filled approximately a third of his first lift with Divisional troops including an entire light artillery regiment and two full field ambulances, while permitting one of his two infantry brigades to be 'trimmed' of almost a third of its strength by Browning's appropriation of the thirty-four Horsas from the Divisional glider allocation. In part this can be ascribed to the structure of British airborne divisions, in which two-thirds of the infantry component was made up of parachute troops, even though the Air Ministry had no intention of providing sufficient aircraft to deliver more than a fraction of them at any one time. Consequently and leaving aside the impact of Browning's interference, as things stood from Urquhart's perspective he had to fill almost a third of his glider lift with Divisional troops because the only infantry available were from the 4th Parachute Brigade. As paratroopers tended to view gliders as a half-step away from outright suicide, turning them into impromptu airlanding infantry would likely have been problematic but not impossible.

However – although it does not appear to have occurred to Urquhart or anyone else – there was a solution that would have permitted him to emulate his more experienced US counterparts and deliver most if not all his infantry component in the first lift. The RAF contribution to the first lift into Arnhem consisted of two formations: Nos. 38 and 46 Groups. The former consisted of six Squadrons of Short Stirlings, two Squadrons equipped with Handley Page Halifaxes and a Squadron of Armstrong Whitworth Albemarles; all were configured as glider tugs, while the Stirlings and Albemarles were also configured to deliver parachutists. No. 46 Group consisted of five RAF and one RCAF Squadrons equipped with C-47s/Dakotas. All these appear to have been configured for parachuting too, given that the bulk of their sorties during MARKET were parachute supply missions. No. 46 Group therefore had sufficient aircraft to deliver most if not all of the 4th Parachute Brigade alongside the USAAF aircraft dropping the 1st Parachute Brigade, while No. 38 Group towed in the 1st Airlanding Brigade's gliders and those earmarked for vital support units. This would have allowed Urquhart to despatch two infantry brigades to secure his primary objective while still keeping the third back to protect the landing area for the second lift. On the downside it would also have meant bumping most of the Divisional units over to the second or possibly third lifts, but of these arguably only the guns of 1st Airlanding Light Regiment RA proved useful and then largely after the original plan had failed and the 1st Airborne Division was trapped and fighting for its life in Oosterbeek. The trick would have been getting Air Vice-Marshal Hollinghurst and the RAF planners to agree to the change in loading schedules. It might have been possible with the support of Brereton, but as a product of the British Army patronage system and thus totally beholden to Montgomery and Browning for his position, Urquhart was likely unwilling if not simply incapable of rocking the boat vigorously enough. However justified, such an action would likely have spelled the end of his Army career.

All this strongly suggests that Urquhart had simply failed to grasp the essential differences between conventional and Airborne operations, and especially that the latter were very much a 'come as you are' affair for which commanders were required to mix, match and balance their units to suit the mission. Lieutenant-Colonel John Frost, commanding the 2nd Parachute Battalion, highlighted the danger of placing non-Airborne commanders in charge of Airborne units:

> However good they might be, they were inclined to think that airborne was just another way of going into battle, whereas in fact the physical, mental and indeed spiritual problems were, when the battle might have to be fought without support from the normal army resources, very different.[86]

The accuracy of this assessment with regard to Urquhart is clear from his plan, and especially the assumption that getting his Division assembled in its entirety was of equal importance to securing and holding the Division's primary objective. As we shall see, Urquhart's decision-making and behaviour once on the ground in Holland further confirmed the veracity of Frost's assessment. These misconceptions ought to have been corrected by Urquhart's senior subordinate commanders, but in practical terms they were little if any more experienced than Urquhart himself. This was arguably most apparent in the case of his senior brigade commander, Brigadier Gerald Lathbury, who had commanded the 1st Parachute Brigade in its attempt to seize the Primasole Bridge on Sicily in July 1943. That particular venture provided little more than an object lesson in how not to carry out an Airborne operation. Nonetheless, Lathbury went on to replicate the same errors in Holland and his plan for seizing the Arnhem bridges resembled a peacetime exercise even more than Urquhart's Divisional scheme. To his credit, Urquhart had noted a tendency toward unwarranted overconfidence on taking command of the 1st Airborne Division that also drew comment from some of his Divisional officers.[87] It was also noted by Sosabowski during a briefing for MARKET at Moor Park at 17:00 on 12 September:

> At the end Urquhart asked: 'Any questions?'. Not one brigadier or unit commander spoke. I looked round, but most of them sat nonchalantly with legs crossed, looking rather bored and waiting for the conference to end. Questions were buzzing round my head, but I quickly sensed that if I started asking questions it would delay the end of the meeting; I would be unpopular with all of them and I did not think that it would be any use anyway.[88]

To be fair, the assembled officer's reticence might have been due in part to the presence of Browning at the briefing[89] and to the ennui resulting from the series of cancelled missions that preceded MARKET. This was certainly Urquhart's view[90] and it was shared by others including Major Philip Tower from 1st Airborne Division's Royal Artillery staff: 'Even the most reluctant of us…who had seen so much fighting already at Dunkirk and in North Africa…were sick of all the cancellations and keen to go.'[91] Nonetheless, that many harboured doubts was also clear from comments made at subsequent lower-level briefings. Lathbury appears to have warned Lieutenant-Colonel Frost that the upcoming battle would be 'some bloodbath', which Frost duly passed on to his 2nd Parachute Battalion officers.[92] After briefing his 4th Parachute Brigade as a whole, Brigadier Hackett presciently informed his battalion commanders and a handful of key officers that they could 'forget all that…Your hardest fighting and worst casualties will not be in defending the northern sector of the Arnhem perimeter, but in trying to get there.'[93] This may have been the same occasion that Captain Nicholas Hanmer, Adjutant of the 10th Parachute Battalion, recalled Hackett predicting that his Battalion would be lucky to lose less than fifty per cent of its officer strength following a morale-boosting visit from Urquhart.[94] Captain Eric

Mackay, commanding A Troop, 1st Parachute Squadron RE, was so unhappy with the Divisional plan that he ordered his men to jump carrying a double scale of ammunition, and personally briefed his entire Troop on escape and evasion techniques.[95] All this was now incidental, however. The die was cast and the 1st Airborne Division was embarking on its first and only full-scale airborne operation with Urquhart's plan, whatever the reservations of his officers.

With the 14 September briefback complete, the Division commanders were cleared to brief their subordinate commanders and authorise final preparations for Operation MARKET, although in some instances the ball was already rolling. The 1st Parachute Brigade held an O Group at the Brigade HQ at Syston on 13 September and issued an Intelligence Summary and Air Operation Order No.1 the same day, while the Brigade's glider element was briefed by the Intelligence Officer at the airfields at Keevil and Tarrant Rushton on 15 September.[96] The pilots of the Glider Pilot Regiment also appear to have been briefed at the same time. Staff-Sergeant Victor Miller from G Squadron recalled being confined to camp at RAF Fairford near Swindon on 15 September, and being briefed by the Squadron commander, Major Robert Croot. Miller and his co-pilot, Sergeant Tom Hollingsworth, then went on to familiarise themselves with their route and the layout of LZ Z, using the maps and aerial photographs issued to each glider crew. In addition, the two pilots had been designated to act as a PIAT team after landing, which obliged them to check and stow the weapon and nine rounds of ammunition in addition to their personal weapons.[97] The morning of Saturday 16 September was spent loading a Jeep and trailer, possibly belonging to the 1st Airlanding Anti-Tank Battery RA, followed by additional briefings, during which Miller learned that he would also be carrying additional passengers. These included an unnamed colonel from 1st Airborne Division Signals, possibly Lieutenant-Colonel Tom Stephenson, a Major Oliver from the Army's public relations office accompanied by a photographer sergeant named Harvey, Stanley Maxted from the BBC and Alan Wood from the *Daily Express*. Miller's reaction was mixed. On the one hand he felt excited at carrying 'such and interesting load', but on the other was concerned that his passengers would be of no help in unloading the Horsa once on the ground.[98]

The men of the 1st Parachute Battalion were allowed thirty-six hours' leave from their billets in Grimsthorpe Castle and Bourne in Lincolnshire on 14 September, followed by a Battalion O Group at Lieutenant-Colonel David Dobie's HQ at 20:00 on Friday 15 September. Troop briefings were held the following day, and one participant recalled the Battalion's officers being unimpressed with the far-flung DZ and unsuccessfully volunteering *en masse* to jump on or adjacent to the Arnhem road bridge.[99] The 2nd Parachute Battalion's O Group at Stoke Rochford established that Major Digby Tatham-Warter's A Company would lead the advance from the landing area.[100] At the Battalion's troop billets near Grantham, Private James Sims from Support Company had been informed that he and two other young soldiers had been struck from the operation, although they were not excused from preparations. Consequently, he spent a hot afternoon practising aircraft exit drills in a Nissen hut while weighed down with his loaded kitbag and other jump kit and equipment, owing to his Platoon Sergeant's obsession with achieving a tight stick. In the event, Sims and his companions were placed back on the roster after three older soldiers appear to have decided that MARKET was another no-go and sneaked off for a night of drinking in nearby Nottingham.[101] While Sims was being stood down and then up, his Battalion commander Lieutenant-Colonel Frost was packing the brass hunting horn he used to rally his men into his combat equipment and instructing his batman to pack his golf clubs and dinner jacket into his staff car in preparation for its despatch to Holland with the Battalion ground party.[102] At Spalding a few miles to the south-east, Lieutenant-Colonel John Fitch's 3rd Parachute Battalion were following the same general process after its stint assisting the local farmers, albeit slightly later. Fitch held his Battalion O Group on Friday 15 September, with troop briefings taking place the following day.[103]

Generally speaking, British units were kept in their camps and billets until D-Day, when they were moved by road to the airfields from which they were to be despatched, although there was at least one officially sanctioned exception: the 2nd Parachute Battalion were shuttled in sealed trucks with a military police escort to a cinema in Grantham on the morning of Friday 15 September, where they were treated to a special screening of the 1941 comedy *Hellzapoppin'*, starring the American comedians Chic Johnson and Ole Olsen. According to Private James Sims, 'It was the funniest film I'd ever seen in my life.'[104] In contrast, US practice was to move units from their sometimes far-flung billets into accommodation on the airfields and carry out briefings and final preparations there. In most instances the accommodation was tented, but the 401st Glider Infantry Regiment was housed at Aldermaston in an aircraft hangar fitted out with bunk beds.[105] Not all units were billeted in their entirety, however. The 3rd Battalion, 501st Parachute Infantry Regiment was lifted from Chilbolton near Winchester for example, while the remainder of the Regiment flew out of Aldermaston twenty miles or so to the north-east near Newbury.[106] According to Gavin, the 82nd and 101st Airborne Divisions' units were locked down in such camps by nightfall on Friday 15 September.[107] Not everyone appreciated the process. Private James Allardyce, who moved from billets in the grounds of Wollaton Park in Nottingham with the rest of the 508th Parachute Infantry Regiment, recalled feeling like a prisoner within the British-guarded barbed wire that surrounded his temporary home, and being unable to shake off the gloomy feeling that he and his comrades 'were like condemned men waiting to be led off'.[108]

It is unclear where Private Allardyce was incarcerated, but it was likely one of the airfields belonging to the 313th or 316th Troop Carrier Groups at Cottesmore or Folkingham in Lincolnshire, or possibly one of the 50th Troop Carrier Wings' three airfields in Nottinghamshire.[109] Much of Saturday 16 September appears to have been taken up with troop briefings. The commander of the 508th Parachute Infantry Regiment's 3rd Battalion, Lieutenant-Colonel Louis G. Mendez, used one briefing to register his dissatisfaction with the USAAF performance in Normandy, where only eight sticks of his Battalion unit were delivered onto the correct DZ. The remainder were scattered up to fifteen miles astray and in an effort to prevent a recurrence Mendez addressed the aircrew present: 'Prior to Normandy, I had the finest combat-ready force of its size …By the time I gathered them together in Normandy, half were gone. I charge you: put us down in Holland or put us down in hell, but put us all down together in one place.'[110]

Not everyone was impressed with the operation as revealed at the briefings. Private John Garzia, who had participated in three combat jumps, thought it 'sheer insanity', while Staff Sergeant Russell O'Neal and Private First Class John Allen, also three-jump veterans, were more concerned with the daylight drop; the former included his fears in a letter home while Allen, who was still recovering from wounds sustained in Normandy, was convinced that the Germans would not be able to miss him in daylight. Private Leo Hart, on the other hand, remained convinced that the operation would be cancelled because of a rumour that 4,000 *SS* troops were stationed in the area of the DZ. The rumour may well have originated with Private Philip H. Nadler from the 504th Parachute Infantry Regiment, in an additional and somewhat unusual attempt to inject some levity into proceedings; when his platoon commander had revealed a model of the Battalion objective labelled 'Grave', Nadler quickly responded: 'Yeah, we know that, Lieutenant, but what country are we droppin' on?' Major Edward N. Wellems, commanding the 508th Regiment's 2nd Battalion, noted another briefer referring to the 'Gravy' bridge, presumably for the same reason.[111]

Matters proceeded in a similar vein 100 miles to the south-west, where the 101st Airborne Division was ensconced on six airfields belonging to the 53rd Troop Carrier Wing at Aldermaston, Chilbolton, Greenham Common, Membury, Ramsbury and Welford, located west, south and east of Newbury in Berkshire. Sergeant George Kosimaki from Division HQ referred in his diary to being briefed on 15 September, and to being issued ammunition and Dutch currency the following day at Greenham Common.[112] At Ramsbury the barbed wire and armed guards also gave Corporal Hansford Vest of the 502nd Parachute Infantry Regiment feelings of incarceration; as Ramsbury was given over exclusively to glider serials, he was presumably part of the 502nd Regiment's glider-borne Jeep lift. If so, he was accompanied by the 502nd's chaplain, Captain Raymond S. Hall, who, much to his chagrin, was medically barred from jumping because of wounds suffered in Normandy. Like most paratroopers, Hall considered gliders to be unsafe in the extreme.[113] First Sergeant Daniel Zapalski from the 502nd Regiment's 3rd Battalion at Greenham Common was also recovering from a leg wound sustained in Normandy, but had better luck in circumventing authority. Banned from jumping by his Battalion commander Lieutenant-Colonel Robert G. Cole, Zapalski had sought out written confirmation of his combat-worthiness from the Regimental surgeon. Cole responded by accusing him of being 'a fatheaded Polack, impractical, burdensome and unreasonable' but allowed the medical verdict to stand. Zapalski thus jumped into Holland with his Battalion.[114] Like many of his comrades, Private Donald R. Burgett of the 1st Battalion 506th Parachute Infantry Regiment had become jaded by 'sixteen false alarms and three dry runs', but his opinion changed on being served a full fried chicken dinner with all the trimmings followed by ice cream soon after arrival at a large tented camp at Chiseldon near Membury. Burgett noted that he had received the same superior USAAF rations immediately prior to jumping into Normandy.[115] Private William J. Stone, part of a forward observer team from Battery B, 321st Glider Field Artillery Battalion attached to the 3rd Battalion 506th Parachute Infantry Regiment, made the same connection at Chilbolton on 16 September on being served a steak dinner followed by fruit cocktail, 'a delicacy in the ETO and when it and steak – which never made our menu – were served, while I wouldn't say that we were being fattened up for the slaughter, the air did take on an ominous quality. My feeling was reinforced when the C-47s began landing as dinner was ending. Those pilots wanted their share of the steak and fruit cocktail.'[116] Private Burgett also noted that the briefing that followed the fried chicken dinner was notably short in comparison with those back in May and June, with just a few maps and none of the detailed discussion, aerial photographs and sand table models employed in the run-up to the D-Day drop.[117]

By the evening of Saturday 16 September the briefings and preparations were largely complete. Staff Sergeant Miller of the Glider Pilot Regiment visited a well-patronised Sergeant's Mess at Fairford, although he drank little so as to be clear-headed for the morning.[118] Having adapted to his new role of lugging sixty pounds of mortar bombs, Private Sims spent the evening in the Other Ranks canteen at Grantham petting a cat that had attached itself to the 2nd Parachute Battalion, while somewhere nearby Sergeant Francis Moncur amassed a large pile of Guilders playing blackjack with his issued Dutch currency.[119] At Ruskington near Sleaford, the commander of the 1st Airborne Reconnaissance Squadron, Major Gough, celebrated his forty-third birthday by visiting his parachute contingent in their billets. The Squadron's glider contingent, consisting of thirty-one armed Jeeps under the Squadron's second-in-command, Captain David Allsop, was ensconced with its gliders and Halifax tugs at Tarrant Rushton in Dorset. According to an eyewitness the mood was quiet and a little sceptical, as part of the Squadron had actually been airborne when a previous operation had been cancelled.[120] At least some of the Pathfinders from the 21st Independent Parachute Company based at nearby Newark were in higher spirits; Corporal Alan Sharman was coated green by a smoke flare ignited by one of his men as a joke, and spent much of the remainder of the night scrubbing off the dye. Some succeeded in circumventing the lock-down order. A number of men from the 1st Parachute Brigade's Signal Section repaired to the Plough Hotel in Syston village, and some members of the 1st Airlanding Anti-Tank Battery appear to have visited a public house in Tarrant Rushton.[121] Many appear to have shared the Reconnaissance Squadron's opinion that the Operation would be cancelled at the last minute. They were wrong.

Brereton had taken the decision to launch MARKET at 19:00 that evening, after receiving a favourable long-range weather forecast. H-Hour, the point at which the 1st Allied Airborne Army would begin to land on Dutch soil, was set for 13:00 in the afternoon of Sunday 17 September 1944.[122] While the rank and file were not aware of this, their superiors were, for Brereton had made his decision known at a final high-level meeting convened by Browning in the early evening of 16 September.[123]

D-Day 00:01 to 14:30

Sunday 17 September 1944

While the men of the 1st Allied Airborne Army were counting down the hours to take-off, their air force counterparts were laying the groundwork for Operation MARKET. During the night RAF Bomber Command sent between 223 and 282 aircraft to strike an anti-aircraft battery and four *Luftwaffe* fighter airfields in a position to interfere with the MARKET fly-in.[1] One of the airfields was recently occupied by a unit equipped with the new Messerschmitt 262 jet fighters, and the bombing cratered the runways sufficiently badly to prevent flying operations.[2] Two Avro Lancasters failed to return from the strike against the anti-aircraft battery, and may have collided after delivering their load; there were no survivors and the fourteen RAF and RCAF aircrew from RAF Nos. 90 and 115 Squadrons thus became the first casualties of Operation MARKET GARDEN.[3] With the coming of daylight a further twenty-three Mosquitoes and 200 Lancasters bombed German anti-aircraft positions along the Dutch coast, paying particular attention to three coastal batteries on the island of Walcheren in the mouth of the River Scheldt. Shortly thereafter the US 8th Air Force joined the fray, despatching up to 852 B-17 bombers to deliver 3,139 tons of ordnance on a fifth airfield and 117 German anti-aircraft positions along the fly-in route; the attack cost a further two B-17s and three escorting fighters lost.[4] While this was going on, the Continent-based British 2nd Tactical Air Force struck targets inland, including German barracks at Arnhem, Cleve, Ede and Nijmegen, followed by 212 fighter-bombers from the US 9th Air Force that attacked the anti-aircraft positions hit earlier by the B-17s. In all, the Allied air forces flew 1,395 bomber and 1,240 fighter sorties during the night of 16 September and morning of the following day.[5]

With take-offs scheduled to begin after 09:00, those so inclined were able to get a full night's sleep. In what was likely the case across the board, the Glider Pilots and RAF aircrew at Fairford were roused by an orderly at 05:00. After shaving in cold water Staff-Sergeant Victor Miller from the Glider Pilot Regiment's G Squadron enjoyed a breakfast that featured bacon and two fresh eggs rather than the usual powdered variety, during which he was joined by his co-pilot Sergeant Tom Hollingsworth; being bleary eyed and dishevelled, Hollingsworth does not appear to have imitated Miller's abstemious behaviour the previous evening. Breakfast was followed by a last-minute briefing with the RAF tug crews, which confirmed the previous day's fine weather forecast and thus that MARKET was on.[6] According to Miller the weather at Fairford was clear but at Membury, twenty miles or so to the south, Private Donald Burgett of the 1st Battalion, 506th Parachute Infantry Regiment stared out into thick fog while enjoying a breakfast of bacon, eggs, fried potatoes, toast, orange marmalade, fruit and coffee.[7]

The MARKET first lift was the largest single concentration of military transport aircraft ever assembled for an airborne operation, with the powered component numbering 1,534 machines.[8] Of these, 332 were Armstrong Whitworth Albemarles, Handley Page Halifaxes,

Douglas Dakotas and Short Stirlings belonging to RAF Nos. 38 and 46 Groups, with the remainder being Douglas C-47s from the USAAF 50th, 52nd and 53rd Troop Carrier Wings.[9] The unpowered component consisted of at least 491 gliders.[10] The bulk of these were British Airspeed Horsas, with a payload of just over three tons, while at least thirteen were General Aircraft Hamilcars with a wingspan of 110 feet and a payload of almost eight tons.[11] All carried British troops or equipment for the 1st Airborne Division, and were towed by RAF aircraft from Nos. 38 and 46 Groups. The remainder were approximately 120 US-built Waco CG4s carrying artillery pieces, Jeeps and equipment for the 82nd and 101st Airborne Divisions. These machines were only available thanks to an extraordinary effort by the US 26th Mobile Repair and Reclamation Squadron based at Cookham Common just west of London. The Airborne landings in Normandy had used up virtually the entire stock of Waco CG4 gliders in the UK and by the beginning of July 1944 normal replacement procedures had provided just over a thousand machines, only sufficient for a single division lift. The 926-strong Squadron therefore set up a three-shift assembly line system on 8 August capable of assembling sixty gliders per day, rising to a peak of 100 on one occasion. Thus by 15 September 2,160 CG 4s were available, ninety per cent of which were deployed for MARKET. This, however, raised the problem of who was to fly them, for by mid-September there were only 2,060 US glider pilots in the UK. After consultation with Major-General Williams, Brereton authorised US gliders to fly into Holland with just one pilot and no co-pilot to take over in an emergency; the reaction of the glider pilots and their passengers to this decree does not appear to have been recorded, but can be well imagined.[12]

The MARKET first lift thus involved over 2,000 aircraft and gliders from twenty-four separate airfields spread across an area fifty miles or more west of London, and 100 miles north of the capital in the East Midlands.[13] Consequently the Air Plan, which involved marshalling this aerial throng, directing it out across the North Sea via two waypoints and ensuring the lead elements were in place to deliver their loads at precisely the same time, was a masterpiece of staff work in its own right. The aircraft were organised using two assembly points: Hatfield north of London for aircraft flying from the western airfields, and March in Cambridgeshire for those flying from airfields in the East Midlands. The glider tugs, which were all based in the west, were scheduled to take off first, partly because they were slower than the parachute transports and partly because of the location of their launch airfields. In order to gain height and formation these serials initially flew west, some as far as the Bristol Channel, before wheeling through 180 degrees and joining the western-based parachute transports carrying the 101st Airborne Division. From there the glider element flew east-north-east for almost 100 miles to rendezvous with the parachute transports carrying the 1st and 82nd Airborne Divisions from the East Midlands over Aldeburgh on the Sussex coast. Once assembled, the aerial armada divided to follow two separate paths to the landing areas in Holland. The Northern Route leading to Nijmegen and Arnhem crossed the Suffolk coast at Aldeburgh, codenamed ANTIGUA, and ran south-east over a ship-borne beacon codenamed TAMPA for around 100 miles to the island of Schouwen just off the Dutch coast, codenamed BERMUDA; the route was also reassuringly marked by the presence of seventeen rescue launches. At approximately the halfway point the formation was to be joined by a further fifty-six glider combinations from Manston in Kent and at this point the British glider component was organised into three adjacent streams one-and-a-half miles apart and occupying a corridor of sky up to 100 miles long.[14] At BERMUDA the route doglegged almost due east to a point just north of Eindhoven, where the stream split again, the aircraft and gliders carrying the 1st Airborne Division peeling off to the north toward Arnhem while those carrying the 82nd Airborne Division continued on to the Grave and Nijmegen landing areas.

The Southern Route, which was assigned exclusively to the 101st Airborne Division, ran east from Hatfield for almost fifty miles to the Essex coast near Harwich. It then veered south-east across the Thames Estuary to the tip of the Kent coast near Margate and then east across the mouth of the English Channel with the route again marked by ten patrolling rescue launches.

After crossing the coast near Ostend the route continued east past Antwerp to a point just south of the Albert Canal where it turned north over Bourg Leopold and the GARDEN jump-off line and headed for the landing areas just north of Eindhoven. After delivering their loads the three sections of the armada were to wheel through 180 degrees and retrace the same route back to their home bases to prepare for the second lift the following day. In addition to the electronic EUREKA beacons, marker and rescue boats stationed on the over water legs to aid navigation, the transport armada also enjoyed extensive fighter cover. The Northern Route was protected by a total of 371 RAF Mosquitoes, Spitfires and Tempests, while the US 8th Air Force provided 548 P-38 Lightnings, P-47 Thunderbolts and P-51 Mustangs to protect the Southern Route.[15] Sixty per cent of the fighters were assigned escort duties, while the remainder provided a rolling *flak* suppression effort for the fly-in.[16]

The 05:00 reveille noted by Staff Sergeant Miller at Fairford appears to have been applied to the British Airborne troops across the board, given that at Grimsthorpe the 1st Parachute Battalion 'arose from sleep at an unwarranted hour' for a relatively leisurely breakfast.[17] At Grantham, Private James Sims from the 2nd Parachute Battalion was sagely advised to 'have a good breakfast as you don't know when you'll get your next meal', and a 'good breakfast' also figured in the 1st Battalion The Border Regiment's account of the early morning of 17 September.[18] The atmosphere for the meal was generally light and confident but not universally so. At Manston in Kent elements of the 2nd Battalion South Staffords and the 1st Airlanding Light Regiment RA were served by WAAFs, and the morale value of the breakfast may have been offset to some extent by the sight of some of the latter crying at the prospect of their customer's imminent departure for battle.[19] With breakfast and presumably muster parade out of the way, the British Airborne units ensconced in their regular billets were trucked to their designated airfields from 07:00. The length of journey varied. The 1st Parachute Battalion travelled fifteen miles from Grimsthorpe to the 61st Troop Carrier Group's base at Barkston Heath, for example, while the 2nd and 3rd Parachute Battalions' billets at Grantham and Spalding were eight and thirty miles respectively from the 314th Troop Carrier Group's airfield at Saltby. The bulk of the 1st Airlanding Brigade appears to have been moved from its base at Woodhall Spa in Lincolnshire to temporary billets nearer the western cluster of airfields housing the RAF's glider tug units in preparation for MARKET; the 1st Border Regiment, for example, were billeted at Burford, six miles from No. 512 Squadron's base at Broadwell.[20]

As they were already at their airfields, the men of the US Airborne divisions went back to their accommodation after breakfast to collect their personal equipment, and then marched or were trucked out to the C-47s and Waco CG4s drawn up alongside runways and perimeter tracks. NCOs in charge of sticks were issued slips with their aircraft number, which was also chalked on the aircraft. The 1st and 2nd Battalions of the 506th Parachute Infantry Regiment at Membury experienced some difficulty locating their C-47s in the fog, and Private Burgett's platoon encountered the additional problem of their sergeant being given an incorrect aircraft number. The troops then went into immediate pre-jump routine, packing and mounting A5 Parapacks, the large padded containers for supplies and heavy equipment carried on special racks beneath the aircraft or delivered via the passenger door in mid-stick. The parachutes attached to the Parapacks were colour-coded for easy identification: red or yellow for ammunition and explosives, blue for rations, green for fuel and white for signals equipment or medical supplies; lights with interchangeable coloured lenses could also be fitted for night drops.[21] Parachutes were trucked out to the aircraft, and Burgett's stick was allotted T7 models, the standard US T5 parachute modified with a quick-release box similar to that employed on the British X-type parachute. The modification was carried out in-theatre by Divisional riggers, as a number of US paratroopers had drowned in Normandy after being dragged into flooded areas by their uncollapsed canopies before they could undo the numerous harness buckles or cut themselves free with the knives most US paratroopers carried for the purpose.

As a Normandy veteran Burgett welcomed the modification, but some of his companions complained vociferously, apparently worried in case the box disengaged prematurely.[22]

It also appears to have been US procedure to issue ammunition at this point, again by truck drop-off, although it is unclear whether this included individual basic loads as well as ammunition for crew-served weapons and explosives. According to Burgett, every man in his stick carried two cans of .30 belt, two bazooka rounds, two mortar bombs, blocks of C2 plastic explosive, blasting caps, lengths of detcord fuse and possibly an anti-tank mine in addition to water, three days' K and D rations, spare clothing, combat equipment and personal weapon, parachute, reserve parachute and Mae West life preserver.[23] While a considerable physical burden that meant most paratroopers were unable to board their C-47s without assistance, this was a logical precaution for troops operating behind enemy lines with tenuous resupply arrangements. It was also standard procedure across the board. Brigadier-General Gavin referred to his troopers from the 82nd Airborne Division loading themselves 'with all the ammunition and anti-tank mines they could carry' as a result of experience in Normandy, and to ordering that an additional 700 anti-tank mines be distributed across each of his three Parachute Infantry Regiments.[24] Neither was this an exclusively US practice. Trooper Arthur Barlow from the 1st Airborne Reconnaissance Squadron used 'dozens of packets of spare Sten gun ammunition' as protective packing for a No.38 radio in his parachute kitbag, for example.[25] Major Michael Forman, commander of B Company, 7th King's Own Scottish Borderers (KOSB) made an unexpected discovery on inspecting his men shortly before take-off from Down Ampney. Virtually every man had augmented his load with so much extra ammunition that Forman feared the additional weight would unbalance their Horsa gliders; he therefore ordered it all to be left behind.[26]

At the British airfields trucks dropped the glider plots, their passengers and sticks of paratroopers off by their aircraft, where they carried out last-minute checks and fitted parachutes. Their mood appears to have been less serious than that of their US counterparts, presumably because the bulk of the preparatory work had already been done. At Fairford, Staff-Sergeant Miller rechecked the instruments and load lashing of his Horsa with his co-pilot Sergeant Hollingsworth and chatted briefly with his passengers while an RAF photographer filmed the scene. Duty done, he then lay down on the dew-wet grass to enjoy the sunshine.[27] Some members of the 1st Airborne Reconnaissance Squadron's glider component spent the run-up to take-off at Tarrant Rushton chalking nicknames and ribald comments on the sides of their Horsas. This graffiti was analysed in a post-battle intelligence report by *Hauptsturmführer* Sepp Krafft, the commander of *SS Panzergrenadier Ausbildungs und Ersatz Bataillon 16*, in an attempt to discern the political conviction of the British troops. It is unclear what National Socialist conclusions were drawn from inscriptions like 'West Ham for the Cup' and 'Get up them fucking stairs'.[28] Morale was boosted at all locations by the liberal distribution from canteen trucks of 'char and wads', slang for hot, sweet tea and bacon sandwiches; Captain Stanley Panter from the 2nd Parachute Battalion spent many hungry days in captivity after MARKET bemoaning the fact that he had abandoned a half-eaten sandwich on the wing of his C-47 at Saltby.[29] Private James Sims' recollections of this period provide an illuminating insight into the atmosphere on the eve of take-off:

> Someone dished out great mugs of tea and bacon sandwiches, and a camera crew on a truck came along and filmed us. We jumped about and waved our mugs in the air. The excitement was beginning to build up, everyone was laughing and shouting; the atmosphere had suddenly become like a school outing or picnic. All our doubts seemed to be swept away in a sudden surge of confidence. At last we were going and we somehow knew that this time there would be no stand-down.[30]

The Airborne throng on the glider lift airfields also contained a few more august individuals. At Harwell the commander of the Glider Pilot Regiment, Colonel George Chatterton, had elected to fly the Horsa carrying Lieutenant-General Browning and noted the light-hearted atmosphere and the studied elegance of his distinguished passenger: 'He [Browning] came to the glider immaculately dressed in a barathea battle-dress with a highly polished Sam Browne belt, knife-edge creased trousers, leather revolver holster, all gleaming like glass, a swagger cane in one hand and wearing kid gloves. He was in tremendous form because he realized that he had reached one of the climaxes in his career. There was immense gaiety everywhere.' Once aboard Browning took station on an upturned Worthington beer crate placed between and just to the rear of the pilot's seats.[31] Major-General Urquhart, who was slated to fly in a Horsa from Fairford, also had a high-ranking pilot, Lieutenant-Colonel Iain Murray, the commander of No.1 Wing The Glider Pilot Regiment. Urquhart was accompanied by his ADC Captain Graham Roberts, Captain George Pare the No. 1 Wing padre, Urquhart's batman Private Hancock, a signaller and two Military Policemen as a personal escort, presumably drawn from the 1st Airborne Division Provost Company; the body of the Horsa was loaded with Urquhart's radio-equipped personal Jeep and two motorcycles for the MPs.[32] As he was preparing to board Urquhart was approached by his Operations Officer, Lieutenant-Colonel Charles Mackenzie, regarding a USAAF query about bombing the Wolfheze mental asylum, located in the woods just east of LZ Z and a six-wagon *flak* train on a siding nearby. The Americans were willing to carry out the attack, but only if 1st Airborne Division took responsibility, which Mackenzie had already done on Urquhart's behalf. The mission was scheduled to be carried out an hour before the landing commenced.[33]

Although it has attracted little if any comment, what came next was to have a direct and detrimental impact on subsequent events at Arnhem, and raises doubts about Urquhart's grasp of precisely what he was involved in. Sources vary as to who initiated the exchange, but according to Urquhart's biography Mackenzie then enquired as to how command of the Division was to devolve in the event of Urquhart being 'put out of battle'.[34] The upshot was that command of the 1st Airborne Division was to devolve in the first instance to the commander of the 1st Parachute Brigade, Brigadier Lathbury, a decision that may have been already communicated in general terms to the Division's senior commanders. Next in line was to be Brigadier Philip Hicks, commanding the 1st Airlanding Brigade, and then the commander of the 4th Parachute Brigade, Brigadier John Hackett. Although Hackett was senior in time-in-rank to Hicks, the latter had more experience as an infantry commander as the former had been a cavalryman before joining Airborne Forces. The controversial aspect here is not Urquhart's decision, but the time at which it was taken. Taking a conventional formation into battle without resolving such basic precautions and ensuring they were disseminated and acknowledged by all concerned would have been questionable, if not negligent. To do so in an Airborne operation was certainly negligent and arguably a dereliction of duty, for the vagaries of tow-rope failure, aero-engine malfunction, enemy action or landing accident meant there was absolutely no guarantee that anyone would reach the landing area in Holland in a fit state to carry out their duties. Urquhart's failure in this regard, and more importantly that of any of his staff or subordinates to advise him of his error, would appear to be a further manifestation of the unwarranted overconfidence that infected the 1st Airborne Division. It also provides additional evidence that Urquhart had not really grasped the fundamental differences between Airborne command and operations and their conventional counterparts. He was shortly to confirm this contention on the ground in Holland.

By 09:00 the fog that had complicated the 506th Parachute Infantry Regiment's march to their aircraft at Membury had dissipated in the sun, and the weather was 'fine and clear except for some broken cumulus cloud'.[35] The MARKET force thus began to take off at 09:45, starting with the glider combinations from the airfields in Berkshire and the West Country.[36] If not already drawn up in staggered rows on the end of runways, the gliders were towed forward onto the runway and attached to their tugs. Horsas used thick, 300-foot-long hemp ropes with an integrated radio-telephone cable to allow speech communication between glider and tug, while the US CG4 employed a nylon cable just under an inch in diameter. Staff-Sergeant Miller's account of a Horsa take-off from Fairford provides a graphic insight into the process that followed:

> We swung into the space just vacated…The ground crew plugged the tow-rope into our glider and the tug. Our glider vibrated in the slipstream from the Stirling…The controller stood with the yellow disc raised. I looked at Tom. O.K. Nodding at the controller, I raised my left thumb. Down flashed the yellow disc. The tug began to creep forward, taking up the slack of the rope. I heard the tug pilot call over the intercom 'Brakes off, Number Two!'…We rolled forward. Shooting a glance to one side, I saw the line of men and WAAFs waving farewell. I raised one arm in reply, and then switched my eyes back to the tug, the tail of which was swinging violently from side to side. I kicked the rudder one way and then the other to take the strain off the Stirling. Glider and tug lined up…I watched the airspeed creep up, forty, fifty, sixty mph…The tail of the Stirling lifted gradually off the ground. Levelling off, I hugged the runway ten feet up. The Horsa trembled under the impact of the tug's slipstream beating up from the runway. It was hard to hold her level. One wing dipped, over went the wheel to correct…Our airspeed clocked 110 mph… We were climbing rapidly, and a moment later the hedge at the end of the runway…slid underneath – we were away.[37]

As the take-offs got underway the glider combinations were lifting off at a rate of one every thirty-five to sixty seconds. All of the 1st Airborne Division's first-lift gliders took off without serious accident, although there were some minor mishaps. One Horsa aborted during take-off at Keevil due to load balance problems. A tractor swiftly towed the Horsa off the runway and around the perimeter track to the rear of the queue where the balance problem was resolved by reorganising the passenger seating; the Horsa was then hitched to another Stirling and towed aloft. At Manston the Horsa carrying Major Robert Cain and his men from B Company, 2nd South Staffords came adrift from its Albemarle tug five minutes after take-off. The glider landed safely in a convenient field after crashing through a fence. Major Cain noted the forced landing was a 'terrible anticlimax after the tension and high spirits of the morning' and that there was a good deal of cursing from his men as they unloaded the lightweight motorcycle and Airborne handcarts full of equipment and supplies for transport back to Manston.[38]

Once aloft the glider combinations flew west, climbing to a height of 2,500 feet before levelling off. Those from Fairford did so for at least fifteen minutes before reversing course to form up, while some continued as far as the Bristol Channel. One of the latter, a Stirling from the Keevil-based No. 299 Squadron towing a Horsa loaded with twenty-one men from the 9th Airborne Field Company RE was unwittingly carrying Operation MARKET's first Army fatalities. The combination was just inland of Weston-super-Mare when the horrified Stirling tail-gunner, Sergeant Wally Simpson, saw the Horsa's tail detach, leaving the fuselage and wings to plunge earthward; fortunately for the tug the tow-rope snapped under the sudden strain. The tug crew subsequently visited the crash site to find the tail section had come to rest on a road and the main body of the Horsa looking 'like a matchbox that had been stepped on'.[39] The reason for the Horsa's disintegration was never ascertained, and may have been connected to the numerous explosive devices the Sappers were carrying. As the rear section of the Horsa fuselage was designed for rapid post-landing removal to ease unloading, it may also have been due to a malfunction of that feature. Not all failures had such deadly results, although some were equally alarming for those involved. Lieutenant Graham Wadsworth, Sergeant George Kay and Trooper

Bill Cook from HQ Troop 1ˢᵗ Airborne Reconnaissance Squadron were lifted from Tarrant Rushton in a Horsa carrying their armed Jeep. As the combination turned over the Bristol Channel, Cook saw a foot-wide strip of fabric tear off from the full width of the glider's port wing, allowing the slipstream to ripple and billow the wing's surface alarmingly. After sampling a bottle of rum belonging to Sergeant Kay, Cook informed Lieutenant Wadsworth, who in turn alerted the glider pilots. The combination duly returned to Tarrant Rushton, where repairs to the Horsa were carried out in less than half an hour, before taking off again in a vain attempt to catch the glider stream. Trooper Cook thus listened to reports of MARKET on the radio that night in his otherwise deserted billet.[40] Another Horsa carrying men from the 7ᵗʰ KOSB from Blakehill or Down Ampney towed by a No. 46 Group Dakota ran into trouble when the tug lost power and then recovered and surged ahead. The slackening and then sudden tension on the tow-rope tore a section out of the port wing that extended into the fuselage roof, and one of the Borderers lost his maroon beret to the slipstream while reporting the extent of the damage. When the tug lost power twice more the pilot decided to abort and cast the Horsa off to land at the US 356ᵗʰ Fighter Group's base at Martlesham Heath near Ipswich. The Americans were not fazed in the slightest at the arrival of a platoon of fully armed and battle-kitted British Airborne infantrymen, as Lance-Corporal Stan Livesey noted: 'The amazing thing is that the moment we stopped and opened the door a PX van, with two American girls, was there waiting for us with coffee and chewing gum – two smashing bits of crumpet they were. Then we were all taken to the officers' mess and fixed up with real ham and eggs.'[41]

In all twenty-two Horsas lost their tow while still over south-east England. Some were cast off by their tugs when the latter suffered engine problems, mostly from the twin-engine Dakotas, which were arguably underpowered for glider towing in comparison with the four-engine bombers employed by No. 38 Group. Most, however, were simply tow-rope failures, many resulting from sudden changes of direction to avoid collision. This was especially the case with combinations taking off from Blakehill Farm and Broadwell, which had converging flight paths, and the problem was exacerbated by poor station keeping in the low cloud that lingered over the airfields in Oxfordshire. The Horsa losses fell disproportionately on the 1ˢᵗ Airlanding Brigade and especially the 1ˢᵗ Border and 7ᵗʰ KOSB, which lost a total of fourteen gliders.[42] The Border's losses included the machine carrying the Battalion commander, Lieutenant-Colonel Thomas Haddon, in the second combination to lift off from Broadwell. After a promising start his Horsa suffered a series of instrument malfunctions that obliged the pilot to cast off and force-land; his passengers were back at Broadwell by midday, arranging a place in the second lift. The Albemarle towing the Horsa carrying Lieutenant John Wellbelove, a CanLoan officer commanding the 1ˢᵗ Border's 13 Platoon, abandoned the tow not long after taking off from Manston when its engines began to overheat; the Horsa landed safely and its passengers whiled away the time waiting for transport watching the aerial armada passing overhead and picking mushrooms. Lieutenant Robert Crittenden's platoon from C Company 1ˢᵗ Border had perhaps the most spectacular experience of the day following a tow-rope failure. Despite the loose end of the rope trying to hammer its way through the glider's plywood side, the pilot managed to bring the Horsa to rest in a cornfield near Braintree in Essex after careering across two fields and through a wire fence and a hedge. The commander of a nearby USAAF base came to the rescue by ferrying Crittenden and his men back to their start point in the American unit's B-26 Marauder bombers, with the Platoon's Airborne handcart being lashed into a bomb bay. All went out with the second lift the following day, bar one man injured in the landing.[43]

The first parachute transports, carrying the Pathfinder units tasked to drop in ahead of the main body to mark the landing areas, left while the glider combinations were still taking off. The 186 men from the 21ˢᵗ Independent Parachute Company tasked to mark the British drop and landing zones departed from Fairford at 10:00 in twelve Short Stirlings from No. 190 Squadron. It was the first time the Pathfinders had jumped from Stirlings, which was a daunting prospect in itself. The exit was a large, coffin-shaped aperture in the floor at the back of the fuselage, which gave a clear view of a heavy U-shaped bar designed to prevent parachute strops fouling the tailplane. On jumping the parachutist's head appeared to barely shave this bar, while the violent slipstream caused severe oscillation when the parachute canopy deployed; an attempt to use the Stirling for training descents in early 1944 resulted in over a hundred qualified paratroopers refusing to jump in spite of all the disciplinary sanctions refusal entailed.[44] For the Arnhem jump the 21st Independent's three platoons were divided into sticks of fifteen or sixteen, at least four members of which were equipped with kitbags containing Eureka beacons and other bulky marker aids; all the marking equipment was carried in triplicate so that any given platoon could carry out the tasks of the other two in an emergency. In order to ensure a swift exit and thus tight stick these men were placed around the aperture to be the first to exit; stick commanders generally placed themselves in the middle of the stick with a senior NCO bringing up the rear. The US Pathfinders took off at 10:25 in six C-47s, two carrying men from the 82nd Airborne Division to Grave and Groesbeek and the remainder carrying the 101st Airborne Division's Pathfinders to Veghel and Son–St. Oedenrode. The time difference may have been due to the British formation attempting to disguise its intent as part of the wider preparatory bombing effort by taking a circuitous route, whereas the US aircraft appear to have dispensed with subterfuge in favour of taking a direct route to their target; the fact that the British Pathfinders were only allotted twenty minutes to carry out their work ahead of the 13:00 deadline for the arrival of the main force supports this assumption.[45]

The main body of the MARKET parachute force began to take off at 11:00, with an aircraft leaving the ground every five to twenty seconds.[46] Eight C-47s carrying the 1st Airborne Reconnaissance Squadron's parachute contingent left Barkston Heath at dead on the hour, the 82nd Airborne Division's transports began taking off from Cottesmore, Folkingham and Spanhoe at precisely 11:09, and the aircraft carrying Support Company 2nd Parachute Battalion at 11:30, ten minutes after the first lift-off from Saltby. The last parachute transport was aloft by 11:55.[47] At that point in excess of 20,000 men, 330 guns, 551 Jeeps and Universal Carriers and 590 tons of assorted equipment were in the sky over southern England.[48] After rendezvousing with the glider serials over Hatfield and March the airborne host shook itself out at a height of 1,500 feet into three parallel streams ten miles apart and up to 100 miles long; in some places it took an hour and a half for the streams to pass a fixed point. By chance Sunday 17 September has been designated a Day of Thanksgiving for RAF Fighter Command's victory in the Battle of Britain, and the noise of the MARKET force drowned out singing and church organs alike, drawing out worshippers and householders within earshot to witness the spectacle. The sight of a vast airborne army en route to strike at the heart of enemy territory bore eloquent witness to the reversal of British fortunes since the dark days of 1940. 1st Lieutenant James J. Coyle from the 2nd Battalion, 505th Parachute Infantry exchanged waves with a group of nuns in a convent courtyard, and the party atmosphere continued aboard at least some aircraft. According to Private Roy Edwards from the 1st Parachute Brigade 'it was like going on a bus outing to the seaside.' Some sang popular songs and more ribald ditties.[49]

The aircraft jockeyed into their final formation as the two streams crossed the coast. On the Northern Route the No. 46 Group Dakotas towing the 1st Airlanding Brigade took the lead as the armada crossed the Suffolk coast at Aldeburgh, trailed by No. 38 Group's various four-engine bombers towing the other British glider-borne elements. Next came the C-47s of the US 50th and 52nd Troop Carrier Wings carrying the 1st Parachute Brigade and the 82nd Airborne Division's three Parachute Regiments and other elements. At the rear came the glider combinations carrying Browning's Forward Corps HQ. The high spirits among the airborne soldiers ebbed somewhat as the flight crossed the hundred miles of water to the Dutch coast. At least one man watched the Suffolk coastline until it disappeared in the distance with tears in his eyes, although most were less overtly emotional. Many men smoked or read newspapers and paperback books, and two paratroopers from the 3rd Parachute Battalion were observed playing chess for the entire crossing. Private Leo Hart, a Normandy veteran from the 82nd Airborne Division, was annoyed by a green paratrooper in his stick asking if the C-47's flimsy aluminium bucket seats were bulletproof.[50] Major Alan Bush, the 3rd Parachute Battalion's second-in-command, later described himself as 'the only person to have vomited my way into Europe. I was sick all the way even though I had flown many times. It wasn't apprehension, because it all went like a practice drop; it was the petrol and oil fumes that did it.'[51] There were also some lighter moments during the crossing. Sergeant Bill Oakes, flying as co-pilot in a 1st Airlanding Brigade Horsa, was horrified to see some of his passengers blithely boiling a mess tin of water on a chemical stove set up on the glider's plywood floor. To make matters worse, the stove was set up next to an Airborne handcart loaded with mortar bombs. When the tea makers and their companions standing by with mugs proved impervious to his anger and alarm Oakes appealed to the first pilot, Staff Sergeant Bert Watkins; Watkins responded with a cheery 'Tell 'em not to forget us when the tea's ready.'[52] Three Horsas were obliged to ditch in the North Sea, two with tug engine problems and one owing to tow-rope failure; all ditched successfully with crew and passengers being picked up by the rescue craft stationed along the fly-in route.[53] One was flown by Staff-Sergeant Cyril Line, who was obliged to cast off when his Stirling tug suddenly lost both starboard engines. Matters were not helped by his passengers beginning to break an escape route through the roof of the Horsa immediately on Line's co-pilot issuing the standby to ditch order. Line just had time to order them to desist as they were weakening the fuselage to the point of collapse before the Horsa hit the sea. The glider broke up on impact, but Line and all his passengers were picked up within minutes by one of the rescue launches.[54] At one point the northern airborne stream found itself flying straight at a formation of B-17 bombers flying a reciprocal course; collision was averted when the US machines climbed to pass above the glider serials.[55]

The B-17s had been engaged in final preparatory bombing missions in Holland, possibly against the German anti-aircraft battery at Wageningen, twelve miles west of Arnhem. A total of twenty-four Douglas Bostons, forty-eight North American Mitchells and fifty de Havilland Mosquitoes from the British 2nd Tactical Air Force bombed a number of targets in and around Arnhem itself. The airfield at Deelen, which had been heavily bombed by the RAF on 3 September, was hit again and a Dutch SS barracks at Ede was attacked at the request of Brigadier John Hackett, whose 4th Parachute Brigade was to land on DZ Y in the second lift on 18 September; Ede lay only a mile or so west of the DZ. The Mosquitoes struck the Willems Barracks in Arnhem proper with considerable accuracy and set it ablaze but some bombs fell in nearby streets, setting a high school and restaurant on fire as well. Arnhem's fifteen firefighters led by Dirk Hiddink were despatched with instructions to let the German-occupied barracks burn while trying to save the surrounding civilian buildings, but the damage was too extensive for their two handcarts of equipment to make much impression. Other aircraft knocked out twelve *flak* positions around the Arnhem road bridge but again some bombs fell wide, hitting the prison, courthouse and the church, convent and school belonging to the Insula Dei Catholic community. A good many civilians in Arnhem and the surrounding area were in church when the bombing began, including 1,200 assembled in the city's *Grote Kerke*. The congregation reacted by standing and singing the Dutch national anthem, accompanied by a hand-pumped organ as the raid had cut off the electricity. The numbers of German casualties are unclear, as are those for the Dutch civilians killed on the morning of 17 September, being folded into the total of 188 killed during the subsequent battle. Thirty-seven Dutch civilians were killed in Wageningen and fifty-nine at Ede. A further ninety were killed in the attack on the *flak* train and mental asylum at Wolfheze authorised in writing by Mackenzie in Urquhart's stead just before the MARKET force began to take off. According to an eyewitness, the attack, apparently carried out by USAAF B-26 Marauders, came in two waves. The first struck the area of the railway station, creating around 200 craters stretching away to the north. The second wave hit the asylum area in the woods just east of LZ Z and walked their bombs on into Wolfheze proper, but did not actually hit the main hospital building occupied by the Germans; forty-six of the ninety civilians killed in or around Wolfheze were asylum patients. In fact the *flak* train posed no threat to the British landing area. Originally employed in removing equipment from Deelen airfield after the RAF bombing on 3 September, the train had been badly damaged by Allied fighter-bombers, which also destroyed or put out of action all six of the 20mm *flak* guns it mounted.[56]

While all this was going on the MARKET force was approaching the Belgian and Dutch coast. Two glider combinations did not quite make landfall. One Horsa, piloted by Captain Wreford Tallentire and carrying part of Browning's Forward Corps HQ, was ineffectually shelled by a German shore battery after ditching off Walcheren Island in the Scheldt Estuary. All aboard were rescued unharmed by a British rescue launch in the evening, and the inaccurate artillery fire proved to have been a deliberate ploy on the part of the gunners, who were impressed Red Army prisoners of Armenian extraction; eight were subsequently executed for sabotage. Lieutenant W. G. Beddowe and his platoon from the 7th KOSB were less fortunate when their Horsa ditched just off the beach. After wading ashore they became MARKET's first Allied prisoners of war.[57] The head of the northern stream made landfall at waypoint BERMUDA over Schouwen Island at around 12:15, approximately 100 miles and forty minutes' flying time from the landing areas. It also brought the aerial armada within range of unsuppressed *flak* guns positioned on Schouwen, which claimed three victims from the 82nd Airborne Division's formation. One C-47 from the 315th Troop Carrier Group, flown by Captain R. E. Bohannan, was set ablaze by tracer rounds igniting the A5 Parapacks slung beneath the fuselage. 1st Lieutenant Virgil Carmichael from the 2nd Battalion 504th Parachute Infantry Regiment watched from the door of his nearby C-47 as Bohannan kept the doomed transport flying long enough for the stick of fifteen paratroopers from Company H to jump followed by crew chief Sergeant T. N. Carter, identifiable by his aircrew-issue white canopy. The latter was barely clear when the C-47 nosed over and bored straight into a flooded area at full throttle, killing Captain Bohannan and the rest of his crew, Lieutenants D. H. Felber, B. P. Martinson and Staff-Sergeant T. P. Epperson.[58] The incident prompted a number of jumpmasters including 1st Lieutenant James Megellas from the 3rd Battalion 504th Parachute Infantry Regiment, to order their sticks to stand and hook up their static lines, an instruction not normally issued until the aircraft was approaching the jump point. Another victim was an unidentified C-47 towing a CG-4, which also appears to have been hit. Major Dennis Munford from the 1st Airlanding Light Regiment RA watched the US glider come apart: 'Men and equipment spilt out of it like toys from a Christmas cracker.' The C-47 tug crash-landed, killing its crew.[59]

Owing to its position at the head of the stream, the British glider contingent soaked up most of the flak that briefly escaped the attention of the escorting fighter-bombers. A member of the 2nd South Staffords who slid his Horsa side-door closed in response to a burst of *flak* prompted amusement from his comrades, but a number of men were wounded by shrapnel passing through the glider's plywood skins and the co-pilot of the 1st Border Horsa flown by Lieutenant-Colonel John Place was struck in the head and killed by a shell splinter. In all, eight Horsas appear to have been lost between the coast and the landing area near Wolfheze. One, carrying a Jeep, trailer and four men from the 1st Airlanding Light Regiment RA disintegrated after a direct hit, and two more, carrying a gun crew from the same unit and a Platoon from the 2nd South Staffords respectively came down near Tilburg, fifty miles south-west of Arnhem; passengers and crews all reached safety over a month later with the assistance of the Dutch Resistance. Two more Horsas carrying 6-Pounder guns from the 1st Airlanding Anti-Tank Battery came down short of the landing area, and rallied late but intact under their own steam.[60] Despite the *flak* and forced landings the formation thundered on, encouraged by frantically waving Dutch civilians, to the final waypoint just north of Eindhoven. There the aircraft and gliders carrying the 1st Airborne Division peeled off to the north toward Arnhem, while the 82nd Airborne Division's transports continued east toward Grave and Groesbeek.

The twelve Stirlings carrying the 21st Independent Parachute Company approached the Wolfheze landing area from the west and delivered their sticks of paratroopers at 12:40 precisely. Their arrival was observed by farmer Jan Pennings and a chauffeur named Jan Peelen. The former was returning to Reijers-Camp Farm in the centre of what was to become LZ S, and assumed the Stirlings were going to bomb the railway sidings again until the parachutes appeared. As he was breathlessly breaking the news to his wife, some of the Pathfinders entered his farmyard and after shaking hands, one paratrooper, possibly Private Alan Dawson, informed him that they would be joined by hundreds more within the next half hour. Peelen was struck by the silence of the Pathfinder's arrival and the disciplined way in which they immediately set about their business.[61] 3 Platoon, commanded by Lieutenant Hugh Ashmore, was tasked to mark LZ S north of the Arnhem-Utrecht railway line for the 1st Airlanding Brigade. Ashmore's men shared the LZ with Major Bernard Wilson's Company HQ section. Nicknamed 'Boy' in a wry reference to his years, Wilson was actually the oldest parachutist in the 1st Airborne Division at the age of forty-five. South of the railway line Lieutenant David Eastwood's 1 Platoon was to mark DZ X for the 1st Parachute Brigade, while the task of marking the adjacent LZ Z for the glider-borne support elements was allotted to Lieutenant Cecil Speller's 2 Platoon. The Pathfinder's drop was accurate and without mishap apart from just two landing injuries, although two Pathfinders had German bullets pass through their equipment during their descent. The few German troops in the vicinity, who were apparently caught eating picnic lunches, either fled or surrendered. Major Wilson began MARKET in style by taking the surrender of several overawed Germans immediately on landing, and sixteen prisoners from a horse transport unit were rounded up near the Reijers-Camp Farm, where Wilson set up his HQ. While this was going on other Pathfinders were marking out the drop and landing zones. Large day-glo panels were pegged out to form each zone's code-letter S, X and Z, along with a letter T to indicate wind direction, augmented by smoke canisters and a EUREKA beacon for each zone. The markers were all offset to counter a slight easterly breeze, in the case of DZ X to prevent parachutists inadvertently drifting into the trees that bordered the DZ, and the EUREKA beacons also had to be set up well clear of the trees to avoid interference. Each of the latter was allotted a small defence group, which remained in place while their Platoon mates withdrew to the woods bordering their landing area. All three zones were marked within the allotted twenty-minute deadline, and after confirming that this was the case Major Wilson ordered the release of a number of carrier pigeons which were supposed to carry word of the unopposed Pathfinder landing back to London. The pigeons initially had other ideas and promptly alighted on the roof of the Reijers-Camp Farm, from where they were eventually dislodged with some well-aimed pebbles.[62]

The glider combinations carrying the 1st Airlanding Brigade arrived dead on time at 13:00, approaching the landing area from the south-west at a height of 2,500 feet. After requesting last-minute course corrections from their tugs, the glider pilots pulled the red-topped release lever and cast off on reaching a point approximately two-and-a-half miles from the LZ. The standard operating procedure was to maintain a gentle glide for two to five minutes after casting off while losing a thousand feet or so of altitude, then a steep dive to avoid enemy fire, levelling off for last-minute adjustments and the landing. Staff-Sergeant Miller's account again gives a good overview of the process:

> The voice of the navigator on the Stirling came over the wire… 'OK number two, when you're ready.' 'Okay number one, thanks.' … 'Good luck number two – out'. My hand slid over the red topped release lever…Height 2,500 feet, exactly right. Airspeed 145 mph. I snapped back the release, and we were free…The airspeed needle slid back, 120, 110, 100 mph. 'Half flap!'…The glider bucked as the great flaps were forced down into the airstream, the speed dropped to ninety, then eighty mph…the altimeter was unwinding fast; already we were down to just under 1500 feet…The field was very close now. Already

I could see several gliders motionless with little figures darting around them…Full flaps! The tops of the trees were rushing up to meet us…My eyes flickered to the airspeed. Eighty mph…I eased back a fraction on the wheel…Now the ground was rushing up…Another glider was coming in alongside…We levelled. The wheels hit once. We bounced about three feet, came down again and held. Tom had already slammed on the brakes…We careered across the ploughed field. Dust rose up and was whipped past the cockpit. The line of trees loomed nearer. I gritted my teeth. The airspeed dropped rapidly, sixty, fifty, forty. The wheels sank into the soft earth which helped us to slow up. I relaxed slightly as we ground to a halt. Before the glider had stopped I turned my head and shouted 'OK boys' to the passengers. We were down to fifteen to twenty mph so I released the wheel, tore at my harness release pins and hurled aside the shoulder and leg straps. We had stopped short of the trees by fifty yard.[63]

The first glider down on LZ S appears to have been that flown by Lieutenant-Colonel Place with his dead co-pilot, which delivered its load from the 1st Border onto the western section of the LZ. The Horsa flown by Major Ian Toler and Staff-Sergeant Arthur Shackleton, carrying the commander of the 2nd South Staffords, Lieutenant-Derek McCardie, was first down on the eastern sector. The pilots had been ordered to run up to the far end of the LZ in order to free up as much space as possible for the gliders coming in behind, but unfortunately the soil was softer on the eastern side and Major Toler's Horsa came to an embarrassing stop in the middle of the LZ.[64] Not all the Horsas landed on LZ S unscathed. The pilot of one glider carrying men from A Company, 1st Border took the instruction to push well forward on the LZ to the extreme, sliding his machine into a barn in the treeline despite applying the brakes and tearing off the wheels. Nobody was injured in that incident, but another from the same Battalion's D Company was hit by automatic fire at the edge of the DZ, which wounded Private Ron Stripp in the arm.[65] The heavily laden Horsas carrying vehicles and guns were susceptible to less happy outcomes as a matter of course. Sergeant George Barton from the 7th KOSB was travelling in a Horsa carrying a Jeep and 6-Pounder anti-tank gun which crashed into trees and ended up with its tail high in the air. The impact killed one pilot and left the badly injured co-pilot unconscious and trapped in the wreckage, while Barton and his unnamed driver were obliged to jump fourteen feet to the ground.[66] Some crashes had a lighter side. Private Alan Dawson from the 21st Independent Company watched a Horsa crash head-on into an isolated tree on LZ S, but on rushing forward to assist what he assumed were casualties he found the glider pilots unscathed and arguing fiercely over the destruction of a thermos flask of coffee.[67]

The vast majority of the 1st Airlanding Brigade's gliders came down safely however, and in a matter of minutes 134 of the scheduled 153 gliders were down on LZ S. After pausing briefly to gather their bearings and unload their Airborne handcarts, the passengers from the Horsas carrying infantry platoons began moving to their rendezvous points (RVs) while avoiding still-landing gliders; as Major Michael Forman, commanding B Company, 7th KOSB recalled, 'The gliders coming in were whistling past us – terrifying!' The 1st Airlanding Brigade's constituent battalions rallied according to their post-landing tasks. As it was to move east and secure DZ Y for use by the 4th Parachute Brigade in the second lift, Lieutenant-Colonel Robert Payton-Reid's 7th KOSB rallied at an RV at the northern end of LZ S; as an additional rally marker the Battalion piper, a Corporal Ford, played 'Blue Bonnets over the Border' for a full twenty minutes. Lieutenant-Colonel McCardie and the understrength 2nd South Staffords rallied to Reijers-Camp Farm in readiness to take over protection of LZ S, while the leaderless 1st Border rallied along the railway line at the southern edge of the landing area in readiness to extend a defensive perimeter around DZ X and LZ Z. Although there was some desultory German fire the general atmosphere was of an exercise, an impression reinforced by the scenery. Captain James Livingstone of the 7th KOSB was struck by its similarity to the area around Woodhall Spa in Lincolnshire, and two young soldiers from the 1st Border decided it was safe and appropriate to pause en route to their RV to brew tea. They were rudely and loudly disabused of this notion by their Battalion Signals Officer Lieutenant Joseph Hardy who 'managed to keep a very straight and very stern face for the few seconds it took them to get on their way, and as soon as they were out of earshot I allowed myself a good hearty laugh. It was a terrific morale booster to see two kids, who, in a situation of that sort, thought the most important thing was a cup of char.'[68]

While the 1st Airlanding Brigade was moving to its various RVs or unloading Jeeps, trailers and guns, the gliders carrying the 1st Airborne Division's other glider-borne elements were landing on LZ Z. Many of these machines carried heavy loads and as a result most ended up clustered at the top end of the LZ, with a number overshooting altogether. One Horsa carrying troops and a Jeep from HQ Troop 1st Airborne Reconnaissance Squadron ended up wedged high in a stand of trees, fracturing the spine of Troop Sergeant-Major Bill Meadows in the process; Corporal Cyril Belcham was obliged to climb out of the Horsa and down a tree to get help after dosing Meadows with morphine.[69] The landing difficulties were compounded by areas of unharvested potatoes making up part of the LZ. Several Horsas' undercarriages collapsed on digging into the soft soil, and at least one ended up with 'potatoes flying around the glider like cannon balls'.[70] Several machines came to sudden and premature halts with their tails high in the air and their noses dug deep into the soil, sometimes trapping the pilots and frequently rendering their loads unrecoverable. Unloading was not straightforward even in perfect conditions. With the Horsa it involved cutting the control cables with specially stowed wire-cutters, undoing four quick-release bolts, removing the tail section and then driving the Jeep and its trailer or gun down specially made aluminium ramps. Unfortunately, the quick-release bolts frequently failed to quick release, obliging the crew to remove the tail section by brute force using axes and hacksaws. If the Horsa had nosed in, the cargo had to be painstakingly reversed out of the large side door just behind the cockpit. In normal conditions it took an average of thirty minutes to unload a Horsa, and the process took much longer in the latter case.

The soft soil was a particular problem for the giant Hamilcars with their payload of over seven tons, and four of the thirteen in the first lift suffered serious landing accidents. One crashed into the railway embankment at the north end of LZ Z, shooting its load of two Universal Carriers out through the nose in a spectacular fashion, one came down heavily and broke up on impact, and two each carrying a 17-Pounder anti-tank gun, prime mover and gun crew dug into the soft soil and flipped over onto their backs with potentially fatal results for their pilots and passengers. Lance-Sergeant Sid Fitchett was strapped into the driver's seat of one vehicle: 'I was left hanging upside down, my right foot broken and trapped under the brake pedal, my head and face almost covered in what I thought was potato soil, and, to make matters worse, a jerrycan had burst, and petrol was covering me all over.' He was eventually pulled free after someone snapped the pedal and despatched to a Regimental Aid Post via Jeep. The hazard was even greater for the pilots, as the Hamilcar's cockpit was located in a blister atop the fuselage and directly over the cargo. The crew of one machine was trapped thus with one pilot dead and the other crushed by the vehicle it was carrying. Despite the frantic efforts of rescuers, which included digging a trench into the cockpit, it took several hours to extricate the injured man from the wreckage, and his injuries were so severe that he died later. In all, eleven men were killed, mostly glider pilots and up to four of them in the Hamilcar accidents. Serious as they were, such incidents were the exception rather than the rule however, and the vast majority of the 284 gliders from the 320 that had departed from the West Country three-and-a-half hours earlier landed safely on LZs S and Z with their cargoes intact in under forty minutes, an impressive achievement.[71]

The 1st Parachute Brigade and other parachute elements assigned to land on DZ X in the first lift were the last to arrive. The sticks of paratroopers were given the signal to stand up, carry out last minute checks on their kit bags, weapon valises and neighbour's parachute before hooking up their static lines approximately twenty minutes from the drop point. The wag behind Private

James Sims tugged on his parachute pack and shouted, 'Blimey, cowboy, this isn't a chute, it's an old Army blanket.'[72] At five minutes out the red warning light mounted by the door came on, and the stick No. 1 took up position in the door with the USAAF crew chief to one side in readiness to assist or unhook the static line of any refusals. Each man's right hand was holding the kitbag attached to his right leg with a special strap, with left hand on the shoulder of the man in front. By the time they reached the jump point the C-47s had adopted a tail-high attitude and throttled back to just above stalling speed, between eighty and ninety knots at an altitude of 600 feet, no mean feat for an entire formation to achieve simultaneously under any circumstances. The jump order was then given by switching the red stand-by light located by the exit to green, backed up with a bell in case of malfunction. The order was transmitted to the man in the door, who could not see the light, by a slap on the back from the stick's No. 2, who also pressed the release for any containers stowed beneath the aircraft before jumping; he was followed as rapidly as possible by the remainder of the stick in order to minimise scattering. It took the average parachutists a mere fifteen seconds to reach the ground, during which he had to ensure his canopy deployed properly, maintain all-round observation to avoid entanglement or collision with other parachutists, release his kitbag on its five yards of cord and execute the appropriate landing drill. Private Sims' landing was not textbook:

> Lieutenant Woods stood framed in the doorway, the slipstream plucking impatiently at the scrim netting on his helmet. The red light glowed steadily and then the green light winked on. 'Go!' The lieutenant vanished. We shuffled along the heaving deck of the Dakota…three…four…five…six…seven…eight…a chap from Maidstone half turned and shouted something with a grin but it was lost in the roar of the engines…nine…ten…eleven…twelve…thirteen…fourteen…the man in front of me hunched over slightly as he went out. Almost before his helmet disappeared I jumped but the slipstream caught me and whirled me around, winding up my rigging lines. I was forced to let go of my kitbag grip in an effort to try and stop the winding up process, for if it reached the canopy I was finished…All around me parachutists were being disgorged from Dakotas and I found myself in the middle of a blizzard of silk. The parachutes were all the colours of the rainbow; it was an unforgettable sight…Luckily the twisting rigging lines had reversed their motion and I spun beneath them as they unwound…[but]…I faced another problem. My right leg hung straight down with the kitbag on it and I was quite unable to reach the grip to pull it up again…We had been told that to land in this way would almost certainly result in a broken leg, and any second I was going to find out. Wham! I hit the deck with a terrific jolt, but all in one piece, and immediately struggled out of my parachute harness, slicing through the cords that held my kitbag to pull out my rifle.[73]

Private Sims had jumped from one of seventy-two C-47s from the US 314th Troop Carrier Group based at Saltby in Leicestershire. The transports were arranged in two trailing formations, the first carrying the 2nd Parachute Battalion and a platoon from 250 (Airborne) Light Composite Company RASC, while the second carried the 3rd Parachute Battalion and part of 16 Parachute Field Ambulance. A further seventy-one C-47s from the US 61st Troop Carrier Group from Barkston Heath arrived only six minutes behind schedule, carrying Brigadier Lathbury's Brigade HQ, the 1st Parachute Battalion, 1st Parachute Squadron RE, the parachute element of Division HQ, the remainder of 16 Parachute Field Ambulance, men from the 1st Reconnaissance Squadron and an Advance Party from the 4th Parachute Brigade. Of this host, five men refused to jump, although one changed his mind after his C-47 went round again. Of the remaining four, a batman from the 1st Airborne Reconnaissance Squadron claimed to be sick and was unhooked by the officer in charge of the stick, an action that saved him from punishment. The other three likely returned to face a court-martial for refusing to obey a lawful order, before being stripped of their Airborne insignia and returned to their units of origin if applicable with the letters LMF (Lack of Moral Fibre) stamped in their paybook. The number of landing injuries is unclear but appears to have been tolerable for an operational jump with full equipment. One sadly unidentified paratrooper, probably a member of the 1st Parachute Battalion, was killed by a parachute malfunction. His demise was witnessed by a number of men from the 1st Border lined out along the railway embankment eating sandwiches from the haversack rations issued on departure: 'One of the paras came down with a "Roman candle" – chute not fully opened… he hit the ground with a bump about 400 yards away. He was first down in that part…One or two of our lads thought of going along to have a look, but in the end no one went.'74

These were very isolated incidents however and like the glider landings, the parachute drop was an impressive achievement in its own right. By 14:08, eighteen minutes after the drop commenced, 2,278 of a planned 2,283 paratroopers were down on DZ X, virtually all of them equipped and fit to fight. An unusual exception was Sapper Tam Hepburn from the 1st Parachute Squadron RE. Having unwisely partaken in a badly cooked fry-up and several bottles of Guinness in his Donington billet the previous night, he suffered from griping bowels throughout the fly-in: 'When I was down on the DZ I dropped my parachute and my trousers in almost the same movement and deposited the first Airborne spoor in the Netherlands.'75

Renkum Heath was a hive of activity as the paratroopers shed their parachute harnesses, unsheathed and prepared their weapons and set about recovering containers or making their way to their unit RVs, which were marked with coloured smoke along the eastern side of the DZ. The atmosphere was again akin to an exercise, with the paratroopers arguably in more danger from stray kitbags than the desultory German small-arms fire. As one participant put it, 'It was what we called a YMCA drop – just like an exercise, with the YMCA canteen wagon waiting at the end.'76 Not everyone was carried away by the relaxed atmosphere, however. As he hurried toward his Battalion rally point Private Sims had an uncomfortable experience: 'Something glinted in the sun not thirty yards away: it was a rifle levelled straight at me. To my relief a very cockney voice shouted "What Battalion mate?" "Second," I croaked. "Over to your right about two hundred yards. OK?" "Thanks a lot," I shouted, "but who are you?" "Independent Company. We're holding the DZ until you're all off it."77 Lieutenant Eastwood, the unidentified Pathfinder's Platoon commander, considered the landing more successful than any of the exercises he had participated in, not least because he was able to locate the 1st Parachute Brigade's commander, Brigadier Lathbury, without difficulty and obtain permission to withdraw his Platoon to the Independent Company RV at Reijers Camp Farm.78

Ten miles to the south, the two C-47s carrying the 82nd Airborne Division's pathfinders dropped their passengers on the Division's landing zones at 12:47. Theodorus Roelofs, a nineteen-year-old Dutchman hiding from the Germans in the family farm near Grave, assisted one group in ascertaining their location; on discovering he spoke some English, Roelofs was recruited as an interpreter and watched in fascination as the Pathfinders took just minutes to mark out the DZ for the 504th Parachute Infantry Regiment's DZ with coloured panels spelling out the letter O and purple smoke markers.79 Having lost one C-47 over Schouwen Island, the vanguard of the 479 C-47s from the US 50th and 52nd Troop Carrier Wings carrying the 82nd Airborne Division arrived over the landing area exactly on schedule at 13:00. The lead formation delivered Colonel William E. Ekman's 505th Parachute Infantry Regiment onto DZ N just south of Groesbeek followed by Lieutenant-Colonel Edwin A. Bedell's 307th Airborne Engineer Battalion, making its first jump as a complete unit, at 13:20. Bedell's engineers were followed fifteen minutes later by another first, as the final parachute serials delivered 544 men, twelve 75mm Pack Howitzers and 700 rounds of ammunition from Lieutenant-Colonel Wilbur Griffiths' 376th Parachute Artillery Battalion, the first time that a US field artillery unit had been dropped accurately and in one location.80 Ekman's Regiment was accompanied by Brigadier-General Gavin who, according to the newly established US Airborne ethos, jumped first from an aircraft in one of the leading serials. Gavin jumped with the same load of ammunition and kit as his men including a Garand M1 rifle, and his serial may well have been flying under the recommended jump height given his subsequent account: 'Although we seemed quite close to the ground, we went out without a second's delay, and we seemed to hit the ground almost at once. Heavily laden with ammunition, weapons, grenades, I had a hard landing whilst the parachute was still oscillating.' Gavin came down near the 307th Engineer Battalion and his landing was indeed hard, for although he did not mention it in his memoir or apparently at the time, the landing damaged several vertebrae and Gavin spent the remainder of the battle in pain. He also found himself under German small-arms fire immediately on landing. Captain William H. Johnson from the Engineers reported that there were a number of Germans in the wood skirting the DZ and that he had killed two personally. Undeterred, Gavin set off for his planned Command Post (CP) location, which lay a mile or so away, initially accompanied by the Engineers but latterly with just his Dutch liaison officer, Captain Arie Bestebreurtje. The CP was reached around an hour after landing, after a brief firefight with a German machine-gun team that ended with Captain Bestebreurtje killing the German gunner with a head shot, and contacting the Dutch Resistance for a situation report via the public telephone system in a house en route.[81]

Next in at 13:13 was Colonel Reuben H. Tucker's 504th Parachute Infantry Regiment, carried in two ninety-strong serials from the 315th Troop Carrier Group.[82] The C-47s delivered the bulk of the Regiment's 1,240 paratroopers and 473 Parapacks to DZ O, just north-east of Grave between the River Maas and the Maas-Waal Canal; eleven C-47s were tasked to deliver Company E from the 2nd Battalion to a small subsidiary DZ on the west bank of the River Maas to secure the western end of the 1,800-foot Grave bridge.[83] The main drop onto DZ O was extremely accurate, as attested by Captain T. Moffatt Burriss, commanding the 3rd Battalion's Company I: 'If ever we made a perfect jump, this was it. All of my company landed exactly on the drop zone. I touched down within a few feet of the assembly point. Within one hour, my entire company was assembled with all equipment and no injuries…None of our practice jumps had ever gone so well.'[84] Unfortunately, this did not apply to the jump onto the supplementary DZ west of the River Maas. It is unclear if the subsidiary DZ was marked by Pathfinders, but ten of the eleven C-47s carrying Company E despatched their sticks up to 1,200 yards short when, for reasons that remain unclear, the Jumpmaster in the lead aircraft pre-empted the green light and ordered his stick to jump, prompting nine of the trailing aircraft to follow suit.[85] The exception was the eleventh C-47 carrying Lieutenant John S. Thompson's stick, where the Jumpmaster waited for the green light. However, noting that the aircraft was over a group of buildings Thompson went against all his training and paused for a few seconds until over open fields before leading his stick out of the door. Fortuitously, the pause delivered Thompson and his stick just 600 yards or so from the western end of the Grave bridge.[86]

The third of the 82nd Airborne's parachute increments, Colonel Roy E. Lindquist's 508th Parachute Infantry Regiment, began jumping onto DZ T, roughly midway between Groesbeek and Wyler, at 13:28.[87] The centre of the 1st Battalion's assembly point, which was marked with red smoke and markers, was relocated slightly after a wooded area on the issued maps and proved to be non-existent; the individual companies rallied to prearranged locations centred on the Battalion marker guided by whistle blasts, bugle calls and, in the case of Company B, a taxi horn liberated in Normandy.[88] Lieutenant-Colonel Louis G. Mendez's 3rd Battalion was dropped a mile north of DZ T but this did not seriously impinge on the Regiment's cohesion and there was no resistance apart from a few *flak* crews and German labour troops in the woods bordering the DZ.[89] However, two sticks from the 1st Battalion's Company A, totalling twenty-two men led by 1st Lieutenant Rex G. Combs, received the green jump light forty-five seconds late and were delivered 2,500 yards astray on the wrong side of the German border near Wyler. Regaining the safety of the Divisional perimeter involved an extended skirmish lasting several hours, during which the paratroopers killed an estimated twenty-one Germans and took a further fifty-nine prisoner. Lieutenant Combs was subsequently awarded the Silver Star for his part in the action.[90] Overall the 82nd Airborne Division's parachute landing was, like that of the British a few miles to the north, overwhelmingly successful. Only a single C-47 had been lost on the fly-in, and 7,277 paratroopers had been delivered in under thirty minutes. Two per cent of the troops, equating to approximately 150 men, sustained landing injuries, of which two were fatal: one man died when his parachute malfunctioned, and the other was killed when struck by a stray Parapack after landing.[91]

The 82nd Airborne's glider increment, consisting of fifty Waco CG4s, was scheduled to arrive thirty minutes after the parachute landing on the swiftly renamed LZ N. The gliders carried a total of 209 men, the bulk of them from Lieutenant-Colonel Raymond Singleton's confusingly named 80th Airborne Anti-Aircraft Battalion equipped with eight 57mm anti-tank guns, Americanised versions of the British 6-Pounder piece; the remaining machines carried nine Jeeps, two trailers and men from Division HQ and other specialist units. Up to two combinations were lost en route, one on crossing the Dutch coast and another south of Vught, but the remaining forty-eight arrived at approximately 13:45. Matters then went awry. For some reason the tugs cut their gliders loose prematurely, and as a result some forty CG4s came down a mile west of the LZ, with only six machines actually reaching it and another landing even farther afield. Two gliders were destroyed on landing and another fourteen suffered varying degrees of damage, but despite this only seven men were injured and all eight guns were recovered in working order. The final arrivals in the 82nd Airborne Division's area were the gliders carrying Browning's Forward Corps HQ, reduced to twenty-nine Horsas after three of the latter and all four Waco CG4s either aborted or were lost en route. Browning's serial began landing on at LZ N at precisely 14:00 and in contrast to the preceding US glider contingent all but one landed squarely on the LZ.[92] Colonel Chatterton brought Browning's Horsa to a stop in a cabbage field only a hundred yards or so from the *Reichswald* Forest and the German border, after striking a power cable that removed one of the glider's nose wheels. The Corps commander's immediate reaction on the Horsa coming to a stop was to exclaim 'By God, we're here, George!' before leaving the glider and running toward the trees in order to become the first British officer to urinate on German territory.[93]

Things did not run quite so smoothly for the 101st Airborne Division, a further twenty-five miles to the south, from the outset. In a foretaste of what was to confront the main body of the 101st Airborne's lift, the four C-47s carrying the Division's Pathfinders flew into intense *flak* that brought one aircraft down in flames, with only four men managing to jump before the doomed C-47 crashed; the stick may have been tasked to mark DZ A-1 for the 1st Battalion 501st Parachute Infantry Regiment, between the River Aa and Willems Canal a mile or so north of Veghel. The remaining three C-47s delivered their sticks accurately and by 12:54, DZ A, two miles south-west of Veghel, and DZs B and C seven miles to the south-west, just north of the Wilhelmina Canal, had all been successfully marked.[94] As we have seen the 424 C-47s carrying the bulk of the 101st Airborne Division's first lift made landfall near Ostend and then flew east past Antwerp before turning north for the Eindhoven landing area. Two aircraft were lost before the formation began its run-in to the drop point, flying over the Albert Canal, Bourg Leopold and the British front line, which was marked with yellow smoke. Thereafter the transports flew directly into light and medium *flak* for the final five minutes of the run-in, which damaged a number of C-47s and shot down fourteen. Only two machines went down before all their stick had jumped, and at least two crews sacrificed themselves by maintaining control of their damaged aircraft until all their passengers were away.

Colonel Howard Johnson's 501st Parachute Infantry Regiment appears to have been the first of the 101st Airborne's units to jump, with Regimental HQ, 2nd and 3rd Battalions dropping accurately onto DZ A, just west of Veghel, at 13:03, three minutes after the designated H-Hour. Lieutenant-Colonel Harry W. O. Kinnard's 1st Battalion was not so fortunate, being delivered three miles north-west of DZ A-1 near Kameren on the east side of the River Aa. Kinnard realised his unit had been misdropped before jumping, but the drop was compact to the extent he was obliged to take avoiding action on the way down, and was able to pinpoint his location with the aid of the excited Dutch civilians that gathered on the DZ to greet their liberators. At the main landing area to the south-west, Colonel John H. Michaelis' 502nd Parachute Infantry Regiment dropped onto DZ B at the northern edge. They were accompanied by Major-General Taylor, who jumped from the C-47 that was carrying the commander of the Regiment's 1st Battalion, Lieutenant-Colonel Patrick Cassidy. He became engrossed in watching a burning C-47 flying nearby and had to be reminded that the green light was on by Taylor.[95] Cassidy's Battalion was also misdropped, being delivered onto DZ C two miles south of its assembly point, but the remainder of the 502nd was dropped accurately onto the correct DZ. Colonel Robert Sink's 506th Parachute Infantry Regiment began jumping onto DZ C at 13:25. The drop was again compact and accurate, the only problem being some slight confusion with the 502nd Regiment's coloured smoke rally signals on the adjacent DZ B. In common with the other MARKET drops, the 101st Airborne's was an overwhelming success even with the loss of fourteen C-47s, with 6,769 paratroopers being delivered in around thirty minutes. Ninety-five per cent of the supplies and equipment dropped was recovered, and the jump casualty rate was again around two per cent. Three men were killed, one while standing in the door of his aircraft and the others were struck by a crashing C-47 during their descent.[96] Overall the drop was the most compact and accurate the Division had ever experienced, including training drops.

As with the 82nd Airborne Division at Nijmegen, the 101st Airborne Division's glider element came in at around 14:00 onto LZ W, which had been inserted between the two parachute DZs. Of the original increment of seventy Waco CG4s, two aborted over England and another ditched in the Channel. At least two and possibly four came down in friendly territory in Belgium, seven came down behind German lines, two collided over the LZ and up to three crash-landed. Approximately fifty-three landed safely, the lead machine in the first serial with the assistance of Corporal James L. Evans from the Division's Artillery HQ. A *flak* hit knocked the pilot unconscious, severely wounded the man in the co-pilot's seat in the thigh and wounded Evans, but the latter managed to take control while the pilot recovered his senses. He then applied a tourniquet to the wounded man's thigh while the pilot brought the glider in safely. The glider lift brought in 252 men, thirty-two Jeeps, thirteen trailers and a war correspondent named Walter Cronkite.[97]

Thus by 14:30, Sunday 17 September 1944 approximately 20,000 Allied airborne soldiers with all their weapons and equipment were on the ground in German-occupied Holland. Operation MARKET had begun, and the Airborne soldiers began the race for their objectives against the German defenders.

6

D-Day 14:00 to 19:00

Sunday 17 September 1944

Like their airborne counterparts in England, the ground units slated for participation in MARKET GARDEN spent the run-up to Sunday 17 September making preparations to resume the advance into Holland. As we have seen, the Guards Armoured Division's tank component had been withdrawn south of the Meuse-Escaut Canal on 13 September and the 5th Guards Armoured Brigade spent the next two days carrying out routine maintenance before beginning preparations for GARDEN on Saturday 16 September.[1] The Division's infantry component, which had defended the Neerpelt bridgehead against *Kampfgruppe* Walther's counter-attack on 14 September, was relieved by the 50th Division the following day. Consequently, while unit briefings for GARDEN had been carried out by 16 September, some Guardsmen were still making their final preparations while the aerial armada carrying the MARKET first lift was flying across southern and eastern England. The 3rd Irish Guards, for example, spent the morning of Sunday 17 September checking weapons and equipment and loading vehicles. Lieutenant Brian Wilson's platoon truck was so crammed with items ranging from spare ammunition to blankets, some of which had to be lashed to the roof, that 'it could scarcely take another toothpick on board'. Wilson's platoon finally climbed aboard their troop-carrying vehicles along with the remainder of the 2nd Company at midday and began the move forward toward the Meuse-Escaut Canal and the GARDEN start line.[2]

This rather leisurely start was due to 30 Corps setting H-Hour for GARDEN at 14:30 on 17 September. This meant that the ground advance was not scheduled to begin until the whole MARKET first lift was on the ground, and thus sacrificed the element of surprise and, arguably more importantly, several hours of precious daylight; sunrise and sunset occurred at 06:13 and 18:47 OST respectively at Arnhem on the day MARKET GARDEN was launched.[3] The mid-afternoon start also militated against the already tight timetable the ground advance was to follow, which envisaged reaching Eindhoven by c.17:00 on Sunday 17 September. To meet this schedule the Guards Armoured Division's lead elements would have to cover approximately seventeen miles in around two-and-a-half hours. While such a rate of advance might have been feasible for tracked vehicles with a top speed of around twenty miles per hour in an unopposed road march, it was somewhat optimistic for an opposed advance into enemy-held territory, especially as the enemy masking the Neerpelt bridgehead was well aware that something was afoot. *719 Infanterie Division* reported continuous vehicle movement on the roads behind the Albert Canal throughout the night of 15-16 September for example, *Kampfgruppen* Richter and Walther reported seeing lights and heavy vehicles moving on the Hechtel-Valkenswaard road to the south, and *Generalleutnant* Kurt Chill predicted a major attack once the British had finished concentrating additional armour within the bridgehead.[4]

It has been claimed that the late start time was due to 30 Corps' HQ not being informed that MARKET was going ahead until 13:00 on 17 September, when the transports carrying the

101[5] Airborne Division were actually passing over Horrocks' forward HQ near the Neerpelt bridgehead.[5] This claim is presumably based in part on the Operation Order issued by 30 Corps HQ on 15 September, which did not specify a start time for GARDEN but instead referred to a generic 'Z Hour' throughout; the latter was defined as the 'time leading troops of divisions taking part in Operation Garden will advance...Z Hour is likely to be the same as H Hour [the beginning of the MARKET landings] and will in any case *not* be earlier [original emphasis]. The exact time of Z will be notified later.'[6] The problem with this is that the official records show that it is highly unlikely that Horrocks was unaware that MARKET was going ahead well before 13:00 on 17 September. 30 Corps HQ signal logs note a request for confirmation that MARKET had been launched as arranged being transmitted at 10:15 and attracting a rapid affirmative response[7] and the news reached the 2nd Irish Guards, the unit selected to spearhead GARDEN, at 12:00.[8] In fact, Z Hour appears to have been fixed for 14:30 at least twenty-four hours before GARDEN commenced, and possibly earlier than that. The 3rd Irish Guards was informed of that start time at an Orders Group during the morning of Saturday 16 September, in accordance with the Guards Armoured Division's allotted tasks and timings.[9] These specifically ordered the lead formation to reach the crossing over the Wilhelmina Canal at Son before dark on 17 September. Both order and intent were clearly understood and explicitly acknowledged by 5th Guards Armoured Brigade on 15 September and again the following day by the Brigade commander, Brigadier Norman Gwatkin. Gwatkin personally signed a declaration of future operations on 15 September which read 'Intention: To reach the area north of Eindhoven 4321 before dark on 17th September in preparation for advance at first light on the following day, 18th September'. A further signed entry in the Brigade War Diary for 16 September reads '5 Guards Armoured will advance to Eindhoven 4218 on D Day preparatory to an advance to the area NUNSPEET on D+1.'[10] The simple fact was that it was not feasible to marshal and keep forces of the scale committed to GARDEN hanging on the start line without a definite start time. It is therefore likely that Horrocks deliberately selected 14:30 as the latest possible time to launch the Operation in order to offset the relatively short lead time, even though it militated against the tight schedule for the advance, and that he did so because 30 Corps was still completing preparations for the attack when MARKET commenced.

This does not appear to have been the case with the very tip of the spear, given that the Irish Guards Group was formed up ready to move by 13:15 on 17 September, having received confirmation that GARDEN was going ahead at 12:00.[11] Any problems likely manifested themselves farther down the line, given that GARDEN involved marshalling 20,000 assorted vehicles with all the traffic control problems inherent in deploying a force of that scale on a restricted road net, exacerbated by the narrow attack frontage. The Guards Armoured Division alone deployed 3,124 vehicles for the initial attack, for example.[12] Apart from the 5th Guards Armoured Brigade all the Guards Armoured Division's constituent and attached units were specifically forbidden to move from their pre-battle harbour areas without explicit authorisation from Division HQ.[13] Marshalling the 9,000-strong bridging train may have been especially problematic, given that it was assembled from units drawn from all across the North-West European theatre; in addition to 30 Corps' organic and division-level Engineer assets, this host included four Army-level formations, two of them Canadian, two GHQ formations and two Mechanical Equipment Platoons. Some elements were only just arriving in the area of Bourg Leopold as GARDEN commenced. The 23rd Field Company Royal Canadian Engineers (RCE) only arrived in the area at 03:00 on 17 September after a two-day, 200-mile drive from St. Omer in the Pas de Calais for instance, and did not link up with other Canadian units slated to participate in GARDEN until 10:40, in the area of Hechtel.[14] The Engineer contingent nevertheless deployed sufficient materiel to bridge all the water obstacles on the GARDEN line of advance twice over, with an additional 2,000 truckloads of equipment being cached at Bourg Leopold, where the Engineer units initially concentrated. The bridging train was divided into twenty individual columns, each organised and equipped to meet a variety of specific contingencies and allotted codenames and convoy serial identification to permit them to be despatched north along the traffic control system if and when required.[15]

Whatever its timings and their ramifications, the basic concept for 30 Corps' plan for Operation GARDEN was relatively straightforward. The Guards Armoured Division was given responsibility for leading the advance north, and to this end moved with six days' rations to hand, and with each vehicle carrying sufficient extra fuel to move a further 250 miles after its integral fuel tanks had run dry.[16] The Guards were to be trailed by the 43rd Division, accompanied by the bridging train. In the event that any of the bridges at the major crossings was destroyed before it could be secured by the airborne troops, the Guards Armoured Division was tasked to move outward and secure the flanks of the corridor while the 43rd Division moved forward to cover the bridging operation, after which the Guards would resume the advance north. Once the Guards Armoured Division reached Arnhem the 43rd Division was to take over the advance, push across the River Ijssel and on to Deventer and Zutphen, while the 50th Division followed on as the Corps' reserve.[17] The axis of the initial break-out from the Neerpelt bridgehead was the Hasselt-Eindhoven highway, and the attack was to be preceded by a preparatory artillery barrage from ten Field and three Medium Royal Artillery Regiments, supported by a Heavy Battery and a Heavy Anti-Aircraft Regiment firing in the ground role, totalling around 350 guns in all. The barrage was to begin at 13:55 with all guns putting down counter-battery fire until 14:15, at which point the ten Field Regiments were to switch to delivering concentrated fire on the approaches to Valkenswaard. At 14:25 the 50th Division's heavy mortars were to thicken the barrage with a ten-minute concentration on known enemy locations, and two minutes later the Field Regiments were to shift their fire again, this time to a point 1,000 yards ahead of the Start Line, extending 1,000 yards either side of the axis of advance. The barrage was to remain static for the two minutes until 14:30 and then begin moving forward at a rate of 200 yards per minute until 14:50, at which point responsibility for fire support was to switch to eleven squadrons of Hawker Typhoon fighter-bombers from the RAF's 2nd Tactical Air Force (TAF).[18] These were to be controlled by specialist RAF Forward Air Control teams codenamed TENTACLES, which linked the Army ground units with the close-support aircraft via radio-equipped 'Control Cars' travelling with the advance, co-ordinated by RAF Forward Control Posts (FCPs) attached to Corps-level HQs.[19] For the initial phase of GARDEN Guards Armoured Division appears to have been allotted three TENTACLES, one travelling initially with the 5th Guards Armoured Brigade, one with 32 Guards Brigade and one with Division HQ, while 30 Corps HQ maintained a single co-ordinating FCP.[20]

Responsibility for the initial break out from the Neerpelt bridgehead was allotted to the 5th Guards Armoured Brigade. Brigadier Gwatkin in turn delegated the initial assault to the tanks and infantry of the Irish Guards Group, consisting of the 2nd Irish Guards and 3rd Irish Guards. The Irish Guards' initial objective was the town of Valkenswaard, approximately seven miles from the Start Line, but this entailed crossing a bridge across the River Dommel, which bisected the Hasselt-Eindhoven highway a mile or so short of Valkenswaard. A hasty reconnaissance by Lieutenant A. R. J. Buchanan-Jardine from the 2nd Household Cavalry had confirmed that the bridge was intact on 11 September.[21] The Shermans of the 2nd Irish Guards' No. 3 Squadron were therefore tasked to secure the bridge, accompanied by two Troops from the 2nd Household Cavalry and a reconnaissance party from 14 Field Squadron RE equipped with a heavy bulldozer as a contingency measure. No. 3 Squadron's Shermans were to be followed by the tanks of Nos. 1 and 2 Squadrons in that order, carrying infantry from the 3rd Irish Guards' Nos. 1 and 3 Companies respectively on their decks, with No. 2 Company bringing up the rear in its organic troop-carrying vehicles.[22] Once No. 3 Squadron and its attachments had secured the Dommel bridge the remainder of the Group was to pass through, clear Valkenswaard and hand the town over to the 1st Dorsets and the 2nd Devonshires, which had been detached from the 50th Division's 231 Infantry Brigade to assist in the opening phase of GARDEN. The Irish Guards Group was then to push on to Eindhoven and link up with the elements of the US 101st Airborne Division holding the crossings over the Wilhelmina Canal north of the city. The advance from Valkenswaard was also to widen into two separate axes. The 5th Guards Armoured Brigade were assigned to continue advancing north along the main highway through the small town of Aalst and into Eindhoven from the south, while 32 Guards Brigade looped to the right along subsidiary routes to enter the city from the east.[23] Both were scheduled to link up with the US airborne troops by nightfall, which occurred at approximately 19:30.[24]

The German units screening the Neerpelt bridgehead were less numerous and less well equipped than the attacking Guards Armoured Division. Having suffered considerable loss during the failed counter-attack on 14 September, *Kampfgruppe* Walther had remained fairly passive with the abortive attempt to destroy the bridge by *Kriegsmarine* combat swimmers with a 500-kilogram sea mine on 15 September being a notable exception.[25] *Oberst* Walther was ordered to resume attacking the bridgehead by *1 Fallschirmjäger Armee* HQ during the evening of 16 September, but unwilling to squander his strength in the face of imminent attack, Walther compromised by authorising a few local probes. It is unclear if these began before Operation GARDEN commenced.[26] The sector of the bridgehead to the west of the Hasselt-Eindhoven road was covered by *Oberstleutnant* Friedrich von der Heydte's *Fallschirmjäger Regiment 6*, while the sector to the east was held by two battalions drawn from *SS Panzergrenadier Regiments 19* and *21* commanded by *Hauptsturmführer* Dr Karl Segler and *Hauptsturmführer* Friedrich Richter respectively; the SS units were part of *Kampfgruppe* Heinke which had been despatched south by *II SS Panzerkorps* on 10 September. The central sector, straddling the Eindhoven road and thus the boundary between the *Fallschirmjäger* and SS contingents was assigned to *Fallschirmjäger Ausbildungs Regiment* Hoffmann and *Luftwaffe Strafbataillon 6*, the former a replacement training unit commanded by *Oberstleutnant* Helmuth von Hoffmann and the latter a penal unit drafted in from Italy. In all, the Germans could muster approximately ten understrength infantry battalions to oppose any Allied advance out of the Neerpelt bridgehead, supported by a handful of towed anti-tank guns and around a dozen *Jagdpanzer* IV tank destroyers from *Hauptsturmführer* Franz Roestel's *SS Panzerjäger Abteilung 10*. The latter were billeted in the village of Borkel-en-Schaft, which was located in a wooded area roughly halfway between the front line and Eindhoven and just east of the Hasselt-Eindhoven road.[27]

Despite their titles *Fallschirmjäger Ausbildungs Regiment* Hoffmann and *Luftwaffe Strafbataillon 6* both contained a large proportion of partially trained *Luftwaffe* ground personnel, and the road blocking force had to be reinforced with up to a company of combat engineers drawn from *SS Panzer Pionier Abteilung 10*. The reinforcement proved to be a wise precaution as the commander of *Luftwaffe Strafbataillon 6*, a Major Veith, was killed by British artillery fire on 16 September along with his adjutant. At around the same time *Major* Helmut Kerutt's *I Bataillon Fallschirmjäger Ausbildungs Regiment* Hoffmann was redeployed into a reserve defensive position to the rear of the main line. Kerutt's *Bataillon* was joined by his *Regiment's* anti-tank company, commanded by a *Hauptmann* Brockes and equipped with eight or possibly nine towed guns. These may have been 75mm *PaK* 40 pieces, although some sources refer to them being captured and refurbished Soviet pieces, designated 7.62 *PaK* 36(r) in German service.[28] Whatever their provenance, Brockes lacked all-terrain prime movers capable of moving his guns over the boggy ground that flanked the Hasselt-Eindhoven road, which obliged their crews to site them where they could be positioned by wheeled vehicles and muscle power. This restricted them to positions a few metres off the main road at best. *Major* Kerutt also organised a tank ambush position as a backstop 2,500 metres behind the front line, manned by thirty men from his HQ defence platoon. The ambush consisted of a number of slit trenches with overhead cover for use by men armed with disposable *Panzerfaust* rocket launchers spaced along the sides of the road. The concealed trenches were supported by machine-gun positions farther out, which were tasked to protect the *Panzerfaust* operators from Allied infantry and to deal with any tank crews attempting to abandon their vehicles.[29]

The GARDEN artillery bombardment commenced on schedule at 13:55 on Sunday 17 September 1944, accompanied by bombing from Allied medium bombers along the line of the Eindhoven road as far as Valkenswaard. The bombs also enveloped Borkel, where *Hauptsturmführer* Franz Roestel's detachment of *Jagdpanzer* IV tank destroyers from *SS Panzerjäger Abteilung 10* was billeted, although it is unclear whether any of the vehicles were damaged.[30] The 2nd Devons and 2nd Irish Guards crossed the start line at 14:35 led by Lieutenant D. K. F. Heathcote's Sherman, which closed to within 300 yards of the barrage and followed it forward into the clouds of smoke and dust kicked up by the shelling.[31] Initially there was little or no resistance, for the barrage had effectively suppressed the German defenders and knocked out all of *Hauptmann* Brockes' anti-tank guns deployed in the forward area, killing many of their crewmen in the process. The dead included Brockes himself, killed by a direct hit on the house commandeered for his HQ, possibly by one of the 50th Division's 4.2-inch mortars. The battery of 105mm guns from *SS Panzer Artillerie Regiment 10* stationed behind the *Fallschirmjäger* positions was also hit repeatedly and badly damaged.[32]

The lack of opposition continued for the ten minutes or so it took for the advance to reach *Major* Kerutt's newly established reserve defensive position, which had escaped the bombardment relatively lightly because it was targeted upon known German locations. Kerutt had been absent at *1 Fallschirmjäger Armee* HQ and only arrived back at his command post as the British tanks approached, but his men manning the tank ambush displayed admirable discipline by allowing most of No. 3 Squadron's Shermans to pass before springing the trap on the rear of the Squadron and the lead vehicles of the following No. 1 Squadron. Nine Shermans and possibly two armoured cars were knocked out in the first two minutes of the action, killing eight men from the 2nd Irish Guards and wounding several more. Some tank crewmen may also have been captured, given that one account refers to some of Kerutt's men rallying to his HQ with prisoners.[33] The rising pillars of greasy black smoke from the knocked-out vehicles and sound of the subsequent battle were obvious to Lieutenant Wilson and his Platoon bringing up the rear of the Irish Guards Group column, despite the ongoing artillery barrage.[34] The surviving tanks from Nos. 3 and 1 Squadrons immediately assumed defensive positions as best they could and laid down fire on the road verges and likely enemy locations while the infantry they were carrying dismounted and set about clearing the German positions. They were assisted by 2nd TAF fighter bombers called in by the TENTACLE accompanying the 2nd Irish Guards HQ. In all, eleven Squadrons of Typhoons from RAF No. 83 Group carried out 116 sorties through the afternoon from 15:12. The margin for error was very small, given that the Typhoons were attacking targets within 200 yards of the lead Guards vehicles and thirty yards either side of the road.[35] In some instances the Typhoons were firing their rockets from behind the 3rd Irish Guards' No. 2 Company at the tail end of the Irish Guards column, and some of the aerial fire reportedly struck the Guards' leading elements.[36]

The fighting along the road was intense. Kerutt's adjutant, *Leutnant* Heinz Volz, referred to his unit losing a large number of killed and missing, some crushed in their slit trenches by tank tracks.[37] Others appear to have decided that discretion was the better part of valour, given that some 250 German prisoners had been captured by 15:30. Around 100 of these were taken by the 3rd Irish Guards, and Lieutenant Wilson reported unescorted prisoners coming down the road from the front with the 'curious shambling gait of the physically frightened', although sympathy had its limits: Wilson also referred to a group of prisoners sitting in a ditch next to a Regimental Aid Post coming close to being 'murdered where they sat' after sniggering at a 'bewildered Devonshire soldier nursing a bloodsoaked hand'.[38] The remaining prisoners appear to have been taken by the 2nd Devons which, after moving past the rear of the Irish Guards Group, became engaged in a protracted fight to clear a wooded area on the east side of the road.[39] The fighting also involved some of Roestel's eight surviving *Jagdpanzer* IVs, which used the dense vegetation flanking the road north of Kerutt's ambush site as concealment for hit-and-run attacks on the advancing Irish Guards tanks.[40] It is unclear if they inflicted any casualties on the advancing Guards vehicles, but the 2nd Irish Guards War Diary referred to a Lance-Sergeant Cowan knocking out a German self-propelled gun and then forcing its crew to point out other targets from the rear deck of his Sherman.[41] By just after 16:00 No. 3 Squadron had reached the edge of 300 yards of open ground leading to the Dommel bridge and the ten RA Field Regiments were requested to repeat the final stage of the artillery barrage for cover. However, the 2nd Irish Guards lead elements were within 200 yards of the barrage line, and a 500-yard withdrawal was deemed necessary for safety reasons if the barrage were to include the edge of the wood overlooking the road from the west. Although the road was two lanes in width at this point, turning the vehicles was a time-consuming process, not least because some sections of the road verge were mined; turning the bulldozer from 14 Field Squadron RE appears to have been especially problematic. The 500-yard withdrawal thus took an hour-and-a-half to complete. This meant the advance and renewed barrage, of twenty minutes' duration and again lifting 200 yards per minute, was not able to commence until 17:39. After an additional five-minute artillery concentration, No. 3 Squadron finally reached the bridge, which was intact and, following inspection by the Engineers, capable of supporting tanks. The Squadron then pushed some of its Shermans across to the north bank of the Dommel and the bridge was declared secured at 18:30.[42]

***

While the Guards Armoured Division was fighting its way along the seven miles to Valkenswaard, the US 101st Airborne Division was enjoying mixed fortunes in seizing its objectives. The most southerly, assigned to Major James L. LaPrade's 1st Battalion 506th Parachute Infantry Regiment, were three bridges over the Wilhelmina Canal near Son.[43] The two smaller bridges had been demolished shortly before MARKET commenced, leaving just the main bridge carrying the highway south to Eindhoven. The 506th Regiment was not informed of the demolitions and the Regimental commander, Colonel Robert F. Sink, only became aware of them after landing in Holland.[44] In the interests of speed Major LaPrade had dispensed with a formal post-jump reorganisation and despatched his men toward the objective in groups of fifteen to twenty as they arrived at the Battalion rally point and thus the entire 1st Battalion was on the move by 14:10, just forty-five minutes after the jump had commenced, and while the 506th Regiment's 2nd and 3rd Battalions were still reorganising on DZ C. The plan was for LaPrade's Battalion to move directly south through the Zonsche Forest that bounded the southern edge of the 101st Airborne Division's main landing area to the Wilhelmina Canal, and then approach the bridges from the west. The remainder of the Regiment was to move east from the DZ and follow the Eindhoven road south through Son to link up with LaPrade's men at the bridges.

The Zonsche Forest was about a mile wide at its eastern end and initially Captain Melvin C. Davis and Company A made good time leading the 1st Battalion through the trees. However, as the paratroopers approached the southern edge of the wood they came under fire from a German anti-aircraft emplacement on the north bank of the Wilhelmina Canal. The fire caused a number of casualties including Captain Davis, many of them due to the airburst effect of 88mm anti-aircraft shells detonating in the treetops. The US advance came to an abrupt halt and it took over an hour for Davis' men to manoeuvre close enough to overrun the emplacement with a bayonet charge. The action cost Company A around a third of its strength, and after a hasty reorganisation Major LaPrade ordered Company B to take over as vanguard and press along the line of the canal toward the bridge.[45] While all this was going on the remainder of the 506th Parachute Infantry Regiment was moving upon Son from the north led by Lieutenant-Colonel Robert L. Strayer's 2nd Battalion, accompanied by Colonel Sink and trailed by Lieutenant-Colonel Oliver M. Horton's 3rd Battalion acting as Regimental reserve. The advance proceeded to the outskirts of Son, where an off-duty German soldier inadvertently pedalled into the lead scouts from Strayer's Company D and while the town proved to be clear of German troops, moving through the streets took a considerable time. The US Official history attributes the delay to a lack of urgency based on the assumption that the swifter moving 1st Battalion would have already secured the objective.[46] However, the real reason appears to have been that the entire civilian population of Son turned out en masse to greet their liberators, blocking the streets and pressing hugs, kisses, cigars, beer and fresh fruit on every paratrooper who came within reach. As a participant's account drily noted, the 2nd Battalion's officers 'had a hard time keeping the men moving'.[47]

On reaching the southern outskirts of Son the 2nd Battalion came under fire from another German anti-aircraft position straddling the road leading to the bridge. This time the paratroopers were able to use buildings to screen their movement, and Private Thomas G. Lindsey from the 2nd Battalion's HQ Company closed to within fifty yards and knocked out one 88mm gun with his Bazooka. The hit on the gun's elevating mechanism killed one of the crew and the remainder were despatched as they tried to escape by Sergeant John F. Rice from Company D. Another gun on the opposite side of the road was also overrun, possibly by elements from Company E, which moved up in support.[48] In all, the fight for the guns took around fifteen minutes, and as Companies D and E pushed on down the last few hundred yards toward the canal they came under small-arms fire from German troops occupying buildings on the south bank, just as elements of the 1st Battalion came into view moving along the canal bank from the right. The paratroopers were within fifty yards of the road bridge when the Germans detonated their demolition charges, dropping both spans into the Wilhelmina Canal. The commander of Company E, Captain Richard Winters, was only twenty-five yards short with his lead Platoon and narrowly avoided injury from falling debris; Lieutenant Sterling Horner found three German soldiers, possibly the demolition party, stunned but unhurt behind the stump of the north pillar. Undaunted, Major LaPrade immediately swam across the canal, accompanied by Lieutenant Millford F. Weller and Sergeant Donald B. Dunning, while some of his men stripped the doors from a nearby barn and manhandled them to the wrecked bridge with the assistance of First Sergeant Carwood Lipton and a party from the 2nd Battalion's Company E. Corporal Gordon Carson, also from Company E, stripped naked despite German fire, performed a perfect racing dive and swam the canal to reach a small boat moored on the south bank, which was then used to ferry groups of paratroopers across to the canal. This small force proved sufficient to drive off the German rearguard and secure the south end of the bridge site. Colonel Sink, who had been trailing the 2nd Battalion with his Regimental HQ, arrived at this time, and it was also now that Sink learned that the two smaller bridges he had been ordered to secure had been demolished before MARKET commenced. Noting that the central pillar of the road bridge was intact, Sink ordered the attached company from the 326th Airborne Engineer Battalion to fabricate a footbridge as quickly as possible to allow the 506th Regiment to cross the canal and move on Eindhoven.[49]

Things ran a little more smoothly north of Son. While Colonel John H. Michaelis and the 502nd Parachute Infantry Regiment's primary task was to protect the Division landing area and provide the Division reserve, his 1st Battalion under Lieutenant-Colonel Patrick Cassidy was tasked to secure St. Oedenrode, just over a mile north-east of the landing area and specifically the four bridges over the River Dommel in the town. After ascertaining that his Battalion had actually been dropped onto the wrong DZ and was thus two miles south of its intended position, Cassidy made his way to the Battalion assembly point, a crossroads 1,000 yards east of DZ A and after a hasty reorganisation set out for St. Oedenrode. Company C led the bulk of the 1st Battalion north along the Son-St. Oedenrode road, while Company B moved east to enter the town via a small footbridge. Company C was stalled by German small-arms fire soon after passing two *Panzer* IV tanks knocked out by fighter-bombers before the drop began, but Company B not only discovered a fifth road bridge across the Dommel they had not been briefed about, but also shot up a party of Germans moving to destroy it before they could lay their charges. The new bridge was secured intact after a firefight with a larger German covering force, while the remainder of the 1st Battalion pushed into St. Oedenrode proper and secured the original four Dommel crossings. After clearing a number of German rear-echelon troops from the town, Cassidy organised a defensive perimeter and despatched a patrol to make contact with Colonel Howard Johnson's 501st Parachute Infantry Regiment, which was tasked to secure the bridges at Veghel, five miles to the north-east.[50]

Matters had followed a similar pattern for the 501st Parachute Infantry Regiment at Veghel.[51] Lieutenant-Colonel Julian J. Ewell's 3rd Battalion was on the move toward its objectives within forty-five minutes of landing, and rapidly secured the town of Eerde, just west of the landing area, and established a blocking position astride the Veghel–St. Oedenrode road just to the south, as planned, by 15:00. Lieutenant-Colonel Robert A. Ballard's 2nd Battalion was equally fast off the mark, with the bulk of the Battalion advancing behind Lieutenant Richard G. Snodgrass' Company D along the main road to secure the road bridges over the Zuid Willems Canal and River Aa, while Company E angled to the north-east to secure the railway bridge over the canal. All three crossings were secured in the face of light resistance by 15:15 and in the process the 2nd Battalion's lead scouts ran into their opposite numbers from Lieutenant-Colonel Harry W. O. Kinnard's 1st Battalion coming into the town from the east, after being misdropped three miles downstream near Kameren. After learning his true location from excited Dutch civilians who flocked to the DZ, Kinnard had set off down the riverside road toward Veghel within an hour of landing, leaving a party of thirty-eight under Captain William G. Burd from HQ Company to gather in equipment and supply bundles and tend eight jump casualties; the party was to follow the remainder of the 1st Battalion as quickly as possible. Around thirty German rear echelon troops and some vehicles were captured going about routine business in the course of the advance, which was spearheaded by a number of paratroopers who commandeered bicycles and other vehicles on their own initiative. Once again the biggest problems came from crowds of enthusiastic Dutch civilians but 1st Battalion was on its two objectives by 16:00 and all the Regiment's objectives were officially reported secured by 16:30.[52]

Besides securing the assigned bridges over the rivers Aa and Dommel and Zuid Willems and Wilhelmina canals, the 101st Airborne Division also went after an additional set of bridges that did not feature in the MARKET guidelines. These were the road and rail bridges five miles west of Son, at the eastern end of the Zonsche Forest and a mile or so south of Best. These bridges were presumably not included because they were not on 30 Corps' direct route to Arnhem and having failed to interest British 2nd Army HQ in their capture, Major-General Taylor unilaterally added them to his Division's list of objectives as an insurance against failure to secure the crossings at Son; it is unclear if the initiative was communicated to 30 Corps. In order to conserve manpower, the mission was originally assigned to a single platoon from Lieutenant-Colonel Robert G. Cole's 3rd Battalion 502nd Parachute Infantry Regiment but at the latter's request the force was increased to Captain Robert E. Jones' Company H, reinforced with a .30 machine-gun section from HQ Company and a Platoon from the 326th Airborne Engineer Battalion. Jones left the landing area intending to bisect the Eindhoven–Best road 1,000 yards south of Best but lost direction in the outskirts of the Zonsche Forest and emerged only 400 yards from the town. The paratroopers immediately became entangled in an extended and costly fight with *FlaK Abteilung* 424 for a crossroads just east of Best and held their own until the arrival of a twelve-truck convoy of reinforcements from *59 Infanterie Division*, which was regrouping at nearby Tilburg after escaping across the Scheldt Estuary.[53] The remainder of the 3rd Battalion was ordered forward to assist Jones at 18:00.[54]

***

Twelve miles further north the 82nd Airborne Division enjoyed similarly mixed fortunes in securing its objectives. The 2nd and 3rd Battalions of Colonel Reuben H. Tucker's 504th Parachute Infantry Regiment, commanded by Majors Edward M. Wellems and Julian A. Cook respectively, were tasked to secure the 1,800-foot, nine-span bridge across the River Maas at Grave, at that time the longest bridge in Europe. Major Cook's 3rd Battalion was also tasked to clear the area around the large Regimental DZ O between the River Maas and the Maas-Waal Canal, and had enjoyed an almost perfect jump. Company H, for example, suffered no jump injuries and lost just six wounded, four before jumping, and the centre man in the first stick landed within ten feet of the predicted spot.[55] The 2nd Battalion's Company E was supposed to be delivered onto a subsidiary DZ on the west bank of the River Maas to secure that end of the bridge, but ten of the eleven C-47s carrying Company E dropped their sticks up to 1,200 yards short of the DZ. The exception was Lieutenant John S. Thompson's stick, which fortuitously landed around 600 yards from the western end of their objective after Thompson delayed jumping by a few seconds in order to avoid landing among buildings. Once safely on the ground Thompson quickly rallied his fifteen-strong band, despatched Corporal Hugh H. Parry to inform his Company commander of his intent and set out for the bridge using water-filled drainage ditches as cover from German fire from the outskirts of Grave and a 20mm anti-aircraft gun mounted in a tower near the bridge.

Thompson's route first brought them into contact with a party of five Germans moving equipment of some kind from a small building toward the bridge. Fearing the party were preparing demolition charges, Thompson stealthily deployed his men before opening concentrated fire upon the unsuspecting Germans, killing four and wounding the fifth; subsequent examination of the bodies showed they had in fact been moving personal effects and equipment. Moving on, Thompson and his men were then approached from the rear by two German trucks moving at speed toward the bridge from Grave. One left the road and crashed after the driver was shot, scattering the unfortunate passengers. The other screeched to a stop and disgorged its load of troops, who promptly scattered and ran under the paratrooper's fire. The *flak* tower was silenced by Private Robert McGraw, who crawled close enough to fire three Bazooka rockets into the gun platform atop it, two of which passed through a firing slit. His companions then scrambled into the tower to find two of the 20mm gun crew dead and a third wounded.[56] After moving in to secure the west end of the bridge Thompson set his men to destroying any electrical equipment and cables that might have been linked to demolition charges and establishing a defensive perimeter to await the arrival of the rest of Company E. The time was approximately 13:45, less than an hour after Thompson had made his delayed exit from his C-47.[57]

The eastern end of the bridge appears to have been defended by another 20mm gun mounted in a tower or possibly atop the bridge superstructure, which might have wreaked considerable havoc on the paratroopers advancing from the main DZ. However, according to Captain T. Moffatt Burriss, commanding the 3rd Battalion's Company I and in the forefront of the rush from the DZ, the Germans were simply overawed by the approach of large numbers of 'crack American troops with a lethal reputation' and chose to surrender, using a discarded undershirt as a makeshift white flag.[58] This may well have been true, although the fact that the Germans had been taking fire from Lieutenant Thompson's men using the 20mm gun captured at the other end of the bridge might also have had some bearing on the matter. Whatever the reason, by 14:30, just an hour and a quarter after the 504th Regiment had commenced its jump, the 1,800-foot Grave bridge had been captured intact, although it would be another hour before paratroopers from the 2nd Battalion crossed from the eastern end. The bridge was not officially declared secure until 17:00.[59] German fire from the southern outskirts of Grave initially prevented the remainder of Company E moving up to reinforce Lieutenant Thompson, but once the juncture was achieved a roadblock was established to prevent German troops approaching from the south. The remainder of Major Wellems' 2nd Battalion appears to have moved to the south bank of the River Maas to clear and secure Grave while Major Cook's 3rd Battalion cleared the area between the River Maas and Maas-Waal Canal and set up a perimeter around the eastern end of the bridge.[60] Company I was part of the latter, and Captain Burriss was approached by one of his men while digging in, who reported finding a 'big lead cable' at the bottom of his foxhole. Burriss identified the find as a major telephone line and, mindful of Standing Orders to disrupt communications wherever possible, ordered his men to cut it, which they did with the enthusiasm soldiers generally reserve for officially sanctioned vandalism. It was not the last Burriss was to hear of the matter.[61]

While all this was going on Major Willard E. Harrison's 1st Battalion 504th Parachute Infantry Regiment was attempting to seize three of the four crossings over the Maas-Waal Canal to the east of DZ O, with a Company being despatched to secure each. No move was made at this time against the fourth and most northerly bridge, the combined road and rail affair at Honinghutie because Brigadier-General Gavin had decreed it a provisional objective to be seized in concert with the 508th Parachute Infantry Regiment from the east, dependent upon 'the development of the fight once the landings were accomplished'.[62] Given the distance from the DZ and that he had only three rifle Companies to draw upon Harrison was doubtless grateful for Gavin's prioritising. In a rerun of events at Son, the bridges at Malden and Hatert were blown in the face of Harrison's paratroopers as they closed in and both companies had to content themselves with securing both banks of the crossing, which was done by nightfall. Captain Thomas B. Helgeson enjoyed better luck at the southern Molenhoek lock bridge. Initially held at bay by heavy fire from German troops positioned on a small island in the centre of the canal, three paratroopers managed to dash across to the east bank where they were joined by a party of seven using a commandeered rowing boat. Captain Helgeson's men succeeded in keeping the Germans on the island pinned down while this little band examined the bridge; this revealed the structure to be fully rigged with demolition charges, which were rendered safe by the simple expedient of severing the electrical wiring. Why the charges were not detonated by the defenders remained a mystery. The Germans on the island were finally dealt with by a patrol from the 505th Regiment, which attacked across a footbridge linking it to the east bank at approximately 18:00. The road bridge was officially declared secure an hour-and-a-half later.[63]

Elements of Colonel William E. Ekman's 505th Parachute Infantry Regiment were also on the move from DZ N less than an hour after landing, and enjoyed arguably the easiest ride in securing its objectives. The town of Groesbeek just north of the DZ was rapidly secured as planned with the assistance of the Dutch Resistance, and a two-Battalion perimeter was established along the southern edge of the Groesbeek Heights overlooking the town and the road and railway line running north to Nijmegen.[64] British intelligence reports had indicated that German armoured units were stationed in the nearby *Reichswald* Forest, just inside the German border to the east of the landing area. A company-sized patrol established that the reports were erroneous and simultaneously obtained more accurate information from Dutch civilians. The news doubtless came as a relief to the lightly armed paratroopers, whose only anti-tank weapons at that point consisted of Gammon bombs, Bazooka rocket launchers, the 700 anti-tank mines Gavin had insisted his paratroopers carry for the jump, and six glider-borne 57mm guns belonging to Battery A, 80th Airborne Anti-Aircraft Battalion.[65] Ekman also despatched patrols to the three crossings on the Maas-Waal Canal to assist the 504th Regiment, one of which was instrumental in finally securing the Molenhoek bridge. Another patrol came close to securing an additional bridge carrying the Nijmegen-Eindhoven railway line over the River Maas near Mook, south-west of the landing area but was foiled by a German demolition party. All the 505th Parachute Infantry Regiment's immediate objectives had been accomplished by 20:00.[66] The 82nd Airborne Division's support elements that landed on DZ/LZ N were equally swift in accomplishing their immediate post-drop tasks. Companies B and D from Lieutenant-Colonel Edwin A. Bedell's 307th Airborne Engineer Battalion protected elements of Division HQ on the move from the DZ, and subsequently provided security for the Division Command Post after its establishment at 17:15, while Company C moved west to contact the 504th Parachute Infantry Regiment on the Maas-Waal Canal. Lieutenant-Colonel Wilbur Griffiths' 376th Parachute Field Artillery Battalion gathered up and assembled ten of its twelve 75mm Pack Howitzers, each of which had been dropped broken down into seven parts; it is unclear what became of the other two guns and they were presumably dropped wide. The Battalion then moved 1,000 yards to a pre-selected firing position within the Division perimeter. Griffiths broke an ankle on landing but resorted to a commandeered Dutch wheelbarrow as makeshift transport around the Battalion gun position. He was so engaged when Gavin called in while checking the status of his units, and jocularly reported his guns' readiness in person. The guns fired their first fire mission in support of the 505th Regiment at 18:00, just four-and-a-half hours after jumping.[67] Finally, the eight 57mm anti-tank guns belonging to the misleadingly named Battery A, 80th Airborne Anti-Aircraft Battalion were parcelled out, with two guns apiece being assigned to each of the Division's Parachute Infantry Regiments. The remaining pair of guns was kept back as a reserve in the vicinity of Gavin's Division Command Post.[68]

Although saddled with the 'most difficult regimental mission of all', the immediate post-drop phase began relatively smoothly for Colonel Roy Lindquist's 508th Parachute Infantry Regiment.[69] The misdropped 3rd Battalion swiftly rallied with the remainder of the Regiment on DZ T, and all three Battalions moved off for their objectives only twenty minutes or so behind schedule. Lieutenant-Colonel Otho E. Holmes' 2nd Battalion moved west from the DZ toward Hatert, leaving Company D to defend the DZ for use the following day. A Platoon despatched to assist the 504th Parachute Infantry Regiment in seizing the nearby bridge was unsuccessful but by nightfall the remainder of the 2nd Battalion had accomplished its initial mission by establishing a blocking position astride the Nijmegen-Mook road. Lieutenant-Colonel Louis Mendez and the 3rd Battalion moved north to secure the highest point of the Groesbeek Heights around Berg-en-Dal, and established an east-facing defensive perimeter covering the villages of Wyler and Beek at the base of the Heights. Mendez was also tasked to secure Beek but this was stymied by the onset of darkness and the task was postponed until the following day.[70]

The northern sector of the 508th Parachute Infantry Regiment's perimeter, linking the 2nd and 3rd Battalions to the west and east respectively, was assigned to Lieutenant-Colonel Shields Warren's 1st Battalion. Warren's initial objective, an area of high ground overlooking the southern Nijmegen suburb of De Ploeg, lay three miles or so north of the DZ and approximately the same distance from the bridges across the River Waal on the north side of the city. Two pre-arranged patrols from Captain Jonathan E. Adams' Company A were on the move toward the objective within thirty minutes of landing, and the remainder of Company A led the 1st Battalion advance within the hour. The move to and occupation of the initial objective was relatively uneventful, with the capture of a handful of German labour troops being the only sign of enemy activity, but it was also accompanied by a noticeable degree of straggling and discarding of equipment and ammunition. Captain Adams subsequently observed that his Company was 'not in the best training shape' and that he was one of the few men still carrying an anti-tank mine when Company A reached the objective. Adams also noted a widespread and unwarranted assumption that the operation would continue in the same easy manner it had begun, which he attributed to a lack of time to fully train and assimilate the large number of replacements posted in to make up losses incurred in Normandy. The Battalion Executive Officer, Captain Benjamin F. Delamater, noted that the same problem across the entire 1st Battalion and particularly the heavily laden 81mm Mortar Platoon, which was obliged to drop out briefly en masse, although they caught up by the time the Battalion reached the objective; Delamater put it down to moving too fast during the post-jump 'let down' period.[71]

Be that as it may, the 1st Battalion was digging in on its objectives within three hours of leaving the DZ and was joined there by Lieutenant-Colonel Lindquist, accompanied by his personal radio operator and two Dutch military interpreters attached to his HQ for the operation. His appearance appears to have been connected to Gavin's verbal pre-jump instructions to despatch a force to secure the Nijmegen bridges 'without delay after landing'.[72] Although Gavin had specified the 1st Battalion for the mission Lindquist had also provisionally warned off the 3rd Battalion, too, as a contingency measure, but the underlying problem was Lindquist's understanding of Gavin's verbal instructions, which Lindquist took to mean he was free to put off moving on the bridges until all his Regimental tasks had been fully accomplished. Consequently, Lindquist instructed Warren to concentrate on digging in on the De Ploeg objective and tying in his flanks with the 2nd and 3rd Battalions while being 'prepared to go into Nijmegen later'.[73] Gavin, however, was looking for a more urgent and literal interpretation of his instructions.[74] In the event Lindquist modified his intentions slightly after several members of the Dutch Resistance turned up at the 1st Battalion's location and reported that the Germans had abandoned Nijmegen leaving the Waal bridges held by an eighteen-strong party of German troops.[75] Lindquist therefore authorised Warren to despatch an 'aggressive patrol' into Nijmegen to check the veracity of the Dutch reports, with instructions to secure the south end of the road bridge if possible. The patrol, commanded by a Lieutenant Robert J. Weaver and consisting of a Platoon from Company C reinforced with the Battalion Intelligence Section and two .30 Machine Gun Squads, was to approach the bridge from the east, presumably using the circuitous route Gavin had drawn up in England to minimise the possibility of becoming disoriented in Nijmegen's streets. Whatever the provenance of its route, Weaver's patrol moved off at 18:30.[76] However, while Weaver and his men were making their preparations Gavin had become aware that Lindquist had not yet moved on the Nijmegen bridges in strength and radioed him 'to delay not a second longer and get the bridge as quickly as possible with Warren's battalion'.[77] With Gavin's intent finally made absolutely explicit, Lindquist called a conference at 18:00 to formulate a plan with Warren and Captains Jonathan E. Adams and Woodrow W. Millsaps, commanding Companies A and B respectively. Reinforced with two .30 Machine Gun Squads and two 81mm mortars, Adams and Millsaps were to advance into Nijmegen and approach the road bridge from the south-east to avoid the possibility of clashing with Weaver's earlier patrol, assisted by a member of the Dutch Resistance; the latter was to guide the paratroopers via the Resistance HQ for the latest intelligence on what was reported to be the control post for demolition charges rigged on the bridge.[78] Matters where then delayed by Dutch reports of a large German force lurking in the woods to the rear of the 1st Battalion's position. The report proved to be erroneous but it took the patrol despatched to verify its accuracy until after dark to confirm the fact.[79]

There was one other unit ensconced in the 82nd Airborne Division's area of responsibility. Lieutenant-General Browning had landed at 14:00 on LZ N with his Advanced Airborne Corps HQ in twenty-nine Horsa gliders stripped as we have seen from the 1st Airborne Division's already limited allotment. After exiting his Horsa and running across the LZ to the *Reichswald* in order to be the first British officer to urinate on German soil, Browning supervised the unloading of his personal Jeep and specifically mounted a hand-sewn Pegasus pennant on the vehicle's front bumper. With these weighty matters attended to the Advanced Corps HQ was established at the southern edge base of the Groesbeek Heights, and radio contact was rapidly established with Gavin's nearby Division HQ, by the simple expedient of handing the Americans a radio set to replace their own, all of which had been damaged on landing.[80] A telephone line was also run out to the 82nd Airborne Division HQ, but the first officer allotted the task, Lieutenant Fuller Gee from the Royal Corps of Signals, lost both legs when his collapsible Welbike ran over a German mine; he died later in the evening. The task was completed by Lieutenant Nick Carter, attached to Browning's HQ from the 101st Airborne Division.[81]

The superfluous nature of Browning's presence in Holland soon became apparent. No contact could be made with the 1st Airborne Division at Arnhem, and contact with British 2nd Army HQ and the main Airborne Corps HQ at Moor Park was of limited utility because Browning's end lacked the trained cipher operators necessary to handle secure transmissions. As Browning himself acknowledged in a post-operation report 'Corps Signals in the field and at Airborne Base were totally inadequate in personnel and equipment and training.' Much of the problem lay in the fact that 1st Airborne Corps HQ overall was only a training and administrative entity with little to no operational function or experience.[82] Browning must have been only too aware of these limitations and the fact that his move to Holland would effectively remove him from the means to exercise effective command, and in that light it is difficult to interpret Browning's actions as anything other than placing his career ambitions ahead of the success of Operation MARKET.

By nightfall on 17 September and thus within six hours of landing, the 82nd and 101st Airborne Divisions had seized the bulk of their initial objectives. A total of eleven bridges had been secured intact across five of the watercourses on the GARDEN line of advance, spanning the River Dommel, the Zuid Willems Canal, the River Aa, the River Maas and the Maas-Waal Canal. Of the remaining two watercourses, both ends of the bridge site over the Wilhelmina Canal near

Son had been secured while efforts were ongoing to seize another crossing near Best, and a move to secure the Nijmegen road bridge across the River Waal was underway, having been delayed by the need to meet Browning's edict placing the seizure of the Groesbeek Heights above securing the river crossings. This was a highly creditable performance by any standard, and was in no small part due to painstaking preparation, aggression and speed displayed by the units involved. The 1st Battalion, 506th Parachute Infantry Regiment was perhaps the fastest off the mark, with elements on the move from the DZ within twenty minutes of the jump, but numerous other units were on the move well within an hour after landing. It is unclear if all the seized bridges were rigged for demolition like the ones across the Maas-Waal Canal at Molenhoek, Malden and Hatert and the Wilhelmina Canal near Son, although it is logical to assume that they were. Consequently, while the US paratroopers thus created their own good fortune to an extent, their success was also in large part down to a combination of surprise and sheer good luck.

This is in no way a criticism of the troops involved, but merely an inescapable consequence of the limitations of the technique employed. Specifically, no matter how well prepared, motivated and swift the parachute troops may have been, it was not generally possible to deliver large numbers of them in daylight sufficiently close to their objectives to permit them to overcome an alert and prepared enemy before the latter could detonate pre-placed demolition charges. The truth of this is clear from events on 17 September when, despite being delivered accurately in a compact landing pattern a mile and one-and-a-half miles respectively from their objectives, the 506th and 504th Parachute Infantry Regiments were still unable to prevent the Germans demolishing their target bridges at Son, Hatert and Malden. What was required was a highly trained and dedicated glider force capable of delivering troops very close to, or even directly onto, spot targets such as bridges. This was not a deficiency specific to the operation in Holland, for such a capability would also have been highly beneficial in Normandy; the la Barquette locks, bridges over the River Merderet and causeway exits from the UTAH landing beaches and the strongpoints guarding their seaward ends were tailor-made targets for such a capability.

However, US airborne doctrine relied overwhelmingly upon parachute insertion as its primary means of delivery, with gliders, their pilots and dedicated passengers being relegated to a subsidiary and subordinate role. USAAF regulations defined US glider pilots as merely the aerial equivalent of truck drivers with no combat role save in 'exceptional circumstances,'[83] while US Glider Infantry soldiers were considered very much second-class Airborne citizens, being denied the hazard pay, special insignia and uniform items enjoyed by their Parachute Infantry colleagues until at least July 1944.[84] More importantly, US glider pilots were not trained in the requisite techniques or to the necessary standard to perform such missions, and the US Army arguably did not attain a capability akin to that provided by the British Glider Pilot Regiment until the advent of the troop-carrying helicopter. The irony was that the British had exactly this capability but chose not to use it for no discernible reason. As we have seen, Operation COMET envisaged a pre-dawn glider *coup-de-main* to seize the Arnhem road bridge but this was dropped from the MARKET plan and Urquhart was unable to persuade Hollinghurst's RAF planners to reinstate it, even with the support of the commander of the Glider Pilot Regiment.[85] It is interesting to speculate how Operation MARKET might have proceeded had specialist glider capability been more readily available and/or properly utilised.

***

The bulk of the 1st Airborne Division's first lift was slated to remain on or near the Wolfheze landing area until the arrival of the Division's second lift, which was scheduled to arrive during the morning of Monday 18 September. As a result, the Divisional units were either tasked to carry out their primary missions in the interim or posted to defend designated sectors of the Divisional perimeter. After securing the drop and landing zones for the main landings and capturing sixteen assorted Germans and a staff car, the 21st Independent Parachute Company dug in without incident around its post-drop RV at the Reijers-Camp Farm for example, covering the northern section of DZ S.[86] The 1st Airlanding Light Regiment RA's Nos. 1 and 3 Batteries were dug in on the eastern side of the landing area ready to provide fire support by 16:30 and when no missions had been received by 18:00 the Regimental commander, Lieutenant-Colonel William 'Sheriff' Thompson, was heard to complain that his men may as well have come in with the second lift. In the event, the Regiment's first shoot was carried out by Lieutenant Keith Halliday and No. 1 Battery against German troops in the vicinity of the Hotel Wolfheze, just east of LZ Z, at dusk. In the meantime Lieutenant Frank Moore from No. 3 Battery took a patrol to investigate reports of brand-new German 105mm guns stored in the vicinity of the Wolfheze mental asylum. The guns were there as reported but Lieutenant Moore decided to leave well alone when one of the pieces proved to be booby-trapped.[87] The guns were subsequently destroyed in place by Captain Roger Binyon and No. 1 Platoon from the 9th Field Company RE on the morning of 19 September.[88]

Not all the Divisional units were so passively engaged. Major John Winchester's 9th Field Company RE lost one officer to enemy fire before it had fully assembled at its post-landing RV; Lieutenant Jerry Wise was hit in both legs, the left arm and face by a German machine-gun located in the woods east of LZ Z but nonetheless managed to reach the RV under his own steam. After regrouping and despatching a number of small detachments to accompany other units as previously arranged, the Company moved off to secure the Hotel Wolfheze, which was earmarked to serve as Company HQ. Captain Roger Binyon's No. 1 Platoon led off at 15:10 accompanied by Lieutenant Roy Timmins and part of No. 2 Platoon, followed by Company HQ and part of No. 3 Platoon twenty minutes later. The HQ group covered only 600 yards before being held up by German machine-gun fire, and after Lieutenant James Steel disappeared without trace after going forward to investigate on a motorcycle, the group pulled back slightly and dug in around a track junction 500 yards east of the Company RV.

Captain Binyon had meanwhile run into problems of his own at the Hotel Wolfheze. Lieutenant Timmins was killed and Sapper Peter Greig seriously wounded in the stomach while performing a flanking attack on the hotel at around 18:00, and Lance-Corporal William Takle was subsequently wounded in turn while trying to assist Greig. Both men died of their wounds the following day.[89] In the meantime a party of six Germans, possibly attempting to outflank Binyon's party, ran into the southern edge of the Company HQ perimeter at around 19:00. Major Winchester's men killed three, claimed three more wounded and captured an MG42; Captain Binyon was ordered to withdraw his party to the Company HQ position around thirty minutes later.[90] Given the timings, the 1st Airlanding Light Regiment's first shoot may have been intended to cover Captain Binyon's withdrawal.

According to the 9th Field Company's War Diary, the Germans killed after bumping the Company perimeter were identified as members of the *Hitler Jugend*, presumably referring to 12 SS Panzer Division, which carried that name as a cuff title. In fact, the dead Germans were more likely members of *SS Panzergrenadier Ausbildungs und Ersatz Bataillon 16*, the replacement training unit billeted three miles or so east of Wolfheze near Oosterbeek. The bombing that preceded the Allied airborne landings prompted *Hauptsturmführer* Sepp Krafft to move two of his three units, the somewhat confusingly numbered 2 and 4 *Kompanien*, out of their billets for impromptu training in the woods and heathland to the north-west in an effort to avoid casualties; 9 *Kompanie*, Krafft's heavy weapons unit, appears to have been left at its billets in or near Arnhem. In so doing Krafft thus inadvertently placed two-thirds of his *Bataillon* between the 1st Airborne Division and its objectives. On observing the landings Krafft moved west and set up a tactical HQ at the Hotel Wolfheze, despatched 2 *Kompanie* to reconnoitre toward the landing area, called 9 *Kompanie* forward to act as a mobile reserve and set 4 *Kompanie* to establishing a line of outposts running inside the woods bordering the landing area centred on the Hotel Wolfheze. After becoming disoriented in the woods and briefly emerging onto the edge of LZ Z, from where they claimed to have hit four gliders with machine-gun fire,

2 *Kompanie* returned to the Hotel Wolfheze and assisted in establishing the outpost line.[91] The timings are unclear but the outpost line appears to have been at least partially in place by around 15:45; the machine-gun fire that held up 9th Field Company's HQ group presumably emanated from elements of *Bataillon* Krafft, given that the northern end of the outpost line covering the Arnhem-Ede railway and parallel Johannahoeveweg road was in place by that time. It was also Krafft's men who rebuffed the 9th Field Company's attempt to secure the Hotel Wolfheze, killing Lieutenant Timmins in the process. In all, *Bataillon* Krafft's initial move toward the landing area thus led to a three-hour skirmish that cost both sides a handful of casualties and prevented the 9th Field Company from occupying its planned HQ location on the eastern perimeter of the landing area. This was not to be the last contact *Bataillon* Krafft had with the 1st Airborne Division on 17 September, although as we shall see, Krafft made much more of the matter than was actually the case.

The dedicated Airlanding infantry units tasked to protect the landing area moved off to their pre-arranged positions soon after reorganising at their RVs and ironically encountered less opposition than Major Winchester's Airborne Sappers. Thanks to his glider allotment being trimmed to provide machines for Browning's Advanced Corps HQ, Lieutenant-Colonel McCardie's 2nd South Staffords arrived in Holland with just his Battalion HQ, B and D Companies and Vickers Medium Machine Gun (MMG) Platoons from Support Company; this total had been further reduced by the loss of two gliders in the fly-in carrying men from B Company. One of the latter, carrying B Company HQ and its commander, Major Robert Cain, aborted over Kent five minutes after take-off and force-landed safely near Canterbury. The other, carrying Lieutenant Roland Sharp and 12 Platoon, came down behind German lines near Tilburg and its passengers spent the next six weeks evading capture until liberated by the British 2nd Army as it advanced to Boxtel. Back at the landing area, Lieutenant-Colonel McCardie's men dealt with two isolated German machine-guns and took twenty German prisoners in return for two dead and seven wounded, all from Major John Phillp's D Company. The wounded included Lieutenant John Hardman-Mountford commanding 21 Platoon, and the casualties may have been sustained in clearing Wolfheze; according to Middlebrook the town was cleared by two Platoons from the 2nd South Staffords.[92] After parcelling out part of the MMG and Mortar Platoons to the Rifle Companies, McCardie's men dug in near Reijers-Camp Farm to protect LZ S with the exception of a Platoon from D Company, which was detached to protect 1st Airlanding Brigade HQ and 181 Airlanding Field Ambulance's Main Dressing Station, occupying houses in the aptly named Duitsekampweg nearby.[93]

The 1st Border, leaderless as the Horsa carrying Lieutenant-Colonel Thomas Haddon had force-landed safely shortly after take-off, came under the temporary command of his deputy Major Stuart Cousens and moved off from its rally position along the Arnhem-Utrecht railway at the bottom of LZ S to four pre-arranged company positions, with each Company accompanied by attachments from Support Company. Major Tom Armstrong's B Company led off as it had been allotted the most far-flung position, just east of Renkum overlooking the road running along the north bank of the Lower Rhine. Four *Kriegsmarine* personnel armed with two MG34s were captured en route, with the prisoners being placed on a Jeep trailer belonging to the MMG Section attached from Support Company; this provoked some irritation from the heavily laden Vickers teams who were routinely forbidden from riding on Jeeps or trailers. Once in Renkum proper, B Company were confronted by a German truck on the main street which yielded several more prisoners after being shot up. The Company then established a defensive perimeter amongst houses and factory buildings including a large brickworks. Establishing radio contact with the remainder of the Battalion proved problematic, and Armstrong was reduced to relaying messages via D Company using a telephone in Renkum police station with the assistance of the Dutch Resistance. Major Charles Breese's D Company trailed B Company before branching off to secure a road junction just east of Heelsum. It, too, was approached by a German truck heading for Heelsum; two of the occupants were killed and the remainder captured. C Company, commanded by Major William Neil, set up south-east of Wolfheze, covering the eastern edge of LZ Z while Major Thomas Montgomery's A Company dug in facing west, straddling a track just south of the Arnhem–Utrecht railway line. Battalion HQ and part of Major Richard Stewart's Support Company occupied positions around Johannahoeve Farm, in the centre of the landing area. Things remained quiet as the glider soldiers dug in for the night, but Major Breese was recalled to Battalion HQ to become acting Battalion second-in-command, with command of D Company devolving to Captain William Hodgson.[94]

The 7th KOSB landed with eight gliders astray, which reduced its strength by three rifle Platoons and a number of organic and attached support elements including three 6-Pounder anti-tank guns. Lieutenant-Colonel Robert Payton-Reid's Battalion had been allotted the 1st Airlanding Brigade's most far-flung mission, that of securing and protecting the as yet unused DZ Y for the second lift, which lay roughly two miles north-west of the main Brigade perimeter. The Battalion moved off at 15:00 led by Major Robert Buchanan's A Company, which was to deploy independently in order to interdict German traffic moving along the Amsterdamseweg linking Ede and Arnhem. The road also marked the northern boundary of DZ Y, and Buchanan's men peeled away and deployed between the *Zuid Ginkel* café at the north-east corner of the DZ and another building, referred to locally as the *Planken Wambuis*, two miles or so to the east. 1 Platoon and Lieutenant Lawrence Kane, a CanLoan exchange officer, were allotted the most westerly sector of A Company's area near the café, reinforced with an anti-tank gun.[95] The remainder of the Battalion moved directly to DZ Y, with Major Michael Forman's B Company capturing a female *Luftwaffe* auxiliary named Irene Reiman and her unnamed boyfriend en route; Ms Reiman was sent back to Brigade HQ where she became an object of much interest among the HQ personnel.[96] On arrival B Company and Major Gordon Dinwiddie's C Company moved straight across the DZ and established Company perimeters on its western edge with B Company to the north. Battalion HQ set up shop just south of an embankment carrying an unfinished motorway that ran across the southern edge of the DZ, with Major Charles Sherriff's D Company nearby as Battalion reserve. The latter's 16 Platoon commanded by another CanLoan officer, Lieutenant Peter Mason, was despatched to occupy a group of buildings in the woods just east of the DZ along with the Battalion second-in-command, Captain George Gourlay.[97]

Apart from the capture of Ms Reiman the move was made without incident, and the 7th KOSB was the only Battalion that did not suffer any fatalities on 17 September. Lieutenant Kane's men were the first to make direct contact with the enemy, although 1 Platoon does not appear to have initially appreciated the reality of their position deep behind enemy lines. As Bren-gunner Private William Anderson put it: 'Shortly after we had taken up position at a bend in the road, we heard a car. It was a pick-up type truck and it passed, *and nobody fired a shot* [original emphasis]. I don't know why. The platoon commander shouted many things at us [including] "When I say fire - ACT!"'[98] There was no mistake when two more vehicles, one of them an ambulance according to Anderson, appeared a little later. The vehicles were carrying men from *Sturmbannführer* Paul Anton Helle's largely Dutch *SS Wacht Bataillon 3*, specifically members of the unit band commanded by an *Oberscharführer* Sakkel which was routinely used as a quick-reaction force, usually to round up downed Allied aircrew.[99] On this occasion *Oberscharführer* Sakkel and his men left their barracks in Ede at around 17:00 in two commandeered vehicles with orders to reconnoitre the woods bordering Ginkel Heath. Ginkel Heath was known to the 7th KOSB as DZ Y and the SS bandsmen were thus soon to encounter a rather different kind of Allied interloper in the shape of the suitably motivated 1 Platoon. Lieutenant Kane's men promptly and comprehensively shot up both vehicles. Sakkel was mortally wounded, an undetermined number of his bandsmen were killed and the remainder fled the way they had come in panic, with some taking the opportunity to desert.[100]

The units tasked to protect the landing area for the second lift were thus on the move within an hour or so of landing, but Brigadier Gerald Lathbury's 1st Parachute Brigade and attached 1st Airborne Reconnaissance Squadron did not move with similar despatch. As we have seen, the entire Brigade was down on DZ X by 14:10 following what one participant described as a 'YMCA drop'.[101] The seemingly routine nature of the drop and lack of tangible opposition created a somewhat relaxed atmosphere, noted in the Brigade War Diary, which explicitly referred to 'everyone [being] rather slow getting off the DZ'. This was exacerbated by the size of the DZ, which made it a relatively long way to the rally points located along its eastern edge; Brigade HQ elements did not begin to arrive at their RV until 14:25, for example.[102] Thereafter it took until 14:45 for the 1st Parachute Battalion to report itself ready for action and for Brigade HQ to report the Brigade eighty per cent complete and in radio contact with the 2nd and 3rd Parachute Battalions. This was followed by an additional delay of half an hour or more while the glider-borne support elements rallied, notably the guns from the 1st Airlanding Anti-Tank Battery RA, presumably because of unloading difficulties.[103] The Brigade's dedicated RASC detachment failed to arrive at all, and Captain William Gell's equivalent from the 1st Airlanding Brigade, No. 3 Parachute Platoon and 3rd Parachute Jeep Section from 250 (Airborne) Light Composite Company RASC with two Jeeps and four trailers loaded with ammunition, was co-opted as an emergency replacement with Captain Gell's agreement.[104] Interestingly, the Brigade HQ's organic transport was last to appear, arriving at the Brigade RV at 15:30.[105] Thus the advance from the DZ did not commence until a full hour or more had elapsed after the landing, with the 2nd and 3rd Parachute Battalions being given permission to move at 15:10 and the 1st Parachute Battalion twenty minutes later at 15:30.[106] The latter had been held back as a reserve until the Brigade HQ's organic transport arrived, and did not actually move off until 15:40.[107] The Brigade HQ column was last to move off in the wake of the 2nd and 3rd Parachute Battalions at 15:45; the additional delay was necessary to sort out transport and to unpack and mount wireless sets, although the latter were not properly netted in before moving.[108] The 1st Parachute Brigade was therefore not on the move toward the Arnhem bridges in its entirety until an hour and thirty-five minutes after landing.

This was a rather tardy performance in the circumstances, especially in comparison with the US parachute units to the south, many of which were on the move toward their objectives in much less than half that time. Even allowing for the somewhat leisurely move to its unit RVs, the Brigade could still have been on the move within thirty-five minutes of the drop had Brigadier Lathbury not deliberately chosen to keep his fully assembled Battalions immobile while the Brigade transport and attachments from the 1st Parachute Squadron RE and the 1st Airlanding Anti-Tank Battery were gathered in; he may also have been awaiting the arrival of a liaison officer from the 1st Airborne Reconnaissance Squadron. Even allowing for that however, the delay cannot be seen as other than needless and ill judged, given that the distance between the landing area and Arnhem made time of the essence. This was certainly the view of at least one of Lathbury's subordinate commanders; Lieutenant-Colonel David Dobie commanding the 1st Parachute Battalion, became increasingly frustrated at being held back for virtually an hour after his Battalion was fully assembled.[109] There was no real need to synchronise the advance because all three Battalions were to advance independently using separate routes and largely without intermediate objectives, and as they were moving on foot the motorised support attachments could have been despatched in their wake when they finally turned up at the RV. Lathbury's insistence that his Battalions wait for specific permission to move cannot therefore be justified on tactical or operational grounds and appears to be the result of his tendency toward micromanagement. This in turn raises the suspicion that Lathbury simply did not fully comprehend the realities of airborne operations, nor the urgency the situation demanded, a suspicion that his plan for the 1st Parachute Brigade's move to and seizure of the Divisional objectives reinforces significantly.

The initial movement phase of Lathbury's plan was a very slight reworking of the COMET scheme, rejigged to include three rather than two parallel lines of advance. Lieutenant-Colonel Dobie's 1st Parachute Battalion was allotted the northern route along the Amsterdamseweg linking Arnhem and Ede, codenamed LEOPARD. The 3rd Parachute Battalion, under Lieutenant-Colonel John Fitch, was assigned the centre TIGER route, which followed the Utrechtseweg running through the centre of Oosterbeek and Lieutenant-Colonel John Frost's 2nd Parachute Battalion was allocated the southern LION route, running along the north bank of the Lower Rhine through the southern outskirts of Oosterbeek and into Arnhem proper. All three Battalions were to launch themselves down their respective routes independently with no provision for scouting ahead; the 1st Airborne Reconnaissance Squadron had been tasked to secure the Arnhem road bridge and Lathbury had rejected Major Freddie Gough's requests to operate in the role for which his unit was trained and equipped.[110] Dividing the Brigade into three along separate and widely spaced routes dispersed the formation's collective combat power, militated against effective co-ordination and effectively ruled out any prospect of mutual support if any or all of the Battalion groups ran into serious opposition. A more sensible arrangement would have been to despatch two Battalions and Brigade HQ along the riverside LION route using the Lower Rhine to protect the right flank, with the third Battalion using the Utrechtseweg/TIGER route to protect the Brigade's left flank. This does not appear to have occurred to Lathbury, however, and his more widely dispersed scheme virtually obliged each Battalion to fight its own battle in isolation and without the benefit of mutual support or control although events intruded before things got that far.

The movement phase of Lathbury's Brigade plan thus resembled a peacetime training exercise rather than a scheme for execution in the face of a live enemy, and that impression is heightened yet further by his intended post-approach march dispositions. Dobie's 1st Parachute Battalion was directed to secure an area of high ground to the north of Arnhem rather than the vital river crossings in the south-east of the city, which meant that Lathbury had effectively disbarred a third of his combat strength from involvement in securing the key objective before his Brigade even left the landing area. Responsibility for securing the river crossings was assigned to Frost's 2nd Parachute Battalion supported by Fitch's 3rd Parachute Battalion. Frost was tasked to secure not only the Arnhem road bridge but the pontoon bridge a few hundred metres downstream, the railway bridge on the outskirts of the city, the German HQ located in Arnhem town hall and to pass a full Company over the river to approach the Arnhem road bridge from both ends simultaneously, a tall order for a single Battalion operating in temporary isolation against a first-rank enemy. Had events unfolded according to plan, a third of the 1st Parachute Brigade would thus have been isolated on the high ground north of Arnhem, a third would have been dispersed in company packets holding the pontoon bridge, the Arnhem rail bridge and the German HQ in the centre of Arnhem respectively, and the remaining third would have been holding the Arnhem road bridge. Given that each of these objectives arguably warranted the minimum of a battalion rather than a company to secure and defend them this was a classic case of trying to do too much with too little, and virtually guaranteed that the 1st Parachute Brigade's sub-units would be isolated, overwhelmed and defeated in detail. They were spread too wide and too thin to defend themselves effectively, let alone secure and hold the Brigade's primary objective.[111] As we shall see, Frost's defence of the Arnhem bridge was hamstrung by a lack of manpower that prevented him establishing a properly defensible perimeter at one end of the structure; it is interesting to note that had Lathbury's plan gone as envisaged this would have remained the case, as only a single battalion would have been available to defend both ends of the bridge.

Lathbury's inadequate planning is routinely ascribed to him being misled by intelligence suggesting the landing would only be faced with minor opposition, often with the caveat that he would have done things differently had he been made aware that elements of II SS *Panzerkorps* were in the area.[112] This does not hold water however, if only because the intelligence did not say any such thing. While the Intelligence Summary attached to the Brigade Operation Order reported there was 'no direct, recent evidence on which to base an estimate of the troops in the immediate divisional area', it also noted that barrack accommodation in the area had a capacity of 10,000 and that troops withdrawn from the fighting front might also be present; this ought to have been sufficient in itself to warrant basing subsequent planning on a worst case scenario.[113] Nor was this the first time Lathbury had exhibited poor judgement in his planning, for his Arnhem plan replicated errors committed in the operation to seize the Ponte Primasole in Sicily in July 1943. On that occasion a landing plan tailored to suit the numerous Brigade objectives spread the 1st Parachute Brigade across four separate DZs and a single glider LZ, which were collectively too far from those objectives but too close together for easy differentiation from the air. Once on the ground the plan again directed a large proportion of the Brigade's strength to subsidiary tasks in breach of the military maxim about identifying and maintaining focus on the primary aim, and dispersed the Brigade in three separate locations across more than five square miles, too far apart to permit mutual support or reinforcement. The root of the problem was that despite being the 1st Airborne Division's senior Brigadier, Lathbury simply lacked operational experience, Airborne or otherwise, having spent most of his war service in Staff appointments at the War Office or overseeing the raising and initial establishment of parachute units. The bulk of his time was thus spent dealing with personnel recruitment and selection, initial training and administration rather than operational matters; the partially self-inflicted fiasco at the Ponte Primasole represented the sum total of his operational experience.[114] Ordinarily, such inexperience could have been offset by guidance from above but as we have seen – and as he was about to clearly demonstrate further – the 1st Airborne Division's commander knew even less about operational Airborne matters than Lathbury.

Lathbury left the landing area at 15:30 in a Brigade HQ Jeep equipped with a No. 22 radio set, accompanied by his Brigade Intelligence Officer, Captain Willie Taylor, and presumably a signaller.[115] Before departing he appears to have decided that the non-appearance of the liaison officer from the 1st Airborne Reconnaissance Squadron meant that the entire unit had failed to arrive in Holland. Rather than attempting to ascertain if this were indeed the case, by despatching a messenger to the Squadron's RV on the adjacent LZ Z for example, Lathbury instead reportedly radioed the 2nd and 3rd Parachute Battalions with a warning and suggestion that they assemble an alternative *coup-de-main* force from their organic motorised transport.[116] Nothing appears to have come of the idea, although this message may well have been the source of the rumour concerning the Reconnaissance Squadron's alleged non-arrival that rapidly ran around the landing area and was to subsequently hamstring the *coup-de-main* effort. Despite having obliged his units to remain immobile for a considerable period Lathbury then set off to urge his units to greater haste in person, beginning with the 2nd Parachute Battalion on the LION route. According to one source, he conferred first with Frost at some point before the 2nd Parachute Battalion reached Heveadorp and thus within the first two miles of its advance.[117]

In fact, the 1st Airborne Reconnaissance Squadron was fully present in Holland and preparing to depart for Arnhem at its rally point on LZ Z, located at the edge of a wood 750 yards south of the Arnhem–Utrecht railway line.[118] At least twenty of the Squadron's allotment of twenty-two Horsas had landed as planned with only four landing casualties, although several Jeeps were damaged and/or trapped in wrecked gliders and four vehicles failed to arrive; the latter may have included vehicles assigned to the liaison officers tasked to report to 1st Parachute Brigade and Division HQs.[119] Fortuitously, most of the damaged and two of the missing vehicles belonged to A Troop, which was to remain at the landing area as Squadron reserve. The *coup-de-main* force lost only three Jeeps, which reduced its strength to twenty-eight operational vehicles. The glider-borne component, commanded by the Squadron's second-in-command Captain David Allsop, was on the ground by 13:35, but did not move off for the Squadron RV until 15:00, apparently due to problems unloading Jeeps from Allsop's glider; they arrived at the rally point fifteen minutes later, at around the same time as Major Gough, who had come in by parachute with the bulk of the Squadron's personnel.[120] The Squadron was thus fully assembled by 15:30 and the *coup-de-main* force moved off for Arnhem ten minutes later, just over two full hours after the glider landing was complete.[121] This was a considerable period given that it took an average of thirty minutes to unload a Horsa, even allowing for the additional time required to unload damaged machines and for the glider and parachute contingents to reach the Squadron RV. It is therefore likely that the Reconnaissance Squadron was infected with the same lack of urgency that had afflicted the 1st Parachute Brigade, and waiting for the arrival of four Jeeps from the 9th Field Company RE tasked to accompany the *coup-de-main* force caused additional delay; unbeknown to Gough and his men the Horsas carrying the Sappers had been allocated to LZ S, and they never did link up with the Reconnaissance Squadron as planned.[122]

The bulk of the Reconnaissance Squadron left its RV at 15:40 with Captain John Hay's C Troop in the lead followed by Major Gough's Tactical HQ, Captain John Park's D Troop and Support Troop, commanded by Lieutenant John Christie. The column's initial route ran across the top corner of LZ Z to a sandy track paralleling the south side of the Arnhem–Utrecht railway and thence east toward Wolfheze. Nurses from the still-burning Wolfheze Mental Asylum pressed information and fresh fruit upon C Troop as they passed, and Sergeant David Christie from 9 Section encouraged a stray German to the rear with a burst of Sten fire while Sergeant Bill Stacey from 7 Section shot another who made a dash for the woods. Once in the northern outskirts of Wolfheze the Squadron crossed the railway tracks at a level crossing and continued east along the Johannahoeveweg still paralleling the railway line, which now ran atop a brush-covered embankment on the right. The two Jeeps of Lieutenant Peter Bucknall's 8 Section assumed the lead from 9 Section at the level crossing as part of the Squadron's standard tactical leap-frogging, travelling a few hundred yards apart. A thousand yards or so east of the level crossing the trees thinned away and the Johannahoeveweg dipped before rising again and entering the northern edge of the woods surrounding the Hotel Wolfheze. Lieutenant Bucknall's Jeep entered the woods at approximately 15:45 and in so doing triggered an ambush set just moments before by elements of *Bataillon* Krafft's *4 Kompanie*; had the Reconnaissance Squadron moved off earlier ahead of the 1st Parachute Brigade as scheduled, it might well have avoided the ambush altogether.[123]

Precisely what happened to the lead Jeep is unclear, but all its occupants including Lieutenant Bucknall were killed and the state and location of the bodies led men from the Squadron who examined the ambush site the following day to believe they had been executed after surrender.[124] 8 Section's second Jeep, commanded by Sergeant Tom McGregor, came under fire as it reached the bottom of the dip and Trooper Richard Minns was hit in the stomach and tumbled from the vehicle. Standard operating procedure called for the trail vehicle to stop and render dismounted assistance but Sergeant McGregor's Jeep was raked by fire from German troops stationed atop the railway embankment to the right as it came to a stop. Sergeant McGregor was killed and the other four men travelling in his Jeep, Lance-Corporal Taffy Thomas and Troopers Arthur Barlow, Reg Haslar and Jimmy Pearce were all wounded and obliged to surrender.[125] Their captors permitted Haslar to be carried but Minns had to be left behind with assurances from a German NCO that he would be dealt with properly in due course. The prisoners were hustled away so quickly that they were gone by the time Lieutenant Ralph Foulkes and 7 Section moved forward on foot to investigate. Foulkes and a Trooper Dodson attempted to drag Sergeant Bill Stacey to safety after he too was hit in the stomach while investigating McGregor's shot-up Jeep, but he proved too heavy and they were obliged to abandon the attempt.[126] There then followed a drawn-out but inconclusive firefight across the dip in the Johannahoeveweg, with the Germans calling down mortar fire on the stalled Reconnaissance Squadron from 16:00.[127]

At approximately 16:30, while the firefight was in full swing, Major Gough received a radio message summoning him to Division HQ immediately. Gough therefore handed over command to Captain Allsop and departed at 16:45, accompanied by his Intelligence Officer Lieutenant Trevor McNabb, the commander of HQ Troop Captain Horace Platt and some men from D Troop.[128] In the event, Gough's departure effectively brought the *coup-de-main* effort to an end. Because he assumed Gough's absence would be a short one, Allsop left matters in the hands of the Troop commanders, with the result that the *coup-de-main* force remained in place until 18:30, when it was ordered to withdraw to the landing area. The source of the order is unclear, although the Squadron's semi-official history claims it was issued by Division HQ.[129] Whatever its source, between the initial ambush and the withdrawal order only C Troop attempted to push forward, and two of its men caught a glimpse of Lieutenant Bucknall's Jeep ablaze in the trees with a body still aboard. Captain Hay ordered a withdrawal to the main Squadron perimeter when the SS tried to outflank him, and an attempt to gather in the wounded by the Squadron Medical Officer, Captain Thomas Swinscow, was also abandoned when the stretcher party was fired on despite displaying a Red Cross flag.[130] As a result Sergeant Stacey and Trooper Minns were left behind; the former consequently bled to death but Minns was still alive the following day when he was discovered by a party from C Troop and removed to an aid post.[131]

Although routine reconnaissance was the Squadron's *raison d'être* there does not appear to have been any attempt to ascertain the strength and extent of the German blocking position or to find an alternate route to Arnhem; as *4 Kompanie* was at the northern extremity of Krafft's outpost line, it may have been possible for the *coup-de-main* force to abandon the Johannahoeveweg route, sidestep to the north and pick up the LEOPARD/Amsterdamseweg route around two miles further west than originally intended. To be fair, this might well have brought them into contact with *Hauptmann* Willi Weber's patrol from 213 *Nachrichten* Regiment and armoured reinforcements from *SS Panzer Aufklärungs Abteilung 9*. However, Gough and then Allsop appear to have been content to exchange fire with largely unseen opponents and passively to endure mortaring at their hands while restricting their activity to recovering the wounded. It is therefore difficult to escape the conclusion that the *coup-de-main* mission was shelved while awaiting Gough's return, and then quietly dropped altogether when he failed to reappear. As with the Squadron's tardiness in leaving the landing area, the precise reason for the Squadron's lack of application is unclear, but it may have been the result of Gough's misgivings over the *coup-de-main* mission being transmitted to and/or shared by the remainder of the Squadron. Be that as it may, the salient but frequently overlooked point is that a mission of potentially vital importance to the Arnhem portion of Operation MARKET was stopped and then abandoned virtually on the edge of the landing area following a skirmish that cost two Jeeps from a total of twenty-eight and a dozen or so casualties. For his part, *Hauptsturmführer* Krafft passed off the ambush of two armed Jeeps and an inconclusive firefight with a relative handful of lightly armed reconnaissance troops as a full-scale attack by two full British companies in his self-serving report.[132]

Gough's summons to 1st Airborne Division HQ came directly from Major-General Urquhart, who arrived without mishap on LZ Z shortly after 13:00. After watching the 1st Parachute Brigade's drop onto the adjacent DZ X at 13:50 Urquhart drove across to confer with Brigadier Hicks at 1st Airlanding Brigade HQ, but Hicks was absent visiting his Battalions. At around this time Urquhart became privy to the rumour that Gough had lost almost all his vehicles and that the *coup-de-main* mission had not gone ahead.[133] At this point it would have been logical to try and establish the veracity or otherwise of the rumour, which should have been relatively easy, given that the Reconnaissance Squadron's Rear HQ under Lieutenant Quarter Master Tom Collier and Captain Michael Grubb's A Troop, the Squadron reserve, were located only a few hundred yards away; it would have taken a messenger a matter of minutes to make the journey.[134] However, Urquhart chose instead to proceed on the totally erroneous and unjustified assumption that the rumour was proven fact and issued the order for Gough to report to Division HQ forthwith via his own and the 1st Airlanding Brigade's signallers. The recall order raises three salient points. First, it strongly suggests that Urquhart had a poor to non-existent grasp of his Division's signals set up, for the Reconnaissance Squadron's vehicles were netted into their own internal frequency with two external links, to the 1st Parachute Brigade and Division HQ, via radio-equipped Liaison Officers. The 1st Airlanding Brigade was netted into a different frequency and was therefore unlikely to be able to contact the Reconnaissance Squadron whatever Urquhart may have wished and it is likely that Division HQ only succeeded in contacting Gough because he was stationary during the protracted firefight, rather than on the move.[135] Second, it suggests that Urquhart had a low opinion of the competence and indeed common sense of Gough and his men. At least a score of the 181 men of the Reconnaissance Squadron took into Arnhem were officers and it is difficult to imagine any combination of circumstances that would prevent at least some of them from finding some way to report any serious impediment to their *coup-de-main* mission to Division HQ.[136] By merely framing the recall order Urquhart was therefore assuming that Gough and his men lacked the wit to make contact. Third, the recall order also assumed that Gough and/or his men were lurking in the vicinity of the landing area, for Urquhart had no way of knowing that they were embroiled with elements of *Bataillon* Krafft a mile or so east of the landing area. Had matters gone as planned, Gough would likely have been well on the way to Arnhem, and possibly in the city itself when the recall order was issued. Urquhart was thus operating on the assumption that it was perfectly acceptable or indeed possible for Gough to motor blithely back and forth across miles of enemy-held territory and that it was equally acceptable to remove him from his command in the middle of what was supposed to be a vital mission.

It is therefore difficult to see Urquhart's summoning Gough to Division HQ as anything other than a poorly thought out knee-jerk reaction to a baseless rumour, and one taken with no effort whatsoever to establish its veracity. It reinforces the contention that Urquhart had not properly grasped the realities of Airborne command, something his next action was to prove beyond doubt. Urquhart had originally intended to remain at Division HQ until the arrival of the second lift on Monday 18 September, but at 16:30 he left in order to carry news of the supposed abandonment of the *coup-de-main* mission to the 1st Parachute Brigade in person, and to urge Lathbury to greater haste.[137] The final prompt for his decision appears to have been Division HQ losing contact with 1st Parachute Brigade soon after the latter left the landing area at 15:30; this was caused in turn by only two of the Brigade's four Jeep-mounted No. 22 Sets arriving in Holland intact. One was acquired by Lathbury and the other was assigned to the Brigade HQ column to control the internal Brigade net. Contact with Division HQ was thus relegated to a lower-powered and shorter-ranged No. 68P Set, which moved out of range shortly after the Brigade moved off from the landing area.[138] Urquhart therefore ordered the Divisional Signals Section to continue their efforts to contact Gough and to direct him on to 1st Parachute Brigade HQ, before departing in his Jeep accompanied by his personal signaller, Corporal Warford, and Lieutenant-Colonel Robert Loder-Symonds, the Division's Commander Royal Artillery (CRA). Quite how Gough was supposed to locate Lathbury when the latter was busy shuttling between his widely separated Battalions by Jeep was not explained. In the event, the recall order not only aborted the *coup-de-main* mission but also permanently separated Gough from his command, for he eventually fetched up at the Arnhem bridge in his fruitless quest to locate Urquhart while his men were eventually subsumed into the defence of the Oosterbeek Pocket after acting as guides and scouting the route into Arnhem.

Although sometimes partially excused on the grounds of Urquhart's growing frustration at his inability to exert control over events, the decision is nonetheless widely and correctly judged to have been a serious mistake.[139] Whatever his personal feelings, Urquhart's place was at Division HQ because the radio communication problems made his presence there more rather than less important; messengers were the only practical alternative method for subordinate units to make contact, and Urquhart should therefore have been in place there ready to react to reports and issue orders as necessary. His decision to take on the role of a lowly HQ messenger was thus another poorly thought-out reaction, and he does not appear to have appreciated the risk he was running by driving around unescorted sixty miles behind enemy lines. As it was, he was lucky not to have suffered the same fate as the *Stadtkommandant* of Arnhem *Generalmajor* Friedrich Kussin, who was killed after his car blundered into the 3rd Parachute Battalion at the junction of the Utrechtseweg and Wolfhezeweg.

Urquhart seriously compounded his error. First, he failed to inform his Operations Officer, Lieutenant-Colonel Charles Mackenzie, of how and where he could be contacted, how long he would be absent and to clarify what measures were to be taken in his absence should the need arise or he fail to reappear. This omission was to exacerbate his earlier failure to clarify and disseminate the Division's succession of command to all those involved. Second, at some point after leaving his HQ, Urquhart ordered Corporal Warford to retune the No. 22 Set mounted in his Jeep from the Division frequency onto that of the 1st Airborne Reconnaissance Squadron and to continue the effort to contact Gough.[140] This was not the effortless process allowed by modern radio equipment but involved partially dismantling the set to replace the delicate tuning crystals, a fiddly job at best and more so in a moving Jeep. Urquhart therefore deliberately severed his only link to his Division HQ, and although it was not apparent at the time, the point when Corporal Warford broke the connection with Division HQ is the moment when Urquhart abdicated command of the 1st Airborne Division.

The consequences of these rash and ill-thought-out decisions lay in the future however, and Urquhart soon caught up with the 1st Parachute Brigade HQ Group and the tail end of the 2nd Parachute Battalion Column as they moved toward the riverside LION route. There he left word of the alleged failure of the Reconnaissance Squadron's *coup-de-main* with Brigade Major Tony Hibbert and urged him on with a shout of 'Hibbert, for God's sake get your brigade moving or the bloody Germans will get to the bridge before us.'[141] After moving up the column in an unsuccessful attempt to talk with Frost, Urquhart then drove north in search of Lathbury and the 3rd Parachute Battalion travelling on the centre TIGER route. At some point Lieutenant-Colonel Loder-Symonds departed to rejoin his own HQ at the landing area, as Urquhart was alone when he caught up with Lathbury at the tail end of the 3rd Parachute Battalion column on the Utrechtseweg just west of Oosterbeek at approximately 18:30.

While Urquhart was committing his series of errors, his opposite numbers were acting in a more speedy and efficient manner. The basis of German reaction to the arrival of the 1st Airborne Division west of Arnhem lay with *Hauptmann* Weber from *213 Nachrichten* Regiment who, after going forward from Deelen airfield to investigate and exchanging fire with the 1st Airlanding Brigade, arranged for what he had seen to be disseminated via the highly efficient *Luftwaffe* communication system. Weber's information appears to have permitted *Obergruppenführer* Wilhelm Bittrich at *II SS Panzerkorps* HQ to issue a Warning Order at 13:40, just ten minutes after receiving word of the landings; this alerted all subordinate units and ordered them to assemble, ascertain the situation in the area of Arnhem and Nijmegen, secure Arnhem and its road bridge, and destroy the airborne landings near Oosterbeek.[142] The Warning Order reached *Obersturmbannführer* Walther Harzer, commanding the portion of *9 SS Panzer Division* remaining in Holland, within the hour. At the time of receipt Harzer was at a formal parade at Hoenderloo, ten miles north of Arnhem, awarding *Hauptsturmführer* Viktor Gräbner of *SS Panzer Aufklärungs Abteilung 9* the Knight's Cross for gallantry in Normandy.[143] Harzer promptly ordered Gräbner to unload his vehicles from the railway flatcars onto which they had been loaded for transport to Germany and restore them to running order immediately. It should be remembered that Gräbner and his men had deliberately rendered their vehicles unserviceable by removing key components in order to avoid handing them over to *10 SS Panzer Division*; by this means Gräbner's *Abteilung* had kept thirty armoured half-tracks, ten eight-wheeled armoured cars and a number of trucks armoured with oil drums filled with sand. Harzer then returned to his own HQ at Apeldoorn to implement the rest of the order. The reactions of his subordinate units were equally swift. All *9 SS Panzer Division's* subordinate units acknowledged compliance with the Warning Order within an hour and were en route to the scene of the action shortly thereafter; *SS Panzerjäger Abteilung 9* left Apeldoorn, sixteen miles north of Arnhem, at around 15:00 and *SS Panzer Pionier Abteilung 9* was away from its billets at Brummen twelve miles distant by 16:30, for example.[144]

Hauptsturmführer Gräbner had his vehicles, the most powerful collection of armour in the immediate vicinity of Arnhem, unloaded and refitted within approximately three hours and his instructions were refined by a further order issued by *II SS Panzerkorps* HQ at 16:30. This directed him to divide his *Abteilung* in two parts: 'Smaller sub-units are to [reconnoitre] towards Oosterbeek, and secure the remainder of the divisions [sic] move to Arnhem' while the main body crossed the Lower Rhine at Arnhem and carried out a reconnaissance of Nijmegen to clarify the situation there.[145] Gräbner complied by despatching the first ten refitted vehicles, which appear to have been *Sd.Kfz.* 250 and 251 armoured half-tracks, toward Wolfheze; it is unclear if they were despatched individually or as a group but by 17:00 at least some of them were stationed along the Amsterdamseweg up to a point a mile or so to the north of Wolfheze. They were to form a serendipitous backstop for *Hauptmann* Weber's patrol from 213 *Nachrichten* Regiment, which had retired to the woods between Wolfheze and the Amsterdamseweg, and was subsequently reinforced by *Hauptsturmführer* Klaus von Allwörden's *SS Panzerjäger Abteilung 9* with its two *Panzerjäger* IV tank destroyers and three composite infantry companies made up of dismounted vehicle crewmen and drafted *Kriegsmarine* personnel.[146] Gräbner led the bulk of *SS Panzer Aufklärungs Abteilung 9* south across the Arnhem road bridge at approximately 18:00.[147] In so doing he also unwittingly missed possibly the sole opportunity to prevent the British seizing the north end of the bridge, for the 2nd Parachute Battalion was closing on its objective at that point; according to one source some of the latter actually saw the *SS* convoy moving across the bridge.[148] The column reached Elst, six miles south of the Arnhem bridge, at c.19:00 after scouting the area either side of the main highway for Allied airborne troops. With no sign of the enemy Gräbner transmitted a situation report, detached a handful of vehicles in Elst for rear security and to act as a radio relay station and then pushed on to Nijmegen in the gathering darkness. He arrived there shortly before 20:00 to again find no sign of Allied activity and the Waal bridges protected by a scratch force of approximately 750 men assembled from a number of reserve and training units stationed in and around Nijmegen by a *Luftwaffe Oberst* Henke from a local *Fallschirmjäger* training HQ.[149]

Bittrich's orders from *II SS Panzerkorps* addressed the immediate situation at Arnhem and Nijmegen, and the arrival of *Generalfeldmarschall* Walther Model, the commander of *Heeresgruppe B*, did the same for the wider battle. Model had been using the Hotel Tafelberg in Oosterbeek as his HQ for four days, and according to one source he left in some haste, abandoning a partly consumed lunch because he was convinced he was the target of the Allied airborne attack.[150] He arrived at *II SS Panzerkorps* HQ at Doetinchem at 15:00 on 17 September, took direct control of Bittrich's formations possibly as early as 17:30, and issued a wide-ranging operation order that confirmed and clarified Bittrich's local counter-measures and framed the future course of the overall battle to defeat MARKET GARDEN. In the south 1 *Fallschirmjäger Armee*, reinforced with Major Berndt-Joachim *Freiherr* von Maltzahn's *Panzer Brigade 107* that was en route to Aachen, and elements of *Generalleutnant* Walter Poppe's 59 *Infanterie Division*, which was fortuitously regrouping at Tilburg after escaping across the Scheldt Estuary with other elements of 15 *Armee*, was to block the British ground advance from Neerpelt and destroy the US landings near Eindhoven. Presumably due to its proximity to German territory, responsibility for dealing with the US landing at Nijmegen was allotted to *Wehrkreis VI*, a rear echelon HQ responsible for replacement and training, located at Münster and commanded by *General* Franz Mattenklott. It was to be assisted by 10 *SS Panzer Division*, which was ordered to move south, secure the Nijmegen bridges and establish a foothold on the south bank of the River Waal for use as a base for further offensive action. Model added the specific proviso that linkage between the Allied lodgements at Nijmegen and Arnhem was to be prevented at all costs. Finally, responsibility for dealing with the British presence north of the Lower Rhine was allotted to 9 *SS Panzer Division's Warnungs Kompanien*, apart from *SS Panzer Aufklärungs Abteilung 9*. With the exception of the detachment despatched to reconnoitre toward Wolfheze, Gräbner's unit was placed under the operational control of 10 *SS Panzer Division* while Harzer received *Hauptsturmführer* Heinrich Brinkmann's *SS Panzer Aufklärungs Abteilung 10* in exchange.[151]

This was speedy and efficient work by any standard and credit for *II SS Panzerkorps'* initial moves is often attributed to a programme of anti-airborne training undertaken by its constituent formations in the summer and early autumn of 1943, notably by *Brigadeführer* Harmel, commander of 10 *SS Panzer Division*.[152] However, given that both Divisions lost approximately three-quarters of their strength in Normandy it is legitimate to question how much influence this training exerted by September 1944. It is therefore more likely that the underlying reason for the speedy reaction of *II SS Panzerkorps'* HQ and its constituent formations was more the general ethos of the *Waffen SS*, with its emphasis on aggression, rapid action and personal initiative at all levels, although these attributes were by no means exclusive to the *Waffen SS*. Model was equally rapid in his appreciation of the situation, and some *Heer* units moved equally swiftly and from farther afield. Major Hans-Peter Knaust's *Panzer-Grenadier Ersatz und Ausbildungs Bataillon 64* 'Bocholt' for one, a replacement training unit for convalescent infantry personnel; it was despatched by *Wehrkreis VI* in response to Model's 17:30 operation order and was in Arnhem by 04:00 on 18 September.[153]

However, while the speed and focus of the German reactions were undeniably impressive, they also included two serious and interlinked errors. The first of these was the containment of the British airborne incursion west of Wolfheze. As we have seen, the 16:30 Order from *II SS Panzerkorps* instructed *SS Panzer Aufklärungs Abteilung 9* to use part of its strength to reconnoitre toward the Allied landing area and made *9 SS Panzer Division* responsible for securing Arnhem against the Airborne incursion. A further Order issued an hour later at 17:30 clarified precisely how this was to be done. Gräbner's detachment was instructed to make contact with *Bataillon* Krafft in order to establish a cordon to the north and east of Wolfheze while *Sturmbannführer* Ludwig Spindler of *SS Panzer Artillerie Regiment 9* was tasked to marshal *9 SS Panzer Division's* various *Warnungs Kompanien* into a single entity to deny access to Arnhem from the west.[154] The idea was thus to mask the British airborne landing by creating a secure shoulder along the line of Amsterdamseweg and a blocking line in the western outskirts of Arnhem to prevent movement to the north or east, with the Lower Rhine acting as a block to the south. This cordon would effectively seal off the 1st Airborne Division until a clearing operation could be mounted moving west from Arnhem through Oosterbeek, Wolfheze and Heelsum. The problem was that establishing the northern shoulder of the cordon on the Amsterdamseweg placed it three miles or more north of the Lower Rhine. Had the blocking line in the western outskirts of Arnhem been set up earlier or at the same time as the northern shoulder this would not have been a problem, but it took Spindler until the early hours of Monday 18 September to gather and deploy his forces there. As a result there was a significant gap in the cordon for around twelve hours, and that gap included two of the Battalion-specific routes allotted to the 1st Parachute Brigade for the move from the landing area to Arnhem.

The second error concerned the Lower Rhine crossings at Arnhem and specifically the road bridge. Model's rapidly formulated operational strategy to counter MARKET GARDEN involved masking off the British airborne landing north of the Lower Rhine to be dealt with later while stopping the Allied ground advance on the River Waal. This was a perfectly logical scheme given the situation and German deployments in Holland but it depended almost totally upon possession of the Arnhem bridges, and especially the road bridge, as a conduit to funnel forces south to the Waal. As the bridges were located in a rear-echelon area sixty miles behind the fighting front their protection had been an internal security matter and the *Stadtkommandant* of Arnhem, *Generalmajor* Kussin, had garrisoned them accordingly. The road bridge was protected by approximately twenty-five teenage and elderly soldiers manning some light *flak* guns and using two concrete towers that formed part of the bridge structure as makeshift defensive bunkers; the railway bridge appears to have been covered by a ten-strong demolition party commanded by an NCO, and a group of gunners manning three 20mm anti-aircraft guns.[155] Kussin may well have intended to reinforce the bridge guards in the face of the British landings, but he was killed in his encounter with the 3rd Parachute Battalion just west of Oosterbeek. The problem here was that despite the wide-ranging nature of his 17:30 Operations Order, Model did not make specific provision to ensure that the Arnhem bridges remained firmly in German hands, apart from placing them in *9 SS Panzer Division's* area of responsibility. The boundary of this area ran from Velp, just north-east of Arnhem, up to and including the road bridge and then along the line of the Lower Rhine to the west; *9 SS Panzer Division* was responsible for the area north of the river and *10 SS Panzer Division* for the area to the south as far as Nijmegen and the River Waal.[156]

Model presumably did not feel it necessary to issue explicit instructions regarding the bridges because *II SS Panzerkorps*' 13:40 Warning Order specifically instructed Harzer that the 'Arnhem bridge is to be occupied by strong security forces' with 'absolute speed'.[157] The problem was that Harzer appears to have made little effort to comply with this part of his orders. While all the Division's *Warnungs Kompanien* were ordered to Arnhem post haste and it would have been a simple matter to specifically order one or more to the road bridge, all were directed either toward the landing area or the western outskirts of the city. This, incidentally, was also in contravention of an order issued by *II SS Panzerkorps* at 16:00, which instructed Harzer to concentrate at Velp to the east of Arnhem before moving on the landing area located to the west of the city.[158] The only unit from *9 SS Panzer Division* to deliberately approach the Arnhem road bridge at this time was Gräbner's *SS Panzer Aufklärungs Abteilung 9*, and he was merely crossing the river to reconnoitre the situation at Nijmegen on behalf of *10 SS Panzer Division*. Gräbner was criticised years after the event by Harmel for failing to reinforce the token force guarding the bridge, and for being cocksure and overly preoccupied with what might have been unfolding to the south.[159] Harmel's criticism was based on the fact that the *II SS Panzerkorps* Warning Order issued at 13:40 specifically instructed *9 SS Panzer Division* about occupying the bridge with 'strong security forces', and failing to do so seriously impacted upon the ability of his own formation to comply with the instructions therein for it to 'assemble, move to Nijmegen and firmly occupy the main bridges, and defend the Nijmegen bridgehead'.[160]

Whilst perhaps understandable, Harmel's criticism nonetheless smacks of wisdom after the event and was rather unfair given that Gräbner was unable to defend himself; he was killed on the morning of Monday 18 September. More importantly, Gräbner's initial orders did not come directly from *II SS Panzerkorps* HQ but via Harzer, who may not have mentioned securing the bridge, and it was not Gräbner's place to second-guess direct verbal orders from his Division commander. Furthermore, Gräbner arguably lacked the strength to provide 'a strong security force' at the Arnhem bridge, especially as he had no idea what situation he might be confronted with at Nijmegen; placing a relative handful of light armoured vehicles and trucks with rudimentary improvised armour in the likely path of a fully functioning British armoured division required a certain amount of steely courage in itself. Harmel may also have been looking to avoid blame, given that *SS Panzer Aufklärungs Abteilung 9* actually came under the operational control of *10 SS Panzer Division* when it was ordered to reconnoitre south to Nijmegen. It is unclear whether in an official or unofficial capacity, but Harmel was actually in Berlin on 17 September, leaving his *Division* under temporary command of *Obersturmbannführer* Otto Paetsch of *SS Panzer Regiment 10*.[161] Harmel was ostensibly negotiating for resources to rebuild his Division and he did not return to reassume command until the early hours of Monday 18 September.[162] This would suggest that Paetsch was rather more culpable in the matter than Gräbner.

The salient point is that the failure to secure the Arnhem road bridge in the immediate post-landing period was a potentially fatal flaw in Model's counter-strategy, and responsibility lay primarily with Harzer. This effectively left the road and railway bridges open for any Airborne elements able to reach them and with the benefit of hindsight it can be seen that Harzer compounded his error, albeit unwittingly, by holding his units along the line of the Amsterdamseweg rather than ordering them to concentrate on sealing the approaches to Arnhem between the Amsterdamseweg and the Lower Rhine. This in turn gave the 1st Parachute Brigade a clear run along the LION and TIGER routes to their objective for the first ten or twelve hours or so after the landing. The initial stage of the Arnhem portion of Operation MARKET was therefore in effect a straight race between the 1st Parachute Brigade and *II SS Panzerkorps* and, by extension, *Heeresgruppe B*. The key question was whether the 1st Parachute Brigade would prove capable of offsetting the self-inflicted tardiness in the immediate post-landing phase by moving with sufficient speed and urgency to take full advantage of Model's and Harzer's errors.

7

D-Day to D Plus 1

19:00 Sunday 17 September to 07:00 Monday 18 September 1944

The 1st Parachute Brigade's race for the Arnhem crossings commenced when Brigadier Gerald Lathbury released his three battalions to advance from the landing area, where they had been waiting for permission to move for the better part of an hour. Lieutenant-Colonel David Dobie's 1st Parachute Battalion received permission to move from Brigade HQ at 15:30, and moved off ten minutes later.[1] It took the heavily laden column around twenty minutes to reach the railway station at Wolfheze, using the same route as the 1st Airborne Reconnaissance Squadron across the top of LZ Z and following the south side of the Arnhem–Ede railway line to the level crossing in Wolfheze. At some point Dobie met Major Gough as the latter was moving back to Division HQ and he warned Dobie about the German presence across his intended route along the Johannahoeveweg to join the Amsterdamseweg/LEOPARD route further east.[2] Dobie therefore decided to strike north from Wolfheze and directed Major John Timothy and R Company to lead the Battalion along the Wolfhezeweg in order to sidestep *Bataillon* Krafft's outpost line.

The Wolfhezeweg ran through open fields for almost 1,000 yards before entering a wooded area. The wooded area was occupied by *Hauptmann* Weber and his patrol from *213 Nachrichten Regiment*, recovering from its skirmish with the 2nd South Staffords at LZ S. R Company made contact at approximately 17:00 and Major Timothy immediately launched a hasty attack that pushed the hapless *Luftwaffe* signalmen back in a series of sharp, close-range encounters.[3] Bren gunner Private John Hall recalled his Platoon commander, Lieutenant Michael Kilmartin, skilfully manoeuvring 1 Platoon through the woods and seeing an NCO cut down while moving forward to secure a German who looked to be surrendering; Hall and his comrades responded with a pact not to take any more prisoners.[4] The Company became dispersed by the fighting, obliging Major Timothy to reorganise before performing a concerted left-flanking attack around the west side of the Wolfhezeweg.[5] The 1st Parachute Battalion's Mortar Platoon, commanded by Lieutenant George Guyon, deployed in a clearing in the woods to render support but his radio set failed at the crucial moment and he was reduced to arranging a chain of men to pass back information from his mortar controller travelling with R Company's lead elements. One of the relay chain was killed and three or four were wounded in the process but despite this and the poor visibility the controller was able to search out likely German locations with accurately placed salvos of mortar bombs, forcing one group of Germans to abandon a truck.[6] The left-flanking attack carried R Company the rest of the way to the Amsterdamseweg but there they ran into armoured vehicles identified as tanks but which were likely the detachment of armoured half-tracks from *SS Panzer Aufklärungs Abteilung 9*. Timothy's men had no answer to this and were obliged to seek whatever cover they could. The resultant fighting went on for five hours or more, during which R Company lost all contact with the remainder of the 1st Battalion and around half its strength killed, wounded and missing, although many of the latter had likely become separated in the undergrowth and darkness.

The fight on the Wolfhezeweg initially also drew in elements of Major Ronald Stark's S Company, but Dobie intervened at 18:00 and ordered a move along a track running east in an effort to bypass R Company's fight and access the Amsterdamseweg closer to Arnhem; radio contact with Major Timothy was lost in the process and the 1st Battalion HQ signallers were also unable to contact 1st Parachute Brigade HQ.[7] The by-passing did not reflect any lack of aggression but was a deliberate tactic to preserve the Battalion's fighting power for securing and holding its primary objective, about which Dobie had briefed his company commanders prior to arrival in Holland, although R Company's rapid and aggressive action against 213 *Nachrichten Regiment* strongly suggests that the 1st Battalion would likely have been capable of dealing with the light armour ranged against them using Gammon bombs and PIATs had it been so ordered, using the wooded terrain and darkness for concealment.[8] After moving east for around an hour Dobie decided to try and access the Amsterdamseweg again. Lieutenant Robert Feltham's 7 Platoon from S Company was leading the Battalion column at this point, and Sergeant Frank Manser was despatched 500 yards or so up a side track to check if the way was clear. It was not, for 300 yards from the end of the track Manser saw 'lots of vehicles, armoured cars, etc., and lots of troops moving about – a company at least, possibly more, obviously getting themselves into defensive positions'.[9] Erecting the blocking line along the Amsterdamseweg was thus in full swing by 19:00, and Manser may have witnessed the arrival of *Hauptsturmführer* Klaus von Allwörden's *SS Panzerjäger Abteilung 9*, given that the Battalion War Diary referred to the Germans being equipped with five tanks and fifteen half-tracks;[10] von Allwörden's force boasted three infantry companies built around 120 dismounted self-propelled gun crewmen augmented with a draft of *Kriegsmarine* personnel, two *Panzerjäger* IV self-propelled guns and a handful of towed 75mm *PaK* 40 pieces.[11]

Sergeant Manser's report prompted Dobie to attempt another sidestep and while this was being organised he despatched Major John Bune, the 1st Parachute Battalion's deputy commander, to guide R Company back to the main Battalion location. By this time it was almost completelyy dark and at 20:00, half an hour after Bune's departure, the Battalion's temporary perimeter was bumped by a German armoured vehicle supported by infantry. The Germans were driven off in the ensuing firefight, which cost the paratroopers six casualties and appears to have gone on until Major Bune returned at 22:00 accompanied by R Company's second-in-command, Captain Peter Mansfield. The latter informed Dobie that Major Timothy had successfully broken contact but was unable to move effectively due to half his force being casualties. Dobie therefore ordered Major Bune to return to R Company, accompanied by the Battalion medical officer, field ambulance detachment and Battalion transport to assist with the casualties and to bring in Major Timothy and the fit portion of his Company to the main Battalion column. In the interim, patrols were despatched to try and find a way through to the Amsterdamseweg, sparking spasmodic fighting and firing in the surrounding woods.[12] Dobie appears to have settled down to wait for Major Timothy, but all that changed at around midnight when the 1st Battalion signallers picked up a clear signal reporting that the 2nd Parachute Battalion had secured the Arnhem road bridge. Major Christopher Perrin-Brown, commanding T Company, was with Dobie when the signal arrived:

I don't think David Dobie replied to the message. He just called an O-Group. He was of the opinion that we were in such a muck in the woods that we would never fight our way through. He said 'I'm not going on to the north of Arnhem; we'll try to get down to help Johnnie at the bridge.'[13]

At 01:00 on Monday 18 September Lieutenant-Colonel Dobie therefore abandoned his attempts to reach the high ground to the north of Arnhem and moved the 1st Parachute Battalion south-east toward the Arnhem bridge, where Lathbury should have sent it in the first place. Guides were left to direct R Company, although the latter never reached the rendezvous; Major Timothy and forty of his men linked up with the 2nd South Staffords and eventually rejoined Dobie in the evening of Monday 18 September, and while R Company's wounded appear to have reached the landing area, Major Bune and the Mortar Platoon were listed as missing and likely fell victim to an encounter with a German patrol.[14] Major Perrin-Brown's T Company led off, moving stealthily through the pitch-black woods. This was no easy task, and matters were compounded by the need to manhandle the heavily laden Jeeps and Bren Gun Carriers with their engines switched off, some towing trailers or 6-Pounder anti-tank guns belonging to the attached Troop from the 1st Airlanding Anti-Tank Battery.[15] After two hours, T Company's lead element, Lieutenant John MacFadden's 9 Platoon, clashed with a group of Germans occupying a track junction. The Germans withdrew after suffering a number of casualties, but Lieutenant MacFadden was badly wounded in the process and subsequently died in captivity.[16] Eventually, the 1st Parachute Battalion column left the woods and appears to have followed a minor road across the Arnhem-Ede railway line into the northern outskirts of Oosterbeek. By this point Dobie's unit had been on the move or fighting for nearly twelve hours non-stop and had suffered around a hundred casualties including eleven dead and a large number of missing, many of whom had simply become separated in the darkness.[17] As Major Timothy pointed out in a post-war interview the missing men 'weren't all killed or wounded. The idea is that you meet up again somewhere but it didn't often happen.'[18]

Having reached Oosterbeek, Dobie decided to access the Utrechtseweg/TIGER route running east as the most direct route into Arnhem proper, with Major Stark's S Company taking the lead. By 04:30 Lieutenant Robert Feltham's 7 Platoon was approaching the point where the Utrechtseweg passed under the embanked railway branch line running south from the main Arnhem-Ede line to the *Oosterbeek Laag* Station and thence over the Lower Rhine. The embankment was occupied by German troops, most likely elements of *Hauptsturmführer* Hans Möller's *SS Panzer Pionier Abteilung 9*, which had been ensconced on the wooded bluff on the east side of the railway line known locally as *Den Brink* since about 18:00 on 17 September. The *Abteilung* numbered in the region of ninety men equipped with at least two *Sd.Kfz.* 251 armoured half-tracks and a collection of weapons and stores scrounged through Möller's contacts at *II SS Panzerkorps* HQ, including a large number of MG42 machine-guns.[19] They may also have been reinforced, given that the 1st Parachute Battalion War Diary referred to S Company coming under fire from mortars and armoured car-mounted 20mm guns. The *SS* allowed the first two paratroopers to pass through the underpass, seized them and then opened fire on the remainder of the lead section when they scrambled back for cover. The rest of 7 Platoon attempted to assault the German strongpoint but was rebuffed by the weight of return fire, losing seven dead and a number of wounded, including Lieutenant Feltham. The firefight went on for around an hour and Major Stark was organising a full company attack when Dobie intervened after meeting Captain Anthony Harrison from the 3rd Airlanding Light Battery RA at around 05:00. Harrison and the Forward Observation (FO) party from his E Troop had accompanied the 2nd Parachute Battalion to the Arnhem bridge, and had been despatched back to the landing area by the Battery commander, Major Dennis Munford, to report the seizure of the bridge to Division HQ and bring the Battery forward in support; the meeting was fortuitous, as Harrison had intended to follow the riverside LION route and only ended up on the Utrechtseweg after taking a wrong turning. On learning that Frost's Battalion was in serious need of reinforcement Dobie decided to sidestep south again onto the riverside LION route. The 1st Parachute Battalion therefore disengaged from the fight that had cost S Company a further thirty casualties and moved south at 05:30.[20]

Lieutenant-Colonel John Frost's 2nd Parachute Battalion moved off for Arnhem at 15:10.[21] Accessing the allotted LION route involved moving south from the Brigade RV to Heelsum, and then east along the Koninginne Laan through the *Doorwerthsche Bosch* forest toward Heveadorp and Oosterbeek. Major Digby Tatham-Warter's A Company led the way, spearheaded by Lieutenant Andrew McDermont's 3 Platoon. Frost had selected A Company as his 'spearhead company' because he considered Tatham-Warter something of a 'thruster'.[22] The latter was certainly something of an eccentric. It is unclear if he carried it into Holland or acquired it after landing but Tatham-Warter spent much of the battle carrying a furled umbrella rather than a weapon, ostensibly as a recognition measure. He had also trained his Company to respond to bugle calls, a measure prompted by his lack of confidence in the issued radio equipment; to this end two men in Company HQ and in each platoon carried bugles and were trained in a number of calls based on those used by Sir John Moore's Light Division in the Peninsular War.[23] A Company was trailed by Major Victor Dover's C Company, followed by Major Douglas Crawley and B Company and then Major Tony Hibbert and the Brigade HQ column. The latter moved off at 15:45 after the Brigade's radio equipment had been unpacked and partly netted in. A Company had barely moved off when a number of German vehicles approached, presumably along a track running south-west from the Hotel Wolfheze. Reacting quickly, Lieutenant McDermont's men went to ground and comprehensively shot them up killing fifteen of the passengers and capturing fifteen more, to Lieutenant-Colonel Frost's slight chagrin: 'As we passed their [A Company's] old positions we found two lorries and three motor-cars in various stages of destruction…It seemed a pity that the vehicles were now unusable but there had been no time to arrange an ambush. It was however an encouraging start.'[24] According to one account, the Germans were a reconnaissance element from *Bataillon* Krafft's *2 Kompanie*.[25] Several other surprised off-duty German soldiers were scooped up by the paratrooper's advance, some of them walking with girlfriends, and Signalman Bill Jukes saw one out for a Sunday afternoon bicycle ride: 'When he saw us, he probably thought his last hour had come. His machine began to wobble until he eventually fell off. We took him prisoner and loaded him and his bike with all our gear and took him along with us.'[26]

The advance through Heelsum was slowed by enthusiastic Dutch civilians eager to greet their liberators but speeded up again as A Company followed the Koninginne Laan into the forest toward Heveadorp, alternating lead platoon as they went. At some point in this stage of the approach march Brigadier Lathbury drove up the column to confer with Frost, informing him of the alleged failure of the 1st Airborne Reconnaissance Squadron's *coup-de-main* to seize the Arnhem road bridge; Lathbury may have also suggested that Frost mount part of his A Company on the Battalion transport as a makeshift replacement. On the other hand, Frost's account refers to the idea occurring before Lathbury arrived, allegedly on gaining information from a POW regarding German strength in Arnhem; he may also have been influenced by Lathbury's alleged radio message transmitted before he left the landing area at 15:30.[27] Either way, according to Frost the sound of the 3rd Battalion having a 'bit of a battle' on the TIGER route to the north was audible during the meeting, which would place it around 17:00. Lathbury then left to harass the 3rd Battalion while Frost appears to have gone forward to confer with Major Tatham-Warter regarding the makeshift transport plan. Tatham-Warter was apparently enthusiastic but while Frost was waiting for the Battalion HQ group to close up, A Company's lead elements ran into opposition as it neared Heveadorp on the eastern outskirts of the Doorwerthsche Bosch forest. Lieutenant John Grayburn's 2 Platoon was in the lead and had taken a left at a T-junction when the remainder of the Company came under rifle fire followed by a few inaccurate mortar bombs. Grayburn immediately put down a smokescreen with his Platoon 2-inch mortar and attacked toward the source of the firing, while Lieutenant McDermont's 3 Platoon moved to seal the opposite flank; this prompted a German withdrawal leaving a number of casualties behind.[28] The 2nd Parachute Battalion War Diary claims it had encountered 'the southern flank of a strong enemy position', but the Germans may have been a small guard force for the nearby Heveadorp ferry across the Lower Rhine.[29] Although it was known to the 1st Airborne Division's intelligence, Frost does not appear to have been made aware of the ferry's existence. While that was perhaps just as well, given the number of missions the 2nd Parachute Battalion had already been tasked with, possession of the ferry with its capacity of eight Jeeps or equivalent would have been a useful additional avenue for the 1st Parachute Brigade to approach its bridge objectives from the south. Whoever the Germans were, they did give Tatham-Warter the satisfaction of hearing his bugle-call communication system functioning properly in action; he may have blown the signal to resume the advance personally in front of Frost, who had come forward to investigate.[30]

The residents of Heveadorp also turned out to greet their liberators, pressing fresh fruit and jugs of milk on the heavily laden paratroopers and twining orange flowers in their clothing and equipment. One elderly gentleman generously offered Frost the use of his car; Frost politely declined by pointing to his personal Jeep a few yards back in the column.[31] The process was repeated with even greater enthusiasm a mile or so further on as the LION route morphed into the Oosterbeekweg and passed into the much larger town of Oosterbeek, where it changed again into the Benedendorpsweg. The 2nd Battalion reached there at some point before 18:00 and A Company's second-in-command Captain Anthony Frank recalled 'the incredible number of orange flowers or handkerchiefs that suddenly appeared like magic' and the 'problem of trying to stop them [Dutch civilians] slowing our men down by pressing cakes, milk etc on them'. Private Sidney Elliot was less concerned with disciplinary matters and more interested in shaking hands, accepting the gifts and being 'lucky enough to receive the odd kiss'.[32] In some instances the proffered beverages were rather stronger than milk and orders were passed down the column forbidding the acceptance of alcohol, although it is unclear to what extent they were obeyed by the independently minded paratroopers. The move through southern Oosterbeek was not totally without opposition, with A Company, still at the head of the Battalion column, receiving some scattered rifle shots as it approached the eastern outskirts of the town. More seriously, a German machine-gun team fired on Private James Sims and the rest of the 2nd Battalion's Mortar Platoon as they passed a tall hedge which was

> ...raked from end to end belly-high by machine-gun fire. Although the enemy could not see us they hit at least three of our lads, one of them with an incendiary bullet. This was the youthful Brum Davis [sic]. The rest of us had already flattened ourselves on the tarmac but my helmet seemed to stick up an awful long way as the bullets swept over us again and again....The firing ceased as the German machine-gun crew departed, having achieved what they set out to do – hold us up.[33]

As the 2nd Parachute Battalion column traversed the southern outskirts of Oosterbeek, Major Victor Dover's C Company peeled off across the riverside polder toward the Battalion's first objective, the bridge carrying the railway line south across the Lower Rhine from the Oosterbeek Laag railway station. Dover was accompanied by Captain O'Callaghan and 2 Platoon from the 9th (Airborne) Field Company RE and had detailed Lieutenant Peter Barry's 9 Platoon to secure the bridge with Lieutenant Ian Russell and 8 Platoon providing a smokescreen with their 2-inch mortar. Access to the bridge was via a long embanked ramp, upon which a train had been abandoned, and it was protected by *flak* positions which had been hit by the RAF as part of the pre-landing preparation; the polder was dotted with dead cows killed in the attack. 9 Platoon had closed to within 500 yards without incident when a solitary German appeared at the southern end, ran to the centre of the bridge and then escaped unscathed despite Lieutenant Barry directing a Bren Group to rake the structure. Prompted by Major Dover, Barry took a nine-man Section forward, climbed the embankment and moved onto the north end of the bridge structure. As there was still no German response Barry told his Section:

> We might as well carry on and capture the whole bridge...We threw a smoke grenade; unfortunately the wind was in the wrong direction, but it gave some cover...We ran across, as fast as we could, through the smoke...We got about fifty yards and then needed to pause; we had a lot of equipment on and soon got short of breath. So I told them to get down. We were just above the water by then. The centre span of the bridge exploded then,

while we lay there, and the metal plates right in front of me heaved up into the air. It was lucky that we had stopped when we did, otherwise we would have all been killed; no one was wounded by the explosion.[34]

German troops on the south bank then opened fire, wounding Barry in the leg and right arm and killing one of his men.

Precisely who was responsible for dropping the railway bridge is unclear. One source credits a mobile detachment from *Bataillon* Krafft, although another refers to a ten-man demolition party commanded by an NCO being billeted in nearby houses on the south bank. The timings, the fact that the soldier who ignited the charge appeared on the south bank and the substantial nature of the charge suggests it was pre-placed, making the latter explanation the most likely.[35] Precisely who ordered the bridge to be rigged for demolition is similarly unclear, given that *Obergruppenführer* Bittrich professed ignorance of any such arrangements to *Hauptsturmführer* Hans Möller shortly after the event.[36] As wiring up major pieces of infrastructure for demolition lay outside *Hauptsturmführer* Krafft's pre-landing replacement training remit and he appears to have lacked the resources and equipment anyway, it was presumably done on the orders of the Arnhem *Stadtkommandant*, *Generalmajor* Kussin, without Bittrich or other commanders being made aware. Whoever was responsible, the destruction of the railway bridge denied the 2nd Parachute Battalion access to the south bank of the Lower Rhine. This in turn frustrated Frost's plan to despatch a company across the river to permit the Arnhem road bridge to be seized from both ends simultaneously and also effectively put the Arnhem pontoon bridge beyond reach, for the centre span proved to be moored inaccessibly on the south bank. Frost was therefore left with no option but to push on into Arnhem toward the north end of the Arnhem road bridge. A combination of circumstances and the planners' failure to inform Frost of the existence of the Heveadorp ferry thus imposed a deleterious and arguably lethal penalty on the Arnhem portion of Operation MARKET.

While C Company was making its unsuccessful bid for the railway bridge Major Tatham-Warter's A Company was experiencing problems in the push into Arnhem. Shortly before 19:00 Lieutenant Robin Vlasto's 1 Platoon led the way through an underpass carrying the LION route under the branch line running south from the Oosterbeek Laag station to the demolished bridge; at this point the Benedendorpsweg became the Klingelbeekseweg. As they rounded a bend just beyond the underpass a German armoured car emerged from a group of buildings flanking the road and opened fire, hitting the men on either side of Vlasto, killing one and seriously wounding the other in the hand. 1 Platoon went to ground while Major Tatham-Warter had the lead 6-Pounder anti-tank gun unhitched from its Jeep and brought into action, but the armoured car reversed out of sight before the crew could open fire. While all this was going on the 2nd Parachute Battalion received another flying visit. Having left Division HQ at some point before 17:00 also with the intention of warning the 1st Parachute Brigade about the alleged failure of the *coup-de-main* against the Arnhem road bridge, Major-General Urquhart travelled along the LION route in pursuit of Lathbury. He came upon the 1st Parachute Brigade HQ column and after passing on word of the Reconnaissance Squadron's alleged absence urged Major Hibbert on with that parting shout mentioned earlier of 'Hibbert, for God's sake get your brigade moving or the bloody Germans will get to the bridge before us'.[37] The comment appears to have been prompted by Urquhart's perception that the Brigade HQ column and rear of the 2nd Battalion were not moving with sufficient urgency, which he also expressed to Frost's Battalion HQ staff after working his way up the column; Frost himself was up at the front of the column overseeing Major Tatham-Warter's efforts to clear the road. On being informed that Lathbury had been last seen heading north to harass the 3rd Parachute Battalion, Urquhart abandoned his intention of speaking to Frost and, deciding that the latter had matters in hand, drove off toward the centre TIGER route in pursuit of the 1st Parachute Brigade's commander.[38] Urquhart, incidentally, was being trailed by the hapless Major Gough seeking to report to his Division commander as ordered. Having missed Urquhart at Division HQ by a matter of minutes, Gough set off down the LION route in pursuit and missed him again at Hibbert's Brigade HQ column by a similar margin.[39]

Back at the head of the 2nd Battalion column Lieutenant Vlasto resumed the advance, initially using a row of buildings as cover, only to come under fire from *Den Brink* bluff overlooking the riverside road from the north. The railway branch line formed a convenient firebreak between Oosterbeek and the western outskirts of Arnhem proper, *Den Brink* dominated that firebreak, and the parkland atop the bluff had recently been occupied by *Hauptsturmführer* Möller's ninety-strong *SS Panzer Pionier Abteilung 9*, which had rushed down from its billets at Brummen, twelve miles north-east of Arnhem.[40] The fire was sufficiently heavy to interfere with further passage along the riverside road, so Lieutenant-Colonel Frost ordered Major Douglas Crawley's B Company to clear the feature at approximately 19:00, in order to permit the remainder of the Battalion to proceed unhindered. The railway line ran through a cutting along the western edge of *Den Brink* and Crawley despatched Lieutenant Peter Cane's 6 Platoon up the cutting as a concealed avenue to get men onto the feature and outflank enemy firing on the riverside road. Unfortunately Möller had stationed one of his numerous machine-guns to cover the cutting as it curved to the east. Lieutenant Cane was killed in the first burst of fire along with an NCO, likely Corporal Edgar Rogers, and Privates Claude and Tom Gronert, twins who had joined up together and received consecutive Army numbers.[41] Major Crawley's B Company remained embroiled with *SS Panzer Pionier Abteilung 9* for the next four hours or so, and a combination of their efforts and the onset of darkness permitted the remainder of the 2nd Battalion to pass along the riverside road unmolested.

Lieutenant-Colonel John Fitch's 3rd Parachute Battalion moved off from the landing area after finally being released by Lathbury at 15:10. Lieutenant James Cleminson and 5 Platoon from Major Peter Waddy's B Company led the way, with the remainder of the Battalion column stretching out for over a mile in their wake. In addition to the Battalion HQ and three Rifle Companies, the column included Lieutenant Edward Shaw and C Troop from the 1st Airlanding Anti-tank Battery RA with three 6-Pounder guns, half of C Troop 1st Parachute Squadron RE under Captain Cecil Cox, a detachment from 16 Parachute Field Ambulance RAMC and an FO party from the 1st Airlanding Light Regiment RA. The column also included two Bren Gun Carriers and a score of Jeeps followed by Major Mervyn Dennison and A Company bringing up the rear. The route from the landing area took the Battalion south through the centre of Heelsum, where it received an enthusiastic reception from the inhabitants, and then east onto the Utrechtseweg/TIGER route, which ran into and across the northern edge of the Doorwerthsche Bosch forest toward Oosterbeek. There was practically no concerted opposition for the first two hours or so of the march, although at least one man was killed, likely by a sniper. Lance-Corporal William Bamsey was moving with Corporal Robert Allen with A Company at the rear of the column:

> We sensed enemy ahead and both paused – me behind one tree, Bamsey at the side of another. A shot rang out from the right. Bamsey collapsed like a puppet whose strings had been cut. I…dashed across and pulled Bamsey behind a tree. He had been shot through the throat, and the bullet had broken his neck.[42]

Twenty-one-year-old Lance-Corporal Bamsey was the 3rd Parachute Battalion's first fatality of Operation MARKET.[43]

At around 17:00, after almost two hours on the move, 5 Platoon was in the vicinity of a crossroads on the Utrechtseweg near the end of the forested area. The lead scouts had just passed the junction when a camouflaged Citroën saloon car emerged from the road running north-west to Wolfheze and made to turn left toward Arnhem. Lieutenant Cleminson's two lead Sections, which were advancing on either side of the road, promptly opened fire and the shot-up vehicle came to a halt in the middle of the road with a body hanging from the front passenger door. 5 Platoon pressed on, 'leaving it for someone else to sort out'.[44] The Citroën was carrying the *Stadtkommandant* of Arnhem, *Generalmajor* Friedrich Kussin, with his batman and driver; 5 Platoon's accurate shooting killed all three men outright. Kussin had been conferring with *Hauptsturmführer* Krafft at the latter's temporary HQ at the Hotel Wolfheze, which lay 800 yards up the side road, and he had rashly disregarded advice from Krafft's men that the Utrechtseweg route back to Arnhem might be unsafe. His two companions paid a high price for their commander's haste, and the bullet-riddled car with Kussin's body hanging from the passenger door became one of MARKET's most enduring images.[45]

Fifteen minutes and a few hundred yards later Lieutenant Cleminson's 5 Platoon had emerged from the woods and was approaching another crossroads among a group of houses at Koude Herberg, approximately halfway to the Arnhem bridge. At that point a German vehicle, likely a half-track mounting a 20mm gun, emerged from a side road and opened fire along with German infantry stationed on either side of the road. They appear to have belonged to *Bataillon* Krafft's mobile reserve, 9 *Kompanie*. The 3rd Parachute Battalion had passed the southern end of the *Bataillon's* outpost line, which now lay a few hundred yards to the north-west. A PIAT team with one of the lead Sections was shot up immediately along with a Jeep towing a 6-Pounder before the crew could unhitch and deploy their gun. Major Peter Waddy and Lieutenant Cleminson tried to organise a flanking movement through the houses but were frustrated by a combination of German fire and the chain-link fencing the locals used to delineate their property boundaries. Attempts to engage the vehicle with Gammon bombs proved ineffective as it remained outside effective throwing range, and an attack by Major Waddy with a Very pistol was equally ineffective. The vehicle then disengaged by pulling back up the side road; according to one account the vehicle crew dismounted briefly to drape one of the British wounded across the front of their vehicle, presumably as a human shield. It or another vehicle then reappeared from another side road near the 3rd Battalion Rear HQ and sprayed the column with fire, forcing the Battalion second-in-command, Major Alan Bush, to take cover behind a tree with a member of the Battalion Intelligence Section. Major Bush made a successful dash for safety, while his companion remained behind and was captured. 9 *Kompanie* then withdrew, taking six prisoners with them. The clash lasted for ten to fifteen minutes and cost the 3rd Battalion five wounded and two killed: Corporal Benjamin Cope and Gunner George Robson.[46]

While Major Waddy was reorganising B Company to resume the advance, Lieutenant-Colonel Fitch was rejigging his plan in an effort to avoid being ambushed again. B Company was to filter west toward Arnhem by moving south of the Utrechtseweg while Major Richard Lewis and C Company did the same to the north, although it is fair to assume that the final decision was not actually made by Fitch. It is unclear precisely when he arrived at the 3rd Parachute Battalion column, but Brigadier Lathbury was present in the aftermath of the clash with *Bataillon* Krafft's mobile reserve and his micromanaging tendencies rapidly came to the fore – he appears to have begun virtually running the 3rd Battalion over Fitch's head. It is therefore likely he badgered if not simply ordered Fitch to despatch C Company to the north, with both men moving to C Company's location in the middle of the column to brief Lewis. Lieutenant Leonard Wright's 9 Platoon was selected to lead the move, and he received short shrift from Lathbury as he tried to brief his men on their new mission: 'I had my O-Group standing by; that was routine. But, before I could start to brief them, I heard the high-pitched voice of the brigade commander…He asked what I was doing, and I replied "Briefing my O-Group sir." He snorted, very sharply, "They don't need briefing, just tell them that's the bloody way. Get Moving!" So I did.'[47] Briefed or not, C Company moved off at 18:00 along a track leading north to the Arnhem–Ede railway line, which Major Lewis thought might provide a protected route to Arnhem proper, while B Company led the remainder of the Battalion column down the Utrechtseweg at around the same time.

While all this was going on Major-General Urquhart had finally caught up with Lathbury and by 18:30 he was conferring with him and the hapless Fitch near *Generalmajor* Kussin's shot-up Citroën. At that point elements of *Bataillon* Krafft opened fire from the woods to the north of the Utrechtseweg with machine-guns and mortars, hitting Major Mervyn Dennison's A Company at the tail of the Battalion column. As the head of the column was already on the move at this point, Dennison's men would likely have contented themselves with returning fire while advancing away from the attackers, but Lathbury had other ideas and ordered Lieutenant Tony Baxter and 3 Platoon to drive the attackers back:

> I had two or three men hit by the first fire. Lathbury and Urquhart were both in the platoon position, taking cover behind a tree. Lathbury knew me and said 'Baxter, collect up your platoon and clear that wood.' I called out to the three section commanders, telling one to take the right, one the left, and the third to come with me. We just spread out and rushed into the trees.[48]

After a sharp exchange during which Lieutenant Baxter's thumb was almost severed by a German bullet, Major Dennison ordered 3 Platoon to withdraw and called an O-Group at the edge of the woods. The SS pushed forward again under another mortar barrage and one mortar bomb landed among the O Group, killing two or three of the assembled Section Commanders and wounding Baxter again in the head and shoulders. Dennison then led A Company forward overrunning several machine-gun positions in two hours of inconclusive fighting before the SS finally broke contact, leaving behind an estimated forty dead and a dozen prisoners; the fight cost A Company eighteen casualties, three of them officers, and at least two dead.[49] In the meantime the remainder of the 3rd Battalion had advanced a few hundred yards into the outskirts of Oosterbeek without meeting any more opposition. Lieutenant Cleminson and 5 Platoon pushed into the grounds of the Hotel Hartenstein, formerly the Staff Mess for *Heeresgruppe B* HQ. Apart from a few Germans seen across the parkland to the rear of the hotel, no opposition was encountered and Cleminson and his men enthusiastically helped themselves to *Generalfeldmarschall* Model's abandoned lunch before being chased out of the building by Major Waddy. An order to halt was then received at around 19:30.

At this point it is convenient to debunk the enduring myth that *Bataillon* Krafft was responsible for blocking the 1st Parachute Brigade's advance into Arnhem. Rboert Kershaw credits Krafft with single-handedly holding up the 1st Parachute Brigade for the entire afternoon, inflicting significant casualties and only withdrawing after dark when threatened with imminent encirclement.[50] However, this appreciation is based solely on Krafft's self-serving version of events, which is also cited in a similar work as an exemplar of German operational efficiency; even Middlebrook, while pointing out the inconsistency between Krafft's account and those of British participants, nonetheless gives the SS commander partial credit for the deed.[51] The problem with this is that Krafft's version of events was not intended to provide an objective record of events for posterity, but rather to ingratiate him with his SS superiors with an eye to personal advancement in true National Socialist fashion. Consequently, Krafft's account is somewhat at variance with the verifiable evidence. As we have seen, Krafft's first contact with the 1st Airborne Division did not involve the 1st Parachute Brigade at all, but was an extended skirmish with the 9th Field Company RE, which was not even seeking to leave the landing area. The second involved ambushing lead elements of the 1st Airborne Reconnaissance Squadron followed by another extended skirmish, and the 'blocking' in that instance was largely self-inflicted. With regard to interfering with the 1st Parachute Brigade, *Bataillon* Krafft had no contact whatever with the 1st Parachute Battalion and its sole contact with the 2nd Parachute Battalion appears to have been

3 Platoon ambushing and wiping out the motorised reconnaissance element from 2 *Kompanie* as the paratroopers moved off from the Battalion RV. Of the two contacts with the 3rd Parachute Battalion, the first held up the advance for less than an hour and the second occurred at the rear of the 3rd Battalion column while the head was actually on the move, away from the attack, toward Arnhem. The SS broke contact on both occasions and as such both incidents amounted to merely harassing rather than blocking the 1st Parachute Brigade's advance.

This begs the question as to why the bulk of the 3rd Parachute Battalion came to a halt in Oosterbeek at 19:30 rather than pushing on into Arnhem. The answer is that the halt was actually self-imposed and the instigator appears to have been Brigadier Lathbury. As we have seen, Lathbury had spent the bulk of his time after leaving the landing area at 15:30 harassing the 2nd and 3rd Parachute Battalions to greater haste. Yet at 19:30, within ninety minutes of pressing if not actually ordering Fitch to detach a third of his combat power and modify his plan of advance in the interests of speed, Lathbury totally reversed tack by halting the 3rd Battalion for the night; the decision was justified in a radio conversation with Major Hibbert two-and-a-half hours later by claiming that he was in contact with the enemy and that the men of the 3rd Parachute Battalion were tired.[52] This was a curious claim, given that the 3rd Battalion was not in contact at that time and as Major Hibbert later pointed out, there should have been no question of halting because the 3rd Parachute Battalion had only been on the ground for five hours and fighting for a fraction of that period.[53] The situation at that point was far from satisfactory, given that the bulk of the 1st Parachute Brigade was only halfway to its objectives at best.[54] Something must therefore have prompted Lathbury's change of tack, and the only significant event up to that point was Urquhart's arrival at the 3rd Parachute Battalion's location, and more specifically his decision to remain there for the night. Urquhart was actually on the verge of departing for Division HQ when *Bataillon* Krafft attacked the tail of the 3rd Parachute Battalion column but then changed his mind, partly because it would involve travelling through unsecured territory in darkness and partly because his Jeep had been struck by a German mortar bomb that seriously wounded Corporal Warford, while leaving the allegedly malfunctioning No. 22 Set undamaged.[55] Urquhart therefore decided to remain where he was on the grounds that he was 'with the brigade charged with the initial thrust to the bridge and thereby usefully placed to give on-the-spot instructions'.[56]

The problem was that Urquhart was not with the Brigade charged with the initial thrust to the Arnhem bridge. He was with an isolated and incomplete Battalion and the Brigade's Tactical HQ consisting of Lathbury, his Brigade Intelligence Officer and presumably a signaller, out of contact with the bulk of its constituent units and with no real idea of their progress or condition. Urquhart was therefore anything but usefully placed or indeed capable of giving on-the-spot instructions, and his decision to remain with the 3rd Battalion column merely compounded his original error of leaving Division HQ without adequate communications or properly clarifying command arrangements during his absence. His reluctance to risk driving through two miles or so of unsecured territory is arguably valid, although by that logic he should not have left the landing area at all. It contrasts with the behaviour of his opposite number with the 6th Airborne Division, Major-General Richard Gale, in Normandy. At around 09:00 on the morning of 6 June 1944 Gale covered a similar distance between Ranville and the Orne bridges on foot and unescorted apart from two of his Brigadiers.[57] Had he been so minded Urquhart could have taken an escort from the 3rd Battalion and walked back to the landing area under the cover of darkness, which would likely have been a safer prospect than motoring around in the stillness of the night in a Jeep.

It is therefore valid to assume that Lathbury halted the 3rd Parachute Battalion for the night, putting his primary mission aside in the process, in order to protect Urquhart. Under normal circumstances this would have been justifiable as it was Lathbury's military duty to protect his superior. The circumstances of the evening of 17 September 1944 were far from normal however, and the onus was therefore upon Urquhart to keep things moving – but he remained little more than a bystander, his passivity allegedly arising from ignorance of the overall situation.[58] Strictly speaking this was true, but given his discussions with Lathbury he cannot have been unaware that the latter had no real idea of his constituent Battalion's progress or location, or that after five hours on the ground his Division's primary objective had not yet been secured. On that basis alone he had no place simply acquiescing to Lathbury's decision to halt for the night. Rather, he should have acted in line with the urgency of the situation and indeed his justification for remaining with the 1st Parachute Brigade, by taking the initiative and issuing 'on-the-spot instructions' for Lathbury to continue to move on Arnhem. Given that the 3rd Parachute Battalion's C Company reached the north end of the Arnhem bridge in the early hours of Monday 18 September it is highly likely that the entire battalion could have done the same, had it been allowed to press on.[59] This would have doubled the size of the infantry force defending the north end of the Arnhem bridge at a stroke, and thus might well have permitted the defenders to hold out until 30 Corps reached them. As it was, Urquhart spent the night of 17-18 September with Lathbury in a house near the Hotel Hartenstein, making frequent but futile checks on the radio communication situation, surrounded by the bulk of the 3rd Parachute Battalion. While they rested, the window of opportunity to reach the Arnhem road bridge was slowly closing, for just two miles or so to the east *Sturmbannführer* Ludwig Spindler was diligently piecing together what was to become an impregnable blocking line in the western outskirts of Arnhem.

Whatever the reason, Lathbury's decision to halt for the night did not go down well. Private Fred Moughton from the 3rd Battalion's HQ Company later lamented being 'held up by twopenny-ha'penny opposition'.[60] Fitch's view is unknown because he was killed two days later, but his second-in-command, Major Alan Bush, regarded the halt as 'the start of the great cock-up' and was convinced that Fitch would have continued moving had he been left to his own devices, probably in the wake of his C Company: 'I felt very sorry for Colonel Fitch. Urquhart needed to get back to Division, and Lathbury wanted to get forward to the bridge. If we had not had those two with us, Fitch would have probably followed C Company around that route to the north, but he could hardly move without the approval of both the divisional and brigade commanders – a hopeless situation.'[61] Brigade Major Tony Hibbert was more forthright in his criticism of Lathbury's decision. Hibbert was at the Arnhem road bridge by about 20:45[62] and unsuccessfully urged Lathbury to despatch the 3rd Parachute Battalion or at least a company each from the 3rd and the 1st Parachute Battalion down the riverside LION route during their radio exchange at 22:00.[63] Hibbert quite rightly pointed out fifty-seven years after the event that there should have been no question of halting after such a short period on the ground and in his view, Lathbury's refusal to move was 'the moment we lost the battle'.[64] It is difficult to disagree with this assessment.

While the 1st Parachute Battalion was trying to bypass German opposition on the Amsterdamseweg/LEOPARD route and the 3rd Parachute Battalion was digging in around the Hotel Hartenstein, the 2nd Parachute Battalion was pushing into Arnhem proper. Screened from the SS atop *Den Brink* by B Company, Major Digby Tatham-Warter and A Company led the way across the Arnhem city boundary at approximately 19:30 accompanied by Lieutenant-Colonel Frost. A and HQ Companies were trailed by Major Hibbert's swollen Brigade HQ column, which by this point had attracted part of the 1st Parachute Squadron RE, a platoon and attached section from 250 (Airborne) Light Composite Company RASC, a two-strong Jedburgh Team, Major Gough and two armed Jeeps from the Reconnaissance Squadron and a party from the 3rd Airlanding Battery RA led by the Battery commander, Major Denis Munford. There were also two units accompanying Hibbert by prior arrangement, Lieutenant-Colonel Eric Townsend and the bulk of 16 Parachute Field Ambulance RAMC and Lieutenant Wilfred Morley's fifteen-strong No.1 Section from the 1st (Airborne) Divisional Provost Company CMP with twenty POWs. Townsend's and Morley's men struck out for their own specific objectives soon after crossing the city boundary. The Field Ambulance was tasked to establish a Main Dressing Station (MDS) for the 1st Parachute Brigade in the St. Elizabeth Hospital and was treating casualties from the 2nd Parachute Battalion at that location by approximately 22:00, using two operating theatres with the assistance of volunteers from the Dutch staff.[65] The Provost Section was tasked to secure the main police station in the centre of Arnhem, presumably to serve as a POW holding facility. They arrived there at approximately 23:00, picking up Sergeant Harry Parker and Private Robert Peatling who had become separated from the 3rd and 2nd Parachute Battalions respectively on the way, after seeking directions from the rather bemused occupants of the Dutch Civil Defence HQ.[66]

After the Arnhem railway bridge had been blown literally in the face of Lieutenant Barry and 9 Platoon, C Company paused to reorganise before setting out for its secondary objective, the primary German HQ in the centre of Arnhem located near the main railway station. Lieutenant David Russell and 7 Platoon led the Company past the bottleneck at *Den Brink* and then came upon a group of German troops disembarking from a bus outside the St. Elizabeth Hospital:

> After a quick whispered briefing by Major Dover, my platoon opened fire with small arms. This resulted in much scuffling, moaning and groaning, shouting – every sign of a party caught by surprise. A number of survivors dived into the shelter of a vehicle against the hospital. The Piat fired on them – more groaning, and the survivors ran off into the hospital entrance. Another Piat was fired which resulted in more cries – 'Nicht schiessen!' and so on.[67]

Russell's men then shot up an approaching white vehicle which proved to be a Dutch ambulance carrying Captain John Tobin from 16 Parachute Field Ambulance. No one appears to have been hurt in the incident, but Tobin was understandably 'very annoyed'.[68] C Company then pushed on to within 600 yards of their objective, and at around 21:30 ran into German troops blocking the Brugstraat in a densely built-up area with no room to deploy. Two paratroopers were killed in the exchange, possibly by fire from an armoured half-track mounting a 75mm gun of some description, perhaps a *Sd.Kfz.* 251/9; the vehicle was knocked out by Private William Saunders from 7 Platoon's HQ element using a 2-inch mortar as a makeshift anti-armour weapon.[69] Despite this, the Company was obliged to fall back and Dover elected to occupy a large building on the north side of the Utrechtsestraat belonging to the PGEM power company, where they remained for the rest of the night.

Lieutenant Grayburn and 2 Platoon continued to lead A Company's advance on the Arnhem road bridge, taking a number of individual Germans prisoner in the first stage of the move. Preoccupied with Major Crawley's fight on *Den Brink*, Frost briefly lost contact with Major Tatham-Warter and his men and had to rush forward accompanied by his Intelligence Officer, Lieutenant Clifford Boiteux-Buchanan; they were guided in the right direction after 300 yards or so by an A Company soldier escorting ten German POWs. Frost was then able to bring the remainder of the 2nd Battalion forward in A Company's wake, with a slight detour to the north end of the pontoon bridge site. The bridge proved to be unusable, with only a section moored to hand on the northern bank, so Frost detached a party from Support Company, probably from the Battalion Assault Platoon, to guide B Company to the site when it broke contact at *Den Brink*, in the hope they could devise some way of crossing the river. Frost then pressed on over the remaining half-mile or so to the road bridge.[70] Grayburn and his men arrived there ahead of him at around 20:00 and A Company reorganised under the bridge's huge north ramp prior to establishing a defensive perimeter. 2 Platoon was then despatched to cover the lower embanked section of the ramp, while 1 and 3 Platoons occupied houses covering the approaches to the bridge. A Company's advance to the bridge had gone extremely well, covering the seven miles from the landing area in just less than five hours at a cost of only a single fatality and a small number of wounded. Frost arrived with HQ and Support Companies while A Company was reorganising. Spirits were understandably high and inevitably generated a considerable hubbub in addition to the noise generated by several hundred men and numerous vehicles in a relatively confined space. Lieutenant Vlasto recalled that things were organized 'amid the most awful row...The CO [Frost] arrived and seemed extremely happy, making cracks about everyone's nerves being jumpy.'[71] Despite the noise, the Airborne interlopers remained undetected, partly because 2 Platoon remained concealed and allowed German vehicles to cross the bridge unmolested, and partly because of the inexperience of the twenty very young or overage German soldiers guarding the bridge. In their ignorance these soldiers remained ensconced inside their makeshift bunkers in the structural concrete towers at each end of the bridge, rather than patrolling. This error was shortly to cost those at the north end their lives.

The first attempt to secure the road bridge was an impromptu effort by Lance-Sergeant Bill Fulton and his Section from 3 Platoon. Ordered to secure the end of the bridge by an unidentified officer, Fulton's seven-strong band made their way onto the bridge ramp via a stairway cut into the embankment and, after pausing for a truckload of German troops to depart, moved along the right side of the structure and took several individual Germans prisoner before Fulton's luck ran out: 'I saw a rifle starting to point at me. I swung round to the right and started firing my tommy-gun. I know I hit him because he fired his rifle as he was falling forward and I caught the bullet in the top of my left leg. I told the section behind me to report back that the bridge was well manned and would need more troops. I managed to crawl behind an iron girder, and eventually a couple of medics came for me.'[72] The second attempt was organised by Major Tatham-Warter and went ahead around the same time Major Hibbert arrived at the bridge with the Brigade HQ column, at 20:45. After blackening their faces and wrapping their steel-shod ammunition boots in strips of material obtained from nearby houses, Lieutenant Grayburn's 2 Platoon stealthily advanced from their positions on the ramp embankment in two files hugging the edges of the roadway. They had penetrated onto the bridge proper and were approaching the improvised bunker when a machine-gun therein opened fire; according to one source the fire was thickened by armoured half-tracks from *SS Panzer Aufklärungs Abteilung 9* shooting from the south end of the bridge.[73] Caught in the open with no cover to hand, the paratroopers had no alternative but to withdraw back to the embankment. There were no fatalities but eight men were wounded including Lieutenant Grayburn, who was hit in the shoulder, but despite this he supervised his Platoon's withdrawal and was the last man off the bridge. One of the wounded, making his way off the ramp and calling loudly for a stretcher-bearer, was confronted and sharply admonished by Lieutenant-Colonel Frost for making noise; according to an eyewitness he responded with 'Excuse me, sir, but I'm fucking well wounded,' in calm and measured tones.[74]

A third attempt at around 22:00 was more successful. A Jeep deftly reversed Sergeant Ernest Shelswell's 6-Pounder gun part way up the ramp embankment, from where it was manhandled onto the ramp facing the bridge. At the same time 1 Platoon used a PIAT to blow a hole in the upper storey of the house they were occupying; the hole was level with the bunker and gave a flame-thrower team from Captain Trevor Livesey's B Troop, 1st Parachute Squadron RE a clear line of fire.[75] Several rounds of armour-piercing shot were then pumped into the bunker, and while the flame-thrower missed the bunker the jet of flame detonated ammunition stored in wooden huts behind it and ignited the paintwork on the bridge superstructure, bathing the north end of the bridge, the ramp and adjacent buildings in orange light. Frost had intended to push men across to the south end of the bridge at that point, but was forestalled by the arrival of a four-truck convoy that made the mistake of approaching tentatively from the south. Tatham-Warter's men opened fire as the convoy neared the knocked-out bunker; at least one of the trucks was also carrying ammunition and the resultant explosion destroyed the vehicle and set the others ablaze. Several of the occupants were killed, others were taken prisoner and a German NCO reportedly charged the British positions and killed one paratrooper with a pistol before being despatched. The destruction of the convoy stymied Frost's plan to push over the bridge altogether, as the combination of blazing vehicles and burning paintwork made it impossible to cross.[76] Despite this setback, Frost had nonetheless succeeded in effectively securing the 1st

Airborne Division's primary objective within six hours or so of leaving the landing area and with only part of his 2nd Parachute Battalion.

While all this was going on the Airborne troops establishing a perimeter facing out from the bridge were also making contact with Germans, few if any of whom were expecting to see the British so far from their landing area. Possibly the first was a 120-strong *Vergeltungswaffe* 2 ballistic missile unit that included *Leutnant* Joseph Enthammer, billeted in a school a few hundred yards from the road bridge. Despite witnessing the parachute drop in the distance, the rocket troops were held back from participating in the counter-measures in light of their specialist nature, and were then ordered to evacuate the area. Assigned to command a seventeen-man rear party, Enthammer was not able to leave the school until around 21:00, by which time it was too late: 'We couldn't have travelled more than 300 to 400 metres before British soldiers stepped out and halted the lorry in the street. What could we do? We were virtually unarmed except for a few rifles. It came as a complete surprise.' Enthammer and his little group were herded into a nearby house and kept quiet about their unit affiliation and recent activities, probably a wise decision given the well-publicised damage V2 attacks were wreaking on London and south-eastern England at that time.[77] The paratroopers also clashed with *SS Panzergrenadier Regiment 21*'s fifty-strong *3 Kompanie*, which had pedalled the twenty-five miles from its billets in Deventer after commandeering bicycles from Dutch civilians at gunpoint. Nineteen-year-old *Rottenführer* Rudolf Trapp, one of the few veterans in *3 Kompanie*, found himself under fire from all directions in the darkened streets under the north ramp and rapidly realised that digging out the paratroopers was going to be 'no easy task'.[78]

A similar clash brought the British presence at the bridge to the attention of the German senior commanders. When Gräbner's reconnaissance unit was despatched to Nijmegen *Hauptsturmführer* Heinrich Brinkmann's *SS Panzer Aufklärungs Abteilung 10* was transferred to *9 SS Panzer Division* in exchange, with effect from 17:30 on 17 September.[79] Brinkmann had already been ordered to patrol along the north bank of the Lower Rhine as far as Emmerich, twenty-five miles upstream from Arnhem, in order to ascertain the extent of the Allied landings. Finding no sign of Allied activity, Brinkmann ordered *Obersturmführer* Karl Ziebrecht's *1 Kompanie*, equipped with a number of captured French Panhard armoured cars dubbed *Panzerspähwagen P204 (f)* in German service, to proceed to Arnhem in line with fresh instructions from *II SS Panzerkorps* to secure the road bridge there. Approaching the crossing at around 20:00 the Panhard's were fired on by Frost's men; taken aback by the unexpected turn of events, Ziebrecht pulled his vehicles back and radioed news of the encounter to *Obersturmbannführer* Paetsch at *10 SS Panzer Division* HQ, who in turn passed it up the chain to *II SS Panzerkorps* and *Heeresgruppe B*.[80] The arrival of the next unit at the bridge highlighted the potentially fatal consequences of the German failure to properly secure the crossing. *Hauptsturmführer* Karl-Heinz Euling's *Bataillon* from *SS Panzergrenadier Regiment 22*, reinforced with *SS Panzer Pionier Bataillon 10* and redesignated *Kampfgruppe* Euling, had been ordered to proceed from its billets at Dieren, eleven miles north of Arnhem, and secure the road and rail crossings across the River Waal in Nijmegen. Some elements appear to have crossed the Lower Rhine just before access to the Arnhem bridge was blocked by the British paratroopers, but the bulk of the unit became embroiled in a fight at the bridge ramp that went on through the night and into the morning of Monday 18 September.

More Airborne troops trickled into the Arnhem bridge perimeter through the remainder of the night. Captain O'Callaghan's 2 Platoon from the 9th (Airborne) Field Company RE, which had been attached to C Company, arrived unscathed and expanded Frost's little band by around thirty men. Major Peter Lewis' C Company from the 3rd Parachute Battalion reached the bridge perimeter at around 03:00 after quite an odyssey. The Company left the remainder of the 3rd Battalion at 18:00, moving along a minor road leading north through the woods to the Arnhem–Ede railway with a Sergeant Mason from Lieutenant Len Wright's 9 Platoon in the lead and Lieutenant Peter Hibburt's 7 Platoon bringing up the rear. Sergeant Mason and his Section captured a German despatch rider and killed two more Germans travelling on another motorcycle before becoming separated from the rest of the Company at some point before reaching the railway. Following a track running parallel to the rail line, 9 Platoon was engaged by a *Kübelwagen* loaded with Germans, losing Private Tindle wounded in exchange for a German POW. The *Kübelwagen* and the rest of its German passengers escaped. A German truck loaded with ammunition which approached from the rear was then ambushed and set ablaze; the driver appears to have been wounded and captured while a single passenger was killed in an exchange of fire that badly wounded Sergeant Thomas Graham, who died later.[81] Meanwhile 7 Platoon had also destroyed an ammunition truck, killing all four passengers and knocked out a half-track also approached from the rear, losing five casualties in the process. At around dusk the Company was reunited and after allowing his men a short rest Major Lewis set his Company off down the railway line toward Arnhem.

Lewis and his men reached the main railway station in the centre of Arnhem at around midnight without incident and then pushed on toward the main square, capturing two Germans on the way. The square was full of German troops and transport but Lewis gambled on the darkness concealing their identity and boldly marched his entire Company openly down the main road leading to the bridge after ordering Lieutenant Gerald Infield's 8 Platoon at the head of the column not to 'engage the enemy or make any hostile moves'. According to Sergeant Mason they were, however, recognised en route by two Dutch policemen, who gave them 'a great welcome'. The bluff carried the paratroopers almost to the bridge before they ran into a German armoured car, which Lieutenant Infield's men knocked out with a Gammon bomb. On reaching the approaches to the bridge Major Lewis concealed his men in roadside shrubbery, 7 and 8 Platoons on the right and 9 Platoon and Company HQ on the left, before going forward with his Platoon commanders to arrange entry into the 2nd Battalion's perimeter. After liaising with Lieutenant Boiteux-Buchanan, Lewis sent his platoon commanders back to bring in their men, and at that point it all went wrong. Lieutenant Infield and 8 Platoon moved without incident but 7 Platoon were surprised and captured by German troops moving to attack the bridge and the Platoon commander, Lieutenant Peter Hibburt, was killed along with one of his sergeants.[82] One of the attackers, who may have been from *Kampfgruppe* Euling, then moved onto the road and called on 9 Platoon to surrender as Lieutenant Wright was holding an O Group prior to moving. When the paratroopers responded with a burst of fire the German's companions raked the shrubbery with a machine-gun, causing several casualties and obliging Lieutenant Wright to order his men to make their way into the perimeter independently; approximately half of them made it safely.[83]

Major Crawley and the 2nd Battalion's B Company broke contact with *SS Panzer Pionier Abteilung 9* atop *Den Brink* at around midnight and met Lieutenant Patrick Barnett's Brigade HQ Defence Platoon and some Sappers from the 1st Parachute Squadron RE at the pontoon bridge site. Frost had sent Barnett's party back after the second abortive attempt to secure the road bridge to try and locate some means of getting B Company across to the south bank, but the effort was abandoned when no boats or other means could be located. All made it safely back into the bridge perimeter at around 05:00 apart from the B Company rearguard, Lieutenant Hugh Levien's 4 Platoon, which was caught moving after first light approximately a mile from the bridge. Sergeant Frank Kemp and another man were wounded, the former seriously in the groin and while Sergeant Herbert Carrier led a small group in a successful dash to the safety of the road bridge perimeter, the remainder of the Platoon were driven back by the weight of enemy fire and became split up in the process. Lieutenant Levien and eleven men took shelter in the house of a Miss Mieke Engelsman on Bakkerstraat with the assistance of a patriotic Dutchman named Jan Brouwer, from where Levien was able to contact Major Crawley via the civilian telephone network.

Not all the traffic ran into the solidifying bridge perimeter. After accompanying the Brigade HQ column into the perimeter, Major Dennis Munford's party was reportedly unable to make contact with the remainder of 3 Battery back at the landing area with their own radios or those of nearby units.[84] Munford then allegedly resorted to making the round journey from the bridge to the landing area and back in two Jeeps, in order to have his radio sets retuned and inform Division HQ that the bridge had been secured.[85] However, another participant's account suggests that this was not actually the case. Bombardier Leo Hall, who served at Arnhem as a signaller with Captain Anthony Harrison's Observation Post (OP) party from E Troop, succeeded in establishing contact with the Battery Command Post at the landing area using a No. 22 set to transmit and a No. 68 back-pack radio set to receive from the attic of the building occupied by Brigade HQ; although he neglected to inform Munford or Harrison of the contact immediately, the former became aware of it and subsequently used the link to register his guns at first light.[86] According to Hall, Munford never left the bridge perimeter on the night of 17-18 September, and he is supported in this by another participant account and the fact that there is no reference to Munford's epic journey in the unit War Diary, as one would expect. The latter does refer to Munford despatching Captain Harrison to contact the Battery and inform Division HQ of developments in person, however.[87] In fact, Harrison appears to have left the bridge perimeter twice, the first time at some point after 22:00, given that Hall refers to hearing ammunition cooking off in the burning store on the bridge in the background. The object of the excursion is unclear, although it may have been in search of Lathbury. Harrison was driven by Bombardier Michael Ogle and accompanied by Hall and Gunners Jock Chrystal and Jock Morrison; all returned safely to the perimeter.[88]

On the second occasion, at some point after 04:00, Harrison was despatched by Munford to carry a situation report to Division HQ and more importantly, to order 3 Battery to move forward into Oosterbeek to place it within range of the bridge.[89] Again driven by Bombardier Ogle, Harrison left the perimeter intending to follow the riverside LION route. However, the pair took a wrong turning in the darkness and ended up on the Utrechtseweg/TIGER route instead and ran into Lieutenant-Colonel Dobie and the 1st Parachute Battalion in the midst of their fight at the railway embankment at around 05:00.[90] After apprising Dobie of the situation Harrison then made his way to the landing area, presumably by following the Utrechtseweg through the 3rd Parachute Battalion's perimeter in the western outskirts of Oosterbeek, although the latter's War Diary makes no mention of his passage. Whatever his route, Harrison reached the landing area without incident. On arrival he left the report on the seizure of the north end of the Arnhem road bridge at Urquhart's vacant HQ, which was spending the night in four abandoned Horsas on LZ Z along with a group of war correspondents, and set 3 Battery's move to Oosterbeek into motion.[91]

Captain Harrison's passage back to the Divisional area was eased by the fact that the units defending the eastern edge of the landing area remained untroubled by German activity. The understrength 2nd Battalion South Staffordshire Regiment, dug in near Reijers-Camp Farm to protect 1st Airlanding Brigade HQ and 181 Airlanding Field Ambulance in the outskirts of Wolfheze, reported that 'no opposition developed in the bn area and all ranks spent a quiet night', and the 9th (Airborne) Field Company RE also referred to passing a 'relatively quiet night' on the eastern edge of LZ Z.[92] The same appears to have been the case with the 1st Border's A Company manning the eastern perimeter to the south of the Field Company and the remainder of the Battalion protecting the western side of the landing area. The exception was B Company, the most far-flung of the 1st Border's units, which was dug in on the outskirts of Renkum at the far south-western corner of DZ X. At some point during the night a group of German troops approached the perimeter of Sergeant Thomas Watson's 14 Platoon, located in the grounds of the local brickworks. Private Edward Peters, who was at that point sharing a slit trench with aptly named fellow sniper Private Eric Borders, recalled hearing foreign voices and the sound of men crossing a barbed wire fence to their front in the darkness. Sergeant Watson ordered his men to open fire after a Very flare revealed a number of German troops to the Platoon's front, and no further German activity was detected for the remainder of the night.[93] Dutch Resistance reports of a sixty-strong German force moving toward Renkum led to Lance-Corporal Albert Wilson's Section from 11 Platoon being despatched to lay an ambush at 21:00. Wilson occupied a house overlooking a promising section of road after rousing two elderly Dutchmen and persuading them into their cellar, but was recalled to the Platoon perimeter at 23:00 after further reports claimed the German force had taken a different road.[94]

This may have been the German force encountered in part by the 1st Border's Signals Officer, Lieutenant Joseph Hardy, who had harassed the two tea-making Privates on LZ S just a few hours earlier. In an effort to alleviate B Company's communication difficulties Hardy was despatched to establish a field telephone link across the two miles separating Renkum from Battalion HQ at Johannahoeve Farm, using a Jeep driven by his Platoon Sergeant, Jock McClusky. While returning to Battalion HQ in the early hours of Monday 18 September after successfully completing the task, they spotted two figures in the road ahead. Perhaps naively, Hardy assumed the figures were British and the Jeep was virtually on top of them before it became apparent they were in fact both German and armed. Reacting quickly as McClusky brought the Jeep to an emergency stop, Hardy vaulted the bonnet with his Sten gun in hand and confronted them with the immortal words 'How's about it chums?' This had the desired effect and the startled Germans allowed themselves to be disarmed and hustled into the back of the Jeep, which McClusky rapidly turned and raced back to B Company's location. Subsequent interrogation revealed that Hardy and McClusky had enjoyed a narrow escape, for the prisoners had been the rearguard of an entire German company that had occupied that stretch of road only moments earlier. Given this, Hardy, probably wisely, decided to remain with B Company for the rest of the night. He then found himself pressed into service as temporary Company second-in-command by Major Armstrong.[95]

Although the 1st Border had no way of knowing it, the appearance and movement of German troops in the vicinity of Renkum was not accidental. The German effort to contain the British landing from the west was assigned to *Generalleutnant* Hans von Tettau, who headed the German training infrastructure in Holland from his HQ located at Grebbeberg, forty miles west of Arnhem. When MARKET began, von Tettau was responsible for a mixed bag of *Heer*, *Kriegsmarine* and *SS* training units which included *Artillerie Regiment 184*, *Schiffsstammabteilung 6/14*, *Bataillon* Krafft, *SS Wacht Bataillon 3* and *SS Unterführerschule* 'Arnheim', a three battalion-strong NCO training unit commanded by *Standartenführer* Hans Lippert; two of Lippert's units, commanded by *Hauptsturmführer* Heinrich Oelkers and *Hauptsturmführer* Walter Mattusch, were already deployed screening the River Waal.[96] *Heeresgruppe B* appointed von Tettau in the late afternoon of 17 September, and his first task was to ascertain the true extent of the British encroachment, given that Airborne landings had been reported at Dordrecht, Tiel, Utrecht and Veenendaal in addition to those near Arnhem. These reports likely resulted, at least in part, from RAF aircraft scattering dummy parachutists in the area of Utrecht on the night of 16-17 September as a disinformation measure, and it was this remit that despatched *Oberscharführer* Sakkel and his bandsmen from *SS Wacht Bataillon 3* into the 7th KOSB's ambush near the *Zuid Ginkel* café just after 17:00.[97] With the exception of *Bataillon* Krafft, which was already engaged on the other side of the British enclave and subsequently transferred to *Sturmbannführer* Ludwig Spindler's command, all of von Tettau's units were thus ordered to redeploy to the wooded area east of Wageningen as the shape of the British landing became clear. The German troops in the vicinity of B Company's location were therefore likely *Kriegsmarine* personnel from *Schiffsstammabteilung 6/14* or possibly *SS* from Lippert's uncommitted *bataillon* commanded by *Hauptsturmführer* Günther Schultze, which received orders to move to the area of Wageningen at 19:00; both units deployed just west of Renkum.[98]

However, von Tettau's deployments impacted first on the 7th KOSB, the bulk of which reportedly spent the hours of darkness patrolling to the west, south and east of DZ Y, apparently without contact. The most pressing problem was poor communications, particularly between the dispersed Company locations. The surrounding woods interfered with radio transmissions, and attempts to establish field telephone lines were stymied by the distances involved and the delicate nature of the assault cable employed.[99] The exception to this was Major Robert Buchanan's A Company, which was deployed to interdict German traffic on the Amsterdamseweg two miles or so from the remainder of the Battalion. Lieutenant James Strang's 4 Platoon, which appears to have been allotted the easterly portion of the Company perimeter, was attacked three times in the course of the night by an unidentified German armoured vehicle. The attacks involved the vehicle illuminating the British position with a spotlight before raking it with 20mm and machine-gun fire while accompanying infantry attempted to infiltrate. 4 Platoon successfully withstood the attacks but Lieutenant Strang and his men were reportedly 'severely shaken by them'.[100] It is unclear where the attackers came from, but they may have been elements of *SS Panzer Aufklärungs Abteilung 9* exceeding their orders by moving along the Amsterdamseweg west of Wolfheze. Whoever attacked 4 Platoon, matters took a more positive course to the west in the vicinity of the *Zuid Ginkel* café, where elements of A Company ambushed *Hauptsturmführer* Ernst Bartsch's 4 *Kompanie* from *SS Wacht Bataillon 3* as it advanced east along the Amsterdamseweg. Caught in the glaring white magnesium light of trip flares, Bartsch's men were stopped cold as was *Obersturmführer* Karl Hink's 3 *Kompanie* when it tried to bypass Bartsch's unit to the south. Buchanan's men inflicted numerous casualties on the hapless *SS*, who withdrew in some confusion into the woods north of the Amsterdamseweg to await reinforcement and daylight.[101] However, in withdrawing as they did the two *SS* units inadvertently exploited a serious flaw in the 7th KOSB's deployment. Offsetting A Company to the east of the main Battalion location left the northern edge of DZ Y unprotected and the *SS* had unknowingly inserted themselves into this weak point, and thus placed themselves perfectly to threaten the rear of the British screen covering the western edge of the DZ. The consequences of this were not to become apparent until daylight on 18 September.

Von Tettau's preparations were thus well in hand by the late evening of Sunday 17 September and he was therefore in a position to issue a Warning Order at 23:15 for a dawn assault, after *Heeresgruppe B* had formally authorised attacks on the British lodgement from the north and west. At 04:00 *Heeresgruppe B* further informed von Tettau that he was to be reinforced with all or elements of *Schiffsstammabteilung 10*, *Fliegerhorst Bataillon 2* and *3*, *Ausbildungs und Ersatz Regiment* 'Hermann Göring', *Sicherheits Regiment 26*, an *SS* battalion commanded by *Sturmbannführer* Eugen Eberwein and *Panzer Kompanie 224* equipped with seventeen captured French tanks.[102] Not all of these units would be available for the attack; *Panzer Kompanie 224* was based eighty miles away at Naaldwijk near Den Haag for example, while *Bataillon Eberwein* was not scheduled to reach the scene of the action until 10:30 on 18 September.[103] All but the armoured unit were however available for integration into the existing attack plan for a general, two-pronged advance into the British landing area. In the north *SS Wacht Bataillon 3* was to push forward across the width of Ginkel Heath using the Amsterdamseweg as a left marker and with *Bataillon Eberwein* pushing along the Arnhem–Ede railway on arrival as a right marker, with the aim of splitting the landing area in two. The southern flank of the attack was to be anchored on the Lower Rhine with *Schiffsstammabteilung 6/14* and *Schiffsstammabteilung 10* tasked to advance along the river bank and clear Renkum with *SS Unterführerschule* 'Arnheim' on the left tasked to do the same to Heelsum. The *Fliegerhorst* units were to occupy the centre to provide a link between the two axes of attack, while *Artillerie Regiment 184* was designated reserve and tasked to support the southern prong of the attack.[104]

The process of redeployment was neither straightforward nor tidy. Bicycles were the only transport available to *Ausbildungs und Ersatz Regiment* 'Hermann Göring' to cover the seventy-odd miles from its billets at Katwijk aan Zee on the Dutch coast, and it also had to travel by night with all the disruption that entailed, to avoid Allied air attack. *SS Unterführerschule* 'Arnheim' was also obliged to rely on bicycles, although two Dutch fire engines were commandeered in Leerdam to carry heavy weapons. *SS Junker* Rudolf Lindemann, an officer candidate with the latter formation, noted a severe shortage of basic items like maps and claimed never to have seen one throughout the battle. This was in stark contrast to the enemy: every man in the 504th Parachute Infantry Regiment was issued with a map of Holland and a larger scale map of their objective and surrounding area, for example.[105] Lindemann was also unimpressed with what he witnessed generally during the move: 'It was really depressing to witness the march to Arnhem – a ridiculous event! More like Napoleon's retreat from Moscow than a military operation.'[106] Lindemann was perhaps being a tad cynical and overly critical, for untidy as it might have been, within eighteen hours of the British landing the Germans were well on the way to sealing off the landing area and thus the bulk of the 1st Airborne Division from its objective. Von Tettau specifically had ascertained the extent and location of the landings, drawn up an attack plan, located and deployed the units to execute it and was poised to launch the equivalent of two brigades along a five-mile front. This was a creditable performance by any standard, and raises some interesting points. First, it showed that the British airborne planners were being optimistic in the extreme when they decided that it was feasible to put two lifts into the same landing area twenty-four hours apart in the face of a first-class enemy. Second, it shows that the *Waffen SS* did not hold the sole monopoly on fast reactions to the unforeseen, and that the *Heer* was at least equally capable of reacting with speed, efficiency and aggression when necessary.

***

The same process was taking place fifteen miles or so away to the east and south of Nijmegen. Although British intelligence reports had insisted on the presence of German armoured units in the *Reichswald* forest adjacent to the 82nd Airborne Division's landing area, the Germans actually had very little in the area to contest the US landings apart from the units protecting the bridges across the various watercourses. As we have seen, *Heeresgruppe B* allotted responsibility for dealing with the US landing at Nijmegen to *Wehrkreis VI*, a rear-echelon formation commanded by *General* Franz Mattenklott from his HQ in Münster. The latter appointed *General der Kavallerie* Kurt Feldt, a First World War veteran and Knight's Cross holder who had recently escaped from the debacle in France, to head the counter-measures. *Heeresgruppe B* assigned Feldt *1* and *2 Fallschirmjäger Divisions*, which were to be assembled at Cleve by the afternoon of 18 September. In the meantime he was to gather and employ whatever he could from *Wehrkreis VI's* resources, and on that authority he therefore devolved operational responsibility to *Generalleutnant* Gerd Scherbening's *406 z.b.V. Division*, an administrative HQ for a number of training and replacement units also based in Münster. Scherbening was informed of his assignment at some point before 21:00 on 17 September, when he issued a warning order to his HQ personnel, and five hours later he ordered a move to an as yet unknown location, scheduled to begin at 08:00 on 18 September. As *406 z.b.V. Division* had been a static administrative entity for some years, the news understandably caused some consternation. Major Rasch, Scherbening's adjutant, noted: 'Only an expert in such matters can appreciate what it means to change from a barracks-based staff organisation, with no equipment or vehicles, and turn it into a mobile field headquarters, all in the space of six hours.'[107] The unknown location turned out to be Geldern, eighty miles west of Münster and just five miles from the Dutch border, and Scherbening was informed that he was to form an *ad hoc* fighting division covering a fifty-mile sector running along the River Maas from Venlo to Nijmegen; this coincidentally corresponded with the entire US section of the MARKET Airborne Corridor.

While Scherbening and Rasch were busy arranging for their move to Geldern, Feldt was busy rounding up units for them to command on arrival. These included an NCO training school, possibly *Unteroffizier Schule Wehrkreis IV*, several *Luftwaffe* ground units and a *pionier bataillon* drawn in from Roermond, among others. In the course of the night a force of approximately 3,500 men equipped with 130 assorted machine-guns and twenty-four mortars had been assembled along a ten-mile line running south from Beek to Wyler and then west around Groesbeek to Mook near the River Maas. The force was divided into three roughly battalion-size battle groups named after their commanders: *Kamfgruppen* Goebel, Greschick and Stargaard. A fourth *kampfgruppe* commanded by a *Hauptmann Freiherr* von Fürstenberg included five armoured cars and three 20mm armed half-tracks gathered in from a training unit, which represented the only armoured support immediately available, and the equivalent of three artillery batteries was concentrated in the area of Zyfflich, midway between and just east of Beek and Wyler. With all this in hand, Feldt redefined the *406 z.b.V. Division's* mission. First, Scherbening was ordered to establish a tactical forward HQ thirty miles to the north of Geldern near Kranenburg, only three miles or so east of Groesbeek. Second, he was ordered to attack the US landing area along the line from Beek to Groesbeek with the intention of securing the Groesbeek Heights and ultimately driving the US troops back across the River Maas. The attack was to begin at 06:30 on Monday 18 September. Given the circumstances, Scherbening's reaction to the order can be well imagined, and he may have been even less impressed had he been aware of Feldt's thinking in issuing it: 'I had no confidence in this attack, since it was almost an impossible task for *406 z.b.V. Division* to attack picked troops with its motley crowd. But it was necessary to risk the attack in order to forestall an enemy advance to the east, and to deceive him in regard to our strength.'[108]

Little if any of this was apparent to the men holding the various sectors of the 82nd Airborne Division's perimeter, however, and most spent a generally quiet night in their positions or patrolling around them. Company E from the 504th Parachute Infantry Regiment's 2nd Battalion, stationed at the western extremity of the perimeter, despatched one such patrol to investigate strange noises emanating from Grave and discovered the German garrison had abandoned the town; the noise proved to be the jubilant Dutch civilian population singing their version of 'Tipperary' in celebration.[109] At the eastern end of the perimeter the 505th Parachute Infantry Regiment experienced an even more unusual incident when a railway train steamed into the Divisional perimeter from Nijmegen at 23:45, took the eastern spur and drove right through the Regimental perimeter before exiting through the 3rd Battalion's positions in Groesbeek, all without a shot being fired. In so doing the train passed close to the 2nd Battalion, which was acting as Divisional reserve, and Division HQ; the locomotive's whistle disturbed Major-General Gavin from a fitful sleep under a tree near his Command Post and prompted a terse enquiry to 3rd Battalion HQ.[110] It is unclear whether it was due to orders from Gavin or from further down the chain of command, but a second train received a rather different reception an hour or so later. By that time the line had been seeded with anti-tank mines and a well-aimed Bazooka rocket scored a direct hit on the locomotive, bringing it to an abrupt halt. The train was carrying German military personnel including a number of female auxiliaries and members of the *Organisation Todt* labour force, all of whom promptly fled into the darkness, to be rounded up later by the paratroopers.[111]

The exception to the 82nd Airborne Division's generally quiet night was Lieutenant-Colonel Shields Warren's 1st Battalion 508th Parachute Infantry Regiment, which, along with Regimental commander Colonel Roy E. Lindquist, was stationed along the northern edge of the Groesbeek Heights overlooking the Nijmegen suburb of De Ploeg, roughly three miles from the road and rail bridges across the River Waal. Warren had been warned off to move on the bridges before the drop but the mission was delayed by Lindquist, who misunderstood Gavin's admittedly rather opaque instructions and assumed that he was free to complete his Regiment's routine tasks before moving on the bridges. Lindquist did, however, authorise Warren to despatch a patrol from Company C to the Nijmegen road bridge to confirm Dutch Resistance reports that it was defended by only a handful of Germans; if this proved to be the case, the patrol was to seize the southern end of the bridge and await reinforcement. However, while preparations for the patrol were underway Lindquist was radioed by Gavin, who resolved his confused priorities by explicitly ordering Lindquist 'to delay not a second longer and get the bridge as quickly as possible with Warren's battalion'.[112] Lindquist therefore convened a conference at 18:00 that ended with Warren being ordered to advance on the Nijmegen road bridge with Companies A and B, commanded by Captains Jonathan E. Adams and Woodrow W. Millsaps respectively, guided by a member of the Dutch Resistance rather than the route mapped out by Gavin back in England. The force was to be reinforced with .30 machine-guns and 81mm mortars along with Warren and a party from HQ Company; according to Adams, he was also to collect additional information en route from the Dutch Resistance. The remainder of the 1ˢᵗ Battalion, consisting of the depleted Company C and part of HQ Company commanded in Warren's absence by the 1ˢᵗ Battalion's Executive Officer, Captain Benjamin F. Delamater, were to remain in place on the Groesbeek Heights with Colonel Lindquist and his Tactical HQ.[113]

The initial patrol was commanded by Lieutenant Robert J. Weaver and consisted of his platoon from Company C, reinforced with the Battalion Intelligence Section and two .30 Machine Gun Squads. Weaver and his men moved off from the 1ˢᵗ Battalion perimeter at 18:30 and approached the road bridge from the east, probably using the circuitous route Gavin had worked out back in England to prevent the attackers becoming lost in Nijmegen's streets. Penetrating as far as the traffic roundabout at its south end known as the *Keizer Lodewijkplein*, Weaver's party ascertained that the bridge was in fact held by *Luftwaffe Oberst* Henke's scratch force of trainee *Fallschirmjäger* NCOs, possibly augmented by that time with two half-tracks from *SS Panzer Aufklärungs Abteilung 9*. As this precluded them from securing the bridge, the paratroopers contented themselves with scouting the extent of the German defences and additional avenues for attack. At some point the element of surprise was lost when the patrol ambushed a truckload of German troops, but it was nonetheless able to remain in the area until 06:00 on 18 September. At that point and having received no further instructions from Warren, Weaver and his men withdrew to the 1ˢᵗ Battalion position on the Groesbeek Heights. It is unclear how many casualties the patrol sustained, but Captain Delamater later referred to several key men from the Battalion Intelligence Section being killed.[114]

The subsequent two-Company move on the road bridge proved to be rather less successful and went awry from the outset. Departure was delayed for two hours while Dutch reports of a large German force lurking in the woods to the 1ˢᵗ Battalion's rear were investigated; when the reports proved to be false, Company A, its Dutch guide and Lieutenant-Colonel Warren, accompanied by part of HQ Company, moved off for the rendezvous with Company B. This was scheduled for 19:00 just south of Nijmegen but Millsaps became lost en route and during the hour when Warren held back, the Dutch guide went off to contact the Resistance armed with Warren's Colt .45 pistol. Neither he nor the pistol was seen again and at 20:00 Warren finally ordered Adams to leave a guide for Millsaps and proceed. The plan was to move north-west into the centre of the city along the Groesbeekseweg and then veer north-east toward the road bridge to avoid becoming entangled with Lieutenant Weaver's earlier patrol, which was supposed to approach the objective from the east. With no moonlight and visibility at less than ten yards, progress was slow and the need to allow scouts to check buildings dominating the route made it even slower. It therefore took the better part of two hours to cover the two miles or so to the *Keizer Karel Plein*, the wooded traffic roundabout where the advance was to veer north-east along the Oranjesingel for the final half mile to the Hunnerpark, an area of parkland astride the bridge ramp. Adams' lead platoon was just two blocks from the roundabout when the scouts literally bumped into German troops, sparking a confused firefight in which the lead platoon commander was wounded and his deputy killed, possibly by friendly fire; according to Adams his Company began firing wildly from both sides of the Groesbeekseweg and Company B, which came up to the tail end of Adams' column at this point, also began firing down the middle of the roadway.[115]

Although the various US commanders involved had no way of knowing it at the time, the outbreak of the confused firefight at c.22:00 on the Groesbeekseweg marked the point where the paratroopers were pipped to the post in the race for the Nijmegen bridge. Just two hours earlier the Waal crossings had only been defended by *Oberst* Henke's scratch force of trainee *Fallschirmjäger* NCOs as Gräbner, finding all quiet at Nijmegen, had moved back north with his vehicles, possibly prompted by reports of the fighting at Arnhem from his rear security detachment at Elst. Reinforcements were on the way, the most substantial being *Hauptsturmführer* Karl-Heinz Euling's *Kampfgruppe* which had been ordered south to Nijmegen in the late afternoon of 17 September but was delayed for over twelve hours after becoming embroiled with Frost's 2nd Parachute Battalion as it secured the northern approaches to the Arnhem road bridge. The first reinforcements actually to reach Nijmegen appear to have been a party of dismounted tank crewmen from *SS Panzer Regiment 10* led by the Regimental commander, *Sturmbannführer* Leo Reinhold, and the advance party of a detachment from *SS Panzer Pionier Bataillon 10* commanded by *Untersturmführer* Werner Baumgärtel. The precise time these units arrived at Nijmegen is similarly unclear, but the evidence suggests that it may have been in the late evening of Sunday 17 September and that they may have been the last German units to cross the Arnhem road bridge before the 2nd Parachute Battalion sealed it off; a number of heavy vehicles were heard passing over the bridge while the British Airborne troops were reorganising beneath the north ramp.[116] Reinhold had been tasked to oversee the defence of the Waal crossings presumably by *Obersturmbannführer* Otto Paetsch, commanding *10 SS Panzer Division* in *Brigadeführer* Harmel's stead while the latter visited Berlin. After receiving a situation report from *Oberst* Henke, Reinhold established his command post just north of the road bridge and had his men dig in on the north bank of the river as a backstop position.[117] The advance guard from *SS Panzer Pionier Bataillon 10* crossed the river to assist Henke's scratch force and its arrival was presumably that heard by Captain Adams, who referred to the sound of German troops hurriedly unloading from trucks located in the streets on the other side of the *Keizer Karel Plein* being audible throughout the initial stages of the firefight there.[118] Adams attempted to push Lieutenant George D. Lamm's 2nd Platoon forward to replace his badly hit lead platoon but was thwarted by the darkness and confused close-quarter fighting; the situation was finally stabilised by Millsaps' Company B occupying a three-storey building overlooking the *Keizer Karel Plein*, from where it successfully rebuffed a dawn counter-attack with the assistance of two 81mm mortars emplaced on the building's flat roof.[119]

Meanwhile, Lieutenant-Colonel Warren had received reports from the Dutch Resistance that the control point for demolition charges rigged on the road bridge was located in Nijmegen's main post office, a few blocks north of the *Keizer Karel Plein*. After two consultations at Warren's command post Captain Adams was ordered to despatch a patrol to filter around the traffic roundabout, seize and destroy the control point and then move on to the road bridge; Adams was to follow with the rest of his Company if the route was clear. Adams assigned the mission to Lieutenant Lamm's 2nd Platoon but at the last minute decided to lead the patrol himself, apparently in frustration because time was growing short and because he did not trust Lamm's competence; Adams' post-action report referred to Lamm being seemingly incapable of understanding verbal instructions even with the aid of a map.[120] The problem was that Adams did not inform his superiors or subordinates of his last-minute decision, and the remainder of his Company was left essentially leaderless until 1st Lieutenant John P. Foley assumed command on the morning of 18 September. Whatever his reasoning, Adams successfully led the patrol to the post office, dodging a first encounter with a *Panzerfaust* on the way. Lieutenant Lamm and six men managed to enter the post office where they killed a number of Germans and smashed what they assumed to be the demolition switches before rejoining the main group with the loss of one man. For his part, Adams suspected that the post office was merely a German HQ of some description rather than a demolition control post, and that the destroyed apparatus were merely light switches. Given that the road bridge does not appear to have been rigged for demolition until the following morning by *SS Panzer Pionier Bataillon 10*, Adams' suspicions were likely justified.[121] The idea of continuing to the bridge was abandoned when the patrol could not make contact with Warren or the remainder of Company A via its SCR 536 radio and also presumably because they were carrying two badly wounded men. The patrol therefore started to move back to its start point but this plan had to be abandoned owing to increasing German activity and the approach of daylight. By dawn avoiding contact with the Germans appears to have driven the patrol to within half a mile of the railway bridge, and Adams and his men were obliged to take shelter with sympathetic Dutch civilians. They remained in hiding for two days, until the area was liberated by troops from the Guards Armoured Division in the morning of Wednesday 20 September.[122]

The fighting at the city centre end of the Groesbeekseweg waxed and waned from 22:00 through to around 08:00 the next morning, and the pre-dawn German attack frustrated Lieutenant-Colonel Warren's final attempt to get the advance on the road bridge moving again.[123] The block at the *Keizer Karel Plein* therefore marked the end of Gavin's first, partly illicit attempt to secure the Nijmegen bridges. The immediate reason for the lack of success was Lindquist's seeming failure to pick up on Gavin's subtle prompting and consequent tardiness in despatching Warren's Battalion, but this was in turn directly attributable to Browning's insistence that securing and holding the Groesbeek Heights be accorded a higher priority than seizing the Waal bridges; without this, Gavin would have been able to dispense with the subterfuge and move on the bridges with a stronger force immediately after landing. Browning's edict was therefore ultimately responsible for squandering the window of opportunity in the first few hours after landing, when the Waal bridges could and should have been seized, before the German defences were properly established. The 82nd Airborne Division, Guards Armoured Division and by extension the 1st Airborne Division were to pay a high price for Browning's faulty prioritising over the coming days.

However, while the 1st Battalion 508th Parachute Infantry Regiment might well have been able to reach and secure the Nijmegen road bridge had it been despatched earlier on 17 September, it is not at all certain it could have held onto it. Warren had only two rifle companies to hand and an understrength Battalion simply lacked the numbers to effectively hold one end of the bridge, let alone the whole structure, as events at Arnhem were to show. The task required at least a full regiment with supporting elements, and a combination of Browning's edict, the need to protect DZ T and the sheer size of the 82nd Airborne Division's perimeter meant that Gavin was simply unable to spare sufficient men in the opening stages of MARKET. It should also be remembered that Model had specifically ordered that linkage between the Allied lodgements on the Waal and Lower Rhine was to be prevented at all costs.[124] His selection of Nijmegen as the *schwerpunkt* of the German effort to counter MARKET meant that any US foothold on the River Waal would have been faced with ferocious and unrelenting attack with everything the Germans could bring to bear, and it is extremely likely that such a response would have overwhelmed an understrength Battalion in short order. At least one US participant was of the same opinion. Writing three years after the event, then Captain Delamater, the 1st Battalion's Executive Officer, stated: 'I believe at least 90% of us fully believed that we could take the bridge with one Bn. had we been able to reach it before dark. I, personally, have since changed my mind to the extent that we could not have *taken and held* the bridge even one day [original emphasis].'[125] Given the ferocity of subsequent German resistance in Nijmegen and the systematic manner in which the British enclave at the Arnhem road bridge was isolated and overwhelmed, it is difficult to disagree with this assessment.

***

Twenty miles south-west of Nijmegen the 101st Airborne Division's 501st Parachute Infantry Regiment was deployed in and around Veghel covering the road and rail bridges across the River Aa and parallel Zuid Willems Canal. The town had been secured by 15:00 with little resistance and around fifty Germans taken prisoner, although the process of establishing a defensive perimeter was again slowed by the understandably ecstatic locals; as the Division's semi-official history put it, 'throngs of civilians gathered around any group of soldiers, chattering and offering them goodies. It became hard to believe that there was still a war to be fought. But, starting from the top and working down, discipline reasserted itself, and the town was organized for all round defence.'[126] In addition, the two Platoons from the 326th Airborne Engineer Battalion that had jumped in with the 501st Parachute Infantry Regiment set about erecting a supplementary crossing over the Zuid Willems Canal, in order to permit two-way traffic when 30 Corps arrived. Men from Lieutenant-Colonel Robert A. Ballard's 2nd Battalion fired on and then captured a German bus loaded with supplies that inadvertently drove into their midst, taking the wounded driver and his four passengers prisoner. The most spectacular incident involved a German light tank of some description and a staff car, which approached a roadblock established on the St. Oedenrode–Veghel road two miles or so west of the latter. The block was manned by Captain Vernon Kraeger's Company G from the 3rd Battalion and the paratroopers initially assumed the vehicles belonged to 30 Corps. On recognising their error they opened fire and scored a direct hit with a Bazooka but the rocket failed to explode and the tank carried on across the Zuid Willems Canal and into Veghel unscathed, despite being peppered with small-arms fire by the surprised paratroopers holding the Canal bridge. Lieutenant-Colonel Kinnard was alerted by radio and deployed Bazooka men to meet the threat, but the tank appears to have turned off to the south between the Canal and the River Aa and disappeared before reaching the 1st Battalion's positions. The staff car was not so lucky. Kraeger's men shot it up after the driver unwisely ignored signals to stop; he was wounded and his passengers, a *Major* and a senior NCO, were captured. Colonel Johnson was reportedly extremely angry over the collective failure to deal with the armoured interloper, and this presumably spurred Kraeger's men to beef up their roadblock by placing logs across the road, with the assistance of some local farmers.[127]

The 501st Regiment's 1st Battalion and a detachment from Regimental HQ had been misdropped three miles downstream near the town of Kameren and Lieutenant-Colonel Kinnard was obliged leave a party of thirty-eight under Captain William G. Burd to gather in equipment bundles and assist Captain David Kingston, the Battalion Medical Officer, with eight jump casualties; they had been gathered in a temporary aid post located in a large stone building near the DZ known locally as the *Kasteel*. Burd's party was attacked by a force of Germans shortly after the remainder of the 1st Battalion had moved off, and the resultant firefight was heard by a Lieutenant Holt moving with the Battalion's rear element. Holt informed Kinnard when he reached Veghel and although initially sceptical, Kinnard sent his Supply Officer, Lieutenant Clark Howell, back to the DZ with a small patrol to clarify matters. Howell duly reported that Burd's party was indeed besieged in the *Kasteel* by a force of around fifty Germans armed with mortars, and his report was subsequently confirmed by stragglers from Burd's party who fetched up at 1st Battalion HQ. Kinnard promptly sought permission to send a company to their aid but Colonel Johnson was unwilling to sanction diverting such a large force and a Platoon led by 1st Lieutenant Louis E. Raffety was despatched shortly before dark instead.[128] The rescuers got as far as Heeswijk, half a mile or so short of the DZ, before bumping into a force of Germans in the darkness. The resulting fight halted the advance and obliged Raffety to order his men to dig in and wait for daylight.[129]

Apart from this, the first part of the night of 17-18 September passed relatively quietly for the remainder of the 501st Parachute Infantry Regiment, with what action there was involving the 3rd Battalion. Lieutenant-Colonel Ewell's men were deployed in and around Eerde, three miles or so west of Veghel, and manning the log roadblock on the adjacent St. Oedenrode–Veghel road. A German staff car and two trucks were ambushed while trying to drive into the town at 19:00 and a German patrol that probed the Airborne perimeter two hours later was driven off, apparently without any US losses. The remainder of the Regiment was deployed to protect the various objectives in and around Veghel proper. Kinnard's 1st Battalion was responsible for the bridges across the River Aa, with Captain Stanfield A. Strach's Company A assigned the road bridge, Company C the railway bridge to the north while Captain Ian B. Hamilton's Company B covered the south-eastern approaches to the town. Kinnard also despatched his Demolitions

Officer, Lieutenant Lee J. Bowers, to destroy a section of railway track a mile east of the railway bridge, thereby pre-empting the problem encountered by the 505th Parachute Infantry Regiment near Groesbeek. Ballard's 2nd Battalion held the Zuid Willems Canal crossings with Companies D and F, commanded by 1st Lieutenant Richard D. Snodgrass and Captain Robert F. Harwick respectively, deployed to protect the road and rail bridges while 1st Lieutenant Frank A. Gregg's Company E covered the north-western approaches astride the Zuid Willems Canal. Gregg's unit appears to have occupied its position after dark, possibly relocating from another site. He and his men were thus unable to properly familiarise themselves with the terrain or register their attached 81mm mortars. The problem was exacerbated by fog that rose from the river and canal after dark.

While the 501st was settling into positions around its various objectives, its German opponents were busy organising their response. As we have seen, *Feldmarschall* Model at *Heeresgruppe B* had set matters in motion at 17:30 with his operation order that gave *Generaloberst* Kurt Student's *1 Fallschirmjäger Armee* responsibility for destroying the US airborne landings in the vicinity of Eindhoven. To this end Student was reinforced with two formations: *Generalleutnant* Walter Poppe's *59 Infanterie Division*, which was regrouping with other elements of *15 Armee* at Tilburg after escaping to German-held territory across the Scheldt Estuary; and Major Berndt-Joachim Freiherr von Maltzahn's *Panzer Brigade 107*, which was en-route to Aachen to help defend the city from the advancing US 1st Army. Student's task was further assisted by an intelligence windfall, in the shape of a briefcase of documents recovered from a Waco CG4 glider that came down near his HQ at Vught. According to Student, the briefcase contained a complete copy of the MARKET operation order that showed 'the dropping zones, the corridor, the objectives – even the names of the divisions involved. Everything!'[130] This seems rather unlikely given the security routinely attached to such sensitive documentation, although all four of the Waco CG4s carrying elements of Browning's Forward Corps HQ were lost on the fly-in, one of which reportedly came down near Vught.[131] On the other hand, seven of the 101st Airborne Division's allotment of seventy Waco CG4s also came down prematurely in Holland, and another source specifically suggests that the information referred only to the 101st Airborne Division and 30 Corps. Whatever the truth of the matter, at 23:30 on 17 September *Heeresgruppe B* issued a report that credited a combination of captured documentation and prisoner interrogation for providing an outline of those Allied formations' proposed tasks, complete with outline orders of battle for each.[132]

It is unclear if it was the result of the captured documentation or a local initiative prompted by the earlier operation order from *Heeresgruppe B*, but the 501st Parachute Infantry Regiment's quiet night came to an abrupt end in the early hours of 18 September. Using the fog to mask their approach, German infantry attacked the elements of Company E deployed east of the Zuid Willems Canal at 02:00, overrunning some outposts and pushing the remainder back to the Company's main line, with a large warehouse becoming the focus of the fighting. In all the Germans launched three separate attacks down the east side of the canal, with the heaviest commencing at 04:00. At one point Lieutenant Joseph C. McGregor's Platoon was driven out of its position and although seriously wounded, McGregor personally covered his men's withdrawal with his Thompson sub-machine gun. By first light E Company had lost seven dead and twenty-six wounded including the Company commander, Lieutenant Gregg, who sustained the first of three wounds he was to suffer in Holland. McGregor was dragged to safety by his men and subsequently awarded the Silver Star for his actions. The fighting east of the Zuid Willems Canal went on all night, and the Germans also launched two additional company-sized attacks against other sectors of the 501st Regiment's Veghel perimeter, which were beaten off.[133]

Things were less fraught back at the main landing area where Major-General Taylor had initially set up his Division command post in the woods to the south of DZ C, manned by thirty-one signalmen who had also jumped with the first parachute lift. This little band was augmented within an hour with the arrival of other Division HQ elements with the glider lift, and radio contact was established with all three of the Division's three Parachute Infantry Regiments shortly after 14:00. By 21:00 Division HQ had been relocated to a more substantial location in a school building in Son proper, and field telephone lines had been run out to the 502nd and 506th Regiments' locations and the Division Artillery HQ. The major drawback was a lack of communications with 30 Corps, initially due to the non-arrival of gliders carrying a detachment of British signallers. Taylor's signallers nonetheless managed to establish communications with the 101st Airborne Division's rear HQ in England, which was in turn able to relay communications with British 2nd Army HQ, but no firm information on 30 Corps' progress was gained and this remained the case when direct contact was established with British 2nd Army later in the night. The British GHQ Liaison Regiment detachment attached to Taylor's HQ did succeed in making direct contact with 30 Corps HQ via their dedicated PHANTOM net, but their signal was not recognised by their opposite number with 30 Corps because of a coding mix-up.[134]

It was also business as usual for Major William E. Barfield and the 326th Airborne Medical Company. The Company's first increment, carried in six Waco CG4s and consisting of fifty-two men including members of the Auxiliary Surgical Team equipped with two Jeeps and two trailers, landed without incident on LZ W at 13:45. A temporary aid post established at the southern edge of the landing area was receiving casualties by 15:00, and surgical operations were being carried out in the Auxiliary Team's two specially equipped tents by 17:00. The Company was relocated to a hospital building in Son by 19:00, and by midnight a total of 107 assorted casualties had been treated.[135]

Most of the remainder of the 101st Airborne Division also enjoyed a relatively quiet night. At Son Company C of the 326th Airborne Engineer Battalion had fabricated a footbridge across the Wilhelmina Canal within two hours of the bridge being blown, but the resultant structure could only support a few men at a time and it took until midnight to pass the whole of the 506th Parachute Infantry Regiment across to the south bank. Colonel Sink was consequently unable to move on Eindhoven at 20:00 as planned, and he postponed the move altogether after Dutch Resistance reports of a German regiment recently arriving in the city; the information was accurate and referred to a *kampfgruppe* from *Ausbildungs und Ersatz Regiment* 'Hermann Göring', elements of which had been occupying the buildings at the south end of the Son bridge when the crossing was demolished.[136] Sink therefore ordered his Regiment to establish a defensive perimeter around the village of Bokt a mile south of the Wilhelmina Canal and wait for daylight. The opportunity for rest was spoiled in the early hours by heavy rain, although some of Sink's men coped better than others. HQ Company commandeered a large barn, and Privates Donald Hoobler and David Webster from Company E negotiated a night in the kitchen of a nearby farmhouse by trading cigarettes and D-Ration chocolate for jars of preserved fruit with the farmer.[137] To the north of the Canal Lieutenant-Colonel Cassidy and the 1st Battalion 502nd Parachute Infantry Regiment spent an equally quiet night in St. Oedenrode, as did Regimental HQ and the 2nd Battalion protecting the landing area for the second lift.

The exception to this general quietude was Company H and latterly the rest of Lieutenant-Colonel Robert G. Cole's 3rd Battalion 502nd Parachute Infantry Regiment. The former was tasked to secure the road and bridges over the Wilhelmina Canal just south of Best but a navigation error brought Captain Robert E. Jones and his men to a crossroads just east of the town where they were drawn into a prolonged fight with *FlaK Abteilung 424* and then a convoy of reinforcements from *59 Infanterie Division*. As word of Company H's fight filtered back to Battalion and then Regimental HQ it rapidly became apparent that securing the Best bridges was too much for a single Company and at 18:00 Colonel Michaelis ordered Lieutenant-Colonel Cole to take the remainder of the 3rd Battalion to assist. Cole appears to have followed the same route from DZ B but was also brought to a halt a mile or so short of Best, this time by mortar and artillery fire that prevented further movement. As the light was starting to fade he therefore ordered his men to dig in for the night and, mindful of the urgency of the situation, radioed

Jones and ordered him to reinforce one of his platoons with the machine-gun and engineer elements and send it to secure the bridges immediately. Jones therefore broke contact, withdrew south-east into the edge of the Zonsche Forest, ordered his men to reorganise and dig in and at around sunset despatched Lieutenant Edward L. Wierzbowski's 2nd Platoon south as ordered. Company H remained isolated in its new location for the remainder of the night, apart from radio contact with Battalion HQ, as a number of patrols sent out by Cole failed to make contact in the darkness; three small patrols despatched by Jones in Wierzbowski's wake were similarly unsuccessful. The Germans had no such difficulty and frequent contacts throughout the night cost Company H a total of thirty-nine casualties.[138]

Lieutenant Wierzbowski was meanwhile experiencing problems of his own. Moving in pitch darkness and then heavy rain was a time-consuming process, made even slower by the need for stealth when crossing the frequent firebreaks in the woods to avoid alerting German machine-guns firing on fixed lines. As a result, the paratroopers did not reach the Wilhelmina Canal until 21:00, and then some 500 yards east of the road bridge; the railway bridge lay three-quarters of a mile beyond. The Platoon spent another hour crawling stealthily along the dyke before Wierzbowski called a halt while he scouted the approaches to the bridge with his point man, Private Joe E. Mann. The pair became cut off by an unwitting German sentry and while they remained undetected other Germans somehow spotted their companions. Around thirty minutes after Wierzbowski had gone forward the remainder of the Platoon was attacked with a number of stick grenades thrown across the canal followed by small-arms, mortar and artillery fire. A number of men began digging in at the base of the dyke but some had become restive during their commander's absence and promptly fled across the open ground for the shelter of the woods to the north. However, Wierzbowski and Mann were able to rejoin the Platoon under cover of the enemy fire, and the Lieutenant led the group back sixty yards along the canal before ordering them to dig in. A swift headcount revealed that the reinforced 2nd Platoon had been reduced to fifteen men and three officers, equipped with a single .30 machine gun with 500 rounds, a Bazooka with five rockets and a mortar of undetermined calibre, likely a 60mm piece, with six rounds. The German mortar and artillery fire finally ceased at 03:00 and Wierzbowski and his somewhat reduced band hunkered down in their muddy foxholes to await daylight in the continuing rain.[139]

By daylight on Monday 18 September Operation MARKET was thus proceeding fairly well, with crossings over six of the eight major watercourses in the Airborne Corridor secured intact within eighteen hours of the landings. At the northern end of the corridor one of the 1st Parachute Brigade's battalions had secured the north end of the Arnhem road bridge over the Lower Rhine and a second battalion was moving to reinforce. In the centre the 82nd Airborne Division had secured the Groesbeek Heights as specifically ordered by Browning, along with the bridge over the River Maas at Grave, one intact bridge and two crossing sites over the Maas-Waal Canal and had penetrated to within a mile of the Nijmegen road bridge. In the south the 101st Airborne Division had secured five bridges over the River Dommel in St. Oedenrode, a further four across the Zuid Willems Canal and River Aa in and around Veghel, and had a Battalion moving to secure the additional road and rail crossing over the Wilhelmina Canal near Son. Virtually complete surprise had been achieved over the German defenders, although the reactions of their higher command levels had been extremely efficient and their counter-measures were starting to make themselves felt, notably at the western side of the 1st Airborne Division's landing area, in Nijmegen and at Veghel and Best. Perhaps most serious was the 101st Airborne Division's failure to capture the first bridge in the chain, over the Wilhelmina Canal near Best, but the site had been secured in readiness for the bridging train accompanying the lead elements of 30 Corps. The problem was that the GARDEN ground advance was not mirroring the speed or efficiency of the airborne troops in the corridor.

***

The Guards Armoured Division's initial objective was the town of Valkenswaard, seven miles from the Start Line, and despite intense fighting with *Fallschirmjäger Ausbildungs Regiment* Hoffmann and *Luftwaffe Strafbataillon 6*, Shermans from the 2nd Irish Guards' No. 3 Squadron had almost reached a small bridge across the River Dommel a mile short of the town just after 16:00 on 17 September. However, the advance was then delayed for an hour-and-a-half while the British lead elements withdrew 500 yards to permit the final stage of the artillery barrage to be repeated to cover the advance across the final 300 yards of open ground, and the bridge was not secured until 18:30. The 2nd Irish Guards Nos. 1 and 2 Squadrons then passed across the bridge and pushed on into Valkenswaard, entering the partially burning town an hour later at dusk to an ecstatic reception from the locals.[140] There does not appear to have been any serious resistance, although the commander of the leading Troop was, perhaps understandably, reluctant to push too far in the gathering darkness; Lieutenant Brian Wilson from the 2nd Company 3rd Irish Guards was travelling with his Platoon on the decks of a Troop of Shermans and overheard a running commentary on his vehicle's radio that reflected the reticence of the lead Troop commander being 'equalled by the insistence of his commanding officer to get a move on'.[141] According to the 2nd (Armoured) Battalion Irish Guards War Diary its Shermans reached the main square at 20:30, capturing a half-track and thirty prisoners in the process.[142]

Lieutenant Wilson and the 2nd Company had started the advance travelling in their trucks at the rear of the Irish Guards Group column. After taking a detour around five knocked-out Shermans, Wilson picked up Lieutenant Edward Ryder from his Battalion and five of his men who had been travelling on one of the knocked-out tanks. The column then came to a stop at some point after 17:00 on a stretch of open road near four abandoned 88mm *FlaK* 36 guns belonging to *schwere FlaK Abteilung 602* and Wilson watched with interest as a Lieutenant Isitt from the 2nd Irish Guards inadvertently fired one of the pieces while trying to remove the breech block to prevent it being put back into action. The gun was fortunately pointing in a safe direction but the recoil struck one of Isitt's men, injuring him in the face and shoulder and the report caused some alarm at the nearby 2nd Battalion HQ.[143] At some point around dusk Wilson and his men transferred onto the rear deck of a number of Shermans, possibly from the 2nd Irish Guards 3rd Squadron, for the final stage of the journey to Valkenswaard and in addition to the exchange between the lead Troop Commander and his commander he also overheard the commander of the 2nd Irish Guards, Lieutenant-Colonel Giles Vandeleur, cancelling an artillery barrage on Valkenswaard because the Gunners were allegedly 'too bloody slow'. Although they were untroubled by the enemy, Wilson's journey proved eventful when his tank ran off the road on the approaches to a bridge and became stuck on an embanked incline. Concerned lest he become separated from the remainder of his Platoon and spurred on by shouted instructions from his Company commander to get a move on, Wilson tried unsuccessfully to flag down other vehicles in the darkness, including a half-track carrying the Division's CRA, which gave him short shrift. In the meantime the tank crew managed to regain the road by piling rocks and earth beneath their vehicle's right track, and Wilson was soon reunited with the remainder of his Company digging in on the north side of Valkenswaard's main square.[144] In all, the day's fighting had cost the 2nd Irish Guards eight dead, an undetermined number of wounded and missing and nine tanks; the 3rd Irish Guards lost eight killed and eighteen wounded.[145]

Wilson need not have been worried about being left behind because despite having covered only around half the scheduled distance by nightfall on 17 September, Guards Armoured Division HQ ordered the Irish Guards Group to halt for the night at Valkenswaard and duly informed 30 Corps HQ of its intention. The Corps commander, Lieutenant-General Brian Horrocks, approved the decision, ostensibly because the Guards Armoured Division 'had had a tough fight'.[146] The order went out to the 2nd Irish Guards at 22:00, with the rider that the advance was to be resumed at 07:00 the following morning.[147] Leaving aside that only part of the Guards Armoured Division had been involved in the fighting and that nine tanks and sixteen fatalities spread across two separate Battalions was arguably not especially compelling evidence of a collective 'tough fight', the most immediate reason for the halt was the failure of the attached units from the 50th Division, the 1st Dorsets and 2nd Devons, to move up and take over responsibility for Valkenswaard from the Irish Guards Group as planned.[148] The 2nd Devons had crossed the start line with the 2nd Irish Guards at 14:35, with half the Battalion deployed on each side of the axis advance. The increment deployed on the western side of the Hasselt–Eindhoven highway made good progress and had reached its initial objective, the hamlet of Heuvel eight miles from the start line and five miles short of Valkenswaard, by 17:30. However, the eastern increment became bogged down clearing woods on their side of the road with the assistance of tanks from the 15th/19th Hussars and as the task was only partially complete by dusk, both halves of the Battalion dug in for the night at their separate locations. The 1st Dorsets remained in their positions near La Colonie until 17:00, when it was supposed to move up to a junction on the Eindhoven road near Heuvel to pass though the 2nd Devons and lead the way into Valkenswaard. Severe traffic congestion prevented the head of the Battalion column from reaching the junction until 18:30, and the tail did not arrive until 21:00 and the Battalion commander was obliged to use a motorcycle to navigate his way through 'double and treble banked traffic' to report the situation to the Irish Guards Group HQ. As further forward movement was virtually impossible in those conditions, the 1st Dorsets were ordered to dig in for night ready to resume the move at daylight on 18 September, in the meantime providing security for 90 Field Regiment RA, which was also caught in the traffic jam moving forward to a new firing location.[149]

The decision to halt for the night in Valkenswaard puzzled friend and foe alike. *1 Fallschirmjäger Armee* HQ, fully aware that it had no means to block the British from continuing their advance on Eindhoven, found the hiatus 'incomprehensible'.[150] Lieutenant Wilson from the 3rd Irish Guards expressed similar sentiments writing fifty-four years after the event: 'It is a sad reflection that we should never have stayed the night in Valkenswaard…Having broken the crust of German opposition…and achieved surprise with the speed of advance, it made no sense to stop, bearing in mind the distance yet to be covered to Arnhem and the river crossings ahead. Another opportunity lost.'[151] Lieutenant-General Horrocks subsequently justified the halt on the grounds that 30 Corps' tanks required maintenance owing to previous hard fighting, but this was highly questionable.[152] Horrocks was presumably referring to the 2nd Irish Guards, given that unit had seen the bulk of the action on 17 September, but Lieutenant-Colonel Vandeleur's unit had been withdrawn across the Albert Canal on 12 September and had thus had the better part of a week to carry out maintenance before GARDEN commenced.[153] In addition, the US-built M4 Sherman tank with which they were equipped was famously reliable with minimal upkeep and should have been more than capable of operating for forty-eight hours without significant crew maintenance.[154]

There was a little more to it, however. The Guards Armoured Division's halt in Valkenswaard was not made of its own volition. Major-General Alan Adair was in fact conforming to Operational Instructions issued by 30 Corps on 15 September, which specifically forbade movement on the main axis of advance after dark, and it is worth quoting the relevant paragraph in full:

There will be NO movement on the main axis during the hours of darkness. The only exceptions to this rule will be i. tactical necessity [or] ii. when a Group Commander is satisfied that his Group can complete its move without disrupting traffic arrangements within two hours of last light. Groups leaguering for the night will probably have to do so on the main road owing to the nature of the ground, though it may be possible for them to pull off into fields adjacent in some places. If units leave the road for leaguering they will leave a representative on the road to indicate the point at which the tail of the column was when it started to leave the road. Following serials will NOT pass this point except under provision of i. and ii. Above [original emphasis].[155]

The order was not disseminated solely to units directly involved in the drive north to Arnhem but also to those operating in a support of the main attack; a copy appears in the War Diary of the 15th/19th Hussars, the British 11th Armoured Division's reconnaissance regiment tasked to secure the right flank of the advance, for example.[156] The existence and widespread acceptance of this instruction explains the seeming equanimity with which the 1st Dorsets and 2nd Devons simply settled down in place with the onset of darkness, despite being collectively well short of their objectives. It also casts a different light on the Guards Armoured Division's rather optimistic intention to 'reach the area north of Eindhoven 4321 before dark on 17th September in preparation for advance at first light on the following day, 18th September'.[157] This would have required the Irish Guards Group to fight through around fifteen miles of German-occupied territory within five hours to link up with the 101st Airborne Division. Despite its uncompromising wording it may have been intended more as a best-case scenario rather than a concrete statement of intent, with the implicit assumption that the advance would simply be temporarily curtailed whenever darkness fell en route.

This is supported by the behaviour of the Irish Guards Group on arrival in Valkenswaard. As we have seen, when Lieutenant Wilson caught up with his parent 2nd Company, all ranks were busy setting in for the night in the town's main square amidst the usual crowd of Dutch civilians enthusiastically greeting their liberators. The crowd steadfastly ignored Wilson's suggestions to take shelter indoors for their own safety until someone noticed that an abandoned German horse-drawn wagon was loaded with bread, butter, cigars, flour, potatoes and sausages; it was swiftly looted and the crowd dispersed rapidly with their booty while Wilson liberated a few loaves of gingerbread for his men. Wilson then retired to the house selected for his Platoon HQ and enjoyed a short sleep in an armchair before being woken by his servant on the arrival of hot food, presumably prepared by the Battalion cooks. Nor was this atypical. Wilson was roused some time later by his Company OC and ordered to take his Platoon across the town to reinforce the Battalion's 3rd Company, which was allegedly under pressure from German troops equipped with half-tracks. On arrival he reported to the 3rd Company HQ to find that the officers 'had obviously decided that there was no further threat. They had just finished dinner and invited me to join them. The bottles were empty, however, and I declined as this was not a moment to be convivial.' With his presence unnecessary, Wilson led his men back to their original positions in the main square where they were finally able to settle down and sleep at 03:30.[158] This does not suggest a unit unexpectedly stymied and looking to push on urgently to the aid of beleaguered Airborne troops, but rather a unit carrying out a routine and possibly pre-planned stop for the night.

Horrocks' thinking in issuing the no move after dark order is curious, although he was merely reflecting the British dictum that tanks only fought by day and used the hours of darkness for maintenance, rearming and crew rest. The origins of this practice are unclear but it dated back to at least January 1941, when Major-General Richard O'Connor, commanding the Western Desert Force, complained of the 'disinclination of [British] armoured forces to take any action at night'. O'Connor's criticism was prompted by an unauthorised night halt by the 4th Armoured Brigade that permitted the Italian *Brigata Corazzata Speciale* to escape from a planned trap near Mechili in Libya.[159] As Horrocks held three separate Corps commands in North Africa between August 1942 and June 1943, he presumably became familiar with the practice at that time. Whenever it began, the cessation was virtually standard operating procedure in Normandy,[160] although there were numerous counter-examples on both sides of the fence by that time. Panther tanks from *SS Panzer Regiment* 12 spearheaded an attack on Canadian troops holding the village of Bretteville l'Orgueilleuse on the night of 8 June 1944 for example, which was stalled owing to a lack of infantry after the Panthers succeeded in penetrating the Canadian defensive perimeter.[161] On a larger scale, Operation TOTALIZE successfully launched four armoured columns assembled from elements of the Canadian 2nd Division and 51st Highland Division along narrow fixed lines of advance against German positions on the Verrières Ridge south of

Caen at 23:30 on 7 August 1944; and more pertinently still, the 11th Armoured Division carried out a night advance to Amiens on the night of 30 August 1944 during the breakout from the Vernon bridgehead across the River Seine.[162] Significantly, the Guards Armoured Division had adhered to the fight by day and halt by night dictum during its own advance from the Seine across Picardy and the Pas de Calais to Brussels.

To be fair, Horrocks had never worked with Airborne Forces and his injunction may have resulted from an imperfect understanding of the realities and urgency of Airborne operations. Whatever his motivation, with dusk at around 19:00 and dawn at around 06:30, he was in effect imposing a mandatory twelve-hour halt in every twenty-four hours on the British advance. This was much more in line with a standard, business-as-usual advance as executed by the Guards Armoured Division in its advance to the Albert Canal and thence the Meuse-Escaut Canal, rather than one to relieve beleaguered Airborne troops before they were overwhelmed. It is therefore difficult to reconcile Horrocks' order with MARKET GARDEN generally and more specifically with his stated intent that 30 Corps should reach Arnhem within forty-eight hours made at his 16 September briefing in the cinema at Bourg Leopold, although his 'if possible' rider is more significant than was realised at the time or thereafter.[163] With 30 Corps hobbled in this way, time was to be an even more crucial element in an operation that already hinged on that factor.

The Irish Guards Group was an hour and eleven miles behind schedule when its tanks rolled into Valkenswaard's main square at 20:30 on the night of 17 September, and Horrocks' no movement after dark order extended this shortfall to twelve hours at a stroke. It remained to be seen if the Guards Armoured Division would prove capable of moving the following day with sufficient despatch to make up at least some of the lost time.

D Plus 1

07:00 to 14:00 Monday 18 September 1944

While the Guards Armoured Division was halted for the night in Valkenswaard and along the road leading north from the Neerpelt bridgeheads, the Germans facing them were busy trying to create some order. Their task was complicated by the fact that not all British units may have been as quiescent as the Guards. *Hauptsturmführer* Friedrich Richter's 150-strong portion of *Kampfgruppe* Heinke had been ordered to withdraw six miles east to the village of Budel in the late afternoon of 17 September, after finding itself isolated on the eastern fringe of the British breakout. At 04:30 the following morning British infantry accompanied by four Sherman tanks penetrated the village past sleeping *SS* sentries while other tanks moved east around Budel to cut the line of retreat to the east. The ensuing fight allegedly lasted for several hours and cost the SS sixty-four killed, wounded and missing before the survivors eventually broke contact and reorganised a mile or so outside Budel before withdrawing a further seven miles east to Weert.[1]

Despite being well aware of the British preparations for the coming blow, the speed and violence of the assault created near total confusion on the German side, worsened by a general shortage of communications equipment. *Kampfgruppe* Walther lost both its internal communication links and contact with *1 Fallschirmjäger Armee* almost immediately, and the latter was therefore unable to effectively control its subordinate units or form a clear picture of the developing situation. Thus it was not until 04:15 on the morning of 18 September that *1 Fallschirmjäger Armee* felt able to inform *Heeresgruppe B* that 'there is no doubt about it, the enemy has broken through'.[2] As we have seen, the *SS* units making up *Kampfgruppe* Heinke had been obliged to withdraw eastward away from the British corridor forming around the Eindhoven highway, apart from the surviving *Jagdpanzer* IVs from *Hauptsturmführer* Franz Roestel's *SS Panzerjäger Abteilung 10*, which had withdrawn north from Borkel in the face of the British advance; they may have been accompanied by the survivors of *Hauptsturmführer* Segler's *Kampfgruppe* from *SS Panzergrenadier Regiments 19*.[3] On the other side of the highway *Fallschirmjäger Regiment 6*'s east flank was left hanging wide open, prompting *Oberstleutnant* von der Heydte to withdraw west in an effort to establish contact with *Generalleutnant* Kurt Chill's *Kampfgruppe* from *85 Infanterie Division*; he was accompanied by the remnants of *Luftwaffe Strafbataillon 6* and *Fallschirmjäger Ausbildungs Regiment* Hoffmann's II *Bataillon*, which had become separated from its parent formation. The withdrawal was made without authorisation, however, and at 08:52 on 18 September Chill was ordered to take von der Heydte's unit 'firmly in hand' and deny him the opportunity for any further such withdrawals. *Fallschirmjäger Regiment 6* and its accompanying survivors were formally placed under Chill's command later that day.[4]

In fact, *1 Fallschirmjäger Armee* was mistaken in its assertion that the British had achieved a breakthrough. The Irish Guards Group had been on the verge of so doing when it entered Valkenswaard at around 20:00, as the British attack had fully pierced the German force blocking the Eindhoven highway and pushed the units flanking the road aside. Consequently, when 30 Corps stopped the advance for the night there was effectively no organised German presence between Valkenswaard and Eindhoven, the suburbs of which lay just six miles or so to the north. However, in the course of the night surviving elements of the blocking force made their way north, in some instances avoiding British troops on the fringes of the breakthrough, and regrouped at Aalst, three miles north of Valkenswaard. Thus by dawn on Monday 18 September 1944 the remnants of two of *Fallschirmjäger Ausbildungs Regiment* Hoffmann's *bataillonen* were deployed along the southern edge of Aalst, supported by a light *flak* platoon equipped with 20mm guns and, according to one source, eleven *PaK* 40 75mm anti-tank guns without prime movers. It is unclear where these pieces came from, as all eight of *Regiment* Hoffmann's anti-tank guns had been destroyed south of Valkenswaard by the British opening bombardment, and British accounts do not refer to encountering such equipment at Aalst. They may have belonged to *SS Panzerjäger Abteilung 10*, which brought up to a dozen *PaK* 40s from Hasselt on or around 6 September 1944, although how they arrived in Aalst without prime movers is unclear. The new blocking position was also supported by one or possibly two surviving *Jagdpanzer* IV tank destroyers from SS *Panzerjäger* Abteilung 10, which were deployed east of the highway covering the approach to Aalst. Command of this depleted band devolved to *Major* Kerutt, as *Oberstleutnant* von Hoffmann had been killed during the previous day's fighting.[5]

The renewed British advance north from Valkenswaard did not have any pre-planned artillery preparation and bad weather precluded close air support. The Irish Guards Group was again assigned to lead off at 07:00, although interestingly 30 Corps' records refer to the advance beginning an hour earlier.[6] In the event neither time was correct because the only element of the Guards Armoured Division to move off at or around the allotted time seems to have been the Division's reconnaissance force, the 2nd Household Cavalry Regiment; Lieutenant Wilson recalled their armoured cars passing through Valkenswaard's main square at some point after 07:00.[7] Whatever time the Household Cavalry left Valkenswaard, Major A. W. P. P. Herbert's C Squadron appears to have been detailed to scout ahead of the Irish Guards Group toward Aalst.[8] In the meantime the Irish Guards Group was somewhat tardier in resuming the advance. After being roused from their billets Lieutenant Wilson and the rest of the 3rd Irish Guards climbed aboard their troop-carrying vehicles, which had been brought forward and marshalled in Valkenswaard's main square and adjacent streets. The Battalion appear to have been ready to move at 07:00 but was delayed by the late arrival of the 1st Dorsets, who were to take over responsibility for the town's defence.[9] The Dorsets had resumed the advance at first light moving first to the village of Hoek, just east of the Eindhoven highway opposite the 2nd Devons at Heuvel, four miles south of Valkenswaard and on the line it was supposed to have reached the previous day. As a result, the 1st Dorsets did not reach Valkenswaard until 09:25, although the records suggest that the 3rd Irish Guards actually moved off twenty-five minutes before the Dorsets finally arrived.[10] The delay may have been the result of a 'considerable traffic jam' on the small bridge over the River Dommel a mile south of Valkenswaard. Recognising that this was likely to become a recurring problem, Lieutenant-General Horrocks issued orders for another bridge to be constructed at the site, with the stipulation that Guards Armoured Division's assets were on no account to be diverted to the task.[11]

The Sherman tanks of the 2nd Irish Guards also appear to have been ready to leave Valkenswaard as planned at 07:00 but their advance was delayed by reports from the 2nd Household Cavalry that Aalst was occupied by German self-propelled guns and a *Jagdpanther*; the report was confirmed by a telephone call to the station master at Aalst, who claimed to have seen the armoured vehicles near the village church.[12] The self-propelled guns were presumably *Hauptsturmführer* Roestel's surviving *Jagdpanzer* IVs but the provenance of the *Jagdpanther* is unclear, not least because German sources do not refer to the presence of such a vehicle in Aalst or the vicinity at that time. It is therefore possible that the 2nd Irish Guards were influenced, consciously or unconsciously, by the experience of the 1st Coldstream Guards at the hands of the first *Jagdpanther* encountered by the Guards Armoured Division during the fighting at Heppen ten days earlier.[13] Whether or not they were, the 2nd Irish Guards' No.2 Squadron did not move off from Valkenswaard until 10:00, three hours after the advance was supposed to have begun, and the timing accords with German reports of British armoured columns appearing in front of Aalst at 10:20.[14] The ubiquitous Lance-Sergeant Cowan from No.2 Squadron added to his previous day's tally by knocking out another German self-propelled gun, while the 3rd Irish Guards pushed *Major* Kerutt and the remnants of *Fallschirmjäger Ausbildungs Regiment* Hoffmann out of their positions in the southern outskirts of Aalst. In the process the 2nd Irish Guards were able to spare Lieutenant William MacFetridge's Troop of Shermans to carry Lieutenant Wilson's platoon to a flanking position guarding a decrepit bridge on the eastern fringe of Aalst, where they spent an uneventful morning; Wilson was able to enjoy a wash and shave courtesy of a Dutch housewife, and watched British artillery reducing a church-like building to rubble, presumably in support of the main advance.[15]

Aalst appears to have been cleared by the late morning but further advance was blocked when armoured cars from the 2nd Household Cavalry's C Squadron ran into four 88mm guns, possibly from *FlaK* Brigade 18, emplaced around a bridge over the River Dommel just north of the town. Artillery was called down but by midday the German guns had proved impervious and Major Herbert was instructed to reconnoitre a route for the Irish Guards Group to bypass the block to the east, while the 2nd Irish Guards' No.2 Squadron 'exchanged shots with the 88s'.[16] In the meantime, two additional moves to speed up the advance were initiated. The Grenadier Guards Group was ordered to bypass Aalst and Eindhoven to the west and move directly to Son, while the 32nd Guards Brigade was instructed to move to Leende, four miles east of Valkenswaard, and then advance north to Helmond via Heeze and Geldrop. The Grenadier's route was scouted by Major F. E. B. Wignall's B Squadron, 2nd Household Cavalry and so successfully that one two-vehicle patrol reached the Wilhelmina Canal at 12:30 and made contact with the platoon from the 506th Parachute Infantry Regiment guarding the Son bridge site. The paratroopers were accompanied by a platoon from the 326th Airborne Engineer Battalion which had been tasked to prepare the site for the arrival of the British relief force. They were able to provide the Household Cavalrymen with details of the gap, bank conditions and bridging equipment necessary to effect repairs, which was relayed back to 30 Corps; the latter in turn ordered a Bailey bridge unit forward from the bridging train concentration area at Bourg Leopold to Valkenswaard in readiness to move to Son as soon as the route was secured.[17] The Grenadier Guards Group were not so fortunate. The area to the west of the Eindhoven highway was riven with numerous small watercourses and while the bridges across them were capable of supporting light armoured vehicles many were unable to support the weight of a Sherman tank, which severely retarded the rate of advance; it took until late afternoon for the Grenadier Guards Group to reach a point level with Aalst. The Welsh Guards Group led the attempted by-pass to the east and appears to have advanced for six miles or so through Heeze before finding Geldrop 'strongly held' by the Germans. This and Dutch civilian reports that Helmond was also 'well garrisoned' led Guards Armoured Division HQ to order the 32nd Guards Brigade to abandon the eastern loop and return to the main axis of advance north from Valkenswaard.[18]

Thus by the afternoon of 18 September the Guards Armoured Division had taken seven hours, over half the available daylight, to push forward around two miles. This might have been understandable had the advance encountered stiff German opposition as 30 Corps' War Diary claimed, but this does not appear to have been the case.[19] As we have seen the Guards Armoured Division was faced by the remnants of a single battalion from a *Fallschirmjäger* replacement training unit, up to ninety per cent of whom were partially or untrained *Luftwaffe* ground personnel pressed into the infantry role, supported by two *Jagdpanzer* tank destroyers and possibly a handful of SS troops, a single alleged *Jagdpanther* and up to a dozen towed anti-tank guns, the majority of which had been mauled by the initial British attack, the crews of which had spent a sleepless night withdrawing north to Aalst. Perhaps understandably *Major* Kerutt's men no not appear to have put up especially stubborn resistance, considering that the British advance had passed through Aalst to bump the German gun emplacements covering the Dommel crossing north of the town within two hours of the 2nd Irish Guards tanks finally moving off from Valkenswaard at 10:00. Neither do the defenders appear to have inflicted any losses on their assailants, for the 3rd Irish Guards War Diary does not record any casualties for 18 September, although the numbers of killed, wounded and missing appear at the end of daily entries before and after that date.[20] Similarly, the 2nd Irish Guards War Diary does not record any casualties or tank losses for that day, although the Guards Armoured Division War Diary refers to a single, unspecified tank casualty.[21] It is difficult to reconcile all this with the urgency of the situation, and it is equally difficult to avoid concluding that collectively the Guards Armoured Division did not really try very hard in the morning and early afternoon of Monday 18 September.

***

Having spent a rainy night at Bokt, a mile south of the Wilhelmina Canal, Colonel Sink's 506th Parachute Infantry Regiment resumed the advance on Eindhoven under clear skies in the early morning of 18 September. Lieutenant-Colonel Horton's 3rd Battalion took the lead with Companies H and I deployed on either side of the Eindhovenseweg and despite coming under German small-arms fire within six hundred yards of the start line the paratroopers made good progress for two miles or so, pushing back or overrunning and killing several small groups of German troops. However, as Horton's men approached the suburb of Woensel their progress was halted by two 88mm guns emplaced among the houses firing directly along the line of the Eindhovenseweg. The guns were part of *Kampfgruppe* Koeppel from *FlaK Brigade 18*, which appears to have been tasked to defend Eindhoven and deployed a number of infantry and mortars to cover the guns. A sniper lodged in Woensel church tower shot and killed Captain John W. Kiley, the 3rd Battalion's Intelligence Officer before being despatched by a bazooka rocket.[22] Deciding that a frontal assault on the German position was likely to be too costly, Sink ordered Lieutenant-Colonel Strayer's 2nd Battalion to move out to the left and continue the advance into Eindhoven, and to try to flank the German guns holding up the 3rd Battalion in the process.

Lieutenant-Colonel Strayer assigned the task of attacking the guns to his Company F, which in turn delegated it to its lead element, Lieutenant Russell Hall's 2nd Platoon, via the Battalion Executive Officer, Captain Charles G. Shettle, who also introduced Russell to a Dutch local who had offered to act as a guide. On the Dutchman's advice Lieutenant Hall infiltrated his men through a block of houses without being detected, capturing three Germans in the process. While crossing a street, Staff Sergeant John H. Taylor and Private Robert W. Sherwood found themselves facing one of the enemy guns located at a crossroads 150 yards away. Taylor emptied his M1 Garand at a party of six Germans approaching the gun, wounding two before the 88mm put three rounds into the building in which the two Americans had gone to ground. After finding a new firing position Sherwood responded with two rifle grenades, one of which landed just five yards behind the gun, followed by another fired by Private Homer Smith from 2nd Squad across the street. In order to remain behind cover Smith was obliged to fire from the shoulder rather than bracing his rifle butt against the ground as recommended, but the grenade scored a direct hit on the gun. The rifle grenadiers were then joined by mortar squad leader Sergeant Frank D. Griffin, who scored another direct hit on the gun with his 60mm mortar despite lacking a bipod and firing with the tube braced between his knees. This blew a German officer off his feet. Taylor then shot the officer in the leg as he scrambled into a nearby house. Another rifle grenade from Sherwood wounded all ten Germans sheltering within. In their haste Lieutenant Hall's men were unaware they were actually facing two guns, until the second pumped three rounds into nearby buildings as the first was knocked out. However, Lieutenant Robert Pardue and the 2nd Squad had spotted the new threat and were already manoeuvring to deal with it. Private Smith fired several rifle grenades and while none actually hit the gun, they were close enough to persuade the gun crew to abandon their weapon after trying to blow the breech with a hand-grenade. Several of the fourteen-strong crew were shot by the pursuing paratroopers as they attempted to flee across nearby sugar beet fields. In addition to the two 88mm guns, the fight cost the German defenders thirteen dead and forty-one prisoners; there were two US casualties.[23]

Overwhelming the gun position was complete by mid-morning. In the meantime the 2nd Battalion had continued pressing into Eindhoven while the rest of the 506th Regiment paused in Woensel. At 11:30 Colonel Sink's signallers, who had set up their equipment in the bazooka-damaged tower of Woensel church, established contact with 30 Corps and learned that the Guards Armoured Division was still bogged down north of Valkenswaard, the first definite word the US airborne troops had received on the progress of the ground advance. At around midday Major-General Taylor arrived from his HQ in Son and on learning of the contact he instructed Sink to inform 30 Corps of the destruction of the Son bridge and request that Bailey bridging equipment be added to the head of the ground column, before enquiring about the 506th's progress into Eindhoven. Colonel Charles H. Chase, Sink's Executive Officer ensconced with the signallers in the church tower, responded by relaying Lieutenant-Colonel Strayer's reply: 'We hold the center of town and we are sitting on the four bridges over the Dommel River.' Taken aback by the unexpected confirmation that his Division's initial mission had been completed with such relative ease, Taylor insisted on climbing the church tower and getting confirmation from Strayer in person.[24] Despite fears of a large German presence in Eindhoven the 2nd Battalion encountered only scattered resistance, largely from individuals armed with rifles. One of them did manage to seriously wound Lieutenant Robert Brewer from Company E in the throat as he unwisely exposed his officer status at the head of his Platoon.[25] *Kampfgruppe* Koeppel maintained a running commentary to *FlaK Brigade 18* as the US paratroopers pressed into the city, which stopped abruptly after reporting that contact had been lost with an unnamed unit and requesting orders for *Panzerabwehr Gruppe* Grunewald.[26] Colonel Sink therefore lost no time moving the 1st and 3rd Battalions of the 506th Regiment into the city where, as liberators of the first Dutch city to be freed from German occupation, they received an even more frenzied reception from the local populace. There was also a palpable difference in the atmosphere, as one US officer noted: 'The reception was terrific…[but the]…air seemed to reek with hate for the German.'[27] In addition to Taylor's surprised approval, the icing on the cake for Sink's Regiment at this point was its first physical contact with the GARDEN relief force, in the shape of the two-vehicle patrol from the 2nd Household Cavalry that arrived at the demolished Son bridge at 12:30.

Five miles west along the Wilhelmina Canal daylight brought little comfort to Lieutenant Wierzbowski and his eighteen-strong band from the 3rd Battalion 502nd Parachute Infantry Regiment, who had dug in between the Canal dyke and a parallel road after an unsuccessful attempt to reach the bridge carrying the Eindhovenseweg Zuid road the previous night. The position was alongside an area of loading derricks while the bridge, a 100-foot-long single-span concrete affair, lay sixty yards to the west, with what Wierzbowski identified as a barracks, surrounded with occupied trenches, situated just twenty yards south of the bridge. Worse, an 88mm gun emplacement was visible 150 yards east up the canal with an ammunition and spares dump located nearby, and more German troops were dug in eighty yards to the north on the other side of the road; the latter fired on any attempt to move toward the bridge. At 10:00 a German soldier accompanied by a man in civilian clothing were spotted approaching the south end of the bridge. The paratroopers allowed the pair to go unmolested as they could not get a clear shot, and they remained in the area for around twenty minutes. In the event the pair were probably setting the timer on a pre-placed demolition charge, for at precisely 11:00 the bridge erupted in a huge explosion that forced the paratroopers down into their foxholes and showered the position with large pieces of debris.

In the course of the morning more enemy troops were also seen moving through the woods beyond the German position to the north; although Wierzbowski had no way of knowing, these were stragglers from the fighting near Best, the sound of which was clearly audible by the canal. A large group approached Wierzbowski's position at one point and an estimated thirty-five were killed after the paratroopers allowed them to close to within fifty yards before opening fire. A rather less welcome but more spectacular manifestation of the fight for Best was a strafing by USAAF P-47 fighter-bombers called in to provide close air support, although the paratroopers escaped unscathed. After the bridge had been blown Wierzbowski despatched Sergeant James Hoyle and Private First Class Joe E. Mann, his point man of the previous night, with the platoon's Bazooka and its five rockets to deal with the ammunition dump and 88mm gun. It is unclear whether Wierzbowski was motivated by concern over the threat posed by the 88mm gun or was seeking to keep his men motivated after the destruction of the bridge, but Mann destroyed the ammunition dump with several rockets and the pair then shot six Germans who tried to interfere. Mann was hit twice in the ensuing firefight but Hoyle succeeded in hitting the 88mm gun with possibly the last remaining Bazooka round before helping Mann back to the relative safety of the main position.[28]

The 502nd Parachute Infantry Regiment's effort to relieve Lieutenant Wierzbowski had continued at dawn on 18 September. As we have seen, the 3rd Battalion's Company H had originally been allotted the task of securing the Best bridges but became embroiled with German troops defending a road junction east of the town and when it eventually became apparent that the task required a larger force Lieutenant-Colonel Cole and the rest of the 3rd Battalion were despatched to assist at 18:00 on 17 September. However, a combination of German mortar and artillery fire and the onset of darkness obliged the newcomers to stop for the night a mile east of Best, just north of the Zonsche Forest. Cole ordered a resumption of the advance at first light on 18 September that succeeded in moving south and linking up with the isolated Company H, but German resistance frustrated subsequent attempts to move west on Best or south to the Wilhelmina Canal bridges and obliged the 3rd Battalion to dig in just inside the edge of the Forest; unbeknown to the paratroopers their opponents had been reinforced during the night by additional elements of *Generalleutnant* Walter Poppe's 59 *Infanterie Division*. The reinforcement was part of the effort by *Generaloberst* Student at 1 *Fallschirmjäger Armee* to contain and destroy the US landings in the vicinity of Eindhoven as ordered by *Heeresgruppe B* the previous day. Another entire regiment detrained near Best at 11:45 on 18 September and while the German units were short of ammunition and in many instances lacked heavy weapons, they were nonetheless sufficiently well-armed and equipped to cause significant problems for the lightly armed Airborne troops.[29] From the US perspective, the checking of Cole's advance showed that the task of clearing Best was also too large for a single battalion, and that the action had evolved from attempting to seize additional bridges into the more critical matter of protecting the western edge of the 101st Airborne Division's landing area for the Division's second lift, which was scheduled to arrive in the early afternoon of 18 September. The 502nd Regiment's commander, Colonel John H. Michaelis, therefore handed control of his 1st Battalion holding the bridges in St. Oedenrode to Division HQ in order to concentrate on the developing fight at Best before ordering Lieutenant-Colonel Steve A. Chappuis to move his 2nd Battalion west, establish contact with Cole's right flank and then pivot left and clear the town from the north-east.

This Lieutenant-Colonel Chappuis duly attempted to do, advancing across newly harvested hay fields with all three of his companies in extended line in the face of mortar, artillery and automatic fire from German troops ensconced behind the Eindhovenseweg Zuid highway to their front. The paratroopers maintained their formation with exemplary courage and discipline, using piles of uncollected hay for concealment:

…each group of two or three men dashing to the next hay pile as it came their turn. It was as if the piles were of concrete. But machine-gun fire cut into them, sometimes setting the hay afire, sometimes wounding or killing the men behind them. That did not stop anyone except the dead and wounded…It was like a problem being worked out on a parade ground. The squad leaders were leading, the platoon leaders urged them on.

Another participant put it more succinctly: 'We had no artillery and the Krauts had beaucoup of it. We lost a quarter of our men that day.'[30] Exemplary courage and discipline could only go so far, and Chappuis was obliged to halt the advance as the casualty toll threatened to render his Battalion combat ineffective, with eight officers and approximately twenty per cent of its men killed or wounded in a matter of minutes.[31] With the 2nd Battalion stopped and reorganising, the Germans ranged behind the highway turned their attention to the 3rd Battalion and also began to infiltrate small groups of infantry into the paratrooper's lines, obliging Cole to call in the P-47s that had strafed Lieutenant Wierzbowski's embattled platoon by the Wilhelmina Canal. The fighter-bombers' first pass also hit Cole's positions, apparently without causing casualties, until the paratroopers deployed fluorescent panels to mark their position. Subsequent passes fell along the line of the highway and beyond as needed, but while this prompted a marked slackening in the weight of German fire, it also brought a grimmer result. Lieutenant-Colonel Cole moved out from the shelter of the trees to obtain a clearer view of the strafing and in the process provided a German rifleman with a clear target; he was shot in the head and killed instantly. Command of the 3rd Battalion devolved to Major John P. Stopka, the Battalion Executive Officer, although he did not learn of the reason for his elevation until later.[32]

In contrast to all this Lieutenant-Colonel Cassidy's 1st Battalion 502nd Regiment enjoyed a relatively quiet morning in St. Oedenrode. *Heeresgruppe B* had also ordered 1 *Fallschirmjäger Armee* to move on the US force holding the town via Schijndel, but the fight at Best meant Student was only able to spare three infantry companies, a police battalion and *Fallschirmjäger Bataillon* Ewald drawn from a local training establishment; another *bataillon* from the same source was directed to Veghel.[33] None of these units were in a position to make contact with Cassidy's Battalion on the morning of 18 September and the only excitement experienced in St. Oedenrode came from what the 1st Battalion later dubbed the 'Incident of the Seven Jeeps'. At some point during the morning Colonel Harold H. Cartwright, a 1st Allied Airborne Army staff officer who appears to have landed in Holland with 101st Airborne Division HQ, led a party of five Jeeps north to investigate the situation at Veghel escorted by a guide from the 501st Parachute Infantry Regiment and two additional Jeeps from the Division Reconnaissance Platoon. All went according to plan until the speeding Jeeps took a wrong turn in the centre of St. Oedenrode, which led the little convoy north through Company C's lines, ignoring attempts to flag it down and on toward German-occupied Schijndel. Three miles further on, the Germans raked the convoy with mortar and small-arms fire that wounded several men, set the lead Jeep ablaze and forced everyone to seek cover in roadside ditches. The exception was the vehicle carrying Colonel Cartwright, which somehow managed to turn around and race back to St. Oedenrode, where Cartwright sought out Cassidy and requested he mount a rescue effort immediately.

The situation placed Cassidy in something of a quandary. The developing German pressure from the west meant that St. Oedenrode could be attacked at any time so he was reluctant to divert a major part of his strength from his primary mission of holding the Dommel bridges, but on the other hand a request from a higher ranking officer from an Army-level command could not be simply ignored either. Cassidy therefore compromised by handing the matter over to one of his most can-do officers, Lieutenant Joshua A. Mewborn from Company C. Mewborn was already on patrol in the area accompanied by a Private First Class Culverhouse and Privates Duval and Edward Leafty Junior, and Cassidy ordered him to take two additional squads and extricate the stalled convoy from its predicament. Heavy German fire forced the rescuers to seek cover around a thousand yards short of the staff party but Mewborn and his three original companions charged forward to the stalled Jeeps. Culverhouse and Duval succeeded in turning and driving two Jeeps to safety while Mewborn and Leafty laid down covering fire, and the latter then covered two medics attending the wounded before assisting in their evacuation. Their withdrawal was covered in turn by the remainder of the rescue party, which Lieutenant Troy Wall led forward to a point where it could put down suppressive fire on the German positions. All the staff party were escorted back to the safety of St. Oedenrode, with the rescue party suffering two wounded in the process.[34]

In the event, Colonel Cartwright and his companions were perhaps fortunate in being diverted from reaching the 501st Regiment's positions at Veghel. As we have seen, Company E from the 2nd Battalion had spent the night fighting off German attacks down the east side of the Zuid Willems Canal to the north of Veghel, which only ceased after daybreak when Lieutenant Gregg was able to mount a counter-attack with his reserve platoon. The Germans then turned their attention to Lieutenant-Colonel Julian Ewell's 3rd Battalion which was deployed in and around Eerde, a mile or so west of the rest of the Regiment in Veghel. The attackers focussed primarily on a roadblock established near the railway station to the north of the town by Company I but were repulsed with the loss of forty-three prisoners, reportedly *Luftwaffe* NCOs; another attack at around midday was similarly handled although the Germans maintained their pressure on the beleaguered paratroopers.[35] There was one final matter to be resolved by the 501st Regiment on the morning of D+1. A platoon-strength patrol led by 1st Lieutenant Louis E. Raffety had spent the night near Heeswijk on the east bank of the River Aa, four miles or so north-west of Veghel. Lieutenant-Colonel Kinnard's 1st Battalion had been misdropped just north of Heeswijk the previous day and a party left behind to gather in supply bundles and tend jump casualties under Captain William G. Burd had been attacked and besieged in a large stone building adjacent to the DZ known as the *Kasteel*. Raffety's patrol made it to within 800 yards of the DZ before German resistance obliged a halt for the night, and Colonel Johnson ordered the patrol recalled when daylight revealed Raffety was in danger of being outflanked and cut off. Kinnard was unwilling to let the matter drop however, and the following day he had a routine patrol from Company C led by Staff Sergeant William DeHuff extend its route to include the *Kasteel*. De Huff reached the DZ without incident and found most of the equipment bundles missing and two abandoned US mortars but no sign of Captain Burd, the clear-up group, Captain Kingston, his medics or the eight jump casualties, apart from a number of bloodied field dressings.[36]

***

The 2nd and 3rd Battalions of the 82nd Airborne Division's most westerly unit, Colonel Reuben H. Tucker's 504th Parachute Infantry Regiment, spent a relatively quiet morning patrolling around their objectives: the 1,800-foot bridge across the River Maas at Grave and the area between the Maas and the Maas-Waal Canal to the east of the town. There was, however, an uncomfortable encounter for Captain T. Moffatt Burriss, whose Company I was dug in just east of the bridge. In the course of the morning a Military Policeman turned up at Burriss' Command Post accompanied by two non-English-speaking Dutch telephone engineers and announced: 'We're here to repair the cable.' The cable in question was a thick, black item discovered by one of Burriss' men the previous day while digging in and mindful of instructions from Regiment to disrupt enemy communications wherever possible, he had ordered it severed. Burriss duly led the trio to the offending foxhole, the bottom of which was covered with 'frazzled wires spilling out of their casing like multicoloured spaghetti' and the sight immediately prompted a good deal of agitation between the telephone engineers who began jabbering excitedly in their own language. At this point Captain Burriss was called away to answer a field telephone call from Colonel Tucker who demanded to know what was going on in the Company I area. Puzzled, Burriss replied that things were pretty quiet and when Tucker mentioned the cut telephone cable he immediately owned up to the deed, citing the Colonel's own instructions about disrupting enemy communications. 'Yes, but I meant locally. You cut the international telephone cable. The 504th was planning to use it for our own communications,' replied the exasperated Tucker. The latter's exasperation was doubtless increased by the fact that General Gavin had explicitly forbidden the destruction of any communication cables bar German field telephone wires in his Field Order No. 11 issued to all the 82nd Airborne Division's units on 13 September 1944.[37] The telephone engineers were still busy splicing wire two days later when Burriss and Company I left for Nijmegen early in the morning of Wednesday 20 September.[38]

Major Harrison's 1st Battalion of the 504th Regiment was dispersed in Company packets along the Maas-Waal Canal, holding the intact bridge captured the previous day at Molenhoek and both banks of the two destroyed bridges at Hatert and Malden that had been demolished before they could be secured. The most northerly bridge across the canal, a combined road and rail affair at Honinghutie, was not approached on 17 September even though it was the most direct route from Grave to Nijmegen, presumably because it lay some way from the 82nd Airborne Division's DZs and because the 504th and 508th Regiments could only realistically be expected to deal with so many objectives at once. As we have seen, Browning's insistence that Gavin secure the entirety of the Groesbeek Heights in addition to the water crossings in the Divisional area had stretched the 82nd Airborne Division to something approaching breaking point. Consequently, Gavin had designated the Honinghutie bridge, codenamed Bridge 10, a provisional joint objective to be secured by the 504th and 508th Regiments as soon as the situation permitted. Major Harrison's contribution to the matter consisted of despatching a platoon north at 12:00 to assist the 508th Regiment's assault on the Honinghutie bridge, which by that time had been secured.[39]

The 508th Regiment's effort to secure the Honinghutie bridge began in the early morning of 18 September when Colonel Lindquist ordered his 2nd Battalion to secure the bridge immediately. Major Holmes delegated the task to Lieutenant Lloyd L. Polette's 1st Platoon from Company F. Approaching the bridge from the south-east at around 06:00 the platoon came within 300 yards of the bridge before the German defenders opened fire. Polette then led a charge that carried the platoon to within 150 yards of their objective but at the cost of twelve killed and wounded. Driven to cover again by the intense German fire, Polette called for reinforcements and 81mm mortar support and set his surviving men to preventing the Germans from moving toward the bridge with small-arms fire; having seen several such attempts Polette surmised that the enemy was attempting to plant demolition charges. Reinforcements arrived at approximately 09:30 in the shape of Lieutenant Thomas Tomlinson's 2nd Platoon from Company E, but the German fire was still too heavy for the paratroopers to move forward and the stalemate continued for another hour. At that point the Germans detonated their demolition charges, which destroyed the railway bridge while leaving the road bridge standing but severely damaged. In the meantime the attackers were reinforced by a section of 81mm mortars, imaginatively utilising a number of Dutch cattle as pack animals and their fire finally suppressed the defence sufficiently for Polette and Tomlinson to mount another charge. The German defences were cleared and the bridge secured by 12:00. The road bridge proved too badly damaged to use, obliging the relief force to use the more circuitous route over the Molenhoek bridge at the southern end of the Maas-Waal Canal, but Lieutenant Polette was nonetheless awarded the Distinguished Service Cross for his actions.[40]

The Platoons from the 2nd Battalion were not the only elements of the 508th on the move in the early morning of 18 September. At around daybreak Brigadier-General Gavin visited Colonel Lindquist at his tactical Regimental HQ overlooking the Nijmegen suburb of De Ploeg, in order to clarify reports that the 1st Battalion had patrols on the Nijmegen road bridge.[41] The actual situation report Gavin received was grim. 'My heart sank. They had failed to get the bridge. The situation of the 1st Battalion was confusing. No one knew what had happened to it.'[42] Determined to clarify the matter Gavin proceeded into Nijmegen in the 1st Battalion's wake, running into Captain Bestebreurtje and a group of around six hundred Dutchmen looking for weapons to allow them to fight alongside their liberators on the way. Mindful that the success of MARKET was by no means guaranteed, Gavin warned them of the penalties of fighting in civilian attire and asked for their assistance in preventing the Germans from demolishing the Nijmegen road bridge by cutting wires and interfering with German access to the structure. He then continued to Lieutenant-Colonel Warren's Command Post near the *Keizer Karel Plein*, arriving while the German dawn attack was in progress. He noted that the 1st Battalion was spread across a number of streets and buildings while the Germans appeared to be growing steadily stronger. In order to prevent the Battalion being overrun Gavin therefore ordered Warren to 'withdraw from close proximity to the bridge and reorganize' before moving off to visit the 505th Parachute Infantry Regiment on the southern sector of the Divisional perimeter.[43]

However, while Warren was breaking contact at the *Keizer Karel Plein* and Lieutenant Weaver's patrol was returning from the *Keizer Lodewijkplein* to the east, the 3rd Battalion 508th Parachute Infantry Regiment was stepping into the breach. As noted earlier Gavin had specified the seizure of the Nijmegen road bridge be assigned to Warren's 1st Battalion, but Lindquist had also warned Lieutenant-Colonel Louis Mendez that his 3rd Battalion might be required to provide additional manpower if circumstances required. Anticipating that this would be the case, Mendez had ordered Captain Russell C. Wilde's Company G to reconnoitre toward the Nijmegen road bridge from the south-east after the Battalion had reorganised, possibly along the circuitous route Gavin had worked out for Lindquist back in England.[44] After 1st Lieutenant Howard A. Greenwalt's 3rd Platoon reached a position overlooking the south-eastern suburbs of Nijmegen without incident, Mendez despatched the remainder of Company G in their wake after dark on 17 September and Captain Wilde set up a defensive perimeter and awaited orders to move on the bridge.[45] It is unclear precisely who finally issued the order. According to the Official History it came out of a meeting between Gavin and Lindquist, presumably during the former's visit to the latter's tactical HQ in the early morning of 18 September, but the same source also refers to Lieutenant-Colonel Mendez claiming to have launched the action on his own initiative.[46] Whoever was responsible, Captain Wilde and Company G left their overnight position to move on the bridge at 07:45.[47] Lieutenant Greenwalt's platoon was assigned the lead and discovered a German hospital shortly after entering the suburbs, possibly the civilian St. Martin's Hospital, which was swiftly searched for arms and left under guard.[48] The precise route the advance followed is unclear but it followed a line toward the *Keizer Lodewijkplein* traffic roundabout at the southern end of the Nijmegen bridge ramp, and as usual the paratroopers attracted enthusiastic attention from crowds of Dutch civilians, many still in their nightclothes.

The paratroopers noted a thinning of the throng the closer they drew to the bridge, and the reason soon emerged. The *Keizer Lodewijkplein* traffic circle lay just south of two areas of parkland called the Hunnerpark and Valkhofpark, the former straddling the Arnhemscheweg leading onto the bridge and the latter containing sections of Nijmegen's medieval defences, and it was here that *Oberst* Henke's scratch force of reserve and training personnel had dug in to protect the Waal road bridge. Two 20mm and one 88mm *FlaK* guns assigned to protect the south end of the bridges from air attack were integrated into the defences and more formal artillery support was organised by *Hauptsturmführer* Oskar Schwappacher, the commander of *SS Artillerie Ausbildungs und Ersatz Regiment 5*. This involved establishing links with *10 SS Panzer Division*'s artillery and redeploying the large calibre *FlaK* guns on the north bank of the River Waal closer to the water's edge to allow them to fire across the river. Schwappacher also took on the role of forward observer in person after walking the ground to familiarise himself with the defensive perimeter, which stretched for almost a mile between the *Keizer Lodewijkplein* and to the south-west the *Keizer Karel Plein*.[49] Henke had received no direct reinforcements at this point apart from the vanguard of the detachment from *SS Panzer Pionier Bataillon 10* the previous evening as *Sturmbannführer* Reinhold had deployed his scratch force of dismounted tank crewman from *SS Panzer Regiment 10* as a backstop on the north bank of the Waal, although more substantial support was on the way.

Responsibility for removing the British force blocking passage over the Arnhem road bridge and defending the Waal bridges was allotted to *Brigadeführer* Harmel when he reported to *II SS Panzerkorps* HQ on his return from Berlin early in the morning of 18 September. With responsibility for the Waal crossings at Nijmegen temporarily devolved to *Sturmbannführer* Reinhold, Harmel concentrated upon dealing with the British enclave in Arnhem and channelling his Division across the Lower Rhine from a tactical HQ near Pannerden, approximately fifteen miles south-east of Arnhem. The channelling employed two ferry sites, although it is unclear if these were functioning prior to 17 September or were set up in response to the loss of the crossings at Arnhem. The smaller was located at Huissen, ten kilometres or so upstream from Arnhem and the larger at Pannerden, where *Hauptsturmführer* Albert Brandt's *SS Panzer Pionier Bataillon 10* employed anything capable of carrying troops, vehicles and equipment over the river. They commandeered canal barges, motor boats, rowing skiffs and even rubber dinghies. According to one account a *Panzer* IV was manhandled across on an improvised raft using ropes and poles, although subsequently Harmel was able to arrange use of a purpose-built, forty-tonne ferry capable of moving tanks and assault guns from a *Heer* pioneer unit.[50] The remainder of *Untersturmführer* Werner Baumgärtel's detachment from *SS Panzer Pionier Bataillon 10* appear to have been among the first to cross, travelling in trucks augmented with commandeered bicycles. On arrival at Nijmegen Baumgärtel's men set about rigging the road and rail bridges for demolition and helping improve the field defences south of the road bridge.[51]

Apart from the interference of the ecstatic Dutch civilians, Company G's initial advance through Nijmegen was largely unopposed for the first 500 yards or so after the field hospital. At that point the paratroopers came under 'intense sniper fire,' which scattered the civilian onlookers and prompted Captain Wilde to sidestep to the right with the remainder of the Company while Greenwalt's platoon provided covering fire, and the latter subsequently overran a partially completed German roadblock while moving forward to deal with the snipers, killing seven Germans.[52] The roadblock was presumably part of an outpost line ordered by *Oberst* Henke and the dead may therefore have been from *Untersturmführer* Baumgärtel's *SS Pionier* detachment. In the meantime Wilde and the other two platoons closed to within approximately 200 yards of the road bridge before coming under small-arms fire from the German troops dug in around the *Keizer Lodewijkplein* at approximately 10:00. Manoeuvring forward into the increasingly heavy fire, Wilde's men pushed forward another hundred yards before attempting a charge, but this failed in the face of direct fire from 20mm and 88mm guns and artillery fire called down by *Hauptsturmführer* Schwappacher. The paratroopers nonetheless continued to work their way through to the buildings at the edge of the *Keizer Lodewijkplein*, but could proceed no further; one group managed to reach the riverbank just east of the bridge with the assistance of a Dutch Resistance member called Agardus Leegsma but were then driven back to the main company location.[53]

While all this was going reinforcements were filtering into *Oberst* Henke's defensive line at the southern end of the Nijmegen crossings, as ordered by *Heeresgruppe B* almost twenty-four hours earlier. *Hauptsturmführer* Karl-Heinz Euling had spent the night and early morning disentangling his unit from the fight at the Arnhem road bridge an element at a time, and after regrouping crossed the Lower Rhine via the ferry at Huissen, travelling in a number of armoured half-tracks again augmented with locally commandeered bicycles. Once across the Lower Rhine Euling moved via Elst to the north end of the Nijmegen road bridge, arriving at around midday. There he had a hurried meeting with local commander *Sturmbannführer* Leo Reinhold, who ordered Euling to cross the Waal and deploy his *Kampfgruppe* to defend the immediate approaches to the southern end of the road and rail bridges.[54] Euling promptly took his half-tracks across the road bridge and established a Command Post just to the west in the Valkhofpark, the highest point in the city. The unarmoured portion of his unit were ferried across the river in rubber dinghies in order to avoid casualties from Allied small arms and mortar fire, although the source of such fire is uncertain, given that the US units in Nijmegen do not appear to have been in direct sight of the bridge or to have had mortar or artillery support. The German defences were augmented over the course of the day with four *Sturmgeschütze* III and up to a dozen *Panzer* IV tanks from Reinhold's unit, *II Bataillon SS Panzer Regiment 10*, which crossed the Lower Rhine via the Pannerden ferry. Reinhold also had some of the 88mm *FlaK* guns emplaced on the north bank of the Waal re-sited to deliver direct fire on the bridges.[55]

It is unclear if Captain Wilde and his men were aware of the arrival of the SS reinforcements, but by midday it was apparent that they lacked the strength to fight through and secure the bridge without reinforcement. The problem was that there were no reinforcements to hand, due largely to the size of the 82nd Airborne Division's area of responsibility. Lieutenant-Colonel Mendez could not spare more men from the 3rd Battalion without jeopardising the defence of the eastern side of the Groesbeek Heights and the 508th Regiment's sole reserve, Captain Frank Schofield's Company C from the 1st Battalion, had already been despatched elsewhere by Colonel Lindquist. Consideration was given to deploying part of the Divisional reserve, the 2nd Battalion 505th Regiment, but the idea was abandoned, presumably because the 505th Regiment had enough on its hands.[56] Captain Wilde and the men of Company G were therefore left to their own devices occupying buildings along the edge of the *Keizer Lodewijkplein*, while events back at the landing area took a dramatic turn.

While Company G had been feeling its way into the eastern suburbs of Nijmegen, the south-eastern section of the 82nd Airborne Division's perimeter had come under attack from *406 z.b.V. Division*, the scratch force commanded by *Generalleutnant* Scherbening formed by combing *Wehrkreis* IV of personnel from NCO schools, replacement and training depots, medically downgraded rear-echelon units and *Luftwaffe* training establishments. In all this effort mustered a force of around 3,500 men equipped with 130 assorted machine-guns, twenty-four mortars and a number of light *flak* guns, divided into four *kampfgruppen*. Support was provided by five armoured cars and three 20mm armed half-tracks integrated into one of the battlegroups and the equivalent of three artillery batteries deployed in the area north-east of Wyler. This was an impressive host given the prevailing conditions, but the vast majority lacked even basic infantry training and there was a chronic shortage of motorised transport, communications equipment and even field kitchens.[57] The attackers were deployed on an attack frontage of around six miles, running through the edge of the *Reichswald* forest south of Groesbeek before curving north-east past Kranenburg, where Scherbening had established his tactical HQ.

The German attack thus straddled the section of the US perimeter held by the 505th and 508th Parachute Infantry Regiments. The former was deployed along a six- to seven-mile frontage, with Major Talton W. Long's 1st Battalion holding the high ground running east from Mook on the River Waal to Bisselt. Major James L. Kaiser's 3rd Battalion held the eastern portion of the line curving north-east through the southern edge of Groesbeek. As the 3rd Battalion's frontage was too wide to maintain a continuous line, Kaiser's men were deployed in small detachments covering road junctions and villages to the south of Groesbeek facing the German border and the *Reichswald* forest.[58] Their key mission was to protect the landing area for the 82nd Airborne Division's second lift, which was originally scheduled to arrive at 10:00 on 18 September; fortuitously as it turned out, Gavin was informed at 08:40 that the lift had been postponed until 13:00 owing to fog over some of the airfields in England.[59] Responsibility for protecting the southernmost of the adjoining landing zones, codenamed LZ N, was allotted to the 3rd Battalion's Company I, which occupied the villages of Breedeweg, Bruuk and Grafwegen along its southern edge. The northern LZ T was covered by 1st Lieutenant Norman MacVicar's Company D from the 508th Parachute Infantry, which had been detached when the remainder of the Regiment moved north to De Ploeg in the late afternoon of 17 September; as with the 505th Regiment, a single company was all that could be spared because of the number of missions allotted to the 508th Regiment; Lieutenant MacVicar was also tasked to protect Lieutenant Kenneth L. Johnson and four men from the Regimental Supply Section as they gathered in equipment bundles and established a central supply dump alongside the Company Command Post, using a cart and team of horses commandeered from a nearby farm.[60] Given the distances involved, the idea was for the US units to act as a warning tripwire to delay the attackers while reinforcements were organised, rather than a blocking force per se.[61]

The German attack began as scheduled just after first light at 06:30, although it does not appear to have been immediately apparent to their opponents because of the attacker's infiltration tactics and the dispersed nature of the American deployments; as one US participant put it, 'the [German] attack developed slowly at first and appeared to be only a series of patrol actions'.[62] This is apparent from the experience of the 508th Regiment's Company D, which was likely the first US unit to encounter the attackers in numbers. After spending the night dug in on the ridge overlooking LZ T from the west, Lieutenant MacVicar summoned his Platoon leaders soon after first light and ordered them to redeploy to three new locations spread along the eastern side of the landing area. The move may have been prompted by the news of the second lift being postponed until the early afternoon, given that it was mentioned during the briefing. However, the redeployment extended the Company frontage to over a mile and located the platoon locations 1,000 yards or more from the Company command post. This had obvious implications for MacVicar's ability to maintain contact with or exercise control over his platoons, together with the shortage of field telephone lines and other equipment that obliged reliance on hand-held SCR 536 radios or runners for communication; with the exception of one SCR 300 set and a single SCR 536, all of Company HQ's communication equipment had been lost when the C-47 carrying the Company Executive Officer and Communication Sergeant was shot down before reaching the jump point.[63]

Matters went awry almost from the outset. Lieutenant Robert L. Sickler's 3rd Platoon was digging in to cover the southern end of LZ T after establishing contact with the 505th Regiment on the right flank when MacVicar ordered him to take two of his Squads and move to the 2nd Platoon's location near Voxhill at the other end of the line, via the Company command post, for further instructions; contact with the other two Platoons had been lost after some scattered shooting from the direction of Voxhill and a cryptic SCR 536 transmission referring to trouble and needing help. MacVicar accompanied Sickler and his men for half the distance with the Company SCR 536 and a runner, at which point he despatched the runner to contact the 1st Platoon and remained in place, presumably in an effort to stay within range of the SCR 536. The remainder of the patrol continued across the Wyler road and a field planted with sugar beet to within 200 yards of a group of farm buildings atop Voxhill before coming under fire from two .30 calibre machine-guns that killed two men and forced the rest to seek cover. At first it was assumed the firing was accidental but when a faster-firing German weapon joined in, it became apparent that the 2nd Platoon had been overrun and Voxhill was held by the enemy. Casualties might have been more severe had the two squads not been well dispersed and without the shelter offered by the furrows, which fortuitously ran at right-angles to the German position. Lieutenant Sickler extracted his men from the trap by ordering his two .30 gun teams to crawl back along the furrows to the road bordering the field, from where they were able to provide covering fire for the remainder of the party to follow the same route, losing two more men in the process. The move fortuitously reoriented the paratroopers to face a flanking attack by two platoons of German troops from the north who employed fire-and-movement tactics to press on after Sickler's men brought them under effective fire. The attack was finally halted 250 yards short of the US positions, but countering this new threat left the American's right flank open to the Germans holding Voxhill, who poured withering 20mm cannon fire into the hapless paratroopers. This swelled the number of casualties including Lieutenant MacVicar; the Company Commander had crawled forward to inform Sickler that the messenger had found no sign of the 1st Platoon. Sickler was thus left the sole unwounded officer in a Company effectively reduced to less than Platoon strength, pinned down from two sides in an increasingly untenable position and running short of ammunition.[64]

The situation was retrieved to an extent by Captain Johnson from the Regimental Supply Section. On observing Sickler's plight from the Company observation post on the ridge, he promptly contacted Colonel Lindquist via the Company SCR 300 and informed him that 'Company D was surrounded on the drop zone, that the enemy was threatening to overrun the regimental supply dump and that the situation was extremely critical'. Captain Johnson then gathered together his Supply Section men and the Company HQ group and reoccupied the 2nd Platoon's overnight position adjacent to the supply dump, approximately 400 yards west of Sickler's patrol. From there he was able to use the stored ammunition to lay down fire sufficiently heavy to deter the German advance and ease the pressure on Sickler's pinned-down platoon. Good use was made of an abandoned 60mm mortar, despite the lack of a baseplate or bipod, and the paratroopers were also assisted by eight *Luftwaffe* fighters which misidentified and strafed the attacking German troops.[65] Captain Johnson's radio call, which appears to have reached the forward Regimental HQ overlooking De Ploeg shortly before 10:00, galvanised Colonel Lindquist into rather more prompt action than he had displayed in getting his men to the Nijmegen road bridge the previous evening. The Regimental reserve, Captain Frank Schofield's Company C, was ordered to march the four miles back to the landing area immediately to secure the start line for a battalion attack. Lieutenant-Colonel Warren was then ordered to break contact in Nijmegen, take the remainder of the 1st Battalion to Company C's location and then counter-attack and clear the landing area of German troops before the arrival of the glider lift at 13:00. This was a rather tall order, given that the landing area lay seven to eight miles away and that Company B, which was still emplaced near the *Keizer Karel Plein*, was out of radio contact. Warren nonetheless ordered the bulk of Company A, which had been withdrawn earlier in the morning, to prepare to move and despatched his Operations Officer, Captain James Dietrich, to brief Company B and lead them back to Lindquist for further orders. Dietrich arrived at Captain Millsaps' command post in the cellar of Nijmegen's town hall at 11:00 and Company B was retracing its route back to the Groesbeek Heights shortly thereafter. To their chagrin the withdrawing paratroopers were again greeted enthusiastically by the unwitting Dutch civilians they had encountered on the way into the city. As Millsaps later recalled:

> One of the saddest, most touching experiences for me up to that time was that pull back from Nijmegen. The natives of the town, undoubtedly thinking the town was being liberated from German rule, came out in the streets shouting and dancing, kissing soldiers, and giving us fruit and handfuls of flowers. We dared not tell them, even if we could have spoken their language, that we were giving the city back to the Germans and moving back to start all over again.[66]

The German attack had a similar impact on the 505th Regiment's frontage along the southern aspects of LZ N, sparking a number of sharp fights as the infiltrators ran up against the scattered US outposts. One notable action involved Staff-Sergeant Clarence Prager, who commanded a small outpost established in the edge of the *Reichswald* forest with Corporal Harry J. Buffone and a number of men, including a Browning Automatic Rifle team. They were swiftly surrounded by a large number of German troops who called on them to surrender and a fierce firefight developed after the paratroopers declined the offer. When the pressure became too much, Prager ordered Corporal Buffone to lead the Browning Automatic Rifle team back to the next outpost while he covered them with his Thompson gun, but Prager was hit in the head and killed; he was subsequently awarded the Distinguished Service Cross for his gallantry, and Corporal Buffone received the Silver Star for his part in the action.[67] Lieutenant Harold L. Gensemer and 2nd Lieutenant Richard H. Brownlee's platoon from Company C had been temporarily transferred to Company B, and unwittingly moved into the advancing Germans while establishing a roadblock near Riethorst; Brownlee had been slightly wounded in a skirmish with a German patrol in the same area in the early hours of 18 September. The outpost had barely finished setting in when it was approached by a *Möbelwagen flak* vehicle from Lieutenant Brownlee's description.[68] The vehicle killed two Browning Automatic Rifle gunners with its 37mm gun when they fired on it and proved impervious to Bazooka rockets, obliging the surviving paratroopers to withdraw to nearby high ground overlooking the outpost site. There they were pounded by German mortar and artillery fire, at least one strafing Messerschmitt 109 fighter and the *Möbelwagen*. The German fire caused numerous casualties and totally demolished a windmill atop the hill occupied by a US Forward Observer, who was unable to hit back effectively because the US guns were restricted to a mere five rounds per fire mission. Additional attempts to knock out the *flak* vehicle with Bazookas and Gammon bombs proved fruitless. Eventually, Gensemer and his men were given permission to withdraw to the main Company B line.[69]

Although it was not apparent to the beleaguered US Airborne troops, their German opponents were suffering problems of their own, due to the variable quality and training of the units committed to the attack. At one point *Generalleutnant* Scherbening was obliged to despatch his adjutant *Major* Rasch to take command of a stalled unit commanded by a *Hauptmann* Gruenenklee attacking toward Groesbeek; these may have been the troops encountered by Lieutenant Sickler and his men near Voxhill. Whether or not, *Major* Rasch discovered that his new temporary command was a replacement unit made up of overage men:

> These were all old boys lying here, veterans of the First World War, who had just been called up to relieve the younger soldiers manning POW camp battalions. Now they too had been put into the front line. Somebody in the line called out to me 'Captain, we've already stormed the Craoneer Heights in 1914!'. 'Ja' I was able to answer. 'Can't you see that it's up to us old boys to run the whole show again.'

Rasch's subtle chiding did the trick and he was to hand the unit back to its original commander shortly thereafter before returning to Scherbening's HQ.[70] Nonetheless, by 11:00 the attack had either bypassed or simply pushed back the US units protecting both landing zones by sheer weight of numbers and German troops were occupying large portions of both; some had re-manned a number of 20mm *flak* guns abandoned the previous day, which by some oversight the US paratroopers had failed to disable. The 1st Battalion 508th Regiment was on the way back from Nijmegen at Colonel Lindquist's order by just after 11:00 to clear LZ T in an effort to rectify the situation, and Gavin set similar counter-measures in motion. First, he ordered the 505th Regiment to attack and clear LZ N, prompting Colonel Ekman to deploy his sole reserve, the understrength Company C, to the western edge of the landing zone. Gavin then gathered up Company D of the 307th Airborne Engineer Battalion, which was guarding the Divisional Command Post near Groesbeek, and personally deployed it on the western edge of LZ T in an effort to seal the gap that had opened up in the Divisional perimeter between the 505th and 508th Regiments.[71] The question was now whether the counter-attack had sufficient strength to clear the landing zones, and whether it could be done before the glider lift arrived at 13:00 and a massacre ensued.

***

Daylight on Monday 18 September saw the north end of the Arnhem road bridge wrapped in a cold mist from the Lower Rhine thick enough to conceal anyone moving in the streets and as a result Private James Sims from the 2nd Parachute Battalion's Mortar Platoon found himself stealthily trailing his Platoon Commander with a roll of signal wire. Sims had spent the night in his slit trench on a small traffic island at the junction of the Weertjesstraat and Eusebiusbinnensingel,[72] overlooked from the north by the house containing the rest of the

Mortar Platoon and Battalion HQ and just west of where the Weertjesstraat ran under the bridge ramp and became the Westervoortsedijk; in the process he had earned the respect of his veteran companion by resisting all efforts to rouse him during a sudden firefight during the night. Lieutenant Woods had summoned Sims to assist in setting up an observation post in a warehouse occupied by the Machine Gun Platoon on the corner of the Kade Straat overlooking the river:

> The mist enveloped us like a cloak – the island had already vanished – but he [Lieutenant Woods] seemed to know where he was going so all I had to do was stick close to him and keep paying out the line…The closer we came to the Machine Gun Platoon the thicker grew the mist, for we were quite near the Rhine…We seemed to be making a hell of a noise with our boots and at every step I expected to be cut down by a panzer grenadier. We were eventually challenged by an alert sapper sentry, who gave as much gen as he could on the position ahead.

The pair eventually reached their destination via a barricaded back door after cutting through an enclosed yard and scaling a six-foot wall, during which the aerial of the radio Lieutenant Woods was carrying became entangled in a line of some kind. The barricade was so effective it took five minutes for the machine-gunners to make a gap big enough for the visitors to pass through. The mission eventually proved futile as their field telephone refused to function and they were unable to make clear contact with the No. 18 set Woods was carrying. The telephone was abandoned in disgust along with the wire Sims had painstakingly reeled out. Both men returned to the Mortar Platoon location.[73]

By this time the equivalent of just over a parachute battalion had gathered around the north end of the Arnhem road bridge, of which only around 385 were infantrymen. The bulk of these were from the 2nd Parachute Battalion's HQ Group, HQ Company, A Company, B Company minus part of 4 Platoon and Support Company, totalling 340 men; the remaining forty-five or so belonged to two incomplete platoons and HQ element from the 3rd Parachute Battalion's C Company. Of the remaining 350 or so, 110 were from 1st Parachute Brigade HQ, the 1st Parachute Squadron RE and 9th Field Company RE provided seventy-five and thirty men respectively, forty were from the 1st Airlanding Anti-Tank Battery's HQ, B and C Troops and a further forty were from 3 Platoon, 250 (Airborne) Light Composite Company RASC. The remainder consisted of twelve men belonging to forward observer elements from the 3rd Airlanding Light Battery RA; two US personnel from a Jedburgh Team; Major Gough and seven men from the 1st Airborne Reconnaissance Squadron; seventeen Glider Pilots; six men from the 1st (Airborne) Divisional Field Park RAOC; five men each from the 1st (Airborne) Divisional Workshop REME and 1st (Parachute) Field Security Section, Intelligence Corps; and two or possibly three Military Policemen from the 1st (Airborne) Divisional Provost Company CMP. In all, this added up to around sixty officers including thirteen majors and 680 Other Ranks, totalling approximately 740 men.[74]

Lieutenant-Colonel Frost oversaw deployment of this force into a perimeter anchored on a 250-yard stretch of the Lower Rhine centred on the road bridge, defended on the eastern side by elements of the 2nd Parachute Battalion's B Company and C Company 3rd Parachute Battalion, the former's Medium Machine Gun Platoon and part of the Brigade HQ Defence Platoon. The western side of the perimeter, defended by other elements of B Company, elements of the 2nd Battalion's HQ and Support Company and the 9th Field Company RE, ran north from the riverside Rijnkade and across the Weertjesstraat for almost 200 yards before curving north-east for just over 100 yards enclosing a right-angle stretch of the Prinsenhof and the city mortuary, which was defended by the RASC platoon. It then ran for 250 yards due east just short of the prison, bisected the Eusebiusbinnensingel that paralleled west side of the landscaped embankment carrying the Nijmeegseweg up to the bridge, the lower end of the embankment itself and the Eusebiusbuitensingel that paralleled the east side of the embankment, before curving south for another 300 yards or so back down to the Lower Rhine. The west side of the embankment was defended by part of the Brigade HQ Defence Platoon, while the east was covered by part of the 3rd Battalion's HQ element and part of a platoon from C Company along with the 1st Parachute Squadron's HQ and A Troop, all occupying the Van Limburg Stirum School. This position also closely overlooked an access slip road from the Nijmeegseweg. The rest of the eastern perimeter including a bulge to the east from the Westervoortsedijk running from the bridge underpass to the riverbank was held by another element of the Brigade HQ Defence Platoon and C Company's 8 Platoon. The remainder of Frost's force was deployed in buildings toward the centre of the perimeter, along the Kadestraat and the parallel Oostraat, the Weertjesstraat, the Prinsenhof and the Eusebiusbinnensingel, mainly to the west of the bridge ramp.[75]

The shape of the British perimeter had been defined the previous night, with the exception of the north-east corner where Captain Eric Mackay and eighteen Sappers from A Troop 1st Parachute Squadron RE had occupied a building known as the Red School on the east side of the embankment at 23:00; Lieutenant Denis Simpson and another twenty-five Sappers from B Troop were ensconced in the Van Limburg Stirum School twenty yards to the south, while a party of ten from HQ Troop and twenty signallers under Lieutenant Donald Hindley occupied a house on the opposite side of the Eusebiusbuitensingel. Observation and fields of fire from the Red School proved to be severely restricted by trees and within fifteen minutes of Mackay's party moving in German troops closed in undetected and threw hand-grenades through the windows before raking the building with machine-gun fire, wounding several Sappers. A confused, half-hour firefight followed, which underlined the vulnerability of the position and Mackay therefore ordered a withdrawal to the Van Limburg Stirum School at 23:45, after he and five Sappers cleared the grounds of the Red School with grenades and Sten fire.[76] The B Troop contingent in the Van Limburg School were not overjoyed at the arrival of their new companions as Sapper George Needham discovered: 'They objected and said "Bugger off, go find your own place," but Captain Mackay, being the man he was, persuaded them in no uncertain terms to let us in, and we started fortifying some of the empty rooms.'[77] According to Lance-Corporal Arthur Hendy from B Troop, the hostility was the result of intense rivalry between the Squadron's three Troops, which was in turn a spin-off from the Troops being semi-permanently attached to individual parachute battalions.[78] The A Troop contingent were all safely in the Van Limburg School by just after midnight, and an attack following the same pattern was repulsed at some point between 02:00 and 03:00.[79] Shortly after that Major Lewis and fifteen men from the 3rd Parachute Battalion's HQ group and 9 Platoon including Captain Wilfred Robinson and Lieutenant Len Wright received a similarly chilly reception; the remainder of the C Company contingent, Lieutenant Gerald Infield and 8 Platoon, occupied the south-eastern portion of the perimeter south of the Westervoortsedijk with elements of the Brigade HQ Defence Platoon.[80] The reason is unclear but there appears to have been bad blood between Major Lewis and Captain Mackay. Although the former was the senior officer present there was no interaction between them, their respective units appear to have operated in isolation despite their proximity, and neither officer mentioned the presence of the other or their men in their War Diary entries or post-battle accounts.[81] While the Airborne troops were busy preparing their perimeter for defence, removing glass and inflammable materials from windows, barricading doorways and stockpiling water in baths and sinks, their opponents were making preparations to dislodge them.

Initially however, the German upper command echelons were handicapped by the same kind of confusion that had reigned in the immediate aftermath of the British ground assault south of Eindhoven. In the early hours of 18 September *II SS Panzerkorps* erroneously informed *Heeresgruppe B* that the Arnhem road bridge had been cleared and was passable to traffic, for example. This was subsequently corrected but with a major underestimation of British strength, considered to be only 120 men. At 04:00 *Hauptsturmführer* Heinrich Brinkmann, the officer tasked to clear the bridge, received the first increment of reinforcements from *Wehrkreis IV*. *Panzer-Grenadier Ersatz und Ausbildungs Bataillon* 'Bocholt' commanded by *Major* Hans-Peter Knaust, a one-legged veteran of the Eastern Front, was a four-company-strong replacement training unit for infantry in the final stage of convalescence following wounds, and Brinkmann immediately set Knaust to relieving the elements of *Kampfgruppe* Euling deployed north of the bridge ramp so they could continue their journey to Nijmegen. By this time Brinkmann's own unit, *SS Panzer Aufklärungs Abteilung 10*, appears to have been deployed to the north and east of the British perimeter while *SS Panzergrenadier Regiment 21*'s fifty-strong 3 *Kompanie*, fresh from pedalling the twenty-five miles from Deventer, was deployed to the west.[82] The former was therefore likely responsible for the attacks on the 1st Parachute Squadron at the Red and Van Limburg Stirum Schools, and the latter for the firefight with the 2nd Battalion's Support Company that had failed to rouse Private Sims. In the meantime Private Sims and Lieutenant Woods set up their observation post in the attic of a building on the corner of the Kadestraat and Weertjesstraat. Dubbed the White House by the paratroopers, it was occupied by A Company and not only provided an excellent view over the rooftops to the southern approaches to the bridge, but also allowed clear radio contact with the Platoon's mortar pits on the traffic island where Sims had spent the night.[83] The same process was taking place 100 yards to the north where Major Denis Munford used the attic of the building occupied by Brigade HQ on the Eusebiusbinnensingel west of the bridge embankment to register the guns of 3 Battery via Bombardier Leo Hall's piggybacked No. 22 and No. 68 radio sets. 3 Battery had relocated to the vicinity of Oosterbeek Old Church at 05:00 to be within range of the bridge, and Munford used six rounds to register the south end of the bridge as target Mike One.[84]

The first intrusion into the airborne perimeter was a municipal refuse lorry loaded with dustbins that drove south past Brigade HQ and turned left onto the Weertjesstraat. It was promptly riddled with fire from both sides of the road and came to stop a few yards from the bridge underpass by the staircase leading up the embankment; the driver and any passengers were probably killed. Next came two trucks carrying troops from *SS Panzer Aufklärungs Abteilung 10*, following in the wake of the dustbin lorry along the Eusebiusbinnensingel west of the ramp. They may have been part of a concerted German attack, but as they were reportedly moving slowly they may have simply been lost. Whatever the reason for their presence, the lead truck tried to accelerate when the paratroopers opened fire and passed the dustbin lorry before slewing at right-angles across the road almost beneath the underpass; the other vehicle, a captured US Dodge ¾-ton Weapons Carrier, attempted to reverse back up the Eusebiusbinnensingel but was brought to a stop outside the building occupied by Brigade HQ.[85] Most of the passengers in these vehicles were killed or wounded before they could exit and those who did were shot down in the roadway. Private Sims recalled the road being carpeted with German dead, and of one badly wounded SS man being shot by a 2nd Battalion sniper from the White House after dragging himself all the way to the top of the embankment. He also reported another German attack from the same direction using a civilian ambulance filled with SS. After being halted by a burst of Bren fire that earned the gunner a rebuke from an officer, 'the back doors of the ambulance sprang open and a dozen fully armed SS men came tumbling out firing automatic weapons from the hip. They charged straight at us… But the Brens and rifles were already at their grim work and not a man survived that desperate attempt. One SS man actually reached the front door of the White House before collapsing on the steps, riddled with bullets.'[86]

The next set of intruders, who appeared after a short but intense German mortar barrage, were less hesitant and more powerful. A group of armoured vehicles which had formed up in the industrial area to the east of the bridge attempted to push along the Westervoortsedijk and under the bridge underpass. British accounts refer to armoured half-tracks led by one or possibly more tanks, but there do not appear to have been any German tanks in the area of the Arnhem bridge at this point. While *Wehrkreis IV* had despatched an armoured unit drawn from

Panzer Ersatz Regiment 6 'Bielefeld' to Arnhem at the same time as Knaust's *Bataillon* 'Bocholt', those vehicles did not arrive in Arnhem until the morning of Tuesday 19 September.[87] The 'tank' was therefore likely one of the French-built Panhard 178 armoured cars operated by the *Obersturmführer* Karl Ziebrecht's *kompanie* from *SS Panzer Aufklärungs Abteilung 10*, designated *Panzer Spähwagen* P204 (f) in German service.[88] Whatever it was, the vehicle got as far as the bridge underpass before coming under fire from a 6-Pounder anti-tank gun, possibly Sergeant Cyril Robson's gun from C Troop stationed at the western end of the Weertjesstraat. The first round not only missed the target but the recoil sent the weapon skidding backwards across the cobbled surface because the spades at the end of the gun trails had not been dug in; the inadvertent movement injured two crewmen. By the time the gun had been manhandled back to its firing position, reloaded and the crew casualties made up by co-opting the Battery clerk, the armoured car had begun to emerge into the open from the gloom of the underpass. The second shot scored a direct hit, slewing the vehicle across the road and setting it ablaze. This brought the following vehicles to a stop, giving the paratroopers ensconced in the buildings on either side of the bridge the opportunity to pour fire into them. It is unclear if any more were knocked out before the SS withdrew, but at least one crewman survived in the burning armoured car and fired on any British movement. Despite shouted appeals to surrender from the paratroopers the gunner refused to bail out and was burned to death as the fire spread through the stricken vehicle.[89]

All this took place in the first two hours or so after sunrise, which occurred at 06:15.[90] There followed a brief period of calm; at this stage Frost reportedly felt that 'everything was going according to plan, with no serious opposition yet and everything under control.'[91] The calm did not last long, and this time the threat came from the other side of the Lower Rhine. *Hauptsturmführer* Viktor Gräbner had raced south to Nijmegen with the bulk of *SS Panzer Aufklärungs Abteilung 9* in the evening of 17 September, only to find the bridges there defended by *Oberst* Henke's scratch force and no sign of Allied activity. After detaching two armoured half-tracks to assist the defence, Gräbner returned to Elst at some point between 20:00 and 22:00; his move may have been prompted by reports of the firefight at the Arnhem road bridge from vehicles left at Elst as a radio relay station. By dawn on 18 September he and his men were back in the vicinity of the Arnhem bridge having left six half-tracks, some or possibly all of which were *Sd.Kfz* 251/9s mounting short 75mm guns, in Elst as a blocking force.[92] Gräbner watched *Kampfgruppe* Brinkmann's unsuccessful attack through his binoculars, and then began to marshal his force to join the fray, even though it ran counter to his orders. This may have been his intention in moving north from Elst or he may have been prompted by the sight of his opposite numbers from the *Frundsberg* being roughly handled, but Gräbner's decision was both unilateral and typically *Waffen SS*, and came as no surprise to his superiors; as *Hauptsturmführer* Wilfried Schwarz, 9 SS Panzer Division's Chief-of-Staff, later commented, 'This was typical of Gräbner – always the first to get stuck in!'[93] Whether he intended to dislodge the British interlopers or merely to rush through the British perimeter to rejoin his parent formation is unclear. Whatever his intention, Gräbner marshalled his twenty-odd vehicles on the approach to the bridge, placing five *Sd.Kfz.* 234 eight-wheeled armoured cars in the van. Next came eight *Sd.Kfz.* 250 armoured half-tracks, followed by eight assorted trucks armoured with sand-filled oil drums, one towing a trailer of some kind, and a solitary *Sd.Kfz.* 10 unarmoured half-track.[94] According to one source there was also a captured British Humber scout-car that Gräbner was using as a personal vehicle.[95]

Gräbner's preparations were spotted by British sentries posted in the upper storeys of the buildings overlooking the river and the vehicles were initially assumed to be the vanguard of 30 Corps. The recognition error was swiftly recognised, however, and Major Munford, ensconced in his artillery OP in the attic of the Brigade HQ building, called down fire on the column using the target co-ordinates established with 3 Battery just after dawn; he ceased fire after the column moved onto the bridge to avoid damaging the structure.[96] The precise time the SS began to move across the bridge is unclear, with times between 08:00 and 09:30 being cited in different accounts.[97] Whenever it commenced, the speed differential between the different types of vehicle soon disrupted the column's integrity and the lead *Sd.Kfz.* 234s not only opened up a significant gap but also easily avoided the still-smouldering wreckage of the four trucks ambushed the previous night, which Frost had assumed would present an effective obstacle.[98] A daisy-chain of mines laid on the road surface also failed to impede their passage, with one vehicle losing a wheel with no noticeable loss of performance, and all five passed down the Nijmeegseweg and through the northern edge of the British perimeter. Although the armoured cars reportedly sprayed the surrounding buildings with 20mm and machine-gun fire there does not appear to have been any response from the Airborne troops, who were presumably waiting for the mines to bring them to a halt before opening fire.

The second increment of Gräbner's force received a much warmer reception. The paratroopers in the upper storeys of the buildings level with the bridge promptly opened fire on the gaggle of half-tracks weaving and squealing across the carriageway and the volume of fire increased as the vehicles moved into view of the British-occupied buildings on either side of the embanked section of the ramp. The small-arms fire became more effective as the drop in elevation exposed the vehicle's open-topped passenger compartments to plunging fire and heavier calibre punch was added by Sergeant Robson's 6-Pounder on the Weertjesstraat and another commanded by a Sergeant O'Neill located on the Eusebiusbinnensingel near the Brigade HQ building. Sergeant Robson's gun was unsighted by the bridge's concrete parapet but spotting by Lieutenant Anthony Cox, the Anti-Tank Battery's Liaison Officer located in the upper storey of a nearby building, allowed Robson to blow part of the parapet away with several armour-piercing rounds and engage the half-tracks as they passed the gap.[99] The latter's collective momentum nonetheless carried them off the bridge proper and a third of the way down the embanked section of ramp until the lead driver lost his nerve, possibly after being wounded, and tried to reverse back out of the storm of fire. The reversing vehicle rammed the next half-track in line and both vehicles became jammed against the parapet on the western side of the bridge, where three more half-tracks collided with them in quick succession, creating a tangle that blocked half the carriageway. The convoy of trucks bringing up the rear, protected by only their rudimentary oil-drum armour, did not get as far as the embanked section of the ramp. At least one, a Renault three-tonner, received a direct hit from either a PIAT or 6-Pounder that totally demolished the cab. The lead truck was brought to a stop over the Weertjesstraat/ Westervoortsedijk underpass and the remainder backed up behind it along the concrete parapet on the east side of the bridge.[100]

The Airborne troops poured a merciless fire into the stalled vehicles with rifles, Stens, Brens and PIATs, augmented with more exotic weapons including the Vickers K guns mounted on Major Gough's reconnaissance Jeep and at least one captured MP40 machine pistol wielded by Corporal Geoffrey Cockayne from the Brigade HQ element, who fired off the bulk of his ammunition after leaving the shelter of the Brigade HQ building with others to gain clearer firing positions. Lieutenant Harvey Todd, a US officer from the attached Jedburgh Team, was credited with picking off eight Germans with his M1 Carbine. Major Munford and a Private Shuttlewood claimed a similar number.[101] The defender's task was eased by several of the shot-up vehicles catching fire, giving their SS passengers and crewmen the unenviable choice of burning to death or braving the hail of fire in the roadway in an attempt to reach safety. A few made it. A signaller in the 2nd Parachute Battalion's HQ building recalled one German emerging from a half-track halted hard against the east parapet and dashing down the embankment and across the Eusebiusbuitensingel to safety.[102] Many others were not so fortunate and the roadway was soon littered with dead SS, some dismembered by bullets and shrapnel and some set ablaze by burning petrol and diesel spilled from ruptured fuel tanks.

Not all the SS who emerged from the clusters of stalled vehicles sought safety. Impressively, some continued to try and push forward down the ramp, as did some vehicles that had not been immobilised in the initial storm of fire. One *Sd.Kfz.* 250 half-track veered off the ramp along a maintenance slip road called the Bleckmanslaan leading down the east side of the embankment. This carried the vehicle past and under the windows of the Van Limburg School and specifically that occupied by Sapper Ronald Emery from the 1st Parachute Squadron's A Troop. Emery allowed the vehicle to pass before firing down into the open top from the rear, hitting the driver and co-driver, and then stood up in clear view to throw a grenade into the vehicle's passenger compartment despite return fire from the half-track's machine-gun; he was subsequently awarded the Military Medal.[103] The last vehicle knocked out in the action was an unarmoured *Sd.Kfz.* 10 half-track, which also attempted to avoid the slaughter on the carriageway by taking the Bleckmanslaan; it, too, was comprehensively shot up and ended up slewed across the road with its front end poking through the roadside railings just a few feet from the Van Limburg School. As it became apparent the assault was being successfully rebuffed the buildings around the ramp echoed to exultant calls of 'Waho Mohammed', the war cry adopted by the 1st Parachute Brigade in North Africa, accompanied by the keening of a jammed vehicle horn.[104]

The attack went on for around two hours before the SS survivors finally admitted defeat and retired south across the bridge to link up with the blocking force at Elst, or possibly German reinforcements moving up to secure the south end of the bridge. Private Sims was involved in the risky business of relaying fire control orders to the mortar pits on the Weertjesstraat by shouting from an upper-storey window after Lieutenant Woods spotted a number of German trucks approaching from the south. Several vehicles were set ablaze before the remainder withdrew in some confusion, helped on their way by the Vickers guns emplaced at the front of the White House.[105] In spite of all this, at least half a dozen SS men remained trapped among the wreckage and were captured by a patrol from the 2nd Parachute Battalion's B Company moving onto the bridge after dark.[106]

Gräbner's impetuous and poorly executed attempt to force a way across the Arnhem road bridge thus achieved little apart from virtually destroying II SS *Panzerkorp's* single most powerful integral unit for no practical return. Around ten armoured vehicles and up to a dozen trucks were left scattered across the north ramp, forming an inextricable block across much of the carriageway along with approximately seventy dead including Gräbner, whose body was never found.[107] In contrast, British losses appear to have been light in the extreme, but while the successful repulse boosted morale it brought no real respite. At 10:00 the house held by Lieutenant Donald Hindley and men from the 1st Parachute Squadron's HQ and Signals Troop on the Eusebiusbuitensingel opposite the Van Limburg School was attacked by infantry moving under covering fire from machine-guns, although the Sappers succeeded in driving the attackers back. An hour later *Kampfgruppe* Brinkmann launched another attack on the east side of the British perimeter, which, apparently learning from the earlier attempt to rush the bridge underpass, was more carefully focussed on securing the crossroads formed by the junction of the Westervoortsedijk, Eusebiusbuitensingel and Oostraat.[108] The blow therefore fell on buildings occupied by Lieutenant Patrick Barnett's Brigade HQ Defence Platoon and Lieutenant Gerald Infield's 8 Platoon from C Company 3rd Parachute Battalion and appears to have involved *Obersturmführer* Ziebrecht's Panhard armoured cars, again reported as tanks by the British. Sergeant Robson's 6-Pounder was credited with knocking out one while another may have fallen victim to a PIAT, and further support was provided by 3 Battery via Captain Henry Buchanan, an artillery forward observer attached to the 2nd Parachute Battalion.[109] By 13:00 the Bren Groups defending the south side of the Van Limburg School had been drawn into the fray, presumably as the German advance brought them into view, and the school was subjected to an hour-long mortar bombardment in response, although one source suggests some of this might have been fire from the 2nd Battalion's Mortar Platoon, which was stopped after the occupants confirmed their occupation with cries of 'Waho Mohammed'.[110]

Not all of the 2nd Parachute Battalion's elements enjoyed such success on Monday morning. Major Victor Dover and C Company had spent the night holed up in the PGEM building on the Utrechtsestraatweg a mile or so north of the road bridge and 600 yards short of its objective, the main German HQ in Arnhem. Following radio contact with Battalion HQ just after dawn the latter mission was abandoned in favour of moving south to join the bridge perimeter via a dogleg to the west to reach the riverside road. The Company moved out the back of the hotel at 07:00 with Lieutenant David Russell's 7 Platoon in the lead but movement was again complicated by the maze of small walled backyards and worse, the dogleg west carried them toward the Municipal Museum and into the area occupied by *Kampfgruppe* Harder as a backstop to Spindler's main blocking line. The paratroopers were quickly spotted and when Lieutenant Russell led a dash across the to the next block he discovered the road was swept by 20mm and machine-guns firing on fixed lines, which deterred the remainder of the Company from crossing, leaving Russell, a Sergeant Campbell and six men isolated. The road was almost certainly the Nachtengaalstraat and attempts to cross were further complicated by high chain-link fencing running along both sides, which the desperate paratroopers tried to breach with PIATs. Private William Saunders used the last of his 2-inch smoke bombs to cover the crossing but the appearance of German armoured vehicles obliged the paratroopers to withdraw farther west, covered by Sergeant Campbell throwing hand grenades at the vehicles from No. 34 Nachtengaalstraat. Eventually the survivors, many of whom were wounded and virtually out of ammunition, were pinned down just 300 hundred yards or so from the 3rd Parachute Battalion's positions near the Rhine Pavilion. Faced with imminent annihilation, Dover surrendered. Three officers and around 100 men thus passed into captivity, equivalent to a third of the 2nd Parachute Battalion's rifle strength. Lieutenant Russell and his little band were more fortunate and succeeded in breaking through the German line to link up with Lieutenant Cleminson's platoon near the St Elizabeth Hospital.[111]

While Frost's party was defending its grip on the north end of the Arnhem road bridge, the remainder of the 1st Parachute Brigade spent the morning trying to reach them. Although the unit War Diary refers to the 3rd Parachute Battalion setting off from its overnight location on the western outskirts of Oosterbeek at 08:30, the move actually began some hours earlier. Lieutenant-Colonel Fitch was still in the unenviable position of running his Battalion with his Brigade and Division commanders looking over his shoulder and the Battalion thus only moved off after consultation with Lathbury and Urquhart. The latter gave Fitch permission to abandon his assigned TIGER/Utrechtseweg route and sideslip south onto the riverside LION route used by the 2nd Parachute Battalion the previous night, and thus to do what he would likely have done nine hours before, left to his own devices. His superior showed no such inclination. At this point Urquhart had been absent from and out of touch with his HQ for over twelve hours. Given the lack of radio communication and his consequent inability to influence or even properly monitor the situation, the logical thing for Urquhart to do on the morning of Monday 18 September would have been to borrow an escort from Fitch and return to the landing area. Instead, he elected to maintain his self-imposed isolation from the levers of command by staying with the 3rd Battalion when it resumed the advance toward Arnhem, as did Lathbury and his Tactical Brigade HQ.

The 3rd Battalion's advance was again led by B Company, spearheaded by Lieutenant James Cleminson's 5 Platoon and accompanied by Fitch and his Tactical Battalion HQ, Urquhart and Lathbury, a party from the 1st Parachute Squadron RE and a single 6-Pounder anti-tank gun. HQ Company came next with Major Dennison's A Company bringing up the rear. The column also included the remaining two 6-Pounders from C Troop 1st Airlanding Anti-tank Battery, a detachment from 16 Parachute Field Ambulance and a Forward Observer party from the 1st Airlanding Light Regiment RA, along with two Bren Carriers and around twenty Jeeps. B Company made good progress in the pre-dawn darkness, moving through Oosterbeek onto the riverside Benedendorpsweg, through the Oosterbeek Laag underpass and up the incline of the Klingelbeekseweg as it rose several yards of elevation to the junction with the Utrechtsestraatweg, without any enemy contact. The advance continued until 5 Platoon reached the Rhine Pavilion,

300 yards or so east of the junction of the Klingelbeekseweg and Utrechtsestraatweg and almost three miles from the Battalion's start point. Major Waddy's Company had therefore covered as much ground as the previous day in around three hours, with Lieutenant Cleminson's 5 Platoon reaching a point just over a mile from the Arnhem road bridge. At this point Lieutenant-Colonel Fitch called a halt because the Battalion column had become separated; as it grew light the German troops occupying *Den Brink* and adjacent buildings had opened fire on HQ Company's lead element, which consequently lost sight of the tail end of B Company. Major Waddy therefore ordered B Company and its companions to take cover in some large houses on the right of the Utrechtsestraatweg backing onto the Lower Rhine and ordered Lieutenant Cleminson and 5 Platoon to withdraw the hundred yards or so back from the Rhine Pavilion to rejoin the rest of the Company.[112] The 1st Parachute Battalion was also on the move in the pre-dawn gloom, following Lieutenant-Colonel Dobie's chance 05:00 meeting with Captain Anthony Harrison, who had informed Dobie that Frost was in urgent need of reinforcement and presumably that the riverside LION route was clear. At that point the 1st Battalion's S Company had been embroiled with elements of SS *Panzer Pionier Abteilung* 9 holding the underpass carrying the Utrechtsestraatweg under the Arnhem–Ede railway line for the better part of an hour, and Major Stark was preparing to launch a full company attack on the roadblock. Dobie cancelled the attack and ordered another side-slip onto the LION route beginning at approximately 05:30. The 1st Battalion therefore broke contact, withdrew into the eastern edge of Oosterbeek to reorganise and then struck south-east to pick up the Benedendorpsweg as it passed through the Oosterbeek Laag underpass. Arriving there at around 07:00 Dobie found the 3rd Battalion's HQ and A Companies still stalled and took them under command; having lost R Company and most of his support elements and attachments the previous night, the 3rd Battalion's 3-inch mortars, Vickers Medium Machine Guns and 6-Pounder anti-tank guns were especially welcome additions.[113]

Up at the head of the 3rd Battalion column near the Rhine Pavilion Lieutenant Cleminson was champing at the bit to continue the advance; as he put it years after the event, 'The Germans were certainly not in major strength yet, and I had only had one serious casualty in my leading section so far that morning.'[114] This, however, was not actually the case, for the Germans were there in sufficient strength and they were deployed in depth across Cleminson's projected line of advance. In fact, 5 Platoon had inadvertently halted only 200 hundred yards short of a *kampfgruppe* made up of the 350-strong SS *Panzer Artillerie Regiment* 9, reinforced with elements from SS *Panzergrenadier Regiments* 19 and 20 occupying a blocking position on the Utrechtsestraatweg and Onderlangs just east of the Arnhem Municipal Museum. A few hundred yards behind them, manning another line running south for around 300 yards from Arnhem's main railway line to the Lower Rhine was *Kampfgruppe* Harder, made up of around 350 dismounted tank crewmen, fitters and logistic troops from SS *Panzer Regiment* 9, augmented with a draft of 100 *Kriegsmarine* personnel. This was the southern section of the *Sperrlinie* or blocking line erected during the night by *Sturmbannführer* Ludwig Spindler to seal off the British airborne force to the west of Arnhem, as ordered by II SS *Panzerkorps* at 17:30 on 17 September. To this end Spindler had been given command of all 9 SS *Panzer Division's Warnungs Kompanien* and other units in the immediate area, including a detachment of unarmed *Reichsarbeitsdienst* workers who had to be armed with captured British weapons.

By dawn on 18 September the northern section of the *Sperrlinie*, running west along the Amsterdamseweg from a point north of Wolfheze to the Dreijensweg and then south along the latter to the Arnhem–Ede railway line, was manned by elements of *Bataillon* Krafft, a *Heer panzergrenadier* unit dubbed *Kampfgruppe* Bruhn, 140 men from SS *Panzerjäger Abteilung* 9 again reinforced with 100 *Kriegsmarine* personnel, the detachment of armoured half-tracks from SS *Panzer Aufklärungs Abteilung* 9 and the patrol from 213 *Nachrichten Regiment*, all collectively designated *Kampfgruppe* von Allwörden. The central section, commanded by

Spindler in person, ran south from the Amsterdamseweg along the Diependaalschelaan past the *Diependaal* ('city district') to the southern spur of the Arnhem-Ede line, then east around *Den Brink* to the area of the St Elizabeth Hospital. This was manned by elements of *Bataillon* Krafft located on the Amsterdamseweg, with *Hauptsturmführer* Hans Möller's 100-strong *kampfgruppe* from *SS Panzer Pionier Abteilung 9* holding the *Diependaal* and *Den Brink* features and the line of the Klingelbeekseweg and Utrechtsestraatweg, with *Obersturmführer* Heinz Gropp and his eighty-five men from *SS Panzer FlaK Abteilung 9* deployed as a backstop in the area of the railway marshalling yard just north of the St Elizabeth Hospital. The southern segment blocking the Utrechtsestraatweg and running down to the Lower Rhine was occupied by *SS Panzer Artillerie Regiment 9* with *Kampfgruppe* Harder deployed as a further backstop as detailed above. Finally, the large brickworks on the south bank of the Lower Rhine opposite the Onderlangs and the steep, scrub-covered bank rising to the Utrechtsestraatweg and the Municipal Museum was occupied by the remnants of *SS Panzer Aufklärungs Abteilung 9* after its abortive attempt to force the Arnhem road bridge.[115] Given the volume of fire subsequently reported from this location there may also have been light *flak* and other German elements stationed there as well. Spindler's *Sperrlinie* totalled in excess of 1,000 men equipped with various types of armoured half-tracks, two *Jagdpanzer* IVs, an 88mm *flak* gun and several 20mm pieces, although these were spread along a frontage of around 9,000 yards.[116]

It was at this point that the British advance began to go awry. Lieutenant Cleminson's short withdrawal to B Company's main location was spotted by *Kampfgruppe* Spindler, which reportedly sent forward an armoured vehicle to investigate; the 3rd Parachute Battalion War Diary refers to B Company coming under 'accurate 88mm fire' and being subsequently attacked by self-propelled guns.[117] The Germans did not close in but were content at this stage to stand off and fire upon any movement on the Utrechtsestraatweg, and attempts to move from the rear of the houses along the river's edge were blocked by machine-gun fire from the brickworks across the Lower Rhine. The paratroopers were thus relatively safe if they remained indoors, although ammunition began to run short as the stalemate continued. The halt permitted the Battalion signallers successfully to establish radio contact, first with Major Lewis' Company at the road bridge and later with the remainder of the 3rd Parachute Battalion column back down the lower Klingelbeekseweg near the Oosterbeek Laag underpass.[118]

In the meantime the 1st Parachute Battalion had come under harassing fire from mortars and artillery as it approached the underpass after taking the stalled portion of the 3rd Battalion column under command at 07:00. The subsequent advance east through the underpass and up the Klingelbeekseweg road appears to have begun at around 08:00 and was supported by the 3-inch mortars and Vickers guns co-opted from the 3rd Battalion column and fire from the 1st Airlanding Light Regiment's 3 Battery; the latter were controlled by the Regiment's commander, Lieutenant-Colonel William 'Sherriff' Thompson, who had come forward to the 1st Battalion's location, possibly accompanied by Captain Harrison and Lieutenant Antony Driver, commander of the Battery's E Troop.[119]

The 1st Battalion's advance was led by Major Christopher Perrin-Brown's T Company, spearheaded by Lieutenant Jack Hellingoe's 11 Platoon. The paratroopers soon came under heavy fire from automatic weapons emplaced on *Den Brink* on the left and a reported four armoured cars, an unidentified tank, and infantry ensconced in houses and a factory on the right between the Klingelbeekseweg and the Lower Rhine.[120] 11 Platoon was obliged to take shelter in houses on the right of the road and Lieutenant Hellingoe accompanied one of his gunners into a roof space:

> Private Terrett, the Bren gunner, bashed some slates off with the Bren and put the gun down on the rafters pointing through the hole. We could see straight away where the fire was coming from, from the houses and gardens up on the higher ground, only 150 to

200 yards away…I told Terrett to get firing and I think he got a couple of mags off at least before the Germans got onto him and a burst hit him. It took the foresight off the gun, took the whole of his cheek and eye away, and we both fell back through the rafters, crashing down into the bedroom below.[121]

With movement on the Klingelbeekseweg impossible, Major Perrin-Brown then tried to move his men through the back gardens, but the chain-link fencing and concrete panel walls dividing the plots slowed progress, and machine-gun fire from the factory buildings closer to the river slowed it yet further and caused numerous casualties; some unfortunates who took shelter behind the concrete panel walls were wounded when the panels proved to be hollow. By about 09:00 the 1st Battalion also became bogged down in an inconclusive firefight, like Fitch's Battalion just a mile or so further up the road.[122]

While the 1st and 3rd Parachute Battalions were battling their way into the outskirts of Arnhem, the remainder of the 1st Airborne Division was looking either to follow in their wake or hold landing areas for the second lift, led by the armed Jeeps of the 1st Airborne Reconnaissance Squadron. Commanded by Captain David Allsop in Major Gough's absence, the bulk of the Squadron was tasked at 06:30 to ensure the Utrechtseweg was clear toward Heelsum before following the road east through Oosterbeek to scout a secure route for Division HQ's move into Arnhem in the wake of the 1st Parachute Brigade. The exception to this was Captain John Hay's understrength C Troop, which, in light of the casualties it had suffered in its extended contact with *Bataillon* Krafft the previous day, was assigned to assist the 2nd South Staffords holding LZ S around Reijers-Camp Farm. Moving in a Squadron column led by Captain John Park's D Troop, the move east commenced at 07:00 and proceeded without incident for the hour it took to pass almost all the way through Oosterbeek. At that point D Troop came under machine-gun fire at the junction of the Utrechtseweg and Grindweg, around 700 yards short of the underpass beneath the railway spur running south to the Oosterbeek Laag station. There were no casualties apart from an unfortunate German motorcycle despatch rider who drove into the line of fire, but the dismounted investigation and resultant clashes north of the Utrechtseweg went on until the afternoon, drew in A Troop and cost the Squadron two seriously wounded casualties while repeatedly failing to locate a clear passage eastward. As Squadron Adjutant Captain Geoffrey Costeloe put it, 'Everywhere we went, we "bumped" [the enemy].'[123] At 16:00 Squadron QM Lieutenant Collier set up a Rear HQ location close to the Hotel Hartenstein to which the Squadron rallied over the next few hours, all being present and digging in by 22:30; according to the Squadron War Diary this was the first opportunity the troops had for a hot meal that day.[124]

While the Reconnaissance Squadron was trying and failing to locate a route for Division HQ, measures were underway to clarify command arrangements at the latter. Urquhart had been absent from his HQ for over twelve hours at this point and the Division Operations Officer, Lieutenant-Colonel Mackenzie, decided it was time to address the situation. As Lathbury was also out of contact the appointment thus fell upon Urquhart's next choice, the commander of the 1st Airlanding Brigade, Brigadier Philip Hicks. Mackenzie therefore set off by Jeep to inform him of Urquhart's delegation at some point between 07:00 and 09:00.[125] The problem was that Hicks was unaware of this arrangement because Urquhart had dealt with the matter off-the-cuff on the steps of his Horsa, rather than in the administrative period of the planning phase when it should have been addressed. Hicks would thus have been perfectly justified in regarding the matter not as an executive order from his superior but as merely a suggestion or proposal from a HQ functionary of lower rank. There was therefore no guarantee that he would step up to take command of the Division and perhaps more importantly, no mechanism to force him to do so. An outright refusal on Hicks' part was not beyond the bounds of possibility because his Brigade was tasked to protect the parachute and landing zones slated for use by the second lift, which was scheduled to begin at 10:00 and Hicks would arguably have been justified in declining command of the Division in favour of the potentially greater responsibility for ensuring the safe arrival of the remainder of the formation. In the event Mackenzie persuaded Hicks to assume command of the Division and after handing over to his Deputy Brigade Commander, Colonel Hilaro Barlow, Hicks moved to Division HQ at approximately 09:15; interestingly, the 1st Airlanding Brigade HQ War Diary records the change occurring almost two hours later, at 11:00,[126] and the transfer does not appear to have been made official until then.[127]

Whatever the precise timing, Mackenzie was also able to persuade Hicks to authorise reinforcements for the effort to reach the Arnhem road bridge, which he appears to have deduced had run into difficulties. Despite the risk in weakening the landing area defences, Hicks' first act as Division commander was therefore to despatch Lieutenant-Colonel Derek McCardie's under-strength 2nd South Staffords toward Arnhem to reinforce the 1st Parachute Brigade, although there is some confusion as to the precise time the 2nd South Staffords moved off.[128] The Battalion column was led by Major John Phillp's intact D Company followed by Major John Buchanan's depleted Support Company, Colonel McCardie's Tactical HQ and the equally depleted B Company under Captain Reginald Foot. Buchanan was missing half his complement of Vickers guns and all his mortars and anti-tank guns, while B Company was missing its commander, Major Robert Cain, and Lieutenant Roland Sharp's 14 Platoon in its entirety: Cain's Horsa had aborted shortly after take-off and landed safely near Canterbury, while Sharp's glider had force-landed behind German lines near Tilburg.[129] The Staffords were also accompanied by Major Ian Toler, the commander of B Squadron, No. 1 Wing The Glider Pilot Regiment with Captain Angus Low's forty-strong 20 Flight. Major Toler had lost contact with his other Flight after landing and decided that accompanying McCardie's Battalion offered the best prospect of establishing contact with Division HQ.[130]

Brigadier Hicks could have been forgiven for refusing Mackenzie's request, for his Brigade was having problems of its own. The day began quietly for Captain Hodgson and D Company 1st Border, deployed in houses around the crossroads just west of Heelsum at the south-western corner of the Division perimeter, but German probes to ascertain the Company's strength and location began shortly thereafter. Lieutenant Alan Green's 20 Platoon became involved in a long firefight after a German patrol was spotted moving in front of its perimeter. Lance-Sergeant Stanley Sears and Bren gunner Private Joe Walker were killed in the exchange and Lieutenant Green and his runner Private Len Powell were obliged to seek cover in a fortuitously located hen house, part of which was shot away from around them.[131] Another group of ten Germans were spotted moving in on 21 Platoon's position by Corporal Alan Fisher, who allowed them to close within a hundred yards before ordering his section to open fire. A subsequent attack by a larger group appears to have penetrated the Platoon perimeter but Lieutenant Philip Holt rallied his men and drove the Germans back with the assistance of the Battalion's mortars emplaced at Johannahoeve Farm and artillery support from 1 Battery, 1st Airlanding Light Regiment.[132] Although D Company had no way of knowing, these small-scale probes, interspersed with mortaring, did not develop into anything more significant during the morning because they were only the northern fringe of *Kampfgruppe* von Tettau's dawn attack by *Schiffsstammabteilung 6/14* and elements of *SS Unterführerschule* 'Arnheim'. The main focus was upon Renkum, a mile or so south-west of Heelsum overlooking the Lower Rhine.

As a result Major Tom Armstrong's B Company, the most far-flung of the 1st Border's units dug in just east of Renkum, unwittingly found itself directly in the path of the German attack. Armstrong's men had been in intermittent contact with the enemy through the night and daylight revealed German troops occupying houses on the edge of Renkum proper approximately 200 yards from B Company's positions. Further investigation by Armstrong and his recently co-opted second-in-command, Battalion Signals Officer Lieutenant Joe Hardy, showed that the German presence had inadvertently cut the Company off from the remainder of the Battalion. An enquiry to Battalion HQ via the field telephone link strung by Hardy the previous night elicited a curt instruction from the Battalion's temporary commander, Major Stuart Cousens, to fight their way out. Up to this point the Germans were oblivious to the presence of the glider soldiers, but while Armstrong and Hardy were debating their next move a German motorcycle combination drew up in the yard of one of the German-occupied houses and a number of men from *Schiffsstammabteilung 6/14* poured out and gathered around it. The opportunity was too tempting to miss and several Bren guns and a dozen rifles opened fire, hitting a number of the sailors and driving the rest back into cover. At around the same time a column of Germans led by an officer was spotted marching out of Renkum toward the brickworks by Private James Longson, manning a Vickers gun from 2 MMG Platoon emplaced in the hayloft above the brickwork's stables. Longson's gun opened fire when the column closed to within 200 yards, again leaving dead and wounded scattered around in the open while the survivors sought cover in the houses flanking the roadway.

However, by opening fire the glider soldiers revealed their presence and the immediate eruption of fighting around the Company perimeter showed that the *Kriegsmarine* troops were in fact deployed in strength all around the glider soldiers. The attached Vickers guns and mortars were instrumental in rebuffing a German attack launched from a nearby paper mill, but the Germans soon identified the location of the British support weapons and laid down accurate suppressive fire in return. Private Longson's gun came under attack from what was assumed to be a sniper who hit the tripod with a round that ricocheted and wounded Longson in the face and another crewman in the shoulder; both men returned to duty after being patched up by the Company Medical Orderly. In order to avoid additional casualties the MMG Platoon's commander, Lieutenant John McCartney, gave permission for the gun to be redeployed to the riverbank.[133] This involved passing the weapon, ammunition and associated equipment out of a back window and across the roof of an adjoining outhouse because German fire made it impossible to use the main front door to the stable. The German fire also prevented the glider soldiers from rescuing three horses fastened in the stalls beneath the hayloft after a German tracer round ignited the hay. The unfortunate animals burned to death, the sound of their passing providing an unearthly aural backdrop to the crump of mortar bombs and the pop and rattle of small-arms fire. The pressure on B Company increased steadily as the morning wore on. German mortar fire destroyed or seriously damaged all the Company's Jeeps, many of the British-occupied houses caught fire and the field telephone link to Battalion HQ was severed, leaving B Company again reliant on radio messages relayed via neighbouring D Company.[134]

In comparison with the situation at Heelsum and Renkum, the remainder of the 1st Border enjoyed a rather less fraught Monday morning, although they did not escape entirely unmolested. At 11:00 a reported thirty German fighters strafed LZ Z, killing seven men from A Company at the north-west corner of the landing area and wounding fourteen more according to Lieutenant Patrick Baillie, commanding the Company's 7 Platoon; the men had apparently assumed the fighters were friendly and moved into the open to deploy their yellow Celanese (acetate) recognition panels.[135]

The other seat of the action lay to the north-east of the main landing area at DZ Y located on the Groote Heide south of the Amsterdamseweg near the *Zuid Ginkel* café. Usually referred to as Ginkel Heath in British sources, the drop zone was protected by the thinly spread 7th KOSB. Although dispersion and radio communication problems had prevented Lieutenant-Colonel Payton-Reid from closely monitoring German activity around his Battalion's extensive perimeter, he divined the German presence at the unprotected northern end of the drop zone. At 06:00 he therefore ordered Major Charles Sherriff's D Company, all but one platoon of which was deployed along the southern and south-eastern aspects of the DZ as Battalion reserve, to attack and clear a small wood overlooking it on the north side of the Amsterdamseweg. Major Sherriff intended to use Lieutenant Peter Mason's 16 Platoon as a firm base around which to manoeuvre the remainder of the Company; Mason's Platoon, accompanied by the Company second-in-command Captain George Gourlay, had spent an uneventful night dug in a few hundred yards east of the DZ around a hutted work camp, which turned out to be partially occupied by Dutch civilians. However, *Obersturmführer* Hermann Kuhne's 5 *Kompanie* from *SS Wacht Bataillon 3* had surrounded the work camp undetected during the night and opened heavy fire on 16 Platoon during the dawn stand to. As the Platoon's radio communications with Company and Battalion HQ were down Captain Gourlay was unable to call for support or indeed issue any warning of the attack, but despite being seriously outnumbered and hampered by the presence of the Dutch civilians, the glider soldiers held out until mid-morning when they were finally overwhelmed and the survivors taken prisoner. By that point seven men including the Platoon sergeant were dead or dying and a further six were wounded, including Captain Gourlay and Lieutenant Mason.[136]

Major Sherriff's first inkling that 16 Platoon was in trouble came when he was fired on from the woods in the direction of the work camp while moving forward to explain his plan to Captain Gourlay. On receiving word of this development Lieutenant-Colonel Payton-Reid ordered C Company at the south-western side of the perimeter to despatch a Platoon onto the DZ to engage the enemy in the area of the work camp, but the effectiveness of this was partially nullified by the long range and rolling terrain and resultant dead ground. Major Dinwiddie's men were not the only Airborne soldiers moving about on the DZ. Lieutenant Hugh Ashmore and 3 Platoon from the 21st Independent Company had left their overnight position at Reijers-Camp Farm in the early morning to mark DZ Y for the arrival of the 4th Parachute Brigade, which was scheduled for 10:00.[137] The work of setting up the EUREKA beacon, pegging out the day-glo marker panels and placing of the coloured smoke markers for the individual unit RVs by the 4th Parachute Brigade's advance parties was hampered by German fire from the east side of the drop zone; the markers were subsequently used as convenient aiming points by the strafing German fighters later in the morning.[138] In the meantime, at 07:00 pressure of time obliged Major Sherriff to give up on 16 Platoon, bypass the work camp and manoeuvre north through the eastern woods and across the Amsterdamseweg to attack his original objective from the north-east. However, moving into the woods cut D Company's radio link with Battalion HQ and brought it into contact with elements of *SS Wacht Bataillon 3*, and the resultant confused fighting went on for the remainder of the morning and into the afternoon. By 09:00 the sound of battle emanating from the eastern woods suggested that the Germans were advancing south, raising the unwelcome possibility of them dominating the DZ when the 4th Parachute Brigade arrived and decimated the descending paratroopers. After several unsuccessful attempts to contact Major Sherriff to clarify the situation, Colonel Payton-Reid despatched his sole remaining reserve into the woods in the wake of D Company, a composite platoon drawn from Support Company led by its commander, Major Henry Hill. Hill reappeared two hours later and reported inflicting a number of dead and wounded on German infiltrators encountered, taking personal credit for two.[139]

Colonel Payton-Reid was obliged to rely on Major Hill's composite platoon because B and C Companies were also engaged, on the north-western and south-western sectors of the drop zone perimeter respectively. The Germans were initially unaware of the presence of Major Forman's B Company and an attached 6-Pounder anti-tank gun commanded by Sergeant George Barton knocked out at least one half-track among a group of vehicles heading back toward Ede on the Amsterdamseweg; the SS who escaped from the stricken vehicle or vehicles were finished off by a Vickers MMG detachment in a nice example of attached Support element co-ordination.[140] When another group of SS were subsequently spotted digging mortar pits north of the Amsterdamseweg Captain John Walker from the 1st Airlanding Light Regiment, who was acting as a forward observer with 7th KOSB, swiftly organised a shoot by No 1 Battery. The resulting salvoes of 75mm fire prompted a hasty withdrawal and no further activity was noted from that area.[141] Fire support also assisted Lieutenant Donald Murray's 5 Platoon after some SS closed in using the surrounding scrub for cover and wounded two men deepening their trench in the open before launching an assault. An unnamed Sergeant commanding a nearby

3-inch mortar detachment noted the situation and rapidly dropped a score of mortar bombs onto the attackers, who promptly broke off their attack. The feat was especially noteworthy because the distance to the target was only half the 500 yards usually considered the minimum for safety, and firing at such close range involved jacking up the mortar's bipod with sandbags to elevate the tube sufficiently.[142]

Despite being a Platoon understrength – as the gliders carrying Lieutenant Charles Doig's 7 Platoon appear to have aborted while still over Britain – B Company was not content to remain passive in the face of German pressure. Major Forman despatched a six-man patrol from 6 Platoon under Sergeant Edward Shaw equipped with the Platoon's 2-inch mortar to deal with a German machine-gun firing from the direction of Ede, just over a mile to the west. After locating a number of likely positions Sergeant Shaw fired off his entire supply of mortar bombs before withdrawing to the relative safety of the perimeter. The mortar gunner, Private Alexander McKay, was killed when his last bomb exploded prematurely after striking an overhead branch.[143]

The fighting also involved Major Buchanan's A Company, deployed along the Amsterdamseweg two miles or so to the east of the main Battalion perimeter. 4 Platoon at the eastern end of the line again came under sustained pressure from German infantry with support from heavy weapons, which eventually obliged Lieutenant Strang to withdraw to the main Company perimeter at the rather too aptly named *Planken Wambuis*.[144] The latter rebuffed German troops pursuing the beleaguered 4 Platoon, inflicting heavy casualties on the attackers as they made repeated attempts to breach the Company perimeter, and took a number of prisoners in the process. At some point the Company second-in-command, Major John Coke, was despatched to reconnoitre the route for the Company's scheduled move back to the main landing area and returned with the heartening news from Brigade HQ that part of the 1st Parachute Brigade had secured the north end of the Arnhem road bridge.[145]

Thus by mid-morning the situation at the landing area was fairly stable, with the defenders holding firm and maintaining control over LZs X and S and more especially DZ Y as ordered. However, although the second lift was scheduled to arrive at 10:00, 'Unfortunately, the aircraft did not appear at their appointed time,' as the 7th KOSB War Diary drily noted.[146] Because the men on the ground in Holland lacked communication with the airfields and higher HQs in Britain they had no idea whether the lift had been delayed or even abandoned altogether. As the aircraft might appear at any moment they had no option but to continue to hold in the face of steadily increasing German pressure and by the early afternoon the scales had begun to tip against the 7th KOSB holding DZ Y. *Sturmbannführer* Paul Helle had deployed most of *SS Wacht Bataillon 3* in the attack against Ginkel Heath, keeping just *Obersturmführer* Johannes Bronkhorst's 1 *Kompanie* and his heavy weapons element commanded by a *Hauptscharführer* Einenkel in reserve; Helle himself set up his HQ in the *Zuid Ginkel* café at the north edge of the landing zone.[147] The SS had pressed south through the eastern woods from the hutted work camp, were holding the line of the Amsterdamseweg and had pushed the glider soldiers back and overrun the north-eastern corner of the drop zone. The German advance appears to have forced part of Major Forman's B Company to fight its way out of near encirclement, with elements of the 1st Airlanding Light Regiment being also caught up in the fighting. Captain John Lee from the Regiment's A Troop was attached to B Company and lost his Jeep trailer in the breakout, and Lieutenant Keith Halliday and a party from B Troop accompanying the 7th KOSB's HQ element was obliged to revert to the infantry role in defence of its allotted sector of the perimeter.[148] By the early afternoon of Monday 18 September 1944 the question was thus rapidly becoming not when the 4th Parachute Brigade would arrive, but whether or not there would be a drop zone for it to use when it did.

D Plus 1

14:00 to 16:00 Monday 18 September 1944

Operation MARKET's second lift was scheduled to deliver the second increment of units to all three of the Allied airborne divisions, utilising 1,676 parachute transports and glider tugs, and 1,205 assorted gliders. Although the total of powered aircraft was around 300 lower than the first lift, the glider total was almost triple and overall the second lift was therefore larger, with a combined total of 2,501 machines. The 1ˢᵗ Airborne Division's share amounted to 455 aircraft and 296 gliders, with the latter lifting infantry from the 1ˢᵗ Airlanding Brigade and guns, vehicles and supplies for a variety of other units; it also included fifteen of the massive Hamilcar gliders, three of which were carrying trailers pre-loaded with ammunition as a resupply experiment.[1] Twenty-five gliders, likely all Horsas, carried loads that had aborted from the first lift. Of the thirteen Horsas carrying elements of the 7ᵗʰ King's Own Scottish Borderers (KOSB) for example, only the five carrying the Battalion MT Section and a single machine carrying a platoon from C Company were originally slated for the second lift.[2] Of the remainder, ten Horsas carried an advance party for the 1ˢᵗ Polish Independent Parachute Brigade consisting mainly of the Brigade Anti-tank Battery, and four Horsas carried men and equipment from two RAF radar teams. The gliders were again towed by a mixture of Albemarles, Halifaxes and Stirlings from No. 38 Group and Dakotas from No. 46 Group. The parachute portion of the Division's second lift, principally Brigadier John Hackett's 4ᵗʰ Parachute Brigade, was again carried exclusively in USAAF aircraft, specifically 123 C-47s and three visually identical C-53s drawn from the 314ᵗʰ and 315ᵗʰ Troop Carrier Groups based at Saltby in Lincolnshire and Spanhoe in Northamptonshire respectively. Finally, thirty-three Stirlings from Nos. 295 and 570 Squadrons based at RAF Harwell in Berkshire were slated to carry out the first routine supply drop for the 1ˢᵗ Airborne Division onto the as yet unused LZ L, half a mile or so east of LZ S.[3]

All the aircraft slated for the second lift appear to have been loaded and ready to fly by the evening of Sunday 17 September. The 4ᵗʰ Parachute Squadron RE despatched working parties the six miles or so from its billets at Glaston and Uppingham to RAF Spanhoe to load containers onto the C-47s from the US 315ᵗʰ Troop Carrier Group that would be carrying them to DZ Y the following day at 17:30.[4] In addition to the routine infantry stores the containers were loaded with engineer-specific supplies and equipment including mines, mine detectors and explosives. The Squadron commander, Major Æneas Perkins, later recalled that loading the containers was problematic because it was 'difficult to decide exactly what should be taken in view of our rather indefinite tasks'.[5] At RAF Blakehill Farm in Wiltshire 5 Flight from D Squadron, No. 1 Wing The Glider Pilot Regiment spent part of the morning loading their Horsas with 6-Pounder guns and Jeeps belonging to the 1ˢᵗ Airlanding Anti-tank Battery RA, supervised by the Flight commander, Captain Alexander Morrison. This involved driving or pushing the Jeeps and guns up a ramp to the glider's side door and then physically manhandling them through ninety degrees into the fuselage where they were secured. With the back-breaking job completed in around thirty minutes, the Glider Pilots were free for the rest of the day and some took the opportunity to 'personalise' their gliders with cartoons, mottos, lewd comments or similar; Morrison returned from checking his unit's gliders to find his own Horsa decorated rather restrainedly by one of his Staff-Sergeants with the Flight badge, a winged Roman numeral five, as a recognition feature.[6] After watching RAF No. 46 Group's Dakotas taking off towing the first lift from RAF Down Ampney in Gloucestershire, Private Albert Blockwell and the rest of the 7th KOSB's MT Section repaired to a recreation tent at around 14:00 to hear about the landings in Holland on the radio. They were then put to the more typically prosaic military work of cleaning up the Battalion's tented camp of the mess left behind by the first lift.[7]

With the lead element of the second lift scheduled to arrive at the landing area in Holland at 10:00 on Monday 18 September, take-offs had to begin soon after dawn and aircrew and troops were roused at around 05:00. After groping their way through the pre-dawn darkness to the cookhouse tent, Private Blockwell and his comrades were disappointed to find that the 'wonderful big pre-invasion meals' they had heard about were not forthcoming and that they would have to make do with the standard breakfast fare of bacon, bread and jam.[8] At Blakehill Farm Captain Morrison made a more worrying discovery on leaving his billet at 05:00 after showering and shaving. The airfield, along with many others across southern England, was blanketed in mist and low cloud, obliging 1st Allied Airborne Army HQ to postpone take-off until conditions improved. Consequently, the 4th Parachute Squadron RE did not leave its billets for RAF Spanhoe until 09:00, while the Glider Pilots Regiment's B Squadron at RAF Manston in Kent commenced its final briefing at the same time.[9] Back at Blakehill Farm Captain Morrison and his men spent a hopeful hour in the cockpits of their Horsas parked around the perimeter track on the basis of early meteorological reports suggesting the mist would lift, before receiving word that take-off had been postponed until midday.[10]

The mist actually cleared around four hours after dawn and the postponement was lifted at 11:00, making the timings roughly the same as the previous day. At RAF Down Ampney the first Dakota from No. 48 Squadron, piloted by Squadron-Leader Peter Duff-Mitchell, took off at precisely 11:00 followed by the remainder of the Squadron at one- or two-minute intervals; all twenty-six Dakotas and their Horsas from the Glider Pilot Regiment's E Squadron, No.2 Wing were aloft by 11:36.[11] It is unclear precisely what time Captain Morrison and 5 Flight took off from Blakehill Farm, but the remainder of D Squadron, consisting of 8 and 22 Flights commanded by Captain Barry Murdoch and Captain Iain Muir respectively, began taking off from RAF Keevil at 11:26, while the Short Stirlings from Nos. 190 and 620 Squadrons towing G Squadron from RAF Fairford started four minutes later.[12] At RAF Manston the Armstrong Whitworth Albemarles from Nos. 296 and 297 Squadrons towing B Squadron's gliders began taking off a little later, at 12:15, because their start point in Kent was a hundred miles or more closer to Holland than the other glider bases. All three units were normally based at RAF Brize Norton in Oxfordshire but had moved temporarily to Manston for the MARKET lift.[13] The parachute transports from the US 52nd Troop Carrier Wing followed a similar timetable. The C-47s from the 314th Troop Carrier Group carrying the 156 Parachute Battalion from RAF Saltby began taking off at 11:00 for example, while the aircraft from the 315th Troop Carrier Group carrying the 4th Parachute Squadron's parachute echelon began taking off from RAF Spanhoe at 12:10; the Squadron's glider element took off from RAF Keevil at 11:45.[14]

Once again, the take-off phase went relatively well. One Horsa, probably from A Squadron, crashed on take-off after the tug aircraft lost power and a further seven Horsas and a single Hamilcar aborted while still over England.[15] The latter, from C Squadron based at RAF Tarrant Rushton, was carrying a 17-Pounder gun from the 2nd Airlanding Anti-tank Battery RA and landed safely at RAF Chilbolton in Hampshire after its Halifax tug developed engine trouble.[16] Staff-Sergeant Proctor's Horsa from B Squadron also landed safely at Ashford in Kent shortly after taking off from nearby Manston,[17] and another Horsa from D Squadron piloted by a Staff-Sergeant Stocker and Sergeant Allen force-landed at the US fighter base at RAF

Martlesham Heath in Suffolk after the towline parted; according to some sources their Stirling tug from 299 Squadron piloted by a Flight-Lieutenant B. H. Berridge or Barridge also landed there, reattached the towline and joined up with a Dakota stream, although the Squadron War Diary refers to Stocker and Allen moving over to the third lift.[18] The remainder of the seven aborts also appear to have landed safely and all were reportedly carried over to the third lift.[19] The parachute transports got away without mishap apart from one aircraft leading a three-aircraft vic from the 314th Troop Carrier Group's 50th Squadron carrying men from 156 Parachute Battalion, which had a lucky escape when a malfunction prematurely deployed a parachute attached to a container stowed in the cargo cells in the underside of the aircraft's fuselage. The unexpected drag seriously affected the machine's trim and releasing the container resulted in the errant parachute canopy becoming entangled with the aircraft's tail wheel. The unknown pilot calmly landed at a convenient airfield in East Anglia with the container streaming behind like a drogue, had the canopy cut free and resumed the flight to Holland with the glider stream after failing to catch up with his original serial.[20]

Originally the intention was to despatch the entire second lift via the Southern Route employed by the aircraft carrying the 101st Airborne Division the previous day, which made landfall near Ostend and ran over Allied-held Belgium. However, during the postponement reports of heavy cloud and rain over Belgium prompted 1st Allied Airborne Army HQ to switch to the shorter Northern Route, which ran south-east for a hundred miles from Aldeburgh before crossing the Dutch coast near the island of Schouwen; a desire to make up time lost to the postponement may also have been a factor. The change of route obliged some rapid redrawing of flight plans and the Operations Record Book of at least one of No. 46 Group's constituent squadrons lists the original coded waypoints and grid references for the Southern Route but refers to crossing the Dutch coast near Schouwen in the subsequent mission précis.[21] Two replacement Dakota crews drafted in to assist No. 575 Squadron at RAF Broadwell did not receive word of the change at all and ended up flying alone across Belgium with the cloud base forcing them progressively lower until RCAF Flying Officer Edward Henry's machine was hit by German anti-aircraft fire on approaching the front line. The *flak* killed Henry and wounded his navigator, Flying Officer Harry McKinley, a US citizen serving with the RCAF. Despite there being no second pilot aboard, after consulting with the glider crew McKinley agreed to continue the mission with the assistance of Warrant Officer Bert Smith, even though neither man had undergone any formal flying training. This courageous decision had to be abandoned when the Horsa, likely from No. 2 Wing's F Squadron, lost an aileron to more *flak* but McKinley and Smith succeeded in towing the damaged glider back to friendly territory where it landed safely near Bourg Leopold. Its passengers included the commander of the 1st Battalion The Border Regiment, Lieutenant-Colonel Thomas Haddon, who had force-landed shortly after take-off the previous day; undeterred by this second glider failure in twenty-four hours, Haddon and his party set out for Arnhem under their own steam. Meanwhile McKinley and Smith managed to keep their Dakota aloft despite McKinley's wound and a large hole in the port side of the cockpit. After an attempt to land at Brussels had been thwarted by low cloud, they finally arrived over Martlesham Heath after a flight lasting two hours and ten minutes. After an unsuccessful attempt to persuade Smith and the aircraft's radio operator to bail out, McKinley performed a bumpy landing that saw the Dakota trundle off the end of the runway and roll unscathed through a row of parked P-47 fighters before coming to rest. The 356th Fighter Group treated these latest in a series of unscheduled visitors to a hero's welcome, after which McKinley found himself the sole occupant of a hospital ward set aside specifically for MARKET casualties near Swindon in Wiltshire.[22]

Of the main formation, two more gliders were lost over the North Sea. Chalk No. 457, a Horsa from D Squadron carried over from the first lift piloted by Lieutenant Norman Adams and an aptly named Sergeant Waterman, ditched and all aboard were swiftly picked up by rescue launches patrolling the route, apart from Lieutenant Adams, who was posted missing presumed drowned.[23] The second was a Hamilcar carrying a 17-Pounder gun and prime mover from the 2nd Airlanding Anti-tank Battery RA, which was cast off when its Halifax tug experienced engine trouble. The giant machine broke up on impact with the sea and again all aboard were rescued bar one unfortunate: Lieutenant Robert McLaren, commanding the Battery's F Troop, was trapped by the gun and drowned.[24] Another Horsa from D Squadron, Chalk No. 596 piloted by Staff-Sergeant Black and Sergeant Hudson, appears to have made landfall safely after casting off over Schouwen due to slipstream problems. Crossing the Dutch coast added German anti-aircraft fire to the existing hazards, as Captain Morrison noted: 'My Second Pilot called out "coast ahead" and there we were passing over the yellow sand dunes of Holland. Our route took us past Schouwen Island...suddenly, five miles ahead, all hell broke loose. German anti-aircraft guns both on the ground and in flak-ships had opened up on the leading aircraft carrying the parachute companies and within seconds they were completely engulfed by angry black puffs.'[25] Unlike the previous day, the second lift placed the parachute drop ahead of the glider landings, with the 314th Troop Carrier Group leading the aircraft stream trailed by the 315th Troop Carrier Group. Both formations passed safely through the coastal anti-aircraft fire unscathed, again in contrast to the first lift. In part this was due to the *flak* suppression effort mounted by RAF and USAAF fighter-bombers, which appears to have continued right up to the landing area. Glider pilots dug in near 1st Airborne Division HQ after landing with the first lift reported seeing 'Mustangs, Thunderbolts and Spitfires' overhead in the mid-afternoon of 18 September shortly before the second glider lift arrived.[26] On the other hand, pilots from the 315th Troop Carrier Group specifically reported seeing no friendly fighters at all after reaching their Initial Point (IP) for the run in to the DZ, when they were at their most vulnerable.[27] The fighters may therefore have been held up dealing with anti-aircraft positions farther back along the route, given that the co-pilot of the C-47 from the 310th Troop Carrier Squadron carrying Brigadier Hackett recalled seeing RAF Typhoons strafing *flak* positions on offshore islands and P-47s shooting up German trucks.[28]

The parachute element's luck continued largely intact until the lead flights reached the vicinity of the River Waal, around twenty miles from the drop zone. As they had passed their Initial Point for the run-in to the drop zone the C-47s were forbidden from taking evasive action and were descending to their jump height of 600 feet, throttling back toward their jump speed of around ninety knots. At this point the formation ran into a concentration of anti-aircraft fire not noted during the first lift. The guns may have been moved in as a result of the same German intelligence windfall that had despatched the *Luftwaffe* fighters to the 1st Airborne Division's landing area at 11:00, as one source suggests.[29] Whatever the origin of the guns, their fire was accurate and at least four transports were shot down in quick succession. Captain Leonard A. Ottaway's C-47 from the 50th Troop Carrier Squadron, which had moved up to replace the aircraft with the malfunctioning container parachute over Suffolk, took a hit in the port wing that set the engine and fuel tank ablaze. On being informed of the damage by an accompanying aircraft, Captain Ottaway jettisoned his containers and went into a steep dive, possibly in an attempt to extinguish the flames. Its passage was noted by Major John Waddy, commanding 156 Parachute Battalion's B Company standing in the door of his own C-47,[30] and 1st Lieutenant Walter D. Nims piloting another C-47: 'He [Ottaway] headed for the ground as if to make a forced landing. His gear came down and he was apparently ready to land but he seemed to be unable to flare out his approach and went right on into the ground, hitting very tail high, buckling the gear and skidding to a stop on its belly...When the plane hit, the gas tank seemed to explode and one wing came half off...The cockpit and cabin were not badly cracked but was on fire when I last saw it.'[31] In addition to Captain Ottaway the C-47 was carrying five crew and eighteen paratroopers from 156 Parachute Battalion's MMG Platoon, all of whom were killed.[32]

The passengers in Captain Warren S. Egbert's C-47 from the 61st Troop Carrier Squadron were more fortunate when it, too, sustained a hit to the port wing; Egbert held the burning aircraft steady while his stick from the 11th Parachute Battalion and two of his crew jumped, but he was killed in the subsequent crash along with his co-pilot and navigator, Lieutenants Jacob Feldman and Horace M. Jerome respectively. One of the paratroopers, Private John Barton, also appears to have been killed by a parachute malfunction in spite of Captain Egbert's gallantry.[33] Captain Frank King, commanding the 11th Parachute Battalion's Support Company, was travelling in the other shot-down 61st Squadron C-47, piloted by Captain George Merz. The stick were making their immediate pre-jump checks when the aircraft was hit and King only became aware of how badly on looking out the door: 'I was horrified to see how low we were – no more than 250 feet. I then put my head out, into the slipstream, and saw that the whole port wing was on fire. I shouted to Sergeant-Major Gartland…and told him to open the little door into the pilot's compartment, which he did, and we saw a mass of smoke and flames.' King promptly ordered the stick to jump even though the light was red, which was considered a serious disciplinary offence, and all but the final three made it through the door barely high enough for their parachutes to open: 'I was told afterwards that one man fell in the doorway and the man behind him jumped over him, but his parachute didn't open. Probably the last men… decided they were too low and stayed with the plane.'[34]

The crash appears to have been witnessed by the 11th Battalion's Medical Officer, Captain Stuart Mawson, who was third in his stick behind Battalion Commander Lieutenant-Colonel George Lea and his batman: 'Then another nearby aircraft started to bank slowly out of formation, dragging a wing with dirty yellow flame and black smoke trailing from the engine, and with horrible inevitability spiralled slowly earthwards…It was…halfway to the ground before men appeared, jettisoning themselves with hopelessly slow precision…the last few had no time, and as the Dakota hit the ground and burst into flames a man was still framed in the doorway.'[35] The stricken C-47 crash-landed in a field just north of the Lower Rhine between Rhenen and Wageningen. Navigator Lieutenant Russell C. Stephens and Radio Operator Technical-Sergeant William Buckley were killed trying to bale out from the forward door but Merz and his co-pilot, Lieutenant Ernest W. Haagensen, escaped from the burning wreck via the roof hatch and assisted one of the 11th Battalion men suffering from burns and possibly Crew Chief Corporal Richard Eastman; King reported the latter killed by the *flak* hit but in a post-war interview Merz referred to him being captured and executed by Dutch SS at some point after the crash. Both pilots were spirited away from the crash site by the Dutch Underground, who also rescued Lieutenant Frederick Hale, pilot of the sole C-47 lost by the 62nd Troop Carrier Squadron on 18 September. Hale baled out via his aircraft's roof hatch with barely enough height for his canopy to deploy, but three members of his crew were killed and it is unclear how many of his stick of paratroopers managed to jump, if any. Having survived a night-time ditching off Sicily during Operation HUSKY following a mid-air collision, the crash was Merz's second lucky escape and he, Haagensen and Hale were sheltered by their Dutch saviours until ferried to safety over the Lower Rhine during Operation PEGASUS on the night of 22-23 October.[36]

The 315th Troop Carrier Group did not suffer as badly as their forebears from the 314th, losing just two C-47s shot down in quick succession to anti-aircraft guns defending the railway yard at s'Hertogenbosch, approximately sixteen miles from the drop zone; the town marked the point where the stream divided into three sub-streams heading for the three divisional landing areas. Lieutenant Thomas T. Tucker's aircraft from the 34th Troop Carrier Squadron was hit first and began to burn; after quickly assessing the situation Tucker ordered his stick and crew to jump before following himself. The stick was probably from No. 4 Platoon, A Company, 10th Parachute Battalion and included Sergeant Keith Banwell, who said only eight men managed to exit the stricken aircraft and their passage to the door was hindered by a number of dead and wounded paratroopers.[37] All landed safely and Lieutenant Tucker and his crew made it safely to Allied territory four days later; the crew's only casualty was crew chief Technical Sergeant Woodrow W. Durbin who suffered a sprained ankle.[38] Lieutenant James H. Spurrier from the trailing 43rd Troop Carrying Squadron was not so fortunate. Lieutenant Spurrier's co-pilot, Lieutenant Edward S. Fulmer, had just noted Tucker's aircraft burning in the formation ahead when their C-47 was hit by a series of 20 or 37mm rounds that set fire to the starboard engine and punched holes in the inner wing and fuselage. At least one round exploded in the navigation compartment behind Spurrier's seat, killing him or rendering him unconscious. The same explosion wounded Fulmer in the leg and back and ignited the fuel tank under the cockpit floor:

> I was flying the plane at the time and was listening out on the VHF radio set and Spurrier was connected to the crew chief on the intercom set. I reached over and shook Spurrier, wanting him to get the fire extinguisher as smoke and flames were coming inside the cockpit. Spurrier sort of slumped over in his seat and I couldn't rouse him. I held the ship level and pulled out of the formation to give my paratroops and other crew men time to get out. I felt the slight jar as the troops left the ship and the flames were burning my face and left side, shoulder and back.[39]

Back in the C-47's troop compartment the stick of paratroopers from B Company, 10th Parachute Battalion were hooked up ready to jump, with Sergeant Albert Spring in the door and crew chief Corporal Russell L. Smith on the intercom, standing by for the green light. Another hit had just shot away the jump light and nearby container-release lever when the aircraft's radio operator, Corporal William T. Hollis, opened the cockpit door to reveal a mass of smoke and flame. Already alerted by the intercom going dead, Smith reacted quickly: 'I ordered the paratroopers to jump. There was some confusion while these men were jumping as one trooper got his foot fouled in the lines. Before they were all out, we had been hit numerous times by small arms and *flak*, and were rapidly losing altitude. I ordered the radio operator to jump and I followed.' Lieutenant Fulmer tried to belly land the burning C-47 near Opheusden between the Waal and Lower Rhine but appears to have lost control after clipping a power line. Spurrier was killed but the wounded and badly burned Fulmer escaped through a side window after failing to unlatch the roof escape hatch and was carried away from the crash site by a local farmer called Willemsen and his two sons; the pilot was subsequently awarded the Distinguished Service Cross and knighted by Queen Wilhelmina of the Netherlands for his courage. Corporal Smith hit the ground just 200 yards from the wreck, injuring his ankle in the process, but Corporal Hollis and one of the 10th Battalion paratroopers, Private Alfred Penwill, were killed by parachute malfunction. The exits were noted by another pilot in the formation:

> The enemy had been firing for about thirty seconds when I noticed Lt. Spurrier's plane nose down slightly and pass below our ship…It was during this time the paratroopers started jumping out…the plane started a slight turn to the left and I noticed one man jump out. His parachute had just started to come out of the pack when he struck the ground. At the same time, a second man jumped out and his chute was hanging in a trail position but I do not believe it had opened enough to check his fall. These last two men used the white type chutes carried by crew members.[40]

The survivors were again sheltered and treated by the Dutch Underground until they could be evacuated to Allied-held territory.[41]

Arrival at Ginkel Heath revealed another unwelcome change from the previous day's drop: as one US pilot put it, 'I could tell before we got to the drop zone that they [the British] were going to be in big trouble. You could see the mortar bursts hitting the ground all over the drop zone. It was not just one or two, it was multiple mortars. It could have been mortars or guns, probably both. You could see it peppering the ground all around.'[42] The throb of hundreds of Wright Cyclone aero engines became audible to the south before the aircraft themselves were visible, and the sound prompted differing reactions at the drop zone. The immediate reaction of some of the German attackers was caught for posterity by an *SS Propagandakompanie* film cameraman, and included riflemen and machine gunners with MG42s and captured Bren guns on anti-aircraft mounts improvised from hastily stacked fruit boxes firing into the sky, backed by a half-track-mounted four-barrelled 20mm *Flakvierling*.[43] One source refers to the Germans aiming specifically at the C-47's doors in an effort to hit the first man in the stick and block the exit for the rest, although this would have been a tall order for even a skilled marksman at the range and speeds involved.[44] Mortar bombs set fire to vegetation at the northern end of the drop zone, although it is unclear whether this was accidental or deliberate. For the British Airborne soldiers charged to protect the drop zone the approach of the parachute transports was the signal to trigger their EUREKA beacon, ignite the coloured smoke pots to indicate wind direction and rally points for the various incoming units, and to launch their last-ditch effort to suppress German interference with the landing. Thus the 7th KOSB's HQ and Support Companies launched a counter-attack on the German troops firing on the aircraft from the woods and the unfinished motorway embankment at the south and south-eastern edges of the drop zone, co-opting Lieutenant Keith Halliday's attached party from the 1st Airlanding Light Regiment to make up the numbers. At the opposite end of the DZ Captain Brian Carr led the 10th Parachute Battalion's advance party forward into the teeth of the German attack in an effort to secure the Battalion rally point near the *Zuid Ginkel* café.[45]

The precise time the jump commenced is unclear. One source says 15:09, but this is around an hour later than the times cited in the various unit War Diaries; the 7th KOSB referred to the drop taking place 'between 14:00 and 15:00' and to 'all parachutists being down' within the time.[46] 156 Parachute Battalion reported the jump commencing at 14:00, the 4th Parachute Squadron RE at 14:20 and the 11th Parachute Battalion at 'approx. 14:30', while the 4th Parachute Brigade HQ does not give a time but refers to the drop being six minutes late. Given all this, it is probably safe to assume that the drop actually began at a few minutes after 14:00, which fits with the approximately three hours-plus flying time of the first lift along the same route.[47] The US transports were flying in a compact formation and the drop was complete with an estimated 1,914 paratroopers being delivered on or near DZ Y in well under thirty minutes; this again accorded with the first parachute lift, which was complete in eighteen minutes. Seven men reportedly failed to jump due to wounds from ground fire or losing their footing as their aircraft took evasive action.[48] Not all the US pilots were happy about giving such passengers another chance by going round again. As one pilot put it: 'I just wanted to get the mission over with. I always told the crew chief that if anyone freezes in the door, you kick him out. I never wanted to go back over the DZ again.'[49] Not all US aircrew appear to have subscribed to this philosophy, however. Corporal David Jones' stick from B Company, 156 Parachute Battalion was delayed when 'one of the relatively new men in the battalion refused to jump and froze in the doorway. An RAF despatcher would have given him a boot in the rear, but the American crew chief didn't, and there was a long delay before he was pulled away.'[50] Whatever their individual philosophies regarding going round again, once their passengers were gone the transport pilots wasted no time getting clear, as described by Captain Bernard Coggins, a navigator with the 43rd Troop Carrier Squadron, 315th Troop Carrier Wing: 'With the green light, all of the paratroopers left the plane without hesitation. I always had a lot of respect for paratroopers, but it was never higher than when they dropped into that preview of hell. There was no hesitation on our part, either. When the last man was out the door, the throttles were pushed to the firewall and we dove for the deck.'[51]

Despite the German ground fire the majority of the paratroopers were unscathed, although many had narrow escapes. One Private from 156 Battalion saw tracer rounds passing close by as he descended and heard one of the other men in his stick being hit, but was prevented from going to his aid on landing by Regimental Sergeant Major Dennis Gay, who correctly if cold-bloodedly ordered him off to join the rest of his Platoon instead. Signalman Arthur Winstanley from the 4th Parachute Brigade Signals Section had an even closer shave. A box containing a carrier pigeon and bag of feed attached to his equipment was half shot away during the descent and as he braced for landing about fifty feet up a mortar bomb exploded to his front right, killing another man from the stick as he touched down.[52] The 10th Parachute Battalion's Quartermaster-Lieutenant Joseph Glover also had an avian-oriented descent. Glover owned a pet chicken named Myrtle he had carried on six training jumps during the summer, on several occasions releasing her during the descent to land under her own steam. In recognition of this Myrtle had been awarded the rank of Parachick and a set of parachute wings worn on an elastic strap about her neck, and Glover had decided that Arnhem would be Myrtle's first combat jump. Both man and Parachick landed safely, the latter in a zippered canvas pouch attached to Glover's parachute harness. Myrtle was then handed over to Glover's batman, Private Joe Scott, for safekeeping before both men began making their way through the confusion to the column of green smoke marking the 10th Battalion's RV at the north-eastern corner of the DZ.[53] Corporal Frederick Jenkins, also from the 10th Battalion, landed in the burning portion of the DZ and avoided being hit by fire from five German machine-guns before almost being killed when heat began to detonate abandoned mortar bombs scattered nearby; a piece of shrapnel wounded the man next to him in the face and Jenkins rendered first aid before helping him off the DZ.[54]

The hostility directed at the new arrivals did not emanate solely from the Germans. After landing unscathed Major John Waddy from 156 Battalion's B Company was confronted on the way to his RV by the irate commander of the 10th Battalion's Battalion Advance Party, Captain Brian Carr: 'You're bloody late. Do you realise we've been waiting here for four hours?' the fulminating Carr observed, before giving an increasingly unsettled Waddy a brief overview of the situation.[55]

In sharp contrast to the training jump atmosphere the previous day, the second parachute lift not only descended into the middle of a battle, but a large number of paratroopers also overshot the DZ. This included the entire final flight of nine C-47s, which had become separated from the main formation during the fly-in, and a number of individual aircraft that despatched their sticks late for a variety of reasons. The most far flung were two sticks from 133 Parachute Field Ambulance RAMC and one from the 4th Parachute Squadron RE, which came down eight miles north of the DZ near Otterlo. A number of men from the 10th Parachute Battalion's D Company, including Company commander Captain Cedric Horsfall, landed two miles wide and Company Sergeant Major Robert Grainger was initially only able to rally fifty-three men at the RV, although Horsfall and the majority of the misdrops were able to reach the Battalion RV with the aid of a Dutch civilian.[56] One stick from 156 Parachute Battalion was in the process of jumping when a *flak* burst threw the paratroopers off their feet. The resultant delay put Private David Dagwell into the trees along the east side of the DZ entangled with the cord from his rifle valise, which was wedged higher up in the tree: 'I was struggling to get my knife free when a movement registered in the corner of my eye…and I wished I were elsewhere as three German soldiers made their way cautiously along the path below…Fortunately for me they were far more interested in the events on the DZ and, after what seemed an age, they disappeared round a bend. When I began breathing again I managed to draw my knife, cut through the cord, slap the release box and let go, to fall on to a soft carpet of pine needles.'[57] Corporal David Jones, whose exit had been delayed by a refusal, ended up 'swinging like a pendulum' in trees north of the DZ with six other members of his stick, and landed among a party of Germans on cutting free from his harness. Fortunately the Germans fled apart from one individual who surrendered, and Jones became the proud possessor of a truck loaded with ammunition. Unfortunately, his intention of delivering the vehicle to his Company commander was thwarted by an unnamed KOSB officer who commandeered Jones and the truck to carry wounded to a medical facility in Oosterbeek; the enforced transfer became permanent and Corporal Jones never did rejoin 156 Parachute Battalion.[58]

Unsurprisingly given the circumstances, the drop suffered a larger proportion of jump injuries than normal. These included the 10th Parachute Battalion's chaplain, Captain Raymond Bowers, who fractured an ankle on landing and Major Æneas Perkins and six men from the 4th

Parachute Squadron RE; Perkins dislocated a shoulder so severely he was obliged temporarily to hand over command to his deputy, Captain Nigel Thomas.[59] Overall, the landing was a significantly more costly affair than the first lift. The first had suffered only a single parachute fatality whereas the landing on 18 September cost the 4th Parachute Brigade approximately thirty, with the 7th KOSB losing around fifteen more killed in the fight to protect the drop zone.[60] The latter included the commander of the KOSB's Support Company, Major Henry Hill, who was killed by machine-gun fire while crossing the motorway embankment at the southern edge of the DZ after leading the counter-attack that drove the Germans back as the drop commenced.[61] The combination of landing injuries, fatalities and scattering made a significant dent in the Brigade's combat power, collectively and to its constituent units. According to the Brigade War Diary, the Brigade was between seventy-five and eighty per cent complete by 15:30 with no contact with the 4th Parachute Squadron RE or 133 Parachute Field Ambulance, while 156 Parachute Battalion reported the absence of two officers and approximately 100 men at the Battalion RV, for example.[62] Brigadier Hackett nonetheless considered his formation to be 'a going concern', presumably in comparison with the somewhat pessimistic briefings he had made to his subordinate commanders before MARKET commenced.[63]

The unwieldy glider combinations also suffered from the attentions of unsuppressed anti-aircraft fire after crossing the Dutch coast, although the first loss appears to have been Chalk No.956 from D Squadron flown by a Staff Sergeant Black and Sergeant Hudson, which was obliged to cast off over the Dutch coastal islands with slipstream problems.[64] A near miss blew the rear door off one Horsa carrying a party from the 2nd Airlanding Anti-Tank Battery, and three of the Gunners linked arms to form a human windbreak against the slipstream roaring through the glider's fuselage.[65] In another Horsa carrying a Jeep and trailer Gunner Robert Christie and two companions from the 1st Airlanding Light Regiment went forward to investigate a series of tearing noises, fearing it was the load coming unlashed: 'I crawled up the floor, between the wheels in their troughs and the skin-and-frame members of the Horsa. Again the noises and sudden shafts of sunlight appeared through jagged holes. It was *flak*. Relieved, we returned to our seats and, as one, removed our steel helmets and sat on them to protect our vital assets.'[66] Flight-Lieutenant James Stark's Halifax tug from No. 298 Squadron lost part of its starboard fin as it approached the Allied front line, without consequence – but not all hits were resolved so happily. One of the Horsas carrying the RAF radar teams folded in half after being struck by a large-calibre shell and two tugs were seen to be shot down: a Dakota from No.512 Squadron and a Stirling from No.570 Squadron. The Dakota, piloted by Squadron-Leader Trevor Southgate, caught fire after being hit, but Southgate cast off his glider before crash-landing near Kesteren, seventeen miles west of Arnhem on the south bank of the Lower Rhine. All aboard were burned, co-pilot Flight-Lieutenant A. E. Saunders especially badly, but all survived, Southgate with a broken elbow and wireless operator Flying Officer J. H. Parry with a broken ankle. All evaded capture with the aid of Dutch civilians and were evacuated to the UK on 24 September 1944.[67] The Stirling, piloted by Pilot-Officer Charles Culling, was not so fortunate. The bomber went out of control and exploded on hitting the ground killing all on board, but the Horsa, carrying RAF radar equipment, landed safely near the south bank of the Lower Rhine; all aboard reached the 1st Airborne Division's lines later via the Heveadorp ferry along with a number of other strays who had landed south of the river.[68] No. 570 Squadron actually lost three machines including Pilot-Officer Bell's plus another in a take-off accident.

In all, fifteen gliders were lost over Holland.[69] At least one more was deliberately cast off when its tug was hit, possibly Staff-Sergeant Coombs' and Sergeant Knowles' Chalk No.964 from D Squadron, which landed at an unidentified US landing area, and three were cast adrift when stress or *flak* severed their towlines. These included a Horsa being towed by a Dakota from No.48 Squadron that came down five miles east-north-east of s'Hertogenbosch, and D Squadron's Chalk No.1011 flown by Lieutenant Stanley Moorwood and a Staff-Sergeant Stevenson, which came down ten miles short of the landing zone.[70] These separations were sometimes a consequence of the turbulence created by bringing so many aircraft and gliders into such close proximity for prolonged periods, a phenomenon sometimes referred to in official reports as 'slipstream trouble'.[71] Captain Morrison experienced the problem during the fly-in:

> There were planes everywhere and I was beginning to ponder if there was enough air space for us all when my reverie was suddenly shattered by the first of many vicious sideslips that were quite terrifying. What had happened was that the slipstream from one of the huge bomber aircraft ahead had created a tremendous air turbulence which had hit only one wing of my glider, forcing it to swing away and to drop drastically. This, in turn, yanked the tail of the tug sideways and down and, if we had not succeeded in bringing our aircraft back onto station by heaving on the control column, the whole combination would have been out of control. Whilst we had been aware of this problem from previous operations, the numbers of aircraft were now far greater than before and this presented a constant hazard which gave pilots a terrible strain of anticipation.[72]

The tugs approached the release point at a height of 3,000 feet to avoid German ground fire, descending to 2,500 feet or lower for the release. Captain Morrison again:

> We approached our Landing Zone at about 1,800 feet, and could see the coloured parachutes of the 1st [Parachute] Brigade dotted around the DZs 'X' and 'Z'…At last I could discern our own field ahead, which had been marked with coloured smoke by the Independent Parachute Company and, when we were ready, my Second Pilot pulled the lever which released the glider. With a crack, the tow parted and our tug, with the rope whipping below, turned away to port for its return journey…I eased back on the column to reduce speed prior to applying the large flaps in the 'half down' position…When the speed had dropped sufficiently, I called for 'full flap' and, as the glider responded, I pushed forward hard on the control column, as far as it would go, until the nose was pointing straight down to just short of the near side boundary of our LZ. 'V5' literally dropped out of the sky and, as with the barn door-type flaps the speed remained constant, I experienced the peculiar sensation of the ground appearing to come right up at me. At 100 feet, I levelled out and then holding her just above the heath, we skimmed toward the far hedge. Eventually the two main wheels connected and, with a roaring noise, we ploughed through the heather in a cloud of dust to run right up to our station where, with a touch on the brakes, we skidded to a standstill. For a moment we sat in complete silence, realising that we were down safely with a perfect landing to the furthest extent of our LZ.[73]

Not all the gliders took such a direct route to the ground. One machine from E Squadron cast off from the extreme eastern side of the glider stream and made a long and unmolested approach that carried it over Arnhem and Deelen airfield. In so doing the pilot unwittingly disproved RAF insistence that the 1st Airborne Division could not be delivered closer to its objectives because of Deelen's allegedly extensive anti-aircraft defences.[74]

The glider landings commenced at approximately 15:00. Captain Morrison's V5 was one of the first of sixty-nine Horsas to land on LZ S, north of the Arnhem-Utrecht railway line centred on Reijers-Camp Farm, most carrying the remainder of the 1st Airlanding Brigade's infantry component and aborts from the first lift. Once again, the glider pilots were ordered to land as far up the landing zone as possible to leave as much room as they could for following machines, but not all managed to comply with the order. Captain Morrison noted that one 'had overestimated his height and…looked as if he would not clear the front hedge…he just made it but only reached a third of the way towards what should have been his final position…the following Glider Pilot, having already committed himself, had to swing to the right to avoid the "shortie" and in doing so, sideswiped the wing of another aircraft, injuring two men.'[75] At least one Horsa had the opposite problem and crossed the whole of LZ S before finally touching down in the trees on its northern edge, almost killing two Glider Pilots from the first lift dug in there:

> The pilot was trying hard to get it on the ground, but only the nose wheel touched, and he could not get the main wheels down. When it became clear to us that his speed was too great…we both jumped out of the trench and tried to move back [but] the tangle of undergrowth and low branches defeated our efforts, and…there was an almighty bang over our heads…a great cloud of dust arose, and when it cleared I saw that I was under the fuselage and behind the nose wheel, and Andy was behind the skid and also under the fuselage. Fortunately for us the undercarriage had not collapsed.[76]

Despite this and the fact that LZ S was littered with gliders from the first lift and resembled 'a crowded car park', there were no serious collisions or injuries. There was also much less interference from the Germans compared with events a mile or so to the west at DZ Y, although Lieutenant Donald Edwards' 17 Platoon from C Company 2nd South Staffords came under machine-gun fire from two separate locations after being despatched to unload a glider that had crash-landed at the north-eastern tip of the LZ; the operation was reportedly carried out successfully following a 'minor platoon action'.[77]

The remaining 204 gliders came down south of the railway on LZ X, which had served as a parachute drop zone the previous day. Most were Horsas carrying men and equipment from Divisional units, accompanied by up to four Waco CG4s and twelve of the giant Hamilcars. Along with a total of eighty-nine passengers spread amongst their cargo, four of the latter were loaded with Bren Carriers belonging to the 4th Parachute Brigade and 2nd South Staffords, three were loaded with stores and ammunition as a resupply experiment and the remaining five were carrying 17-Pounder guns and prime movers from the 2nd Airlanding Anti-tank Battery. A sixth Hamilcar carrying a 17-Pounder was hit by anti-aircraft fire and came down short of the LZ.[78] Again, most landed safely, although one of the Hamilcars crashed while landing. According to Captain Barry Ingram, commanding the 1st Border's Mortar Group, the machine was already in flames when it struck a stand of trees and two Bren Carriers were thrown clear as it went end over end before coming to rest. At least one Horsa also crashed into trees, injuring some of its passengers.[79] However, the most serious threat came from German troops who had infiltrated through the woods on the western edge of the LZ between the Border's A and D Companies. The 1st Border's C Company appears to have been redeployed from the eastern side of the LZ to Johannahoeve Farm to assist Captain Ingram's mortars in suppressing the interlopers and the Battalion's temporary commander, Major Stuart Cousens, later recalled that the salvoes of mortar bombs had to be carefully timed so as to avoid striking the gliders in mid-air, which he referred to as 'a successful and amusing game'.[80] Even so, the infiltrators, likely from *Standartenführer* Hans Lippert's *SS Unterführerschule* 'Arnheim', shot up at least three Horsas as they landed. Two carried elements from Divisional units, REME personnel and a Jeep from the Divisional Motor Transport Repair Section and men from the 1st Airlanding Light Regiment RA respectively. The German fire killed two Gunners and wounded a third in the latter, and killed both pilots and a Jeep driver in the former as well as seriously wounding the Repair Section commander, Lieutenant Harry Roberts; the German fire was sufficiently heavy to keep Roberts and his companions pinned down near their glider for a considerable period.

The third Horsa, carrying men and equipment from the RAF radar teams, was hit by small-arms fire on its final approach that wounded the pilot and set the glider on fire; the passengers survived the landing but both machine and load were burned out. As we have seen, the other two Horsas carrying the RAF radar equipment had been lost during the fly-in, one destroyed by anti-aircraft fire and the other cast adrift south of the Lower Rhine when its tug was shot down. The sole survivor, piloted by Staff-Sergeant John Kennedy, landed safely but in the contested portion of the LZ. This and a lack of manpower and motor transport made it impractical to unload the equipment, so after consultation between Staff-Sergeant Kennedy and the ranking RAF officer, a Flight-Lieutenant Richards, the decision was taken to destroy it in situ with demolition charges to prevent it falling into German hands. Most of the hapless technicians thereafter found their way to Division HQ on foot.[81] Quite how the RAF party and their crated equipment were to be moved from the LZ had all gone according to plan is unclear, and it is therefore difficult to fathom the justification behind their despatch onto what was likely to be a contested landing area that was to be abandoned as rapidly as possible. The inclusion of the radar detachment in the second lift was a waste of equipment and resources, and the episode provides a clear illustration of the peacetime exercise mentality that characterised much of the MARKET planning.

That aside, the vast bulk of the 204 gliders came down intact onto LZ X and with only eight fatalities: two Gunners from the 1st Airlanding Light Regiment, a REME driver from the Divisional Motor Transport Repair Section, four Glider Pilots and a soldier from the 10th Parachute Battalion's glider component. The advance party and anti-tank battery from the 1st Polish Independent Parachute Brigade all arrived safely with their guns and equipment, and the ammunition resupply effort was particularly successful. The 1st Airlanding Brigade's three infantry Battalions were allotted a fifteen-Jeep convoy apiece, each vehicle towing two trailers loaded with ammunition, along with an additional RASC unit equipped with a further eighteen Jeeps and trailers to provide each Brigade with a reserve ammunition train. All three of the Hamilcars carrying ready-loaded trailers of ammunition also landed safely, although one machine was captured by the Germans before it could be unloaded. Unloading the remaining two was complete by 17:30.[82]

In the meantime the remainder of the resupply effort was taking place half a mile or so east of LZ S, involving thirty-three Short Stirlings from Nos. 570 and 296 Squadrons from RAF Harwell tasked to deliver eighty-six tons of supplies in 803 containers and panniers onto the as yet unused DZ L.[83] Lieutenant David Eastwood's 1st Platoon, 21st Independent Parachute Company had marked the drop zone in the early morning of 18 September and held on until the drop finally commenced at 15:30, despite almost losing their EUREKA beacon to the strafing *Luftwaffe* fighters and the sound of tracked vehicles in the woods to the east; these were likely half-tracks from *SS Panzer Aufklärungs Abteilung 9* or *Panzerjäger* IVs from *SS Panzerjäger Abteilung 9* holding the line of the Amsterdamseweg, which ran just to the north of and parallel with the DZ.[84] The supply-carrying bombers had a more fraught time. One Stirling was obliged to abort the mission, probably before reaching Holland and the remainder had to run the gauntlet of German anti-aircraft crews alerted by the passage of the parachute and glider elements, although only one was shot down. Pilot-Officer D. H. Balmer's aircraft from 570 Squadron caught fire after being hit by flak near Stampersgat, shortly after crossing the Dutch coast. Balmer, a Canadian serving with the RCAF, ordered his crew to bale out but only five made it before it was too low for further exits. The remainder survived the crash-landing near Ouidenbosch, from where they were swiftly spirited away by Dutch civilians (including a Catholic priest) and handed over to the Underground. Nine of the ten-man crew survived; seven, including Pilot-Officer Balmer, successfully evaded capture and two were taken prisoner. The sole fatality was Corporal Alfred Barker, one of two RASC despatchers aboard, who died later of head injuries sustained during the crash-landing.[85] The remainder of the bombers appear to have succeeded in delivering their loads, although it is unclear how much was retrieved by the waiting RASC Jeep and trailer teams. The Official History refers to the supply drop onto DZ L being '80 per cent successful', but another source claims that only twelve of the eighty tons delivered were recovered.[86] The latter is quite possible given that DZ L lay outwith the 1st Airlanding Brigade's protective perimeter and that the German blocking line along the

Amsterdamseweg lay only a short distance beyond its northern boundary. Whether or not, the 1st Airborne Division's second lift cost a total of ten aircraft. The RAF lost twelve dead along with two Stirlings and two Dakotas from Nos. 570 and 48 Squadrons, while their US counterparts lost seventeen men and six C-47s, one each from the 43rd, 50th and 62nd Troop Carrier Squadrons and two from the 61st Troop Carrier Squadron.[87]

***

The 82nd Airborne Division's share of the second lift amounted to 454 Waco CG4s towed by C-47s from the US 50th and 52nd Troop Carrier Wings; the latter's contribution appears to have consisted of the 313th and 316th Troop Carrier Groups based at RAF Folkingham and RAF Cottesmore respectively. As Brigadier-General Gavin had taken in all his Division's infantry component in the first lift, the bulk of the aircraft were carrying the Division's artillery component, consisting of thirty-six 75mm Pack Howitzers and eight 57mm anti-tank guns, the former belonging to the 319th and 320th Glider Field Artillery Battalions and 456th Parachute Field Artillery Battalion, and the latter belonging to the confusingly labelled 80th Airborne Anti-Aircraft Battalion. The remaining CG4s were loaded with ammunition, transport for all three of the Division's Parachute Infantry Regiments and elements of Division HQ, the 307th Airborne Engineer Battalion, the 307th Medical Company, the 40th Quartermaster Company and the 782nd Ordnance Company. In total the armada amounted to 1,899 men, 206 Jeeps and 123 trailers, in addition to the forty-four guns, and began taking off at approximately 11:00.[88] At least four and possibly seven gliders dropped out of the glider stream before reaching the Continent. Two aborted but landed safely while still over England, one after the machine began to come apart and one after a 'crazed' passenger pulled the tow release, and the crews and passengers of two more were rescued after ditching in the North Sea.[89] For many of the passengers in the CG4s there was initially something of a carnival atmosphere until the armada crossed the Dutch coast, although for Private First Class John McKenzie from the 456th Parachute Field Artillery Battalion the fun stopped almost immediately after take-off. As a paratrooper, Private McKenzie likely had reservations about travelling in a glider and these were doubtless exacerbated by flying without a qualified co-pilot due to a shortage of glider pilots: 'I was seated in the co-pilot's seat and could see everything through its wide Plexiglass front. Just after take-off, the pilot gave me a few additional quick lessons in how to land a glider in case he was killed or wounded. This though, terrified me even more than the threat of being hit myself.' The experience of Corporal David Click from Battery B, 320th Glider Field Artillery Battalion, who was making his first glider flight, was probably more typical:

> I was having the time of my life, watching the fighter plane escort, and looking at all of the ships in the English Channel. I didn't sit in my seat or buckle my safety belt, like the veterans of the Normandy invasion did – that is, until we came over the coast of Holland. A German flak barge opened up on us with anti-aircraft fire. The first shell exploded near my glider and almost turned us over. I immediately knew what it was to be scared. I sat down, buckled up, and shut up. This war business had become quite serious.[90]

Although Corporal Click and his companions had no way of knowing it, the situation at their destination in Holland, the adjoining landing zones near Groesbeek, had moved beyond 'quite serious' through the actions of *Generalleutnant* Gerd Scherbening's *406 z.b.V. Division*. Attacking from out of the Reichswald forest at dawn, the Germans had advanced onto the northern LZ 'T' from the east, recapturing and re-manning a number of light *flak* guns and overrunning the bulk of the defenders from Company D, 2nd Battalion 508th Parachute Infantry Regiment. The latter's surviving Platoon under Lieutenant Robert L. Sickler was pinned down in an open beet field near Voxhill and was only saved from annihilation by the Battalion's Assistant Supply Officer, Captain Kenneth L. Johnson, who marshalled his small supply detachment and Company D HQ personnel to lay down heavy fire on the attackers after radioing a warning to Regimental HQ. In the meantime the bulk of the 1st Battalion, 508th Regiment was force marching back from De Ploeg and the outskirts of Nijmegen at Colonel Lindquist's orders, following Captain Johnson's timely warning. Scherbening's men had also pressed into LZ N from the south despite the 505th Regiment deploying its reserve company on Gavin's orders while he scraped together men to plug the gap that had opened up in the Divisional perimeter between the 505th and 508th Regiments; as Captain Johnson put it in his post-war account of the action, 'by noon it [the landing area] was principally occupied by the enemy.'[91]

Fortunately for the incoming glider lift, the tide was about to turn. The lead element of the 1st Battalion 508th Regiment, Captain Frank Schofield's Company C, reached the woods along the northern edge of LZ T without incident where they were joined at or just after midday by the remainder of their Battalion. Despite the fatigue of carrying out an eight-mile forced march Lieutenant-Colonel Warren paused only to hold a brief orders group with his Company commanders before launching his attack onto the landing area with Companies B and C abreast, the latter on the right, followed by Battalion HQ and then his depleted Company A. The attack appears to have commenced shortly before 13:00 and involved the lead Companies pushing through thick woods and cutting gaps in a stout wire fence before emerging into the open and shaking out into formation.[92] Initially, the advancing paratroopers were in dead ground but on crossing the crest they attracted a storm of German fire including the 20mm weapons at Voxhill, which caused a brief pause before the line pushed on either side of the farm.[93] They were spotted equally swiftly by Lieutenant Sickler's beleaguered platoon, who initially assumed they were German reinforcements and opened long-range fire until the newcomers were properly identified. The advancing troops from Company C subsequently returned the favour as they closed on the pinned Company D men, who lacked orange smoke grenades to advertise their identity. One of Sickler's men was shot and the error was only recognised when Company C actually assaulted into the roadside position.[94]

The two Companies from the 1st Battalion swept systematically across the DZ, eliminating German positions or putting their occupants to flight. First-Sergeant Leonard L. Funk was especially prolific, leading a small group from Company C in knocking out four 20mm *flak* guns and three larger pieces, killing fifteen Germans in the process; Funk was awarded a Distinguished Service Cross for his action to join a Silver Star and Purple Heart he had earned in Normandy.[95] Captain Schofield then had his 60mm mortar teams plaster the Germans occupying the bypassed farm buildings at Voxhill before carrying out a platoon attack, supported by another platoon from Company B led by Captain Woodrow W. Millsaps. The situation was complicated by the presence of some US medics and jump casualties from the previous day in one of the buildings, but the paratroopers persuaded over seventy Germans to surrender by detonating grenades and Gammon bombs against the outer walls of the German-occupied buildings. The fight for LZ T only cost the 1st Battalion of the 508th Regiment two to five dead and nine or ten wounded, with four of the latter coming from Colonel Warren's HQ group, hit by 20mm fire while observing the fight from a rise. The 2nd Battalion's Company D lost its 2nd Platoon in its entirety killed or captured and Lieutenant Sickler's 3rd Platoon five dead and six wounded, in addition to the Company commander 1st Lieutenant MacVicar, who was wounded in the head. The missing 1st Platoon turned up in Groesbeek, after being cut off and attaching itself to elements of the 505th Regiment. The Germans lost an estimated fifty dead, 149 prisoners and sixteen 20mm guns.[96]

The German pressure on the southern sector of the Divisional perimeter meant that Colonel Ekman's 505th Parachute Infantry Regiment had only managed to keep back a single, understrength Company as a reserve. This was Captain Anthony S. Stefanich's Company C from the 1st Battalion, which had already detached its 3rd Platoon under Lieutenant Harold L. Gensemer to reinforce Company B at Riethorst; the latter was involved in repulsing a German attack there at 13:00.[97] Despite the pressure, Ekman held Company C back until 13:30 before launching it in a do-or-die attack to clear LZ N before the arrival of the second lift gliders. As Ekman himself put it, 'I carefully guarded against pre-commitment…with the pre-planned intention of launching a rapid initial attack which would disconcert the enemy and force him to fall back, with the attack so timed that the landing zones would be cleared.'[98] Stefanich's men swept across the LZ in line abreast, and their bold action had the anticipated effect; as the Company Executive Officer Lieutenant Jack Tallerday recalled: 'The C Company troopers were firing and the Germans were running away from us…It looked like a line of hunters in a rabbit drive and the Germans looked like rabbits running in no particular pattern.'[99] The first gliders began to land while Company C was still clearing the landing zone, and one machine overflew Captain Stefanich's command group before coming to rest near the southern edge of the LZ where German troops in the nearby fringes of the *Reichswald* forest immediately raked it with machine-gun fire. Stefanich immediately led a party under Lieutenant Gus Sanders forward to assist but was hit in the process and died a few minutes later, despite the best efforts of one of his medics, as Sanders looked helplessly on. The medic was reduced to tears at his failure to save him, and the loss was keenly felt across the unit.[100] As Private Arthur 'Dutch' Schultz put it, 'I felt like I lost an older brother…He was a born leader who led by example, not by virtue of rank. To the men of C Company, he was both our leader and our friend.'[101] Command of Company C devolved to Captain Tallerday. In the meantime Company I of the 3rd Battalion 505th Regiment's fight to hold the southern edge of the landing area reached a peak while the gliders were landing, with a reported eleven German tanks emerging from the *Reichswald* forest. However, the new threat receded in the face of pinpoint fire from the 376th Parachute Field Artillery Battalion's 75mm Pack howitzers, which knocked out five vehicles and prompted the remainder to withdraw; Company I then launched a counter-attack that drove the remaining attackers back into the forest and permitted the paratroopers to reoccupy their original roadblock positions.[102]

The precise time the gliders began to arrive is unclear. According to Gavin the landing began at 14:00 and was complete by 14:30, but one source refers to the first glider casting off from its tug at 'approximately 14:31', and another to the landings beginning at 'approximately 15:00'; as there was only a single formation of glider tugs the 14:00 timing tallies best with the take-off and flight times.[103] Whenever they arrived, the landing did not run smoothly. Eleven gliders had already been obliged to cast off over Holland but well short of the landing area after they or their tugs were hit by anti-aircraft fire; the passengers of seven subsequently reached Allied territory with the assistance of Dutch civilians and members of the Dutch Resistance, six of them bringing all their equipment with them.[104] Matters were compounded as the formation approached the landing area and ran into heavier than expected *flak* that brought down eight C-47s and damaged over a hundred more.[105] Despite this the landings on the northern LZ N were largely accurate, with all but a handful of machines coming down within a mile-and-a-half of the landing zone. The experience of Captain Herman L. Alley from Battery A, 456th Parachute Field Artillery Battalion, who flew in the co-pilot's seat in Glider No.58 towed by a C-47 from the 441st Troop Carrier Group, was likely typical after a whimsical false start. The glider's pilot, 2nd Lieutenant Ned H. Yarter, cast off immediately after take-off from RAF Langar with a rudder malfunction. He repaired the malfunction with a pair of pliers and a coat hanger borrowed from some bemused military policeman, hooked up to the original tug and set down on LZ N with the remainder of Battery A. 'German artillery was working over the landing zone as we landed. The glider landed at about seventy miles per hour, plowing through a potato field. The landing tore up the nose of the glider and the fabric ripped. I had a lapful of dirt and vegetables. The rough landing also caused the clamshell release mechanism to jam, and we couldn't get my Jeep out. We got out of the glider quickly and took shelter until the artillery rounds moved away from us.' The clamshell release proved jammed beyond repair and the nose of the CG4 had to be cut away with an axe taken from Alley's Jeep.[106]

Things did not run so smoothly at LZ T, where only ninety gliders landed accurately, the remainder releasing either prematurely or late. Of the thirty-eight gliders carrying the 319th Glider Field Artillery Battalion's Battery A that reached the approach to the landing area, only six actually came down on LZ T. Of the remainder, thirty cast off prematurely and landed under heavy fire from light *flak* five miles short of the LZ, one landed on DZ O to the west in the 504th Regiment's area, and one overshot the landing area altogether and came down near German-occupied Wyler. Battery B had more success, although eight CG4s from the third serial, carrying seven officers and forty-two men, also overshot both LZs to come down in the vicinity of Wyler; only four men eventually made their way to US-held territory, with the rest being killed or captured. The 320th Glider Field Artillery Battalion fared even worse. Between twenty-four and thirty of the tugs from the ninth serial carrying Battery A released their charges early, obliging the gliders to land five miles south-east of LZ T. Despite this, only four artillerymen and nine glider pilots were missing and the remaining 160 artillerymen defended in place before making their way into the Divisional perimeter after dark, bringing twenty-two Glider Pilots, ten Jeeps and two 105mm howitzers with them. Of the forty gliders carrying Battery B only twenty-one landed on or near LZ T as planned. One cut loose for unknown reasons forty-five miles short, nine came down twelve miles south-east of the landing area and were never heard of again and a further nine overshot to land near Wyler, although all but two officers from the latter increment managed to fight their way into the Divisional perimeter, but without their vehicles and equipment.[107]

Despite all this the artillery units came through the landing fit to fight, recovering thirty of thirty-six howitzers and seventy-eight Jeeps from a total of 106. The 456th Parachute Field Artillery recovered ten of its twelve 75mm Pack howitzers and twenty-three of thirty-three Jeeps, the 319th Glider Field Artillery all twelve 75mm pieces and twenty-six out of thirty-four Jeeps. The 320th recovered eight of its twelve 105mm howitzers and twenty-nine of thirty-nine Jeeps. Battery D of the 80th Airborne Anti-aircraft Battalion fared best of all, recovering all eight of its 57mm anti-tank guns and eight out of nine Jeeps.[108] In all, the lift brought in 1,600 men, 177 Jeeps, 106 trailers and 211 tons of supplies, at a cost of three dead and forty-two wounded from those that landed on or close to the landing area.[109]

The final increment of the 82nd Airborne Division's second lift was scheduled to arrive twenty minutes after the glider landing, although one source refers to a thirty-minute delay. Between 130 and 135 B-24 heavy bombers from the 93rd, 446th, 448th and 489th Bombardment Groups had been pressed into service to drop 285 tons of assorted supplies onto the landing area, apparently utilising bomb bays and packs loaded inside the aircraft for despatch via waist and belly hatches. As the crews had no prior experience with such missions the approach flight was made at 1,500 feet, descending to 300 feet for the drop, although the volume of anti-aircraft fire on the approaches to and over the drop point appears to have come as an unpleasant surprise. Four B-24s were shot down and a further thirty-eight were damaged, and the *flak* was blamed for a widespread scattering of the supplies, with some bundles landing five miles astray. Not all supplies were delivered onto the glider landing area, and some of the scattering was very small-scale and hazardous to the recipients, as Captain Carl W. Kappel, the commander of Company H, the 3rd Battalion of the 504th Regiment recalled: 'B-24 Bombers brought in resupply at DZ "O" at 16:20. Drops were at a very low altitude but poorly concentrated...In this resupply it so happened that boxes of rations, detached from parachutes, struck company and platoon CPs, burst open, and scattered rations all through the company area in true foxhole delivery.'[110] Nonetheless, overall around eighty per cent of the supplies, equating to approximately 261 tons, were eventually recovered, although gathering the bundles in took a considerable time; this may explain why some participant accounts place the total nearer sixty per cent.[111]

***

The 101st Airborne Division's share of the second lift also totalled 450 CG4 gliders, towed by C-47s from the 53rd Troop Carrier Wing and was once again assigned to LZ W, tucked between the previous day's parachute drop zones just west of the Son-St. Oedenrode road. Unlike Gavin, Major-General Taylor chose to leave his Division's artillery component for the third lift, and most of the second lift gliders were assigned to carry the bulk of Colonel Joseph P. Harper's 327th Glider Infantry Regiment, consisting of the regimental HQ, Lieutenant Roy L. Inman's 2nd Battalion and Lieutenant-Colonel Ray Allen's 1st Battalion, 401st Glider Infantry Regiment.[112] The lift also carried part of the Division Artillery HQ, an advance party from the 377th Parachute Field Artillery Battalion, the remainder of the 326th Airborne Engineer Battalion, the Division Signal Company and Division Medical Company, and elements of the 426th Quartermaster Company and the 801st Ordnance Maintenance Company. The second lift consisted of 2,656 troops, 156 Jeeps, 111 trailers and two bulldozers.[113] Take-off began at 11:20 with the lead C-47 piloted by Colonel William B. Whitacre, the commander of the 434th Troop Carrier Group, towing a CG4 piloted by Lieutenant Victor B. Warriner. The lead glider was also carrying the second lift's most illustrious passenger, the 101st Airborne Division's deputy commander, Brigadier-General Anthony C. McAuliffe; McAuliffe had specifically requested the services of both pilots and travelled in the CG4's co-pilot seat.[114]

At least ten CG4s were obliged to abort while still over England, apparently due to towline failure. Three more ditched in the North Sea with all their passengers being picked up by the waiting rescue launches and another was obliged to make a forced landing on Schouwen as a result of stability problems; all aboard were captured. A further eight CG4s went astray over Holland en route to the LZ and those that reached their destination had their fair share of adventures. Technician 4th Class Andrew E. Rasmussen from the 506th Parachute Infantry Regiment had been grounded by an ankle injury incurred in Normandy and volunteered to fly into Holland as co-pilot in a CG4 loaded with an ammunition trailer and a supply of maps. He was unimpressed by the brief five-minute tutorial on how to fly the machine and the smell of whiskey on the pilot's breath, and his discontent increased when the latter appropriated both the available *flak* jackets for himself, wearing one and using the other as a seat cushion. Rasmussen emerged unhurt after a landing that involved a near collision with another glider, crashing through a wooden fence and skidding across a drainage ditch; he walked away from the machine vowing 'it would be a cold day in Hell before he ever climbed into another glider.' Flight Officer Roy C. Lovingood found himself wrestling to counteract a left wing so heavy that it took all his strength to keep the machine level. The reason for the problem became apparent shortly after making landfall over Holland when a *flak* shell passed clean through the wing without exploding and a large quantity of water gushed out of the resulting hole. The trim problem resolved itself instantly and it transpired that the wing had filled with rainwater after an inspection cover had been left off during a pre-flight check.[115]

Eventually 428 CG4s reached the landing zone, beginning at approximately 14:30.[116] The machine carrying Technical Sergeant Robert M. Bowen from the 1st Battalion 401st Glider Infantry Regiment's Company C was struck repeatedly by small-arms fire near Eindhoven: 'There was a loud crack beside my head. I flinched and looked at Frank McFadden, one of my scouts who was pressed up against me. The bullet had torn through the fabric on the side of the glider, whistled between our heads and exited out the roof…Bullets were now ripping through the wings and…ailerons [and] through the glider's honeycombed wooden floorboard and glanced off the two cloverleaves of 81mm mortar ammunition that we were carrying tied down to the flooring.' In the event Bowen and his companions landed safely after their CG4 'hit the ground with a crash, bounced a few times and streaked across the field with the brakes locked and tearing up turf' before coming to a halt.[117]

The glider carrying the 101st Airborne Division's deputy commander had an equally interesting fly-in. Colonel William Whitacre's C-47 received a hit during the run-in to the release point that set the starboard engine on fire. When the understandably alarmed Warriner relayed the fact via the telephone line woven into the tow line, the usually calm and considered Whitacre responded with a testy 'Warriner, I know that goddamned engine's on fire. Now you just fly your glider and let me fly this airplane.' Warriner was equally discomfited to notice that Brigadier-General McAuliffe had slept through the emergency, only waking after Warriner had cast off as the glider made its final approach. More by luck than good judgement the CG4 came to a rest just fifty yards from the spot McAuliffe had indicated in the pre-flight briefing, and Warriner managed to keep a straight face as the General congratulated him on the accuracy of his landing.[118]

The second lift delivered 2,579 men, between 146 and 151 Jeeps, 109 trailers and both bulldozers to LZ W, at a cost of fifty-four dead or missing and twenty-three injured. According to the 101st Airborne Division's semi-official history, the lift was considered to have been ninety-five per cent successful.[119] The subsequent resupply drop by 121 bombers was deemed less successful, with less than half the supplies being recovered.[120]

Thus by the late afternoon of Monday 18 September 1944 the second lift for all three of Operation MARKET's airborne divisions was safely on the ground in Holland. This left the 82nd and 101st Airborne Divisions lacking just their organic glider infantry and artillery components respectively, while the 1st Airborne Division was present in its entirety apart from the Divisional tail. While the latter's third lift was scheduled to deliver the 1st Polish Independent Parachute Brigade to DZ K, south-east of the Arnhem road bridge, and the Brigade's glider-borne elements and the US 878th Airborne Aviation Engineer Battalion to LZ L on D+2, those units were attachments rather than organic elements of the Division. With the bulk or all of their strength on the ground, the MARKET airborne divisions were now free to concentrate on attaining those primary objectives that had not been secured on 17 September.

10

D Plus 1

16:00 to 23:59 Monday 18 September 1944

Although the 7th KOSB had been fighting to hold DZ Y since dawn on Tuesday 18 September, the fact could not be relayed to higher HQs and airfields in Britain owing to the lack of communications; consequently the parachute increment of the 1st Airborne Division's second lift remained blissfully unaware that a battle was raging at their destination, an unwelcome surprise to both the aircrew from the US 314th and 315th Troop Carrier Groups and their passengers from the 4th Parachute Brigade. Captain Bernard Coggins, a navigator with the 315th Troop Carrier Wing's 43rd Squadron, recalled later: 'I don't know what hell looked like [sic], but I got a preview. Earlier groups had already dropped, and there were explosions all over the drop zone, which was now host to a large brush fire.'[1] The shock was much more immediate for the paratroopers, and the experience of Captain Stuart Mawson, the 11th Parachute Battalion's Medical Officer, doubtless spoke for many:

> Then I looked down quickly because, although after leaving the plane there had been an immediate healing contrast of quiet, I could now again hear the sound of explosions, and I looked in horror as the piece of ground on which I was shortly to land erupted in tulips of black smoke. 'Oh, my God,' I found myself shouting out loud, 'they're shelling the DZ.'[2]

Unsettling as descending into the middle of a battle might have been for the parachute soldiers, the arrival of the 4th Parachute Brigade had an even more profound impact on their German opponents. Despite being roughly handled and rebuffed repeatedly through the previous night, by the afternoon of 18 September *SS Wacht Bataillon 3* was beginning to make progress in its attack against the Ginkel Heath perimeter, but the arrival of an additional 2,000 British paratroopers in a matter of minutes reversed that at a stroke. At the south-eastern edge of the DZ 6 *Kompanie* was scattered and its commander, *Obersturmführer* Hugo Fernau, was captured, likely by the 7th KOSB's Support Company. *Obersturmführer* Hermann Kuhne's 5 *Kompanie*, deployed around the hutted work camp in the woods east of the DZ, disintegrated after Kuhne lost his nerve and abandoned his men in panic, while *Hauptsturmführer* Ernst Bartsch's 4 *Kompanie* and *Obersturmführer* Karl Hink's 3 *Kompanie*, which had been pressing onto the north-eastern portion of the Heath, were overwhelmed and destroyed by a tide of paratroopers intent on reaching their rally point. At the northern edge of the drop zone *Obersturmführer* Bronkhorst's 1 *Kompanie* put up a brief fight from a farm near the *Zuid Ginkel* café before retreating hastily westward toward Ede, possibly covered by fire from *Hauptscharführer* Einenkel's heavy weapons detachment; the latter reportedly engaged the advancing paratroopers with its 20mm guns and mortars until it was in danger of being outflanked, upon which it conducted a fighting withdrawal northward. The disintegration of *SS Wacht Bataillon 3* was hastened by a literal and metaphorical absence of leadership, for *Sturmbannführer* Paul Helle had decided that the middle of a battle was an appropriate time to take a sleep on a convenient table in the *Zuid Ginkel* café. He awoke to find his temporary HQ under attack by paratroopers from Lieutenant-Colonel Kenneth Smyth's 10th Parachute Battalion, which had been allotted the café as its RV. Helle promptly fled the scene and turned up alone at the Ede HQ of a supporting formation, *Sicherheit Regiment 42*, later that day.[3]

The SS presence on and around the drop zone appears to have had most impact on the 10th Parachute Battalion due to the presence of Helle's HQ, reserve *kompanie* and support element on or adjacent to its RV; as the commander of the Battalion Advance Party, Captain Brian Carr later drily pointed out, 'Our Battalion R.V. was actually in the hands of the enemy and had to be cleared before the battalion could rendezvous. That was one exercise that we had not practised.'[4] Carr led a last-minute counter-attack that drove the SS back and allowed a slightly relocated RV point to be established, marked as prearranged with a green smoke marker; Brigadier Hackett noted it burning near the Amsterdamseweg approximately ten minutes after landing.[5] Some of Lieutenant-Colonel Smyth's men went into action immediately on landing including a Sergeant Shaw, who rounded up a party of twenty men and attacked a German position that had fired on him while descending, killing a number of SS and leading ten prisoners to the Battalion RV. Lieutenant Patrick Mackey, commander of A Company's 4 Platoon, had been the third man to jump and rallied a number of his men including Sergeant Banwell, despite German machine-gun fire. The group set about stalking one of the German weapons spotted near an abandoned woodcutter's cart located just off the DZ. Lieutenant Mackey was killed along with his Platoon Sergeant Frank Bennett whilst charging the gun. Command of 4 Platoon then devolved to Sergeant Banwell as the Platoon 'successfully secured their revenge'.[6] Back at the relocated Battalion RV Lieutenant-Colonel Smyth was among the first to arrive, having jumped in the Battalion's lead chalk along with his Intelligence Officer, Captain John Henry. He was swiftly joined by members of Henry's Intelligence Section and the Battalion deputy commander, Major George Widdowson, followed shortly thereafter by Major Francis Lindley, OC Support Company, with Medical Officer Captain Gareth Drayson, Lieutenant Joseph Glover with Myrtle the Parachick and a number of other HQ personnel. Next came the bulk of Support Company; the latter was completed, bar the absence of two MMG teams and part of the Anti-tank Platoon, by the arrival of Lieutenant Roy Dodd from the Mortar Platoon with four Jeeps that had come in by glider. Lieutenant-Colonel Smyth reported the 10th Parachute Battalion ready to move within ninety minutes of landing, but the fight to clear the north-east corner of DZ Y went on for some time and the area remained dangerous, not least owing to the thick smoke from the burning gorse; Liaison Officer Lieutenant Harold Roderick was killed in the process of reporting the securing of the 10th Battalion's RV to 4th Parachute Brigade HQ, for example.[7]

The experience of the remainder of the 4th Parachute Brigade appears to have been less fraught. 11th Parachute Battalion reported that the 'drop and assembly went according to plan', while Lieutenant-Colonel Sir Richard Des Vœux's 156 Parachute Battalion laconically noted that 'opposition was encountered'; he also reported being assembled at the Battalion RV at the north-western corner of the drop zone by 14:30, with 'two officers and 100 men missing as casualties and stragglers'.[8] The Brigade HQ advance party appears to have gone astray in the confusion given that Brigadier Hackett despatched Captain Robert Temple from his Brigade staff to mark its RV with a blue smoke pot, while the 4th Parachute Squadron RE rallied without loss apart from six jump casualties including the Squadron commander Major Æneas Perkins, who suffered a dislocated shoulder. The Sappers lost most of their carefully packed containers.[9] The most problematic unit was Lieutenant-Colonel William Alford's 133 Parachute Field Ambulance, which had a third of its parachute component dropped astray north of the DZ. The two missing sticks included the unit second-in-command Major Brian Courtney, a surgeon, two medical officers and a number of orderlies.[10] Despite this Alford assembled his remaining four sticks and set up a Brigade Main Dressing Station (MDS) at the *Zuid Ginkel* café once the 10th Battalion had cleared the area; their presence at that location was eventually reported to Hackett by Captain

Colin Harkess, the Brigade RASC officer, at some point after 15:15. By that time the 10th, 11th and 156 Parachute Battalions were in radio contact with Hackett's Forward Brigade HQ and contact was subsequently established with the 4th Parachute Squadron RE. According to Hackett 'By 1530 hrs, [4th Parachute] Bde was a going concern – 75 to 80 per cent strong.'[11]

The collapse of *SS Wacht Bataillon 3* had an equally serious knock-on impact on the southern prong of *Kampfgruppe* von Tettau's attack, which had made good headway against the 1st Airlanding Brigade in the area of Renkum and Heelsum. Elements of *SS Unterführerschule* 'Arnheim' had penetrated between the 1st Border's A and D Companies on the western edge of the LZ and shot up at least three Horsas as they landed; it took a partial redeployment of C Company from the east side of the perimeter and supporting fire from the Battalion's organic mortars and the 1st Airlanding Light Regiment RA to suppress the infiltrators. However, the primary focus of the German effort was against the 1st Border's B Company in the eastern outskirts of Renkum by *Schiffsstammabteilung 6/14* and elements of *SS Unterführerschule* 'Arnheim'. The German troops had inadvertently closed around the British positions during the night while deploying to attack LZ X and B Company announced its presence by opening fire on its unsuspecting neighbours shortly after daylight. The resultant fight raged on through the morning but by 14:00 all the Company's Jeeps and those belonging to the attached elements from 2 MMG Platoon and the 2nd Airlanding Anti-tank Battery had been damaged or destroyed and fire had forced the glider soldiers out of some of their buildings. Permission to retire toward the main Battalion location was sought via the radio link with D Company as the field telephone line laid by Lieutenant Hardy the previous night had been cut. By the time permission was granted the Company was all but surrounded in the area of Major Armstrong's HQ, but fortuitously the latter backed onto the riverbank, and a riverside path several feet lower than the surrounding land offered a perfect concealed escape route. Major Armstrong therefore instructed the MMG Platoon to break down its Vickers guns to be man-packed out and ordered the Airlanding Battery detachment to spike their anti-tank guns in place, as moving them was impossible without Jeeps. A rear guard organised from 11 Platoon and commanded by Lieutenant Stanley Barnes held off the German attackers with the assistance of Lieutenant Hardy and Sergeant Hendry Burr while the rest of the Company made their way down to the riverside in small groups and then away to the east along the concealed path.

Sergeant Burr was killed but the remainder of the rearguard succeeded in slipping away just before the Germans made their final assault. Hearing the volume of enemy fire increase, Lance-Corporal Albert Wilson from the rearguard climbed the riverbank to investigate and 'nearly had a heart attack' at the size of the German force assaulting his erstwhile position. The rearguard rejoined B Company safely and after reorganising, Armstrong led his men north-east toward Heelsum and the main Battalion location, enduring some mortaring near the southern outskirts of the town en route at around 17:00.[12] The eight-hour battle cost B Company at least four dead and an unknown number of wounded. Lieutenant Hardy was awarded a Military Cross and Sergeant McClusky a Military Medal for their gallantry during the action. The fight at Renkum had a more significant impact than Major Armstrong or his men realised however, for their stand effectively prevented the southern prong of *Kampfgruppe* von Tettau's attack from interfering with the arrival of the second lift gliders onto LZ X. Nor were the attackers able to capitalise on their eventual success in clearing Renkum, for by the time it was complete the collapse of *SS Wacht Bataillon 3* to the north-west had left them with a dangerously exposed left flank. *Generalleutnant* von Tettau was therefore obliged to order *Standartenführer* Lippert and *SS Unterführerschule* 'Arnheim' to hold in place and cover their northern flank while *Sicherheit Regiment 26*, commanded by a *Major* Knoche, moved up to replace Helle's unit and complete its mission of clearing Ginkel Heath and the woods bordering its eastern edge. The attack was therefore suspended, to be resumed on Tuesday 19 September.[13] Although von Tettau and his staff had no way of knowing it, their attack would be moving into a vacuum because with the second lift safely on the ground, the 1st Airlanding Brigade was scheduled to move east to its Phase II locations.[14]

Back at DZ Y Brigadier Hackett was making the unwelcome discovery that the formation he had raised in Egypt twenty-one months earlier was to be dismembered.[15] Despite the lack of communication with Lathbury and Urquhart, by the morning of 18 September Lieutenant-Colonel Mackenzie, the 1st Airborne Division's Operations Officer, had divined that the 1st Parachute Brigade had run into difficulties and he therefore persuaded Brigadier Hicks, the Division's newly installed temporary commander, to despatch reinforcements. Lieutenant-Colonel McCardie's understrength 2nd South Staffords were thus detached from the 1st Airlanding Brigade and moved off toward Arnhem in the mid-morning with orders to advance through Wolfheze and into Arnhem along the TIGER/Utrechtseweg route.[16] However, word came through at 14:20 that McCardie had been held up by strong opposition. This was indeed the case. The South Staffords had run into the German blocking line that had held up the 1st Parachute Battalion in the early hours of the morning. Hicks therefore issued a revised set of orders at 14:30 which assigned additional reinforcements from the second lift to assist the 1st Parachute Brigade's stalled advance. Thus the second increment of the 2nd South Staffords was directed to join McCardie as soon as it arrived, and Brigadier Hackett was to detach Lieutenant-Colonel Lea's 11th Parachute Battalion to act in support.[17] According to one source, Hackett received word of the impending removal of one of his battalions from his Brigade Major, Major Bruce Dawson, who had come in with the Brigade HQ Advance Party in the first lift.[18] However, while Hackett's War Diary account refers to the arrival of the 'BM' at his HQ shortly after landing, it does not refer to him passing on any such news, and Dawson appears to have been involved in the effort by the 7th KOSB's HQ and Support Companies to clear the south-eastern portion of the DZ; it is therefore difficult to see how he could have been privy to a decision taken at Division HQ while the 4th Parachute Brigade's drop was underway.[19] Either way, Hackett received official notification of Hicks' orders from Mackenzie, who left Division HQ at 15:00 and arrived at Hackett's location thirty minutes later, after calling in at the 1st Airlanding Brigade's HQ to pass on the order despatching the 2nd South Staffords second lift toward Arnhem.[20] On arrival at Hackett's Tactical HQ Mackenzie informed him that Hicks was now commanding the Division in Urquhart's unexplained absence before passing on Hicks' order transferring the 11th Parachute Battalion to the 1st Parachute Brigade with immediate effect. The order not only directed the 11th Battalion to move immediately to Division HQ for further instructions, but also appears to have instructed Hackett to abandon his pre-existing movement plan and dictated his order of march from the DZ along the Arnhem–Ede railway line.[21]

Although Hackett's War Diary account does not reflect it, the peremptory removal of one of his Battalions without consultation appears to have rankled, not least because the order came from an officer of equal standing but less time in rank and technically therefore a subordinate.[22] As Hackett was ignorant of Urquhart's last-minute arrangement for the succession of Divisional command, neither was he obligated to regard Hicks' orders as binding and his co-operation was again likely due in no small measure to Mackenzie's powers of persuasion. However, Hackett's co-operation only appears to have extended to agreeing to the transfer of the 11th Parachute Battalion, and then only after the Brigade had moved from the DZ in its entirety. As he put it himself, Hackett's initial intention was 'to move the Bde…in towards the centre of Div activity as quickly as was compatible with the retention of its coherence'.[23] This was to be achieved by moving the Brigade along the Arnhem–Ede railway to the crossing at Wolfheze, where it was to rendezvous with its glider-borne elements and pause for the remainder of the night before pushing on with its mission of securing the high ground north of Arnhem at first light. For its part, the Division HQ War Diary glossed over Hackett's disinclination to co-operate by noting that 'He [Hackett] decided…to adhere to his original plan for carrying out his task which remained substantially unchanged.'[24] This was not to be the end of Division HQ interfering with the execution of the 4th Parachute Brigade's plan, as Hackett was to discover.

That lay some hours in the future however, and Hackett's Brigade HQ moved off at 17:00 as planned to join the 7th KOSB HQ in the south-eastern corner of the DZ.[25] The Brigade's constituent units were also ready to move by or shortly after 17:00. 156 Parachute Battalion moved off from its RV in the north-west corner of the DZ on the hour, led by Major Geoffrey Powell's C Company. 133 Parachute Field Ambulance was to follow once it was able to move the casualties gathered at the *Zuid Ginkel* café, protected by the 10th Parachute Battalion. The task of protecting the Brigade's rear was assigned to the 4th Parachute Squadron RE, which moved to a point on the railway line a mile south of the DZ and established a defensive perimeter to cover the Brigade column from the west; from there Captain James Smith and his twenty-one-strong 1 Troop departed to accompany 156 Parachute Battalion in its role as Brigade spearhead.[26] The 11th Parachute Battalion also experienced interference from the scattered remnants of *SS Wacht Bataillon 3*; Captain Mawson linked up with a small group from HQ Company hunting *SS* stragglers led by Major Dan Webber. Lieutenant-Colonel Lea had established his Battalion HQ in an underpass beneath a partly constructed motorway using a Jeep bonnet as a map table, while the remainder of the Battalion reorganised in a large clearing on the south side together with approximately forty German prisoners. Mawson found himself treating the Battalion second-in-command, Major Richard Lonsdale, who had been wounded in the right hand during the fly-in. Lonsdale became irate when Mawson suggested he report to the Brigade Dressing Station for treatment and, insisting the wound was 'only a scratch', he demanded Mawson 'Stop flapping around like a wet hen…Bind the blasted thing up now and make me serviceable.'[27] It is unclear when the order transferring the 11th Battalion to Lathbury's Brigade reached Lea, and one source refers to him being summoned to Hackett's HQ to be briefed by Mackenzie, possibly after Hackett's HQ moved to the south-eastern corner of the DZ.[28] However the transfer order was transmitted, the 11th Parachute Battalion took its place in the 4th Parachute Brigade column at approximately 17:30 for the first stage of its move, with Major David Gilchrist's A Company in the lead.[29]

Once the second parachute lift was down and the 4th Parachute Brigade was clear of the DZ, the 7th KOSB's next mission was to secure the landing zone selected for the third glider lift near the village and farm of Johannahoeve, four miles or so to the east and just across the Arnhem–Ede rail line from Oosterbeek. To that end 1st Airlanding Brigade HQ issued provisional verbal orders at 15:15 for a move at 19:00, dependant on liaison with Hackett. However, there was some confusion in relaying the order within the Battalion and Major Robert Buchanan's A Company moved off from its positions near the *Planken Wambuis* immediately on receipt and had marched two miles or more along the Amsterdamseweg before the error was discovered.[30] Interestingly the incident does not figure in the 7th KOSB War Diary, possibly because A Company's absence contributed to the German penetration onto the north-eastern corner of the DZ. The inadvertent British withdrawal also handed the Germans control of a section of the Amsterdamseweg near Reijersheide and the opportunity to occupy the woods south of the road on the north-east edge of LZ S, and thus within striking distance of the Divisional units concentrated in and around Wolfheze. The War Diary does record Major Buchanan's Company re-establishing contact with the Battalion at some point between 06:00 and 09:00 on the morning of Tuesday 19 September, however.[31] Be that as it may, in the meantime the Battalion had to cover the 4th Parachute Brigade's move from the DZ and Lieutenant-Colonel Payton-Reid made the most of the enforced delay by ordering his men to prepare a hot meal from their 24-hour ration packs, their first since landing the previous day. While this was underway the Battalion was joined by Lieutenant Charles Doig's 7 Platoon from B Company and CanLoan Lieutenant Albert Wayte with C Company's 10 Platoon, which had come in with the second lift.[32] They were followed at 18:00 by D Company after its day-long close-quarter fight in the woods led by a slightly wounded Major Sherriff, who reported the death of CanLoan Lieutenant Albert Kipping from 15 Platoon.[33] Reorganisation complete and hot meal consumed, the 7th KOSB moved off in the gathering darkness at 19:00 with Major Michael Forman's B Company in the lead, following the Arnhem–Ede railway line in the wake of the 4th Parachute Brigade; in the process it encountered 'considerable congestion' from the latter's units and transport in the vicinity of Wolfheze that took several hours to negotiate.[34]

The 7th KOSB's march from Ginkel Heath was part of an overall move by the entire 1st Airlanding Brigade to its Phase II locations which began, by design or coincidence, with 181 Airlanding Field Ambulance's Main Dressing Station (MDS). Originally set up in houses near the 1st Airlanding Brigade HQ in Wolfheze, the volume of casualties had overflowed into a nearby factory by Monday afternoon and the decision was taken to move the MDS to the Hotel Tafelberg in Oosterbeek. Ferrying casualties began at 15:00, using a bus and a captured German ambulance restored to working order by the 9th (Airborne) Field Squadron RE, and continued through the night with 'no patients being left behind', although the War Diary suggests that some particularly serious cases may have been left with volunteer orderlies.[35] The remainder of the Brigade began the move to their Phase II positions located on a line running from Johannahoeve down to the Lower Rhine at Heveadorp, at 19:00. The northern end was assigned to the 7th KOSB, which was to deploy north of the Arnhem–Ede railway line to protect LZ L. Lieutenant-Colonel John Place's battalion-size No.2 Wing The Glider Pilot Regiment, standing in for the detached 2nd South Staffords, occupied the middle section of the line centred on Point 63.5 near a large house or hotel called the *Graftombe*, leaving the southern sector running down to Heveadorp to Major Cousens and the 1st Border.[36] The 1st Border began its move east to the vicinity of Heveadorp by the light of gliders burning on LZ Z with Major Thomas Montgomery's A Company in the lead, but shortly after moving off Lieutenant Patrick Baillie's 7 Platoon came under machine-gun fire while crossing a ploughed field. The fire killed at least one man, pinned the Company down and delayed the entire Battalion for around an hour, despite a Sergeant Kerr knocking out two German machine-guns with hand-grenades after his Sten jammed.[37] The 7th KOSB's move to Johannahoeve along the Arnhem–Ede railway line made good progress until it ran into the congestion near Wolfheze caused by the 4th Parachute Brigade's transport element and attached anti-tank guns, which delayed the KOSB until after midnight. In contrast to this, No.2 Wing enjoyed an uneventful move of a little over a mile and was in its new location by 20:00.[38] Moving with the Glider Pilots and accompanied by Captain Roger Binyon's No.1 Platoon from 9th (Airborne) Field Squadron RE and a Troop from the 1st Airborne Reconnaissance Squadron, Brigade HQ also had an uneventful move to the Hotel Bilderburg, a few hundred yards west of the *Graftombe*, where it was happily ensconced by 20:00. The disadvantages of the hotel – being an obvious target, constructed largely of glass and located on the forward edge of the Brigade line – appear to have paled into insignificance in view of the fact it was 'in true Airlanding Brigade tradition…the most luxurious building in the area'.[39]

The 4th Parachute Brigade's Main HQ was also supposed to move from DZ Y at dusk to a house near the Wolfheze crossing, while the Brigade Tactical HQ consisting of Hackett, Brigade Major Dawson and a signals element remained at the DZ. At around 18:00 Hackett was joined by the Brigade HQ motor transport element guided by Lieutenant Frederick Lock from the Divisional Provost Company, who had jumped in with the 4th Parachute Brigade's Advance Party the previous day.[40] In the meantime the Main HQ relocated instead to the Hotel Buunderkamp, located in the woods south-east of Ginkel Heath, 500 yards or so north of the Arnhem–Ede railway line on the fringe of LZ S. The reason for the change of venue is unclear and may have been due to congestion on the track paralleling the north side of the railway line but whatever the reason, Hackett and his Tactical HQ also moved to that location at 18:45.[41] It is worth noting at this point that Hackett had done an exemplary job of commanding the 4th Parachute Brigade in the face of an opposed landing and the onset of darkness, especially in comparison with Lathbury's performance in the relatively benign conditions prevailing the previous day. The most far-flung element of Hackett's Brigade appears to have been Sergeant W. Griffiths and 3 Platoon from A Company, 156 Parachute Battalion, which remained at the *Zuid Ginkel* café protecting a party of non-ambulatory casualties, while Lieutenant-Colonel Alford and 133 Parachute Field Ambulance were ordered to move on to Wolfheze and join 181 Airlanding Field Ambulance operating from the sanatorium there. Alford's men were shepherded clear of the landing area by Colonel Smyth's 10th Parachute Battalion, which was then ordered to set in for the night in the woods just off the south-eastern corner of DZ Y near the Main Brigade HQ at the Hotel Buunderkamp. It is unclear whether this was due to the difficulty of moving through the wooded terrain in darkness or to reinforce the 4th Parachute Squadron RE as Brigade rearguard. The fact that the 10th Battalion deployed initially north of the Amsterdamseweg before moving to the overnight position, and that Smyth was tasked to resume his advance along the Brigade axis toward Arnhem in the early hours of the following morning, suggests the latter.[42]

Whatever the precise reason for its location, the 10th Parachute Battalion did not passively occupy its overnight position, for Colonel Smyth ordered an intensive programme of patrols to dominate the area around it. This was a wise precaution given the confused situation and because there were many Germans in the surrounding area, not all of them survivors of the collapse of *SS Wacht Bataillon 3*. Sergeant Banwell was reconnoitring the area around 4 Platoon's initial location with Corporal George Cuthill when they happened upon a laagered German armoured vehicle with a sentry maintaining an ineffectual watch while the remainder of the crew cooked a meal.[43] The paratroopers stealthily obtained a PIAT and knocked the vehicle out, presumably killing or dispersing the crew in the process. Nor was the patrolling restricted to senior NCOs. Banwell was leading 4 Platoon south across the Amsterdamseweg to the Battalion overnight position when 'He stumbled on a strange sight – in the woods, Lt. Col. Smyth, surrounded by twenty men of the 10th, was arguing violently with a German officer and a similar number of enemy troops. The two patrols had come face to face so suddenly that not a shot was fired. In excellent English the German stated "I consider you our prisoners!" Colonel Smyth was just as vehement in his counter-claim. Suddenly both patrols dispersed their own way.'[44]

While the 10th Battalion's patrols were clashing with the Germans around their overnight perimeter, Major Gilchrist and A Company were leading the 11th Parachute Battalion east to join the 1st Parachute Brigade. Having trailed 156 Parachute Battalion from the DZ, Lieutenant-Colonel Lea struck off on his own after linking up with the 11th Battalion's glider-borne transport and a detachment of anti-tank guns from the 2nd (Oban) Airlanding Anti-tank Battery near LZ S. Heading for Division HQ, which had relocated to the Hotel Hartenstein in Oosterbeek at 17:00, the Battalion column crossed the Arnhem–Ede railway line at Wolfheze, where the inhabitants again lined the road to greet their liberators.[45] As Captain Mawson recalled:

> The faces of the younger women and children were bursting with smiles and cheers and laughter…The road was strewn with trampled flowers, and dogs and little children ran beside the column…They pressed upon us cups of water and rosy apples…and everywhere the Churchill 'V' sign was used as a currency of friendship and greeting.[46]

The Battalion marched on south-east along the Wolfhezeweg past the Hotel Wolfheze and then east along the Utrechtseweg into Oosterbeek where matters devolved to 'sitting on our backsides for several hours on a grassy bank near the [Hotel] Hartenstein' as the commander of the lead Company put it;[47] interestingly the delay is not mentioned in the Battalion War Diary, which merely details the Battalion order of march and that it 'marched all night'.[48] The reason for the delay is unclear, with one source suggesting it might have been due to Hackett arguing with Hicks over the deployment of his Brigade. This is doubtful however, given that the 1st Airlanding Light Regiment's 3 Battery reported the 11th Battalion passing its location near the riverside Oosterbeek Old Church at 22:00, and that Hackett did not visit Division HQ at the Hotel Hartenstein until after 23:00.[49] The delay was therefore more likely due to the need to brief Lieutenant-Colonel Lea and to give the Dutch Underground time to organise local civilians to guide his Battalion.

The third of Hackett's Battalions was also pushing on into the gathering darkness. 156 Parachute Battalion linked up with its glider-borne element near the Wolfheze railway crossing at some point before 20:00, minus two Jeeps lost in a Horsa that had force-landed in the sea, and then moved off eastward along the track paralleling the railway line.[50] Hackett had instructed Lieutenant-Colonel Des Vœux to halt for the night at around 18:30, to permit pre-dark reorganisation in readiness to resume the advance along the railway at first light.[51] Des Vœux had his own ideas however and, apparently encouraged by the lack of opposition, resumed the advance at 20:00 with Major Powell's C Company still in the lead. The unopposed progress continued for the hour or so it took to cover another two miles, although warning of what was to come was received from an unnamed 7th KOSB officer in the process. Presumably a member of an advance party given the timings, he informed the paratroopers that the Germans had set up a 'strong outpost line' ahead in the vicinity of the Dreijensweg which ran north for roughly a mile from the Oosterbeek Hoog railway crossing to the Amsterdamseweg. At 21:00 Sergeant J. R. Black's 10 Platoon ran into an ambush approximately 400 yards short of the Hoog crossing, which scattered and pinned down the platoon in the darkness; the ambushers may have been from *SS Panzerjäger Abteilung 9*, and a stray round from the firefight killed A Company Clerk, Private George Tansley, further down the Battalion column.[52] Major Powell promptly despatched Lieutenant Brian Willcock and 11 Platoon to carry out a left-flanking movement, but when Willcock was also halted by heavy fire Powell deduced that the enemy line was too strong to be carried by an impromptu night attack. Colonel Des Vœux concurred with this assessment when he came forward to investigate the hold-up and ordered a general withdrawal to a wood a few hundred yards west of Johannahoeve to await daylight. Hackett's HQ could not be informed of 156 Battalion's unilateral advance and subsequent check or its post-withdrawal location owing to a communications breakdown of some kind, an omission that was to cause some confusion the following day.[53]

In the meantime Hackett was having a fight of sorts back at Wolfheze. At approximately 23:00 Major James Linton from the 2nd Airlanding Light Battery arrived at Hackett's HQ at the Hotel Buunderkamp bearing further orders from Division HQ. These again diverted the Brigade from its pre-existing mission, this time to secure a different area of high ground in the woods to the east of LZ L. Hackett responded by climbing into his Jeep and driving the four miles or so to the Hotel Hartenstein. Ostensibly this was because Major Linton was unable to answer queries about timings and co-ordination, but Hackett was doubtless also looking to confront Hicks in order to make clear his dissatisfaction with what he famously described as 'an untidy situation'. However, while the two Brigadiers may have exchanged harsh words, Hackett does not appear to have openly challenged Hicks' right to command and neither did he avoid having his mission amended to securing a mile-long ridge of high ground linking the Arnhem–Ede railway and the Amsterdamseweg. Dubbed the *Koepel* (Dome) after a building located on it, the ridge lay around 1,000 yards east of the Oosterbeek Hoog railway crossing and its seizure was intended to be the first stage in opening a route into Arnhem from the north in order to bypass the German line blocking the Utrechtsestraatweg and Onderlangs. Hackett did however secure Hicks' agreement to the transfer of the 7th KOSB to the 4th Parachute Brigade as a replacement for the 11th Parachute Battalion, presumably on the grounds that the Airlanding unit's mission of protecting LZ L placed it in close proximity to the parachute brigade's forming-up point for the advance to the *Koepel* ridge. For his part, Hicks was doubtless unhappy at seeing his already reduced formation being further dismembered, and insisted that Hackett permit the 7th KOSB to complete its existing mission before redeploying it. With that Hackett returned to his own HQ to draw up plans and orders for his Brigade's shift in focus, arriving there at 01:30 on Tuesday 19 September.[54]

While all this was going on around the landing area, the bulk of the 1st Parachute Brigade was continuing its attempt to fight through *Sturmbannführer* Spindler's *Sperrlinie* in the western outskirts of Arnhem. The most forward element was Major Peter Waddy's B Company, 3rd Parachute Battalion, which, accompanied by Lieutenant-Colonel Fitch's Tactical HQ, Brigadier Lathbury, Major-General Urquhart, the detachments from the 1st Parachute Squadron RE and C Troop 1ˢᵗ Airlanding Anti-tank Battery, was occupying several houses on the right of the Utrechtsestraatweg backing onto the Lower Rhine, just west of the St. Elizabeth hospital. The remainder of the 3ʳᵈ Battalion column had become separated near the Oosterbeek Laag underpass, almost a mile back down the Klingelbeekseweg; they were taken under command by Lieutenant-Colonel Dobie's 1ˢᵗ Parachute Battalion when it approached the underpass at around 07:00. Major Waddy's men had been observed entering the riverside houses by elements of *Kampfgruppe* Spindler and a stalemate ensued, with the Germans standing off and bringing down heavy fire on any attempt to move from the front of the houses from armoured vehicles stationed outside Gammon bomb range on the Utrechtsestraatweg, and from the rear by 20mm and possibly 37mm automatic weapons emplaced in a brick factory compound on the opposite bank of the Lower Rhine. Sergeant Gus Garnsworthy engaged one of these with his 6-Pounder gun with unknown results, although his gun was subsequently put out of action by German mortar fire that began at around 13:00; Sergeant Garnsworthy, his crew and C Troop's commander Lieutenant Edward Shaw were then obliged to take shelter in the nearest house.[55]

Ammunition supply became an increasing concern as the stalemate wore on and Colonel Fitch used a brief radio contact with the 1ˢᵗ Parachute Battalion, likely in the late morning to midday, to relay instructions for his A Company to join him with additional ammunition 'at any costs'; the Battalion War Diary suggests that preparation for such an effort were already underway when the order was received.[56] The order bore fruit at around 15:00 when Lieutenant Herbert Burwash and a party of up to forty drawn from his Assault Platoon and A Company arrived at Major Waddy's location after fighting their way up the Klingelbeekseweg, accompanied by a Bren Carrier loaded with ammunition driven by Lieutenant Leo Heaps, a CanLoan officer attached to the 1ˢᵗ Battalion. According to his own account, Heaps was ordered to the Arnhem road bridge with a Jeep-load of ammunition on the orders of Major Hugh Maguire, the Divisional GSO2 (Intelligence) and was sequestered by Colonel Dobie en route.[57] The ammunition was distributed around the Battalion's location on Colonel Fitch's order, but Major Waddy and his Company Sergeant Major Reginald Allen were killed by mortar fire while assisting in the unloading. The incident was witnessed by the Battalion second-in-command, Major Alan Bush: 'Peter Waddy had no need to go out, but he was very impetuous…I saw him killed. There was just a blinding flash and…there he was, prostrate. There was not a mark on him – killed outright by blast.'[58] Groups of Germans then began to infiltrate into the B Company location from the west. Major Bush, ensconced in a house with Lathbury and Urquhart, spotted one group but refrained from opening fire to avoid endangering his superiors. Another group were fired on by a Bren further up the Utrechtsestraatweg as they passed the house occupied by Sergeant Garnsworthy and Lieutenant Shaw and the latter shot two that tried to enter with his Sten gun: 'One fell into the house; one fell outside. The one inside was wounded – hit in the stomach. I made him as comfortable as I could in a chair, but I couldn't do much because there was firing at the rear of the house, and it was obvious that we had to get out.'[59]

At this point B Company was still a going concern, having lost only a handful of casualties during the stand-off and having been resupplied with ammunition courtesy of Lieutenant Heaps. However, the appearance of the German infiltrators raised the prospect of being cut off from the remainder of the 3ʳᵈ Battalion and Lieutenant-Colonel Fitch decided to make another attempt to break through to the Arnhem road bridge, abandoning the Utrechtsestraatweg route in favour of moving through the houses west of the St Elizabeth Hospital to the railway marshalling yard and then following the tracks east. The break-out was to be led by Lieutenant Burwash's party, followed by Fitch's Tactical HQ and B Company, with the 1ˢᵗ Parachute Squadron contingent bringing up the rear. Despite the volume of German fire the paratroopers successfully crossed the bullet-swept Utrechtsestraatweg but the gridwork of streets on the other side were also occupied by elements of *Kampfgruppe* Spindler, specifically from *Obersturmführer* Heinz Gropp's *SS Panzer FlaK Abteilung 9*. Lieutenant Burwash thus ran into fire from numerous machine-guns and mortars and the entire 3ʳᵈ Battalion was again pinned down with Fitch, Burwash and around seventy men occupying houses on one side of a street with the remainder, also numbering around seventy, holding the other. Both groups fought on independently, with the Germans again preferring to stand off and fire on any movement. The commander of the second group, the 3rd Battalion's Intelligence Officer Lieutenant Alexis Vedeniapine, distinguished himself by moving repeatedly between the houses occupied by his men over a two-hour period with 'complete disregard for his own safety'. The firing died down toward nightfall, although German armoured vehicles then approached the British positions but restricted their contribution to firing large amounts of tracer ammunition down the open streets with their machine-guns before withdrawing; this was likely intended to clarify the contested area for the benefit of the German infantry occupying the surrounding buildings. As the German quiescence might have been preparation for a night attack the paratroopers held in place in the darkness, while Colonel Fitch drew up another scheme for finding a way through to the Arnhem road bridge, which involved moving back to the Rhine Pavilion for another attempt along the riverside Onderlangs road.[60]

While all this was going on Major-General Urquhart was busy compounding his existing errors of judgement. Having decided to remain with the 3rd Parachute Battalion when it resumed its advance to Arnhem rather than travelling the two miles or so back to his HQ at the landing area, Urquhart had spent 18 September moving three miles in the opposite direction before becoming pinned down on the Utrechtsestraatweg with B Company. That wilfully separating himself from the Divisional levers of command might not have been the wisest course appears to have occurred to him then; in contrast to his earlier justification of placing himself where he could control events to some extent, Urquhart admitted in his account that 'As a divisional commander mixed up in a battalion encounter, and personally situated somewhere in the middle of the column at that, I was in the worst possible position to intervene too much.'[61] Urquhart therefore decided to make his way back to his HQ in the late afternoon while Lathbury, under the erroneous impression that the bulk of his Brigade was fighting nearer the centre of Arnhem, decided to move forward. The decision appears to have been made in the run-up to Colonel Fitch's attempted move north across the Utrechtsestraatweg, given that the 3rd Parachute Battalion War Diary refers to Urquhart and Lathbury's decision to leave and pursue their own routes.[62] For his part, Fitch was doubtless happy at the prospect of being left to fight his Battalion without his Brigade and Division commanders looking over his shoulder.

The two senior commanders, accompanied by Lathbury's Intelligence Officer, Captain William Taylor, appear to have moved across the Utrechtsestraatweg with the rest of the B Company group at approximately 16:00 before striking off on their own. However, they soon became disoriented in the maze of walled backyards and ended up in a house occupied by Lieutenant James Cleminson and 5 Platoon, who warned his illustrious visitors that his was the 3rd Battalion point platoon and that everything in their direction of travel was German-held. Cleminson then set about organising a section to act as escort but Urquhart had other ideas and launched himself out into the open roadway shouting 'Come on Gerald [Lathbury], we must go and have a look.' He was trailed by Lathbury, Taylor and an appalled Cleminson reportedly calling in turn 'For goodness sake don't, you will only run into a lot of Germans.' Cleminson assumed that at least some of his men would follow but they too had other ideas; as Cleminson subsequently commented, 'My men thought we were mad, and rather sensibly did not follow.'[63] Running across open streets swept by enemy fire was a risky business and before long Lathbury was hit in the leg and back, with one round chipping his spine. His companions managed to manhandle him into the relative safety of No. 135 Alexanderstraat to render first aid, where Lathbury repeatedly insisted his companions leave him and make good their escape; they were obliged to do just that after Urquhart shot a passing German with his pistol. Leaving Lathbury in the care of the Dutch householders the three surviving officers made off again, this time eschewing the open streets in favour of the maze of walled backyards and ended up with the householder of No.14 Zwarteweg, Mr Anton Derksen, who warned that more German troops were approaching and ushered them to the relative safety of his attic. After carrying out a cursory search of the house that fortunately did not include the attic, the Germans set up a section position in front of No. 14 that included an anti-tank gun or an armoured vehicle depending on the account, which was parked directly outside the front door.[64] Urquhart and his companions were therefore trapped in their attic, as Lieutenant Cleminson discovered when he stealthily ventured downstairs at around nightfall.

Urquhart's move to regain his Division HQ was therefore another poorly thought-out and executed decision in the chain that began with his impetuous and needless departure from his HQ the previous day, and he continued in the same vein while debating possible courses of action with Cleminson and Taylor. According to Cleminson, Urquhart 'held a very democratic discussion between the three of us as to what we should do next', during which Cleminson suggested 'that the only sensible thing for us to do was to sit tight in the attic until first light... if we went downstairs and were lucky enough to avoid the [German] section, which was at the front of the house, we were unlikely to get back into our own lines without being shot by one side or the other. The IO [Taylor] agreed with me.'[65] However, this was perhaps understating Urquhart's stance in the exchange, given that his own account refers to suggesting an attack on the armoured vehicle with hand-grenades and using the resultant confusion as cover for their escape, and that he was 'outvoted' by his companions' obvious and indeed understandable lack of enthusiasm for the idea.[66] While he may not have mentioned it at the time, Cleminson later admitted to being less than impressed with his Division Commander's behaviour: 'I have never understood how the General and the Brigadier could be quite so foolhardy as to advance through their own front-line, and subsequently all General Roy would say was that he had lost touch by wireless...and wanted to see for himself. Well he certainly did!'[67]

At this point Urquhart had been absent from and out of touch with his HQ for over twenty-four hours, leaving the 1st Airborne Division effectively leaderless. This state of affairs is usually excused on the grounds that Urquhart's initial decision to leave his HQ in the manner he did was ill-judged but understandable, given his desire to see what was happening, and that he simply became an unwitting victim of events thereafter. As we have seen, however, this explanation simply does not hold water, not least because Urquhart's poor decision-making predated arrival in Holland, and leaving his HQ on a baseless rumour once there, did nothing to help him see anything. On the contrary, it simply removed him from what communication links and command systems there were, and the series of events he subsequently became a victim of were all self-generated by faulty reasoning and decision-making. All this makes it difficult to escape two interlinked conclusions. First, it is no exaggeration to say that Urquhart did not make a single correct decision between arriving at his Horsa at RAF Fairford in the early morning of Sunday 17 September and becoming incarcerated in the attic of No.14 Zwarteweg. Second, he was simply out of his depth in the first phase of Operation MARKET, having failed to grasp the essential differences between Airborne and conventional ground operations. To be fair this was not totally Urquhart's fault, given that he had harboured doubts about his suitability and that circumstances and illness had conspired against him grasping those essential differences in the period between assuming command of the 1st Airborne Division in January 1944 and embarking for Holland. Ultimate responsibility lay with those who elevated him to that command, and the episode is a damning example of the deleterious consequences that could arise from the promotion-via-patronage system endemic in the British Army of that time and arguably since.

Lieutenant-Colonel Dobie's 1st Parachute Battalion spent 18 September fighting its own battle in virtual isolation, despite being located only around a mile from Urquhart and Fitch. After taking the cut-off portion of the 3rd Battalion column under command near the Oosterbeek Laag underpass at 07:00, the 1st Battalion's advance came to a halt a few hundred yards east of the underpass at around 09:00 in the face of fire from weapons emplaced on *Den Brink* on the left and houses and a factory ahead on Klingelbeekseweg; German fire from the latter direction was reportedly thickened by four armoured cars and a tank of some kind, which were likely

Kampfgruppe Möller's *Sd.Kfz* 251 half-tracks. The 1ˢᵗ Battalion's lead element, Major Christopher Perrin-Brown's T Company, was therefore obliged to take shelter in houses on either side of the road, and fire from the factory and the light-calibre *flak* weapons emplaced across the river also stymied attempts to move through backyards and gardens. The advance then stalled for several hours while the paratroopers reorganised, and the fact that the 1ˢᵗ Battalion had been moving and fighting virtually non-stop for eighteen hours likely also had some bearing on the hiatus. The factory area, located on the right between the Klingelbeekseweg and the Lower Rhine and consisting of a number of brick buildings and chimneys set amongst scrub-covered spoil heaps, was identified as the major obstacle to further advance, but an attack in the early afternoon was rebuffed, largely by 20mm fire from the brickworks across the river.[68]

Lieutenant-Colonel Dobie then set about organising a co-ordinated effort following discussion with the ranking 3ʳᵈ Battalion officer, Major Mervyn Dennison of A Company; Dennison appears to have been in the process of organising his own attack when Fitch relayed his radio demand for immediate reinforcement and resupply. As Dobie had commandeered the 3ʳᵈ Battalion's support platoons the plan was for the remainder of the 3ʳᵈ Battalion column, consisting of Dennison's A Company and Lieutenant Burwash's Assault Platoon, to attack along the high ground on the left of the Klingelbeekseweg with Major Perrin-Brown's T Company on their right; Lieutenant Eric Davies' twelve-strong 10 Platoon was tasked to attack up the road, briefed by Dobie in person, while Lieutenant Hellingoe's 11 Platoon was instructed to simply 'clear the factory' by Major Perrin-Brown.[69] The attack was again supported by mortars, Vickers guns, artillery fire from the Light Regiment's 3 Battery and at least one of the attached 6-Pounder anti-tank guns; the latter scored a direct hit on a German bunker in the factory area causing a number of casualties and may also have been responsible for knocking out a German armoured car.[70] The attack began at around 14:00 and as we have seen, the 3ʳᵈ Battalion contingent succeeded in fighting its way through to B Company's location. In the process Major Dennison was knocked unconscious by the blast from a mortar bomb and then seriously wounded in both arms in a hand-to-hand encounter that obliged him to hand over command to Lieutenant Burwash; Dennison was later awarded the Military Cross for this and his actions against *Bataillon* Krafft west of Oosterbeek the previous day.[71] The T Company contingent went forward in a rapid advance despite the enemy fire. Lieutenant Hellingoe's 11 Platoon, numbering around forty after Major Perrin-Brown rounded up some reinforcements, charged straight through the scrub-covered spoil heaps toward the factory buildings, some shouting the 1ˢᵗ Parachute Brigade's North African war cry 'Waho Mohammed'. Hellingoe pressed on despite being wounded in the right foot but was brought low by another hit in the left ankle; according to his citation for a Dutch award he refused to be evacuated until the sharpshooter had been located and dealt with.[72] He was dragged to safety by his Platoon Sergeant John Richards, who exposed himself to heavy enemy fire for twenty minutes to do so. Richards then suppressed an enemy position in one of the factory buildings with a hand-grenade, reorganised the Platoon under cover of smoke and then continued the advance.[73] Two or three others including Hellingoe's batman, Private Geoff Baker, were also hit, possibly after the factory had been cleared: 'Returning, we noticed a German half-track marked with a Red Cross between us and the river but we did not take a lot of notice. We should have done as it opened up with a machine gun and I was one of two or three wounded...with a shattered shin.'[74] Private Baker was helped to safety by a member of 10 Platoon but subsequently lost his leg.

Lieutenant Davies and his depleted 10 Platoon made it up the incline without suffering any casualties, although a Bren gunner was killed by a hit in the face shortly afterward in an exchange with Germans holding nearby houses. Most of the houses were also occupied by Dutch civilians, some of whom provided the reorganising paratroopers with food and drink until increasingly heavy German fire drove them to shelter; Davies set his Platoon medic to treating a young girl shot through the thigh while his men held back her 'berserk' mother. Despite being down to only eight or nine men by this point, Davies nonetheless pushed on up the Klingelbeekseweg but ran out of luck while directing another Bren gunner onto a German machine-gun position: 'Old soldiers say that you never see the one that hits you. I did – it was a tracer…coming over in a flat arc from our right flank. The bullet went through the top of both my legs, severing the sciatic nerve in my right leg on the way. A second bullet then went through my small pack and wounded me in the neck.'[75]

While this was going on Major Ronald Stark's S Company was hit with what was described as a 'light attack' from the rear near the Oosterbeek Laag underpass; the attackers were presumably infiltrators from the SS atop *Den Brink* and were beaten off with the loss of six British casualties. The attack east up the Klingelbeekseweg had cleared the factory and carried the advance halfway up the slope toward the junction with the Utrechtseweg, but T Company was reduced to just twenty-two men in the process. Major Perrin-Brown therefore amalgamated the remnants of 10 and 11 Platoons and with all his platoon commanders dead or wounded, divided the resulting grouping in two and placed an experienced platoon sergeant with each; he then took command of one group and placed his Company second-in-command, Captain James Richie, in charge of the other. The attack up the Klingelbeekseweg was then resumed and reached the junction with the Utrechtseweg at 15:00, which was secured with the help of the 3rd Battalion mortars in the face of intense fire from German machine-guns, mortars and what was identified as an 88mm gun.[76] Perrin-Brown's little band and the remainder of Dobie's Battalion then pushed along the south side of the Utrechtseweg for over an hour, moving past the Rhine Pavilion and through the houses recently vacated by the 3rd Parachute Battalion in the face of numerous snipers and machine-guns. Private Douglas Charlton recalled that 'there were bodies of our 3rd Battalion lying everywhere. Officers and NCOs were running in and out of houses trying to chivvy men along; some had stayed behind to comfort dead or dying comrades.'[77]

The advance was halted at the approaches to the next road junction, a fork in front of the St Elizabeth Hospital 400 yards east of the end of the Klingelbeekseweg; the left prong carried the Utrechtsestraatweg uphill toward the Municipal Museum while the right prong carried the Onderlangs down to and along the riverside. Enemy tanks were reported ahead on the Utrechtseweg and the light *flak* guns emplaced in the brickworks on the south bank of the Lower Rhine again made their presence felt. But on this occasion support was available and Lieutenant Antony Driver called down suppressive fire from 3 Battery's 75mm Pack Howitzers along with Dobie's co-opted mortars and Vickers guns, which knocked out two *flak* guns on the riverbank; the Vickers' gunners were credited with 'good work' after hitting a number of running Germans. In an effort to maintain momentum Dobie switched his advance to the north side of the Utrechtsestraatweg at 17:00, crossing the road under cover of smoke and moving through the backyards to avoid the worst of the German fire; this too attracted heavy machine-gun and mortar fire that eventually brought movement to a halt by the St Elizabeth Hospital, and left the paratroopers cut off from the Battalion vehicles. An attempt to bring them up was abandoned with the loss of a Bren Carrier.[78] The portion of T Company with Sergeant Richards appears to have been reduced to just three men in the process of clearing a German position and Richards was subsequently awarded the Military Medal for this and his earlier actions at the factory on the Klingelbeekseweg. As another member of T Company, Lance-Sergeant John Fryer, put it: 'We couldn't get past them because it was like daylight with all the tracer fire…The fire was coming from the hospital and from across the Rhine where there was a brickfield and factory. Every move we made the Germans had us under fire.'[79] However, the 20mm fire from across the Rhine did not deter Fryer from dropping his equipment and running out into the open to the aid of a wounded Sergeant named Collis; interestingly, the German fire ceased while Fryer hauled the bulky Collis onto his shoulder and carried him to safety, although it is unclear whether the pause was deliberate or due to a fortuitous magazine change.[80]

By 18:30 the 1st Parachute Battalion had effectively fought itself to a standstill and in the process had been reduced to around a hundred men with little remaining ammunition. At that point contact was again made with the force holding the Arnhem road bridge, presumably via

Bombardier Leo Hall's jury-rigged No. 22 and No. 68 sets, and Dobie was again ordered to get through to the road bridge at all costs. The order came from Frost, who had assumed command of the 1st Parachute Brigade on learning that Lathbury was missing, and he instructed the 1st and 3rd Battalions to form a force of at least company strength and push through to the bridge by midnight. Isolated at the road bridge with problems of his own, Frost had no way of knowing that by this time neither battalion had the strength or wherewithal to do any such thing, but Dobie nonetheless set about organising a move back across the Utrechtseweg to 'try right down on [the] river bank', using darkness as cover against the guns emplaced in the brickworks on the south bank. This appears to have worked to some extent, but movement was again hampered by closer German guns sweeping all the roads and side streets with automatic fire.[81]

Help, however, was at hand in the shape of Lieutenant-Colonel McCardie and the first-lift portion of the 2nd South Staffords. On leaving its overnight position at LZ S at around 10:00 the South Staffords had made for the Utrechtseweg and was in Oosterbeek within two hours despite an ineffectual strafing near the Hotel Wolfheze. There it came upon a party of between forty and sixty stragglers from the 1st Parachute Battalion gathered in by the commander of R Company, Major John Timothy; McCardie took Timothy's band under command and reinforced him with Major Toler and his B Squadron Glider Pilots before pushing on.[82] D Company emerged from the eastern outskirts of Oosterbeek at 13:00 and promptly ran into fire from elements of *Kampfgruppe* Möller positioned in buildings along the Utrechtseweg backed by automatic weapons on the *Mariendaal* feature and the embanked railway spur. Major Phillp's men immediately set about clearing the route but McCardie was wary of being drawn into a costly and drawn-out fight and began seeking an alternative way through the streets onto the riverside LION route. The advance was resumed at 17:30, covered by D Company, and within two hours McCardie's Tactical HQ and depleted B and Support Company had passed through the Oosterbeek Laag underpass and up the Klingelbeekseweg into Arnhem, making contact with Dobie near the junction with the Utrechtsestraatweg at 20:00. Although he appears to have deferred to Dobie's greater knowledge of the local situation, McCardie felt it unwise to resume the advance with only his understrength B Company and between seventy and a hundred exhausted paratroopers, preferring to wait until the rest of his Battalion caught up. The two officers therefore drew up a compromise plan to resume the advance at 01:00, in order to allow time for Dobie's exhausted men to reorganise and rest, and for the remainder of the 2nd South Staffords to catch up.[83] Dobie's men appear to have been left to rest although not all benefited, as Private Charlton recalled:

> Someone made tea, and we ate from our ration packs; we also ate bottled pears from the cellar of the house we had occupied. Then I was detailed to go with a sergeant and four men back along our route to look for stragglers. I had been on the move without sleep for more than forty hours and was none too pleased. It was dark now, and we found medics patching up the wounded along the way as well as many reluctant heroes hiding in the houses; these were directed to our new position or they joined us.[84]

The next increment of the 2nd South Staffords arrived at around midnight. Major Phillp and D Company began to break contact at 18:30 in order to follow in McCardie's wake. This took some time and in the process they were fortuitously joined by Major Thomas Lane and A Company, the lead element of the Battalion's second lift. Lane assumed overall command as senior in rank but was unwilling to proceed through the Oosterbeek Laag underpass without any idea of what was on the far side. He therefore went forward in person to clarify the situation and having found and conferred with McCardie near the Rhine Pavilion, returned to lead the party forward, deploying D Company on the north side of the Utrechtseweg opposite B Company on the south, while A Company deployed along the line of the road behind them.[85] The passage of the remainder of the South Staffords' second lift, consisting of the Battalion Main HQ under Major John Commings, Major Philip Wright's C Company, MMG and anti-tank elements, the Battalion's twenty-five Jeeps and trailers and Major Robert Cain with B Company's HQ element, was not so straightforward. After leaving the landing area at around 17:30, a pause at the Hotel Hartenstein resulted in Division HQ appropriating a number of the Mortar Platoon's Jeeps and the anti-tank element being detached to assist the 1st Border. In exchange a section from the 9th (Airborne) Field Company RE was attached to Major Cain's party for the trip to the Arnhem road bridge while Lieutenant Donald Edwards and 17 Platoon also appear to have been sequestered. The South Staffords column then became separated in the congestion on the Utrechtseweg, apparently due to the 11th Parachute Battalion insinuating itself into the column behind A Company, and unwittingly ran into *Kampfgruppe* Möller's guns firing on fixed lines down the roadway in the darkness. Major Commings was thus obliged to emulate Colonel McCardie by withdrawing and seeking an alternative route, with the added complication of turning two dozen Jeeps and trailers in pitch darkness, an operation which took several hours and carried on into the early hours of Tuesday 19 September.[86]

It is difficult not to sympathise with Dobie and McCardie and especially the former, who had been operating totally without guidance or support for the entire thirty-five hours since leaving DZ X at 15:30 on 17 September. Both Battalion commanders were functioning in a vacuum with no effective contact, guidance or support from higher up the chain of command and no clear information about the situation, friendly or enemy. The man who should have been supporting and controlling their efforts was temporarily paralysed as a result of wounds to the legs and lower back only a few hundred yards away at No. 135 Alexanderstraat. The man responsible for putting him there and indeed with overall responsibility for Dobie, McCardie and everyone else from the 1st Airborne Division on the ground in Holland was also impotently sequestered in the attic of No.14 Zwarteweg within a stone's throw of the action, as a result of his own impetuosity and poor judgement. While the reins of command had been passed to Hicks at 09:15 on the morning of Monday 18 September, this did not herald any major shift away from the existing Division plan despite the vastly changed circumstances, although to be fair the scope for revision was limited during Hicks' tenure, as the 1st Airlanding Brigade was fully committed to protecting the landing area for the inbound second lift, and then covering the eastward move of the numerous Divisional units and securing LZ L for the third lift.

There was scope for revision with regard to the 4th Parachute Brigade however, specifically by cancelling its existing and now superfluous mission in favour of employing it in its entirety to reinforce the drive for the Division's primary objective, Hackett's objections notwithstanding. This was even more the case because by 15:00 Division HQ was aware that the 1st Parachute Brigade's drive to the Arnhem road bridge had gone seriously awry and that only a fraction of a single battalion had reached that primary objective.[87] A full Brigade attack with artillery support from the Airlanding Light Regiment along the axis of the Utrechtseweg ought to have been feasible by midnight if not earlier, given the actual timings and movements of the Brigade's constituent units after landing; the 11th Parachute Battalion was in the eastern outskirts of Oosterbeek by around 20:00 for example, and 156 Parachute Battalion had covered a similar amount of ground by 21:00.[88] Such an attack would have had good prospects for success as the *c.* 100-strong element of *Kampfgruppe* Möller occupying the embanked railway spur was holding not only the embankment but also the *Mariendaal* (a historic country estate) and *Den Brink* features and the line of the Klingelbeekseweg facing the Lower Rhine. Darkness reduced the effectiveness of the German automatic weapons located on the high ground, as is clear from the relative ease with which British units passed through the Oosterbeek Laag underpass after nightfall, and a breakthrough along the Utrechtsestraatweg would have outflanked and/or exposed the rear of the units manning the southern section of Spindler's *Sperrlinie*. Indeed, it might well have unhinged the entire blocking line and created a corridor down to the Arnhem road bridge through which the remainder of the Division could have passed. This situation would not apply indefinitely however, for German reinforcements and tactical redeployments were slowly but surely tipping the balance against the British and would eventually render the blocking line impregnable; as *Hauptsturmführer* Wilfried Schwarz, *9 SS Panzer Division's* chief-of-staff, put it: 'As reinforcements arrived, it dawned on us that we might succeed… Dozens of commanders reported to me at divisional headquarters, and these I parcelled out to the front.'[89] The British situation was therefore analogous to that pertaining twenty-four hours earlier, when more energetic leadership could have seen the bulk if not all of the 1st Parachute Brigade safely into Arnhem before Spindler could erect his blocking line.

Unfortunately for the Arnhem portion of MARKET such leadership was again not forthcoming, because Hicks was satisfied to follow the existing plan with the minor adjustments of despatching reinforcements piecemeal to the 1st Parachute Brigade and slightly refocusing the 4th Parachute Brigade's mission to secure the *Koepel* ridge, and even then only in direct response to events. This strongly suggests Hicks saw his role as a temporary and essentially passive caretaker under Mackenzie's close supervision until Urquhart returned to resume command, and the appropriateness of this approach was doubtless reinforced by an erroneous late evening report that Urquhart was with the 2nd Parachute Battalion near the Arnhem road bridge.[90] Aside from the fact that the situation demanded a rather more pro-active and vigorous attitude, the problem was that Hick's stewardship was a combination of business as usual with a tendency toward learned behaviour response. For example, following receipt of another erroneous report in the late evening of 18 September that the force at the Arnhem road bridge had been overrun, at 01:00 in the morning of 19 September, Hicks ordered Dobie to abandon the effort to reach the bridge and withdraw to Oosterbeek, only to reverse his decision ninety minutes later.[91]

There does not appear to have been much effort to clarify the situation or confirm the accuracy of incoming reports. At 23:30 for example, an unnamed officer from the 2nd South Staffords reportedly arrived at Division HQ with the accurate news that the 1st and 3rd Parachute Battalions had been reduced to a combined strength of 150 men commanded by Lieutenant-Colonel Dobie, that the Staffords' two lead companies were under fire near the Rhine Pavilion from the south bank of the Lower Rhine, along with the inaccurate information that Urquhart and Lathbury were with the 2nd Parachute Battalion at a grid reference on the south side of the Arnhem road bridge, and that the South Staffords were 'out of touch' with Dobie's force.[92] The identity of the messenger and source of his information is unclear, although he may have been despatched by Dobie following interception of a radio transmission from an artillery forward observer at the bridge monitored at some point after 23:00, presumably to ensure Division HQ was aware that Frost's force was still holding out.[93] The errors may also have been the result of poor transcription, given that several orders and reports from Division HQ recorded in other unit War Diaries do not appear in the Division HQ Diary. The essential point here is that no effort appears to have been made to seek verification for this report, even though darkness significantly reduced the danger in passing back and forth through the Oosterbeek Laag underpass, and there were no entries in the Division HQ War Diary at all between 23:30 on 18 September and 07:25 the following morning. So Hicks appears to have been happy to remain ensconced at Division HQ diligently overseeing the execution of an increasingly outmoded and irrelevant plan while the 1st Airborne Division's final chance to complete its primary mission of securing a passage across the Lower Rhine ebbed slowly away.

By midnight on Monday 18 September, thirty-four hours after landing, the surviving bulk of the 1st Parachute Brigade was still stalled just over a mile short of its primary objective, with the remainder of the 1st Airborne Division backing up behind it. There were also some scattered elements caught in the German-occupied space between Dobie's men and the road bridge perimeter. Lieutenant John Dickson, commanding the 3rd Parachute Battalion's Mortar platoon, found himself alone after leading a charge that branched off along the lower Onderlangs road and carried him 750 yards beyond the St Elizabeth Hospital. Coming to a halt by the harbour area near the pontoon bridge site, Dickson gathered up two other stray members of the 3rd Battalion and took shelter in a nearby house where they were obliged to emulate Urquhart by taking refuge in the roof space when German troops occupied the lower floors.[94] Another group led by Major Anthony Deane-Drummond, second-in-command of the Division Signals Section and a veteran of the Tragino raid in February 1941 (the first ever British parachute raid on enemy territory), were holed up nearby. Deane-Drummond had left the landing area with his batman at 07:30 on 18 September to inform the 1st Parachute Brigade HQ of a new HQ radio frequency; the change, which may have been a daily routine, was necessary to avoid interference from a more powerful British transmitter.[95] In the process he came across a leaderless group from the 3rd Parachute Battalion, likely in the vicinity of the Klingelbeekseweg and led them forward before also being halted near the harbour. Unable to return to British lines, Deane-Drummond instructed his force, by now reduced to around twenty, to break up into small groups, lay low and rendezvous after dark for another attempt to reach the bridge; this may have been the source of Dickson's two 3rd Battalion men. Deane-Drummond then led a group of three including his batman into a nearby house that was also subsequently occupied by a party of Germans intent on turning it into a strongpoint. The outnumbered paratroopers were therefore obliged to lock themselves in a lavatory at the rear of the house; fortunately the Germans made no attempt to investigate the locked door beyond a cursory rattle of the handle.[96]

Although they had no way of knowing it, the two groups of paratroopers had become entangled in a tactical withdrawal by the southern section of the German blocking line. The British presence in the vicinity of the St Elizabeth Hospital was too close to the German positions to permit timely response to renewed British attacks, so Spindler ordered *SS Panzer Artillerie Regiment 9*, *Kampfgruppe* Harder and elements of *SS Panzergrenadier Regiment 20* to withdraw to a new line located at the eastern end of a stretch of scrub-covered ground sloping up from the riverside Onderlangs road to the Utrechtsestraatweg, just short of the harbour area and pontoon bridge site. Approaching the new line thus involved crossing half-a-mile of open ground covered from the north by elements of *Kampfgruppe* Möller and probably *SS Panzer FlaK Abteilung 9* deployed on the Utrechtsestraatweg and along the far side of the railway cutting running along atop the slope, and from the south by the automatic weapons emplaced in the brickworks on the other side of the Lower Rhine. Any British attack would therefore be channelled into a funnel 250 yards wide at most, every inch of which was exposed to fire from automatic weapons and mortars. The deadly tactical efficiency of the German redeployment would not become apparent until the 1st and 3rd Parachute Battalions attempted to resume their attack in the early hours of Tuesday 19 September.

Deane-Drummond and Dickson thus represented the furthest penetration by the bulk of the 1st Parachute Brigade toward the Arnhem road bridge at this time, but at least two other Airborne contingents were even closer to that objective. A group of eleven men from 4 Platoon, B Company, 2nd Parachute Battalion under Lieutenant Hugh Levien were holed up in a house on the Bakkerstraat just outside the bridge perimeter, having become separated when the remainder of B Company moved into the perimeter from the pontoon bridge site just before dawn. Levien had been able to speak to his Company commander, Major Douglas Crawley, via the civilian telephone network but was unable to move because their location was surrounded by German troops. The other group was Lieutenant Wilfred Morley's fifteen-strong No.1 Section 1st (Airborne) Divisional Provost Company, which had been occupying Arnhem's main police station half-a-dozen blocks north of the bridge perimeter since around 23:00 on 17 September. The MPs were accompanied by Sergeant Harry Parker and Private Robert Peatling from the 3rd and 2nd Parachute Battalions respectively, who had been picked up on the march into Arnhem. Twenty German POWs were locked securely in the cells and a number of enthusiastic Dutch policemen were in attendance. Sergeant Henry Callaway was left in charge after Lieutenant Morley and Lance-Corporal Jock Keddie departed for the Arnhem bridge at around midnight. The pair successfully reached 1st Parachute Brigade Main HQ and met up with a Dutch interrogation officer as planned, but the Dutchman was shot on the return journey and German fire drove Morley and Keddie back into the bridge perimeter, where they were assigned to the Brigade HQ defence force.

Back at the police station the remainder of No. 1 Section settled down to sleep after sharing their cigarette and chocolate rations with the Dutch police, who had been starved of such luxuries under German occupation. Overall there was an air of optimism, as Lance-Corporal Jack Coates noted: 'It was quiet in the town and it seemed we had cracked it. All we had to do was dig in and hold out for a couple of days.' The optimism evaporated at dawn with the sound of the 1st and 3rd Parachute Battalions' battle to the west and the appearance of large numbers of SS troops in the streets around the police station. Sergeant Callaway promptly deployed his little band in defensive positions around the building and after surreptitious reconnaissance by the Dutch police had established that the surrounding streets were also full of SS it was decided that the policemen should depart for their own safety, although some may have returned briefly during the day with updates on German activity. The Germans made no effort to enter the station through the closed front doors, although two opportunist SS men broke in after smashing a window and made off with an unattended small pack, fortunately without spotting the owner lurking nearby, and at least one other SS man was deterred from interfering with the police cars parked in the station courtyard by a burst of Sten fire, which again elicited no further response. Callaway initially told his men to stand by to leave at midnight and preparations were set in hand including wrapping ammunition boots in strips of blanket to deaden their sound. The move was abandoned however, possibly after Callaway had visited the bridge perimeter in search of Lieutenant Morley, and No. 1 Section and their hungry and increasingly truculent POWs settled down for their second night in the police station.[97]

At the Arnhem road bridge Private James Sims had an eventful afternoon in the White House on the corner of the Kadestraat and Weertjesstraat. Ordered to prepare a stew from the dehydrated meat and biscuits in their ration packs by Lieutenant Woods, Sims ventured out to collect water from a standpipe in the yard amidst a full-scale firefight, to the cheers from paratroopers occupying the surrounding buildings, and then set to work with a mess tin and hexamine cooker. The subsequent concoction proved inedible however, to the extent that Lieutenant Woods poured it away after a single mouthful in favour of sharing a bar of ration chocolate with the crestfallen Sims. A fire order on a German mortar position detected behind a nearby building proved more successful, with the enemy weapon and its crew being 'tossed into the air', possibly by a secondary explosion, but the pair were then obliged to abandon their attic observation post by German counter-fire that blew out the rear windows and sent shrapnel tearing through the roof tiles. On descending they discovered Sergeant McCreath from the Mortar Platoon attempting to set up a radio, who reported that the remainder of the Platoon were still happily ensconced in their house and mortar pits across the Weertjesstraat. Shortly thereafter, at around 16:00, they were joined by Lieutenant-Colonel Frost on a tour of inspection. As well as speaking individually to the White House defenders, Frost had someone check the condition of some barges, presumably located along the riverside Rijnkade; the report came back that the barges were too badly damaged for use, prompting Frost to comment 'That's that, then, we'll stay where we are.'[98]

By this point the reality of being under siege had tempered Frost's earlier optimism, not least because German artillery, mortar and small-arms fire had made movement between the British-occupied buildings a hazardous undertaking. Frost was also becoming concerned over a developing shortage of ammunition. The scales carried by the paratroopers were being rapidly depleted in the close-range, house-to-house fighting and the small reserve carried into the perimeter by the contingent from 250 (Airborne) Light Composite Company RASC had been distributed by nightfall; under normal circumstances a resupply would then have been drawn from Division stocks but that source was still situated on the wrong side of the Oosterbeek Laag underpass. To conserve the available ammunition as far as possible Frost therefore prohibited sniping and engaging targets of opportunity by ordering that firing be restricted to defending against direct assaults at close range.[99] Food supplies were also running short as the paratroopers only carried ration packs for forty-eight hours, and the houses in the perimeter yielded nothing more than a small number of fresh apples and pears, although this may have varied between buildings and the guile and scrounging abilities of the men occupying them; Private Sims for example recalled the house occupied by the Mortar Platoon was 'simply bursting with preserved foods, sweets, chocolates and drinks of all kinds'.[100] In the midst of all this Frost found himself elevated to a somewhat truncated command of the 1st Parachute Brigade after Brigade Major Hibbert reportedly learned from Dobie that Lathbury was missing, presumably in the early evening. Hibbert therefore formally requested Frost to assume command of all units in the bridge perimeter and Frost duly handed command of the 2nd Parachute Battalion contingent to his second-in-command, Major David Wallis, before moving next door to the Brigade HQ building on the Eusebiusbinnensingel. At 18:30, following a radio report that the 1st and 3rd Parachute Battalions were held up near the St Elizabeth Hospital, he made his only effort to exert control over the elements of the Brigade outside the bridge perimeter with his abortive instruction for Dobie to despatch a flying column to the bridge.[101]

There was little overt German activity on the western side of the bridge perimeter at this point, presumably because the German units there were preoccupied with establishing a watertight block to the 1st and 3rd Parachute Battalions' advance. Venturing out into the open on the western side of the bridge ramp remained hazardous though, as Private Sims discovered when Lieutenant Woods left briefly to confer with Frost. Sergeant McCreath promptly ordered him to fetch his small pack from the Mortar Platoon house. Unable to refuse a direct order, Sims dropped to the Kadestraat from a six-foot-high window to retrieve McCreath's pack, his fall cushioned by a handy German corpse, and attempted a high-speed dash across the Weertjesstraat but was greeted by the ripping snarl of a German machine-gun as soon as he emerged into the open: 'My legs seemed to turn to water, for the rate of fire was so rapid that it appeared as if the bullets were tearing up the ground behind me faster than I could possibly run.' Fortunately, he was able to dive headlong into a mortar pit dug into the traffic island before the machine-gunner adjusted his aim, interrupting the mortar crew drinking a brew from a liberated fine china tea service. Sims' explanation for his interruption prompted a forthright 'the Scotch bastard, why didn't he go himself?' and gained him a share of the hot, sweet tea before the crew gave him a collective boost out of the mortar pit for the final leg to the safety of the Mortar Platoon house. The errant small pack was located despite the fumes from a host of hexamine stoves. Sims was not destined to deliver it. Travelling back to the White House via the slit trench where he had spent the previous night, he was waylaid by Sergeant Joe Hamilton, who was disinclined to listen to Sims' explanation and ordered him to remain in the trench on pain of being shot. Sims and Sergeant McCreath's small pack consequently stayed put.[102]

The Germans remained more active on the eastern side of the perimeter. *Kampfgruppe* Brinkmann, or more likely elements of Major Knaust's *Bataillon* 'Bocholt', finally succeeded in overrunning one of the three buildings held by Lieutenant Infield's 8 Platoon from the 3rd Parachute Battalion on the south side of the Westervoortsedijk; this appears to have then obliged the men from the Brigade HQ Defence Platoon to withdraw from another building on the north side of the road.[103] The pressure was also maintained against the elements of the 1st Parachute Squadron RE and C Company 3rd Parachute Battalion holding the Van Limburg Stirum School at the north-eastern tip of the perimeter. In the mid-afternoon German troops stationed in the houses on the Eusebiusbuitensingel began firing into the School's east-facing rooms, initiating a duel with the Bren gunners stationed on that side of the building that went on through the afternoon. The paratroopers had designs on machine-guns, food and cigars spotted in the *Sd.Kfz.* 250 half-track knocked out on the Bleckmanslaan by Sapper Emery that morning, but the Germans had other ideas. At 19:30 tracer ammunition was used to set light to the unarmoured *Sd.Kfz.* 10 half-track resting against the Van Limburg Stirum School's west wall while a flame-thrower did the same to the armoured *Sd.Kfz.* 250. Ninety minutes later the Red School was also set ablaze after the Germans had made the rooms on the north side of the Van Limburg School temporarily untenable by firing light mortar bombs through the windows. Sparks and embers from the Red School spread the fire to the roof of the Van Limburg School and the heat from the burning vehicles damaged the west wall, but the fire was brought under control by 23:50 despite 'spasmodic' German machine-gun fire; the burning vehicles were finally extinguished with demolition charges. By this point, defence of the Van Limburg School had cost the Parachute Engineers two dead and twelve wounded; The 3rd Parachute Battalion contingent's casualties are unclear.[104]

Apart from their effort against the Van Limburg School German activity appears to have fallen away with nightfall and the Airborne soldiers took full advantage of the lull. At this point the bridge force was still in fairly good order, apart from the looming ammunition shortage, having lost an estimated ten dead and thirty wounded. Frost redeployed part of the 2nd Battalion's B Company from the west to the east side of the perimeter in response to the German incursion along the Westervoortsedijk.[105] He also organised what he dubbed a 'mobile storming party' around Major Gough's two Reconnaissance Squadron Jeeps and the 2nd Battalion's Bren Carrier as a further countermeasure, and when no new German incursion was forthcoming Gough was given an even more hazardous mission. The 1st Polish Independent Parachute Brigade was scheduled to land on DZ K, just south of the road bridge, the following day, and fearing a massacre Frost detailed Gough to lead his storming party across the bridge to greet them. Gough was understandably less than enthusiastic about undertaking what Frost himself characterised as a suicide mission that might win Gough his family's fifth Victoria Cross.[106]

There was also more overtly aggressive British activity. As Private Sims recalled, with the onset of darkness 'our lads came to life; out went the riflemen, cocky and confident, looking for Jerry. At night we had moral, if not material, superiority.'[107] The Airborne soldiers also needed light for their prowling and defence. The burning Red School illuminated the east side of the bridge ramp and Frost ordered a small building on the corner of the Eusebiusbinnensingel and Weertjesstraat to be set alight to illuminate the west side. The flames spread to the adjacent Brigade HQ building and possibly that occupied by the 2nd Battalion HQ too, before being brought under control. Though they did provide sufficient illumination for the defenders to see 'to shoot at two hundred yards'.[108]

In addition to partially redeploying to the east side of the perimeter, B Company also mounted a twelve-strong standing patrol on the bridge. Consisting mainly of the 4 Platoon contingent that had reached the bridge at dawn, the patrol was led by Company second-in-command Captain Francis Hoyer-Millar, because all B Company's Platoon commanders were dead, wounded or missing. Lieutenant Peter Cane from 6 Platoon had been killed the previous night at *Den Brink*, Lieutenant Levien was holed up behind German lines on the Bakkerstraat with his group from 4 Platoon and Lieutenant Colin Stanford had been wounded in the head in the afternoon while surveying the area around 5 Platoon's position with binoculars; Hoyer-Millar had been present when Company Sergeant Major William Scott had somewhat indelicately announced, 'Mr Stanford's had his chips.' Wary of venturing into the pool of intense darkness beyond the top of the ramp, Hoyer-Millar led the way with a fragmentation grenade and was surprised and gratified when five SS men, three of them wounded, came forward to surrender; Private Donald Smith discovered another SS man lurking beneath a knocked-out vehicle and took him prisoner as well.

Moving around in the darkness was of course a dangerous business. A nervous Bren gunner loosed a burst at the patrol, possibly as Hoyer-Millar deployed it on either side of the bridge, and he responded with an annoyed 'Stop firing that bloody Bren gun. It's only me!'[109] Major David Wallis, the recently installed commander of the 2nd Battalion, was not so fortunate. Approaching the rear of a building on the south side of the Weertjesstraat while checking his positions, he was challenged and then hit in the chest by a burst from a Bren belonging to the

9th Field Company RE, possibly because his response was insufficiently clear. Major Wallis was killed instantly and his passing obliged Frost to appoint Major Tatham-Warter, the commander of A Company, in Wallis' stead over the head of B Company's Major Crawley, who was senior in rank.[110] Frost noted some resentment from the latter but selected Tatham-Warter because of his greater familiarity with the bridge perimeter positions.[111]

***

Sixty miles or so south of Arnhem the Grenadier Guards Group's attempt to by-pass the fighting in Aalst by following the route scouted by the 2nd Household Cavalry was obstructed by a series of water crossings that were unable to bear the weight of their Sherman tanks. As a result the Grenadiers had only drawn level with Aalst by nightfall, at which point they received word that the 101st Airborne Division had secured Eindhoven. The flanking move appears to have then been abandoned and the Grenadier Guards Group moved back onto the Valkenswaard–Eindhoven road and on to Son, although the precise timing of the move is unclear owing to 30 Corps' embargo on movement on the main axis of advance during the hours of darkness. In the meantime, the Irish Guards Group's problem with the German roadblock on the River Dommel north of Aalst resolved itself just after 17:00, when the gunners manning the four 88mm guns abandoned their positions and thereby left the road to Eindhoven open.[112] The Irish Guards column then motored up to the city, arriving at around 18:00 and reaching the blown bridge at Son at 19:00.[113] The column was led by elements of the 2nd Household Cavalry and the 2nd Irish Guards tanks, with the lead infantry element being Lieutenant Brian Wilson's Platoon from the 3rd Irish Guards travelling on the decks of Lieutenant William MacFetridge's Troop of Shermans. The infantrymen had been abruptly shaken from their bucolic bridge guard near Aalst shortly after being stood down, and Wilson noted the signs of recent combat along the road, which gave way to US paratroopers and then a tumultuous welcome from Eindhoven's civilian inhabitants: 'The long street was packed with people, jostling, pushing, waving, hysterical with happiness. Above their heads was a moving sea of waving handkerchiefs, hats, hands, little flags, paper streamers.'[114]

Lieutenant Wilson appears to have been the point Platoon for the entire Guards Armoured Division by the time the Irish Guards column reached the blown bridge at Son, where the guard detail from the 506th Parachute Infantry Regiment also appears to have entered into the celebratory mood; on reaching the bank of the Wilhelmina Canal Wilson was greeted by a group of paratroopers on the other bank 'with their arms full of children', before being tasked to cover the right flank of the crossing point with the rest of his No.2 Company.[115] The Bailey bridging unit had been ordered forward over the twenty miles from Bourg Leopold to Valkenswaard after the 2nd Household Cavalry made first contact at Son at midday, and was then 'rushed forward' a further twelve miles up the newly opened road to Son; construction began at 21:00. By nightfall the Irish Guards Group was at Son, the Grenadier Guards Group was en route and the remainder of the Guards Armoured Division was stretched out behind them. The Welsh Guards Group had branched eight miles north-east of Valkenswaard to Geldrop in the suburbs of Eindhoven while the Coldstream Guards Group had moved into Valkenswaard in the afternoon, where it remained while Division HQ decided whether to direct it onward through Eindhoven to Son or through the Welsh Guards to Helmond, seven miles beyond Geldrop. Much of the Division's tail was still in Belgium, and it was estimated that it would take another six hours on 19 September to pass them all across the GARDEN start line near the Meuse-Escaut Canal; the latter provides a graphic illustration of the sheer scale of Operation GARDEN.[116]

With Eindhoven taken and the spearhead of the Guards Armoured Division at Son, Colonel Robert F. Sink's 506th Parachute Infantry Regiment had achieved its initial objectives, and its constituent Battalions spent a relatively quiet night. The main threat came from the jubilant Dutch civilians who took every opportunity to show their appreciation to their liberators, cheering, asking for autographs and photographs and pressing food and drink upon the delighted paratroopers. Private 1st Class David Webster from the 2nd Battalion's Company E later wrote that this was 'the most sincere thanksgiving demonstration any of us were to see, and it pleased us very much'. His Company commander, Captain Richard Winters, put things more succinctly: 'It was just unbelievable.'[117] North-west of Eindhoven the 1st Battalion, 502nd Parachute infantry Regiment spent a relatively quiet Monday under Division control at St. Oedenrode, apart from the 'Incident of the Seven Jeeps', but matters were less benign for the 2nd and 3rd Battalions near Best. Lieutenant Wierzbowski and his little band from the 3rd Battalion remained cut off near the demolished bridge over the Wilhelmina Canal and the remainder of the 3rd Battalion, commanded by Major John P. Stopka after Lieutenant-Colonel Robert G. Cole had been killed by a sniper earlier in the day, managed to push west in the face of heavy fire from German units in and around Best and establish a roadblock on the Eindhoven-Boxtel road. Lieutenant-Colonel Steve A. Chappuis' badly depleted 2nd Battalion launched a further attack south-west from the Zonsche Forest at 17:00 intended to secure the Canal bridge and relieve Lieutenant Wierzbowski. Chappuis was unaware the Germans had demolished the bridge six hours earlier. The 2nd Battalion covered around 1,000 yards before coming under heavy fire from 88mm guns emplaced on the canal, which obliged the paratroopers to withdraw back into the woods to reorganise in readiness to resume the attack at dawn the following day; on the upside the attack may have assisted the 3rd Battalion's push to the Eindhoven-Boxtel road by distracting the Germans at Best.[118]

Lieutenant Wierzbowski's Platoon therefore spent another isolated night on the bank of the Wilhelmina Canal broken up by three brief contacts with friendly forces. A British armoured car, presumably from the 2nd Household Cavalry, appeared on the south bank of the canal, followed by a disoriented patrol from Company E in the early evening and then by Lieutenant Nicholas D. Mottola's Platoon from Company D, which had become separated in the fighting near Best. The patrol departed but did not regain the main US line until the following morning while the British armoured car, which had been providing Wierzbowski with fire support, also departed with the arrival of Lieutenant Mottola's Platoon. Although it had declared its intent to remain at the bridge site the latter departed in some disorder across the canal when attacked during the night and did not rejoin the 2nd Battalion until two days later, leaving Lieutenat Wierzbowski and his depleted band to continue their lonely vigil without support.[119] The 101st Airborne Division's most northerly unit, Colonel Howard R. Johnson's 501st Parachute Infantry Regiment, was set in around Eerde and Veghel straddling the Zuid Willems Canal and appears to have had a quieter night, presumably as a result of roughly handling several determined German attacks through the previous night and morning. Johnson was concerned that his 3rd Battalion was too isolated at Eerde on the western edge of the Regiment's area and thus ordered Lieutenant-Colonel Julian Ewell to withdraw the three miles or so into Veghel, where the 3rd Battalion became the Regimental reserve.[120]

After the last-minute clearing of LZ N and T just in time for the arrival of the second lift, the 82nd Airborne Division's sector of the Airborne Corridor remained active through the night of 18 September, with only the 504th Parachute Infantry Regiment at the western end of the Division's area having a relatively quiet time. The 505th and 508th Parachute Infantry Regiments nonetheless continued to hold their assorted bridges and maintained their other tasks. The exception to this was the 508th Regiment's disjointed push toward the Nijmegen bridges, which had to be reduced and then abandoned in order to allow the 2nd Battalion to counter the German encroachment onto the Division's landing areas just ahead of the arrival of the second lift; Captain Russell C. Wilde's Company G from the 508th Regiment's 3rd Battalion had been ordered into Nijmegen to resume the mission at dawn on 18 September, but were again stopped at the *Keizer Karel Plein* traffic roundabout and after fruitless attempts to get forward were ordered back to Berg-en-Dal to become the 3rd Battalion reserve at some point during the night.[121] Perhaps the most serious development in the area was another example of interference, on this occasion alloyed with indecision, from Major-General Browning. Thus far Browning's contribution to proceedings had consisted of crossing the LZ immediately on landing to urinate on German soil, theatrically unfurling a specially embroidered Pegasus pennant on his jeep and impressing the Americans with his immaculate Guards turnout, as his Forward Corps HQ had proved unable to make contact with any stations except the 82nd Airborne Division's HQ and his own HQ at Moor Park owing to a shortage of cipher operators.[122] However, at 15:30 and thus shortly after the second lift was safely down, Browning took his first and only independent command decision of Operation MARKET GARDEN, by approaching Gavin and requesting him to refocus his efforts from securing the Groesbeek Heights in their entirety to seizing the Nijmegen bridges as quickly as possible.[123] As the Guards Armoured Division was due to reach Nijmegen by 18:00 and neither officer appears to have been aware that the GARDEN force was at this point a long way behind schedule, this was not before time and it is interesting to speculate what Gavin made of being ordered to do what he would have done at the outset, left to his own devices.

Gavin responded in his unfailingly correct manner by rapidly drawing up a plan for a three-pronged assault using the 508th Parachute Infantry Regiment, reinforced with a battalion from the 504th Parachute Infantry Regiment. When presented with the plan Browning initially endorsed it but he then vacillated and reverted back to his original flawed preoccupation with holding the Groesbeek Heights in their entirety on the grounds that 'the retention of the high ground South of Nijmegen was of greater importance' than securing the crossings over the River Waal.[124] While critical of Browning's decision making, Powell attempts to put the best face on Browning's action by suggesting that his behaviour was due to him lacking 'a worthwhile job to perform in Holland [and that] he was also short of the machinery with which to do such a job'.[125] This of course overlooks the fact that Browning also lacked the requisite skills and experience for the task, given that platoon command on the Western Front during the First World War was hardly an apprenticeship for multi-division corps command, Airborne or otherwise, and that he had deliberately placed himself in that invidious position for reasons of personal ambition. Powell also suggests that Gavin may have been 'somewhat in awe' of Browning because of his age and reportedly 'brilliant' reputation as a junior officer during the First World War, although this is rather unlikely. Gavin's memoir clearly concurs with a warning from Ridgway about Browning's Machiavellian nature when he served briefly at COSSAC HQ in London in November 1943.[126] More importantly, Gavin accurately and presciently noted in his diary on 6 September 1944 that Browning lacked the 'standing, influence and judgement' that came from operational command experience, that his staff was 'superficial' and that British senior Airborne commanders generally lacked 'know how' because 'never do they get down into the dirt and learn the hard way'.[127] The obvious exception to this accurate assessment was Richard Nelson Gale, although Gavin may not have had any contact with him whilst serving at COSSAC HQ or after becoming commander of the 82nd Airborne Division.

The Grenadier Guards Group and the 2nd Battalion 505th Parachute Infantry Regiment were shortly to pay a high price for Browning's operational ineptitude.

D Plus 2

00:01 to 12:00 Tuesday 19 September 1944

Constructing the Bailey bridge at Son took around nine hours with the Sappers and co-opted helpers working through the night from 21:00 on 18 September, and the bridge was complete and ready to take traffic just after first light the following morning. The lead elements of the Guards Armoured Division, the armoured cars of the 2nd Household Cavalry Regiment, then crossed to the north bank of the Wilhelmina Canal at sunrise, which occurred at 06:16 on 19 September; it is unclear if the Household Cavalry crossed at the first opportunity or whether they held back for full daylight.[1] The reconnaissance elements were followed by the Grenadier Guards Group from the 5th Guards Armoured Brigade consisting of the 1st (Motor) Battalion and 2nd (Armoured) Battalion Grenadier Guards, apparently trailed by the Guards Division Armoured Division's Tactical HQ accompanied by Corps commander Lieutenant-General Horrocks, while the Irish Guards Group brought up the rear, crossing the Wilhelmina Canal at 10:00.[2] With the 101st Airborne Division easing the way the GARDEN force made much swifter progress than the previous two days. The 2nd Household Cavalry covered the twenty-four miles or so to Grave at the edge of the 82nd Airborne Division's area, where the 504th Parachute Infantry Regiment were holding the bridge over the River Maas, in just over two hours, arriving at 08:25. The Grenadier Guards Group arrived there around ninety minutes later at 10:00 and were in the vicinity of Nijmegen an hour later, despite being diverted to cross the Maas-Waal Canal near Molenhoek; the more direct crossings at Malden and Hatert had been destroyed before the 504th Parachute Infantry Regiment could seize them on 17 September and the 508th Parachute Infantry Regiment was still in the process of securing the most northerly combined road and rail crossing at Honinghutie. The Irish Guards Group came in last at 14:00 and was directed to Malden, just north of the Molenhoek crossing.[3] Behind this, the rest of the Guards Armoured Division was on the move along the length of what was to become the Airborne Corridor. The 5th Guards Armoured Brigade was trailed by the Guards Armoured Division Main HQ, which moved off from Valkenswaard at 07:00, followed by the Coldstream Guards Group and Welsh Guards Group from 32 Guards Brigade, the lead elements of which halted at Zeeland, six miles or so short of Grave, at just after midday; the Guards Division Main HQ and 30 Corps Tactical HQ appear to have halted in the same vicinity for four hours. Farthest back and the earliest to start was the 15th/19th Hussars Group. This was a temporary independent formation consisting of the Cromwell-equipped 15th/19th Hussars from the 11th Armoured Division, reinforced with a Squadron of armoured cars and a battery of self-propelled 25-Pounder guns which was to be placed under command of the 101st Airborne Division. The Hussars moved off from a concentration area near Neerpelt in Belgium at 06:00 and reached Eindhoven at 10:00 where part of the Group was detached to assist the 506th Parachute Infantry Regiment, while the remainder continued to Son, arriving an hour later.[4]

On arrival the 15th/19th Hussars' Cromwell tanks were divided up and assigned to the 101st Airborne Division's constituent units and, with contact with the GARDEN force established,

Major-General Taylor set about consolidating his hold on the southern stretch of the Airborne Corridor. South of the Wilhelmina Canal Colonel Sink set his 506th Parachute Infantry Brigade to widening the base of the Division's area at Eindhoven, with Lieutenant-Colonel Oliver M. Horton's 3rd Battalion being despatched toward Winterle, six miles or so to the west, while Lieutenant-Colonel Robert L. Strayer's 2nd Battalion moved toward Helmond, eight miles to the east. The former was recalled en route after the British 12 Corps moving up on the west flank of the GARDEN force had taken responsibility for that sector, while the latter was also recalled when Colonel Sink received word that German armour was moving in that area.[5] The armoured force was *Panzer Brigade 107*, commanded by *Major* Berndt-Joachim *Freiherr* von Maltzahn, which had originally been destined for service on the Eastern Front before being redirected to Aachen and then to face the new Allied airborne incursion at Eindhoven, detraining at Venlo over the period 16-18 September 1944.[6] It was a formidable force consisting of *Panzer Abteilung 2107* equipped with thirty-six Panther tanks, *Panzergrenadier Bataillon 2107* mounted in *Sd.Kfz* 251 half-tracks supported by *Panzerjäger Kompanie 2107* equipped with eleven *Panzerjäger* IVs, *Panzer Pionier Kompanie 2107*, also mounted in half-tracks and *FlaK Zug 2107* equipped with four *FlaK Panzer* IV *Wirbelwind* self-propelled 37mm guns; the other units may also have included organic light *flak* vehicles in their organisation.[7] The official US accounts suggest that the 2nd Battalion was withdrawn before contact, but Captain Winters' Company E, reportedly accompanied by half a dozen Cromwell tanks, ran into a German counter-attack just after passing through the town of Nuenen to the usual ecstatic greeting from the local civilian population. After a sharp exchange of fire that knocked out four of the 15th/19th Hussars' Cromwell tanks, Company E fell back to Nuenen and organised a hasty defence that held the German attack and eventually prompted *Panzer Brigade 107* to shift its line of advance to the north, along the line of the Wilhelmina Canal. Company E remained in place until dark and then withdrew to an overnight position in the outskirts of Eindhoven at Tongelre; the day's fighting cost the Company fifteen casualties.[8]

On the north bank of the Wilhelmina Canal the fight to seize the bridge near Best from *59 Infanterie Division* and *Kampfgruppe* Rink continued. Colonel Michaelis ordered Lieutenant-Colonel Chappuis' 2nd Battalion 502nd Regiment to resume the attack toward the bridge at 06:00, which was done despite crossfire from German troops stationed in woods to the north and along the line of the canal to the south. The attack continued until the patrol from Company E that had reached Lieutenant Wierzbowski during the night regained contact with the 2nd Battalion and informed Lieutenant-Colonel Chappuis that the bridge had been destroyed, but not, apparently, that the party from the 3rd Battalion were still holding the north end. Chappuis duly passed the news up to Regimental HQ and was ordered to withdraw to the attack start point and set up a defensive line, which then rebuffed two German counter-attacks in the course of the morning; the 3rd Battalion's Company G also rebuffed German probes into the eastern face of the Zonsche Forest from the direction of the landing area.[9] In the meantime Major-General Taylor had despatched one of the 101st Airborne Division' deputy commanders, Brigadier-General Gerald J. Higgins, to take command of the effort at Best along with the 2nd and 3rd Battalions from the 327th Glider Infantry Regiment, a Squadron of tanks from the 15th/19th Hussars and a small artillery detachment from that unit's independent Group. All this came too late for Lieutenant Wierzbowski and his little band however, who had been finally overwhelmed by a German attack at first light that used the low-lying river mist for concealment before shooting Private Lawrence J. Koller in the head and launching a flurry of hand-grenades into the paratroopers' position. Two were thrown clear, one hit the party's .30 machine-gun before exploding and blinding gunner Private Robert Laino, who nonetheless threw out another grenade that hit his knee while another landed in a trench occupied by several casualties including Private First Class Joe E. Mann. Despite his arms being bandaged due to multiple wounds suffered the previous day, Mann fell back on the grenade to save the other occupants of the trench; he was posthumously awarded the Medal of Honor for his self-sacrifice. Virtually out of ammunition, on the verge of being overrun and with only three of his fourteen surviving men unwounded, Lieutenant Wierzbowski ordered Private First Class Anthony M. Waldt to attach a grubby handkerchief to the barrel of his M1 and the stubborn defence of the north end of the Best bridge came to an end.[10]

Brigadier-General Higgins' reinforced attack down the Eindhoven-Boxtel road went in at 14:00, although part of the 3rd Battalion 502nd Parachute Infantry attacked without orders and ahead of schedule. Despite this the push south along the road down the road was an overwhelming success, with the presence of the 15th/19th Hussars' tanks being the decisive factor. A party of seventy-five Germans surrendered to the 502nd Regiment's 3rd Battalion virtually as it moved off rising to over a hundred before the attack was fully underway, and the tanks flushed numerous other prisoners from the roadside ditches and vegetation as they moved on. After the previous two days' bitter fighting *Kampfgruppe* Rink and 59 *Infanterie Division* succumbed to a 'festering disintegration' and the advance to the canal thus reverted to a mopping-up operation, although not all the Germans appear to have been happy with their comrades' behaviour; Lieutenant-Colonel Chappuis reported seeing some would-be prisoners being machine-gunned by their own side as they moved to surrender to his men from the 2nd Battalion. The sheer number of prisoners became a problem for the attackers as the advancing paratroopers lacked the numbers to guard them and continue on. The 2nd Battalion had taken 700 prisoners by 16:00 for example, and the 3rd Battalion was obliged to press its cooks, messengers and other supernumerary personnel into an emergency guard detail under the Battalion executive Officer, Captain Frank Lillyman, until sufficient Military Police could be mustered. A total of between 1,100 and 1,400 prisoners were taken, between 300 and 600 German dead were counted on the battlefield and while Best remained in German hands, the virtual destruction of *Generalleutnant* Poppe's 59 *Infanterie* Division bolstered the security of the 101st Airborne Division's western flank. In a neat postscript Lieutenant Wierzbowski and the survivors of his platoon also finally made it back to friendly forces, having persuaded the German medical personnel at the aid post where they had been receiving treatment to surrender.[11]

The two Battalions from the 327th Glider Infantry Regiment, again bolstered by tanks from the 15th/19th Hussars, had simultaneously pushed through and cleared the Zonsche Forest, including a cluster of buildings at the southern edge, and advanced up to the bank of the Wilhelmina Canal. The process was again aided by poor German morale that enabled the glider soldiers to persuade most to surrender; in some instances captured German NCOs were despatched forward to bring groups of their countrymen out; some of the prisoners were fleeing from the 502nd Parachute Infantry Regiment's parallel advance down the Eindhoven–Boxtel road to the west. The operation netted 159 prisoners and the US units involved did not suffer a single casualty.[12] Five miles to the west of the Zonsche Forest Lieutenant-Colonel Patrick Cassidy's 1st Battalion 502nd Parachute Infantry Regiment was busy defending the crossroads town of St. Oedenrode against elements of 59 *Infanterie Division* and a scratch force made up of reserve and internal security units. On the southern sector Company A rebuffed two German attacks. A patrol led by Lieutenant Maurice LeGrave probed a German *bataillon* position near Donderdonk three miles to the south-west before engaging a German patrol and returning to the Battalion perimeter with a prisoner.

The most serious fighting of the day occurred to the north of St. Oedenrode and again involved British armour, albeit under somewhat different circumstances. After being warned by the Dutch Resistance of an impending early morning attack Captain Fred Hancock, commanding Company C, despatched a pre-emptive fighting patrol up the Schijndel road led by Lieutenant Harry Larson. Larson succeeded in blocking the initial German advance but was then attacked in turn by a reinforced enemy detachment and at 11:00 was obliged to withdraw; the whole of Company C was then drawn into the ensuing fight. With his Battalion already stretched to man its perimeter Lieutenant-Colonel Cassidy had no reinforcement to offer Captain Hancock but the day was saved by Sergeant Patrick McCrory, whose Sherman had dropped out of the Irish Guards Group due to a mechanical malfunction as it passed through St. Oedenrode. Although his tank was restricted to moving at walking pace, Sergeant McCrory readily agreed to help and set off up the Schijndel road with Private John J. O'Brien serving as a temporary loader and Sergeant Roy W. Nickrent riding on the rear deck as an observer. Arriving just as the Germans were preparing to assault Company C, Sergeant McCrory knocked out three 20mm guns pinning down Captain Hancock's men at 150 yards range, a camouflaged gun position of some kind and a German ammunition truck that tried to escape; in the process Sergeant Nickrent was obliged to jump off the rear deck by small-arms fire and took three Germans prisoner and Private O'Brien was killed while firing a borrowed Sten gun from the turret hatch. The Sherman then led Company C forward for around 500 yards until Lieutenant-Colonel Cassidy, wary of being drawn into a larger fight, ordered Captain Hancock's Company to reoccupy its initial roadblock positions. The paratroopers were subsequently reinforced by three Cromwell tanks from the 15th/19th Hussars, allowing Sergeant McCrory to return to awaiting REME assistance. On being thanked for his vital contribution he replied 'When in doubt, lash out', an axiom that the 1st Battalion subsequently adopted as an unofficial motto. The fight on the Schijndel road cost the Germans thirty dead and fifty-three captured; US casualties are unclear.[13]

Tuesday 19 September 1944 was also supposed to see the arrival of the 101st Airborne Division's third lift, although that did not occur as planned. The third lift was scheduled to include 385 Waco CG4 gliders divided into ten separate serials carrying 2,310 men from the 1st Battalion 327th Glider Infantry Regiment, Division Artillery HQ, 321st Glider Field Artillery Battalion, 377th Parachute Field Artillery Battalion, 907th Glider Field Artillery Battalion and the confusingly named 81st Airborne Anti-aircraft Battalion, half of which was equipped with 57mm anti-tank guns. In addition to personnel, the gliders were loaded with 136 Jeeps, sixty-eight guns, seventy-seven trailers of ammunition and over 500 jerrycans of fuel. The lift was to follow the southern route across the mouth of the English Channel and across Belgium and began taking off at 11:30 into 'barely passable' flying conditions that led to the final serial being recalled after take-off. Despite the recall and a cloud ceiling of 700 feet, two CG4s collided whilst approaching the emergency glider landing area at Membury in Berkshire, killing all on board both machines. Visibility dropped to zero as the preceding serials approached the British coast, obliging the glider pilots to use the tilt of their tow-rope and telephone links with the tugs for guidance; some tugs extended visibility slightly to around half a mile by dropping to an altitude of a hundred feet once over the open sea. Seventeen CG4s were obliged to ditch and a further thirty-one were released or suffered broken tow-ropes after making landfall over Belgium. Some combinations strayed outside the safe corridor and were greeted with intense flak and small-arms fire that downed seventeen C47s at altitudes too low for the crews to escape by parachute; approximately half the CG4s from the shot-down tugs reached LZ W. In addition, 170 tugs returned to their UK airfields with extensive battle damage and a further five were so badly shot up they had to be scrapped after making emergency landings at Brussels. One tug squadron released fifteen gliders ten miles short of the LZ, a further twenty-six gliders disappeared without trace over the Continent and eighty-two combinations were unable to locate the LZ and returned to their airfields in England.

As a result of all this only 209 gliders landed on LZ W, where eleven men were killed in landing accidents and a further eleven injured. Just 1,341 men were delivered as scheduled, the largest contingent of 554 belonging to the 1st Battalion 327th Glider Infantry Regiment while the 907th Glider Field Artillery Battalion suffered the worst losses with only twenty-four men arriving safely and without any of their twelve 105mm Howitzers because the entire serial carrying the guns had turned back; only forty guns arrived at the LZ along with just seventy-nine Jeeps. The gliders that had returned to England were not despatched again until 23 September, although the artillery complement was expanded in the interim; a Battery from the 377th Parachute Field Artillery Battalion was dropped in the following day. Badly depleted as they were, the glider guns were a welcome addition to the 101st Airborne Division's firepower. The infantry component that had made up the first two lifts was badly in need of artillery support and anti-tank weapons as the fight for the Airborne Corridor developed.[14] The 1st Battalion 327th Glider Infantry Regiment 'spent the night unloading the gliders and protecting the piled equipment from bands of marauding Germans'.[15]

In the 82nd Airborne Division's area of responsibility Major-Generals Browning and Gavin greeted the Grenadier Guards Group in person at the Grave bridge at 10:00 and at some point before the GARDEN force arrived Browning reversed his position to inform Gavin that the 'Nijmegen bridge must be taken today. At the latest tomorrow'; again, it is interesting to speculate on what the invariably correct US commander made of this latest *volte-face*.[16] The link-up with the GARDEN force was celebrated in some style with Browning being a Grenadier himself, and the commanders of the 1st and 2nd Grenadier Guards Battalions, Lieutenant-Colonels Edward Goulbourn and Rodney Moore respectively, were swept off to a venue at Overasselt three miles toward Nijmegen where they were joined by the commanders of the 5th Guards Armoured Brigade and the Guards Armoured Division, Brigadier Norman Gwatkin and Major-General Allan Adair. After a brief situation report from Gavin and Browning the assembled officers discussed plans for an attack to seize the Nijmegen bridges before the Airborne and Grenadier commanders departed for Gavin's Command Post near Groesbeek to finalise the attack plans.[17] Maintaining the 82nd Airborne Division's huge perimeter stretched the Division's infantry force to the full, and this was exacerbated by losses incurred in the fighting; by nightfall on 19 September Company A from the 1st Battalion 508th Parachute Infantry Regiment had been reduced to two Officers and forty-two Other Ranks, for example.[18] Gavin had intended to make up the shortfall with the 325th Glider Infantry Regiment, but that unit's arrival was postponed and then cancelled because of the same bad weather that had played havoc with the 101st Airborne Division's glider lift.

With the arrival of the GARDEN force Gavin nevertheless felt secure enough to deploy his Division reserve for an attack toward the Nijmegen bridges and Lieutenant-Colonel Benjamin Vandervoort's 2nd Battalion 505th Parachute Infantry Regiment was mated with elements of the Grenadier Guards Group for a two-pronged attack, scheduled to commence as soon as possible that afternoon. The two columns were to be guided by members of the Dutch Resistance who assured their liberators that Nijmegen was lightly held by the Germans, who would likely surrender at the sight of the Grenadier's tanks; in the meantime the 1st Grenadier Guards temporarily became the 82nd Airborne Division's reserve in exchange for Vandervoort's Battalion.[19] In addition, Gavin took the opportunity presented by Tuesday's period of relative calm to rationalise his deployments, most noticeably by ordering Colonel Reuben E. Tucker to move the bulk of his 504th Parachute Infantry Regiment north-east from Grave to relieve the 2nd Battalion 508th Parachute Infantry Regiment holding the *Jonkerbosch* woods overlooking the Honinghutie bridge. Tucker left a Company from the 2nd Battalion to guard the Grave bridge while his 3rd Battalion was directed to an area near Malden to become the Division reserve; it is unclear if this was in addition to, or as a replacement for, the 1st Grenadier Guards. Colonel William E. Ekman's 505th Parachute Infantry Regiment enjoyed a similarly quiet Tuesday, patrolling around its positions on the south-eastern sector of the Divisional perimeter.

The most fraught day was endured by Colonel Roy E. Lindquist's neighbouring 508th Parachute Infantry Regiment holding the eastern sector of the Division perimeter on Ekman's left. The 508th Regiment's 1st Battalion held the landing zone north-east of Groesbeek for the aborted glider lift until 18:00 and cleared and held a stretch of high ground overlooking the main Nijmegen–Cleve road near Wyler, while the 3rd Battalion did the same along the stretch running north-west to Ubbergen. In the course of the day the 508th Regiment was rejoined by its 2nd Battalion come hotfoot from the north-western tip of the Division perimeter, which occupied a stretch of the Berg-en-Dal feature on the 508th Regiment's right flank overlooking the landing area and the Wyler road. The Regiment was also reinforced with a platoon from Company D, 307th Airborne Engineer Battalion, which was used to reinforce the 3rd Battalion's roadblock near Beek.[20]

***

Fifteen miles north of the 508th Parachute Infantry Regiment's roadblock near Beek, enemy activity around the British perimeter at the north end of the Arnhem road bridge largely fell away with the onset of darkness on Monday 18 September, bringing a measure of respite to beleaguered Airborne soldiers within. The exception to this was the Van Limburg Stirum School on the east side of the embanked bridge ramp, held by elements of the 1st Parachute Squadron RE and C Company, 3rd Parachute Battalion. After their attempts to eject the Airborne defenders failed, as mentioned earlier the Germans set fire to two knocked-out half-tracks on the Bleckmanslaan slip road at 19:30 and ninety minutes later set the adjacent Red School ablaze as well. It is unclear if this was intended to illuminate any British attempts at reinforcement or simply to burn the defenders out, but embers quickly spread the blaze to the roof of the neighbouring Van Limburg School. It took until 23:50 to bring the fire under control, in part by extinguishing the burning vehicles with demolition charges.[21] Forty minutes later the Germans mounted a determined attack on the north and east sides of the school, lobbing grenades through all the ground-floor windows and firing rifle-grenades into those on the first floor, and in the confused fight that followed the attackers manhandled a machine-gun onto a windowsill and swept the room and hallway with fire. The Germans were not driven back until 01:15, and the paratroopers then abandoned the school's ground-floor rooms, barricading the doorways leading into the central hallway and knocking loopholes through partition walls to allow fire from room to room if necessary. At 02:00 the south-west corner of the school was hit at first-floor level by what was likely a *Panzerfaust* launched from the bridge ramp, which blew away sections of the south and east walls along with part of the floor and roof. The violence of the detonation left those within stunned for several minutes but the Germans did not follow up with an immediate assault and the defenders were able to reorganise and move their wounded to the relative safety of the cellar without interference.

An hour or so later an estimated sixty German troops gathered in the darkness under the south wall of the school, talking casually and making no effort at concealment. Their error is frequently attributed to them becoming disoriented in the darkness but this is doubtful given the Van Limburg School's isolated location and the still-burning Red School next door, and it is more likely that the Germans took the lack of British reaction to the *Panzerfaust* as a sign that the building had been abandoned. Whatever the reason, Major Lewis and Captain Mackay stealthily had their men manning the south-facing second- and third-storey windows prepare to use grenades, while Lieutenant Dennis Simpson from B Troop organised a human chain to pass more grenades and Gammon bombs back from the men covering the unthreatened north side of the school. On command they then rained the grenades down onto the Germans below. Lieutenant Len Wright from C Company recalled Major Lewis 'running from one room to another, dropping grenades and saying to me that he hadn't enjoyed himself so much since the last time he'd gone hunting'.[22] Not all the grenade throwing went as planned, however. After moving into a passageway with a barricaded but unmanned window, Lance-Sergeant Norman Swift 'threw a 36 grenade through the window: 'At least that was my intention. Imagine my horror when the grenade hit the wooden crosspiece of the window, bounced back and landed amongst the piled-up furniture!' Fortunately, Swift was alone in the corridor and managed to dive through a doorway with a warning shout before the grenade went off.[23] The defenders then poured fire from rifles, Stens and at least six Bren guns into the unfortunate Germans, in some instances standing on window sills to get a clearer shot, to the accompaniment of the 1st Parachute Brigade's 'Waho Mohammed' war cry. An estimated eighteen to twenty Germans were killed or wounded in the storm of grenade fragments and small-arms fire and the rest fled into the darkness. The defenders do not appear to have suffered any casualties in the incident, and it brought German activity around the Van Limburg School to a halt for the rest of the night.[24]

The German concentration upon the Van Limburg School was likely the result of the building's relative isolation, and their general quiescence elsewhere around the bridge perimeter during the night of 18-19 September was probably due to a shortage of manpower – and exhaustion.

Kampfgruppe Brinkmann had been in the fight since around 20:00 on 17 September for example, while Major Knaust's *Panzer-Grenadier Ersatz und Ausbildungs Bataillon* 'Bocholt' had borne the brunt of the fighting on the east side of the perimeter throughout the 18th. The latter was likely the more in need of rest and reorganisation given that it had been obliged to attack without support from weapons of sufficient calibre to make an impression on the substantial buildings occupied by the British. The only heavy weapons available up to this point appear to have been two 100mm or 150mm artillery pieces deployed in the direct fire role against the 2nd Parachute Battalion's HQ building on the Eusebiusbinnensingel from the traffic island just north of the bridge ramp. Lieutenant-Colonel Frost recalled the impact of the shells and the serious damage they inflicted on the fabric of the building as being a 'rude shock' to those on the receiving end. Fortunately for the defenders, the guns quickly came under counter-fire from the 2nd Battalion's 3-inch mortars, which killed several crewmen and possibly damaged one of the guns; Lieutenant-Colonel Frost reported one piece being towed to safety around a corner from where 'it troubled us no more.'[25]

By this point overall responsibility for retaking the Arnhem road bridge had devolved from *Hauptsturmführer* Brinkmann to *Brigadeführer* Heinz Harmel, commander of 10 SS Panzer Division, who, on returning from a trip to Berlin in the early hours of Monday 18 September, also found himself tasked to prevent the Allies seizing the Waal crossings at Nijmegen. Despite being obliged to shuttle back and forth between the Lower Rhine and the Waal via the crossings at Huissen and Pannerden, Harmel spent sufficient time at Arnhem on Monday to appreciate that while the eventual result was likely inevitable, digging out the British would nonetheless be difficult, time-consuming and costly in lives for both sides. In the early morning of Tuesday 19 September he therefore had the recently captured Lance-Sergeant Stanley Halliwell from the 1st Parachute Squadron RE carry a request for a meeting to Frost; Harmel appears to have mistaken Halliwell for a sergeant-major. Halliwell may have been wounded in the arm. As no truce was in effect Halliwell was obliged to dash forward shouting for his compatriots not to shoot him when his German escort became embroiled in a firefight and then spent ten fraught minutes braving the fire-raked streets searching for Frost who, perhaps predictably, told him to tell Harmel to 'go to Hell'. Understandably wary of relaying such a response and despite having given Harmel his parole to return, Halliwell opted to remain with his comrades in the perimeter. For his part Harmel appears to have anticipated that there would be no British surrender and no returning 'sergeant-major'.[26]

In the meantime the balance had swung further against Frost's embattled band with the arrival of the second increment of reinforcements ordered up by *Wehrkreis IV* twenty-four hours earlier. Drawn from *Panzer Ersatz Regiment 6* 'Bielefeld', *Panzer Kompanie* Mielke was a driver training unit named for its *Leutnant* commander equipped with six *Panzer* III and two *Panzer* IV tanks. Obliged to detrain at Zevenaar where there was a suitable unloading platform, Mielke's unit arrived in Arnhem in the early hours of the morning after a ten-mile road march and was assigned to Knaust, presumably because the industrial area to the east of the road bridge provided better room to manoeuvre than the narrow streets to the west and north; Knaust's command was then upgraded to *kampfgruppe* status. The German attack was resumed after daylight and may have begun with an attack supported by Brinkmann's reconnaissance vehicles, given that PIAT-gunner Private Robert Lygo was awarded the Military Medal for driving off three armoured cars that approached the building held by A Company's 3 Platoon at the junction of the Westervoortsedijk and Ooststraat.[27] Be that as it may, Mielke's *Panzer* IVs appear to have approached the fight via the Westervoortsedijk with one being knocked out around 200 yards east of the road bridge ramp, next to the industrial buildings wrested from Lieutenant Infield's 8 Platoon the previous day. The vehicle likely fell victim to Sergeant Robson's 6-Pounder 300 yards away on the Weertjesstraat, and may have been unaware of its proximity to the British positions given that it ended up facing away from the bridge; it also appears to have been reversing when an armour-piercing shot penetrated its *schürzen* side-armour and snapped the right track. The second *Panzer* IV was also knocked out on the Westervoortsedijk a hundred yards or so closer to the bridge by three hits to the hull front that set it alight. The vehicle came to rest with a pipe bridge linking buildings on either side of the road collapsed across its engine deck, although it is unclear whether this occurred at the time or later.[28]

Whether by accident or design *Leutnant* Mielke's *Panzer* IIIs were deployed out of sight of the British anti-tank guns on the riverside Nieuwekade (New Quay), although at least some of the paratroopers were aware of their presence. Presumably prompted by the engagement with the *Panzer* IVs, Private Cecil Newell was ordered to accompany an unnamed officer with his PIAT to 'see if there were any tanks about'. Using the bridge support pillars on the riverside road for cover, Newell stepped out to peer down the Nieuwekade: 'Well! There were about 20 tanks, or so it seemed, all lined up facing us with their crews standing waiting. I thought to myself I don't know what you're [the officer] going to do, but I know what I'm doing! I sneaked back round the pillar and there he was coming back round on his side.'[29] Suitably chastened, Newell returned to his slit trench and the officer disappeared whence he had come. The *Panzer* IIIs advanced to the attack shortly thereafter. Private Len Hoare from the 2nd Battalion's Mortar Platoon recalled a tank appearing under the bridge ramp only fifteen yards or so from his mortar pit at the junction of the Weertjesstraat and Eusebiusbinnensingel, which knocked out a nearby 6-Pounder, likely Sergeant Robson's gun, and machine-gunned the mortar pit before withdrawing. The machine-gunning set light to the primary mortar bomb charges stacked near the mortar pit and wounded Hoare in the left wrist; as he was already wounded in the right arm he was given first aid in the Mortar Platoon house before being removed to the Aid Post in the cellar of the Brigade HQ building.[30]

Meanwhile three *Panzer* IIIs set about shelling the large house occupied by Lieutenant Andrew McDermont and 3 Platoon on the corner of the Ooststraat and Westervoortsedijk flanking the bridge. The house linked the east and west sides of the British perimeter and was thus vital to its integrity, but the German fire was so intense that Captain Anthony Frank, who had taken over A Company when Major Tatham-Warter was elevated to Battalion command, gave Lieutenant McDermont permission to withdraw from the rear of the building and set up under the bridge ramp.[31]

The German attacks on the bridge perimeter after daylight on Tuesday morning again concentrated primarily upon the eastern side, presumably because the German units on the opposite side were still preoccupied with blocking the remainder of the 1st Parachute Brigade near the Municipal Museum and St Elizabeth Hospital. However, the compact nature of the bridge lodgement meant there was a certain amount of overflow and the easterly concentration was probably not especially noticeable to the Airborne soldiers. After an especially intense mortar bombardment Private James Sims, still ensconced in a Mortar Platoon slit trench on the Weertjesstraat with Sergeant McCreath's small pack, witnessed a German infantry attack from under the bridge ramp that reached the front of the White House before fading away. One of the attackers fell wounded just ten yards from Sims and a British stretcher-bearer was shot down as he attempted to render assistance, an act which elicited a collective 'howl of rage' from the paratroopers who witnessed it. Shortly thereafter Sims discovered, via a shouted enquiry from the upper storey of the Mortar Platoon house, that he was the sole occupant of the traffic island, everyone else having been withdrawn to the relative safety of the surrounding buildings. Braving German fire that struck his small pack, Sims reached the safety of the Mortar Platoon house, which by this time had been fully barricaded for defence. Despite the Germans cutting off the mains water supply morale remained high, thanks to an abundant supply of wine and spirits. The telephone lines were not cut, however, and when Sims inadvertently reached out for a jangling receiver in the hallway his wrist was seized by a Sergeant with the words 'That's Jerry ringing up, but the lady of the house isn't at home. Got it?'[32]

Back at the western outskirts of Arnhem the remainder of the 1st Parachute Brigade and reinforcements spent the dark early morning hours of Tuesday 19 September preparing to resume the effort to break through to the Arnhem road bridge. Lieutenant-Colonel Dobie and Lieutenant-Colonel McCardie had come up with a joint plan to lead the survivors of the 1st Parachute Battalion and the South Staffords' A, B and D Companies forward again at 01:00 but this was abandoned on the hour when Division HQ ordered a withdrawal to Oosterbeek. It is unclear if the timing was coincidental but the withdrawal order was the result of Hicks' knee-jerk reaction to an erroneous report that Frost's force at the bridge had been overwhelmed. While preparations for the withdrawal were underway the 11th Parachute Battalion arrived at Dobie's location on the Utrechtseweg after its eight-hour march from the landing area. Dobie does not appear to have been enamoured with the withdrawal order and when it was rescinded at 02:30 he immediately called an O Group with McCardie and Lieutenant-Colonel Lea. Dobie's Intelligence Officer Lieutenant Vladimir Britneff, described the meeting: 'The scene was, I suppose, dramatic – a darkened, bullet-shattered house with Col McCardie and others sitting and standing round a table lit by a single candle; a wireless set whistling in the background.'[33] Dobie made clear his determination to reach the embattled Frost before first light and outlined a straightforward scheme to achieve that objective. The c.140-strong remnant of the 1st Parachute Battalion was to attack along the Onderlangs riverside road while the 2nd South Staffords did the same along the upper Utrechtsestraatweg toward the Municipal Museum, with the 11th Parachute Battalion moving up behind Dobie's battalion. The start time for the attack was set for 03:30.[34]

Just a matter of yards from where Dobie, McCardie and Lea were making their arrangements, Lieutenant-Colonel Fitch was implementing his own scheme to get the surviving 140 men from the 3rd Parachute Battalion through to the Arnhem road bridge. The first stage began at 02:30 with a silent, house-by-house withdrawal to the Rhine Pavilion, controlled by the officers and NCOs commanding each group. The move was completed without casualties despite the paratroopers coming under machine-gun fire on two occasions, although their success was doubtless assisted by the German withdrawal earlier in the night. After regrouping at the Pavilion, Fitch then led his much-diminished Battalion eastward through the darkness along the riverside Onderlangs road. All went smoothly until the lead elements approached the new German line, as unwittingly witnessed by Major Deane-Drummond and Lieutenant Dickson. The paratroopers then came under intense mortar and machine-gun fire that rapidly inflicted a dozen casualties including the Battalion Liaison Officer Lieutenant Stanley Dean and Regimental Sergeant Major John Lord, both of whom were evacuated to the St Elizabeth Hospital. Unable to proceed in the face of such intense fire or to identify its source, Fitch decided to withdraw to the Rhine Pavilion to regroup at around 04:00 for another attempt after daylight. To that end he despatched his second-in-command, Major Alan Bush, and Captain Geoffrey Dorrien-Smith from B Company, to the rear; it is unclear whether they were tasked to prepare a rally point, an intermediate covering position, or both.[35]

By this point the larger attack organised by Dobie was also underway, with the depleted 1st Battalion contingent crossing the start line and heading down the Onderlangs at 04:00, thirty minutes behind schedule. The late start was attributed to an unspecified delay by the 2nd South Staffords, although the latter actually moved off up the Utrechtsestraatweg later still.[36] While Dobie was ignorant of Fitch's near-simultaneous attack, the volume of German fire less than a mile ahead must have alerted him to the presence of friendly troops to his front, and before long wounded and stragglers from Fitch's unit were passing back through the advancing 1st Battalion, including a passing encounter between Dobie and Captain Dorrien-Smith. The two officers had served together in the 3rd Parachute Battalion in North Africa and a jovial 'Good morning!' from Dobie drew a testy 'Where the hell do you think you're going?' from Dorrien-Smith. 'I'm going up there' replied Dobie, to which Dorrien-Smith responded 'I wouldn't do that if I were you. It's full of mortars and machine-guns.' 'How do you know?' queried Dobie. 'Because I've bloody well been there' retorted Dorrien-Smith and Dobie's attempt to gently chide him with, 'Well, come and show us,' was equally unsuccessful as Dorrien-Smith disappeared into the darkness with a curt 'Not bloody likely.' According to Lieutenant Britneff, Dobie was 'quite infuriated' to learn that his planned route was likely blocked, although the sound of the 3ʳᵈ Battalion's rebuff ought to have made that clear. He may therefore have been annoyed about losing the element of surprise to Fitch.³⁷

Whatever the reason for his annoyance, Lieutenant-Colonel Dobie elected to push on – although in reality he had little option. As there was no communication link with Colonel McCardie apart from runners, halting at this point would have potentially left the South Staffords to carry on alone. The 1ˢᵗ Parachute Battalion's advance paralleled both sides of the Onderlangs with Major Stark's S Company moving along the riverside to the right while Major Perrin-Brown's T Company moved along the scrub-covered slope to the left, apparently trailed by R Company and Dobie's command group; the remainder of HQ Company had been left to follow up behind the South Staffords. Dobie's two lead Companies were down to around platoon strength by this time, while R Company consisted of the fifty or so stragglers gathered up by Major Timothy in Oosterbeek the previous day; Major Toler and his party of forty B Squadron Glider Pilots were initially retained by Lieutenant-Colonel McCardie and then released at 03:30 to return to Division HQ, presumably in line with standing orders for the highly trained pilots to be safeguarded whenever possible.³⁸ The 1ˢᵗ Parachute Battalion advanced for thirty minutes or so before being detected, probably as it drew level with the Municipal Museum up on the Utrechtsestraat to the left. At that point the Germans illuminated the riverside area with flares and opened fire with mortars, automatic weapons and infantry guns, some of which were mounted on half-tracks stationed among the houses on the high ground, as noted by *Hauptsturmführer* Möller on the Utrechtsestraat not far from the Rhine Pavilion: 'There was rifle fire and machine guns rattled continuously. Muffled "dumpfs" signalled the barking of mortars…Flares rose steadily to our left, something like 400 to 500 metres away, where there was open ground down to the Rhine.'³⁹ The fire intensified with first light and some of the Germans were close enough to lob hand-grenades down onto the T Company men below. At around this time R Company appears to have passed through Major Perrin-Brown's men to deal with a troublesome strongpoint; Private Bryan Willoughby recalled being joined by another company as the advance faltered in the face of a 'very determined Spandau machine-gun. I heard an order given by an officer from the newly joined company – "Take that gun out!" There was a pause; nothing happened; then a rush accompanied by shouts of "Waho Mahomed" followed by complete silence. I was glad not to be involved in that.'⁴⁰

The 2ⁿᵈ South Staffords parallel advance up the Utrechtsestraatweg did not proceed as planned; the glider soldiers did not leave their forming up positions just west of the St Elizabeth Hospital until thirty to forty-five minutes after the 04:00 deadline. The reason is unclear but Colonel McCardie may have held back in the hope that the remainder of his second lift would arrive before the attack commenced. If so, he almost got his wish, for Major Commings' party finally came up to the rear of the 11ᵗʰ Parachute Battalion on the Utrechtsestraat at around 05:00, just minutes after the attack commenced.⁴¹ The attack was led by Major John Phillp's D Company followed by Captain Reginald Foot and B Company, with Major Thomas Lane's A Company bringing up the rear. The attack force numbered approximately 340 men, including McCardie's HQ element, Captain Arthur Willcocks and Lieutenant Jack Reynolds with No.1 Mortar Platoon carrying their weapons and ammunition in Airborne handcarts, and Lieutenant David Russell and a small group from the 2ⁿᵈ Parachute Battalion's C Company; the latter had volunteered to join the attack in an effort to rejoin their parent unit at the Arnhem road bridge.⁴² D Company led the way past the brightly lit and Red Cross-bedecked St Elizabeth Hospital, the illumination surreal amidst the debris and dead from earlier fighting, and on up the leafy, tree-lined incline of the Utrechtsestraat. The elevation there gave a clear field of view over the Lower Rhine and Arnhem proper, and Lieutenant Russell recalled seeing 'big fires near the road bridge, an awesome sight with a church tower silhouetted against the flames and the greying sky'.⁴³ Initially, the only sign of opposition encountered came from random bursts of automatic fire, some from

German elements in the houses facing the St Elizabeth Hospital who quickly withdrew through the hospital grounds, and some from machine-guns and 20mm weapons firing on fixed lines down the Utrechtsestraat or across it from side streets on the left. The narrow attack frontage left little room for manoeuvre, an ironic turn of events later noted by Sergeant Norman Howes from the South Staffords' A Company: 'It was totally unlike any other action. We had spent months and months practising battalion attacks on a 400- to 500-yard front, and the battalion finished up attacking up a street no more than fifty yards wide.'[44]

Major Phillp's men ran into the main German line at 05:00, not far past the St Elizabeth Hospital. The first clash likely involved men from Möller's SS *Panzer Pionier Abteilung* 9 and Lieutenant Ernest Roebuck's 21 Platoon and began with a sustained burst of machine-gun fire that killed Roebuck, inflicted a number of other casualties and forced the rest of 21 Platoon to seek cover; a Lance-Sergeant Cockayne attached to the Platoon had a lucky escape when a German bullet pierced the front of his Airborne helmet without injuring him.[45] Captain Ernest Wyss, D Company's second-in-command, played an inspirational role in keeping the attack moving while brandishing his trademark walking stick: 'Yet still, Captain Wyss ran up and down totally ignoring all the stuff and metal flying about him, his voice growing ever hoarser… Where men flagged or hesitated he was there. You just could not crawl and watch him stand upright; you had to follow his lead.'[46] Inspirational it may have been but such blatant disregard for personal safety could not go on indefinitely; Wyss was mortally wounded and died the following day. In around thirty minutes of ferocious house-to-house fighting D Company drove the Germans back 300 yards along the Utrechtsestraat, but at a cost of forty per cent of its strength including four of its six officers; in addition to Roebuck and Wyss, Major Phillp was shot in the stomach and CanLoan Lieutenant James Erskine from 19 Platoon was also badly wounded.[47] With D Company rendered incapable of continuing without consolidation and reorganisation, Lieutenant-Colonel McCardie pushed B Company through to take the lead at c.05:30. At this point the Utrechtsestraat angled up and away from the river, with the right side bordered by the landscaped and wooded parkland sloping down to the riverside. Captain Foot's men were able to use the top of the slope for cover against fire from Germans stationed in the buildings on the left of the road, although this appears to have exposed them to German overshoots from the 1st Parachute Battalion's fight down on the Onderlangs.

By 06:00 B Company had pushed the Germans back another 300 yards or so to the Municipal Museum, where the Utrechtsestraat began to curve right back toward the river; for some reason the South Staffords referred to the museum as 'the Monastery'. However, by this point losses were again impinging on combat effectiveness – and B Company had already lost its HQ element and a full rifle platoon during the fly-in on 17 September. Wary of committing his remaining available rifle company and unaware that his missing C Company and support elements were to hand just west of the St Elizabeth Hospital, Colonel McCardie therefore decided to establish a firm base and seek reinforcement from the 11th Parachute Battalion before resuming the attack. Some elements of B Company and Lieutenant Russell and his little band from the 2nd Parachute Battalion therefore moved into the museum along with Battalion HQ under Captain John Chapman and the Battalion Medical Officer, Captain Brian Brownscombe, who established his RAP in the cellar with the assistance of Chaplain Alan Buchanan. The remainder of B and D Companies occupied a large wooded hollow in the slope just west of the museum flanked by a narrow cobbled track running down to the Onderlangs, where they were joined by Captain Willcocks and Lieutenant Reynolds with their mortars looking to provide fire support for Dobie's attack down on the riverside. Finally, McCardie ordered up Major Lane's A Company; Company HQ and Lieutenant Clowes and 10 Platoon moved into the museum while Lieutenant William Withnall's 7 Platoon and Lieutenant Alan Barker's 8 Platoon occupied three houses opposite the museum after driving out the German defenders, accompanied by elements from the Mortar Group. Three half-tracks, one of them mounting a 20mm gun and likely from *Obersturmführer* Gropp's *SS Panzer FlaK Abteilung 9*, withdrew east along the Utrechtsestraat before Withnall and Barker's men; the *flak* vehicle may have been shot up and abandoned in the street by the east end of the museum. A Company HQ and at least one platoon also moved into the museum proper.[48]

Back at the junction of the Utrechtsestraat and Onderlangs Lieutenant-Colonel Fitch and the remnants of the 3rd Battalion had completed their withdrawal to the Rhine Pavilion, making contact with Major Stark's company from the 1st Battalion and an unidentified Company from the 2nd South Staffords in the process. As we have seen, Major Bush, Captain Dorrien-Smith and a second party had also made contact with Dobie and the remainder of his Battalion before joining Fitch. With his force concentrated, Fitch abandoned his plan of establishing a strongpoint at the Pavilion in favour of assisting Dobie's attack, and the 3rd Battalion moved off in the wake of Dobie's Battalion at around first light with Lieutenant Burwash and A Company in the lead followed by Battalion HQ and a party from the 1st Parachute Squadron under Captain Cecil Cox, with Dorrien-Smith and B Company bringing up the rear.[49]

The area of the Rhine Pavilion remained busy after their departure, however. Lieutenant John Williams, the 1st Parachute Battalion's Motor Transport Officer, had gathered a up around fifty men from his Battalion with the transport just west of the Pavilion, Lieutenant Albert Turrell, HQ Company's second-in-command, had brought up the 1st Battalion's second lift component to the same area during the night, and elements of the 11th Parachute Battalion were also in the area preparing to provide support for Dobie and McCardie's attacks.[50] At around 07:00 they were joined by a more illustrious visitor in the shape of Major-General Urquhart, accompanied by Captain Taylor and Lieutenant Cleminson. The German withdrawal during the night of 18-19 September had removed the German presence in front of No. 14 Zwarteweg and the three officers took their leave shortly after first light, moving stealthily through the deserted streets back toward the Pavilion, 'where jeeps and parts of the 1st and 3rd Battalions were milling around'.[51] After ascertaining the location of Division HQ, Urquhart swiftly commandeered a Jeep for the short drive to the Hotel Hartenstein while Cleminson sought out 5 Platoon. Arriving at 07:25, Urquhart was greeted by Operations Officer Lieutenant-Colonel Mackenzie with 'We had assumed, Sir, that you had gone for good.' Urquhart's batman Private Hancock took the edge off the somewhat downbeat greeting by producing a mug of tea and hot shaving water while Urquhart waited for Brigadier Hicks to return from a visit to the 1st Airlanding Brigade.[52]

In the meantime the 1st Parachute Battalion had overrun outlying German positions on the open ground by the river with bayonets and grenades, taking a number of prisoners and reaching a road junction just short of the harbour. A combination of daylight and physical proximity finally permitted the attacking paratroopers to see the enemy positions plaguing them, although this was a double-edged sword, as Sergeant Frank Manser from S Company's 7 Platoon discovered:

I reached nearly to the houses at the end of the open area. I was fired on there, but for the first time I could see where the fire was coming from. They were about ten yards away in a sandbagged position, possibly a section position with several different weapons…I fired back…but I ran out of ammunition, and that is when they hit me…I felt them shoot off the haversack on my back, then I was wounded in the left arm and under the heart – two separate shots.[53]

At 05:00 Major Timothy and R Company were ordered to deal with the fire coming from the high ground to the left, and Sergeant Dennis Barrett from 1 Platoon led a small group up the slope and into the German-occupied houses. There they drove back some half-tracks with Gammon bombs and overran two infantry guns, killing the crews and rolling the weapons down the slope to prevent them being re-manned before taking cover in the houses when the half-tracks moved forward and reopened fire. Something of a stand-off ensued, with the vehicles wary of coming too close and provoking another shower of Gammon bombs.[54]

Down at the riverside the remainder of the 1st Battalion were unable to make any headway in the face of the hellish crossfire from the German positions blocking the Onderlangs road to its front, the high ground to the left and the brickworks across the river; the firepower of the latter had been augmented by elements of *SS Panzer Aufklärungs Abteilung 9* which had survived Gräbner's ill-fated attempt to force the Arnhem road bridge the previous day. Lacking radio contact with his Company commanders and deducing from the lack of firing that the South Staffords' effort on the left had been stymied, Dobie went forward to Major Timothy's location at around 06:00 in search of a sheltered position in which to regroup; in the process he was wounded in the head, eye and arm by grenade fragments.[55] By this point the 140 men who had crossed the start line with Dobie two hours earlier had been reduced to just thirty-nine; Major Timothy's composite R Company was worst hit with just six survivors, Major Perrin-Brown's T Company was down to eight, Dobie's Battalion HQ to ten and Major Stark's S Company to fifteen.[56] As remaining out in the open could only result in total annihilation, Dobie ordered a move into the houses on the high ground to the left at 06:30. The order came too late for Major Stark's party, which was pinned down in some abandoned German trenches closer to the river and appears to have been overwhelmed there. Gaining shelter in the houses involved running the gauntlet of Germans throwing grenades from the upper stories, fragments of which wounded Private Willoughby as he tried to reach Major Timothy as the latter gestured from a house further up the street; Willoughby was subsequently taken prisoner. Private Thomas Davies and a group from the 1st Battalion's Mortar Platoon fought their way into the rear of one house and drove the occupying *SS* up to the first floor after a brief but bitter hand-to-hand fight. Major Perrin-Brown and just seven men made it into another house while Dobie and five men including Major Timothy entered another, which proved to be occupied by a large group of Dutch civilians.[57]

The shelter was illusory. German armoured vehicles soon moved up and began firing into the British-occupied buildings while *SS* infantry moved in to clear the interlopers house by house. Dobie's party, four of whom were wounded, were taken prisoner when *SS* troops entered their house at around 07:30.[58] Private Davies' group held out despite the close-range fire until they were virtually out of ammunition and after burning maps and any other documents that might prove useful to their captors, waited patiently to surrender in an increasingly unsettling silence. Finally, 'a stark shadow fell across the doorway and a young German soldier, closely followed by two companions, appeared. They could not have been older than seventeen. Their guns jerking about in their hands expressed their nervous and excitable mood as they shouted "Hinder hoc" [sic], their eyes darting quickly about the dimly lit room. I am certain that one careless or thoughtless move on our part would have been suicidal. They would surely have blasted us to ribbons.' Davies and his comrades passed the notoriously vexed hurdle of having their surrender accepted and were hustled out of the back of the house through more *SS* troops standing by to renew the attack and onto trucks for the first stage of the journey to *Stalag IV-B* near Mühlberg in south-eastern Germany.[59] Some paratroopers tried to evade capture by going it alone, but not all succeeded in reaching the temporary safety of the Rhine Pavilion. Private John Hall, a Bren gunner with Sergeant Manser's 7 Platoon, decided to try and swim the Lower Rhine, and after discarding his weapon and webbing somehow made his way down to the riverbank unscathed. He was waylaid there by a paratrooper who had been wounded in the foot: 'I removed his boot - a bloody mess, I thought - then I gave him a morphine injection. As I started to bandage him up, I suddenly heard a voice. Looking up, I saw a German SS, a light machine-gun pointing at me…Perhaps he thought I was a medical orderly…I didn't ask.'[60]

Colonel Fitch had followed in the wake of the 1st Battalion for around 250 yards when casualties from the latter began to pass back through the advancing 3rd Battalion. He then attempted to provide fire support for Dobie's unit and when this proved impossible owing to thick vegetation he personally reconnoitred an alternative location higher up the slope to the left rear, but that too suffered from restricted visibility. In the meantime his Battalion was also losing men to German fire, although the Germans initially concentrated mainly on Dobie's men, and the 3rd Battalion casualties may therefore have been caused by overshoots.

The situation changed drastically for the worse at 07:30 when, with Dobie's attack contained, the Germans turned their full attention to the 3rd Battalion, raking its exposed position with fire from mortars and automatic weapons; the 20mm guns once again proved especially deadly. Private George Marsh from the Battalion Signals Platoon recalled a single 20mm round removing a friend's arm. While the unit War Diary assumed the fire came from armoured cars, it may have been from the light *flak* guns emplaced in the brickworks across the river, which had a panoramic view of every inch of the riverside killing ground.[61] By the time Fitch returned from a second unsuccessful reconnaissance the fire was so heavy that the Battalion was being destroyed in place, so he called together his surviving officers – Adjutant Captain Ernest Seccombe, second-in-command Major Alan Bush and Intelligence Officer Lieutenant Alexis Vedeniapine – for what was to be his final O Group as commander of the 3rd Parachute Battalion.

Sitting at the most forward point of the 3rd Battalion's advance with his back to the bursts as German mortars systematically quartered the slope, Fitch calmly ordered that 'every officer and man would make his way back…by the best way he could. No question of fieldcraft this; the whole area seemed covered by fire and the only hope of getting out safely was by speed.'[62] The officers were then dismissed to spread the word and supervise where necessary. Major Bush recalled finding 'about thirty of our men and told them to run straight back to the pavilion. One or two were badly injured in the arms or shoulders, and I told these to go straight up the slope to St Elizabeth's Hospital…I expected to see the Colonel and the other officers in the pavilion soon after, but they didn't arrive.'[63] In fact Bush was the only participant of the O Group to survive unscathed. Captain Seccombe lost both legs to a mortar bomb shortly after ordering Private George Marsh from the Battalion Signals Platoon to retune to the BBC for news of the relief force before moving on: 'I had the earphones on but could still hear a large explosion behind me. A mortar bomb had fallen and blown his [Seccombe's] legs off. I was sickened by the sight but ran over the road on which the 20-millimetre gun was firing and found some medics, who brought a stretcher.'[64] Colonel Fitch was killed by another mortar bomb that also drove splinters into Lieutenant Vedeniapine's chest and back; the seriously wounded Intelligence Officer nonetheless appears to have made it back to the Pavilion area under his own steam.[65] On reaching the Battalion rendezvous Major Bush set about rallying the survivors of the approximately 140 men who had withdrawn silently from north of the Utrechtsestraatweg in the early hours of the morning, but he was only able to locate a slightly wounded Captain Dorrien-Smith, Captain Cox from the 1st Parachute Squadron, around twenty unwounded men and a number of wounded in adjacent houses; these included A Company's Sergeant Major Watson and Lieutenant Vedeniapine. On hearing the latter's report, Major Bush immediately extended his search to the open area east of the Pavilion in an effort to locate Fitch's body and any other survivors from the attack. In the process he was cut off by German troops but evaded capture to regain British lines in Oosterbeek on Thursday 21 September.[66]

The attacks into the western outskirts of Arnhem in the early morning of Tuesday 19 September can justifiably be considered the death ride of the 1st Parachute Brigade, although it was remarkable in itself that the participating units were able to continue for as long as they did. Dobie's 1st Parachute Battalion had been fighting and moving virtually non-stop for the thirty-six hours or so since Major Timothy's R Company had bumped *Hauptmann* Weber's patrol from 213 *Nachrichten* Regiment just north of Wolfheze at 17:00 on 17 September. During that time the 548 men the Battalion had taken into Holland were reduced to around 150 excluding stragglers, and while the 3rd Parachute Battalion had spent less time on the move, it too had been reduced from 588 to around 140 men over the same period, again excluding stragglers plus C Company at the Arnhem bridge.[67] These losses were incurred in some of the most intense and sustained close-quarter fighting of the war, yet the two Battalions not only remained functional but continued to pursue their primary mission after their commanders had been killed or captured and virtually up to the point of extinction; by 09:00 all that remained of the 1st Parachute Battalion was approximately seven officers including padre Captain Talbot Watkins and 200 stragglers and men from the second lift gathered by the Battalion Motor Transport Officer Lieutenant John Williams. At 09:30 Williams conducted a personal reconnaissance into Arnhem using an armed Jeep likely commandeered from the 1st Airborne Reconnaissance Squadron, accompanied by Lieutenants Leslie Curtis and Albert Turrell. Ninety minutes later he launched yet another attack along the Onderlangs that was subsumed by a stronger German advance moving in the opposite direction.[68]

All this shows that there was little wrong with the 1st Airborne Division at the battalion level or below – all was achieved in isolation, with little to no guidance or support from further up the chain of command. Had Dobie not been tasked with an arguably needless peripheral mission and had Fitch been allowed to get on without interference, it is highly likely that the 1st and 3rd Parachute Battalions would also have inadvertently exploited the flaws in the initial German counter-deployments and reached the Arnhem road bridge like Frost's 2nd Parachute Battalion and the 1st Parachute Brigade column. With a full brigade on the objective, the Arnhem portion of Operation MARKET might well have turned out rather differently. Instead, a combination of inadequate if not inept planning, needless micro-management and deficient leadership squandered the advantage conferred by enemy errors and in the process doomed the 1st Parachute Brigade's constituent units to fight themselves to destruction against a skilfully executed defence that proved impervious to focussed aggression and raw courage alike.

As we have seen, the first stage of II SS Panzerkorps' strategy to counter the 1st Airborne Division had been to block and contain the interlopers along the line of the Amsterdamseweg and in the western outskirts of Arnhem, in order to seal off the Arnhem road bridge. This had been achieved by the morning of 19 September and 9 SS Panzer Division therefore moved to the second stage by launching a counter-attack to push the Airborne incursion back to the west. The catalyst was likely not the destruction of the 1st Parachute Brigade as the Germans were not privy to the detail of the British situation at that time, but to the arrival of reinforcements and specifically a detachment from *Sturmgeschütze Brigade 280* commanded by *Major* Kurt Kühme. An independent *Heer* unit with an integral *panzergrenadier* component and recovery unit, the *Brigade* had been withdrawn to rest and refit in the vicinity of Apenrade in Denmark after suffering severe losses in the fighting at Tarnopol in the Ukraine in April 1944, and was en route to Aachen by rail when orders from *Heeresgruppe B* diverted Major Kühme's *kompanie* to Arnhem.[69] It is unclear precisely where *Major* Kühme and his vehicles detrained but the convoy, consisting of seven *Sturmgeschütze* (StuG) IIIs, three more heavily armed *Sturmhaubitze* (StuH) 42s and a lone *Sd.Kfz.* 251/8 ambulance half-track, road marched into Arnhem from the north. After travelling under the Zijpse Poort bridge and across the Willemsplein and Nieuweplein, the convoy then turned right onto the eastern end of the Utrechtsestraat, where the armoured vehicles lined out nose-to-tail along the leafy suburban street just 700 yards or so east of the Municipal Museum. The precise time the assault guns arrived on the Utrechtsestraat is also unclear but shadows on photographs of their drive through the city show it was well after sunrise, which occurred at 06:16.[70] From there *Hauptsturmführer* Schwarz, 9 SS Panzer Division's Chief-of-Staff, parcelled the vehicles out, with one three-vehicle *Zug* being assigned to *Kampfgruppe* Harder down on the riverside Onderlangs and a second to *Kampfgruppe* Möller a few hundred yards further up the Utrechtsestraat. The arrival of these vehicles represented a step-change in the capability available to the various *kampfgruppen* manning the southern end of *Sturmbannführer* Spindler's *Sperrlinie*. Hitherto a general lack of weapons heavier than light *flak* had obliged them to attempt to take on their British opponents face-to-face, an extremely hazardous and potentially costly process in the face of such an aggressive and ferocious foe.

The arrival of armoured vehicles mounting weapons of 75mm and 105mm calibre conferred the ability to stand off and simply demolish the occupied buildings with impunity.

While the 2nd South Staffords were consolidating their firm base in and around the Municipal Museum Lieutenant-Colonel McCardie had set about obtaining reinforcements from the 11th Parachute Battalion, despatching a runner to bring Lieutenant-Colonel Lea to a meeting on the front steps of the St Elizabeth Hospital. Lea arrived at or shortly before 08:00 with some of his officers and it was decided that the 11th Battalion should move north to the railway cutting and then attack east along it, apparently with a tentative start time of 09:00; the South Staffords were to resume their push along the Utrechtsestraat once the 11th Battalion's attack had developed. McCardie was joined on the steps by Major Commings and Major Cain who, having finally arrived with the South Staffords' Main HQ, transport and B Company's second lift echelon at around 05:00, were looking to rejoin their Battalion; Cain was especially keen to reassume command of B Company. McCardie greeted them with the rather unsettling news that he was running short of officers and inaccurately informed Cain that both Major Philip and Captain Foot had been killed.[71] McCardie then led Cain and Commings east toward the Battalion firm base where they came upon Adjutant John Chapman and a mixed group from the Battalion occupying slit trenches on the corner of either the Bovenover or Sint Elisabethshof. Captain Chapman had occupied the location, apparently on his own initiative, in an effort to suppress German flanking fire interfering with movement along the Utrechtsestraat; McCardie ordered him to abandon that mission and then led the whole group across the road for the shelter of the wooded slope en route to the museum.[72]

Although the fact was likely hidden by the ambient noise, the breathing space won by the 2nd South Staffords had run out and the battle on the Utrechtsestraat was reigniting. German mortar fire had been growing heavier and at around 08:00 the remnants of D Company holding part of the wooded hollow by the museum were attacked from the south-east by a company-size force. The attack was repulsed but the Germans maintained the pressure by infiltrating small groups through the vegetation on the slope behind the museum, and more especially against the buildings occupied by Major Alan Lane's A Company on the other side of the Utrechtsestraat.[73] Major Cain peeled off from McCardie's group to join B Company in the hollow where he was greeted by a wounded but very much alive Captain Foot, who informed him that Major Philip was also alive but had been evacuated for medical treatment. Cheered by the news, Cain did the rounds of his depleted Company before being summoned by runner to the museum, where he joined Colonel McCardie, Major Commings, Major Lane, Captain Chapman and Lieutenant David Longden in

> …an empty room for a conference. McCardie's eyes kept closing and he was clearly burnt out. He did not seem capable of a decision…John Commings said 'Poor Colonel'…The CO told us of the plan for the 11th Battalion's attack north of us and it was eventually agreed (but not decided) that we should push on timing our attack to coincide with [the] 11th Battalion. McCardie called David Longden, the Intelligence Officer and, together with the adjutant, Captain Chapman, retired to get out orders for our attack.[74]

Circumstances were conspiring against Colonel McCardie's intentions, and not solely from the German perspective. Back at the Hartenstein Hotel Major-General Urquhart had been briefed on the situation within an hour of his tea and shave and it rapidly became apparent that the original Division plan had been almost totally overwhelmed by events. The 1st Airborne Division's third lift, scheduled to arrive later that day, was a matter of immediate concern because LZ L had not yet been secured by the 7th KOSB and the 1st Polish Independent Parachute Brigade's DZ K and the supply drop DZ V were both firmly in German hands, the former a mile south of the Arnhem road bridge and the latter a mile or so north-west of Arnhem alongside the Amsterdamseweg. Urquhart's biography makes much of the fact that his attempt to change the two DZs was frustrated because the radio message failed to get through for some unspecified reason, although the 1st Airborne Division's signal logs show that links to the War Office, British 1st Airborne Corps HQ and British 2nd Army HQ via the Phantom net were all open and functioning at the time.[75] That aside, it is unclear precisely where else the Polish Brigade's drop could have been diverted to, as all the zones used by the first and second lifts had been abandoned in the pre-planned move to the 1st Airborne's Phase II positions the previous night and thus lay outwith the Divisional perimeter. Furthermore, had matters in the UK unfolded as planned, the bulk if not all of the third lift would likely have been airborne en route to Holland by the time Urquhart sent his request to change DZs, which would therefore have been too late. In the circumstances the best solution would have been to cancel the third lift altogether, but Hicks and Mackenzie appear to have considered such a decision to be beyond the remit of temporary Division command, and Urquhart was still in self-imposed isolation near the St Elizabeth Hospital at the time the decision needed to be made. As we shall see, bad weather saved Sosabowski's Brigade for a further two days, but the episode further illustrates the consequences of Urquhart's wilful separation from the levers of command.

Urquhart's twofold reaction to events in the vicinity of the St Elizabeth Hospital had the greatest effect on McCardie and the South Staffords. First, after expressing regret at not tarrying to impart some order on the situation at the Rhine Pavilion and thereby second-guessing arguably his first correct decision since landing in Holland, Urquhart decided to despatch Colonel Hilaro Barlow, deputy commander of the 1st Airlanding Brigade, to take control of the effort to break through to the Arnhem road bridge.[76] Barlow appears to have been informed of his new appointment by Hicks in person when the latter returned to his Brigade HQ at the Hotel Bilderburg at 09:00. Barlow departed for the St Elizabeth Hospital an hour later in a Jeep accompanied by his batman, Lance-Corporal Raymond Singer. At this point the Airlanding Brigade HQ was packed and standing by to move east to a new location in Oosterbeek and the pair may have narrowly missed being strafed by the German fighters that attacked the assembled transport.[77] Colonel Barlow reached the vicinity of the Rhine Pavilion but there his luck ran out. Captain John McCooke from the 2nd South Staffords' A Company had been sent back to ensure that his Battalion transport did not come forward of the Pavilion and he described what happened:

> Colonel Barlow appeared there with his batman and asked me about the situation in front. I decided to go forward with him. Heavy mortaring started, and we made a dash for one of the houses which back onto the river…As I ran, I heard a crash behind me and was slightly injured in the leg by a mortar-bomb fragment. I collapsed in the doorway of the house we were making for. No one followed me in…I went upstairs and looked out of the bedroom window. There I saw what I can only describe as a mess on the pavement – which I presumed was Colonel Barlow – and a dead body behind that which must have been his batman.[78]

Incidentally, the 2nd South Staffords transport column was eventually guided back to the Divisional HQ area by Lieutenant Lennard Withers MC from Support Company. After a detour to avoid German machine-gun fire from the *Mariendaal*, the men reached the Hotel Hartenstein where they were allocated an area by the tennis courts at the rear.[79]

Urquhart's attempt to impose order on the effort to break through to the Arnhem road bridge was thus undone by Colonel Barlow's death, and his second action, or reaction, impacted even more directly upon Lieutenant-Colonel McCardie and his Battalion. Concerned at the mounting cost of feeding units into the fight along the Onderlangs and Utrechtsestraat piecemeal, Urquhart decided to halt the process until Barlow had assumed command and clarified the situation. The

11th Parachute Battalion was therefore ordered to remain in place until further orders, the order arriving at Lieutenant-Colonel Lea's HQ at the St Elizabeth Hospital at approximately 09:00, while preparations for the attack in support the 2nd South Staffords were well underway, with Major David Gilchrist's A Company deployed on the start line just east of the hospital. As a result the bulk of the 11th Battalion remained in place west of and in front of the hospital awaiting further instructions from Division HQ while Gilchrist and A Company remained isolated without orders or explanation east of the hospital, with Company HQ located on the south side of the Utrechtsestraat and its three platoons in buildings on the north side. Although visibility was severely restricted by a hedgerow and the slope, the position was largely secure from German direct fire but remained vulnerable to mortar fire; one bomb killed Company Sergeant-Major George Ashdown and wounded the Company second-in-command Captain Peter Perse. Gilchrist also made the unwelcome discovery that he was virtually without anti-tank weapons; all the Company's PIATs and ammunition had been loaded into a trailer for the march from the landing area and the Jeep to which the trailer was attached had been borrowed by the Battalion Padre, Captain Henry Irwin. The PIATs presumably stayed missing as Padre Irwin was killed the following day, and Major Gilchrist was shortly to rue the absence of the weapons.[80]

Lieutenant-Colonel McCardie and the 2nd South Staffords were left hanging in their firm base around the Municipal Museum, waiting for a supporting attack that never came. Had their opponents remained dormant this might not have been a problem, but as we have seen the Germans were maintaining the pressure against A Company on the north side of the Utrechtsestraat and D Company in the wooded hollow next to the museum, backed by increasingly heavy mortar fire. The latter was countered to some extent by the 2nd South Staffords' No.1 Mortar Platoon. Major Cain returned from the Battalion O Group to find Lieutenant Reynolds had set up his section of 3-inch mortars in the hollow: 'They were trying to hit some Jerries who were less than one hundred yards away. Jack [Reynolds] was on top of the monastery (museum) observing and Willie [Captain Willcocks] was shouting fire orders to the mortars. They were taking the secondary charges off the bombs and firing them almost straight up into the air. It was almost as dangerous to us as it was to the Germans.'[81] The target was a number of German troops moving along the riverside, who were also engaged by Cain's B Company with small-arms while CanLoan Lieutenant Albert Boustead led D Company's 19 Platoon forward to clear the wooded slope behind the Municipal Museum.

Up to this point the 2nd South Staffords had been holding their own, but the scales began to tilt inexorably against them at around 09:00 when *Sturmgeschütze Brigade 280* entered the fray. British accounts almost invariably misidentified the unit's assault guns as tanks, although this was an understandable error in the circumstances and the more so because the *StuGs* were liberally decked in foliage to deflect the attention of Allied fighter-bombers. The three vehicles allocated to *Kampfgruppe* Möller moved up to a point on the Utrechtsestraat near the PGEM building a little short of the British positions, where they pivoted left in a herringbone pattern facing out over the wooded slope, although contemporary photographs suggest their view was seriously restricted by the foliage.[82] The formation was therefore likely intended to permit the infantry support to deploy unmolested behind the vehicles, and the pause to permit co-ordination with the vehicles allocated to *Kampfgruppe* Harder down on the riverside, given that the 2nd South Staffords War Diary suggests that the *StuGs* attacked the British positions on the Utrechtsestraat and lower Onderlangs simultaneously. Lieutenant Russell from the 2nd Parachute Battalion saw the arrival of one of the former from his vantage point in the eastern end of the museum, likely the caretaker's flat: 'I suppose it was about mid-morning when I saw the outlines of a large tank through the garden gate. I warned the company commander, who sent a PIAT forward to cover the road; we stayed upstairs. The tank milled around, treating the world in general to bursts of MG and big dollops of gunfire. We were, as yet, untouched.'[83] Down on the wooded slope the vehicles were heard before they were seen, as noted by one of the

Arnhem

D Company men holding the wooded hollow: 'We heard a rattling of tank tracks, we had been told on a briefing to expect our tanks on the second day of the operation and it gave our hearts a terrific lift when someone shouted "Our tanks are here!" Imagine our horror when we saw the black crosses painted on them.'[84]

The 2nd South Staffords had no anti-tank guns to hand because Lieutenant-Colonel McCardie had despatched his eight 6-Pounders back to Division HQ with the rest of the Battalion transport, and the onus for countering the new armoured threat therefore fell on the Battalion's PIAT gunners. Lieutenant Russell in the Municipal Museum saw the A Company PIAT he had ordered up score a direct hit on a *StuG* manoeuvring on the Utrechtsestraat, while Lieutenant Georges Dupenois from B Company 'particularly distinguished himself by his bold use of this weapon' on the wooded slope behind the museum, where he drove back a *StuG* firing high-explosive shells into the hollow working in tandem with another, sadly unnamed, PIAT gunner.[85] The Germans responded by increasing the volume of mortar fire while the assault guns stood off to reduce the risk from the PIATs but continued to shell the British positions. The fire into the hollow became so intense that Lieutenant Reynolds' mortar section was obliged temporarily to abandon its weapons; Reynolds himself was injured by a flying branch that broke his pipe and removed his two front teeth.[86] Any attempted advance toward the hollow by the *StuG*s was met by Dupenois and his running mate until the latter was knocked out by a mortar bomb. They had been playing a cat-and-mouse game worked out with Major Cain and the commander of Support Company: 'Jock Buchanan and I were drawing the fire and trying to get ammunition for Georges…When a tank appeared, we got four Brens firing on it with tracers. That shut the tank up, because the commander couldn't stand up in the turret. As soon as we let off a Piat at it, we'd move back, and then the German shells would explode below us. We were firing at 100 to 150 yards' range.'[87] At one point Dupenois stood fully exposed to steady his weapon atop a fencepost before scoring a direct hit on the target vehicle's flank, and he was also involved in a fight against at least one *StuG* concealed behind convenient hedgerows firing directly on B Company's positions from the Utrechtsestraat. The target was likely a *Zug* command vehicle, given Cain described the radio aerial that betrayed its presence as being crowned with 'a thing like a flue brush' and while Dupenois' blind shot missed the target and partially demolished a building behind it, the near miss persuaded the *StuG* to pull back.[88]

The 2nd South Staffords' PIAT gunners thus succeeded in keeping the German armoured vehicles at bay, but while they scored numerous hits their bombs lacked sufficient punch to knock out or even seriously damage the assault guns. Flank hits were absorbed by the vehicles' *schürzen* side armour plates and their frontal armour appears to have been impervious, given that *Major* Kühme's *StuG* shrugged off a direct hit to the right of the gun mantlet with just a dent and loss of some *zimmerit* anti-mine paste; in fact *Sturmgeschütze Brigade 280* did not lose its first vehicle until the following day and only after coming up against 6-Pounder guns closer to Oosterbeek.[89] The problem for the 2nd South Staffords was that keeping the *StuG*s at bay rapidly depleted the available stock of PIAT bombs, with Lieutenant Dupenois alone expending an estimated ten to twenty rounds.[90] More seriously, while the impact of the PIAT bombs was enough to make the armoured vehicles keep their distance, it did not prevent them from standing off and pumping high-explosive shells into the South Staffords' positions in the hollow and on the Utrechtsestraat. Slowly but surely, the German pressure began to tell and Lieutenant-Colonel McCardie was obliged to move his HQ to a new location a hundred yards west of the museum; he also approached Major Lane about withdrawing A Company into a tighter perimeter centred on the Municipal Museum and despatched a runner back to the St Elizabeth Hospital to guide Major Wright and C Company forward to the main Battalion location.[91]

At 10:15 the Germans renewed their attack, having refined their tactics and teamwork. Still wary of the PIATs the *StuG*s began operating in pairs and the vehicles down on the Onderlangs concentrated their fire on the hollow to cover SS infantry filtering up the wooded slope toward the rear of the museum. B Company was nonetheless able to rebuff the infiltrators with the personal assistance of Major Cain, who spotted one group:

> An NCO was beckoning on a section of six or seven who were in line abreast and in enfilade to us. I indicated to a Bren gunner who fired and missed them…the NCO moving rapidly out of sight. The rest were beautifully bunched. I grabbed a Bren…layed on the bunch and fired half a magazine. As I fired I could see them crumple up. I then let them have the other half of the magazine and there was no further movement.[92]

Cain then went in search of more PIAT bombs, the quest carrying him back to Battalion HQ where his description of events in the vicinity of the museum cast doubt on the plan to tighten the Battalion perimeter around it and prompted McCardie to go forward with Cain to see for himself. By this time the hollow was under constant shellfire and German infantry were pressing into the southern edge, as noted by Corporal Perry: 'Bullets and shells were coming from all directions. We were firing at some Germans who had appeared at the bottom of the dell and had knocked them about badly…the dell was a mess, full of [British] dead and wounded.'[93] On reaching the lip of the hollow the two officers were greeted by the gruesome sight of one of Cain's 'old originals. Only his head and face were untouched. The rest of him was unrecognisable as human – a straggly mess of churned up, bloody clothing with pieces of dead white flesh here and there. Other pieces of him and his clothing were hanging on nearby bushes.'[94] Seeing the hollow was untenable, McCardie gave Cain permission to withdraw and after a brief discussion Cain decided to seek the shelter of buildings on the other side of the Utrechtsestraat behind the houses held by A Company.[95] It was at this juncture, between 10:50 and 11:30, that the supply of PIAT bombs finally gave out, removing the South Staffords' only effective protection against the *StuGs*.[96]

Over on the western side of the Division perimeter some of the other elements of the 1st Airlanding Brigade enjoyed a generally quieter Tuesday morning. Brigade HQ was scheduled to move from the Hotel Bilderburg to a new location 800 yards to the south-east at Valkenburg on the outskirts of Oosterbeek, which was reconnoitred by a member of Brigade staff at 05:00. This proved unnecessary however, as Brigadier Hicks selected a different site shortly after resuming command of the Brigade at 07:30. This was within Oosterbeek proper, just south of the Utrechtseweg and a few hundred yards south of the Hotel Hartenstein, proximity to which probably influenced Hicks' decision. The Brigade HQ column was packed and ready to move from the Hotel Bilderburg by 08:00 when the area was strafed by a number of German fighter aircraft, but the column escaped unscathed and the HQ was established in its new location by 09:00.[97] It was joined shortly thereafter by Major James Dale DFC and C Squadron from the Glider Pilot Regiment's No. 2 Wing, which had passed the night dug in with Lieutenant-Colonel Place and the rest of No. 2 Wing around Point 63.5, just south of the Arnhem–Ede railway line. The Glider Pilots had spent 'a disturbed night with considerable firing coming from direction of railway line, but no attack developed'. C Squadron was detached to provide security for 1st Airlanding Brigade HQ at 09:00, while the remainder of No. 2 Wing began moving to a new location in the outskirts of Oosterbeek thirty minutes later, also enduring an apparently ineffectual strafing by German fighters en route. Place's force was reduced again following receipt of an urgent instruction from Division HQ, which led to Major Anthony Murray and F Squadron being detached at 11:00 to establish a standing patrol along the edge of a wood north-east of the Hotel Hartenstein, presumably as a security measure for Division HQ.[98]

The 1st Border had a less easy passage to its Phase II locations. The Battalion's dusk withdrawal from LZ Z was stymied shortly after moving off when A Company ran into German machine guns emplaced across the Battalion route. The contact delayed the withdrawal for around an hour and although there was no further enemy interference when the advance was resumed after full darkness, moving tactically through three miles of largely wooded terrain in the inky blackness proved to be a time-consuming business. As a result the 1st Border was not dug in on its new locations until 05:15, nine hours after moving off.[99] Battalion HQ was located only 800 yards or so west of the Hotel Hartenstein, which allowed runners, notably signaller Private George Attenborough, to get around the ongoing radio communication problems.

Major Cousens' force was swelled by the arrival of two 17-Pounder and five 6-Pounder anti-tank guns. Precisely when these weapons arrived is unclear, as is the provenance of the former, although they were reportedly from 1st Airlanding Brigade HQ; the 6-Pounders were presumably those sequestered from the South Staffords' second lift column by Division HQ at 17:30 the previous day, and were returned to their parent Battalion at 11:15.[100] The Battalion frontage remained quiet, although Brigade HQ relayed reports of large numbers of German troops moving through Heelsum and other points west of the Battalion location at 09:45, and at 11:00 an NCO from 156 Parachute Battalion reported the presence of two armoured vehicles near the Arnhem–Ede railway line just north of A Company's location. In addition, C Company came under mortar fire at some point, which reportedly killed Lieutenant Alan Roberts' batman, a Lance-Corporal King, and wounded several other men.[101]

Not all of the 1st Airborne Division's units in and around the Divisional area were holding fast or moving east however, for Brigadier Hicks had tasked the 1st Airborne Reconnaissance Squadron to scout west toward Heelsum and north to the Amsterdamseweg to ascertain German strengths and locations; this was the source of the information received by the 1st Border from Airlanding Brigade HQ. To this end the Squadron left its overnight harbour area near the Hotel Hartenstein at 06:30 and headed west along the Utrechtseweg in the pre-dawn darkness with Captain Michael Grubb's A Troop in the lead, followed by Captain John Park's D Troop and then Squadron HQ and Support Troop. Captain Allsop established a Tactical HQ on the Utrechtseweg shortly after 07:30, 500 yards or so west of the junction with the Wolfhezeweg and just forward of the 1st Border's outposts while A and D Troops continued west and then south into the Doorwerthsche Bosch forest to commence their work.[102] Within three hours, details of German activity were being relayed from the individual Sections manning an observation line established just west of the Breedeweg around 1,000 yards short of Heelsum, with A Troop covering the northern section running between the Utrechtseweg and the Van der Molenallee and D Troop from the latter to just south of the Koninginne Laan. The line was established without incident apart from an exchange of fire between Lieutenant Douglas Galbraith's 2 Section and a reported *Panzer* IV at around 09:00 just north of the Utrechtseweg, although the Tactical HQ party was alarmed into a 'spirited siting of defensive pits' by a passing RASC soldier who claimed large numbers of German troops were approaching. In the event the HQ party escaped unscathed with the exception of Trooper Andrew Auld, who was wounded in the leg, and the German advance along the Utrechtseweg failed to materialise, although the Squadron's Polsten Gun Section was deployed as a precaution.[103] Radio reports of German movements in the area of Renkum were being received by 10:00, which appear to appear to have prompted Allsop to move his Tactical HQ back to a new location near the Hotel Bilderberg, adjacent to the gun pits occupied by the 1st Airlanding Light Regiment's 1 and 2 Batteries.[104]

The Squadron's secondary mission of reconnoitring north to the Amsterdamseweg was allotted to Captain John Hay's understrength C Troop, as it had scouted the area around LZ S the previous day. Leaving the harbour area at 06:30 with the remainder of the Squadron, C Troop then branched north-west up the Wolfhezeweg, passed through Wolfheze, crossed the Arnhem–Ede railway line and reached the junction with the Amsterdamseweg without incident. Further progress was then blocked by German mortar fire that forced a hasty independent withdrawal, during which Captain Hay's Jeep became briefly bogged down and some vehicles were strafed by *Luftwaffe* fighters. After reorganising in Wolfheze the Troop moved off along the Duitsekampweg running across the bottom of LZ S toward the Hotel Buunderkamp, in order to approach the Amsterdamseweg further west through the woods near *Planken Wambuis*. In the process Lieutenant Cecil Bowles' 9 Section successfully stalked, captured and interrogated three stray Germans spotted near the Buunderkamp before passing them back to Hay's HQ Section, which in turn somewhat hopefully despatched them back unescorted toward British lines. The dense woodland obliged the Jeeps to move in column behind scouts on foot, passing through a culvert under the incomplete motorway paralleling the railway and a number of abandoned construction huts before finally approaching the Amsterdamseweg. Lieutenant Hubert Pearson, who had been assigned from HQ Troop to make up for Sunday's casualties, climbed a tree to gain a view of the main road and discovered that, 'as far as he could see, enemy armoured vehicles were moving slowly from the west in the direction of Arnhem.' Hay was unable to report this because while the remainder of the Squadron were enjoying unexpectedly clear communications, C Troop had lost radio contact shortly after turning onto the Wolfhezeweg. The volume of German traffic on the Amsterdamseweg precluded that route and it was also becoming increasingly apparent that they were not alone in the woods. Lance-Corporal Albert Palmer and Trooper Jimmy Cooke had detected signs of recent German presence at the motorway culvert whilst scouting ahead of the main column, and stealthy movement was becoming audible to the rear. C Troop therefore had little choice but to hold quietly in place and await developments.[105]

While the 1st Airborne Reconnaissance Squadron had been settling into its night harbour area near the Hotel Hartenstein, the 7th KOSB had finally broken clear of the congestion caused by the 4th Parachute Brigade's transport echelon near Wolfheze at 01:00. The Battalion then moved in column along the track paralleling the north side of the Arnhem–Ede railway line with B Company in the lead, trailed by D Company, Battalion HQ and Support Company with C Company bringing up the rear. Tasked to protect LZ L for the third lift, the Battalion's initial objective was the farm and village of Johannahoeve at the south-east corner of the zone and a mile or so north-west of Oosterbeek. From there B Company were to move north-east and secure a road junction on the Dreijenseweg 1,000 yards north of the Oosterbeek Hoog railway crossing while C Company occupied Point 565 in the woods midway between B Company and the railway line. B Company's advance was somewhat cautious until Lieutenant-Colonel Payton-Reid went forward and directed Major Forman to speed up and the Johannahoeve objectives were then reached and secured without incident, although the Battalion War Diary referred to 'a certain amount of enemy MG and gun fire' and 'air strafing'; 4th Parachute Brigade HQ also referred to encountering 'hostile bombing during the night with flares'.[106] Matters proceeded less smoothly thereafter, however. Major Dinwiddie and C Company pushed on and were climbing the wooded slope leading to Point 565 when they bumped into dug-in German machine guns; unable to locate them in the darkness, Dinwiddie elected to establish a temporary perimeter and resume the attack after daybreak. B Company ran into similarly 'stiff opposition' en route to the Dreijenseweg junction at around 04:00 and suffered a number of casualties in repeated but vain efforts to outflank the German positions; the casualties included the commander of 5 Platoon, Lieutenant Donald Murray, who was posted missing.[107] At that point Colonel Payton-Reid intervened and ordered Major Forman to withdraw to Johannahoeve, around which he had established a loose Battalion perimeter by first light, with Major Sherriff's D Company dug in just to the north and C Company still holding its position near Point 565. At some point after 06:00 the Battalion was rejoined by Major Buchanan and A Company, which had become separated following a misunderstanding the previous afternoon; it is unclear where the latter were deployed on rejoining the Battalion, but the War Diary suggests it was in the 500 yard deep strip of woods separating the Amsterdamseweg and LZ L.[108]

In the event, Colonel Payton-Reid's decision to set in at Johannahoeve proved fortuitous, for at 08:00 the 7th KOSB was officially transferred to the 4th Parachute Brigade and Brigadier Hackett visited Payton-Reid's HQ at around the same time to announce the transfer and deliver new instructions.[109] The 10th and 156 Parachute Battalions were scheduled to advance and secure the western end of the *Koepel* ridge in the course of the morning, and Hackett therefore ordered Payton-Reid to maintain a firm base for the parachute Battalions to manoeuvre around in tandem with the 7th KOSB's existing mission to protect LZ L for the third lift. In line with the latter D Company was redeployed to the north-west corner of the LZ with A Company on its left flank, while B Company and Battalion HQ at Johannahoeve protected the landing area from the south and east. C Company was to hold in place near Point 565 while 156 Parachute Battalion moved through to secure the height en route to *Koepel* and then follow in the paratrooper's wake to secure their gains, and Payton-Reid was also instructed to maintain close contact with both parachute units and to 'assist them in any way possible'. Once its redeployments were complete the 7th KOSB remained in place, although its positions appear to have been noted by enemy observers on the high ground to the east. All the Battalion's locations were heavily shelled in the course of the morning, which set fire to most of the houses in Johannahoeve village, and the Battalion also attracted the attention of German fighter aircraft, which made a series of strafing attacks at around 11:00 that inflicted at least seven casualties on a KOSB patrol caught moving on the LZ.[110]

On returning to the Hotel Buunderkamp from Division HQ at 01:30, Hackett had spent the next few hours drawing up orders to conform with Hicks' instructions for an advance eastward between the Arnhem–Ede railway line and the Amsterdamseweg. Employing the track paralleling the north side of the railway line as the Brigade axis, Hackett's new objective was to secure the *Koepel* ridge and establish a firm left flank anchored on the main road, with the 4th Parachute Squadron continuing as Brigade rearguard. 156 Parachute Battalion and its attached Troop from the 4th Parachute Squadron RE was tasked to secure the *Koepel* ridge while the 10th Parachute Battalion set up the firm flank astride the Amsterdamseweg approximately 1,000 yards west of the junction with the Dreijenseweg. The unforeseen problem with this plan would be co-ordination, for 156 Parachute Battalion was occupying a firm base in woods 800 yards short of Johannahoeve and around two miles further east than Hackett was expecting. The discrepancy was due to Lieutenant-Colonel Des Vœux ignoring Hackett's instructions to halt at dusk the previous evening in favour of pushing on along the Arnhem–Ede railway to within 400 yards of the Oosterbeek Hoog station. There the Battalion's lead element ran into the same well-sited German positions that were to stop the 7th KOSB securing Point 565 and the south end of Dreijenseweg six hours or so later; Des Vœux was unable to inform Brigade HQ of the situation or his actual location because communications with Brigade HQ had broken down. For its part, the 10th Parachute Battalion had set in for the night near Hackett's Brigade HQ just off DZ Y, and was consequently looking at an approach march of at least three miles to its assigned location astride the Amsterdamseweg. This meant that 156 Parachute Battalion would be operating without support until the remainder of the 4th Parachute Brigade closed up from its overnight positions west of Wolfheze.

It took 156 Parachute Battalion until 03:00 to disengage and reorganise in the firm base west of Johannahoeve, and Hackett's new orders for the seizure of the *Koepel* ridge were received ninety minutes later.[111] Lieutenant-Colonel Des Vœux's consequent plan envisaged securing this objective in three bounds and gave Major Geoffrey Powell's C Company responsibility for securing the ridge surmounted by Point 565 as the first bound, supported by Major John Waddy's B Company. The second bound tasked Major John Pott's A Company to move around Powell's left flank, advance up the wooded incline and across the Dreijenseweg to secure the Lichtenbeek feature, after which B Company was to push on and occupy the *Koepel* ridge. It is unclear when the attack began but C Company had secured Point 565 without encountering resistance by 07:00 although B Company, deployed in support south of the railway line, fired on German troops and armoured vehicles spotted near the south end of the Dreijenseweg.[112] The 156 Battalion War Diary surprisingly makes no mention of the 7th KOSB's C Company, although A Company's commander noted their presence on the left flank.[113] Colonel Des Vœux and Major Pott then came forward to Powell's location in an effort to spy out the ground for the next bound but the foliage was too dense for effective observation.[114] They were joined briefly at this point by Brigadier Hackett, who stressed the urgent need to break through to Frost's beleaguered force at the road bridge, before departing for his HQ. Major Pott returned to brief his platoon commanders, Lieutenants Lindsay Delacour and Stanley Watling and Captain Ian Muir from the Glider Pilot Regiment. The latter had been attached to A Company with his thirty-strong 22 Flight from D Squadron as compensation for Sergeant Griffiths' 3 Platoon, which had been detached to protect casualties on DZ Y. A Company also had a 6-Pounder attached; it is unclear whether the gun came from 156 Battalion's Support Company or H Troop, 2nd (Oban) Airlanding Anti-tank Battery, assigned to support the Battalion. The briefing does not appear to have included the previous night's warning that the Germans had established a 'strong outpost line' along the Dreijenseweg from the stray KOSB officer or that B Company had seen armoured vehicles moving on the southern end of the Dreijenseweg.[115] Presumably it was discounted due to C Company's easy passage and Hackett's urging haste. Major Pott began his move around C Company's left flank at 08:30, following a firebreak angling through the trees toward the Dreijenseweg.[116]

The German positions which had blocked the advance of 156 Parachute Battalion and the 7th KOSB during the night of 18-19 September were actually defensive outposts dubbed *sicherungen* (literally, 'fuses') deployed to cover likely avenues of attack; another *sicherung* located at Johannahoeve farm appears to have withdrawn without making contact. The outposts were intended to hold in place long enough to divine enemy intentions before withdrawing to the main *sperrlinie* or blocking line, which followed the course of the Dreijenseweg with positions on the roadway and further uphill, notably along a stretch flanked on its eastern edge by a by a ten-foot bank. The line was manned primarily by *Panzergrenadier Ausbildungs und Ersatz Bataillon 361*, a *Heer* replacement training unit based at Wuppertal commanded by *Hauptmann* Hans Bruhn, a Knight's Cross holder who had lost a leg on the Eastern Front in 1942. Despatched by *Wehrkreis IV*, Bruhn's 525-strong *Bataillon* arrived in Arnhem on 18 September after a 100-mile journey by road and rail. *II SS Panzerkorps* then assigned it to *Sturmbannführer* Spindler, who in turn directed it to the Dreijenseweg sector. There Bruhn also took command of the detachment from *SS Panzer Aufklärungs Abteilung 9* and *Hauptsturmführer* von Allwörden's *SS Panzerjäger Abteilung 9* which had been deployed along the Amsterdamseweg since the early evening of 17 September. This added ten assorted armoured half-tracks, two *Panzerjäger* IV self-propelled guns, several towed anti-tank guns and three infantry companies totalling in excess of 120 men to Bruhn's strength. The vehicles were sited among the trees concealing the defensive positions to cover the approaches to the Dreijenseweg or in some instances patrolling back and forth along the roadway, while one of von Allwörden's *Panzerjäger* IVs was stationed at the junction of the Amsterdamseweg and Dreijenseweg along with a *PaK* 40.[117]

Major Pott and A Company were thus walking into a carefully sited and camouflaged defensive line more than twenty-four hours in the making, supported by over a dozen armoured vehicles and manned by more personnel than 156 Parachute Battalion's total strength. The scene was therefore set for a rerun of the 1st Parachute Brigade's experience just over two miles to the south-east. 4 Platoon got as far as the approaches to the Dreijenseweg when three machine-guns located just west of the road opened fire. Lieutenant Watling's men immediately charged forward through the crossfire and reached the road but were then obliged to seek cover in the shallow roadside ditch. Major Pott set about organising a left-flanking attack using 5 Platoon's riflemen and Captain Muir's Glider Pilots as the assault group covered by Lieutenant Delacour's Bren Groups, but the Bren gunners found it difficult to locate targets among the foliage, as Sergeant Andrew Thorburn discovered:

> It was far too quiet. We were behind little heaps of cut logs. You couldn't see anything but the trees, and I was certain there were snipers hidden in them. I wanted to spray the trees

ahead of us before we started, but before I could do so, Lieutenant Delacour was hit by the first shot fired…I told him to lie still but he jumped up…He was immediately hit again, right across the middle. All hell let loose then. I opened fire with the Bren, firing off about five magazines, spraying the trees, but I couldn't see any effect of my fire.[118]

Lieutenant Delacour had been hit initially in the neck and had jumped up to shout a warning; according to Sergeant Thorburn his exact words were 'Major Pott. Fix bayonets. Charge!' Whatever the wording, Delacour paid a high price for his impetuosity, as he bled to death while the battle raged around him. Major Pott's assault group had also been drastically reduced by a German machine-gun post positioned in a hollow on the left flank that pinned down the Glider Pilot platoon, wounding Captain Muir and mortally wounding one of his Section commanders, Lieutenant Sydney Smith.[119] Sergeant Louis Hagen, a German Jew serving under the pseudonym Lewis Haig, closed to within twenty yards of the German position in a single-handed attempt to silence it before being obliged to seek cover, and then spent some time listening to the crew bickering before making his escape.[120]

Major Pott pressed home the attack with 5 Platoon under Sergeant Charles Gilmour, crossing the Dreijenseweg before pivoting right and assaulting along its axis, rolling up German positions on both sides of the road in a series of brutal encounters with bayonets and grenades. The task was complicated by one or more half-tracks on the right firing down the line of the roadway and along the shallow bordering ditches, inflicting more casualties on 4 Platoon sheltering there; this fire may have killed Lieutenant Watling as he attempted to lead his men over the Dreijenseweg to join the assault and the Company second-in-command, Captain Terence Rogers, was also killed while mopping up German positions east of the road.[121] The half-tracks pulled back when the paratroopers closed on their location but continued to lay down fire, and Pott lost more men attempting to stalk the vehicles with grenades in lieu of PIATs. Private Martin Carney succeeded in locating and bringing forward a 4 Platoon's Bren team but the gunner, Private Alfred Trueman, was killed trying to lay down suppressive fire on a half-track, and Sergeant George Sheldrake was badly wounded whilst doing the same with a 2-inch mortar.[122] The British attack finally ebbed with the Glider Pilots pinned down west of the Dreijenseweg and 4 Platoon pinned down in the roadside ditch, both with numerous wounded, while 5 Platoon was extended south along the road in pursuit of the elusive and deadly half-tracks.[123] The sheer ferocity of the British response nonetheless came as a most unpleasant surprise for their opponents as noted by *Sturmann* Alfred Ziegler, a motorcycle despatch rider from *SS Panzerjäger Abteilung 9* attached to Bruhn's HQ: 'I was with Bruhns [sic] when the [German] position first showed signs of cracking. In some places our men had to adopt isolated "hedgehog" positions with all round defence, while some small groups of enemy managed to infiltrate through our lines.' Thoroughly alarmed and unaware that his force outnumbered the attackers, Bruhn urgently despatched Ziegler toward Arnhem in search of reinforcements.[124]

In the meantime Colonel Des Vœux had decided to enact the third stage of his plan without waiting for confirmation of A Company's progress to the Lichtenbeek feature. Major Waddy and B Company were thus despatched at 09:00 to move around A Company's left flank, across the Dreijenseweg and on to the *Koepel* ridge. At this point A Company was still moving through the woods prior to making contact and Des Vœux appears to have assumed that Major Pott had secured his objective with little to no resistance, given that he assured Waddy that there were only a 'few snipers about'. That this was far from the case became increasingly apparent as B Company moved up the firebreaks in A Company's wake, in part from the increasing volume of fire audible from the fight on the Dreijenseweg but also from more graphic evidence noted by Waddy: 'When we moved up, it was obvious that A Company had received tremendous casualties; there were wounded coming back in Bren carriers and dead chaps lying at the side of the ride, and I passed a complete platoon headquarters all killed.'[125] This was likely Captain

Muir's HQ group, given that at that time B Company appears to have come within range of the well-camouflaged German positions west of the road at around the same time. As Private Ronald Atkinson put it 'we walked right into it, fire from above, from our flanks and even from behind'.[126] The result was also similar as Bren gunner Private Edward Reynolds discovered on going to ground: 'I couldn't see where the Germans were and had to fire at where their fire seemed to be coming from. Things got quite bad. One of the first to be hit was the Number Two on my Bren, Private Ford. Suddenly he was laid on the ground, stone dead, with three little bullet holes in the throat...The platoon lost four or five men.'[127] There was also the added distraction of a Glider Pilot emerging from the undergrowth offering to guide the lead platoon to the German positions before disappearing whence he came. Private Atkinson considered him lucky not to have been shot by both sides. His sudden appearance raised suspicions of a German plant and no one followed, the paratroopers being leery of a trap. In fact the mysterious Glider Pilot was Sergeant Hagen, who, having escaped from under the German machine-gun post, was looking to eliminate it; he was eventually able to pass his information on to an officer from 156 Battalion, although it is unclear if it was acted upon.[128]

Having reached the point where the Battalion had run into the German outpost line the previous night, B Company began pushing up the firebreak toward the Dreijenseweg with a platoon deployed either side, closely followed by Major Waddy and his HQ group. The advance covered another 500 yards or so, accompanied by the growing sound of heavy engines, the rattle and squeal of tracks and shouting from the road ahead and in the trees on the flank. These were not the vehicles from *SS Panzer Aufklärungs Abteilung 9* that had interfered with Major Pott and his men. In his search for reinforcements *Sturmann* Ziegler came upon an *SS* light *flak* unit equipped with an undisclosed number of half-tracks mounting single and quad 20mm weapons, which he led back to the Dreijenseweg; they were joined by a similarly equipped *Heer* unit, although it is unclear if it came up with Ziegler or arrived subsequently. Bruhn immediately deployed the half-tracks in hastily surveyed locations to bolster his defensive line and the shouting noted by the advancing paratroopers was these vehicles being manoeuvred into position by their crews. From a German perspective the *flak* vehicles arrived in the nick of time and as the two lead British platoons approached a clearing just short of the Dreijenseweg they came under murderous crossfire from numerous 20mm weapons. From his trail position Major Waddy noted the German weapons were 'firing high-explosive shells, and these had a deadly effect, bursting in the trees and flinging out small splinters, so that even though...men were on the ground trying to crawl forward, they were still getting killed or wounded'.[129] One of those wounded was Private Atkinson, as he assisted a wounded stretcher bearer with a casualty: 'Then it happened. Something struck me at the back of my neck; it felt like a back heel from a cart horse. I remember feeling to see whether I still had a head on my shoulders and then looking at my hands and tunic sleeves covered in blood – my own blood! I dashed to the rear, to the first-aid post, moaning and groaning all the way'.[130]

Despite the casualties Waddy immediately set about organising a renewed push across the clearing and appears to have been joined in the process by Battalion HQ and Captain Thomas Wainright's Support Company, which had moved from Point 565 at 09:30.[131] It is unclear whether Colonel Des Vœux had ordered the move believing he was following in the wake of a progressing advance, or because B Company had been stalled. Whichever, Waddy launched a dash across the clearing to coincide with the arrival of fighter aircraft overhead, which he assumed to be RAF but proved to be *Luftwaffe*, part of the wide-ranging strafing attack that occurred at around 11:00; interestingly, while the 156 Battalion War Diary refers to the strafing inflicting heavy casualties on B Company, this does not figure in Waddy's account.[132] The renewed attack got across the clearing but was stalled again just short of the Dreijenseweg by a wall of German fire, which obliged around thirty survivors to seek cover. Waddy then became drawn into an attempt to stalk one of the *flak* half-tracks, accompanied by Captain Wainright and some men from B Company. They succeeded in closing to within a few yards of the vehicle. The man next to Waddy was preparing throw a phosphorous grenade when he was shot through the head by a German sharpshooter covering the half-track from a tree above their heads. Waddy had left the captured MP40 he routinely carried as a personal weapon with his HQ Group and attempted to engage the sharpshooter with his .45 automatic pistol but was shot in the groin for his trouble and fired at again as he attempted to crawl away. He was subsequently carried to safety by Private Ben Diedricks, one of a score of Rhodesian soldiers serving with 156 Battalion, and was eventually ferried by Jeep to 181 Airlanding Field Ambulance's MDS at the Hotel Tafelberg.[133] The Battalion War Diary, incidentally, incorrectly reported that Waddy had been fatally wounded.[134]

Thus by mid to late morning on Tuesday 19 September one of the 4th Parachute Brigade's two available battalions was fully engaged with *Hauptmann* Bruhn's force on the Dreijenseweg, and the second was rapidly following in its wake. Lieutenant-Colonel Smyth's 10th Parachute Battalion had left its overnight position near the Hotel Buunderkamp at some point between 03:00 and 04:30, with Captain Cedric Horsfall and D Company in the lead.[135] According to the unit's semi-official history, the Battalion was at seventy per cent of its strength with the absent portion including two officers killed and four more missing. 'The woods behind them were ablaze', presumably resulting from the activities of the Battalion patrols.[136] In line with Hackett's new orders the Battalion was heading for a point roughly a thousand yards west of the junction between the Amsterdamseweg and the Dreijenseweg, where it was to establish a firm left flank for the Brigade's advance on the *Koepel* ridge. The three-mile approach march, which took around five-and-a-half hours, went to plan and D Company reached the Battalion's designated position at 10:00. However, instead of establishing a defensive perimeter, Colonel Smyth pushed on down the Amsterdamseweg toward Arnhem. It is unclear why Smyth appears to have carried on with his original mission of advancing into Arnhem rather than conforming to Hackett's revised orders. One account suggests that it may have been due to an unrecorded order by Hackett, but this is unlikely given that the latter's account shows he was under the impression that the 10th Battalion was in place in its flank position as late as midday.[137] Smyth was unable to clarify matters as he died on 26 September from wounds sustained five days earlier. Whatever the reason, D Company led the Battalion on along the Amsterdamseweg toward Arnhem, keeping to the right-hand side of the road while the Battalion transport closed up along a track from the south. Captain Horsfall's lead platoon was moving abreast of La Cabine water pumping station on the opposite side of the road, approximately 300 yards short of the junction with the Dreijenseweg and the first Jeep in the transport column was negotiating its way onto the main road when the advance ran into the northern end of *Hauptmann* Bruhn's blocking line.

Intense machine-gun fire from the German outposts covering the road drove D Company to ground and a *Panzerjäger* IV sited to fire along the line of the Amsterdamseweg scored a direct hit on the lead Jeep, Colonel Smyth's personal vehicle driven by Glider Pilot Captain Barry Murdoch. The shell was presumably an armour-piercing round as it set the vehicle ablaze rather than demolishing it as a high-explosive projectile would have done; Murdoch miraculously escaped unharmed. Captain Horsfall immediately launched the standard left-flanking attack obliging Lieutenant John Procter and 9 Platoon to 'get across the road first, but there was a self-propelled gun firing straight down it from time to time. It seemed fairly quiet, so we put one man across to see what it was like. The SP fired just then, and the shell blew the man's head off, a most unlucky shot for him. The rest of us lined up and galloped across without any more casualties.'[138] In the meantime A Company deployed in the woods north of the Amsterdamseweg, while B Company moved up in reserve. The German automatic fire penetrated back to the Battalion HQ group, as noted by Adjutant Nicholas Hanmer:

We had been moving fairly quickly, and it happened suddenly…The company ahead may have tried to outflank the opposition…but the fire was so heavy that they had to dig in, and so did we. You dig rather quickly in those circumstances. Quite a lot of the fire was coming through to us. The CO couldn't do much at that stage because the fire was so heavy.[139]

Digging in proved fortuitous, for D Company's attempt to outflank the German outposts provoked a heavy mortar barrage, possibly including fire from multi-barrel *nebelwerfer* rocket launchers, which inflicted a number of casualties including Lieutenant Procter, who was struck in the upper arm by a fragment that broke the bone. Procter had been wounded previously while serving in North Africa and again in Italy and his somewhat jocular passage to the aid post under his own steam was witnessed by Lieutenant John Clarke, the Battalion Signals Officer, who was conferring with Colonel Smyth and Captain Hanmer: 'Grinning, he [Procter] called out "I'm sorry about this. It always happens to me. I've lost my sense of humour about getting wounded. I'm not laughing any more".'[140] The Germans appear to have walked their mortar fire along the line of the Amsterdamseweg and a horse pulling a cart commandeered by the Signals Platoon to carry the spare radio batteries bolted in panic from a near miss; it is unclear if the batteries and a portion of the Battalion's ammunition reserve, which had also been loaded onto the cart, were recovered.[141]

Rather than immediately launching a flanking attack, Lieutenant-Colonel Smyth instructed D Company to maintain contact with the enemy and despatched his Intelligence Section to scout the extent and location of the German positions. He then ordered Lieutenant Roy Dodd's Mortar Platoon to suppress the German fire and went forward with his HQ Group to D Company's line; Corporal Harry Dicken from the Intelligence Section was with Smyth opposite the pumping station when one of its buildings was demolished, likely by a salvo from a *nebelwerfer*: 'I was about ten yards from Colonel Smyth in this action…From my position I could see across the road to a two-storey pumping station with a tiled roof. While we were looking in this direction, there was a double explosion, and the tile roof lifted, and over a period of almost a minute the tiles cascaded to the ground. Colonel Smyth drily remarked "The landlord won't like that".'[142] Lieutenant Dodd's 3-inch mortars made some impression on the enemy but the effort rapidly depleted the ammunition supply. The drawn-out firefight between D Company and the German outposts also appears to have drawn in elements of B Company. The experience of Private George Taylor from 8 Platoon illustrates the intensity of the firefight:

> We were held up by some Germans…and we kept exchanging fire with them. The [Bren] barrel got so hot that we had to urinate on it to cool it down before we could change it; the hot urine spurted back on to me. We were in shallow shell-scrapes on the edge of a wood about fifty to seventy-five yards from the Germans and we eventually decided that we had to move out. It was just then that Nick Walter, the Number One on the Bren was killed – just the one hit in the temple…I had to take the Bren from him and leave him; he was still in the firing position.[143]

The Intelligence Section's reconnaissance appears to have prompted Colonel Smyth to try and bypass the German units blocking passage along the Amsterdamseweg to the north after seeking and receiving authorisation from 4th Parachute Brigade HQ. According to Hackett's War Diary account, Smyth also intended to disengage before executing his move.[144] The move was to be led by the Battalion second-in-command Captain Lionel Queripel and A Company from the north side of the Amsterdamseweg: A Company's commander, Major Patrick Anson, had been aboard one of the C-47s lost in the run-in to the DZ the previous day, likely that piloted by Lieutenant Thomas T. Tucker from the 34th Troop Carrier Squadron.[145] However, the flanking movement does not appear to have developed beyond A Company preparing to move on the north side of the road and the despatch of a three-man patrol led by Sergeant Keith Banwell to scout the area immediately to A Company's front. The patrol returned safely, albeit after almost being cut off by German troops, and reported spotting five tanks and four trucks including two fuel tankers in a compound east of the pumping station.[146] The delay in executing the flanking movement was due to the arrival of German light *flak* vehicles on the 10th Battalion's frontage, which Smyth appears to have erroneously assumed were attempting to push along the Amsterdamseweg through the British line. This was not the case, as Corporal Dicken recalled: 'We were told – Battalion HQ at least – to line the road to ambush them but not to fire until ordered. The enemy stopped short of the wood, spread out and began to plaster us with every weapon they had.'[147] Rather than attempting to move down the Amsterdamseweg the Germans were likely modifying their approach to take advantage of the relatively open ground between the woods occupied by the paratroopers and the north end of the Dreijenseweg, in order to avoid being stalked, as had occurred in the fight with 156 Parachute Battalion to the south. Once again, the heavy-calibre German automatic fire pinned the paratroopers in their hastily dug shell scrapes or other cover and effectively prevented any attempt to break contact.

Having departed as 156 Parachute Battalion's attack toward the *Lichtenbeek* feature was getting underway, Brigadier Hackett does not appear to have been aware of the deterioration of the situation along the Dreijenseweg as the morning wore on, and consequently applied himself to routine business. Brigade HQ had already moved from the Hotel Buunderkamp at 07:30 to a new location just east of the Wolfheze crossing, trailed thirty minutes later by the rearguard 4th Parachute Squadron RE led by the newly returned Major Perkins; he had dislocated his shoulder on landing and had spent the night in the care of 133 Parachute Field Ambulance.[148] On returning to his HQ from Point 565, Hackett was joined at some point between 08:45 and 10:30 by Lieutenant-Colonels Mackenzie and Loder-Symonds, who confirmed the transfer of the 7th KOSB to Hackett's command and presumably briefed him on the overall situation.[149] They also brought news of Urquhart's recent return and a request for Hackett to visit Division HQ if he 'was not pressed', failing which Urquhart would come out to 4th Parachute Brigade HQ later in the day. Although he felt obliged to decline the invitation Hackett welcomed the news of Urquhart's return, commenting at the time 'that things were now looking tidier', and used the same phrase in a post-war interview: 'My feelings were that Roy [Urquhart] was back and a firm hand was in charge at last. Things were looking tidier. I had no quarrel with the conduct of operations now.'[150] Quite how much of Hackett's satisfaction stemmed from the fact that Urquhart's return removed the irksome necessity of serving under Hicks is uncertain.

Hackett then set about bringing the remainder of his Brigade forward. The precise timing is unclear but 133 Parachute Field Ambulance was ordered to move from Wolfheze sanatorium to join 181 Airlanding Field Ambulance at the Hotel Tafelberg in Oosterbeek. Brigade HQ moved again at 11:00, to a track junction in woods just south of the Arnhem-Ede railway line 500 yards or so south-west of Johannahoeve and was 'badly strafed' en route by German fighters, albeit without suffering any casualties.[151] German aircraft also overflew the 4th Parachute Squadron RE leading Captain Henry Brown, commanding No. 3 Troop, to believe his unit was under attack from

…three or four German Messerschmitts. There was a certain amount of panic. Those sappers close to me jumped into a convenient bomb crater. I did too and we kept our heads down. I thought I had taken the right action [but] the planes were firing at 156 Battalion which was about two miles ahead of us. There had been no need to take cover…I resolved from now on to make some attempt at taking sensible action under fire.[152]

With the excitement over, the Parachute Squadron followed in the wake of Brigade HQ at 11:30, moving along the sandy track paralleling the Arnhem-Ede railway line.[153] Captain Brown commandeered an abandoned farm cart discovered at the side of the track to ease his men's burden of No. 75 Hawkins Mines: 'Because we were rather heavily loaded with small anti-tank mines (each man carried two in his pouches) I ordered everyone in my Troop to load up the cart with the mines. They were about the size of a thickish paperback book…In all there must have been about sixty mines each containing about two pounds of explosive. It was an easy task for three men to haul the cart along the firm level sandy track.'[154] Brown also noted a 'considerable amount of firing ahead' and the unsettling sight of casualties from the fight on the Dreijenseweg being ferried back aboard Bren Carriers. The Squadron's destination was a track junction by a small wood alongside the railway line, just under a mile east of the Wolfheze crossing, and after a pause the Sappers were ordered to dig in along the northern edge of the wood, facing out across LZ L; No. 3 Troop left its farm cart of Hawkins mines in cover just off the track while Captain Brown liaised with a unit of Glider Pilots occupying adjacent positions. With that, the 4th Parachute Brigade, along with the remainder of the 1st Airborne Division, was in position to await the arrival of the third lift.

D Plus 2

12:00 to 23:59 Tuesday 19 September 1944

By midday on Tuesday 19 September 1944 the bulk of the 1st Airborne Division was collectively centred on Oosterbeek, with individual units either in the process of moving on Arnhem or occupying Phase II positions east of the landing areas used by the first and second lifts. The exception to this was the 1st Airborne Reconnaissance Squadron, the bulk of which, Captain Michael Grubb's A Troop and Captain Park's D Troop, was occupying a mile-long observation line in the Doorwerthsche Bosch forest 1,000 yards or so east of Heelsum. Initially, things remained quiet in the northern sector and Captain Grubb led a small patrol to a nearby group of houses at the request of an elderly Dutch civilian to deal with an alleged collaborator; the target had disappeared and Grubb and his men had to make do with the hospitality of his more patriotic neighbours. At around 14:00 a German bicycle *bataillon* appeared on the Utrechtseweg but turned south into the forest before reaching A Troop's section of the line, apart from a party of five stragglers who missed the turning and were ambushed by Lieutenant John Stevenson's 1 Section. Two survivors hid in the roadside foliage and were taken prisoner by Trooper Kenneth Hope when his Section moved up to render assistance: 'One of the Germans had extended one arm only, and I thought "My God, the bastard's giving us a Nazi salute!" Then I realised that he was shot through the shoulder and upper arm.'[1] The pair may have been those despatched back to Captain Allsop's Tactical HQ for interrogation where they arrived at 15:30.[2] Another group of Germans on foot was ambushed nearby later in the afternoon, but the trap was sprung too early and they escaped unscathed apart from abandoning a wheeled machine-gun of some kind in the road. Further south, D Troop fought two sharp encounters in the vicinity of its Troop HQ location near the Koninginne Laan beginning at 13:00. Thereafter, matters developed into a stealthy and potentially deadly game of hide-and-seek for the reconnaissance soldiers as large numbers of German troops moved past the deployed Sections in the dense undergrowth, as Lance-Corporal Robert Thomson recalled: 'Most of the time we couldn't see the Germans at all, but we knew that they were there because we could hear them moving through the woods all around. They made a lot of noise.'[3]

Captain Allsop had established the Squadron's Tactical HQ just inside the Division perimeter adjacent to the 1st Airlanding Light Regiment's gun pits near the Hotel Bilderberg, from where it relayed reports from the elements farther west to Division HQ, although the location proved to be only marginally less hazardous than the front line. When a reported ten *Luftwaffe* fighters strafed the area at 13:50 the Squadron War Diary noted an 'intense barrage of Sten gun fire from R.A.s – endangers Tac HQ more than the planes'.[4]

Captain Allsop left his HQ at 12:30 to escort Major-General Urquhart to the Arnhem-Ede railway line en route to 4th Parachute Brigade HQ, and moved from there to the woods north-west of the Division perimeter at 14:15 in an effort to re-establish radio communication with Captain John Hay's C Troop. Links to the latter had been lost shortly after it had left the

Squadron in order to reconnoitre the Amsterdamseweg north of Wolfheze at around 07:00. The third lift supply drop came in while the signaller worked and one Short Stirling reportedly crashed nearby after being hit by German anti-aircraft fire. After forty minutes or so the attempt was abandoned and Allsop returned to the Tactical HQ location on the Utrechtseweg near the junction with the Wolfhezeweg at 15:00.[5]

Although Captain Allsop had no way of knowing it, C Troop would likely have been unable to respond even had radio contact been established. After being prevented from reaching the Amsterdamseweg via the Wolfhezeweg by German mortar fire, Captain Hay's force sidestepped to the west and succeeded in gaining sight of the road from the dense woodland a few hundred yards from the *Planken Wambuis*. The Amsterdamseweg proved to be full of German troops and vehicles, some of them armoured, moving toward Arnhem. While there was no actual contact, the sound of movement in the woods to the rear suggested the Troop's line of retreat had also been blocked. The degree to which this was the case became apparent when the third lift aircraft appeared at shortly before 16:00 and the woods erupted in gunfire, as 9 Section's Sergeant David Christie recalled: 'We must have come right through and passed by several of their positions, and it left us in no doubt that to go back by the way we had come was now definitely out.'[6] Gambling that the Germans on the Amsterdamseweg would be preoccupied and that the noise of the aircraft and anti-aircraft fire would mask the sound of the Jeeps, Captain Hay decided on a bold dash eastward down the main road for the mile-distant junction with the Wolfhezeweg. Jeeps were thus swiftly loaded, weapons checked and with a final order of 'If fired upon, don't stop – keep going,' C Troop's seven Jeeps crunched and bounced their way out of the woods and onto the Amsterdamseweg with Captain Hay's vehicle in the lead. Next came Troop Sergeant Fred Winder's Jeep, followed by Lieutenant Hubert Pearson and then 9 Section's vehicles driven by Lieutenant Cecil Bowles and Sergeant David Christie, with Lieutenant Ralph Foulkes and 7 Section bringing up the rear. The little convoy was soon moving at speed and matters proceeded well for the first half mile or so until the relatively open heathland flanking the road gave way to a beech wood, where the 7th KOSB's A Company had ambushed the motorised Quick Reaction Force from *SS Wacht Bataillon 3* in the early evening of 17 September. At that point a small group of gesticulating Airborne soldiers appeared in the trees at the roadside and seconds later the head of the convoy ran full tilt into a hail of small-arms fire from the left-hand side of the road.

Hit numerous times when the ambush was initiated, Captain Hay's Jeep swerved back and forth across the carriageway before careering off the road and colliding with a tree; the fate of the passengers is unclear. The remaining drivers speeded up and began jinking across the width of the road in an effort to throw off the enemy's aim while their passengers returned fire with every weapon they could muster. Sergeant Christie hunched down in the driver's seat so Lance-Corporal Bert Palmer could fire the vehicle's Vickers K machine gun across the width of the vehicle and over his head. The return fire made little difference, as firing with any accuracy from the wildly manoeuvring Jeeps was virtually impossible and because of the sheer number of ambushers; Sergeant Christie recalled them lining the road so closely he could have spat upon them and Trooper James Cooke recalled there were 'hundreds of them, laid three deep on each side of the road'.[7] This suggests the ambush was a hasty affair organised by a passing unit rather than a deliberate planned arrangement, but the technicality made little difference to the men on the receiving end. Lieutenant Pearson's Jeep disintegrated, possibly after being struck by a large calibre round, scattering human and mechanical debris in all directions. Next in line, Lieutenant Bowles' vehicle was struck by a concentrated burst of fire that knocked out the engine, lightly wounded Bowles in the foot, knees and hand and may also have killed Lance-Corporal Alan Baker and Trooper Frederick Brawn travelling in the back.[8] Bowles deliberately ran the Jeep off the road into a ditch and managed to escape into the woods despite his wounded foot, while an unconscious trooper, Gerry Fergus, was thrown clear by the impact. Sergeant Christie was obliged to run his Jeep onto the grass verge to avoid collision when Bowles' vehicle suddenly decelerated, narrowly missing a concrete milepost. Trooper Raymond McSkimmings was hit in the head and killed outright at around the same time; his body was thrown into the roadway by Christie's evasive manoeuvres.[9] The final two Jeeps in the convoy managed to avoid the ambush altogether. Seeing events unfolding to his front, Lieutenant Foulkes was able to lead his Section off the road up a convenient firebreak, where the shot-up vehicles from *SS Wacht Bataillon 3* had been dragged clear of the road.

Of the five Jeeps that entered the ambush zone, only Sergeants Winder's and Christie's vehicles passed out of the far side, the former by some fluke totally unscathed. Both reported to the Squadron Rear HQ location at 16:20 without further incident.[10] QM Lieutenant Collier was present when the survivors arrived: 'They were very, very shaken, and I remember sitting them down with their backs to some iron railings and pumping rum and strong tea into them.'[11] Trooper Cooke discovered Trooper McSkimmings' brain matter spattered across his vehicle's map cases and Bren. Trooper Stanley Tickle from Sergeant Winder's Jeep appears to have been so traumatised that he drifted away unnoticed and was killed several days later while wandering in a dazed state.[12] By this point the Breedeweg observation line had begun to outlive its usefulness. At the northern end of A Troop's sector Lieutenant Galbraith's 2 Section was strafed by half-a-dozen German fighters at 15:00, apparently without suffering casualties, and an hour later D Troop's high-stakes game of hide-and-seek came to an abrupt end when the Germans attacked the Squadron's locations at the south end of the Breedeweg, obliging Captain Park to withdraw north-east along the Italiaanseweg to the relative safety of the 1st Border's D Company location just south of the Utrechtseweg, before reaching the Squadron Rear HQ at 17:00.[13] Captain Allsop ordered A Troop back to his Tactical HQ location at the same time. Thirty minutes later both elements also withdrew to the Hotel Hartenstein. Allsop was summoned to Division HQ on arrival and at 18:00 A and D Troops were despatched to provide outposts for the north side of the Division perimeter on the line of the Arnhem-Ede railway, A Troop at the north near the end of the Oranjeweg, north-east of the Ommershof position occupied by the 21st Independent Parachute Company, and D at the north-eastern corner of Oosterbeek between the Lebretweg and Schelmseweg. Captain Grubb's Troop were back at the Rear HQ at 22:00 after an uneventful stint of observation apart from suffering three wounded to a German mortar bomb and Troop Sergeant Henry Venes puncturing a Jeep tyre with a negligent discharge from his Sten gun. Captain Park and D Troop had a more eventful time inflicting a number of casualties on a German patrol on the Schelmseweg at around 19:00 and observing a number of others thereafter, before withdrawing to the main Squadron location at 23:30.[14]

While the Reconnaissance Squadron was performing its tasks west of the Division perimeter, the 1st Border continued to enjoy a relatively quiet time in the woods just west of Oosterbeek. C Company's position around the junction of the Utrechtseweg and Wolfhezeweg came under intermittent mortar fire, although the only casualty appears to have been 17 Platoon's Airborne handcart; according to a Lance-Corporal Payne the cart, containing the unit's reserve ammunition and two boxes of compo rations, was destroyed by a direct hit in the early afternoon.[15] A Company and Battalion HQ were strafed by a dozen *Luftwaffe* fighters at 15:00, again without sustaining casualties. A number of supply panniers from the RAF resupply mission reportedly landed in the Battalion area an hour later, two narrowly missing Lance-Corporal Payne and a Private Braithwaite. The pair had been despatched with a Bren to cover C Company's flank and were engaged in knocking loopholes in the walls of a boiler house near some large greenhouses when 'all hell was let loose. Two containers on the end of red parachutes came crashing into the greenhouses.'[16] At 17:30 Battalion HQ relocated to a new position in woods 500 yards to the south-east for reasons that are unclear and ninety minutes later elements from *Kampfgruppe* von Tettau made contact with all four Company locations.[17]

Despite making fairly good progress in the area of Renkum and Heelsum in the afternoon of 18 September, *Kampfgruppe* von Tettau's attack on the 1st Airborne Division's landing area had been brought to an abrupt halt by the collapse of *SS Wacht Bataillon 3* at the hands of the

British second lift on DZ Y, which in turn left the German left flank dangerously exposed. It then took *Generalleutnant* von Tettau's three subordinate *Kampfgruppen* the whole of 19 September to reorganise and feel their way across the now abandoned landing area. In the north *SS Wacht Bataillon 3*'s replacement *Sicherungs Regiment 26*, a two-*Bataillon* military police unit commanded by a *Major* Knoche, was tasked to advance east along the Amsterdamseweg accompanied by three *Flammpanzer B2 (f)* tanks attached from *Oberleutnant* Albert May's *Panzer Kompanie 224*. May's unit had arrived at the scene of the action at 16:30 after an eighty-mile road march from its base at Naaldwijk near Den Haag. It was equipped with sixteen captured French *Char B* tanks, fourteen of them modified by replacing the glacis-mounted short 75mm gun with a flame-thrower, and a single Somua S35 that served as May's command vehicle.[18] In the centre of the advance *SS Bataillon Eberwein* had been tasked to advance along the line of the Arnhem–Ede railway and secure Wolfheze, while *Standartenführer* Lippert and *SS Unterführerschule* 'Arnheim' cleared Heelsum and pushed into the woods running east to Heveadorp and Oosterbeek. Some of *Panzer Kompanie 224*'s vehicles may also have been attached to the latter two units at this point, but it was likely Lippert's men that attacked the Reconnaissance Squadron's D Troop and made contact with the 1st Border's various Company perimeters at 19:00.[19]

The contacts were easily rebuffed and thus likely reconnaissance probes at best, but they highlighted a potentially serious flaw in the 1st Border's dispositions. The Battalion's four Companies were strung along a two-and-a-half-mile line running south-west from A Company's position around the junction of the Valkenberglaan and the Graaf van Rechterenweg just short of the Arnhem–Ede railway line, to B Company's perimeter around the junction of the riverside Fonteinallee and the northward-looping Italiaanseweg around a mile west of Heveadorp. In the centre, C Company was dug in on the Utrechtseweg at its junction with the Wolfhezenweg, 1,500 yards from A Company, with D Company located in the woods 500 yards to its south-west. These locations were too far apart to provide mutual support and their relative isolation and the density of the surrounding woodland also rendered them vulnerable to German infiltration. Major Cousens therefore ordered a withdrawal to shorten the Battalion line at some point after 19:00, which involved pulling B, C and D Companies back abreast of A Company on a line running south along the Valkenberglaan (Valkenberg Avenue), across the Utrechtseweg and along the Van Borsselenweg down to the Lower Rhine. As the most far-flung unit Major Tom Armstrong's B Company moved first, following a roundabout route that involved marching eastward through Heveadorp's darkened streets then north through D and then C Companies, locations before striking south again along the Van Borsselenweg to the junction with the Benedendorpsweg, 300 yards or so north of the river. There B Company dug in, apart from a single platoon detached to establish a position overlooking the riverside Veerweg 500 yards west of the main perimeter. D Company followed, establishing a perimeter on the Van Borsselenweg midway between the Utrechtsestraatweg and B Company's location, while C Company set in around the Utrechtseweg–Van Borsselenweg crossroads. The new positions were still less than ideal, with C and D Companies occupying thick woods and B Company facing the same with the houses and gardens of the western outskirts of Oosterbeek to its back, but the move was completed by 22:45 and the Companies despatched patrols to dominate the approaches to their new locations.[20]

While the 1st Border was busy reorganising its frontage a more determined foe was finally putting paid to the 1st Parachute Brigade's attempt to push into Arnhem along the Utrechtseweg on the east side of the 1st Airborne Division's congealing perimeter. The early morning attacks along the riverside Onderlangs road had reduced the 1st Parachute Battalion to around 200 survivors and stragglers rallied by Lieutenant John Williams, the Battalion Motor Transport Officer who, apparently undaunted, promptly set about organising another attack. Launched at 11:00, this effort progressed for a hundred yards or so before running into elements of *Kampfgruppe* Harder moving in the opposite direction in the face of which the paratroopers were obliged to withdraw, first to area of the Rhine Pavilion at 12:30, and again to the crossroads of the Utrechtsestraatweg and Diependalstraat 400 yards west of the Onderlangs junction, at 14:00. There they hastily set about preparing the surrounding buildings for defence. The 3rd Parachute Battalion was even more badly reduced, to around sixty men led by Captain Geoffrey Dorrien-Smith and Captain Cecil Cox from the 1st Parachute Squadron RE, augmented by a party of 120 men from across the 1st Parachute Brigade gathered up by Lieutenant William Fraser, the 3rd Battalion's Liaison Officer. This force joined the 1st Battalion group at the crossroads at some point after 14:00 along with four 6-Pounders and one 17-Pounder gun from the 1st Airlanding Anti-tank Battery.[21] However, while *Kampfgruppe* Harder may have been responsible for blunting the final British attack along the Onderlangs, the SS unit's mission was supporting and staying abreast of *Kampfgruppe* Möller's advance on the high ground on its right flank, rather than pursuing the paratroopers westward. It was likely this stricture that permitted the remnants of the 1st and 3rd Parachute Battalions their relative breathing space to withdraw and reorganise.

From mid to late morning the focus of the fighting therefore shifted up the slope from the Onderlangs to the Utrechtsestraat, where the 2nd South Staffords were facing attacks on their firm base in and around the museum from *Kampfgruppen* Harder and Möller and more seriously, six assault guns from *Sturmgeschütze Brigade 280*; Battalion HQ and parts of A and B Companies were in the museum proper, the remainder of B Company and D Company held a large wooded hollow on the slope to the west and the bulk of A Company occupied three houses facing the museum on the other side of the Utrechtsestraat. The glider soldiers rebuffed repeated attacks by German infantry and succeeded in keeping the StuGs at bay with PIATs until some point between 10:50 and 11:30 when the supply of PIAT bombs ran out. Major Cain from B Company made this unwelcome discovery whilst seeking a resupply, when the CSM of Support Company 'bluntly informed him that there were none left in the whole area'.[22] By this point German fire from the Onderlangs side had rendered the wooded hollow untenable and the survivors were withdrawn across the Utrechtsestraat and behind the houses held by A Company. Major Cain had sought and received permission for the withdrawal from Colonel McCardie, although one source suggests that Chaplain Buchanan was involved as well.[23] Whoever was involved in the decision, the withdrawal was covered by CanLoan Lieutenant Kenneth Taylor and a handful of men from 11 Platoon equipped with one or possibly two Bren guns, although moving to A Company's location proved be little if any improvement; the house occupied by Lieutenant Alan Barker and 8 Platoon for example was on fire, 'with the roof and one side burning fiercely although the men were still firing back from the unburnt portion of the house'.[24] The withdrawal from the hollow may also have allowed a large group of SS to enter the Municipal Museum from the rear, possibly via a breach in the outer wall created by shellfire. The interlopers were confronted by an unsuspecting Sergeant Norman Howes from A Company:

> I went downstairs to check on the ammo supply and spoke to CSM Vic Williams…I remounted the wooden steps to the first floor to my platoon position… imagine my shock on seeing, instead of my platoon, German troops, two of them facing me as I entered the room, each with rifles in hand…I weighed up the odds and threw myself back down the steps. At the bottom was an upright piano…I got down behind it. At least one grenade was thrown, and the two Germans then came down the steps to check me out. I shot the first; I am not sure if I hit the second as he got up the steps. I shouted to the Dutch people who were there that the Germans were in the building and reported to CSM Williams in the corridor.[25]

The SS were prevented from reinforcing their lodgement by fire from the A Company men on the opposite side of the Utrechtsestraat, but they were helpless to prevent the StuGs standing off and pounding the museum. Lieutenant David Russell and his party from the 2nd Parachute

Battalion watched one assault gun making its way along Utrechtsestraat pumping shells into the houses around the museum and then into their position in the caretakers quarters at the east end of the building: 'Up came another tank in our rear and started on our building, the first two rounds taking off the living room which we had just left.'[26] The German shellfire rapidly rendered the museum untenable. Sergeant Howes intercepted half-a-dozen unarmed men from his platoon attempting to flee and directed them to collect new weapons from the pile discarded by the wounded at the entrance to the cellar RAP, but the group were prevented from taking shelter below by Chaplain Buchanan looking to protect the RAP's neutral status.[27] Despite this, the defenders still on their feet do appear to have ended up fighting among the wounded, and at least some of the latter were less than impressed. Corporal Arthur Stretton from D Company recalled the wounded' were on the ground floor with us' while Private Montgomery from A Company recalled being forced 'from the upper floors of the museum down to the cellar. Here the floor was covered in dead and wounded…we continued to fire on the Jerries from time to time. Unfortunately the fire returned was twice as much as we put out and the wounded shouted things like "Leave the bastards alone"!'[28] By this point the writing was on what remained of the wall and Lieutenant Russell described the end:

I had a quick conference at the foot of the stairs with the Staffords' company commander and other officers; the ground floor was full of wounded. Were we to fight on with small arms against tanks, try to break out, or surrender? We decided that as our object… was impossible and as the building was being systematically demolished and there was nowhere to break out to, we should surrender. I chucked my Sten over a hedge, buried my pistol, and walked out with a handkerchief.[29]

With the Municipal Museum taken, the Germans continued to push along the Utrechtsestraat killing, capturing or driving back the rest of the 2nd South Staffords. The houses opposite the museum were cleared so effectively that 'no one from A Coy on the north side of the road got away.'[30] Lieutenant Jack Reynolds from No.1 Mortar Platoon went into captivity with a number of men from his unit in some style, defiantly giving an *SS Propagandakompanie* cameraman filming the event an emphatic V-sign and in the process creating one of Operation MARKET's most enduring images. Next to be overrun was the 2nd South Staffords Battalion HQ, which had been moved back a hundred yards or so from the museum ; according to the unit War Diary it 'disappeared completely and it is believed, although still unconfirmed, that they were run down by a tank while in the act of withdrawing'.[31] In fact, Colonel McCardie had been caught moving in the opposite direction after observing two *StuGs* driving unmolested down the Utrechtsestraat: 'I was trying to get to A Company, to find out why the hell they weren't shooting at those tanks, and I suppose that something must have fired at me. At any rate, I found myself under about two feet of earth with two Germans pointing Schmeissers at me.'[32] McCardie had vowed never to be taken prisoner but in fact the only officer to escape from what he later described as 'the South Staffs' Waterloo' was Major Cain.[33] Driven out of the building he occupied with other survivors of the fight in the dell by fire from likely the same pair of assault guns that had attracted Colonel McCardie's attention, Cain took shelter in the deep air-raid trenches occupied by Captain Chapman and his mixed group earlier, accompanied by a Corporal Perry and two other men. The group became separated when an approaching *StuG* plastered the area of the trenches from fifty yards. Corporal Perry and his two companions made a break for it and reached the edge of the railway cutting before working their way west to the relative safety of Oosterbeek. Cain rolled over and over until he fell over the lip of a twenty-foot drop into the yard of the St Elizabeth Hospital. The impact knocked him out for ten minutes, after which he made his way through the hospital building to British-held territory, where he linked up with the South Staffords' uncommitted C Company just west of the Rhine Pavilion.[34]

Cain had also passed a warning of what was coming to the 11th Parachute Battalion's A Company en route; the paratroopers were still holding their lonely vigil on the start line for the cancelled supporting attack just east of the St Elizabeth Hospital, as Major Gilchrist recalled: 'Some of the South Staffs fell back through us. I met Major Cain, who said, "The tanks are coming; give me a Piat." I had to apologize that we hadn't any. So the South Staffs disappeared down the hill behind us, hotly pursued by German tanks and infantry. We were outflanked and couldn't engage the tanks, but we were engaging the infantry.'[35] As the Germans had refined their co-operation, this merely attracted the attention of the *StuGs*, and their fire soon obliged A Company to abandon its position adjacent to the railway cutting. Major Gilchrist and around twenty men took shelter in the same deep air-raid trenches used by Major Cain, pursued by the *StuGs*, which again closed to under fifty yards to pound the trapped paratroopers. Attempts to engage the vehicles with Gammon bombs were unsuccessful and after fifteen minutes of absorbing German fire with no means to reply, Gilchrist ordered his group to make a break for the railway cutting: 'That was quite hairy, because the railway cutting was fifty or sixty feet deep. There was a German tank on a bridge over the railway further up, shooting down the railway. We were young and fit in those days and we moved like hell, down the bank, over the rails and up the other side. A few men were hit by the tank's machine gun, but most of us got across.'[36] The respite proved short-lived, for the area north of the cutting was not held by elements of the 4th Parachute Brigade as Gilchrist had assumed but by the Germans, likely elements of *SS Panzer FlaK Abteilung 9*, and Gilchrist's little band were obliged to surrender. Most of A Company was also captured and only Lieutenant Arthur Vickers from 1 Platoon and a handful of men managed to break through to British-held territory.[37]

The destruction of the bulk of the 2nd South Staffords and Major Gilchrist's A Company appears to have been complete by the beginning of the afternoon, given that at around 12:00 the 11th Parachute Battalion's HQ received 'a message to the effect that the attack on the [Arnhem] bridge had been repulsed, and that the German armour was sweeping round to the North to cut us off'.[38] The news prompted Lieutenant-Colonel Lea to redeploy his B Company to cover the Battalion's left flank facing the railway cutting and Major Guy Blacklidge and his men duly occupied the buildings covering a crossroads north-west of the St Elizabeth Hospital, likely the junction of the Alexanderstraat and the Oranjestraat leading to a bridge across the railway cutting; Major Blacklidge emphasised the importance of the Company's mission by ordering his men to 'grenade all enemy tanks and shoot up all infantry'. The move came in the midst of other preparations. At 11:00 Colonel Lea had received new instructions from Division HQ, ordering him to launch a new attack in support of the 4th Parachute Brigade's advance into Arnhem along the Amsterdamseweg. The attack involved moving north across the Arnhem–Ede railway cutting, lining out along the Heijenoordseweg linking the railway line and the Amsterdamseweg and then attacking west to secure a wooded ridge referred to as the Heijenoord-Diependaal feature by the British.[39] Lea also decided to secure *Den Brink* on his left flank to act as a pivot for his attack, and he co-opted the remainder of the 2nd South Staffords to carry out the task. As we shall see, the South Staffords did indeed end up acting as a pivot for the 11th Battalion, but not quite in the way Lea envisaged.

Having arrived from the landing area just too late to join the rest of the 2nd South Staffords in their ill-fated attack up the Utrechtsestraat, Major Philip Wright and C Company had spent the morning waiting for orders near the Rhine Pavilion. At some point Major Wright went forward to contact Colonel McCardie, leaving Captain John Dickens in charge. Wright then went missing and had actually been killed, possibly when Battalion HQ was overrun.[40] As the ranking officer Major Cain therefore assumed command of C Company, the other elements of the South Staffords which had come in with the second lift and around a hundred survivors from the fight at the Municipal Museum who had rallied in the vicinity. Some of the latter had been gathered up near the junction of the Utrechtseweg and Onderlangs by Regimental Sergeant

Major Slater. At least one, a Private Millward, had been captured while undergoing treatment in the St Elizabeth Hospital: 'I had been hit in the arm, and was getting it seen to, when a German appeared and took us prisoner. The German for some reason left us for a minute, so I jumped out of the window and headed back the way we had come.'[41] Major Cain may also have been responsible for a radio request to Division HQ to return the South Staffords' anti-tank guns, which had been sequestered en route from the landing area the previous evening.[42] Half of the survivors were placed under Captain Ralph Schwartz, the Battalion Adjutant, and the remainder under Company Sergeant Major William Robinson from B Company. This gave Cain a force roughly equivalent to five rifle platoons, augmented with Lieutenant James MacDonnell's No.1 MMG Platoon which had come in with C Company on the second lift. The War Diary account suggests that Colonel Lea may have assigned the mission of seizing *Den Brink* before Major Cain arrived, although another source refers to Cain attending an O Group with Lea.[43]

Whoever was initially responsible, Major Cain began by despatching Lieutenant John Badger's 18 Platoon to secure a firm base at the north-west corner of the Arnhem prison compound, at the eastern foot of the high ground. He then deployed the MMG platoon with 18 Platoon to provide cover before leading the rest of his force straight up the wooded slope. The feature appears to have been largely evacuated by *SS Panzer Pionier Abteilung 9*, given that the only opposition encountered was machine-gun fire from the southern end of the feature, which was quickly and effectively suppressed by Lieutenant MacDonnell's Vickers guns. *Den Brink* was thus secured, probably before 13:30, and the glider soldiers set about digging in. The amount of tree roots made it slow-going and most were still above ground when the Germans retaliated with an intense ten-minute mortar bombardment, the effect of which was exacerbated by bombs exploding in the branches overhead. The mortaring caused a number of casualties and the dead included Lieutenant Badger, who had just arrived with his platoon from the firm base by the prison when the bombardment commenced.[44]

Colonel Lea had been organising his move across the railway, closing the 11th Battalion up along the line of the Zuidelijke Parallelweg, which, as its name suggests, ran along the edge of the railway cutting. In addition what was described as a 'weak company' in the South Staffords' War Diary was deployed on the northern edge of *Den Brink* after the mortar bombardment, passing across Major Cain's front to his left flank.[45] Colonel Lea also summoned his B Company up to the Battalion RV from its crossroad covering position, arriving in person via Jeep at around 13:30 and ordering Major Blacklidge to move north up the Oranjestraat to the RV; Lieutenant James Blackwood recalled seeing Lea holding an O Group as he arrived at the Battalion RV with 6 Platoon.[46]

Back at the Utrechtseweg, *Kampfgruppe* Möller pushed west as far as the St Elizabeth Hospital before pausing. The hiatus is usually explained as a measure to permit the Germans to regroup and clear their gains properly, as described by Sergeant James Drew: 'A vehicle came up and down the street with a loud hailer shouting "Come out, you South Staffords, with your hands up. You are surrounded, and there is no way out." We stayed in the cellar…Eventually the cellar door was kicked open, and a German threw an object on the cellar floor…After several minutes I looked and saw that it was a house brick. He was, indeed, the finest German that I had never met. We were then taken prisoner of war.'[47] However, the evidence suggests the primary reason for the pause was to ascertain the best route to continue the advance, and at least one *StuG* probed down the Utrechtseweg as far as the anti-tank screen covering the firm base just west of the Utrechtseweg–Onderlangs junction. The appearance of the German vehicle saw Gunner Eric Milner from C Troop, 1st Airlanding Anti-tank Battery tasked to evacuate an abandoned 6-Pounder gun still hitched to a Jeep at the front of the St Elizabeth Hospital: 'I had to turn the Jeep round first, as it was facing the tank, which was still some distance away. Just as I turned, the tank saw me and fired, but the shells were going over my head. I looked around and saw… the shell bounce off a bump in the road…There was one more fright for me; as I drove to safety, I ran over power cables in the road with blue flashes everywhere.'[48]

Another gun sited on the road was not so lucky, as witnessed by a signaller from the Airlanding Light Regiment: 'I saw to my right the front end of a tank…and I was drawn into a general rush down towards an anti-tank gun sited in front of some park railings…The gun No.1 was yelling to people to get out of his line of fire, but too late; the tank got in first, and I was almost knocked over by the blast that left the gun crew spread-eagled.'[49] Gunner Len Clarke's gun from E Troop, 2nd Airlanding Anti-tank Battery, which was deployed in a front garden facing up the Utrechtseweg, fired on a *StuG*, likely the same vehicle, after a brief argument between Clarke and his Troop commander Lieutenant Robert Glover about who was going to lay the gun; Glover won the argument by dint of his rank and reportedly scored three hits before ordering the gun to redeploy.[50] The assault gun may therefore have been at least damaged, given that subsequent reports suggest *Kampfgruppe* Möller was subsequently accompanied by two rather than three vehicles.[51]

It was thus clear that further advance westward along the Utrechtseweg would involve tackling a rather more potent foe, but *Hauptsturmführer* Möller had located another line of attack along the edge of the railway cutting behind the St Elizabeth Hospital, which would bypass the anti-tank screen; German activity on this axis may have prompted the midday warning to the 11th Parachute Battalion that saw B Company deployed to the junction of the Alexanderstraat and the Oranjestraat.[52] Whether or not, at some point around 13:30 the Germans commenced a heavy, accurate and prolonged mortar bombardment of *Den Brink* and, more importantly, on the 11th Battalion's forming-up position, which caused numerous casualties. Caught in the open the paratroopers were obliged to take cover wherever they could and it was at this point, with the paratroopers at their most disorganised and vulnerable, that *Kampfgruppe* Möller attacked along the Zuidelijke Parallelweg. Colonel Lea's men may have been able to counter an infantry assault but they had no effective counter to the assault guns as the Battalion's attachment from the 2nd Airlanding Anti-tank Battery was still located down on the Utrechtseweg, although one report refers to Captain Albert Taylor from the 2nd Airlanding Light Battery RA bringing a commandeered 6-Pounder gun into action in the 11th Parachute Battalion area and scoring hits on two separate German vehicles.[53] The 11th Parachute Battalion War Diary refers to an order to withdraw to Oosterbeek and to B Company setting up a covering position around a crossroads on the line of withdrawal, but it is unclear where any such order came from, given that Lieutenant-Colonel Lea was wounded and captured in the action; the rearguard was credited with holding back the German advance with the aid of an attached 17-Pounder gun, which reportedly knocked out one of a pair of German tanks.[54] The evidence therefore suggests that the 11th Parachute Battalion was simply overwhelmed and destroyed in place and that the War Diary was understandably attempting to put the best face on it. Whether or not, only around 150 men managed to break away toward Oosterbeek, in small groups or on their own initiative, trailed by B Company.[55]

Up on *Den Brink* Major Cain noted the mortar fire falling on the 11th Parachute Battalion and became aware of that unit's collapse when parties of paratroopers began falling back through his lines. The tide began with an understrength company that had passed across Cain's front earlier and carried some of the 2nd South Staffords with them in the confusion. The fleeing paratroopers were closely followed by *Kampfgruppe* Möller's attached *StuG*s, which began to advance up the wooded slope from two points on the east side of the feature.[56] Once again the South Staffords were essentially helpless in the face of the armoured vehicles, for there were no PIATs to hand and the request for the return of the Battalion's organic Anti-tank Group had gone unanswered. Ironically, the commander of the 2nd South Staffords' Support Company, Major John Buchanan, went forward from Division HQ after a frustrating night 'twiddling his thumbs' to assess the situation for himself. He arrived just in time to help impose some order on the retreat and was joined shortly thereafter by one of his anti-tank platoons, possibly that commanded by Captain Geoffrey Woodward, and Lieutenant Alexander Harvie's No.2 MMG Platoon. Faced with the imminent destruction of the remainder of his Battalion, Major Cain had little option but to abandon *Den Brink* and retire south-west before the German advance. The decision was not taken lightly as Major Cain later recalled: 'It would have been a sheer waste of life to remain there. I had no orders to retire, but I remembered what had happened at the monastery. I felt extremely dejected. I knew that our particular effort to get through to the bridge was a failure and that we had been thrown out of the town.'[57] The cost of acting as a pivot for the 11th Parachute Battalion's thwarted attack had been high; according to Cain, his combined force of C Company and two composite platoons had been reduced to between thirty-five and forty men by the time he ordered the withdrawal.[58]

By this time *Kampfgruppe* Harder was also pressing in along the Utrechtseweg and the prospect of being trapped between the two German units prompted a general withdrawal by the British elements east of the Oosterbeek Laag railway spur, although some men had fallen back from the earlier fighting at the Municipal Museum. At least four men from the 2nd South Staffords got as far as Oosterbeek old village, two of them via a hijacked civilian bicycle, where they were taken over by a gun detachment from the 2nd Airlanding Anti-tank Battery dug in by the Oosterbeek Old Church. Another group of eight passed all the way through the Division area to Westerbouwing, where they were co-opted by the 1st Border.[59] The beginnings of the general retreat were witnessed by Lieutenant-Colonel Thompson, commander of the 1st Airlanding Light Regiment RA, when two Jeeps careered past his attempts to flag them down on the lower Benendendorpsweg road near his 3 Battery positions by the Oosterbeek Old Church; ironically, Thompson was surveying the area with an eye to moving his entire Regiment into the 3 Battery location as their existing position near the Hotel Bilderberg was dangerously close to the western edge of the Division perimeter.[60] He therefore ordered the road blocked with two Jeeps and instructed his officers to prevent any further retreat past the Church, using force if necessary.[61] Back to the east Major Buchanan assumed command of a leaderless group of around sixty South Staffords on the Klingelbeekseweg, which grew to around 300 in short order and included paratroopers from the 1st, 3rd and 11th Parachute Battalions. The numbers swelled yet further when Buchanan led his party west as many of the South Staffords including Major Cain had used the bridge over the Oosterbeek Laag underpass as a rally point after falling back from *Den Brink*; it is unclear if this was by chance or design.[62]

Colonel Thompson had by now been alerted to the full magnitude of the retreat by a radio message from a forward observer attached to one of the withdrawing units. Alarmed by the prospect of his guns being left on the front line with no protection, he went forward in a Jeep to investigate, accompanied by Major Robert Croot from the Glider Pilot Regiment's G Squadron, and the pair met Buchanan and Cain's combined party on the Benendendorpsweg around 500 yards west of the Oosterbeek Laag underpass.[63] After a hurried conference Thompson placed Buchanan in charge of the parachute unit survivors and ordered him to establish of a defensive perimeter around the nearby junction with the Acacialaan. The 3rd Parachute Battalion contingent, commanded by the irascible Captain Dorrien-Smith, occupied the centre of the line on the junction, with Lieutenant John Williams and the 1st Parachute Battalion to the south and Major Peter Milo and the 11th Parachute Battalion to the north around a crossroad a hundred yards or so up the Acacialaan. Major Robert Cain and the 2nd South Staffords occupied houses just west of the junction, overlooking the Rosander Polder stretching away toward the Lower Rhine and the destroyed railway bridge. The various contingents were in their assigned locations by 14:30.[64] Colonel Thompson then departed for Oosterbeek proper, where he arranged for food and ammunition to be despatched to what the 2nd South Staffords dubbed the Station Oosterbeek blocking position, and visited the 1st Airlanding Brigade's HQ in an effort to secure reinforcements and particularly additional officers. Brigadier Hicks assured Thompson he would assign Major Richard Lonsdale, the 11th Battalion's second-in-command who had been wounded in the hand during the fly-in, and Major John Simonds, commanding the South Staffords' HQ Company, who had spent the night in the Division HQ area.[65] Lonsdale and Simonds do not appear to have been sent out until the following morning, but in the immediate term Hicks was also presumably responsible for despatching Major James Dale and his Glider Pilots from C Squadron to establish an outpost line along the Oosterbeek Laag railway spur at around 15:30; the Glider Pilots had been providing security for the Airlanding HQ since 09:00 that day.[66]

Most of the retreat was channelled along the Benedendorpsweg toward Oosterbeek village but some retired west along the Utrechtseweg including men from the 2nd South Staffords, the 11th Parachute Battalion and Lieutenant Glover's E Troop from the 2nd Airlanding Anti-tank Battery. The latter group paused at the crossroads with the Stationsweg running north to the Oosterbeek Hoog railway crossing and Pietersbergseweg running south to the Hotel Tafelberg. The latter, the Hotel Schoonoord and the Hotel Vreewijk on opposite sides of the crossroads were occupied by 181 Airlanding Field Ambulance and 133 Parachute Field Ambulance as a Divisional MDS, while Division HQ in the Hotel Hartenstein lay only 500 yards further west along the Utrechtseweg. At this point the small party thus appears to have been all that stood between the German units in the western outskirts of Arnhem and the heart of the 1st Airborne Division, temporarily reinforced by Lieutenant Donald Edwards' 17 Platoon from the 2nd South Staffords' C Company, which had spent the night near Division HQ.[67] E Troop's presence rapidly proved fortuitous; Lieutenant Glover was hastily approached by one of the South Staffords deployed further up the Stationsweg who announced that there were 'some bloody Tiger tanks coming'. Glover and reluctant volunteer Gunner Clarke quickly prepared a Jeep to investigate but before the 6-Pounder could be hitched up a 'small tank' nosed out of a side road 250 yards up the Stationsweg; it withdrew after Clarke reportedly scored a direct hit but another appeared shortly thereafter:

> We were going to move the gun…but had only manhandled it halfway across the road outside the Schoonoord Hotel when I saw a tank …appearing over the top of a small rise…I shouted 'Turn the gun, drop the trail and get out of the way'.…I fired three shots at the tank and hit it…Then another came up to pass it, and I hit that as it was passing with another three shots and stopped that. Every time I fired, the gun moved back about fifteen feet because the spade end of the trail wasn't dug in; we were only on the cobbled street.[68]

It is unclear what type of vehicles these were. One source suggests that they had infiltrated west from *Den Brink* but this was unlikely given *Sturmgeschütze Brigade 280* does not appear to have lost its first vehicle until the following day. They may therefore have been the armoured vehicles fired on at the south end of the Dreijenseweg near the Oosterbeek Hoog station by 156 Parachute Battalion's B Company earlier in the day.[69] Wherever the vehicles came from, Gunner Clarke's efforts had the desired effect and there was no further German activity from that quarter.

There was therefore little to stop a determined German thrust into Oosterbeek in the wake of the British retreat from the outskirts of Arnhem, but fortunately for the 1st Airborne Division their opponents had problems of their own. The *ad hoc* German units had also been moving and fighting virtually non-stop for up to forty-eight hours and more importantly, they also had the task of clearing their newly occupied territory – not all the Airborne troops succeeded in joining the general withdrawal to Oosterbeek, and not all of them gave up without a fight. Private Fred Morton from the 3rd Parachute Battalion's MMG Platoon was with seven men under a corporal who ambushed an estimated company of German troops and what was reported as a Tiger tank that passed the pair of barricaded terrace houses they occupied, likely on the Klingelbeekseweg. The initial burst of fire killed seven or eight German infantry, but the paratrooper's single Gammon bomb missed what was probably a *StuG* and intense machine-gun fire from the vehicle drove them upstairs. An hour-long stand-off then ensued, during which two of the defenders were killed making a break for the Lower Rhine via the back door and three more were seriously wounded, one in the stomach. Morton and his comrades were then persuaded to surrender by the German vehicle commander:

He told us we had fought well and that we would be treated well…We came out of the front door but had to step over two Germans we had killed. Their mates didn't take that too kindly. The man ahead of me was hit across the head with a rifle butt, and I got it across the arm. I think it was the tank officer who stopped that. We asked if we could go back for our wounded, but they said they would send their own men in for them.[70]

The Germans were also faced with the problem of rounding up, guarding and moving up to 1,700 prisoners, some of them wounded. Not all were especially cowed either, as Corporal Arthur Hatcher, a member of 16 Parachute Field Ambulance captured at the St Elizabeth Hospital, recalled: 'They herded us all into a corridor but then they had to wait for a lull outside before they could move us out. We were all sat down…with guards standing over us, and somebody started singing "There'll Always Be an England", and everyone joined in. We were still full of confidence and thought we would be relieved any minute and we would be top dog again. The Germans didn't like it, but they didn't stop us.'[71]

With the Germans fully engaged east of the Oosterbeek Laag railway spur, the remnants of the 1st Parachute Brigade were left in relative peace to lick their wounds and reorganise. The hiatus was a welcome respite for the paratroopers and glider soldiers had been moving and fighting virtually non-stop for between twenty-four and forty-eight hours, and the resupply of food and ammunition organised by Colonel Thompson was equally welcome. Despite the piecemeal nature of the retreat discipline remained firm and the return to order after the confusion and isolation of battle also appears to have been well received. An unnamed NCO from the 11th Parachute Battalion said to Thompson, 'Thank God we've got some orders at last; now we'll be alright.'[72]

Men continued to trickle into the defensive perimeter on the Benedendorpsweg junction singly or in small groups as the afternoon wore on into evening, some bringing vehicles and equipment. Sergeant Norman Howes and some men from the South Staffords' A Company came upon two SS with a captured jeep, for instance, 'complete with a Vickers machine gun and a loaded trailer…We took possession of this valuable item and, on arrival, handed it over to Major Buchanan.'[73] By the late evening the position was occupied by around 400 men, 116 to 120 from the 1st Parachute Battalion, forty to forty-six and 150 from the 3rd and 11th Parachute Battalions respectively, and between eighty and a hundred from the 2nd South Staffords.[74] Another party of around fifty South Staffords was despatched to Oosterbeek Old Church to provide security for Colonel Thompson's guns; the latter's Regimental HQ and 1 and 2 Batteries arrived in the area of the Oosterbeek Old Church at 18:30 in a hasty move prompted by German infiltration into their former location near the Hotel Bilderberg.[75] Support was provided by the 2nd South Staffords' MMG and 6-Pounder Platoons which had come up with Major Buchanan, augmented with an unknown number of 6-Pounders and a single 17-Pounder from the parachute unit attachments. However, the Germans appear to have been aware of the new British position and it was not left entirely unmolested. At approximately 14:30 the area was 'heavily stonked' by mortars and *nebelwerfer* rockets, and at 18:00 artillery fire demolished two of the five houses occupied by the 11th Parachute Battalion's B Company, killing several men.[76] The fire was not all one way; Major Cain scattered German troops moving around the train abandoned near the demolished railway bridge using one of his attached Vickers guns.[77]

While the 1st Parachute Brigade's attempt to push through to the Arnhem road bridge was coming to an end east of Oosterbeek, the process was being repeated in the woods north of the town. There the 4th Parachute Brigade was attempting to bypass the impasse along the riverside route by pushing into Arnhem from the north-west, with 156 Parachute Battalion tasked to secure the *Koepel* ridge overlooking the city while the 10th Parachute Battalion secured its left flank on the line of the Amsterdamseweg. By midday 156 Parachute Battalion's effort to secure the intermediate *Lichtenbeek* feature had been stopped along the line of the Dreijenseweg running north from the Oosterbeek Hoog railway station. On the left Major John Waddy's B Company had been brought up short by murderous crossfire from newly arrived light *flak* vehicles that reduced the Company strength to thirty; the casualties included Major Waddy, who was wounded in the groin. The initial attack, by Major John Pott's A Company on the right, had reached the Dreijenseweg and cleared a number of German positions astride it before degenerating into a game of cat-and-mouse with German half-tracks; ironically the ferocity of Pott's assault was responsible for the Germans bringing up the *flak* guns that decimated B Company. In an effort to avoid being pinned down and destroyed, Major Pott led the survivors of his Company north-east and unexpectedly reached his objective on the *Lichtenbeek* summit without further opposition at around 13:30. At least three paratroopers were so badly wounded they had to be hidden in the undergrowth for recovery later; one of these men, Sergeant George Sheldrake, recalled Pott apologising and saying a prayer over them before moving on.[78] The Germans soon became aware of the tiny enclave in their rear but Major Pott led a counter-charge that rebuffed the first German attempt to dislodge them. This reduced the British able-bodied strength to six, which proved too few to carry out another counter-charge around thirty minutes later. Pott was hit in the right hand and left thigh, fracturing his femur, in the attempt. The Germans then overran the British position and marched away the British walking wounded, leaving Pott with assurances he would be collected later. This did not happen and after being tended by a small party including his batman, whom he then ordered to make their way to safety, Major Pott spent eighteen hours alone on the ridge before being discovered and carried to safety by Dutch civilians.[79]

Brigadier Hackett appears to have spent the morning unaware of the gravity of the situation facing his 10th Parachute Battalion pinned down near La Cabine pumping station, or of the 156 Battalion's deteriorating situation on the Dreijenseweg. That changed with a message from Lieutenant-Colonel Des Vœux reporting that two separate company attacks on the *Lichtenbeek* feature had been repelled with heavy casualties and that as a result 156 Parachute Battalion had 'for the moment shot its bolt'. Hackett responded by ordering Des Vœux to pull back and consolidate at Point 565. Des Vœux appears to have taken the opportunity to despatch the attached No.1 Troop back to the 4th Parachute Squadron RE.[80] Luckily, Point 565 was still occupied by companies from 156 Parachute Battalion and the 7th KOSB and forming of the firm base was underway, if not complete, by 14:00.[81] Hackett's situation was resolved by the arrival of the 1st Airborne Division's commander, possibly while he was dealing with the message from Des Vœux, although Hackett's account suggests he may have been informed of an upcoming attack by the 1st Airlanding Brigade to secure the Oosterbeek Hoog railway crossing by Division HQ beforehand; though there is no mention of such a message in the Division HQ War Diary.[82] As we have seen, Urquhart had left his HQ at the Hotel Hartenstein at 13:30 in one of the Reconnaissance Squadron's armed Jeeps escorted by the Squadron's default commander, Captain David Allsop. As moving along the north side of the railway was judged unsafe the vehicles halted on the south side and Urquhart crossed the embankment on foot, arriving at Hackett's HQ just south-west of Johannahoeve between 14:00 and 14:20 after being strafed by German fighters on the way.[83] Concerned by reports of the 1st Parachute Brigade's lack of progress and German armour approaching from the north, Urquhart brought instructions for Hackett to abandon the effort to move into Arnhem via the *Koepel* feature and withdraw south of the Arnhem–Ede railway line in order to consolidate the Divisional perimeter against attack from the east. The move was to be covered by the 7th KOSB, which was still tasked to hold LZ L for the third glider lift. Once this was accomplished, there was the prospect of a renewed 4th Brigade advance east along the Utrechtseweg to link up with the detached 11th Parachute Battalion before securing the Heijenoord-Diependaal feature north of the railway line, providing the situation was favourable and with Urquhart's explicit approval.[84] Hackett's War Diary implies the idea of 'cutting losses' north of the railway line and reorienting his Brigade advance along the Utrechtseweg was his.[85]

Whoever was responsible, the idea of maintaining or resuming the advance into Arnhem had been overtaken by events, for the 1st Parachute Brigade and attachments were being driven out of Arnhem as Hackett and Urquhart conferred. With regard to the more immediate matter of the withdrawal south of the railway line, Hackett was understandably concerned about the obstacle the railway embankment posed to vehicular traffic, the more so because the Oosterbeek Hoog crossing was in German hands while the Wolfheze crossing, over a mile to the west, had been abandoned as part of the Division's Phase II plan. According to Middlebrook, Urquhart announced he would order Brigadier Hicks to secure the Oosterbeek Hoog crossing, and this was passed on in person when Hicks appeared at Hackett's HQ during the meeting.[86] However, while Hackett's War Diary account records Hicks' arrival, agreement and departure, there is no mention of Hicks's absence or any planning for an attack in the 1st Airlanding Brigade War Diary.[87] It is also difficult to see what troops Hicks was supposed to perform the attack with, given that the 7th KOSB was holding LZ L, the 1st Border was fully occupied maintaining the western side of the Divisional perimeter and the only troops on the eastern face were a relative handful of survivors from the fighting in the outskirts of Arnhem proper; this was also around the time Lieutenant-Colonel Thompson was meeting with Hicks at the latter's HQ in an effort to garner reinforcements and supplies for the emergency backstop position on the Benedendorpsweg. It is possible Hicks may therefore have turned up at 4th Parachute Brigade HQ in search of Urquhart after speaking to Thompson, but the clash of timings and more especially the lack of mention in any but Hackett's War Diary account is puzzling. Either way, the episode strongly suggests that Urquhart had yet to fully grasp the reality of the situation he and his reduced Division were facing.

Hackett set about organising his general withdrawal as soon as Urquhart departed for Division HQ at approximately 15:00, but he appears to have then been distracted by a message from Division HQ reporting that the 1st Airlanding Brigade had suffered either a reverse or threat of such south of the railway line. Hackett's reaction to this news was to order the 10th Parachute Battalion to break contact immediately, withdraw west and secure the railway crossing at Wolfheze.[88] The precise timing of the order to the 10th Battalion's is unclear but was likely shortly after 15:00, given that the information from Division HQ reportedly arrived at 'about 1500 hrs', and that the 10th Battalion was only part way across the landing area when the glider landing commenced just after 16:00.[89] Orders for the general withdrawal were issued at 16:00 to the commanders of the 7th KOSB and 4th Parachute Squadron RE, Lieutenant-Colonel Payton-Reid and Major Perkins respectively, in person at an O Group at Hackett's Forward HQ, and via radio to Colonel Smyth and 156 Parachute Battalion at the same time. The paratroopers were given fifteen minutes to move, the KOSB thirty and the latter was also tasked to cover the withdrawal and provide protection for Major Perkins in getting all 4th Parachute Brigade and Polish motor transport south across the railway embankment.[90] Although it was not apparent at the time, these precautions were to prove simultaneously fortuitous and potentially disastrous.

As it was, the order to break contact reached the 10th Parachute Battalion while it was pinned down astride the Amsterdamseweg by fire from numerous German machine-guns, mortars and under attack by armoured vehicles near La Cabine pumping station. Adjutant Nicholas Hanmer, schooled in the principle that disengagement while under attack was akin to suicide, was appalled and shouted across to Colonel Smyth 'We can't withdraw from here – the Jerries are all around us', to which his Battalion commander responded laconically 'We've got our orders – let's get going.'[91] Captain Queripel's A Company was brought across the Amsterdamseweg under cover of smoke and the Battalion began to withdraw south-west through the woods toward LZ L, covered by elements of D Company, although the attackers fell upon Major Peter Warr's B Company as it prepared to move. This sparked a close-quarter fight during which Warr shot a German officer demanding his surrender from 'six yards range'.[92] Despite this and a number of men becoming separated in the confusion, the bulk of the 10th Battalion drew clear into the open landing zone despite German fire; Captain Hanmer noted that there was 'much fire from the northern edge and it caused many casualties…Lieutenant Miles Henry, the Intelligence Officer, was walking next to me when he was hit by a burst of machine-gun fire. I remember that he was hit in the back by such a heavy burst that bits of haversack were coming out of his front. I wanted to put his body in the jeep, but the CO said we had to leave him.'[93] Lieutenant Henry had been assisting Sergeant-Major Robert Grainger in carrying a Lance-Corporal Horton, who had been wounded in the kneecap and thigh. All three men were felled by the same burst of fire. Henry was 'knocked fifteen feet' by the impact, Horton was wounded for the third time and Grainger was wounded in the ear by a round that pierced his Airborne helmet; the latter two recovered but Henry died later of his wounds.[94] It was around this time, with the 10th Parachute Battalion stretched out diagonally across the landing area, that the third lift began to arrive.

The first element of the third lift to approach Arnhem, albeit only slightly ahead of the glider lift, was the 164-strong resupply flight heading for DZ V, almost two miles east of LZ L on the north side of the Amsterdamseweg. Consisting of 101 Stirlings from RAF No. 38 Group and sixty-three Dakotas from No. 46 Group, the supply flight had taken off when visibility improved after midday, using the shorter southern route in an effort to make up for lost time; this took the formation over Kent and across the Channel to Ostend before turning north at Ghent and flying up the airborne corridor at 1,500 feet. Two aircraft, both Stirlings, were lost in the fly-in. Flight-Sergeant Ray Hall's machine from No. 295 Squadron was hit by anti-aircraft fire after straying too close to the German front line near Ostend and crashed killing all eight men aboard.[95] The second, from No. 190 Squadron, was also brought down by *flak*, again with no survivors. This was just the beginning.

By the time the supply flight neared Arnhem, the Germans had pulled together an integrated anti-aircraft defence system around the city, linked into the extensive *Luftwaffe* early warning system. Observers in German-held Dunkirk were able to identify Allied transport formations using the southern cross-Channel route and warn of their approach up to an hour before they reached Arnhem. In conjunction with the *Luftwaffe* liaison officer attached to *II SS Panzerkorps*, this permitted 300 fighter aircraft from *3 Jagd-Division* to be vectored onto air and ground targets as required from airfields at Dortmund, Paderborn and Gutersloh among others; the *Jagd-Division* had been temporarily released by *Oberbefehlshaber (OB) West* to participate in operations in Holland, and it was this initiative that prompted the widespread strafing attacks on the 1st Airborne Division. The warning system and intelligence also proved useful on the ground, with the arrival of *Luftwaffe Oberstleutnant* Hubert von Svoboda and his *FlaK Brigade* early on 19 September. Apparently consisting of the 88mm gun-equipped *FlaK Regiment 46* augmented with smaller detachments equipped with 20mm, 37mm and 105mm pieces, the Brigade had travelled the sixty or so miles from its various static locations in the Ruhr towed by a variety of vehicles including gas-powered trucks and agricultural tractors. On arrival three detachments were assigned to *9 SS Panzer Division*, and were presumably the source of the light *flak* guns that had turned the tide for *Kampfgruppe* Bruhn on the Dreijensweg. As a further centralisation measure von Svoboda was placed in command of all anti-aircraft units in the Arnhem area.[96]

As a result, No. 46 Group's Dakotas flew into a wall of anti-aircraft fire as they approached DZ V from the south at their drop height of 900 feet. Two machines from the front of the formation were shot down almost immediately. One, from No. 575 Squadron, went down in a German military cemetery just north of Arnhem while the other, flown by Pilot-Officer Leonard Wilson from No. 271 Squadron, narrowly missed a number of 20mm guns deployed on the Amsterdamseweg alongside the DZ; Wilson was killed but his navigator and three of the RASC despatchers aboard managed to bale out.[97] RCAF Pilot-Officer Brock Christie from No. 48 Squadron belly-landed his stricken machine near Wolfheze by the railway spur running north to Deelen airfield without fatalities, although three of the four RASC despatchers were injured by unsecured supply panniers; all aboard were captured apart from Christie and his co-pilot. The fourth Dakota to be hit was piloted by Flight-Lieutenant David Lord, also from No. 271 Squadron, ten minutes or more south of Arnhem, the *flak* setting the starboard engine ablaze and damaging the fuselage. Lord maintained heading by formating on Wing-Commander Basil Coventry's Dakota from No. 512 Squadron, so closely that the latter's radio operator, Flying-Officer Stanley Lee, feared they would collide. Lord maintained station while Coventry overflew DZ V without delivering his load, possibly having figured out that the DZ was in German hands, and remained in place as the anti-aircraft fire grew more intense and Coventry wheeled round for a second run, this time onto LZ S. Both machines succeeded in dropping their loads before disaster overtook Lord's Dakota, as described by Flying-Officer Lee: 'Then a white aircrew parachute came from it, and at the same time the wing broke and the Dakota seemed to fold around the starboard engine, with the two wing tips almost meeting. The wing dropped off, and the rest of the aircraft half-rolled on to its back and dived into the ground. There were no more parachutes.'[98] The wreckage landed near Reijers-Camp Farm with all crew still aboard except the navigator, Flight-Lieutenant Harry King, who was thrown clear when the aircraft broke up; he linked up with men from the 10th Parachute Battalion after landing. Flight-Lieutenant Lord was awarded a posthumous Victoria Cross but the supplies delivered at such cost likely fell into German hands, as LZ S had been abandoned the previous night as part of the 1st Airborne Division's move east to its Phase II locations.[99]

No. 38 Group fared even worse, losing six Stirlings during the run in or shortly afterwards. Two pilots were killed at the controls of their aircraft, Wing-Commander Peter Davis, commanding No. 299 Squadron and Squadron-Leader John Gillard from No. 190 Squadron; the former's aircraft was destroyed when anti-aircraft fire ignited containers full of petrol loaded in the bomb-bay.[100] Another Stirling piloted by Flying-Officer Geoffrey Liggins, also of No. 299 Squadron, was hit in a port engine and tried to put down on the Lower Rhine but came to rest behind a dyke near Driel on the south bank. The crew were pulled from the burning wreck by Albert, Cora and Reit Baltussen and three members of a Red Cross team from Driel with great difficulty as all the crewmen were injured, the bomb aimer and wireless operator especially badly: the former had suffered two broken arms and a mangled foot and the latter had a broken back. The ambulatory airmen were swiftly concealed before German troops arrived to investigate, some in a nearby brickworks and others in a handy culvert, while the two seriously injured men were transferred to the town hospital by horse and cart where they were cared for by the town's female physician, a Dr. Van de Burg.[101] A seventh Stirling crash-landed in Holland, and an eighth and two Dakotas made emergency landings in Belgium. In all, nine Stirlings and four Dakotas were shot down and of the 100 men aboard them fifty-two were killed or subsequently died of wounds, thirty-nine were captured, six parachuted into the coalescing Airborne perimeter at Oosterbeek, and three evaded capture to reach friendly territory. Of the 152 aircraft that returned to base, ninety-seven had sustained *flak* damage. Some of the lost personnel had been travelling as sight-seeing passengers including a staff officer from No. 38 Group HQ, Squadron-Leader Cecil Wingfield, and the only Royal Navy sailor to die at Arnhem, Air Mechanic Leonard Hooker, who was on leave and flying with a friend from No. 196 Squadron.[102]

To add insult to terrible injury the vast bulk of the supplies delivered at such cost were lost because DZ V was in German hands, as were the drop and landing zones used for the first and second lifts. Urquhart's warning and request for a change of venue, transmitted in the morning, had not been acted upon and attempts to attract the attention of the supply aircraft using 'yellow smoke, yellow triangles and every conceivable means' were unsuccessful, not least because the aircrew had been briefed to treat such distractions as enemy ruses and ignore them.[103] The matter was complicated by the fact that *9 SS Panzer Division* HQ had obtained a copy of the British ground marking instructions from a captured officer. These were swiftly translated by the Division intelligence officer, *Hauptsturmführer* Gerhard Schleffler, and put to good use. According to one estimate 369 of the 390 tons of supplies delivered on 19 September fell into German hands, and British supplies became an important element in supplying the German units engaging the 1st Airborne Division for the remainder of the battle.[104] A *Luftwaffe* NCO involved in the ground fighting referred to his comrades undertaking 'discovery tours' in search of stray British containers, the contents of which placed them on '"separate rations" and [they] were no longer required to rely on their field kitchens. The best and finest tinned food that you only dared dream of – cigarettes and chocolate to go with it of course – all these treasures fell from the sky.'[105] Watching the misdrop was perhaps most agonising for Lieutenant Cecil Speller and his men from the 21st Independent Parachute Company's No. 2 Platoon, who were tasked to set up the EUREKA homing beacon and markers on the inaccessible DZ V, although the Company's unofficial history refers to the Pathfinders assisting RASC crews in recovering some supplies.[106] The latter were presumably from 250 (Airborne) Light Composite Company RASC and the commander of the latter's 2 Platoon, Captain Desmond Kavanagh, also mounted a motorised attempt to reach the German-held DZ employing four Jeeps and trailers and around twenty-four men from his Platoon. The plan was for a high-speed run out from Oosterbeek across the Oosterbeek Hoog railway crossing, but the lead vehicle was hit by a large-calibre round from the south end of the Dreijenseweg shortly after crossing the tracks. The following Jeeps were travelling too fast to avoid the resultant wreckage and the entire convoy became entangled in the ensuing pile-up. Five men were killed in collisions or in the firefight that followed including Captain Kavanagh, who was last seen covering his men's withdrawal with a Bren gun.[107]

The parachute element of the third MARKET lift, consisting of Major-General Stanislaw Sosabowski's 1st Polish Independent Parachute Brigade, was therefore fortunate not to be delivered to its scheduled drop zone just south of the Arnhem road bridge as planned. Brigade HQ, the 2nd Battalion and part of the 3rd Battalion were to be carried by the US 314th Troop Carrier Group from its base at Saltby in Leicestershire, while the 315th Troop Carrier Group lifted the 1st Battalion and the balance of the 3rd from Spanhoe, twenty miles to the south in Northamptonshire.[108] The Poles embarked on the hour's drive from their billets around Stamford and Peterborough at 06:00 in anticipation of a 08:00 departure, given that the aircrew briefing was scheduled for 05:00.[109] The airfields were wrapped in fog however, and take-off was postponed until 10:00, leaving the keyed-up paratroopers kicking their heels around the C-47s. The Poles were a matter of some curiosity to the US personnel, as the commander of the 310th Troop Carrier Squadron noted: 'I didn't have much personal contact with the Polish paratroopers. They impressed me as being mad as hell at the Germans…they had a personal grudge, and were eager to get on with what they had to do. They didn't speak my language, and I didn't speak theirs.'[110] The Poles' discontent was heightened by knowledge of the concurrent Warsaw Rising, which had begun on 1 August. The language barrier fed the resultant frustration when take-off was postponed again until 15:00; while the fog had lifted and conditions looked clear from the ground, the cloud base was too low for the C-47s to form up safely after take-off. Frustration then boiled over in at least one instance when the drop was finally cancelled until 10:00 the next day: 'They scrubbed the flight for the Poles on September 19th, and the Polish paratroopers were very, very upset. One of them pulled a knife on Captain Sitarz and went after him. It happened very fast, and the two were pulled apart. I guess he went after Sitarz because he represented some kind of authority. He was not making an idle gesture. There was blood in his eye.'[111] Disgruntled and deflated, the Poles were trucked back to their billets at 17:00, leaving Brigade Quartermaster Lieutenant Stefan Kaczmarek with the unenviable task of obeying an angry Sosabowski and persuading his British counterparts to despatch compo rations to the various Brigade locations. It was, Kaczmarek recalled later, 'one of the most difficult moments that I experienced in the war', although he was gratified to find the rations waiting when the paratroopers reached their billets.[112]

Mist and low cloud also delayed the glider lift's planned 07:45 take-off at Down Ampney, Keevil and Tarrant Rushton, an initial two-hour postponement was extended until the weather cleared sufficiently to commence take-offs at around midday.[113] The lift consisted of forty-three gliders, thirty-five of which were Horsas carrying elements of Sosabowski's Brigade. Ten of them were loaded with 6-Pounder guns and fifty-three gunners from the Anti-tank Battery under Lieutenant

Jerzy Halpert; Battery commander Captain Jan Kanty Wardzala and the remainder of the Battery personnel were parachuting in while Halpert was flying in Chalk No. 131 with Bombardiers Nosecki and Roman Kabat. The remaining nine gliders, eight Horsas and a single Hamilcar, were carry-overs from the second lift flown by Glider Pilots from A, B, D and E Squadrons.

Five machines, all Horsas, were lost before making landfall on the Continent. Staff-Sergeant Howard and Sergeant Davy returned to base shortly after take-off when their tug became unserviceable while Staff-Sergeant Aldridge and Sergeant Wright force-landed near Little Marlow, 100 miles or so east of Keevil; Aldridge broke a leg and ankle and was taken to Taplow hospital. Chalk No. 1026 also force-landed at Manston in Kent, although in that instance Staff-Sergeant Stocker and Sergeant Allen emerged unscathed, while Staff-Sergeant Baake and Sergeant Garratt came down in the sea; both men were rescued and returned to base the following day. Staff-Sergeant Henry Blake and Sergeant Lee in Chalk No. 144 were carrying Sergeant Boleslaw Nachman, Lance-Corporal Marian Boba, Cadet Sergeant Edward Holub and presumably a Jeep, given that Nachman and Boba were Sosabowski's drivers. The tow-rope parted when Blake lost station with his tug while flying through cloud and the Horsa just made landfall near Ostend, clipping a roof before crashing to earth and injuring Holub.[114] A further seven gliders were lost in the flight across Holland, six due to their tow-ropes being severed by shrapnel and one after a *flak* shell scored a direct hit on the Horsa's Perspex nose, killing both pilots and causing the machine to disintegrate in mid-air.[115] Another shell burst beneath Lieutenant Halpert's Horsa, 'sending splintered pieces of the floorboards and shrapnel into the ceiling and tearing Nosecki's trousers. Seeing the bombardier's smoking and torn pants, Halpert called to him, and asked if he was hurt. Nosecki felt around and as he replied that he was okay, the glider's pilot let out a groan and grabbed his chest. Putting his bloodied hands back on the control column the pilot insisted that he would get the glider down safely.'[116]

Only an estimated thirty of the forty-three gliders reached their release point at around 16:00, twenty-eight carrying Poles and two with carry-overs from the second lift; both the latter were likely carrying men from the 7th KOSB.[117] Their arrival thus coincided with that of the supply flight, which appears to have attracted the bulk of the anti-aircraft fire. The gliders cast off at the standard 2,500 feet but their rapid descent quickly carried them well below the supply aircraft's 900-foot drop altitude, where they were screened from many guns by buildings and trees. A number of gliders were nonetheless hit by light *flak* and small-arms fire, and one was shot down just short of the LZ as witnessed by an inhabitant of Oosterbeek: 'There was an explosion – the nose of the glider seemed to have been shot off – and I saw soldiers and items of equipment, a jeep perhaps and other items, all falling out. It was a terrible sight.'[118] The same incident may have been witnessed by Polish War Correspondent Marek Swiecicki, who had come in with the second glider lift, although he identified the culprit as a German fighter rather than *flak*. Swiecicki was awaiting the gliders on the railway embankment that formed the southern edge of LZ L near a group of dug-in KOSBs, admiring the peaceful view over the empty field and especially the 'cool and quiet wood' at the other side of the LZ. This bucolic idyll vanished abruptly with the appearance of the gliders, when Swiecicki saw his cool and quiet wood 'erupt in fire. Everything: mortars, machine guns, and even individual rifles…it was very bad…this beautiful field became a curse to those on it.'[119] Most of the Polish gliders made good landings despite suffering numerous hits on the way down; Sergeant Ronald Driver from A Squadron put his Horsa down safely despite having part of its landing gear shot away, for example. Not all were so fortunate. Swiecicki saw one Horsa nose into the ground; this was probably the same incident involving a Horsa piloted by Staff-Sergeant John West and Sergeant James Bonham from C Squadron witnessed by Sergeant Driver:

> The pilot made a perfect touchdown, but suddenly its nose dug in, throwing up a wave of earth that obscured the fuselage, so that only the tail could be seen sticking up at a crazy

angle…We started frantically to dig away the soil, clods of earth, pieces of plywood and Perspex etc., until we came across a piece of uniform and pulled out one of the pilots. He was, of course, dead. We redoubled our efforts to find the other but were unsuccessful.[120]

What happened next was largely dependent on which part of the LZ the individual glider came to rest. Staff-Sergeant Ralph Bishop found the 'crackle of small arms fire' the only overt sign of enemy activity while his Horsa's tail was detached and the Jeep within unloaded.[121] The experience of others was more fraught, however. After assisting in the uneventful unloading of a Jeep and trailer from Chalk No. 120, Lieutenant Waldemar Grabowski despatched Bombardier Jozef Oprych on a motorcycle to spread a rally order; a strafing Messerschmitt 109 shot the motorcycle from under Oprych, badly wounding him in the leg and leaving him pinned down by fire from the woods to the north. Lieutenant Halpert and Bombardier Nosecki's Chalk No. 131 ended up near the north edge of the landing zone with Nosecki firing a Bren at German troops in the nearby woods while Halpert tended the wounded pilot. Nosecki also heard Oprych's cries for help and after dealing with the Germans firing on the wounded man was able to direct a passing Jeep carrying British medical orderlies to Oprych's location.[122]

Arguably the most unfortunate were the two Horsas carrying the British carry-overs from the second lift. Through an oversight the glider pilots had not been issued with amended flight plans and came down as originally intended on German-held LZ S. Sergeant Jock Macdonald's Horsa from E Squadron, likely carrying part of the 7th KOSB Mortar Platoon, was immediately surrounded and all aboard were taken prisoner; as Sergeant Macdonald put it later, 'It was just a damned debacle; we were just sitting ducks waiting to be plucked.' The occupants of the other glider appear to have managed to reach friendly territory.[123] Back on LZ L the initial stage of the landing progressed reasonably well despite the German strafing and ground fire, and the withdrawal of the 10th Parachute Battalion across the landing area does not appear to have been particularly problematic either. As Captain Nicholas Hanmer noted: 'The gliders were coming in from the south, but it was a large piece of ground, and there was no need to get out of their way.'[124] The situation was considered sufficiently secure for part of the 7th KOSB's B and D Companies to leave their positions on the south-eastern and north-eastern edges of the LZ respectively to assist with unloading the gliders. The 7th KOSB War Diary noted, 'From the Bn's point of view there was nothing, at this time, to indicate that we had more than a temporary check, nor that any change of plan was imminent.'[125] All that changed when elements of *Kampfgruppe* Krafft emerged from the woods lining the north side of the landing zone.

After its fights with the 1st Airborne Reconnaissance Squadron near Wolfheze and the 3rd Parachute Battalion column west of Oosterbeek in the afternoon and evening of 17 September, *Bataillon* Krafft had been withdrawn north to Deelen airfield to reorganise. At some point Krafft's 2 *Kompanie* was transferred to *Kampfgruppe* Möller in exchange for two *Kriegsmarine* units, *Flottenstamm Regiment 1* and *Marine Regiment 642*, and 10 *Kompanie* from *Polizei Regiment 3*. The expanded unit was also upgraded to *Kampfgruppe* status and moved to a north-western suburb of Arnhem before being tasked to advance on *Kampfgruppe* Bruhn's right flank in the afternoon of 19 September 1944. According to one source, Krafft's initial objective was the line of the Amsterdamseweg, after which he was to exploit southward to the Arnhem–Ede railway line, although another refers to the latter being the objective from the outset.[126] Whichever, the advance began in mid to late afternoon and Krafft's men reached the Amsterdamseweg at some point before 16:00 before pushing into the 500-yard-wide strip of woods on its southern boundary. The 7th KOSB's A Company was deployed on the north-west sector of the landing area perimeter but the German line of advance appears to have passed between it and D Company in the north-east corner and Krafft's men were thus able to engage the withdrawing 10th Parachute Battalion and then the gliders as they appeared from the south; Krafft ordered his 4 *Kompanie* and *Obersturmführer* Günther Leiteritz's 9 *Kompanie* to move forward and attack immediately.

The emergence of the German troops onto the landing zone caused considerable alarm, not least because they were accompanied by at least one vehicle, as witnessed by Captain Hanmer: 'I saw a German wheeled vehicle come out of the trees, right up to one glider, and it fired straight into the glider; it all looked pretty horrific.'[127]

Responsibility for marking the landing zone lay with Lieutenant David Eastwood and No. 1 Platoon from the 21st Independent Parachute Company, which had spent the night at the Company's overnight location, a large house called *St. Paulastichting* just south of the Arnhem–Ede railway line, approximately 500 yards west of the Oosterbeek Hoog station. Staking out the marker panels, deploying the wind-indicator smoke pot and setting up the EUREKA homing beacon was complete by 09:30, thirty minutes before the gliders were scheduled to arrive, with operator Private Tommy McMahon and another Pathfinder using a convenient dung heap as camouflage for the beacon. The Platoon then dug trenches inside the woods bordering the LZ, apart from Sergeant Ronald Kent and No.1 Section, which established an outpost on the northern edge; this was handed over to an unidentified scratch force of KOSBs shortly before the gliders arrived.[128] The Pathfinders were also tasked to guide the Poles off the landing zone, but this proved less than straightforward. While the Poles may have been expecting some ground fire, they were not expecting to land in the midst of a fighting withdrawal with enemy troops and vehicles debouching onto the LZ, and they can therefore be forgiven for sometimes shooting first and asking questions later.

Interestingly, the 21st Independent Company accounts make no mention of such occurrences despite referring to members of No. 1 Platoon 'haring around' among the surviving Poles and pilots directing them south to the strip of woodland bordering the railway line.[129] Company Sergeant Major Lashmore from the 10th Parachute Battalion's Support Company was last seen running toward a group of Poles waving a yellow silk identification panel, and Cholewczynski refers to some Poles firing on men from the KOSB as they came forward to assist in unloading, while others ran toward Krafft's men in search of cover.[130] The language barrier compounded the problem as many of the Poles were unable to understand advice and instructions shouted by their British counterparts; a group of Glider Pilots interviewed by Cholewczynski years later remembered being fired on by Poles after shouting for them to 'come' in a cod-Polish accent, without realising how similar this sounded to the German '*komm*'.[131] Nor was the friendly fire all Pole-on-British or vice versa. The 10th Battalion's QM, Lieutenant Joseph Glover, who was organising a water point on the LZ, saw Lieutenant Paddy Radcliff from the Battalion's MMG Platoon killed by one of his own guns.[132] This may have been troops moving near the 4th Parachute Brigade's Forward HQ shooting wildly in response to intense German fire from the north, as noted by Hackett.[133]

The Germans did not have it all their own way. *Obersturmführer* Leiteritz was killed with a large number of his men by concentrated fire from the 7th KOSB's D Company and Battalion HQ after pushing 9 *Kompanie* too far out into the open LZ; the KOSB War Diary refers to Major Alexander Cochran and Drum-Major Tait personally killing twenty Germans with Bren guns while another account refers to Provost-Sergeant Andrew Parker making good use of a Vickers.[134] The Pathfinders of No. 1 Platoon also wrought 'considerable execution' among the advancing Germans with their three Bren guns, and Lieutenant Eastwood despatched Sergeant Ron Kent and Private Paddy Gamble to try and raise a counter-attack from British troops seen withdrawing west along the line of the railway; their request was refused by an unidentified officer who insisted his orders were to 'get back to Wolfhezen [sic] and regroup and that's where we're going'.[135]

In the absence of assistance Lieutenant Eastwood therefore held on until it was clear the Germans were about to launch a major attack on his location, then withdrew directly south across the railway embankment to the relative safety of the dense woods between the railway line and the Utrechtseweg. A Polish officer attempted to co-opt some of the Pathfinders into manhandling a 6-Pounder onto the embankment; he was disabused of the notion when they pointed out that there was no ammunition for the gun – and it was missing a breechblock. Eastwood headed east toward Oosterbeek after conferring with an unnamed officer heading for Wolfheze in a Jeep and regained the Independent Company's main position on the Graaf Van Rechterenweg shortly after nightfall.[136] Predictably, Krafft's self-serving after-action report referred to the unfortunate Leiteritz meeting a hero's death after suffering 'some very bad luck with his tactics', and again exaggerated the British strength ranged against him in order to cover the fact that his attack did not push as forcefully as it could have; the KOSB's fire was not part of a series of 'concentric counter-attacks on both flanks' as claimed, but was actually the precursor to a British withdrawal west across the landing area in the wake of the 10th Parachute Battalion.[137] Nonetheless, Krafft's attack had done a good job of interfering with the glider landing. Of the eight 6-Pounder guns that made it to the landing area, only three and a total of five Jeeps were unloaded from the estimated twenty-eight gliders that put down on LZ, and one of the guns was commandeered from Lieutenant Halpert by a British officer before leaving the landing area.[138] The remaining gliders were abandoned to be looted and some burned by the SS, who remained active on the LZ until dusk.

The understandable concentration on the drama and confusion of the Polish glider landing has obscured the more important question of precisely how the 4th Parachute Brigade found itself in the extremely vulnerable position it did, especially as Hackett had worked out the details of the withdrawal across the Arnhem–Ede railway line with Urquhart relatively well in advance. The reasons lie in the manner in which the withdrawal was implemented. The initial catalyst for it was information 'received from Div about 1500 hrs [that] indicated some reverse or at least threats of such in [the] area south of ry [railway]', to quote Hackett's War Diary account.[139] But the Division HQ War Diary makes no mention of such a message and the western side of the Divisional perimeter remained quiet until about 19:00. Hackett's immediate reaction to this information was based on two things: his understandable concern that neither the Wolfheze nor Oosterbeek Hoog railway crossings were in British hands, and Reconnaissance Squadron reports of enemy activity in the area of Renkum and Heelsum on the 1st Airlanding Brigade's front. Based on this, he ordered '10 Bn to disengage forthwith and make for WOLFHEZEN [sic] ry crossing, seize and hold it for Bde to cross if necessary'.[140] This was not a new idea, for Hackett had raised it in his discussion with Urquhart and filed it away as a backstop option in case the mysterious 1st Airlanding Brigade attack failed to secure the Oosterbeek Hoog crossing.

The problem here is that Hackett's War Diary account does not provide timestamps for specific events and more importantly, appears to leaven abbreviated notes taken at the time with material gleaned after the event. Separating these elements reveals two different narratives. While some parts seem to show he was aware of the 10th Parachute Battalion's situation, other parts and the course of events strongly suggest that this was not the case, and that Hackett was under the erroneous impression that the 10th Parachute Battalion was passively occupying its assigned blocking position on the Amsterdamseweg around a thousand yards west of the Dreijenseweg in the face of light opposition, rather than pinned down and under serious attack near La Cabine pumping station. Hackett's War Diary cites the map reference for the former location and explicitly mentions the 10th Parachute Battalion three times prior to ordering it to Wolfheze, saying it had suffered 'a few cas – but [was] holding [its] own and consolidating', secondly that '10 Bn reported enemy attacks from NE by some inf and normal SP' and thirdly, '156 and 10 reported continuation of fire by one or two SP guns which had been intermittent since about 0830. 10 Bn reported 5 tracked vehs probably SP guns'.[141] None of these observations reflect the gravity of the 10th Parachute Battalion's situation, and the picture of relative quiet it paints would explain why Hackett felt it appropriate to issue a snap order for immediate execution. The reality was that it took at least an hour for the 10th Parachute Battalion to break contact and commence its move, and that delay led to it becoming entangled in the order for the implementation of the general Brigade withdrawal across the Arnhem–Ede railway line.

As we have seen, the order for the withdrawal was issued via an O Group and radio message at 16:00, around an hour after Hackett discussed and finalised the details with Urquhart. The problem in this instance was not the withdrawal per se, but the speed with which it was to be carried out: 156 Parachute Battalion was ordered to move within fifteen minutes of receipt of the withdrawal order and the 7th KOSB within half an hour. These were very short lead times by any measure, let alone for units in close proximity to, or in contact with, the enemy and the 7th KOSB's deadline actually meant starting to abandon the landing zone before the third glider lift was down and clear, given that the gliders only began to land after 16:00. The haste again appears connected to the alleged message from Division HQ regarding the reverse or threat thereof on the western side of the Divisional perimeter, and again seems based on an assumption of relative calm. To be fair, the 7th KOSB's situation *was* calm when Lieutenant-Colonel Payton-Reid left Johannahoeve for Hackett's O Group, but on returning to his HQ he found 'D and A Coys had been strongly attacked and close and fierce fighting was still in progress', courtesy of *Kampfgruppe* Krafft.[142] For his part, Hackett appears to have also been unaware of 156 Parachute Battalion's true situation, for while his War Diary account records ordering the Battalion to consolidate at Point 565 as it had 'shot its bolt', it then refers to promising its support to Hicks for the attack to secure the Oosterbeek Hoog crossing, it records intermittent fire from self-propelled guns and, most curiously of all, that the situation was 'noticeably satisfactory E toward ARNHEM'.[143] This was far from reality for a Battalion reorganising after having two of its three rifle companies decimated by a superior enemy who was preparing to counter-attack; the 156 Battalion War Diary refers to being attacked by enemy patrols, presumably from *Kampfgruppe* Bruhn, at the time the withdrawal order was received.[144] Implementing Hackett's order thus obliged the 7th KOSB and 156 Parachute Battalion to replicate the 10th Parachute Battalion's ordeal by compelling them to withdraw whilst in contact with the enemy.

This then was the series of assumptions, misconceptions and errors of judgement that placed the 4th Parachute Brigade in the worst possible position, with all its constituent units and support elements withdrawing simultaneously at short notice in the face of a fully functioning, and in some instances advancing, enemy. As an unnamed, experienced and angry participant put it, 'You just can't get up and rush away from the enemy in daylight like that…You just can't bloody well do it.'[145] The fight to break contact on the Amsterdamseweg and subsequent enemy fire and clashes while moving across the LZ reduced the 10th Parachute Battalion to around a third of its strength, while the German patrols harassed 156 Parachute Battalion's withdrawal from Point 565 at around 16:15 and may have pursued the paratroopers westward; whether or not, the confusion generated by the urgency of the situation led to 156 Battalion becoming divided in two.[146] The 7th KOSB's C Company made 'an orderly and comparatively easy withdrawal' from Point 565 without incident, but Battalion HQ and D Company then suffered casualties in the fight with *Obersturmführer* Leiteritz's 9 *Kompanie*. A Company was lost virtually in its entirety for Major Buchanan was unable to withdraw south via the LZ as ordered, presumably because of Krafft's presence, so after breaking contact reportedly moved east instead. Caught in the open between areas of woodland, the bulk of the Company and the attached 10 Platoon from C Company was obliged to surrender, with only around thirty men from the rearguard managing to escape.[147] As the Battalion War Diary presciently noted at the time, 'What occurred on the A Company front is shrouded in mystery since no representatives of that Coy appeared at the [Battalion] RV and it can only be assumed that they…were overrun by superior numbers.'[148]

The most serious problems seem to have been connected to the 4th Parachute Brigade's transport elements, the bulk of which appear to have been channelled along the track paralleling the north side of the railway line near Hackett's Forward HQ. The track became jammed with Jeeps and trailers interspersed with the occasional Bren Carrier and high German fire from the fight on the LZ prompted some wild firing in response, especially when German skirmishers approached the south edge of the LZ. Colour-Sergeant Tony Thomas from 156 Parachute Battalion recalled it was 'a good old jam, like Piccadilly Circus at its worst. Some men were abandoning their vehicles and climbing over the embankment, but that was foolish because they stuck out like a sore thumb and were easy targets.'[149] Matters came close to descending into outright panic and Brigade HQ officers had to be sent out in an effort to restore order; as Hackett himself put it, the HQ officers were obliged to employ 'great energy and even violence… to prevent some confusion'.[150] According to Urquhart's account the 'confusion' may have spread as far south as Division HQ:

> There were small parties of hurrying soldiers, obviously uncontrolled, and then twenty or more, under a young officer, dashed across the lawn in front of the Hartenstein shouting 'The Germans are coming!' With Mackenzie, I moved to intercept them. They were young soldiers whose self-control had momentarily deserted them. I shouted at them, and I had to intervene physically…We ordered them back to the positions they had deserted, and I had a special word with the tall young officer who in his panic had set such a disgraceful example.[151]

The 4th Parachute Brigade only avoided being overrun and destroyed on and around LZ L principally because the Germans lacked the strength and application to press home their advantage. The fact that British discipline held firm in the overwhelming majority of instances was also crucial, as were the sterling efforts of Major Æneas Perkins and the 4th Parachute Squadron RE. Perkins had carried out a personal reconnaissance of the railway embankment most of the way to the Wolfheze crossing immediately after Hackett's O Group and ascertained that it was too steep for vehicles to negotiate apart from two points: a brick and concrete drainage culvert running under the embankment 250 yards east of the Wolfheze crossing which was just wide enough for a Jeep, and a livestock track running up the embankment fortuitously close to where Captain Henry Brown's No. 3 Troop was dug in on the south edge of the LZ. Perkins therefore ordered Lieutenant James Cormie's No. 2 Troop to secure the south end of the culvert and No. 3 Troop to supervise the north end and the farm track; Captain Brown chose to remain at the latter and despatched Lieutenant Norman Thomas and half the Troop to the culvert. At around this time Perkins was informed that the Wolfheze crossing had been secured, possibly by elements of the 10th Parachute Battalion. The crossing should have been in German hands but *SS Bataillon Eberwein* had been badly strafed by *Luftwaffe* fighters as it approached Wolfheze proper around 16:00 and the resultant confusion significantly delayed the German advance; some of the 7th KOSB's transport passed unscathed through the village via the level-crossing after overshooting the improvised crossing points at around this time.[152] Perkins ordered Captain James Smith's No. 1 Troop to take charge of the Wolfheze crossing and sent the Bren Carriers and heavier anti-tank guns there while directing the bulk of the Brigade's Jeeps to the livestock track and culvert. Progress was slow at the culvert as the opening was barely wide enough for a standard Jeep. Those fitted with stretchers proved particularly problematic as the casualties and side-mounted stretchers had to be unloaded, and the delay was compounded by a number of vehicles becoming bogged in the sandy soil at the north end. Captain Brown's party passed half a dozen Jeeps and two 17-Pounders over the livestock track, using eight men to bounce their wheels over the individual rails, and some especially intrepid Jeep drivers managed to coax their vehicles across individually at less steep stretches of embankment.[153]

Major Perkins' Sappers were principally protected in their work by the 7th KOSB's B Company. Lieutenant-Colonel Payton-Reid had assigned the task to Major Michael Forman as his unit was closest to the crossing sites. The remainder of the Battalion successfully broke contact and withdrew across the LZ as ordered shortly after the 16:30 deadline, although in the confusion some elements crossed the railway immediately rather than proceeding west to the Wolfheze crossing as ordered.[154] B Company engaged the German skirmishers from the wood where the 4th Parachute Squadron RE had dug in the previous night. Lance-Corporal O'Neill Berry from Lieutenant Charles Doig's 7 Platoon opened fire with a Bren on a loaded farm cart parked near the track because he 'believed it could be shielding the enemy so…I opened up with a heavy burst of fire. The next instant all I could see was a blinding, hot, searing flash, followed by a deafening explosion. I ducked as bits of trailer and wheels showered among us. I could feel them clattering on my helmet.' Reacting quickly, Lieutenant Doig then led a counter-attack that drove the surviving Germans out of the wood.[155] The cart was actually the one commandeered the previous day by Captain Brown to carry No. 3 Troop's allotment of Hawkins Mines, and contained in the region of 120 pounds of high explosive. Ironically, the blast almost did for Brown as he stood atop the embankment nearby supervising the livestock track crossing: 'Suddenly there was a terrific explosion and I was blown off my feet backwards on to the rails. I was stunned and I think momentarily knocked out…Fortunately my steel helmet protected my head as it hit the railway line. I pulled myself together feeling rather groggy and looked for my team of men.'[156]

Major Forman's B Company was not alone in covering the withdrawal, for others also turned to fight on their own initiative. The Polish 6-Pounder and crew taken from Lieutenant Halpert's depleted Battery was commandeered by Captain Peter Barron from the 2nd Airlanding Anti-tank Battery, who appears to have ordered the Poles to dig in close to the railway embankment near the Wolfheze crossing; according to Hackett the gun was abandoned and Barron 'put a useful scare-the-crows shoot against the advancing Bosche'.[157] It is unclear if he was acting on orders, on his own initiative or was simply cut off, but Captain Queripel and a group from the 10th Parachute Battalion's A Company occupied another finger of woodland projecting into the landing zone midway between Major Forman's position and the Wolfheze crossing, where they were joined unbidden by a number of men from other units. Wounded in the face during the earlier battle on the Amsterdamseweg, Queripel was wounded again in both arms in the ensuing fight, likely by German mortar fire, and on at least one occasion returned a German stick-grenade thrown into the drainage ditch being used as a makeshift trench by the paratroopers. When the position became untenable Queripel ordered the survivors of his little band to withdraw without him despite their protests, and was last seen providing covering fire with his automatic pistol and hand grenades gathered from the remainder of the group. He was posthumously awarded the Victoria Cross for his gallantry.[158] The ferocity of the British resistance and the onset of darkness concealed what was happening from *Generalleutnant* von Tettau to the west and *Hauptmann* Bruhn and *Hauptsturmführer* Krafft on the spot, and the opportunity to destroy the 4th Parachute Brigade and push into the virtually undefended heart of the 1st Airborne Division's area thus slipped away unnoticed. Krafft did not miss the opportunity for more self-aggrandisement however, and wrote up what can be described as a hesitant pursuit and harassment at best as a daring action against a superior force that had to be broken off due to 'concentric [British] counter-attacks on both…flanks'.[159]

Whilst Forman, Barron and Queripel's little bands and doubtless other sadly unrecorded groups and individuals stubbornly battled the Germans on the landing zone, much of the remainder of the 4th Parachute Brigade slipped across the railway to temporary safety in the woods to the south. Despite the confusion and urgency of the situation the crossing was also carried out relatively quickly. Hackett stayed back to supervise the evacuation accompanied by his Intelligence Officer, Captain George Blundell, and a detachment from the Brigade Defence Platoon under Captain Edmund James. The remainder of Brigade HQ was despatched to establish a defensive perimeter at Point 232, a track junction 200 yards or so south of the railway; the move was complete by dusk.[160] The 2nd Airlanding Anti-tank Battery lost three guns and a large number of personnel including the commander of X Troop, Lieutenant George Paull, but four 6-Pounders from G and H Troops reached Oosterbeek safely, along with two of X Troop's 17-Pounders. The latter were probably those bounced across the rail tracks by

Captain Brown's party. Another 17-Pounder was reportedly abandoned atop the embankment when the crew was hit by German machine-gun fire, and one source refers to a fourth using the Wolfheze crossing.[161]

The infantry units were in a more sorry state. Lieutenant-Colonel Smyth arrived in the fortuitously unoccupied Wolfheze with around eighty men from the 10th Parachute Battalion including Major Peter Warr and Captain Benjamin Clegg from B Company and Quartermaster Lieutenant Glover. They were joined by a party led by Major George Widdowson and Adjutant Captain Hanmer, which swelled Smyth's force to about 250 including a number of men from other units, and another group led by Captain Cedric Horsfall from D Company turned up near Point 232 in the small hours of the following morning. Smyth set about preparing the village for defence while Major Warr drove around the streets in a Jeep warning the residents to take shelter; many preferred to move out into the surrounding woods.[162] Lieutenant-Colonel Des Vœux led 156 Parachute Battalion over the embankment near the livestock track but a mix-up led to half of B Company, a platoon from C Company and the whole of Support Company continuing along the railway line to Wolfheze, where they fell in with the 10th Parachute Battalion. The remainder, around 270 strong, reached Point 232 at around 19:00 and were ordered to dig in along a line running north to the railway line, where they endured intermittent mortar fire and rebuffed several German patrols.[163] After successfully breaking contact on the northern edge of the LZ, the 7th KOSB headed for a pre-arranged rendezvous in the woods south of the railway line about a mile east of the Hotel Wolfheze, although there was again confusion in crossing the embankment and C Company appears to have used the Wolfheze crossing. The latter was nonetheless present at the RV by c. 17:30 along with D Company, reduced to two Platoons, and a few men from B Company. On being informed that Major Forman and the bulk of B Company were located nearby, Colonel Payton-Reid conducted an unsuccessful personal search that almost ended in him being cut off by German patrols. The object of the search had in fact rallied to the Hotel Wolfheze proper, where they remained awaiting orders until the afternoon of the following day. In the meantime Colonel Payton-Reid had also been unsuccessful in another quest to locate Hackett's Brigade HQ for further instructions and at that point he decided to cut his losses. Despatching Battalion second-in-command Major John Coke ahead to contact 1st Airlanding Brigade HQ for orders, he led his depleted Battalion eastward through the woods, arriving at Division HQ without further enemy contact at 19:00.[164]

This suggests that it may have been feasible for the remnants of the 4th Parachute Brigade to move straight back to the Divisional perimeter rather than spending the hours of darkness isolated in Wolfheze and the woods east of the town. It is unclear who was responsible for the decision to halt. Hackett's War Diary account suggests the decision came from Division HQ:

I discussed at some length with Div by RT advisability of moving during the night towards our final location. I wanted to get integrated into the Div & fear anie [sic] Cooper business in the trees. I was quite happy to stay but would have preferred to move to a villa near final location at say 2300 hrs, by then 10 Bn would be fit to do so in good order. Div deprecated a move but said I was to send recce parties in by night and follow at first light. I saw nothing to be gained out of recce parties in the dark and it was agreed in the end that I should move the Bde at first light.[165]

However, while Urquhart's account refers to Hackett organising his brigade 'for a march at first light into the divisional area' there is no mention of such a discussion or, more importantly, any issuing of instructions.[166] This is also the case with the official records, with the only reference to the 4th Parachute Brigade in the Division Signals record being routine notations regarding radio contact and signal strength taken mid-morning and late evening.[167] More pertinently, the Division HQ War Diary does not refer to such a discussion either, only to the

4th Parachute Brigade being unable to disengage at 19:25 after crossing the Arnhem–Ede railway line and that the opposition encountered 'would prevent movement during darkness'; a second entry four-and-a-half hours later reported that Brigade HQ and 156 Parachute Battalion had succeeded in reaching an unspecified 'pre-arranged area', presumably Point 232 east of Wolfheze, but were out of touch with the 10th Parachute Battalion.[168] This contradicts Hackett's version, particularly with regard to the 10th Battalion being ready to move by 23:00, as do the Battalion accounts; the 156 Parachute Battalion War Diary specifically refers to being ordered 'to leaguer for the night in a Bde perimeter' at 19:00, and the 10th Parachute Battalion account states that it was not in place until midnight.[169] This all suggests that the remnants of the 4th Parachute Brigade were actually in no fit state to move again after the initial withdrawal from LZ L, and that Hackett was likely guilty of wishful thinking and attempting to put the best face on a bad situation. Be that as it may and apparently unavoidable as it was, holding in place near Wolfheze was to have serious repercussions the following day.

By 18:00 the 4th Parachute Squadron RE was free to make its own withdrawal south across the railway line. Major Perkins' HQ, No. 2 Troop and Lieutenant Thomas' portion of No. 3 Troop therefore moved south to the *Sonnenburg* house on the Division perimeter around 500 yards west of the Hotel Hartenstein. They were mortared en route and on arrival were missing ten men, including Squadron Intelligence Officer Lieutenant George Harris and Squadron Sergeant-Major E. S. J. Marriott. Captain Brown's half of No. 3 Troop had withdrawn from the livestock crossing on their own initiative, under the understandable assumption that their commander had been killed when the cart full of Hawkins mines exploded. On recovering consciousness Brown had actually been swept along in the general withdrawal in a dazed state and fetched up at Division HQ, where he was serendipitously reunited with his men. Staff officers then directed them to the north side of the solidifying Divisional perimeter held by Major Bernard Wilson and the 21st Independent Parachute Company. By 18:00 Brown had been personally guided by Wilson to a sector at the north-east corner of the perimeter just north of the latter's HQ, a large house set in parkland called the *Ommershof*. The Sappers were busy digging in an hour later when they were joined by Captain Smith and No. 1 Troop accompanied by Squadron second-in-command Captain Nigel Thomas, who then assumed command of the entire RE contingent.[170] According to Lieutenant Kenneth Evans from No. 1 Troop, Captain Thomas was unhappy with the Sapper's allocated position on the very north-west corner of the perimeter because it was 'an attrition position protecting the Independent Company'; on the other hand Captain Brown made no reference to any displeasure on Thomas' part in his account of a conversation with the latter regarding the RE contingent's dispositions.[171]

Possibly the most forlorn element of the withdrawal was the Polish 6-Pounder anti-tank gun commandeered by Captain Barron. The Poles appear to have been left to their own devices on the wrong side of the rail line, where they were joined by the badly wounded Bombardier Oprych. He had not been evacuated by the British medical orderlies as his friend Nosecki had assumed, and had spent two hours crawling across the landing zone before stumbling on his comrades in their gun pit. At dusk there was an exchange of fire with a self-propelled gun that appeared from the direction of the Wolfheze; given the location and timing it may have been a *Flammpanzer B2 (f)* from *Panzer Kompanie 224* attached to *SS Bataillon Eberwein*. Whatever it was, the vehicle withdrew after the Poles scored two hits but not before destroying their Jeep with a near miss. With no way of moving their gun, no sign of further guidance or support and further German attack seemingly imminent, the crew decided to get out. After removing and hiding the 6-Pounder's breechblock, the Polish gunners made their way over the railway line, carrying the unfortunate Oprych between them, and spent the remainder of the night dodging German patrols in the woods west of Oosterbeek.

Lieutenant Halpert's remaining four Jeeps and two 6-Pounders enjoyed better luck, reaching the Hotel Hartenstein before being despatched north to join the other five Polish guns that had come in with the second lift the previous day. By dusk they were digging in alongside their comrades on the Oranjeweg, 300 yards north of Division HQ, where the crew of one gun became an object of considerable interest to Captain Thomas' detachment from the 4th Parachute Squadron RE dug in nearby.[172]

By dusk on Tuesday 19 September the 4th Parachute Brigade's effort to penetrate into Arnhem from the north had thus been fought to a standstill, although the British units ensconced in the city had no way of knowing it. Lieutenant Hugh Levien and his eleven-strong party from the 3rd Parachute Battalion's B Company, which had taken shelter with Dutch civilians on the Bakkerstraat after becoming separated during the move into the bridge perimeter at dawn on Monday, had been obliged to surrender. At the central police station the fifteen members of No. 1 Section, 1st (Airborne) Divisional Provost Company remained in place under Sergeant Henry Callaway, accompanied by Private Robert Peatling from the 2nd Parachute Battalion and Sergeant Harry Parker from the 3rd. Despite being completely surrounded by large numbers of German troops, the Military Policemen remained undetected through the day despite shooting and wounding a lone German who attempted to climb the gate into the station yard, and after the prisoners in the cells broke a window and shouted unsuccessfully for help. The only other excitement appears to have been the arrival of two Dutch civilians laden with loot from adjoining shops; they were arrested briefly and then permitted to leave after promising to return with food. This relative calm ended when Sergeant Callaway and an unnamed companion climbed onto the station roof to monitor developments at around 16:00. For reasons that remain unclear one of the pair decided to fire on a nearby party of Germans with a Sten gun, prompting them to storm the police station half an hour later. Sergeant Callaway was killed in the ensuing fight in circumstances that are similarly unclear, with one participant reporting his death in the courtyard entrance, a second at the bottom of the station's main staircase and another claiming he was shot after capture. However Callaway was killed, the rest of No. 1 Section were captured apart from Lance-Corporal Wally Whitmill, Sergeant Parker and Private Peatling. The Lance-Corporal and Sergeant managed to escape detection as the Germans cleared the building by hiding in separate locations and slipped away after dark. Peatling took shelter in the attic where he remained in hiding for forty-two days until discovered by Dutch policemen, one of whom delivered him to the Dutch Resistance where he remained until the end of the war.[173]

At the Arnhem road bridge the non-appearance of the 1st Polish Independent Parachute Brigade on the polder south of the bridge was doubtless greeted with some relief by Major Gough, who had been tasked to storm across the bridge to meet them with his two Reconnaissance Squadron Jeeps and the 2nd Battalion's Bren Carrier. The Poles' absence appears to have remained unknown at Division HQ until Division HQ Signals attempted to establish contact with a No. 22 set tuned to the Polish Brigade's command frequency at 18:02; unsurprisingly the Signals' War Diary said no contact was made, and that subsequently they were informed by an unnamed source that the Polish Brigade's drop had been cancelled.[174]

Tuesday afternoon also began relatively quietly for Private James Sims, safely ensconced in the Mortar Platoon house after his solitary night on the Weertjesstraat traffic island. Tasked by Sergeant Jackman to familiarise himself with the layout of the house and to make himself generally useful, Sims took the opportunity to pick over the rifled remnants of the house for souvenirs before taking post at an upstairs rear window where he overheard a clash with a German patrol, likely involving other elements of Support Company on the other side of the Prinsenhof: 'I could only see out of the top of the window because a large wardrobe had been pulled in front of it. Down the side-road from which I had entered the garden, a battle was going on between airborne and German patrols. Shots, screams, the explosion of hand-grenades and the chattering of automatic weapons drifted up.'[175] The growing shortage of ammunition meant risking moving in the open between buildings, and after being fortified with cherry brandy by Sergeant Smith, Sims found himself recovering an abandoned Bren gun from the traffic island. Both Sims and the gun made it back to safety but Smith's disgust on seeing there was no magazine attached to it suggests he was more interested in ammunition than the weapon. Signalman George Lawson was also ordered to collect ammunition, in this instance from A Company HQ in the White House. Unable to locate Signalman Tony Wareham to assist as ordered, Lawson scrounged a handy shopping basket and raced across the empty street at a speed that 'broke all Olympic records'. After collecting thirty loose rounds and being chivvied by Major Tatham-Warter he was brought up short on the return journey by 'the clatter of boots. I had one up the spout ready if it was a German. But it was Tony and he bellowed out, "Why the hell didn't you wait for me?" and we had an argument, under that bridge, "effing and blinding" at each other. We got that over and scarpered back to our post.'[176]

The pressure on the other side of the bridge ramp was more intense and sustained, as the Germans pressed their advantage on the more isolated British units holding the east side of the perimeter. The 1st Parachute Squadron RE's HQ element holding houses on the Eusebiusbuitensingel fought a three-hour battle during the morning with German infantry and three *Panzer* IIIs from *Panzer Kompanie Mielke*, supported by their fellow Sappers from A Troop and men from the 3rd Parachute Battalion's C Company across the road in the Van Limburg Stirum School. The tanks withdrew after HQ Troop commander Lieutenant Donald Hindley scored a hit on one with a Gammon bomb, leaving their supporting infantry to take shelter in the adjacent house. Fifteen of them were killed by the School garrison whilst attempting to withdraw in small groups over the following hour-and-a-half, and at around midday the latter also eliminated a German mortar team to the north of the School, after patiently waiting for the enemy crew to finish setting up their weapon.[177] Closer to the river sustained fire from other *Panzer* IIIs had obliged Lieutenant Andrew McDermont's 3 Platoon to withdraw from their position on the corner of the Ooststraat and Westervoortsedijk with permission from Captain Tony Frank, but this was not well received by the 2nd Parachute Battalion's newly installed commander: 'Digby Tatham-Warter came walking calmly across from Battalion HQ with his brolly, quite unconcerned about any danger. He was very angry with me for letting McDermont's platoon come back and ordered me to retake the house. I got McDermont's platoon together – fifteen to twenty men only – and they set off from underneath the bridge, all very tired, just shrugging their shoulders and going back.' Captain Frank chose to accompany the attack and the house was duly retaken, although Lieutenant McDermont was wounded in the stomach; Frank dosed him with morphine before evacuation and then took command of the house in time to rebuff a German counter-attack from along the bridge ramp that left four of the attackers dead. Lieutenant McDermont succumbed to his wound three days later.[178]

The mortar knocked out by the garrison of the Van Limburg School pointed to a shift in German tactics, presumably initiated by *Brigadeführer* Harmel. From around midday the British-occupied buildings were targeted in turn by German mortars, artillery and tanks in order to set them on fire before a return to the routine bombardment of the British pocket; the 1st Parachute Squadron recorded eleven direct hits on the Van Limburg School between 12:30 and 15:00, for example.[179] The process had begun the previous afternoon, when the buildings on the riverside Rijnkade occupied by the 2nd Battalion's MMG Platoon were shot up by German light *flak* guns deployed on the south bank of the Lower Rhine; the 20mm fire demolished the flimsier sections of the block and tracer ammunition set fire to what remained, obliging the Vickers teams to hastily evacuate.[180] The Germans also renewed their effort to drive the 1st Parachute Squadron's HQ element out of its foothold on the east side of the Eusebiusbuitensingel, and engaged the Van Limburg School with machine-guns infiltrated into the buildings opposite; the School garrison spent the afternoon identifying and eliminating them one by one. At 16:30 the Germans set light to the block of houses including that occupied by the Squadron HQ, but Lieutenant Hindley's men managed to keep the flames at bay. By 17:00 the only building around the bridge not burning was the Van Limburg School, thanks partly to its isolation and partly to the efforts of a firefighting party stationed on the flat roof tasked to extinguish embers before they could take hold.[181]

Events took a double turn for the worse two hours later with the arrival of two Tiger I tanks from *schwere Panzer Kompanie Hummel*, the arrival of which was likely due to the influence of *Feldmarschall* Walther Model. The commander of *Heeresgruppe B* had been monitoring events at Arnhem closely, visiting *Obersturmbannführer* Harzer's Division command post on the Heselbergherweg in the northern outskirts of Arnhem daily from 18 September; as this was only three kilometres north of the Arnhem road bridge he was likely also aware of the problems encountered by *Brigadeführer* Harmel in clearing Frost's force from the northern end of the structure.[182] The *Kompanie's* fourteen Tiger tanks had entrained at its base in Paderborn around 08:00 and had to unload after twenty-four hours on the move at Bocholt, fifty miles short of Arnhem, owing to damage to the track ahead. Only two vehicles, commanded by a *Leutnant* Knaack and *Feldwebel* Barneki, managed to complete the subsequent road march without breaking down and were assigned to *Kampfgruppe* Brinkmann on arrival in Arnhem in the early evening.[183]

The two Tiger tanks approached the bridge ramp from the north at *c.* 19:00. According to the 1st Parachute Squadron War Diary, one drove onto the ramp, halted and began firing on the Van Limburg School with its main gun at thirty yards' range. The high-velocity 88mm shells blew off the north-west corner of the building at first-floor level, and several passed straight through the structure.[184] Sapper George Needham was on the staircase leading to the attic relaying information from an observing officer when the first shell struck: 'Suddenly, there was a terrific explosion underneath this flight of stairs…We had been used to small-arms fire and mortaring, but it was absolutely stunning when this huge explosion took place. There was dust everywhere, and it took several seconds before I realized what had happened…It says a lot for the quality of Dutch building that the school didn't collapse.'[185] The subsequent movements of the Tigers are unclear. Private James Sims referred to Tiger tanks and supporting infantry moving onto the bridge proper 'trying to bulldoze their way past the still-burning enemy armour blocking the road'; this may refer to the Tiger that shelled the Van Limburg School, although it is unclear how Sims could have seen this from his vantage point in the Mortar Platoon house on the Weertjesstraat.[186] The vehicle's movements for the reported thirty minutes they remained in action are unclear.[187] One Tiger appears to have driven along the Eusebiusbuitensingel on the left of the ramp and shelled the block on the corner of the latter and the Westervoortsedijk occupied by a mixed group from the Division Signals Section and the RAOC Ordnance Field Parks detachment. Private Kevin Heaney was from the latter:

> A shell came whooshing through the open bedroom window and hit the back of the house. The back wall became a pile of rubble, and the floor fell in. One of the signallers, resting on a bed in the back bedroom, came down with the floor and was trapped… his back was broken. Sergeant Mick Walker…climbed down to give him a morphine injection…We then took shelter in the cellar and started hoping for the best.[188]

The other Tiger was likely responsible for bringing the fight spectacularly into the relatively quiet western side of the bridge perimeter.

After his dash to recover the abandoned Bren gun Private Sims was assigned watch at one of the Mortar Platoon house's upper front windows, which involved reclining on a nest of coats and sharing a box of chocolate liqueurs with an adjacent paratrooper. Initially the major distractions were chunks of burning roof timber crashing to the street below and a 'wild eyed soldier' who burst into the bedroom to warn of the fatal consequences of looting rosaries from the house, before disappearing equally suddenly; Sims' veteran companion dismissed the self-appointed messenger as a 'daft bastard'. A stream of tracer bullets then flayed the face of the White House on the opposite side of the Weertjesstraat, held by elements of A Company HQ and the 1st Parachute Squadron's B Troop. Sims took this to be the Germans warning the occupants to evacuate, although it may merely have been a fire control measure to clarify the target in the smoke and dust. Whichever, the occupants responded with a burst of Bren fire and after a five-minute pause a large-calibre shell 'hit a top storey near the roof and the entire building seemed to shake itself like a dog. We could plainly see the riflemen and airborne engineers, caution thrown to the winds, kneeling openly inside the blasted windows, pouring fire down at the Germans.'[189] Sims refers to the shell coming from a self-propelled gun despite having no direct sight of the vehicle, although Corporal Horace Goodrich, a Bren gunner from 1st Parachute Brigade HQ also reported a narrow escape from that type of vehicle: 'The enemy brought up a self-propelled gun to shell our building...After getting off two short bursts, I observed what had all the appearance of a golden tennis ball at the mouth of the SP gun. The next moment I was lying on my back covered in dust and debris.'[190] However, German-based accounts and photographic evidence only record the presence of *SS Panzer Aufklärungs Abteilung 10's* light armour and *Panzer* III & IV tanks from *Kompanie Mielke* at the north end of the Arnhem road bridge and while it is perfectly possible that a self-propelled gun of some kind was present at this time, the evidence strongly suggests that one of *Panzer Kompanie Hummel's* vehicles was responsible for shelling the White House; Frost, for example, refers to German heavy tanks being responsible for shelling the adjacent 2nd Battalion HQ building.[191]

The Tiger was therefore firing either down the length of the Eusebiusbinnensingel or more likely given subsequent events, under the bridge ramp from the Eusebiusbuitensingel. Wherever it came from, the second shell to strike the White House finished the matter, as witnessed by Private Sims:

> We watched in horrified silence as the walls appeared to breathe out before the whole structure collapsed. The roof and floors fell inside and a towering column of flame shot into the sky. A cut-off scream marked the end of many gallant riflemen and engineers. The sudden collapse of such a solid-looking edifice was a terrific shock to our morale, and when...a stream of tracer lashed over our house...we all jumped to our feet and turned towards the door – only to find Sergeant Jackman standing there grinning at us.

Jackman, who had assumed command of the Mortar Platoon on the assumption that Lieutenant Woods had been killed in the White House, told Sergeant Maurice Kalikoff to choose six volunteers to hold the house before ordering the remainder out to dig slit trenches in the back garden. The move proved counter-productive for Sims, who was badly wounded in the left leg by a mortar bomb as he began digging.[192] In the event, the evacuation of the Mortar Platoon house was also somewhat premature, for while the Tiger tanks had inflicted severe damage on the British positions, this was not all one way. By this point there appear to have been two serviceable 6-Pounder anti-tank guns in the bridge perimeter, Sergeant Robson's on the Weertjesstraat and Sergeant O'Neill's on the Eusebiusbinnensingel near the Brigade HQ building. One weapon was machine-gunned whilst attempting to engage the Tigers and it is unclear which gun was responsible for what followed, as Frost's account suggests PIAT gunners may also have been involved.[193] *Leutnant* Knaack's Tiger was hit at least twice, once on the turret, which reportedly injured Knaack and his gunner and once through the muzzle brake of the 88mm gun, rendering it unserviceable; one source suggests the 6-Pounder was manned by an *ad hoc* crew made up of Major William Arnold, commander of the 1st Airlanding Anti-Tank Battery, Battery Captain Arvian Llewellyn-Jones, B Troop commander Lieutenant Philip MacFarlane and a Sergeant Colls.[194] Whoever was responsible, the damage prompted both Tigers to withdraw, with Knaack's vehicle then being sent back twenty-five miles to Doetinchem for workshop repair; *Feldwebel* Barneki's Tiger was to return to the fray the following day.[195]

The withdrawal of the Tigers brought the German attacks on the bridge perimeter to a close for the day, although the effects of the fighting lingered. By 21:00 the fire in the buildings along the Eusebiusbuitensingel was burning out of control and Lieutenant Hindley was obliged to evacuate the survivors of the 1st Parachute Squadron's HQ element to the British-held buildings on the other side of the bridge ramp. It is unclear if any of Hindley's party had been killed, but the Parachute Squadron contingent in the Van Limburg School had lost a dozen wounded in addition to the two dead and twelve wounded from the previous day.[196]

Overall, the day's fighting cost the bridge garrison an estimated nineteen killed and up to 150 wounded including Major Tatham-Warter for the second time, Captain Frank, who handed command of A Company to Lieutenant John Grayburn, and the 2nd Battalion's Padre Captain Bernard Egan.[197] The German mortar fire and shelling abated with the onset of darkness and the Airborne soldiers settled down for their second night at the bridge. The scene was graphically described by Sapper Tom Carpenter from his position on the Weertjesstraat: 'The area around the bridge was becoming a sea of flame. The roar and crackle of flaming buildings and dancing shadows cast by the flames was like looking into Dante's inferno.'[198] The fires had also spread to the two major churches near the British positions and the passing of the night was marked at irregular intervals by the tolling of one of the church bells as it swung freely in the draught generated by the flames.[199]

***

While the 1st Parachute Brigade was being driven out of the western outskirts of Arnhem toward Oosterbeek and the 4th Parachute Brigade was retiring across LZ L through the gliders from the 1st Airborne Division's third lift, Major-General Gavin was launching his first properly configured and officially sanctioned attempt to reach and secure the road and rail bridges over the River Waal in Nijmegen, employing Lieutenant-Colonel Benjamin Vandervoort's 2nd Battalion 505th Parachute Infantry Regiment and part of the Grenadier Guards Group. Gavin's plan involved dividing this force in two, with each group responsible for one of the bridges. The smaller West Force commanded by Grenadier Guards' Captain John Neville was made up of Captain Taylor G. Smith's Company D from the 505th Regiment, augmented by a Troop of four Sherman tanks from the 2nd Grenadier Guards No. 3 Squadron and an infantry platoon from the 1st Grenadier Guards No. 2 Company. They were tasked to secure the railway bridge. The larger East Group was allotted the primary task of seizing the road bridge and appears to have been jointly commanded by Lieutenant-Colonel Vandervoort and the commander of the 1st Grenadier Guards, Lieutenant-Colonel Edward Goulbourn. The Force was made up of the 505th Regiment's Company E commanded by Lieutenant James E. Smith and Captain Robert H. Rosen's Company F, supplemented by the remainder of No. 3 Squadron and No. 2 Company, numbering three Troops of Shermans and three infantry platoons. The Force was to rendezvous at the Hotel Sionshof around four miles south of Nijmegen, divide up into its respective Force columns and proceed to a small traffic island on the Groenestraat on the outskirts of Nijmegen. From there the West Force would peel off and take a circuitous route around the edge of the city to approach the railway bridge from the south-west, while the East force moved north and east through the city toward the road bridge. The attack was scheduled to begin at 15:30.[200]

Each Force was to be accompanied by a dozen members of the Dutch Resistance to guide the tanks and paratroopers through Nijmegen's streets to their objectives, and their reports regarding German strength and determination vary according to source, with one referring to warnings of strong positions around the road bridge backed by anti-tank guns while another claims the Dutch reported that Nijmegen was not strongly garrisoned and that the defenders would likely withdraw at the sight of the Grenadier Guards' tanks.[201] In fact, the former was more accurate, as discussion with the various elements of the 508th Parachute Infantry Regiment that had pushed into Nijmegen from 17 September would have revealed. By 19 September, overall responsibility for the defence of the Nijmegen bridges was still vested in *Sturmbannführer* Leo Reinhold, but he had moved *Luftwaffe Oberst* Henke east to command the railway bridge, leaving *Hauptsturmführer* Karl-Heinz Euling in charge of the road bridge. Deployed to cover the railway bridge proper, the large rail marshalling yard to its immediate south and the Kronenburgerpark just east of the latter, *Kampfgruppe* Henke was made up of a *kompanie* of trainee *Fallschirmjäger* NCOs from *Fallschirmjäger Ausbildungs und Ersatz Regiment* 'Hermann Göring', three *kompanien* from *406 z.b.V. Division* and a number of combat engineers totalling between 500 and 750 men. *Kampfgruppe* Euling consisted of the latter's *bataillon* from *SS Panzergrenadier Regiment 22* and *Untersturmführer* Werner Baumgärtel's detachment from *SS Panzer Pionier Bataillon 10*, elements of *SS Panzer Aufklärungs Abteilung 9*, augmented with another *kompanie* of trainee *Fallschirmjäger* NCOs from *Ausbildungs und Ersatz Regiment* 'Hermann Göring' and four 88mm and eight 20mm *flak* guns from *schwere FlaK Bataillon 572*. Artillery support was provided by *SS Panzer Artillerie Regiment 10* and *SS Artillerie Ausbildungs und Ersatz Regiment 5* ensconced north of the River Waal. Euling's men were securely entrenched in the Valkhofpark and adjacent Hunnerpark at the south end of the bridge ramp, the latter straddling the Arnhemscheweg running from the *Keizer Lodewijkplein* and across the bridge. In addition, numerous buildings on the approaches to the road bridge had been turned into strongpoints and the approach roads were covered by anti-tank guns. The area between the bridges was occupied by *Kampfgruppe* Melitz, made up of a number of internal security and rear echelon units. In all, the bridges were defended by approximately 2,000 German troops.[202]

Lieutenant-Colonel Vandervoort's Battalion rendezvoused with the Grenadier Guards detachment at the Hotel Sionshof in the early afternoon and while the East and West Forces were forming up into their columns the Dutch Resistance reported that the main post office in Nijmegen, located just north of the *Keizer Karel Plein*, contained a German HQ and the control point for demolition charges rigged on the road bridge.[203] This had in fact been addressed during the night of 17-18 September by Captain Jonathan E. Adams and a patrol from the 1st Battalion 508th Parachute Infantry Regiment, but the success had gone unacknowledged as Adams and his men had been subsequently cut off and remained in hiding with Dutch civilians until 20 September. A third *ad hoc* column was therefore formed under Grenadier Major George Thorne, consisting of a Troop of Shermans, two platoons from the No. 2 Company and a platoon of paratroopers; it is unclear which column these elements were drawn from, although the Airborne platoon was reportedly selected by Major-General Gavin by the simple expedient of commandeering the first platoon he came across.[204] The advance to Nijmegen commenced thirty minutes behind schedule at 16:00, the delay possibly due to the last-minute reorganisation of the post office group, with the East and West Forces travelling together on one route, possibly along the Heyensdalsweg or Groesbeekseweg, while Major Thorne's group followed a parallel track a mile or so to the west.[205] Travelling on the back of the Grenadier's Shermans was a welcome novelty for the normally foot-slogging paratroopers, and the move into the outskirts of Nijmegen was again marked by an ecstatic welcome from the local Dutch civilian population, which Lieutenant James J. Coyle from Company E likened to a 'victory parade'.[206]

In the event Major Thorne's column secured the post office after rapidly navigating the warren of narrow streets thanks to the Dutch Resistance guides members, knocking out an anti-tank gun on the way. The post office proved devoid of Germans or demolition apparatus however and Major Thorne then elected to move independently on the road bridge with two Shermans and an infantry platoon; it is unclear if the latter were Grenadiers or paratroopers. This little force reached the approaches to the *Keizer Lodewijkplein* traffic circle before coming under heavy fire from the SS holding the Hunnerpark and after suffering a number of casualties and lacking room to manoeuvre Thorne withdrew to the post office to await further orders; he was reinforced at some point by Major Harry Stanley and the 1st Grenadier Guards' No. 4 Company.[207] Captain Neville's Western Force enjoyed less success, although the circuitous route successfully avoided enemy contact until the column reached an underpass carrying the road under the railway marshalling yard around 200 yards from the target bridge. Captain

Neville elected to rush tanks and some of Company D through the underpass while Captain Smith passed the remainder of Company D over the underpass and through the marshalling yard, as the yard was bounded by an embankment too steep for the tanks to negotiate. It was at this point that things went awry.

The advance through the underpass was stopped dead when anti-tank guns knocked out two Shermans in quick succession as they emerged into the open and the supporting paratroopers were similarly blocked by intense fire from machine-guns emplaced to the front and on the flanks, while the movement through the marshalling yard was stymied by a combination of fire from machine-guns, a tank concealed within the yard and the difficult terrain created by the numerous buildings and large numbers of freight cars; the attendant confusion was worsened by the presence of a large number of Dutchmen, some just boys, sporting Orange armbands and weapons abandoned by Allied casualties. With the way ahead blocked, Captain Neville ordered a withdrawal to regroup and then tried to outflank the German defences to the east by moving along a street flanking the Kronenburgerpark, likely the Kronenburgersingel, which initiated a bout of house-to-house fighting, during which the paratroopers were attacked from the rear by a group of Germans with two manhandled 20mm *flak* guns. The fighting went on into the night at a cost of numerous casualties and another Sherman, which was hit and left burning by an anti-tank gun; when Captain Smith finally withdrew Company D to set in for the night Private First Class Frank Billich and two companions were inadvertently left behind in a house on a side street, where they were obliged to hide in the cellar with the civilian occupants when German troops moved into the upper floors.[208]

In the meantime the East Force had pushed into Nijmegen toward the road bridge as rapidly as possible, paying no heed to its flanks, and continued until it was slowed by *Kampfgruppe* Euling's outpost line occupying key buildings and road junctions south of the *Keizer Lodewijkplein*. Lieutenant-Colonel Vandervoort then deployed Companies E and F in line abreast and set about clearing a corridor two blocks wide oriented toward the road bridge. The paratroopers methodically cleared each individual block from the inside out by moving through attics and across the rooftops in order to minimise casualties, fighting numerous close-quarter encounters in rooms, stairwells and backyards while the Grenadier Guards tanks dominated the streets and reduced any strongpoint that proved too tough for the paratroopers. Both British and US commanders commented on the seamless nature of the co-operation between the paratroopers and the Grenadier Guards' tanks despite the former's lack of experience with tanks and dearth of preparation time; as Vandervoort put it '…it was amazing how beautifully the tankers and troopers teamed together…It was testimony to their combat acumen as seasoned veterans – both Yanks and Tommies.'[209] After three hours of brutal fighting the paratroopers had reached and cleared some of the buildings overlooking the *Keizer Lodewijkplein*, although this exposed them to direct fire from the German heavy weapons emplaced north of the traffic circle and artillery fire controlled from the same area. The British official record refers to two infantry platoons, possibly from the 1st Grenadier Guards, having a building blown from under them by 88mm guns after they revealed their position by firing on Germans spotted moving around the road bridge ramp, and Corporal Earl Boling from the 505th Regiment recalled the German guns methodically demolishing the buildings he and his comrades were seeking to use as cover once there were no Shermans to occupy their attention.[210] The lack of Sherman targets was due to those first two vehicles the Grenadiers pushed out across the traffic roundabout being immediately knocked out by anti-tank guns located in the Hunnerpark, or possibly sited on the far bank of the River Waal, and two more may have been lost in the subsequent fighting; the dead crewmen included Troop commander Lieutenant John Moller.[211]

The indirect fire was not all one way, however. An 81mm mortar platoon from the 505th Regiment dug its deep mortar pits in the only open area available, the old Daalseweg cemetery half a mile south of the *Keizer Lodewijkplein*, from where it was able to bring down heavy fire on the Hunnerpark area, disrupting German passage across the bridge.[212] The mortars fired 1,650 rounds over the course of the two-day battle for the road bridge, and the macabre location drew ribald comment from passing British troops, who jocularly accused the mortar crewmen of being 'fucking Yank grave-robbers'.[213]

By this point it was becoming fully dark and Lieutenant-Colonel Goulbourn was getting close to halting the operation for the night. The semi-official Grenadier Guards history, whilst acknowledging that the 2nd Grenadier Guards had lost a single Sherman and that 1st Grenadier Guards had suffered 'practically no losses', a verdict supported by the unit's War Diary, also declared that 'at no stage in the battle did the forces directed on the two bridges look like being able to rush them or even seriously disturb the German defences'.[214] This was certainly true of the railway bridge but not at the road bridge, where Lieutenant-Colonel Vandervoort took a rather different view. By his own account his internal and external radio communications were functioning perfectly, he had plenty of ammunition apart from 60mm mortar bombs, Companies E and F had suffered minimal casualties and were deployed in readiness on the edge of the *Keizer Lodewijkplein*, and there was a reserve of a dozen uncommitted Shermans drawn up in cover just behind the traffic circle. The 2nd Battalion 505th Parachute was therefore poised to push on, clear the Hunnerpark and secure the road bridge in its entirety.[215] However, this was not to be, for Lieutenant-Colonel Goulbourn advised his superiors that it would be wiser to pause and consolidate the gains thus far, bring up reinforcements and work out a less hasty and more considered plan, which is what happened, to Vandervoort's disappointment. In isolation the incident merely reflects a disparity in outlook, between aggressive Airborne assault troops and their more conservative conventional counterparts, but by this point the GARDEN force was still significantly behind schedule and circumstances were starting to swing against the 1st Airborne Division just twelve miles or so farther north. The incident therefore provides yet another example of the Guards Armoured Division operating in an unhurried, business-as-usual manner rather than with the urgency the situation clearly required, and it represents yet another missed opportunity.

Major-General Gavin's preference had always been to secure the Nijmegen bridges from both ends simultaneously, but he had been frustrated in this by the fact his Division lacked the resources and that the Germans had presciently removed all boats from the vicinity. Nonetheless, Gavin had been working assiduously on a scheme to that end even before Vandervoort's and Goulbourn's men began their approach to the bridges, and the link up with 30 Corps potentially provided a means of overcoming the lack of boats. Gavin revealed his thinking to Browning, Major-General Adair and Lieutenant-General Horrocks at 30 Corps' Tactical HQ, which had been set up in a school building near Malden. By this point Gavin must have been feeling the strain because he had been moving virtually non-stop between his various Regimental, Battalion and in some cases Platoon commanders for over fifty hours, advising, cajoling and inspiring by personal example – not forgetting the fact that he had fractured two spinal discs in a hard landing on 17 September. None of this was apparent to his fellow senior commanders, given that Horrocks referred to Gavin as 'a tall, good looking American General…unlike the popular cartoon conception of the loud-voiced, boastful, cigar chewing American' when he arrived at the Tactical HQ.[216] The precise timing of the meeting is unclear but occurred in the late afternoon or early evening according to one source, and it is thus unclear if Gavin had intended to reveal his scheme as an adjunct to the 505th Parachute Infantry Regiment's drive to the bridges in any case, or whether it was in response to the decision to halt that drive for the night, although the fact that launching a river crossing was reportedly the rationale for bringing the 504th Parachute Infantry Regiment up from Grave to the Jonkerbosch woods, just three miles from the River Waal, suggests the former.

Gavin broached the subject by asking Horrocks if the 30 Corps column included any boats. After some discussion with his staff Horrocks confirmed there were approximately twenty-eight collapsible assault boats somewhere in the Guards Armoured Division column and Gavin responded by announcing that if he were provided with the boats he would push the 504th Parachute Infantry Regiment across the River Waal to secure the road and rail bridges from the north in conjunction with a renewed effort from the south.[217] When Horrocks and Browning concurred, Gavin returned immediately to Groesbeek to finalise his plans and select a crossing place before summoning the commander of the 504th Parachute Infantry Regiment, Colonel Reuben H. Tucker, at 23:00 to discuss the upcoming operation; as Tucker was away from his HQ the summons was answered by the 504th Regiment's Executive Officer Lieutenant-Colonel Warren R. Williams, who duly relayed the news back to his Regimental commander. At this point there was not much to relay, apart from the fact that the 504th would be carrying out a river crossing operation at some point the following day; the timings were uncertain as no arrival time for the assault boats had been fixed, although Gavin expressed the hope that things might get underway before dawn, 'if.the boats arrived, and if the Germans were cleared as far as the riverbank, and if everything could be organized'. It was, as Gavin admitted in his memoir, 'a very iffy situation'.[218]

***

While the fight for the Nijmegen bridges was in full swing, events thirty miles to the south came close to severing the Airborne Corridor near its base. As we have seen, the advance of *Major* Berndt-Joachim *Freiherr* von Maltzahn's *Panzer Brigade 107* had been blocked in the late afternoon at Nuenen, five miles east of Eindhoven, by a hasty defence conducted by Company E 506th Parachute Infantry Regiment and Cromwell tanks from the 15th/19th Hussars. Seeking to bypass the blocking force *Major* von Maltzahn side-stepped his line of advance to the north-west, into the area bounded on the right by the Wilhelmina Canal and, wary of running into strong Allied forces, elected to lead with a reconnaissance in force intended to secure the bridge at Son in order to establish a foothold north of the canal. The *Brigade* thus concentrated in the woods around Molenheide, four miles east of Son, from where a reported six Panther tanks from *Panzer Abteilung 2107* supported by infantry from *Grenadier Regiment 1034* from *59 Infanterie Division* were despatched along the Wilhelmina Canal toward Son at or a little before 17:00.[219]

Reports of German armour 'massing to the southeast' reached Major-General Maxwell D. Taylor's Division HQ at Son at around 17:00; according to one account Taylor was alerted by Panthers firing on the town church tower and the school being used as Division HQ among other targets.[220] Taylor promptly despatched his Adjutant Lieutenant-Colonel Ned D. Moore to investigate, accompanied by Lieutenant Frederick Starrett, an aide to Deputy Division Commander Brigadier-General Anthony McAuliffe (who had just arrived at the HQ in McAuliffe's Jeep), Lieutenant Rodney B. Adams from the 502nd Parachute Infantry Regiment, Dutch Liaison Lieutenant Dubois, ten men from Division HQ and a Bazooka team from the 506th Regiment platoon guarding the Bailey bridge consisting of Private J. J. McCarthy and an unnamed companion. The patrol crossed to the south bank and travelled around 200 yards before a camouflaged Panther burst from the trees onto the Canal tow-path 300 yards further on and opened fire on the bridge, trapping Lieutenant-Colonel Moore's patrol between the advancing Germans and the bridge defences. The attack began at around 17:15 as a column from the Guards Armoured Division's A Echelon was crossing the bridge and a Panther round hit a truck from Q Battery, 21st Anti-Tank Regiment RA; this broke the column and set the truck ablaze on the bridge, lighting up the surrounding area in the gathering dusk and the attackers subsequently increased the illumination by setting fire to a barn and haystack fifty yards south of the Canal. Private McCarthy fired off all three of his Bazooka rounds, scoring an ineffectual hit on a Panther before his assistant gunner was killed and he and Lieutenant-Colonel Moore were forced to take shelter in a convenient hole, where they were trapped as an oblivious German platoon dug in around them. The pair remained there until the illumination dimmed sufficiently to allow them to crawl through the German position to safety at around 22:00. Some of the patrol, including Lieutenant Adams, leapt into the canal to escape. Adams was drowned in the attempt, while Lieutenant Starrett gathered the remainder and established a defensive line along the road after also ineffectually attacking a Panther with a hand-grenade in the nearby woods and escaping the vehicle's retribution. This party also managed to regain safety at around 22:00 but not before being fired upon by the paratroopers on the north bank, who mistook the patrol for Germans in the light from the burning truck, obliging Starrett to despatch a messenger over the bridge to clarify the situation. To add insult to injury, the attackers also pushed Brigadier-General McAuliffe's Jeep into the Canal.[221]

Meanwhile one of the Panthers began firing on the school housing Division HQ from across the Canal. One shell destroyed the field telephone switchboard, although radio communications were maintained unbroken by Technician Fifth Class Gordon B. Gissenass, who remained at his post throughout the fight. The Division HQ personnel and Signal Company were organised into a hasty defensive perimeter augmented by men from the 326th Airborne Engineer Battalion and Battery C 377th Parachute Field Artillery, while Major-General Taylor drove up to the nearby landing area where he gathered up a party from the 1st Battalion 327th Glider Infantry Regiment, which was engaged in unloading the gliders from that day's lift and, more crucially, a 57mm anti-tank gun from the 81st Airborne Anti-aircraft Battalion's Battery B. The gun was deployed on the north bank of the canal in time to engage the Panther firing on the Division HQ school and scored a hit that blew off the vehicle's spaced armour plates and penetrated the hull, leaving it burning and slewed at an angle across the canal tow-path.[222] A second Panther was knocked out at close range by a Bazooka team and also began to burn, and the momentum of the German attack then fell away. Leaving behind covering groups that periodically exchanged small-arms fire with the paratroopers through the night, the Panthers withdrew toward their jumping-off point at Molenheide, while some elements of *Grenadier Regiment 1034* withdrew northward to rejoin *59 Infanterie Division* north of the Wilhelmina Canal. Behind them the men of the 101st Airborne Division were left relieved but puzzled as to why the Germans had not pushed their advantage and seized the bridge. The German side of the matter is unclear, although the darkness, unfamiliar terrain and unexpected arrival of reinforcements are cited as contributory factors; for their part Taylor's intelligence section put it down to *Panzer Brigade 107*, having been slated for service on the Eastern Front, being 'a little bit skittish about its return to combat on the Western Front'.[223] Whatever the underlying reason for the failure to press home the attack on the night of 19 September, the 101st Airborne Division would be seeing more of *Major* von Maltzahn's formation, and perhaps sooner than expected.

D Plus 3

00:01 to 12:00 Wednesday 20 September 1944

The night passed slowly for the men of the 1st Airborne Division holding out in the buildings around the north end of the Arnhem road bridge, punctuated by occasional periods of light rain and the random tolling of a church bell swinging free in the warm breeze created by the nearby fires. Some took the opportunity to rest as best they could while some of those on watch or whose duties required them to remain alert resorted to the issued Benzedrine tablets.[1] These were necessary because the Airborne soldiers were by this point verging on exhaustion, having been moving and fighting virtually non-stop for over sixty hours, and food was running out. The forty-eight-hour ration the troops had landed with and the immediate unit resupply were all but gone, obliging them to fall back upon what could be found in the buildings they occupied. The Mortar Platoon house proved to be well stocked with preserved foods, fruit and chocolate liqueurs for example, whereas the Brigade HQ building, as mentioned earlier, held only a few apples and 'some particularly juicy pears' according to Lieutenant-Colonel Frost; another house also yielded sufficient water to keep the defenders going for another day or so.[2] Ammunition was running critically short, despite Frost's order the previous day prohibiting firing at targets of opportunity or sniping; Lance-Sergeant Harold Padfield in the Van Limburg School was down to a handful of rounds for his Browning pistol, for example.[3] Although Frost referred to patrols again being despatched to probe and harass the surrounding German positions, the majority of the defenders appear to have remained ensconced in their buildings, not least because the fires lit up the streets like daylight, making movement in the open extremely hazardous even in the temporary absence of German mortar and artillery fire. Frost himself spent the night prowling the Brigade HQ building, monitoring the Brigade signallers as they attempted to make contact with Division HQ. At one point he discussed the deteriorating situation with Major Gough in the now roofless attic, specifically the best direction for a breakout to prevent the growing number of wounded from becoming involved in a fight to the finish. He later broke his own injunction on random firing by shooting at a pair of indistinct figures in the darkness with a borrowed rifle.[4]

Frost's concern for the casualties was justified for while the lightly wounded remained with their units to continue the fight, by this point the bridge perimeter was also housing around 200 more seriously wounded men, some of them critically. Conditions permitting, battlefield casualties from conventional British Army units followed a three-stage evacuation process, from Battalion-level Regimental Aid Post (RAP) to Casualty Clearing Station (CCS) to Advanced Dressing Station (ADS) and thence on to field or permanent military hospitals or military wings located within civilian establishments dependent on the severity of the injury. However, the isolated nature of airborne operations obliged Airborne units to employ a truncated, two-stage process that began with evacuation to a battalion-level RAP followed by despatch to a Main Dressing Station (MDS) run by a Parachute or Airlanding Field Ambulance; these had doctors, surgical teams and nursing personnel to provide care until relieved by ground forces.[5] 16 Parachute Field Ambulance had established an MDS at the St Elizabeth Hospital to serve the 1st Parachute Brigade plan, but circumstances obliged the bridge perimeter to rely upon Captain James Logan and the 2nd Parachute Battalion RAP, assisted by the 1st Parachute Brigade's Medical Officer Captain David Wright; it is unclear if the latter was posted to the Brigade on a permanent basis post or if he was on a temporary secondment from 16 Parachute Field Ambulance. The cellars under the Brigade HQ building on the corner of the Eusebiusbinnensingel and Weertjesstraat were pressed into service as a combined triage, operating theatre and hospital ward, as described by Private James Sims:

> The scene was a grim one. The floors were carpeted with dead and badly wounded airborne soldiers…The two medics set me down on a table in…the room adjoining the cellars and reported my arrival to Captain Logan who…came over and examined me… [My] wound was cleaned and I was given an injection while an orderly scribbled details of my treatment on a tie-on label which he attached to my camouflage jacket. As Captain Logan applied a shell dressing he seemed to recede from me with astonishing rapidity and I passed out…When I came to I found myself in a very small vault off the main cellar. It must have been some sort of archway because my head and feet nearly touched the brick. There was no direct illumination, only a ghastly half-light which filtered in from the main cellar.[6]

Up at ground level the Germans resumed the attack against the British perimeter, shortly after a damp and drizzly dawn, with artillery and mortar bombardment. When the direct fire attacks began they were initially focussed on the hitherto lightly treated west side of the bridge ramp rather than to the east. Captain William Gell and his men from 250 (Airborne) Light Composite Company RASC holding buildings on the Prinsenhof at the north-western tip of the bridge perimeter had been largely screened from direct fire by the imposing prison wall to their front, but daylight revealed the Germans had blown down a section of the wall at some point during the night. The RASC men braced themselves for an infantry assault but the Germans began firing an artillery piece through the gap instead, as witnessed by Driver James Wild: 'The first shot hit the corner of the roof. It didn't explode there because the only resistance it had was the slates on the roof, but it left a hole nearly two yards across…I think one man was killed and one wounded. We decided to get out, down to the ground floor, when the second shell exploded against the front wall of the room we had been in; we would all have been killed if we had still been there.'[7] The house held by Lieutenant Patrick Barnett and part of the Brigade HQ Defence Platoon on the Eusebiusbinnensingel by the bridge ramp received similar treatment from an unidentified tank, possibly *Feldwebel* Barneki's Tiger I from *schwere Panzer Kompanie Hummel*. The paratroopers were rapidly disabused of the notion that the sound of tank engines heralded the arrival of 30 Corps when the first shell punched into the corner of their building, and they were soon obliged to abandon their position as the house was systematically demolished around them; one man was killed, Lieutenant Barnett was seriously wounded in the head and US Jedburgh officer Lieutenant Harvey Todd was blown out of his position but otherwise unhurt.[8] The incident was likely that witnessed by *Sturmann* Horst Weber: 'The roof fell in, the top two storeys began to crumble…the whole front wall fell into the street revealing each floor on which the British were scrambling like mad. Dust and debris soon made it impossible to see anything more. The din was awful, but even so above it all we could hear the wounded screaming.'[9]

The fighting was therefore well underway again when 1st Parachute Brigade HQ finally established contact with 1st Airborne Division HQ at the Hotel Hartenstein. It is frequently assumed that the contact was made via radio although this is emphatically denied by

Bombardier Leo Hall from the 1st Airlanding Light Regiment's 3 Battery, who was manning his jury-rigged No. 22 and No. 68 sets in the attic of the Brigade HQ building; on the other hand, an entry in the 1st Airborne Division Signals War Diary does refer to contact being established 'with 1st Para Bde for a few minutes' at 08:40.[10] The main contact between the two HQs occurred twenty minutes earlier and was made via the civilian telephone network rather than by radio. The Division HQ War Diary refers to a report from Brigade Major Tony Hibbert, and implies he was speaking to a HQ functionary. In fact, the conversation appears to have been between the Division commander and Major Gough after Gough had identified himself to an understandably sceptical Urquhart as the 'man who is always late for your "O" groups', to which the Division commander responded with a somewhat unsettling 'My goodness! I thought you were dead.' Gough reported that the north end of the Arnhem road bridge was in British hands, that it was intact albeit blocked by shot-up enemy vehicles and covered by fire. He used a town plan to clarify which buildings were British-held and urgently requested reinforcements and a surgical team. Urquhart's response was not encouraging: after attempting to explain the gravity of the situation at Oosterbeek without going into detail, Gough was informed that there was little prospect of assistance from the remainder of the Division. According to Urquhart's account his exact words were 'I'm afraid you can only hope for relief from the south. For the moment we can only try to preserve what we have left.' Gough responded by pointing out the situation at the bridge was 'pretty grim' but that the defenders would do their best.[11] The 1st Parachute Brigade made another report at 09:25, presumably again using the civilian telephone network, informing Division HQ that the bridge perimeter was under continuous tank attack and that the whole area around the north end of the bridge had been 'devastated'.[12] The report was probably delivered in this instance by Frost, who refers to a conversation with Urquhart in his personal account.[13]

Although the Germans had opened a new front against the British perimeter opposite the prison, their main effort came once again from the industrial area east of the bridge ramp. Observers in the Van Limburg Stirum School noted German activity around the crossroads formed by the junction of the Westervoortsedijk and Eusebiusbuitensingel for two hours after 07:00 and a major German attack began from that quarter at 09:15.[14] The Germans had augmented their firepower by emplacing artillery to the south bank of the Lower Rhine, which was engaged by the 1st Airlanding Light Regiment from its new emplacements around the Oosterbeek Old Church on several occasions from 07:00, directed by Major Munford in the attic of the Brigade HQ building.[15] According to Urquhart, the British fire was so accurate that the Germans turned their light *flak* guns against nearby church steeples on the assumption that they harboured observer teams.[16] The Germans also deployed at least one large-calibre gun in the direct fire role against the east side of the British perimeter, as noted by *Rottenführer* Rudolf Trapp from SS *Panzergrenadier Regiment 21*: 'An artillery piece was trundled into our street from the Battalion Knaust behind us…It was the biggest gun I've ever seen, and was manhandled up along the side of the Rhine.'[17] The gun appears to have been brought into action against the buildings backing onto the bridge underpass held by elements of Major Douglas Crawley's B Company, likely those on the corner of the Nieuwekade and Ooststraat. Trapp covered the gun 'by shooting up the British positions along the street with long protracted bursts from my machine-gun…It fired seven to eight shots directly at it'; the SS then stormed the ruins and found 'the occupants, about a platoon strong, all dead lying in slit trenches and prepared positions'.[18] The German attack thus overran the British enclave on the Ooststraat and pushed the survivors, a group from 1st Parachute Brigade HQ, augmented with half a dozen men from 1st (Airborne) Divisional Field Park RAOC led by Captain Bernard Briggs, back to a makeshift barricade beneath the underpass.[19] By 09:40 the Germans were therefore back in possession of the bridge underpass for the first time since the evening of Sunday 17 September and they promptly set about rigging it for demolition, presumably with the intention of dropping the overpass section of the bridge in order to block access from the south.[20]

Up to this point the German intent had been to recapture the bridge intact in order to use it as a conduit to channel reinforcements south to the fight on the River Waal at Nijmegen, in line with the operations order issued by *Feldmarschall* Model via *II SS Panzerkorps* HQ at 17:30 on 17 September. Demolishing even a small section of the bridge, one relatively easy to repair, was therefore a major change of tack, which was presumably prompted by the attack toward the Nijmegen road bridge by the Grenadier Guards Group and the 2nd Battalion, 505th Parachute Infantry Regiment, in the late afternoon of 19 September.[21] Although this tied in with Model's other injunction that the Allied forces at Arnhem and Nijmegen were to be prevented from linking up at all costs, the change is nonetheless curious because there does not appear to be any mention of it in German accounts; and in view of the fact that the SS defending the approaches to the Nijmegen bridge comprehensively rebuffed the afternoon attack. It must also have been apparent to their counterparts at the Arnhem road bridge that the British defenders were reaching the end of their tether. On the other hand, Urquhart refers to an SS officer captured and interrogated by Frost's men claiming to have been tasked to destroy the bridge, and British sources are absolutely clear that the Germans began preparing the overpass for demolition as soon as they took possession.[22]

The Airborne response to the German capture of the underpass was characteristically swift and aggressive. Within twenty minutes Lieutenant John Grayburn and his fifty-strong group built around the survivors of the 2nd Parachute Battalion's A Company had retaken it at cost of several casualties, including Grayburn himself, who had already been wounded on 17 September; he quickly returned to the fray after having his new wounds dressed. With the underpass back in British hands Lieutenant Donald Hindley and five Sappers from the 1st Parachute Squadron's HQ Troop were able to remove the fuses from the demolition charges, a task Hindley later described as 'a nerve-racking experience, working a few feet away from a large quantity of explosives which could be fired at any moment'.[23] A see-saw battle then developed as the equally determined Germans recaptured the underpass at 10:20 and set about replacing the fuses, prompting another attack by Grayburn and his men forty minutes later, by this time reduced to thirty, again supported by Hindley and three surviving Sappers who were now tasked to remove the demolition charges altogether. It is unclear if this was done, although the fact the overpass remained intact after the Germans recaptured it for the final time at 11:30 with the support of a tank suggests that the Sappers were successful. The Airborne party had no counter to the tank and while some escaped a number were captured, including Lieutenant Hindley – who had been wounded in the face and shoulder – his Squadron Sergeant Major, and another unnamed Sapper. Lieutenant Grayburn was killed by machine-gun fire from the tank whilst standing in the open with his back to the vehicle supervising the withdrawal; his body fell into the Lower Rhine and was not recovered until 1948. He was posthumously awarded the only Victoria Cross awarded to a member of the Arnhem bridge force.[24]

Three miles or so to the west of the Arnhem road bridge, Oosterbeek proper had remained relatively calm through 19 September despite the fighting that raged to the north and east, and business thus continued as usual through the night at the various formation headquarters located only 600 yards or so south of the Arnhem–Ede railway line. 1st Airlanding Brigade HQ, located in houses close to Division HQ, was informed of the contact with the 4th Parachute Brigade's via a liaison officer from Division HQ at 02:30 and that the 7th KOSB was to return to the Airlanding fold two-and-a-quarter hours later; the latter was presumably relayed by radio, given that the Airlanding Brigade HQ was the only contact Division Signals were able to make, as reported at 02:00 and again at 04:40.[25] At 01:40 Division HQ received a message from 1st British Airborne Corps Rear HQ at Moor Park requesting a new location for the Polish Independent Parachute Brigade's drop, which had been rescheduled for the afternoon of 20 September. The request presumably resulted from Urquhart's request for a change of venue on the morning of 19 September and four grid references were duly transmitted delineating an area just east of Driel, directly south of Oosterbeek on the opposite side of the Lower Rhine and just under three miles west of the original DZ K.[26] Although the Division HQ War Diary makes no mention of it, the idea seems to have been to bring the Poles across the Lower Rhine via the Heveadorp ferry, located at the northern edge of the new drop zone. The ferry was still functional at this point and ferryman Pieter Hensen had been carrying normal Dutch commuter traffic back and forth until at least 18 September, along with Airborne strays from south of the river including one of the RAF early warning radar crews from the second lift; Major John Winchester and a party from his 9th Field Company RE had surveyed the ferry and jetty in the late morning of 19 September while searching for diesel barges for future bridging operations. No barges were found but a group of seven, mainly from the 2nd South Staffords, were brought across from the south bank by a Corporal Hey.[27] By the early hours of 20 September the bulk of B Company, 1st Border was dug in on the Westerbouwing high ground overlooking the ferry terminal, with CanLoan Lieutenant John Wellbelove's 13 Platoon deployed 500 yards to the front straddling the riverside Veerweg; the Platoon Scout Section consisting of Corporal Cyril Crickett, Bren Gunner Private Philip Hulse and sniper Private Thomas McDonald was dug in on the road leading down to the ferry.[28]

Surprisingly, the decision to change the Polish Brigade's drop zone has attracted little comment despite the fact that it amounted to delivering Sosabowski's men onto an unsurveyed, unmarked and unprotected DZ and hoping for the best – the Polish Brigade had no organic Pathfinder capability and the 21st Independent Parachute Company was unable to reach the proposed landing area. Perhaps more importantly, neither Urquhart nor Moor Park had any idea of the conditions of the ground or enemy dispositions south of the river and they could therefore have been delivering the Poles squarely into the lap of a fully prepared enemy. Urquhart can perhaps be excused given his proven dearth of airborne experience and increasingly desperate need of reinforcement, but the staff at Moor Park ought to have known better, and should arguably have been looking to cancel the Polish drop unless, or until, more favourable conditions prevailed. Such a cancellation would likely not have gone down well with the keyed-up Polish paratroopers, but that would have been preferable to sacrificing their lives on the altar of wishful thinking. As it was, 1st Airborne Corps was merely channelling Browning's arrogant and vindictive attitude toward the Poles, prompted by the Polish Government-in-Exile's stubborn refusal to cede control of Sosabowski's Brigade to him for the two years before March 1944, and which was to find even more blatant expression at the end of Operation MARKET GARDEN.[29] Be that as it may, the change of drop zone was relayed to Sosabowski at his HQ at Stamford in Lincolnshire at 08:45 by the Brigade Liaison Officer, Lieutenant-Colonel Richard Stevens, along with orders to move to the north bank of the Lower Rhine via the Heveadorp ferry; the ferry was to be secured by the 1st Parachute Brigade, which was also to protect the crossing and provide guides. Consequently, the 'many days and nights of staff work, the map studies, and the briefings, were all thrown out the window' and within thirty minutes Sosabowski had drawn up a hasty plan and was briefing his Brigade staff officers. By 10:00 the staff officers were passing on the briefing to unit and stick commanders at Saltby and Spanhoe; the lift had been scheduled to begin taking off at that time, but poor weather had again prompted a three-hour postponement.[30]

Having successfully sealed off the British outpost at the Arnhem road bridge and fought the relieving force to a standstill doing it, the Germans now turned their attention to eradicating both. *Heeresgruppe B* ordered the total evacuation of Arnhem's civilian population on 20 September, informing the city's mayor that this was to be completed from south to north in four-day increments; the only exceptions were police, fire service and hospital personnel, and non-ambulatory sick and wounded. The decision was prompted in part by the fact that the sizeable civilian presence was a drain on the German supply chain, not least because the city had been without water or electrical power since 18 September, and because the Germans were aware that elements of the civilian population were openly aiding the British. More pertinently from an operational perspective, measures were also implemented to streamline the rather convoluted command and control arrangements. Hitherto *Heeresgruppe B* had been obliged to communicate with *9 SS Panzer Division* via *Obergruppenführer* Wilhelm Bittrich's

II SS Panzerkorps, and with *Kampfgruppe von Tettau* via *Wehrmachtbefehlshaber Niederlande*, frequently utilising the Dutch telephone network owing to a shortage of radios. *Feldmarschall* Model addressed these cumbersome arrangements by subordinating von Tettau's command to *II SS Panzerkorps* and establishing a direct link between *Obersturmbannführer* Harzer's *9 SS Panzer Division* HQ and *Heeresgruppe B*. This permitted reinforcements to be despatched directly to the fighting front from Germany, among the first of which were *Festung MG Bataillon 37* and *MG Bataillon 41*; the former had only been raised at Wandern in Germany on 10 September.[31] *Heeresgruppe B* also offered *9 SS Panzer Division* the services of *Artillerie Regiment 191* providing it could provide transport to move its twenty-four 105mm guns from its refitting area at Zutphen, twenty-five miles north-east of Arnhem. Harzer swiftly arranged a relay with his handful of vehicles and he also elevated the Regiment's HQ to *Artillerie Kommandeur (ArKo)* status, with responsibility for all artillery units operating in *9 SS Panzer Division*'s area in the same way *FlaK Brigade* von Svoboda had been given control of all anti-aircraft assets the previous day. With his reinforcement and support needs thus at least partially addressed, Harzer set about organising attacks against the Oosterbeek pocket in line with orders from *II SS Panzerkorps* on 20 September, scheduled to commence on Thursday 21 September; the delay was to permit *Kampfgruppen* von Tettau and Spindler to close up to the western side of the coalescing British perimeter.[32]

There was to be no respite for the British in the interim however, for just after 07:00 the Germans commenced a bombardment of the entire British Divisional area with mortars, artillery and rocket launchers which Urquhart described as 'the heaviest mortar stonk yet'.[33] The bombardment coincided with a conference at the Hotel Hartenstein HQ at 08:00, although precisely who attended is unclear; the primary sources only refer specifically to the presence of Lieutenant-Colonel Iain Murray from the Glider Pilot Regiment's No.1 Wing and Captain David Allsop from the 1st Airborne Reconnaissance Squadron.[34] Lieutenant-Colonel Thompson from the 1st Airlanding Light Regiment also attended and was formally placed in charge of THOMPSON Force, as the *ad hoc* grouping he had rallied to protect his guns down on the Benedendorpsweg the previous afternoon was dubbed; he may have been accompanied by Majors Richard Lonsdale and John Simonds, the 11th Parachute Battalion's second-in-command and commander of the 2nd South Staffords' HQ Company respectively, who had been assigned to Thompson the previous afternoon.[35] According to the latter, the conference 'mainly dealt with supplies' but given the intent to shuttle the 1st Polish Independent Parachute Brigade across the Lower Rhine, the Heveadorp ferry also likely featured in the discussion. As it did not figure in the original briefing material passed to the 1st Airborne Division, Urquhart only appears to have become aware of the ferry's existence after his return to Division HQ on 19 September, likely via the Dutch Resistance; this presumably prompted the survey of the ferry and landing stage carried out by Major Winchester and his party from the 9th Field Company RE the previous day.[36] The only interruption to Urquhart's conference appears to have come from Major Gough's 08:20 telephone call from the Arnhem road bridge. Others were not so lucky. A German salvo straddled the nearby building occupied by 1st Airlanding Brigade HQ and at least one projectile scored a direct hit on the room where Brigadier Hicks was holding his own conference; Hicks was unhurt but Staff Captain Edward Moy-Thomas, Brigade Intelligence Officer Captain Raymond Burns, Brigade Signals Officer Captain Stuart Blatch and Lieutenant Antony Thomas, commander of the Brigade HQ Defence Platoon, were all killed.[37] The culprit was likely a 150mm *nebelwerfer* rocket launcher from *SS Werfer Abteilung 102*; half an hour before the incident the 1st Airborne Reconnaissance Squadron reported two such weapons firing from the north-east.[38]

Down on the lower Benedendorpsweg road the forward elements of what was to become THOMPSON Force spent a largely uneventful night in its Battalion positions around the Acacialaan junction. According to the 3rd Parachute Battalion War Diary, the night was 'reasonably quiet and most men were able to obtain a few hours badly needed sleep'.[39] Not everyone was asleep. At 03:30 the 11th Parachute Battalion despatched a patrol to investigate the

Oosterbeek Laag underpass, which ascertained that it was held by a German mobile patrol; it is unclear if the information was obtained by contact or stealth.[40] All that changed abruptly at 08:00 when *Kampfgruppe* Harder resumed the attack along the Benedendorpsweg, hitting the 1st and 3rd Parachute Battalion positions straddling the road, in the former instance against the sector held by Lieutenant Leslie Curtis and S Company, and across an area of open ground to the east of the 11th Parachute Battalion's position on the Acacialaan.[41] The attackers were initially concealed by a combination of thick river mist and dust and smoke from the bombardment, and were accompanied by at least two vehicles from *Sturmgeschütze Brigade 280*, again misidentified as tanks. The Germans doubtless expected the assault guns to be their trump card again but that did not prove to be the case, in part because the reduced visibility prevented the *StuG*s identifying the British positions and standing off out of PIAT and Gammon bomb range as they had done on the Utrechtsestraat and Den Brink the previous day. There was also the presence of two alert and fully manned 6-Pounder guns located at the Acacialaan-Benedendorpsweg junction commanded by Lance-Sergeant John Baskeyfield from the 2nd South Staffords Anti-tank Group. The guns appear to have been deployed close together with Baskeyfield's piece covering both roads while Lance-Sergeant Mansell covered the Benedendorpsweg. Baskeyfield and his crew waited until the lead vehicle was within 100 yards' range before pumping at least six rounds into it. This brought the vehicle to a halt by blowing off the right gear differential and subsequent hits set it ablaze; the second *StuG* appears to have decided discretion was the better part of valour and turned right off the Benedendorpsweg accompanied by its covering infantry.[42]

With their armoured support removed, the burden fell on the German infantry and the restricted visibility sparked a series of close-quarter encounters such as that experienced by Private James Gardner from the 1st Parachute Battalion:

> They came at us with all the fury they could muster. We got out of our trenches to meet the infantry…we could not see one another after a while – it was a mixture of dust, smoke and fog. I felt oddly alone, when out of the smoke…a figure emerged with rifle and bayonet out in front of him. I waited a while to be sure who was there. At about four to five feet I could see by the helmet that he was one of 'theirs'. I turned to face him, but he stopped in his tracks and, realizing who was confronting him, turned and scarpered back into the smoke.[43]

At 11:00 the *StuG*s renewed the attack, possibly encouraged by improved visibility and three vehicles broke through into the 1st Parachute Battalion's sector on the British right flank. At least one and possibly more appear to have fallen victim to Lance-Sergeant Baskeyfield's 6-Pounder despite most of his and Lance-Sergeant Mansell's gun crews having been killed or wounded in the course of the morning, and he also accounted for a half-track mounted 20mm gun from *SS FlaK Abteilung 9* that was rash enough to show itself by the demolished railway bridge.[44] A number of German infiltrators succeeded in penetrating the 1st Battalion perimeter under cover of the armoured attack, and Lieutenant Curtis and HQ Company's second-in-command Lieutenant Albert Turrell led patrols to clear them.[45]

Lieutenant-Colonel Thompson was at this time rationalising his command arrangement. Major Simonds was set to organising a new defensive perimeter just east of Oosterbeek Old Church, initially using the fifty or so 2nd South Staffords deployed to protect the 1st Airlanding Light Regiment's gun positions; this force was subsequently augmented with the remaining hundred or so South Staffords under Major Cain deployed on the Benedendorpsweg, which came under Simonds' command at 10:30. Cain was ordered to move his men to a building dubbed the Laundry just north of the Oosterbeek Old Church, with the exception of the South Staffords' MMG and Anti-tank elements, which remained at the Acacialaan position. Their place was taken by a party from the 11th Parachute Battalion which had withdrawn into Oosterbeek proper the previous day, with the changeover complete by midday.[46] The withdrawal to the new line was not quite the soft option it appeared, for the area around the Oosterbeek Old Church was far from quiet. The Light Regiment's gun positions had been subject to heavy mortaring throughout the morning from 07:00 with 3 Battery's Command Post receiving a direct hit from a 150mm *nebelwerfer* rocket at 11:00, fortunately without casualties, and 1 Battery was similarly hit later in the day.[47] Back at the Benedendorpsweg–Acacialaan junction Major Lonsdale took over command from Major Buchanan and the units defending the line there then became part of LONSDALE Force. The precise time Lonsdale assumed command varies between unit accounts, simply because it took time for him physically to get around the unit HQs to inform them of the new arrangement; the 11th Parachute Battalion reported the handover taking effect at 'around 12:00', the 3rd Parachute Battalion 12:30, and the 1st Parachute Battalion 14:00.[48]

Matters took a similar turn at the north side of the Division perimeter, where a defensive line had been hastily erected just south of the Arnhem–Ede railway during the previous evening. Initially manned by his 21st Independent Parachute Company, the line was commanded by Major Bernard Wilson from his HQ in the Ommershof, a large house set in parkland on the south side of the Graaf Van Rechterenweg.[49] The line had been augmented by a number of units from 18:00, starting with the 4th Parachute Squadron's No. 1 Troop and part of No. 3 Troop commanded by Captain Nigel Thomas; the remainder of the Squadron was dug in near the Sonnenberg on the west side of the Division perimeter.[50] Major Peter Jackson and E Squadron from the Glider Pilot Regiment's No.2 Wing arrived next at some point before 20:30, and Jackson was subsequently reinforced with an additional sixty Glider Pilots, thirty drawn from C Squadron and thirty strays from No. 1 Wing who had failed to locate their parent unit after coming in with the second lift; the newcomers were tasked to fill the gap on E Squadron's flank and maintain contact with the 1st Border's A Company.[51] Lieutenant Eastwood and No. 1 Platoon regained the 21st Independent Company fold at the Ommershof after dark. Last to arrive was Lieutenant-Colonel Payton-Reid and his depleted 7th KOSB. Major Coke, the Battalion second-in-command, was waiting with orders in the vicinity of the Hotel Hartenstein, which were confirmed by a Staff officer from Division HQ in person, presumably because the KOSB were still technically under 4th Parachute Brigade command. Carrying out a preparatory reconnaissance of the proposed new position, liaising with Major Wilson and then moving the tired glider soldiers proved to be a long business and it was midnight before the 7th KOSB was digging in at its new location.[52]

Colonel Payton-Reid had been ordered to extend the line eastward to just short of the Stationsweg and chose to centre his position on the Hotel Dreyeroord, which his men christened the White House. C Company was given responsibility for the west and part of the north and southern sectors, D Company the east side and the rest of the north, and the depleted B Company contingent was allotted the remainder of the southern sector. The Battalion's MMG Sections deployed facing the direction of immediate threat toward the railway, the anti-tank guns were deployed to cover the approaches of all four quadrants and the 3-inch mortars adjacent to the White House with the RAP inside. The perimeter was established by 01:00 despite the darkness and patrols were then despatched to check the railway embankment and houses in the immediate vicinity, not least because there was a 400-yard gap in the line between the KOSB perimeter and that of the 4th Parachute Squadron. Stand to was ordered at 04:30 and C Company then despatched CanLoan Lieutenant Martin Kaufman and 11 Platoon with a Vickers Section to mount a standing patrol on the railway, while Lieutenant Joseph Hunter and 13 Platoon from D Company performed a similar function in houses to the east. Colonel Payton-Reid called a 'co-ordinating conference' at 06:00 where he reviewed the situation and stressed that the Battalion's perimeter was to be 'held inviolate' and that every opportunity was to be seized for offensive action. Administrative matters were also discussed, and Payton-Reid 'authorised the issue of rations from the Compo Packs on a one-third basis'.[53] The 4th Parachute Squadron RE contingent had spent a relatively peaceful night in their trenches near the Ommershof, although the attached Polish 6-Pounder was withdrawn after daylight without explanation; the removal was presumably due to the presence of the 7th KOSB's anti-tank element.[54]

The German ground assault on the Graaf Van Rechterenweg line began at 08:00 with a company-strength attack on the 4th Parachute Squadron supported by two *Sd.Kfz.* 250 armoured half-tracks, likely from *SS Panzer Aufklärungs Abteilung 9*. The attack was beaten off, although one 3 Troop Sapper was shot dead while standing close behind Captain Henry Brown, allegedly by a sniper; the enemy's attention may have been attracted by Brown's maroon beret, which he had taken to wearing as a morale booster for his men in lieu of his camouflaged Airborne helmet. The men took a different view and persuaded Brown to cover the beret with his face veil.[55] At around 10:00 the German mortar bombardment grew heavier and a self-propelled gun of some kind, possibly a *Panzerjäger* IV from *SS Panzerjäger Abteilung 9*, drew up on the Graaf Van Rechterenweg directly in front of 3 Troop and began firing down the road at the 7th KOSB's positions around the White House: 'It stopped about 120 yards from us and began firing…We were amazed to realise that we could see the white hot shell flashing past our eyes only a few yards to our front…We opened up with our Bren gun and rifles and Sapper Grantham fired a couple of PIAT bombs at the gun. It eventually stopped firing and withdrew to the north, well screened by the trees.'[56] The German bombardment was not to be so easily deflected and one salvo of mortar bombs killed two Sappers and severely wounded Captain Thomas in both legs; he was evacuated to the nearest RAP with three or four other men wounded in the same incident but died around thirty minutes later, shortly after being visited by Captain Brown.[57]

On the 7th KOSB frontage the Vickers Section attached to Lieutenant Kaufman's standing patrol on the railway engaged a large group of the enemy in a wood north of the line at around 09:00. C Company commander Major Gordon Dinwiddie went forward with Lieutenant Alexander Crighton from the KOSB Mortar Group, who brought down effective fire until he was shot and killed, again allegedly by a sniper.[58] The Germans then began to outflank the standing patrol's location, eventually obliging Lieutenant Kaufman to withdraw into the main Battalion perimeter via D Company's frontage. While this was going on one of the KOSB 6-Pounder anti-tank guns knocked out what was reported as an armoured car but was likely one of the *Sd.Kfz.* 250 armoured half-tracks involved in the earlier attack on the 4th Parachute Squadron, given that a vehicle of that type was damaged and abandoned on the Graaf Van Rechterenweg.[59] Another 6-Pounder under Lieutenant Alexander Hannah was despatched with a Platoon from B Company to cover the Stationsweg just south of the Oosterbeek Hoog crossing and ended up fighting what was described as a Tiger tank 'towing a flame-throwing apparatus'; as the only Tiger tanks in the area were engaged at the Arnhem road bridge at this time, the vehicle was likely a *Flammpanzer B2 (f)* from *Panzer Kompanie 224*. Whatever it was and whoever it belonged to, the vehicle was reportedly knocked out and the crew killed by the courageous efforts of the gun crew and especially a Corporal Watson and a Private McWhirter. Back within the Battalion perimeter it had become apparent that the White House was too exposed for the Battalion RAP and Colonel Payton-Reid therefore ordered it relocated to a more protected house even though the house lacked running water. The transfer appears to have been supervised by Battalion second-in-command Major John Coke and involved repeatedly running the gauntlet of increasingly heavy German mortar, artillery and small-arms fire; Major Coke was wounded in the leg during the move.[60]

Things were less active on the lower half of the 1st Border's frontage along the western face of the Divisional perimeter. B Company was untroubled in its location on the Westerbouwing Heights overlooking the Lower Rhine and the Heveadorp ferry terminal, apart from intermittent mortaring and some small-scale probes against the outpost held by Lieutenant Wellbelove's 13 Platoon and Sergeant Thomas Watson's 14 Platoon on the main Company perimeter; given the generally poor standard of fieldcraft exhibited by the German troops encountered by the Reconnaissance Squadron in the area, the contacts may have been accidental. The sound of tracked vehicles was clearly audible to the west and the glider soldiers thus needed little prompting to deepen slit trenches and generally improve their defences.[61]

There was nothing accidental about D Company's contact during the morning, however. The thick woods around the Company's location on the Van Borsselenweg midway between the Utrechtseweg restricted visibility so much that Company commander Captain William Hodgson decided to despatch Lieutenant Jack Bainbridge and 19 Platoon to establish a combined standing patrol and observation post at a junction on the Van der Molenallee several hundred yards in front of the main Company location. The junction was reached without incident but Lieutenant Bainbridge was unable to signal his safe arrival or relay information, as the two signallers attached to the Platoon were unable to contact Company HQ with their No. 18 set. Perhaps more importantly, the absence of 19 Platoon obliged the remaining three platoons to extend their frontage and a German patrol was able to infiltrate the British perimeter via an area of uncovered dead ground between Lieutenant Alan Green's 20 Platoon and Lieutenant George Brown's 22 Platoon; the interlopers were able to shoot up two Jeeps belonging to a 6-Pounder Gun Section and made good their escape before the glider soldiers could react. The two Platoons were obliged to reorganise their positions to prevent a recurrence, fortunately without further interference from the enemy.[62]

The relative quiet did not extend to the northern half of the 1st Border's frontage. At 10:00 a group of German infantry supported by two armoured vehicles, reportedly a tank and a self-propelled gun, were spotted approaching A Company's location near the Graftombe by Corporal Walter Collings, whose Scout Section from 10 Platoon was deployed covering tracks through the woods; the vehicles were probably from *Panzer Kompanie 224*. Collings quickly divined the vehicles' line of approach and set up an ambush with a PIAT, but as the tank emerged into view 10 Platoon's commander and Platoon Sergeant, Lieutenant Edmund Scrivener and Sergeant John Hunter, emerged around a bend farther down the track; the commander of the lead German vehicle and Sergeant Hunter were both killed in the ensuing exchange of fire.[63] According to Collings' account Sergeant Hunter 'fell right beside me. The officer lost his mind and was running all over the place, the tank still firing.'[64] Lieutenant Scrivener's account was different: 'I heard what sounded like a thousand tin cans being rattled. Curious, I strolled to the end of an avenue of trees and looked along it. Coming toward me were two Tiger tanks and their supporting infantry. My sergeant and I dashed behind a coal shed just in time. The tank fired a couple of shells into the other end, but it must have been full of coal. Unfortunately my sergeant made a run for it. They shot him down before he had gone five paces.'[65] Whichever, the death of the lead vehicle commander appears to have dampened German enthusiasm, as they withdrew rather than pressing forward.

Corporal Collings was involved in beating off another German attack shortly thereafter:

> We were guarding a path in a different part of the woods when three truck loads of Germans started coming down, we engaged them, then all was quiet, then they felled a couple of trees across the path. I had my binoculars and could see them crawling behind the fallen trees, so I got Jack sighted on the spot from which they had emerged, and every time one came out I'd call to Jack and he would let go with his replacement Bren gun and the Germans soon gave up that idea.[66]

10 Platoon also had repeatedly to clear enemy infiltrators from a large house to the front of the Platoon position. Corporal Thomas Edgar led several such expeditions before being shot entering the back door of the house, prompting a Private Beardsall to empty an entire Bren magazine into the building; further investigation yielded a single German body. Corporal Edgar was evacuated to the Battalion RAP but subsequently died from his wounds.[67] The Border's C Company, dug in around the Koude Herberg junction where the Van Borsselenweg ran south from the Utrechtseweg, also came under pressure from elements of *SS Unterführerschule* 'Arnheim'. The attack began with intense fire from mortars and a *nebelwerfer* that interfered with

efforts to evacuate the non-ambulatory wounded from the positions occupied by Lieutenant Alan Roberts' 16 Platoon; these may have included casualties caused by a near miss to one of the attached 6-Pounder guns which killed Private James Wells and wounded Sergeant French and Private Jock McKinley in the head and leg respectively. The bombardment was followed by a ground attack on 16 Platoon supported by one or possibly two tanks, again, likely *Flammpanzer B2 (f)* tanks from *Panzer Kompanie 224*. The attack was nullified with the assistance of an unnamed officer from the Royal Engineers, presumably from the 9th Field Company RE dug in on C Company's left flank, given that the Field Company War Diary refers to enemy tanks being involved in the morning fighting.[68] The Germans retaliated by setting fire to the thatched roofs of several houses to the front of Lieutenant Roberts' position and using the smoke to cover a second assault, which was also driven off. The glider soldiers were unable to prevent a number of Dutch civilians sheltering in the houses being burned to death.[69]

The German attacks from the north against the line on the Graaf Van Rechterenweg were the work of *Kampfgruppen* Bruhn and Krafft, which had closed in on Oosterbeek from the *sperrlinie* along the Dreijensweg and across LZ L, while the enemy pressing against the 1st Border's A Company from the west belonged to *SS Bataillon Eberwein*. As noted, the latter made up the centre of the German front moving in from the west, having been tasked the previous day to clear Wolfheze and advance along the line of the Arnhem-Ede railway, accompanied by tanks from *Panzer Kompanie 224*. Although the 1st Border Company was unaware of the fact, the pressure could have been a good deal more acute: Hackett's 4th Parachute Brigade HQ and the depleted 10th and 156 Parachute Battalions were still at large near Wolfheze, and thus inadvertently distracted a good portion of *SS Bataillon Eberwein's* attention from the Divisional perimeter. According to Hackett the Brigade was on the move by 06:15, although this may have referred to the HQ element, given that 156 Parachute Battalion did not report receiving the movement order until forty-five minutes later.[70] Hackett's plan was to follow a wooded track south-west from the Point 232 overnight position to a larger track called the Breedelaan that ran almost due south past the Hotel Bilderberg to the Utrechtseweg, and then move east to the Hotel Hartenstein. The approximately 270-strong 156 Battalion was to take the lead followed by Hackett's HQ and Brigade Troops with the c. 250-strong 10th Battalion bringing up the rear. Hackett also organised what he dubbed an 'advance group' to act as a vanguard made up of men drawn from all units and commanded by Captain Reginald Temple from the Brigade Staff; according to one source the group also included a number of Glider Pilots.[71]

Matters went awry virtually from the outset. The advance group came under fire almost immediately on moving off, possibly from a German ambush, and likely before the Brigade column had shaken out properly. Captain Temple was wounded in the right arm in the exchange and Hackett was obliged to despatch a protective screen of HQ personnel commanded by Captain Edmund James to cover the advance group's withdrawal into the Brigade HQ portion of the column.[72] 156 Parachute Battalion was then directed to lead the move along another track toward the Breedelaan, moving off at 07:00. Lieutenant-Colonel Des Vœux placed the officerless A Company in the lead followed by Major Michael Page's HQ Company, Major Geoffrey Powell's C Company and with badly depleted B Company bringing up the rear, totalling approximately 270 men. The Breedelaan was reached without incident and the column made good progress until some point between 07:15 and 08:00, when it reached a track junction around 300 yards short of the Utrechtseweg and just west of the Hotel Bilderberg.[73] A Company was then brought to a halt by intense automatic fire from the houses grouped around the junction. While A Company attempted to fight through, Colonel Des Vœux ordered C Company to perform a right flanking movement around the blockage. Powell's men reached a position overlooking the Utrechtseweg and shot up a number of halted half-tracks, but were then also stopped approximately 200 yards short of the road by fire from German troops dug in on the opposite side. This caused a number of casualties including the commander of 11 Platoon, Lieutenant William Donaldson, whose death left Powell as C Company's sole officer. He formed a defensive perimeter and rebuffed two German counter-attacks, but ammunition began to run short and when Powell returned to Battalion HQ in person to obtain a resupply, Colonel Des Vœux ordered him to bring his Company back to the main Battalion location on the Breedelaan. The move appears to have been complete by 10:00.[74]

By this point Hackett realised that the scale of opposition 'was not the odd patrol I had thought but a force moving EAST along axis either WOLFHEZEN – main rd – or HEELSUM main rd, whose left our adv gp must have bumped on first moving off'. He ordered Lieutenant-Colonel Smyth to deploy the 10th Battalion to cover the right rear of the column while 156 Battalion continued to push along the line of the Breedelaan.[75] To complicate matters, Urquhart came up on the Brigade net while all this was going on and ordered Hackett to attend the 08:00 conference at Division HQ, although this at least provided Hackett with the opportunity to inform the Division commander of his situation.[76] By 10:00 156 Battalion had secured the track junction in the face of constant fire from German mortars and anti-tank guns, the latter being used against any building captured by the paratroopers, but the Battalion lost over half its strength in the process. C Company was reduced to forty men, HQ Company to thirty, A Company to fifteen and B Company to just six, although Hackett estimated German losses were five times higher.[77] In the meantime a series of 'small exploiting attacks' led by Brigade Major Bruce Dawson, presumably using Brigade HQ personnel, had identified an opening in the surrounding enemy to the east. Hackett decided to reorient his axis of movement by side-slipping into the gap as far as another track called the Valkenberglaan before striking south again for the Utrechtseweg, and ordered 156 Battalion to hold in place while the 10th Parachute Battalion took the lead. 156 Battalion interestingly characterised its part in the new scheme as covering '10 Bn's withdrawal to the Div perimeter'.[78] Colonel Smyth appears to have been rather slower moving off than Hackett had anticipated, reportedly because the 10th Battalion's 'starting org was not over strong'. This was perhaps because Smyth was approaching the end of his tether, as shown by a conversation between him, the commander of HQ Company Major Charles Ashworth, and QM Lieutenant Joseph Glover at 03:00 that morning; according to Glover, Smyth said 'Look, I think we've had it. I've lost my command and I don't know where we are. I think you'd better get in pairs and decide if you want to stick with me or go it on your own.' After some discussion the two officers decided to stick with their Battalion commander.[79] Once underway the move appears to have proceeded rather too swiftly. Hackett noted: 'Comms bad and when they did start they pushed on without much regard to the rest of the coln [sic] which lost touch with them and ultimately got divided in two.'[80]

The 10th Battalion's semi-official account puts things rather differently, referring to slow progress due to having to 'overcome a certain amount of opposition from enemy tanks' and to receiving a radio message from Hackett just after turning south onto the Valkenberglaan at midday that ordered Smyth to 'pull the plug' and speed things up.[81] Smyth reacted by ordering his men to fix bayonets and charge, although it is unclear whether the charge was directed southward toward the Utrechtseweg or east toward the Sonnenberg. Whatever the direction, the charge carried the paratroopers clear of the enemy and the woods, although the dead included D Company's commander, Captain Cedric Horsfall.[82] Once within the relative safety of the Division perimeter the much-reduced Battalion formed up and marched up to the Hotel Hartenstein. Their arrival at 13:10 was witnessed by Urquhart:

I saw the remains of the battalion as it turned off the main road, following the line of trees into the HQ area. The men were exhausted, filthy, and bleeding; their discipline was immaculate…Their commander, Lieutenant-Colonel Ken Smyth, his right arm bandaged where a bullet had struck, reported breathlessly: 'We have been heavily taken on, sir. I have sixty men left.' 'What has happened to Hackett?' I asked. 'He'll be here as soon as they can disengage…They were in rather a mess in the woods up there.'[83]

The move had cost the 10th Battalion around 190 killed or missing, comparable to the 179 men lost by 156 Battalion in its vain attempt to force a passage down the Breedelaan. The difference was that Colonel Des Vœux's Battalion, along with Hackett and Brigade HQ, were still embroiled in the mess in the woods, and would remain so for several hours.

***

Fifty miles to the south at Son the end of the German Tuesday evening attack along the Wilhelmina Canal sparked a furious bout of redeployments and defence building that lasted into the early hours of Wednesday 20 September. In the immediate aftermath of the attack the 1st Battalion 327th Glider Infantry Regiment was brought down from the landing area to establish a defensive perimeter south of the Wilhelmina Canal, reinforced with two more 57mm anti-tank guns from the 81st Airborne Anti-Aircraft Battalion and augmented by a 'narrow minefield' laid by a platoon from the 326th Airborne Engineer Battalion. As the partial delivery of the third lift had left the glider battalion understrength, the 2nd Battalion 506th Parachute Infantry was brought up from Eindhoven and deployed east of Son on the north side of the Canal, and at 05:00 the 15th/19th Hussars were also put on standby to move south over the Son bridge to assist if necessary.[84] These precautions proved to be prudent as *Panzer Brigade 107* renewed the attack along the south side of the Wilhelmina Canal at 06:15, on the assumption that the US defenders would not be expecting an attack on exactly the same point so soon, and because *Major* von Maltzahn considered a daylight attack feasible owing to the amount of self-propelled *flak* deployed by his formation – around 250 assorted 37mm, 20mm and 15mm weapons.[85] The attack once again came during a US reconnaissance effort, this time involving two Jeeps carrying Captain T. P. Wilder and nine men from the Division Reconnaissance Platoon, who were despatched to locate the German concentration area and ascertain how and where they were moving men and vehicles across the canal. Departing while it was still dark, Captain Wilder's party came upon an unidentified British Colonel after a mile or so, likely Lieutenant-Colonel Anthony Taylor commanding the 15th/19th Hussars, who was on the same mission in an armoured scout car. The three vehicles therefore travelled together for another mile or so before Taylor stopped in the pre-dawn gloom to allow a 150-strong party of what he assumed were US troops to cross the road. The infantry were in fact Germans and realised that the vehicles were enemy as Taylor and Wilder tried to quietly reverse back to where the road was wide enough to turn their vehicles around. The scout car and Jeeps then escaped unscathed under a fusillade of German fire, and the Captain Wilder set up two mutually supporting machine-gun posts back down the road toward Son that successfully held the German column back until the Reconnaissance Platoon was relieved later in the day.[86]

Back at the Son bridge *Panzer Brigade 107's* 06:15 attack fell on the sector occupied by Captain Walter L. Miller's Company C from the 327th Glider Infantry Regiment, which, due to the fragmented glider lift, consisted of just the Company HQ element, 1st Platoon and the Company mortar and machine-gun squads. The attackers overran and wiped out an outpost that nonetheless managed to raise the alarm in the process, but Miller managed to rebuff the German infantry by keeping control of the few shallow ditches leading toward the bridge site by switching his men back and forth across his sector, while the 57mm anti-tank guns kept the accompanying Panthers at bay; the attackers were also constrained by a lack of cover and room to manoeuvre because of the Canal. *Major* von Maltzahn then launched an additional assault on the 1st Battalion 506th Parachute Infantry north of the Wilhelmina Canal before renewing the attack on Captain Miller's sector at around 07:15, employing more infantry and eight Panthers, which was only held by reinforcing Miller with a platoon-and-a-half from the 326th Airborne Engineer Battalion and co-opted HQ elements from the 506th Regiment en route to join the 1st Battalion north of the Canal. The day was saved by the arrival of ten Cromwells from the 15th/19th Hussars from the 05:00 stand to. The first two vehicles ran onto the US minefield despite attempted warnings from Company C. Captain Miller was blown off the rear deck of one vehicle and then wounded in the leg by German machine-gun fire. In a sharp exchange of fire the British tanks knocked out four Panthers in exchange for another Cromwell. By the late morning the attack was over and, having failed again to reach Son or the bridge over the Wilhelmina Canal and losing ten per cent of its strength, *Panzer Brigade 107* withdrew eastward to regroup and work out a more integrated plan of attack.[87] They were followed at 11:45 by a sweep to clear the area east of the Eindhovenseweg up to the River Dommel as far as Bokt to open the road to traffic, carried out by the 327th Glider Infantry Regiment's Companies A and C reinforced with a platoon from the 1st Battalion 506th Regiment and supported by the 15th/19th Hussars' seven surviving Cromwells; three of them followed the sweep line while the remaining four covered the flank with fire from the Eindhovenseweg. The action cost the 101st Airborne Division two dead and twenty-eight wounded and while German casualty figures are unclear, the Airborne soldiers and Hussars took eighty-five German prisoners. It also underscored the vulnerability of the location, so while the Division service area remained at Son with the 326th Airborne Engineer Battalion as security, Division HQ temporarily relocated at 08:30 to Wolfswinkel, just over a mile north of Son, and then to a permanent site in the castle at St. Oedenrode at 16:00.[88]

While all this was going on the remainder of the 327th Glider Infantry Regiment was taking responsibility for protecting the artillery and support units in the Division area and LZ W for future use. To that end, the 2nd Battalions swept the Zonsche Forest prior to setting up a defensive position on the eastern side and embarking on an intensive programme of patrolling, while the 3rd Battalion was made responsible for gathering supplies and forwarding them to Division HQ; this led to an afternoon skirmish with a German patrol that penetrated onto the LZ, which was driven off after suffering a number of casualties. Similarly, the 2nd and 3rd Battalions 502nd Parachute Infantry Regiment were to be reunited with the Regiment's HQ and 1st Battalion at St. Oedenrode and made responsible for that area. The withdrawal from east of Best was delayed by accurate German shelling until counter-battery fire from the 377th Parachute Field Artillery Battalion suppressed the German guns and prevented German reinforcements reaching Best from the north, and the two Battalions finally moved off at 17:00, although their destination had suffered from 'spasmodic but heavy shelling' throughout the day. The 1st Battalion's Command Post was hit by an artillery salvo just after midday that killed four men and wounded two more, compelling Lieutenant-Colonel Cassidy to relocate to a factory cellar. In the late afternoon the Division HQ advance party came under direct fire from German self-propelled guns while preparing the castle for its new role as the Division Command Post. Cassidy responded by personally sallying forth into the growing dusk with a platoon from his Company A and two of the 15th/19th Hussars' tanks, and successfully drove off the enemy guns.

Another hot spot in the 101st Airborne Division's area on 20 September was the east bank of the River Aa north of Veghel, involving Lieutenant-Colonel Harry W. O. Kinnard's 1st Battalion 501st Parachute Infantry Regiment. In order to keep the enemy off balance the 501st Regiment's commander, Colonel Howard R. Johnson, authorised Kinnard to carry out a Battalion sweep to eliminate the enemy from the area between Veghel and Heeswijk, four miles to the north along the parallel River Aa and Zuid Willems Canal. As the 1st Battalion's Company C was already ensconced in the area of Heeswijk and nearby Dinther on outpost duty, Kinnard intended to have it seal the northern end of the area by securing bridges over the River Dommel and Zuid Willems Canal directly west of Heeswijk, while Companies A and B moved north in-line abreast, with Company A between the watercourses and Company A on the right between the River and the Veghel-Heeswijk road. The attack began at 09:30 and ran into the German main line of resistance thirty minutes later; by 17:30 the manoeuvring force had pushed the Germans back out of two sets of prepared positions into the kill zone prepared by Company C to their rear. The fight cost the 1st Battalion four dead and six wounded, the dead including Lieutenant Henry J. Pulhaski from Company A, killed on going forward to investigate a white flag. The action inflicted forty dead and the same number wounded on the enemy. A further

418 Germans surrendered. The attackers then set up individual Company perimeters in the vicinity of Dinther and Heeswijk where they remained unmolested through 21 September. The remainder of the 501st Regiment also had a relatively quiet day, with the 2nd Battalion in Veghel processing the prisoners coming back from the 1st Battalion's fight while the 3rd Battalion conducted patrols around Eerde to the west, which noted the Germans digging in around Schijndel. Of more immediate concern was the supply situation, as fuel was running short and the K and D Rations brought in on 17 September were all but exhausted; only thirty per cent of the latest supply drop had been recovered and many paratroopers were thus becoming increasingly short of food despite the best efforts of the local civilian population, especially those farthest from the Division service area at Son. On the other hand, the morning of 20 September brought a solution to the plight of the mounting number of Airborne casualties, with the arrival of a convoy of thirty ambulances and four 2½-ton trucks, which carried the casualties south to the 24th Evacuation Hospital at Bourg Leopold in Belgium. This shuttle continued throughout the remainder of the Operation, apart from temporary halts caused by the Germans cutting the road south.[89]

***

In the 82nd Airborne Division's area to the north, Major-General Gavin spent the small hours of Wednesday 20 September working out the details of his scheme to secure the Nijmegen road and rail bridges across the River Waal. The scheme was relatively simple but relied upon speed and bold application to head off the developing impasse by securing both ends of the bridges. The effort against the south end of the road and rail bridges was to be resumed by the West and East Forces, while Colonel Tucker and the 504th Parachute Infantry Regiment was to advance north from the Jonkerbosch wood and clear the three miles up to the crossing point on the River Waal, just east of the confluence between the Maas-Waal Canal and the River Waal. Gavin had selected that spot as the canal provided a covered embarkation point and a calmer area for the paratroopers to familiarise themselves with the assault boats rather than the fast-flowing open river; the boats were to be crewed by men from the 307th Airborne Engineer Battalion. On the downside the crossing point was 1,500 yards downstream from the railway bridge and a further 1,000 yards from the road bridge, although the distance would hopefully keep the boats clear of the German defences protecting the bridges. Artillery support was to be provided by the 504th Regiment's organic 81mm mortars, the 376th Parachute Field Artillery Battalion, which Gavin had relocated to bring the crossing site within range, and the Guards Armoured Division's 153 Field Regiment RA equipped with twenty-four Sexton self-propelled 25-Pounder guns. Direct fire support was to be provided by two 57mm anti-tank guns from the 80th Airborne Anti-Aircraft Battalion and the Sherman tanks of the 2nd (Armoured) Battalion Irish Guards, which were to line the south bank and shoot the paratroopers across; it is unclear if the tanks were also to assist in the clearing of the area up to the crossing point. The major question mark hung over the arrival of the assault boats, which Gavin had hoped would be delivered before daybreak to allow the crossing to begin under cover of darkness, although this somewhat optimistic hope was dashed at some point during the night when word reached Gavin's HQ that the boats would not arrive until at least midday. The crossing would therefore have to take place in full daylight and thus in full view of the Germans manning the defences on the north bank of the River Waal.[90]

Back at the *Keizer Lodewijkplein* Lieutenant-Colonel Vandervoort's paratroopers from Companies E and F, 2nd Battalion 505th Parachute Infantry Regiment spent the night shoring up their hold on the buildings adjacent to the traffic circle and patrolling to probe the German positions and dominate the flame-illuminated streets, again sparking numerous no-quarter fights between small groups in darkened rooms and alleyways. As muzzle flash tended to attract unwelcome attention firing was kept to a minimum and many encounters were decided with rifle butts, bayonets or trench knives; one party from Company E resorted to exactly those means to empty a group of occupied slit trenches.[91] Their opponents were engaged in similar activities. A six-man German patrol approached the house occupied by Corporal Earl Boling and his Squad and attempted to storm the building when the paratroopers engaged them with a hand-thrown rifle grenade. One German almost gained entry via the window guarded by Boling after he fumbled changing magazines on his Browning Automatic Rifle; the interloper was shot several times in the face at point-blank range by Private George Wood using a Beretta pistol he had picked up as a souvenir in Sicily.[92] Rank meant nothing: when another German patrol approached the house occupied by Lieutenant-Colonel Vandervoort's HQ they were cut down by his men firing through the 'lace curtained front door and windows'.[93] The fighting may have been sharp and brutal by necessity but there was also the occasional flicker of humanity. Sometimes men were taken prisoner rather than killed, and at one point in Company E's sector the Germans requested and were granted a short local ceasefire to evacuate some wounded; the paratroopers stood watching their opponents work, albeit with weapons at the ready.[94]

Shortly after distributing the order to suspend the attacks toward the rail and road bridges Lieutenant-Colonel Goulbourn was summoned to 5th Guards Armoured Brigade HQ, where Brigadier Gwatkin informed him that the Grenadier Guards Group and the 505th Regiment were to be responsible for resuming the effort the following day, and that US troops would be conducting a river crossing to the west of Nijmegen supported by tanks from the Irish Guards Group. For some reason Gwatkin's instructions also differed somewhat from Gavin's stated intent, for Captain Neville's West Force was to remain in place rather than renewing its drive for the railway bridge and act as a flank guard for the drive on the road bridge and the proposed river crossing to the west. As he was leaving Gwatkin's HQ, Goulbourn overheard a snippet of conversation from a staff officer, reporting that the Irish Guards tanks would no longer be required at 08:00 as planned. This was likely connected to the delay in getting the assault boats to the head of the Guards Armoured Division's column, but Goulbourn interpreted it to mean that the river crossing to the west had been cancelled. He therefore returned to his HQ via Lieutenant-Colonel Vandervoort's Command Post under the false impression that his attack toward the road bridge was to be the sole effort to cross the River Waal that day.

Lieutenant-Colonel Goulbourn's scheme for 20 September was a two-stage affair. The first stage involved the 2nd Battalion 505th Parachute Infantry's Companies E and F holding in place masking the Hunnerpark on either side of the *Keizer Lodewijkplein* while the Grenadier Guards Group expanded the attack frontage on their left toward the River Waal; the expansion would take in the entire north-west side of the Valkhofpark and Hunnerpark, which would mean the SS defenders would have to protect themselves from three directions at once. With this complete, the second stage was to be a co-ordinated and simultaneous attack by Guardsmen and paratroopers intended to pinch off the SS defences at the south end of the road bridge in their entirety and allow the entire structure to be secured. To that end Major Harry Stanley's No. 4 Company, presumably accompanied by Major George Thorne's column and possibly reinforced with a Troop of Shermans, was to extend its frontage to the right from the post office and link up with Vandervoort's paratroopers on the left of the *Keizer Lodewijkplein*. Goulbourn's No. 2 Company, also reinforced with a Troop of tanks, was to move in on Stanley's left and Captain the Hon. Vicary Gibbs King's Company on his left, also reinforced with four Shermans. The repositioning was scheduled to begin at 08:15.[95] Although it took longer than expected, by 14:00 the 1st Grenadier Guards three Companies had not only completed the repositioning but had pushed east and cleared the area of narrow streets up to the Lindenberg along the western edge of the Valkhofpark, including the large police station and convent buildings; in doing this they liberated Captain Jonathan E. Adams and his men from the 1st Battalion 508th Parachute Infantry Regiment, who had been in hiding since the initial abortive attempt to seize the road bridge on the night of 17-18 September.[96] With stage one of his scheme completed, Lieutenant-Colonel Goulbourn conferred with Lieutenant-Colonel Vandervoort on the details for the co-ordinated assault on the SS defences covering the south end of the bridge, which was scheduled to go in at 15:30.[97] While all this was going on the men of the Companies E and F, whilst remaining alert, turned their attention to the pressing matter of food as the K and D Rations brought in on 17 September had run out the previous day and no resupply had reached Vandervoort's Battalion. The paratroopers made up the shortfall by helping themselves to the tame rabbits and vegetable patches that abounded in the Dutch suburban back gardens and 'GI rabbit stew' became the plat du jour. Although it likely did not overly worry the hungry Airborne recipients, the quality appears to have been variable; Lieutenant-Colonel Vandervoort remarked that he did not 'recall that it qualified as gourmet'.[98]

While the 2nd Battalion 505th Parachute Infantry Regiment was watching and dining at the *Keizer Lodewijkplein*, the Regiment's 1st and 3rd Battalions were facing a resurgent threat on the south and east faces of the 82nd Airborne Division's perimeter, along with the 508th Parachute Infantry Regiment. On 17 September *Wehrkreis VI*, an administrative HQ located at Münster, had been charged with dealing with the US landing near Nijmegen and operational responsibility was devolved to *General* Kurt Feldt, who was given two *Fallschirmjäger* Divisions with which to complete the task. These formations had to be concentrated at Cleve as their constituent units were located at a variety of locations across western Germany however, and while this was being done Feldt had despatched *Generalleutnant* Gerd Scherbening and the *406 z.b.V. Division* to attack the US perimeter in the morning of 18 September; Scherbening's men rapidly overran the sparsely defended landing area and it took strenuous counter-attacks by elements of the 505th and 508th Regiments to eject the interlopers in time for the 82nd Airborne Division's glider lift in the mid-afternoon, inflicting a crushing defeat on the motley collection of German units. However, by 20 September the main body of *Korps* Feldt's force had reached the front and was poised to deliver a violent and co-ordinated attack along the entire eastern aspect of the 82nd Airborne Division's already stretched perimeter, in tandem with an attack on the southern aspect from out of the *Reichswald* forest by *General der Fallschirmtruppe* Eugen Meindl's *II Fallschirm Korps*. The attack was intended to capture the Groesbeek Heights via this pincer movement before clearing the area between the high ground and the Maas-Waal Canal, and securing Nijmegen.[99]

The attack from the east was assigned to two formations. *Luftwaffe Major* Karl-Heinz Becker's *Kampfgruppe* was essentially the cadre of the badly mauled *3 Fallschirmjäger Division* made up of the remnants of *Fallschirmjäger Regiments 5, 8* and *9* augmented with recently drafted recruits totalling around 700 men, together with the Division's surviving reconnaissance, engineer, anti-tank and *flak* elements and five assault guns from *Fallschirm Sturmgeschütze Brigade 12*. Becker's eastern attack force was augmented with a *Heer Kampfgruppe* commanded by *Hauptmann* Clemens *Freiherr* von Fürstenberg consisting of a reserve *aufklärungs abteilung* equipped with armoured half-tracks, a small *flak* detachment with two 20mm and one 88mm guns and *Infanterie Bataillon* 'Isphording', around 500 men in total. *Kampfgruppe* Becker was to attack and clear Wyler before pushing west across the US landing area and onto the Groesbeek Heights, while on the right *Kampfgruppe* von Fürstenberg was to attack and clear Beek before pushing into Nijmegen to relieve *Kampfgruppen* Euling and Henke holding the Waal bridges; both formations were then to push on and clear the east bank of the Maas-Waal Canal as far north as the Honinghutie bridge. The attack on the southern aspect of the US perimeter was also assigned to two formations. *Kampfgruppe* Geschick was to advance north-west along the Grafwegen-Groesbeek road, envelop and secure the latter before pressing onto the Groesbeek Heights and linking up with *Kampfgruppe* Becker. To achieve this *Major* Geschick commanded a *Luftwaffe Festung Bataillon*, a so-called 'ear battalion' made up of overage conscripts with hearing problems attached from *406 z.b.V. Division*, backed with a number of 20mm, 37mm and 88mm *flak* guns from *4 FlaK Division* divided into two groups configured for ground support, totalling just under a thousand men. Finally, *Luftwaffe Oberstleutnant* Hermann's *Kampfgruppe*, consisting of *Fallschirmjäger Lehr Regiment 21* augmented with a *kompanie* of

Flemish *Waffen SS*, supported by some 20mm and 88mm *flak* guns again configured for direct fire support and the guns of *Fallschirm Artillerie Regiment 6*. This force was reinforced with *Kampfgruppe* Goebel, which had been ejected from Mook by elements of the 1st Battalion 505th Parachute Infantry Regiment in the late afternoon of 18 September. *Kampfgruppe* Hermann was tasked to attack north out of the *Reichswald* forest up the east bank of the River Maas, secure Riethorst and Mook and then push on and seize the Molenhoek bridge over the Maas-Waal Canal, thereby blocking the flow of Allied supplies and troop reinforcements into Nijmegen and severing the Airborne Corridor.[100]

The attack on the east side of the US perimeter began before first light with an artillery and mortar bombardment on the hilltop position occupied by two Platoons from Company A 508th Parachute Infantry Regiment, reinforced with a Platoon from Company G commanded by Lieutenant John P. Foley, and a probe against an outpost to the front of the position. The bombardment ceased just after first light and an estimated *kompanie* of *Fallschirmjäger* from *Kampfgruppe* Becker attacked the US position, some of whom pressed forward to within five yards of the defender's five .30 machine-guns before being stopped. At one point an immaculately dressed German officer came forward and demanded that the US commander surrender his men and assemble them on the road in front of the hill, to which Lieutenant Foley replied, 'If you want me come and get me!' The fight went on for an hour before the *Fallschirmjäger* broke contact and withdrew to regroup. The attack to the southern sector began later, at 11:00. *Kampfgruppe* Geschick subjected Major James L Kaiser's 3rd Battalion 505th Parachute Infantry Regiment to a concentrated bombardment from its assorted *flak* guns before a fierce attack that pushed Major Kaiser's outposts back half a mile to the outskirts of Groesbeek before the paratroopers were able to impose a pause. To the west *Kampfgruppe* Hermann treated Major Talton W. Long's 1st Battalion 505th Regiment to a similarly concentrated bombardment thickened with *nebelwerfer* rockets before attacking up the main road to Nijmegen, concentrating a complete *bataillon* on each village to ensure overwhelming numerical superiority. The German advance rolled over a roadblock at Plasmolen manned by Company B, from which only Private Albert Mallis escaped before moving on the half mile or so to Riethorst, which was defended by two platoons from B and C Companies. The first German assault was rebuffed with the assistance of ten 75mm Pack Howitzers, but a subsequent attack drove the US paratroopers out of the village; the survivors regrouped on the wooded Kiekberg hill to the east, from where they continued to harass German traffic on the main road. *Kampfgruppe* Hermann then pushed on another two miles to Mook, which was defended by two platoons from Company B. After a vicious house-to-house fight one US platoon was pushed back out of the town while the other went to ground in the cellars and continued the fight despite being overrun.[101] By the early afternoon of 20 September the south-eastern quadrant of the 82nd Airborne Division's perimeter was thus again on the verge of being overwhelmed in a rerun of events two days earlier, and the Germans were on the verge of reaching the bridge over the Maas-Waal Canal at Molenhoek. Drastic action was required if they were to be prevented from severing the Airborne Corridor.

Six miles or so to the north-west of the 82nd Airborne Division's landing area, the 504th Parachute Infantry Regiment spent the small hours of 20 September 1944 absorbing the fact they had been slated for an assault crossing of the River Waal and making preparations. According to one source they were collectively 'flabbergasted' and many viewed the prospect with something short of enthusiasm; while the views of the rank-and-file are unclear, the Regiment's officers were quite forthright. Lieutenant Allen McClain from the 3rd Battalion recalled, 'If ever I had wanted to be somewhere else…it would have been then.' His Battalion commander, Major Julian Cook, was reportedly 'dumbfounded' and Cook's Operations Officer, Captain Henry B. Keep, considered that 'the odds were very much against us'. The sentiment was echoed by Lieutenant John Holabird from the 307th Airborne Engineer Battalion's Company C, which was tasked to crew the assault boats for the crossing: 'I still hoped – or believed – the mission would be called off before we left; that we would wait around there until dark and then be sent back.'[102] Colonel

Tucker had other ideas and issued his orders at 06:00. The move north to the crossing site was to be led by Major Edward N. Wellems' understrength 2nd Battalion, consisting of just Company D and HQ Company, as Companies E and F were deployed protecting the Grave bridge and crossings over the Maas-Waal Canal; Major Wellems' men were also to provide security for the crossing site. Major Cook's 3rd Battalion was second in the column, tasked to spearhead the river crossing and presumably accompanied by Captain Wesley D. Harris' Company C, 307th Airborne Engineer Battalion, while Major Willard E. Harrison's 1st Battalion brought up the rear and were to be ferried over the River Waal in the wake of Major Cook's Battalion.

The move to the River Waal began at 07:30 with Company D in the lead, under orders from Colonel Tucker to avoid contact if at all possible in order to avoid alerting the Germans to what was going on. As a result it took Company D around four-and-a-half hours to navigate a path to the crossing site, and the paratroopers, despite orders, were nonetheless obliged to deal with some individuals or small groups of Germans encountered en route. Company D reached the crossing point at around midday and the remainder of the 504th Regiment followed without incident; on arrival the paratroopers were deployed into an area of low ground shielded from enemy observation by factory buildings and the riverside dyke.[103] The crossing had been provisionally scheduled to commence at 11:00 but this was put back to 13:30, so the keyed-up paratroopers settled down to await the arrival of the assault boats.

14

D Plus 3

12:00 to 23:59 Wednesday 20 September 1944

After a largely uneventful march from the Jonkerbosch woods, Colonel Rueben H. Tucker and the 504th Parachute Infantry Regiment had reached the launch point for their assault crossing of the River Waal by around midday. As the assault boats were still en route, the paratroopers were deployed into an area of low ground where they were screened from view by the riverside dyke and adjacent factory buildings. On arrival the commander of the 307th Airborne Engineer Battalion's Company C, Captain Wesley D. Harris, went to investigate the proposed loading site on the Maas-Waal Canal. Major Julian Cook, the commander of the 3rd Battalion, ascended to the ninth floor of a nearby power station accompanied by his Operations Officer, Captain Henry B. Keep, and his Company commanders to get a look at the crossing point. The sight was not a reassuring one.

The first obstacles were on the south side of the Waal, consisting of the dyke and a 150-yard stretch of mud beach to reach the water's edge. On the far bank there was 800 yards of totally open ground between the water's edge and a broad, 30-foot-high dyke carrying the Oosterhoutsedijk riverside road that angled away from the river to the west. The Germans were dug in on and behind the dyke in a network of trenches, bunkers and automatic weapon emplacements, which were reinforced to the east by the Fort Beneden Lent.[1] This was a brick defensive work complete with moat, constructed in the mid-nineteenth century to protect the Nijmegen river crossing, and the 20mm *flak* guns mounted there and those emplaced on the railway bridge were ideally positioned to deliver enfilade fire into the crossing site. The bridge defences, which consisted of thirty-four machine-guns, two 20mm *flak* guns and an 88mm dual-purpose piece, were to prove especially deadly.[2] Unsurprisingly, Captain Keep recalled that the first view of the crossing site drew gasps from the assembled officers and Captain T. Moffatt Burriss, the commander of Company I, thought the upcoming operation 'looked like a suicide mission'.[3] This impression was heightened when a formation of Allied transport aircraft passed overhead heading north and a 'veritable wall of small arms and *flak* greeted them from the area north of the Waal'.[4]

Major Cook's party appear to have been joined by Browning, Horrocks, the commander of the 2nd Irish Guards Lieutenant-Colonel Giles Vandeleur and a retinue of staff-officers and observers, along with Gavin and Colonel Tucker and his staff. The precise timing of the conference is uncertain, but it occurred at some point between midday and 13:30, when Gavin was called away to address the rapidly deteriorating situation in the south-eastern sector of the 82nd Airborne Division's perimeter.[5] The meeting was another study in contrasting battlefield sartorial styles, as noted by Glider Pilot Colonel George Chatterton, who presumably attended as part of Browning's entourage. Chatterton noted one Guards officer in suede shoes perched on a shooting stick, while three more sported suede chukka boots, corduroys and old school scarves, in contrast to the more warlike appearance of Colonel Tucker, 'who was wearing a helmet that almost covered his face. His pistol was in a holster under his left arm and he had a knife strapped to his thigh.' Tucker also conformed to Horrocks' popular American stereotype by chewing a cigar that he only removed occasionally 'long enough to spit'; Chatterton was amused to note that 'faint looks of surprise flickered over the faces of the Guards' officers' every time he did so.[6]

One of the senior officers, presumably Gavin, briefed the assembled officers on the details of the crossing, which was now scheduled to begin at 15:00, dependent on the arrival of the assault boats. A flight of eight Typhoons was to strafe the German positions on the north bank with bombs and rockets beginning at 14:45, simultaneously with a ten-minute supporting bombardment by artillery and mortars. At 14:55 the barrage would switch to white phosphorous ammunition for a further ten minutes to create a smokescreen and thereafter would only respond to specific fire requests called in by the paratroopers on the north bank; to this end Forward Observer teams from the 504th Regiment's 81mm Platoon and the 376th Parachute Field Artillery Battalion were to accompany the first wave. Direct fire support was to be provided by two 57mm anti-tank guns from the 80th Airborne Anti-Aircraft Battalion and twenty-four Irish Guards Sherman tanks; the latter were tasked to hit identified enemy targets with high-explosive rounds and address any gaps in the smokescreen with smoke rounds; Lieutenant-Colonel Vandeleur ran a line from his Jeep into the power station so he could use his vantage point to control his vehicles' fire.[7] As the expected thirty-three assault boats were insufficient to carry the 3rd Battalion in its entirety, Major Cook selected Companies H and I, commanded by Captains Carl W. Kappel and T. Moffatt Burriss respectively, to make up the first wave accompanied by a Battalion Command Group, a Squad of Engineers from the 307th Airborne Engineer Battalion commanded by Lieutenant John Holabird tasked to neutralise demolition charges on the bridges, Forward Observer teams from the 376th Parachute Field Artillery Battalion, and the Regiment's 81mm mortar platoon. Company I was to assault and clear the dyke and establish a defensive line to protect the crossing point, Company H was to attack and clear Fort Beneden Lent and Company G was to follow in the wake of Company H on crossing. Major Willard E. Harrison's 1st Battalion was to take over Company I's line on the dyke and the 3rd Battalion was then to move east to the Nijmegen–Arnhem road where Company G was to establish a roadblock facing north while Companies H and I attacked south along the road toward the road and railway bridges respectively.[8]

Major Cook departed with Colonel Tucker to brief his men and they were informed by Captain Harris that the current at the mouth of the Maas-Waal canal was too rapid to allow laden assault boats to access the River Waal in a safe and orderly manner; Harris therefore recommended that the assault boats be manhandled over the riverside dyke and launched directly onto the river, even though this would be in full view of the enemy. This was accepted by Tucker and Cook as it was assumed the smokescreen would provide cover. The 3rd Battalion moved up into the lee of the riverside dyke where they were organised into boat parties of thirteen and settled down to wait for the assault boats. Major Cook was approached by the 504th Regiment's chaplain, Captain Delbert Kuehl, who insisted on accompanying the first wave on the grounds that he had to accompany his men on what he, too, viewed as a 'suicide mission'. Captain Keep reported there was little conversation among the men during the wait, and some were fatalistic; Lieutenant Virgil F. Carmichael, the 3rd Battalion's Intelligence Officer, saw Lieutenant Harry F. Busby from Company I light a cigarette with an expensive lighter and then jettison the lighter and the rest of the pack, commenting that he would no longer need them.[9] Lieutenant James Magellas, a platoon leader from Company H, recalled that many men opted to catch up on sleep. This display of *sang froid* made a highly favourable impression on Lieutenant-General Horrocks, who congratulated Colonel Tucker in his usual urbane manner: 'My God look at 'em…They make an assault river crossing in a very short time…but here they lay some of 'em fast asleep! What wonderful troops.'[10] While the 1st and 3rd Battalions prepared, Company D provided security around the concentration area and Lieutenant Edward T. Wisniewski was hit by a sniper while leading one patrol and bled to death as German fire prevented medics from going to his aid despite their use of a Red Cross flag. Wisniewski was a popular officer and word of the manner of his death reportedly stiffened the resolve of some of the paratroopers waiting to cross.[11]

The assault boats finally arrived at some point between 14:40 and 14:50.[12] They were hurriedly unloaded by the men of the 307th Airborne Engineer Battalion who were to crew them, and who were unimpressed by the 20-foot-long plywood-bottomed vessels with their green canvas concertina sides. Lieutenant John Holabird, who had spent the night hoping the crossing would be called off, was 'momentarily stunned' at the sight of the flimsy yet heavy craft, and his reaction was shared by some of the 3rd Battalion's paratroopers when they were drafted in to help assemble and load the boats. The initial reaction of Private First Class Walter E. Hughes from Company I, a pre-war seaman, was one of 'complete horror' at the prospect of employing such craft on a fast-running river.[13] Captain Burriss overheard one of his men commenting, 'I can't even swim. Oh shit, I'm in big trouble.' Another enquired as to the whereabouts of the Boy Scouts that came with the toys, while Lieutenant Magellas was reminded of the craft he used for lake fishing trips back in Wisconsin.[14] To make things worse, only twenty-six assault boats had been delivered as one truckload had been destroyed en route, which meant a hasty reorganising of the boat parties that allotted some boats sixteen to eighteen passengers in addition to the three engineer crewmen, and not all came with their full complement of eight paddles.[15] With the boats erected and loaded Major Cook blew his whistle at 15:00 to signal the start of the crossing, and the individual parties lifted their boats and began moving toward the riverside dyke. The move was none too soon as the Germans, alerted by the activity, began to drop artillery shells into the vicinity of the staging area.

Merely carrying the boats, which weighed between 300 and 400 pounds before loading across the 150 yards to the river was no mean feat in itself and the task was complicated by the gradient of the dyke and the soft sand it was constructed from. The crossing ran into its first obstacle before clearing the far side of the dyke, in the shape of a tall chain-link fence topped with barbed wire that barred the way to the water's edge. Captain Kappel and Lieutenant Magellas blew down two supports with Gammon bombs before pushing a section of it flat and the boat parties then had to cover another hundred yards that included a three-foot high ridge and a stretch of thick, ankle-deep mud before reaching the water; Captain Keep's party simplified the process by allowing their assault boat to slide down the dyke and sliding after it. Loading and launching the vessels then brought its own problems. Captain Kappel had to rescue a Private Legacie from his party from drowning as his assault boat was launched, Captain Keep's boat grounded briefly on a mudbank and Lieutenant Carmichael's vessel spun in circles until he provided counter-paddling from the rear to keep it on course.[16] Despite all this the first wave was launched successfully and the little armada began to make its bobbing and circling way across the river, fighting the eight-knot current. In an attempt to ease matters for the men paddling his assault boat Major Cook set up a rhythm by chanting 'Hail Mary Full of Grace' and Chaplain Kuehl followed his lead with 'Lord, thy will be done'; on a less ecclesiastical note Captain Keep employed a 'one-two-three-four' chant from his stint of competitive rowing at Princeton University.[17]

Up until 100 yards of so out the crossing had only come under random small-arms fire but at that point the wind began to open gaps in the smokescreen on the north bank, possibly made more likely by the launch taking longer than planned; the Germans opened fire on the hapless assault boats with every weapon they could bring to bear. Private First Class Everett S. Trefetheren likened the result to a 'school of mackerel on the feed'.[18] The Engineer steering Captain Burriss' assault boat was hit in the wrist and then decapitated by a 20mm round, as was the man alongside the frantically paddling Chaplain Kuehl. The result of hits from larger-calibre rounds was devastating. Sergeant Albert A. Tarbell had just made eye contact with Private Louis Holt in a nearby vessel when Holt's boat was obliterated by a direct hit. Lieutenant Magellas lost half his platoon to another mortar bomb.[19] The floors of the surviving assault boats were soon carpeted with dead or wounded paratroopers slumped in several inches of water and blood, while those still physically capable paddled frantically with oars, rifle butts, helmets or their bare hands. It took between fifteen and twenty-five minutes for the assault boats to reach the north bank, and then up to 500 hundred yards downstream of their intended landing point owing to the current. A number of boats had to be abandoned as they were too badly damaged for reuse; according Captain Kappel only eight were in a fit state to return to the south bank.[20]

Not everyone paddled all the way. Captain Kappel jumped overboard into the shallow water and pushed his assault boat, which by now only contained two or three unwounded men, for the last thirty yards. Lieutenant Ernest Patrick Murphy's vessel was swamped by a near miss a similar distance out. All aboard made it to the shore including Private Joseph Jedlicka, a non-swimmer who landed upright on the riverbed and stolidly walked up the slope to safety still carrying his slung BAR and a can of ammunition in each hand.[21]

On reaching the north bank, the first to make landfall overran a number of waterside German positions, killing around fifty.[22] They then went to ground where they could to shelter from the incessant German crossfire, some in the lee of a convenient low embankment by the water's edge; others, including Captain Kappel, raced several hundred yards up the beach before finding shelter. Once under some semblance of cover the paratroopers paused to gather breath and wits and, as the chaos of the crossing had swept away formal unit organisation, gravitated to the nearest officer or NCO while clearing their weapons of river mud, securing equipment and distributing ammunition in preparation for the next move. The exceptions to this were Captain Hyman D. Shapiro, the 3rd Battalion's Assistant Medical Officer and Chaplain Kuehl, who busied themselves aiding the wounded along the water's edge, administering first aid and morphine and either putting into or leaving aboard the most serious cases on the assault boats moving back across the Waal; Chaplain Kuehl was wounded himself by mortar bomb fragments as he went about his work. The able-bodied plus a number of wounded then charged across the 800 yards to the dyke, intent on exacting retribution for what they had suffered during the crossing, under the continuing enfilade fire from the German automatic weapons sited in Fort Beneden Lent and the railway bridge; the automatic weapons behind the dyke were unable to depress sufficiently to hit the attackers as they drew closer. The paratroopers overran a number of outposts and despatched those within with bayonets and after a brief pause at its base, swarmed onto the dyke killing every German they found before pushing on to clear the network of positions behind the dyke, again with grenades and bayonets. The ruthless nature of the fight was well illustrated by a comment by Captain Kappel when subsequently chided by other 3rd Battalion officers regarding the small number of prisoners taken by Company H in the action: 'You captured yours. We shot ours.'[23]

By 15:45 the dyke had been secured and Captain Burriss and Company I had established a defensive perimeter to protect the crossing point as ordered and despite having been wounded in the right side during the crossing, Burriss set off with a group of men toward the railway bridge in the wake of Captain Kappel and Company H, who had already moved off eastward. After overrunning a German position dug into an orchard, Company H came under fire from the Fort Beneden Lent and Captain Kappel despatched Lieutenant Magellas' platoon to deal with it. Approaching from the north, Magellas laid suppressive fire on the fort's parapet and despatched Sergeant Leroy Richmond across the moat to investigate; when Richmond reported there was a drawbridge on the south side, Magellas led a charge across it, cleared the parapet killing around a dozen of the garrison, destroyed the 20mm guns emplaced there and drove the survivors into the lower reaches of the fort. As he lacked the numbers for a systematic clearing he then withdrew, leaving a .30 machine-gun team posted inside the drawbridge to keep the garrison bottled up and pressed on to rejoin Company H; the machine-gunners were relieved later in the day by the 1st Battalion, which then cleared the fort properly.

In the meantime Captain Kappel had reached the railway embankment at around 16:00, behind which the survivors from the fight at the dyke were regrouping and an impasse developed after attempts by the paratroopers to penetrate through underpasses beneath the line and charging over the top were rebuffed. Lieutenant Richard LaRiviere from Company I had reached the north end of the railway bridge via some ditches by the riverbank at around 17:00 and secured it after a brief fight. He was then joined by a succession of individuals and groups of paratroopers as they gravitated south in an attempt to bypass the block on the railway embankment, including Captain Kappel and the bulk of Company H, Captain Burriss and his party, and Major Cook, who had become separated from most of his Battalion Command Group. After Kappel's men had captured a fortified position built into the bridge structure partway across, taking Company H's first prisoners of the day in the process, Major Cook reported the capture of the 3rd Battalion's primary objective to Colonel Tucker by radio at 17:40 and requested tanks be despatched to the north bank immediately.[24]

While Colonel Tucker's 504th Regiment was carrying out its epic river crossing, Lieutenant-Colonel Vandervoort's 2nd Battalion 505th Parachute Infantry Regiment was continuing a watching brief along the south side of the *Keizer Lodewijkplein* traffic circle just south of the Nijmegen road bridge, although in some instances this brief was interpreted somewhat aggressively. Lieutenant James J. Coyle from Company E took a party of men including Corporal Thomas Burke, Corporal Earl Boling and Private John L. Gill to stalk a dual-purpose 88mm gun located in a street off the *Keizer Lodewijkplein* that had shelled the houses occupied by Coyle and his men during the previous day's fighting. Moving cautiously into an attic that overlooked the gun, the paratroopers drove the crew off the gun with rifle fire, killing one, and prompting the rest to abandon the gun and withdraw into the Hunnerpark. Thereafter matters went awry. Sergeant Ben Popilsky was shot dead while trying to join the group, Private Gill was badly wounded by Germans occupying an adjacent house and Corporal Burke was killed in an attempt to drag him to safety; in the end Lieutenant Coyle was obliged to blow out the back wall of the German-occupied house with a Bazooka before his party was able to withdraw to the main Company E position. The episode cost Coyle's platoon three dead and one wounded and it is unclear if the Germans re-manned the 88mm gun.[25] On the left of Colonel Vandervoort's position Lieutenant-Colonel Goulbourn's morning reorientation of the 1st Grenadier Guards had been successfully accomplished and in the early afternoon of 20 September he made some last-minute adjustments in readiness for the attack at 15:30. As the Grenadier's attack frontage was narrow and further constricted by rubble-filled streets, Goulbourn reduced his attack to a two-company affair, dividing his centre No. 2 Company up between his other two. On the left Captain the Hon. Vicary Gibbs' King's Company was tasked to secure the Valkhofpark and specifically the mound topped by the ruins of Nijmegen's ancient citadel, which, riven with tunnels, was the highest point in the city. On the right Major Harry Stanley's No. 4 Company was to secure a cluster of buildings on the boundary between the Valkhofpark and the Hunnerpark that included the Haus Robert Janssen, which *Hauptsturmführer* Karl-Heinz Euling had appropriated as his *Kampfgruppe* HQ. Lieutenant-Colonel Vandervoort's paratroopers were to attack the portion of the Hunnerpark west of the Arnhemscheweg, Lieutenant James E. Smith's Company E on the right assaulting directly across the *Keizer Lodewijkplein* into the corner of the park from the south while on the left Robert H. Rosen and Company F went in from the north-west across the Sint Jorisstraat; the remainder of 2nd Battalion was to provide supporting fire from the rooftops opposite the Hunnerpark.[26]

The 1st Grenadier Guards attack appears to have begun on schedule at 15:30 and ran into trouble almost immediately. The commander of the King's Company, Captain The Hon. Vicary Gibbs, was killed in the opening minutes of the attack and a newly arrived Lieutenant M. Dawson was obliged to take over.[27] The boundary of the Valkhofpark was blocked by barbed wire covered by machine-guns but the Guardsmen cut through an unguarded section of wire and passed two platoons through the gap, who penetrated to within fifteen yards of the mound before being spotted. A vicious ninety-minute close-quarter fight ensued with elements of *SS Panzer Pionier Bataillon 10* before most of the SS were driven off the mound, but heavy

German fire then prevented the Guards from pushing on to the road bridge, which was now in plain sight. Major Stanley's No. 4 Company was stopped by intense automatic fire and lost four of its supporting Shermans within minutes of leaving the start line and, after consultation with Lieutenant-Colonel Goulbourn, reoriented its axis of attack slightly to the right. The renewed effort by No. 4 Company then broke through into the Valkhofpark close to the *Keizer Lodewijkplein* and at the same time unhinged the right flank of the *SS Panzergrenadiers* in the Hunnerpark facing Company F.[28] Matters appear to have gone awry initially on the US attack frontage, as according to one source Captain Robert H. Rosen launched Company F's attack on the left of the *Keizer Lodewijkplein* prematurely, without permission from Lieutenant-Colonel Vandervoort or tank support, likely at around 15:00 given the subsequent sequence of events. Captain Rosen moved his men into the front and backyards around a street leading to the Hunnerpark, likely the Gerard Noodstraat, and then led a charge across the Sint Jorisstraat in person accompanied by the twenty or so men who heard him give the order. The attackers reached the edge of the Hunnerpark before being stopped by a wall of German defensive fire and the survivors, many of them wounded, fell back the way they had come. The dead included Captain Rosen who expired after being wounded in the face; he was seen running to the rear clutching his wound by Sergeant Spencer Wurst. Command of Company F was assumed by the senior platoon commander, Lieutenant Joseph Holcomb.[29]

The need for Company F to regroup following the premature attack may have delayed Lieutenant-Colonel Vandervoort launching his full assault on the Hunnerpark; this would explain the 16:40 start time cited in the US official history, and also the strength of the initial German reaction to the attack on the Valkhofpark, if the 1st Grenadier Guards went in as originally scheduled at 15:30.[30] On the right, Lieutenant Smith led Company E's 1st Platoon in a charge straight across the *Keizer Lodewijkplein* covered by fire from 2nd Platoon. The rush carried the paratroopers into the south-east corner of the Hunnerpark where they set about clearing the German trenches with grenades and bayonets. On the left, Company F left the shelter of the buildings and formed an extended line along the line of the Sint Jorisstraat and once all the paratroopers were in the open the Germans in the Hunnerpark opened fire with every weapon they could muster at ranges between twenty-five and 150 yards. The Company lost Lieutenant Holcomb killed and at least two platoon commanders severely wounded in a matter of minutes: Holcomb was shot through the head, possibly by a sniper, Lieutenant Bill Savell was shot through both arms and 1st Lieutenant John Dodd was so severely wounded in the body by a 20mm round that his platoon medic administered an overdose of morphine to ease his suffering. Despite this, F Company succeeded in penetrating into the southern edge of the park and set about clearing the trenches and gun positions in a flurry of merciless close-quarter fights. Their progress may have been eased by the appearance of the Grenadier Guards No. 4 Company, and more especially its supporting Sherman tanks, on the paratrooper's left flank, following Major Stanley's renewed push from the west.[31] The formal link-up of the Grenadier Guards No. 4 Company and Vandervoort's Company F occurred on the riverside embankment just west of the road bridge ramp, in the gathering dusk at around 18:30.[32] Organised German resistance in the area had ceased at some point before this, when *Hauptsturmführer* Euling's HQ in the Haus Robert Janssen at the south-eastern corner of the Valkhofpark was attacked by a platoon from No. 4 Company. The platoon was commanded by Lieutenant Adriaan Slob, a Dutch national who had escaped to Britain earlier in the war. After an inconclusive fight that included tanks firing point-blank into the building, Lieutenant Slob decided to burn the building down with phosphorous grenades rather than engage in a bloody room-to-room fight, after which the HQ was ignored.[33] Ironically, the events at the south end of the Nijmegen road bridge mirrored those twelve miles or so to the north, where the gallant defenders of the Arnhem road bridge by Lieutenant-Colonel Frost's force were coming to a similar conclusion.

There remained the task of physically taking the Nijmegen bridges. Captain Kappel and Company H from the 3rd Battalion 504th Parachute Infantry had secured the north end of the railway bridge by 17:40, and shortly thereafter Captain Neville's West Force renewed its push for the south end of the railway bridge. *Kampfgruppe* Henke appears to have been unaware of the US presence on the north bank of the River Waal and the renewed attack prompted around 300 men to fall back across the railway bridge, only to be faced by Captain Kappel's men, who had deployed two captured machine-guns and two Browning Automatic Rifle teams to fire down the length of the bridge. The guns engaged the approaching mob of Germans as they passed the fort built into the bridge structure, from which Captain Kappel thickened the fire with Gammon bombs, driving the Germans back into the middle of the span. Kappel then despatched a German prisoner to persuade them to surrender and when he was shot by SS among the throng, the guns resumed their fire, sweeping systematically back and forth across the width of the bridge, prompting a number of desperate men to jump into the River Waal; 267 bodies were later counted on the bridge.[34] In the meantime, Captain Burriss, Lieutenant LaRiviere and a small party had pressed east along the river and after a two-hour journey that involved tackling a houseful of Germans with a Gammon bomb, shooting up a German car full of Dutch currency, clearing two 88mm *flak* emplacements and taking a petrified lone sentry prisoner, arrived at the deserted north end of the road bridge at 19:00. Burriss immediately despatched Lieutenant LaRiviere onto the bridge with Private James Musa and another paratrooper to search for demolition charges, despite small groups of Germans making their way across the bridge from the clearly audible fight at the south end and fire from snipers ensconced high in the bridge structure. They were only partway across the span when a tank began to cross from the south end and assuming it was German, LaRiviere and his men hurriedly rejoined Burriss and the main group and prepared to engage the approaching vehicle with Gammon bombs, the only anti-armour weapon the little band had to hand.[35]

At the south end of the road bridge a Troop of Shermans commanded by Sergeant Peter Robinson had been held in readiness for a dash across the bridge once *Kampfgruppe* Euling's grip had been loosened. A first attempt at 18:00, prompted by Major Cook's 17:40 signal that did not make clear he was referring to the railway bridge, was driven back into cover by intense anti-tank fire, including shots from an 88mm dual purpose gun near the north end of the bridge.[36] The attempt was reportedly ordered by the commander of the 2nd Grenadier Guards, Lieutenant-Colonel Rodney Moore, which suggests that Sergeant Robinson's Troop was outwith the control of Lieutenant-Colonel Goulbourn and under the direct command of 5th Guards Armoured Brigade HQ or higher. In addition, Goulbourn had left that HQ the previous night under the impression that the assault crossing over the River Waal had been cancelled until a future date. The evidence further suggests that Major Cook's signal was the first intimation that Goulbourn and by extension Vandervoort had that theirs was not the sole effort and that the assault crossing had actually been carried while their renewed push on the road bridge was underway. Consequently, 'what has since been characterized as a finely synchronized operation was…the coincidental convergence of two separate attacks…with the same objective'.[37]

A second attempt to push across the road bridge was launched at 18:30 and Sergeant Robinson led his Troop, accompanied by a scout car carrying Lieutenant Anthony Jones from 14th Field Company RE, across the *Keizer Lodewijkplein* and up the Arnhemscheweg onto the bridge while the fight for the Hunnerpark was still in full swing. The number of tanks that reached and crossed the bridge is unclear, with one source claiming two were knocked out while accessing the bridge ramp while others refer to all four tanks crossing safely and to Sergeant Robinson changing vehicles en route as a non-penetrating hit had knocked out his radio.[38] However many tanks there were, Robinson's gunner knocked out an 88mm gun emplaced just off the north end of the bridge in an initial exchange of fire on entering the bridge. After clattering the length of it, shrugging off fire from German troops ensconced in the bridge superstructure and jinking through concrete barriers on the carriageway, he dealt with at least one more anti-tank gun – possibly a *StuG* – and a number of German infantry near the north ramp before drawing up to where Captain Burriss and his party were deployed in ditches on either side of the Arnhem–Nijmegen road. As the tank crewmen had no idea there were friendly troops in the vicinity they almost shot them up as well, before recognising their distinctive M1 helmets. The understandably relieved paratroopers swarmed over the Shermans in greeting and Captain Burriss joyfully informed Robinson's gunner, Guardsman Leslie Johnson: 'You guys are the most beautiful sight I've seen for years!' The time was 19:15 on Wednesday 20 September and the Nijmegen road bridge, along with the adjacent railway bridge, was finally in Allied hands.[39]

Sergeant Robinson had no way of knowing but his progress across the road bridge was being monitored by *Brigadeführer* Heinz Harmel, commander of *10 SS Panzer Division*, from atop a bunker in Lent at the north end of the bridge. The commander of *Heeresgruppe B*, *Generalfeldmarschall* Walther Model, had categorically forbidden the destruction of the Nijmegen bridges because he considered them vital for a subsequent German counter-offensive, although this was not universally accepted by the commanders tasked with their preservation. *Obergruppenführer* Bittrich for one, commanding *II SS Panzerkorps*, was sceptical that any such counter-offensive was likely to materialise and felt that the bridges should have been demolished as a precautionary measure. His view was shared by Harmel, who resolved to destroy the road bridge rather than allow it to fall intact into Allied hands. The bridge had been wired with at least 500 pounds of explosive in specially configured demolition charges on 8 September as part of the general preparations to meet the Allied ground advance, although not all the charges were laid and wired as doing so would have prevented traffic moving freely across it.[40] Harmel had *SS Panzer Pionier Bataillon 10* run a firing trigger for the charges out to a specially constructed bunker at Lent at the north end of the bridge that was permanently manned, and a party of *Untersturmführer* Baumgärtel's men were also charged with maintaining the integrity of the charges and their all-important wiring. Watching through binoculars in the gathering dusk, Harmel waited until the British tanks were in the middle of the span before ordering the duty *SS Pionier* to detonate the charges.

Nothing happened. A second working of the detonator firing circuit elicited the same lack of response and the commander of *10 SS Panzer Division* watched helplessly as the tanks advanced down the north ramp. Harmel withdrew to his HQ in Bemmel, where he learned that the railway bridge had also fallen intact, and ordered his staff to organise blocks on the roads leading to Arnhem from Lent and Elst with the remnants of *SS Panzer Regiment 10* and *SS Panzergrenadier Regiment 22* and whatever other forces they could muster. He then telephoned *II SS Panzerkorps* and instructed the staff officer who replied, 'Tell Bittrich that they're over the Waal.'[41] Why the emplaced demolition charges failed to detonate is an ongoing mystery. The deed of cutting the command wires is popularly attributed to a member of the Dutch Resistance named Jan van Hoof who reportedly sneaked onto the bridge and cut the wires on 18 September before being killed the following day. On the other hand Captain Burriss had ordered his men to cut all the wires they could find on reaching the road bridge, Lieutenant Jones cut a number of wires leading to the emplaced charge when he followed the tanks onto the bridge and they may also have been cut by mortar and artillery fire. Whoever was responsible, it was extremely fortunate for Sergeant Robinson, who was later awarded the Distinguished Conduct Medal for his part in the action; two of his men received the Military Medal.

The link-up between the 504th Regiment's paratroopers and the Grenadier Guards' tanks did not bring the fighting at either end of the bridge to an immediate halt. Captain Burriss's little band was joined by other elements of the 3rd Battalion 504th Parachute Infantry Regiment, including Major Cook, who set about clearing elements of *SS Panzer Pionier Bataillon 10* from the immediate area around the bridge ramp. The fighting lasted until midnight while the foothold on the north bank of the Waal was reinforced by more Shermans from Sergeant Robinson's No. 1 Squadron, the M10 tank-destroyers of B and C Troops, Q Battery 21st Anti-Tank Regiment RA at around 19:30, followed later by two companies from the 3rd Irish Guards.[42] Back at the south end of the bridge, isolated pockets of German troops continued to fight on in the parkland by the bridge ramp. At the citadel mound in the Valkhofpark, *Hauptsturmführer*

Krüger, the Forward Observer for *SS Artillerie Ausbildungs und Ersatz Regiment 5*, continued to call in artillery fire via radio and then Verey lights until contact was lost at 19:30 and then organised a last-ditch defensive position in the trenches around a first-aid bunker until his third wounding in the action put him out of commission. The position was finally overwhelmed at around 20:30 and SS survivors claimed that Krüger and a number of other SS prisoners were executed by their captors. At the Haus Robert Janssen HQ in the adjacent Hunnerpark, *Hauptsturmführer* Euling and sixty survivors of the earlier assault had withdrawn to the rear of the blazing building where they remained unmolested until the fire finally drove them out at 22:30. Euling then organised a breakout, leading the party on a circuitous route north through the Valkhofpark to the River Waal and thence eastward under the bridge ramp and on to safety; he was subsequently awarded the Knight's Cross in recognition of his leadership during the battle in Nijmegen.[43] The cost of the fight for the parkland was heavy on both sides. The 505th Regiment's Company F lost nineteen dead and fifty wounded clearing the Hunnerpark for example, and ended the fight with only fifty men still fit to fight. Almost all of the approximately 600-strong German force holding the parkland at the south end of the road bridge was killed, along with another eighty on the bridge or in the fight to extend the foothold in Lent.[44]

At the north end of the road bridge Major Cook's paratroopers had fully expected the Guards Armoured Division to push on immediately for Arnhem, just ten miles up the road, and their elation slowly turned to anger as the growing British force remained immobile. Lieutenant Ernest Patrick Murphy from the 3rd Battalion 504th Regiment climbed aboard Sergeant Robinson's tank and urged him to move, only to be informed by the otherwise willing Robinson that he had no orders to do so. Captain Burriss was reportedly so furious he threatened the deputy commander of No. 1 Squadron, Captain The Lord Peter Carrington, with his Thompson Gun; Carrington wisely dropped inside his tank and locked the hatch. Having paid in blood to secure the bridges their ire was understandable, and it was shared by their Regimental commander Colonel Tucker who was overheard in an acrimonious exchange with an unknown British major in a Command Post near the bridge ramp.[45] The depth of Tucker's anger is apparent from Gavin's recollection of visiting Tucker in the early morning of 21 September: 'Tucker was livid. I had never seen him so angry… His first question to me was, "What in the hell are they doing? We have been in this position for over twelve hours and all they seem to be doing is brewing tea." I did not have an answer for him.'[46] The puzzlement was shared by at least one British officer. Lieutenant Brian Wilson's platoon from the 3rd Irish Guards had been among the first to cross the road bridge in the wake of Sergeant Robinson's Troop, and after a night of immobility Wilson unsuccessfully sought enlightenment at his 2nd Company HQ: 'As far as I could discover…Nijmegen was fairly well cleared…The situation at Arnhem remained desperate. Yet the GAD did not move.'[47] The Americans' incomprehension was matched by their German opponents. In Harmel's view the British failure to advance rapidly north from the Nijmegen bridge squandered the last chance to reach the British Airborne troops who were at that time still clinging to the north end of the Arnhem road bridge, because at that time there were virtually no German troops between Nijmegen and Arnhem; that remained the case for up to sixteen hours until the Germans were able to fully access the Arnhem bridge at midday on 21 September and begin to channel reinforcements south. By halting after securing the Nijmegen road bridge the Guards Armoured Division and by extension 30 Corps effectively handed the hard-won initiative back to *II SS Panzerkorps*, which used the time to once again erect an effective defence where none had existed, as the Irish Guards Group discovered when it finally attempted to resume the advance at 13:30 on 21 September.

Quite why the Guards Armoured Division failed to push on after crossing the Nijmegen road bridge remains controversial and is almost invariably attributed to the difficulty in passing reinforcements up the Airborne Corridor and to Major-General Adair's formation being too badly stretched in defending the Corridor between Veghel and Nijmegen, the 82nd Airborne's perimeter, having supported the fight to secure the Nijmegen bridges. It has been said Adair was reluctant to launch his tanks into unknown territory, although the opposite claim that he delayed the advance after seeing the terrain north of Nijmegen is rather unlikely given that it was almost dark when the Nijmegen road bridge was taken, and Adair cannot therefore have had a clear look at what lay ahead until after dawn on 21 September, almost twelve hours after the event.[48] To be fair, the 2nd Grenadier Guards tanks required refuelling and replenishment after the fight to secure the road bridge, although given the urgency of the circumstances this ought to have been achievable with some application. More importantly, the 2nd Irish Guards appear to have been available and capable of continuing the advance after its fire support mission for the 504th Parachute Infantry Regiment's river crossing, given that it moved across the bridge in the early hours of 21 September, where the 3rd Irish Guards were already in place to act in their customary support role. However, it is difficult to avoid at least the suspicion that the failure to press on was simply another manifestation of the Guards adhering to the same modus operandi they had followed from the outset of Operation GARDEN, again, with no acknowledgement that extraordinary times required extraordinary measures. Over and above that, the root of the problem was a failure by the British senior commanders: as Powell points out, maintaining a reserve for unforeseen circumstances or exploitation is a basic military principle at every level of warfare but this, for whatever reason, was not done at Nijmegen.[49] Even if a full-scale push north was not feasible it ought to have been possible for the Guards Armoured Division to expand the thousand yards or so cleared by Lieutenant-Colonel Tucker's paratroopers; this would have provided a wider base from which to launch a subsequent drive and might well have disrupted the Germans in establishing their defences. The Guards Armoured Division and by extension 30 Corps thus stand condemned not for failing, but for failing to try. In the event the 1st Airborne Division, the 43rd Division – and ironically the Guards themselves – were to pay a high price for that failure over the next few days.

Major-General Gavin had been called away from the 504th Parachute Infantry Regiment's crossing point at 13:30 by a frantic call from his Chief-of-Staff Lieutenant Robert Wienicke, reporting that a renewal of the German attack on the south-eastern section of the 82nd Airborne Division's perimeter was on the verge of overrunning Beek, Wyler and Mook and the Molenhoek bridge. Gavin drove immediately to his HQ at Groesbeek where he was surprised to find an unannounced Major-General Matthew B. Ridgeway, commander of the US 18th Airborne Corps. Ridgeway had travelled up the Airborne Corridor on his own initiative, apparently without any legitimate reason other than discontent that the two US Airborne divisions were under Browning's command – and more generally piqued at Browning being appointed over him to deputy command of the 1st Allied Airborne Army. Having more important things to attend to than glad-handing unheralded senior commanders, and given that Ridgeway was engaged in discussion with his staff officers, Gavin instructed Lieutenant Wienicke to pass on his apologies at having to leave and promised to return as soon as possible before leaving for Mook. This was not the end of the matter. Two weeks later Gavin received a letter from Ridgeway accusing Gavin of a 'flagrant breach of military courtesy' by failing to acknowledge his Corps commander's presence. Gavin responded in his invariably correct manner by explaining the rather obvious extenuating reasons for his behaviour and tendering his resignation from command of the 82nd Airborne Division and from further command in the US 18th Airborne Corps, even if this entailed a reduction in rank; unsurprisingly his offer was not taken up and the matter appears to have been quietly dropped.[50] It is interesting to speculate on what Gavin made of being hindered by two egocentric and self-serving senior commanders during arguably the most demanding and complex military operation he had fought in.

On the northern outskirts of Mook near a railway underpass Gavin found the only thing seemingly standing between the advancing elements of *Kampfgruppe* Hermann and the Molenhoek bridge was a single rather shaken paratrooper with a Bazooka, a single Sherman tank from the 1st (Armoured) Battalion Coldstream Guards and a daisy chain of mines laid across the road. As Gavin watched, the Sherman backed onto one of the mines while manoeuvring, losing a track. He ordered his aide, Captain Hugo Olsen, and a Sergeant Wood to engage the advancing

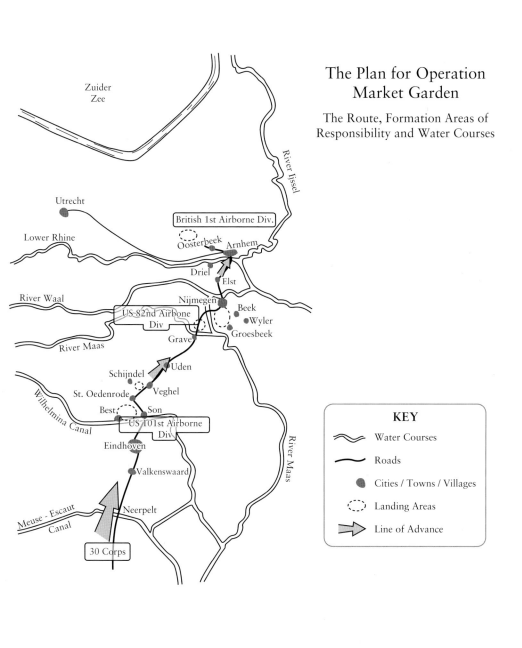

The Plan for Operation
Market Garden

The Route, Formation Areas of
Responsibility and Water Courses

Zuider
Zee

River IJssel

Utrecht

Lower Rhine

British 1st Airborne Div.

Oosterbeek Arnhem

Driel

Elst

River Waal

Nijmegen

Beek

US 82nd Airborne
Div   Wyler

Groesbeek

Grave

River Maas

Uden

Schijndel

St. Oedenrode   Veghel

Wilhelmina Canal

Best   Son

US 101st Airborne
Div

Eindhoven

River Maas

Valkenswaard

Meuse - Escaut
Canal   Neerpelt

30 Corps

KEY

Water Courses

Roads

Cities / Towns / Villages

Landing Areas

Line of Advance

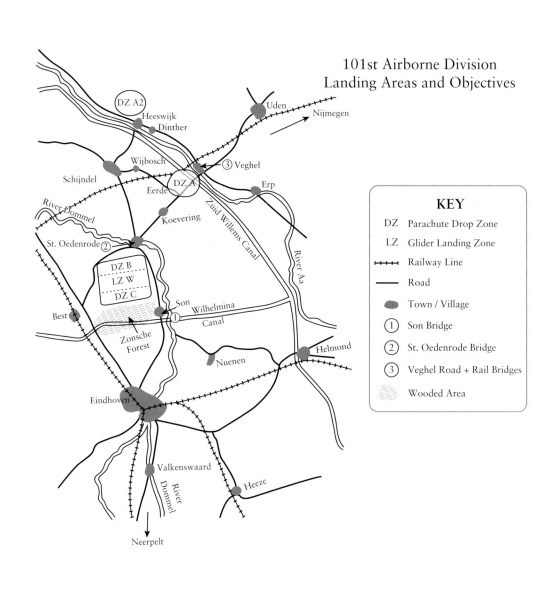

101st Airborne Division
Landing Areas and Objectives

DZ A2

Heeswijk
Dinther

Uden

→ Nijmegen

Wijbosch

③ Veghel

Schijndel

Erp

Eerde

DZ A

River Dommel

Koevering

Zuid Willems Canal

River Aa

St. Oedenrode ②

DZ B

LZ W

DZ C

Son

Wilhelmina Canal

Best

Zonsche Forest

Helmond

Nuenen

Eindhoven

Valkenswaard

River Dommel

Heeze

Neerpelt

KEY

DZ   Parachute Drop Zone

LZ   Glider Landing Zone

├┼┼┼┤   Railway Line

───   Road

⬤   Town / Village

①   Son Bridge

②   St. Oedenrode Bridge

③   Veghel Road + Rail Bridges

〰〰   Wooded Area

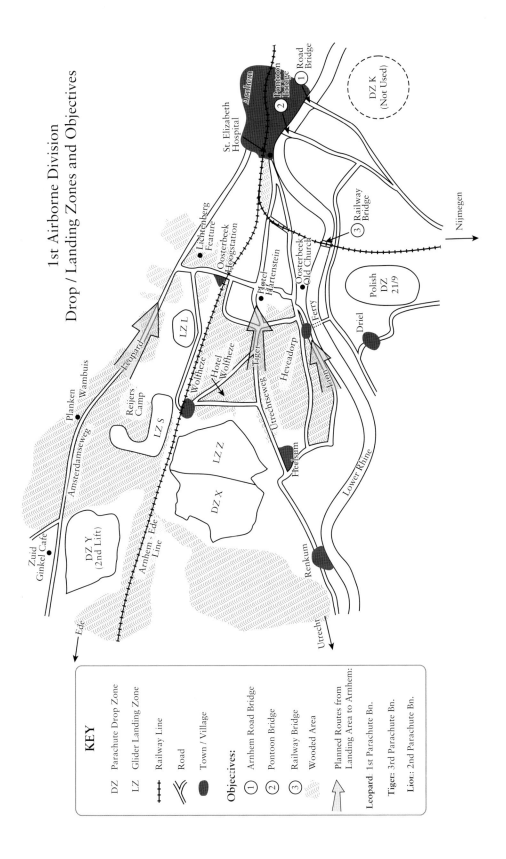

1st Airborne Division
Drop / Landing Zones and Objectives

KEY

DZ Parachute Drop Zone

LZ Glider Landing Zone

╾┼┼┼╾ Railway Line

⅄ Road

⬤ Town / Village

Objectives:

① Arnhem Road Bridge

② Pontoon Bridge

③ Railway Bridge

⬛ Wooded Area

⬆ Planned Routes from
   Landing Area to Arnhem:

Leopard: 1st Parachute Bn.

Tiger: 3rd Parachute Bn.

Lion: 2nd Parachute Bn.

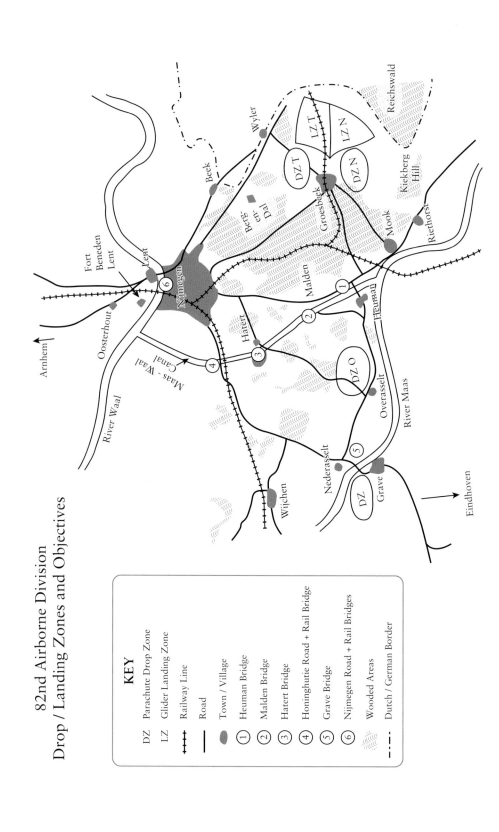

82nd Airborne Division
Drop / Landing Zones and Objectives

KEY

DZ   Parachute Drop Zone
LZ   Glider Landing Zone
━━━ Railway Line
━━━ Road
▰   Town / Village
①   Heuman Bridge
②   Malden Bridge
③   Hatert Bridge
④   Honinghutie Road + Rail Bridge
⑤   Grave Bridge
⑥   Nijmegen Road + Rail Bridges
⋙   Wooded Areas
─··─ Dutch / German Border

Reichswald

Wyler

Beek

LZ T

LZ N

DZ T

DZ N

Kiekberg Hill

Berg-en-Dal

Groesbeek

Mook

Riethorst

Fort Beneden Lent

Lent

Nijmegen

⑥

Malden

①

②

Heuman

Oosterhout

Arnhem

River Waal

Maas-Waal Canal

④

Hatert

③

DZ O

Overasselt

River Maas

Wijchen

Nederasselt

⑤

DZ

Grave

Eindhoven

The Arnhem Road Bridge
Perimeter 17–20 September 1944

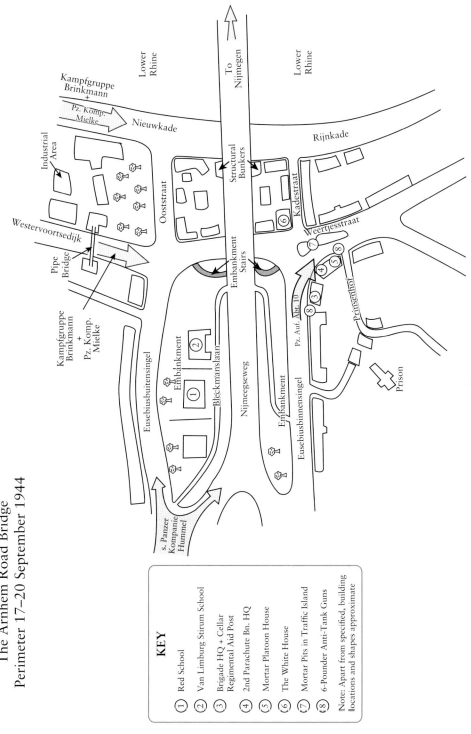

Lower Rhine

Lower Rhine

To Nijmegen

Kampfgruppe Brinkmann
+
Pz. Komp. Mielke

Nieuwkade

Rijnkade

Industrial Area

Structural Bunkers

Ooststraat

Kadestraat

Weertjesstraat

Westervoortsedijk

Embankment Stairs

Pipe Bridge

Kampfgruppe Brinkmann
+
Pz. Komp. Mielke

Eusebiusbuitensingel

Embankment

Bleekmanslaan

Nijmeegseweg

Embankment

Pz. Auf. Abt. 10

Prinsenhof

Eusebiusbinnensingel

Prison

s. Panzer Kompanie Hummel

KEY

1. Red School
2. Van Limburg Stirum School
3. Brigade HQ + Cellar Regimental Aid Post
4. 2nd Parachute Bn. HQ
5. Mortar Platoon House
6. The White House
7. Mortar Pits in Traffic Island
8. 6-Pounder Anti-Tank Guns

Note: Apart from specified, building locations and shapes approximate

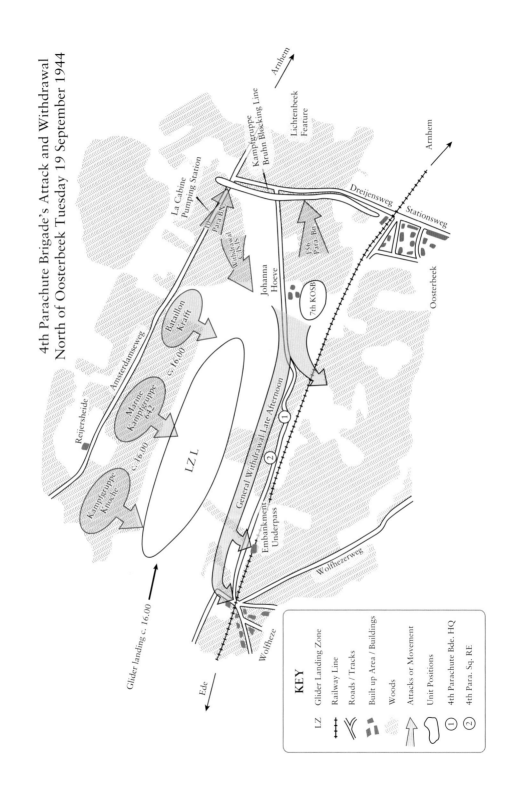

4th Parachute Brigade's Attack and Withdrawal
North of Oosterbeek Tuesday 19 September 1944

KEY

LZ	Glider Landing Zone
	Railway Line
	Roads / Tracks
	Built up Area / Buildings
	Woods
	Attacks or Movement
	Unit Positions
①	4th Parachute Bde. HQ
②	4th Para. Sq. RE

Reijersheide

Amsterdamseweg

Kampfgruppe Knoche

Marine Kampfgruppe 642
c. 16.00

Bataillon Kraft
c. 16.00

LZ L

Glider landing c. 16.00

Ede

Wolfheze

Wolfhezerweg

Embankment
Underpass

General Withdrawal Late Afternoon

②

①

7th KOSB

Johanna Hoeve

Withdrawal CLSS

10 Para BN

La Cabine Pumping Station

156 Para Bn

Kampfgruppe Bruhn Blocking Line

Lichtenbeek Feature

Dreijensweg

Stationsweg

Arnhem

Arnhem

Oosterbeek

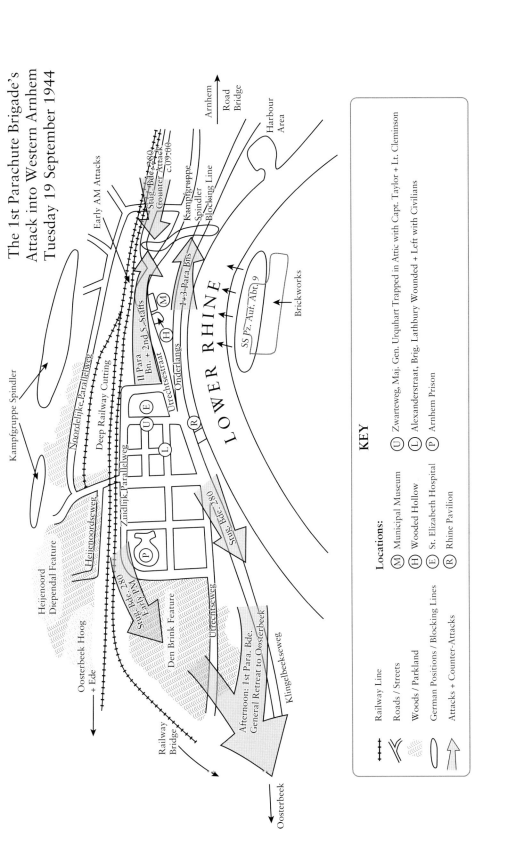

The 1st Parachute Brigade's Attack into Western Arnhem Tuesday 19 September 1944

Kampfgruppe Spindler

Heijenoord Diependal Feature

Oosterbeek Hoog + Ede

Early AM Attacks

Noordelijke Parallelweg

Deep Railway Cutting

Stug. Bde. 280 Counter-Attack c.09:00

Kampfgruppe Spindler Blocking Line

Arnhem Road Bridge

Harbour Area

Railway Bridge

Heijenoordseweg

Zuidlijk Parallelweg

Stug. Bde. 280 Early PM

Den Brink Feature

Utrechtseweg

Klingelbeekseweg

Afternoon: 1st Para. Bde. General Retreat to Oosterbeek

Oosterbeek

II Para Bn. + 2nd S. Staffs

Utrechtsestraat

Onderlangs

1+3 Para Bns

LOWER RHINE

Stug. Bde. 280

SS Pz. Aut. Abt. 9

Brickworks

KEY

- Railway Line
- Roads / Streets
- Woods / Parkland
- German Positions / Blocking Lines
- Attacks + Counter-Attacks

Locations:

- (M) Municipal Museum
- (H) Wooded Hollow
- (E) St. Elizabeth Hospital
- (R) Rhine Pavilion

- (U) Zwarteweg, Maj. Gen. Urquhart Trapped in Attic with Capt. Taylor + Lt. Cleminson
- (L) Alexanderstraat, Brig. Lathbury Wounded + Left with Civilians
- (P) Arnhem Prison

The Fight for the Nijmegen Bridges
19–20 September 1944

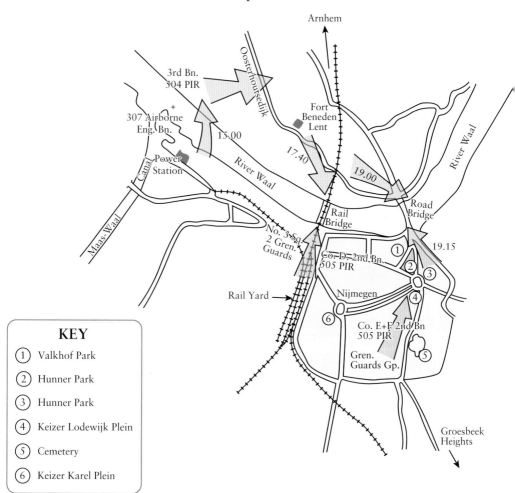

KEY

1. Valkhof Park
2. Hunner Park
3. Hunner Park
4. Keizer Lodewijk Plein
5. Cemetery
6. Keizer Karel Plein

The 'Island' between the River Waal + Lower Rhine 20–26 September 1944

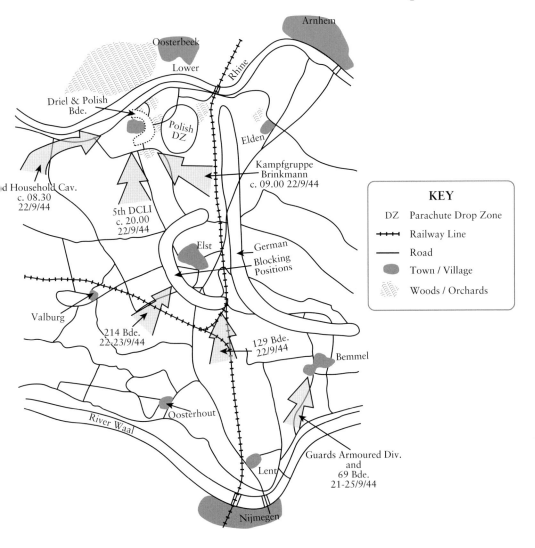

KEY

DZ	Parachute Drop Zone
+++	Railway Line
—	Road
	Town / Village
	Woods / Orchards

Arnhem

Oosterbeek

Lower

Rhine

Driel & Polish Bde.

Polish DZ

Elden

Kampfgruppe Brinkmann c. 09.00 22/9/44

d Household Cav. c. 08.30 22/9/44

5th DCLI c. 20.00 22/9/44

Elst

German Blocking Positions

Valburg

214 Bde. 22-23/9/44

129 Bde. 22/9/44

Bemmel

Oosterhout

River Waal

Guards Armoured Div. and 69 Bde. 21-25/9/44

Lent

Nijmegen

The Oosterbeek Pocket
22–26 September 1944

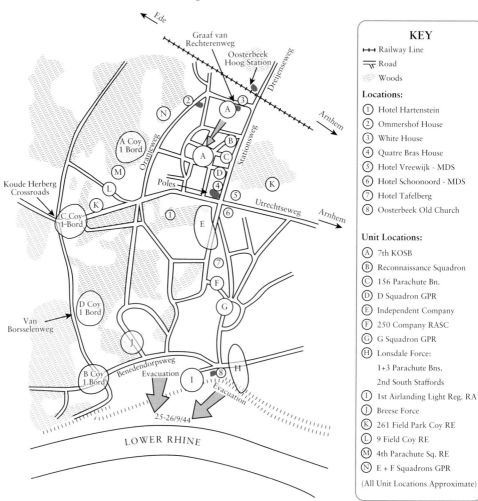

Ede

Graaf van
Rechterenweg

Oosterbeek
Hoog Station

Dreijenseweg

Arnhem

A Coy
1 Bord

Oranjeweg

Stationsweg

Koude Herberg
Crossroads

C Coy
1 Bord

Poles

Utrechtseweg

Arnhem

Van
Borsselenweg

D Coy
1 Bord

Benedendorpsweg

B Coy
1 Bord

Evacuation

Evacuation

25-26/9/44

LOWER RHINE

KEY

⊢•⊣ Railway Line

⊤⊤ Road

Woods

Locations:

① Hotel Hartenstein

② Ommershof House

③ White House

④ Quatre Bras House

⑤ Hotel Vreewijk - MDS

⑥ Hotel Schoonoord - MDS

⑦ Hotel Tafelberg

⑧ Oosterbeek Old Church

Unit Locations:

Ⓐ 7th KOSB

Ⓑ Reconnaissance Squadron

Ⓒ 156 Parachute Bn.

Ⓓ D Squadron GPR

Ⓔ Independent Company

Ⓕ 250 Company RASC

Ⓖ G Squadron GPR

Ⓗ Lonsdale Force:

1+3 Parachute Bns.

2nd South Staffords

Ⓘ 1st Airlanding Light Reg. RA

Ⓙ Breese Force

Ⓚ 261 Field Park Coy RE

Ⓛ 9 Field Coy RE

Ⓜ 4th Parachute Sq. RE

Ⓝ E + F Squadrons GPR

(All Unit Locations Approximate)

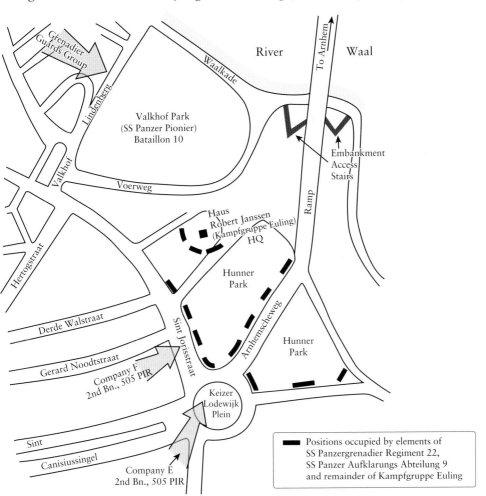

Grenadier Guards Group

River Waal

To Arnhem

Waalkade

Lindenberg

Valkhof Park
(SS Panzer Pionier)
Bataillon 10

Valkhof

Embankment
Access
Stairs

Voerweg

Ramp

Haus
Robert Janssen
(Kampfgruppe Euling)
HQ

Hunner
Park

Hertogstraat

Arnhemscheweg

Hunner
Park

Derde Walstraat

Sint Jorisstraat

Gerard Noodtstraat

Company F
2nd Bn., 505 PIR

Keizer
Lodewijk
Plein

Sint

Canisiussingel

Company E
2nd Bn., 505 PIR

Positions occupied by elements of
SS Panzergrenadier Regiment 22,
SS Panzer Aufklarungs Abteilung 9
and remainder of Kampfgruppe Euling

Above: 1. A 'blizzard of silk'; C-47s from the US 61st and 314th Troop Carrier Groups delivering 2,278 men from the 1st Parachute Brigade onto DZ X north of Heelsum in the afternoon of Sunday 17 September 1944.

Left: 2. Some of the 150 gliders delivered onto LZ Z by aircraft from RAF Nos. 38 & 46 Groups on the afternoon of Sunday 17 September 1944 scattered across the north-east corner of the landing zone. Most are Airspeed Horsas but three of the larger General Aircraft Hamilcars with a payload of over seven tons can be seen to the right of the white building; four of the thirteen Hamilcars in the first lift suffered serious landing accidents, two due to the soft soil.

Opposite bottom: 3. The view today across Ginkel Heath or DZ Y looking south from the Amsterdamseweg and Zuid Ginkel café where the 4th Parachute Brigade dropped as part of the 1st Airborne Division's second lift in the afternoon of Monday 18 September 1944. The Brigade dropped into a fierce battle between the 7th Battalion King's Own Scottish Borderers, which had been tasked to hold the DZ, and *SS Wacht Battalion 3* and the unexpected arrival of *c.* 2,000 paratroopers caused the SS unit to break and scatter in confusion.

Right: 4. Heavily laden US paratroopers pose on the steps of a C-47 prior to take-off.

Below: 5. British Glider infantrymen, possibly from the 1st Airlanding Brigade, wearing their distinctive maroon berets, camouflaged Denison Smocks and carrying their Airborne pattern helmets pose for the camera.

6. A 20mm flak gun at the German barrier defences in Arnhem.

7. A 3-inch mortar crew from the 1st Battalion The Border Regiment during the fighting on the west side of the Oosterbeek Perimeter. The crew are, from left to right, Private McDowell, Corporal Tierney & Corporal Knight.

Left: 8. 'An ambitious and manipulative empire-building bureaucrat *par excellence*': Lieutenant-General Frederick Arthur Montague Browning, Commander of the British 1st Airborne Corps and Deputy Commander of the 1st Allied Airborne Army.

Right: 9. Major-General Roy Urquhart, Commander of the British 1st Airborne Division, at the rear of the Hotel Hartenstein which served as his HQ for the bulk of the Battle of Arnhem. Note the Airborne trailer at the extreme right and the maroon and light blue Pegasus Divisional Pennant flying from the lance to Urquhart's right; the Pennant was removed from the lance and carried across the Lower Rhine by Urquhart's batman, a Private Hancock, on the night of 25–26 September 1944.

Below: 10. The Hotel Hartenstein today. It now houses the Airborne Museum 'Hartenstein' dedicated to the Battle of Arnhem.

11. Paratroopers from the US 82nd Airborne Division, possibly from the 2nd Battalion 505th Parachute Infantry Regiment, stand guard over wounded German prisoners at the south end of the Nijmegen road bridge.

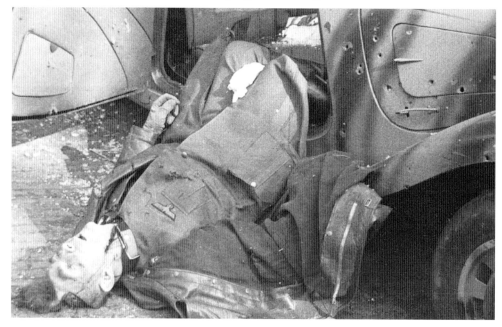

12. The *Stadtkommandant* of Arnhem, *Generalmajor* Friedrich Kussin, who was killed along with his batman and driver in the late afternoon of Sunday 17 September 1944. Kussin had been conferring with *Hauptsturmführer* Sepp Krafft at the Hotel Wolfheze and appears to have been returning to his HQ in Arnhem when his camouflaged Citroën saloon ran into Lieutenant James Cleminson's 5 Platoon from the 3rd Parachute Battalion at the junction of the Utrechtseweg and Wolfhezeweg.

Germans from a nearby embankment and despatched his driver back to the Coldstream Guards Group with a request for immediate tank support.⁵¹ In fact the 1ˢᵗ Battalion 505ᵗʰ Regiment was already reorganising and Regimental commander Colonel William E. Ekman, already mindful of the threat to the Molenhoek bridge, had deployed his Company A reserve and tanks from the 1ˢᵗ Coldstream Guards were already on the way. As a result, Ekman was able to launch a counter-attack under an hour after Mook had been overrun that, after some bitter house-to-house fighting, had retaken the town by nightfall and pushed *Kampfgruppe* Hermann back the way it had come; Colonel Ekman only called off the pursuit because his men were running out of ammunition. A further German withdrawal during the night allowed the paratroopers to reoccupy Riethorst and re-establish the roadblock at Plasmolen the following morning. The day's fighting cost the 1ˢᵗ Battalion 505ᵗʰ Regiment thirty-three dead, seventy-six wounded and seven missing; German casualties are unclear but *Kampfgruppe* Hermann did not figure in subsequent German attacks on the 82ⁿᵈ Airborne Division's perimeter.⁵²

Once he was satisfied Colonel Ekman had matters in hand at Mook, Gavin drove north to see the situation on the eastern aspect of the Divisional perimeter. After a morning of bombardment from artillery and mortars, in the early afternoon *Kampfgruppe* von Fürstenberg attacked the two US platoons holding Beek, one from Company I 508ᵗʰ Parachute Infantry Regiment and one from Company D 307ᵗʰ Airborne Engineer Battalion. The US force was commanded by Corporal Robert Chisolm as all the detachment's officers and senior NCOs had been killed or wounded the previous day securing the town. In a 'stunning display of junior leadership' Chisolm co-ordinated the defence of the town until direct fire from several 20mm *flak* vehicles and an intensive artillery barrage heralded the final German assault. He then organised an orderly withdrawal back onto the Berg-en-Dal ridge, personally acting as rearguard.⁵³ It appears to have been Corporal Chisolm's recently arrived party that Gavin encountered digging in after arriving at the Berg-en-Dal, where German small-arms fire had obliged him to crawl across the crest to reach the forward slope. Lieutenant-Colonel Louis G. Mendez, commander of the 3ʳᵈ Battalion 508ᵗʰ Regiment, informed Gavin that his men had blocked the advance of *Kampfgruppe* von Fürstenberg's armour, reported to number eight tanks and as many assorted half-tracks, by knocking out one of the latter on a sharp S-bend on the road leading uphill from Beek, thereby blocking the road. Mendez also told Gavin that he had only been able to impede the German advance thus far by constantly switching his platoons between locations as new threats developed, and he was unsure how long he could continue to do so. Reinforcements were desperately needed, but the non-arrival of that day's glider lift meant Gavin simply had no resources to give. Fortunately, the situation was saved by von Fürstenberg curtailing the attack with the onset of darkness and a spoiling attack on Beek from the south by Lieutenant Louis G. Toth's Company H from the 508ᵗʰ Regiment at some point after 19:00. After becoming fragmented after penetrating into the town in darkness, Company H renewed the attack at first light on 21 September and after reinforcement with elements from Companies F and G and making four separate attacks in the course of the day, Lieutenant Toth finally secured Beek at 18:00.⁵⁴

The 3ʳᵈ Battalion's stubborn defence also appears to have alleviated the pressure on the 1ˢᵗ Battalion 508ᵗʰ Parachute Infantry Regiment from *Kampfgruppe* Becker along with Captain Woodrow W. Millsaps' Company B, which was holding Wyler to the east of the main 1ˢᵗ Battalion frontage. The action began when one of Captain Millsaps' roadblocks was approached by a truck carrying German infantry at 08:00, which began to burn after being hit by one of the 57mm anti-tank guns from Battery B 80ᵗʰ Airborne Anti-Aircraft Battalion attached to Company B. The Germans responded by moving in on the town with more and more troops including a machine-gun *kompanie*, which Millsaps managed to keep at bay with fire from the 319ᵗʰ Glider Field Artillery Battalion. The Germans then brought up *StuGs* likely belonging to *Fallschirm Sturmgeschütze Brigade 12*. The two 57mm anti-tank guns from the 80ᵗʰ Airborne Anti-Aircraft Battalion were unable to move to engage them because of intense German machine-gun fire.

By the early afternoon the German pressure on Captain Millsaps' little band was continuing to grow, almost all of the two Jeep-loads of ammunition Company B had brought with it had been expended and a resupply attempt by the Battalion Supply Officer Lieutenant Peter L. Kelley had been beaten back by enemy fire. Wyler was under direct fire from the *StuGs* and increasing indirect fire from heavy artillery. The pressure continued to mount and by around 15:00 Millsaps was obliged to inform Lieutenant-Colonel Shields Warren bluntly that if he was not given permission to withdraw to an earlier intermediate position just south of Wyler, then Company B would be overrun and wiped out; this was granted by the Battalion Executive Officer Major Benjamin F. Delamater, although it took over an hour to carry out the withdrawal as all Millsaps men were wounded and he refused to leave the non-ambulatory cases behind. The withdrawal was covered by fire from tanks, presumably from the 1st Coldstream Guards, but the fire initially fell on Company B's new location, reportedly killing and wounding several of the paratroopers before a bed sheet was used to advertise the friendly location to the tanks. At dusk, permission was granted for a further withdrawal to the main 1st Battalion line and Major Delamater went forward to act as a guide. The withdrawal took all night as, once again, Captain Millsaps refused to abandon his non-ambulatory wounded. As there were insufficient able-bodied men to move all the wounded at once, they had to be moved in a series of relays using doors, planks or whatever was available. There were no stretchers. Despite all this the withdrawal was successful and Company B was back within the 1st Battalion lines by dawn on 21 September.[55]

At this point, with the GARDEN ground force passed through the US sector of the Airborne Corridor and across the River Waal, we shall leave the US Airborne formations. It was certainly not the end of the matter for them. The 508th Parachute Infantry Regiment retook Beek on 21 September after a day-long fight and a resupply drop at 15:00 that day alleviated the supply situation somewhat. Overall, the 82nd Airborne Division remained in place in the area between the River Maas and River Waal until it was finally withdrawn from Holland on 11 November after fifty-six days of continuous action during which it suffered a total of 1,432 killed, wounded and missing. To the south, the 101st Airborne Division was kept extremely busy maintaining its sector of the Airborne Corridor, repeatedly attacking northward toward Schijndel and Koevering to keep the enemy off balance and away from the road to Grave, with Sergeant Patrick McCrory's mobility-impaired Sherman from the Irish Guards Group again rendering assistance to the 502nd Parachute Infantry Regiment on 21 September. On the morning of Friday 22 September a two-pronged German attack near Veghel succeeded in cutting the road, which by this time the men of the 101st Airborne Division had dubbed 'Hell's Highway', and the traffic flow north was stopped until midnight. The constant German attacks along the 101st Airborne Division's sector obliged the various Regimental commanders to juggle their units constantly in reaction to the latest threat, a process Major-General Taylor referred to as 'Indian fighting'. The Division moved north to man a sector on the Lower Rhine on 3 October and remained there until finally withdrawn at the end of November after seventy-two days in the line, during which time the Division lost a total of 2,118 men killed, wounded and missing. All that lay in the future however, and the focus will now be on events north of the River Waal.

***

By midday on Wednesday 20 September the 1st Airborne Division's most westerly element was the remnants of Brigadier Hackett's 4th Parachute Brigade, located just a few hundred yards west of the Division perimeter. Having performed a fighting withdrawal across LZ L north of the Arnhem–Ede railway the previous evening, Brigade HQ, the badly depleted remnants of the 10th and 156 Parachute Battalions and the isolated B Company 7th KOSB had spent a relatively undisturbed night in the woods east of Wolfheze. However, continuing their withdrawal to friendly territory the following day led to them becoming entangled with *SS Bataillon Eberwein* as it closed up on the British perimeter from the west. Major Michael Forman and B Company 7th

KOSB remained in place near the Hotel Wolfheze awaiting orders, where they were joined in the course of the morning by a stray party from 156 Parachute Battalion led by Lieutenants Dennis Kayne and Jeffrey Noble from 8 and MMG Platoons respectively. After becoming separated the previous day the paratroopers had spent the night in the nearby woods before being driven out earlier in the morning by German tanks. They were accompanied by a number of wounded including 156 Battalion's second-in-command Captain Hector Montgomery and Lieutenant Ronald Wood from 6 Platoon; their arrival boosted B Company's strength to around 130 men.

With nothing heard by early afternoon Major Forman decided to strike south-west on his own initiative, and thus unwittingly began moving directly into *Kampfgruppe* von Tettau's concentration area. The British force covered less than a mile through the woods before finding itself surrounded by two full companies of fresh German troops equipped with mortars while crossing a large clearing. Forman immediately set about organising an attack to fight his way out of the trap but changed tack when a check revealed that his men had virtually no ammunition:

> The options left to me were to cross 200 yards of open heather under fire from the Germans, being shot at from behind, losing half the men going across the open and with the prospect of heavy hand-to-hand fighting with the Germans if we did get across – or to surrender. I decided not to say 'every man for himself' but to tell them to surrender, which I did, making it my responsibility.[56]

Lieutenant Kayne just had time to relay the news to his men and discard his identity discs to conceal his Jewish faith before the Germans 'came up to us and we laid down all our arms on the ground. It was a terrible feeling to realize that this is what it had come to, that first-class troops had come to this. There were at least 200 Germans, looking quite fresh and smart and well armed.'[57] Although the decision appears to have been generally accepted as the correct course in the circumstances, not everyone concurred, as noted by Lieutenant Noble:

> I personally didn't agree to the surrender and took to the woods again with some of my parachutists. But the Borderers surrendered, and that was probably the right decision, because some 130 men lived to see the end of the war, whereas if we had fought it out most of them probably would have died. I don't think it would have affected the Battle of Arnhem, because we were completely isolated. It wouldn't have had any impact on anything at all.[58]

At the same time the 10th and 156 Parachute Battalions were losing two-thirds of their strength in their effort to reach the Division perimeter. While the 10th managed to reach safety just after midday via a last-ditch bayonet charge, the 156 Battalion and 4th Parachute Brigade HQ remained caught up around a track junction on the Breedelaan 500 yards west of the 1st Border's lines. 156 Battalion led a withdrawal north-east from the junction at 13:00 and as soon as the paratroopers were clear Hackett called down a 'troop stonk' on either side of the new Brigade axis from the 1st Airlanding Light Regiment via the Regiment's second-in-command, Major George de Gex, who had been with Brigade HQ since the previous day; the shelling was repeated and reportedly achieved 'good results'.[59] Despite this, the constant German small-arms fire, already heavy from the south and south-west, increased in intensity and wounded a number of men. Brigade Major Bruce Dawson was hit in the right shoulder and Lieutenant-Colonel Derick Heathcoat-Amory from GHQ Liaison Regiment sustained serious wounds to the shoulder and leg. Ironically, the latter had taken two days' leave to participate in the operation as an unofficial Liaison Officer. Brigadier Hackett later drove the Jeep carrying his stretcher to safety when an adjacent vehicle loaded with mortar bombs caught fire.[60] Lieutenant-Colonel Des Vœux reported the approach of tracked vehicles and Hackett was somewhat discomfited to discover from Major Annesley Haynes, commander of the 2nd Airlanding Anti-tank Battery, that there were no 6-Pounder anti-tank guns available because they were either 'hopelessly stuck' or had been abandoned as no tow vehicles had been available during the withdrawal from LZ L; the only anti-tank weapon to hand was a single PIAT with one bomb.

The 156 Battalion War Diary refers to being 'encircled by S.P. guns and motorised infantry' 600 yards or so from the start point, while Hackett suggests there were two or possibly three vehicles, tentatively identified as *Panzer* IIs. One closed to within 400 yards before being driven off by intense small-arms fire, and a second that ventured closer had a track blown off by a No. 75 Hawkins Grenade. According to Hackett the vehicles were 'rather windy' but their accompanying infantry were not, and numerous close-quarter fights whittled away at the British strength. Brigade Major Dawson was killed while rallying men scattered by the German vehicles, along with Brigade Intelligence Officer Captain George Blundell. Colonel Des Vœux lost his second-in-command Captain Thomas Wainright wounded and Adjutant Captain Michael Gibbs missing.[61] Despite this, the column continued moving until confronted by a 'cup shaped depression containing up to 30 Germans'; the hollow was approximately thirty yards across and roughly circular.[62] Hackett promptly summoned Major Geoffrey Powell to an impromptu conference standing upright behind a tree despite small-arms and mortar fire and, after giving Powell a brief précis of the situation, ordered him to take the hollow despite the situation meaning no covering fire could be provided. Although he kept his views to himself, Powell was less than enthusiastic about his new task, not least because by this point his C Company had been reduced to around twenty-five men with him as the sole officer. This paucity of numbers was alleviated somewhat when Major Michael Page insisted on accompanying Powell with the dozen or so survivors from his HQ Company, and the attackers were also joined by a group of unknown size from A Company.[63]

The charge was successful as the German defenders withdrew without a fight, abandoning their wounded in the process, although Powell was obliged to appropriate a German sub-machine gun of some description to replace his Sten after it jammed in the heat of the action. While this was going on the remainder of the stalled column was being dismembered and overrun by German infantry supported by up to three tanks, leaving Hackett to rally those survivors able to reach the hollow. Colonel Des Vœux was mortally wounded in the attempt, as reported by Sergeant Andrew Thorburn who came upon him leaning against the base of a tree. When asked if he needed assistance the badly wounded officer responded 'No. Move forward. The enemy is in front of you; they need you there.'[64] Approximately 150 men succeeded in reaching the hollow, drawn from 156 Battalion's A, C and HQ Companies, various elements of Brigade HQ and a group from the 10th Parachute Battalion.[65] According to Hackett the latter group was twelve strong. The overall total included around thirty men from 156 Battalion including Intelligence Officer Lieutenant Piers St. Aubyn, along with Majors Page and Powell (the latter elevated to command of 156 Battalion), Captains Reginald Temple and Peter Barron from Brigade Staff and the 2nd Airlanding Anti-tank Battery respectively, Brigade Staff Captain Hubert Booty and Major George de Gex from the 1st Airlanding Light Regiment, who was appointed acting Brigade Major. Ammunition was short and in some instances weapons too, with some including Hackett utilising captured German weapons.[66] The paratroopers nonetheless withstood constant German fire and repeated attacks through the course of the afternoon involving a single armoured vehicle, although the Germans were leery of coming within grenade range. The paratroopers launched a number of counter-forays that inflicted numerous casualties and reportedly netted forty German prisoners, with Hackett leading at least one charge against a German machine-gun position wielding a rifle and bayonet.[67] The constant German pressure reduced the British strength by around half, the dead including Major Page, who was shot peeping over the lip of the hollow whilst attempting to pinpoint a troublesome German position.[68]

By 16:30 the position had become untenable and Hackett decided on a dash for the Division perimeter at 17:00, taking the lead himself, accompanied by Major de Gex. The tactic worked and approximately seventy men reached the section of the Divisional perimeter held by A Company, 1st Border, losing around six men in the retreat.[69] The paratroopers appear to have come in near the Sonnenberg, given that Hackett's account refers to reorganising in positions occupied by Major Æneas Perkins and part of the 4th Parachute Squadron RE.[70] According to Powell, one of the first 1st Border officers he came across while rallying the survivors of 156 Battalion was concerned lest the battleworn appearance of the paratroopers affect his men's morale and requested Powell to 'Please move your filthy lot away from here'.[71] The 'filthy lot' numbered just fifty men and three officers. By 18:30 Powell had overseen a resupply of weapons and ammunition and reorganised them into two composite platoons.[72] Hackett reported to Urquhart in person at the Hotel Hartenstein at 18:50, where he also linked up with his Brigade RASC Officer, Captain Colin Harkness, with an undetermined number of men. According to Hackett's account Lieutenant-Colonel Smyth and approximately forty men from the 10th Parachute Battalion were also at Division HQ, although both Urquhart's and the 10th Battalion's semi-official accounts suggest that by this time Smyth and his men had been despatched to occupy houses at the Utrechtseweg–Stationsweg crossroads. Whichever, Hackett was instructed to take command of the eastern side of the solidifying Division perimeter effective from the following morning and in the meantime to 'take a night's rest'. This he did in the Hotel Hartenstein after visiting 156 Battalion, possibly to relay orders from Urquhart, and establishing his Brigade HQ in a wooded section of the hotel grounds.[73]

While *SS Bataillon Eberwein* was busy harrying the 4th Parachute Brigade into Oosterbeek, other elements of *SS Unterführerschule* 'Arnheim' were preparing to continue the assault on the 1st Border's C Company at the Koude Herberg junction, where the glider soldiers were reorganising after driving off the German morning attack. The reorganisation had its lighter moments. CSM Leslie Fielding and an ammunition resupply party from HQ Company came under 'vigorous attack' from a pair of belligerent geese en route to C Company's location, and despite the near-constant mortar fire the ammunition party were reportedly 'far more intimidated by the birds than by the enemy'.[74] The renewed SS attack at 15:00 pushed at least part of C Company out of their positions with the assistance of two ex-French flame-thrower tanks attached from *Panzer Kompanie 224*, their shock value prompting a number of C Company men to abandon their positions and withdraw to D Company's location to the south. They were pursued, rounded up and led back to their positions by an irate Lieutenant Alan Roberts from 16 Platoon, while CSM Stringer was obliged to retrieve boxes of small-arms ammunition from the Company ammunition reserve after a mortar bomb set the dump ablaze. Major William Neill rallied the Company and launched a counter-attack that regained the lost ground, and when the *Flammpanzer B2s* attempted to outflank the reoccupied position they were attacked with a PIAT and grenades by a Private Webster.[75] Both tanks were subsequently knocked out, one outside a restaurant on the Koude Herberg junction by a direct hit on the front plate from one of the Battalion's organic 6-Pounders attached to C Company; the crew appear to have escaped. The other tank attempted to sidestep C Company's position through the trees to the north of the Utrechtseweg and reached the Sonnenberglaan, only 500 yards or so from the Hotel Hartenstein. At that point it was hit by a 17-Pounder gun from Lieutenant George Paull's X Troop, 2nd (Oban) Airlanding Anti-tank Battery. The projectile sparked a catastrophic explosion that severed the vehicle's left track, unseated the turret, blew off the engine compartment covers and presumably killed the crew.[76] The 17-Pounder was directed by Lieutenant-Colonel Robert Loder-Symonds, the 1st Airborne Division's Commander Royal Artillery, who left his HQ dugout nearby in the grounds of the Hotel Hartenstein to assist.[77] The Germans attacked again at 19:30 but were beaten off, presumably because they lacked armoured support, and C Company enjoyed a quiet night apart from 'occasional mortar fire of nuisance value only'.[78]

Matters also remained quiet on D Company's frontage apart from the persistent mortar fire, but the fight on the Utrechtseweg prevented Captain Hodgson from evacuating his wounded up the Van Borsselenweg to the Battalion RAP; in addition, the front differential on the Company's stretcher-carrying Jeep was damaged by a hit of some description, making it almost impossible to steer. The driver had to return the load of casualties to his start point and a temporary aid post was established in the cellar of D Company HQ. The exception to this relative calm was the experience of Lieutenant Jack Bainbridge and 19 Platoon, who were maintaining the standing patrol-cum-observation post at a junction on the Van der Molenallee several hundred yards in front of the main D Company positions. Bainbridge remained in place until late afternoon, despite his attached signallers being unable to establish contact with D Company HQ on their No. 18 set. At that point 19 Platoon's location was unwittingly approached by a group of German bicycle troops accompanied by an armoured car; the car was knocked out by a well-placed PIAT bomb and small-arms fire scattered the bicycle troops into the woods. With his location compromised and unable to pass reports back to Company HQ, Lieutenant Bainbridge decided to carry out a phased withdrawal, placing half the Platoon under Sergeant Thomas Northgrave. However, the groups lost contact with the onset of darkness and then became further scattered by contact with German troops also moving through the woods. Many of the patrol were killed, captured or lost as a result although some did reach safety; the attached radio men, Signallers Ronald Graydon and Ernest Hamlet, struck off on their own and reached C Company's location without incident, for example. For their part Lieutenant Bainbridge, Sergeant Northgrave and Corporal Atherton spent two days dodging the enemy, at one point almost being stepped on by an enemy patrol, before spotting a maroon beret through the foliage and making a dash for safety.[79]

B Company's location overlooking the Heveadorp ferry remained unmolested apart from the ever-present mortar fire, although it received reinforcement of a kind during the afternoon in the shape of Captain Maurice Heggie and approximately fifteen Sappers from the 9th Field Company's No. 3 Platoon. Detailed to protect the Heveadorp ferry, Heggie's men dug in 500 yards west of B Company's location and in the evening ferried Captain Douglas Green, the Adjutant of the 1st Airborne Division's Royal Engineers HQ, across the Lower Rhine to carry a situation report to 30 Corps.[80] Captain Green left the Hotel Hartenstein at 17:40, apparently escorted by Divisional Operations Officer Lieutenant-Colonel Charles Mackenzie; the 9th Field Company's commander, Major John Winchester, may also have been present given that he visited 1st Airlanding Brigade HQ at 18:30 to ascertain if the ferry were still in British hands and departed to reconnoitre it on learning that was the case.[81] Captain Green either reached the ferry or crossed the river at 19:55; the War Diary wording is unclear.[82] A subsequent medal citation refers to Captain Green being obliged to swim back to the north bank after the ferry was sunk partway across by enemy fire and finally completing the crossing in a small rowing boat.[83] There is no mention of this in the 9th Field Company War Diary, although the Royal Engineers HQ Diary says that the ferry was 'still running but enemy starting to dispute ground' at 21:10.[84] Either way, Captain Green eventually made contact with friendly forces north of Nijmegen early the following morning after traversing ten miles of German-held territory, and successfully passed his sitrep to 30 Corps' HQ.[85]

On the north face of the Division perimeter on the Graaf Van Rechterenweg the German attacks against the 4th Parachute Squadron detachment had died away by 15:00 and the Sappers promptly took the offensive themselves. Captain Henry Brown, who had been elevated to command of the detachment following the death of Captain Thomas, authorised Lieutenant Kenneth Evans from 1 Troop to lead a fighting patrol to deal with a self-propelled gun observed in the woods 100 yards to the west. The patrol returned after waiting vainly in ambush for an hour. Lieutenant Evans enjoyed more success on a subsequent patrol north to the railway embankment at 18:00. After spotting a company or more of Germans north of railway line, the patrol shot up another group gathering recently dropped supply panniers for no loss and passed the location of the German dump on to Division HQ via 21st Independent Parachute Company's HQ at the Ommershof on returning. Shortly afterward the Sappers heard 'the sound of an artillery salvo screaming overhead and exploding in the vicinity of the dump, to our great satisfaction'.[86]

Captain Brown had overseen the dispersal of a group of Germans on the detachment frontage with a well-aimed PIAT bomb fired by Sapper William Grantham, and then dealt with two visitors to his small corner of the perimeter. The first was Major-General Urquhart, who had determined 'to maintain physical contact with as many of the units in the perimeter as I could, partly in the hope that my presence might help morale and also because I wanted to get the picture absolutely right'.[87] He therefore travelled up the Oranjeweg in a Jeep driven by his ADC, Captain Graham Roberts, in search of Major Wilson's HQ in the Ommershof. However, the north end of the Oranjeweg lay in the no-man's-land between the 4th Parachute Squadron's lines and *SS Bataillon Eberwein*, and the officers were forced to seek shelter in the roadside ditch after shouted warnings from Brown and his men. While Urquhart made his way to the Ommershof on foot, Captain Roberts set about turning the Jeep for the return journey by driving up to the junction with the Graaf Van Rechterenweg, as witnessed by Captain Brown:

He drove down the sloping narrow track turned right and over-accelerated. The jeep swung into an uncontrollable skid on the sandy roadway and came to a shuddering halt with a massive thump as the front wheels slammed into a boulder. Graham was catapulted over the windscreen hitting it with his forehead and knee as he flew through the air…I shouted for him to get clear because of sniping and he limped to the five strand wire fence, hopped over and disappeared to join the General in the house.[88]

There Roberts reported the loss of the Jeep with the immortal words 'I'm afraid, sir, that it's a complete write off,' before being despatched to the MDS at the Hotel Schoonoord to have his head and leg injuries treated; Urquhart presumably returned to the Hotel Hartenstein on foot.[89]

Back on the Oranjeweg the call went out to recover Urquhart's maps and other papers from the wrecked Jeep and Captain Brown arranged covering fire to allow CSM James Stewart from the 21st Independent Company to cross the fence and do the retrieving; the Division Signals War Diary revealingly refers to the vehicle's radio also being salvaged and repaired.[90] At some point before 15:00 Brown received his second visitor, Lieutenant Norman Thomas from 3 Troop. Thomas had been despatched from the main 4th Parachute Squadron location at the Sonnenberg in the late morning to gather situation reports from CRE Lieutenant-Colonel Edmund Myers at Division HQ and Captain Brown.[91] The visit to the Ommershof detachment was also a reconnaissance for a visit by the Squadron commander, Major Perkins, planned for the following day; for his part Captain Brown reported back that his detachment was short of ammunition and running even shorter of food, as the forty-eight-hour rations the Sappers had jumped in with were all but gone.[92] Although Captain Brown's account makes no mention of it, the Squadron War Diary refers to the Germans renewing the attack at nightfall and continuing for around an hour before retiring into the darkness. German casualties are unclear, while the Sappers lost an unnamed Other Rank.[93] At some point during the afternoon the 21st Independent Company wiped out a group of around fifty fully armed Germans that emerged from the woods in front of their positions, apparently after a shouted exchange with Corporal Hans Rosenfeld, a German Jew serving with the Independent Company under the alias John Peter Rodley and known to his comrades as Max. It is unclear if the Germans emerged after being duped into believing the Pathfinders wished to surrender or were looking to surrender themselves, and the shooting may have begun with a Bren gun firing from the Glider Pilot positions on the Company's flank, although testimony from members of the Independent Company make it clear they were only holding their fire until all the enemy were clearly in view. Whatever the truth of the matter, most of the German party were hit and only a few survivors were seen crawling back into the woods. As the Independent Company's semi-official account put it, 'the whole thing was somehow unsatisfactory'.[94]

While the 7th KOSB at the eastern end of the Graaf Van Rechterenweg does not appear to have been directly attacked during the afternoon, a general firefight that involved all the Battalion's weapons continued throughout the afternoon, with PIATs being employed to good effect as an anti-sniper weapon. However, the enemy tactic of deliberately targeting the houses inside the KOSB perimeter by shelling and/or burning began to tip the scales against the glider soldiers. Shells from a German self-propelled gun sited out of the view of the Battalion's 6-Pounders forced Major Gordon Sherriff's D Company HQ and other elements to evacuate their building for example; as communications difficulties rendered him unable to act as a forward observer, Captain John Walker from the 1st Airlanding Light Battery volunteered to join the fighting and was pressed into service as D Company second-in-command. The German tactic also caused Lieutenant-Colonel Payton-Reid and Medical Officer Captain Brian Devlin some concern in light of the growing number of casualties housed in the Battalion RAP, which had already been evacuated from the Hotel Dreyeroord/White House during the morning. It was therefore decided to relocate the RAP again, under the Red Cross flag, to a house outside the Battalion perimeter, beginning with the walking wounded. The party ran into a German patrol and were captured; the haul included Captain Devlin and Battalion second-in-command Major John Coke, who had been wounded in the leg during the first evacuation. The capture appears to have gone unobserved from the main Battalion location. The stretcher cases had to remain within the Battalion perimeter with all the dangers that entailed.

Colonel Payton-Reid called an O Group in the late afternoon to issue orders for the night. As well as tightening the perimeter positions these included patrolling the gaps between Company locations, and C and D Companies were also tasked to despatch fighting patrols to the south and north of the Battalion location respectively. C Company was considered secure due to a four-foot wire fence running across its frontage, but D Company's position was more problematic, partly because it was overlooked from the nearby woods and semi-illuminated by burning buildings, and partly because it was dominated by the abandoned White House. Major Sherriff favoured pulling well back from the latter and establishing a shortened line, but while Colonel Payton-Reid was willing to sanction this during daylight to ease the burden on his understrength B Company, he insisted that the White House and existing line be held during the hours of darkness; Major Sherriff thus had no option but to comply, and Captain Walker volunteered to occupy the deserted hotel with a small party. Payton-Reid inspected the Battalion perimeter in person after dark, accompanied by his Intelligence Officer, Lieutenant Alexander MacKenzie, presumably in lieu of Major Coke and while doing so they received a graphic illustration of the Battalion's vulnerability to infiltrators. They were discussing matters with Major Sherriff inside D Company's perimeter when they were approached in the darkness by a soldier who addressed them in German. Major Sherriff immediately 'jumped at his throat' and the ensuing struggle prevented his companions getting a clear shot until both groups jumped back to avoid a German grenade. There was then a flurry of shots, one of which hit Lieutenant MacKenzie in the leg while Sherriff 'eliminated' his opponent unaided. The firing was followed by 'a fearful wailing, as of somebody in death agonies...on investigation, it was found that someone had shot a goat!'[95]

The Germans maintained the pressure against LONSDALE Force on the Benedendorpsweg at the south-east corner of the perimeter. On the left flank the 11th Parachute Battalion was obliged temporarily to abandon its positions around the junction of the Acacialaan and the Hogeweg at around 15:00 as a German self-propelled gun located behind a ridge to the east systematically demolished the houses; when the shelling ceased the paratroopers moved back, with B Company occupying the garden of the demolished house at the crossroads while A Company occupied a group of farm buildings east along the Hogeweg.[96] The vehicle may have been the one stalked by Captain Frank King and two men from Support Company on Major Lonsdale's orders, in the course of which King was wounded while trying to take a German infantryman covering the vehicle from an adjacent house prisoner:

> He astonished me. He was rather fat and was carrying his rifle at the trail; he didn't look particularly dangerous. But he was a good soldier and was fooling me. He just tilted the

rifle up and fired it one-handed, hitting me in the chest…I did what I had been trained to do aiming at 'the centre of the visible mass' – which was quite extensive – and killed him.

Captain King's companions had meanwhile despatched two more Germans in an upper room and discovered that 'they could look down on top of the SP gun…There was a young German officer with his head out of the hatch. We dropped a Gammon bomb on to it, killing the officer and causing the SP to withdraw rapidly.' The trio then withdrew themselves but in the process Captain King was wounded again in the leg by splinters from a grenade that also badly wounded one of his companions.[97] B Company remained unmolested but at around 18:00 the Germans attacked the farm after infiltrating between the company locations and setting fire to some haystacks, forcing the A Company contingent to withdraw into a nearby field.[98]

Down on the Benedendorpsweg Lieutenants Curtis and Turrell from the 1st Parachute Battalion were obliged to lead another patrol to clear infiltrators at 1500, and an hour later the Germans emplaced an infantry gun in a defilade position near the *StuG* knocked out that morning. The gun 'made things most unpleasant' for the 3rd Parachute Battalion until fire from a 3-inch mortar forced its withdrawal. This may have been connected to a 'heavy attack' against the 1st Battalion section of the line at 16:30 involving several armoured vehicles supported by intense enfilading fire from machine-guns emplaced on the embankment running up to the destroyed railway bridge; this caused the paratroopers 'considerable casualties' including Lieutenant Curtis, who was killed.[99] Lance-Sergeant John Baskeyfield from the 2nd South Staffords Anti-tank Group was also a fatality that afternoon. He had continued to man his 6-Pounder despite the remainder of his crew being killed or wounded and being wounded in the leg. Baskeyfield refused to be evacuated for medical treatment and his fire kept the German vehicles at bay; when his own gun was damaged by enemy fire he crawled across and took over Lance-Sergeant Mansell's unmanned 6-Pounder on the other side of the road and continued to fire single-handed while shouting encouragement to the men manning nearby positions until he was killed. He was awarded a posthumous Victoria Cross.[100] At around 18:00 the Germans infiltrated a machine-gun team and a number of riflemen into a house in the 3rd Battalion's forward positions; these were dealt with by a well-placed shell from a 6-Pounder followed by an assault led by Lieutenant Alastair Clarkson, the 1st Parachute Battalion's Liaison Officer, which cleared the interlopers at the cost of two wounded. The 18:00 attack that drove the 11th Battalion's A Company out of the farm buildings at the east end of the Hogeweg extended across the 1st and 3rd Battalion's frontage, with several of the houses occupied by the 3rd being set ablaze in the process.[101]

After a full day of fighting the Benedendorpsweg–Acacialaan position had become untenable and Major Lonsdale therefore asked Lieutenant-Colonel Thompson for permission to withdraw. It is unclear precisely when the request was made but it appears to have been before 18:00, given that 1st Airlanding Brigade HQ reported the 11th Parachute Battalion had been ordered to establish a post west of the Acacialaan at 18:15. The order resulted from Brigadier Hicks visiting the 11th Battalion, presumably in response to Major Lonsdale's request, while making the rounds of his Brigade units beginning with the 1st Border at 15:00 and then the 7th KOSB and an unnamed group of Glider Pilots, possibly from D or G Squadrons. He then called in at Division HQ where he reported that he was 'not confident of the OOSTERBEEK area as 11 Para Bn are in a very nervous state'.[102] Lonsdale was granted permission to withdraw and the 1st and 3rd Parachute Battalions moved south-west across the Benedendorpsweg into the open polder at 19:00 and 18:45 respectively, the former under covering fire from a 6-Pounder and a Vickers MMG. The 11th Parachute Battalion moved at around the same time but eastward toward Oosterbeek Old Church, with the two Company groups moving in covering bounds. All three units successfully broke contact without the enemy realising that a withdrawal was taking place and the 3rd and 11th Parachute Battalions did so without incurring any casualties; the 1st Parachute Battalion reported losing approximately thirty casualties in the course of the day including three killed, but it is unclear if any of these were sustained during the withdrawal.[103] The 1st Parachute Battalion took up position behind a dyke running south-east from the Benedendorpsweg to the river with Lieutenant Alastair Clarkson and HQ Company in the centre, R and S Companies on the left under QM Lieutenant Thomas Brown, and Lieutenant Albert Turrell and T Company on the right. The remainder of the night was 'spent in digging deep trenches in water-logged ground'. The 3rd Parachute Battalion contingent took up position farther along the dyke to the south-east and were similarly occupied.[104] The 11th Parachute Battalion, the remnants of which were now 'thoroughly mixed', appear to have been located in the area of Oosterbeek Old Church; according to Middlebrook it had been selected to act as Lonsdale's reserve, although there is no reference to this in the 11th Parachute Battalion War Diary. If it were the case, then Hicks may have had a hand in the matter, given the concerns he expressed to Division HQ about the Battalion's morale.[105]

Wednesday 20 September thus saw extensive combat around much of the coalescing British perimeter in spite of *Obergruppenführer* Bittrich's intention of using the day to permit Harzer and von Tettau's units to close up to Oosterbeek. Harzer's men nonetheless missed the virtually undefended gap of around 1,000 yards on the eastern side of the British perimeter astride the Utrechtseweg; according to Lonsdale the gap was to be plugged by the 4th Parachute Brigade, but none of Hackett's units were available until the mid to late afternoon.[106] The sole German foray into the centre of this gap came in the late morning, likely led by at least one of *Sturmgeschütze Brigade 280's* vehicles, possibly one of those allocated to *Kampfgruppe* Harder. The vehicle moved along the Utrechtseweg as far as the crossroads with the Stationsweg where 181 Airlanding Field Ambulance's transit location at the Hotel Schoonoord had become a centralised Division MDS by default, gathering in other medical units and personnel in the process. The Schoonoord itself housed Lieutenant-Colonel Arthur Marrable's command post, a reception centre, an operating theatre complete with pre and post-operative wards and a minor injury treatment centre with its own ward located in the garage building at the rear of the hotel, while Section Officer Captain James Doyle established a centre for non-surgical casualties in an adjacent school on the Paasbergweg. Lieutenant-Colonel Alford's 133 Parachute Field Ambulance also set up a surgical centre in an adjacent building, while the glider-borne element of 16 Parachute Field Ambulance established a facility for the less severely wounded in the Hotel Tafelberg, a few hundred yards south of the Schoonoord on the Pietersbergseweg.[107] Although the buildings appear to have been displaying the Red Cross the German vehicle fired four rounds into the Hotel Schoonoord's upper storey where two wards had been set up; the shells blew off part of the roof and turned wards into an 'absolute shambles' according to Colonel Marrable. The casualties included 181 Airlanding Field Ambulance's Padre, Captain Bernard Benson, who was severely wounded in the right arm and head; he died of his wounds a week later.[108]

The SS then sprayed the building with machine-gun fire before despatching infantry to investigate, who entered the Hotel Schoonoord via the rear entrance. Their arrival was witnessed by the 11th Parachute Battalion's Medical Officer, Captain Stuart Mawson, who was assisting Captain Clifford Simmons in amputating Padre Benson's right arm with an improvised saw:

> I straightened up and raised my arms above my head, tissue forceps still in my left hand, needle holder in my right, since I was staring wide-eyed at an automatic sub-machine gun levelled straight at my chest. I stood rooted in this attitude, my eyes travelling slowly down the spotted camouflage smock…taking in the hand grenades dangling from the belt, and…the peremptory line of the mouth, the begrimed face and bloodshot, tired-looking, but very alert eyes beneath the coal-scuttle helmet.[109]

Colonel Marrable was able to persuade the ranking German officer to leave the staff and non-ambulatory casualties unmolested, but a party of forty lightly wounded from the minor injury treatment centre in the Hotel Schoonoord garage were marched away to captivity; Marrable was assigned his own personal guard whilst inside the hotel and the Germans maintained a large armed presence throughout the hotel until early evening.[110] At that point the task of guarding the medical staff and several hundred casualties passed to 'one lonely Corporal who was left as sole guard of the whole outfit…[who]…established himself on a chair in the hall with a tommy-gun across his knees, with his eyes darting anxiously from side to side as if he were watching a tennis match'.[111]

The British medical facilities were occupied at some point between 11:00 and midday, with 1st Airborne Division HQ being informed of the fact at 13:30.[112] The latter despatched Lieutenant Colin Macduff-Duncan, a junior liaison officer attached to Division HQ from the 7th KOSB, to confirm the report, which Macduff-Duncan did by taking a Bren Carrier through the German lines to the MDS and back despite heavy German fire.[113] He was followed by Colonel Marrable at 14:45, who reported the capture in person to 1st Airlanding Brigade HQ and that the medical staff and doctors were being allowed to go about their business unmolested.[114] Whatever the precise timing, the Germans do not appear to have made any effort to advance farther west past the Utrechtseweg–Stationsweg crossroads. Had they done so the entire future course of the battle might have been changed, given that the 1st Airborne Division's HQ lay only 500 yards further along the Utrechtseweg surrounded by a variety of Divisional and Brigade support and logistics elements; even a limited attack into the area could therefore have fatally fragmented the coalescing British perimeter before it solidified. According to Middlebrook the German advance along the Utrechtseweg was reined in by fear of British 17-Pounder anti-tank guns but this does not really fit with Harzer's twenty-four-hour closing-up period, although the ferocity of British resistance had doubtless generated a healthy respect among their opponents by this point. Given their apparent reluctance to continue the advance it is more likely that the German troops that occupied the Hotel Schoonoord were not a deliberate probe but elements of *Kampfgruppe* Harder that had become separated during the 08:00 attack on the Benedendorpsweg, and simply lacked the initiative and/or manpower to press farther west. Whether or not, Harzer's apparently hands-off approach to sealing off the bulk of the 1st Airborne Division in Oosterbeek pitched his units into the occupied sectors of the British perimeter by largely following the previous day's lines of advance. In so doing they missed the wide-open western side of the perimeter, and Harzer therefore missed the opportunity to decapitate and scatter the 1st Airborne Division before it could establish a coherent and integrated defence. The omission condemned the Germans to several more days of brutal, costly and arguably avoidable attritional fighting, during which the British came close to establishing a bridgehead across the Lower Rhine. It ranks alongside holding the blocking line along the Amsterdamseweg on the night of 17 September and thereby allowing the 1st Parachute Brigade a clear run to the Arnhem road bridge as one of the major errors in the German handling of the Arnhem portion of MARKET GARDEN.

The open window of opportunity on the east side of the perimeter closed over the course of the afternoon of 20 September. After reporting to Urquhart at the Hotel Hartenstein at 13:10, Lieutenant-Colonel Smyth and his sixty survivors from the 10th Parachute Battalion were directed to occupy buildings overlooking the Utrechtseweg–Stationsweg crossroads. The precise time of the move is unclear as the 10th Battalion party may have been allowed to rest for a while at the Hartenstein, and QM Lieutenant Joseph Glover may also have been despatched to reconnoitre the new location beforehand.[115] On arrival the paratroopers occupied three buildings, commanded by Colonel Smyth, Major Peter Warr, who had been elevated to Battalion second in command, and Lieutenant Peter Saunders from D Company's 18 Platoon. Major Warr captured a *Panzer* IV tank soon after arrival after disposing of its dismounted crew with his Sten gun; the vehicle was reportedly parked as a trophy outside Colonel Smyth's building.[116] QM Lieutenant Glover was almost co-opted into collecting supply containers whilst at the Hotel Hartenstein, but was ordered up to the crossroads in the nick of time by HQ Company commander Major Ashworth and travelled forward with Major Francis Lindley from Support Company with two Bren Carriers loaded with Vickers guns and ammunition, along with Colour-Sergeant Wainright, Sergeant Bentley and Privates Charlton and Wainright. A third Bren Carrier carrying Corporal Burton withdrew after coming under heavy fire, temporarily separating the Corporal from his section. On arrival Glover joined Lieutenant Saunders but was then assigned a fourth house with a Sergeant Hughes and seven men.[117]

Major Ashworth had organised a Bren Carrier and three Jeeps with trailers loaded with supplies intended for the 10th Parachute Battalion but the convoy took a wrong turn soon after leaving the grounds of the Hartenstein and ended up in German-held territory. As Private McEwan travelling on the last trailer recalled, the enemy held their fire until the convoy stopped to take stock:

> At that moment the Germans really hit us…The bren-carrier was hit immediately…I saw Major Ashworth stand up as if to get out, but a burst of fire hit him and he just toppled over. The leading jeep driver…whipped his jeep and trailer right round…and managed to get away. The next driver and ours received bursts…Some of the lads jumped into the front gardens, but the Germans were in the houses and they started throwing grenades onto the lads from the windows…those of us who were left had no alternative but to make a withdrawal as best we could, which we did in pairs and managed to get back into the perimeter.[118]

On returning to the Hotel Hartenstein McEwan appears to have been co-opted into another resupply effort by Major Warr, using another Bren Carrier but that too was knocked out on the second run out to the Battalion position.[119] Matters appear to have quietened down with the onset of darkness, although a constant watch had to be maintained to prevent German infiltrators closing up to lob hand-grenades through the ground-floor windows of the 10th Battalion houses, and around midnight there was an exchange of fire after a Corporal Wyllie challenged a German car of some type that attempted to pass down the side of the Battalion HQ building, only to find itself blocked in by Major Warr's trophy *Panzer* IV. Corporal Burton, by this time reunited with his Section and about to hand over the guard, was wounded in the knee, Major Lindley was hit in the leg by grenade fragments after moving into the open to investigate, and Corporal Wyllie escaped with two bullet holes in his maroon beret; it is unclear whether the German car and its occupants escaped.[120] Major Powell and his fifty survivors from 156 Parachute Battalion were also despatched at 18:30 to occupy houses on the Stationsweg at the junction with the Dennenkampweg, with the Reconnaissance Squadron's A and D Troops occupying strong points on the left adjacent to the 7th KOSB, and Glider Pilots from D Squadron on the right. The paratroopers were in place by 19:30, with the Battalion's two composite platoons occupying the north-east and south-west corners of the junction, after which the night passed 'without any incidents'.[121]

The other significant events at the 1st Airborne Division's main location on Wednesday 20 September involved reinforcement and resupply. In the English East Midlands the paratroopers of Sosabowski's 1st Polish Independent Parachute Brigade had arrived at Saltby and Spanhoe at 08:45 to learn that their drop zone had been relocated and that their 10:00 take-off had been postponed for three hours owing to fog and drizzle across southern England. The wait in the wet grass alongside the USAAF C-47s was all the more frustrating because the cloud ceiling seemed sufficiently high for take-off to the paratroopers, who could also hear and catch occasional glimpses of aircraft in the murk. The waiting was mirrored in Holland by Captain Ludwik Zwolanski and the Polish Brigade's liaison group attached to the 1st Airborne Division HQ. The group had left in the pre-dawn darkness heading for the Heveadorp ferry, accompanied by a radio operator and War Correspondent Swiecicki. The party paused near the Oosterbeek Old Church and talked to Captain Alfons Mackowiak, the Polish Brigade's artillery liaison officer, who had been acting as an observer for the Airlanding Light Regiment before taking shelter in an artillery battery command post. This was probably the one belonging to the Light Regiment's 3 Battery, located in a house cellar near the Oosterbeek Old Church. The German bombardment resumed at that time, 07:00. The Poles were informed of the three-hour postponement whilst ensconced in the cellar and remained there until after the building above the cellar was badly damaged by a *nebelwerfer* rocket at 11:00; on emerging to return to the Hotel Hartenstein Captain Zwolanski's party discovered that their radio operator had been badly wounded and his radio damaged beyond repair.[122]

Back at Saltby and Spanhoe, take-off was postponed for another hour at 13:00 but shortly afterward the paratroopers were ordered to board their C-47s, which started engines at 13:40 and began manoeuvring around the taxi ways and onto the runway ready for take-off. At 13:55 take-off was cancelled and the transports began moving back to their dispersal locations. The drop was postponed for another twenty-four hours because of the fog and drizzle across southern England; the cloud ceiling over the English Channel was only 9,000 feet.[123] The frustration of the keyed-up Poles at being pulled back at virtually the last minute can be well imagined and was abundantly clear to their US hosts, as observed by a pilot from the 34th Troop Carrier Squadron at Spanhoe: 'When it was canceled [sic] a second time, they were really pissed. They wanted to fight, they wanted to get over there and fight. Some of them thought that we didn't want to take them or something.'[124] The crew of at least one C-47 was advised to remain in their cockpit until the paratroopers had disembarked and dispersed by their crew chief. The tension simply became too much for one member of the Polish Brigade's Engineer Company, who committed suicide with his Sten gun after disembarking; his comrades were trucked back to their billets around Stamford and Peterborough at 17:00.[125] On the up side Brigade Quartermaster Lieutenant Kaczmarek had less problems organising rations for the disgruntled Brigade, and the delay allowed the Brigade Staff to develop their hurriedly cobbled together operational plan properly; to that end Sosabowski despatched Lieutenant-Colonel Stevens to gather all available information on the 1st Airborne Division's situation.[126]

Captain Zwolanski and his liaison party had sallied forth again from the Hotel Hartenstein for the Heveadorp ferry, this time travelling by Jeep. After calling in at 1st Airlanding Brigade HQ where they collected a guide and, curiously, a haversack full of apples the party travelled to the positions occupied by the 1st Border's B Company. There they settled down to wait in slit trenches overlooking the Heveadorp ferry, which was still held at this point by Captain Heggie's detachment from the 9th Field Company RE. There they remained until after 17:00 when word was relayed via 1st Border HQ that the drop had been postponed for a further twenty-four hours and the disappointed Poles retraced their journey back to the Hotel Hartenstein yet again. The postponement was perhaps fortunate for while the ferry remained intact until the late evening, War Correspondent Swiecki noted the Germans were regularly sweeping the crossing with fire that had reduced the timber ferry dock to a splintered wreck.[127]

While the Polish paratroopers were whiling away their time at Saltby, Spanhoe and Oosterbeek, aircraft from RAF Nos. 38 and 46 Groups were carrying out the 1st Airborne Division's latest supply drop. According to Middlebrook, Urquhart's request for a new supply drop point had been received and approved, presumably via contact with Airborne Corps Rear HQ at Moor Park at 01:20 or 07:20 that morning, although thirty-three aircraft were still directed to deliver their loads to LZ Z, which now lay over two miles outside the western edge of the 1st Airborne Division's perimeter.[128] As all three Stirling bases put up approximately thirty-three aircraft it is unclear which was so assigned, although Middlebrook may have been referring the No. 48 Squadron, which put up sixteen Dakotas briefed to deliver their loads onto DZ V; their RAF Down Ampney running mates from No. 271 Squadron may have been similarly tasked.[129] Whichever, the new supply drop zone was centred on the Utrechtseweg–Stationsweg crossroads just 200 yards west of the Hotel Hartenstein and was to be marked with orange smoke, although there does not appear to have been any centralised marking effort. Worse, by the time the first drop commenced the drop point was at least nominally in the hands of the SS troops holding the Division MDS at the Hotel Schoonoord. For reasons that are equally unclear but presumably connected to the weather, the supply drop was to be delivered in two increments, the first provided by No. 38 Group. Seventeen Short Stirlings from No. 295 Squadron and a further sixteen from No. 570 Squadron began to take off from RAF Harwell at 11:30; two more machines aborted due to mechanical defects. They were joined twenty minutes later by another thirty-three Stirlings from Nos. 196 and 299 Squadrons, seventeen from the former and sixteen from the latter, flying from RAF Keevil, again with two aborts due to mechanical failure.[130] The remaining sixty-three aircraft had an uneventful flight across the Channel apart from one machine from No. 196 Squadron, which either ditched or crash-landed among friendly forces in the Airborne corridor, depending on the account.[131]

As on the previous day, the problems began as the formation approached Oosterbeek at just before 14:00 and came within range of *FlaK Brigade* Svoboda's guns, as noted by RAF Warrant Officer Joseph Corless flying in a Stirling from No. 299 Squadron:

> We got a very hot reception with all kinds of rubbish coming up at us…We managed to drop the containers, but one of the hampers jammed in the hatch and the wireless operator and flight engineer were jumping up and down on it in an effort to free it when we were hit in both elevators, rear turret and fuselage…we were by now in a very unhealthy nose-up attitude, with both the pilot and myself doing our utmost to raise the air speed, which was fast approaching stalling speed. We managed to achieve this, got rid of the hamper and limped home feeling that it had been our lucky day.[132]

The aircrew's task was complicated further by the unclear ground marking to mark the drop point and the Germans may have compounded matters by aping the Airborne troops' efforts. The result was pointed out by Warrant Officer Bernard Harvey flying in another machine from the same Squadron: 'We were briefed to drop on orange [smoke] candles but we found orange candles all over the place. So we just pitched the stuff where we thought best as long as it was on the far side of the Rhine. That was the best we could do.'[133] Not everyone succumbed to the hit and hope approach, however. Pilot-Officer Karl Ketcheson, the Canadian bomb-aimer in a third No. 299 Squadron Stirling, refused to release his load on the first pass because he could not properly distinguish the drop point; he was killed on the second run by the only German round to strike the aircraft.[134]

In all, the four squadrons in the first supply flight lost seven aircraft shot down, five of them from No. 196 Squadron.[135] The remaining two aircraft came from Nos. 295 and 299 Squadrons, the former flown by NZRAF Pilot-Officer Neil Couper, who force-landed after being hit by *flak* over the drop zone. Couper was killed but the remainder of his crew survived, with one crewman and two despatchers being captured and the remaining four crewmen making their way to friendly territory.[136] An eighth Stirling from No. 570 Squadron sustained damage to two engines and came down prematurely at RAF Benson in Oxfordshire, landing safely despite two flat tyres.[137] A substantial proportion of the materiel delivered at such cost fell into enemy hands; as the 1st Airborne Division War Diary noted the drop had 'limited success owing to small perimeter, despite efforts by every available man to collect'.[138] The thirty surviving machines from RAF Harwell were back on the ground by 16:00 followed by their twenty-four compatriots from RAF Keevil thirty minutes later.[139]

The second and larger supply flight involved thirty-three Stirlings from No. 38 Group and sixty-three Dakotas from No. 46 Group, which began taking off while the first flight was still over Oosterbeek. Thirty-two aircraft from the latter's No. 48 Squadron and sixteen from

No. 271 Squadron commenced take-off from RAF Down Ampney at 14:15, followed twenty-five minutes later by thirty-one Dakotas from Nos. 512 and 575 Squadrons flying from RAF Broadwell; the third increment of seventeen Stirlings each from No. 190 and No. 620 Squadrons began taking off from RAF Fairford at 14:45, although one machine may have aborted.[140] The flight again appears to have been uneventful until the run-in to Oosterbeek for the drop, which commenced at around 17:00. The Stirling contingent lost five machines shot down, three from No. 190 Squadron and two from No. 620 Squadron with the entire crew of eight aircrew and two despatchers from one of the former being killed, along with two Dakotas from No. 512 Squadron. Identifying the drop zone again proved problematic, as recalled by Warrant Officer Arthur Batten aboard one of No. 190 Squadron's Stirlings: 'Things had changed dramatically and recognition from an aircraft was practically impossible. You could see men waving and sheets being laid out but you had lost them in smoke or woods by the time you came round again to drop.'[141] In spite of this and the anti-aircraft fire the aircrew stuck courageously to the task: the Stirlings of Nos. 190 and 620 Squadrons delivering a total of 696 containers and 116 panniers between them, for example.[142] Ironically the units tasked to deliver their loads onto the German-held DZ V fared better than those that pressed on into Oosterbeek or LZ Z, with No. 271 Squadron losing no aircraft while No. 48 Squadron suffered just one damaged; Dakota KG423 lost its starboard engine to *flak* but its pilot, Flying-Officer Martin Mackay, maintained control and returned to Down Ampney on one engine. The 256 panniers delivered by No. 48 Squadron went straight into the German logistics effort.[143] Despite this 1st Airborne Division HQ noted that the second drop was more successful, as did the Division RASC element tasked to gather and distribute the supplies, although the latter also noted that the 'number of rations collected [was] sufficient only for one third rations to be issued'.[144] Of the machines that delivered them, No. 48 Squadron's sixteen aircraft were the first to reach home along with the sixteen from No. 271 Squadron, landing at Down Ampney by 19:15; the twenty-eight surviving Stirlings landed at Fairford fifteen minutes later, beating Nos. 512 and 575 Squadrons twenty-eight Dakotas to RAF Broadwell by three minutes.[145]

Just three miles to the east of the supply drop's target, events at the Arnhem road bridge were ratcheting down to what was becoming an inevitable conclusion. By the afternoon of Wednesday 20 September the bulk of Frost's much reduced force was hemmed into three adjacent locations around the northern ramp. The 2nd Parachute Battalion's B and Support Companies occupied the buildings and gardens inside the angle of the Eusebiusbinnensingel and Weertjesstraat, along with their Battalion HQ and 1st Parachute Brigade HQ, elements of a variety of support units and over 200 wounded gathered in the Regimental Aid Post (RAP) in the cellar of the Brigade HQ building. On the opposite side of the Weertjesstraat toward the Lower Rhine the survivors of the various elements driven back from east of the bridge including personnel from the 2nd Battalion's A Company, Brigade HQ, Signals and RAOC detachments were sheltering in the area between the bridge underpass and the Kadestraat. The only British presence remaining east of the ramp was the Van Limburg School held by elements of the 1st Parachute Squadron RE and the 3rd Parachute Battalion's C Company.

At around 13:30 Frost was discussing organising a fighting patrol to extend the perimeter northward toward the prison with Major Douglas Crawley in the back garden of the house occupied by the latter's B Company on the Weertjesstraat. Both men were felled by a mortar bomb; Frost was badly wounded in the right shin and left ankle whilst Crawley was hit in both ankles and the right arm.[146] They were evacuated to the relative safety of Major Logan's RAP and command of the bridge force devolved to Major Gough on Brigade Major Hibbert's recommendation and with Frost's agreement.[147] Interestingly, Gough must have been responsible for contacting Division HQ at 14:40 to request information regarding ground relief and the arrival of the Polish Brigade before informing them of the change of command just over an hour later; these contacts appear to have been made via the civilian telephone line, given that Division Signals reported its Base set unusable owing to jamming at 14:00.[148]

The Germans meanwhile renewed their effort to eradicate the approximately thirty-strong British force holding the Van Limburg School. At 14:00 a Tiger I, possibly accompanied by a 105mm self-propelled gun, approached the school from the north-east. This may have been *Feldwebel* Barneki's vehicle although two more of *schwere Panzer Kompanie* Hummel's Tigers had reached Arnhem by this point; all three had been assigned to *Kampfgruppe* Knaust.[149] Whoever commanded it, the Tiger began to systematically pump shells into the school's upper storey from a range of eighty yards. One of the first projectiles detonated beneath the upper-storey room where Major Lewis and Lieutenant Wright from the 3rd Parachute Battalion were resting, wounding the former in the left shoulder and thigh and giving the latter traumatic amnesia, presumably from the concussion.[150] Within ten minutes the school was on fire in four separate locations and the entire south-east corner and much of the south and east faces had been demolished, and by 14:30 the whole of the two upper storeys were ablaze.[151] The able-bodied defenders moved down to the cellar, taking the wounded including Major Lewis with them, although Captain Mackay was determined to continue the fight as recalled by one of his men, Lance-Sergeant Norman Swift: 'Captain Mackay told me to gather together any Gammon bombs the lads had left and he and I would try and get the Tiger tank under one of the school walls. To my relief, after collecting together a few bombs in a canvas bucket, when we were going up the main staircase the ceiling of the landing collapsed putting a stop to that idea.'[152] The school had thus become untenable but even in these dire straits the unexplained antipathy between Major Lewis and Captain Mackay continued, and the latter unilaterally decided it was time to leave and continue the fight from elsewhere. He ordered the wounded brought up from the cellar, the non-ambulatory cases on doors or mattresses pressed into service as makeshift stretchers, and organised a covering group armed with four Bren guns under Lieutenant Denis Simpson.

The plan appears to have been to evacuate the wounded to the Red School building on the bridge ramp twenty yards or so north of the Van Limburg School, which had been occupied briefly by Captain Mackay and his A Troop in the late evening of Sunday 17 September; for some reason the Sappers appear to have referred to the building as the library.[153] This involved not only manoeuvring the makeshift stretchers across the open ground between the building but also lifting them over the brick wall that surrounded the Red School. At least two casualties were killed in this process, a C Company paratrooper by mortar bomb shrapnel and a Sapper by machine-gun fire. A third man, possibly a helper rather than a casualty, was also killed by a gunshot wound to the head whilst climbing over the wall. According to the 1st Parachute Squadron War Diary the move was complete by 14:45, cost four dead and raised the number of wounded to thirty-five, while a further two men from Lieutenant Simpson's covering party were also killed by mortar fire. It is unclear if all the wounded were evacuated by the time Captain Mackay returned to the Van Limburg School to collect Lieutenant Simpson and his rearguard. The German fire grew heavier and Simpson and some of his men were wounded outside the school as they began their move; Mackay then ordered Simpson to surrender with the wounded and led nine unwounded Sappers to the houses on the east side of the Eusebiusbuitensingel. The escapees included Lance-Corporals Arthur Hendy and Joseph Malley and Sapper Ronald Emery, who were aided in their dash by the Tiger tank briefly turning its attention to other buildings to the west.[154] The decision to abandon the wounded did not go down well with all Mackay's men, one of whom later recalled: 'Some of us felt that was the time an officer should have stayed with his men, and I was one of those who stayed with the wounded. It had reached the stage where each individual had to decide whether to stay with his wounded comrades or clear off.'[155]

At around this point Major Lewis announced it was time to raise the white flag, prompting his second-in-command Captain Wilfred Robinson to ask if the able-bodied paratroopers could make a break for it rather than surrender; when Lewis concurred Robinson also led a small group east across the Eusebiusbuitensingel, although it is unclear what became of them.

Major Lewis then made a brief speech congratulating the surviving defenders on their steadfast performance but insisting the situation made surrender inevitable. He then despatched a Sapper onto the bridge ramp with a white flag, who was promptly felled by a burst of machine-gun fire across the legs. The Germans accepted the surrender at around 15:10, allegedly after the errant machine-gunner was summarily executed by his commander for firing on the white flag, and one badly wounded Sapper being despatched by his captors as a mercy killing.[156] The British wounded and those who chose to remain with them were on their way into captivity by 20:00.[157] By that time the Sappers who had escaped across the Eusebiusbuitensingel had also been captured. Lance-Corporal Arthur Hendy was taken after routing a group of SS in a brief firefight following which he 'started moving through the back gardens only to run into a group of SS soldiers who didn't run away! I was soon taken prisoner.'[158] Captain Mackay and five of his men ran into another group of German infantry gathered around *Kampfgruppe* Knaust's other two Tiger tanks in the streets east of the Eusebiusbuitensingel at around 15:15 and after a skirmish during which one of the Sappers was killed, Mackay ordered his party to split up and make their own way back to the British enclave west of the bridge ramp. The tactic proved of little use however, for the Germans began to systematically quarter the area in search of any Airborne fugitives. Lance-Sergeant John Humphries and Corporal Charles Weir were taken together, and Mackay was discovered by a party of SS whilst asleep under a rose bush whilst awaiting darkness. The irascible Captain played dead when kicked in the ribs but erupted in anger when one of the SS men bayoneted him in the buttocks, and he narrowly avoided being shot after brandishing his empty Colt .45 automatic whilst berating his captors with the immortal words 'What the bloody hell do you mean stabbing a bayonet into a British Officer?' All the evaders had been rounded up by around 15:45.[159]

While the Germans were dealing with the Van Limburg School, the British to the west of the bridge ramp were busy regrouping all able-bodied defenders in the area around the Brigade HQ building bounded by the Eusebiusbinnensingel, Weertjesstraat and Prinsenhof. Major Tatham-Warter and his trademark furled umbrella therefore braved the 100-yard journey across the bullet- and shrapnel-swept Weertjesstraat to the group sheltering in the area between the bridge overpass and the Kadestraat. It is unclear precisely how this was communicated, but he ordered them to run the gauntlet of the Weertjesstraat and regroup in the gardens behind the Brigade HQ building. Some, like Signalman George Lawson, made the passage safely, albeit with some delay: 'I heard the shout "Every man for himself". A group of us made a dash for it. We had to go through a mortar barrage first; that's where young Waterston got hit...Several of the others were hit, too; I was hit in the face by shrapnel...A group of us then tried to cross the open road, but four or five were mown down by machine-gun fire. I turned back and took refuge in one of the burnt-out buildings – how long for, I don't know, but I was forced to get up because my gas cape and my smock were burning from the hot stone; my arse was almost on fire.'[160] Others, like Private Kevin Heaney from the RAOC Ordnance Field Parks detachment, were less successful:

I reached the corner of a garden and had to negotiate a wall. I saw several chaps being picked off as they went over. I remember one hit in the forehead and one in the chest...A hand-grenade came over the wall and exploded; the chap behind me had a great big hole in the neck and blood was gurgling out. I put my field dressing round his neck...I managed to make my way into the rubble of the houses nearby; six of us gathered in the remains of a hallway.

The group attempted to surrender using Private Heaney's vest as a makeshift white flag but four were mown down after emerging; Heaney and one of the wounded 'got back into the house and sat in the rubble. We could hear mortar fire on the nearby houses, walls falling, heard our own men trapped, calling for help. We were there about two hours...Later on, the Germans came in, rescuing the trapped men and taking them prisoner, and this great big German came and took the two of us also.'[161]

Most of those who reached the relative safety of the rendezvous area north of the Weertjesstraat were set to occupying or digging slit trenches sited to allow fire between the buildings onto the bridge ramp, alongside other able-bodied defenders not occupying the Brigade HQ and adjacent buildings. Private Henry Sullivan from the 2nd Battalion's A Company discovered a cache of bottles whilst digging in, some full of wine and others containing two Guilders and a half; the former was quickly consumed and one coin was retained as a souvenir.[162] The Germans appear to have maintained the pressure on the western British enclave with mortar and artillery rather than small-arms or direct assaults for much of the afternoon as they concentrated their efforts on the Van Limburg School, and the British were able to maintain contact with the main Divisional area at Oosterbeek. As we have seen, 1st Airborne Division HQ was informed of Frost's wounding, Major Gough's accession to command and that 'the [bridge] party can hold out until tomorrow' at 15:45, and ninety minutes later that the fuses had been removed from German demolition charges at the north end of the bridge; the final message reporting '4 Tiger Tks and one Recce crossed main br from NORTH to SOUTH at 1815 hrs' was received at the Hartenstein ten minutes after the event.[163] The latter report is curious as German sources do not refer to *schwere Panzer Kompanie Hummel* or *Kampfgruppe* Brinkmann crossing the bridge until the morning of Thursday 21 September, and because Major Munford's final transmission to the Light Regiment's HQ at the Oosterbeek Old Church at 19:00 reported that the bridge was 'blocked with German half-tracks, armoured cars etc'.[164] It is unclear whether the reports were transmitted via the civilian telephone network or via radio, although at least two sets belonging to the 1st Airlanding Light Regiment's 3 Battery were still operating from the Brigade HQ building by the late afternoon of 20 September; Bombardier Leo Hall's jury-rigged No. 22 and No. 68 radio sets from E Troop in the attic and a No. 22 set from 3 Battery HQ on the floor below manned by Gunner Dennis Bowles.[165] There was also a third No. 22 set belonging to 1st Parachute Brigade HQ with which Major Hibbert made brief contact with 30 Corps during the morning, although it is unclear if that set was still functioning by late afternoon. There was possibly another radio that may have belonged to the 1st Airborne Reconnaissance Squadron; Private James Sims reported seeing a 'powerful radio transmitter' set up at the bottom of the stairs when he was assisted up from the RAP in the cellar to use the toilet. As Major Gough was operating the set it may have been a No. 76 transmitter removed from a Reconnaissance Squadron Jeep.[166]

By the late afternoon/early evening the Germans renewed their assault, with *Rottenführer* Rudolf Trapp's party from *Panzergrenadier Regiment 21* closing up to the western face of the British perimeter. Their gains may have included the Mortar Platoon house on the corner of the Prinsenhof and Weertjesstraat, given that Trapp referred to being close enough to hear shouted entreaties from German prisoners incarcerated in the cellar of the Brigade and 2nd Battalion HQ buildings.[167] More importantly, all the British 6-Pounder anti-tank guns had either been knocked out or rendered u/s by small-arms fire – Private James Sims recalled seeing one badly damaged gun and its dead crew in front of the Brigade HQ building – and the supply of PIAT bombs had run out the previous day. This permitted German tanks to motor back and forth at will.[168] One, likely a Tiger I from *schwere Panzer Kompanie Hummel*, repeated the drill used against the Van Limburg School as described by Brigade Major Hibbert: 'The tactic was to fire high explosive into the sides of the building to break the wall down then fire smoke shells through that, and of course the smoke shells have got phosphorus in them, [and] the phosphorus sets light to anything inflammable in the house.'[169] Being set back from the Eusebiusbinnensingel, the Brigade HQ building had enjoyed a degree of protection from the buildings to each side, but the Germans were now able to bring their direct fire weapons to bear with impunity. Gunner Dennis Bowles was in contact with 3 Troop at the Oosterbeek Old Church from the top floor when the shelling began: 'There was a big bang and a lot of dust, and that put the wireless out of action. Back at the battery they heard the set go dead in the middle of my transmission and when they returned to England they reported that I was "missing presumed killed".[170] The 'big bang' may have been from a 150mm field gun that Brigade Major Hibbert had seen being brought into action protected by German tanks, and Bowles may have been in the process of calling down fire upon it, given that Hibbert referred to the radio link with the Airlanding Light Regiment at the Oosterbeek Old Church breaking down before the request was complete.[171] The field gun reportedly pumped three rounds into the attic and may have prompted Major Munford's final transmission to 3 Battery at 19:00, which reported his being 'blown off the top storey'.[172] The same flurry of shelling may also have brought Bombardier Hall's occupancy of the Brigade HQ attic to an end:

> Suddenly Munford appeared in the Attic; it would be late afternoon, Wednesday... 'Come on!' he said; 'We're evacuating the building.' I got up. 'What about the set?' I asked. His reply was terse and unmistakable: 'Fuck the set!' But I turned back to switch it off to save the battery...Suddenly, everything happening within a second, a shell-burst fragment caught my hip, flinging me into the down-well of the stairs. My right leg and buttock were paralysed, useless; warm blood trickled down the lower sensitive parts. Munford and two others carried me down into the cellar for a dressing and eventual placing alongside the other wounded.[173]

The severe constriction of the British perimeter made abandoning burning buildings a perilous rat run, and in the case of the Brigade HQ building this was made so much worse by the position of approximately 300 wounded in the RAP in the cellar, as it became apparent that the fire could not be controlled. A start on evacuating the casualties to the building held by Captain Gell and his RASC party adjacent to the prison appears to have been made, which was the only British-held building not burning; but progress was slow, as reaching it involved traversing the entire width of the backyard area under heavy mortar fire.[174] Captains Logan and Wright appear to have broached the idea of arranging a truce to permit an evacuation with Colonel Frost when the building came under direct fire. The walking wounded were moved out of the cellar before the fire reached critical proportions.[175] When Captain Logan returned and warned that the expanding fire meant something would have be done 'fairly quickly' to assist the non-ambulatory cases remaining in the cellar, Frost ordered he and Gough to make the necessary arrangements. Logan made contact with the Germans by the simple and courageous expedient of unbolting the Brigade HQ building's imposing front doors and walking into the open under a flag of truce; it is unclear whether this was a Red Cross or white flag. Despite Gough's fears that the SS would simply open fire irrespective of the flag, the ploy worked and a two-hour truce was arranged at approximately 20:00.[176] Private James Sims heard one of the medical officers explaining the gravity of the situation to a German officer at the cellar entrance, and witnessed what followed including a potentially catastrophic incident as the first German descended the stairs:

> Suddenly a badly wounded paratrooper uncovered a Sten gun he had kept hidden ready to blast the Germans as they appeared. He was quickly overpowered by the equally badly wounded men on either side of him...he first to enter the cellar was an officer wearing a greatcoat and steel helmet...He looked tired and drawn, and was obviously shocked by what he saw...He rapped out orders...More and more German troops appeared. They picked up the wounded with great care and began to clear the cellar.[177]

The evacuation came in the nick of time. Colonel Frost was waiting for his batman to procure a stretcher but a German NCO decided the situation was too urgent for such niceties and half-carried and half-dragged him out of the cellar and through the burning building, assisted by some British battle-shock casualties.[178] Private Sims had a closer call: 'A huge Canadian press photographer was in the cellar with us...He lifted me as though I were a child and carried me upstairs. The ground floor was well ablaze and the whole building was about to cave in. As the Canadian stepped outside...he had to jump to one side, for a massive piece of flaming timber hurtled down from the roof. Large chunks of brickwork and concrete were also coming down, adding to the danger of the evacuation.'[179] The casualties were carried across the Eusebiusbinnensingel and laid out on the grass embankment of the bridge ramp in readiness for transport to the St Elizabeth Hospital, among other destinations. The whole area was lit up like daylight by the burning buildings. Sims recalled a German machine-gun team dug into the embankment successfully demanding some of the casualties be moved from their line of fire, and was amazed 'to see the change in the [surrounding] area...All the houses and warehouses we had held were completely destroyed by fire.'[180] Frost, now on a stretcher next to Major Crawley, watched the burning 2nd Battalion HQ building collapse in spectacular fashion before commenting 'Well Doug, I'm afraid we haven't got away with it this time,' to which Crawley responded 'No sir, but we gave 'em a damn good run for their money.' Frost also noted the German prisoners who had been incarcerated in the British-held buildings gathered nearby were 'not seemingly overjoyed at their liberation'.[181] Their lack of enthusiasm was likely due to their SS liberators intent to rearm them as a handy source of reinforcement, although at least some managed to evade this fate. *Leutnant* Joseph Enthammer and his V2 rear party were able to use their status as members of a *Kriegsentscheidenden Waffen* (Decisive Weapons) unit as inscribed on their pay books to justify immediate return to their parent unit. Enthammer observed, 'We were lucky, therefore, not to be recruited into the ranks of the SS!'[182]

While rendering assistance with the wounded, the Germans also looked to turn the truce to their advantage where possible. They swiftly appropriated around ten Jeeps that had survived in working order behind the Brigade HQ building despite Major Gough's protests, claiming the vehicles were necessary to shuttle the wounded to hospital.[183] Colonel Frost saw them being used for this purpose, although the skill of the new owners was sometimes less than optimal.[184] Private Sims and his companions 'had a few laughs at their efforts...with the Jeep, which bucked all over the road like a mustang, to ribald shouts of Ride him, cowboy!' At the other side of the British perimeter Major Hibbert was almost run down by another German-driven Jeep near the prison.[185] At the other end of the scale the Germans also took at least one Bren Carrier in working order, as witnessed by Sims; in this instance the driver's proficiency led his audience to assume that Private George Hines, a particularly skilled driver from the Mortar Platoon, had been pressed into service, until Hines identified himself among the wounded.[186] The Germans also took the opportunity to reconnoitre the British positions in readiness for the resumption of hostilities. To this end *Rottenführer* Trapp from *SS Panzergrenadier Regiment 21* 'walked with a companion through the British positions right up to the bridge. There we saw the result of Graebner's attack.' This was probably the first inkling the Germans fighting at ground level had of the carnage wrought upon *SS Panzer Aufklärungs Abteilung 9* on the morning of Monday 18 September.[187]

The Germans attempted to persuade the Airborne soldiers to give up, with one greatcoated officer circulating among their slit trenches handing out cigarettes likely obtained from a British supply container while doing so. The SS also simply moved some of their men into more advantageous positions. In one instance Major Tatham-Warter despatched B Company's German-speaking second-in-command, Captain Francis Hoyer-Millar, to protest: 'I found an officer in a long dark leather coat...I warned him that if his men continued, we might have to open fire. He, in turn, kept stressing that there was no hope for us and that we should surrender. I told him there was no chance of that and that we were confident our ground forces would soon be up to relieve us.'[188]

Despite their protests, the British were indulging in similar behaviour themselves, for they were virtually at the end of their tether when the truce was called. Major Hibbert indicated the moment when he thought the game was up: 'At 8 o'clock I realised that our little battle was finished. We just didn't have the ammunition. When the other side can run tanks right up to your front window with no chance of you retaliating, there comes a moment where you can't go on.'[189] Frost had discussed the idea of relocating the men still capable of fighting to another location with Gough the previous day, although it is unclear whether the final decision was made before or during the truce.[190] The 2nd Battalion was allotted the task of holding in place by the bridge ramp while the remainder of the able-bodied troops, most if not all of whom came from the 1st Parachute Brigade HQ column, were to move to a convent school just north of the existing perimeter under cover of the truce, from where they were to break out toward the main Division position; Major Hibbert was carrying out a personal reconnaissance of the location when he was almost run down by the German-driven Jeep.[191] As the group numbered around 120, the troops presumably made their way to the school individually or in small groups to avoid attracting attention, and Major Gough was present at one point to give the would-be evaders a few words of encouragement, as recalled by Corporal Dennis Freebury: 'Major Gough, with his arm in a sling…gave us a pep talk. It was a bit like Hollywood. He said, "I want you to go out, do your best and see if you can get back to our own forces – and just remember that you belong to the finest division in the British Army." Nobody cheered or anything like that, but it made one feel good.'[192] The evaders were then left with Major Hibbert. Gough had elected to return to the bridge perimeter and remain with the 2nd Battalion party.

Back at the bridge, the Germans began carrying the British wounded across the ramp to the shelter of the east side, in parallel with moving small groups away in the commandeered Jeeps. The move was presumably in readiness for the end of the truce, although it may also have been prompted by an unknown Bren gunner in a cellar by the collapsed White House firing on a group of German troops drawn up on the Eusebiusbinnensingel. The burst not only scattered the Germans but came close to hitting the British wounded laid out on the embankment, drawing a chorus of shouted British protests that appears to have stopped him. Despite this and the bitter no-quarter nature of the fighting, the Germans remained strictly correct in their behaviour and in many instances went further. Colonel Frost referred to the SS being 'very polite and complimentary', while Sims exchanged anecdotes with a decorated Normandy veteran. Sims also recalled being given hot coffee, bread and sausage, and a share of a captured British can of condensed milk by three different SS men. The truce appears to have come to an end as the last of the wounded were lifted over the embankment, given that Frost saw the SS moving off 'to take up positions for battle again [and] heard weapons being loaded and orders being given'. Once on the other side of the ramp Frost and a number of other stretcher cases were loaded aboard a German half-track for transit to the St Elizabeth Hospital. British trust of the Germans nonetheless had its limits. Sims turned down the offer of a stretcher from a smiling German NCO, 'as all the stretcher cases were being carried down a road leading to the river. I declined his offer, lest I be dumped in the Rhine…Two other wounded paratroopers hung my arms round their necks and we struggled along under the northern end of the bridge.'[193] While their wounded comrades limped or were driven away for treatment, the remnants of the 2nd Parachute Battalion were settling in for the last act. Captain Hoyer-Millar's thoughts at the time illustrate the general feeling as the truce wound down: 'I was as scared that night as at any time. How could it have been otherwise – completely surrounded by burning buildings and enemy… But there was indeed a strange feeling of exhilaration mingled with pride and bitterness. We were still there after three full days and nights and, incredibly enough, alive and in one piece – though it seemed improbable that we would remain thus for much longer.'[194]

It was around this time that the last British radio message was transmitted from the bridge perimeter. The operator was presumably Gough, given that Ryan refers to him using a radio after the evaders had departed, and that the radio Private Sims saw Gough using on the stairs of the Brigade HQ building before the truce appears to have been the only functioning set left in the bridge perimeter. The transmission does not appear to have been picked up by 1st Airborne

Division HQ or 30 Corps, but it was noted by monitors at 9 *SS Panzer Division* HQ in the north-eastern outskirts of Arnhem. According to *Obersturmbannführer* Harzer, the last two sentences were 'Out of ammunition. God Save the King'.[195]

The truce marked the effective end of organised British resistance at the Arnhem road bridge. It is unclear whether it was due to a resumption of the bombardment, German infiltration up to and into the British perimeter, or a combination, but the 2nd Parachute Battalion contingent was unable to hold or in some instances even reoccupy their pre-truce positions. Major Tatham-Warter attempted to counter this by dividing his force with Major Francis Tate from HQ Company and dispersing for the night outside the perimeter, with the intention of reoccupying their positions at dawn. According Ryan the plan originated with Gough, who intended to re-concentrate 'in a half-gutted building by the riverbank', presumably in the area of the Rijnkade and Kadestraat.[196] The tactic backfired as German infantry began systematically quartering the area in the early hours of Thursday morning and eliminated the isolated pockets of paratroopers as they came on them. Major Tate and a number of his men were killed in one such clash and others, such as the group led by Lieutenant Thomas Ainslie from HQ Company, were trapped and called on to surrender: 'Some of my group had already been hit, so I yelled back in German "Don't shoot. There are wounded in here." And we walked across the street into captivity.' His captors then distributed presumably looted Dutch cigars and both groups engaged in what Ainslie referred to as a 'matey chat'.[197] A few men attempted to evade on their own but all appear to have been captured. These included Major Gough, who was apprehended by a German patrol near the municipal waterworks after attempting to hide beneath a woodpile. He too was congratulated when interrogated by a German officer shortly after capture, who also praised the Airborne troop's skill and experience in street fighting; Gough responded drily 'No, this was our first attempt. We'll do much better next time.'[198] The approximately 120-strong party of evaders from the Brigade HQ Column fared no better after leaving the convent school. The party divided up into groups of ten, each headed by an officer, stealthily exiting the school at intervals. Lieutenant Todd from the US Jedburgh team led the way at 02:00 on the morning of Thursday 20 September. Major Hibbert led the last group out of the school before dawn, including Major Munford and Major Tony Cotterell, a reporter from the Army Bureau of Current Affairs. It is unclear what became of the others but Hibbert's group only made the 300 yards or so to the vicinity of Arnhem cathedral before it became apparent that the German cordon was impenetrable and Hibbert therefore ordered them to hide, presumably intending to try again after dark. Some men were barricaded into the bedroom of a convenient house, two hid in a tool shed in the yard, Munford fastened himself inside a wooden crate and Cotterell and Hibbert climbed into the outside coal bin. All were discovered and taken prisoner.[199]

Thus ended the 1st Parachute Brigade's epic battle to hold the north end of the Arnhem road bridge. Of the approximately 740 men who had reached the bridge on the evening of Sunday 17 September, around eighty-one had been killed or mortally wounded, equivalent to eleven per cent of the total force. Almost half these deaths, thirty-seven in total, occurred in the final twenty-four hours of the battle when the Brigade's attached anti-tank guns had been knocked out and the supply of PIAT bombs had been expended, leaving the Airborne soldiers effectively pinned in their positions by German armour and artillery fire with no effective means of response.[200] Approximately 280 men had been wounded, and had the Germans not agreed to the truce on the evening of Wednesday 20 September a good number of them would likely have joined the death toll. Nor was the killing confined to the battleground around the north bridge ramp. While the *SS* behaviour toward their opponents was almost always exemplary, there were nonetheless lapses. Private James Sims saw a badly burned member of the Dutch resistance dragged from the British column and summarily executed while being marched away from the bridge, and shortly afterward witnessed an altercation when an unknown paratrooper refused to hand over his wallet during a search: 'His searcher pulled out a pistol and shot him dead. He then looked through the wallet and, finding nothing of military importance, carefully replaced it on the dead body.'[201]

Nonetheless, the Airborne troops had held the north end of the Arnhem road bridge for just over three days, a full day longer than tasked, and in so doing had complicated and slowed the flow of reinforcements and materiel south to the main German blocking position at Nijmegen for another twelve hours or more: the first German unit to use the recaptured Arnhem road bridge, *Kampfgruppe* Knaust, was not able to cross until the early afternoon of Thursday 21 September, and the area around the north end of the bridge was not considered fully cleared until the early evening of that day.[202] The number of German casualties is unclear, in part due to the *ad hoc* nature of the units involved and the piecemeal manner in which they were fed into the fighting, but the British destroyed at least thirty German vehicles including eight armoured half-tracks, at least one armoured car and two *Panzer* IV tanks, and damaged an undetermined number of other tanks, including a fifty-six ton Tiger I.

British discipline and morale remained firm to the end, although there was some understandable frustration at not managing to hold on until relieved. Frost referred to the failure as 'desperately disappointing', while Private Sims recalled: 'the thought that we had fought for nothing was a natural one…The hardest thing to bear was the feeling that we had just been written off.'[203] Given 30 Corps' and more specifically the Guards Armoured Division's unhurried performance, such feelings were both understandable and arguably justified, but it is not usually appreciated that a significant portion of responsibility lay closer to the Airborne home. As we have seen, Brigadier Lathbury's plan for securing and holding the Arnhem bridges was more akin to a peacetime training exercise, as it debarred the 1st Parachute Brigade's three battalions from providing mutual support, with one battalion isolated on high ground to the north of the city and the other two spread across three widely spaced bridges and a German HQ in the city centre. In the event, Frost's defence of the north end of the Arnhem road bridge was hamstrung by a lack of manpower as the approximately 740 men to hand were insufficient to establish a properly defensible perimeter; this would have also been the case had Lathbury's plan unfolded as envisaged, given it would have spread two battalions over at least four and possibly seven separate locations, seven if troops were deployed at each end of the three bridges. In addition, Lathbury was responsible for nullifying the fortunate turn of events that permitted Frost to concentrate on defending a single bridge by preventing more troops from reaching the road bridge, with his order halting the 3rd Parachute Battalion on the western fringes of Oosterbeek for the night of 17-18 September. With the 3rd Battalion present at the bridge, it might have been possible to expand the defensive perimeter to more tactically advantageous positions farther from the bridge. On the other hand, it is also relevant to consider that the British defence was assisted to an extent by their opponents, specifically their prioritising the erection of blocking lines to the south and west above properly protecting and then recapturing the Arnhem road bridge. Had the Germans deployed a proportion of the men and equipment despatched south, to the River Waal at Nijmegen or west to the outskirts of Arnhem, then Frost's party may well not have been able to hold out as long as they did.

The defence of the Arnhem road bridge can nonetheless be justifiably labelled as a military epic, and it is fitting to give the final word to the man who commanded the last stage of the defence, Major Digby Tatham-Warter: 'The [2nd Parachute] Battalion had fought with the utmost gallantry, in inconceivably difficult conditions, and had denied the use of the vital Bridge to the enemy for 80 hours.'[204]

15

D Plus 4

00:01 to 16:00 Thursday 21 September 1944

While *Kampfgruppen* Brinkmann, Knaust and the rest were finally eliminating the British presence at the north end of the Arnhem road bridge, the remainder of the 1st Airborne Division was having a generally quieter time around Oosterbeek. On the western face of the perimeter, the 21st Independent Company, 1st Border, Glider Pilots and Sappers from the 9th Field Squadron spent an uneventful night apart from some nuisance mortaring, although Major Peter Jackson's E Squadron from the Glider Pilot Regiment's No. 2 Wing was pulled back from its position in the woods into alignment with F Squadron on the right and the 1st Border's A Company on the left at 03:30.[1] The same was the case on the opposite side of the perimeter, with the 10th and 156 Parachute Battalions and the 1st Airborne Reconnaissance Squadron also reporting an uneventful night, while at the south-eastern end 1st and 3rd Parachute Battalions spent the hours of darkness digging slit trenches in the waterlogged polder behind a dyke running south-east from the Benedendorpsweg.[2]

Not everyone was resting or digging. CanLoan Lieutenant Leo Heaps had attempted to break through to the Arnhem road bridge with a Jeep-load of ammunition in the afternoon of Monday 18 September, and at some point after dark on 20 September he was asked to repeat the feat, apparently by Major-General Urquhart in person. The details of the effort are unclear. According to Urquhart it involved 'Three Bren carriers…loaded with ammunition and other sorely needed gear'; of these, one broke through the German outer line but failed to reach the bridge, one was knocked out by a shell and the third was obliged to abandon the mission by German fire.[3] However, Heaps' account refers to two Jeeps provided by Lieutenant-Colonel Henry Preston, the Division Assistant Adjutant and Quartermaster General. The vehicles, which were loaded with assorted ammunition, were manned by Heaps, Dutch Captain Martin Knottenbelt, apparently on attachment from No. 10 (Inter-Allied) Commando, US Lieutenant John Johnson from the 306th Fighter Control Squadron, and two unnamed Glider Pilots. The party left the Hotel Hartenstein at around midnight and headed south toward the 1st Border positions overlooking the Heveadorp ferry, intending to cross the Lower Rhine and approach the road bridge from the south, as driving through the eastern outskirts of Arnhem was, quite rightly, considered impossible. Approaching through dense river mist that reduced visibility to a matter of feet, Heaps discovered that the ferry terminal was undefended and the ferry itself was listing at an angle twenty yards or so out into the river. The two Glider Pilots disappeared while investigating an unexplained noise and a chance encounter with a lone Sapper searching for a wounded comrade explained the lack of defenders. Captain Heggie's detachment from the 9th Field Company RE had been attacked by a larger German force using the mist as cover only half an hour earlier; the attackers were rebuffed but the fight cost the Sappers around half their strength with at least one man, Sapper Gilbert Gwilliam, killed. Heggie therefore decided to abandon the ferry and withdraw with the eight survivors to the main Company location, where they arrived at around 09:00.[4] After climbing out along the cable to examine the ferry and ascertaining that the winding mechanism was jammed, likely beyond repair, Heaps gave up and returned to the Hotel Hartenstein where he reported to Lieutenant-Colonel Mackenzie at 03:40. The news was relayed to 1st Airlanding Brigade HQ ten minutes later and the ammunition on the Jeeps was issued to the 11th Parachute Battalion instead.[5]

While Lieutenant Heaps was being baulked in his mission some units were engaged in more conventional activity. 1st Airlanding Brigade HQ ordered the 11th Parachute Battalion to send patrols toward 'the road-rail bridge', presumably the Oosterbeek Laag underpass, at 05:45, although it is unclear if the order was carried out.[6] In fact, the bulk of British patrolling activity was centred on the northern face of the perimeter where the 4th Parachute Squadron RE despatched Captain James Cormie and four men on a patrol of unknown duration at 23:30 on 20 September.[7] The busiest unit in this regard was the 7th KOSB on the 4th Parachute Squadron's right flank, however. A programme of local patrols intended to prevent German infiltration between the Battalion's locations commenced at midnight, backed by fighting patrols from C and D Companies led by CanLoan Lieutenant James Taylor from 12 Platoon and Lieutenant Joseph Hunter from 13 Platoon. Taylor ranged to the south in search of Battalion Medical Officer Captain Brian Devlin and the walking wounded but found no sign of the medical party as they had been captured the previous afternoon while relocating the RAP, unbeknown to the remainder of the Battalion. The patrol did detect enemy activity and preparations for an attack on the Battalion location however, while Lieutenant Hunter's patrol confirmed that the Germans were also present in strength in the houses and gardens north of the Graaf Van Rechterenweg toward the railway and in the woods on the other side of the line; this information was used to lay down a pre-emptive concentration on the German positions by the Battalion's mortars and Vickers guns after stand to at 04:30. When no enemy attack was forthcoming, the Battalion was stood down at 06:30 and Lieutenant-Colonel Payton-Reid ordered a one-third-scale ration issue to allow all ranks a hot meal. While this was underway CSM Drummond took a Bren Carrier patrol south along the Stationsweg and ascertained that the route was open to allow evacuation of the Battalion wounded; Drummond was also informed of the fate of Captain Devlin and the walking wounded by an unnamed sniper who had witnessed their capture. A shuttle service was then organised using two Jeeps marked with Red Cross flags to move the non-ambulatory wounded from the Battalion location to the Division MDS at the Hotel Schoonoord, which continued through the day.[8]

While the Airborne soldiers on the Oosterbeek perimeter were resting or patrolling their opponents were busy preparing to launch the concentric attacks on the British positions ordered by *Obergruppenführer* Bittrich at *II SS Panzerkorps* on 20 September. In light of experience gained thus far *Obersturmbannführer* Harzer ordered 9 *SS Panzer Division's* various *kampfgruppen* to regroup and form 'penetration groups' based where possible around specialist *Sturmpionier* elements. These were to carry out narrow frontage attacks on the eastern side of the British perimeter with the intention of penetrating the British line under cover of close fire support from *Sturmgeschütze Brigade 280's* assault guns and other self-propelled heavy weapons; the attacks were also to be launched in a series of successive echelons to maintain the pressure.[9] Harzer's units also received replacements, although the recipients were somewhat ambivalent about the quality of their new personnel as recalled by *Hauptsturmführer* Hans Möller, commanding *SS Panzer Pionier Abteilung 9*:

On 20 September, the engineer battalion received the promised replacements from the *Reichsarbeitdienst* [and] the navy and Luftwaffe. The replacements had no combat experience whatsoever and were totally inexperienced in street fighting. Nevertheless we were glad to have them…and in time they integrated completely, becoming good and reliable comrades.[10]

The northern and eastern faces of the British perimeter were designated the *schwerpunkt* of the coming attack under the overall control of *Kampfgruppe* Spindler, who consequently retained the bulk of the available armoured vehicles. The northern sector was allotted to *Kampfgruppe* Bruhn, which included *Panzergrenadier Ausbildungs und Ersatz Bataillon 361* supported by the surviving *Sd.Kfz.* 250 armoured half-tracks from *SS Panzer Aufklärungs Abteilung 9*, up to two *Panzerjäger* IVs from *SS Panzerjäger Abteilung 9* and presumably the self-propelled light anti-aircraft guns from the unnamed *SS* and *Heer flak* units drafted in to block the 4th Parachute Brigade's attack on the Dreijensweg on Monday 18 September; two *Möbelwagen* anti-aircraft vehicles armed with 37mm FlaK guns from *SS Panzer FlaK Abteilung 9* were also available, while a third was detached to support the units attacking the eastern side of the perimeter, *Kampfgruppen* Harder and Möller.[11] The former was to continue to press along the riverside Benedendorpsweg toward the Oosterbeek Old Church and the Westerbouwing Heights overlooking the Heveadorp ferry terminal while the latter, having reorganised after clearing *Den Brink* and the surrounding area east of the railway spur, was to advance west down the Utrechtseweg supported by *Sturmgeschütze Brigade 280's* assault guns and possibly two *Sd.Kfz.* 251 armoured half-tracks belonging to *SS Panzer Pionier Abteilung 9*.[12]

On the west side of the perimeter *Kampfgruppe* von Tettau was also receiving reinforcements, some of which were still en route. After bicycling the seventy-plus miles from Katwijk-am-Zee near Den Haag, *Oberleutnant* Artur Worrowski's *Bataillon* from *Luftwaffe Ausbildungs und Ersatz Regiment* 'Hermann Göring' had spent the night of 19-20 September at Wolfheze before moving up to the British perimeter on the Westerbouwing Heights the following night for example, while *Fliegerhorst Bataillon 3* was still en route near Utrecht.[13] Von Tettau's preparations were further complicated by *Wehrmachtbefehlshaber Niederlande* (Wehrmacht Commander Netherlands) making his formation responsible for preparing defences south of the Lower Rhine to block any Allied breakout from Nijmegen, and to guard against any further airborne landings north of the river. *Fliegerhorst Bataillon 2* and *Schiffsturmabteilung 10* were therefore detached from *Standartenführer* Lippert's *SS Unterführerschule* 'Arnheim' to man the new line located along a canal midway between the Lower Rhine and the Waal running fifteen miles west from Elst to Ochten. The anti-airborne mission was allotted to a newly created *Kampfgruppe* Knoche made up of the latter's *Sicherheits Regiment 26* reinforced with *FlaK Abteilung 688*.[14] The western side of the British perimeter was therefore set to be attacked by units including *Bataillon* Worrowski, *SS Bataillonen* Eberwein, Schulz and Helle from *SS Unterführerschule* 'Arnheim', with *Bataillon* Krafft in reserve, supported by up to two *Panzer B2 (f)*, fourteen *Flammpanzer B2 (f)* and a single *Panzer 35S (f)*, all from *Panzer Kompanie 224*; the latter unit had lost two Panzer B2 (f)s in the attack on C Company 1st Border near the Koude Herberg junction the previous day. Finally, artillery support for the renewed attack was to be provided by the newly created area *Artillerie Kommandeur (ArKo)*, operating from the headquarters of *Artillerie Regiment 191*, who oversaw a busy night stockpiling and distributing ammunition and co-ordinating targeting priorities in anticipation of the assault, scheduled to begin at 08:00, equivalent to 09:00 Ordinary Summer Time employed by the British.

The German preparatory bombardment commenced up to three-and-a-half hours before the attack, with timings staggered to fall on different sections of the British line. The 1st Border's entire frontage was hit first, just after dawn at 05:30, with the bombardment falling especially heavily on A and C Companies and Battalion HQ astride and north of the Utrechtseweg.[15] The 9th Field Company RE, dug in south of the road between C and D Companies, came under fire markedly more accurate than that of the previous day at around the same time, which destroyed a parked Jeep and trailer at 06:00, while the 1st Airlanding Light Regiment's gun positions in the vicinity of the Oosterbeek Old Church came under increasingly heavy mortar fire from the same time.[16] Similarly accurate fire from mortars and *nebelwerfer* rocket launchers began to fall on the Divisional area from 06:50, with Division HQ and HQ Royal Engineers at the Hotel Hartenstein referring to the 'morning hate' beginning at that time.[17] The nearby

HQ RASC received a direct hit at 07:00 that killed two men and the Glider Pilot Regiment's B Squadron lost Sergeants Dennis Andrews and Denis Raggett killed and Captain Angus Low, Staff-Sergeant Watt and Sergeants Consterdine and McCarthy wounded; the fire prompted the Glider Pilots to reinforce slit trenches with overhead cover during the course of the day.[18] The German mortar and artillery fire also began to fall on the units defending the east side of the perimeter at around the same time; 156 Parachute Battalion reporting its forward platoon on the Stationsweg-Dennenkampweg junction being heavily shelled at 07:00 while further south on the Benedendorpsweg the 1st Parachute Battalion also referred to the 'morning hate' commencing at 07:30.[19] The bombardment eased somewhat on the 1st Airlanding Brigade HQ location at 10:00, allowing the 9th Field Company to complete a temporary slit trench command post with overhead cover for use while more permanent accommodation was prepared in a nearby outhouse cellar. The Division HQ area continued to be hard hit through the day however, and an ammunition dump near the Hotel Hartenstein was set ablaze at 10:05.[20]

The German bombardment provided a backdrop to Major-General Urquhart formalising his own defensive dispositions via an O Group called at 09:00, although the 1st Airlanding Brigade War Diary erroneously refers to the meeting taking place at 07:30; the timing may refer to the time Brigadier Hicks left his own Brigade HQ in the woods south of the Hotel Hartenstein, rather than the time of the actual meeting.[21] The precise list of attendees is unclear but presumably included Brigadiers Hackett and Hicks and representatives from the various Divisional units, attachments and detachments such as the commander of the Glider Pilot Regiment's No. 1 Wing, Lieutenant-Colonel Murray.[22] By the morning of Thursday 21 September Urquhart was compelled finally to acknowledge that the operation had no prospect of achieving his Division's specific objectives. The only remaining option was to maintain a foothold on the north bank of the Lower Rhine, in the hope 30 Corps would be able to close up to the river and establish a crossing before the 1st Airborne Division was totally overwhelmed. What remained of the Division was corralled into a thumb-shaped perimeter projecting north just over a mile from the Lower Rhine. The base of the perimeter ran for just under a mile west from the Oosterbeek Old Church along the Benedendorpsweg paralleling the riverbank 500 yards or so to the south, with a bulge westward to include the Westerbouwing Heights overlooking the Heveadorp ferry. The western side of the perimeter was predominantly wooded and ran almost directly north along the Van Borsselenweg to the junction with the Utrechtseweg, before veering north-east to the Ommershof at the western end of the Graaf Van Rechterenweg. The apex ran east for approximately a quarter of a mile along the latter to the junction with the Stationsweg, paralleling the Arnhem-Ede railway line just a few hundred yards to the north. The eastern side of the perimeter then ran south through the houses and other buildings that formed the centre of Oosterbeek, following the Stationsweg south to, and across, the Utrechtseweg, where it became the Pietersbergseweg, on to the Weverstraat and south to the junction with the Benedendorpsweg just east of Oosterbeek Old Church. The pocket, which the Germans were to dub the *Hexenkessel* (witches' cauldron), contained a mixture of woodland, built-up terrain, gardens and parkland – along with approximately 3,600 Airborne soldiers, around a third of whom were infantrymen, and 2,500 Dutch civilians.[23]

This then was the place where Urquhart and the 1st Airborne Division were to fight a conventional defensive infantry battle while awaiting relief. Ideally, the perimeter would have included the north end of the Heveadorp ferry as the metalled roads running to both terminals made it an ideal location for erecting a Bailey bridge or similar. This would at least have been in line with the 1st Airborne Division's general mission to 'establish a sufficient bridgehead to enable the follow-up formations of 30 Corps to deploy north of the Lower Rhine'.[24] Having not known of the existence of the ferry earlier, Urquhart was by this point well aware of its importance. This is clear from his specific reporting of possession of the northern terminal to 1st Airborne Corps Rear HQ at Moor Park in the mid-afternoon of Wednesday 20 September. Urquhart has been criticised subsequently for failing to ensure that the ferry terminal was included within his defensive perimeter.[25] This specific criticism is unjustified, however. The western side of the perimeter was on the line of the Divisional Phase II plan, and had settled there as the Division's planned move into Arnhem was stymied. The east side congealed where the remnants of the 1st Parachute Brigade regrouped after being driven out of the western outskirts of Arnhem, and the northern face settled in a similar manner following the 4th Parachute Brigade's rebuff on the Dreijensweg north of the Arnhem-Ede railway line. The 1st Airborne Division's location was thus shaped by circumstances, if not actually dictated by enemy action, largely because Urquhart had ceded the initiative through his needless absence from the levers of command for the first forty hours of the operation. He therefore had little if any input into where his Division was finally brought to bay.

Even if this had not been the case, the ferry terminal could not have been included in the perimeter without moving the west side forward a considerable distance, which was simply not feasible against the ever-increasing strength of *Kampfgruppe* von Tettau, and its location on the south-western fringe of the perimeter was not really defensible either. In order to stand against the armoured vehicles the lightly armed Airborne troops required buildings to use as strongpoints, but the terrain in the vicinity of the terminal consisted of woods and open polder, the only defensible feature in the immediate area being the Westerbouwing Heights, which overlooked the ferry from several hundred yards to the north. The fact that the 1st Border's B Company were driven off this feature by a combined tank-infantry assault during the course of the day proves the point.

Urquhart decided to retain his HQ at the Hotel Hartenstein, protected by Lieutenant Alfred Butterworth's Division HQ Defence Platoon, Lieutenant Donald Edwards' 17 Platoon from C Company 2nd South Staffords, and B and G Squadrons from No. 1 Wing The Glider Pilot Regiment led by Majors Iain Toler and Robert Croot respectively; G Squadron was deployed on the eastern side of the Hartenstein grounds, which by this point also formed the eastern sector of the main Divisional perimeter.[26] The Glider Pilots had been withdrawn to the Hotel Hartenstein from the western side of the perimeter the previous day to form an emergency reserve, apart from Captain Terence Miller's 3 Flight from B Squadron deployed with the 1st Airlanding Light Regiment on the high ground near the Oosterbeek Old Church, which Urquhart also chose to leave in place; he later referred to the Glider Pilots 'performing magnificently as infantry' in his account of the battle.[27] Responsibility for the Divisional perimeter was divided in two, with the 1st Airlanding Brigade being allotted the western sector, a logical arrangement given that the bulk of that formation was already defending the Phase II line along the Van Borsselenweg. To defend his sector, which also included the northern stretch of the perimeter along the Graaf Van Rechterenweg, Brigadier Hicks thus had command of the 1st Border, the 9th Field Company RE, the elements of the 1st Parachute Squadron RE that had not reached the Arnhem road bridge, No. 2 Wing The Glider Pilot Regiment, the 21st Independent Parachute Company, the 4th Parachute Squadron RE, the 7th KOSB and the 1st Airborne Reconnaissance Squadron.

Command of the shorter eastern sector was allotted to Brigadier Hackett's 4th Parachute Brigade HQ, manned by the 10th Parachute Battalion, 156 Parachute Battalion, THOMPSON Force consisting of the Airlanding Light Regiment, the remnants of the 2nd South Staffords and 3 Flight from B Squadron The Glider Pilot Regiment, LONSDALE Force consisting of the 1st, 3rd and 11th Parachute Battalions, and D Squadron The Glider Pilot Regiment.[28] According to Hackett's War Diary account, the units deployed on the eastern sector totalled approximately 500 men; the total for the western sector is unclear.[29]

In addition to establishing his Brigade HQ on the Pietersbergseweg, Hackett requested and was assigned Major David Madden from the Division Staff to replace Brigade Major Bruce Dawson, who had been killed the previous day during the 4th Parachute Brigade's fight to regain the Divisional perimeter. The appointment did not last long; Major Madden was killed by mortar fire at 10:00 near the Oosterbeek Old Church while accompanying Hackett on a visit to the southern end of his new command immediately after the Divisional

O Group. Lieutenant-Colonel Thompson, commander of the Airlanding Light Regiment and THOMPSON Force, was wounded in the stomach in the same incident and Madden was attempting to render assistance when hit. Thompson's responsibilities were inherited by Major Lonsdale and his units were incorporated into LONSDALE Force.[30]

While Urquhart's O Group was underway, the 1st Airborne Division began receiving its first specifically targeted external artillery support, although guns from the 84th Medium Regiment RA had reportedly been firing general harassing missions north of the Lower Rhine from just after midnight.[31] At 09:00 Captain Christopher MacMillen from 1 Forward (Airborne) Observation Unit RA attached to 1st Airlanding Brigade HQ established contact with the 64th Medium Regiment RA as it was relocating to a new firing position near Nijmegen.[32] It is unclear whether MacMillen was located at 1st Airlanding Brigade HQ or the 1st Airlanding Light Regiment's 1 Battery Command Post, but he lost no time fine-tuning the connection using the HQ Royal Artillery's No. 19 HP set. Coming up on the 64th Medium Regiment's net using the call sign 'PCS' at 09:35, MacMillen requested urgent artillery support after introducing himself as 'the people you are trying to meet' and being identified as part of the 1st Airborne's Royal Artillery establishment by the Regimental Adjutant, Captain D. W. Scrimgeour.[33] He then ordered ranging from 211 Battery's 4.5-inch guns as soon as they came on line at 10:35, targeted just west of the Westerbouwing Heights; but there was a further delay at 11:00 when 43rd Division HQ interceded to demand additional proof of MacMillen's identity.[34] The situation was resolved by the serendipitous presence of Major-General Urquhart and Lieutenant-Colonel Robert Loder-Symonds, the Division CRA, at MacMillen's location. Their presence appears to have been prompted by the contact with the Medium Regiment being reported to Division HQ at 09:45; Urquhart and Loder-Symonds arrived at 1st Airlanding Brigade HQ forty-five minutes later with a list of suggested targets.[35] Loder-Symons was personally acquainted with Captain Scrimgeour and was able to authenticate MacMillen's transmissions were indeed originating from the 1st Airborne Division by confirming his wife's forename – Merlin – and favourite sport – falconry.[36] By 11:30 MacMillen had transmitted a list of ten targets south and west of the Westerbouwing Heights to be engaged in rotation, although numbers seven through ten proved to be out of range.[37] Urquhart described what followed as 'one of the most exciting and remarkable artillery shoots I have ever experienced. From a range of about eleven miles, these gunners proceeded to answer our calls with a series of shoots on targets…some of which were no more than a hundred yards out from our perimeter line.'[38] 211 Battery addressed the range problem by moving its guns forward 4,000 yards to hastily scouted new firing positions, and the available firepower was augmented by 212 Battery's 5.5-inch guns from 13:00 and three hours later by 155mm guns belonging to 419 Battery attached from 52 (Bedfordshire Yeomanry) Heavy Regiment RA.[39]

Directing fire from the 64th Regiment onto the vicinity of the Westerbouwing Heights was not driven solely by that sector of the 1st Airborne Divisional perimeter being within range of the guns. German troops had been preparing to move against the 1st Border's A, C, D and HQ Companies on and north of the Utrechtseweg from shortly after first light on 21 September, but the attack appears to have been delayed by fire from the 1st Airlanding Light Regiment.[40] However, the Germans then refocused their attacks on the southern half of the British line starting with Major Thomas Armstrong's B Company at the southern end of the 1st Border's line overlooking the Heveadorp ferry from the Westerbouwing Heights. This switch is sometimes assumed to have been a deliberate attempt to prise the 1st Airborne Division away from the Heveadorp ferry and the Lower Rhine generally, but in reality the action was not thought through in that way. *Oberleutnant* Artur Worrowski's 600-strong *Bataillon* from *Luftwaffe Ausbildungs und Ersatz Regiment* 'Hermann Göring' had only arrived from Katwijk-am-Zee during the night of 19-20 September and spent 20 September searching for non-existent 'paratrooper stragglers' near Ginkel Heath before moving up to the 1st Airborne Division's western face during the night of 20-21 September. The fruitless hunt for stragglers was presumably responsible for

B Company remaining relatively unmolested the previous day.[41] *Bataillon* Worrowski's attack, under the overall command of an *Oberst* Schramm and supported by four of *Panzer Kompanie 224*'s former French vehicles, went in on schedule at 08:00 German time on 21 September, albeit with no briefing or objectives save the order to move in the general direction of the unlocated British positions. As a result, Worrowski's men did not so much attack B Company as stumble across it while moving east along the Van der Molenallee, as recalled by an NCO named Herbert Kessler: '[They]…turned off the road to the right on to a forest trail, where they halted, packed closely together. So far as they could see there was no trace of the enemy. But this was to change rather soon. The soldiers were sitting on their bicycles without a care in the world when they were surprised by a murderous machine gun fire from the flank. Some of them did not have enough time to take cover somewhere on the ground…After the initial shock was overcome, the inevitable order came, "company attack!"'[42]

Three of B Company's rifle Platoons were dug in around the Westerbouwing Restaurant just south of the point where the Van der Molenallee became the Benedendorpsweg, with 11, 13, and 14 Platoons covering the north, west and southern aspects respectively. 12 Platoon was dug into an orchard a hundred yards or so down a slope to the east as Company reserve, where Major Armstrong had established his HQ in an adjacent farmhouse. The Germans appear to have chosen to halt directly in front of and downhill from Lieutenant Stanley Barnes' 11 Platoon, and the source of the machine-gun fire reported by Kessler was probably an outpost manned by Lieutenant Barnes and a Bren team consisting of Lance-Corporal Albert Wilson and Privates Harry Bragg and Davidson. The outpost held until the Bren jammed and resisted all attempts to clear it, including using the baseplate of a No.36 grenade as a makeshift hammer against the Gun's cocking-handle. Private Bragg was killed and the three survivors withdrew up the hill toward 11 Platoon, passing an unidentified artillery Forward Observer Officer calling down fire on the advancing Germans on the way; Lance-Corporal Albert Wilson from 11 Platoon recalled the latter 'coming through the trees like a crowd at a football match'.[43]

With the brake provided by the British machine-gun fire removed, the German advance overwhelmed 11 Platoon by sheer weight of numbers and overran a 6-Pounder gun before it could engage the *Panzer B2 (f)* tanks accompanying the attack. Some of Lieutenant Barnes' men fell back down the slope toward 12 Platoon and Company HQ pursued by the tanks, while the German infantry pushed south into the restaurant perimeter, taking 13 Platoon in the right flank and 14 Platoon from the rear. The commander of 13 Platoon, CanLoan Lieutenant John Wellbelove, was killed alongside Private Francis Jarvis in the confused fighting, along with the commander of 14 Platoon, Sergeant Thomas Watson.[44] A number of glider soldiers were captured when the restaurant was secured and Kessler witnessed them being marched to the rear: 'Even a cursory glance at the first enemy soldiers revealed that these indeed belonged to a select unit. The lads were tall as trees, well fed and well equipped.'[45]

The tanks were tackled single-handedly by PIAT gunner Private George Everington from 12 Platoon, who scored a direct hit on the lead vehicle, setting it ablaze and forcing the crew to bail out via the turret. Everington then reportedly knocked out two more *Panzer B2 (f)s* using the corpse of a cow for cover, the third after it turned away just short of the British positions; the fourth tank withdrew back up the slope with its accompanying infantry, presumably at the sight of Everington's handiwork.[46] Major Armstrong and Company Sergeant-Major Ernest McGladdery rallied the survivors from the three overrun platoons including 13 Platoon Sergeant Terry and Corporal Cyril Crickett with 13 Platoon's Scout Section and Corporal Ian Hunter from 14 Platoon. After despatching Lieutenant Arthur Royall's 12 Platoon back to establish a backstop position east of the municipal gasworks, Major Armstrong led the survivors forward up the slope in a counter-attack that reached the restaurant position before being stopped by heavy German fire. Major Armstrong, Sergeant Terry and Corporal Crickett were taken prisoner, the latter two wounded in the chest and hand respectively. CSM McGladdery was reportedly killed, although he may have died of wounds the following day, and Corporal Hunter was wounded in the back and legs while reloading an abandoned PIAT.[47] Some of the survivors fell back to 12 Platoon's location where they were organised into a composite platoon by Lieutenant Barnes, while others retreated north as far as 1st Airlanding Brigade HQ.[48]

B Company had no direct communication with Battalion HQ as the woods interfered with radio signals and the telephone line laid during the night by the Battalion Signals Platoon had been cut, presumably by the mortar and artillery fire.[49] Consequently, Battalion HQ was informed by the B Company second-in-command, Lieutenant Patrick Stott, that the Company had been overrun, while 1st Airlanding Brigade HQ appears to have been made aware by a number of unarmed stragglers that pitched up there. Lieutenant Stott had been despatched to Battalion HQ on the Utrechtseweg with a situation report at some point before 09:00, with the round trip taking the better part of two hours. He therefore arrived back at 12 Platoon's deserted orchard location in the lull after Major Armstrong's ill-fated counter-attack. He only realised what had occurred on seeing a *Panzer B2 (f)* moving down the slope toward the former Company HQ farmhouse as he made his way to the restaurant in search of his comrades. The vehicle was knocked out by Privates Devlin and Fitzgerald deployed in the woods north of the Benedendorpsweg while Stott took shelter in a convenient slit trench; it is unclear whether Devlin and Fitzgerald were manning a 6-Pounder gun or a PIAT. Stott then made his way back to Battalion HQ to report B Company's apparent disappearance.[50] On receiving the news, temporary Battalion commander Major Cousens promptly organised a fighting patrol tasked to sweep the woods south of D Company's location to the Benedendorpsweg and then regain B Company's positions. The patrol was commanded by Major Dennis Morrisey and Captain Robert Reese, OC HQ Company and second-in-command of A company, although its strength is unclear; according to the Battalion War Diary it comprised the reformed stragglers and two platoons from HQ Company, whereas Green's account refers to it being approximately eighteen strong and including Lieutenant Stott and Lieutenant Joseph Tate, the Battalion Liaison Officer.[51]

Lieutenant Tate was killed in the initial sweep south to the Benedendorpsweg by a German who appeared to be attempting to surrender, and another three Germans were despatched with a grenade in a subsequent encounter.[52] Major Morrisey then led an attack across the road that reached B Company's former positions but again lacked the strength to push on and the attackers were obliged to withdraw to regroup and evacuate casualties. These included Major Morrisey, who was badly wounded in the back; he was succeeded by Major Richard Stewart from Support Company, who continued to patrol on the north side of the Benedendorpsweg to protect the 1st Border's left flank with the assistance of an unidentified group of Glider Pilots. Stewart's little force received a resupply of ammunition courtesy of a Private Knott, who drove a loaded Bren Carrier south from Battalion HQ through the German bombardment. The vehicle was knocked out on the return journey but Knott escaped unscathed and delivered eight German prisoners before volunteering to repeat the run with more ammunition and food.

It is unclear if Major Stewart assumed command of, or indeed was aware of the presence of, the remnants of B Company, Lieutenant Royall's 12 Platoon near the gasworks and Lieutenant Barnes' approximately thirty-strong composite platoon dug in near the tennis court of a large house called the *Dennenord* a few hundred yards east of B Company's former farmhouse HQ. The composite platoon had suffered a number of casualties in an abortive attempt to evict a German machine-gun post located in a summer house in the gardens.[53] By midday on Thursday 21 September the 1st Airborne Division had thus lost control of the Westerbouwing Heights along with access to the Heveadorp ferry and was relying on a relative handful of men scattered across at least three locations to hold the south-western sector of the Divisional perimeter. Fortunately for the 1st Airborne Division, their opponents were in no condition to press their advantage. *Bataillon* Worrowski had paid a high price at the hands of the glider soldiers and the 64th Medium Regiment including the destruction of at least three of *Panzer Kompanie* 224's vehicles, exacerbated by a combination of inept leadership and lack of training. *Oberst* Fritz Fullriede, commander of *Ausbildungs und Ersatz Regiment* 'Hermann Göring' observed:

'In the attack on Westerbouwing the Worrowski battalion lost all its officers except a lieutenant, and half its other ranks. These casualties were due to a certain Colonel Schramm who was in command of this operation and had forbidden the use of heavy weapons because he was afraid his own men would be hit. The idiot preferred to let hundreds of them die.'[54] The dead appear to have included *Oberleutnant* Worrowski, and the *Bataillon* bearing his name needed to regroup and reorganise before it could be fed back into the battle.

The main German attack on the remainder of the 1st Border finally got underway in the afternoon of 21 September. Captain William Hodgson's D Company, which had enjoyed a relatively quiet time the previous day, was heavily mortared during the morning. A number of men from the south-facing 21 Platoon were killed, including the Platoon Commander, Lieutenant Philip Holt;[55] the survivors were withdrawn to the Company HQ location on the east side of the Van Borsselenweg to form a reserve. The remainder of D Company, consisting of Lieutenant Alan Green's 20 Platoon and Lieutenant George Brown's 22 Platoon, reinforced with two 6-Pounder guns from Lieutenant Anthony Howe's 25 Anti-tank Platoon, were deployed on the other side of the Van Borsselenweg facing west into the dense woods. Apart from the mortaring the morning passed relatively quietly, although a precursor of what was to come occurred around midday, when at least two heavy tracked vehicles were heard moving in the woods to the Company's front. The Division RASC element had only gathered in sufficient rations from the previous day's resupply drop to allow a one-third issue of Compo rations, which D Company's cooks stretched into a communal stew; this was the Company's first hot meal for some time and Lieutenant Brown supervised distribution to the Platoon locations.[56]

The ration party was moving in the open between positions when they were machine-gunned by a *Panzer B2 (f)* that emerged from the trees on 22 Platoon's right flank, killing Lieutenant Brown.[57] The tank advanced obliquely behind a hedge bordering a field projecting west into the woods, firing its machine-gun into the British positions as it went, while the second vehicle could be heard moving across the Platoon's front heading for the dead ground used by the German infiltrators the previous morning. The first tank was engaged by a Bren and then a PIAT manned by a Private Parker, who scored a direct hit but with no discernible effect. The nearest 6-Pounder could not be brought to bear, so Lieutenant Howe led Corporal Thomas Langhorn's crew to the second gun sited at the rear of 22 Platoon's position, which was hastily manhandled to face the threat, which by this point had closed to within twenty yards. Corporal Langhorn was killed by small-arms fire while steadying the gun muzzle, and his death so incensed the remainder of the crew that they pumped six armour-piercing shots into the tank as it broke through the hedge before they were manhandled away from the gun. The *Panzer B2 (f)* was stopped by the first hit and then burst into flames, killing the crew. In the meantime Lieutenant Green was wounded while leading a PIAT team forward to ambush the second tank, possibly by friendly fire from the Battalion's mortars and a defensive barrage from the Airlanding Light Regiment. The barrage nevertheless had the desired effect and the second tank and its supporting infantry broke off the attack and withdrew. That left D Company with Captain Hodgson as the sole unwounded officer, for while Lieutenant Green was able to continue in the line, Lieutenant Howe was wounded in the latter stages of the action badly enough to require evacuation to the Aid Post in the cellar of the Company HQ building. There he found himself lying under an unexploded mortar bomb lodged in the ceiling.[58]

The German attack also fell on the remainder of the 1st Border's frontage. At C Company's positions astride the Koude Herberg junction on the Utrechtseweg, Corporal John Swann led a party of six against an estimated platoon of Germans attempting to outflank one of the Company's positions, dispersing them with grenades and a bayonet charge that earned Corporal Swann the Military Medal. Some infiltrators nonetheless must have succeeded in interfering with C Company's rear links, given that Major Neill ordered HQ Company to clear the woods between the two locations; CSM Leslie Fielding swept the area with a fighting patrol made up of pioneers, signallers and anyone else available, which killed two snipers. A Company was also attacked in the early afternoon after a morning enduring a lack of food and water and dealing with a mounting number of wounded who could not be safely evacuated from the Company Aid Post. The attackers made an 'awful noise' as they came through the trees, presumably in an effort to boost morale, while the glider soldiers held their fire until they were within thirty yards in order to conserve ammunition. Despite suffering heavy casualties the Germans nonetheless regrouped and attacked twice more before fading back into the woods. As the trees were again interfering with radio communications the commander of the 1st Border's Mortar Platoon, Captain Barry Ingram, resorted to a human chain for passing back fire support requests from the Rifle Companies. Ingram had the requests called out to his position at the bottom of the garden behind the Battalion HQ house, which he then shouted to 1 Mortar Platoon's commander Lieutenant Michael Holman stationed in the open twenty-five yards away, who in turn shouted them across the mortar pits, all the while under artillery and mortar fire and exposed to the ever-present infiltrators.

The attacks also spilled over onto the units flanking A Company. The 4th Parachute Squadron RE element on the left reported killing at least a score of attackers with Bren fire and grenades while the Glider Pilots from E and F Squadrons reported a day of 'continual attack' and mortaring that caused a 'considerable number' of casualties. This included coming under fire from a self-propelled gun infiltrated into the woods to the detachment's front with a number of infantry, which the F Squadron contingent forced back in the afternoon with a counter-attack.[59]

On the north-west tip of the perimeter Captain Henry Brown and the 4th Parachute Squadron's Ommershof detachment were again receiving visitors, this time in the shape of an 08:00 visit from Squadron commander Major Æneas Perkins as arranged the previous day. Perkins briefed Brown on the situation, relayed praise for his Brown's performance from Major Wilson from the adjacent 21st Independent Company and delivered some rations, 'which were much appreciated even though they were lamentably meagre', before embarking on a tour of the detachment's positions.[60] By this point the constant German mortar fire had rendered such activity a risky business and Major Perkins was badly wounded in the neck and throat by fragments from a mortar bomb while talking to Lieutenant Kenneth Evans from 1 Troop, who was also wounded in the left elbow; both men were treated in the aid post in the Ommershof before being evacuated to the MDS at the Hotel Schoonoord. Command of the Squadron therefore devolved to Captain John Cormie with effect from 09:15.[61] Captain Brown was then left to his own devices, beating off a German attack at 11:00, warning a nearby Bren manned by Sappers Randall and Parker to conserve ammunition in the process, and posting a newly acquired PIAT assigned to Lance-Corporal Michael Flannery to the west of the Graaf Van Rechterenweg–Oranjeweg junction, ten yards or so from Brown's slit trench. At around 15:30 a group of men and a gun of some kind were spotted on the Graaf Van Rechterenweg a hundred yards to the west. Fearing they were lost Poles redeploying a 6-Pounder, Brown ordered Flannery to display his fluorescent recognition panel. The group response was a hail of machine-gun fire, one round of which took a chunk from the bomb ready-loaded in the PIAT; fortunately the maltreated ammunition did not detonate. Meanwhile the German gun, which may have been the same weapon that prompted the counter-attack by the F Squadron Glider Pilots, also opened fire on the British position, killing Lieutenant Michael Eden from 2 Troop and wounding three other men. In the event an undaunted Lance-Corporal Flannery retrieved the situation by unloading the damaged bomb from his PIAT and engaging the enemy gun; his fourth round scored a direct hit and prompted the German crew to abandon their weapon.[62]

The main German effort on the northern sector of the perimeter was against the adjacent positions held by the 7th KOSB. The 7th KOSB's pre-dawn mortar and machine-gun bombardment did not deter *Kampfgruppe* Bruhn from launching its attack on schedule at 09:00, advancing through the woods into the vicinity of the abandoned Hotel Dreyeroord/White House from where they could enfilade the positions along the Graaf van Rechterenweg and fire directly into D Company's positions. One of the Anti-tank Groups' 6-Pounder guns located near the gates of the hotel was particularly exposed, with all the crew being killed or wounded by machine-gun fire. The situation was resolved by Sergeant Dennis Keyes who, despite intense enemy fire, crawled out to the gun, closed the trails and prepared it for movement before hitching it up to a Jeep that towed it to safety; it is unclear whether Sergeant Keyes was also responsible for bringing up the Jeep but his actions led to him being awarded the Military Medal.[63] D Company initially attempted to suppress the Germans with small-arms and PIAT fire and by infiltrating small patrols into the German-held woods to identify enemy strongpoints, but by late morning the growing pressure prompted Colonel Payton-Reid to order Major Sherriff to counter-attack and drive the Germans back. Lieutenant Joseph Hunter's 13 Platoon reoccupied the White House and provided covering fire while a platoon borrowed from C Company commanded by Sergeant Clifford Wilson performed a right-flanking attack across the Stationsweg. The attack cleared the Germans from the east side of the perimeter and forced them into the houses and gardens on the north side of the Graaf van Rechterenweg where the glider soldiers were able to inflict a number of casualties, although they suffered losses themselves; Lieutenant Hunter was killed while performing a reconnaissance in the wake of the action. The wounded included the commanders of C and D Companies, Majors Dinwiddie and Sherriff, Sherriff for the second time. The counter-attack was concluded by midday and German activity died away apart from the constant artillery and mortar bombardment. Lieutenant-Colonel Payton-Reid was visited in the course of the afternoon by Liaison officers from the 21st Independent Company and the Reconnaissance Squadron. The latter brought a warning order from Airlanding Brigade HQ instructing the Battalion to prepare for a withdrawal to narrow the 400-yard gap on the left between its location and the 21st Independent Company's positions, providing Payton-Reid considered it feasible.[64] He did, providing the move was co-ordinated to avoid the Independent Company being left exposed.[65]

The respite was only temporary, however. Colonel Payton-Reid called an O Group at 16:30; attendees included Captain James Livingstone in Major Dinwiddie's stead as OC C Company, a twice wounded Major Sherriff – even though he had been supplanted at the head of D Company by Lieutenant William Lamond from HQ Company's Signals Platoon – Major Alexander Cochran from HQ Company acting as Battalion second-in-command and the Adjutant, Captain David Clayhills. In light of the seemingly imminent relocation Colonel Payton-Reid decided to cut his HQ down to the bare minimum and post the remaining HQ and Support Company personnel to reinforce the rifle companies; Captain Livingstone and Lieutenant Lamond's command appointments were confirmed along with that of Captain James Dundas, who had been leading the B Company contingent since Major Forman had gone missing during the evening of 19 September. It was at this point that the Germans launched another attack, heralded by an intense mortar barrage; according to the 7th KOSB War Diary the attack began while the O Group was underway and Colonel Payton-Reid cut the meeting short to investigate.[66] Captain Brown from the 4th Parachute Squadron provides a different version of events, however. Brown became aware of the German attack on his neighbours from a 'terrific commotion along [the] Graaf van Rechterenweg' and more importantly, when some KOSBs fell back through his lines; these included a 'rather large officer with a wild look on his face…shouting "The Germans are coming, the Germans are coming"'. After persuading the officer to return whence he had come by shouting and waving his pistol, Brown made his way to the 21st Independent Company's command post to warn Major Wilson of developments where he found Wilson with 'a good looking sandy haired Lieutenant Colonel. They were enjoying a glass of whisky. The unknown officer was introduced to me as Lieutenant Colonel Payton-Reid commanding the 7th KOSB. I told my story in half a dozen words. Payton-Reid was off like a shot.'[67]

The German attack came from the east across the Stationsweg in at least company strength and pushed deep into the KOSB's perimeter, capturing the White House and occupying the recently vacated British slit trenches around it. Sergeant George Barton's 6-Pounder was overrun in the initial rush: 'I managed to fire only two rounds of high explosive before the Germans were upon me. My Sten then jammed, and I stood alone, in the open, waiting to be killed. But the Germans just rushed straight past me.'[68] The German advance penetrated as far as the rear of C Company's positions, which appear to have brought it to a halt as recalled by Captain Livingstone:

> They came across – running and shouting – to within about twenty yards of us before I opened fire. I killed an awful lot of Germans then, with my Sten. There was a big tree in front of me, and there was one German who was on his knees, wounded, but still preparing to fire. I remember David Clayhills, the Adjutant, who was standing by the side of the hotel, shouting 'Kill the bastard!' and I did so.[69]

At this point Colonel Payton-Reid appeared on the scene, rallying his men, ensuring every possible weapon was brought into action and arranging 'a two-minute crescendo' with the Battalion 3-inch mortars firing on the woods, Support Company's Vickers Guns on the German-occupied slit trenches and the Anti-tank Group's 6-Pounders on the White House proper. He then led a counter-attack in person, spearheaded by CanLoan Lieutenant James Taylor's 12 Platoon augmented by a number of stragglers Taylor had rallied whilst retreating across the hotel grounds. The attackers were also reinforced by a party of stragglers rounded up and led back to the White House perimeter by Division HQ liaison officer Lieutenant Colin Macduff-Duncan.[70] The Battalion War Diary notes that the resultant bayonet charge 'came at a most opportune moment, so far as the Bn was concerned, when everyone had reached a state of extreme exasperation at the continuous shelling and sniping. As a result, when the GERMANS showed themselves the BORDERERS rose in their wrath and slew them, – uttering the most blood-curdling howls meantime.'[71] The charge had the desired effect, as recalled by Private Henry McClusky: 'I have never screamed aloud so much. It was hell. Fortunately, Jerry took to his heels and ran, leaving behind a terrible scene of dead and wounded – dreadful!'[72]

The KOSB counter-attack was over by about 17:30 and succeeded in driving the Germans out of the perimeter, but at heavy cost. Major Cochran, whose body was found head to head with a slain German officer on the White House veranda, was among the dead along with Provost Sergeant Andrew Graham, who had also participated in the morning counter-attack and was reported as being 'well on the way to winning a VC' when he was killed.[73] The wounded included Major Sherriff with his third wound of the battle, this time to his thigh, sustained after leaving the RAP to take part in the bayonet charge; Captain James Coulthard commanding the Battalion MMG Group; 11 Platoon's commander Lieutenant Martin Kaufman, and Captain Ronald Bannatyne and Lieutenants Alexander Hannah and Arthur Sharples commanding the Battalion Anti-tank Group and its 1 and 2 Platoons respectively.[74] Lieutenant Sharples was likely the officer carried to the Ommershof by Private Alan Dawson from the 21st Independent:

> There was a KOSB lieutenant with a lot of wounds, in the neck, chest and stomach; he was covered in blood…I picked him up in my arms and carried him to the house where our Company HQ was…There was a lot of lead flying about, but I got him there, and 'Doc' Taylor took him under his wing straight away. I went back to my position but I wished I had found out after the war whether he survived. He was only young.

Lieutenant Sharples died of his wounds later that day.[75] By this point all the Battalion's Company commanders had become casualties, only one CSM and a handful of senior NCOs were left and the Battalion RAP was again 'completely filled up' by casualties from the day's fighting. The medical situation was alleviated by the serendipitous arrival of Captain John Buck RAMC from 156 Parachute Battalion to replace the 7th KOSB's Medical Officer Captain Brian Devlin; as we have seen Captain Devlin had been captured the previous afternoon, unbeknown to his Battalion.[76]

The units assigned to Brigadier Hackett's command on the east side of the 1st Airborne's perimeter were also hard pressed in the course of 20 September. On the line of the Stationsweg running south from the 7th KOSB's corner position Major Powell's group of survivors from 156 Parachute Battalion had increased to sixty and were ensconced in buildings at the north-east and south-west corners of the crossroads formed by the junction of the Stationsweg, Dennenkampweg and Cronjéweg. Powell had also been placed in command of the Reconnaissance Squadron's A and D Troops, although these were not located on the Stationsweg proper but on streets to the west behind 156 Battalion's location. A Troop HQ was located in a large house on the Mariaweg close to Major Powell's HQ with other elements occupying a large house and bakery on the other side of the road, while D Troop were ensconced in two houses on the Steijnweg 200 yards or so to the west.[77] 156 Battalion came under heavy mortar and artillery fire from 07:00 but there was no direct attack on its two strongpoints, although German troops were subsequently spotted infiltrating into the Divisional perimeter on either side of the Battalion's position; they were likely the left flank of *Kampfgruppe* Bruhn's attack on the 7th KOSB.[78] The two Reconnaissance Troops took a more proactive role, despatching patrols to comb the surrounding area for German-held locations and especially mortar positions. Lieutenant John Stevenson's patrol from A Troop unwittingly passed close to houses used as a forming-up point for the main German attack at 09:00; Trooper Alfred Webb later saw the attackers 'pouring out of those same houses. We realised then that the bastards could have been watching us all the time….and probably held their fire so as not to give away their positions.'[79] At 10:00 a self-propelled gun was heard manoeuvring nearby and an hour later shelled A Troop HQ and 2 Section's locations before being reportedly knocked out by a PIAT manned by Sergeant Gwyn Williams and Trooper Frank Mann.[80] D Troop HQ also acted as an observation post to control the 1st Airlanding Light Regiment's guns, and called in artillery fire on a German armoured vehicle, possibly that engaged by A Troop's PIAT, spotted to the north at 11:00.[81]

An hour later both the Reconnaissance units were attacked by the German infantry who had bypassed 156 Battalion's location. Lieutenant Stevenson and 1 Section were driven out of the bakery on the Mariaweg after the attackers closed up under intense machine-gun fire and lobbed bundled stick grenades through the windows although it was retaken at 13:00 in a counter-attack organised by A Troop's commander, Captain Michael Grubb. Grubb arranged covering fire from small-arms and a PIAT initiated by a long whistle blast, along with smoke to cover the approach to the bakery before leading a charge across the road; No. 36 grenades were posted through the windows prior to entering and Corporal James Taylor recalled Captain Grubb cursing unrestrainedly when the ring became separated from the pin on his grenade.[82] The bakery was cleared and reoccupied, only to be abandoned again later in the afternoon after catching fire, eventually burning to the ground.

The building held by Lieutenant Douglas Galbraith and 2 Section had reportedly come under fire from a German tank, and by 14:30 Grubb had been obliged to gather all three of his Sections into a tight perimeter around his Troop HQ.[83] An attack on D Troop on the Steijnweg began with a determined assault supported by mortar fire and an armoured half-track on the house occupied by Lieutenant John Marshall and 10 Section on the northern side of the Troop perimeter. Marshall's right hand was almost severed by a hand-grenade or mortar bomb, he was shot in the left shoulder and then wounded in the face as he emerged into the back garden to clarify the situation with Trooper Jeffrey Williams; Williams was also wounded in the left shoulder and back as a number of Germans came over the rear garden wall. Marshall managed to crawl back into the house and ordered a Trooper Smith to withdraw to Troop HQ before taking shelter under the kitchen sink; Trooper Williams and at least four others including Trooper Bert Pegnall were taken prisoner. At 13:00 the focus of the German attack shifted to the adjacent position held by Lieutenant William Hodge's 11 Section. This too was swiftly overwhelmed, with Hodge and a number of his men being taken prisoner along with the badly wounded Marshall, who emerged into the garden again only to find it occupied by a crowd of

Germans and their prisoners. Marshall heard Hodge exclaim 'Oh! Look what you've done to my friend!' before passing out; he was evacuated to a hospital in Apeldoorn where his hand was amputated. The Germans then appear to have abandoned their gains, given that Lieutenant Alan Pascal's 12 Section ran four patrols out to 10 and 11 Section's former positions from 16:30 to collect up abandoned weapons and ammunition.[84] While all this was going on Major Powell and the 156 Battalion contingent was left largely unmolested while firing on the German infiltrators moving past their location. The exception was the composite Platoon stationed on the north-east corner of the crossroads, which lost an undetermined number of casualties to heavy fire from mortars, machine-guns and a self-propelled gun or tank that began at 14:00.[85]

The central section of the eastern perimeter was held by the 10th Parachute Battalion. Lieutenant-Colonel Smyth and his sixty survivors of the fight in the woods west of Oosterbeek initially occupied three buildings around the Utrechtseweg–Stationsweg crossroads. This placed the Division MDS located in the Hotels Schoonoord and Vreewijk on the Utrechtseweg–Stationsweg crossroads directly in the front line, so the 10th Battalion therefore extended its perimeter around 150 yards further east along the Utrechtseweg, to the junction with the Annastraat running to the south. QM Lieutenant Joseph Glover and his group turned a large former restaurant on the latter junction into a strongpoint while another party, headed by Battalion second-in-command Major Peter Warr, accompanied by Colonel Smyth, occupied another house belonging to Mrs Bertje Voskuil, who had taken to the cellar with a score of her neighbours. The remaining third of the 10th Battalion, commanded by Lieutenant Peter Saunders, appears to have remained in the Battalion's original positions back at the Utrechtseweg–Stationsweg crossroads.[86] It is unclear when the move took place as the 10th Parachute Battalion's semi-official history makes no mention of it and while Brigadier Hackett's Brigade War Diary account refers to it occurring in the afternoon of 21 September, this is likely another of his *ex post facto* insertions.[87] The evidence suggests that the move forward was carried out in the early hours of 21 September, given that the 10th Battalion was occupying the Utrechtseweg–Annastraat position when the German attacks commenced at around 08:00.[88] More pertinently, Captain Stuart Mawson recalled being awakened from a well-earned sleep in an under-stairs cupboard in the Hotel Schoonoord at 04:00 by an orderly who informed him 'our lads have returned and we're back in our own lines.'[89]

Whenever it moved forward, the 10th Battalion was attacked by a rested, regrouped and reinforced *Kampfgruppe* Möller supported by assault guns from *Sturmgeschütze Brigade 280* and possibly two armoured half-tracks from *SS Panzer Pionier Abteilung 9*.[90] The attacks began at around 08:00 according to QM Lieutenant Glover and followed the usual pattern, with German infantry infiltrating around buildings on foot and bringing up *StuGs* to batter British strongpoints as they were discovered. The German vehicles were understandably wary of British 6-Pounder guns dug into the floor inside buildings for protection.[91] *Sturmgeschütze Brigade 280* was also handicapped by the quality of some of their reinforcements, as recalled by *Rottenführer* Wolfgang Dombrowski:

A Sturmgeschutz III was attached to my section. It had a motley crew, there was a Wehrmacht NCO in charge, a Luftwaffe man – probably the loader – and two other army men. We were making really good progress...until we eventually came under fire from infantry supported by an anti-tank gun. The crew...panicked when the vehicle was hit. Even though the damage was only superficial the gun abruptly reversed into a side street where the crew baled out over the rear and fled. Only the NCO remained with us – somewhat disgusted.[92]

This was not quite the end of the story. Major Warr called across and suggested that Glover investigate, as he had served for twelve years as a ranker in the Royal Armoured Corps, and the QM Lieutenant and some of his men duly braved the winnowing fire and gained possession of the abandoned vehicle. In a fraught period that saw the assault gun fired on by friend and foe alike, Glover managed to start the engine and elevate and depress the main gun, to the alarm of Dombrowski and the vehicle's erstwhile commander, while one of his companions employed the machine-gun mounted on the roof. However, Glover noted a fuel leak and, more importantly, was unable to engage the gear to move the vehicle; he also had his false teeth knocked out by the concussion from hits on the vehicle's armour before giving up the vehicle for the relative safety of the disused restaurant.[93] The *StuG* remained where it had been abandoned, a potential threat to both sides until the Germans overran the area again in the early evening and it was towed away for repair.[94]

The defenders were able to keep Dombrowski and his comrades back for a while, at some points reportedly with the assistance of artillery fire from the 64th Medium Regiment; but before long another assault gun was brought up and began pumping shells into the British-occupied buildings; one shell saw QM Lieutenant Glover unceremoniously dumped into the ground floor after a hit caused the upper floor of his building to give way. In the early afternoon the pounding and pressure from German infantry compelled a partial withdrawal from the Voskuil house back to the crossroads to regroup, under cover of smoke and fire from QM Lieutenant Glover's group. Major Warr continued playing a deadly cat-and-mouse game between the houses with his party until badly wounded in the thigh, when he was taken down into the relative safety of the Voskuil cellar. According to Lance-Corporal George Wyllie, Colonel Smyth was in the meantime visited by Brigadier Hackett who stressed the importance of holding the corner houses.[95] This appears to have been the catalyst for a counter-attack led by Major Francis Lindley and accompanied by Colonel Smyth; Lindley last saw him wounded and 'lying in the road beside a garden gate'. Lieutenant Saunders may have been killed in the same action.[96] Smyth had been paralysed from the waist down after being shot in the stomach, and was also removed to the Voskuil cellar. The Germans entered the Voskuil house and killed or drove out the remaining paratroopers after a vicious hand-to-hand fight that was clearly audible to the terrified civilians sheltering below. They then tossed two grenades down the steps into the cellar. Mrs Voskuil was saved by Private Albert Willingham, who lay over her as she was tending Major Warr: he was killed, Mrs Voskuil was hit in the legs. Major Warr was wounded again in the shoulder and a number of civilians were also wounded including Mrs Voskuil's husband and nine-year-old son. The Germans then entered the cellar and took the paratroopers present prisoner while Mrs Voskuil harassed the Germans into providing a doctor to treat Smyth; he subsequently died of his wounds on 26 October.[97] The Germans then turned their attention to QM Lieutenant Glover's position despite a charge by the paratroopers that briefly recaptured the Voskuil house. Glover was wounded in the hand shortly afterward and departed for the MDS when the heavy bleeding could not be staunched; he was wounded again en route, this time in the right calf.

The survivors of QM Lieutenant Glover's party had to withdraw to the east side of the Utrechtseweg–Stationsweg crossroads at around 20:00 after the disused restaurant was blasted and set ablaze by fire from a *StuG*; a Private Banks reportedly continued firing a Bren from the upper storey until the building collapsed beneath him.[98] The withdrawal took place at about 20:10 and was covered by a shoot from the 64th Medium Regiment targeted upon the Utrechtseweg east of the junction and the woods to its north-east; the Gunners had broken up an attack against the 1st Border's section of the western perimeter an hour earlier, dropping shells as close as 100 yards to the glider soldiers' front.[99] Precisely where the 10th Battalion's survivors came to rest is unclear, but it was likely two buildings to the east of the MDS area, and it is also unclear whether they were located to the north or south of the Utrechtseweg. The 10th Parachute Battalion numbered around fifty all ranks by this point, led by Captain Peter Barron from the 2nd Airlanding Anti-tank Battery and FOO (Forward Observation Officer) Lieutenant Kenneth White from the 2nd Airlanding Light Battery, as all the 10th Battalion officers had been killed or wounded severely enough to be evacuated out of battle. Some of those remaining on the line were also nursing wounds; Captain Barron had been wounded in the shoulder and hand on

Wednesday 20 September, for example. The 10th Battalion survivors were out of contact with 4th Parachute Brigade HQ, which prompted Brigadier Hackett to despatch a night patrol from the Brigade HQ Defence Platoon in an effort to locate them. The patrol failed to locate any sign of the survivors but Hackett 'still had hope' for his missing Battalion.[100]

On the south-eastern section of the British perimeter *Kampfgruppe* Harder resumed its push along the line of the riverside Benedendorpsweg at 09:00 when approximately a *kompanie* of German infantry accompanied by three tanks appeared on the polder near the destroyed railway bridge. They approached the right-hand sector of the 1st Parachute Battalion's line dug in along the dyke south of the road, held by Lieutenant Albert Turrell and T Company. The attackers were rebuffed with small-arms and artillery fire called down by Captain William Caird from No. 1 Forward Observation Unit RA. The Germans responded with an intense ninety-minute *nebelwerfer* barrage, the effect of which, whilst 'highly unpleasant', was largely nullified by the Battalion's deep trenches and thus inflicted few casualties; though liaison officer Lieutenant Alastair Clarkson was killed.[101] The Germans also pushed along the Benedendorpsweg proper, close to the Airlanding Light Regiment's gun positions near the Oosterbeek Old Church. B Troop's commander, Lieutenant Keith Halliday, was killed by tank fire at 11:00 while manning an observation post, A Troop's Command Post was engaged by a *StuG* an hour later and 1 Battery had to clear German infiltrators located in houses overlooking its gun pits.[102]

In the early afternoon the Germans turned their attention to Major Robert Cain and his approximately eighty-strong contingent from 2nd South Stafford's deployed at the Laundry just north of the Oosterbeek Old Church; the remainder of the Staffords, around fifty men under CanLoan Lieutenant Philip Hart, were dug in closer to the Old Church protecting the Airlanding Light Regiment's gun positions.[103] As had become his SOP, Major Cain immediately commandeered a PIAT and set about stalking two German armoured vehicles accompanied by an unnamed private, who was presumably employed as an ammunition bearer. Cain's fire was initially directed by Lieutenant Ian Meikle from the Light Regiment's B Troop, who was acting as a forward observer from a nearby upper storey until he was killed by a shell from the lead vehicle. Cain held his position despite almost being crushed by a toppling chimney pot, which scared off his companion. He eventually disabled the *StuG* after being wounded by return fire from its machine gun. He was then injured when a PIAT bomb detonated prematurely while stalking the second vehicle: 'It blew me over backwards, and I was blind. I was shouting like a hooligan. I shouted to somebody to get onto the Piat, because there was another tank behind. I blubbered and yelled and used some very bad language. They dragged me off to the Aid Post.'[104] In the event Cain's vision cleared shortly after arrival and he insisted on returning to the front line against medical advice.[105]

Despite the best efforts of the 2nd South Staffords the Gunners had a rough time of it, especially B Troop. The latter lost a number of men including Command Post Officer Lieutenant Christopher Fogarty to the tank attack from the east that killed Lieutenant Meikle. The vehicle Major Cain was stalking when he was wounded was knocked out by one of the Light Regiment's guns firing over open sights, possibly that commanded by a Sergeant McBain from F Troop, and the Gunners also came under fire from German infiltrators in the woods to the west of the gun positions. As the casualty toll included all of B Troop's officers killed, Battery Captain Basil Taylor and Command Post Officer Lieutenant Carmel Leitch had to be drafted in from 2 Battery, along with a number of men, to make up numbers. In the late afternoon Captain Anthony Harrison from 3 Battery led a patrol to suppress an enemy machine-gun post established in the municipal gasworks west of F Troop's gun positions; the patrol appears to have failed in its objective, given that Captain Harrison spent twenty minutes pinned down by German fire before being obliged to dash back to 3 Battery's lines.[106] With *Kampfgruppe* Harder rebuffed to the east and *Bataillon* Worrowski to the west, the southern extremities of the 1st Airborne Division's perimeter remained intact but were pressed almost back to back. The Oosterbeek pocket was thus on the brink of being prised away from the Lower Rhine and its sole remaining potential avenue for relief and reinforcement.

D Plus 4

16:00 to 23:59 Thursday 21 September 1944

While the 7th KOSB were counter-attacking to regain their positions on the Graaf van Rechterenweg and the South Staffords were stalking *Sturmgeschütze* in the vicinity of the Laundry north of the Lower Rhine, the first of two aerial events to take place on 21 September occurred. Unlike the previous day's effort, Thursday's resupply drop was concentrated into one late afternoon increment, albeit with take-offs staggered to spread the arrival of aircraft over the drop zone across two-and-a-half hours. Curiously, the 1st Parachute Battalion and Division HQ War Diaries refer to supply drops occurring at 11:00 and 12:45 respectively, even though the first take-off only commenced three minutes after the former time and the latter was between fifteen and forty-five minutes short of the minimum flying time from the UK airfields to Oosterbeek.[1] Be that as it may, the supply effort involved sixty-three Stirlings and fifty-five Dakotas, totalling 118 aircraft. The Dakota contingent included No. 233 Squadron and No. 437 Squadron RCAF, which had been diverted from supply flights to Belgium in lieu of Nos. 512 and 575 Squadrons; the substitution appears to have been made in the late morning due to the low number of serviceable aircraft available from the RAF units based at Broadwell.[2] First away were twenty-one Stirlings from Nos. 295 and 570 Squadrons from Harwell at 11:03, followed thirty-seven minutes later by the same number of Stirlings from Nos. 196 and 299 Squadrons flying from RAF Keevil. The third increment of Stirlings, fifteen machines from Nos. 190 and 620 Squadrons, took off from RAF Fairford at midday, six machines following at 16:00; the reason for the staggered take-off is unclear. The first increment of twenty-five Dakotas from Nos. 48 and 271 Squadrons took off from Down Ampney at 13:10, followed twenty minutes later by twenty-five machines from Blakehill Farm belonging to the co-opted Nos. 233 Squadron and 437 Squadrons RCAF; five Dakotas took off from Blakehill Farm at 13:40, two of which aborted with load problems, although these may not have been involved in the Airborne resupply effort, given there is no reference to the event in the Operational Record Books of the Squadrons involved.[3] According to one source 1st Airborne Division HQ had requested the supply drop be targeted on the Hotel Hartenstein, but the Dakotas of Nos. 48 and 271 Squadrons at least were still briefed to drop on DZ V, which had never actually been in British hands and by now lay the better part of a mile outside the Oosterbeek perimeter.[4]

The flight was uneventful until the final leg up the Airborne Corridor, where a significant gap had developed in the protective fighter cover, which No. 48 Squadron referred to as being 'very scarce and very late'.[5] This was due in part to USAAF fighters being tasked to cover other missions including bombing raids on the synthetic oil plant at Ludwigshafen and railway marshalling yards at Mainz and Koblenz, and in part to bad weather over eastern England that grounded approximately half of the UK-based RAF contingent. The resupply mission could have been escorted by fighters from RAF 2nd Tactical Air Force squadrons based on the Continent, but the commander of the 1st Allied Airborne Army, USAAF Lieutenant-General

Lewis H. Brereton, had forbidden those units from operating over the Airborne Corridor to avoid control issues.[6] German fighters from *3 Jagd-Division* were thus able to shoot down around half-a-dozen Stirlings on the fly-in without interference, carrying on their attacks until in sight of the Oosterbeek perimeter where *FlaK Brigade* Svoboda took over; as No. 48 Squadron reported 'Very heavy flak and tracer was met over and near to the DZ, also at HERTOGENBOSCH, BOXTEL and KEELSAN [sic]'.[7] The transports were not solely at peril from *flak* and fighters. An RASC despatcher fell to his death from one of No. 233 Squadron's Dakotas presumably as it took evasive action, while one of No. 48 Squadron's machines, possibly that flown by RCAF Warrant-Officer David Webb, was brought down over Oosterbeek after being struck on the wing by a supply pannier dropped by another aircraft; most of the crew were killed.[8] Another container packed with 6-Pounder ammunition free-dropped onto the 1st Airlanding Brigade's HQ after a parachute malfunction, and the resultant explosion wounded a number of men from the Brigade Provost Section.[9] The German fighters pounced again as the transports flew the return leg across Holland after delivering their loads, shooting down several of the slower Dakotas. These included one piloted by future show-business personality Flight-Lieutenant Jimmy Edwards from No. 271 Squadron, who elected to crash land on learning two of his RASC despatchers had been too badly wounded to bail out, and two machines from No. 48 Squadron flown by Flying-Officer Finlay and Flight-Sergeant Webster.[10] The surviving machines landed at their home bases between 18:15 and 20:15. Fourteen Stirlings and nineteen Dakotas failed to return to base, although two Stirlings landed elsewhere in the UK and two Dakotas landed at Brussels. In all, thirteen Dakotas were subsequently verified as being lost due to enemy action.[11] Once again the majority of the supplies dropped into German hands; Major-General Urquhart referred to the Germans using the captured ground marking instructions translated by *Hauptsturmführer* Schleffler from *9 SS Panzer Division* HQ, and possibly employing a captured EUREKA beacon too.[12]

The second aerial contribution was on a much grander scale. In the East Midlands the 1st Polish Independent Parachute Brigade had spent another restless night in its billets around Stamford and Peterborough, and likely none more so than Brigade commander Major-General Stanislaw Sosabowski. Unhappy with the near total lack of information on the situation in Holland and increasingly suspicious that his formation was to be sacrificed to reinforce failure, Sosabowski had contemplated refusing to allow his Brigade to take-off without written confirmation of his orders; he had also written letters of protest addressed to Lieutenant-General Brereton and Major-General Browning. Having failed to contact Brereton directly by radio, Sosabowski informed Lieutenant-Colonel George Stevens, the Polish Brigade's British liaison officer that he would not take off for Driel without an accurate situation report. Stevens returned from Moor Park at 09:00 on 21 September and handed Sosabowski a signal purportedly from the 1st Airborne Division timed at 04:30 confirming that the Heveadorp ferry was in British hands.[13] This was not the case, for as we have seen Captain Heggie's detachment from the 9th Field Company RE had abandoned the ferry at around midnight on 20 September, and 1st Airborne Division HQ had been aware of the fact from 03:40 on 21 September, when Lieutenant Heaps reported the failure of his resupply mission. Furthermore, there is no reference to any such signal in the 1st Airborne Division HQ or Division Signals War Diary. While Urquhart had been in communication with Moor Park at 04:15, 05:45 and 06:25, none of these signals explicitly mentioned the ferry, although the 06:25 message did erroneously refer to positions being unchanged; the only signal referring to holding the ferry prior to the Polish drop was sent thirteen hours earlier at 15:05 on Wednesday 20 September.[14] The Division Signals War Diary only lists losing contact with a No. 22 set issued to Captain Heggie's party at 03:45 on 21 September.[15] The signal would therefore appear to that from the previous day presented as a current situation report. It is unclear if Stevens or Brereton were complicit in the deception, although the latter telephoned Sosabowski shortly after Stevenson handed over the signal. Whether that was the case or not, it is difficult to avoid the conclusion that Sosabowski was deliberately handed inaccurate information to allay his objections and ensure his Brigade dropped into Holland. Subsequent events were to confirm his suspicions that his formation was indeed being sacrificed to reinforce failure.

Sosabowski's men had again been trucked from their billets to Saltby and Spanhoe where the 52nd Troop Carrier Wing had provided a total of 114 C-47s for the lift, sixty machines from the 314th Troop Carrier Group based at the former and fifty-four from the 315th Troop Carrier Group at the latter.[16] The weather looked bad on arrival, with heavy mist blanketing the airfields, although Lieutenant Albert Smaczny, the commander of the 3rd Battalion's 8th Company, recalled being able to see C-47s parked on the edges of the runways 400 yards away. The weather report cited visibility of between one and two miles with clouds stacked in layers from 150 to 9,000 feet.[17] Despite this the mission was approved, with take-off scheduled for midday and went ahead after a one-hour postponement following reports of clear weather over the Channel. The first serial of fifty-four C-47s drawn from the 34th, 43rd, 61st and 62nd Troop Carrier Squadrons thus took off at 13:10. The initial plan was to form up and fly beneath the cloud ceiling, which was estimated to be 1,500 feet, but when the ceiling began to drop the C-47s were forced to climb through the clouds to clear skies at around 8,500 feet, according to 2nd Lieutenant Robert L. Cloer from the 34th Troop Carrier Squadron, who likened the transports emerging from the cloud to 'bugs popping out of a mattress'.[18] The second serial, made up of twenty-seven C-47s from the 309th and 310th Troop Carrier Squadrons and thirty-three aircraft from the 32nd and 50th Troop Carrier Squadrons, began taking off just over an hour later, at 14:27. By this point the clouds were an estimated 2,000 feet with a lower ceiling of approximately 800 feet, and the C-47s were obliged to fly a series of ninety-degree turns in near-zero visibility until they too emerged into the clear. The process was hazardous and not solely because of the proximity of other transports. Flight Officer Robert O. Cook's C-47 from the 43rd Troop Carrier Squadron barely missed a collision with a B-17 bomber descending through the same cloudbank; Cook's crew chief, who had been maintaining collision watch through the C-47's astrodome, claimed that the bomber passed so close he was able to 'see the 50 calibre shells in the ball turret'.[19]

The weather continued to deteriorate as the transports formed up and headed off toward Holland and the decision was taken to cancel the mission. For some reason not all the aircraft had been issued with the correct radio codes and around two-thirds either did not receive the recall signal or could not decipher it despite repeated transmission. Those that did were then faced with renegotiating clouds stretching virtually down to ground level, and put down on the first airfield they saw; as 2nd Lieutenant Charles Voeglin from the 43rd Troop Carrier Squadron put it to his co-pilot, 'Get ready to put the gear down as soon as I yell, and any runway I see, we're going straight in.' All the C-47s appear to have landed safely, albeit scattered far and wide across southern England. Lieutenant Voeglin put down on an unidentified B-17 base, where he was surrounded by suspicious military police. One machine ended up in Ireland.[20] Once on the ground the aircrew had again to face the ire of their keyed-up and disappointed Polish passengers. Lieutenant Cloer's crew chief suggested he and the remainder of the crew remain in the cockpit until the paratroopers had cleared the aircraft as they were 'in a pretty foul mood', a position Lieutenant Voegelin had some sympathy for: 'The Polish paratroopers were so disappointed. They were completely befuddled and frightened, but just wanted to get over there and fight instead of being back in England. All they wanted to do was kill Germans.'[21] Forty-one aircraft were recalled, fourteen from the 314th and twenty-seven from the 315th Troop Carrier Groups.[22] The remaining seventy-three C-47s, which included all but two of the machines from the 309th and 310th Troop Carrier Squadrons and two from the 43rd Troop Carrier Squadron, continued their journey along the southern route over the tip of Kent, across the Channel and over Belgium, dropping to 1,500 feet after making landfall. Unlike the preceding British resupply flight, the US formation does not appear to have been troubled by German fighters, thanks to the efforts of a ninety-strong escort of P-47 and P-51 fighter-bombers, which reportedly fought off a fifty-strong enemy force. Twenty German aircraft were claimed shot down for the loss of three P-47s and three more damaged, one beyond repair; all three shot down pilots were listed as missing in action.[23] One C-47 was hit by anti-aircraft fire on crossing German lines and despatched its stick of fourteen paratroopers from Brigade HQ over friendly territory before turning back for England.[24] The remaining seventy-two transports continued up the Airborne Corridor and after wheeling to run parallel with the Lower Rhine and descending to a drop height of approximately 800 feet, the lead C-47 arrived over the landing area just east of Driel at 17:08. Within seventeen minutes 957 paratroopers were delivered onto DZ K, with the last man touching down at 17:25.[25]

The last leg of the flight brought the C-47s into range of *FlaK Brigade* Svoboda's guns, however. The result was graphically described by 2nd Lieutenant James R. Wilson, the navigator in Lieutenant Cecil Dawkins C-47 from the 310th Troop Carrier Squadron: 'We were all in beautiful formation and ready to drop, and we came on in and then everything erupted. I mean fire from every direction. That DZ had mortar fire hitting the ground all over the place. I looked up and saw *flak* cars on that railroad track, and they had 40mms, and they were firing directly at us.' 1st Lieutenant Oliver J. Smith from the same Squadron was flying further back in the formation: 'We slowed down, put out some flaps, cut the left engine and were flying along at 90 mph when the whole ground opened up. You couldn't see for tracers.'[26] According to some pilots, including the commander of the 310th Squadron, Lieutenant-Colonel Henry G. Hamby, the Polish paratroopers were not as swift as they might have been in clearing their aircraft. According to Hamby, on average '18 paratroopers would exit a C-47 in about 18 seconds. The Polish troopers had these heavy equipment bags that had to be pushed out the door ahead of each trooper, and it seemed that it took forever.' Similarly, 1st Lieutenant Monroe Zartman referred to being 'in drop mode for the longest minute of my life'.[27] In part this may have been due to Sosabowski's policy of restricting his men to synthetic parachute training after their training and qualification jumps in order to minimise parachuting casualties, but there were sometimes other reasons for the tardiness; the entire stick in Lieutenant Smith's aircraft were knocked off their feet by a shell that came through the underside of the fuselage for example. Smith had to hold his course and speed while the Poles sorted themselves out and jumped.[28] The formation was consequently late in turning right and therefore overflew rather than passed west of Elst, which was fully occupied by German troops preparing to block the Allied ground advance from Nijmegen; one pilot likened the blizzard of fire the transports attracted to 'a pinball machine gone mad'.[29]

Five of the seventy-two C-47s were brought down over DZ K or in the immediate vicinity, all after despatching their sticks. Two of them belonged to the 309th Troop Carrier Squadron. Lieutenant C. C. Biggs' machine exploded on impact, killing everyone aboard while Captain F. K. Stephenson crash-landed in woods after catching fire; all the crew escaped without serious injury. The other three downed machines belonged to the 310th Squadron. Lieutenant Kenneth Wakely and his entire crew were killed when their C-47 also exploded on impact while Lieutenant Jacob Boon's machine was hit just after despatching its stick and crash landed near the DZ. Although all but the pilot were wounded, the crew escaped the wreck before it exploded and Boon was awarded the Silver Star for assisting his injured co-pilot from the burning cockpit. 1st Lieutenant Cecil Dawkins was wounded in the face and head during the run-in by *flak* that also set fire to his port wing fuel tank. Dawkins nonetheless despatched his stick of paratroopers though the streamer of flame licking along the port side of the fuselage and then had his crew bail out. He survived the subsequent crash and was captured but his crew landed safely and reached Allied territory.[30] Lieutenant Smith's C-47 from the 310th Troop Carrier Squadron almost crashed after a hit briefly knocked out the flight controls and wounded his radio operator and crew chief, but Smith managed to regain control and landed safely at an airstrip near Eindhoven where medics from the 101st Airborne Division rendered aid to the wounded aircrew. Subsequent examination of the aircraft revealed the right rudder and trim control cables had been severed, the elevator cable was only attached by three strands and over 600 holes had been punched in the airframe.[31] Lieutenant-Colonel Smylie C. Stark, the commander of the 309th Squadron, was hit in the chest by a bullet that passed through the instrument panel; his issue *flak* vest absorbed the impact but he was injured in the face and rendered unconscious by fragments of the instrument panel leaving his co-pilot, Captain Julius H. Petersen, to nurse the aircraft home. Lieutenant-Colonel Hamby's C-47 took a series of hits as the last paratrooper exited that knocked out his port engine and wounded every other member of the crew but Hamby; he managed to nurse the damaged machine to a safe landing at Brussels, where an inspection revealed it was riddled with 120 holes.[32] Flight-Officer Cook from the 43rd Troop Carrier Squadron also fetched up at Brussels after having his rudder pedal, hydraulic lines and fuel gauges shot away. Landing therefore involved the C-47 careering without brakes between parked aircraft before colliding with a partly demolished hangar. The crew all emerged unhurt and then departed with the cash from their escape kits to find a hotel on the orders of an unnamed colonel from another unit, possibly Lieutenant-Colonel Hamby. As Cook put it later, the mission had been 'a hell of a trip, but as I have to admit, Brussels was a good city to have fun in.'[33]

The Polish drop was observed by Captain Zwolanski and the Polish Brigade's liaison group from a gun pit in the 1st Airlanding Light Regiment's location, again accompanied by War Correspondent Swiecicki. The view of the DZ was partially obscured by the high dyke on the south bank of the Lower Rhine, but the arrival of the C-47s was heralded by the hum of engines and the growing crackle of German anti-aircraft fire. As soon as the parachutes began to blossom behind the aircraft, Zwolanski's radio operator, Cadet Corporal Pajak, began transmitting on the prearranged frequency 'Hallo Kuba, Hallo Kuba, this is Roman, can you hear me?'[34] The first aircraft over the DZ was that carrying Brigade Quartermaster Lieutenant Stefan Kaczmarek, which had emerged from the clouds over England into clear but empty skies and set off for Holland solo. As a result Kaczmarek and his stick were dropped just west of Driel alone and several minutes ahead of the rest of the drop; he was therefore probably exaggerating only slightly when he later claimed 'every gun on the ground seemed to be aimed at me.' His stick nonetheless landed safely and recovered one of their supply containers, located the other and was busy interrogating a German straggler found sheltering in a nearby house when the remainder of the Brigade began jumping on the other side of the village.[35] Major-General Sosabowski's experience was typical:

An exploding anti-aircraft shell burst too near for comfort, bouncing the plane to one side...The green bulb shone ghostlily [sic] above the door space and simultaneously the Jumpmaster shouted 'GO!'...the plane bucked as a crash under the belly indicated the first of the equipment containers had dropped...The leading man pushed out a bundle of folding bicycles and in an instant flung himself into space. Number Two, Three Four... Then it was my turn...I leaned forward, grasped both sides of the door and as the slipstream tried to push me back, I stepped with my left foot into nothingness...I felt the tug of the parachute webbing on my shoulders – I was floating down. All round me, as far as the eye could see, other paratroopers were descending.[36]

The Poles' reception was similar to that of the 4th Parachute Brigade three days earlier. Every German with a line of sight poured fire into the parachute-filled sky. The result was vividly recalled by medic Lance-Corporal Bayzli Borowik: 'We were under fire from machine-guns while we were in the air...The tracer bullets looked like arrows with smoke behind them; one man's kitbag was hit in the air and burst into flames.'[37] Corporal Wladijslaw Korob's parachute canopy was riddled with holes during his descent; he landed next to a decapitated colleague. Major-General Sosabowski had a similar experience after landing close to a watercourse; while running for cover he came upon the spread-eagled body of one of his men: 'He lay on the grass, stretched out as if on a cross, a bullet or piece of shrapnel had neatly sliced off the top of his head.'[38]

Landing on DZ K would have been fraught at best, given that it was riven with dozens of water-filled drainage ditches and criss-crossed with wire fences, orchards and copses. The Poles had to cope with the additional hazards of mortar fire quartering the landing area and crossfire from machine-guns in the outskirts of Elst to the south and on the railway embankment that marked the east edge of the DZ; the fire was thickened by elements of *Kampfgruppe* Knaust as they drove south along the Arnhem–Elst road en route to the blocking position being established at Elst.[39] Major-General Sosabowski's Brigade HQ and Staff rallied intact and rapidly established radio communications with the Brigade's sub-units, although the news this brought was not good. The Poles' 3rd Battalion, which likely landed on the eastern side of the DZ, appears to have been hardest hit. Some of the paratroopers clashed with parties of German troops immediately on landing and German fire prevented them from recovering most of their containers. The 7th Company was missing its commander and forty men, obliging Lieutenant Wieslaw Szczygiel from the Engineer Company to take command and while the 8th and 9th Companies, commanded by Lieutenant Albert Smaczny and Captain Ignacy Gazurek, appear to have fared better, Battalion HQ was only able to muster twenty men under a Lieutenant Slesicki. The missing included the 3rd Battalion's commander, Captain Waclaw Sobocinski, so Captain Gazurek took command of a severely depleted 3rd Battalion consisting of fewer than 200 men.[40] The number was so low in part because the Polish parachute battalions were significantly smaller than their British counterparts to begin with – under 400 men each.[41]

Even more serious was the non-arrival of the 1st Battalion in its entirety. Major Marian Tonn had landed at Spanhoe at around the same time as the remainder of the Brigade were jumping at Driel where he was joined by all but four of the C-47s from the 34th and 43rd Squadrons carrying his Battalion and two carrying sticks from the 2nd Battalion; another eleven aircraft carrying men from the 3rd Battalion had returned to RAF Saltby. As we have seen, the missing aircraft were scattered across southern England by the weather, and Tonn described the operations room at Spanhoe as 'frantic' as he and his USAAF counterparts tried to make sense of the situation.[42] It was to be another two days before the 1st Battalion and other residual elements of the Polish Brigade were dropped in Holland.

Despite the volume of German fire only four paratroopers had been killed in the Driel drop and twenty-five or so injured; ten had suffered sprains or broken bones from bad landings, the others were presumably wounded by German fire. The Poles had also taken eleven German prisoners in the course of the landing, including five deserters who had been hiding in the crypt of Driel church, two of whom were conscripted Poles.[43] The Polish casualties were initially treated by members of the Brigade's ninety-strong Medical Company and then cared for by Dutch civilians from Driel who turned a disused school in the centre of the village into a makeshift hospital. The initiative was led by Cora Baltussen, who had donned her Red Cross armband and pedalled out to the landing area to render assistance as soon as she saw the parachutes descending. She was taken aback to discover the paratroopers were Polish rather than British; for their part the Poles had been briefed not to trust the local civilian population and remained aloof until a Private Cooney from the British 2nd Parachute Battalion, who was receiving treatment at the Baltussen house for an injured ankle, vouched for their trustworthiness to Sosabowski in person. The latter then moved his HQ in the Baltussen house where he questioned Mrs Baltussen closely about the situation and especially the condition of the Heveadorp ferry.[44] After a conference with his officers Sosabowski despatched a fifteen-strong patrol from the Brigade's Engineer Company, headed by Captain Piotr Budziszewski and Lieutenant Kaczmarek, to investigate the ferry terminal. The patrol reached its objective just after dark at around 19:00: 'We stood on the ramp and Captain Budziszewski shouted a big "Hello", but there was no reply from the other side. Then he put up a flare, but as soon as it lit up, there broke out a hell of a fire from the opposite bank…The firing went on for about five minutes and we could hear it ricocheting off the stones…We returned to Driel when the firing stopped and reported.'[45]

By 21:00 the entire Polish Brigade had moved up to a flood dyke overlooking the Lower Rhine, with Brigade HQ located in a convenient barn while the paratroopers searched vainly in the darkness for some means to cross the river.[46] Despite repeated attempts Sosabowski's signallers were unable to contact their British counterparts. The problem appears to have been due to mismatched radio frequencies, given that the Division Signals was unable to make contact on the Polish command or rear links after the landing and that the Brigade's liaison group near the Oosterbeek Old Church also failed to establish contact.[47] The Polish Brigade's first contact with Urquhart therefore came when Captain Zwolanski swam the river from the 1st Airlanding Regiment's battery positions at around 22:00. He carried a message informing Sosabowski that a counter-attack had been arranged to clear a section of the north bank to permit his Brigade to cross the river using reconnaissance boats and rafts constructed from Jeep trailers; this prompted Sosabowski to call a midnight conference to organise the order of crossing.[48]

***

Fifteen miles or so south of Arnhem the Germans were busy organising a new defensive line on the River Waal, prompted by the loss of the Nijmegen bridges in the evening of Wednesday 20 September. The German units that had finally overcome Lieutenant-Colonel Frost's force holding the east end of the Arnhem road bridge were despatched southward from midday on Thursday 21 September, in compliance with orders from *II SS Panzerkorps*. *Obergruppenführer* Bittrich, already concerned at the Allied incursion across the River Waal, who decided that the arrival of the 1st Polish Independent Parachute Brigade at Driel in the late afternoon of 21 September was part of a pincer movement to isolate *10 SS Panzer Division*. He therefore reorganised priorities and unit boundaries to meet both the perceived new threat and that developing from Nijmegen. *Brigadeführer* Heinz Harmel's *10 SS Panzer Division* was ordered to establish a blocking line from which to counter-attack the Allied lodgement north of the Waal. The line was to run west from Bemmel, four miles north-east of the Nijmegen road bridge, to Oosterhout and then north to Elst on the main road to Arnhem, with Elst forming the boundary with *9 SS Panzer Division*. The line was manned by the surviving *Sturmgeschütze* III and *Panzer* IVs from *Sturmbannführer* Reinhold's *II Bataillon SS Panzer Regiment 10*, a roughly half-strength *SS Panzergrenadier Regiment 22* and the approximately battalion-strength *Kampfgruppe* Hartung, made up of *Heer* reservists. Additional reinforcement from *SS Panzergrenadier Regiment 21* arrived in the course of the day and from the mid- to late afternoon the western end of the line could also call upon the armoured units belonging to *9 SS Panzer Division* redeployed to Elst following the fight at the Arnhem bridge; it is unclear who had direct control over these units.[49]

Obersturmbannführer Walther Harzer's orders involved extending *9 SS Panzer Division*'s responsibilities south of the Lower Rhine, initially by establishing a defensive line south of the Arnhem road bridge centred on Elden. This was subsequently extended to setting up an east-facing blocking position along the length of the railway line running between Arnhem and Nijmegen, to be manned by a new *ad hoc* formation dubbed *Sperrverband* (blocking group) Harzer. Confusingly, the new formation was actually commanded by a *Heer* officer, *Oberst* Egon Gerhard, as Harzer was fully occupied with *9 SS Panzer Division*'s ongoing fight against the 1st Airborne Division at Oosterbeek; Gerhard also brought his existing HQ from *Panzergrenadier Ersatz Regiment 57* with him to his new appointment. This formal sub-division of *9 SS Panzer Division*'s responsibilities was ordered by *Heeresgruppe B* as a deliberate command streamlining measure, and *Sperrverband* Harzer was consequently tasked to take control of all units belonging or assigned to *9 SS Panzer Division* operating south of the Lower Rhine. These initially included *Hauptmann* Otto Schörken's *Grenadier Ersatz und Ausbildungs Bataillon (motorisiert) 60*, *MG Bataillon 41*, *Kampfgruppen* Kauer and Köhnen from the *Luftwaffe* and

Kriegsmarine respectively and a Dutch *Waffen SS* unit, *III Bataillon, Grenadier Regiment 1* 'Landsturm Nederland'. Commanded by *Hauptsturmführer* Adalbert Stocker, the Dutch unit had been placed in reserve by Harzer on arrival in Arnhem on 20 September after pedalling the seventy miles from its training base at Hoogeveen in northern Holland.

The southern end of *Sperrverband* Harzer's line was assigned to two units that had played the major role in clearing the British foothold at the north end of the Arnhem road bridge. *Kampfgruppe* Brinkmann, built around the armoured cars and half-tracks of *SS Panzer Aufklärungs Abteilung 10* and augmented with elements from *SS Panzergrenadier Regiment 21*, had been involved in the fight at the Arnhem bridge from the outset, was reinforced with the surviving elements of *SS Panzer Aufklärungs Abteilung 9*, which had been marooned south of the Arnhem road bridge since the evening of 17 September. *Kampfgruppe* Knaust had originally consisted of Major Hans-Peter Knaust's *Panzer-Grenadier Ersatz und Ausbildungs Bataillon 64* 'Bocholt' augmented with *Panzer Kompanie* Mielke from *Panzer Ersatz Regiment 6* 'Bielefeld', which had been reduced to six *Panzer IIIs* in the course of the fight at Arnhem. However, by the time it moved south at around midday on Thursday 21 September Knaust's unit had been substantially reinforced, being assigned *schwere Panzer Kompanie Hummel* with its dozen Tiger I tanks and eight Panther tanks belonging to the recently re-equipped *I Bataillon SS Panzer Regiment 10*.[50] *Kampfgruppen* Brinkmann and Knaust thus collectively comprised the most powerful armoured unit available to *II SS Panzerkorps*, and were deployed in the vicinity of Elst as a local contingency reserve but during the night of 21-22 September new orders directed an attack against the new parachute landing at Driel. The task was allotted to *Kampfgruppe* Brinkmann, according to one source because its light armoured vehicles would not impose too much strain on the fragile road network of the Betuwe, as the locals referred to the lozenge-shaped island between the Lower Rhine and the Waal; the fact that Knaust's tanks were better employed facing a prospective Allied armoured advance from Nijmegen rather than chasing down lightly armed paratroopers also likely played a role in the allocation.[51] The terrain and tactical situation made redeploying *Kampfgruppe* Brinkmann's vehicles toward Driel a difficult and time-consuming process, and the attack was delayed until the late morning of the following day as a result.[52]

On the British side of the Nijmegen bridgehead 30 Corps had also issued fresh orders for operations on 21 September. In addition to establishing security for the Nijmegen bridges, the Guards Armoured Division was instructed to 'Advance earliest possible…at maximum speed' for Arnhem in line with the original GARDEN concept and in order to bring 'assistance' to the 1st Airborne Division; this was an interesting order of priority in the circumstances, albeit one that continued the general lack of emphasis on the Airborne end of the operation that had characterised the Guards Armoured Division's orders and behaviour from the outset. The designated axis of advance was oriented along the line of the Arnhem–Nijmegen railway line through Ressen, just under five miles north of the bridges, with 'operational traffic' permitted to use the main road running north through Elst. If enemy resistance on the designated axis proved too stiff, the Division was also authorised to sidestep to the west and make contact with the 1st Airborne Division directly across the Lower Rhine.[53] In the event, security for the bridges was provided by pushing two companies from the 3rd Battalion Irish Guards over the Waal soon after the bridge had been secured, followed at 03:00 on 21 September by a Squadron of tanks from the 2nd (Armoured) Battalion Irish Guards. The newcomers discovered an abandoned German map detailing enemy positions and despite the armoured cars of the 2nd Household Cavalry Regiment probing around the perimeter, the new bridgehead remained unmolested apart from 'fairly heavy' artillery and mortar fire as *10 SS Panzer Division* concentrated upon erecting its blocking line.[54]

The order to attack did not percolate down to the Irish Guards Group slated to carry it out until the late morning of 21 September, and the projected start time of 11:00 did not impress when it did. Lieutenant-Colonel John Vandeleur, who had his own reservations about the advance, nonetheless issued the attack order to Captain Roland Langton, commanding No. 1 Squadron, 2nd Irish Guards, in person at 10:40, just twenty minutes before the attack was scheduled to commence with the injunction to 'go like hell and get on up to Arnhem'. For his part Langton could not believe that 'they were actually going to launch this thing in twenty minutes' and not merely because of the extremely short notice; he was also concerned that the only briefing materials were a single captured map and an aerial reconnaissance photograph of an anti-aircraft site near Elst, and there was also a paucity of support.[55] In contrast to previous days, the attack was to be supported by a single artillery unit, the 153rd Field Regiment RA from the Guards Armoured Division's Support Group, equipped with Sexton self-propelled 25-Pounders.[56] However, while the short notice and paucity of support may have been a surprise, it is difficult to see why the advance order should have been, given the prevailing circumstances and especially given the fact that the Irish Guards Group had been in place on the north bank of the River Waal for at least seven and possibly up to eleven hours.

Much is made of the fact that the Guards Armoured Division's tanks and infantry were in need of rest and replenishment after the fight to reach and secure the Nijmegen bridges, but this refers to the Grenadier Guards Group, which had been involved in that fight for two days; the Irish Guards Group had been in Division reserve since reaching the Son bridge on 18 September.[57] Nor do the Irish Guards appear to have been involved in actively protecting the bridges once across the Waal. Lieutenant-Colonel Reuben Tucker's 504th Parachute Infantry Regiment had deliberately pushed forward to establish a perimeter around a mile from the bridges to create space to marshal a further advance and Lieutenant Brian Wilson from the 3rd Irish Guards 2nd Company recalled crossing the Nijmegen road bridge and setting in close to the bridge near the Grenadier Guards tanks that had rushed the bridge, along with a troop of M10 Achilles anti-tank guns from the 21st Anti-Tank Regiment RA. Wilson also recalled patrols of US paratroopers constantly roaming through his location while 'for our part, we just sat in our positions all night.'[58] The Irish Guards Group's reconnaissance seems to have been limited to observing the area after daylight and unanimously deciding that the terrain was 'a ridiculous place to try to operate tanks'.[59] D Squadron, 2nd Household Cavalry Regiment, carried out what reconnaissance was undertaken after crossing the Waal at some point shortly after 04:30. Household Cavalry patrols thus scouted the main road toward Elst, where four 88mm guns were pinpointed, and Bemmel to the north-east and Valburg to the west. Progress on all axes was dammed up because *10 SS Panzer Division* had managed to erect a blocking line, as detailed above, by daylight on 21 September.[60]

This had not been the case earlier, however, as for several hours after the capture of the bridges there were only two coherent German positions between Nijmegen and Arnhem; *Sturmbannführer* Leo Reinhold's recently relocated *Kampfgruppe* HQ in Bemmel, four miles north-east of the bridges, and a single battery and HQ from *Hauptsturmführer* Oskar Schwappacher's *SS Artillerie Ausbildungs und Ersatz Regiment 5* in Oosterhout, four miles west of Bemmel.[61] As *Brigadeführer* Heinz Harmel later put it: 'The English drank too much tea…The four panzers who crossed the bridge made a mistake when they stayed in Lent. If they had carried on their advance, it would have been all over for us.'[62] Harmel's assessment was arguably a little pessimistic given that *SS Panzer Regiment 10's II Bataillon*, equipped with a dozen *Panzer* IV tanks and four *StuG* IIIs, was being ferried across the Lower Rhine from the night of 18-19 September.[63] Furthermore, reaching Arnhem would also have brought the Irish Guards Group into contact with the Tiger tanks of *schwere Panzer Kompanie Hummel*. On the other hand, a determined thrust might at least have disjointed the implementation of *II SS Panzerkorps'* defensive plan in the *Betuwe*, prevented *Sperrverband* Harzer from interfering with the 1st Polish Independent Parachute Brigade and thereby expedited a more rapid and concentrated relief effort across the Lower Rhine to the Oosterbeek Pocket. None of that happened because the Irish Guards Group remained immobile for the hours of darkness and beyond, as the Guards Armoured Division had collectively and consistently done since Operation GARDEN commenced; as Lieutenant Wilson put it, 'The situation at Arnhem remained desperate. Yet the GAD did not move.[64] In a replay of events north of the Lower Rhine on the night of Sunday 17 September, the opportunity to maintain the initiative by pushing on toward Arnhem again ebbed away in inactivity while the Germans used the windfall respite to organise their blocking line.

The attack order from 30 Corps was not implemented for over two hours after the designated 11:00 start time, allowing Harmel and his men around six hours of daylight to fine-tune their defensive preparations. The Irish Guards Group finally attacked at 13:30 with No. 1 Squadron in the lead followed by the remainder of the 2nd Irish Guards carrying infantry from the 3rd Irish Guards on the decks of their Shermans.[65] The advance up the line of the Arnhem-Nijmegen railway proceeded well for around two miles, until the lead tanks approached Ressen and came into range of the German blocking line.[66] At that point at least three of the lead tanks were knocked out in rapid succession; Captain Langton, travelling further back in the column in his Daimler scout car, saw 'a Sherman sprocket wheel lift lazily into the air over some trees up ahead'.[67] The advance then came to an abrupt halt. The 3rd Irish Guards infantry deployed from their tanks but were pinned down by German machine-gun, mortar and artillery fire, as were Captain Langton and his Battalion commander Lieutenant-Colonel Giles Vandeleur when they moved forward to investigate. Artillery support from the 153rd Field Regiment proved ineffective as two of the Regiment's three batteries were en route to new positions, and for reasons that are unclear no Forward Observer team was travelling with the advance either; a developing shortage of artillery ammunition may also have contributed to the poor artillery response.[68] The slack ought to have been taken up by close air support and some Typhoon fighter-bombers were overhead despite bad weather closing a number of the 2nd Tactical Air Force's forward airfields in Belgium. However, the Irish Guards Group was unable to communicate with the aircraft because the radio set in the only available Tentacle forward air control vehicle was unserviceable. Even if that had not been the case, the Typhoon's utility would have been limited because Allied air activity north of the Waal was prohibited in the afternoon to avoid interfering with the 1st Polish Independent Parachute Brigade's drop at Driel.[69]

Semi-official and secondary sources give the impression that an afternoon of hard fighting followed the advance being stalled, constrained by terrain that prevented tanks from manoeuvring or indeed leaving the roads, while the infantry's attempts to advance or outflank the German defences were pinned down and rebuffed.[70] However, the official records cast a different light on proceedings: 'At 1330 hours the advance started and at 1350 hours it finished.'[71] Much is made of the unsuitability of the terrain in both participant and historical accounts, typified by Lieutenant-Colonel Giles Vandeleur in an exchange with the commander of the Irish Guards Group: 'If we send any more tanks up along this road it's going to be bloody murder.'[72] Ironically, given the Guards Armoured Division's proven preference for halting operations at dusk and not restarting until the following midday or early afternoon, the Division's semi-official history refers to the German defences being insuperable due to the dearth of artillery, air support and 'without cover of darkness'.[73] The terrain was undoubtedly difficult but the repetitive and uniform manner in which it is cited to excuse the lack of progress raises suspicions of protesting too much, not least because German armoured vehicles, both those with narrower tracks and thus inferior flotation and those that weighed a great deal more than the Guards' Shermans, 'were able to deploy off road to good effect'.[74] As ought to have been abundantly clear from daylight observation, the terrain required an infantry-led approach, but there were insufficient infantry on hand to implement it. The Guards Armoured Division's semi-official history gives the impression that the 2nd Irish Guards tanks may have only been accompanied by a single infantry company from the 3rd Irish Guards, with the remainder of the Battalion presumably still deployed to guard the north end of the Nijmegen bridges.[75] Even had that not been the case, the atypical Guards Armoured Division practice of pairing armoured and infantry battalions by regimental cap badge meant only a single infantry battalion would have been available for a task that ultimately required the better part of a brigade. As a result, apart from an abortive attempt to outflank the German positions to the east by a company commanded by Major J.S.O. Haslewood, the rest of the afternoon passed in something of a stand-off until 18:30, when the Irish Guards Group predictably pulled back to a night harbour area 1,000 yards from the scene of the day's action. Infantry reinforcements were available from the 1st Welsh Guards, which spent the period from 13:00 to 17:00 sitting on the tanks of the 2nd Welsh Guards lined out on the Nijmegen road bridge but they were not called upon, again presumably due to the self-imposed habit of only operating units with the same cap badge. The Welsh Guards Group was eventually ordered forward toward Oosterhout on the Irish Guards' left flank at 17:00, presumably as a nod to the 30 Corps' instruction to sidestep to the west if the direct route to Arnhem proved too strongly defended. The move was equally short-lived, as the Welsh Guards were also ordered back to a harbour area near the Nijmegen road bridge at dusk, after a brief fight that reportedly saw three German tanks knocked out. The clash was likely with *Panzer Kompanie* Mielke from *Kampfgruppe* Knaust, which reported losing two *Panzer* IIIs in Oosterhout in the late afternoon or early evening of 21 September.[76]

The Irish Guards Group did not try particularly hard on the afternoon of Thursday 21 September, despite clear orders from 30 Corps and the urgency of the situation, although this was entirely consistent with the pattern of late starting and ceasing operations promptly at dusk adhered to by the Guards Armoured Division from the beginning of Operation GARDEN. Arrival at Nijmegen appears to have added another dimension to this unhurried attitude however, which underlay the uniform protests from the Guards Armoured Division's senior commanders that the terrain between Nijmegen and Arnhem was unsuitable for tanks. The Division commander, Major-General Allan Adair, commented that 'to get along that road was obviously first a job for infantry', while Lieutenant-Colonel John Vandeleur made pretty much the same point to Captain Langton when ordering him to hold in place after the advance was stopped in the early afternoon.[77] The clear inference was that the Guards Armoured Division had done enough and that it was time for another formation with more infantry to take over, specifically the 43rd Division, which was making its way up the Airborne Corridor from the Neerpelt bridgehead.

This attitude was not shared universally across the Guards Armoured Division, however. Lieutenant Brian Wilson from the 3rd Irish Guards later considered it 'shameful' that his Division had remained immobile for eighteen hours after the Nijmegen bridges had been secured.[78] Lieutenant John Gorman MC, a Troop commander in the 2nd Irish Guards, was equally forthright, and his comment is worth quoting in full:

> We had come all the way from Normandy, taken Brussels, fought halfway through Holland and crossed the Nijmegen bridge, Arnhem and those paratroopers were just up ahead and, almost within sight of that last bloody bridge, we were stopped. I never felt such morbid despair.[79]

The more laissez-faire attitude at the upper echelon of the Guards Armoured Division's chain of command prevailed however, and another precious twenty-four hours were allowed to slip by while the 1st Airborne Division continued to fight for its life.

***

While the Irish Guards were stalled before Ressen and the 1st Polish Independent Parachute Brigade was landing and reorganising, their counterparts on the north bank of the Lower Rhine were carrying out what would become the final two voluntary adjustments to the Oosterbeek perimeter. In the late afternoon the 7th KOSB had been ordered to withdraw to a narrower frontage in a wood behind their existing positions in order to reduce the 400-yard gap on the

Battalion's left flank with the 21st Independent Company, although compliance was delayed by the German attack at 16:30. Lieutenant-Colonel Payton-Reid carried out the move in the immediate aftermath of his successful counter-attack while the enemy were still off balance and to take advantage of the remaining daylight; the move proved to be additionally fortuitous because the day's fighting had reduced the 7th KOSB's strength to 150 all ranks.[80] In addition, a burning Jeep had set fire to the building housing the overflowing Battalion RAP, putting the casualties at risk from the flames and detonating ammunition stowed in the vehicle. The wounded were therefore evacuated by Jeep to either the 21st Independent Company's RAP or the Division MDS at the Hotel Schoonoord, while the new position was reconnoitred by Captain David Clayhills, who had been elevated to Battalion second-in-command. The moved commenced at around 18:00 with B and D Companies covering toward the east and was carried out without incident, with all movable equipment being brought out apart from a number of Jeeps damaged by artillery and small-arms fire. The Battalion's left flank was then tied into the 21st Independent Company's position and two 6-Pounders and a Mortar Section were deployed in the latter's perimeter, which was considered to be 'of great assistance'. Another 6-Pounder was deployed in the 4th Parachute Squadron's location.[81]

While Payton-Reid's men were digging in Urquhart held a conference at his HQ and decided to contract the northern face of the Divisional perimeter yet further, giving sole responsibility for the sector to the 7th KOSB and withdrawing the Independent Company and Captain Henry Brown's detachment from the 4th Parachute Squadron into the Division reserve.[82] Colonel Payton-Reid only became aware of the decision when the Independent Company received its withdrawal order at some point before 21:30; the order did not go down well with Major Wilson, who was of the view that his Ommershof location could have been held 'indefinitely'.[83] Payton-Reid sought clarification from 1st Airlanding Brigade HQ via a 'long and fruitless' radio exchange that ended with Captain Colin Macduff-Duncan being sent forward to Payton-Reid's location with a map trace of the new line on the Ommershoflaan, around 200 yards south of the Battalion's original position on the Graaf van Rechterenweg. The move began at 21:30 and was again carried out without incident, with the Battalion setting up a three-sided perimeter around Battalion HQ and Mortar Group; the 6-Pounder guns were deployed covering the roads leading into the position from north, east and west, while the MMG Group's Vickers were set up in woods on the Battalion's left flank, also covering the northern approaches. To the east the Battalion's flank was tied into the positions on the Stationsweg occupied by the Reconnaissance Squadron and 156 Parachute Battalion, and to the west with the Glider Pilots from E and F Squadrons.[84]

The other adjustment occurred on the eastern face of the Division perimeter and not solely at Urquhart's behest. *Kampfgruppe* Möller had maintained the pressure on the west-central sector for most of the day and by 18:40 had reoccupied the area around the MDS in the Hotels Schoonoord and Vreewijk on the east side of the Utrechtseweg–Stationsweg crossroads, although it is unclear if they actually entered the makeshift hospitals. In the process Möller's men drove back the remnants of the 10th Parachute Battalion to just east of the crossroads by 20:10.[85] The planned British withdrawal took place to the south of the crossroads in the sector held by LONSDALE Force. The 1st and 3rd Parachute Battalions held back *Kampfgruppe* Harder from the sodden polder south of the Benedendorpsweg until mid-afternoon, when Major Lonsdale gained permission to withdraw them to a section of the Divisional perimeter held by Major Cain and the 2nd South Staffords near the Oosterbeek Old Church. The 3rd Parachute Battalion moved first at 15:30, presumably because it occupied the most far flung section of the line, followed thirty minutes later by the 1st Parachute Battalion; the latter lost eight casualties to heavy enemy fire in doing so.[86] The withdrawal was covered by an artillery barrage, although it is unclear if the shelling came from the Airlanding Light Regiment, the 64th Medium Regiment, or both.[87]

On reaching the relative security of the new line the paratroopers were permitted a brief respite in the blacked-out Oosterbeek Old Church during which they were treated to a morale-bolstering speech delivered from the pulpit by Major Lonsdale in person, his head swathed in a field dressing and with one arm in a sling:

> You know as well as I do there are a lot of bloody Germans coming at us. Well, all we can do is to stay here and hang on in the hope that somebody catches us up. We must fight for our lives and stick together. We've fought the Germans before – in North Africa, Sicily, Italy. They weren't good enough for us then, and they're bloody well not good enough for us now. They're up against the finest soldiers in the world. An hour from now you will take up defensive positions north of the road outside. Make certain you dig in well and that your weapons and ammo are in good order. We are getting short of ammo, so when you shoot you shoot to kill. Good luck to you all.[88]

It is unclear if the two Parachute Battalions attended the Oosterbeek Old Church together or separately, but the fact that Lonsdale went to the trouble of writing out the speech on a dismounted door placed conveniently in sight of the pulpit suggests multiple reading. Whichever, the paratroopers cleaned their weapons, catnapped and ate whatever rations they had left as they lounged in the old wooden pews. The scene was witnessed by Major Alan Bush, the 3rd Parachute Battalion's second-in-command, who proudly commented on seeing the 'filthy, tired men cleaning their rifles – well trained men those were'.[89]

Major Bush had just regained the Division perimeter after becoming separated during the fight on the riverside Onderlangs on 18 September, and as ranking officer found himself promoted to command the 1st Parachute Brigade, albeit a shadow of the formation which had landed with such confidence five days earlier. The 1st Parachute Battalion mustered approximately 100 men commanded led by Lieutenant Albert Turrell and the Battalion FOO Captain William Caird; the latter had assumed command after Lieutenant John Williams was wounded, presumably during the withdrawal to the church. The 3rd Parachute Battalion was in even worse shape, numbering just forty-three men including Lieutenant James Cleminson and another unidentified officer, possibly Lieutenant Philip Evans from the 2nd South Staffords' C Company. It is unclear precisely who was in command of the 3rd Battalion at this point, as the irascible Captain Dorrien-Smith, who had assumed command of the 3rd Battalion on its withdrawal to Oosterbeek on the afternoon of 19 September, had been killed at some point on 21 September. In addition, Major Bush could call upon the services of around a dozen Glider Pilots from D Squadron, two men from the 2nd Parachute Battalion and one from the 1st Airlanding Anti-tank Battery. With their brief respite over, the 3rd Parachute Battalion contingent joined Major Cain's group from the 2nd South Staffords dug in near the Laundry where they spent yet another night digging in. The larger group from the 1st Parachute Battalion occupied a new position in houses and gardens north of the Benedendorpsweg where it was heavily shelled and mortared at 21:00. A quiet night followed. The day's fighting had cost the 1st Parachute Battalion two dead and ten wounded; the total presumably included the eight casualties sustained during the late afternoon withdrawal to the Oosterbeek Old Church.[90]

Whilst not decisive, II SS Panzerkorps attacks on the 1st Airborne Division's perimeter had nonetheless yielded useful results by nightfall on 21 September. While the attacks against sections of the east and western faces of the perimeter had been rebuffed, the northern face had been pushed back several hundred yards, in part because of the poor defensive quality of the Graaf van Rechterenweg position. Ground had also been gained on both sides of the base of the perimeter, where LONSDALE Force and the 1st Border's B Company were almost back-to-back, raising the prospect of pinching the British perimeter away from the Lower Rhine altogether. The Allied crossing of the River Waal at Nijmegen and more immediately the arrival of the bulk of the 1st Polish Independent Parachute Brigade south of the Lower Rhine rendered this objective the more important, and *Bataillon* Worrowski's driving back of the elements of the 1ˢᵗ Border holding the north end of the Heveadorp ferry helped toward that objective, albeit inadvertently.

On the other hand, the day's fighting had also shown that the British Airborne troops at Oosterbeek were no less skilled and aggressive than those encountered at the Arnhem road bridge, and the brutal fighting necessary to combat them was taking an increasing toll on the German units involved. *Sturmann* Alfred Ziegler, the motorcycle despatch rider from *SS Panzerjäger Abteilung 9*, recalled his 120-strong contingent being reduced to a mere twenty-one in the course of the day. This prompted the commander of *Kampfgruppe* Bruhn to send a message to *Hauptsturmführer* von Allwörden warning him that if he did not withdraw his few surviving men left in the line, 'there would be none of the original tank destroyer crews left'. Wary of British artillery and mortar fire, Ziegler took a novel approach when given time to rest: 'I dug a hole near the bridge over the railway line, pulled my motorcycle [combination] over the top of it for protection against overhead shrapnel and fell asleep at the bottom of it.'[91]

Whilst his units were busy reorganising and resting, *Obersturmbannführer* Harzer was making good use of the direct link between *9 SS Panzer Division* HQ and *Heeresgruppe B*. On receiving complaints from Harzer that his men lacked the means to assault the British-held houses effectively, *Generalfeldmarschall* Model immediately ordered a supply of flamethrowers brought forward from supply dumps and assigned Harzer *Pionier Lehr Bataillon 9*, a specialist unit trained and equipped for house-to-house fighting; the *Bataillon* was flown into Deelen airfield by a shuttle of Junkers 52 transports on the nights of 21-22 and 22-23 September.[92] Despite the rising cost, the German attacks on the 1ˢᵗ Airborne Division's perimeter were slowly bearing fruit, and were therefore to continue the following day, incorporating lessons from the fighting at the Arnhem road bridge as well as those gained at Oosterbeek.

D Plus 5

00:01 to 23:59 Friday 22 September 1944

On the south bank of the Lower Rhine the 1st Polish Independent Parachute Brigade spent the early hours of Friday 22 September waiting to move across the Lower Rhine to Oosterbeek. Major-General Sosabowski was joined at 01:00, during or shortly after the end of his midnight conference, by Lieutenant David Storrs from the 1st Airborne Division's HQ Royal Engineers. Storrs had been supervising a party of Sappers from the 9th Field Company under a Lance-Sergeant Green attempting to convert Jeep trailers into rafts from 20:00 the previous evening.[1] It is unclear if Storrs swam the river or crossed in an inflatable reconnaissance boat, but he announced that one of the improvised rafts was 'almost completed' and reiterated the report delivered earlier by Captain Zwolanski that the British would launch a covering attack to secure a section of the north bank along with details of a proposed new crossing site east of the Heveadorp ferry terminal. Sosabowski therefore had his men in place at the proposed crossing site by 02:00 despite German artillery fire, and there the exhausted paratroopers settled down to wait. By 03:00, with no sign of the rafts or the covering attack, Sosabowski decided that there was 'no possibility of crossing at this night' and ordered a move back to Driel, which was completed by 05:30. Once there the largely intact 2nd Battalion formed an all-round defence perimeter while the badly understrength 3rd Battalion acted as a reserve, with two platoons deployed in outposts to the south and south-east.[2] Lieutenant Storrs returned to the north bank, accompanied by Captain Zwolanski and the Polish Brigade's British liaison officer, Lieutenant-Colonel George Stevens. Stevens arrived at the Hotel Hartenstein at 05:15 and after giving a situation report presented Major-General Urquhart with a gift:

> He [Stevens] had no news about XXX Corps' efforts to effect our relief, but he had considerably brought a copy of Thursday morning's *Times* which he pressed into my hand with due aplomb. 'You will find there are some references to the operation, sir,' he said...Not by what it said, but because it was in my hands, *The Times* lent a momentary and purely artificial security to our position; it represented our first link with the outside world.[3]

The morale boost generated by Lieutenant-Colonel Stevens' copy of *The Times* was reinforced an hour later at 06:17 and again at 07:40 by signals from 1st Airborne Corps HQ at Moor Park. The first informed Urquhart that the 43rd Division would be taking over from Guards Armoured Division at first light and would be advancing to the Oosterbeek [Heveadorp] ferry; the second reiterated the 43rd Division's line of advance, that it had been ordered to 'take all risks to effect relief today' and that 'if situation warrants you should withdraw to or cross the ferry'.[4] The latter caveat provides an early intimation that the commander of the 43rd Division, Major-General Ivor Thomas, had not properly grasped the rapidly deteriorating reality of the 1st Airborne

Division's plight; Urquhart expressed his suspicion that this was the case at the time, which was subsequently confirmed to be absolutely correct.[5]

Whilst Urquhart did not become aware of it for some hours, another link with the outside world occurred shortly thereafter, albeit on the other side of the Lower Rhine. During the night of 21-22 September Major-General Sosabowski ordered the commander of the 3rd Battalion's Reconnaissance Section, 2nd Lieutenant Jerzy Bereda-Fialkowski, to take a patrol south toward Nijmegen in an effort to make contact with the Allied troops that had crossed the River Waal in the evening of 20 September. After selecting three men and drawing additional ammunition and possibly commandeered bicycles, Lieutenant Bereda-Fialkowski led his little band out of the Driel perimeter through the hamlet of Honingsveld at 06:00 toward Elst, four miles or so to the south, using the pre-dawn gloom and early morning mist for cover. On reaching a point just north of Elst the patrol settled down for a time to observe. They estimated German strength in Elst at approximately fifty men, possibly buttressed with armoured vehicles; four German tanks were observed moving west from the northern outskirts of Elst and a pair of armoured cars moving north toward Driel. Bereda-Fialkowski then side-slipped toward Valburg, three miles to the west, where they found no sign of the German tanks or Allied troops but received the usual rapturous welcome from the locals. After enjoying the adulation for a while the patrol pushed on toward the village of Andelst, a further three miles to the west. It was at this point they were overtaken on the misty road by a quartet of British reconnaissance vehicles.[6]

The vehicles, two Daimler Dingo Scout Cars and two Daimler Armoured Cars, belonged to 5 Troop, C Squadron 2nd Household Cavalry Regiment commanded by Captain Lord Richard Wrottesley. An expedient unit formed by amalgamating personnel from the Life Guards and Royal Horse Guards initially dubbed the Household Cavalry Training Regiment, the unit was renamed the 2nd Household Cavalry Regiment and assigned to the Guards Armoured Division in September 1941 before being reassigned to the British 2nd Army as a Corps-level reconnaissance asset in July 1943. It served in that role with the British 8 and 30 Corps following the D-Day landings and, in a presumably coincidental hat tip to its origin, spearheaded the Guards Armoured Division's advance up the Airborne Corridor, making first contact with the US 101st and 82nd Airborne Divisions in the process. After reaching the 82nd Airborne Division's perimeter south of Nijmegen in the morning of 19 September, C Squadron spent two days escorting truck convoys moving materiel from a captured German supply depot at Oss, eighteen miles west of Nijmegen, before receiving fresh orders in the evening of Thursday 21 September. The Squadron was to scout ahead for an attack across the *Betuwe* scheduled to begin at 10:00 by the 43rd Division, which was to take over the lead for Operation GARDEN from the Guards Armoured Division, and specifically make contact with the Polish Parachute Brigade reportedly holding the crossing place at Driel.[7]

The task of establishing contact with the Polish paratroopers was assigned to Captain Wrottesley's 5 Troop, Lieutenant Arthur Young's 2 Troop and a third Troop commanded by a Lieutenant H. S. Hopkinson. As Elst on the main route between Nijmegen and Driel remained in German hands, the plan was to bypass the town to the west before looping north to Driel via the network of smaller roads. 5 Troop led the way across the Nijmegen road bridge at first light on Friday 22 September. Using the mist and early morning gloom for cover the little convoy passed through the Allied lines near the village of Oosterhout and followed the north bank of the River Waal before angling inland to pass through Valburg and westward toward Andelst where they overtook Lieutenant Bereda-Fialkowski's patrol; as the British vehicles had already encountered German troops on the road, the Polish paratroopers were perhaps lucky not have been shot up. After warning his British counterpart of the presence of German armour in the vicinity, Lieutenant Bereda-Fialkowski departed southward to reconnoitre the bank of the Waal; he and his patrol returned safely to the Driel that night.[8] Captain Wrottesley's vehicles angled north to Heteren and then east to the sector of the Driel perimeter held by the Poles' 4th Company, arriving at some point between 08:00 and 08:50; by that time Operation MARKET

GARDEN had been underway for approximately four days and eighteen hours.[9] Fortuitously, Sosabowski was with 4th Company, in the midst of ordering a redeployment of Lance-Sergeant Cadet Hrechorow's platoon from a bakery building to a position on a dyke, from where they could simultaneously control the road and overlook the riverbank. The armoured vehicles were then escorted to Sosabowski's HQ in the centre of the village, where Captain Wrottesley transmitted a situation report that included his route.[10] Although a radio link had finally been established between Sosabowski's HQ and the Hotel Hartenstein at 09:05, Urquhart does not appear to have become aware of the arrival of the 2nd Household Cavalry patrol until 11:20, and then via a signal from 2nd Army HQ via the PHANTOM net.[11]

Lieutenant Young and 2 Troop reached Driel around an hour after Captain Wrottesley. According to one source he was despatched following a summons from Wrottesley, but another gives the strong impression that all three Troops left the Nijmegen bridgehead either simultaneously or in succession; the hour gap suggests that Young may have been scouting an alternate route and homed in on Driel after receiving Wrottesley's situation report.[12] Whichever, Young reported passing knocked-out German tanks near Elst, presumably victims of the fighting with the 2nd Welsh Guards at Oosterhout in the early evening of Thursday 21 September.[13] The reconnaissance vehicles also picked up a number of aircrew who had force-landed south of the Lower Rhine, and machine-gunned a number of Germans spotted on the north bank of the river while travelling along the elevated riverside road near Heteren on the final stretch into Driel.[14] The good luck enjoyed by Wrottesley and Young did not extend to Lieutenant Hopkinson's Troop, bringing up the rear with C Squadron HQ in tow. The concealing mist lifted whilst the Troop was on the move and it immediately came under fire from German armoured vehicles, possibly the tanks spotted by Lieutenant Bereda-Fialkowski's patrol, or a rocket launcher of some description, depending on the account. The lead vehicle, a Daimler Dingo scout car, was hit by at least one round that killed the driver, Trooper Harold Read from the Life Guards, and set the vehicle ablaze. Lieutenant Hopkinson dismounted from his own vehicle and attempted to render assistance, but the intensity of the blaze drove him back and the surviving British vehicles were obliged to retire the way they had come, still under German fire. According to one account the retiring armoured cars forced the Jeep carrying Brigadier Hubert Essame, commanding 214 Infantry Brigade, off the embanked road paralleling the River Waal; their haste was presumably due to the fact that German guns located in nearby Oosterhout had a clear view of the road.[15] The indirect route to Driel was thus closed and unusable in broad daylight, although the success of Captain Wrottesley and Lieutenant Young showed it was possible at night or in reduced visibility.[16]

Welcome as the arrival of the 2nd Household Cavalry patrols at Driel was, they weren't going to shield the Polish Brigade from German attention. At 09:00 Sosabowski ordered Captain Siudzinski's Transport and Supply Company to gather in the unrecovered containers from the drop zone, in part because the commander of the Brigade's Engineer Company, Captain Piotr Budziszewski, reported that some of his containers contained USAAF rescue dinghies that he had obtained through unofficial channels. In addition, 2nd Lieutenant Arkady Bandzierz from the 4th Company was ordered to ascertain the contents of up to thirty containers spotted in the open fields to the west of Driel, drop shorts from the 1st Airborne Division's supply lifts. This attracted the attention of German observers on the north bank of the Lower Rhine, and Lieutenant Bandzierz was eventually compelled to abandon his mission after being repeatedly pinned down by very accurate mortar fire.[17] In the meantime Captain Siudzinski's men gathering in the Brigade's containers on DZ K also came under German attack, but in a more direct manner. Having played a major role in recapturing the Arnhem road bridge, *Kampfgruppe* Brinkmann had been ordered south by *II SS Panzerkorps* at midday on 21 September to help block the Allied incursion over the River Waal, along with *Kampfgruppe* Knaust; both units were intended to act as a collective local contingency reserve located in the vicinity of Elst. However, during the night of 21-22 *September II SS Panzerkorps* issued new orders for an attack upon the new parachute landing near Driel, a task that was in turn devolved to *Kampfgruppe* Brinkmann, in part as its armoured cars and half-tracks were less likely to damage the *Betuwe*'s fragile road network than *Kampfgruppe* Knaust's tanks.[18] The order was easier said than done and not just because of the poor going on the waterlogged polder that comprised much of the *Betuwe*. Brinkmann's vehicles had travelled to the area of Elst via the main Arnhem to Nijmegen road but moving on Driel involved crossing the embanked railway line paralleling the road to the west; the only crossing appears to have been in Elst proper and was thus unusable due to the proximity of British troops after the Guard's Armoured Division's abortive attempt to push on to Arnhem on Thursday 21 September. Passing even relatively light armoured cars and half-tracks over the embanked railway line presented a major challenge, overcoming which a German senior signals NCO from a unit stationed on the embankment considered an 'amazing achievement' in itself.[19] As a result of all this *Hauptsturmführer* Brinkmann was not able to begin his attack on Driel until 10:00 on Friday 22 September.[20]

The German approach was concealed by the river mist and the SS were thus able to close up unseen on Captain Siudzinski's recovery party, which had been augmented by a group from the Brigade Signals Company led by 2nd Lieutenant Zdzislaw Detko, complete with a captured German horse and cart. The recovery party were pinned down by a sudden deluge of German machine-gun fire, some seeking shelter in a convenient roadside ditch, but the mist proved to be a two-edged sword and many of the Polish paratroopers were able to use it as cover to regain the safety of the Driel perimeter. They included Private Piotr Wawiorko who braved the fire in order to free the terrified horse from its traces. Some of the paratroopers were so badly scattered by the German attack and the mist that they did not regain the Polish perimeter until the early afternoon.

The two 3rd Battalion platoon outposts were rolled up in a similar fashion to the recovery party. The outpost to the south-east of Driel commanded by 2nd Lieutenant Richard Tice, a US volunteer serving with the Polish Brigade, was overrun after the attackers infiltrated through an orchard at the rear of the farm, calling out in English to confuse the defenders. Tice was hit in the chest in the initial storm of automatic fire and died shortly afterward, and his men were obliged to withdraw under heavy fire from machine-guns and mortars. The other outpost to the south, commanded by 2nd Lieutenant Waclaw Urbanski, came under direct attack from six half-tracks advancing north from Elst; having nothing to counter such a threat the paratroopers promptly withdrew into the main Driel perimeter, which came under intense mortar bombardment as they arrived. The attacking vehicles closed to within a hundred yards of the 2nd Battalion's perimeter before being temporarily halted by a torrent of small-arms fire that hit a number of the dismounted SS. It was at this point that Sosabowski arrived on his commandeered lady's bicycle leading Lieutenant Young's Daimler Armoured Car, having persuaded the reluctant British officer that his primary mission of simply reporting via the radio would be somewhat impeded if the Germans overran the village. A few rounds from Young's 2-Pounder gun deterred the lightly armoured half-tracks from advancing further, and the attackers paused to take stock of the situation while continuing the mortar bombardment.[21]

Meanwhile Sosabowski had also been sending out patrols to ascertain the strength and dispositions of the enemy around Driel, possibly in line with requests from the 43rd Division relayed via the Household Cavalry patrols.[22] At 11:00 Lieutenant Albert Smaczny was ordered to take his forty-nine-strong 8th Company west to Heteren to ascertain if the village were held by the enemy, with the secondary mission of freeing a party of British prisoners reportedly held there. Thirty minutes later the parachute component of the Brigade Anti-tank Battery was sent off in the opposite direction to reconnoitre to the riverbank and establish German strength in the vicinity of Elden. Both patrols returned safely. Lieutenant Smaczny reported that there were no enemy forces in Heteren, where he and his men had received the usual rapturous reception from the local civilian population with the unusual twist of a mayoral speech and being presented with the ornate key to the town hall; the Dutch also informed Smaczny that

British prisoners were hidden in the town but were best left in concealment until after dark in order to avoid revealing the identity of those involved from German collaborators. The Anti-tank detachment returned with a captured German officer, an RAF NCO, two men from the 1ˢᵗ Airborne Division and confirmation that the area east of the Arnhem–Nijmegen railway embankment was 'strongly held by the enemy'.[23]

***

As we have seen the arrival of the Polish Brigade at Driel and the Allied capture of the Nijmegen bridges had shaped a major German reorganisation south of the Lower Rhine, and it also led to a re-appreciation of the effort against the 1ˢᵗ Airborne Division north of the river. *II SS Panzerkorps'* orders *to 9 SS Panzer Division* on 22 September instructed *Obersturmbannführer* Harzer to maintain the existing strategy of concentric attacks against the British in order to 'annihilate them as soon as possible'. *Sperrverband* Harzer was thus to 'operate offensively' from its blocking line in the *Betuwe* to prevent any link up between Allied forces advancing out of the Nijmegen bridgehead while the units investing the British perimeter at Oosterbeek were to intensify their efforts; it was considered 'particularly important that the remaining British forces north of the river Rhine are quickly destroyed, and the enemy bridgehead there cleared'.[24] Harzer therefore opted to modify the pattern that had developed piecemeal as the German forces had tightened their grip on the corralled 1ˢᵗ Airborne Division into a deliberate strategy of concentric attack all along the British perimeter, attacking during the hours of daylight with infantry, armour and artillery while pounding it with mortars and artillery fire during the hours of darkness.

Responsibility for attacking the western face of the British perimeter had been devolved from von Tettau to *Standartenführer* Michael Lippert, commanding *SS Unterführerschule* 'Arnheim'. Additional responsibility did not equate to additional reinforcement however, and Lippert was still principally reliant upon *SS Bataillonen* Eberwein and Schulz from his own unit, the *Luftwaffe Bataillon* Worrowski and the part-Dutch *SS Bataillon* Helle, supported by the remaining *Panzer B2 (f)* tanks from *Panzer Kompanie 224*. The axis of advance of attack was once again eastward along the Utrechtseweg toward the Koude Herberg crossroads, and then south-east through the wood toward the Lower Rhine. *Kampfgruppe* Bruhn remained responsible for the northern face while the four *SS kampfgruppen* formed from elements of *9 SS Panzer Division* continued to attack from the east. *Kampfgruppe* Harder was tasked to push along the riverbank to the municipal gasworks near the Heveadorp ferry terminal, and thus prise the British enclave away from the Lower Rhine; *Kampfgruppe* von Allwörden was to continue battling to penetrate the British line between the Oosterbeek Old Church and the Utrechtseweg–Stationsweg crossroads; *Kampfgruppe* Möller was to continue to press west along the Utrechtseweg; and *Kampfgruppe* Spindler to push against the British line along the Stationsweg between the Utrechtseweg–Stationsweg and the Stationsweg–Dennenkampweg–Cronjéweg crossroads.[25] Finally, the recently created *ArKo 191* was augmented with *SS Werfergruppe* Nickmann, consisting of two batteries of *Nebelwerfer* multi-barrel rocket launchers drawn from *SS Werfer Abteilung 102*, commanded by *Hauptsturmführer* Alfred Nickmann.[26] The weapons were noted for not only their fearsome explosive effect but also the psychological impact of their noise, which led to them being dubbed 'Moaning Minnies' by British troops; *Rottenführer* Wolfgang Dombrowski from *Kampfgruppe* Möller recalled British Airborne prisoners emerging from cellars 'with their nerves shot to pieces' by exposure to *Nebelwerfer* fire.[27]

The 1ˢᵗ Airborne Division was also reorganising as well as its increasingly meagre resources allowed. The rationalisation of the north-facing sector of the Division's perimeter, ordered by Major-General Urquhart in the evening of 21 September, was carried out in the period between the late evening of that day and the very early hours of Friday morning.[28] After some confusion over its precise destination, the 7ᵗʰ KOSB, which now had sole responsibility for the north-facing sector, began moving back to the shorter and more defensible line along the Ommershoflaan at 21:30. The other two units manning the sector did not move until the early hours of the following morning. Despite receiving orders reassigning it to the 4th Parachute Brigade at some point after 18:00 on 21 September, Major Bernard Wilson and the 21st Independent Company did not begin to withdraw from its Ommershof position until 01:00; the delay may have been due to Wilson's dissatisfaction at being ordered to abandon a position he considered to be 'indefinitely' defensible. Be that as it may, the move was not completed without incident. One man refused to leave the security of his slit trench until his Section sergeant 'persuaded' him at pistol point while Private Maurice May disappeared during the move, presumably becoming separated in the pitch darkness. The Company reached the vicinity of Hackett's HQ at 02:30, where they were permitted to rest before moving up to their new position on the eastern face of the perimeter at around 05:00.[29] The second unit was Captain Henry Brown and his approximately thirty-five-strong detachment from No. 3 Troop, 4th Parachute Squadron RE, which was destined to become the 4th Parachute Brigade's reserve. The initial order to withdraw to Division HQ at the Hotel Hartenstein was not relayed by the disgruntled Major Wilson until 01:30 and Brown was also initially reluctant to abandon his 'securely dug in' position, although he subsequently acknowledged the wisdom of the order.[30] After holding a hurried O Group and instructing Captain James Smith to oversee the burial of Captain Thomas and the other fatalities incurred in the Ommershof fighting, Brown made his way back to the Hotel Hartenstein accompanied by Lance-Corporal Dai Morris. There he was informed that his party was not to rejoin the rest of the 4th Parachute Squadron on the western face of the perimeter but was to remain under command of the Division CRE, Lieutenant-Colonel Edmund Myers, whilst being seconded to act as reserve for Brigadier Hackett. He was then directed to Hackett's HQ just east of the Hartenstein on the Pietersbergseweg from where he was led to a new location midway between the two HQs by Captain Reginald Temple, a former member of the Squadron serving with the 4th Parachute Brigade staff. The move was completed by 04:00 although the Sappers were advised not to dig in until dawn, when daylight would aid the selection of effective fire positions.[31]

The 7th KOSB was fully established in its new position on the line of the Ommershoflaan forming the northern face of the Oosterbeek perimeter by 01:00, with individual Companies responsible for maintaining contact with their neighbours and patrolling to keep their frontages clear. Strongpoints were established in houses supplemented with slit trenches where necessary, although with the Battalion's strength standing at around 150, some buildings could only be garrisoned by two men. After stand-to at 04:30 Lieutenant-Colonel Payton-Reid spent two hours inspecting the perimeter and ordering modifications where necessary; the most significant of these involved C Company despatching CanLoan Lieutenant James Taylor and 12 Platoon to occupy a narrow strip of woodland just to the Company's front. The positions then received a second inspection from Brigadier Hicks, who warned Colonel Payton-Reid that he might be facing a 'trying day' and informed him that 30 Corps might well be across the Lower Rhine during the night. In the event, Hicks' warning proved to be unfounded; 'Contrary to expectations this day passed off more quietly than we have become accustomed to.'[32] The quiet time was presumably due to a combination of the drubbing meted out to *Kampfgruppe* Bruhn on the Graaf van Rechterenweg and around the Hotel Dreyeroord/White House the previous day, and the resultant, understandable caution in closing up to the KOSB's new positions after the Battalion's surreptitious relocation. Artillery and mortar fire increased over the course of the day, however, as the Germans pinpointed the KOSB's new positions, and the tiled roofs of the British-occupied houses were targeted with 20mm fire, presumably from the light *flak* guns co-opted by *Kampfgruppe* Bruhn and employed with deadly effect on the Dreijensweg on 19 September. On this occasion the weapons were not judged especially effective despite their 'alarming noise' and the KOSBs assumed the fire was intended to curtail observation, but it might also have been intended to allow tracer rounds to set fire to exposed roof timbers or flammable material stored in attics and dormer rooms. The German fire prompted many inhabitants of the hitherto untouched suburb to abandon their homes, although contact with German ground troops did not occur until the late afternoon or early evening, when B and C Companies drove off what were likely reconnaissance probes. At 19:00 the Battalion began to shift to its night dispositions, which were intended to prevent enemy infiltration into the Battalion's thinly spread positions. Fighting patrols were despatched to roam the area outside the perimeter and pairs of men were posted in every house along the Ommershoflaan to act as sentries; the sentry posts were to be visited at regular intervals by internal patrols, which could be alerted to any enemy attempts to penetrate the perimeter.[33]

The 7th KOSB's night move allowed it to escape the resumption of the German mortaring and shelling around dawn, but the bombardment fell heavily on other units, those manning the perimeter and within it. At 07:30 the ill-starred 1st Airlanding Brigade HQ was struck again by a salvo of German fire which caused a number of casualties including the Brigade RASC Officer, Captain Leslie Lockyer, and Lieutenant Ralph Schwartz from the 2nd South Staffords, who was acting as Brigade GSO III; both officers were evacuated to the Hotel Schoonoord, where Captain Lockyer's left leg was amputated. It is unclear if Brigadier Hicks was present or visiting his units at the time, but the incident prompted a relocation of the HQ at 09:00 to a site in woods around 500 yards south of the Hotel Hartenstein, complete with a detachment of Glider Pilots and two 6-Pounder guns from the South Staffords for close protection; a platoon from the 9th Field Company RE that had been held at Brigade HQ for the latter purpose was released at the same time to rejoin its parent unit on the west side of the Division perimeter.[34] The German barrage on the 1st Border's positions on the south-west face of the perimeter recommenced at 05:45. The pounding from artillery, mortars and direct fire from self-propelled guns swiftly destroyed all the vehicles in the vicinity of Battalion HQ with the exception of two Jeeps and a motorcycle, and at 09:10 a direct hit set fire to the Battalion ammunition dump. A party of men led by Regimental Sergeant Major (RSM) Albert Pope and Company Sergeant Major (CSM) Leslie Fielding managed to save a quantity of small-arms ammunition and mortar bombs before the flames detonated a stock of explosives. The resultant explosion stripped leaves and branches from the surrounding trees and mortally wounded RSM Pope, who died after being removed to the Battalion RAP.[35] German mortars then used the residual burning and smoke as an aiming mark, 'so that any movement from slit trenches resulted in casualties'.[36]

The 1st Border's B Company had been virtually wiped out on the Westerbouwing Heights by *Bataillon* Worrowski in the morning of 21 September and as a result the Battalion's left flank was held by a handful of men scattered across three locations. These were an *ad hoc* group patrolling north of the Benedendorpsweg led by Major Richard Stewart from Support Company and two surviving elements from B Company, Lieutenant Arthur Royall's 12 Platoon and a composite platoon formed from survivors commanded by Lieutenant Stanley Barnes. The B Company men were located south of the road, with Barnes' party occupying the grounds of a large house called the *Dennenord* a few hundred yards east of the B Company's original position, and 12 Platoon was dug in just east of the municipal gasworks to block passage along the riverbank. At 12:00 the 1st Border's acting second-in-command, Major Charles Breese, was despatched to take command of the 1st Airlanding Brigade's left flank accompanied by two depleted platoons from A Company commanded by Lieutenant Robert Coulston and a Sergeant Davidson, along with a small group of B Company stragglers commanded by Lieutenant Patrick Stott. Breese was also allotted a party of thirty men detached from the 2nd South Staffords earlier that morning, commanded by CanLoan Lieutenant Arthur Godfrey; it is unclear if the party was originally intended to assist in protecting Division HQ, act as part of the Division reserve, or was intended to reinforce the 1st Border from the outset.[37]

The new grouping was dubbed BREESE Force in honour of its commander, and may not have initially included 12 Platoon. According to the 1st Border's semi-official history it took Lieutenant Royall some time to discover BREESE Force was occupying the woods north of the Benedendorpsweg and after doing so, he 'went across from time to time to exchange information'.[38] It is unclear if he realised it but Lieutenant Royall was also assisted by two more elements. The remnants of the 11th Parachute Battalion had been redeployed as a back-stop south of the Benedendorpsweg facing south-west toward the municipal gasworks at 11:00 on the orders of 1st Airlanding Brigade HQ, from where it beat off a number of German attacks from the area of the gasworks, despite the most intense enemy mortar fire the Battalion had yet experienced. A subsequent Airlanding Brigade order at 15:00 for Lieutenant James Blackwood and B Company to attack and clear a group of German-occupied farm buildings near the gasworks was countermanded by Major Breese when he learned of it. The attack was intended to be the first step in a BREESE Force effort to retake the Heveadorp ferry terminal to assist the ferrying of the 1st Polish Independent Parachute Brigade across the Lower Rhine, but was cancelled at 21:45 owing to difficulties registering the fall of shot for a covering artillery fire plan.[39] The second element was a party of anti-tank gunners from the 1st Independent Polish Parachute Brigade who had also been redeployed to cover the rear of the 1st Border's line with their two remaining 6-Pounder guns in the early morning of 22 September. One, located at the junction of the Benedendorpsweg and Kneppelhoutweg, was knocked out by a marauding *Sturmgeschütze* but the other spent the morning using high-explosive shells to keep the Germans from establishing machine-guns in a small copse overlooking the polder running down to the Lower Rhine. The gunners switched to armour-piercing rounds when the Germans turned their attention to a brick building near the municipal gasworks for the same purpose, and had virtually demolished it by the afternoon. The gun and surviving gunners were withdrawn to a position near the Oosterbeek Old Church at sundown.[40]

Fortunately, given its depleted nature, Major Breese's section of the 1st Border perimeter enjoyed a relatively peaceful Friday, in part due to the efforts of the 11th Parachute Battalion and the Polish anti-tank gunners and because *Bataillon* Worrowski was reorganising after its rough handling the previous day. This, however, was not the case along the rest of the 1st Border's frontage. Captain William Hodgson and D Company spent the entire day under mortar and shell fire. Lieutenant Alan Green was sharing a slit trench with Private Len Powell when a mortar bomb fell into the trench, striking Powell on the back of the leg before coming to rest without detonating; Powell gingerly lifted it from the floor of the trench and threw it clear. The bombardment was backed with continuous pressure against the Company's positions along the Van Borsselenweg, likely from SS *Bataillon* Schulz, which had almost surrounded D Company by 16:00 and reduced it to thirty-five men led by Captain Hodgson and a lightly wounded Lieutenant Green. The Battalion War Diary proudly noted, 'There was no withdrawal.' On the right at C Company's position around the Koude Herberg junction on the Utrechtseweg and A Company to its north also stood firm against SS *Bataillon* Eberwein and in some instances took the fight to enemy. Lieutenant Alan Roberts from C Company's 16 Platoon and Sergeant W. C. Thompson were notable in leading patrols into the surrounding woods, the former returning from one foray with two captured German machine-guns and a quantity of ammunition after his patrol had killed their former owners. A Lance-Corporal Cavaghan from the Signals Platoon also distinguished himself by laying a telephone line through enemy-occupied territory to Battalion HQ after the Company's radio link failed. The German attacks died away after 19:30, although harassing fire from mortars continued through the night; this was fortunate given that ammunition, along with food and other supplies, were described as 'non-existent' by this point.[41]

The situation was especially problematic for the 1st Border's Medical Officer, Captain John Graham-Jones, who was unable to evacuate his wounded to the Divisional Main Dressing Station (MDS) in Oosterbeek due to the German bombardment and had to deplete his meagre stock of medical supplies instead. This became an official arrangement after Colonel Graeme Warrack, the Divisional Assistant Director of Medical Services, informed Graham-Jones that there would be no further medical evacuations from the front line because the MDS was no longer able to provide better treatment than the RAPs and there were no longer any Jeeps available for casualty transport anyway.[42] There was no Friday supply drop, the reason for which is unclear. Seventy-three Stirlings and up to sixty-six Dakotas were fully loaded and ready to depart by midday, but take-off was cancelled for the day by Airborne Corps Rear HQ at 12:15, with the aircraft ordered to remain loaded and await further orders.[43] One source suggests the cancellation was based on the assumption that the arrival of the GARDEN ground force on the south bank of the Lower Rhine rendered it superfluous, although the hiatus may also have been connected to mounting RAF concern at the number of aircraft being lost on the resupply missions; to that end the commander of No. 46 Group, Air Commodore Lawrence Darvall, flew to Brussels on Friday 22 September in an unsuccessful attempt to have fighter aircraft drop supplies ferried in to Brussels by his Dakotas.[44]

In line with rest of the Airborne soldiers manning the Oosterbeek pocket the 1st Border's men were left reliant on whatever rations they had left or whatever food they could scavenge. Lieutenant Joseph Hardy from the Battalion Signals Platoon released his sole remaining carrier pigeon with a jocular message for 1st Airborne Corps Rear HQ to prevent it being killed and eaten; his ploy was successful as the pigeon survived to deliver its message to Moor Park where it became a 'nine days wonder'. A scrawny-looking chicken Hardy saw wandering by in search of food was not so lucky. The unfortunate fowl was swiftly despatched, gutted, plucked and deposited in a galvanised bath along with whatever scraps of ration-pack biscuits, bully beef, concentrated oatmeal and other food and water the troops involved could muster before being set to cook, garnished liberally with sand and grass thrown up by the bombardment. The garnish and ring of soap suds around the rim of the bath did not put off the hungry contributors, who considered the end result to be 'the epitome of home cooking'.[45]

Pressure was maintained along the northern sector of the western perimeter by the partly Dutch SS *Bataillon* Helle. E and F Squadrons from No.2 Wing, The Glider Pilot Regiment reported holding their positions despite constant and heavy mortar and artillery fire throughout the day, although 'Continual casualties caused…[the]…line to become dangerously thin.' E Squadron, on the 1st Border's right flank, was reinforced with a 6-Pounder anti-tank gun of unknown origin and Lieutenant-Colonel John Place relocated No.2 Wing HQ at 19:00 hours to a location on the Hartensteinlaan or Nassaulaan just north of the Hotel Hartenstein.[46] The relocation may have sparked an incident recalled by then thirteen-year-old Henke Capelle, who, it will be recalled, had been sheltering for several days with the rest of his family and the neighbouring Mager family in the cellar of his home, No. 35 Nassaulaan:

> One dark evening all the inhabitants of the houses at the end of our street were ordered by the Englishmen to leave their cellars and prepare to leave our fighting zone. There we stood in the middle of the street, I guess some twenty people with a few bags and cases, looking helplessly around – nobody knew in which direction to go. Suddenly a British officer turned up, 'What the hell are you people doing here?' 'We were told to assemble and leave, but have no idea where to go.' Our answer obviously amazed him. 'Back to your cellars on the double! Standing here is life-threatening, for you, too. There is absolutely no possibility for you to get out of here. We are all in this precarious foothold.' I now believe that it was just a rumour or misinterpretation that caused this episode.[47]

The unit on No. 2 Wing's right flank, Captain John Cormie's 4th Parachute Squadron RE, dug in near the Sonnenberg, was attacked by some of *Panzer Kompanie 224's* flame-throwing tanks at 09:10. Fortunately for the Sappers, the tanks were not adequately protected by *Bataillon* Helle and experienced some difficulty in identifying the British positions among the trees and undergrowth. One of the vehicles, likely *Kompanie* commander *Oberleutnant* Alfred May's personal Somua S35, ran over a daisy chain of twelve No. 75 Hawkins Anti-tank Grenades that were set off by Sapper William Coulsting. The resultant explosion killed some of the crew and the vehicle was totally destroyed when flames from the subsequent fire detonated its ammunition.[48] The attack was repulsed by 11:15 at a cost of five British casualties; another vehicle which was observed firing its flame gun on the Squadron frontage twenty minutes later was reportedly crippled by a PIAT. The Germans then fell back on pounding the British positions with artillery and mortars until launching an infantry attack at 16:10.[49] According to Lance-Corporal Maurice Weymouth and Sapper Arthur Ayers some of the attackers may have donned Denison smocks and maroon berets as a ruse to allow them to close on the British positions, although another eyewitness pointed out that SS camouflage smocks and helmet covers appeared very similar to British Airborne kit. Some recalled the Germans calling out claiming to be Poles.[50]

Be that as it may, the German attack was repelled by concentrated fire from six Bren guns, although one group of SS managed to outflank the Sappers' position by infiltrating through the woods south of the Sonnenberg and came within ten yards of the position occupied by Sappers Philip Hyatt and J. Bromilow before being spotted. Bromilow called a warning and threw a grenade, but the explosion drove some of the Germans forward rather than back. Hyatt left his slit trench to attack a German machine-gun team with a pistol and hand grenades, killing several and driving off the remainder. Hyatt then took possession of the abandoned weapon and dragged one of the enemy wounded to the relative safety of the British perimeter; the wounded prisoner died before he could receive treatment but Hyatt was subsequently awarded the Military Medal for his part in the episode.[51] Like their Glider Pilot neighbours, the 4th Parachute Squadron positions held firm until the German attacks died away with the onset of darkness. Although the Airborne soldiers had no way of knowing, they had also claimed a high-level SS scalp, albeit not actually on the battlefield. *Sturmbannführer* Paul Helle, the commander of *Bataillon* Helle, had begun a less than spectacular performance by narrowly escaping capture while sleeping in the *Zuid Ginkel* café during the fight against the 4th Parachute Brigade's drop onto DZ Y in the afternoon of 18 September, and matters did not improve thereafter; as *Standartenführer* Lippert noted at the time: 'Helle was not a field officer of any experience, and had little idea of his own situation, never mind that of the enemy.'[52] Helle's lack of competence was unsurprising given that SS *Wacht Bataillon 3* had been formed primarily to administer and guard the concentration camp system in Holland, but the losses sustained by his unit and probably more importantly by *Panzer Kompanie 224* led to Lippert relieving Helle of his command on 22 September. The decision was confirmed by Helle's superior, *Obergruppenführer und General der Polizei* Hanns Rauter, who also removed SS *Wacht Bataillon 3* from the Arnhem fighting; *Bataillon* Helle was disbanded and its surviving personnel were integrated into SS *Bataillon* Eberwein.[53]

Events followed a similar pattern on the east face of the Divisional perimeter. The German bombardment on LONSDALE Force's positions by the Oosterbeek Old Church resumed at 06:30, followed thirty minutes later by platoon-strength infantry attacks from *Kampfgruppe* Harder on the 1st and 3rd Parachute Battalions' positions. These attacks were repulsed without loss but both units were attacked again by infantry reportedly supported by two tanks, at 09:00 and 11:00 respectively. The armoured vehicles, probably StuGs from *Sturmgeschütze Brigade 280*, were driven back by anti-tank guns while the supporting infantry were repulsed with small-arms and accurate 3-inch mortar fire directed by Sergeant Harold Whittingham from the 1st Battalion's Mortar Platoon.[54]

The remnants of the 11th Parachute Battalion were pulled out of the line at 09:00 for a 'much needed rest, clean up and food' at the Oosterbeek Old Church. As we have seen, the rest lasted until 11:00, when 1st Airlanding Brigade HQ ordered the Battalion redeployed south of the Benedendorpsweg as a backstop to BREESE Force, facing south-west toward the municipal gasworks, where it spent the day rebuffing German infantry attacks from the vicinity of the municipal gasworks.[55] The 2nd South Staffords' position near the Laundry also came under mortar and artillery bombardment from early on, although this did not prevent Captain John Dickens gathering the party of thirty men under CanLoan Lieutenant Arthur Godfrey, also destined to be reinforcements for BREESE Force.[56] For his part, Major Cain again armed himself with a PIAT and resumed his tank stalking activities when the Germans turned their attention to the Laundry position and had another lucky escape whilst tackling what was reported as a Tiger tank but was again likely a *StuG*, as the only Tiger unit in the area had been despatched south to Elst. Whatever the target vehicle, on Cain's sixth shot the bomb detonated prematurely as it left the PIAT and the resultant explosion knocked him out and ruptured both his eardrums. On recovering consciousness he nonetheless insisted on returning to his command after basic first aid, with his sole concession to his damaged ears being to stuff them with strips torn from a field dressing.[57]

The 1st Airlanding Light Regiment continued to provide artillery support from its gun positions located just behind LONSDALE Force despite the German bombardment, although responsibility for 1 Battery's guns had to be divided up between 2 and 3 Batteries due to officer casualties. All twenty-one of the Regiment's guns remained in action and the link with 64th Medium Regiment remained extant. The guns were controlled by Major James Linton from 2 Battery and Captains John Lee and Raymond Stevens from 1 Battery and No. 1 Forward Observation Unit respectively. 2 Battery was menaced by a German armoured vehicle in the afternoon, but the threat was nullified by a tank-hunting party of Glider Pilots led by Major Robert Croot from G Squadron, which reportedly destroyed one vehicle.

Not all the RA casualties occurred at the Light Regiment position. Major Arthur Norman-Walker was present at the 1st Airlanding Brigade HQ in the late afternoon, although it is unclear in precisely what capacity: the Brigade HQ War Diary refers to him commanding 1 Battery as the Brigade's dedicated battery, while the Light Regiment records refer to him commanding 3 Battery at this point. Major Norman-Walker was killed at around 17:00 during a particularly fierce bout of German mortar fire, ironically just as the Brigade HQ's new command post with overhead protection was being completed. He was replaced by Captain Basil Taylor from 2 Battery and Captain Christopher McMillen from No. 1 Forward Observation Unit, McMillen carrying a radio set.[58]

To the north of LONSDALE Force Major Wilson and his 160 men from the 21st Independent Company moved up to the perimeter from their rest position near 4th Parachute Brigade HQ at 05:00. No. 1 Platoon took up position on the west side of the Stationsweg north of the junction with the Utrechtseweg opposite the overspill MDS in the Hotel Vreewijk. The buildings entered included No. 8 belonging to a Mr and Mrs Kremer, who had a twelve-year-old daughter, Ans, and an eleven-year-old son, Sander. Mrs Kremer prevailed upon a group of her liberators to pose for a photograph with her house guestbook; the group included Sergeants Norman Binnick and Benjamin Swallow, a Corporal Jeffries, Corporal Hans Rosenfeld, Lance-Corporal James Cameron and Privates Frank McCausland and H. Mitchell from 1 Platoon and Captain Stanley Cairns from D Squadron GPR, with another unidentified Glider Pilot.[59] No. 3 Platoon occupied houses to the south along the Pietersbergseweg opposite the main MDS location in the Hotel Schoonoord, and No. 2 Platoon along the northern stretch of the adjacent Paasbergweg, with Major Wilson establishing his HQ in a house at the junction between them.[60] The Pathfinders' right flank was held by 250 (Airborne) Light Composite Company RASC's two parachute platoons commanded by Captain John Cranmer-Byng, which had been seconded to Hackett by HQ RASC at 03:00, presumably because the paucity of supplies rendered their primary role superfluous. The remainder of the RASC Company relocated to 1st Airlanding Brigade HQ to act as a reserve for Cranmer-Byng's detachment.[61] The left flank was held by 156 Parachute Battalion reinforced with fifteen Glider Pilots from D Squadron totalling around a hundred men, ensconced in the substantial houses along the west side of the Stationsweg, and to their left the 1st Airborne Reconnaissance Squadron occupied the very north-eastern tip of the perimeter.[62] With the exception of the constant German mortar and artillery fire the latter appears to have had a relatively restful Friday.

Major Wilson and the Independent Company were also left largely unmolested apart from mortar fire, possibly because *Hauptsturmführer* Möller's men were unsure of their exact positions, and the Pathfinders spent the relative respite digging trenches in the gardens and preparing the buildings for defence by bolting doors and window shutters, smashing the glass from front windows and removing roof tiles to create loop holes for observation and sniping.[63] Brigadier Hackett spent the morning moving between his units although his recollections are somewhat at odds with at least some of those he visited. According to Hackett's account in the 4th Parachute Brigade War Diary '…attacks on 10 Bn and 156 were almost constant during this day 22 Sep and use of SP guns got bolder during the day'; the 156 Parachute Battalion's War Diary however referred to the day being '…fairly quiet with steady sniping and mortaring and occasional attacks from an SP gun'. Be that as it may, Hackett also found the positions occupied by Captain Cranmer-Byng 'rather far back' for his liking and he therefore ordered the RASC contingent to move further forward, presumably to the east side of the Pietersbergseweg.[64] The source is unclear but at some point early in the morning Hackett learned that Captain Barron and the survivors of the 10th Parachute Battalion were occupying buildings east of the MDS location on the Stationsweg–Utrechtseweg crossroads, although it is unclear whether they were located north or south of the Utrechtseweg. Hackett therefore ordered contact with the 10th Parachute Battalion to be restored along with links to 156 Parachute Battalion, and also appears to have instructed Major Wilson to push his section of the line eastward across the Stationsweg and Pietersbergseweg to make link up with the 10th Battalion party. Wilson does not appear to have been overly impressed with this idea, given that he made no effort to implement Hackett's orders until the late afternoon. At 16:00 Nos. 2 and 3 Platoons despatched patrols eastward across the Pietersbergseweg but their progress was blocked by intense machine-gun fire from German strongpoints located around 400 yards from the British perimeter. One of the first casualties was Bren gunner Private James Fiely from No. 2 Platoon who 'went down with his head blown off by a Spandau' on turning a corner, according to his assistant gunner Private Thomas Scullion. Two more Pathfinders were wounded in the exchange, after which both patrols returned to their starting positions.[65] The 10th Battalion party was successfully relieved by the Pathfinder's No. 3 Platoon in the early hours of Saturday 23 September on Hackett's explicit orders, and in spite of Major Wilson's objections that the position was too isolated.[66]

Hackett was also concerned with protecting the MDS at the Hotels Schoonoord and Vreewijk and thus called in to see Lieutenant-Colonel Marrable at the former during the morning of Friday 22 September. At some point later in the day a *StuG* drew up outside the Hotel Schoonoord and a German officer informed Marrable that the German forces would open fire on the MDS if it were not evacuated forthwith. On hearing of this Hackett relayed the ultimatum to Urquhart, apparently in person; Urquhart reportedly decided that it 'appeared unjustified to evacuate' the MDS at that time.[67] Harsh as it sounds, Urquhart's response was merely acknowledging the simple fact was that there was no suitable alternative location within the 1st Airborne Division perimeter, and almost certainly insufficient manpower or vehicles to carry out the task even if there had been. Hackett relayed Urquhart's decision to Marrable, likely in the aftermath of the 21st Independent Company's abortive attack at 16:00. His arrival at the Hotel Schoonoord, which came amid premature celebrations over mistaken Dutch Underground reports that Allied tanks had entered Arnhem, was witnessed by Captain Stuart Mawson: 'The excitement was still at its height when, almost unnoticed, a small man, with a grey, dusty face, in full, begrimed battle order, and a Sten gun slung over his shoulder, came in through the front door straight in to the hall.' Hackett took Marrable aside into an unoccupied operating room and according to Marrable's subsequent briefing to his own officers, tersely informed him that no Allied tanks were anywhere near Arnhem, any approaching tanks would therefore be German and that the MDS was about to be caught up in an inch-by-inch fight to maintain a foothold north of the Lower Rhine. He also appears to have recommended that all arms in the hotel be collected and placed under guard in an adjacent garage order to comply with the Geneva Convention. This may just have been an initiative by Marrable to deal with the increasing stockpile of weapons being brought into the MDS by or with casualties.[68]

With the remains of his Division compressed into the Oosterbeek perimeter, Major-General Urquhart occupied himself with attempting to marshal reinforcements from Sosabowski's

Brigade and ensuring that the higher command echelons were aware of the urgency of the situation in Oosterbeek. He despatched his Operations Officer, Lieutenant-Colonel Charles Mackenzie, across the Lower Rhine to impress this on Browning and Horrocks in person, and to survey the south bank of the river for crossing points suitable for use by DUKWs and other transport; the Division CRE Lieutenant-Colonel Edmund Myers was to accompany Mackenzie. The framing of Mackenzie's mission shows Urquhart was not convinced that his superiors had properly grasped the gravity of the 1st Airborne's situation, doubtless prompted by the exchange of signals with 1st Airborne Corps HQ earlier that morning. This is clear from his parting comment to Mackenzie: 'Above all, do try and make them realize over there what a fix we're in.'[69] The despatch of such senior officers via an extremely risky daylight crossing of the Lower Rhine reinforced the point. The two officers left the Hotel Hartenstein at 12:10 and crossed the river using one of a handful of serviceable inflatable rubber dinghies, dubbed reconnaissance boats, which Myers had fortuitously hidden near the Oosterbeek Old Church; according to one source they were escorted to the departure point by an unnamed 'large sergeant-major' armed with a Bren gun.[70] The crossing, with Mackenzie paddling, was uneventful apart from some inaccurate German machine-gun fire and complete by around 13:00. Mackenzie then had to identify himself to an apparently hesitant reception committee consisting of one of Sosabowski's officers and an unidentified British liaison officer, presumably Lieutenant-Colonel George Stevens, by walking towards them waving a handkerchief.[71] The four men then travelled to Sosabowski's HQ in Driel on commandeered bicycles, arriving at some point before 13:50, given that the Poles radioed news of their arrival at that time.[72] Lieutenant-Colonel Mackenzie was slightly put out by the Poles' preoccupation with their fight around Driel rather than attending to their guests and their mission. Sosabowski's chief of staff, Major Ryszard Malaszkiewicz, was shocked 'by the sight of the British officers. Their uniforms were filthy, and their faces were haggard and unshaven. Even more shocking was the fact that divisional staff officers, rather than junior officers had crossed the river as messengers. All of this underlined the straits in which the 1st Airborne Division found itself.'[73] Mackenzie lost no time emphasising the 1st Airborne's desperate need for reinforcement to Sosabowski while discussing arrangements for ferrying the Poles across the river that night; Sosabowski responded with a few questions regarding the means before summoning the commander of his Engineer Company, Captain Piotr Budziszewski, to discuss the technical details with Myers. Mackenzie then approached Captain Wrottesley seeking a lift to Nijmegen and on learning this was impossible because the Germans had cut the road, used an armoured car radio to contact 30 Corps HQ and, via onward transmission, Browning's Forward Corps HQ. Transmitting in clear, presumably for effect, Mackenzie explained the 1st Airborne's desperate need of ammunition, rations and medical supplies in front of an increasingly stunned Wrottesley, and rounded things off by bluntly stating that the Division would be unable to hold out for more than twenty-four hours without resupply and reinforcement.[74] The message appears to have been received in person by Lieutenant-General Horrocks, who assured Mackenzie that 'Everything will be done to get the essentials through.'[75]

With the way south still blocked by the Germans, Mackenzie was unable to proceed to Nijmegen as planned. He was thus obliged to spend the remainder of the day kicking his heels in Driel while Lieutenant-Colonel Myers assisted Captain Budziszewski and the Polish Brigade's Engineer Company in surveying the riverbank and 'trying to acquire boats and improvise rafts' for the coming night's river crossing.[76] Nor was the Driel perimeter an especially secure location, for the German attacks from the direction of Elst continued through the day. At 14:00 a German attack supported by half-tracks closed to within 250 yards of the Polish 6th Company's positions before being driven back by the Polish cross-fire, although one of the 2nd Household Cavalry's Daimler Armoured Cars was obliged to withdraw in turn by the volume of German return fire when it ventured forth to assist the paratroopers. After a brief truce to collect their wounded the SS renewed the assault, this time with the assistance of what was reported as a tank but which may have been one of *SS Panzer Aufklärungs Abteilung 10*'s French *Panzerspähwagen P204 (f)* armoured cars. Whatever it was, the Polish paratroopers responded by firing their PIAT anti-tank launchers at high elevation to maximise the weapon's range, a desperate ploy that succeeded, as a lucky near miss prompted the mystery vehicle to withdraw back into the orchard from which it had emerged. By 18:00 *Kampfgruppe* Brinkmann appears to have had enough and withdrew toward Elst under cover of an hour-long barrage from mortars, artillery and *nebelwerfer* rocket launchers, at least some of the rocket launchers located on the north bank of the Lower Rhine.[77] The day's fighting on the Driel perimeter cost the Poles seven dead, including 2nd Lieutenant Tice, Lieutenant Stanislaw Slesicki and Sergeant Antoni Salwuk.[78]

Major-General Sosabowski was continuing to make arrangements for the coming night's crossing of the Lower Rhine. Captain Budziszewski estimated it would be possible to pass up to 200 men across the river during the hours of darkness, using the three aircraft emergency rubber dinghies recovered from the landing area and at least three more inflatable reconnaissance boats provided by the 9th Field Company RE. Equipment was to be moved on rafts fabricated from barn and house doors by a party under Sergeant Wojciech Juhas; it is unclear what became of the British attempt to fabricate rafts from Jeep trailers. Enemy action aside, the most serious threat to these flimsy craft was the Lower Rhine's rapid current, which the Polish engineers measured to be flowing at a rate of almost one and a half metres per second. Sosabowski informed Urquhart of the arrangements via a radio-telephone exchange at 15:50, presumably via the link established between the Polish HQ and the Hartenstein that morning.[79] He also decided to put his badly depleted 3rd Battalion across first, with Lieutenant Smaczny's forty-nine-strong 8th Company in the lead. Smaczny, who had barely finished digging a slit trench after his patrol to Heteren, was therefore summoned to Sosabowski's farmhouse HQ where he was briefed on the location of the crossing and ordered to move up to the riverbank at dusk to keep watch for British-manned craft. Somewhat unsettlingly, Sosabowski ended the briefing by staring intently at Smaczny for several seconds before shaking his hand.[80] Smaczny and his men moved up to the dyke overlooking the crossing point at some point after 21:00.[81]

More substantial reinforcement was heading for the Polish lodgement at Driel. As we have seen, the 2nd Household Cavalry's task was to scout ahead of a planned attack out of the Nijmegen bridgehead by the 43rd Division. It is unclear if Sosabowski was aware of this, although he may have been informed by Captain Wrottesley, but the 1st Airborne Division was informed of developments over the course of Friday morning via a series of radio signals. The source of the first, received at 03:20, is unknown but warned that the 43rd Division would be coming up on the frequency used by 1st Airborne Corps HQ at Moor Park and provided the required call signs.[82] As we have seen, this was followed by two messages on that frequency received at 06:17 and 07:40 that informed Urquhart that the 43rd Division would be taking over from Guards Armoured Division at first light, aiming at the Oosterbeek ferry, and that the 1st Airborne Division was to be ready to 'withdraw to or cross the ferry' if necessary.[83] A third message, received at 11:20, came from British 2nd Army HQ via the PHANTOM net and informed Urquhart that the 43rd Division had been ordered to launch a two-pronged attack at 10:00 employing 129 and 214 Infantry Brigades, and that a patrol from the 2nd Household Cavalry had made contact with the Poles at Driel.[84] It was this signal that appears to have prompted Urquhart to despatch Lieutenant-Colonels Mackenzie and Myers across the Lower Rhine tasked to impress the gravity of the 1st Airborne Division's situation upon 30 Corps.

***

The 43rd Division had been moving up the Airborne Corridor in the wake of the Guards Armoured Division since the early morning of Wednesday 20 September, after being ordered up to Nijmegen by 30 Corps HQ as per the original GARDEN plan. The Division's lead formation, 130 Infantry Brigade, crossed Joe's Bridge across the Meuse-Escaut Canal near Neerpelt at 14:45, passed through Eindhoven between 16:35 and 17:25 before halting for the night just south of Grave at 23:00, in part because the Division column had become 'very spread out'. A fifty-mile road march that terminated eight miles short of Nijmegen and south of the River Maas had thus taken 130 Brigade around nine hours, and the Division's other formations took similar amounts of time to road march relatively short distances. 214 Infantry Brigade took the six hours between 18:00 and 23:59 to cover the twenty-five miles between Hechtel and Eindhoven for example, while 129 Infantry Brigade did not even reach Joe's Bridge until 01:35 on Thursday 21 September, after which it took just under fifteen hours to cover the thirty-two miles to Veghel, arriving at 15:55.[85] This tardiness does not appear to have been due to enemy action, for although German activity did interfere with traffic in the Corridor from first light to between 10:00 and 11:00 on 20 September, this was cleared before the 43rd Division's units were on the move, and Guards Armoured Division HQ reported that overall traffic was not delayed by enemy action during that day. In part the delay arose from some of the 43rd Division's leading elements being sequestered by 30 Corps. The 43rd Reconnaissance Regiment was commandeered for around thirty hours for flank protection duty before reaching Eindhoven for example, while on arrival at Nijmegen 130 Infantry Brigade had two battalions detached to assist the Guards Armoured Division in clearing the city.[86]

Nonetheless, Major-General Thomas' formation ought to have been able to cover the ground between Neerpelt and Nijmegen faster than it did. The 30 Corps' injunction forbidding movement on the main axis of advance during the hours of darkness had been lifted on 19 September and the 43rd Division was also given special priority on the route, with a heavy anti-aircraft unit destined for Eindhoven and the 1st Airborne Division's seaborne tail being frozen in place to allow the Division to pass.[87] The reason for the unhurried rate of progress may therefore have lain with the 43rd Division's commander himself. Commissioned into the Royal Artillery in 1912, Major-General Gwilym Ivor Thomas was awarded the Military Cross and Bar and the Distinguished Service Order whilst serving on the Western Front during the First World War. After attending both the Army and Royal Navy Staff Colleges in the interwar period, he served at the War Office as Deputy Director for Recruiting and Organisation and then Director of Organisation before assuming command of the 43rd Division in March 1942. Thomas was selected for the command on his reputation as a 'pusher', presumably based on his posts at the War Office and brief artillery appointments at brigade, division, and corps level between 1939 and 1942, a view supported by the 43rd Division's assault crossing of the River Seine on the night of 25-26 August 1944. However, an eyewitness who accompanied 30 Corps in the advance across Europe observed Thomas at work and described him as by nature 'cautious and methodical and his troops followed his example',[88] the very characteristics that appear to have held back the Division's progress to Nijmegen. In addition, Thomas was also reportedly difficult to work with on account of his cold and acerbic character, a trait that was to become increasingly apparent beginning with his peremptory and unrealistic instruction to the 1st Airborne Division to be prepared to withdraw over the Heveadorp ferry in the early morning of Friday 22 September.[89] In this specific instance the methodical approach of the 43rd Division unnecessarily added another twenty-four-hour delay to the Division's pre-planned assumption of the lead in the advance to Arnhem, and provided yet another example of the overall lack of urgency that had been the leitmotif of MARKET GARDEN from the outset.

The 43rd Division's Tactical HQ passed through 130 Infantry Brigade in the vicinity of Uden, approximately seventeen miles south-west of Nijmegen, at 03:45 on 21 September and presumably arrived in the area of the city with or before that formation at some point before 08:30; the remainder of Division HQ arrived at 20:30.[90] The Division was thus in place to receive orders for the following day from 30 Corps, instructions to secure the Arnhem road and 'with maximum speed to contact 1 Airborne Div area Oosterbeek ferry...subsequently passing one brigade group over Nederrijn'.[91] Major-General Thomas responded by issuing his own orders at 22:30 on 21 September for an advance north out of the Nijmegen bridgehead the following day, employing two brigades. On the left, Brigadier Hubert Essame's 214 Infantry Brigade, reinforced with Sherman tanks from the 4th/7th Dragoon Guards, a Troop of self-propelled 17-Pounder anti-tank guns commanded by a Lieutenant Bellamy and support from a Troop of self-propelled 25-Pounder guns and a Royal Artillery Field Regiment, was to cross the River Waal at 07:00 via the Nijmegen railway bridge and angle north-west to Driel. On the right, Brigadier Gerard Mole's 129 Infantry Brigade, reinforced with three Squadrons of Sherman tanks from the 13th/18th Hussars, was to cross the River Waal via the Nijmegen road bridge no earlier than 10:00 and advance up the Nijmegen–Arnhem road to secure the Arnhem road bridge.[92]

129 Brigade's advance to Nijmegen does not appear to have been prosecuted with the urgency the orders suggested or the situation required. The methodical approach march mandated by 43rd Division HQ meant the Brigade took over thirty hours to cover the sixty-odd miles from Neerpelt and as a result did not reach Nijmegen until 11:00 on 22 September.[93] While the remainder of the Brigade stayed south of the River Waal, Lieutenant-Colonel E. L. Luce's 4th Wiltshires and tanks from 13th/18th Hussars crossed the river at some point after midday and advanced straight up the west side of the Nijmegen–Arnhem railway line toward the station at Ressen, with Major A. D. Parsons' A Company in the lead. The railway line ran through an area of close country and orchards incised by five-foot-wide drainage ditches, where *10 SS Panzer Division* had established its defensive line the previous day, and Major Parson's men became embroiled in a vicious, small-unit infantry battle at close quarters, with armoured support largely precluded by the ditches and the SS stubbornly contesting every inch of ground. Lieutenant-Colonel Luce tried to outflank the SS positions by pushing his B and C Companies forward but they too were pulled up by heavy German fire, as was an attempt to push tanks along the main road running parallel to the railway line at last light. British infantry losses were heavy, along with up to four Shermans from the 13th/18th Hussars and two more from the 2nd Irish Guards. The 5th Wiltshires crossed the Waal in the evening and expanded the attack frontage by pushing up the east side of the railway line, but when the fighting ceased for the night at around 22:00, the British advance remained 400 yards short of Ressen station and with barely fifty yards separating the British and German front lines.[94]

Brigadier Essame's 214 Infantry Brigade enjoyed a more rapid approach march to Nijmegen, although events outwith its control conspired to nullify the time saved. Moving off from Hechtel in Belgium at 18:00 on Wednesday 20 September, the Brigade passed through Eindhoven at midnight on 20 September to reach Uden, midway between Veghel and Grave at 09:45 the following morning; lead elements reached a harbour area west of Nijmegen at 11:30 on Thursday 21 September, a journey time of seventeen-and-a-half hours to cover around seventy miles.[95] The Brigade was then briefed by Major-General Thomas in person, who reportedly stressed the need for the utmost speed and ordered a battalion group pushed across the River Waal at 14:00. At this point things began to go awry. The Brigade's lead unit, Lieutenant-Colonel H. A. Borradaile's 7th Somerset Light Infantry was unable to access the Nijmegen railway bridge before 15:00 because strengthening work was being carried out, and the structure was not cleared to support tanks until 16:15. For some reason part of the Battalion's A Echelon crossed the Waal via the road bridge, but when the bulk of the Battalion finally moved off at 15:30 for a concentration area near the south end of the Nijmegen railway bridge, it became entangled with elements of the Guards Armoured Division and the ever-present crowds of celebrating Dutch civilians in the outskirts of the city. As a result, the 7th Somersets did not reach the concentration area until 19:30, and only then because Colonel Borradaile ordered his Battalion to temporarily abandon its vehicles and move on foot. The Brigade move across the Waal was thus postponed until the following morning as darkness overtook events.[96]

In the meantime Brigadier Essame had gone forward over the Waal to reconnoitre the ground and discuss matters with his opposite number from 5 Guards Armoured Brigade, Brigadier Norman Gwatkin. The latter identified the village of Oosterhout as the western pivot of the German defensive line and therefore the key to breaking through to Driel; the newly arrived 1ˢᵗ Battalion Welsh Guards had put in an attack on the village between 17:00 and dusk on Thursday 21 September that reportedly knocked out three German tanks before being called off with the onset of darkness. Essame appears to have intended to move his lead battalion across the Waal during the night in readiness for a first-light attack to take advantage of the early morning river mist, and remained north of the river for the night in anticipation. He was therefore not best pleased at the 7ᵗʰ Somerset Light Infantry's failure to cross the River Waal as ordered on 21 September and greeted Lieutenant-Colonel Borradaile with a terse 'Where the hell have you been?' when the Battalion finally crossed the Nijmegen railway bridge at 07:00 on Friday 22 September.[97] The 7ᵗʰ Somerset Light Infantry's D Company, commanded by Major Sidney Young, was tasked to carry out a hasty attack on Oosterhout at around 10:00. Major Young was badly wounded whilst carrying out his pre-attack reconnaissance. The attack then ran into stiff resistance from SS infantry supported by at least one tank, and an attempt to outflank the village from the east by another company was also rebuffed. A deliberate battalion attack was then organised, preceded by a forty-minute barrage employing brigade-, division- and corps-level artillery carried out despite an 'alarming shortage of artillery ammunition'. The 7ᵗʰ Somerset Light Infantry's A and B Companies went in at 15:20 supported by a troop of Sherman tanks from A Squadron, 4ᵗʰ/7ᵗʰ Dragoon Guards and Oosterhout was cleared and secured in 100 minutes of fighting. Two German tanks were knocked out, a third captured intact along with an 88mm gun, and 139 'sullen' SS troops taken prisoner. British casualties for the day numbered nineteen wounded including Major Young, who died of his wounds two days later.[98]

While Oosterhout was being cleared and secured the remainder of 214 Infantry Brigade, the 1ˢᵗ Battalion The Worcester Regiment and the 5ᵗʰ Duke of Cornwall's Light Infantry (DCLI), remained at their concentration area awaiting the order to move; the DCLI was tasked to move through the 7ᵗʰ Somersets and on to Driel once Oosterhout was secured, while the Worcesters were to protect the left flank of the advance by securing Valburg, just over two miles west of Elst. The enforced inactivity for the better part of two days frustrated many. Lieutenant-Colonel George Taylor, commanding the 5ᵗʰ DCLI, was acutely aware that Operation GARDEN was around seventy-two hours behind schedule at this point, and he was unable to see 'what was holding everything up'. His anxiety was assuaged to some extent by the arrival of a staff Major from 30 Corps HQ at around midday on Friday 22 September. The staff officer informed Taylor that his Battalion column was to be joined shortly by two DUKW amphibious trucks loaded with supplies for the 1ˢᵗ Airborne Division. He explained the gravity of the Airborne formation's situation and stressed that the DUKWs were to be despatched across the Lower Rhine immediately on arrival at Driel.[99] The idea of using DUKWs actually appears to have originated with Taylor, who suggested it when Lieutenant-General Horrocks invited suggestions whilst visiting 214 Brigade's concentration area the previous day, although Horrocks' response at the time gave the impression he had dismissed the idea out of hand. The two heavily laden DUKWs arrived as promised at 15:00 but Taylor expressed doubts as to whether the two loads were sufficient to his Intelligence Officer, Lieutenant David Willcocks.[100]

The 5ᵗʰ DCLI crossed the River Waal while the 7ᵗʰ Somersets were still fighting in Oosterhout, which was cleared less than two hours before sunset; the western edge of the village was actually secured by B company 5ᵗʰ DCLI as a forming-up point for the Battalion's advance to Driel. On past GARDEN precedent the approach of darkness ought to have signalled a cessation of operations until the following day, but not in this instance. It is unclear whether it was a brigade-, division- or corps-level initiative or even a unilateral battalion-level decision, but what came next provides an example of the flexibility, lateral thinking and improvisation which had been conspicuously absent from the ground advance up the Airborne Corridor to date. Despite the fading daylight Lieutenant-Colonel Taylor scrapped his existing plan for the advance to Driel to take advantage of the fleeting gap in the German defences created by the fall of Oosterhout, and rejigged his Battalion for a rapid advance via the route followed by the 2ⁿᵈ Household Cavalry Regiment's armoured cars that morning. The 5ᵗʰ DCLI was hurriedly divided in two. An armoured column consisting of Colonel Taylor's command group, A and D Companies commanded by Majors Parker and John Fry and a Medium Machine Gun platoon was formed. It used the Battalion's integral armoured troop carriers and the Sherman tanks of Major Richards' B Squadron, 4th/7th Dragoon Guards as troop transports. The remainder, Major Hingston's B Company and Major Arthur Kitchen's C Company, were to follow on in a second column, moving largely on foot with the Battalion's support personnel and unarmoured wheeled transport.[101]

The impromptu reorganisation took time and the armoured column did not move off into the gathering dusk until some point after 19:00. They went despite Lieutenant-Colonel Taylor spotting two Tiger tanks to the north of Oosterhout shortly beforehand. The risk was considered worth taking as the Battalion route ran west from the village but was courageous nonetheless, especially given the near-mythical status accorded to the Tiger tank by Allied forces at that time; Colonel Taylor instructed Lieutenant Willcocks, who also saw the enemy vehicles, to withhold the information to safeguard morale. Taylor later justified his decision on the grounds that delay would have squandered the window of opportunity created by the capture of Oosterhout: 'If we had waited five minutes more...I knew the road would have been closed again.'[102] Moving with all available speed the armoured portion of the column moved west along the north bank of the River Waal to Slijk-Ewijk, then north-west to Valburg where the column had to contend with crowds of enthusiastic Dutch civilians, primed by the earlier passage of Lieutenant Bereda-Fialkowski's bicycle patrol and the 2nd Household Cavalry's armoured cars. From there the column veered north directly to Driel and the 5th DCLI's vanguard reached the southern outskirts of the village at around 20:00, having covered around ten miles in approximately thirty minutes.[103] This puts the time taken for the relatively benign road march to Nijmegen into perspective. What could have been achieved had the Guards Armoured Division displayed a similar degree of urgency and flexibility upon securing the Nijmegen road bridge in the evening of 20 September, or if the formation had displayed more application in its eventual attack toward Bemmel in the afternoon of 21 September?[104]

The 5th DCLI's run into Driel was undoubtedly rapid, and especially so in comparison with the GARDEN advance to that point, but it did not run totally smoothly and involved two serious incidents, the first of which would be classed as a Blue-on-Blue today. The approach of the British armoured column was heard by the Polish paratroopers in Driel, first by a patrol from the 2nd Battalion probing south along the Dorpstraat in search of *Kampfgruppe Brinkmann*, and then by the men of the 4th Company dug in covering the southern sector of the Polish Brigade's perimeter. Sergeant Michal Iwaskow was concerned that a renewed German attack employing heavier armour would overwhelm the lightly armed paratroopers, as their organic anti-tank guns were north of the Lower Rhine.[105] Lieutenant Young was therefore prevailed upon to investigate with his armoured vehicles, accompanied by Sergeant Iwaskow and Lieutenant Lukjan Zuchowski, second-in-command of the 5th Company. Recognising the distinctive silhouette of a Sherman tank Young quickly ordered his vehicles to ignite yellow smoke grenades, the standard friendly recognition sign, while the paratroopers deployed their cerise Day-Glo recognition panels. It was at this critical juncture that the lead Sherman, commanded by a Corporal Reboulf, ran over an anti-tank mine laid earlier by the paratroopers, as did the following tank. Reboulf's crew, having spotted Young's armoured vehicles, reacted swiftly to the perceived attack with two armour-piercing rounds. The first grazed the left side of Lieutenant Young's Daimler Armoured Car, tearing off the mudguard and spare wheel and blowing an otherwise unhurt Sergeant Iwaskow into a roadside ditch. The second struck the Daimler Dingo Scout Car commanded by Corporal 'Mac' McNeill on the right side of the glacis and decapitated the driver, Trooper Reginald Holmes; he was buried in Driel churchyard with full military honours the following day.[106] Assuming the tanks were manned by German troops, Lieutenant Zuchowski immediately set about stalking them with a PIAT team but the potentially calamitous confrontation was averted by Lieutenant Young, who had dismounted to move forward with Zuchowski; on hearing English voices emanating from the halted Shermans he was able to rein in the paratroopers and presumably identify himself to the tank crewmen, and thus prevent further fratricide.[107]

The second incident occurred at the tail of the armoured column at around the time the head reached Driel. The route from Valburg to Driel involved negotiating road junctions and a motorcycle despatch rider was stationed at these junctions to ensure all adhered to the correct route, as per standard operating procedure. At one crossroads dubbed *De Hoop* (The Hope) by the locals the bulk of the armoured column had passed on toward Driel when another group of vehicles approached from the direction of Elst. Assuming they were friendly vehicles travelling by a different route, the despatch rider signalled them onto the road to Driel and it was only when they drew abreast he saw they were marked with black crosses. The vehicles were actually three Tiger I tanks from *schwere Panzer Kompanie Hummel* from *Kampfgruppe* Knaust and at least two Panthers from *SS Panzer Regiment 10*, accompanied by around a dozen infantry and a motorcycle outrider; the British despatch rider managed to pass the tanks and raised the alarm at Driel.[108] Had the German vehicles arrived at the junction very slightly earlier or later there would have been carnage; as it was they slotted into a lucky gap that had opened up in the 5th DCLI armoured column because A Company in the rear was unable to keep up with the speedier vehicles ahead of it. In addition, A Company's portion of the column had also become spaced out; by the halfway point between Valburg and Driel Major Parker's Jeep, two M3 Half-tracks and a 15-Hundredweight Bedford truck had drawn 600 yards ahead of the slower Bren Carrier driven by a Private Rogers transporting Company Sergeant Major (CSM) Reg Philp and a Private Tucker. The last vehicle in the column, another Bren Carrier carrying Lieutenant J. Olding, trailed another 200 yards behind CSM Philp.

Major Parker's group thus came upon the enemy tanks at speed and although they did not see their black cross markings until actually overtaking them, the British vehicles were able to accelerate out of danger and reached Driel unscathed; the Germans could not have recognised them. At the tail end of the A Company column CSM Philp's Bren Carrier almost made it past the tanks as well, but Private Rogers was obliged to perform an emergency stop when the two lead tanks veered across the road and stopped, leaving the Carrier touching the front of one of them. Showing remarkable presence of mind CSM Philp put a burst of fire into one of the turret crew who attempted to speak to them, using a captured German MG of some kind according to one account, before ordering his men to abandon the Carrier for the shelter of the reed-filled roadside ditch. Fortunately for the Riflemen, they were too close for the tank to bring its bow or co-axial machine-guns to bear, although CSM Philp banged his head on the tank's main gun barrel as he went over the side of the Carrier. After ascertaining the strength of the German force Philp made his way south accompanied by Private Rogers to warn the unarmoured column of the danger. As the last Carrier in the group had witnessed events with sufficient time to stop he was preceded by Lieutenant Olding, who suggested Lieutenant Bellamy deploy his 17-Pounder anti-tank guns as a precaution. The latter remained in place until Major Kitchen and C Company came up. It was decided to detour the soft-skin column to the west to avoid the German tanks. The detour was carried out successfully and the two parts of the Battalion were reunited at Driel at around 21:00, although the German tanks may have clashed with Major Hingston's B Company at some point.[109] In the meantime, Major Parker, correctly surmising that the German tanks would at some point return to Elst, had organised an anti-tank ambush close to *De Hoop* crossroads where the tanks had first appeared. It is unclear precisely when the party set out or when the ambush was sprung, but it was probably after 21:00, given that the party was accompanied by CSM Philp after he rejoined A Company. After leaving a platoon to act as a firm base midway between Driel and the crossroads, the ambush party moved on to a suitable stretch of road, possibly where CSM Philp had abandoned his Bren Carrier. No. 75 Hawkins mines were placed across the road at the forward end of the kill zone, which was covered by six PIATs briefed to volley-fire on Parker's order when the lead Tiger tank reached the mines; another chain of mines was to be pulled across the road behind the tanks to prevent them reversing out of danger. Small-arms fire was strictly forbidden unless the ambush group was attacked by enemy infantry, in order to avoid muzzle flashes giving away the ambushers' location, and total silence was enforced as the Riflemen settled down to wait.

The ambush's first victim was a German motorcycle combination from Elst, which was destroyed after running over one of the mines. The convoy of tanks eventually approached the ambush site from the opposite direction led by a motorcycle, with the lead tank firing flares every thirty seconds to illuminate the road ahead; Major Parker construed this as an indication that the tank crews were 'windy'. Whether or not, once the unfortunate motorcyclist had detonated a mine Major Parker ordered all six PIATs to fire on the lead tank, likely a Tiger, just as it reached the mines, which put it out of action immediately. The PIAT gunners, after some very rapid cocking and reloading, meted out the same treatment to the second tank after it moved past its running mate and detonated a mine. The third Tiger tried to reverse away from the ambush but ran over the daisy chain of mines that had been pulled across the road behind it and was thus immobilised before also being knocked out by a PIAT wielded by a Private Brown, who closed to within a few yards to ensure hitting the target. The last two tanks, likely Panthers, also attempted to reverse out of danger but were abandoned by their crews after the vehicles slipped off the edge of the road in the darkness and confusion; one appears to have become bogged in the deep roadside ditch while the other toppled right over onto its roof.[110] After reorganising the ambush party moved back to Driel via the firm base location, but not before CSM Philp moved systematically down the row of tanks ensuring they were properly knocked out by dropping grenades into their open hatches. There were two known casualties. Private Brown, who had only recently joined the 5th DCLI, strayed too close to the target when despatching the third Tiger and received a serious eye wound from flying debris. His last words before losing consciousness whilst being evacuated by Jeep were reportedly 'I don't care, I knocked the ****** out.' He was subsequently awarded the Military Medal for his actions.[111] The second casualty was CSM Philp, who was wounded in the face by a shell splinter whilst moving between the immobilised tanks as Allied artillery, alerted by the noise and light generated by the ambush, had begun to shell the nearby crossroads. Undaunted Philp continued his self-appointed task, and he was later awarded the Distinguished Conduct Medal in recognition of his actions on 22 September 1944.[112]

The lead element of the GARDEN relief force finally reached the south bank of the Lower Rhine five days and six hours after the Irish Guards had crossed the start line from the Neerpelt bridgehead at 14:35 on Sunday 17 September. This was seventy-seven hours behind schedule and around thirty-six hours after Lieutenant-Colonel Frost's party holding the north end of the Arnhem road bridge had finally been overwhelmed. The question was now whether supplies and reinforcements could be channelled over the Lower Rhine with sufficient speed to prevent the 1st Airborne Division's shrinking enclave at Oosterbeek from suffering the same fate as Frost's force.

D Plus 6

00:01 to 23:59 Saturday 23 September 1944

The second attempt to ferry the 1st Independent Polish Parachute Brigade across the Lower Rhine to reinforce the 1st Airborne Division's Oosterbeek perimeter was scheduled to begin at some point after 21:30 on the night of Friday 22 September. The precise start time varies between accounts, but the unit selected to be first across, Lieutenant Albert Smaczny's forty-nine-strong 8th Company, moved up to the crossing site between 21:00 and 22:00. It is unclear if they were accompanied by the rest of the 3rd Battalion or if they moved up later. Smaczny was thus in place to see the arrival of the horse and cart carrying the first of the three improvised rafts constructed by Staff Sergeant Wojciech Juhas' party and the rather noisy unloading onto the road atop the riverside dyke that followed. The raft was manhandled down to the water's edge and handed over Smaczny's men who quietly carried it a few yards out into the river before carefully lowering it to the surface, whereupon it promptly sank. The paratroopers fished the raft out and tried again with the same result; it transpired that the raft was constructed from an oak barn door which was simply too heavy to float. The Polish end of the reinforcing effort was thus left reliant upon three bright-yellow aircraft emergency rubber dinghies, two two-seaters and a single four-seater scrounged by Captain Piotr Budziszewski's Engineers back in England and recovered earlier that day from the Brigade DZ. With his men lined out in the lee of the riverside dyke to await developments, Lieutenant Smaczny watched members of the Brigade's Engineer Company inflate their three dinghies and then waited, chewing a blade of grass to lessen his craving for a cigarette, until a small, dark-coloured dinghy paddled by a lone British officer emerged out of the gloom.[1]

Carrying out the British end of the river crossing had been assigned to Captain Henry Brown and his party from No. 3 Troop 4th Parachute Squadron RE, fresh from its new role as the 4th Parachute Brigade reserve. Brown was summoned to the Hotel Hartenstein by the Division CRE, Lieutenant-Colonel Edmund Myers, late on Friday morning, where he was ordered to make arrangements to ferry Polish troops across the Lower Rhine from Driel. The briefing took place immediately before Myers departed for Driel with Lieutenant-Colonel Charles Mackenzie en route to 30 Corps HQ, and in uncomfortable circumstances, with Captain Brown lying atop Lieutenant Colonel Myers in his slit trench as they sheltered from a sudden German mortar bombardment.[2] After collecting the vessels that Myers had cached earlier – six Army-issue two-seater dinghies and a larger RAF dinghy likely salvaged from a downed aircraft – Brown told off between twelve and twenty-four of his Sappers for the mission, selecting older men for their superior stamina.[3] The party moved off for the Lower Rhine at 19:45 in two Jeeps loaded with the deflated dinghies, reels of marker tape and drums of signal wire, accompanied by an unnamed liaison officer from 1st Airborne Division HQ equipped with a radio. On reaching the water's edge Brown organised a defensive perimeter around his chosen crossing point, a 400-yard stretch of bank located among a series of protective stone groynes projecting out into the river. He then paddled alone across the Lower Rhine to establish contact, making landfall in front of Lieutenant Smaczny and his men, being welcomed 'by a group of Poles some of whom I could just understand'.[4] After ascertaining the Polish preparations Brown quickly informed Smaczny that he intended to run the six smaller dinghies back and forth along individual lengths of signal wire, carrying two men per crossing, with the larger craft making their own way in between. Once across, the Poles would be escorted to the Oosterbeek Old Church by a group of Glider Pilots detailed to act as guides under Lieutenant Brian Bottomley, No. 1 Wing's Intelligence Officer; they were assisted, apparently unofficially, by Captain Alfons Mackowiak from the Polish Liaison Team attached to 1st Airborne Division HQ. The Poles asked Brown to take a Polish officer back with him to liaise over the crossing, although one source refers to the return passenger being a signaller. Whatever the identity of any passenger, Brown returned safely to the north bank where he received an enthusiastic welcome from his men, who had decided that they would not see him again.[5]

The crossing appears to have begun at 23:00, with the first increment of Lieutenant Smaczny's men employing the Polish craft in the wake of Captain Brown.[6] Staff Sergeant Juhas paddled the lead dinghy with a shovel, as the Poles had not managed to purloin paddles when appropriating their dinghies. The crossing took around forty-five minutes; 1st Airlanding Brigade HQ reported the arrival of Polish paratroopers at the 1st Airlanding Light Regiment's location by the Oosterbeek Old Church at 23:45.[7] At least one more increment that included Lieutenant Smaczny appears to have crossed using the Polish dinghies while the British Sappers were still organising their own craft, and the Poles' use of their own craft appears to have brought them onto the north bank earlier than anticipated. This is suggested by the fact that 1st Airlanding Brigade HQ reported Poles missing the guides from the Brigade Defence Platoon because they had landed at the wrong place, although Captain Brown's account makes no mention of it.[8] This may have been why Lieutenant Smaczny's party was reportedly guided away from the crossing point to 1st Airlanding Brigade HQ rather than the Oosterbeek Old Church by an unidentified Glider Pilot, who unwittingly gave the Poles a dramatic introduction into the realities of the Oosterbeek pocket, *der Hexen Kessel* (the Witches' Cauldron). Despite repeated reassurances that he knew the way, the alleged Glider Pilot appears to have become disoriented in the dark streets after passing through an impressively silent and alert British platoon location. Lieutenant Smaczny recalled hearing the sound of cooking pots and voices in what he thought was Dutch before a German sentry called the alarm and the ensuing blizzard of small-arms fire from German troops ensconced in buildings on both sides pinned the party down in a narrow, glass-and rubble-strewn street. The Poles were only able to break contact after Smaczny organised a volley of hand-grenades and put down covering fire with his Sten gun. The Glider Pilot guide was killed in the process and one of Smaczny's men was wounded in the thigh. On trying to retrace their steps the Poles were then pinned down for several fraught minutes by fire from the British platoon they had passed through earlier, until Lieutenant Smaczny managed to establish their identity by hollering over the noise of the gunfire. The Lieutenant commanding the British position, perhaps unsurprisingly, had no knowledge of any reinforcing effort across the Lower Rhine, but had one of his men finally led Smaczny and his men to their proper rendezvous point at the Oosterbeek Old Church. There they found a number of other men from the 8th Company and were able to snatch some sleep.[9]

Back at the crossing point things were not going well for Captain Brown. The plan to haul pairs of dinghies back and forth had to be abandoned as the signal wire was not strong enough to withstand the current, and simply snapped once the dinghies left the sheltered waters between the stone groynes. The Polish paratroopers thus had to be ferried across individually and more precious time was lost as the current tended to carry the craft downstream on the southern leg, obliging the rowers to drag them laboriously across the sodden polder back to the crossing site. The larger, four-seat RAF craft proved 'very difficult to control and almost impossible to steer' and one sank just after leaving the south bank, its passengers swimming to safety. The other was carried a mile or more downstream by the current before running onto the north bank; the men aboard eventually made their way back to the relative safety of the Oosterbeek perimeter. Suspecting that something was afoot the Germans began firing machine-guns across the river and dropping mortar bombs along both banks and into the water, followed by rocket salvos from SS *Werfergruppe* Nickmann located behind the Oosterbeek Laag railway embankment east of the crossing point.[10] The rowers applied themselves fully to their task: Lieutenant David Storrs from HQ Royal Engineers, who turned up to help after the crossing was underway, reportedly made twenty-three round trips in the course of the night for example. But the Sappers had been fighting virtually non-stop since arriving with the second lift five days earlier, and Captain Brown unsurprisingly noted a diminution of his Sappers' performance as the night passed, to the extent he was obliged to patrol the defensive perimeter around the crossing point repeatedly kicking their feet to keep them awake. Brown also had an additional problem in the shape of an unidentified Polish liaison Officer, who constantly pestered the harassed and increasingly tetchy Sapper Captain for greater speed. When Brown's patience finally ran out he pointed his Browning pistol at the Pole and said quietly 'If you don't fuck off, I'll shoot you.'[11] This did the trick as the liaison Officer promptly disappeared, to be replaced shortly thereafter by Lieutenant Henri Podzorski, the Polish liaison Officer attached to 4th Parachute Brigade HQ; Brown suspected Podzorski had approached him at the behest of the unnamed liaison officer to establish if the Sapper Captain was still in his right mind.[12]

Matters did not proceed as planned with the two DUKWs loaded with supplies. Having been briefed on the urgency of the 1st Airborne Division's situation and on speaking to Lieutenant-Colonel Mackenzie on arrival at Driel, Lieutenant-Colonel Taylor wanted to push straight on to the Arnhem road bridge with the DUKWs. He was dissuaded on learning that there had been no contact from that quarter for around thirty-six hours, and presumably also on being informed that *Sperrverband* Harzer was securely dug in along the Arnhem–Nijmegen railway embankment between Driel and the road bridge. Taylor thus accepted Major-General Sosabowski's assurance that measures would be taken to get the supplies across the Lower Rhine as rapidly as possible.[13] The dykes, ditches and sodden polder along the river line were impassable to the unwieldy amphibious vehicles however, as ascertained by the earlier survey by Captain Budziszewski and Lieutenant-Colonel Myers. The only option was the paved road leading down to the Heveadorp ferry, several hundred yards west of the crossing point and likely outside the Polish perimeter. Guiding the DUKWs down such a narrow roadway would have been a tricky business in daylight, let alone on a moonless night with the tactical situation precluding the use of lights, and according to one source matters were complicated further by thick riverside mist. The result was predictable, with both DUKWs running off the edge of the paved surface and becoming inextricably bogged in the deep roadside ditch. Had the vehicles made it across the river and delivered their supplies, they might have made a significant difference in the number of Polish paratroopers shuttled into the Oosterbeek pocket. As it was, the DUKWs appear to have remained bogged in place for the remainder of the battle and while it is unclear what became of the supplies they were carrying, it is highly unlikely they made their way across the Lower Rhine, given the ongoing dearth of craft, personnel and time.[14]

The personnel ferrying effort was running out of steam despite the best efforts of all involved. At 03:00 Captain Budziszewski returned to Sosabowski's HQ in Driel to report that it would be impossible to move much more than the forty-nine men of 8th Company before dawn. Most - and possibly all but one - of the dinghies had been lost to enemy fire, accidents or the current and the 8th Company had suffered fifteen per cent casualties whilst waiting on the south bank, mostly killed. Sosabowski therefore ordered the understrength 3rd Battalion to return to its positions at 04:00.[15] It is unclear if there was any coordination between the Poles and Captain Brown, but the latter also terminated the effort and withdrew the 4th Parachute Squadron party to the Oosterbeek Old Church at some point between 04:00 and 05:00. It then transpired that one of the RE party, Lance-Corporal Michael Flannery, had been inadvertently left on the south bank. Brown returned to the river with a reconnaissance boat and personally retrieved the missing man – that success did little to dispel a general feeling that the Sappers had failed in their mission.[16] Just fifty-two men had been ferried across the Lower Rhine in the four hours or so from 23:00 although only thirty-six, all from Lieutenant Smaczny's 8th Company, appear to have made it to the rendezvous at the Oosterbeek Old Church.[17] The remainder either ended up in different parts of the 1st Airborne Division perimeter or were drowned, killed or wounded during the crossing or on reaching the north bank; the wounded were shuttled back to Driel, presumably to avoid burdening the 1st Airborne Division's already overstretched medical resources.[18]

***

Saturday 23 September in Oosterbeek dawned grey, rainy and blanketed in river mist, with first light marked by a resumption of the German bombardment.[19] On the western face of the Airborne perimeter the 1st Border's positions along the Van Borsselenweg came under fire at 05:20 followed an hour-and-a-half later by the units in the vicinity of the Laundry and Oosterbeek Old Church at the southern extremity of the eastern face.[20] Shells and mortar bombs began to land in the area of the Hotel Hartenstein at approximately 07:30 and, in an unwelcome contrast to the previous day, with a particularly heavy strafe on the 7th KOSB's positions along the Ommershoflaan on the north face of the perimeter at the same time.[21] The bombardment heralded a resumption of the German strategy of concentric attacks against the 1st Airborne Division's perimeter, beginning with the positions held by elements of Major Bernard Wilson's 21st Independent Parachute Company on the west side of the Utrechtseweg–Stationsweg crossroads.

The survivors of the 10th Parachute Battalion, led by Captain Peter Barron from the 2nd Airlanding Anti-tank Battery, had been cut off by *Kampfgruppe* Möller in the evening of Thursday 21 September and were still holding a position east of the Utrechtseweg–Stationsweg crossroads and thus outside the Divisional perimeter to the front of the 21st Independent Company. Major Wilson considered the position too far forward to be tenable, a not unreasonable view given that two attempts to reach the 10th Battalion party the previous afternoon had been beaten back by German fire, but Brigadier Hackett was insistent that Wilson relieved and then maintained the outpost, ostensibly because it protected the Divisional Main Dressing Station (MDS) located in the Hotels Schoonoord and Vreewijk. Hackett may also have been motivated by the fact that the 10th Parachute Battalion was an original constituent of his 4th Parachute Brigade, while Major Wilson's unit was not; interestingly, Hackett does not appear to have informed Division HQ of the substitution either, as there is no mention of it in the Division HQ War Diary, which refers to the forward position being held by the 10th Battalion several hours after it had been relieved.[22] Major Wilson was reluctantly obliged to order Lieutenant Hugh Ashmore and No. 3 Platoon to relieve the marooned paratroopers, with the changeover being complete by 03:00.[23] The relief appears to have been carried out without incident and the 10th Parachute Battalion party was assigned a reserve position on the Utrechtseweg just west of the crossroads near Hackett's Brigade HQ to snatch some rest. The Battalion's semi-official history described the scene: 'The rain had ceased and as the stars again became visible the small band of 10th Battalion defenders was withdrawn from its shell-shattered positions to a new group of houses to the west.'[24] They were joined at around 06:30 by Lieutenant Smaczny and his men from the 1st Polish Independent Parachute Brigade, who had been led up from the Oosterbeek Old Church by the wounded but still functioning Captain Barron.[25] He and Lieutenant White were subsequently relieved as temporary commanders of the 10th Battalion party, which was handed over to Lieutenant William Grose from the 11th Parachute Battalion; Grose had been serving as a Junior Liaison Officer at Division HQ and was reassigned at around 07:35.[26]

Major Wilson's objections to maintaining the outpost on the Utrechtseweg proved to be justified. Possibly provoked by the relief activity, *Kampfgruppe* Möller attacked the Pathfinder's

No. 3 Platoon at 07:15, using the tactics developed in the fight at the Arnhem road bridge. In pouring rain and covered by a thick phosphorous smoke screen to prevent the main British positions at the Utrechtseweg-Stationsweg crossroads from interfering, two *Sturmgeschützen* and what was reported as a *Panzer* IV tank began systematically to pump shells into the British-held houses until they collapsed, forcing the surviving Pathfinders to abandon their inadequate shelter. The unit War Diary implies that their subsequent withdrawal to the main British line at the crossroads was ordered by Major Wilson, but the semi-official history suggests it resulted from a less formal or orderly impulse. Several men were wounded or killed by the German pounding, the dead including Sergeant Dennis Martin. Others including Sergeant Paddy Cockings and his Section were taken prisoner.[27] A number of men managed to withdraw to No. 1 Platoon's positions on the crossroads, among them Lieutenant Ashmore and Sergeant Ernest Thompson, who had reportedly killed a number of German infantry with an improvised Gammon bomb as they moved into the garden of the collapsed building; he was described as 'quite berserk' on arrival at No. 1 Platoon's location. Private Francis Hillier also made it back to the crossroads despite being wounded and was hit again in the throat when he returned to assist an injured comrade. He died of his injuries after the engagement.[28] The fight for the outpost was over by 08:40.[29]

The Germans then renewed their assault along the entire eastern face of the 1st Airborne Division's perimeter, although the precise degree of co-operation between the various units involved is hazy. After a particularly heavy artillery bombardment *Kampfgruppe* Harder's attacked again along the riverside Benedendorpsweg against the positions held by LONSDALE Force, the remnants of the 2nd South Staffords and the 1st and 3rd Parachute Battalions protecting the 1st Airlanding Light Regiment's 75mm Pack Howitzers. The attack followed the pattern of the previous day, with 'continuous small engagements with venturesome tanks' and German infantry 'more hesitant in making close-range attacks', although the constant sniping and frequency of the attacks made up for any lack of application; as the 3rd Parachute Battalion War Diary put it, attacks 'were so frequent between this period and the time of withdrawal that it is impossible to give full details of each attack'.[30] The thinly spread defenders received what reinforcements were available. At 11:00 the 11th Parachute Battalion contingent was recalled from its backstop position covering the municipal gasworks to the Oosterbeek Old Church for 'food and weapon cleaning' before being assigned new positions stretching west from the church, while the 1st Parachute Battalion were reinforced by twenty-one Glider Pilots at 20:00; it is unclear which Squadron the party were drawn from.[31] The Airlanding Light Regiment's 1 and 2 Batteries located just north and north-west of the Oosterbeek Old Church emerged unscathed from the constant mortaring and *StuG* attacks, although a *StuG* knocked out a pack howitzer belonging to 3 Battery dug in west of the Church. It is unclear if this occurred before or after Captain Anthony Taylor took command of 3 Battery in place of Major Arthur Norman-Walker, who had been killed by German mortar fire at 1st Airlanding Brigade HQ the previous day. Twenty of the twenty-one pack howitzers the Regiment had landed with on 17 September still remained in action.[32] In an effort to increase close protection for the Airlanding Regiment, the 11th Parachute Battalion's B Company, commanded by Lieutenant James Blackwood, was detailed to act as a 'protection unit' for the guns.[33]

Kampfgruppe Harder's attacks in the vicinity of the Oosterbeek Old Church were held until the Germans broke contact covered by an especially heavy barrage at 18:00, but not without cost.[34] The total number of British casualties in unclear but Lieutenant James Cleminson, who had spent the night of 18-19 September in the attic of No.14 Zwarteweg with Major-General Urquhart, was wounded and evacuated to the MDS at some point during the day; he was the last original Battalion officer still serving with the 3rd Parachute Battalion contingent.[35] Major Guy Blacklidge, who may have been commanding the 11th Parachute Battalion at this point, was killed by German artillery fire near the Oosterbeek Old Church to which the German artillery paid regular attention, presumably because its tower provided a convenient aiming point in the heart of the British positions.[36] Major John Simonds from HQ Company, 2nd South Staffords also died during the day, apparently whilst undergoing treatment for serious wounds sustained on 19 September.[37]

After eliminating Lieutenant Ashmore's outpost and regrouping, *Kampfgruppe* Möller resumed its push along the Utrechtseweg against the 21st Independent Company's main positions, specifically targeting that held by Lieutenant David Eastwood's No. 1 Platoon on the Stationsweg running north from the junction with the Utrechtseweg, approaching through the park on the east side of the Stationsweg. However, in this instance the attack was less effective, perhaps initially owing to the smokescreen interfering with the armoured vehicles' targeting abilities, but more importantly because the Pathfinders employed a counter-tactic of their own. It is unclear if it was the result of a centrally generated order but Sergeant Benjamin Swallow ordered his men out of the fortified Hotel Strijland at No. 6 into the hotel grounds and Sergeant Ronald Kent did the same from No. 4 next door. This allowed the defenders to avoid the worst effects of the sustained close-range shelling from the German armoured vehicles and to engage the German infantry on a more equal footing when they moved in to mop up, although the subsequent fight was still fierce. Private John Avallone was killed manning a Bren in the grounds and Sergeant Swallow was severely wounded after reoccupying the hotel proper, to the extent he died of his wounds almost three weeks later.[38] No. 1 Platoon also lost Corporal Hans Rosenfeld, who was reportedly killed by a mortar bomb whilst sheltering in his slit trench, although another account refers to him being struck in the neck by a ricochet of some kind.[39] Sergeant Thompson, the berserker from No. 3 Platoon, was also killed, one of the fifteen dead and wounded suffered by No. 3 Platoon that day.[40]

The traffic was not all one way. An unnamed cook from No. 2 Platoon, which was holding positions on the Pietersbergseweg opposite and to the right of the MDS in the Hotel Schoonoord south of the crossroads, reportedly knocked out a *StuG* with a borrowed PIAT and Private Avallone was credited with shooting up a German ammunition truck on the Utrechtseweg and setting it ablaze. The vehicle must have become disoriented to end up in the front line, and it was not the only instance of such confusion during the fight. Private Alfred Jones from No. 1 Platoon recalled a motorcycle combination blithely pulling up outside the house next door to the one his Platoon was occupying and a German officer dismounting to approach the building. Both officer and driver were hit and wounded when Jones and his comrades recovered from their surprise and opened fire. The German casualties were subsequently recovered and evacuated across the Utrechtseweg to the MDS by an unnamed Medical Officer.[41]

The German attack also extended north from the Utrechtseweg–Stationsweg crossroads to the houses on the Stationsweg held by Major Geoffrey Powell and his hundred-strong contingent from 156 Parachute Battalion, including fifteen Glider Pilot reinforcements from D Squadron, and on their left A and D Troops from the 1st Airborne Reconnaissance Squadron commanded by Captain David Allsop from his HQ near the Hotel Hartenstein. In addition to the constant mortar and artillery bombardment the houses came under heavy and sustained machine-gun and small-arms fire from 08:00, with infantry attacks from the area of woodland east of the Stationsweg. An assault gun from *Sturmgeschütze Brigade 280*, likely a *Sturmhaubitze (StuH) 42*, was roaming among the British-occupied buildings west of the Stationsweg.[42] Trooper Frank Mann from the Reconnaissance Squadron's A Troop resolved to ambush the vehicle using the Troop's single PIAT, accompanied by 2 Section Sergeant Gwyn Williams. The pair took up position in a slit-trench opposite the burned-out bakery on the junction of the Mariaweg and the Paul Krugerstraat; the trench was so deep that Williams acted as a human platform for Mann to kneel on. When the *StuH* duly appeared after around half an hour, Mann waited until it was only a few yards away before letting loose with the PIAT and succeeded in blowing off one of its tracks, although the German crew promptly responded with a 105mm shell that exploded just in front of the trench. Both men were temporarily buried but dug their way out, losing the PIAT in the process, and reached the shelter of a nearby house despite intense fire from the immobilised vehicle's MG34 that killed and wounded Glider Pilots occupying an adjacent trench. The German crew abandoned their vehicle and Trooper Mann was subsequently awarded a US Distinguished Service Cross for his courageous action.[43]

In the meantime Brigadier Hackett had a brief 'tete a tete' [sic] at 09:00 with Captain Allsop in the latter's slit trench presumably after visiting the 21st Independent, and he may have also called in to see Major Powell and 156 Parachute Battalion en route given the contiguous nature of the various unit positions.[44] At 10:00 Captain John Park and the Reconnaissance Squadron's D Troop holding the north-east shoulder of the perimeter came under sustained infantry attack supported by what were wrongly described in the unit War Diary as Mark VI tanks.[45] Whatever the armoured vehicles actually were, they knocked out a 6-Pounder anti-tank gun emplaced in a shop window 200 yards behind D Troop HQ that unsuccessfully engaged them, wounding Lance-Corporal Robert Thomson and another D Troop Bren gunner posted as protection.[46] The vehicles resumed the attack at 11:00 by systematically demolishing a forward outpost occupied by a Trooper Smith with two unnamed companions and commanded by Sergeant James Pyper. The latter later recalled how 'the momentum of the shells carried them straight through both the outer and inner walls of the house, just as if the structure were made of cardboard.' The two unnamed defenders were wounded in the course of the demolition.[47] Although the unit War Diary and semi-official Reconnaissance Squadron account makes no mention of it, Sergeant Pyper braved the machine-gun and shell fire to request the assistance of stretcher bearers at D Troop HQ before returning to the demolished outpost and was carrying his wounded comrades back in person when the stretcher bearers arrived; he was subsequently awarded the Military Medal for his gallantry and additional acts the following day.[48] Sergeant Pyper and the other unwounded survivor of his group, Trooper Smith, were then withdrawn to Troop HQ. Having eliminated Sergeant Pyper's outpost, German infantry then attacked the main D Troop house on the Cronjéweg from the east at 15:00. The attack was rebuffed but a further effort from the east and north an hour later was more successful and at 16:30 the close-range shelling obliged Captain Park to order a withdrawal to another house 150 yards to the south. The attack cost two wounded, reducing D Troop to Captain Park, Lieutenant Alan Pascal and thirteen Other Ranks including Sergeant Pyper and Trooper Smith. At 17:00 Captain Allsop, who had himself been wounded by shrapnel earlier in the afternoon but 'made do with first-aid in order to remain at his post', appears to have ordered Captain Park to retake his original position.[49] This was done at 17:30 without a fight as the Germans had withdrawn toward their original position, presumably to regroup for the night. The D Troop contingent then set about consolidating their old position with fresh trenches before maintaining listening posts through the night from 22:00.[50]

On Captain Park's flank the bakery and adjacent house held by Captain Michael Grubb's A Troop came under attack from a *StuG* that approached from the rear of the house at midday, which may have been the same vehicle that demolished Sergeant Pyper's outpost, taking advantage of the breach thus created in the British line. Its arrival was inadvertently witnessed by Captain Grubb from the back garden: 'I walked up through the vegetable plot...when I suddenly realized that there was a great long gun barrel, poking over the hedge at the bottom. It was either a tank or an SP gun, so I hastily withdrew.' The *StuG* moved forward into the garden and began firing into the house. Corporal James Taylor recalled how 'a great gaping hole suddenly appeared beside him', while Lieutenant Douglas Galbraith was blown down the stairs, unscathed but rendered permanently partially deaf by the blast.[51] The shelling again rapidly rendered the house untenable and A Troop fell back under heavy fire across the Mariaweg to two houses on the De la Reijweg, with Trooper Ronald Spicer carrying his rifle in one hand and a large, newly brewed container of tea in the other. Captain Grubb was seriously wounded in the foot during the withdrawal; according to the Troop War Diary he was evacuated to the MDS and command of A Troop devolved to Lieutenant Galbraith, but another source refers to him declining to be evacuated and continuing in command until the following day.[52] Whichever was the case, A Troop fought a series of brief engagements with German patrols from 14:00 onward, during which it lost another man wounded. One of the Troop's new positions consisted of a loft above a brick wash house connected to the house next door by a 'mousehole' knocked through the brickwork, occupied by Troopers Spicer, Kenneth Hope and Stanley Sutherby. The trio accounted for a number of German infantry moving between buildings by firing from slits in the timber superstructure, including an especially tall individual who inexplicably stopped in full view in an adjacent alleyway. He was felled by a burst of fire from Trooper Sutherby and 'screamed for what seemed ages'; according to Lieutenant John Stevenson the Recce soldiers were unable to reach the German casualty because of sniper fire and resorted to singing 'Lili Marlene' in an effort to comfort him.[53]

The adjacent position on the Stationsweg occupied by 156 Parachute Battalion also came under attack at midday, first by what was reported as a Panther tank, disabled by the paratroopers' single PIAT.[54] The tank was replaced by a *StuG* that proceeded to systematically demolish the houses and as the Battalion's PIAT had been lost or damaged and the shelling was causing 'considerable casualties', at 14:00 Major Powell ordered a withdrawal to a line fifty yards behind the Battalion's existing position. A counter-attack an hour later led by Captain Raymond Stevens from No.1 Forward Observer Unit RA was repulsed by heavy German fire, with Captain Stevens reported killed in the attempt.[55] In fact, he was badly wounded in the arm and abdomen and over several hours managed to crawl to the house occupied by Lieutenant Stevenson and Sergeant Maurice Riches from the Reconnaissance Squadron's A Troop, where he died in the early hours of 24 September despite the best efforts of Sergeant Riches and some Dutch civilians sheltering in the cellar.[56] With the failure of the counter-attack 156 Battalion dug in on the new line, where it was left unmolested by the Germans for the rest of the day, apart from very heavy mortar fire.[57]

An ever more acute problem for the 1st Airborne Division was the treatment and safety of its steadily increasing number of casualties. By 23 September, nine separate locations within the perimeter contained approximately 1,300 casualties and those locations were increasingly coming under fire as the perimeter contracted under German pressure. Major Guy Rigby-Jones from 181 Airlanding Field Ambulance had a narrow escape when the games room in the Hotel Tafelberg he was using as an operating theatre was hit by an artillery shell that destroyed all the surgical equipment. The Hotel Tafelberg was also serving as the HQ for the Division's Assistant Director of Medical Services, Colonel Graeme Warrack. On another occasion a German mortar round blew in one of the Tafelberg's bay windows, injuring the already wounded Major John Waddy from 156 Parachute Battalion in the foot, prompting an incensed Colonel Warrack to take to the street shouting 'You bloody bastards! Can't anybody recognise a Red Cross?'[58] The MDS located in the hotels Schoonoord and Vreewijk, approximately 300 yards north-east of the Hotel Tafelberg straddling the Utrechtseweg–Stationsweg–Pietersbergseweg crossroads, was especially vulnerable, as *Kampfgruppe* Möller's advance along the Utrechtseweg had put it directly on the front line, which interfered with both side's tactical freedom. From the German perspective the MDS buildings effectively masked sections of the British line, channelling or outright blocking lines of attack and preventing them from exerting control over the crossroads; at the same time the 21st Independent Company holding the houses immediately west of the MDS complained that the MDS buildings provided the Germans with a covered conduit to approach the British positions. The Germans demanded the evacuation of the MDS on Friday 22 September, which was rejected by Major-General Urquhart on the not unreasonable grounds that there was simply nowhere else to relocate the facility within the slowly shrinking British perimeter. The Germans maintained the pressure on that sector of the perimeter the following day however, again using the MDS as a lever. In the early afternoon of Saturday 23 September Captain Stuart Mawson, the 11th Parachute Battalion's Medical Officer who was serving as a surgeon at the MDS, witnessed the Hotel Schoonoord being occupied by members of an SS Regiment 'of the toughest fibre. Aggressive and determined, and preoccupied entirely with the exigencies of battle, they appeared hardly to notice the sorry plight of the wounded, pushing them roughly out of the way to make room for their machine gun emplacements, and brooking no interference from those Medical Corps men who had the temerity to remonstrate with them.'[59]

Captain Mawson was imprisoned under armed guard for a time in the MDS's makeshift operating theatre with Captain Clifford Simmons from 181 Parachute Field Ambulance and a number of other medical personnel, until they persuaded their captors to allow them upstairs to tend the casualties in the wards. On the way up he witnessed an extended argument between hospital commander Lieutenant-Colonel Arthur Marrable speaking calmly but determinedly with two SS officers, citing the Geneva Convention and the equality of treatment the MDS staff had provided to wounded German POWs.[60] One of the officers was probably *Hauptsturmführer* Dr Egon Skalka, 9 SS *Panzer Division*'s Senior Medical Officer, who had been despatched by *Obersturmbannführer* Harzer to arrange an evacuation of the MDS; Skalka was at this time running the St Elizabeth Hospital in the outskirts of Arnhem employing its original British medical staff and medical supplies gathered from British resupply drops.[61] Skalka also appears to have been the officer who subsequently engaged Captain Mawson in French conversation on a ward after enquiring about the number of wounded in the MDS. After a discussion on the efficacy of different medication and treatments, the German officer admitted his reliance on captured British airdropped medical supplies and generously offered Mawson a Players cigarette from the same source.[62] Lieutenant-Colonel Marrable's quiet but determined diplomacy initially paid off, the threat to the MDS being lifted at 13:30 on the proviso that the British troops in the immediate vicinity refrained from firing. According to Captain Mawson the Germans also agreed to provide food and medical supplies, arrange evacuation of the seriously wounded as soon as possible and to remove their troops in the Hotel Schoonoord apart from sentries posted to prevent the ambulatory British casualties rejoining the fight, by 17:00. A German medical officer and a number of orderlies were also to remain to assist their British counterparts through the coming night and to help in any evacuation the following day.[63] Over the course of the afternoon the SS did provide a quantity of supplies and cigarettes, removed their own wounded and a number of the more serious British casualties to ease the burden on the MDS, and by the 17:00 deadline had assembled their fighting troops, described by Mawson as 'a formidable looking bunch', in the hallway of the Hotel Schoonoord in readiness to withdraw.[64] It was at this point that matters went awry as the SS came under small-arms fire whilst leaving the rear of the hotel, which drove them back inside for shelter. It is unclear whether the firing came from the 21st Independent Parachute Company, an unidentified group from the 1st Polish Independent Parachute Brigade lodged nearby or even possibly German units, but the incident instantly dissolved the SS goodwill.[65] One senior SS NCO called Colonel Marrable a 'dirty swine' before threatening to shoot him, and the potentially murderous situation was only eased slightly by an intercession from the SS medical officer and Lieutenant-Colonel Marrable coolly walking out into the rear parking area where the SS had come under fire.[66]

The MDS had also been a matter of discussion higher up the British chain of command. At around midday Brigadier Hackett was summoned to parley with a German officer, accompanied by a *StuG* or half-track. The German announced that a major attack was about to be launched and requested Hackett withdraw his forward positions 600 yards in order to avoid the German preparatory bombardment falling on the MDS; Hackett responded by arranging another meeting at 15:00 before relaying the German request to the Hotel Hartenstein in person.[67] Granting the German request was simply not possible as Hackett's HQ was only eighty yards west of the Utrechtseweg–Stationsweg crossroads, 1st Airborne Division HQ was around 250 yards further on, and the embattled western side of the perimeter only a half mile beyond that. Consequently, ceding any ground to the Germans along the Utrechtseweg ran the risk of splitting the Divisional perimeter in two.

If Hackett was looking for guidance or advice from his superior on the matter he was to be disappointed. Urquhart told him, 'You will have to do as you think best, I am not going to influence you.' After some thought Hackett acknowledged that the MDS would 'have to take its chances', to which Urquhart replied 'That is the conclusion I would have come to.'[68] This lack of support from his commander bothered Hackett for many years after the event, although he eventually came to the view that Urquhart was 'displaying his trust in the judgement of a subordinate rather than avoiding an awkward issue'.[69] Hackett returned to the arranged 15:00 meeting with the German officer and politely declined his request, and despite the German threat no bombardment of the MDS sector was forthcoming.

The fact that Hackett's rejection of the German proposal did not trigger the threatened bombardment was likely down to Lieutenant-Colonel Marrable's continuing quiet diplomacy inside the Hotel Schoonoord, but as we have seen co-operation there ceased abruptly when the SS troops were fired upon at around 17:00. The upshot was a new ultimatum demanding that the British evacuate a number of positions on the Utrechtseweg west of the crossroads up to and including a small building being used as an RAP by 19:30; failure to do so would see the entire area – including the MDS – subjected to concentrated mortar fire. According to the 4th Parachute Brigade War Diary the MDS promptly relayed news of the ultimatum to Brigadier Hackett, who this time changed tack. Presumably due at least in part to the German demand being more realistic, Hackett exercised his judgement in favour of the approximately 600 casualties and ordered the positions immediately adjacent to the MDS, held by the 21st Independent Parachute Company and the unidentified group from the 1st Polish Independent Parachute Brigade, to be evacuated; this was complete by 19:00.[70] Given his hands-on command style and past precedent, one would have expected Hackett to have relayed his withdrawal instruction to Major Wilson, the Poles and the MDS in person, but there is no reference to any such instructions or withdrawal in the 21st Independent Company War Diary or semi-official account, or in Mawson's MDS account. Nor does Hackett appear to have informed Division HQ of his decision, even though he attended a meeting with Urquhart, Brigadier Philip Hicks and Lieutenant-Colonel Robert Loder-Symons at the Hotel Hartenstein at some point between 19:00 and 20:00.[71] There is no reference to the 17:00 German ultimatum in the Division HQ War Diary or Urquhart's account of the battle; the only mention of the MDS in the War Diary for Saturday 23 September refers to the initial German ultimatum at 13:00, although curiously the entry for 15:27 the following day ends with an order from Major-General Urquhart for the then commander of the 4th Parachute Brigade to 'stand fast' in the face of renewed German threats to bombard the Hotels Schoonoord and Vreewijk.[72]

In fact, the evidence suggests that credit for the lack of German response to the rejection of the 17:00 ultimatum belongs to Lieutenant-Colonel Marrable, apparently without any involvement or input from Brigadier Hackett. The commander of the MDS perambulating around the open area at the rear of the Hotel Schoonoord only slightly mollified the SS, who threatened to call up tanks to bombard the MDS if a guarantee that they would not be fired on again was not forthcoming. Marrable therefore decided the only way to prevent a recurrence was to 'make personal contact with these [British] troops and put them in the picture', and persuaded Captain Mawson to approach one of the identified 'trouble spots', while he dealt with the other. The unfortunate Mawson thus found himself approaching the 21st Independent Company's positions bearing a Red Cross flag attached to a broom handle given to him by a Dutch nurse, and after being held briefly at Sten point by suspicious Pathfinder sentries Mawson was ushered into the presence of the irascible Major Wilson, who greeted him with a terse 'Who the devil are you?' The meeting went downhill after Mawson relayed Marrable's request, to which Wilson responded 'I'm damn well not budging an inch from here. The boot's on the other bloody foot. The damned Germans fired on us and that's why we fired back...What do you doctors think this is, drawing room tea at the vicarage?' When Mawson continued to argue his point about the agreement with the SS and the order from Division HQ to render the MDS area neutral, Wilson exploded again: 'That's enough, I don't give a damn what the Germans say, and I don't trust 'em more than I would a rattlesnake. I told you. The circumstances [of the Division HQ order] have changed.' Wilson eventually partially relented, through a combination of Mawson's suggestion that they contact the Hotel Hartenstein to clarify the official approach and sympathy for Mawson as a parolee POW. The medical officer was instructed to tell Lieutenant-Colonel Marrable that 'we will evacuate tonight, provided it can be done without loss. If the Germans so much as fire a pistol, they've had it.' On returning safely to the Hotel Schoonoord with his broom handle and Red Cross flag, Mawson discovered that Colonel Marrable had elicited the same reaction and caveated agreement from the Poles, although it is unclear if the promised evacuations actually took place. Whether or not, the SS troops in the Hotel Schoonoord withdrew without further incident shortly after dark, and the immediate area of the MDS remained relatively quiet for the rest of the night.[73]

While the MDS staff and the casualties in their care were being used as bargaining chips by *Kampfgruppe* Möller, the Germans were also maintaining the pressure on the remainder of the Oosterbeek perimeter. On the northern face the 7th KOSB had enjoyed a relatively quiet Friday as their night withdrawal to new positions on the line of the Ommershoflaan had broken contact with *Kampfgruppe* Bruhn and thus put the attackers on the back foot. However, the Germans spent the night of 22-23 September pinpointing the KOSB's new positions and Saturday reprised the heavy fighting on the Graaf van Rechterenweg two days earlier. The day began quietly for the glider soldiers with no enemy activity during the two-hour Battalion stand-to from 04:30, during which Lieutenant-Colonel Payton-Reid visited the Battalion positions and ordered all ranks to have a hot meal and a shave, using water drawn from a functioning pump discovered within the Battalion perimeter the previous day.[74] The quiet ended at 07:30 when a heavy German artillery, mortar and *nebelwerfer* barrage descended upon the length of the 7th KOSB's two-company frontage, augmented with machine-gun and small-arms fire that grew in intensity and rendered movement outside houses and slit trenches hazardous in the extreme. The German ground attack commenced during the bombardment. On the right side of the KOSB line a German tank reportedly accompanied by a self-propelled gun introduced B Company to the new German tactic of standing off and systematically shelling the houses to the point of collapse; in this instance the Company's attached anti-tank gun was unable to interfere because a falling tree rendered the weapon unserviceable, injuring several of the crew. The KOSBs occupying the houses rapidly employed the counter-tactic of temporarily abandoning their posts for the shelter of the surrounding slit trenches, from where they rebuffed the German infantry moving in to mop up before reoccupying their posts indoors.[75]

On the left half of the 7th KOSB's line CanLoan Lieutenant James Taylor and 12 Platoon were occupying a narrow strip of woodland just to the front of C Company's line and were attacked by infantry supported by a self-propelled gun and what were reported as armoured cars; these may have been the *flak* half-tracks employed with such deadly effect on the Dreijenseweg on 19 September. Using the trees for cover the German vehicles subjected 12 Platoon to concentrated 20mm fire until they were pushed back to the main C Company line. The Germans then occupied the strip of woodland and established a machine-gun post firing down the street, possibly the Steijnweg, acting as a divider between B and C Companies. The commander of C Company, Captain James Livingstone, ordered 12 Platoon to retake their lost position after organising support from the Battalion's mortars and MMGs and this was done with heavy casualties being inflicted on the German interlopers; the action cost 12 Platoon an unknown number of dead and half a dozen wounded, including Lieutenant Taylor.[76] C Company's line was re-established by 13:00, although 1st Airlanding Brigade HQ War Diary refers to a heavy German attack beginning just before 15:00 being rebuffed with the assistance of artillery from south of the Lower Rhine; simultaneous German shelling initially led the KOSBs to believe the friendly barrage was falling short.[77] The Battalion's attached anti-tank guns made the Germans keep their distance by reportedly scoring several hits on individual vehicles and using HE projectiles against infantry in the surrounding woods. The work of locating and eliminating German infiltrators continued until dark. Lieutenant-Colonel Payton-Reid and acting RSM Sergeant Russell Tilley from E Squadron the Glider Pilot Regiment managed to escape unscathed after inadvertently walking into a group of German troops occupying British slit trenches, but Battalion Adjutant Captain David Clayhills was not so lucky. He was hit three times by a German machine-gun while conducting a reconnaissance and had to be evacuated to the increasingly overcrowded Battalion RAP run by Captain John Buck RAMC from 156 Parachute Battalion and the Battalion padre, Captain James Morrison. Colonel Payton-Reid had another close shave whilst conferring with Captain George Steer from the Battalion Mortar Group and Drum-Major Andrew Tait when the slit trench they were occupying received almost direct hits from two German shells in quick succession.[78] Drum-Major Tait was injured to the extent of requiring evacuation to the RAP, Colonel Payton-Reid received a minor wound and Captain Steer was, perhaps unsurprisingly, reported as being 'severely shell shocked'. An element of bitterness appears to have begun to creep into the fighting at this point, with the Battalion War Diary referring to the deliberate targeting of three of the Battalion's stretcher bearers by German snipers; as a result a number of the Battalion's wounded could not be collected until after dark.[79]

On the north-western sector of the 1st Airborne's perimeter Captain John Cormie and the 4th Parachute Squadron RE, along with fellow Sappers from the 9th (Airborne) Field Company RE, 261 (Airborne) Field Park Company and Glider Pilots from No. 2 Wing's E and F Squadrons, did not come under such sustained attack in their positions near the Sonnenberg. The only formal German attack was an infantry-only affair that began at 13:15 and which was not pressed particularly hard, probably because of the lack of armoured support.[80] According to Sapper Arthur Ayers from the 4th Parachute Squadron's 3 Troop, the Germans 'would approach to within grenade throwing distance then retreat back into the trees'.[81] Once again, the unremitting German bombardment proved to be at least as dangerous as their direct attacks. Lieutenant Norman Thomas was deafened by a mortar bomb that burst on the lip of his slit trench, badly wounding the other occupant, and a Sapper Mackintosh was wounded in the forehead by shrapnel whilst scrambling for cover; Lieutenant Thomas' hearing was permanently damaged and Sapper Mackintosh subsequently lost the sight in his left eye. As the MDS was no longer able to receive casualties the wounded had to be retained and treated in the cellar of Squadron HQ, as graphically described by Sapper Ayers on visiting the cellar for a rest: 'I was unprepared for the sight that met my eyes, most of the floor space was covered with wounded men, laying on the cold stone floor. Some, in spite of medical help were dying, others lay unconscious with their white faces staring at the ceiling, wincing even as they slept.'[82]

Captain James Smith, commanding the 4th Parachute Squadron's 1 Troop, was knocked unconscious by a ricocheting mortar bomb that struck him square in the chest as he moved through the woods near the Sonnenberg. Remarkably, on regaining consciousness he discovered that while the mortar bomb had not detonated, the impact had punctured the brandy flask carried in a breast pocket; he was furious at the loss of the precious liquid.[83] The Squadron War Diary refers to losing between four and eight Other Ranks wounded and five killed during the course of the day.[84] The dead included Sapper Bernard Higgins and Sapper Leonard Rawlings, both from 2 Troop.[85]

The 9th Field Company RE and No. 2 Wing GPR endured a relatively quiet Saturday because they were coincidentally occupying the eye of the storm that was to engulf the remainder of the western side of the 1st Airborne Division's perimeter. The 1st Border was still largely holding the positions on the Phase II line it had occupied in the early morning of Tuesday 19 September on moving from LZ Z. On the right of the line Major Thomas Montgomery's A Company was holding what was now the north-west shoulder of the Division perimeter, with Major William Neill's C Company to the south straddling the Utrechtseweg near the Koude Herberg crossroads. The wooded section of the frontage between the Companies was occupied by the 9th Parachute Company RE and No. 2 Wing GPR, and C Company's line extended into the woods southward along the line of the Van Borsselenweg to link up with D Company, oriented along the same line. The remaining section of the perimeter running down to the Lower Rhine had originally been manned by B Company, but Major Armstrong's unit had been driven off the Westerbouwing

Heights by *Bataillon* Worrowski in the morning of 21 September and was virtually wiped out in the process. The survivors, Lieutenant Arthur Royall's 12 Platoon and a composite platoon commanded by Lieutenant Stanley Barnes, were dug in east along the riverside Benedendorpsweg near the municipal gasworks and the *Dennenord* house respectively; another *ad hoc* force commanded by Major Richard Stewart from Support Company was maintaining a roving patrol along the Benedendorpsweg. The open left flank created by the destruction of B Company was filled by BREESE Force.

The night on the western perimeter passed relatively quietly with the cessation of direct German attacks at around 19:30 on Friday 22 September, which gave way to the by now standard harassing mortar and artillery fire, and at 02:00 A Company received fourteen reinforcements from Division HQ reserve as partial recompense for the two depleted Platoons detached to BREESE Force.[86] The German barrage resumed in full force along the entirety of the 1st Border's frontage at 05:20 and continued throughout the morning, falling particularly heavily upon the remnants of B Company at the southern end of the line.[87] The barrage killed Lieutenant Coulston, with command devolving to a Sergeant J. Davidson.[88] Infiltrators were mostly kept at bay by British patrols roving between B Company's locations but even then one enemy group managed to occupy B Company's RAP on the *Dennenord*, which was being run by the Dutch occupants of the house. The interlopers were promptly evicted by Corporal Thomas Edgar, who entered the house alone, killed most of them with his Sten gun and drove out the rest; he was killed later in the day by a wounded German officer.[89] The remainder of the 1st Border's line came under direct attack from SS *Bataillonen* Schulz, Oelkers and Eberwein, supported by self-propelled guns and *Panzer Kompanie 224's* flame-throwing tanks. D Company suffered repeated attacks that reduced its strength to just twenty-five by the onset of darkness. They were cut off and surrounded, with radio the only contact with the rest of the Battalion; this ceased as the supply of batteries ran down and several attempts to re-establish contact via patrols after dark were unsuccessful.[90] C Company came under direct attack at around midday but managed to maintain its position astride the Utrechtseweg until a further German attack at 17:30, supported by self-propelled guns, pushed deep into the Company's positions. The interlopers were driven out in a fierce counter-attack organised and led by Company commander Major William Neill despite his being wounded four times in the course of the day's fighting, which restored the Company line by 19:20. Major Neill then led a fighting patrol from 19 Platoon in pursuit of the retreating Germans that attacked and overran a German strong point located in some houses by a crossroads, possibly at the Koude Herberg. Neill provided covering fire for the assault using a Bren gun resting on the shoulder of Private Robert Lee, and was subsequently awarded the Distinguished Service Order for this and his performance across the whole nine-day battle. Lance-Corporal Douglas Payne was badly wounded in the face and left side by a German mortar bomb during the action, severely enough to be left for dead by his withdrawing comrades; he made his own way back to C Company's lines after regaining consciousness, but was wounded again by machine-gun fire as he reached safety.[91]

The epicentre of the 1st Border's Saturday fight was at the extreme right of the Battalion's frontage. The German attack on A Company's sector of the perimeter began at 09:30, reportedly carried out by 'Rumainian SS' and again supported by *Panzer Kompanie 224's* flame-thrower tanks. By midday the attackers had turned A Company's northern flank with enemy tanks pushing deep into the Company's positions and were threatening to overrun that entire section of the Divisional perimeter.[92] Battalion HQ was made aware of the gravity of the situation via a calm and collected radio message from A Company HQ: 'Flame throwing tank in the area, and shelling the company headquarters – all officers and N.C.O.s killed or wounded – What shall we do?'[93] The message coincidentally arrived at Battalion HQ at the same time as Captain Barry Ingram, commander of the 1st Border's Mortar Group, who was probably reporting that Lieutenant Michael Holman's 23 Platoon was redeploying into the infantry role as its 3-inch mortars had all been put out of action by a combination of enemy action and lack of ammunition. Acting Battalion commander Major Stuart Cousens ordered Captain Ingram to clarify A Company's situation, accompanied by his runner, a Private Gordon, and a party of ten men from A Company led by a Sergeant H. Burton; it is unclear if the latter were stragglers or had been deployed away from their parent Company. After passing through the 4th Parachute Squadron's lines, Ingram approached A Company's positions with Private Gordon in time to see an unaccompanied *Flammpanzer B2 (f)* knocked out by glider soldiers using grenades. He came upon A Company's second-in-command Captain Charles Wilson, who was badly wounded by shrapnel before he could brief Ingram on the situation.[94]

A swift appreciation showed that A Company consisted of around sixty-five men from a variety of units including a Vickers MMG Section, equipped with two Bren guns and a PIAT with three rounds of ammunition. Captain Ingram swiftly organised this force to face a German infantry assault, holding fire until the inexperienced and bunched-up attackers were at point-blank range while crossing an open stretch of ground to the front of the Company HQ house. The result was reportedly a 'massacre', after which the glider soldiers collected two M34 machine-guns, a rifle, two pistols and a quantity of ammunition from the fallen enemy to augment their own almost depleted stock. On returning to Battalion HQ to report, Ingram was joined by Lieutenant Lennard Withers from the 2nd South Staffords accompanied by Sergeant Rogers with a 3-inch mortar with nine HE and three smoke rounds. Ingram appointed Withers his second-in-command and on returning to A Company lines had Sergeant Rogers drop two HE and a smoke bomb upon a thatched cottage he suspected was being employed as a German HQ; the smoke round set the roof on fire as intended and the Vickers Gun inflicted a number of casualties as the enemy evacuated the blazing building. In all, four separate German attacks were rebuffed over the course of the day, with All Ranks in A Company and beyond playing their part. A Lance-Corporal Steele addressed the Company's lack of anti-tank grenades by venturing into no-man's land alone to recover a supply container, while Acting Intelligence Officer Lieutenant Douglas Skilton and Company Sergeant Major Connett repeatedly carried ammunition to the fighting positions through continuous small-arms and artillery fire. Some of the ammunition thus distributed was brought up from the depleted Battalion HQ dump by Company Sergeant Major Leslie Fielding, who also witnessed the Vickers MMG team indulging in a collective 'wee pee' to fill their weapon's barrel jacket owing to a lack of water; Fielding then assisted an unnamed sergeant in an unsuccessful attempt to mortar a dismounted German tank crew with a PIAT. For his part, in addition to moving between his new command's fighting positions, Captain Ingram with Lieutenant Withers and two unnamed men put out a fire started by a mortar hit on some stored ammunition that threatened to spread to the trees surrounding the Company HQ house; he also ensured the transmission of hourly radio situation reports to Battalion HQ as well as tendering reports in person at least twice during the day.[95]

All did not go well between Captain Ingram and his acting Battalion commander. At some point Major Cousens instructed Ingram to pull A Company back to a new position closer to Battalion HQ. Ingram was not keen, not least because the new location was under constant German artillery fire, but he was badgered into agreeing with the caveat that the considerable number of wounded in the cellar of A Company HQ were evacuated to safety. He visited the Battalion RAP in person to arrange the evacuation. As we have seen, Medical Officer Captain John Graham-Jones had been unable to evacuate his casualties to the MDS through lack of serviceable Jeeps and because the MDS location had become the front line, and Ingram was thus greeted by 'an evil smell of unwashed bodies, dirty dressings and foetid air' in an RAP packed with wounded men. After accidentally treading on the Battalion Padre, Captain The Reverend John Rowell, Ingram located a sleeping Captain Graham-Jones, who was pummelled awake just long enough to inform Ingram that evacuating the A Company wounded to the RAP was 'impossible'. On returning to Battalion HQ, Ingram therefore apologised to Major Cousens but declined to withdraw to the new location because that would involve abandoning A Company's wounded to the Germans and would probably incur a large number of additional casualties in the process. He stuck to his decision even when threatened with a future court-martial, maintaining that Cousens' order was unreasonable; the two officers 'eventually parted on the worst of terms'.[96]

The very southern tip of the western perimeter was occupied by Lieutenant Smaczny and his party from the 1st Polish Independent Parachute Brigade's 8th Company. The Poles had been withdrawn from their reserve position on the Utrechtseweg at approximately 08:00, reportedly after accurate German mortar and artillery fire that wounded several of their number and rendered the ruined house they were occupying untenable. They were then despatched west by an unnamed Lieutenant-Colonel from the 1st Airlanding Brigade.[97] The new position was adjacent to a large house called *Transvalia* and was intended to fill the gap between the Lower Rhine and BREESE Force and the 1st Border's B Company positions in the woods, as well as blocking any German move along the Benedendorpsweg from Heveadorp. Despite constant small-arms, mortar and artillery fire, Lieutenant Smaczny had a daisy chain of No. 75 Hawkins Anti-Tank Grenades laid across the road and set his men to digging slit trenches in the grounds of the house.[98] The neighbouring British units do not appear to have been impressed with their efforts: they reported the Poles losing around half their number to the barrage. According to 1st Airlanding Brigade HQ the losses were due to poor digging skills and battle inoculation, and the 1st Border's semi-official account also refers to the Poles being reluctant to dig slit trenches.[99]

On investigating noises emanating from the *Transvalia* Lieutenant Smaczny discovered that the cellar was packed with British casualties being cared for by a Dutch woman, possibly the housekeeper, and her teenage daughter using whatever meagre means were to hand. The Polish officer promptly collected morphine syrettes from his party to aid the most seriously wounded while one of his men donated a large slab of beef cut from a convenient dead cow in lieu of rations; in return the woman gave Smaczny information on nearby German positions and later gave his men some beef stew left over after feeding the casualties. After an attempt to summon a doctor to assist the casualties they were evacuated to a safer location in the afternoon, presumably to the Division MDS, in a small convoy of medical Jeeps flying Red Cross flags. The Germans ceased fire while the Jeeps went about their business, and it took the convoy two round trips to remove all the casualties.[100]

By the time the casualty evacuation took place Lieutenant Smaczny's little band had not only been under constant small-arms and artillery fire, but had also been menaced by German armoured vehicles. During the morning two unidentified vehicles, likely *Char* B tanks from *Panzer Kompanie 224*, approached the *Transvalia* along the Benedendorpsweg from Heveadorp. The Poles had nothing to counter the behemoths apart from a single PIAT, but the day was saved by the appearance of a 6-Pounder gun from the direction of the Oosterbeek Old Church, manhandled into a firing position by its crew; the gun may have been the same piece belonging to the Polish Brigade's Anti-Tank Battery that had spent Friday 22 September keeping back enemy infiltration near the gasworks, possibly commanded by a Corporal Pawalczyk. The gun scored a direct hit on the lead vehicle, damaging it and prompting both to make a hasty exit the way they had come, as did the 6-Pounder. Another *Char* B approached from the same direction an hour before the medical evacuation, standing off while a marksman picked off the No. 75 Mines stretched across the road with a rifle. Smaczny had left the mines unconcealed on the advice of a British officer, reportedly to allow future reinforcements to locate them easily, but the tank showed no inclination to close on the Polish position after dealing with the mines and presumably retired the way it had come.[101] The Germans had also been maintaining the pressure with infantry, obliging Lieutenant Smaczny to withdraw an outpost on the Benedendorpsweg, and they also succeeded in establishing a machine-gun post between the *Transvalia* and the woods to the north, cutting the Poles' link with the Border Regiment troops. Lieutenant Smaczny therefore despatched a fighting patrol via a circuitous route tasked to explain the situation to the 1st Border and then attack the German post from the north, while he led a diversionary attack from the *Transvalia* with a dozen men at 17:30 to draw the enemy post's fire.

The ruse worked and the fighting patrol overran the post from the rear, killing the occupants and capturing two machine-guns. Thereafter the night was relatively quiet apart from sporadic German mortar and artillery fire, and the Poles took the opportunity to work in the darkness, stealthily improving their positions and burying their dead.[102]

On the other side of the hill the 1st Border's solid defence of the western face of the Divisional perimeter again had an impact beyond the battlefield level. *Sturmbannführer* Paul Helle, the commander of *Bataillon* Helle, had been relieved of his command for incompetence the previous day, and the Saturday fighting led to the commander of *Panzer Kompanie 224*, *Leutnant* Alfred May, being called before *Generalleutnant* von Tettau to explain the loss of six of his tanks, over a third of *Panzer Kompanie 224's* strength, in the three-day period 20 to 22 September for no return.[103] The interview revealed that one of the primary reasons for the losses was the failure of supporting infantry to protect the tanks from their opposite numbers, and confirmed von Tettau's suspicion that all-arms inexperience was the root cause. He therefore ordered the implementation of a crash course in tank-infantry co-operation and the creation of dedicated tank protection units. In addition, May's surviving tanks were forbidden to operate individually, and they were to operate only in support of SS *Bataillonen* Eberwein and Schulz, as those units contained a good proportion of combat-experienced troops.[104]

***

The Saturday resupply drop came in, again in a single late-afternoon increment employing seventy-three Stirlings and fifty Dakotas that had originally been loaded for the previous day's cancelled effort.[105] The Squadrons from RAF No. 46 Group were first away, apart from Nos. 512 and 575 Squadrons based at RAF Broadwell. 575 Squadron temporarily relocated to Evere airfield near Brussels that day in line with an abortive scheme to have fighter aircraft deliver supplies suggested by the Group Commander, Air Commodore Lawrence Darvall, intended to reduce losses among the Dakotas. 512 Squadron spent the day transporting freight, also to Brussels.[106] The first aircraft slated for the Oosterbeek resupply drop, seventeen Dakotas from No. 233 Squadron, began taking off from Blakehill Farm at 13:17 followed three minutes later by fifteen aircraft from the recently drafted-in No. 437 Squadron RCAF; next came eighteen Dakotas from Down Ampney beginning at 13:36, thirteen of them belonging to No. 48 Squadron and the remainder from No. 271 Squadron.[107] The Stirlings from No. 38 Group began taking off first from RAF Keevil, led by thirteen machines from No. 196 Squadron at 14:00 followed by thirteen machines from No. 299 Squadron fifteen minutes later. This overlapped events at RAF Fairford, where eleven aircraft from No. 620 Squadron took off at 14:07 followed thirteen minutes later by eight machines from No. 190 Squadron. Last, albeit only by a few minutes, came the contingent from RAF Harwell with twenty-eight aircraft split evenly between Nos. 295 and 570 Squadrons commencing take-off from 14:32; the last machine lifted off at around 14:43. The entire process of putting the better part of 200 machines into the air from six different locations took approximately ninety minutes.[108]

The flight across the North Sea and up the Airborne Corridor appears to have been uneventful, although Flight-Lieutenant P. I. Burden's Dakota from No. 233 Squadron aborted after turbulence from another aircraft caused a sudden drop in altitude that displaced its load.[109] The flight enjoyed extensive fighter cover that extended right up to Oosterbeek; 1st Airlanding Brigade HQ reported 'activity by our rocket-firing Typhoons' while No. 1 Wing Glider Pilot HQ reported seeing Thunderbolts and Mustangs suppressing German *flak* with the understandably bitter rider that the 'only time our fighter aircraft are seen in this area is when supplies are being dropped'.[110] Details of the RAF effort are unclear, but the USAAF effort was huge, with a total of 586 P38, P47 and P51 fighter-bombers, largely from the US 8th Air Force, being deployed to strafe German *flak* and other positions in support of the resupply and reinforcement flights for all three Airborne divisions. They kept a reported 150 *Luftwaffe* fighters away from the vulnerable transports, claiming between twenty-seven and thirty-five *Luftwaffe* machines shot down in return for a loss of four P47s and ten P51s, with a further one of each type being damaged beyond repair; in addition, twenty-five P47s and ten P51s suffered lesser damage, with one pilot wounded in action and another ten posted missing.[111] The fighter effort was noted by most units involved in the 1st Airborne Division resupply. No. 48 Squadron commented that 'All crews were very glad and cheered to see good fighter cover' and Nos. 233 and 437 Squadrons expressed similar sentiments, with the latter referring to friendly fighters dealing 'promptly' with German *flak* positions that revealed themselves west of the Drop Zone. In contrast No. 570 Squadron reported that 'fighter support was again poor'; as the latter was one of the last away its aircraft may have arrived at Oosterbeek after the fighter-bombers had departed.[112]

No. 46 Group appears to have profited most from the *flak* suppression effort given that all aircraft from Nos. 233 and 271 Squadrons returned safely to base, though not entirely unscathed. Nine of No. 233 Squadron's seventeen aircraft received varying degrees of damage whilst in the vicinity of Oosterbeek, the most serious being Warrant Officer K. G. Cranefield's machine, which had a two-foot-diameter hole blown in its starboard wing. Cranefield was also seriously wounded in the knee and thigh but refused morphine in order to remain conscious for the landing at Blakehill Farm, as co-pilot Flight-Sergeant B. A. Stapleford was not fully qualified on the Dakota; Cranefield was subsequently awarded the Distinguished Flying Cross.[113] Of No. 271 Squadron's five-strong contingent only Flying Officer J. R. Nicoll's machine received slight damage from light *flak* north of Drop Zone V, shrapnel from which also wounded one of the despatchers in the leg.[114] Approximately half of No. 437 Squadron RCAF's fifteen machines returned with light damage from small-arms fire and one, piloted by Flying Officer William Paget, was shot down and crashed south-west of Driel; Paget and his crew of three RCAF personnel were killed along with four RASC despatchers.[115] Two of No. 48 Squadron's aircraft also failed to return. One, flown by a Warrant Officer S. McLaughlin, was badly damaged by anti-aircraft fire but force-landed safely near Eindhoven. The other, flown by Pilot Officer Ralph Pring, was shot down near the Drop Zone possibly by a German fighter, given that a crew member in another aircraft reported seeing an FW 190 pursuing an unidentified Dakota. Flight-Sergeant Derek Gleave was the navigator on Pilot Officer Pring's aircraft:

> There were flames in the cockpit, and I was burnt on the hands and face. The pilot was absolutely marvellous. He saw this field and said 'I'm going to land there.' He must have been burned as well. I was struggling to open the escape hatch, which was right above me. I got it open all right but that caused a further rush of fire through the cockpit area, although we were nearly on the ground by then…I was the first out, and the wireless operator [Warrant Officer James Springsteele RCAF] and second pilot [Sergeant Henry Colman RCAF] followed me. As far as I know, the pilot never got out; he may have been wounded by the flak.[116]

Pilot Officer Pring had put the Dakota down on the polder close to the railway bridge, and all three men were hit by German small-arms fire after escaping from the burning wreck. Warrant Officer Springsteele was killed instantly, Flight-Sergeant Gleave was shot twice in the stomach and Sergeant Colman was hit multiple times. Eventually the two survivors were attended by German medical personnel who, after a shouted argument with the shooters, evacuated them to the St Elizabeth Hospital. Sergeant Colman died the following day.[117]

Most of No. 38 Group's six Squadrons benefitted from the close fighter support. All seven of No. 190 Squadron's Stirlings returned to Fairford unscathed apart from minor damage, while eleven of No. 196 Squadron's thirteen-strong contingent landed safely at Keevil. Flying Officer W. A. Sparks' aircraft was damaged by anti-aircraft fire near Oosterbeek and crash-landed sixty miles to the south near Valkenswaard; Flying Officer Sparks was injured along with his wireless operator, Flight-Sergeant J. E. Herring. The Stirling piloted by Flying Officer J. A. Norton was struck by *flak* over the drop zone that injured flight engineer Sergeant F. Gill and blew off part of the port outer propeller, obliging Norton to land the damaged machine at Manston in Kent. Five of the remainder sustained varying degrees of light damage to nose, fuselage and in one instance the bomb bay, while Flying Officer F. T. Powell's aircraft suffered a punctured port tyre but landed safely.[118] Flight Lieutenant E. P. Byrom's machine from No. 295 Squadron also suffered damage to one of its inner engines, which obliged a forced landing at Ghent from which all the crew emerged unhurt.[119] Several of No. 299 Squadron's crews referred to not seeing any anti-aircraft fire at all, although there were complaints about aircraft releasing their loads too high and obliging those flying behind at the correct altitude to take evasive action to avoid being struck by the falling panniers and containers. Nonetheless, four machines suffered minor *flak* damage and Pilot Officer I. T. Rowell's aircraft was shot down after dropping its load; Rowell and two members of his crew were wounded, one seriously, but all were safely evacuated to the UK.[120]

By this point *FlaK Brigade* Svoboda possessed in excess of thirty-three 88mm pieces supported by at least eight 37mm and twenty-nine 20mm automatic *flak* guns, operating under a new centralised tactic of throwing up a concentrated barrage across the transport's line of approach, rather than permitting gun commanders to engage individual aircraft as they saw fit.[121] The guns were unable to fully engage whilst the escorting Allied fighter-bombers were in the vicinity, but once the fighters moved on, the transports toward the tail end of the stream were increasingly exposed to their fire. The resultant upsurge in anti-aircraft fire appears to have hit No. 620 Squadron first, which noted that 'shortly before reaching the dropping zone, the stream of aircraft ran into severe A.A. fire', badly damaging a number of aircraft. All returned safely to Fairford apart from the Squadron commander, Wing-Commander D. H. Lee DFC, who crash-landed near Ussen, just south of the River Maas twenty-five miles south-west of Oosterbeek; Lee and his entire crew emerged unscathed and were back with their Squadron within forty-eight hours.[122] By the time No. 570 Squadron's aircraft at the rear of the stream approached the dropping area the German blocking barrage was fully established and the Stirlings flew into a wall of shell bursts and tracer that claimed four Stirlings in quick succession. Pilot Officer William Kirkham's machine was hit over the drop zone and crashed near the *Planken Wambuis* on the Arnhem–Ede road just north of LZ S, killing all on board apart from Air Gunner Flight-Sergeant G. Wood and one of the RASC despatchers, Driver S. Badham.[123] Flying Officer William Baker RCAF's Stirling crashed at Panoramahoeve, just south of the Arnhem–Ede railway six miles west of Oosterbeek, killing everyone on board.[124] Flying Officer C. M. Beck RCAF's machine was severely damaged and crashed on the south bank of the Lower Rhine at Heteren, three miles west of Driel; Beck and his Wireless Operator, Sergeant S. Wheatley, survived the crash and evaded capture but the remaining five members of the crew were killed.[125] *Flak* damage that wounded the two RASC despatchers also obliged Squadron Leader R. W. F. Cleaver to crash-land on the south bank of the Lower Rhine but without injury or loss of life, and the whole crew subsequently returned to the UK. Two more machines failed to make it back to Harwell. Flying Officer B. S. Murphy's Stirling was severely damaged but managed to limp 130 miles before crash-landing at Ghent in Belgium while Flying Officer G. J. H. Burkby made it across the English Channel to force-land at Manston; neither crew suffered any casualties. Three of the eight Stirlings that made it back to Fairford were also damaged, one badly and another to the point it appears to have been written off; an Air Gunner and Wireless Operator from two separate machines were also wounded.

The Friday 23 September resupply effort thus cost two Dakotas and four Stirlings shot down in the vicinity of Oosterbeek, with several more crash or force-landing along the Airborne Corridor, across Belgium and as far away as Kent. Approximately thirty-three RAF and RASC personnel were killed and a smaller number wounded. The pity was that the vast bulk of the supplies delivered at such cost again did not reach the intended recipients, a fact those involved appear to have been fully cognisant of; No. 570 Squadron considered it 'rather an expensive effort especially in view of the fact that the troops were not getting a great percentage of the supplies'.[126] This was not solely due to the slowly shrinking and already relatively tiny Airborne perimeter at Oosterbeek. The precise drop zones the bulk of the Squadrons were aiming for are unclear from the records, although No. 299 Squadron referred to 'dropping on DZ flashing "A"' and other signals, while No. 437 Squadron RCAF reported being guided by Verey lights and a 'drop here' sign of some description.[127] However, Nos. 48 and 271 Squadrons at least were still being briefed to deliver their loads onto DZ V, which had never actually been in British hands and lay over a mile outside the Oosterbeek perimeter to the north-east; this meant that at least 269 panniers and seventeen medical bundles were – if dropped accurately – delivered into German-held territory.[128] Only a fraction of the dropped materiel was recovered by its intended recipients, some and possibly all by elements of the 1st Airlanding Brigade, and duly passed on to Division HQ at the Hotel Hartenstein.[129] There the materiel remained as there was no practical means of distributing it, not least because the detachment of 250 (Airborne) Light Composite Company RASC responsible for such work had been seconded to 4th Parachute Brigade HQ as infantry reinforcements the previous day.[130] Even if that had not been the case the task would not have been achievable as the constant German bombardment and shortage of manpower ruled out manual distribution, while the streets within the perimeter were ' so blocked by falling trees, branches and houses that movement in jeeps [was] virtually impossible. Jeeps [were] in any case practically out of action'.[131] As we have seen, the beleaguered Airborne troops were being forced to gather and employ captured enemy weapons and ammunition by this point, and to forage for whatever food they could find to eke out the last remnants of their rations. The seriousness of the food situation is well illustrated by an evening entry in the 1st Airlanding Brigade HQ War Diary: 'A ration distribution, the first at Brigade HQ, worked out at one sardine and some biscuits per man.'[132]

The Saturday supply drop was preceded by a small piece of unfinished business. As we have seen, after repeated cancellations the 1st Polish Independent Parachute Brigade had finally taken off for Holland at 13:10 aboard 114 C-47s from the US 314th and 315th Troop Carrier Groups on Thursday 21 September, but when worsening weather prompted a recall only forty-one transports aborted the drop owing to a signal mix-up. Two of the returning aircraft carried sticks from the 2nd Battalion, eleven from the 3rd Battalion and the rest from the 1st Battalion, apparently in its entirety; one machine with a faulty radio reportedly overshot its home base in the cloudy murk and ended up in Ireland.[133] Major Marian Tonn, commander of the 1st Battalion, took command of the Polish strays and was ordered to have them at their respective airfield at 12:00 the following day in readiness for an afternoon take-off. By that time Major Tonn had received two rebuffs, the first to his seemingly reasonable request that all the outstanding Polish sticks be concentrated at a single airfield. It is unclear if the refusal originated with the USAAF or British liaison staff, but the latter were reportedly responsible for refusing a Polish request for fresh parachutes, on the grounds that those available had sat for several days in damp and wet conditions and were thus likely to malfunction. The unnamed British liaison officer responded by pointing out that the parachutes were in good order and countered by asking if Tonn was refusing to allow his men to jump; Tonn denied this but announced he would lodge an official protest in case any of his men were killed by parachute malfunction. A third and arguably more serious rebuff occurred thirty minutes after Tonn had arrived at RAF Spanhoe, when he was informed that he and his men were not to be dropped at Driel but at the US DZ O near Grave, around twenty miles distant and on the wrong side of the River Maas from the remainder of their Brigade. Tonn promptly protested to the commander of the 315th Troop Carrier Group, who replied that the matter was out of USAAF hands, after which Tonn was handed written orders and maps by the unnamed British liaison officer, who also informed the Polish commander that he would be met by another British liaison officer on the ground at Grave. Tonn's concern was understandable, but the German anti-aircraft fire that had greeted the main Polish drop on

21 September – and more importantly that against the British supply drop on 23 September – suggests the decision to deliver the Poles farther south was the correct one. As it turned out, the drop was cancelled at 13:00 and the Polish paratroopers were trucked the weary ten miles or so back to their billets once again.[134]

Major Tonn and his 559 men finally got away at 13:45 in the afternoon of Saturday 23 September, carried in forty-one C-47s drawn from the 315th Troop Carrier Group, along with 219 parachute packs of supplies and equipment.[135] The flight across the North Sea and up the Airborne Corridor was uneventful and the Poles dropped onto DZ O at 16:43 or 16:47 depending on the account.[136] They were preceded by a glider landing carrying reinforcements for the 82nd Airborne Division on the same landing area, which sandwiched the Polish drop with a second increment of a hundred Waco CG4s that commenced landing just seven minutes after the last Polish paratrooper was down. High winds across the DZ caused a number of landing injuries, but the Poles and their containers were clear of the landing area before the gliders started coming in. Within an hour Major Tonn had been met by a British Lieutenant-Colonel from Browning's Forward Corps HQ accompanied by a US officer, who took him to 82nd Airborne Division HQ where he was ordered to proceed to a wooded area near Malden, seven miles or so to the east, and await further orders. While briefing his men for the move Tonn was approached by another US officer, who informed him a Polish officer was looking for him. This was Captain Kazimierz Dendor, a Polish liaison officer also attached to the Forward Airborne Corps HQ. Dendor was unable to arrange transport for Tonn and his men to reach the rest of the Brigade, but promised to return with more information the following day; he also agreed to get word of the 1st Battalion's arrival to Sosabowski, although the Brigade War Diary suggests he did not manage to do so.[137] New orders came through placing Tonn under command of the 82nd Airborne Division until further notice, and the Poles were provided with US rations and tasked to protect a newly arrived US anti-tank unit for the night.[138]

***

On the south bank of the Lower Rhine 30 Corps spent Saturday 23 September consolidating and expanding its bridgehead over the River Waal at Nijmegen. As described, by midnight the previous day the 43rd Division had established a solid presence on the north bank of the River Waal with Lieutenant-Colonel George Taylor's 5th Duke of Cornwall's Light Infantry (DCLI) safely ensconced in Driel with the 1st Polish Independent Parachute Brigade, following its encounter and successful ambush of the Tiger and Panther tanks from *schwere Panzer Kompanie Hummel* and *SS Panzer Regiment 10* near the *De Hoop* crossroads. The remainder of Brigadier Hubert Essame's 214 Infantry Brigade, the 1st Battalion The Worcester Regiment and 7th Battalion Somerset Light Infantry, were occupying Valburg and Oosterhout respectively on the bridgehead perimeter. As the various delays meant that its objectives for Friday had not been achieved, 30 Corps issued a new set of instructions. The 5th Guards Armoured Brigade was to take over the eastern sector of the bridgehead perimeter and keep an armoured regiment on standby to support the 43rd Division, while the the 43rd was to protect the Nijmegen bridges, capture Elst, strengthen the tenuous link with the 1st Airborne Division and reconnoitre westwards between the River Waal and the Lower Rhine.[139] The orders may have been issued while Lieutenant-General Horrocks was temporarily cut off from his HQ whilst reporting to the commander of the British 2nd Army, Lieutenant-General Sir Miles Dempsey, at Veghel. A major attack by *Panzer* Brigade 107 and 59 *Infanterie* Division on 22 September cut the Nijmegen road between Veghel and Uden and it remained closed until it was reopened by elements of the 101st Airborne Division and the 32nd Guards Brigade Group in the afternoon of the following day; Horrocks appears to have issued a more detailed set of instructions on regaining his HQ.[140]

Major-General Ivor Thomas had originally intended 214 Brigade to head the 43rd Division's push north to Driel whilst Brigadier Gerard Mole's 129 Infantry Brigade advanced up the

Arnhem–Nijmegen highway to secure the Arnhem road bridge, but the fighting on 22 September had left those formations dispersed and needing time to regroup. 214 Brigade were spread across Driel, Oosterhout and Valburg and 129 Infantry Brigade were straddling the River Waal with one battalion bogged down in front of Ressen just north of the Nijmegen bridges. For 23 September Thomas therefore reorganised his unit assignments and ordered Brigadier Ben Walton's 130 Infantry Brigade, which had recently regrouped south of the Waal after its constituent battalions had been released from guarding the bridges at Grave and Neerbosch and assisting in clearing Nijmegen. Walton was instructed to reach the Lower Rhine by following the 5th DCLI's route to Driel via Valburg, with his Brigade travelling in DUKW amphibious trucks. It is unclear if the vehicles were provided specifically for the mission or whether they had been in use hitherto. Walton was reinforced with Sherman tanks from the 13th/18th Hussars. These vehicles had been attached to 129 Brigade for the attack toward Ressen but were redeployed because the close country and wide drainage ditches on that axis severely restricted their utility. A number of vehicles carrying twelve, fourteen or sixteen collapsible canvas assault boats were also attached to 130 Brigade for the advance to the Lower Rhine; the precise number varies between sources.[141] The vessels, which were reportedly the survivors of the US 504th Parachute Infantry Regiment's epic assault crossing of the River Waal on Wednesday 20 September, were accompanied by 3 Platoon, 204 Field Company RE, which was specially trained in river crossing techniques.[142] For its part, 129 Brigade was to continue to push against the German blocking line north of the Nijmegen bridges toward Ressen, while 214 Brigade was to clear the way for 130 Brigade by having the 7th Battalion Somerset Light Infantry vacate Oosterhout no later than 06:30 and then attack Elst in conjunction with the 1st Battalion The Worcestershire Regiment no earlier than 10:00, supported by tanks from the 4th/7th Dragoon Guards. Finally, 43 Reconnaissance Regiment were to probe westward beyond Valburg to assess German strength in the area between the Waal and Lower Rhine.[143]

130 Brigade crossed the River Waal after first light in heavy rain and mist, with Lieutenant-Colonel Basil Coad's 5th Battalion Dorsets in the lead followed by Lieutenant-Colonel Dennis Talbot's 7th Hampshires. Brigadier Walton's HQ came next, followed by Lieutenant-Colonel Gerald Tilley's 4th Dorsets Regiment to which were attached the vehicles carrying the assault boats.[144] The column passed along the elevated riverside road, through Slijk-Ewijk and into Valburg without incident, apart from some difficulty manoeuvring the DUKWs on the narrow embanked roads. All went well until the column approached a crossroads at Valburg, where German observers called down an artillery barrage intensified with direct fire from German tanks in Elst to the east. The shellfire hit a number of DUKWs and split the 5th Dorset's section of the column, with Lieutenant-Colonel Coad and approximately half his Battalion continuing unscathed to arrive at Driel at 11:30 while the rest of the Brigade came to a halt and sought cover. There then followed several hours of delay while the infantry debussed and made their way through the artillery fire via the deep drainage ditches alongside the road, whilst the DUKWs and other vehicles made best speed along the carriageway under covering fire from the Brigade's organic anti-tank guns and a mortar smokescreen; the latter were likely employed because the 43rd Division's artillery was fully engaged supporting the attack on Elst. As a result, 130 Brigade did not reach its assigned position on the Lower Rhine near Driel until the late afternoon. The reunited 5th Dorsets deployed on the bank of the Lower Rhine, probably to the east of Driel, the 7th Hampshires occupied Heteren to the west of Driel and Brigadier Walton set up his HQ at Homoet, four miles or so to the south-west, with the 4th Dorsets nearby in Brigade reserve.[145]

The delay at Valburg adversely affected 214 Brigade's attack on Elst. The waterlogged ground restricted much of Brigadier Essame's transport to the roads, and as the only route to the Brigade assembly area ran through Valburg it became entangled in 130 Brigade's traffic jam. The attack on Elst could not therefore go in as scheduled, although Brigadier Essame had some difficulty in getting Major-General Thomas to understand the situation via radio, prompting the Division commander to go forward to assess the situation in person. He arrived just as

Essame was holding a final pre-attack meeting with his commanders over a snooker table in a local hostelry, as the traffic situation had finally been resolved. The area was still under German artillery fire and Thomas' arrival coincided with a salvo that blew out all the hostelry windows and caused a number of casualties outside the building; Thomas expressed his dissatisfaction with the location of the meeting with his 'normal brevity and force' before a second salvo 'brought the conference to an even speedier conclusion' than was customary.[146] The attack went in at 16:55. Attacking over drier ground from the west, Lieutenant-Colonel Robert Osborne-Smith's 1st Worcesters led with D Company in front supported by Shermans from C Squadron 4th/7th Dragoon Guards, and by nightfall the Battalion was firmly ensconced in the western outskirts of Elst, having knocked out two Panthers and a Tiger getting there. On the right, the 7th Somerset Light Infantry had more difficulty rendezvousing with its vehicles and tank support after the infantry component had pushed forward on foot owing to the boggy nature of the attack frontage but nonetheless reached its objective, a crossroads south-west of Elst, against 'slight opposition'. Lieutenant-Colonel Borradaile therefore pushed his D Company on to secure another crossroads on the main Nijmegen–Arnhem road and thus inadvertently severed the main German line of communication with the units blocking the advance northward from the Nijmegen bridges. The development was of little immediate assistance to 129 Brigade's continuing push toward Ressen but within an hour D Company had captured or shot up 'two despatch riders, a 20mm A.A. gun complete with crew, an artillery officer and a ration truck'. Confused fighting continued through the night.

The 43rd Reconnaissance Regiment's A and C Squadrons had pushed north from Slijk-Ewijk through light resistance from German rear echelon troops to reach the Lower Rhine at Randwijk, just west of Heteren, while B Squadron set up midway and cleared the area around Zetteren. As a result 'the main axis of the [43rd] Division through Valburg could therefore be considered as reasonably secure at last light.'[147] By this point the GARDEN advance was over ninety hours behind schedule, and despite the passing of twenty-four hours since British lead ground elements had reached the Lower Rhine, there had been little progress in getting succour to the embattled 1st Airborne Division fighting for its life on the north bank.

The imminent arrival of the 43rd Division in the vicinity of Driel did permit Lieutenant-Colonel Mackenzie, the 1st Airborne Division's Operations Officer, to proceed with his mission of impressing the urgency of the situation in Oosterbeek upon Browning and Horrocks in person. Mackenzie, it will be recalled, had crossed the Lower Rhine to Driel with the Division's Commander Royal Engineers (CRE), Lieutenant-Colonel Edmund Myers in the early afternoon of 22 September but they were unable to proceed as the Germans were still blocking the way to Nijmegen. However, the mist and rain on Saturday morning encouraged the commander of one of the Troops from the 2nd Household Cavalry Regiment in Driel, Captain Lord Richard Wrottesley, to risk a run back the eighteen miles or so to the Nijmegen bridgehead. Captain Wrottesley's decision may also have been influenced by the arrival at Driel of a Captain Watson from Browning's Forward Airborne Corps HQ at 09:00.[148] According to his account, Major-General Sosabowski was not overly impressed with Watson's questioning, on the grounds he had 'sent plenty of information already'. The relayed instructions from Browning for the Poles to lead a third attempted river crossing that night did not go down well either, although he kept his reservations to himself and agreed, providing more boats were forthcoming, along with a resupply of food and ammunition. Watson responded with assurances that as many boats as needed would be provided by the 43rd Division, along with support from long-range artillery.[149] Sosabowski was also mollified to learn that his missing 1st Battalion had returned safely to the UK when its transports had been recalled on 21 September and would be delivered to Holland as soon as possible; as we have seen, Major Tonn and his men were to be delivered to US DZ O near Grave, south-west of Nijmegen, at around 16:43.[150]

Lieutenant-Colonel Mackenzie's passage back to Nijmegen, possibly travelling on the back of one of Captain Wrottesley's Daimler Armoured Cars, was eventful.[151] The convoy of two armoured and two scout cars made good progress until reaching a crossroads partially blocked by a wrecked German armoured vehicle, possibly *De Hoop* crossroads where the 5th DCLI had carried out its successful tank ambush the previous night. Captain Wrottesley had dismounted from the lead Armoured Car and guided the driver around the obstacle when a German tank reported as a Tiger approached the junction. The second Daimler Armoured Car carrying Mackenzie exchanged shots with the tank but overturned whilst reversing as the road verge collapsed beneath its seven-ton weight. The tank then withdrew but the approach of German infantry obliged Captain Wrottesley to make a dash for Nijmegen for help while the two Daimler Scout Cars, one of them carrying Lieutenant-Colonel Myers, withdrew the way they had come, also in an effort to summon assistance. Mackenzie and the two crewman from the overturned vehicle, armed with a single Sten gun between them, hid under a pile of cuttings in an adjacent turnip field. There they managed to evade the searching Germans despite one enemy soldier approaching to within feet of their hiding place, only to come under fire from friendly troops when Wrottesley returned accompanied by British tanks. The friendly fire was fortunately poorly aimed and Mackenzie and Myers were then delivered to Browning's Forward Corps HQ without further incident. The HQ had been located in a 'large and comfortable house' in the southern outskirts of Nijmegen from the afternoon of Wednesday 20 September, and a thoroughly wet and frozen Mackenzie was provided with a hot bath by Browning's chief-of-staff, Brigadier Gordon Walch.[152]

The bath and short stay in the warmth and safety of the Forward Corps HQ does not appear to have been of much restorative benefit, given that Browning described both officers as 'putty coloured, like men who had come through a Somme winter'.[153] According to Lieutenant-Colonel Walch and his staff Browning was 'disgusted' with the 43rd Division's tardy performance and with Major-General Thomas in particular, and was anxious to hear Mackenzie's report because his knowledge of events and conditions north of the Lower Rhine was 'apparently very vague'. The records show, however, that Urquhart's communications had been relaying the deterioration and urgency of his situation quite clearly; Browning's avowed, 'public' dismay was therefore due at least in part to the growing realisation that his exercise in self-promotion to shore up his Airborne credentials was turning into a monumental failure.[154] Mackenzie obliged with a full and frank account of events and current conditions at Oosterbeek, which ended: 'if there's a chance of the 2nd Army getting to us we can hold – but not for long. There isn't much left.' Browning reportedly listened in silence before assuring Mackenzie that he had not given up hope and that plans were being implemented to get reinforcements and supplies across the Lower Rhine during the coming night. According to Brigadier Walch, Browning went on to temper this encouraging news: 'I do remember Browning telling Charles that there did not seem to be much chance of getting a good party across,' although it is unclear on what, if anything, this assessment was based (and what a 'good party' would represent).[155]

Perhaps unsurprisingly, Mackenzie left Browning's HQ with the feeling that he had failed to convey the gravity of the 1st Airborne's situation properly, partly because 'a messenger bearing bad news is always presumed to be exaggerating'. He was also struck by the 'ambivalence of thinking there'.[156] To be fair, there was not much Browning could do officially, given that Lieutenant-General Horrocks and 30 Corps had assumed control of operations on reaching Nijmegen, with decision-making powers thus passing to Horrocks and the commander of the British 2nd Army, Lieutenant-General Sir Miles Dempsey; on the other hand, there is no evidence of Browning actively promoting the needs of his formation fighting on the other side of the Lower Rhine either.[157] Mackenzie's disquiet was shared by Myers, and both men were additionally concerned over the marked lack of urgency they saw on display on their subsequent visits to 30 Corps and 43rd Division HQs. Mackenzie went on to attend an Orders Group at 130 Brigade HQ at Homoet at some point before 19:00, after which he appears to have returned to Driel.[158]

With the cessation of the crossing effort at 04:00 Sosabowski's 3rd Battalion had returned to its positions in Driel, with Lieutenat Smaczny's 8th Company being initially replaced by men from

Captain Siudzinski's Transport and Supply Company, augmented with some HQ personnel. Lance-Corporal Boleslav Kuzniar returned to find his former slit trench had been replaced by a shell crater, the shell having killed the man who had taken over the trench on his departure. Kuzniar set about digging a replacement and then prevailed upon the Dutch family in a nearby farmhouse for hot water to allow him to wash and shave.[159] The arrival of the 43rd Division in the vicinity appears to have mitigated the threat of ground attack, although a German patrol probed the 4th Company's positions, reportedly using a Dutch civilian as cover for its withdrawal.[160] At least one German fighter strafed the Polish positions, shooting up a farm building occupied by signaller Privates Adamowicz and Wawiorko; neither man was injured but Wawiorko was badly shaken up. There was no let-up in the German artillery fire. 2nd Lieutenant Jozef Kula's platoon from the 1st Battalion was relocated into an orchard to further reinforce the 8th Company gap and came under *nebelwerfer* fire whilst digging in. The paratroopers were presumably spotted by SS *Werfergruppe* Nickmann, located just across the river behind the Oosterbeek Laag railway embankment, and repeated salvoes of 150mm rockets drove the paratroopers back into the orchard, partly demolished a barn and wounded at least one man; he was saved from being killed by a pair of heavy-duty wire cutters attached to his webbing, which partly deflected a large piece of shrapnel.

The German shelling paid particular attention to the Driel church tower, which the Poles were using as an observation post, and a sustained barrage scored twenty hits on the building in quick succession, killing a member of a Polish burial detail.[161] The paratroopers enjoyed a measure of respite and revenge in the afternoon with the arrival of the Allied fighter-bomber cover for the Oosterbeek resupply drop, which prompted the German artillery to cease fire to avoid attracting attention. The Poles climbed out of their slit trenches for a better view of RAF Typhoons strafing *Sperrverband* Harzer's positions behind the Arnhem–Nijmegen railway embankment with rockets and cannon fire; as Major-General Sosabowski recalled, 'the fighters emptied their cannons at every likely target; the noise was horrific and dust drifted over the whole area, choking the men and obscuring the view'.[162] The Poles also watched helplessly as the tail end of the RAF resupply flight flew into the unsuppressed German anti-aircraft fire. They gathered in some supply containers that dropped short into the Driel perimeter; signaller Private Wawiorko recalled sorting through ration cans in search of corned beef and being disappointed to find only Canadian-made potato soup and some kind of pudding. The respite from the German artillery fire was short-lived, and resumed with greater intensity at around 16:30 once the fighter-bombers had made way for the supply drop and the latter was complete.[163] On a lighter note, 23 September was the third anniversary of the formation of the Polish Parachute Brigade in 1941. Major-General Sosabowski had understandably forgotten the significance of the date but his staff had not, and he was waylaid into a room by an aide to find them 'gathered around an iced cake commemorating the Brigade Anniversary. I was deeply touched and surprised that they had remembered in the midst of battle'.[164]

Following his discussion with Captain Watson and the orders for the Polish Brigade to lead a third river crossing that night, Sosabowski called a staff meeting at 10:00. It is unclear if Watson was still present, but an RAMC Brigadier from Browning's Corps HQ who arrived in Driel with or after Watson discussed obtaining medical supplies and evacuating the Polish wounded with the Brigade Medical Officer, Major Jan Golba.[165] Sosabowski then despatched his Chief of Staff, Major Ryszard Malaszkiewicz, to chase up the boats and rations pledged by Captain Watson using a Jeep supplied by the 4th/7th Dragoon Guards; according to one source the vehicle and driver was the first direct assistance the Polish Brigade had received from the 43rd Division since the 5th DCLI had reached Driel at 20:00 on 22 September.[166] Major Malaszkiewicz made his way over the four miles or so to Homoet – driving cross-country over tulip fields at one point to avoid a trio of dug-in German tanks reported by medical troops encountered en route – to Brigadier Walton's 130 Brigade HQ. On arrival he was shocked by the contrast between conditions at Driel and the British HQ, which had 'so many telephone lines and tents, it looked like a peacetime maneuver'. Malaszkiewicz was more impressed with Brigadier Walton, the Polish officer found him 'combative...and wanting to continue the advance' but lacking the orders to do so.[167] The talks between the two officers regarding boats, artillery support and supplies proved to be both cordial and fruitful, although it is unclear if the discussion was part of or separate from the 130 Brigade Orders Group attended by Lieutenant-Colonels Mackenzie and Myers.

Major Malaszkiewicz reported back to Major-General Sosabowski at Driel at 19:00, informing him that Brigadier Walton would provide twenty-four large assault boats capable of carrying between sixteen and eighteen men apiece, which would be delivered to Driel by 20:30.[168] According to the British official records the vessels were to be handed over 'with personnel to operate them' and the 43rd Division's semi-official history specifies men from 204 Field Company RE and the 5th Dorsets Regiment, while Cholewczynski refers to 'Canadian sappers attached to the Wessex division'.[169] There is some confusion here, for despite the unequivocal evidence from the War Diary of the RE unit involved, Major Malaszkiewicz clearly reported that the Poles would have to provide crews for the assault boats themselves, as cited in the Polish Brigade War Diary; Major-General Sosabowski also referred to receiving the 'rather surprising news that we would have to supply the crews as well'.[170] Whatever the rationale for that, artillery support would be provided by guns from the 43rd Division and 30 Corps controlled from the riverside dyke at Driel, and an issue of rations was to be delivered in the course of the evening.[171] Sosabowski promptly called a staff conference also attended by Lieutenant-Colonel Mackenzie, an unnamed Royal Artillery officer from 30 Corps, and possibly Lieutenant-Colonel Myers; the three may have travelled back from Homoet with Major Malaszkiewicz. Captain Budziszewski's Engineer Company was tasked to organise the crossing and man the assault boats, and a warning order was issued to the remainder of the Brigade to sort men into boatloads of eighteen with ammunition, heavy weapons and other equipment spread across the groupings to expedite rapid loading and unloading and to offset the impact of possible boat losses. The outlook for artillery support was less positive, with the RA officer from 30 Corps stressing that supporting fire would have to be restricted due to a shortage of ammunition; he later expressed concern that artillery fire was likely to be ineffective owing to the close proximity of friend and foe, after observing the lower portion of the Oosterbeek perimeter from the south bank of the Lower Rhine.[172] Sosabowski held a commander's briefing at 21:30 where he laid out the Brigade's order of embarkation for the crossing. The remaining elements of the 3rd Battalion were to cross first, followed by Brigade HQ, the various Brigade specialist elements, the 2nd Battalion and finally the Engineer Company bringing up the rear; the commanders were then dismissed to brief their men.[173] On returning to the 3rd Battalion area, temporary commander Captain Ignacy Gazurek informed 2nd Lieutenant Kula that his misplaced party from the 1st Battalion would be accompanying his men on the crossing and rounded off with the cheery observation that 'across the river our skins will be better thrashed than here'.[174]

With his commanders dismissed, Sosabowski continued to discuss the situation with an unknown British officer according to 2nd Lieutenant Szczesny Relidzinski, who had been sleeping in the attic above the meeting room. The unknown British officer may have been Lieutenant-Colonel Mackenzie given the timings, and according to Relidzinski the Polish Brigade commander expressed serious concern about his troop's tiredness, and lack of ammunition and food: 'Unless supplies come today, it's difficult to even talk about crossing. The soldiers cannot go hungry...we cannot even guess about anything on the other side.' The very tired-sounding British officer responded by assuring Sosabowski that the promised supplies would arrive as arranged.[175] Assuming the anonymous British officer was Lieutenant-Colonel Mackenzie, the overheard discussion must have taken place shortly before he returned to Oosterbeek at 23:00 via a boat organised by Major John Winchester from the 9th (Airborne) Field Company RE and again rowed by Lieutenant Storrs.[176] On arrival at the Hotel Hartenstein at 23:45, Mackenzie opted to keep his disquiet over Browning's poor grasp of the gravity of the situation and the marked lack of urgency displayed by 30 Corps and the 43rd Division to himself, a somewhat presumptuous action in the circumstances and one that was arguably beyond his remit as Divisional GSO1. He restricted his report to detailing the imminent second attempt to ferry the Poles across from Driel that night and that the 43rd Division were planning to establish a brigade bridgehead on the north bank of the Lower Rhine to allow the Royal Engineers to construct a bridge for reinforcements.[177] His moral dilemma aside, Mackenzie was likely relieved to regain the relative quiet and safety of the Oosterbeek perimeter after a day that had involved having an armoured car topple from under him and subsequent near capture by German infantry, meeting with two Corps, one Division and one Brigade commander, smoothing over a potential Anglo-Polish dispute and crossing a wide and fast-running river in pitch darkness under enemy fire.

Meanwhile Captain Budziszewski's Engineers were busy organising the Polish Brigade's crossing of the Lower Rhine. A concentration area was established in an orchard set back behind the tall riverside dyke with paths to two embarkation points around 300 yards beyond the dyke across the mudflats at the water's edge. One crossing point, which had been employed the previous night, was controlled by 2nd Lieutenant Mieczyslaw Grünbaum and 2nd Lieutenant Stanislaw Skulski, while the other, 500 yards to the west, was controlled by Lieutenant Jan Dawidowicz. Lieutenant Wieslaw Szczygiel, who was in overall charge of the crossing, oversaw the laying of white tapes to mark the paths after dark, and had some men wade out into the river at the crossing points to check the depth while Captain Budziszewski established his Company Command Post in a shell-damaged house north of the dyke.[178] The remainder of the Brigade had by now withdrawn from its positions and concentrated in Driel proper in anticipation of the arrival of the assault boats at 20:30 and while they did not appear as scheduled, the promised ammunition and rations were delivered at around 21:00.[179] The food appears to have been a mix-and-match effort using emergency rations; Lance-Corporal Kuzniar from the 3rd Battalion reported being issued with a can of sweets of unknown provenance, a bar of US D Ration chocolate and a cube of pemmican dried meat.[180] If Kuzniar's experience was typical it suggests that the victuals were emergency rations hastily gathered in by 43rd Division QMs, augmented with what were described as 'locally canned preserves', which the paratroopers picked through for the most edible; it is unclear if the local produce came up with the emergency rations or had been procured by the Poles themselves. Many of the heavy cans were abandoned unopened in the streets of Driel as the paratroopers sought to minimise their burdens, which suggests that Sosabowski may have been overcooking his men's hunger, so to speak.[181] With the rations distributed the bulk of the 1st Polish Independent Parachute Brigade moved off for the orchard concentration area at some point between 22:30 and 23:00, leaving behind a small party to guide the assault boats forward when they finally arrived.[182] Sosabowski's men were thus poised to make their third consecutive attempt to bring a measure of relief to the embattled 1st Airborne Division on the north bank of the Lower Rhine.

D Plus 7

00:01 to 23:59 Sunday 24 September 1944

Major-General Sosabowski and the portion of the 1ˢᵗ Polish Independent Parachute Brigade on the south bank of the Lower Rhine gathered in Driel for their third attempt to cross the river to reinforce the 1ˢᵗ Airborne Division at around 20:00 on Saturday 23 September 1944. The eighteen assault boats promised by 130 Brigade did not materialise as arranged at 20:30 but a delivery of food, consisting of a variety of emergency rations gathered up and forwarded by 30 Corps augmented with local produce, did. Once this largesse had been distributed, the paratroopers moved off for the concentration area marked out by Captain Budziszewski's Engineer Company, leaving a party to bring the assault boats forward when they arrived; it is unclear if the carrying party was drawn from the Engineer Company or from the wider Brigade. The paratroopers moved silently through the rainy darkness along a muddy track that paralleled the riverside dyke, partly illuminated by a nearby burning farm building. The firelight revealed a number of containers from that afternoon's supply drop dangling from nearby trees, although there was no attempt to collect them. On arrival at the concentration area, which encompassed the edge of an orchard and a stretch of polder in the lee of the riverside dyke, the Poles split into their pre-arranged boat groups and settled down to wait in the wet grass.[1] They were joined at some point by Major-General Sosabowski, who established a forward HQ by the dyke from which to monitor the crossing.[2]

The British side of the crossing was controlled by the 1ˢᵗ Airborne Division CRE Lieutenant-Colonel Edmund Myers assisted by Major Hugh Maguire from Division HQ, who was recently returned to duty after being wounded; Maguire was commanding a party drawn from the 1ˢᵗ Airlanding Brigade's Defence Platoon tasked to guide the Poles to an area of slit trenches where they were to spend the night.[3] The Poles were also planning to provide their own security. Men from Captain Budziszewski's Engineer Company were briefed to cross in the initial wave to provide security on the north bank and assist in turning the assault boats around.[4] A primary source suggests that Lieutenant Henry Brown and a party of twenty Sappers from the 4ᵗʰ Parachute Squadron RE accompanied by a Lance-Sergeant Lake from the 9ᵗʰ (Airborne) Field Company RE were again involved, although this appears to be unlikely.[5] Some of the Poles already on the north bank of the Lower Rhine were certainly involved. Captain Ludwik Zwolanski spent the first part of the night in the cellar of the Hotel Hartenstein with the rest of the Polish Liaison Team before moving off for the riverbank at just before 02:00, accompanied by War Correspondent Marek Swiecicki. Behind them Major-General Urquhart was reportedly communicating with Sosabowski via the radio set operated by a Cadet Corporal Pajak, although there is no mention of such contact in the official records or either senior officer's personal accounts. Zwolanski and Swiecicki were preceded by Captain Alfons Mackowiak, also from the Liaison Team, who, as an artillery officer, had been working with the 1ˢᵗ Airlanding Light Regiment; Mackowiak had also acted as a seemingly unofficial guide during the previous night's crossing.[6]

The assault boats finally arrived in Driel between 00:20 and 00:30 on a number of DUKWs whose drivers wasted no time in departing once their cargo had been unloaded. The arrival of the vessels was just the beginning of the Pole's problems. The commander of 130 Brigade had promised Sosabowski's Chief-of-Staff twenty-four large assault boats capable of carrying sixteen to eighteen men apiece. However, the DUKWs delivered just twelve collapsible wood and canvas assault boats reassigned from the 4th Dorsets, reportedly as previously indicated survivors from the assault crossing of the River Waal by the 504th Parachute Infantry Regiment on 20 September. The vessels had a total capacity of around sixteen men and as the Poles intended to crew each boat with four of Captain Budziszewski's Engineers, the number of passengers was reduced accordingly.[7] While the Polish accounts give the impression that they crewed the craft themselves, at least some appear to have been manned by Sappers from 3 Platoon, 204 Field Company RE from the 43rd Division's divisional assets, which moved up from a harbour area at the north end of the Nijmegen road bridge at 21:00 on 23 September.[8]

The craft substitution rendered the Pole's careful division of men and equipment into boat parties redundant and they were thus obliged to reorganise in the concentration area with darkness, the need for stealth and sporadic German mortar and artillery fire hampering officers and NCOs in identifying and reordering men and equipment; the process was further complicated by tired paratroopers falling asleep during the process. Consequently, it was over two hours before the reorganisation was complete and the crossing could commence, covered by the Polish Brigade's mortars and the 43rd Division's artillery, the latter reportedly firing at maximum range; one source also refers to the 4th/7th Dragoon Guards' Sherman tanks firing across the river.[9] Carrying the 200-pound assault boats in addition to their personal weapons, kit and other equipment, the first dozen boat parties made their way down the slippery polder, manhandled the boats over the dyke and across the sucking mud to the water's edge at 03:00.[10] The parties may also have included more men than the vessels could actually carry to ease the burden; Lance-Corporal Boleslav Kuzniar recalled the boat he helped carry and launch being filled up as he struggled with a kit-bag filled with signals equipment and having to find a place on another, for example.[11]

German observation of the crossing site was assisted by illumination from the burning building on the south bank, the blazing roof timbers of which War Correspondent Swiecicki likened to 'an apocalyptic cross'.[12] This was increased with liberal use of flares and by opening and igniting a main at the Oosterbeek municipal gas works just west of the crossing point, which Major-General Sosabowski assumed to be the result of Allied or German artillery setting fire to a building.[13] The volume of German artillery and mortar fire increased as soon as the Poles left the cover of the dyke to move down to the water's edge, inspissated with sustained machine-gun fire from weapons sited on both banks to cover embarkation and debarkation points and the intervening stretch of river itself. On the south bank Major-General Sosabowski recalled seeing an assault boat floating 'empty and abandoned downstream, because all the crew had been killed or wounded', while on the northern polder Captain Zwolanski and War Correspondent Swiecicki watched German tracer rounds from both sides of the river converge on one unfortunate assault boat and follow it all the way across, before swinging back to engage another vessel.[14] The boat may have been the one carrying Lance-Corporal Kuzniar, which reached the middle of the river before being fully illuminated by a flare popping overhead and then raked with tracer rounds that set fire to the vessel's canvas sides and wounded one paratrooper in the arm. The horrified pause the incident elicited was ended by an angry order from the rear of the boat that set all the occupants rowing as fast as they could.[15] The initial waves of the crossing carried Captain Ignacy Gazurek and men from his 3rd Battalion including the Battalion Padre, Reverend Hubert Misiuda; Gazurek had refused the Padre permission to accompany the Battalion on the not unreasonable grounds that carrying unarmed passengers was a waste of effort, but Misiuda ignored the order and sneaked aboard one of the assault boats in the confusion. In another boat 2nd Lieutenant Leon Prochowski, a Platoon commander in the 9th Company, was wounded in the leg by a round that passed through the man rowing in front of him.[16]

On reaching the north bank the assault boats rapidly unloaded their passengers, who required little urging, and repeated the hazardous journey back across the bullet- and shrapnel-frothed water to collect another load, carrying casualties back with them. Major-General Sosabowski recalled that 'files of stretcher bearers trudged past' his Forward HQ en route to the Brigade Main Dressing Station in Driel whenever he emerged to check on progress.[17] The boat parties were relentlessly organised and chivvied by the officers controlling the embarkation points, Engineer Lieutenants Dawidowicz and Grünbaum. The latter was especially active, briefing and leading parties to the river, assisting with loading and launching boats and on occasion successfully urging the men on with un-officerlike profanity; he was wounded in the face by a shell fragment shortly before the crossing was halted.[18] Thanks to their efforts and despite the intensity of the German fire the bulk of the 3rd Battalion was across the river within an hour and the Brigade specialist elements and HQ began to cross. The assault boat ahead of that carrying Private Zbigniew Raschke from Brigade HQ sank after being caught in crossfire which then riddled Raschke's vessel, hitting 2nd Lieutenant Waclaw Jaworski multiple times and Lance-Sergeant Tomasz Lepalczyk in the head, killing both men.[19] The boat carrying Captain Jan Kanty Wardzala, the commander of the Brigade's Anti-tank Battery and Brigade QM Lieutenant-Colonel Marcin Rotter made landfall safely on the north bank but after being carried downstream by the current. All were taken prisoner, possibly after a brief firefight, by German troops who appear to have allowed the Poles to unload and the assault boat to depart before revealing themselves; the prisoners included an unfortunate and unnamed private who, ironically, had been put aboard the boat by Lieutenant Zbigniew Bossowski, the Anti-tank Battery's Supply Officer with specific orders to look after Captain Wardzala, 'no matter what'.[20] The also unnamed Engineer Corporal who had paddled the boat reported his suspicion of what had happened to Captain Budziszewski on returning to the south bank, who responded with a blunt 'You must row harder.' Budziszewski was wounded in the hand by a shell burst just moments later as he returned the salute of another reporting paratrooper.[21]

The Poles stubbornly continued to push men across the river until first light began to grey the sky, although traffic was channelled to just one of the crossing points toward the end, possibly because the other had been accurately registered by *SS Werfergruppe* Nickmann. Unsurprisingly in the stress and confusion, some of the Poles reportedly 'went astray' on reaching the north bank and ended up in the 1st Airlanding Regiment's perimeter near the Oosterbeek Old Church, presumably because the church had been the designated rendezvous for the previous night's crossing.[22] This group included Lance-Corporal Kuzniar and his companions, who saw the church silhouetted against the skyline after moving inland; this may have been further upstream than intended, given that they crossed an area carpeted with German dead and reported spotting the church to their west.[23] It may also have included men gathered by Captain Mackowiak, who repeatedly exposed himself to enemy fire to call out to paratroopers struggling with their burdens through the sticky mud extending up from the water's edge; after gathering a group between thirty and forty strong he handed them over to Captain Zwolanski and War Correspondent Swiecicki, who in turn led them to unspecified British positions near the Oosterbeek Old Church. This group may also have included Lieutenant Prochowski who, on reaching cover, took the opportunity to pull the bullet from his still-functioning leg with his fingers and apply a field dressing to the wound.[24] Likely the last boat to reach the north bank carried 2nd Lieutenant Szczesny Relidzinski and some of his men from the Brigade HQ Signal Section, which landed at just before 05:00.[25]

Precisely who issued the order that brought the crossing to a halt is unclear. Major-General Sosabowski takes the credit in his memoir, but participant testimony suggests it was actually the Deputy Brigade Commander, Colonel Jan Kaminski. Private Piotr Wawiorko, who was attempting to follow his Section commander with a kitbag full of signals equipment, recalled Colonel Kaminski standing at the water's edge shouting over the noise of bursting shells for the paratroopers to break off and get back into cover; Wawiorko also recalled being waylaid and accused of cowardice by Sosabowski while falling back across the polder until he explained that he was only following orders.[26] Whoever issued the order, the Poles' third effort to cross the Lower Rhine and reinforce the Oosterbeek perimeter ceased at 05:05 in the morning of Sunday 24 September 1944, leaving Major-General Sosabowski, part of Brigade HQ and the 2nd Battalion still on the south bank of the Lower Rhine. There were also ten men from the Anti-tank Battery and all the Other Ranks from the 3rd Battalion's Mortar Platoon. The latter had become separated from their commander, Lieutenant Jan Kutrzeba, when their heavily laden Airborne handcarts had become bogged in the soft polder; Lieutenant Kutrzeba thus arrived on the north bank with no command. His men were amalgamated with the anti-tank gunners under Lieutenant Tadeusz Rembisz and attached to the 2nd Battalion.[27] Tired and bedraggled after a sleepless night under German fire, the paratroopers and their commander once again retraced their steps to their recently vacated positions in Driel in the grey dawn. While the results may not have met hopes or expectations, the Poles had once again done their very best with the poor hand they had been dealt. Perhaps the most fitting comment on their efforts is the much-quoted observation by the man who had controlled the effort on the north bank, CRE Lieutenant-Colonel Myers:

> I can find no fault with their attempts; they did as much as they could. They had not been trained in river crossings, and the Arnhem plan had not envisaged one, and no one had any proper boats. But the less said about their watermanship the better.[28]

A total of 153 Poles reached the north bank of the Lower Rhine in a combat-ready state, excluding an unknown number of killed and wounded who, as we have seen, were immediately evacuated back across the river by returning boats;[29] the Platoon from 204 Field Company RE also lost two men missing and an NCO wounded in the course of the night, with the latter presumably being evacuated to the Polish Brigade Forward Dressing Station.[30] Including the casualties may explain the figure of 200 men cited by Major-General Sosabowski and reported in the British official records, a conjecture supported by the arrival of an additional forty casualties at the Polish Brigade MDS in Driel during and in the aftermath of the crossing; fortuitously, a reconnaissance party from 163 Field Ambulance had escorted the medical portion of the Polish Brigade's seaborne tail to Driel late in the evening of 23 September.[31] 1st Airlanding Brigade HQ cited a lower figure of 125, which may exclude Poles who made their own way into the 1st Airborne Division's perimeter and thus went unrecorded.[32] Of the 153, ninety-five were from the 3rd Battalion, forty-four from the Anti-tank Battery and fourteen from various Sections of Brigade HQ.[33] They were initially concentrated in the *Hemelsche Berg*, an area of woodland just north of the Benedendorpsweg and adjacent to the 1st Airlanding Light Regiment's gun pits; the location included a two-storey convalescent home called the *Hemeldal* set in landscaped grounds with two large ornamental ponds, which prompted the British to refer to the area as 'the ponds'.[34] Captain Zwolanski directed Captain Gazurek and the 3rd Battalion to the woods to the north of the *Hemeldal* while the anti-tank gunners, now commanded by Lieutenant Mieczyslaw Mikulski following Captain Wardzala's capture during the crossing, and the Brigade HQ personnel, occupied or dug slit trenches around the building. Brigade Signals Officer Captain Julian Karasek and his platoon colonised the building itself, where the cellar proved to be filled with Dutch civilian wounded to whom Karasek donated a satchel full of medical supplies he had come upon after landing.[35]

The area was quiet when the Poles arrived, although the guides from the 1st Airlanding Brigade reported that their charges were 'difficult to control and were very noisy, causing alarm to all troops in the vicinity'.[36] The Poles appear to have found their new hosts rather less concerned. Corporal Cadet Adam Niebieszczanski from the Signals Platoon unsuccessfully tried to pass off some of his canned rations to a British neighbour, a rather surprising result given the shortage of food in the Oosterbeek perimeter, while one of his comrades was more than happy to exchange one of his hand-grenades with another British paratrooper for the considerable sum of £5.[37] Despite the shelling in Driel the quiet lulled the Poles into a false sense of security, with Captain Zwolanski having to urge members of the Signal Section to dig in while 2nd Lieutenant Bossowski from the Anti-tank Battery had to specifically order his men to break out their entrenching tools.[38] The routine commencement of the German bombardment at around 07:00 therefore came as an unpleasant surprise and caused a number of casualties, including the unitless Lieutenant Kutrzeba, who was killed by shrapnel whilst sheltering in a covered slit trench.[39]

The Pole's original plan had been to deploy their Battalions as complete units and for the Anti-tank Gunners to rejoin the 6-Pounder guns and crews that had come in with the glider lift on Tuesday 19 September. However, on making contact with the ranking officer from the glider lift, Lieutenant Wladyslaw Mleczko, Lieutenant Mikulski discovered that there were only four Polish guns still functioning and that these were either embedded with, or had been appropriated by, British units, rendering the reinforcements superfluous.[40] In the event the decision was taken out of the Poles' hands, and Captain Zwolanski appears to have led the entire newly arrived contingent to the area of the 1st Airborne Division HQ at 09:00; interestingly, there does not appear to have been any thought of reuniting Lieutenant Smaczny and the 8th Company contingent at the *Transvalia* with their parent 3rd Battalion. Zwolanski also despatched two of Lieutenant Mikulski's to help man anti-tank guns and transferred a further three, all armed with Bren guns, to the 3rd Battalion contingent. It is unclear if this minor reorganisation occurred before or after arrival at the Hotel Hartenstein. Captain Gazurek and his ninety-four men were then assigned to the 4th Parachute Brigade HQ on the eastern side of the perimeter, while Lieutenant Mikulski and his forty-three Anti-tank Gunners were assigned to the 1st Airlanding Brigade to fight as infantry on the western side; the HQ personnel appear to have been allotted to the Division reserve.[41]

***

The night began relatively quietly at the Hotel Hartenstein but at 01:20 the hotel and the immediate vicinity came under a heavy and sustained mortar barrage that continued for over an hour; according to the Royal Engineers HQ War Diary it ceased at 02:57 precisely. The Germans may by this point have become aware that the hotel was the site of the 1st Airborne Division's HQ, either through direct observation by the elements of *Kampfgruppe* von Tettau from the west, or possibly from monitoring signals traffic. Whatever the reason, the rest of the night appears to have remained quiet until the regular German bombardment of the Airborne perimeter recommenced just after dawn at 07:29.[42] The daylight threat was not solely from German artillery, rocket launchers and mortars, as the proximity of the front line to the west and north-west of the Hotel Hartenstein rendered the hotel and surrounding area susceptible to small-arms fire. The Division Commander Royal Artillery, Lieutenant-Colonel Robert Loder-Symonds, and his Brigade Major Philip Tower narrowly escaped being hit in the entrance to the Royal Artillery HQ bunker in the hotel grounds for example, by what was reported as a sniper, prompting the HQ to move its wireless sets deeper underground and redirect the aerials through the bunker roof. The Division Signals section reported that 'things were very difficult at Div HQ throughout the day owing to… the fact that [hotel] entrances were covered by enemy snipers.'[43] At 05:35 1st Airborne Division HQ received a sitrep from British 2nd Army HQ via the PHANTOM net which summarised the 43rd Division's activities on the south bank of the Lower Rhine, detailing 129 and 214 Brigades efforts toward Ressen and Elst respectively. More importantly, it also informed Major-General Urquhart that 130 Brigade was to assault across the river in the vicinity of the Heveadorp ferry with two battalions that night. A Class 40 bridge was then to be constructed across the river over which 129 and 214 Brigades were to reinforce and expand the bridgehead to the east and west.[44]

Although it reiterated the information provided by Lieutenant-Colonel Mackenzie on his return to the Hotel Hartenstein shortly before midnight on Saturday, receiving official confirmation of imminent reinforcement likely lifted Urquhart's spirits, at least until he was called to the radio to speak to his opposite number commanding the 43rd Division, Major-General Ivor Thomas. The timing of the conversation is unclear but was probably in the late morning or early afternoon. It did not go well.[45] Anxious to stress the gravity of his situation Urquhart informed Thomas that the 1st Airborne Division was 'being very heavily shelled and mortared *now* from areas very close to our positions'. This drew an impatient 'Well, why don't you counter-mortar them? Or shell them?' from Thomas, to which Urquhart angrily replied 'How the hell can we? We're in holes in the ground. We can't see more than a few yards. And we haven't the ammunition.'[46] Urquhart was understandably angered by the exchange which, although he wrote it off as a facet of Thomas' character, he also considered showed Thomas 'had not got the situation clear at all'.[47] In itself Thomas' response displayed a breathtaking lack of insight into the reality of what was happening on the north bank of the Lower Rhine for a serving division commander, to say nothing of his appreciation of the likely capabilities of an airborne formation after fighting alone and virtually unsupported for almost a week, especially as Urquhart had transmitted numerous reports of the 1st Airborne Division's deteriorating situation. Taking into account the 43rd Division's failure to render more than token assistance to the Poles and the general lack of urgency displayed by the Division after reaching the south bank of the Lower Rhine, Thomas probably considered what was happening just across the river to be of tangential concern to him at best. In this he was merely reflecting a shift in priorities higher up the British chain of command, for at some point late on Saturday 23 September, Lieutenant-General Dempsey at British 2nd Army HQ 'delegated authority to Commanders 30 Corps and 1 Br Airborne Corps to withdraw 1 Airborne Div if and when considered advisable'.[48] As we shall see, this delegation effectively sealed the fate of the 1st Airborne Division.

Roughly a mile south of the Hotel Hartenstein at the riverside end of the perimeter Lieutenat Smaczny and his men from the 8th Company spent a relatively quiet night despite the presence of German troops within a hundred yards or so of the *Transvalia*, interrupted only by sporadic mortar fire and shelling. Once it was fully dark the paratroopers were able to leave their trenches to stretch cramped limbs, and the opportunity was also taken to gather and bury the dead. The Poles do not appear to have been aware of the renewed crossing by their comrades until later on Sunday morning, when rumours circulated that around 200 of their comrades had made it across to the north bank. They were however aware of the upsurge in German fire down at the river in the early hours; the overwhelming feeling was of relief that the fire was not falling on them. Smaczny was worried that the shortage of food and water would affect his men's morale, but an early morning tour of the positions around the *Transvalia* found them in good fettle, with two of his NCOs busy amending the date on the grave marker they had made to reflect the fact that they had survived into a new day. There does not appear to have been a recurrence of the German tank probes along the Benedendorpsweg, but in the afternoon the adjacent 1st Border requested Smaczny to provide a reconnaissance patrol. Ten men under a Lance-Corporal Bielawski were duly despatched to the 1st Border HQ where an unnamed British Major guided them through the woods to the patrol jump-off point on a country lane, likely the Van Borsselenweg. The Poles moved westward through the woods for approximately 400 yards before coming under intense machine-gun fire that killed the patrol point man, Private Mieczyslaw Krzeczkowski.[49] Having located the enemy front line, Bielawski and his men marked the location of Private Krzeczkowski's body and fell back to the *Transvalia*, from where Lieutenant Smaczny forwarded a report to 1st Border's HQ.[50]

Later in the afternoon a formation of Dakotas approached the Oosterbeek perimeter from the south, crossing the river and dropping a number of supply containers in the woods north-east of the *Transvalia*, despite some of the 8th Company paratroopers energetically waving their day-glo identification panels; the containers were also seen by members of the Polish Brigade HQ element dug in around the *Hemeldal* and one loaded with PIAT bombs came down in the positions occupied by D Company 1st Border on the Van Borsselenweg.[51] The provenance of the aircraft is unclear. According to one source there were four machines belonging to No. 575 Squadron, which had temporarily moved to Brussels to shorten the journey time to the Airborne perimeter on Saturday 23 September, and were part of a twenty-one-strong flight that delivered 235 panniers of food and ammunition and thirteen bundles of bedding to a DZ west of Grave.[52] However, the No. 575 Operational Record Book differs on the number of aircraft involved in both the Brussels detachment and 24 September mission, and makes no mention of any aircraft being despatched to Oosterbeek.[53] On the other hand, No. 620 Squadron's official record refers to despatching five machines from Fairford to drop supplies in northern Holland in support of the Airborne operation. Although only one succeeded in delivering its load and the success of the mission was reportedly compromised by 'much ground activity at the dropping zone'; the problem for identification in this instance is that all resupply flights from UK bases to Oosterbeek were supposed to have been suspended on 23 September, the aircraft were Stirlings rather than Dakotas and they took off long after dark, at between 22:30 and 23:00.[54] Wherever the aircraft had come from, Lieutenant Smaczny despatched a patrol to retrieve the closest containers while he led a party of six men in a noisy feint attack to distract the German's attention. The ploy succeeded and the patrol returned with three containers retrieved at a cost of two wounded; on opening their booty back at the *Transvalia* the 8th Company men were disappointed to find one container packed full of 9mm ammunition and the other two with No. 75 Hawkins Anti-tank Grenades without fuses, rather than the food and cigarettes the paratroopers had been hoping for. Heavy German shelling throughout the night prevented them from sleeping properly.[55]

The relatively quiet day enjoyed by Lieutenant Smaczny and his men may have been due to the Germans on the southern end of the western perimeter concentrating their attention on BREESE Force in the woods just north of the *Transvalia*. German infantry accompanied by one or possibly two tanks penetrated into the BREESE Force perimeter; the timing of the attack is unclear but it may have been connected to German infiltration around D Company at around midday or even as late as 19:35.[56] Whenever the attack developed, Sergeant Sidney Clark and his detached 7 Platoon from A Company were tasked to mount a counter-attack to restore the line. The Platoon was pinned down initially by German small-arms fire from deeper in the wood, but Sergeant Clark led his men forward despite the enemy fire, using hand-grenades to suppress the enemy and drive them back. The advance then brought the glider soldiers into contact with a hull-down tank, possibly a *Char* B from *Panzer Kompanie 224*, which was firing into the main British position. Despite *Generalleutnant* von Tettau's instruction on improving infantry protection for tanks the previous day, 7 Platoon was able to isolate the vehicle while Sergeant Clark replenished his supply of grenades by gathering more from his men. He then arranged covering fire, successfully stalked and climbed aboard the unprotected tank before forcing open the turret hatch and dropping several grenades inside, all the time under heavy enemy fire. The tank abruptly ceased fire and began to burn; it is unclear if any of the crew escaped. Sergeant Clark was subsequently awarded the Distinguished Conduct Medal for his actions.[57]

The previous day's fighting had left the 1st Border's D Company cut off from the rest of the Battalion and reduced its strength to twenty-five All Ranks including the only two officers still mobile, Company commander Captain William Hodgson and Lieutenant Alan Green, both of whom were wounded but still functioning. However, while the depleted Company continued to hold its position, it had simply too few men to block its entire frontage along the Van Borsselenweg. As a result a platoon-strength force of German troops succeeded in setting up a position in the woods east of D Company's location, occupying a number of vacant slit tranches around a crossroads from where they infiltrated in small groups across a track toward 1st Airlanding Brigade HQ; ironically the HQ had been moved there on 22 September after twice being badly hit by German artillery fire in its initial location close to the Hotel Hartenstein.[58] A Bren belonging to the Brigade Signals Section inflicted a number of casualties on those crossing the track and a party commanded by Lieutenant George Austin, an RA officer attached to the Airlanding Brigade HQ and Sergeant-Major Leslie Morgan from the Army Physical Training Corps attempted to clear the crossroads but failed to dislodge the interlopers; both Lieutenant Austin and Sergeant-Major Morgan were killed in the fighting.[59] Later in the afternoon a group of twenty Glider Pilots commanded by Lieutenant Robert Boyd from C Squadron launched another attack but was unable to close in because two German tanks were covering their infantry comrades from a nearby track junction; a subsequent attempt to tackle the tanks by members of the Brigade HQ Defence Platoon equipped with PIATs also failed, losing the weapons and incurring a number of casualties.[60] Medium artillery from the south side of the Lower Rhine, likely the 5.5-inch guns from the 64th Medium Regiment RA, was then brought into play, although the guns had to be registered individually by Captain Anthony Taylor from the Airlanding Light Regiment's 3 Battery owing to the proximity of friendly troops. According the Brigade HQ War Diary, following two concentrations of fire at 18:46 and 18:57 the enemy 'kept quiet for the rest of our stay in ARNHEM'.[61] Nonetheless D Company remained cut off, with Lieutenant Jack Bainbridge being wounded whilst attempting to regain contact with the rest of the Battalion, and the Germans launched a direct attack on the isolated Company at 19:35; the attack was repelled but the fighting reduced D Company's strength to nineteen All Ranks as the Company entered its second night in isolation.[62]

After a day of artillery and mortar fire the 1st Border's A and C Companies also came under direct attack at 19:05, the late timing possibly due to the depredations those units had inflicted upon German attackers the previous day.[63] The new attack was paralysed on C Company's front thanks to the commander of the 1st Border's Signals Platoon, Lieutenant Joseph Hardy, who had been relaying fire orders to the 1st Airlanding Light Regiment after the Battalion's assigned Forward Observer had been killed; he was subsequently replaced by Captain John Walker from the 1st Airlanding Light Battery RA. In the meantime Hardy somehow found himself in direct contact with a US artillery unit near Nijmegen and promptly called in a sustained barrage just to the front of C Company's positions that stopped the attack and prompted the attackers to withdraw; the incident provided a welcome boost to the hard-pressed and increasingly battle-weary glider soldiers.[64] The cessation of the German attacks with the onset of full darkness was fortunate: the 1st Border's food reserves were now totally exhausted and its ammunition reserve reduced to just 2,500 rounds of .303 ammunition. Fifty per cent of C Company were by this time using captured enemy weapons.[65] On the upside, C Company's frontage did receive some reinforcements. Guided by Glider Pilots, Lieutenants Bossowski and Mikulski and their party of forty-two reassigned Polish Anti-tank Gunners occupied a number of slit trenches in the edge of the wood overlooking a farm track and area of pastureland behind C Company's line, close to the Utrechtseweg near a villa called the *Valkenburg*. This appears to have been taken over as C Company's Command Post and Lieutenant Bossowski discovered it contained a functioning piano, which was played by a young British officer when he crossed to liaise with his 1st Border counterparts. The Poles drove off a number of curious German troops who appeared on the pasture to their front with a few bursts of Bren fire.[66]

The Germans also maintained the pressure against the perimeter on the north side of the Utrechtseweg in addition to the constant mortar and artillery fire that wounded a Sapper from 261 Field Park Company RE and two more from the 4th Parachute Squadron RE. Another source refers to the latter unit also losing at least three dead in the course of the day.[67] Two of the dead were likely killed during the early morning artillery barrage, as recalled by Sapper Stanley Holden from No. 3 Troop: 'In a trench a few yards away were two bodies…They were both decapitated but the man in front had part of his chin left and there were bits of flesh strewn about…somebody suggested getting their dog tags but there were no takers for such a gruesome job'.[68] The third fatality, Sapper Thomas Cunningham from 1 Troop, was hit later while seeking additional bombs for PIAT gunner Sapper William Grantham and subsequently died of his wounds; Captain Roger Binyon from the 9th Field Company RE was also killed in the fighting to maintain the perimeter, while stalking a tank with a PIAT in the woods to the north of his unit's location.[69]

The heaviest pressure was directed against the Glider Pilots from E and F Squadrons holding the north-western shoulder of the perimeter. An attack at 12:30 by two flamethrower tanks from *Panzer Kompanie* 224 inflicted a number of casualties on the defenders before the vehicles were reportedly knocked out by 17-Pounder guns; it is unclear whether the latter came from the 1st or 2nd Airlanding Anti-tank Batteries, although all anti-tank guns including the 17-Pounders in the Divisional area had been concentrated into a single Group on 19 September.[70] The attack was held but Lieutenant-Colonel Place approached the 7th KOSB holding the north face of the perimeter and asked them to redeploy in more depth to provide a backstop for the Glider Pilot's line, which Lieutenant-Colonel Payton-Reid agreed to do.[71] This was a prescient move, as the Germans renewed their attack at 14:07, this time coming in from the right flank to the north, and at 17:00 the Glider Pilots were obliged to withdraw from the woods and take up position in houses along the Oranjeweg.[72] It is unclear how the withdrawal impacted upon the 1st Border's A Company on the Glider Pilot's left flank, but 261 Field Park Company despatched three men to reinforce the 4th Parachute Squadron although one was wounded and evacuated in the process or shortly thereafter.[73]

On the northern aspect of the perimeter the 7th KOSB spent a more active night along the Ommershoflaan than their western neighbours, thanks to determined German infiltration. The KOSB's roving patrols moving between the occupied houses clashed repeatedly with the infiltrators between midnight and 04:30, and a fighting patrol led by Company second-in-command Captain James Dundas and Lieutenant William Lamond from the Battalion Signals Platoon had to be despatched to drive off a group attempting to dig in close to B Company on the right of the Battalion's two-company frontage. Daylight revealed that the Germans had taken the opportunity to lodge numerous snipers and machine-gun teams inside the KOSB perimeter, some entering through a gap on the Battalion's right flank where contact had been lost with the 1st Airborne Reconnaissance Squadron's D Troop. Lieutenant-Colonel Payton-Reid's men spent the morning locating and clearing the interlopers, with D Company CSM James Swanston, Sergeant John Nattrass and a Sergeant Wilson playing a prominent role despite Swanston and Wilson having been wounded the previous day. The clearing operation cost the KOSB a number of additional casualties. This explains why Colonel Payton-Reid agreed to the Glider Pilots' early afternoon request to rearrange the line in more depth. The precise location of the new consolidated position is not clear from the Battalion War Diary, but the front of the new location appears to have involved redeploying B Company westward to man houses along the north side of the Bothaweg, D Company in the houses on the south side of that street along with the Battalion RAP, while C Company occupied houses on the north side of the next street, the Paul Krugerstraat.[74]

From this block, which was around 150 yards deep north to south, 'it was felt we could put up a stiff defence and from which we could inflict considerable casualties on any enemy', although only half- a-dozen houses could be actually occupied in each row because by this point the Battalion's strength had been reduced to just seven Officers and under a hundred Other Ranks.[75] The Glider Pilots' withdrawal from the woods back to the Oranjeweg at 17:00 exposed the left flank of the 7th KOSB's new position and ceded the enemy a concealed forming-up point just fifty yards or so from the KOSB line. The KOSB's 3-Inch mortars attempted to head off German attack preparations by bombarding likely points but with limited success. They began to lay a smokescreen in preparation for an attack an hour or so after the Glider Pilots' withdrawal. The day was saved by Captain John Walker from the 1st Airlanding Light Regiment, who was acting as Forward Observer for the Battalion, although his effectiveness had been reduced by the fighting on much of the perimeter being too close for the 1st Airlanding Light Regiment's 75mm Pack Howitzers to bring fire to bear.[76] Captain Taylor called in concentrations from the medium guns of the 64th Medium Regiment RA at 18:11 and 18:20.[77] This had the desired effect: 'The Bn stood to until after dark awaiting it [the attack], but, although there were signs of activity, it did not materialise.'[78]

Captain David Allsop's 1st Airborne Reconnaissance Squadron was holding the north-eastern sector of the perimeter and came under heavy and sustained mortar and artillery fire from around 06:30. The Squadron HQ, located at the junction of the Utrechtseweg and Oranjeweg 200 yards or so west of the Hotel Hartenstein, reported the bombardment as having 'no comparison with anything which has come our way previously'.[79] It also claimed a noteworthy scalp from outwith the Reconnaissance Squadron. Brigadier John Hackett had paid another early morning visit to Captain Allsop, in this instance to arrange guides to bring in the Polish paratroopers assigned to HACKETT Force, as the eastern face of the perimeter was sometimes called; he was hit in the stomach and thigh by mortar fragments at 07:40 whilst making his way back to his own HQ at the height of the bombardment.[80] The commander of No. 1 Wing GPR, Lieutenant-Colonel Iain Murray, was immediately elevated in Hackett's stead within the hour, while Major Ian Toler from B Squadron took command of No. 1 Wing at 09:55. Hackett officially handed over command to Lieutenant-Colonel Murray in the Division RAP at around 14:00, where he was visited by Major-General Urquhart before being evacuated to the MDS at the Hotel Schoonoord for treatment.[81] Back at the Utrechtseweg–Oranjeweg junction, the barrage lulled at 09:30 before resuming at 10:15, and was reportedly 'even more fierce than the previous plastering'.[82] The enemy fire originated from the west with the orders and the sound of bombs leaving mortar tubes being clearly audible emanating from the woods near the Sonnenberg. The bombardment continued until around 14:00, when the appearance of Hawker Typhoon fighter-bombers from the 2nd Tactical Air Force's No. 83 Group forced another pause; the Group flew twenty-two sorties to the Oosterbeek pocket on 24 September and was able to access the pocket because there were no resupply flights scheduled for the day.[83] The bombardment resumed at 15:30 with the departure of the RAF aircraft and was replaced fifteen minutes later with direct fire from what was reported as a self-propelled gun firing from the woods near the Sonnenberglaan in support of a German infantry attack on the perimeter there; when the enemy withdrew into the woods the HQ was then subjected to alternating mortaring and heavy machine-gun fire until the onset of darkness at 19:30, the source of which could not be ascertained. By this time Captain Allsop and his men were out of contact with A and D Troops as well as Division HQ, just 200 yards or so away across the Utrechtseweg. Four HQ personnel became casualties in the course of the day, at least one of whom was killed. Trooper Alfred Odd was sharing a slit trench with Trooper Michael Gassett and was killed by a single gunshot to the head while searching for a sniper with binoculars.[84]

Out at the north-eastern sector of the perimeter Captain John Park's D Troop had been reduced to two officers and thirteen Other Ranks by the previous day's fighting, which was why the Germans were able to infiltrate into the 7th KOSB's right flank. D Troop lost two more casualties early on when a patrol to draw water from a nearby well came under intense machine-gun fire at 07:00; the gun was registered on the well and had killed a number of earlier would-be users.[85] German patrols then began to push into the perimeter around D Troop's location from 10:00 and ninety minutes later launched a heavy attack under cover of a 'terrific' mortar barrage. The attackers were held, although Captain Park, Lieutenant Alan Pascal and Trooper Thomas Walker were all killed during the fighting; according to Sergeant James Pyper the three were occupying the same slit trench and were decapitated by the blast and shrapnel from a mortar bomb.[86] The appearance of the Typhoons in the afternoon prompted the attackers to cease their activities temporarily to avoid being targeted and also provided the beleaguered Airborne soldiers with a welcome morale boost, as noted by Sergeant William Bentnall: 'We were treated to an attack by rocket firing Typhoons…fearsome things, with a shark's head and teeth painted on the undernose, and rockets screaming.'[87] The German attack inevitably resumed once the fighters withdrew and the remaining D Troop men fought on until their ammunition ran out; the position was finally overrun at around 18:00. Sergeants Pyper and Bentnall were taken prisoner along with four other unnamed men; it is unclear what became of the other four members of the Troop. This was not the end of the story for the Sergeants and their party, however. Quickly escaping from incarceration in a nearby house on the Steijnweg, the six took refuge from the rain and patrolling Germans in a wrecked shop farther down the street where they discovered a cellar stacked with potatoes. After all had attacked the raw vegetables (not recommended in normal circumstances), Sergeants Bentnall and Pyper left the four with the potato pile and moved into an upstairs room. Pyper took shelter behind an overturned table and Bentnall crawled beneath a settee. They were joined by a party of Germans also seeking a comfortable spot to spend the night. The darkness saved the Reconnaissance NCOs from detection, although Sergeant Bentnall spent the remainder of the night with his nose ground into the floor and a spring digging into his spine thanks to the German occupying the settee above him; he crammed a rag into his mouth to stifle a cough.[88]

Just a hundred yards or so to the east, A Troop had spent the early hours digging trenches in the rain around the houses it now occupied on De la Reijweg, sited and supervised by Lieutenant Douglas Galbraith; the latter also appears to have taken command of the Troop at some point during the morning after Captain Michael Grubb, who had been badly wound in the foot the previous day during the withdrawal from its position on the Paul Krugerstraat, finally agreed to be evacuated to the MDS.[89] Although the sound of armoured vehicles was noted first thing, German activity during the morning appears to have been restricted to intense mortaring, sniping and machine-gun fire alternating with aggressive probing, presumably intended to pinpoint A Troop's new positions. Trooper William Fraser recalled it was 'difficult to know where to go to be safe, because the Germans were firing all the time, in through the windows or any holes in the walls' and that the enemy tracer ammunition looked like 'firework sparklers', while out in the garden of the same house Troopers Kenneth Hope and Ronald Spicer were pinned down for a considerable period by very accurate rifle fire, the source of which they were unable to locate. The early afternoon respite created by the RAF Typhoons also applied to A Troop, with Corporal James Taylor witnessing the rocket attack on the German-held house as enjoyed by D Troop, albeit from closer quarters, given that he reported the blast effect made him feel 'as if my head were freewheeling'.[90] The Germans launched a full-scale assault once the fighter-bombers departed at around 15:30 and while Lieutenant Galbraith and his men managed to maintain their positions and repulse the attackers, it was a close-run thing. One of the A Troop houses was hit by a large-calibre projectile, possibly a 105mm shell from a *Sturmhaubitze* 42, which blew a four-foot-wide hole in the wall, stunning Trooper Stanley Sutherby who was standing in the doorway and prompting a stampede to escape the building. Trooper Fraser was standing near the bottom of the stairs: the next thing that happened was a terrific bang, and I was hit…I staggered up and tried to make for the door, but it was difficult, because I couldn't see properly.' Badly wounded in the head and bleeding profusely, Trooper Fraser staggered outside and tried to enter the slit trench occupied by understandably alarmed Troopers Hope and Spicer; at that point Lieutenant Galbraith appeared and calmly enquired 'Where the bloody hell do you think you're all going – now just bloody well settle down,' thereby quelling a potential panic before it could take hold. With the German attack repulsed A Troop was obliged to consolidate into a more concentrated location at the southern end of the De la Reijweg, where they became intermingled with men from the similarly compressed 7th KOSB.[91]

The adjacent Stationsweg positions, held by Major Geoffrey Powell's party from 156 Parachute Battalion and the 21st Independent Company straddling the Utrechtseweg junction, appear to have been left unmolested through the morning apart from intense mortaring, machine-gun fire and sniping. The Independent Company reported coming under fire from *nebelwerfers*, 88mm guns, *StuGs* and snipers who had apparently infiltrated behind No. 1 Platoon's positions via the MDS, and also mortar bombs containing phosphorous being used to set fire to the British-held houses.[92] Reinforcements were on the way for the beleaguered Pathfinders however, for at 11:00 the initial increment of paratroopers from the Polish Brigade's 3rd Battalion arrived at the positions occupied by Lieutenant David Eastwood's No. 1 Platoon, where they were to man the sector of the perimeter on the Stationsweg running north from the Utrechtseweg junction. This included No. 2, a large mansion called the *Quatre Bras* overlooking the junction and No. 8 belonging to the Kremer family; by this point the Kremer's cellar was also sheltering thirty-three civilians from adjacent houses that had been destroyed or rendered uninhabitable by the fighting.[93] The Poles' unexpected and somewhat noisy arrival came as a surprise to No. 1 Platoon. Private William Mollett noted them moving into the rear of the house next door occupied by Sergeant Ron Kent's Section who heard 'the chatter of many voices, sounding very like German…[which]…sent me scuttling downstairs with my Sten gun at the ready'.[94]

The Poles' journey to their new position had not been a smooth one. After being gathered near Division HQ at 09:00, Captain Gazurek and his men were led through the southern portion of Oosterbeek to 4th Parachute Brigade HQ by No. 1 Wing GPR's Intelligence Officer Lieutenant Brian Bottomley, losing at least one man en route; Lieutenant Bottomley may have been brought in as staff by the newly installed Lieutenant-Colonel Murray, who briefed Captain Gazurek on his role and guided him toward his new positions.[95] In order to reach the Stationsweg the Poles had to cross to the north side of the Utrechtseweg, and a point twenty yards west of the Utrechtseweg–Stationsweg junction was selected, where a rise in the road partially deflected German fire coming down the road. Here Captain Gazurek organised the order of crossing with Lieutenant Mieczyslaw Pudelko's 7th Company leading, followed by the Battalion HQ elements and 2nd Lieutenant Leon Prochowski's Platoon from the 9th Company bringing up the rear. The paratroopers were sent across in small numbers in an effort to avoid attracting German attention and Captain Gazurek was one of the first across, moving with elements of 2nd Lieutenant Waclaw Urbanski's platoon, accompanied by Corporal Jan Towarnicki from the Battalion HQ element armed with a Bren gun. Private Mikolaj Bzowy from Urbanski's platoon was hit in the stomach while crossing and died later that day.[96]

Moving behind the buildings Captain Gazurek reached the back garden of the *Quatre Bras* where he made contact with the Pathfinders within and took shelter from German machine-gun fire with the first of his men; their reportedly noisy arrival was presumably what had alarmed Sergeant Kent, together with the machine-gun fire from German troops involved in the nearby fight with the Reconnaissance Squadron on De la Reijweg. Accompanied by Corporal Towarnicki, Captain Gazurek then led the 7th Company north in person through the back gardens and into and through the Kremer house, where he sent Towarnicki back to guide those following before scaling the six-foot wall dividing the Kremer garden from its neighbour. This took Captain Gazurek close to the line of British occupation, and he was killed by a shot to the head; he had removed his Airborne helmet before beginning the climb, something he had expressly forbidden his men from doing during training.[97] The 3rd Battalion men did not take the death of their commander well. According to Sander Kremer, two enraged Poles appeared at the cellar door threatening to kill his father, who had been seen burning personal documents upstairs, which the Poles assumed was a signal to the enemy; they were dissuaded and ordered away by an unnamed Polish officer cadet.[98] Command of the 3rd Battalion contingent should have passed to Lieutenant Pudelko but he deferred to Bereda-Fialkowski, who had been acting as Captain Gazurek's adjutant, on the grounds that the latter had been briefed and it was thus Bereda-Fialkowski who oversaw the deployment into the houses on the Stationsweg. The *Quatre Bras* and No. 4 were occupied by 2nd Lieutenants Francisz Kowalczyk and Prochowski's Platoons from the 9th Company, Lieutenant Bereda-Fialkowski and the Battalion HQ personnel moved into the Hotel Strijland at No. 6, 2nd Lieutenant Jozef Kula's stray Platoon from the 1st Battalion took over the Kremer house and Lieutenant Pudelko and Lieutenant Urbanski's Platoon from the 9th Company moved into No. 10. The next two houses were occupied by Glider Pilots from D Squadron, to whom the Poles sent six men equipped with a PIAT as reinforcements, including Lance-Corporals Kuzniar and Karol Matlak who were assigned to the last house in the row held by a party of seven Glider Pilots commanded by an unnamed captain.[99]

Lieutenant Eastwood and No. 1 Platoon were formally relieved by the Poles at midday, and after regrouping in a downstairs room the Pathfinders moved back across the Utrechtseweg to the Independent Company's HQ. The Platoon made the crossing in a single group under cover of a smoke grenade and suffered only one casualty, Private Thomas McMahon, who was wounded in the foot.[100] The Polish paratroopers then settled in for a relatively uneventful day, apart from the constant fire from machine-guns and mortars, as the intermingled nature and proximity of the German positions spared them the attention of the less precise *nebelwerfers* and artillery, although there was a continual stream of Polish casualties nonetheless. Lance-Corporal Konstanty Wesolowicz was killed by machine-gun fire in the back garden of Stationsweg No. 6 whilst foraging for water. Private Emil Mentlik was killed by a sniper whilst manning an upstairs window in the Kremer house; the impact of the round reportedly threw the unfortunate paratrooper clear across the room.[101] The Poles were shooting back. Corporal Franciszek Wieczorek was narrowly missed by a burst of machine-gun fire that tore up the wall by the attic window he was manning with a Bren gun in the attic of Stationsweg No. 6. Carefully quartering the parkland east of the Stationsweg with binoculars, Corporal Wieczorek spotted wisps of smoke rising from an innocuous clump of bushes and put a full thirty-round magazine into it; he was gratified to see German stretcher bearers removing two bodies from the clump a short while later.[102]

The bulk of the 21st Independent Company was still occupying the positions on the south side of the Utrechtseweg it had occupied in the early morning of Friday 22 September. No. 3 Platoon, commanded by Lieutenant Hugh Ashmore, was deployed in houses along the Pietersbergseweg running south from the Utrechtseweg facing the MDS in the Hotel Schoonoord, with Lieutenant John Speller's No. 2 Platoon on their right along the Paasberg, which angled to the south-east and then south to the sector held by two platoons from 250 (Airborne) Light Composite Company RASC. Major Wilson's Company HQ was located from just after 12:00 in a house on the junction of the Pietersbergseweg and Paasberg between the two Platoons, with Lieutenant Eastwood's No. 1 Platoon resting nearby.[103] At 14:15 Major Wilson reported to 4th Parachute Brigade HQ that German troops were moving up from the south on No. 2 Platoon's right flank, apparently having bypassed the RASC contingent. Lieutenant-Colonel Murray responded by requesting LONSDALE Force stand-by to launch a counter-attack in support, which was reportedly ready by 14:30 and asked Major Wilson if a medium artillery shoot was feasible; Wilson responded at 14:45, pointing out his No. 2 Platoon was mixed up with the enemy and suggesting the barrage be brought down 200 yards to the front of the RASC Company's positions.[104] Major Wilson correctly divined that the German objective was the Casualty Clearing Station (CCS) in the Hotel Tafelberg, located to the right rear of No. 2 Platoon. As this would provide the enemy with a covered access into the British perimeter, Wilson cut short No.1 Platoon's brief rest and deployed Lieutenant Eastwood and his men on the right-hand side of the equally understrength No. 3 Platoon as a potential backstop. No. 3 Platoon was further reinforced by a party of eight Glider Pilots of unknown provenance armed with a number of Bren guns. The Pathfinders were unable to prevent the Germans securing the Hotel Tafelberg, but they then paused and made no effort to press further.[105]

Measures were being undertaken to at least partially ameliorate the increasingly acute medical situation in the Oosterbeek perimeter, focussing on the Divisional MDS located in the Hotels Schoonoord and Vreewijk on the Stationsweg-Utrechtseweg-Pietersbergseweg crossroads. *Kampfgruppe* Möller's advance west along the Utrechtseweg had put the MDS exactly on the front line, with both sides complaining that the other was taking illegal advantage of the situation. The SS were especially vociferous in this regard, and occupied the Hotel Schoonoord from early on Saturday afternoon until just after dark, although they did provide food and medical supplies as well as evacuating some of the most serious cases. By the night of 23-24 September the 1st Airborne Division's senior medical officer, Assistant Director of Medical Services (ADMS) Colonel Graeme Warrack, had decided that 'the battle could no longer continue in this fashion', with medical facilities being caught up in the fighting despite displaying Red Cross flags; one location, possibly the CCS in the Hotel Tafelberg where Colonel Warrack had set up his HQ, was reportedly hit six separate times by artillery, one strike setting the building on fire and forcing the evacuation of 150 casualties.[106] On the not unreasonable grounds that being a live prisoner of war was better than being a dead casualty, Colonel Warrack decided that the best solution was to come to an arrangement with the Germans that would allow the evacuation of the most serious cases for treatment at the German-run St Elizabeth Hospital in Arnhem, although this would require permission from the 1st Airborne Division's commander. Warrack therefore presented his case to Major-General Urquhart at the Hotel Hartenstein at 09:30 on 24 September in what he described as 'a long crack with the Commander…[that]…explained how unhealthy things were down our way'.[107] After hearing Warrack out, Urquhart concurred and authorised him to approach the Germans but only on the strict proviso that on no account 'must the enemy be allowed to think that this was a crack in the formation's position…[and]…on condition that the Germans understand you are a doctor representing your patients – not an official emissary from the division'.[108] Warrack promptly sought out two men to accompany him, Dr. Gerrit van Maanen, a Dutch civilian doctor working in the Hotel Tafelberg, and the Dutch military liaison officer assigned to the 1st Airborne Division, Lieutenant-Commander Arnoldus Wolters, to act as an interpreter; in order to conceal his potentially extremely dangerous status, Wolters assumed the identity of a fictitious Canadian officer named Johnson.[109]

The three men began by calling into the Hotel Schoonoord to allow Colonel Warrack to contact his opposite number from 9 *SS Panzer Division*, *Hauptsturmführer* Dr Egon Skalka, who had been instrumental in the evacuation of serious casualties from the MDS the previous day; Skalka was also running the St Elizabeth Hospital on the outskirts of Arnhem as a joint facility, employing its original British medical staff from 16 Parachute Field Ambulance RAMC and medical supplies gathered from British resupply drops.[110] *Hauptsturmführer* Skalka not only agreed to approach his Division commander, but also magnanimously offered to drive Warrack and Wolters to meet him in person using a captured Airborne Jeep. He refused to allow Dr van Maanen to accompany them, presumably because he was a civilian. As 9 *SS Panzer Division* HQ was located in a commandeered school on the Hezelbergheweg in Arnhem, the journey involved traversing not only the scene of the recent fighting on the east face of the Oosterbeek pocket but also the detritus and destruction from the 1st Parachute Brigade's epic but abortive fight to reach the Arnhem road bridge; Lieutenant-Commander Wolters found the sight 'sad and miserable', although he and Warrack were likely more immediately concerned with Skalka's aggressive driving style. On arrival Skalka was obliged to reassure an angry *Obersturmbannführer* Walther Harzer that his roundabout route and speedy driving had obviated the need to blindfold the emissaries before he and Harzer sat down to talk with the Airborne officers, with Warrack introducing Wolters as the Canadian Johnson. The character of what followed differs between accounts, with Harzer describing the discussion as mutually conciliatory in tone. He said he agreed to Warrack's proposal and a truce for it to be carried out. However, according to Wolters, Harzer initially 'refused to even consider a truce' and after some discussion with chief-of-staff *Hauptsturmführer* Wilfried Schwarz and other senior members of the Division staff, it was decided to present the matter to higher authority. The emissaries were left with a plate of meat and onion sandwiches and a bottle of brandy, which Warrack ordered Wolters not to imbibe on an empty stomach; the sandwiches were the first proper food either of the Airborne officers had tasted for some time.

Higher authority was the commander of II *SS Panzerkorps*, *Obergruppenführer* Wilhelm Bittrich, who happened to be present at Harzer's HQ. Entering hatless in his trademark long leather coat, trailed by Harzer and his staff amidst a flurry of salutes, Bittrich greeted the Airborne emissaries by quietly expressing regret that Britain and Germany were at war. He then listened in silence to Warrack's proposal before giving his consent for the truce and evacuation. The agreement was thus reached in a matter of minutes by around 10:30, only an hour or so after Warrack had initially broached the matter with Major-General Urquhart; Bittrich also handed Warrack a bottle of brandy to pass on to his Division commander with his compliments, before leaving as swiftly as he had arrived. *Hauptsturmführer* Dr Skalka promptly set about rounding up vehicles to carry out the evacuation, leaving Warrack and Wolters to be escorted back to British lines by another SS medical officer in the same Jeep, now decorated with a large Red Cross flag; Skalka also generously allowed the Airborne officers to fill their pockets with captured British morphine ampoules and other medical supplies before leaving. The departure from the SS HQ was greeted with extra relief by Wolters, as at one point during the discussions *Hauptsturmführer* Schwarz had pointedly commented that he did not 'speak German like a Britisher'. The SS escort also allowed a detour on the way back to British lines to allow Warrack to visit the St Elizabeth Hospital where he was greeted by surgeons Major Cedric Longland and Captain Alexander Lipmann-Kessel from 16 Parachute Field Ambulance RAMC, and the senior Dutch civilian surgeon Dr. Van Hengel. They were all anxious for news on the progress of the battle; Warrack obliged before warning the surgeons to expect an increase in the flow of casualties when the evacuation of the Division MDS commenced later in the day. He then returned to his HQ in the Hotel Tafelberg to be greeted by 'a packet of mortaring'.[111]

The truce was arranged to begin at 15:00 although Colonel Warrack does not appear to have informed Division HQ of the arrangement until the evacuation had been underway for almost two hours, assuming it did begin at 15:00, as the sources are unclear.[112] Nor does he appear to have informed the Airborne units immediately adjacent to the MDS, although the beginning of the truce was marked by a cessation of the German bombardment. Surgeon Captain Stuart Mawson referred to the sudden 'exaggerated silence' against which 'the call of birds could be heard taking their rightful place in the scheme of things on a sunny September morning'.[113] On the north side of the Utrechtseweg-Stationsweg crossroads the Poles fired on any German who exposed himself in the vicinity of the MDS, including an NCO who was rash enough to point his weapon toward the Polish positions while standing next to an ambulance. This continued until Lieutenant-Colonel Marrable crossed to the *Quatre Bras* and took 2nd Lieutenant Kowalczyk to task, which was reportedly the first the Poles had heard of any local ceasefire; Kowalczyk duly passed word to acting Battalion commander 2nd Lieutenant Bereda-Fialkowski, who immediately forbade any more firing toward the MDS.[114]

For their part the Germans appear to have used the truce to continue their effort to extend control over the area around the MDS, and there was an armed German presence inside the medical facility from at least the early morning. According to the Division War Diary, an unnamed BBC correspondent who left one of the MDS buildings to fetch water for the wounded under a Red Cross flag returned to find around 150 armed German troops in the hospital; the correspondent was presumably either Guy Byam or Stanley Maxsted, the two BBC members of the ten-strong press team attached to the 1st Airborne Division.[115] The Polish semi-official account refers to German troops occupying a temporary ward upstairs in the Hotel Schoonoord and drawing fire from the nearby Poles when they set up a machine-gun in one of the windows. The situation was reportedly resolved by an unnamed British doctor who manhandled the weapon away from the window and ordered the SS to leave the ward forthwith; it is unclear if they complied.[116]

On the south side of the Utrechtseweg the 21st Independent Company reported the arrival of two *Panzer* IVs in front of No. 3 Platoon's positions on the Pietersbergseweg followed shortly afterward by a message to Major Wilson, delivered via an unnamed British medical officer from the CCS in the Hotel Tafelberg. The demand was simple: the Pathfinders were to abandon one of the houses they occupied or the tanks would blast them out. Major Wilson informed Division HQ of the development at 15:27, although somehow the message became a threat to shell the CCS in the Hotel Tafelberg rather than the 21st Independent's position; the message nonetheless prompted a 'stand fast' order from Major-General Urquhart.[117] Wilson responded to the Germans with his customary bellicosity by agreeing to abandon the house provided the Germans reciprocated by withdrawing all their troops from the immediate vicinity of the

MDS, pulled their tanks back for a mile and refrained from further activity until the casualty evacuation from the MDS was complete; failure to comply would prompt the Pathfinders to hold onto the disputed house and destroy the two tanks. To back this up, Wilson despatched a Private Dixon, the Army Catering Corps cook attached to No. 3 Platoon, to stalk the tanks with a PIAT. Dixon scored a direct hit on one of the vehicles, detonating its ammunition and igniting a fire that lasted for several hours; the second tank then decided discretion was the better part of valour and withdrew whence it had come.[118] Despite this, Major Wilson 'agreed locally' to evacuate one of his houses in return for the Germans withdrawing a *StuG* from a crossroads adjacent to the MDS at around 19:00.[119]

In the meantime the evacuation of casualties from the hotels Schoonoord and Vreewijk was going ahead as arranged. The arrival of *Hauptsturmführer* Dr Skalka's six vehicles, each capable of carrying four stretcher cases each, was witnessed by a rather unimpressed Captain Mawson:

> The ambulances scarcely deserved the name, being a hotch-potch of battered commercial vehicles distinguished only by large Red Crosses on their sides and tops. They wound their way jerkily along the torn-up road, following a serpentine and unpredictable route to avoid the holes, and fetched up in an untidy line outside the Schoonoord, having first advanced to the crossroad where they performed a wide, sweeping turn to bring them back facing the way they had come.

Lieutenant-Colonel Marrable described the commandeered German fleet as 'ramshackle boneshakers…hardly fit to carry a healthy man let alone a sick and wounded one', but also correctly surmised that the vehicles were likely all the Germans had been able to scrape together.[120] After a brief discussion between Colonel Marrable and *Hauptsturmführer* Dr Skalka the process of carrying the stretcher-bound wounded through the hotel's main entrance to the waiting vehicles began; all of them were loaded and driven as a convoy, making an undetermined number of round trips over the course of the truce. The process of checking the casualties off the hospital roll and despatching them out to the waiting transport was supervised by Colonel Marrable in person from the entranceway, in part to deter armed German troops from entering the MDS.

The most serious cases were moved first, including Brigadier Hackett, who was optimistically masquerading as a corporal to increase his future chances of escape. On arrival at the St Elizabeth Hospital Hackett was triaged by an SS surgeon who, based upon a superficial examination consisting of poking the stretchered casualty with his foot, assessed him as not worth treating. He was nonetheless examined by Captain Alexander Lippmann-Kessel from 16 Parachute Field Ambulance, and when he was unable to locate any exit wounds the SS surgeon again opined that stomach and head wounds should be given an injection and left to die; both exchanges were noted by the fully conscious Hackett, who spoke German.[121] In the event Captain Lippmann-Kessel ignored his opposite number's advice and went on to remove several mortar bomb splinters from Hackett's stomach and sealed fourteen perforations in his lower intestine, thereby saving his life.[122] Back at the Hotel Schoonoord, Colonel Marrable surreptitiously initiated a deliberate slowing of the evacuation process when the most urgent cases had been evacuated in a covert effort to keep the less seriously wounded casualties in the MDS so they could be liberated by 30 Corps when it finally pushed across the Lower Rhine. Captain Clifford Simmons from 181 Parachute Field Ambulance dubbed the process 'Operation Dilly-Dally' and explained to Mawson that the idea was to 'make everything take twice as long as usual; twice as long to get the Germans' meaning if they tell you something, twice as long to lift a stretcher, twice as long to carry it, twice as long to put it down. Bandages must fall off and any other damn thing you can think of tried on.'[123] It is unclear how many casualties were eventually evacuated by the Germans, or how many were successfully held back at the MDS by the go-slow effort.

Despite the trials and tribulations involved in serving in the MDS Captain Mawson saw the evacuation of the patients as the 'dissolution of the cement that bound us all together' and he decided it was time to rejoin his parent unit, the 11th Parachute Battalion; his decision was likely also prompted at least in part by Captain Simmons pointing out that the Germans were likely to co-opt the MDS medical staff, as they had at the St Elizabeth hospital. Mawson thus sounded out a Sergeant Dwyer and Private Adams from the 11th Battalion who were also serving in the Hotel Schoonoord before approaching Colonel Marrable for permission, although Dwyer announced that he had already raised the matter with Adams and would be departing that night whether Marrable agreed or not. However, Mawson was side tracked by fruitlessly trying to persuade the Dutch nurse who had improvised the Red Cross flag for his foray to the 21st Independent Company the previous evening to leave the MDS. She refused to leave unless Mawson and his companions accompanied her into hiding. Mawson was then buttonholed by Colonel Marrable who asked for time to think about the request. Mawson went ahead with preparations with Dwyer and Adams in the meantime, but approaching Marrable again proved to be his undoing as the latter was in the middle of a discussion via interpreter with *Hauptsturmführer* Dr Skalka, whom Mawson had literally bumped into a little earlier. Skalka was asking Marrable to provide a German-speaking doctor to assist with the evacuated casualties, who were reportedly resisting German attempts to assist them owing to the language barrier. Disregarding Marrable's insistence that he had no suitable personnel available, Skalka spotted Mawson standing to one side, clapped him on the shoulder and, recalling their conversation in French the previous day, announced that he would come and help. After retrieving his Denison smock, webbing and maroon beret from the escape cache with Sergeant Dwyer's assistance, Captain Mawson joined Skalka in the back seat of his staff car, where the German officer greeted his new assistant with the immortal words 'Ah well, my friend. Now, for you the war is finished, would you like a cigarette?' It is unclear if Sergeant Dwyer and Private Adams were successful in leaving the MDS but they do not appear to have escaped from the wider Oosterbeek perimeter, given that Mawson saw both men working in a German medical facility set up in a barracks near Apeldoorn shortly after the battle. Mawson ended the war serving as a Medical Officer at a satellite POW labour camp administered from *Stalag IV G* at Oschatz near Dresden in eastern Germany.[124]

The sector to the immediate south of the Hotels Schoonoord and Vreewijk was held by Captain John Cranmer-Byng and two parachute platoons from 250 (Airborne) Light Composite Company RASC, backed by Glider Pilots from Major Robert Croot's G Squadron protecting the northern aspect of the 1st Airlanding Light Regiment's gun positions around the Oosterbeek Old Church as part of LONSDALE Force. The RASC Company may therefore have been forced back or overrun, given that the 1st Parachute Battalion also serving with LONSDALE Force to the south reported German tanks breaking through into a sector to their north.[125] For its part LONSDALE Force continued to hold the south-eastern sector of the perimeter shielding the 1st Airlanding Light Regiment's gun positions, and more importantly preventing *Kampfgruppe* Harder from advancing along the riverside Benedendorpsweg and pinching the 1st Airborne Division's perimeter away from the Lower Rhine. The unit War Diaries of the various units involved all tell a similar story of intense and incessant mortar and artillery fire covering German attacks with infantry and armoured vehicles. The 11th Parachute Battalion reportedly spent the day clearing snipers that had infiltrated into the area north of the Oosterbeek Old Church, while the 2nd South Staffords operating near the Laundry had the satisfaction of watching while the Light Regiment's guns '...smashed up a German MG post in the roof of a house 300 yds away up the road towards STATION OOSTERBEEK', presumably referring to the Weverstraat running north from the Benedendorpsweg.[126] The 1st Parachute Battalion reported coming under increasingly heavy fire from German tanks and self-propelled guns that had broken through to the north of its positions along with infiltration by snipers from the same source, and to despatching Lieutenant Albert Turrell to take command of the 3rd Parachute

Battalion contingent at 14:00 after it lost its last officer. The last 3rd Battalion officer, Lieutenant James Cleminson, had been wounded and evacuated the previous day, after which command may have devolved to Lieutenant Philip Evans from the 2nd South Staffords' C Company; Evans was wounded and evacuated in turn at some point before 14:00.[127]

Echoing the 1st Parachute Battalion account, the 1st Airlanding Light Regiment reported two self-propelled guns firing into 1 Battery's positions throughout the day and demolishing most of the Airborne-held houses in the immediate vicinity. By this point the Germans were so close that the Regiment's pack howitzers could only engage over open sights in most instances, ammunition for the guns had become 'very scarce' and all the Regiment's motor transport had been rendered unserviceable; as the Regimental War Diary rather understatedly put it, the 'situation at the end of the day was becoming critical'.[128] The breakthrough north of the Oosterbeek Old Church on the line of the Weverstraat was presumably carried out by *Kampfgruppe* Möller, and had the potential to fragment if not simply destroy the integrity of the 1st Airborne Division's increasingly tenuous perimeter. The fact that it did not and that the hard-pressed Airborne remnants comprising LONSDALE Force were able to keep back *Kampfgruppe* Harder's drive along the riverside Benedendorpsweg suggests that the two SS *Kampfgruppen* were suffering from the same problems with tank-infantry co-operation that were plaguing *Kampfgruppe* von Tettau on the west side of the Airborne perimeter. By Sunday 24 September the 1st Airborne Division had been on the ground in Holland for eight days with minimal resupply, and its constituent units were reaching the end of their logistical tether. 1st Airborne Division HQ acknowledged that a 'Shortness of serviceable weapons, particularly P.I.A.Ts. for dealing with tanks and SP guns, [was] becoming a very serious handicap' and ammunition supplies were running down to exhaustion; as we have seen the 1st Border had fewer than 3,000 rounds of .303 ammunition for example, and some units were having to employ captured German weapons and ammunition as a stop gap.[129] Food supplies had also run out in some instances The 1st Airlanding Light Regiment War Diary noted that 'rations were conspicuous by their absence', while the 2nd South Staffords reported that the men were 'by this time getting very exhausted from lack of sleep and food'.[130] This was not universal however. Glider Pilot Staff-Sergeant Sergeant Victor Miller from G Squadron still had access to tinned ration pack sausages and tea for Sunday breakfast for himself and a companion in the grounds of the Hotel Hartenstein, and studiously ignored the gaze of hungry German prisoners incarcerated in the nearby hotel tennis court as he prepared the meal.[131] Elsewhere in the hotel grounds a Sergeant Dear, possibly from the Army Catering Corps, 'did sterling work by producing food and cooking it in a hole they had made, at all hours of the day' for the HQ Royal Artillery contingent, assisted by Lieutenant-Colonel Loder-Symonds' batman, a Gunner Templeman.[132]

The source of Sergeant Dear's food is unclear but in some instances unit feeding was augmented or totally drawn from Dutch civilian provisions located in the houses within the Oosterbeek perimeter. Sergeant Henry Venes from the 1st Airborne Reconnaissance Squadron, acknowledged as one of A Troop's most proficient foragers, came upon a cache of tea, porridge, salt and sugar, which he immediately carried to a house where 156 Parachute Battalion maintained a cooking fire and proceeded to make a thick porridge cake and brew the tea. Unfortunately, he accidentally added the salt to the latter, leading an outraged Trooper James Bruce to spit out the brew and indignantly declare that 'if the Gerries don't do us in, that bastard [Venes] will!'[133] The freebooting Pathfinders from the 21st Independent Company were especially successful in their collective foraging activities as noted by the unit War Diary:

> By this time no rations were available and water was very scarce...[but]...most of the houses occupied by the Company or nearby had some tinned food stored in the cellars. Also most houses had tame rabbits. H.Q. were fortunate to find a bath half full of water.

Raids for food and water were made by night…It was therefore possible to have two meals of a sort each day and sufficient water was found for one brew of tea. Wine was the only other liquid and a fair supply was discovered.[134]

The 7th KOSB were equally successful in this regard, primarily due to the larger scale efforts of Sergeant Russell Tilley from E Squadron, The Glider Pilot Regiment, who chose to remain with the Battalion after landing rather than rallying to his own unit and appointed himself to a number of roles during the course of the battle, including assisting in the Battalion RAP and acting as Lieutenant-Colonel Payton-Reid's bodyguard. He also organised a central kitchen that provided a daily hot meal for every man in the Battalion, using foodstuffs ferreted out from abandoned houses and vegetables gathered from gardens; this, 'together with his infectious optimism, was a great help to general morale'. Sergeant Tilley was subsequently awarded the Distinguished Conduct Medal.[135]

***

On the opposite side of the Lower Rhine, Sunday 24 September saw partial resolution of the stalemate north of the Nijmegen bridges. The Guards Armoured Division continued to hold the east side of the Waal bridgehead but was reinforced by Brigadier Fergus Knox's 69 Infantry Brigade, seconded from the 50th (Northumberland) Division, which moved up on the Guards' left flank and launched a three-battalion attack intended to secure Bemmel in the afternoon. The 5th East Yorks were held up on the right of the attack frontage between De Pas and Ressen but the Brigade's other two units, the 6th and 7th The Green Howards, secured Ressen and Merm in the south-eastern outskirts of Elst in the face of light opposition, and after dark established contact with the 7th Battalion Somerset Light Infantry from 214 Infantry Brigade on the railway line just south of the town.[136] The Somersets had spent the day fighting through the western half of Elst in the face of similarly light opposition alongside the 1st Worcesters, although the latter faced more determined resistance; as the 43rd Division semi-official history noted: 'The enemy consisted of Waffen SS. Every house seemed to contain a German with an automatic.'[137] The day's fighting cost the 1st Worcesters ten dead including at least one Company commander, Major Mowbray Souper.[138] Both of 214 Infantry Brigade's Battalions were on the Arnhem–Nijmegen railway line by nightfall, and the link-up with 69 Infantry Brigade effectively pinched 129 Infantry Brigade out of the British line, although the 4th and 5th Battalions The Wiltshire Regiment reportedly remained in contact with the enemy on the Brigade's frontage south of Elst.[139]

As we have seen in the late evening of 23 September British 2nd Army 'delegated authority to Commanders 30 Corps and 1 Br Airborne Corps to withdraw 1 Airborne Div if and when considered advisable'.[140] The reason for the delegation was presumably because Dempsey thought Horrocks and Browning were better placed to expedite matters, which was also the reason for Horrocks' subsequent summons to 2nd Army HQ at St. Oedenrode in the morning of 24 September. This would also explain why Horrocks first travelled north from his HQ in Nijmegen to Driel to see the situation on the Lower Rhine for himself. He was joined en route or on arrival by Major-General Thomas, Lieutenant-Colonel George Taylor, commander of the 5th DCLI, and Lieutenant-Colonel Edmund Myers, the 1st Airborne Division's Commander Royal Engineers; Myers was tasked to assist the 43rd Division's river crossing effort, and appears to have remained on the south bank of the Lower Rhine when Lieutenant-Colonel Mackenzie returned to Oosterbeek shortly before midnight on 23 September.[141] The party viewed the crossing site from the battered church tower in Driel, accompanied by Major-General Sosabowski who had been woken from a well-deserved sleep by the unannounced arrival of the 30 Corps' commander and his party. Horrocks' intentions on receiving his newly delegated authority vary according to the source. According to his own account and the official record, Horrocks intended to continue the effort to reinforce and ultimately relieve the 1st Airborne Division. To that end Major-General Thomas was ordered to carry out another assault crossing of the Lower Rhine that night involving a minimum of one and preferably two battalions from his Division, along with supplies and the remainder of the Polish Brigade if time permitted; Thomas was also to reconnoitre west along the Lower Rhine to locate another crossing site to permit the 43rd Division to carry out another assault crossing in order to outflank the German forces besieging the Oosterbeek perimeter.[142]

This intent was largely in line with the situation report from British 2nd Army HQ received by 1st Airborne Division HQ at 05:53 that morning.[143] However, the 43rd Division semi-official account presents a rather different picture of Horrocks intent and the subsequent orders he issued, which is worth citing in full:

> Lieut.-General Horrocks faced the facts. The position held by the Airborne Division had no military value. It was merely a nebulous area in the wooded hills with very little control over the river bank, which ran dead straight for over half a mile. The enemy held the high ground overlooking the river and the approaches to it. It would therefore be impossible to bring bridging lorries down to it in daylight. Even if a bridge were built it would still be under small-arms fire from the opposite bank both above and below the bridging site. He [Horrocks] therefore instructed 43 Division to carry out the evacuation.[144]

The final decision was to be taken at a conference at 43rd Division HQ at Valburg later that morning. Although it offered cold comfort to the Airborne soldiers clinging to the Oosterbeek enclave it is difficult to dispute the dispassionate logic of the appreciation despite it arguably overplaying the difficulties of continuing the effort to support the 1st Airborne Division; the complaints regarding the difficulties in forcing a bridge across the Lower Rhine could be applied as a counter to attempting any assault river crossing, including the 43rd Division's crossing of the River Seine near Vernon on 25 August, for example. It was also thoroughly in keeping with the general lack of urgency and application displayed by 30 Corps collectively from the start of Operation GARDEN.

The variance between accounts strongly suggests that Horrocks had already reached a conclusion as to what the situation required but chose to mirror the 2nd Army's position until he had seen the situation first-hand, at which point he exercised his newly delegated authority to bring matters to a close. Horrocks was also likely hedging his bets a little because openly calling a halt to the relief effort would effectively make him responsible for the failure of MARKET GARDEN; this would explain his initially paying lip service to the original 2nd Army position and making a token show of continuing the effort to push across the Lower Rhine. It also suggests that Horrocks may have misled his superior Dempsey about his intentions. The decision to cease the reinforcement effort and withdraw the remnants of the 1st Airborne Division across the Lower Rhine was taken at a conference at the 43rd Division HQ at Valburg at around midday on 24 September, where Horrocks authorised Thomas to contact Urquhart and make arrangements to commence the withdrawal at a mutually agreed time. However, according to Dempsey's personal diary, when Horrocks attended the subsequent meeting at British 2nd Army HQ at St. Oedenrode later that day, he was still considering pushing a brigade from the 43rd Division across the Lower Rhine, and the final decision on continuing or giving up the foothold on the north bank of the Lower Rhine would not be taken until the following night of 25-26 September.[145] This narrative appears in the British Official History, and was passed up the British chain of command at the time; hence Montgomery informed CIGS Field-Marshal Sir Alan Brooke that 'if we suffer heavy casualties tonight in trying to get across [the Lower Rhine]…I shall probably give it up and withdraw 1 AB.'[146] An alternative explanation could be that Thomas simply lied about the timing and tone of his orders from Horrocks and initiated his own solution without authorisation, possibly with the connivance of Urquhart. This is not a very likely scenario however, not least because the evacuation plan, codenamed Operation BERLIN, was reportedly a joint effort between Thomas and the British 2nd Army's Chief of Staff, Major-General Harold Pyman. Given his character Thomas was an unlikely candidate to indulge in such maverick, unilateral behaviour. The crux of the matter is not whether the 1st Airborne Division would be withdrawn across the Lower Rhine, as all command levels south of the river had accepted or were moving toward accepting the fact as inevitable, the major variable being the degree of public acknowledgement. The crux is whether Horrocks deliberately misled his superiors regarding the timing of the withdrawal. The evidence suggests that he did for the reasons cited above, and that his superiors did not subsequently press the matter either. With obfuscation to this degree at the time it is scarcely surprising that the debate as to why MARKET GARDEN failed and who was responsible rumbles on after nearly seventy-five years; the pity of Horrocks' deception is that it was to involve the needless sacrifice of the remainder of the Polish Parachute Brigade and a battalion from 130 Infantry Brigade to buttress against and deflect the blame.

Horrocks' visit to the 43rd Division area appears to have had a secondary purpose. This was the creation of a scapegoat for the failure of MARKET GARDEN, and the chosen candidate was Major-General Stanislaw Sosabowski. The British GARDEN commanders appear to have either arrived north of the River Waal with a definite dislike of Sosabowski, or developed one shortly thereafter. This is apparent in the 43rd Division's semi-official history: 'It must be recorded that General Sosabowski's attitude was the reverse of co-operative' with regard to the river crossing on the night of 23-24 September, for example.[147] However, it is difficult to see the basis for this dislike given that Sosabowski's only direct contact with the 43rd Division had been with Lieutenant-Colonel George Taylor when the 5th DCLI arrived in Driel in the evening of 22 September, and then with 130 Infantry Brigade HQ via his Chief of Staff, Major Ryszard Malaszkiewicz, the following day. The Polish commander's behaviour at the Valburg Conference on 24 September was also criticised, with claims that Horrocks was obliged formally to rein in the Polish officer's truculent behaviour.[148] As we shall see, the Polish version of events at Valburg is somewhat at variance with this but that aside, it is unclear on what this hostility was based. There was no direct contact between Sosabowski and Major-General Thomas or Lieutenant-General Horrocks prior to their arrival in Driel in the late morning of 24 September just an hour or two before the Valburg conference, and given the geographic location of their various commands it is difficult to see how they had any contact prior to MARKET GARDEN. The exception to this lack of contact, however, was Browning, for whom the Polish commander had been a long-standing and persistent irritant from November 1941 through his involvement in Polish attempts to prevent Browning absorbing the Polish Parachute Brigade into his Airborne fiefdom.[149] More recently, Sosabowski had stood in the way of Browning's determination that the Airborne invasion of Holland go ahead at all costs by vociferously and repeatedly questioning the wisdom of Operation COMET, to the point of requesting that his orders be confirmed in writing, and then raising similar objections to MARKET. It would seem that that the high-level British enmity toward Sosabowski was based upon Browning briefing Horrocks and Thomas against the Polish commander. It may also be significant that Browning was the only British commander of equal or superior rank Sosabowski had contact with before the Valburg Conference, via Captain Watson from Browning's Forward Corps HQ, who visited Driel in the morning of 23 September.

The scapegoating of Sosabowski began amicably enough. Horrocks arrived unannounced at Sosabowski's HQ in Driel at 10:00, to find the Polish commander snatching some sleep after his third sleepless night trying to get his Brigade across the Lower Rhine.[150] According to Sosabowski, Horrocks entered the room whilst he was still rising and greeted him with a warm handshake and the news that the Polish Brigade's 1st Battalion was in the process of being ferried to Driel from the 82nd Airborne Division's area, where it had been dropped the previous day.

For his part the Polish commander was pleased to see his first high-ranking British officer since arriving in Holland three days earlier; he and his staff 'all took a very good view of his coming into the front line'. In response to a request for 'full details of the situation' Sosabowski gave the 30 Corps commander and his party a detailed appreciation that encompassed both sides of the Lower Rhine as well as showing him the site of the Poles' attempted crossings and another possible site that might be of use if employed immediately, all presumably done from Driel church tower.[151] Horrocks reportedly reciprocated by informing Sosabowski that his Brigade was to make another crossing that night alongside an effort from the 43rd Division, and stressing that it was vital that supplies be pushed across to the beleaguered Oosterbeek perimeter; the only alternative to this would be to withdraw the 1st Airborne Division across the Lower Rhine.[152] The 30 Corps' commander then requested that Sosabowski attend the conference at the 43rd Division HQ at Valburg later that morning, where the full details of the night's operation would be revealed before taking his leave 'smiling and waving at my troops'.[153] Sosabowski followed at 11:30, travelling in a Jeep recently acquired by the Brigade's British Liaison Officer, Lieutenant-Colonel George Stevens. Stevens accompanied Sosabowski along with his adjutant and interpreter, Lieutenant Jerzy Dyrda, who was somewhat perturbed to discover that the vehicle was to be driven by Sergeant Wojciech Juhas from the Engineer Company who 'had long had a reputation as a crazy driver'. Despite the latter racing along the narrow farm roads at over fifty miles per hour and coming under German machine-gun fire at one point, the party reached Valburg safely, although Dyrda and Stevens had been obliged to cling on for dear life to avoid being pitched from the rear of the wildly careering Jeep.[154]

What happened next again varies according to the source. Sosabowski's account, which claims that he arrived at Valburg shortly before Horrocks, is neutral up to the point where Horrocks announced the details of that night's river crossing, which involved the Polish Brigade continuing at their existing crossing point and also providing a battalion to cross at the Heveadorp ferry site in the wake of the 4th Dorsets. The problem was not with the Polish redeployment per se but the way it was announced. Thomas, although equal in rank to the Polish commander, bluntly informed Sosabowski that his 1st Battalion was to accompany the Dorsets, to which the Pole replied 'Excuse me General, but *one* of my Battalions selected by *me* will go there [original emphasis]'. The potential flashpoint was reportedly headed off by 'some soothing words from Horrocks' although thereafter Thomas refused to speak to Sosabowski, issuing instructions via Lieutenant-Colonel Stevens even though he was standing right next to the Polish commander, and he left the conference without shaking hands or acknowledging Sosabowski's existence.[155] As we have seen, the 43rd Division's semi-official history paints a rather different picture, beginning with the blunt declaration that 'General Sosabowski's attitude at the conference cannot honestly be described as cordial'. There is no reference to any exchange between the Polish commander and Thomas, but the former's response on hearing the plan for the night's crossing was reportedly to declare 'I am General Sosabowski, I command the Polish Para Brigade. I do as I like.' Horrocks' reply was hardly conciliatory: 'You are under my command. You will do as I bloody well tell you.' Sosabowski responded, 'All right. I command the Polish Para Brigade and I do as you bloody well say,' after which the conference 'continued on more formal lines'.[156]

The two accounts are clearly at variance, not least because the sentences in the British version expressing open criticism of Sosabowski appear rather disjointed and contrived, as does the wording of his alleged comments. More importantly, however, the British version of events does not square with a third account from a participant at the Valburg Conference. According to Sosabowski's adjutant/interpreter Lieutenant Dyrda, Horrocks and the rest of the British officers were already gathered outside the meeting tent when Sosabowski arrived and Thomas behaved in a cold and distant manner toward him from the outset. Next, Horrocks refused to allow Dyrda to accompany his commander into the conference tent on the grounds that the Polish commander spoke English well enough, and he only relented when Dyrda appealed to Browning to intercede. The tent was laid out with a single long table with seating for the British attendees along one side and a single chair for Sosabowski on the other but no seat for Dyrda. Horrocks ordered him to stand behind his commander; the Polish Brigade's liaison officer, Lieutenant-Colonel Stevens, was seated on the British side of the table. Dyrda, perhaps presciently, thought the seating arrangements were more suited to a trial than a military conference, and subsequent events supported his view. With Lieutenant Dyrda translating, Horrocks began the conference by announcing that he was executing orders from Dempsey to establish a strong lodgement on the north bank of the Lower Rhine, then outlined that this would be done via two crossing points, before handing over to Thomas to fill in the details. Thomas then not only informed Sosabowski that he was to continue the crossing at the same place as previously, but that one of his Battalions would be removed to cross near the Heveadorp ferry after the 4th Dorsets and that he was to be effectively placed under the command of Brigadier Walton from 130 Infantry Brigade, who was in charge of the crossings overall; according to one source Dyrda chose not to pass the latter point on to his commander.[157]

Despite his humiliating treatment Sosabowski waited until Thomas had finished before proposing a full Division crossing farther west near Renkum and pointing out that not only would crossing near the Heveadorp ferry be under the guns of the Germans occupying the Westerbouwing Heights, but that the crossing on the planned scale 'would change nothing' and would be 'an unnecessary sacrifice of soldiers'. He closed by pointing out that as the Polish Brigade commander, he should have been allowed the courtesy of selecting which of his units would be detached to cross with the 4th Dorsets. All this fell on deaf ears. Thomas simply rose and stated, 'The crossing will take place as I said, at the locations I stated, and will begin at 22:00 hours'. Sosabowski tried again, this time speaking in English that became more fluent as he went on, talking over Thomas when he tried to interrupt to point out that the 1st Airborne Division had been holding out in Oosterbeek for eight days and that 'the best sons of England are dying there, for no effect'. Again, this was to no avail for Sosabowski was then interrupted by Horrocks, who announced, 'The conference is over. The orders given by General Thomas will be carried out. And if you, General, do not want to carry out your orders, we will find another commander for the Polish Para Brigade who will carry out orders'. As the meeting broke up Thomas added one final twist of the knife by totally ignoring the Polish commander despite him standing close by while issuing the orders for the night's operation to Lieutenant-Colonel Stevens. When Stevens passed on the orders to Sosabowski the Polish commander acerbically enquired when the hapless Liaison Officer would be taking over command of the Polish Brigade.[158] Although perhaps aimed at the wrong target, Sosabowski's bitterness was both understandable and excusable. His contemptuous treatment would have been reason enough, but Sosabowski was also likely the only man in the conference tent who had been in recent close contact with the enemy and seen first-hand the results of trying to perform a river crossing with insufficient numbers, equipment or support. In the event, his assessment of the coming night's crossing was to prove to be absolutely correct.

This puts a rather different complexion on the matter than that provided by Sosabowski's personal and the 43rd Division semi-official accounts, and with the benefit of hindsight it is difficult to see the treatment meted out to Sosabowski as anything other than the prelude to the full-scale blame-shifting that occurred after MARKET GARDEN was concluded. Nor was the Valburg Conference the end of the matter that day, for as the meeting was breaking up Browning invited Sosabowski to his Forward Airborne Corps HQ in Nijmegen. According to one source the invitation was to allow the Polish commander to celebrate Mass, but the course of events make it more likely that the purpose was to allow Browning to inform Sosabowski about the decisions taken at Valburg in his absence.[159] Sosabowski began by dining with Browning in the Staff Officer's Mess after dropping Lieutenant Dyrda at a nearby Officer's Mess, during which Sosabowski was 'bombarded with questions about the battle' by curious members of the Corps HQ staff; Sosabowski mentally compared the lunch, served on china plates, to the more basic repast he would have enjoyed back at his own HQ at Driel.[160] When the pair retired to discuss business after the meal Browning began by reiterating that his Airborne Corps was subordinate to 30 Corps, that the primary task at this juncture was keeping the road open between Eindhoven and Nijmegen and gathering in both formations' vehicles; Browning may have been in temporary command of 30 Corps at this point as a German attack had severed the road near Veghel, obliging Horrocks to remain at 2nd Army HQ at St. Oedenrode until the following day.[161] Anxious to push the points he had made at the earlier conference, Sosabowski again urged a full divisional crossing west of Driel and was reportedly 'thunderstruck' when Browning countered this by announcing that the upcoming crossing might fail due to a lack of equipment, adding 'because it is impossible to get the equipment up to the river' when Sosabowski queried the announcement. The discussion then deteriorated as Sosabowski bluntly pointed out the price the 1st Airborne Division was paying 'every hour and every minute' and urged Browning to make a final worthwhile effort, while Browning simply repeated the point about keeping the road open before bringing the meeting to a close.[162]

Before detailing Sosabowski's reaction to his unofficial meeting with Browning and subsequent developments, and given Browning's claim that there was insufficient bridging equipment and that it was not possible to get the equipment that was available up to the Lower Rhine, we should investigate what river crossing personnel and equipment was potentially available to 30 Corps at this moment. The GARDEN order of battle included a Special Bridging Force (SBF) made up largely of Engineer and Service Corps units gathered from across 21st Army Group and including the only Canadian units involved in MARKET GARDEN, totalling approximately 9,000 personnel and 2,277 vehicles. This force was initially concentrated at Bourg-Leopold near the GARDEN start line, where a huge dump of equipment was established for despatch up the Airborne Corridor. The SBF was in turn divided into three Army Group Royal Engineers (AGRE), each of which was assigned to crossings on specific watercourses; the 11th AGRE was responsible for the River Maas, the 1st Canadian AGRE for the Maas–Waal Canal and River Waal, and the 10th AGRE for the Lower Rhine. The AGREs in turn controlled specifically configured bridging columns for each crossing. The column assigned to the Mass–Waal Canal contained 483 vehicles carrying the components for two Class 40 Bailey pontoon bridges while that for the River Waal consisted of 380 vehicles carrying nine Class 40 rafts, to be followed by a single Class 40 Bailey pontoon bridge within seven days. The column assigned to the Lower Rhine consisted of 536 vehicles carrying a single Class 9 Folding Boat Equipment (F.B.E.) bridge to be followed by a single Class 40 Bailey pontoon bridge within twelve days; the initial arrangements on the Waal and Lower Rhine were to be augmented with additional Class 40 Bailey barge bridges within thirteen to eighteen days.[163] Preparation and provision of river-crossing personnel and equipment for Operation GARDEN was thus thorough and plentiful and although it is unclear precisely where all the various elements of this host ended up along the Airborne Corridor this nonetheless begs the question as to what was available at the head of the Airborne Corridor after the GARDEN force crossed the River Waal.

In fact, there were at least four specialist engineering units on or north of the River Waal within fifteen miles and thus striking distance of the crossing point near Driel. Two of these belonged to the 43rd Division. Major Thomas Evill's 204 Field Company RE arrived at a point three-and-a-half miles south-west of Nijmegen at 11:00 on 21 September, after moving off from a harbour area near Hechtel at 16:45 the previous day. The seventy-two-mile journey took just fifteen hours and forty-five minutes and the Company halted from 03:00 to 05:30 near St. Oedenrode, a rate of progress that suggests that traffic movement up the Airborne Corridor was smoother and swifter at this juncture than popularly portrayed.[164] The Company then remained in that general area until the morning of 24 September, apart from being stood to for a series of proposed crossing operations. The Company's 3 Platoon was despatched to assist 214 Infantry Brigade with a proposed attack across the Lower Rhine at 18:00 on the day of arrival before being released by the 7th Somerset Light Infantry at 22:30 when the crossing was postponed, although it did not arrive back at the Company harbour until the late afternoon of the following day due to traffic congestion north of the Waal bridges.[165] At 15:15 on 22 September the bulk of the Company moved to another harbour area close to the south end of the Nijmegen railway bridge to participate in the pending assault crossing over the Lower Rhine. Although as we have seen, in the event only the Company's 3 Platoon went forward at 21:00 on 23 September to assist with the Polish Brigade's third attempt to cross the river.[166] The second 43rd Division unit was Major Anthony Vinycomb's 260 Field Company RE, which moved off from a harbour area just south of the Albert Canal at 18:00 on 20 September and arrived at a harbour area near Nijmegen at 10:00 the following day after an all-night road march. There the Company learned that its projected task of bridging the Rivers Maas and Waal had been rendered superfluous by the 3rd Battalion, 504th Parachute Infantry Regiment's seizure of the Nijmegen bridges in the afternoon of 20 September, and remained there awaiting orders until 25 September.[167]

The other two units were from the Canadian contribution to the SBF, the No. 1 Army Group Royal Canadian Engineers commanded by Colonel C.J. 'Spike' Bermingham and specifically from one of that formation's two sub-formations, Lieutenant-Colonel N.I. Byrn's 1st Canadian Army Troops (CAT), Royal Canadian Engineers (RCE) made up of three RCE Field Companies and an RCE Field Park Company.[168] The 20th Field Company RCE, commanded by Major A.W. Jones, was actually on the move before MARKET GARDEN commenced, leaving Arques in the Pas de Calais at 07:30 on 16 September and travelling via Brussels to a harbour area near Eksel, just south of the Meuse-Escaut Canal, at 06:30 on 17 September. There the Canadian Sappers discovered that while they had no specific mission, they were likely to be given the task of erecting a Bailey bridge across the River Maas and carrying out 'an assault ferrying job' over the Lower Rhine using Class 9 or Class 40 rafts.[169] After spending four days at Eksel the Company moved to Nijmegen at 10:30 on 21 September, linking up with a bridging train en route. The convoy was shelled near Uden, with Sapper G.A. Topping being evacuated to a US field hospital after being badly wounded by shrapnel, before reaching a temporary bivouac area on the outskirts of the city at 19:00. They discovered via an O Group at 22:00: 'We still don't know whether or not there is a job for us. The assaulting corps wants its own engineers to handle the rafting and bridging so we may have come on a wild goose chase.'[170] The following day the Canadians were ordered to despatch a party to reconnoitre the crossing site on the Lower Rhine in readiness to ferry tanks across the river on Class 40 rafts, and on 23 September the Company officially came under command of the 43rd Division's CRE, Lieutenant-Colonel Mark Henniker, on one-hour notice to move.[171] On 24 September the Company's organic transport and the bridging train, totalling 483 vehicles, were marshalled to move by midday but the move was cancelled at 13:30 and the increasingly disgruntled Sappers were stood down to their bivouac site.[172] Events unfolded in a similar vein for the second Canadian unit, Major Mike Tucker's 23rd Field Company RCE, which left St. Omer at 07:45 on 16 September, also moving via Brussels, before arriving at a harbour area near Hechtel at approximately 10:30 the following day.[173] At 12:10 on 21 September the 23rd Company moved off for Nijmegen again in company with a bridging train, although the timings and locations cited suggest it might have been the same train as that accompanied by the 20th Field Company RCE. Whether or not, Major Tucker and his men arrived at their new harbour area south of Nijmegen at approximately 17:00 where they remained, apart from despatching a reconnaissance party to the Lower Rhine the following day and commencing a move forward on 24 September that was cancelled at approximately 13:00; again, this may have been the move with the bridging train marshalled by the 20th Field Company on that day.[174]

This shows that Browning was being economical with the truth in his claim that there was insufficient equipment as there were at least four specialist bridging units and at least one complete bridging train in place at Nijmegen by 21 September, arriving hard on the heels of the seizure of the Waal road and rail bridges and not caught up in the oft-cited traffic congestion farther south in the Airborne Corridor. These units were thus in position to move up to the Lower Rhine in the wake of 130 Infantry Brigade's advance to Driel in the morning of 23 September and they were actually marshalled and preparing to make that very move on 24 September when it was cancelled at about 13:00. Moving the bridging train up to the Lower Rhine was clearly problematic before 214 Infantry Brigade succeeded in pushing back the German forces overlooking the road through Valburg by last light on 23 September, but it is difficult to see why at least some if not all the Field Companies could not have been moved up in their entirety to assist the Poles in their river crossing efforts on the nights of 22-23 and 23-24 September, given that the Sapper units were able to despatch reconnaissance parties to the river and remembering the Platoon level assistance rendered by 204 Field Company RE on the night of 23-24 September. It is also difficult to see how moving the equipment up to the riverbank would have been much more difficult than in any contested river crossing, although the state of the ground and the fact the Germans held the ground overlooking the proposed crossing site as part of the ring around Oosterbeek supports Sosabowski's suggestion of utilising a crossing site farther west. Quite why the bridging units' collective move on 24 September was cancelled is unclear, but the timing does support the contention that Horrocks had decided to cut his losses and evacuate the Oosterbeek pocket rather than push across the Lower Rhine before the Valburg Conference, irrespective of his claimed intentions communicated to Dempsey at British 2nd Army HQ. To be fair, Horrocks' reluctance may have been due to a lack of resources for while Sosabowski repeatedly recommended a Division-strength crossing, which was likely the minimum force necessary to make a difference, at this point 30 Corps did not have a Division available. Half of the Guards Armoured Division was busy maintaining the eastern side of the Waal bridgehead along with 69 Infantry Brigade from the 50th Division; the remainder of both Divisions were employed in maintaining the Airborne Corridor south of Nijmegen. 129 and 214 Brigades from the 43rd Division were engaged in clearing Elst and maintaining the western half of the Waal bridgehead, thus leaving only 130 Brigade to form a bridgehead over the Lower Rhine, with no immediate prospect of reinforcement. However, there does not appear to be any reference to Horrocks pointing this out in the official or semi-official records and 30 Corps' general lack of push from the outset of MARKET GARDEN, combined with the seeming lack of urgency after crossing the River Waal creates the distinct impression that as far as 30 Corps' senior commanders were concerned, all bets were off when the 1st Airborne Division failed to provide the crossings at Arnhem – the GARDEN force had done its bit by reaching the Lower Rhine, and whatever was happening on the north bank of the river was not really their concern.

Major-General Sosabowski was still noticeably agitated when Lieutenant Dyrda and Sergeant Juhas picked him up from Browning's HQ to return to Driel; it is unclear if they were still accompanied by Lieutenant-Colonel Stevens. When Sosabowski related the details of the meeting to Lieutenant Dyrda the adjutant pointed out, not mincing his words, that even suggesting there was any reluctance to aid the 1st Airborne Division might have lost friends among the senior British commanders if not actually created enemies, although Sosabowski's treatment at Valburg strongly suggests that this was already the case before the Polish commander set foot in the conference tent. Sosabowski, perhaps understandably, did not take Dyrda's analysis well and the remainder of the journey back to Driel passed in a rather frosty silence.[175]

There are two key points to note with regard to Browning's comments during the meeting at Nijmegen. First, as none of this appears to have been raised while Sosabowski was present at Valburg there was presumably an earlier meeting before he arrived, at which Horrocks confirmed his intention to withdraw the 1st Airborne Division on the night of 25-26 September and authorised Thomas to carry it out. This supports the contention that Sosabowski was only present to lay the groundwork for a subsequent scapegoating, as it is difficult to see any other purpose in his being there, given his treatment. Second, the comments show that while Horrocks may have concealed his precise intentions from Dempsey, he had not confined knowledge of them only to his subordinates at the 43rd Division because of Browning's presence at the Valburg Conference. This raises the additional suspicion that 2nd Army HQ may have been aware of Horrocks' intent despite official pronouncements, and that Browning had thus willingly acquiesced to the abandonment of one of his subordinate formations. Writing a decade-and-a-half after the event, Sosabowski laid responsibility for the failure of the effort to relieve the 1st Airborne Division firmly upon Browning, claiming that he argued against Horrocks' scheme for a larger-scale crossing on 25 September to Dempsey, who in turn passed it on to Montgomery, who then decided to 'call the whole thing off'.[176] Given his Machiavellian tendencies it would be surprising had Browning not been involved to some degree, but this appears to grant him far too much influence, not least because he is unlikely to have wished to maintain a high profile as the operation he had single-mindedly ensured would go ahead to be the capstone of his Airborne career crumbled. More importantly, Sosabowski's appreciation misses that Montgomery, with admittedly uncharacteristic reticence, does not appear to have been involved in the decision-making process and, as we have seen, authority to continue or end the effort to relieve the 1st Airborne Division was devolved by 2nd Army to Horrocks and Browning. The two British Corps commanders were not equals, however, Browning being officially subordinate. It was thus Horrocks who attended the conferences at Dempsey's 2nd Army HQ at St. Oedenrode while Browning remained in Nijmegen. It would therefore appear that it was actually Horrocks who ultimately took the decision to initiate Operation BERLIN at the Valburg conference and bring matters to a close.

In the meantime the die was cast and preparations went ahead through the afternoon and into the early evening of 24 September for that night's river crossing. Lieutenant-Colonel Gerald Tilley's 4th Dorsets had been in reserve near 130 Brigade HQ at Homoet, four miles south-west of Driel, since the late afternoon of the previous day.[177] 130 Brigade HQ issued a Warning Order to the 4th Dorsets at Midday and the Battalion Intelligence Officer reported to 130 Brigade HQ for orders at 14:00. Lieutenant-Colonel Tilley then took his Company commanders forward to Driel to view the prospective crossing from the church tower at 16:00 and may then have attended an O Group at 130 Brigade HQ thirty minutes later, although the Battalion War Diary makes no reference to him so doing.[178] He briefed his own officers at 18:00. The Battalion's task was two-fold: to enlarge the bridgehead on the north bank of the Lower Rhine, and to expedite the passage of supplies to the 1st Airborne Division. The immediate objective was a disused factory approximately 600 yards from the water's edge and the Battalion was to cross in four waves, A and B Companies followed by C and D, then Battalion HQ followed by S Company bearing the Battalion support weapons and supplies for the Airborne troops; the supply effort was to be augmented by four or six DUKWs once the 4th Dorsets were across, manned by troops from the 7th Royal Hampshires commanded by a Major Rooke.[179] However, Middlebrook refers to the amphibious vehicles being manned by twenty men from 181 Airlanding Field Ambulance RAMC's Seaborne Echelon commanded by the unit Quartermaster Lieutenant John Tiernan and a Lieutenant Tansell RASC from 133 Parachute Field Ambulance. The vehicles were carrying three tons of medical supplies gathered from the Seaborne Echelon of the 1st Airborne Division's three Field Ambulances by Lieutenant-Colonel Martin Herford commanding 163 Field Ambulance RAMC, whose activities are described in more detail below.[180] The assault boats for the crossing, which were still en route up the Airborne Corridor, were to be manned by Sappers from 1 and 2 Platoons, 204 Field Company RE, which had moved up to Valburg from a harbour area near the Nijmegen railway bridge.[181] Fire support was to be provided by small-arms and mortars from 130 Brigade's other two battalions, the 5th Dorsets and 7th Hampshires on the 4th Dorsets' right and left respectively, Vickers Guns from the Divisional MG Battalion the 8th Middlesex, a Squadron of tanks from the 13th/18th Hussars and all three of the 43rd Division's Royal Artillery Field Regiments. The crossing was to commence at 22:00.[182]

The 4th Dorsets involvement in the upcoming river crossing was not greeted with enthusiasm. Lieutenant-Colonel Tilley began his briefing to his assembled officers with the comforting words, 'Gentlemen, we've bought it this time.' The commander of C Company, Major Philip Roper, recalled thinking it unlikely that he and his men would be returning from the operation, although he attempted to safeguard morale when briefing his own men by stressing that the crossing was 'an important job to help the airborne people'.[183] Be that as it may, the Battalion moved off for its assembly area, orchards several hundred yards from the water's edge near the Heveadorp ferry terminal, at 19:30 in darkness and under cold, drizzling rain and intermittent German mortar and artillery fire. Taking cover from the fire in the darkness broke up the Dorsets' column into a number of small parties that had to be reorganised in Driel before continuing the move up to the assembly area.[184] The infantrymen were preceded by Sappers from 204 Field Company RE, all three Platoons of which had moved up to a harbour area near Valburg at 16:00; 1 and 2 Platoons then moved up to the crossing point in readiness to man the assault boats at 19:15, leaving 3 Platoon on stand-by to assist if required.[185]

While 130 Brigade and the 43rd Division were making their preparations, an officer from one of 30 Corps' attached units was also making a small-scale crossing of the Lower Rhine on his own account. Lieutenant-Colonel Martin Herford's 163 Field Ambulance had been slated to cross the Lower Rhine with the Poles on the night of 23-24 September with a quantity of medical supplies, but it hadn't happened through lack of boats. Concerned at the increasing severity of the medical situation in the Oosterbeek perimeter, Herford sought and obtained permission from Major-General Thomas to take a quantity of medical supplies across the Lower Rhine and crossed the river at 14:30 in a single assault boat loaded with the supplies and adorned with a Red Cross flag. He was accompanied by Captain Percy Louis from 133 Parachute Ambulance's sea tail and four unnamed medical orderlies. The party landed on the north bank near Heelsum, three miles downstream from the Heveadorp ferry site; it is unclear whether this distance was deliberate or due to the current. On landing Lieutenant-Colonel Herford set out alone with the Red Cross flag and made contact with the local German forces, who allowed Captain Louis, the medical orderlies and two stray Polish paratroopers to return to the south bank; it is unclear if the Germans appropriated the medical supplies or despatched them back across the river too. The subsequent fate of the Other Ranks is unknown but Captain Louis was killed at some point later that day, possibly during the night's river crossing. Herford remained with the Germans who would not agree to allow further deliveries of medical supplies across the river but did permit him to contact the senior German medical officer in the Arnhem area. The upshot of this contact was the establishment of a hospital in a Dutch Army barracks near Apeldoorn, seventeen miles north of Arnhem, where the 250 surviving members of the 1st Airborne Division's medical staff treated 1,700 British Airborne casualties. Herford served as deputy commander of the hospital under the 1st Airborne's ADMS, Colonel Graeme Warrack, and was subsequently awarded the Distinguished Service Order for his conduct.[186]

Matters proceeded in a similar vein at Driel where Major-General Sosabowski briefed his commanders at 17:00, informing them that the crossing was scheduled to commence at 22:00.[187] The 2nd Battalion and Brigade HQ would cross at the original site while Major Tonn's 1st Battalion and accompanying portion of the 3rd Battalion commanded by Captain Sobocinski would cross further west at the Heveadorp ferry site behind the 4th Dorsets. At this point Major Tonn and the 1st Battalion contingent, between 551 and 565 men, were at Valburg having boarded a convoy of thirty-three trucks at Malden just after 15:30 for the journey up the Airborne Corridor.[188] There the trucks left the Poles, apart from four vehicles retained to carry the parachute containers in which the paratroopers' heavy weapons, ammunition and signals equipment were still packed. After failing to contact Polish Brigade HQ by radio Major Tonn led his contingent in a road march over the five miles or so to Driel, the paratroopers carrying the remainder of their equipment because the rutted road rendered the Airborne handcarts useless. They arrived at Driel at 19:30 where Lance Sergeant Cadet Boguslaw Horodeczny was waiting to lead them to Sosabowski's HQ. The Brigade commander listened to Tonn's report on his adventures after being recalled from the Polish drop on 21 September before briefing the newcomer on his part in the British portion of that night's crossing efforts.[189] It unclear what time Major Tonn led his men across to the concentration area for the Heveadorp crossing, although it was reportedly after a short rest, but the 2nd Battalion and Brigade HQ moved off for their well-worn crossing site at 21:00. They appear to have been preceded by the Brigade's Engineer Company, now commanded by Lieutenant Wieslaw Szczgiel after Captain Budziszewski had been wounded. They had laid out the path to the water with white tape and readied the three collapsible wood and canvas assault boats that had survived the previous night's crossing.[190]

Now, with the keyed-up troops waiting in the darkness things again went awry, with the assault boats once more failing to arrive as arranged. According to the 43rd Division semi-official account the craft were carried aboard five trucks. Two of these apparently ran off the embanked road and became stuck in the roadside ditches while two more took a wrong turn at a junction in Valburg and drove into German lines in Elst. Another account refers to the captured vehicles belonging to a Canadian unit, although there is no mention of the incident or indeed any involvement with that night's crossing in the 20th and 23rd Field Company RCE War Diaries. The single vehicle that reached its destination reportedly arrived with boats but no paddles and ended up with the Polish Brigade, although again, there is no mention of this in the Polish Brigade War Diary or other Polish accounts.[191] At 21:45 Brigadier Walton therefore postponed the crossing for three hours until 01:00 and instructed the Polish Brigade to return the vessels left over from the previous night's crossing to the 43rd Division, although Sosabowski refers to the order coming from Major-General Thomas via Lieutenant-Colonel Stevens in person.[192] The 43rd Division's semi-official account took another snide and unsupported swipe at Sosabowski and his men, asserting that 'The Poles were unco-operative' although there is no evidence to suggest that this was actually the case.[193] According to Sosabowski, the order to hand back the three assault boats was delivered as a request by Stevens after he had passed on the postponement order: 'Are you willing, sir, to give up the boats held by you and hand them over to the Dorsets, so that the main assault can be put in?' Sosabowski agreed, albeit reluctantly as he thought there was a good chance of getting his 2nd Battalion and Brigade HQ across to the Oosterbeek perimeter.[194] For his part Lieutenant Szczgiel recalled the unannounced arrival of an unknown British captain at the Polish crossing site baldly stating 'You are to give up the boats,' which he promptly did after radioing Captain Budziszewski at Brigade HQ to ensure it was permissible to 'give up the toys'; the British officer was a Captain Dawes from the 5th Dorsets, who shuttled the craft across to the Heveadorp crossing site aboard vehicles of some description, possibly Universal Carriers.[195] The Polish crossing was cancelled at 22:45, and the weary Polish paratroopers again wended their way back to their positions in and around Driel. Lieutenant Szczgiel led his men back to their slit trenches dug around the cattle barn that served as the Engineer Company HQ, where he settled himself into a convenient trough set in the concrete floor and quickly fell asleep.[196]

Major Tonn and the 1st Battalion were still tasked to follow the 4th Dorsets across at the Heveadorp ferry site, however, and British infantrymen and Polish paratroopers alike continued to wait amongst the dripping apple trees in their orchard assembly areas as the clock ticked on past midnight and carried Operation MARKET GARDEN into its ninth day.[197]

D Plus 8

00:01 to 18:00 Monday 25 September 1944

Precisely when the single truckload of paddleless assault boats and the vessels retrieved from the Polish Brigade arrived at the Heveadorp ferry site is unclear, but Lieutenant-Colonel Tilley and the first wave of the 4th Dorsets began the task of manhandling their craft through the rain-dripping apple trees and across the soggy polder to the water's edge before the rescheduled start time an hour after midnight; each vessel was crewed by two Sappers from 204 Field Company RE and their infantry passengers were divided into boat parties of ten men with ammunition and supplies for four days.[1] The first wave was preceded by a twenty-minute bombardment from the 43rd Division's three RA Field Regiments thickened with fire from the infantry and tank units deployed along the riverbank to the east and west of the departure point. This was a tactic dubbed 'the Pepperpot' invented by Major-General Thomas, which involved every weapon in the Division from rifles to anti-tank guns firing at known or suspected enemy locations. It was intended to inflict casualties at best and psychological damage at worst, the latter being confirmed by prisoner interrogation. The Pepperpot became a set 43rd Division drill administered and controlled by Lieutenant-Colonel Mervyn Crawford, commander of the 8th Middlesex, the Division Machine Gun Battalion.[2] The artillery barrage perhaps set fire to two factory buildings in the woods near Heveadorp village, which unfortunately illuminated the crossing area, although the Germans may have simply set fire to the buildings themselves to provide illumination once the barrage indicated the landing area, in the same way they had ignited the main at the Oosterbeek municipal gasworks the previous night. The barrage alerted the Germans to the imminent crossing and provoked an immediate mortar counter-barrage backed by the ubiquitous automatic weapons firing on fixed lines targeting the lines of approach on the water and likely embarkation points on the south bank.

The '1st Flight' of craft across the river departed the south bank on schedule at 01:00, carrying Lieutenant-Colonel Tilley's tactical Battalion HQ and men from A and B Companies commanded by Majors James Grafton and Michael Whittle respectively. Each Company was also accompanied by a two-man Forward Observer team drawn from 112 Field Regiment RA with Captain Thomas Rose and his signaller accompanying Major Grafton's HQ; the identity of the teams accompanying the other Companies is unclear.[3] Some of the vessels were hit by German small-arms and mortar fire that caused a number of casualties but most landed unscathed despite the German fire, although they had become split up during the crossing and came ashore in scattered pockets and farther downstream than planned owing to the fierce current; according to the 1st Airborne Division HQ War Diary the Dorsets made landfall 1,000 yards west of the Oosterbeek perimeter.[4] While a combination of the scattering, darkness and enemy fire prevented the incoming units from assembling, their place of arrival proved fortuitous as it brought them ashore behind the concentration of German troops manning the west side of the Oosterbeek perimeter. The troops manning the positions overlooking the river were actually *Kriegsmarine* personnel from *Korvettenkapitän* Theodor Zaubzer's *10 Schiffsstammabteilung* and those in the immediate vicinity of the landing initially withdrew onto the wooded Westerbouwing Heights after lobbing grenades at the interlopers.[5]

At some point the Sappers also began ferrying men from C and D Companies and one source refers to men from all five of the 4th Dorset's Companies being present on the north bank. However, the small number of assault boats involved, the short duration of the crossing effort and the fact that only approximately 300 men were lifted across during that period strongly suggests that whatever Companies were represented on the north bank, they were far from present in their entirety.[6] The commander of D Company, Major Tony Crocker, was wounded in the leg by German automatic fire at the embarkation point, so seriously that the limb had to be amputated subsequently. Command of his Company then appears to have devolved upon Captain Ronald Hall, who made three unsuccessful attempts to cross the river: the first two assault boats were obliged to return to the south bank after being holed by mortar fragments and small-arms fire and the third was carried off by the current and cast up some distance downstream, again on the south bank.[7] The crossing also included a small party from the 1st Border made up of Battalion commander Lieutenant-Colonel Thomas Haddon, his batman, a Lance-Corporal Nolan, the Battalion Intelligence Officer Lieutenant Ronald Hope-Jones, and Private Kelly. The Horsa carrying Haddon and part of his HQ group had been obliged to abort from the first lift over the UK following a series of instrument malfunctions and his attempt to fly in with the second lift the following day ended when his Horsa force landed near Bourg Leopold after it and its Dakota tug were damaged by *flak*. Haddon and his party spent the next week moving up the Airborne Corridor in an effort to rejoin their Battalion on their own initiative and arrived at the south bank of the Lower Rhine at some point on Saturday 23 September.[8] The 1st Border party was accompanied by Major Patrick Anson, the commander of A Company, 10th Parachute Battalion whose transport had reportedly been shot down during the second lift's run-in to DZ Y on Ginkel Heath, who was also seeking to rejoin his unit.[9]

The fortunes of the men from the 4th Dorsets were in many cases dependent upon where they alighted onto the north bank. On the right of the landing frontage and thus closest to Oosterbeek Major Grafton managed to gather a party from A Company including Captain Rose and his signaller, which he successfully led along the riverbank and into the Airborne perimeter via the sector held by BREESE Force. By 06:00 this party and possibly another of unknown provenance was located in the vicinity of the 1st Airlanding Light Regiment's gun positions near the Oosterbeek Old Church, from where they despatched a Liaison Officer to the Hotel Hartenstein at 08:40.[10] After liaising with the Light Regiment Captain Rose and his signallers established a radio link to their parent unit, 112 Field Regiment RA, which relieved some of the pressure upon the sole existing line to 64 Medium Regiment RA and thereby allowed an increase in artillery support for the beleaguered Airborne troops. Captain Rose was badly wounded in the shoulder by German machine-gun fire later in the day whilst observing from the porch of the Oosterbeek Old Church, and died at some point the following day.[11] The Dorsets that came ashore on the left of the landing frontage came up against rather stiffer opposition. Four assault boats carrying men from B Company including Major Whittle landed 100 yards or so east of the blazing factory buildings near Heveadorp and were immediately attacked with hand-grenades by German troops manning the top of a steep, 100-foot-high bank overlooking the river. After gathering a party of around thirty men including Lieutenant Dennis McDermott, Major Whittle launched an assault up the bank that drove the Germans back and secured the crest at a cost of half the party becoming casualties; the survivors immediately set about digging in on their new location.[12]

Lieutenant-Colonel Tilley also reached the crest of the slope after landing, presumably accompanied by his tactical Battalion HQ after leading a headlong charge up the slope shouting 'Get them with the bayonet!' He was reportedly struck on the head by a grenade in the rush and suffered a slight wound from the subsequent detonation.[13] In the process he appears to have lost contact with the remainder of his Battalion and remained isolated throughout the hours of darkness. Lieutenant Hope-Jones from the 1st Border party came in with the second flight east of the Heveadorp ferry terminal after his assault boat had reportedly turned 'in a complete circle' midway across after the crew realised the vessel was heading too far upstream. He was confronted by the same 'steep and thickly wooded slope' that had confronted the Dorsets' B Company. He then became separated from the remainder of his boat party after returning to the vessel with a signaller to retrieve a forgotten radio battery. While searching for his own party he ran across a 'rather frightened platoon of Dorsets' who reportedly 'looked on him as a gift from heaven, obviously expecting to be led safely...into the arms of their Battalion'. Despite considering himself hardly 'qualified to do the job' Hope-Jones nonetheless led the group up the slope despite much slipping and sliding in the loose sandy soil until they were challenged by German troops manning the crest; he then led his new charges in a rush that cleared and secured the enemy position. Whilst reorganising after the assault Hope-Jones discovered that the stray party of Dorsets included a Platoon officer, which he not unreasonably decided absolved him of any further responsibility for them. He therefore struck off eastward on his own in search of the Airborne perimeter and his Battalion.[14] Irrespective of their location and situation, the men who succeeded in reaching the north bank were effectively abandoned to their own devices at 02:15 when the crossing effort was suspended reportedly due to 'HVY enemy pressure', just an hour and fifteen minutes after the crossing effort had commenced. It is unclear if the order originated with Brigadier Walton at 130 Brigade HQ or further up the British chain of command.[15] The effort was then switched to passing supplies for the 1st Airborne Division across the Lower Rhine, although this also proved to be less than successful. Three of the DUKWs either did not arrive at the crossing point or were unable to access the water due to the steep bank depending on the source, but the remaining three vehicles succeeded in crossing the river carrying approximately two tons of ammunition, food and the medical supplies gathered by Lieutenant-Colonel Herford. They were again carried downstream by the current and then became stuck in deep mud on exiting the water around 1,000 yards west of the Oosterbeek perimeter, from where two of the RASC drivers, a Corporal Varney and Driver Chilton, swam back to the south bank in an unsuccessful bid to secure assistance.[16] 1st Airborne Division HQ became aware of the supply effort at 06:05 and reported being unable to distribute the supplies in the 'ducks', due to a combination of enemy action and lack of transport, at 09:40; given that the stranded vehicles lay the better part of a mile outside the Oosterbeek perimeter the former factor was key, and the supplies were presumably appropriated by the Germans.[17]

The onset of daylight proved to be a mixed blessing for the marooned Dorsets in their isolated pockets along the north bank. Lance-Corporal Wally Smith and his Bren team were part of a group that had dug in on the riverbank in the darkness. Daylight found them exposed to merciless fire and a rain of hand-grenades from German troops overlooking them from higher ground that killed Smith's gunner, Private Harold Wyer, and over time reduced their number to around ten, pinned down along 200 yards of the riverbank. The Dorsets maintained the unequal struggle until their ammunition was exhausted at some point in the morning, after which the survivors 'lay doggo' and awaited nightfall.[18] After reaching the crest of the slope Major Whittle managed to gather in a number of men from several Companies but failed to make contact with Lieutenant-Colonel Tilley or any formed elements of the Battalion. He therefore led the B Company party forward to a more defensible location deeper in the woods, or behind a bank midway between the river and the wooded high ground depending on the account, where they remained for the rest of the day.[19] Major Philip Roper and twenty of his men from C Company also took a more aggressive approach by moving deeper into the woods at first light in an effort to locate other men from the Battalion. The party included Private Aubrey Steirn who had a narrow escape during a sudden, close-range encounter:

> I was in the lead when a machine-gun opened up on me from a very short distance. I was knocked over…I came to in one piece, apart from a facial wound and badly bruised shoulder where a burst of fire had 'clipped' me and left metal fragments in my uniform.

The German position was overrun and eliminated while Private Steirn was recovering and the party moved on, gathering up more scattered elements of the Battalion including Lieutenant-Colonel Tilley.[20]

Obergruppenführer Bittrich at *II SS Panzerkorps* became aware that the British were mounting a reinforcement effort across the Lower Rhine at 05:15 when *Wehrmachtbefehlshaber Niederlande* forwarded a signal from *Kampfgruppe* von Tettau informing the higher HQ that 'the enemy has crossed the Rhine at Kasteel Doorwerth and Heveadorp after heavy artillery fire' and that 'counter-measures have been initiated'. Another signal at 06:10 reported that the crossing had taken place only at the 'Driel ferry' crossing, was in battalion strength and had penetrated *Schiffsstammabteilung 10's* sector. Moving with his customary swiftness *Generalleutnant* von Tettau launched *Oberstleutnant* Shennen's *bataillon* from *Sicherungs Regiment 26* in an immediate counter-attack, supported by two *kompanien* from *Fliegerhorst Bataillon 1* and *SS Kompanie* 'Moll', which proceeded to clear the 'incursion'.[21] Major Roper's party from C Company was surrounded after occupying some abandoned German trenches and Lieutenant-Colonel Tilley took the decision to surrender to save further loss of life. While all this was going on Lieutenant Hope-Jones had abandoned his solo attempt to reach the Airborne perimeter and linked up with another group of Dorsets, which came under small-arms and mortar fire while he was digging in; this ceased with the arrival of British and German officers who informed the party that Lieutenant-Colonel Tilley had ordered a surrender and led them to the C Company location. There he discovered Lance-Corporal Nolan and Private Kelly, the former badly wounded in the stomach; Hope-Jones administered a dose of morphine and helped Kelly get him to a Dressing Station. There was no sign of Lieutenant-Colonel Haddon, who had also embarked on a solo attempt to reach the Airborne perimeter; he was captured in the attempt.[22] *Kampfgruppe* von Tettau subsequently identified the British attackers as belonging to the 43rd Division which had 'moved by foot march from Nijmegen' and reported that 'the enemy has high losses. 140 are taken prisoner, including nine officers and the battalion commander, a colonel'.[23]

Thus the 4th Dorset's valiant effort to reinforce the beleaguered Oosterbeek perimeter came to a premature end after seventy-five minutes, during which time just seven Officers and 298 Other Ranks reached the north bank of the Lower Rhine; of these, thirteen were killed, approximately 200 were captured and five from 204 Field Company RE were wounded.[24] The 43rd Division's semi-official account gives the distinct impression that the effort went on through the whole of the night and characterised it as a period of 'heroic struggle against hopeless odds'; interestingly, the 204 Field Company RE War Diary also wrongly refers to the ferrying operation not ceasing until dawn.[25] On the other hand Middlebrook noted 'a lack of push about the operation from the highest level of the 43rd Division downwards' and characterised the aborted crossing as a 'sacrifice'.[26] Given the evidence the latter view is nearer the mark, although it pitches responsibility a little low on the chain of command, for as we have seen, the commander of 30 Corps had personally involved himself in the 43rd Division's activities north of the River Waal from 23 September, when he and Browning were given the authority to terminate Operation MARKET and withdraw the 1st Airborne Division across the Lower Rhine if required. On that basis neither Brigadier Walton nor Major-General Thomas can have been responsible for the planning, execution or premature termination of the Sunday night crossing. This is clear from the fact that 30 Corps specifically ordered the crossing to be pared down from an already inadequate two battalions on the night of 23-24 September (amended to 'two companies' in a subsequent order) to a single battalion effort on the night of 24-25 September; even had it reached the north bank intact, a single battalion could not have 'relieved the pressure on the [1st Airborne] bridgehead' as intended in any meaningful way.[27] It is difficult to see how this would not still have been the case even if 130 Brigade had crossed the Lower Rhine in its entirety. The 1st Airborne Division required immediate reinforcement including armour to stand a chance of survival, and that was not in the offing as 30 Corps did not specifically instruct the 43rd Division to begin reconnoitring possible sites for a full-scale crossing of the Lower Rhine until 25 September, when the decision to withdraw the Airborne formation had already been taken.[28] It therefore looks as though the 4th Dorset's crossing was never intended to succeed from the outset. Rather, it appears to have been intended as a token gesture to allow Lieutenant-General Horrocks to claim that reinforcing the 1st Airborne Division and maintaining a foothold on the north bank of the Lower Rhine was impossible, and thus provide justification for the withdrawal decision; this would also explain the rendering down of the reinforcement effort to the inadequate level of a single battalion. Lieutenant-Colonel Tilley and the 4th Dorsets were therefore sacrificed not in a serious effort to bring succour to the Airborne troops struggling in Oosterbeek, as has been routinely claimed, but on the altar of political expediency for the benefit of the upper echelons of the British chain of command.

Possibly the last man to reach the north bank of the Lower Rhine in the early morning of Monday 25 September was Lieutenant-Colonel Edmund Myers, the 1st Airborne Division's Commander Royal Engineers, who had been assisting the 43rd Division with its latest crossing effort; he reportedly crossed the river aboard one of the three DUKWs loaded with Lieutenant-Colonel Herford's supplies and then made his way upstream along the riverbank into the Airborne perimeter.[29] Myers arrived at the Hotel Hartenstein at 06:05 carrying two letters for Major-General Urquhart, one from Major-General Browning and one from the commander of the 43rd Division, Major-General Thomas.[30] Thomas informed Urquhart that the 2nd Army plan was no longer to establish a bridgehead across the Lower Rhine west of Arnhem, but to withdraw the 1st Airborne Division back across the river. According to Urquhart's account the withdrawal was to be an arrangement between himself and Thomas 'on a date to be agreed', but the 1st Airborne Division HQ War Diary reflected the urgency of the situation by adding a caveat that it was to be carried out when the Airborne formation 'could no longer hang on'. Ironically, given that MARKET GARDEN was intended to open the way for an advance eastward across the North German Plain, the withdrawal was codenamed Operation BERLIN.[31] Perhaps unsurprisingly the 43rd Division's semi-official account claims that the decision to launch BERLIN was taken by Thomas alone, who then ordered Urquhart to comply via a radio message.[32] That aside, Urquhart took two hours to consider the matter, although the writing was pretty much on the wall. As described, the Airborne units holding the perimeter had been reduced to mere shadows of their former selves with the survivors virtually out of food and ammunition and the Dorsets' crossing of the Lower Rhine had failed to materially alleviate the situation; furthermore, the evacuation of the Division MDS from the Hotels Schoonoord and Vreewijk had effectively removed access to anything more than basic medical treatment for the mounting number of casualties. The perimeter itself had been compressed to its limit, with the Germans to the west being within small-arms range of the Hotel Hartenstein while those to the east had made inroads that threatened to fragment it altogether. A report from the Airlanding Light Regiment suggested the enemy there were about to launch a concentrated effort to cut the perimeter off from the Lower Rhine.[33] With the caveat that the evacuation should be launched when the 1st Airborne could no longer hang on thus pretty well fulfilled, Urquhart responded to Thomas' letter at 08:08 via the radio link with the 64th Medium Regiment RA, with the request that BERLIN had to be carried out that night before summoning his senior commanders to a planning conference at the Hotel Hartenstein at 10:30.[34]

***

While the Dorsets were struggling across the Lower Rhine and the hungry and exhausted Airborne troops manning the Oosterbeek perimeter took the opportunity to snatch a little rest, the Germans were busy reorganising and integrating reinforcements. *Obersturmbannführer* Harzer had persuaded *Generalfeldmarschall* Model that the liberal use of artillery to reduce the Oosterbeek pocket would be more effective, quicker and less costly in German lives than digging out the stubborn British defenders with tanks and infantry; Harzer may also have been trying to compensate for his relative lack of manpower, given that the fight at Oosterbeek was low on the priority list for reinforcement. *Heeresgruppe B* therefore instructed the overall area artillery command, dubbed *ArKo 191*, to employ all its 110 guns and *SS Werfergruppe* Nickmann's two batteries of *Nebelwerfer* rocket launchers in systematically raking the British perimeter, which had now shrunk to less than two square kilometres in extent.[35] On the west side of the perimeter *Generalleutnant* von Tettau rationalised his *Kampfgruppe* by withdrawing the hodge-podge of internal security and rear-echelon units to Elden and Velp where they were to regroup and form a reserve; combat operations remained the responsibility of *Luftwaffe Bataillon* Worrowski on the sector abutting the Lower Rhine with *SS Bataillonen* Eberwein and Schulz to its left linking in with the elements of *9 SS Panzer Division* covering the northern aspect of the perimeter, presumably still supported by the surviving tanks from *Panzer Kompanie 224*.[36] *Standartenführer* Lippert had been relieved of overall command of these units by von Tettau, reportedly because von Tettau was no longer willing to tolerate the outspoken and critical behaviour of his *SS* subordinate. Who replaced Lippert is unclear.[37] On the eastern side of the Pocket *Obersturmbannführer* Harzer carried out a more in-depth reorganisation, particularly of the units responsible for the line running south from the Utrechtseweg to the Lower Rhine: *Kampfgruppen* Möller, von Allwörden and Harder. These units were broken up into small combat groups that were augmented with assault pioneers from *SS Panzer Pionier Abteilung 9* and *Pionier Lehr Bataillon 9*, the latter a specialist urban combat demonstration unit *Heeresgruppe* B had flown into Deelen airfield on the nights of 21 and 22 September.[38]

Monday morning dawned with heavy rain over the Oosterbeek perimeter.[39] The by now customary early-morning mortar and artillery barrage began to fall on the 1st Border's positions on the western face of the perimeter at 06:00 and the south-eastern sector including the 1st Airlanding Light Regiment's gun positions around the Oosterbeek Old Church appears to have come under fire at around the same time.[40] The barrage was not universal across the entire perimeter however, with the 7th KOSB on the northern face reporting a 'quiet period [that] continued until about 1100 hours'.[41] On the western face of the perimeter the bombardment heralded a resumption of the German pressure upon the 1st Border's stubbornly held positions along the Van Borsselenweg, with 1st Airlanding Brigade HQ reporting: 'No major attack was put in anywhere but under its cover parties started infiltrating at all points and the morning was very sticky everywhere.' This included the environs of Brigade HQ itself, where a group of infiltrators occupied houses midway between the Brigade HQ and the Hotel Hartenstein and had to be eliminated by the Glider Pilots providing security for Brigade HQ commanded by Major James Dale DFC.[42]

At the southern end of the line abutting the Lower Rhine the survivors of B Company, Lieutenant Arthur Royall's 12 Platoon dug in near the municipal gasworks and Lieutenant Stanley Barnes composite platoon dug in near the *Dennenord*, repelled several German attacks over the course of the day and while armoured vehicles were clearly audible moving around in the woods to the north of their location, they did not put in an appearance. The constant German artillery and mortar fire proved to be more deadly. Lieutenant Barnes and his men had begun began taking temporary shelter from the rain in the garage of the *Dennenord* from where they could still cover their assigned frontage and the Platoon Commander was thus engaged with Lance-Corporal Ginger Wilson when a shell exploded in the doorway to the garage, killing four men standing just inside and badly wounding Lieutenant Barnes in the foot. The unscathed Lance-Corporal Wilson promptly carried the wounded officer round to the cellar of the

Dennenord where B Company's Aid Post was located and assisted a medical orderly in trying to staunch the bleeding with field dressings and then an abandoned Denison smock.[43]

On the Van Borsselenweg D Company 1st Border, by now reduced to just nineteen men, was still holding its position despite being cut off from the remainder of the 1st Border for two days. At some point in the morning Company commander Captain William Hodgson despatched Corporal Alan Fisher to report to Battalion HQ before overseeing the setting up of the Company's No. 18 wireless set in the open by Privates Ron Graydon and Joseph Maguire in an effort to establish contact. A heavy German mortar concentration fell just as the already wounded Hodgson left the shelter of the Company HQ building and he was wounded again so severely he died the following day.[44] Private Maguire was also wounded and another Company signaller, Corporal Lawrence Cowin, was killed by a direct hit on his slit trench.[45] Apparently missing Battalion HQ, Corporal Fisher arrived at the 1st Airlanding Brigade HQ at 14:30 and after making his report was immediately sent back to D Company with orders for an immediate withdrawal to a track east of the Van Borsselenweg.[46] This Corporal Fisher did but his arrival coincided with a heavy German mortar barrage and as he was only able to contact a few men he assumed the Company was in the process of being overrun; he therefore led the handful of men he had located back to Brigade HQ and reported that D Company had been under heavy attack at 15:30 and was presumed to have been overrun at 16:00.[47] This was not the case. The fatal wounding of Captain Hodgson during Corporal Fisher's absence left Lieutenant Green as D Company's sole functioning officer. By this point the situation of the Company's wounded had become critical as medical supplies were almost exhausted, so following a discussion with his surviving senior NCOs it was decided to try to arrange a temporary ceasefire to allow the wounded to be evacuated. However Lieutenant Green was fired upon as he attempted to approach the nearest German positions before being caught in a mortar barrage, in the course of which he sustained a further four wounds. With that, the surviving nineteen members of D Company pulled into a tighter perimeter around the wounded and settled down to hold out until relieved or overrun, which is presumably why Corporal Fisher failed to locate them.[48]

Along the remainder of the 1st Border's frontage running up to the Utrechtseweg C Company was heavily bombarded from 06:00 but German attacks were reportedly broken up by Allied artillery fire. Details are sketchy and subsequent events suggest the seeming lack of German push during the daylight hours was due to *SS Bataillonen* Eberwein, Oelkers and Schulz switching to night attacks. The official and participant accounts from the units holding the line north of the Utrechtseweg, 261 Field Park Company RASC, 9th (Airborne) Field Company RE, 4th Parachute Squadron RE, the 1st Border's A Company and the Glider Pilots from E and F Squadrons are similarly sketchy, and understandably focus on preparations for the night's evacuation.[49] On the northern aspect of the perimeter *Kampfgruppe* Bruhn appear to have been similarly quiet, given that the 7th KOSB reported that despite spending the night in 'some trepidation' in expectation of a final enemy effort at dawn, their frontage little happened until around 11:00. At that point the Battalion's block position straddling the Bothaweg and Paul Krugerstraat came under 'an extremely heavy concentration of shelling', presumably connected to *ArKo* 191 implementing the order from *Heeresgruppe B* to systematically rake the entirety of the Oosterbeek pocket. German ground activity was confined to movement in the woods to the west of the KOSB's positions, and was kept at arm's length by a combination of sniping and machine-gun fire augmented with mortars and artillery.[50] The latter appears to have been provided by the 64th Medium Regiment RA, possibly again controlled by Captain John Walker from the 1st Airlanding Light Regiment, which fired concentrations into the vicinity of the western and northern aspects of the perimeter at 11·47, 12·45 and 13·45.[51] However, Bren Gunner Private Robin Holburn reported an attack by unsupported German infantry across a cabbage field in the vicinity of the KOSB's block position. The enemy went to ground among the vegetables after Holburn and another unnamed gunner fired off several magazines and inflicted numerous casualties. An NCO remained on his feet exhorting his men to rise and continue the attack; after watching for a few seconds Holburn recalled, 'I fired and hit him with a burst of fire and he dropped to the ground. At this, and among cries from the wounded, the rest scurried or crawled back behind other houses.'[52]

The relative German inactivity did not extend to the eastern side of the perimeter. On the north-eastern corner the 1st Airborne Reconnaissance Squadron's A Troop came under intense small-arms and machine gun fire from 07:30, in line with *Obersturmbannführer* Harzer's intent to break in the western aspect of the British perimeter. The intense fire permitted German patrols to move around and up to the houses held by the Reconnaissance Troop at the junction of De la Reijweg and Steijnweg, which were attacked with bundled stick grenades as an improvised breaching device. The fighting cost the defenders two wounded, and the pressure became so great that Lieutenant Douglas Galbraith, the sole functioning A Troop officer remaining, ordered his men to abandon the buildings at 09:00 in favour of the slit trenches he had wisely had dug in the gardens the previous night. There A Troop waited to be overrun by the inevitable final German attack but was not forthcoming, reportedly due to the presence of RAF Hawker Typhoons overhead. Despite the intensity of the fighting there were still Dutch civilians sheltering in the area. Trooper Ken Hope, who had been posted in a house covering the roadway, was startled by a noise behind him but instead of a German infiltrator he was confronted by an aged couple standing in the cellar doorway 'looking at the shambles of what had probably been their best room. The old lady was sobbing, and tears streamed down her wrinkled face.' She and her dazed husband were gently ushered back into the cellar by Troop Sergeant Henry Venes.[53] On the Reconnaissance Squadron's right Major Geoffrey Powell and his hundred-strong group from 156 Parachute Battalion and Glider Pilots from D Squadron remained in the box position just back from the Stationsweg they had been obliged to withdraw to the previous day. They held on despite repeated German attacks supported by *StuGs* and heavy mortar fire until 14:00, when Major Powell was given permission by 4th Parachute Brigade HQ to 'withdraw to the house North of the main rd' due to the isolated nature of his position; the location was on the north side of the Utrechtseweg and the move was part of a consolidation by Lieutenant-Colonel Murray in preparation for that night's withdrawal over the Lower Rhine.[54]

Lieutenant Bereda-Fialkowski's Poles had spent a tense night after an unnamed British medical officer from the Hotel Schoonoord relayed an ultimatum from the Germans at just before 18:00; this demanded an immediate evacuation of the Polish-held houses or tanks would be brought up to level the buildings. Lieutenant Bereda-Fialkowski contacted Captain Zwolanski at the Hotel Hartenstein for guidance. Zwolanski's blunt if honest response was not encouraging: 'You cannot surrender, you cannot withdraw, and we cannot give you any help.' The Poles responded accordingly. In the *Quatre Bras* house overlooking the Utrechtseweg-Stationsweg junction Corporal Jan Towarnicki collected all the available Gammon Bombs and used the plastic explosive from some to create a larger charge, which was in turn attached to a plank to allow it to be shoved beneath any tank moving across the junction; a party of seven men commanded by a 2nd Lieutenant Kowalczyk who were occupying slit trenches in the narrow lawn in front of the house were to deploy the weapon. The remaining Gammon Bombs were stored on the upper floor of the *Quatre Bras* to be thrown down onto the decks of any armoured vehicles that came within range. Just before dark another explosive charge was used on the brick wall dividing the back gardens of Stationsweg Nos. 8 and 10. The explosion had the startling side-effect of blowing out all the remaining window glass in the two houses, but the resultant breach completed a network of shallow communication trenches linking the rear of the five Polish-occupied houses on the Stationsweg. At No. 8 Lieutenant Bereda-Fialkowski ordered the Kremer family and the thirty-three Dutch civilians sheltering there from the fighting back into the cellar with strict instructions to remain totally silent, cover the cellar windows and to refrain from showing any lights. The Poles were perhaps understandably concerned about the damage a collaborator among the civilians could cause, but the paratroopers nonetheless handed over what chocolate and sweets they could muster to the Dutch children, and Officer Cadet

Mieczyslaw Jurecki reassured Mrs Kremer that British tanks would arrive shortly. Elsewhere the Poles set about preparing what food they could find. In the *Quatre Bras* house Corporal Towarnicki despatched one of his men to collect a bucket of water from a nearby well which, after the paratroopers had partially slaked their thirst, was boiled up with the contents of a large bag of bran discovered in the house earlier; Towarnicki augmented this meagre fare with three cans of oxtail soup he had been hoarding in his webbing small-pack.[55]

The German tank attack failed to materialise, although a single tracked vehicle did approach the Polish positions in the darkness coming to a halt just short of the Utrechtseweg–Stationsweg junction by the Hotel Vreewijk, where the commander engaged nearby German troops in a conversation audible over the idling engine. Lieutenant Kowalczyk led a party of his men stealthily forward from their trenches in front of the *Quatre Bras* across the junction and attacked the vehicle with a Gammon bomb. It is unclear if the subsequent explosion damaged it but the vehicle immediately reversed away from the junction while spraying the *Quatre Bras* with machine-gun fire; it then fired several more bursts west along the Utrechtseweg before withdrawing. Kowalczyk and his men also withdrew to their trenches, apparently unscathed. Although the Poles remained on the alert the vehicle did not return and the rest of the night passed relatively quietly apart from regular rounds by Lieutenant Bereda-Fialkowski and the noise of heavy calibre shells from 30 Corps' artillery falling just behind the German positions straddling the Utrechtseweg to the east.[56] This continued after daybreak, when the Poles moved back into the buildings from the slit trenches, and the German bombardment was soon augmented by direct fire from *Sturmgeschütze Brigade 280*'s vehicles. Many of the German projectiles passed clean through the houses without exploding, which led to speculation that the vehicles were employing anti-tank shells due to a shortage of high-explosive rounds.

The British heavy artillery shells also began falling closer to the Polish positions, making the buildings quake alarmingly. One shell, presumably a smaller calibre German projectile, burst in the parlour of the house serving as Bereda-Fialkowski's command post, demolishing a heavy green brocade sofa and scattering the burning debris around the room. The flames were quickly extinguished by the occupants, although Corporal Stanislaw Lewicki sadly noted that the damage included a container of Genever gin gifted to the paratroopers the previous day that, 'neither tasted or enjoyed, had soaked into the plaster that covered a once-luxurious rug'.[57]

On the Poles' right the Pathfinders from Major Wilson's 21st Independent Company also appear to have spent a relatively quiet night after rebuffing German demands to evacuate the house on the Pietersbergseweg and subsequent destruction of a *Panzer* IV by the PIAT-wielding Company cook, Private Dixon. The by-now routine morning bombardment of the Pathfinder's positions was classified as 'very heavy' by the unit War Diary and included a number of white phosphorous mortar bombs that ignited a number of fires in the buildings occupied by the Pathfinders and those adjacent. German ground activity in the morning consisted of attempts to infiltrate through No. 2 Platoon's positions along the Paasbergweg on the right of the Company frontage.[58] No. 1 Platoon and especially Bren-gunner Private Sidney Humphries were able to assist in repelling the would-be interlopers from its central position on the junction of the Pietersbergseweg and Paasbergweg. Private Humphries fired on and hit a German spotted by one of the Platoon NCOs standing in the open on the Annastraat just east of their location, only to see a previously concealed Red Cross armband as the man fell; after a pause Humphries not unreasonably justified his error by pointing out that the German had 'asked for it – standing in the open like that'.[59] By 11:55 Major Wilson was able to report that his situation had 'stabilised and that any enemy who infiltrated were either dead or withdrawn'. A direct attack on No. 3 Platoon's positions on the Pietersbergseweg facing the Hotel Schoonoord in the afternoon was also rebuffed.[60]

While the fighting on and north of the Utrechtseweg was hard, the heaviest German attack of Monday 25 September, which came close to fragmenting the Airborne perimeter, came in against the sector south of the 21st Independent Company and involved the most formidable armoured vehicles deployed against the 1ˢᵗ Airborne Division to date. After serving in some of the heaviest fighting on the Eastern Front in the first half of 1944, Major Eberhard Lange's *schwere Panzer Abteilung 506* was ordered to withdraw to Ohrdruf in central Germany on 15 August. There the unit was re-equipped with forty-five Tiger II heavy tanks over a three-week period ending on 12 September and after a short period of training was despatched to the Western Front by rail, arriving at Zevenaar during the night of Saturday 23 September. There at least two of the *Abteilung's* sub-units, each equipped with fourteen tanks, were unloaded to join *II SS Panzerkorps* while *1 Kompanie* and the *Abteilung* HQ element carried on to Aachen, although they too may have been unloaded to road march to the railway stations at Apeldoorn and Zutphen for onward despatch to join the fighting against the US 1ˢᵗ Army. Of the remainder that definitely detrained at Zevenaar, *2 Kompanie* commanded by a *Hauptmann* Wacker was despatched south to Elst to join *10 SS Panzer Division* while Hauptmann Otto's *3 Kompanie* embarked on the fifteen-mile road march to Oosterbeek to join *9 SS Panzer Division*.[61] On arrival Otto's vehicles appear to have been parcelled out to the units pressing against the south-eastern sector of the British perimeter, *Kampfgruppe* Harder and *Kampfgruppe* von Allwörden and possibly *Kampfgruppe* Möller, the new arrivals may also have been integrated with the elements of *Sturmgeschütze Brigade 280* already operating with the various *kampfgruppen*, given British accounts of the Monday fighting.

The German bombardment on the southern half of the Airborne perimeter was noted as being especially heavy, although reports of the time it commenced varied between units and locations. The 1ˢᵗ Airlanding Light Regiment referred to heavy mortaring from the early morning for example, while the 1ˢᵗ Airlanding Brigade HQ, located just a few hundred yards to the north, referred to heavy mortaring and shelling breaking out at around 10:00 after a 'comparatively quiet morning'.[62] The ground attack began at 10:00, although some reports refer to it beginning at 11:00 or in the early afternoon, the disparity likely being due to the attackers reaching the various British unit locations at different times.[63] The target of the thrust was again the previously penetrated section of the eastern perimeter between the 21ˢᵗ Independent Parachute Company and LONSDALE Force. The 1ˢᵗ Parachute Battalion account noted: 'On this day the perimeter was widely breached to the North of us, and the enemy was moving in our left flank in force. A considerable number of tanks inside the perimeter.'[64] One Tiger II, accompanied by three *StuGs* and possibly a section of infantry, penetrated two-thirds of the way across the British perimeter, into the rear area of its western face. The infantry were eliminated after occupying a group of houses midway between the 1ˢᵗ Airlanding Brigade HQ and the Hotel Hartenstein by a party of Glider Pilots from C Squadron commanded by Major James Dale DFC and Bar, who had been providing protection for the Brigade HQ since Tuesday 19 September.[65] The armoured vehicles came even closer to the Airlanding Brigade HQ after regrouping at a track junction 100 yards or so south, with the Tiger reportedly coming to a halt 'with its nose just visible round the corner of the gate'. As the HQ was protected by a concealed 6-Pounder anti-tank gun the arrival of the sixty-eight-ton behemoth did not cause undue alarm, until it was discovered that the 6-Pounder's breech had been damaged by mortar fire, rendering it inoperable. Another gun was then hastily brought up and fired three rounds in quick succession that 'immobilised the tank but did not destroy it'. The presence of the 6-Pounder 'deterred the enemy for the rest of the day', while the damaged Tiger was towed away by another tank after dark.[66]

The most serious fighting of the day actually took place in the vicinity of the Oosterbeek Old Church as the German units facing the south-eastern sector continued their efforts to prise the Airborne perimeter away from the Lower Rhine. The 1ˢᵗ Airlanding Light Regiment's 3 Battery had moved into the immediate vicinity of the Church on Monday 18 September, where it was joined by the rest of the Regiment the following afternoon. Regimental HQ occupied a building on the north side of the Benedendorpsweg just opposite the Church with 1 Battery's gun positions immediately adjacent to the north and 2 Battery located just to the west, while 3 Battery was deployed on the south side of the Benedendorpsweg almost directly west of the Church.

LONSDALE Force was deployed around the Light Regiment's location, with a composite group made up mainly of men from the 2nd South Staffords commanded by Major John Simonds dug in to the immediate south of the Church; another group of Staffords commanded by Major Robert Cain was located north-east of the Church covering 1 Battery's gun positions and a third group, dubbed 'LONGSTOP', was dug in just west of 3 Battery's location. The much-reduced 1st, 3rd and 11th Parachute Battalion contingents were located straddling the Benedendorpsweg to the east of the Church and the north of 1 and 2 Battery's gun positions was protected by G Squadron Glider Pilots commanded by Major Robert Croot. The location also included two Vickers Medium Machine-Guns and two 3-inch mortars deployed in the immediate vicinity of the Church, up to five 6-Pounder anti-tank guns and a single 17-Pounder.[67] According to Middlebrooks's account the crisis point of the German attack came with the arrival of tanks after a supporting shoot from 30 Corps' artillery, but the primary source material suggests this was not the case as the 1st Airlanding Light Regiment record refers to being 'subjected to a heavy Tank attack' at the outset of the attack at 10:00.[68] Within the hour the Gunners informed 1st Airlanding Brigade HQ that they were 'being very heavily attacked' and made an emergency request for 'immediate infantry support and PIATs'. As the Airlanding Brigade HQ had no assistance to offer, the request was passed on to the Hotel Hartenstein, which responded honestly if equally unhelpfully by pointing out that 'nothing could be found for them and that they must hang on'.[69] The Light Regiment's 1 Battery bore the brunt of the initial assault from the north during which A Troop was reportedly overrun by three Tiger tanks despite a Sergeant Daly, a Gun Commander from B Troop, reportedly knocking out an unidentified vehicle. The adjacent 2 Battery appears to have been attacked initially by infantry whose heavy fire prevented the crews from operating their guns and then, just as the Gunners were organising a counter-attack to drive the interlopers back, by tanks that overran the Battery position.[70] One vehicle stood off and pumped shells into the house serving as the Battery Command Post, where Gunner William Speedie stuck steadfastly to his assigned duty whilst manning the Battery control set, as related by Gunner Robert Christie from C Troop:

> As the house was tumbling he came on the air and, in a clear and controlled Scots voice, went through the proper procedure for closing down control and passing those duties to an out-station. What he did was straight out of Signals Training – All Arms, and this while the building was literally coming down around him.[71]

The fight for 2 Battery's position also saw the destruction of the sole Tiger II lost in the Oosterbeek fighting by *schwere Panzer Abteilung 506*, at the hands of two men from C Troop. A Tiger and *Sturmgeschütze* attached to *Kampfgruppe* von Allwörden approached the east of 2 Battery's position from the direction of the Weverstraat near the junction with the Benedendorpsweg and brought C Troop's gun pits and Command Post under intense machine-gun fire at around 11:00. The latter consisted of a slit trench with overhead cover, occupied by Gun Position Officer Lieutenant Adrian Donaldson with Lance-Bombardier Percy Parkes and Gunner Christie manning the Troop wireless sets. Lieutenant Donaldson left the trench and collecting Lance-Bombardier James Dickson en route, crawled 100 yards under intense machine-gun fire to a 6-Pounder gun with a dead crew. The pair brought the gun back into action. After firing eight or nine rounds the gun was demolished by a direct hit that rendered Donaldson unconscious, although Dickson was able to move him into cover. When Donaldson recovered his senses the two men crawled back across the bullet-swept ground to one of C Troop's 75mm Pack Howitzers, also with a dead crew, where Dickson fired the four armour-piercing rounds there and then continued to bore-sight, load and fire the gun's supply of HE ammunition at the Tiger single-handedly, while Donaldson collected three more armour-piercing rounds from another gun pit. Dickson fired off two of these rounds, one of which blew off the tank's right track, before the gun jammed; he then collected a PIAT from C Troop's vehicle park and attacked the Tiger again, reportedly without success. The source of the damage is unclear, but the immobilised vehicle also sustained damage to the muzzle brake of its 88mm gun and caught fire at some point. The two Gunners eventually withdrew to 3 Battery's location as German infantry overran 2 Battery's gun pits, although Donaldson returned later in the day to ensure no wounded had been left behind and removed the sights and breech blocks from the abandoned guns. Lieutenant Donaldson was awarded the Distinguished Service Order for his part in the incident and Lance-Bombardier Dickson the Military Medal.[72]

The survivors of 2 Battery withdrew into the nearby woods and the attackers then pushed south across 1 Battery's location to surround the adjacent Regimental HQ, obliging the HQ personnel to withdraw to 3 Battery's Command Post after destroying their equipment.[73] The fighting pushed deeper into LONSDALE Force's positions as the day progressed, drawing in the Parachute Battalion contingents straddling the Benedendorpsweg and the South Staffords dug in south of the road by the early afternoon. The Airborne soldiers appear to have been equal to the task of dealing with their opposite numbers as noted by the 11th Parachute Battalion, which reported that it had 'engaged the [German] infantry with bren [sic] and rifles, and handled them severely'.[74] The real problem was the tanks and assault guns that accompanied them as pointed out in the 2nd South Staffords War Diary: 'our PIAT amn was completely exhausted – and all but one of the ATk guns were out of action, so that further prolonged defence particularly against enemy armour was out of the question.'[75] In the event the day was saved by the 5.5-inch guns of 64 Medium Regiment RA and possibly other artillery units from 30 Corps. It is unclear precisely who called in the guns, although the 64 Medium Regiment War Diary and Urquhart's biography suggests it was the 1st Airborne's CRA, Lieutenant-Colonel Robert Loder-Symons.[76] Whoever was responsible, the Medium Regiment began its involvement in the fight by shelling a point south of the Benedendorpsweg 300 yards east of the Oosterbeek Old Church at 13:35, followed ten minutes later by shelling the junction of the Benedendorpsweg and Kneppelhoutweg 400 yards north-west of the Old Church, reportedly in response to a 'Main attack developing'. A target dubbed MZ39, presumably in the vicinity of the Old Church, was engaged at 14:50 and again at 15:15, on the latter occasion 'repeated with everything available [as] requested by 1 A/B Div. Situation quite serious'. This was presumably the point where Lieutenant Donaldson and Lance-Bombardier Dickson had gone after the Tiger, after which the German assault appears to have ebbed. Lieutenant-Colonel Loder-Symons' station informed 64 Regiment that the attack had 'more or less died down' and that a Tiger tank had been disabled at 15:56. The hiatus appears to have been temporary, however, given that MZ39 was hit once more at 16:55 and 17:11 in response to '1 Tiger tank re-attacking' and again at 17:34, 18:35 and 19:30 in response to German attacks.[77]

The general consensus on the Airborne side was that 30 Corps' artillery had saved the day: 'The position was becoming desperate when a stonk from 30 Corps artillery came down exactly in the right place, on whose orders I don't know.'[78] However, the close-quarter nature of the fighting also made the artillery assistance a double-edged sword. The 1st Parachute Battalion reported that the enemy mortar and artillery fire 'was made more unpleasant because many British shells from south of the river were landing in our area, but these did providentially quieten the tanks'.[79] The 2nd South Staffords War Diary was more direct: 'Things looked rather serious until 25 pdrs and medium guns from south of the river laid down a barrage in front of the forward troops. It was in fact uncomfortably close and we suffered some casualties from our own shell fire but the Germans had got pretty close too and the barrage completely broke up their attack.'[80] This was not quite the end of the matter for the South Staffords however, as some of the retreating enemy infantry occupied a partially demolished house around fifteen yards from the Glider Soldiers forward post, provoking a sharp but inconclusive exchange of hand-grenades. When this failed to dislodge the interlopers one of the South Staffords' officers persuaded a functioning and still manned 75mm Pack Howitzer, possibly from 3 Battery, to put a HE round into the building at a range of seventy yards. The house promptly collapsed in a shower of dust and sparks with only one of the occupants being seen to escape. The Gunners then employed their 75mm guns, presumably from the Airlanding Light Regiment's 3 Battery given that the other two Batteries had been overrun, to drive off some tanks that began firing into the rear of the South Staffords' positions; the departure of the vehicles was seen as the 'final crisis'. The dead from the fight included Major John Simonds, OC of HQ Company, who commanded the contingent of South Staffords dug in south of the Old Church.[81]

While the tenacity of the Airborne troops and the efficiency and accuracy of the Gunners played a key role in holding the German attack on the south-eastern aspect of the Oosterbeek perimeter on 25 September, it is important to acknowledge an additional factor. The fight at Oosterbeek was existential for the 1st Airborne Division – but this was not the case for their opponents. Once *II SS Panzerkorps* had blocked and secured the approaches to the Arnhem road bridge and *Heeresgruppe* B had implemented measures to seal off the Airborne corridor south of the Lower Rhine it became a matter of secondary importance, and the German units involved were left largely to their own devices. The elements of *9 SS Panzer Division* were badly understrength from the outset, and while the patchwork of *Heer*, *Kriegsmarine*, *Luftwaffe* and *SS* units drafted in during the first two or three days of the battle were largely up to strength, the majority lacked infantry experience and their numbers were rapidly whittled down when they came into contact with the aggressive and more tactically adept Airborne troops. Thereafter there was little significant reinforcement, which consisted primarily of armour from *Sturmgeschütze Brigade 280* and *Panzer Kompanie 224*, which arrived on 19 and 20 September respectively and *schwere Panzer Abteilung 506*, which arrived on the 24th; foot reinforcements included the *Luftwaffe Bataillon* Worrowski and the amalgamated *Pionier Lehr Bataillon z.b.V.* and *Pionier Bataillon 26* arriving on 21 and 22 September.[82] As a result *9 SS Panzer Division* and *Kampfgruppe* von Tettau had sufficient armour and infantry strength to make inroads into the Airborne perimeter but lacked sufficient manpower to properly exploit or indeed hold onto any gains made. This explains the German pattern of fighting during the hours of daylight and then withdrawing with the onset of darkness, which repeatedly allowed the Airborne troops a breathing space to rest and reorganise in readiness for the next assault the following day. The pattern continued almost up to the end of the battle for Oosterbeek, although it shifted slowly as attrition and compression of the Airborne perimeter began to tilt the odds toward the attackers, and there was a switch to night attacks just as the remnants of the 1st Airborne Division executed its withdrawal across the Lower Rhine. This in no way devalues the skill, tenacity or courage of the Airborne soldiers who had achieved more than ought to have been militarily or humanly possible in their defence of the Oosterbeek perimeter, but it does explain why they were able to hold out as long as they did in the face of seemingly overwhelming German strength.

The 1st Airborne Division had pretty much reached the end by this point and its ability to withstand more attacks on the scale of Monday's assault was doubtful; indeed, Urquhart had already furnished 1st Airlanding Brigade HQ 'with a warning of what action was to be taken in the event of the Div being overrun' the previous day.[83] It was therefore not before time when Operation BERLIN was scheduled to take place that night.

***

On the south bank of the Lower Rhine Lieutenant-General Horrocks' intentions for 25 September remained largely the same as they had been since 30 Corps had established the bridgehead north of the River Waal six days earlier. The Guards Armoured Division, with 69 Brigade still under command, was tasked to capture Bemmel and 'continue to operate northeast to push the enemy out of range of [the] Nijmegen bridge' in order to permit reinforcements and supply transport to make full and unfettered use of the crossing. The 43rd Division was tasked to 'complete the capture of Elst', conduct the evacuation of the 1st Airborne Division and 4th Dorsets across the Lower Rhine including a deception operation, to 'reconnoitre and plan' for a possible crossing on the stretch of the Lower Rhine between Renkum and Wageningen, six miles west of Oosterbeek, and to hold a brigade in reserve.[84] As the link-up of 214 and 69 Brigades to the south of Elst effectively pinched 129 Brigade out of line, Major-General Thomas elected to withdraw 129 to form the reserve as instructed, but not before the 4th Wiltshire ascertained that the Germans had abandoned their positions blocking the way to Bemmel, which they had occupied since 21 September.[85] 214 Brigade secured Elst with the support of the 4th/7th Dragoon Guards' Sherman tanks in the course of a day of 'protracted and bitter' fighting, during which two Tiger tanks and six Panthers were reportedly knocked out. The vehicles were presumably from *schwere Panzer Kompanie Hummel* and *SS Panzer Regiment 10*.[86] The town was finally secured by the 1st Worcesters, with their opponents withdrawing north toward Arnhem; 214 Brigade then pushed out patrols to around a mile east of the Arnhem–Nijmegen railway line.[87] The latter was also the scene of a potentially fatal miscalculation during the afternoon by D Company, 5th DCLI. Suspicious of a number of rail freight carriages abandoned on the line outside Elst, D Company brought them under fire with an anti-tank gun. It transpired that the stationmaster in Elst had placed the carriages outside the town because they were loaded with German ammunition. The subsequent explosion destroyed the carriages, flattened a stretch of the railway embankment and demolished several nearby houses in which British troops were sheltering from the rain; it is unclear if the incident caused any friendly casualties.[88]

In Driel, Major Tonn's 1st Battalion and the contingent from the 3rd Battalion rejoined the Polish Brigade after their planned crossing in the wake of the 4th Dorsets was cancelled at 04:00, with Brigade HQ issuing instructions as to the positions the newcomers were to occupy an hour later; the newcomers passed cigarettes and ammunition to their predecessors.[89] In the event the aborted crossing with the 4th Dorsets proved to be the final direct Polish involvement in MARKET GARDEN, for at midday a Warning Order from Airborne Corps HQ put the Brigade on stand-by for a move to an unspecified new location for an unspecified task at 09:00 the following day; it also announced the intention to evacuate the north bank of the Lower Rhine, with further details following at 17:30. Major-General Sosabowski was shocked at the imminent unexplained redeployment of his Brigade as he had expected to be involved in a further crossing attempt, but he nonetheless disseminated the Warning Order to his Battalion heads at a Commander's Conference at 18:00, which was confirmed by 43 Division an hour later.[90] There was no let-up in the heavy German mortar and artillery bombardment of Driel however, which caused the Polish paratroopers 'heavy casualties'. One shell scored a direct hit on the building occupied by the Brigade Staff but there were no casualties as an earlier near miss had prompted the occupants to withdraw to the cellar. The exception was Major-General Sosabowski who was asleep in an upstairs room: the shell actually detonated in the room but the Polish commander somehow escaped unscathed.[91]

To the west of Driel 130 Brigade remained in place around Brigade HQ at Homoet making fruitless attempts to contact the 4th Dorsets on the north bank. A Major Eyre assumed command of the bulk of 4th Dorsets Battalion south of the river in Lieutenant-Colonel Tilley's absence, and he gave an overall briefing on the upcoming evacuation at 15:00. A Captain Hall was to be despatched to the north bank to co-ordinate with the contingent there, who were to be ferried back to a sorting area set up in an orchard near the riverbank from where wounded personnel were to be evacuated for treatment, while the able-bodied moved to the Company locations occupied before the crossing effort. The route from the sorting area was marked with white tape with each Company supplying guides to attend the sorting area and during the afternoon the Battalion Intelligence Section took over an observation post on the riverside overlooking the planned crossing point.[92] 130 Brigade's left flank was secured by 43 Reconnaissance Regiment with the 12th King's Royal Rifle Corps from the 8th Independent Armoured Brigade Group under command, and the newly withdrawn 129 Brigade also appears to have been located in the same vicinity. According to the British official record and the 43rd Division account Lieutenant-Colonel W.G. Roberts' 5th Wiltshire was assigned overall responsibility for the deception operation, although a more recent source refers to it being carried out under the auspices of 43 Reconnaissance Regiment.[93] Whoever was in charge, the deception involved gathering a collection of mortar and medium machine-gun platoons carried on Bren Carriers accompanied by several empty DUKWs and a number of vehicles from an unidentified bridging train carrying pontoons and other bridging equipment. The column openly approached the Lower Rhine at the village of Heteren, three miles west of Driel, as dusk fell and then spent an hour firing mortars and assorted machine-guns across the river to create the impression that another crossing was being mounted.[94] The effect upon the Germans on the north bank is unknown, but the idea and execution certainly impressed the instigators. The 43rd Division's semi-official account claimed: 'The deception undoubtedly gave the impression that the crossing attempted the previous night was being repeated further west and thus contributed to the success of the withdrawal.'[95]

Preparations to receive the Airborne evacuees once they reached the south bank of the Lower Rhine were underway. At 09:00 the commander of the 1st Airborne Division's 1,000-vehicle Seaborne Echelon, Major R. D. Sellon, was summoned to a conference at 1st Airborne Corps HQ at Nijmegen.[96] The plan was to set up a transit area at a barn on the southern outskirts of Driel close to a Casualty Clearing Post (CCP) manned by 130 Field Ambulance, where the evacuees would be provided with blankets and hot food before being transported to a larger reception centre in Nijmegen.[97] Major Sellon was placed in charge of organising the reception centre and was instructed to set up and staff it sufficient to clothe, feed and accommodate 2,000 men.[98] Two adjacent buildings, either schools or hostels depending on the source, were commandeered in the eastern outskirts of Nijmegen for the purpose. One of the buildings was capable of accommodating 1,200 men and the other, dubbed the 'Pagoda' due to the shape of its roof, had a capacity of 800. Major J. A. Jessop and Major J. C. H. Eyles, Adjutant of the 1st Parachute Brigade and the Deputy Assistant Adjutant & Quartermaster General (DAA&QMG) of the 4th Parachute Brigade respectively, were assigned responsibility for the larger building while Major W. A. Balmer, DAA&QMG to the 1st Airlanding Brigade, was allotted the smaller.[99] By 15:00 blankets, clothing, rations, GS rum and stretchers, the latter presumably for use as makeshift beds, had been delivered to the reception centre from 30 Corps stocks while the transit area was visited an hour later by Major Henry Richard, the commander of the RAMC detachment from 1st Airborne Division HQ's Seaborne Echelon.[100] All preparations were complete by 22:00, including arrangements at the reception centre for 'preliminary documentation to find out the names and units of survivors'.[101]

Major-General Thomas' plan for the evacuation, which was to be carried out under the command of Brigadier Walton and 130 Brigade, involved two crossing sites, one roughly opposite the Oosterbeek Old Church where the Poles had made their crossings on the nights of 22-23 and 23-24 September and the other at the Heveadorp ferry terminal, where the 4th Dorsets had crossed the previous night.[102] Four Sapper Field Companies, two British and two Canadian, were tasked to carry out the ferrying with the two eastern sites being manned by the 23rd Field Company RCE and 260 Field Company RE. The Heveadorp site was manned by the 20th Field Company RCE but there is some confusion as to which British unit shared that crossing point with the Canadians. The 20th Field Company RCE War Diary specifically refers to it being tasked with 204 Field Company RE, but that unit's War Diary makes no mention of being involved in the evacuation, merely referring to its constituent platoons returning to their respective harbour areas after the previous night's activities and being involved in road repairs south-west of Driel. The only possible involvement is indicated by a cryptic reference to 'Four men from 3 Pl under comd of RAMC ferrying men from far bank of river'.[103] However, the British official record, the 43rd Division's semi-official account and Sliz's work on the Canadian involvement quite clearly state that the western crossing site was manned by the 20th Field Company RCE and 553 Field Company RE, the latter being one of the 43rd Division's organic Divisional units.[104] The pairing of the units was deliberate in order to make the best use of the different craft with which the units were equipped. The arrangement originated with Lieutenant-Colonel Mark Henniker, the 43rd Division's CRE, who argued his case with a sceptical Major-General Thomas at the Divisional O Group for Operation BERLIN. According to Henniker, Thomas 'was unbelievably ill-informed about the behaviour of boats in a swiftly flowing river' and he did not take having the realities of the situation pointed out well either: 'He [Thomas] looked at me with astonishment and increasing displeasure as I told my tale, but it seemed to me prudent to warn him of the worst before he heard of it from spectators the following morning.'[105] Thomas yielded grudgingly and the ferrying operation was run according to Henniker's detailed template.[106]

The two British Field Companies were equipped with the standard canvas-sided assault boats while the Canadians were equipped with storm boats. At twenty feet long and with a capacity of around a dozen men the storm boats were larger than the assault boats employed hitherto, their all-plywood construction rendered them considerably more robust and most crucially they employed a fifty-horsepower Evinrude outboard motor. This of course made them faster than the oar-propelled assault boats and the absence of oarsmen freed up more space for passengers and equipment.[107] There is some confusion regarding the actual number of craft involved depending on the source. According to the 43rd Division account the British units deployed sixteen canvas assault boats to each of their two sites and the Canadians twenty-one storm boats to each, giving a total of thirty-two and forty-two craft respectively.[108] The British official record on the other hand cites figures from 130 Brigade and is adamant that the true overall total across the two locations was sixteen assault boats and fifteen storm boats. Sliz's more recent research puts the total number of storm boats at twenty-two, with fourteen allocated to the 23rd Field Company RCE and eight to the 20th Field Company RCE; the figure of sixteen assault boats each is likely accurate given that 260 Field Company RE reported employing eight of the craft.[109]

The commanders of the four Sapper units attended an O Group called by Lieutenant-Colonel Henniker at 10:00 at 43rd Division HQ at Valburg. It is intriguing – perhaps ironic – that Henniker had served as the 1st Airborne Division's CRE in Sicily and thereafter until August 1944 when he transferred to the 43rd Division, recommending Lieutenant-Colonel Edmund Myers as his successor. The transfer away from the Airborne fold was reportedly due to Henniker's increasingly negative attitude during the period June to September 1944, when the 1st Airborne Division was repeatedly placed on stand-by for aborted missions.[110] The Sapper commanders were informed of the decision to evacuate the Oosterbeek perimeter that night and that the Canadian storm boats were intended to play the primary role as their outboard motors made them better able to cope with the strong current. No details of the upcoming operation were provided as these were to follow at another O Group at 130 Brigade HQ at Homoet at 17:00, although Major Tucker from the 23rd Field Company RCE was informed that 'he could only rely on his own resources to deploy the [storm] boats to their launch sites'; the Canadians appear to have addressed this by temporarily co-opting a number of vehicles from 551st General Transport Company RASC, which was part of one of the 2nd Army's bridging trains.[111] The Engineers were to concentrate near the railway station in Valburg, five miles south of Driel, where they would remain until dark. In the meantime Major Tucker inspected the concentration area accompanied by Lieutenants Russell Kennedy and Robert Tate, Sergeant Donald Barnes and Sapper Buck McKee. The latter four were then despatched north to liaise with 130 Brigade, familiarise themselves and reconnoitre the routes and likely crossing sites while Major Tucker returned to the Company location at Nijmegen to brief the rest of the unit and organise the move to the concentration area. It is unclear if the reconnaissance party proceeded straight from Valburg or returned to Nijmegen first.

The 23rd Field Company RCE moved off from its harbour area in Nijmegen at 14:00 in a thirty-seven-vehicle column, with the Company personnel travelling in three Jeeps, two wireless-equipped scout cars, twelve three-ton trucks and two kitchen lorries; of the remainder seventeen vehicles were carrying storm boats and their outboard motors and a single three-ton truck carried two Sections from the 10th Field Company RCE, each made up of an electrician, four engine fitters and two carpenters to make any necessary running repairs to the storm boats during the evacuation.[112] The thirteen-mile journey to Valburg was slow due to the complicated route, the narrow roads with their impassable verges and deep ditches and the proximity of the enemy, but the convoy reached the concentration area near Valburg railway station without significant mishap after an hour and three-quarters at 15:45. It was fully dispersed and parked by 16:30 on an area of hard standing near the station and concealed on an adjacent tree-lined street.[113] The 20th Field Company RCE moved off from Nijmegen in eighteen vehicles including two kitchen trucks at 14:30; it is unclear if the column travelled with the other Canadian Field Company or independently, and when it arrived.[114] In the event the 17:00 O Group at 130 Brigade HQ did not get underway until 17:45 as Lieutenant-Colonel Henniker was 'unavoidably delayed' but this was perhaps fortunate as Lieutenants Kennedy and Tate from the scouting party did not arrive at Homoet until 17:15.[115] Lieutenant Kennedy briefed the assembled commanders on the three locations he had selected as crossing points and the preparations necessary to make them usable. At the eastern location this involved building a bridge from the road into the riverside orchard where the 23rd Field Company RCE's fourteen storm boats and seventeen Evinrude outboard motors were to be unloaded ready for manhandling over two dykes to the water's edge. While the western location was more accessible, it required white tapes to be laid as a guide from the point on the road where the 20th Field Company RCE's eight storm boats were to be unloaded, four of them complete with motors and other equipment fitted, through an orchard and over three separate dykes, one of them twenty feet high; additional guidance was to be provided by Bofors guns firing tracer across the river to mark the left and right boundaries of the Heveadorp crossing lane.[116] The operation was to begin at 21:00 with a covering bombardment on the north bank intended to keep the enemy occupied and to mask the noise of unloading and other preparations from the Sappers. The first assault boat scheduled to launch at 21:30 with the first storm boat following ten minutes later and in an effort to conceal what was afoot the trucks carrying the storm boats were forbidden to move before the onset of full darkness at 19:30.[117]

Lieutenant-Colonel Henniker terminated the O Group at 18:15 and the Sapper officers rejoined their units to complete preparations for the last act of Operation MARKET GARDEN.[118]

Evacuation

D Plus 8 to D Plus 9
18:00 Monday 25 September 1944 to
06:00 Tuesday 26 September 1944

Major-General Urquhart took two hours to consider the letters carried across the Lower Rhine by Lieutenant-Colonel Edmund Myers from his opposite number Major-General Thomas at the 43rd Division and his direct superior Lieutenant-General Browning at 1st Airborne Corps. After snatching a few moments of pre-bombardment quiet in the shattered remnants of the Hotel Hartenstein's once pristine gardens he informed Thomas at 08:08 via the radio link to the 64th Field Regiment that Operation BERLIN had to be implemented that night. Twenty minutes later he transmitted a message to Browning via the Phantom link that included the warning that 'Even comparatively minor offensive [enemy] action may cause complete disintegration'; the message had been encoded the previous night by the Division's GHQ Liaison Regiment officer, Lieutenant Neville Hay.[1] With the messages transmitted Urquhart summoned his senior commanders to a commander's conference at the Hotel Hartenstein at 10:30.[2] In the meantime he turned his attention to the mechanics of the upcoming withdrawal and evacuation with his Chief-of-Staff, Lieutenant-Colonel Charles Mackenzie, taking the Allied evacuation from Anzac Cove at Gallipoli on the night of 19-20 December 1915 as a template. Urquhart had studied the operation in detail for a promotion exam as a junior officer.[3] As Urquhart himself put it, the intent was to work out 'the simplest possible plan to get the chaps out of the perimeter during the few hours that were available to do so' and to that end he planned the withdrawal 'like the collapse of a paper bag. I wanted small parties…to give the impression we were still there, all the while pulling downwards and along each flank.'[4] The evacuation was to be covered by 30 Corps artillery using a complex fire-plan supervised by the 1st Airborne Division's CRA, Lieutenant-Colonel Robert Loder-Symonds. The plan was drawn up and encoded into Slidex in 'two huge messages' for transmission to 43rd Division by Brigade Major RA Major Philip Tower and Lieutenant Patrick de Burgh from Division HQ RA. The task took six hours and was made more onerous and time-consuming as the final signal had to be returned after receipt by 43rd Division to be double-checked because 'Slidex keys…[had]…proved a stumbling block throughout the battle owing to faulty "tie up" in [the] planning period.'[5] In the event the signal was acknowledged as accurate to the 'great relief' of all involved; Major Tower later recalled 'It was a Slidex signal the like of which I had never done before and I have never done since – all done in poor conditions.'[6]

Most of the attendees at Urquhart's 10:30 commander's conference were likely already present in the Hotel Hartenstein, specifically Lieutenant-Colonel Mackenzie, CRA Lieutenant-Colonel Robert Loder-Symonds and CRE Lieutenant-Colonel Myers. They were joined by Brigadier Philip Hicks, commanding the 1st Airlanding Brigade and western side of the Oosterbeek perimeter and Lieutenant-Colonel Iain Murray from No.1 Wing GPR, who had taken command of the 4th Parachute Brigade and the eastern side of the perimeter on 24 September, after Brigadier John Hackett was wounded. Hicks reportedly arrived out of breath after being obliged to sprint across the Hartenstein's back lawn, which was covered by a German machine-gun.[7] The conference may also have included Major John Winchester commanding the 9th (Airborne) Field Company RE, given that he returned to his Company on the north-west sector of the perimeter at around 11:00 with details of the withdrawal plan.[8] The conference was inadvertently joined by the Division ADMS Colonel Graeme Warrack, who had come into Division HQ to brief Urquhart on the casualty situation, and his adventures behind German lines connected to transferring the most serious casualties from the Division CCS to the St Elizabeth Hospital the previous day. Urquhart informed him of the evacuation prior to the conference commencing, including his decision that all the Division's doctors would be expected to remain on the north bank with the wounded. This made Warrack the first officer of the Division outside the staff and senior commanders to learn of the withdrawal; the first Other Rank appears to have been Signalman James Cockrill attached to Division HQ who overheard the terse 'Operation Berlin is tonight' signal, albeit without realising its significance.[9] The news of the imminent withdrawal left Warrack 'downcast and unhappy. Not because I had to stay – I had an obligation to the wounded – but because up to this moment I had expected the Division to be relieved in a very short time.'[10] After garnering some details and covering his disappointment with his customary smile, Warrack left to start his own preparations for the withdrawal.

Urquhart opened the conference with the simple announcement 'We are to clear out tonight' before laying out the withdrawal plan in detail.[11] The covering bombardment from 30 Corps' artillery using the fire-plan then in the process of being drawn up by Major Tower and Lieutenant de Burgh was to commence at 20:30 with the evacuation across the Lower Rhine scheduled to begin ninety minutes later, the delay being intended to mask the withdrawal of the units farthest from the Lower Rhine. The units were to move along two routes running east and west of the Division HQ area, with the 4th Parachute Brigade responsible for placing guides along the former and 1st Airlanding Brigade along the latter. The routes converged near the gun positions occupied by the 1st Airlanding Light Regiment's 3 Battery west of the Oosterbeek Old Church, with the route from there across the polder to the embarkation area at the river's edge being marked with white tape. All ranks were to muffle their footwear using whatever means available and move along the routes in groups of fourteen to facilitate rapid loading onto the evacuation craft; these groups were expressly forbidden from engaging any enemy encountered en route unless absolutely unavoidable, partly to avoid alerting the Germans to what was going on and partly to avoid friendly casualties in any outbreak of firing. On arrival at the water's edge the parties were to take shelter in the lee of the bank and wait their turn.[12] After assigning Myers the task of selecting the withdrawal routes and arranging the 'ferry service' over the river and assurances from Loder-Symonds that 30 Corps' artillery would be up to the task of covering the evacuation, Urquhart brought the conference to a close by announcing that

> ...news of the evacuation should not be broken until it was absolutely necessary to do so...there was always the likelihood of exhausted men falling into German hands and coming under interrogation. Further, when once men start to look over their shoulders their effectiveness is reduced. Only those who had to know were told now of the plan.[13]

The Division challenge and password for BERLIN was JOHN/BULL.[14] On the western half of the Oosterbeek perimeter some of those who needed to know were informed of the upcoming evacuation by Brigadier Hicks via an O Group at 1st Airlanding Brigade HQ at 13:30, although unit records refer to the meeting taking place at 13:00, 14:00 and 15:00 depending on the source.[15] The attendees included Lieutenant-Colonel Robert Payton-Reid from the 7th KOSB, who travelled from his Battalion's location in a Bren Carrier, the acting commander of the 1st Border Major Stuart Cousens accompanied by the Battalion Adjutant Captain Colin Douglas, the commander of No. 2 Wing GPR Lieutenant-Colonel John Place, and Major Charles Breese commanding BREESE Force.[16] The 4th Parachute Squadron RE appears to have been briefed in two increments at different times, with the bulk of the Squadron at the Sonnenberg location being briefed by Major Winchester from the 9th (Airborne) Field Company RE at 14:00, while the detachment closer to Division HQ were included in the 4th Parachute Brigade O Group.[17] Brigadier Hicks' plan allotted BREESE Force the task of holding its positions and providing a covering screen through which the rest of units on the western half of the perimeter would withdraw along a route marked in white tape by the 9th (Airborne) Field Company RE.[18] The first to move would be the 7th KOSB, which was scheduled to withdraw from its box position straddling the Bothaweg and Paul Krugerstraat at 21:15; D Company 1st Border was supposed to move off from its location on the western edge of the perimeter at the same time but when contact was lost later in the afternoon it was assumed the beleaguered Company had been overrun; Lieutenant Green and his little band were thus left isolated and without orders in the woods near the Van Borsselenweg.[19] Brigade HQ was to move next at 22:40, presumably accompanied by Major Dale and his Glider Pilots from C Squadron, followed by the rest of the Glider Pilots from No. 2 Wing and the re-roled Polish anti-tank gunners, and then the 1st Border; for some reason the No. 2 Wing War Diary refers to the Glider Pilots starting their move out of sequence at 21:00.[20] Once all the above had passed through its positions BREESE Force was to withdraw to the river, although the timing is uncertain. The need for silence and stealth was again emphasised and the withdrawal was to include walking wounded from the unit RAPs while non-ambulatory cases were to be left behind to be gathered in by the Division Field Ambulance personnel the next day; the latter were to remain with their charges on the north bank. All ranks were to carry their personal weapons and ammunition 'but no surplus eqpt carried. Everything left behind was to be destroyed so as to be rendered unusable'.[21]

Disseminating instructions for the withdrawal did not flow quite so smoothly on the eastern side of the perimeter. Lieutenant-Colonel Murray called a Brigade O Group at the Hotel Hartenstein at 13:00 attended by around half a dozen commanders including Captain Brown from the 4th Parachute Squadron RE and probably Major Ian Toler commanding No. 1 Wing GPR in Murray's stead, Major Hugh Bartlett and Captain James Ogilvie commanding B and D Squadrons GPR respectively.[22] Major Lonsdale sent word that it would be impossible to get anyone through to Division HQ from his location due to the heavy German attack on the south-eastern sector of the perimeter, while Major Wilson warned that he might be late or unable to attend at all due to German snipers.[23] In the event Major Wilson does appear to have reached the Hotel Hartenstein at 16:00 where he was given details of the withdrawal and informed that the Independent Company was to act as rearguard for the east.[24] By this point LONSDALE Force was reportedly cut off from 4th Parachute Brigade HQ except for runners. A warning order for the withdrawal appears to have arrived via this runner at 16:00. Major Alan Bush from the 3rd Parachute Battalion was tasked to make 'preliminary arrangements' for the withdrawal in case more detailed orders did not appear.[25] Implementation of Urquhart's edict on not breaking news of the withdrawal to the rank-and-file until absolutely necessary was patchy. 156 Parachute Battalion was informed at 13:00 for example. Major Geoffrey Powell found the news 'an appalling blow. I thought of all the men who had died and then I thought the whole effort had been a waste.' Powell nonetheless requested and received permission to withdraw to a less isolated position in readiness at 14:00, presumably on the Utrechtseweg to the west of the Polish positions on the junction with the Stationsweg, although the new position put the paratroopers in close contact with the enemy on their left flank.[26] At the other end of the scale LONSDALE Force did not receive the withdrawal instructions until 22:30, just an hour before it was to move.[27]

Most units received warning and/or more detailed instructions in the late afternoon or early evening. The 1st Parachute Battalion received a warning order at 17:00 and full instructions three hours later for example, the 11th Parachute Battalion a detailed warning at 18:00 and the 1st Airborne Reconnaissance Squadron received orders at 19:30, which were distributed to the Troops at 20:00.[28] In fact Lieutenant Galbraith and A Troop were ahead of the loop in this regard, having been ordered by 4th Parachute Brigade HQ to withdraw from their exposed position at the junction of De la Reijweg and Steijnweg at 15:00, to the Utrechtseweg at the junction with the Mariaweg. The move took thirty minutes and on arrival the Reconnaissance Troop was amalgamated with a group of Glider Pilots, possibly from D Squadron, before Lieutenant Galbraith was briefed on the evacuation at 16:00. Sergeant Henry Venes was then despatched at 17:30 to make contact with 156 Parachute Battalion, which had also been withdrawn from the exposed north-eastern sector, in preparation for a collective move down to the Lower Rhine, with Major Powell and his men coming into the A Troop position at 19:00.[29] As with so many aspects of their involvement in Operation MARKET the Poles within the Oosterbeek perimeter appear to have been treated largely as an afterthought. At the *Valkenburg* villa behind C Company 1st Border's lines Lieutenant Zbigniew Bossowski and his re-roled anti-tank gunners were approached by two unidentified British officers who notified them of the imminent evacuation with a vague description of the route to the Lower Rhine; the 'only firm instruction was that the Poles would be informed when they could withdraw'.[30] Down at the riverside *Transvalia* Lieutenant Smaczny and his party from the 8th Company were treated in a similarly offhand manner by an unnamed RE Major, possibly Major Winchester from the 9th (Airborne) Field Company, who informed Smaczny that he was to withdraw at 00:30 but only after receiving permission via a runner. The British Major then refused Lieutenant Smaczny's offer of a Polish guide to expedite matters; this was deemed unnecessary as the RE officer promised to return with the orders in person if necessary. Smaczny viewed this arrangement as a 'virtual sentence of extermination' although he refrained from passing on the instructions or his misgivings to his men to safeguard morale.[31] Up on the Stationsweg the evacuation order was brought to 2nd Lieutenant Bereda-Fialkowski at a little before 18:00 by Captain Zwolanski in person, accompanied by three unnamed British officers, one of whom was Scottish and wearing a kilt according to 3rd Battalion radio operator Private Jan Szubert; this was probably Major Ogilvie from D Squadron GPR and formerly of the Gordon Highlanders, who was photographed wearing a kilt during the battle.[32] Zwolanski informed Bereda-Fialkowski that the 3rd Battalion was to form the rearguard for the north-eastern sector of the perimeter before withdrawing at 22:00, along with instructions on abandoning unnecessary equipment. He then departed for the Hotel Hartenstein with his three companions. Private Szubert recalled one of the British officers pausing at the doorway to look back at the Polish paratroopers before disappearing into the gloom with the farewell, 'God help you.'[33]

Major-General Urquhart left Division HQ to walk the withdrawal routes in person, dodging the German bombardment as he did so; he was seen taking shelter, possibly near the Laundry on the south-east sector of the perimeter, by a Sergeant Calladine from the 2nd South Staffords.[34] The time between being warned or briefed for the withdrawal and moving off was spent rendering equipment that was to be abandoned unserviceable and making personal preparations: blackening faces for camouflage, wrapping issue Ammunition Boots in strips of blanket or curtains obtained from abandoned houses to muffle the sound of metal studs, and ensuring weapons and personal equipment did not rattle when moving. Artillery and anti-tank gun crews were additionally burdened with the sights and breech blocks from their weapons, which were to be dumped into the Lower Rhine. The Polish paratroopers from the 3rd Battalion on the Stationsweg fastened their Celanese panels to the back of their Denison smocks as a recognition measure.[35] For some it was about appearances and entailed shaving. An unnamed Sergeant directed Private Robert Downing from the 10th Parachute Battalion to a used razor and ordered him to have a dry shave on the grounds that 'We're crossing the river and by God we're going back looking like British soldiers.' Similarly, Lieutenant-Colonel Murray instructed Major Toler to clean up a little, presumably after the 13:00 O Group, because 'We don't want the army to think we're a bunch of tramps' and provided his own razor and a 'dab' of lather; Toler grudgingly complied and recalled that it was 'amazing how much better I felt, mentally and physically'.[36] The men of the 1st Airborne Reconnaissance Squadron HQ also received a morale boost at 20:30 with the issue of rations reportedly from Division HQ equating to half a tin of stew, one bar of chocolate and a small packet of biscuits per man, although the recipients of this largesse had only twenty minutes to enjoy it before moving off.[37] Major Winchester handed over command of the 9th Field Company to Captain Stephen George from the 1st Parachute Squadron RE at 19:45 and set out to mark the western withdrawal route with white tape, accompanied by four Sappers; the task also included marking the route from the rendezvous point near the Oosterbeek Old Church to the water's edge.[38] Marking the eastern withdrawal route was tasked to Captain Maurice Priest from G Squadron GPR assisted by Lieutenant Herbert Fuller from B Squadron GPR and a Squadron Sergeant-Major Watt, also presumably from B Squadron.[39] According to Staff-Sergeant Victor Miller, Glider Pilots from G Squadron located near the Hotel Hartenstein were detailed to act as guides along the routes at a briefing by the commander of G Squadron's 24 Flight, Captain Robert Walchli, apart from two volunteers tasked to remain guarding the 200 German prisoners incarcerated in the Hotel Hartenstein's tennis court 'until about midnight'; Major-General Urquhart had specifically ordered the guard to be maintained at his commander's conference that morning, and until 01:30 rather than midnight.[40] The final preparation came courtesy of the weather, for by around 18:00 it was raining heavily with high winds, ideal conditions to mask Major-General Urquhart's collapsing paper bag.

The first units to move appear to have done so up to an hour before the covering artillery barrage from the 43rd Division commenced. The 1st Airborne Divisional Signals left the Hotel Hartenstein at 20:00 after an hour of last-minute burning of documents and rendering equipment unserviceable, the exception being the unit registers and War Diary, which were carried away. The Base radio set and another set linked to 130 Brigade were to continue operating as a disinformation measure after the rest of the unit had withdrawn at the hands of Signalman James Cockrill, who volunteered or was detailed for the duty depending on the account; he was also reportedly wounded, although he later attempted to swim the Lower Rhine. Most of the Signals' fourteen-strong parties reached the river unscathed and were ferried safely to the south bank despite German mortar fire on the embarkation area.[41] Lieutenant Galbraith's A Troop from the 1st Airborne Reconnaissance Squadron began to move off from the Utrechtseweg–Mariaweg junction at 20:00, crossing the Utrechtseweg in pairs to rendezvous at 4th Parachute Brigade HQ from where the final leg of the journey down to the Lower Rhine was to begin.[42] They were followed fifteen minutes later by Major Powell and 156 Parachute Battalion who appear to have headed straight for the river rather than rendezvousing first at the 4th Brigade HQ. The column, led by the Battalion Intelligence Officer Lieutenant Piers St. Aubyn and QM Lieutenant Thomas Bush, made it over the Utrechtseweg unscathed despite German machine-gun fire, but then became separated in the woods south of the Hotel Hartenstein when 'one slow thinking fellow…released his hold on the smock of the man ahead' and did not pass back word of what had happened. The front section of the column reached the embarkation point without mishap while the rear section, which included Major Powell, became aware of its predicament thanks to an 'irate Corporal Rosenberg'. Major Powell led the party away from an encounter with an enemy machine-gun post and reached the riverbank east of the embarkation point and waded downstream to it, passing a holed and beached assault boat with a dead crew on the way. Overall a dozen men became casualties during the move.[43]

Just a few hundred yards up the Utrechtseweg the second Division HQ increment departed the Hotel Hartenstein at 20:30, consisting of the HQ Royal Engineers and No. 1 Wing GPR HQ. HQ RE appears to have reached the Lower Rhine without incident apart from CRE Lieutenant-Colonel Myers and an unnamed Other Rank being slightly wounded, presumably by enemy mortar fire. The HQ personnel were reportedly safely across the river by 21:15 with just one wounded casualty. Myers remained behind to supervise the crossing.[44] He had been joined at 20:40 by Captain Michael Green, the HQ RE Adjutant who had swum the Lower Rhine on Wednesday 20 September with a situation report for 30 Corps and reached the Nijmegen bridgehead after a ten-mile trek through German-held territory; Green had made several unsuccessful attempts to rejoin his comrades in Oosterbeek in the ensuing days and after finally reaching the north bank remained to assist Lieutenant-Colonel Myers.[45] After a quiet start masked by the rain the No. 1 Wing column came under machine-gun and mortar fire at 21:20 and was then broken up; the Glider Pilots finally reached the embarkation point at 22:05.[46]

The 1st Airborne Reconnaissance Squadron HQ left its positions at the junction of the Utrechtseweg and Oranjeweg near the Hotel Hartenstein at 20:50 divided into four groups led by acting Squadron commander Captain David Allsop, Squadron Adjutant Captain James Costeloe, Squadron QM Lieutenant Tom Collier and Liaison Officer Lieutenant Alexander Lickorish; Captain Allsop was the last man to leave the position. The groups were supposed to withdraw in turn at three-minute intervals on receiving word from the preceding group, although Lieutenant Lickorish's group did not and only discovered its neighbour had departed when Corporal 'Tommy' Trinder from the Squadron Intelligence Section investigated the ongoing delay on his own initiative. The route crossed the Utrechtseweg and passed through the pitch-black woods to the south of the Hotel Hartenstein, with the Reconnaissance Troopers hanging onto the man in front's Denison smock, sometimes perilously close to unsuspecting German positions. Trooper Stanley Collishaw saw Germans playing cards through a carelessly lighted window in a nearby house while Squadron Medical Officer Captain Douglas Swinscow recalled quietly passing 'a little tent with a light burning inside it – a German tent'. Captain Costeloe's group was less fortunate, being 'slightly dispersed' by close-range machine-gun fire after bumping a German outpost, and Squadron QM Sergeant George Holderness was shot dead by a German he mistakenly approached while gathering in the stragglers.[47]

The survivors from D Troop were also on the move despite being unaware of the withdrawal order, after spending the day surrounded by Germans in the wrecked shop on the Steijnweg. Waiting until after dark, at 20:00 Sergeants Bentnall and Pyper emerged first after instructing the other four Troopers to follow in pairs if things remained quiet, but only the two Sergeants made it back into the Airborne perimeter where they linked up with friendly troops, possibly Glider Pilots, at 20:30. Learning of the evacuation they joined a party making its way to the river and crossed to the south bank in the early hours of 26 September; Sergeants Bentnall and Pyper may have been the only members of the forty-strong D Troop to reach safety.[48]

***

On the south bank of the Lower Rhine the 23rd Field Company RCE's immediate preparations involved installing a vehicle bridge over a roadside ditch to access the riverside orchard selected as the Company's unloading point, and a three-ton truck carrying the necessary stores and equipment along with a Section from the Company's 2nd Platoon commanded by Lieutenant Robert Tate and including Corporal George Robinson and Sapper Donald Sommerville was despatched at 18:45. The orchard and single-track road upon which Lieutenant Tate was obliged to unload the truck were in full view of the Germans atop the Westerbouwing Heights on the north bank but overall the shelling was routine and did not significantly interfere with the work, although the Sappers were occasionally obliged to take cover in the water-filled ditch. The bridge was complete at around 20:00.[49] In the meantime the remainder of the 23rd Field Company RCE had sent out guides to man the road junctions on the route and had been joined by the contingent from the 20th Field Company RCE, which left its own location at 18:30.[50] The two Companies' vehicles were combined into a twenty-four-vehicle column, of which seven vehicles – a single scout car, three Jeeps and three trucks carrying personnel – belonged to the 23rd Field Company.[51] It is unclear from the official records how the remaining seventeen vehicles temporarily co-opted from the 551st General Transport Company RASC, which carried a total of twenty-two storm boats, were divided between the two Canadian Field Companies, but one source suggests that the 20th Field Company had seven trucks, five loaded tactically with a storm boat and engine apiece, one loaded with three storm boats and the seventh carrying the other Evinrude motors. The remaining ten trucks carried the 23rd Field Company's equipment, five loaded tactically with a boat and engine apiece, three trucks carrying three storm boats each and two trucks loaded with outboard motors.[52] All the boat-carrying vehicles also appear to have carried personnel from their respective Companies, some of whom actually travelled in the vessels. The column was arranged with 23rd Field Company's boats at the front followed by the 20th Field Company's boats, with the 23rd Field Company Jeeps and scout car between the two increments and the three personnel trucks bringing up the rear.[53]

The Canadian column moved off from Valburg at 19:15 leaving Captain Donald McIntyre and Lieutenant Charley Aspler in charge of the 23rd Field Company personnel and the dozen vehicles not selected for the operation, to the chagrin of the two officers.[54] The journey proceeded smoothly despite German illumination with flares and shelling that cost the Canadians a single casualty when a piece of spent shrapnel struck a Sapper Black on the elbow with sufficient force to temporarily paralyse the limb. Things went awry when the 23rd Field Company branched off for the eastern crossing point, as the three personnel trucks at the rear of the column missed the turning and carried on in the wake of the 20th Field Company; Major Tucker was initially unable to despatch a vehicle to recall them: the three Jeeps had already crossed Lieutenant Tate's bridge into the orchard, the bridge was blocked by a truck that had partially slipped off the roadway and the single-track road behind it was blocked by the other nine boat carriers. The wayward vehicles were later located and led back by Lieutenant John Cronyn.[55] The 20th Field Company column reached the western Heveadorp crossing point at some point after 20:10 where it linked up with 553rd Field Company RE with its assault boats. While the vessels were being unloaded in another convenient orchard the 20th Field Company's commander, Major A. W. Jones, went forward with a Sapper to mark the route to the water's edge with white tape, using a compass for guidance in the darkness.[56] The route to the Heveadorp crossing point involved crossing a twenty-foot-high winter dyke with forty-five-degree earthen banks, topped by a single track road bounded on each side by a metal-posted wire fence, a summer dyke half that height close to the water and an additional two flood banks located between the dykes. Not only did the heavy rain and repeated passage turn the slopes of these obstacles into a quagmire, they were also under enemy fire, as recalled by one of the 20th Field Company's Platoon commanders, Lieutenant W. W. Gemmell: 'You couldn't just walk across that dyke. Jerry had, I'd say, about six or seven M.G.'s on the northern bank; you had to spot the tracers and duck over when they went past.'[57] Despite being fully exposed to illumination from German flares and machine-gun fire the two fences were dealt with by Sapper Harry Decker Thicke, who cut the wire strands and then removed at least one of the metal posts with a shovel before assisting with carrying the first storm boat down to the water; he was subsequently awarded the Military Medal.[58] By 21:30 the Canadian storm boats and RE assault boats were located behind the lower summer dyke closest to the water's edge, ready to launch at 21:30 as scheduled.

Back at the eastern crossing site things continued to go badly for the 23rd Field Company. The first truck across the bridge into the orchard unloading point misjudged the turn, put a wheel off the road and became stuck in the soft ground. According to Sapper Donald Somerville there was 'a tank nearby, so we asked if they would fire a few rounds from the machine gun to kill the noise of the truck engine, as it tried to back up.'[59] The vehicle remained stuck fast, however and, mindful of the time pressure and the danger of the column remaining stationary on the open road, Lieutenants Russell Kennedy and James Martin took the decision to tip it off the road, thereby allowing the rest of the column to gain the shelter of the orchard while Lieutenant Cronyn took off in pursuit of the errant personnel trucks in a Jeep.[60] In order to allow the trucks to keep up on the return journey Lieutenant Cronyn made the error of illuminating the small station keeping light on his Jeep's rear axle:

> I looked back to see if I could see the trucks…and actually saw an 88 shell ricochet off the road in a shower of sparks between the jeep and the truck following …without exploding. It went into the next field where it finally did explode. It was apparent that the Germans were able to see even our small axle lights and were firing at us over open sights.[61]

While the storm boats were being unloaded in the orchard under Lieutenant Kennedy's supervision, Lieutenant Cronyn and Lieutenant Martin were tasked to clear the 500-yard route to the water's edge over the two dykes and mark it with white tape. The crossing point itself consisted of a stretch of mud beach with two inlets twenty and sixty yards wide to the west and east respectively, divided and bounded by stone groynes extending thirty yards or so out into the river. The smaller inlet was designated as the boat launch point while the larger inlet was to act as a servicing and holding area for reserve storm boats and making running repairs; Major Anthony Vinycomb's 260 Field Company RE occupied the adjacent inlet downstream to the west and possibly the one next to that. Major Tucker set up his Command Post on the servicing and holding inlet while Sergeant George King set up a refuelling station 100 yards back from the launch inlet, and a RAP was established in a culvert under the summer dyke opposite the launch point manned by a Lance-Corporal Roseborough and Sapper McDonald. Lieutenant Kennedy was responsible for getting the storm boats from the orchard to the inlets assisted by Lieutenant Tate, unloading was to be controlled by Lieutenant Cronyn on the south bank while Lieutenant Martin was to cross the river and supervise loading on the north bank.[62]

Unloading the storm boats from the trucks was a difficult task complicated by the darkness and rain. They weighed 900 pounds apiece and the Evinrude outboard motors 198 pounds; it took eight men to unload each vessel and the task was hampered initially by a shortage of manpower until Lieutenant Cronyn returned with the missing personnel trucks.[63] Moving the boats over the 500 yards from the orchard to the lee of the ten-foot-high summer dyke was even more challenging, with each vessel requiring a carrying party of sixteen to eighteen men employing lengths of steel pipe threaded through cast iron hoops attached to the hulls. The twenty-foot-high winter dyke proved to be a formidable obstacle as the 'heavy rain softened the ground and the churning of men's feet as they struggled over with the stormboats soon created a slippery mess which lent no footing whatsoever. Hand ropes were fixed, but even with these the going was extremely difficult.'[64] Lieutenant Kennedy, who accompanied the first carrying party commanded by Corporal George Robinson, remembered it was 'unbelievably difficult to climb…and we left men to fix hand ropes over it'.[65] The difficulty was compounded by fire from German machine-guns, mortars, artillery and *nebelwerfers* stirred up by the British covering barrage, which commenced at 21:00. As Sapper Donald Somerville recalled, 'the Germans were firing machine guns at us; the tracers bouncing off the dyke wall seemed to go right through your legs.'[66] The artillery and mortars proved to be an even worse problem as near misses understandably prompted the carrying parties to drop their burdens and seek cover; several boats were damaged this way and that carried by Corporal Robinson's party was holed after being inadvertently dropped on one of the clumps of rocks scattered along the taped pathway, although the damage does not appear to have been discovered until the vessel was launched. Despite this the first storm boats were delivered to the lee of the summer dyke where one of the maintenance Sections from the 10th Field Park Company RCE attached the outboard motors; the other Section had been assigned to the 20th Field Company at the western crossing point.[67] Just west of the Canadian crossing point 260 Field Company RE had a slightly easier time moving its lighter canvas-sided assault boats to the water's edge. Each vessel could be manhandled by a team of ten men, although the German small-arms and artillery fire rendered the task no less dangerous. Nonetheless by 21:30 the British and Canadian vessels were in place ready to launch and commence the evacuation as scheduled.[68]

The artillery fire-plan to cover the 1st Airborne Division's withdrawal to and across the Lower Rhine began at 21:00, although two sources refer to it commencing ten minutes before the hour and another fifteen minutes after the hour.[69] The evacuation fire-plan was delivered by all three of the 43rd Division's organic artillery units, 94, 112 and 179 Field Regiments RA with an ammunition allotment of 200 rounds per gun and a further 100 rounds per gun was provided to be fired in support of the deception operation at Heteren, although it is unclear which unit was involved.[70] The bombardment was intensified by fire from 84 Medium Regiment RA and possibly 64 Medium Regiment RA from 5 Army Groups Royal Artillery (AGRA) operating under 30 Corps control. 84 Medium Regiment reported firing a total of '20 rpg [rounds per gun] spread over 2½ hours engaged in sp [support] of 43 Inf Div', while 64 Medium Regiment reported firing six separate fire missions on coded targets between 21:00 and 22:58, when all radio contact was finally lost with 1st Airborne Division.[71] This tallies with Middlebrook, who refers to the fire-plan consisting of 'Intensive fire from every available regiment...for the first three hours, followed by "spasmodic concentrations" for the next five [hours]'.[72] The weight and ferocity of the fire-plan doubtless brought comfort to the embattled Airborne soldiers who had endured days of bombardment from German mortars and artillery, although some rounds inevitably fell short inside the British perimeter; Staff-Sergeant Victor Miller divedr beneath a wrecked Jeep under a series of short rounds whilst acting as a guide on the route to the Lower Rhine, and to add insult to injury he discovered he had 'plunged into some dung'.[73]

***

Unsurprisingly, the British bombardment prompted a response from the Germans, which interfered with the British withdrawal in at least one instance. Major Wilson briefed his officers from the 21st Independent Parachute Company on the upcoming withdrawal at 18:00, the plan being to disengage quietly from the Company positions on the Pietersbergseweg and Paasbergweg under cover of the British bombardment and move to a Forming Up Point (FUP) in a cabbage field just west of the Pietersbergseweg, before moving down to the river at 21:45 in a Company column, Lieutenant David Eastwood's No. 1 Platoon in the lead. The process commenced at 19:45 with the most forward elements being withdrawn within the Company perimeter but for most it was a nervous period of waiting for the order to move; Sergeant Stanley Sullivan passed the time in the school occupied by No. 1 Platoon by chalking 'WE'LL BE BACK' in large underlined block letters on one of the blackboards.[74] The fire-plan included a concentration on a patch of woodland south of the Independent Company's location held by the Germans, presumably as a result of their push into the perimeter earlier that day. The German response came fifteen minutes later when the 'the enemy...put down everything he had into our area, making the forming up of the Company very difficult and hazardous'.[75] The Germans pressed forward and set fire to the houses occupied by the Company under cover of darkness, possibly a facet of their new tactic of night fighting.

Despite this the Independent Company appears to have withdrawn to the FUP without incident, although despite the heavy rain some of the Pathfinders may have fallen asleep while lying in the cabbage field and the move to the embarkation point began fifteen minutes late, at 22:00. The planned order of march may also have been modified or abandoned, given that part of No. 1 Platoon under Sergeant Ron Kent and another party commanded by Sergeant Richard Wilkin were left behind at the FUP when the Company moved off; the error was discovered when the two Sergeants came together whilst seeking to clarify the prolonged delay in moving. In the event the abandonment proved a good thing as the two Sergeants led their men into the woods, located the white tape for the western route and reached the Benedendorpsweg west of the Old Church without further incident at 23:30.[76] Matters did not run so smoothly for the remainder of the Company, which bumped a German outpost in the wood and came under fire from two machine-guns; Major Wilson and Lieutenant John Horsley, who was on attachment from the Border Regiment, were both hit and other members of the lead Section may also have become casualties. The Pathfinders discouraged the guns with hand-grenades while Captain Robert Spivey, the Company's second-in-command, reformed the column and reached the Lower Rhine without further incident after taking a dog-leg to the west to avoid the outpost.[77] Both increments of the Independent Company waited separately on the riverside polder to be called forward to the embarkation point, although at least one man, Private Kenneth Roberts, attempted to swim the fast-flowing river and was drowned in the attempt.[78] Major Wilson, who became separated during the incident in the wood where he received grazing wounds to his nose and eye, reached the embarkation point under his own steam and rejoined the Company on the south bank; Lieutenant Horsley died of his wounds on 27 September 1944.[79]

On the western side of the perimeter the 7th KOSB, among the most far-flung of the 1st Airlanding Brigade's units, was first to move off from its position straddling the Bothaweg and Paul Krugerstraat as scheduled at 21:15, with C Company and Battalion HQ in the lead, followed by D Company and then B Company acting as rearguard. The Battalion's non-ambulatory casualties were to be left in the Battalion RAP under the care of the Battalion Medical Officer and Padre, Captain John Graham-Jones and Captain The Reverend John Rowell; the walking wounded were supposed to accompany D Company but for some reason they did not appear at the FUP as ordered.[80] The first stage of the withdrawal, to the 1st Airlanding Brigade RV on the Benedendorpsweg west of the Oosterbeek Old Church, did not go as planned. The Battalion column stayed clear of the Oranjeweg and Steijnweg running south to the Utrechtseweg to avoid roving German patrols and machine-guns firing along them on fixed lines, and instead followed a route through the gardens of the houses on the Nassaulaan and the Hartensteinlaan reconnoitred by a Corporal Munro from the Battalion Intelligence Section. As it negotiated this route the column ran into 'an extremely heavy shelling concentration' that caused a number of casualties and cut off the tail of the column as men sought cover and became separated in the darkness.[81] The bulk of the Battalion successfully crossed the Utrechtseweg but then became disoriented in the thick woods to the south of the Hotel Hartenstein after falling in with a guide leading a group of unidentified paratroopers. Lieutenant-Colonel Payton-Reid solved this by striking off on his own, marching to a compass bearing with the assistance of Captain John Walker from the 1st Airlanding Light Battery RA who was acting as replacement FOO for the 7th KOSB; this brought the Battalion column to the 1st Airlanding Brigade HQ from where it was able to access the western route to the Brigade RV on the Benedendorpsweg, possibly with the assistance of the HQ given that it remained in place until 23:00.[82] Whether or not, the 7th KOSB column reached the Brigade RV exactly on schedule at 22:15 and from there followed the white tape across the polder to the embarkation point.[83]

The RE contingent on the north-west sector of the perimeter moved off at the same time as the 7th KOSB just as a heavy German artillery bombardment began to land on that sector. The main body of the 4th Parachute Squadron RE led by Lieutenant Norman Thomas fell back through the positions of the 9th (Airborne) Field Company at 21:15, followed five minutes later by a covering party commanded by Captain James Cormie.[84] The two groups made their way straight to the Lower Rhine independently, arriving at 22:15 and 22:30 respectively, where Captain Cormie made contact with Captain James Smith from the Squadron's 1 Troop. Both parties reported losing an unknown number of men missing en route; it is unclear if this was due to enemy action or as a result of men simply getting lost.[85] The 9th (Airborne) Field Company followed at 21:27, moving in parties of approximately fifteen, each under a Sergeant or Senior NCO, the first of which reached the Lower Rhine at 22:30.[86] They were accompanied by approximately fourteen men from 261 (Airborne) Field Park Company RE, the bulk of whom made it to the Lower Rhine although a Sapper Page was wounded en route and Sapper Lennox

Anderson was killed by a mortar bomb. Sapper Kenneth Clark may also have been killed during the withdrawal.[87]

The 1st Border was scheduled to begin its withdrawal at 20:00 with the despatch of a reconnaissance party to the Lower Rhine to set up a Battalion RV point. Battalion HQ, S Company and the walking wounded from the Battalion RAP were to move off at 22:40, followed by A company at 22:50 and C Company ten minutes after that but things went awry when Captain Barry Ingram and A Company moved back temporarily to occupy the positions vacated by the RE contingent. The German shelling of the Sappers' location proved to be the precursor for a German attack as *Kampfgruppe* von Tettau took up the new night-fighting tactic and a combination of the bombardment and German infantry attacks rapidly took a serious toll of the glider soldiers; on conferring with his second-in-command Lieutenant Lennard Withers, Captain Ingram discovered that the fighting had halved his effective strength to twenty-two men in under an hour. With no sign of a let-up Ingram decided staying in place until 22:50 as ordered would simply lead to A Company being destroyed in place and he therefore went back to Battalion HQ accompanied by a Private Kerwin to seek permission to withdraw earlier; Lieutenant Withers was instructed to lead the Company to the river if Ingram did not return within forty-five minutes.[88] Captain Ingram found the HQ occupied by Lieutenants Joseph Hardy and Michael Holman from the Battalion from the Signals and Mortar Platoons respectively, with no sign of acting Battalion commander Major Stuart Cousens, who had presumably departed early for the embarkation RV with S Company and the walking wounded; 1st Airlanding Brigade HQ noted that 'Other units in the order of the march had not adhered to their timetable' and departed earlier than scheduled.[89] Ingram therefore sought out the commander of C Company, Major William Neill, and arranged for A Company to fall back to Battalion HQ and act as a temporary backstop for Major Neill's Company, after which he returned to the perimeter. He had some difficulty retracing his steps in the darkness. He appears to have led A Company back to the Battalion HQ location but found it impossible to act as a rearguard there due to German pressure. On coming across an immobile line of men waiting in the woods, he struck off for the Brigade RV with his Company in tow. After clambering over several dykes and wading through waist-deep water Major Neill eventually located the RV where Major Anthony Blake, the Brigade Major, directed them onto the soggy riverside polder where they joined 'a long serpentine queue…for all the world like a cinema queue'.[90]

The 1st Border's C Company also appears to have come under German attack but held on in its positions astride the Utrechtseweg until 23:00 as ordered. At that point Major Neill put in an attack to put the enemy off balance before neatly breaking contact and withdrawing toward the river ten minutes later, becoming the Battalion rearguard in the process; the Company appears to have reached the Brigade RV without further incident.[91] In so doing Major Neill's unit appears to have neglected to inform the re-roled Polish anti-tank gunners to the rear of his Company location of his departure. After tiring of waiting in the darkness for the word to move, Lieutenant Bossowski visited the C Company Command Post in the *Valkenburg* house in search of clarification, only to find it empty and abandoned. Understandably a 'little disgusted at the "misunderstanding"', Bossowski held a brief conference with Lieutenant Mikulski, gathered his men and set off through the rain-lashed woods in the direction that seemed most likely to bisect the withdrawal route. Unfortunately, this took the Poles to the brink of entering the German lines before Bossowski got an inkling that something was amiss; he halted the column and on retracing his steps located the path leading to the Lower Rhine and was able to join the expanding throng on the riverside polder.[92] Back with the 1st Border, the remnants of B Company and BREESE Force were presumably scheduled to withdraw after C Company at some point after 23:00, but Major Breese was summoned to Brigade HQ at 22:00; the reason is unclear but after he had been absent for two hours Lieutenant Patrick Stott made his way around the various positions ordering the men to begin moving down to the river. Major Breese then returned and announced that they were to remain in place for a further hour and this was done despite difficulties in recalling the men in the darkness. In the meantime the 1st Airlanding Brigade HQ left its location for the Brigade RV on the Benedendorpsweg at 23:00 with the men holding hands to avoid becoming separated in the darkness. On arrival Brigadier Hicks and his party discovered that that 'units which should still have been in position were already moving past'. They were followed by BREESE Force, which found itself at the very back of the queue on the polder.[93]

***

The boats began moving across the Lower Rhine from the south bank as scheduled, although there were some minor variations to the plan. As nothing was known about the situation opposite the Heveadorp ferry crossing site it was decided to despatch a single craft over the Lower Rhine to gauge the situation, and that it would be tactically prudent for it to be an assault boat from 553 Field Company RE rather than a storm boat with its noisy Evinrude outboard motor. The assault boat, commanded by Sergeant Frederick Petrie, was launched precisely on schedule at 21:30 and took just ten minutes to reach the north bank in the face of 'incessant machine gun fire from three enemy posts' and illumination from a burning factory building near Heveadorp village, repeating the tactic employed over the previous two nights.[94] On arrival Sergeant Petrie found the riverside mudflats deserted apart from two men from the 4th Dorsets who had been hiding in one of the mired DUKWs from the previous night's crossing. On reaching the south bank these stragglers, 'advised us that there were no other personnel on the far bank'.[95] Another assault boat was immediately despatched to verify this and returned empty and Sergeant Petrie made a second crossing at 23:30 with the same result, although in the meantime a party made the passage from the north bank using an assault boat abandoned there during the previous night's crossing; this may have been the group from the 1st Border that included Private Wilfred Oldham.[96] Sergeant Petrie was awarded the Military Medal for his actions that night and for rescuing a wounded officer under fire during the crossing of the River Seine in August 1944.[97] Operations were suspended for an hour at 01:00 owing to friendly mortar fire falling on the disembarkation area, and another assault boat crossed at 02:00 and returned carrying two men before operations were permanently cancelled an hour later at 03:00, partly because of the lack of passengers and more immediately because the volume of German machine-gun and mortar fire made it too dangerous for the Sappers to operate on the water or exposed riverbank.[98] In around five hours, forty-eight men came across the Lower Rhine through the western crossing point, twenty-five via 553 Field Company's assault boats; the remainder either made their own way across like Private Oldham's party or were carried downstream from the eastern crossing site by the current.

The lack of demand for the Sapper's services at the western crossing point was simply because the bulk of the 305 men from the 4th Dorsets who crossed the Lower Rhine the previous night had been killed or captured in the course of the day, and the Airborne troops were simply unable to reach the crossing point because the Heveadorp ferry site had been outwith the 1st Airborne Division's perimeter since the 1st Border had been driven off the Westerbouwing Heights on Thursday 21 September; it is unclear whether Urquhart's HQ had not informed 30 Corps that this was the case or whether 30 Corps had been informed but chose to ignore the fact; either way, the result was the needless risking of lives and more importantly a waste of resources that would have been better deployed at the eastern crossing point. The 20th Field Company RCE thus did not make a single crossing at Heveadorp. The 03:00 cancellation was unfortunately not the end of the story for the Canadian Sappers. At 03:30 they were ordered to send four of their storm boats to assist at the eastern crossing site, which meant carrying the craft back over the summer dyke and reattaching their outboard motors before relaunching them. The first boat was struck by a mortar bomb and sunk as it was launched, the second made it upstream halfway to the eastern crossing point before being forced to beach on the south bank by intense machine-gun fire; the outboard motor then refused to start and the crew were forced to abandon it, wading through waist-deep mud to safety. The two remaining storm boats were not launched as the effort was abandoned with the approach of first light. Major Jones made some trenchant observations on the employment of his unit in the final paragraph of his report on the 20th Field Company's involvement in the evacuation.[99]

Matters ran more according to plan at the eastern crossing site opposite the Oosterbeek Old Church. It was again decided to deploy the more stealthy assault boats first to clarify the situation on the north bank and the first of 260 Field Company's eight craft, commanded by Lieutenant Alan Bevan, was launched at 21:30 as scheduled. It reached the north bank after ten minutes of intense paddling against the current, where Lieutenant Bevan made contact with the waiting Airborne troops and was swiftly loaded and returned with the first party of evacuees; Lieutenant Bevan remained on the north bank to liaise with Lieutenant-Colonel Myers' loading control party. The return of the first assault boat to the south bank was witnessed by Lieutenant-Colonel Henniker, who had been pacing the shore after watching Lieutenant Bevan's craft disappear into the 'inky darkness': 'I do not know how long the interval was, but perhaps after ten or fifteen minutes, though it seemed longer, there came across the darkness the sound of dipping paddles. Then I saw a boat. It held a dozen men. I could recognize their airborne-pattern helmets. What a welcome sight it was!'[100] All eight of 260 Company's boats were launched and moving back and forth across the river in short order, with Lieutenant-Colonel Henniker witnessing the arrival of around sixty men from the north bank in a relatively short period.[101] Despite the best efforts of the Sappers manning the craft the current carried the assault boats up to 200 yards downstream on each leg of the journey, obliging the crews to carry them back along the bank to the embarkation/disembarkation points.[102] There was also some friction over loading wounded individuals as the Sappers had been ordered to prioritise able-bodied evacuees whereas the Airborne troops were looking to bring out their walking wounded and gave them priority by despatching them to the head of the queue. According to Ryan, members of LONSDALE Force visited the RAP in the vicarage near the Oosterbeek Old Church before withdrawing to the river and 'took as many of the walking wounded as they could'; this may have been connected to Captain The Reverend Talbot Watkins, the 1st Parachute Battalion's Padre, leading a party of around fifty wounded to the embarkation point from the same location.[103] The result was some understandably acrimonious exchanges before the boat crews accepted that the Airborne troops were not going to comply; one Airborne Sergeant recalled that one boat crew refused to load his wounded friend until he threatened them with his rifle.[104] The engine of the storm boat Private Arthur Shearwood from the 11th Parachute Battalion obtained a place on failed and the Canadian crew suggested their passengers employed rifle butts as paddles while it was coaxed back into life. Private Shearwood tapped the man in front and suggested he start paddling; the man pointed at his bandaged shoulder and replied 'I can't, I've lost an arm.'[105]

There was also the enemy machine-gun and mortar fire to contend with. One assault boat was reportedly 'hit by a shell', presumably close to the south bank as the 'crew and cargo' reached the shore safely. At least one other assault boat crew were not so lucky; Ryan recounts how when his fifteen-strong party from 156 Parachute Battalion reached the Lower Rhine Major Geoffrey Powell saw a boat 'bobbing up and down in the water, sinking lower as the waves hit against. Powell waded out. The boat was full of holes and the sappers in it were all dead.'[106] Two men from 260 Field Company RE were awarded the Military Medal for their actions during the evacuation, Sergeant Fred Hilton for making numerous crossings and remaining on the north bank for three hours organising embarkation and Sapper Arthur Denmark for making over twenty crossings without relief.[107]

Events were worse for the 23rd Field Company RCE. When the first storm boat was launched at 21:30 it began leaking badly, having been holed on rocks during the carry down to the water's edge. The second boat, crewed by Lance-Corporal Daniel Ryan, Sapper Harold Magnusson and Sapper Leslie Roherty, carried Lieutenant James Martin to liaise with the Airborne side. It was launched fifteen minutes later and promptly disappeared with its crew, possibly after suffering a direct hit from a mortar bomb according to two witnesses.[108] The third storm boat, commanded by Lance-Corporal James McLachlan, left at 22:15 followed at 22:35 by a fourth crewed by Corporal Sidney Smith, Sapper David Hope and Sapper Neil Thompson. The latter was capsized by a near miss from a mortar bomb as it headed fully laden for the south bank. Most of the men in the boat were killed including Sappers Hope and Thompson but five were thrown clear including Corporal Smith, who was kept afloat by air trapped inside his greatcoat. A borrowed assault boat commanded by Sergeant George Willick was later despatched to search for Lieutenant Martin's craft.[109] Lance-Corporal McLachlan's boat eventually reappeared after nearly an hour loaded with wounded, possibly from Padre Watkins' party from the vicarage RAP. It returned for another load as soon as the vessel was emptied. The first few boatloads may all have contained at least a proportion of wounded due to the Airborne troops giving them priority; Sergeant Sandy Morris noted that the 'boats that came back were mostly full of wounded'.[110] This caused delay as it took longer to embark wounded men, and the problem was compounded by the fact that many walking wounded weren't walking. Lieutenant-Colonel Henry Preston, one of the 1st Airborne Division staffers supervising the loading, referred to wounded being laid on the bottom of the storm boats 'amongst the boots of the others',[111] while on the other side of the Lower Rhine Sergeant Morris recalled carrying wounded from the boats and lying them on the beach in the rain with 'nothing to cover them'; Lieutenant Cronyn also recounted comforting a badly wounded paratrooper whilst waiting for a stretcher party to carry him off the beach.[112]

***

Back on the north bank the Polish 3rd Battalion contingent was scheduled to withdraw at 22:00 and Lieutenant Bereda-Fialkowski had ordered his men to make their way from the houses on the Stationsweg to the *Quatre Bras* house on the junction of the Utrechtseweg and Stationsweg in readiness. However, before the move began and possibly provoked by the British bombardment, the Germans attacked the *Quatre Bras* house at 21:30 with machine-guns and hand-grenades using flares for illumination. Lieutenant Kowalczyk's men replied in kind; Corporal Towarnicki put out a hail of fire from a downstairs corner window, reloading his Sten gun with magazines provided by Private Marian Nowak and on occasion exchanging weapons provided from the same source. The German attack died down as the flares began to gutter out although there was still firing from both sides and Lieutenant Bereda-Fialkowski immediately ordered the rest of his men to concentrate in the adjacent No. 4 in readiness to move through the *Quatre Bras* and across the Utrechtseweg. The move involved filing though a window opening after Bereda-Fialkowski, during which one paratrooper was shot and progress faltered when someone shouted that the Lieutenant had been killed; Bereda-Fialkowski scotched this with an angry rejoinder from across the yard and after a pause in the *Quatre Bras* the entire party reached the relative safety of the woods on the south side of the Utrechtseweg. Lieutenant Bereda-Fialkowski's decision to withdraw when he did was shrewdly judged, for the Germans appear to have attacked the Poles' positions again shortly afterward and swiftly divined where the paratroopers had gone. Lance-Corporal Kuzniar heard shouting back on the Stationsweg followed by a volley of flares and mortar bombs dropping into the wood; a paratrooper next to Kuzniar was seriously wounded in the neck by mortar fragments and had to be left behind. The rest of the journey to the embarkation point appears to have gone without incident and the Poles joined the throng on the riverside polder. Seeing that there was no chance of securing a crossing as a group, Lieutenant Bereda-Fialkowski cut his men loose by announcing 'Men, each is on his own…We shall meet in Driel.' The 3rd Battalion contingent then broke up into small groups to work out their next move, at least two of which appear to have found their own way across the Lower Rhine. Some of Lieutenant Jozef Kula's men called him to an abandoned boat of some description, which they then launched and paddled across to the south bank.

Lance-Corporal Kuzniar, accompanied by Lance-Corporal Cadet Grzelak and two unnamed companions, also located an abandoned boat under an overhang in the riverbank. Paddling with two small shovels they found in the craft, the four Poles headed for a red boat beached on the south bank but accurate machine-gun fire obliged them to take to the neck-deep water just short of the beach and swim to the shelter of the red craft; timing their move to when the gun was at the opposite end of its sweep, the four made a dash for and over the summer dyke to safety, although in the tumble down the far side Kuzniar's Sten gun struck a painful blow on Grzelak's leg, to the latter's annoyance.[113]

The last HQ increment left the Hotel Hartenstein from 22:00, beginning with HQ Royal Artillery. After destroying its radio equipment CRA Lieutenant-Colonel Loder-Symonds and Brigade Major RA Major Philip Tower led a party of thirty down to the embarkation point, arriving at 23:45. RA HQ Intelligence Officer Lieutenant Hilary Barber was late and appears to have made his own way to the river, possibly with Signals Officer 2nd Lieutenant George Marshall, while Lieutenant de Burgh was wounded, captured and somehow taken to the MDS; he escaped and swam the Lower Rhine the following day. RA HQ clerks Sergeant Dear and Lance-Bombardier Cole were also captured after failing to get a boat.[114] Major-General Urquhart and the Division HQ element moved off from the hotel at 22:30, leaving the wounded accrued at that location in the cellar in the care of Lieutenant Derrick Randall, the HQRA Medical Officer.[115] The senior commanders burned their personal papers as part of their preparations for departure and Major-General Urquhart wrapped his boots in curtaining obtained by Private Hancock, who had been his batman since serving with the 2nd DCLI in 1940. Urquhart also passed a bottle of whiskey around that had lain forgotten in his pack so the assembled officers could enjoy a 'nip' and received Benzedrine tablets in exchange from an unnamed Sergeant-Major, possibly Company Sergeant-Major Reginald Field from the Division HQ Defence Platoon; the tablets were pocketed and also forgotten. The Division commander then visited the wounded in the cellar in person to wish them well before meeting up with his group for the journey down to the river.[116] This included Division Chief-of-Staff Lieutenant-Colonel Charles Mackenzie, Operations Officer Major Gordon Grieve, ADC Captain Graham Roberts and Major Anthony Murray, commanding F Squadron GPR; the latter two were wounded but had escaped from the Division MDS after the Germans occupied the Hotel Schoonoord, possibly at the prompting of ADMS Colonel Warrack, by simply walking out past the guards carrying blankets and a medical pannier and purloining a parked Jeep.[117] The group also included Private Hancock, who slipped out without Urquhart's knowledge immediately before departure and purloined the maroon and light blue Pegasus pennant that had flown from a lance on the back lawn of the Hotel Hartenstein whilst the building had served as Urquhart's HQ.[118] The journey to the riverbank, with Lieutenant-Colonel Mackenzie in the lead, passed without incident apart from the random German mortaring and small-arms fire and a whispered conference about whether or not to throw a grenade at a German post. On arrival Urquhart's party merely settled down in the rain-lashed riverside mud to wait for a boat, although Mackenzie appears to have 'slipped away' briefly on his own account and returned to inform Urquhart that Myers was rearranging the evacuation schedule in the erroneous belief that around half the boats had been lost in the first hour of the evacuation.[119]

The fact that Major-General Urquhart simply blended into the crowd at the embarkation point has gone largely unremarked or has been seen as a positive; Middlebrook holds it up as evidence of an atmosphere of equality amongst all ranks during the evacuation, for example.[120] However, this overlooks the fact that Urquhart was still the formation commander and ranking officer in the Oosterbeek Pocket, and he should therefore have been monitoring the operation as a matter of course, even if that involved delaying his own departure, rather than remaining inactive while Mackenzie went soliciting information on his own account. Urquhart's behaviour was therefore poor leadership at best and raises the suspicion that he essentially considered his responsibility for the members of the 1st Airborne Division to have ended on drawing up the evacuation plan and handing it to Lieutenant-Colonel Myers for execution, a contention that is reinforced by his behaviour on reaching the safety of the south bank of the Lower Rhine. It is difficult to imagine his opposite number at the 6th Airborne Division for the Normandy landings, Major-General Richard Gale, behaving in such a fashion. Urquhart's behaviour also contrasted poorly with more specific examples, one of which he must have been aware of. Given that he based the Oosterbeek withdrawal plan on the Gallipoli evacuation, Urquhart must have been aware that Major-General Stanley Maude, commander of the British 13th Division, came out on the very last boat from the last beach to be evacuated near Cape Helles.[121] Three more examples were more immediate. Brigadier Hicks, commander of the 1st Airlanding Brigade, was initially reluctant to make the crossing to the south bank until he could be sure all his men were safe, before being persuaded that 'such honourable gestures were not practicable' according to Brigade Major RA Major Philip Tower. Major Richard Lonsdale remained at the embarkation point until all his men from LONSDALE Force were away; by this time the crossings had been called off and Lonsdale was obliged to swim the river despite his wounds.[122] Perhaps even more pertinently, *Hauptsturmführer* Heinrich Oelkers established a lodgement on the south bank of the Lower Rhine near the Heveadorp Ferry on 1 October 1944, which was evacuated after ten days of near constant bombardment and infantry attacks; Oelkers was almost literally the last man out, crossing the river in the last, badly holed inflatable dinghy to leave the south bank.[123]

Urquhart's party was called forward to board a storm boat a little after midnight. First the vessel had become stuck in the mud and, as the outboard motor lacked a reverse gear, had to be pushed off; this was done by Private Hancock, who slipped into the water to perform the deed and then reboarded the moving vessel despite complaints from some of those onboard that it was 'overcrowded already'.[124] The motor then cut out part-way across, likely due to the rain penetrating the motor's electrics, and the boat drifted for what seemed 'an absolute age' before it was restarted. The final indignity occurred after the vessel gained the relative safety of the groynes of the disembarkation area on the south bank. Having crossed the mudflats to the summer dyke Urquhart began to pull himself over the concrete obstacle when

> …there was an ominous snap…[and]…the voice of Graham Roberts came out of the gloom near by [sic] solemnly inquiring whether I was intact. 'It's all right' I said. 'It's only my braces.' Even in these circumstances, when my chief reaction was one of heartfelt relief, it was an annoying indignity. When we set out down the road beyond the dyke, I was holding my trousers up.[125]

The collapsing bag strategy also worked well on the recently contested south-eastern aspect of the perimeter. The support units pulled out first, with the 1st Airlanding Light Regiment RA receiving the order to move from Captain Ronald Hayward, the Electrical and Mechanical (EME) Officer at HQ RA, who carried the order in person from the Hotel Hartenstein.[126] 1, 2 and 3 Battery moved first at around 22:00 followed by Regimental HQ; as 3 Battery was the only portion of the Regiment to remain in its gun positions after the fighting earlier in the day, the others likely concentrated there before moving off; the sights and breech blocks had been removed from the Regiment's guns after the last of the 75mm ammunition had been fired off earlier.[127] Lieutenant Wladyslaw Mleczko and his 3 Troop from the Polish Brigade's Anti-tank Battery moved off at the same time. The Troop had been deployed on the Benedendorpsweg from Wednesday 20 September, and appears to have lost the last of its four 6-Pounder guns in the Monday fighting. Lieutenant Mleczko had despatched Bombardier Stanislaw Nosecki to pass the word of the upcoming evacuation to his men in their dispersed locations with orders to concentrate at the Oosterbeek Old Church ready to move off at 22:00, although most were already aware courtesy of adjacent British units. Before moving off into the darkness and deluge Lieutenant Mleczko briefed his men that if they had not gained passage on a boat by 03:00 it was every man for himself and they were to either swim for it, as Mleczko intended to do, or 'take a chance and wait for whatever might happen'. In the event there was no need for the domesday scenario as Lieutenant Mleczko, Bombardier Nosecki and around a dozen anti-tank gunners who had come in on the third glider lift made the crossing to the south bank at 02:00 after a lengthy wait.[128]

The infantry units manning the perimeter began to withdraw around an hour later, beginning with the LONSDALE Force units straddling the Benedendorpsweg east of the Oosterbeek Old Church. The 1st Parachute Battalion withdrew from its positions at 23:00 after silencing some unspecified enemy activity, taking its walking wounded and leaving the non-ambulatory cases 'where the enemy would find them'; the entire party was reported as being on the south bank by 04:00.[129] The 3rd and 11th Parachute Battalion pulled out thirty minutes later, the former numbering around thirty effectives, all of whom reportedly reached the safety of the south bank accompanied by an unknown number of walking wounded; the remaining casualties were ensconced in a cellar, the location of which was passed to the RAP.[130] The 11th Parachute Battalion rendezvoused at the Oosterbeek Old Church before moving off, possibly under the command of Lieutenant James Blackwood. Details are sparse as Lieutenant Blackwood was wounded at some point and as he noted in the 11th Parachute Battalion War Diary, 'I cannot say how 11 Bn fared. I was blind with blood and field dressing and lost touch with my men in the darkness, crossing the river myself with 1st Bn personnel'; according to Middlebrook seventy-two paratroopers from the Battalion were evacuated.[131] Last out was the 2nd South Staffords party, which was detailed to withdraw no earlier than 23:45 and 'thus had the honour of covering the withdrawal'.[132] Equipment that could not be carried out was smashed in place at 23:30 and Major John Buchanan commanding Support Company passed the word to move to the South Staffords dug in near the Oosterbeek Old Church. A newly shaven Major Robert Cain from B Company did the same for the contingent at the Laundry. The withdrawal to the embarkation point went without incident apart from the usual random German mortaring and machine-gun fire and appears to have been concluded quickly, given that Lieutenant Donald Edwards and the remains of C Company's 17 Platoon reportedly joined the back of the queue for a boat at 01:00.[133] The honour of being the last away led to an unclear number of South Staffords still being on the north bank when the crossing was ended at dawn, but between 124 and 139 members of the 2nd South Staffords crossed the Lower Rhine to safety.[134]

At the disembarkation point on the south bank the number of casualties being ferried across the river or sustained during the crossing rapidly became a major problem. As the Canadians had not been briefed to expect wounded no reception arrangements had been made and the 23rd Field Company's two-man RAP in the culvert under the summer dyke struggled to cope; over the course of the night Lance-Corporal Roseborough and Sapper McDonald treated sixty-nine stretcher cases and 100 walking wounded. Many of the Canadian Sappers gave up their greatcoats for use as blankets or improvised stretchers.[135] The unexpected burden also impacted on the 23rd Field Company's ability to perform its primary task; as the unit War Diary put it, 'Caring for all these casualties proved a great drain on man power of the Coy and prevented adequate relief for the boat carrying parties and boat crews.'[136] This, together with the numbers of able-bodied evacuees moving along the route from the riverside and churning up the ground, likely explains why although the first increment of storm boats was launched at twenty-minute intervals. It took until 03:00 to get all fourteen craft into the water; salvaging the three vessels from the truck overturned at the entrance to the orchard unloading site caused further delay.[137] Casualty-handling arrangements had been made but further up the chain of command, at a conference at 130 Brigade HQ at Homoet at 07:00 on 25 September and a second at Nijmegen at 12:30; the attendees included 1st Airborne Corps Deputy Director Medical services Brigadier Arthur Eagger, the DDMS from 30 Corps, Major Henry Richards commanding the RAMC detachment from 1st Airborne Division HQ's Seaborne Echelon, and the acting commander of 163 Field Ambulance in the absence of Lieutenant-Colonel Herford, a Major Mackenzie. 163 Field Ambulance was to operate an MDS at Valburg while 130 Field Ambulance from the

43rd Division was to set up a Casualty Collection Post (CCP) near the evacuee transit area in the south-west outskirts of Driel, and also establish an RAP in the orchard near the disembarkation point.[138] However, the latter was only intended to handle any casualties incurred during crossing or while operating the disembarkation point and the number of casualties rapidly began to back up there, as noted by Brigadier Eagger and Major Richards when they visited the RAP at 23:30, which was also under heavy mortar fire. The problem was a lack of transport to move the casualties down the medical evacuation chain, which led to the CCP at Driel also being obliged to retain casualties.[139] The situation was alleviated initially by the trucks from the 551st General Transport Company RASC, which began to ferry casualties back once its vehicles had shed their loads of storm boats, assisted by 3-ton trucks from the 5th Dorsets according to Sliz.[140] The problem was reportedly solved eventually by a fleet of forty medically adapted Jeeps gathered at the CCP by the 43rd Division's Assistant Quarter Master General (AQMG) Lieutenant-Colonel J. McCance, as these were the only vehicles that could '…master the narrow, slippery roads back from Driel.'[141] This was presumably the pool of vehicles from which the 43rd Division's Deputy Assistant Director Medical Services promised to provide some 'ambulance cars' for Major Richards when he visited the CCP at 01:00, and the source of the five ambulance Jeeps that Richards procured to move casualties back from the orchard RAP.[142] The Jeeps, reportedly in conjunction with the 'genius for administrative improvisation' of Lieutenant-Colonel McCance and the 43rd Division ADMS, Colonel K. A. M. Tomory, appear to have ultimately done the trick as by 05:00 casualties were 'being cleared fairly well' despite enemy mortar fire on the area around the CCP and nearby roads.[143]

The constant German machine-gun and mortar fire may have fallen disproportionately on the disembarkation point owing to German observers on the Westerbouwing Heights opposite. Sergeant George King running the Canadian refuelling point recalled German flares repeatedly illuminating the beach: 'the water was just boiling with machine-gun fire, 88's would burst in the air…Every time a flare went up, we dove under the water. The river was boiling, just boiling!'[144] Alarming as it may have been the German fire on the south bank does not appear to have been particularly effective, given that the Canadian Sappers stationed on the south bank suffered only four wounded in the course of the operation. Sappers D. E. Francis and J. P. LeTouqueux were wounded by a mortar bomb near Major Tucker's Command Post on the beach. Sergeant Donald Barnes and Lieutenant Kennedy's driver Sapper Ronald McKee were hit by shell fragments in the orchard; Sapper McKee died later that night after being evacuated, likely in the CCP at Driel.[145]

The exemplary behaviour of the Airborne soldiers awaiting passage has been commented upon in most accounts of the battle. The 1st Border War Diary noted that 'The discipline of the Bn was beyond praise, especially during the long wait on the "flats".' Cholewczynski noted that 'the Poles constantly marvelled at the Red Devils' discipline as they patiently waited for evacuation.'[146] Unsurprisingly given the ordeal they had undergone for the previous nine days the discipline was a little brittle, however, and the Airborne soldiers were sometimes callous when it came to the boats. Lieutenant-Colonel Preston recalled the reaction to a storm boat drawing into the bank, men 'scrambling and heaving themselves into it from all directions… In a moment the boat had filled with men, and those still trying to clamber in were prevented from doing so by those already there [and] were falling into the water or onto the shore.' Preston was nonetheless able to restore order with a whispered warning that the vessel was in danger of capsizing.[147] During a lull in the shelling Sergeant David Christie from the 1st Airborne Reconnaissance Squadron recalled a loud scream, reportedly from a drowning man, elicited a response of 'If he has to die, why the hell should he make such a bastard noise about it?' from another man in the queue, concerned lest the noise attract German fire.[148] The Sappers' official records are critical. The 260 Field Company War Diary refers to 'Difficulty in marshalling airborne troops for loading in spite of officers & NCOs on far bank supervising job', while the 23rd Field Company War Diary noted that it was 'impossible to regulate the number of passengers carried in the boats … in many cases they had to be beaten off or threatened with shooting to avoid having the boat swamped.'[149] Such threats were the exception rather than the rule, although the Airborne troop's discipline became more ragged as time went on and the fear of being abandoned on the north bank grew.

As 260 Field Company's assault boats plied their way back and forth across the Lower Rhine their numbers diminished over time. As we have seen one craft was hit by a shell and two more were swamped by the wake from Canadian storm boats, which were capable of twenty knots when moving unladen; the unit War Diary refers to the Canadian boats being a 'nuisance' in this regard and to some men being lost from one of the swamped craft, although it is unclear if the missing men were 260 Field Company personnel or evacuees. A combination of the current, fatigue and an increase in the strength of the wind obliged an increase in the assault boat crews from four to six at some point, with a concomitant reduction in lift capacity; by 05:00 this made the assault boats 'practically unmanageable' and the effort was called off an hour later. The Sappers were reportedly 'extremely tired but pleased' with their efforts, although there was apparently some resentment when a radio report announced, two days later, 'that the job was done by Canadians'.[150] Nonetheless, the bulk of the lifting across the Lower Rhine fell upon the 23rd Field Company due to the larger capacity and motorised nature of its equipment The number of storm boats was again reduced over the course of the night, and all fourteen of the 23rd Field Company's craft were never operating simultaneously. According to a Private Charlton from the 1st Parachute Battalion, by 02:00 the boats 'had reduced to six or seven', while Lieutenant Cronyn claimed there were likely 'no more than three or four in use at [any] one time'.[151] This could have been because the storm boats were damaged by enemy fire or rough handling while the craft were being carried across the dykes, because the craft had to be replaced after being holed by striking underwater obstacles when beaching or by enemy fire during the crossings. The five craft held in reserve were therefore rapidly used up.[152] There was also the matter of refuelling, which was required after approximately an hour's running and temporarily removed storm boats from the cross-river shuttle. This was no easy task in the rain-sodden zone of fire and a good deal of petrol was lost in transit between the orchard and the refuelling point on the beach; as Sapper William Richardson put it, 'We spilled so much that I think we lost more than we brought forward.'[153]

The biggest brake upon the Canadian Sapper's activities in fact proved to be the fifty-horsepower Evinrude outboard motors.[154] The Evinrude was a US-produced civilian item that had performed satisfactorily during training in the UK and in carrying the 10th Canadian Infantry Brigade across the Seine at the end of August 1944, but which was found wanting in the prevailing conditions on the Lower Rhine on the night of 25-26 September. The problem was inadequate waterproofing that allowed the heavy rain and backwash created by beaching the vessels at speed to penetrate the motor's electrical circuits and spark plugs, which resulted in multiple and repeated failure of the motors.[155] This was especially dangerous in mid-crossing and not just due to the fast-running current, as the heavily laden craft were vulnerable to swamping by movement from their passengers or, like the unpowered assault boats, the wash from their fully powered brethren; Lieutenant John Stevenson from the 1st Airborne Reconnaissance Squadron noted that the storm boat that carried him across the Lower Rhine had only half an inch between the water and the gunwales.[156] Hitching a tow from a functioning craft presented the same risk swelled by a much slower rate of progress in the face of the current and enemy fire, although it was done successfully on at least one occasion. The motor of the craft carrying Private John Crosson from the 7th KOSB failed to start after loading at around 02:00: 'Another boat came alongside to load up. Our sapper persuaded its pilot to give us a tow across. This was very slow progress [and] it seemed like ages before a bump was felt as both boats arrived on the south bank.'[157] The waterlogged motors were swapped out for functioning items by men from the maintenance Section from the 10th Field Park Company RCE who then carried them to a small hole in the riverbank dubbed 'the Shop', where Lance-Corporal Arthur Gamble and Sapper

Earl Fisher dried out the electrics and spark plugs, immersing the plugs in a pan of burning petrol. The work of swapping out, drying and restarting the malfunctioning motors continued all night.[158] The engine failures also prompted spectacular outbursts of foul language from the operators. As Major Alan Bush from the 3rd Parachute Battalion remembered, after the motor of his storm boat cut out in midstream, 'I thought I had heard every oath in the English language but I heard a few new ones from those Canadians until they got it going again.'[159] Lieutenant Stevenson had a similar experience when the motor on his storm boat refused to start after loading: 'the Canadian engineer pulled at the lanyard to start the outboard motor, but nothing happened…All the time he was pulling away, he kept saying "The bastard – the bastard – the bastard" when suddenly it "phut-phutted" into life and we were away.'[160]

The Canadian Sappers made in the region of 150 round trips across the Lower Rhine in the course of the night; the unit War Diary declared: 'All of the boat crews were magnificent, and only gave up their ferrying when their boats were no longer operable or else when they were exhausted and had to be ordered from the beach.'[161] The capacity of the storm boats was ten, although it is unclear if this included the three-man crew employed by the Canadians, but the average load brought across was sixteen and, in one instance, thirty-six. Surprisingly in the darkness some storm boat crews spotted and rescued Airborne soldiers attempting to swim to safety. Sergeant Alf Roullier from the 1st Airlanding Light Regiment became disoriented while attempting the swim and was grabbed by the scruff of the neck by a crewman of a passing storm boat who then lifted him into the craft and assured him he was 'almost home'. Signalman James Cockrill from Division HQ Signals underwent the same process and 'nearly cried when I found out I was back where I started' when the empty boat then grounded on the north bank; the storm boat then carried him to safety along with a full load of evacuees. Private Alfred Dullforce from the 10th Parachute Battalion made it all the way across the river under his own steam stripped naked but still carrying his .38 pistol, only to make landfall in front of two Dutch women. They proved to be the less embarrassed about the encounter, and Dullforce made his way to Driel clad in a multicoloured skirt and clogs.[162] Not all the swimmers were so lucky. Captain James Ogilvie from D Squadron GPR, who had helped relay the withdrawal order to the Poles on the Stationsweg, drowned while attempting the swim with another Glider Pilot, allegedly due to the weight of his sodden kilt.[163]

The men of the 23rd Field Company more than lived up to the accolades in the 23rd Field Company after-action report. Corporal George Robinson, who had helped construct the access bridge into the orchard concentration area before carrying the first storm boat over the dykes, also carried the last vessel down to the river at 03:30 and then commanded it for six round trips until it was put out of commission. This may have been the craft reported as making a final trip despite being holed and which sank just short of the south bank in water shallow enough for all aboard to wade ashore.[164] Corporal James McLachlan, who made the first successful crossing of the night, was relieved with his crew after making fifteen round trips that lifted approximately 210 men to safety. The leader in this regard, however, was Sapper Raymond LeBouthillier. When his crew was relieved after fourteen crossings Sapper LeBouthillier refused to rest and instead joined another crew and made a further twelve trips across an unbroken five-hour period, during which his vessels lifted over 500 men from the north bank. He made a speciality of leaping from the storm boat to physically prevent it beaching too hard to offset the Evinrude motor's lack of a reverse gear, and to prevent the backwash from a fast beaching from swamping the engine. On several occasions he deliberately directed his boat to the outer edges of the crossing lane and called out for any Airborne troops unable to make it to the embarkation point, and only desisted when exhaustion led to a direct order to leave the beach. Sapper LeBouthillier's performance was justifiably rated as 'outstanding' and he was awarded the Military Medal in recognition of his actions.[165]

The precise number of Airborne personnel the 23rd Field Company lifted from the north bank of the Lower Rhine is unclear as the record sheets were destroyed by the rain, but the unit War

Diary estimated 2,400 to 2,500 while the British Official History written in 1968 cites a figure of 2,587, which ties in with Middlebrook's total from the individual unit returns.[166] It also ties in with the reception arrangements in Nijmegen for the evacuees by the 1st Airborne Division's Seaborne Echelon, which initially allowed for accommodation of 2,000 men in two buildings but had to expand into a third in the early morning of 26 September.[167] Be that as it may, the official figure of 2,398, which appears to have originated with Urquhart's 1958 account of the battle, is regularly cited elsewhere including the semi-official 10th Parachute Battalion account published in 1965, and more recently by Fairley and Middlebrook. The figure breaks down to 2,163 personnel from the 1st Airborne Division and attached units, 160 Poles and seventy-five men from the 4th Dorsets.[168] The total also included a number of RAF personnel shot down in the resupply flights, a Dutch Jew named Isaäc de Vries who acted as a guide for a group from LONSDALE Force, and an unnamed elderly German prisoner who insisted on remaining with his captors from the 21st Independent Company.[169] Whatever the precise figure, the expertise, application and sheer courage of the British and Canadian Sappers had achieved what ought to have been impossible in the circumstances.

***

Once across the river the evacuees from the 1st Airborne Division first faced the trek to the transit area at Driel through the rain and continuing German mortar and shellfire, although in some instances this barely registered in the relief of being in relative safety. As the 7th KOSB War Diary put it, 'Once on the other side it seemed one had reached a haven, and, despite mud and fatigue, all trudged the four miles to DRIEL with light hearts if somewhat heavy footsteps.'[170] More immediate liquid refreshment also appears to have been available en route; although it does not figure in other accounts. Lieutenant Stevenson from the Reconnaissance Squadron clearly recalled a Salvation Army mobile canteen van operated by a 'grey haired woman' dispensing hot tea on the road between the disembarkation point and Driel.[171] The route to the transit area was poorly marked, although the problem was swiftly rectified after the first evacuees began to arrive from 22:30 and guides were provided and a sentry posted to help succeeding parties.[172] Not everyone appears to have reported to the transit area after crossing the river. Captain David Allsop and Sergeant Patrick Quinn from the Reconnaissance Squadron, accompanied by a Dutch NCO attached to the Squadron met en route, visited what was likely the 130 Field Ambulance CCP west of Driel as Captain Allsop had been wounded in the thigh during the crossing. The trio then headed for Nijmegen and ended up being provided with porridge and a straw bed by a Dutch farmer before hitching a ride into Nijmegen the following day, where Captain Allsop was taken in by 10 Casualty Clearing Station.[173] Similarly, the 2nd South Staffords Diary makes no reference to the transit area at Driel, just to a 'weary 9 miles to cover' in the rain before reaching Nijmegen and linking up with the Division seaborne tail.[174]

The initial trek to the transit area had its lighter moments. Trooper Stanley Collishaw from the Reconnaissance Squadron teamed up with a fellow boat passenger after struggling together across the riverside dykes and the pair passed the journey being 'very free with the expletives'. On entering the barn at the transit area where hot food was being served, Collishaw discovered his companion was a Major and apologised for his foul language, to which the officer replied 'Don't talk bloody rubbish, we're all the same here...I was at Dunkirk, but this lot's a fucking sight worse!'[175] According to the 43rd Division's semi-official account the transit area was organised and manned by Major G. R. Hartwell and D Company 5th Dorsets, although Major Richards RAMC from the 1st Airborne's seaborne echelon also appears to have been involved. The facilities were somewhat restricted, with illumination in the barn being provided by the headlights of a Jeep, but the effort was well received by the wet, tired and hungry Airborne soldiers.[176] The 1st Parachute Battalion reported being given 'a rum ration and [a] great welcome from the 43rd Division'. The 7th KOSB noted that 'tea, rum and blankets were dished out, under excellent arrangements made by 30 Corps, and all were most acceptable.'[177] Lieutenant Henry Brown from the 4th Parachute Squadron RE recalled 'a well lit interior where I was struck by the warmth of the air, the smell of unwashed exhausted bodies, soaked uniforms and food!' He remembered a mug of piping hot tea with a shot of rum and a modest ration of stew, the portion size being dictated by medical concerns of the possible negative effect of large amounts of food on shrunken stomachs.[178] However, satisfaction may have waned later as the transit area ran out of blankets and food at 05:00, and not everyone was especially enamoured of Driel; for some unknown reason Lieutenant Stevenson from the Reconnaissance Squadron dubbed the town 'the most miserable place on God's earth'.[179]

The original plan had been to shuttle the evacuees from the transit area to Nijmegen by motor transport, which was the case for some units. The 1st Parachute Battalion reported being transported in DUKWs for example, No. 1 Wing GPR reported being moved in 'Ducks' and Jeeps and the 1st Border was carried in trucks, but there was insufficient transport to maintain a constant shuttle, possibly because vehicles had been diverted to move casualties away from the riverside RAP and the CCP in Driel. As a result some units were carried part of the way, like the 7th KOSB, and others had to march the entire distance to Nijmegen, which appears to have been the case with the 2nd South Staffords.[180] In some instances a darker edge emerged as the Airborne evacuees passed elements of the Guards Armoured Division on the road. Captain Roland Langton of the 2nd Irish Guards recalled taking an involuntary step back and feeling 'almost embarrassed to speak' as the filthy, battle-worn survivors trudged past him; another unnamed Guardsman was asked 'Where the hell have you been, mate?' and a quiet response that the Guards had been fighting for five months drew 'Oh? Did you have a nice drive up?' from another Airborne soldier.[181] On the other hand the men of the Reconnaissance Squadron again injected some humour into the situation. Lieutenant Douglas Galbraith and Sergeant Henry Venes commandeered a wicker supply hamper in an effort to avoid the rain as it was large enough to go over both of them if they moved one behind the other, with vision possible to the front through the weave; the pair thus set off for Nijmegen 'looking for all the world like a wickerwork pantomime horse'.[182] The transit area remained open until 08:30 after which the nearby CCP, which was reportedly almost clear of casualties by this point, assumed responsibility for processing and despatching any additional evacuees to the reception centre in Nijmegen until it too was closed later in the morning.[183]

The first Airborne evacuees began to arrive at the larger reception centre building in Nijmegen at 23:30, while the Airlanding Brigade staff at the smaller Pagoda building reported receiving their first customers at 03:00. The time difference was presumably due to the larger venue being filled first before the overspill was directed to the Pagoda.[184] The 7th KOSB War Diary well summed up the prevailing mood among the Airborne evacuees as a whole: 'At NIJMEGEN the survivors of the Bn were welcomed by our own "Seaborne Tail", under Major RD SELLON, who had made most detailed preparations for their comfort and well-being. All were soon refreshed, fed and sent to bed to enjoy their first real sleep for 10 days.'[185] Similarly, the 21st Independent Company semi-official account reported the reception centre provided the evacuees with a 'sumptuous meal' with no queuing along with plentiful supplies of brandy and cigarettes: 'Whoever prepared the reception of the battle's survivors was indeed thoughtful…Every man through whose hands the battle-weary passed showed a consideration and understanding of what their guests had endured.'[186] There were also some happy reunions and unusual sights. When Major Cain from the 2nd South Staffords entered one of the reception centre buildings he was greeted by Brigadier Hicks with 'Well there's one officer, at least, who's shaved' to which Cain replied 'I was well brought up Sir.' Lieutenant Peter Scott-Malden from Division HQ arrived at the centre 'clad in several yards of flannel secured by a belt'; after a large bowl of Irish stew and two tumblers of Cointreau he slept for twelve hours straight.[187] In the event the two commandeered buildings proved insufficient to hold all the evacuees and a nearby police barracks was also pressed into service, manned and administered by the 1st Airlanding

Light Regiment's seaborne tail commanded by Captain A. J. A. Hanhart.[188] The evacuees were not totally out of the line of fire, for in the morning a bomb from a German aircraft landed in the courtyard of the Pagoda building, injuring an unknown number of men and setting fire to three Airlanding Brigade vehicles parked there, which were all written off.[189]

The highest ranking member of the 1st Airborne Division to avoid both the transit area and the reception centre was its commander. Having survived the crossing and his snapped braces and accompanied by his ADC Captain Graham Roberts, Major-General Urquhart spoke briefly with Lieutenant Colonel Henniker on the road leading away from the winter dyke.[190] The pair then made their way over the five miles or so to 130 Brigade HQ at Homoet where Urquhart unsuccessfully attempted to procure transport before moving on for another three miles to the 43rd Division's forward HQ in Valburg, where Captain Roberts' unkempt appearance 'was not received with any warmth'.[191] Urquhart's fixation on obtaining transport was not connected to checking on the progress of the evacuation or the welfare of his men as might have been assumed. In fact, he does not appear to have visited the reception centre in Nijmegen at all on the day of the evacuation or thereafter and limited his activities in this regard to holding a Commanders Conference at 14:30, which appears to have largely endorsed the work already done by the Divisional seaborne echelon. He did find time for an 'extravagant' dinner party held in his honour at 1st Airborne Corps HQ that evening, however.[192] Urquhart did visit the transit area later on the morning of 26 September at the beginning of a round of 'courtesy calls' to 'those who had been closest to us in the battle', which included Lieutenant-General Horrocks, Major-General Thomas and the 64th Medium Regiment RA whose commander, a Lieutenant-Colonel Hunt, was absent from his HQ, although the time of the visit is unclear and as we have seen the transit area closed at 08:30.[193] For his part Major-General Browning did visit the reception centre in Nijmegen to attend a parade at 17:00 on 27 September, although interestingly only six of the thirty-seven Airborne War Diaries examined refer to the fact. All this lay in the future however, and by his own admission Urquhart's motivation in seeking transport was quite straightforward; it was because he was 'keen to get back as soon as possible to report to General Browning'.[194]

The transport problem solved itself with the arrival of Browning's ADC Major Harry Cator at 43rd Division HQ, who whisked Urquhart and Roberts off in a Jeep through the pouring rain to Nijmegen and the comfortable Senior Officer's Mess at the Advanced Airborne Corps HQ where Browning was quartered. On arrival Urquhart was shown into a room in the Senior Officer's Mess while Cator departed to fetch Browning, who appeared after twenty minutes fully dressed in his usual immaculate Guards attire 'as if he had just come off parade'. Urquhart then reported his failure: 'The Division is nearly out now. I'm sorry we haven't been able to do what we set out to do.' Quite how Urquhart knew about the progress of the evacuation having left the crossing point somewhat peremptorily and while it was still underway is unclear. Browning magnanimously responded by saying 'You did all you could. Now you had better get some rest,' before offering Urquhart a drink and presumably disappearing back to his bed.[195] In the circumstances Urquhart would have been more than justified in rounding on Browning and acquainting him with a few home truths; certainly as commander of a Division extricating itself from encirclement he ought to have had more pressing concerns than racing through the night to report like an errant schoolboy. Instead he simply classified the encounter as a 'totally inadequate meeting', although he appears to have kept this opinion to himself for over a decade-and-a-half while reportedly becoming increasingly amazed at the memory of it as time went on.[196] At the time, however, Urquhart simply allowed himself to be shown to a comfortable bedroom in an adjoining house where an orderly brought him tea and dry battledress from Major Cator to replace his own soaked attire, and he lay down on a bed 'that was too comfortable...[where]...Sleep did not come easily'.[197] There is something deeply unedifying about the spectacle of Browning sleeping comfortably between clean sheets while the survivors of the 1st Airborne Division were struggling and in some instances dying to extricate themselves from a situation largely of his making just a few short miles to the north, although the spectacle of their Division commander availing himself of similar facilities is only marginally less unedifying, if at all. The First World War stereotype of red-tabbed donkeys urging lions to the slaughter from the comfort of opulent chateaux was rather less prevalent than popular perception assumes, but the spirit of that behaviour was certainly alive and well and on clear display in Nijmegen on the night of 25-26 September 1944.

Back at the crossing point the work of ferrying the Airborne evacuees across the Lower Rhine became increasingly hazardous with the onset of dawn; despite this Major Tucker ordered Sergeant George King to take out the last boat at the 23rd Field Company's crossing point but perhaps fortunately Sergeant King was unable to coax the vessel's Evinrude motor into life.[198] As it became apparent that the effort would have to be terminated, at least one and possibly two of the last storm boats across were loaded with lifebelts, which were dumped on the north bank before the evacuees boarded, for any who wished to swim for it.[199] The growing light not only made it easier for the Germans to see and fire upon the storm boats, but also concealed the muzzle-flash of their weapons that had been used to target counter-fire to suppress or knock them out during the night. At 04:00 the 43rd Division artillery began a pre-planned firing of smoke ammunition onto the north bank and the Sappers also ignited smoke pots in an effort to conceal the storm boats, but the benefit was limited as a morning breeze rapidly dissipated the smoke.[200] It did cause some alarm among the Germans however, who initially assumed they were under gas attack.[201] As the light level increased Lieutenant-Colonel Henniker decided that the risk to the boat crews was too much and therefore 'called a halt to the operation' after speaking to Lieutenant-General Thomas via field telephone.[202] The precise time of the halt is unclear. Henniker does not cite a time in his account, the 20th Field Company RCE War Diary unhelpfully reports that 'the show was called off at first light', the 23rd Field Company cites a time of 04:15 and the 260 Field Company 06:00.[203] Whatever the time of the cessation order, the Sapper units at the eastern crossing point began to move their equipment away from the riverside launching site for loading and transport back to the concentration area in Valburg, although this was not quite the end of the story.

The despatch of the final storm boat from the orchard at around 03:00 effectively put Lieutenant Kennedy out of a job, and with Major Tucker's permission he scoured the shoreline for a craft with which to assist in the evacuation. He was refused permission to use an abandoned assault boat as Major Tucker rightly considered the current too strong for it to be effective, but he then came upon an abandoned storm boat with a failed motor that had been carried downstream from the launch point by the current. Kennedy managed to coax the motor back into life and prevailed upon Major Tucker to provide a crew in the shape of a Lance-Corporal H. D. Gillis and Sapper David McCready before starting across the river at some point between 04:30 and 05:00. On arrival on the north bank Kennedy and his crew came face to face with a new and unexpected hazard as the discipline of the Airborne soldiers awaiting the boats began to break down; after jumping ashore Lieutenant Kennedy found himself being 'pushed backwards by an uncontrollable mass of men'. His immediate reaction was to draw his Browning pistol before simultaneously realising that he could not in all conscience shoot any of the mob, and that they could not see the gesture in any case.[204] The incident was witnessed by 2nd Lieutenant Szczesny Relidzinski from the Polish Brigade Signals Company, who also saw a British officer attempting to reason with the mob by shouting 'Soldiers, you are British, behave like gentlemen'; the officer may have been Major Anthony Vinycomb, commander of 260 Field Company who had crossed to the north bank to help organise the crossing.[205] Whoever he was, the shouted entreaty was ignored, the mob swept forward onto the storm boat and Lieutenant Kennedy 'went down with the ship – in four feet of cold water'. The resultant pause to bale out the water, while no easy task on the slippery and steeply sloping bank, allowed Lieutenant Kennedy to impose a measure of order and the vessel was loaded without further incident, although it had to be rowed across to the south bank using rifle butts as the dousing had put the motor out of commission again; as a result the craft came to rest downstream in the 260 Field Company area.[206] On the way in,

Kennedy's crew spotted an assault boat and another storm boat abandoned in an adjacent bay in the groynes and when the storm boat's engine was started the three Sappers agreed to make another trip with the functioning storm boat towing the other two craft in sequence. This time the 'paratroopers were organized in line', the loading went quickly and efficiently and three full boatloads of evacuees were brought across safely.[207]

By this point the light had grown to the extent that the storm boats were clearly visible on the water but, knowing there were still a large number of Airborne soldiers waiting to be lifted from the north bank, Lieutenant Kennedy and Sapper McCready determined to make another trip while Lance-Corporal Gillis declined to take part in what he not unreasonably considered to be a 'suicide mission'. Dispensing with the assault boat Lieutenant Kennedy towed the engineless storm boat back to the north bank in the face of increasingly heavy and accurate German machine-gun and mortar fire, plucking Lieutenant Relidzinski from his attempt to paddle across the river en route. This time Kennedy was ready for the indiscipline that had sunk him earlier; according to Private John Ranger from D Company 1st Border he fired a shot from his pistol and shouted 'If you try to rush the boats, I will use this on you' before announcing 'Sorry this is our last run, we will not be returning.'[208] In relatively good order twenty-five evacuees packed themselves into Sapper McCready's engineless craft while an even more astounding thirty-six were crammed into Lieutenant Kennedy's. The latter was so overloaded that Kennedy was unable to operate the Evinrude motor's rope-starter until some passengers leaned out over the side to give him room and predictably, the motor then refused to start. Increasingly agitated at the delay the men aboard McCready's vessel cut the rope linking the two storm boats despite Kennedy's warnings not to do so, while a heavily outnumbered McCready looked on. The slow-moving vessel attracted a storm of German fire as it crawled painfully slowly across the river, and only nine of the twenty-five men aboard survived to make landfall on the south bank; a further four were killed scrambling up to or over the summer dyke and Sapper McCready was wounded.[209] Back on the north bank Lieutenant Kennedy finally got his motor to start: 'The blunt bow of the storm boat was so close to the water that I didn't dare use much power for fear of…driving her under…A single projectile hit the man who was jammed under my right elbow, with a sound like the blow of a club. He jerked once and never moved again. The bow of the boat hit the beach and 10 seconds later the dead paratrooper and I were alone.'[210] For their courage and dedication during the long night of the evacuation across the Lower Rhine Lieutenant Kennedy was awarded the Military Cross and Sapper McCready the Military Medal.[211]

Lieutenant Kennedy's storm boat grounded on the south bank of the Lower Rhine in full daylight at 07:20 on Tuesday 26 September 1944. At that point Operation BERLIN, and by extension Operation MARKET GARDEN that had necessitated it, effectively came to an end.

Aftermath and Reflections

The end of Operation BERLIN was not the end of the story in Oosterbeek. A significant number of Airborne soldiers were still on the north bank of the Lower Rhine when the evacuation effort was called off. The 1ˢᵗ Airborne Division HQ War Diary cites a figure of 300, but the 260 Field Company record refers to 200 and an eyewitness at the embarkation point, Private John Ranger from the 1ˢᵗ Border, estimated there were half as many again when Lieutenant Kennedy's storm boat departed on its last southbound crossing.[1] Interestingly, if not surprisingly given the number of eye-witness accounts to the contrary, Lieutenant-Colonel Henniker's account claims that at the time of the last trip 'no more Airborne soldiers were found awaiting passage to the south bank'.[2] Whatever the precise number of men abandoned on the north bank, the more important point was that the vast majority of Airborne personnel had been successfully evacuated because the 1ˢᵗ Airborne Division's deception and withdrawal plan tailored to carry out that most difficult of military manoeuvres, breaking contact without alerting the enemy, had exceeded expectations. The Germans had thus remained oblivious to what was occurring under their noses. As late as 09:30 *II SS Panzerkorps* had informed *Kampfgruppe* von Tettau that 'the enemy made another attempt to break out to the east in the early morning hours but was repulsed,' presumably referring to the clashes involving the 21ˢᵗ Independent Company and the 1ˢᵗ Parachute Battalion as they withdrew to the embarkation point.[3] Eager to capitalise on the previous day's progress the Germans renewed their assault on the British perimeter at first light and it rapidly became apparent that they were pushing against an open door. By 10:25 *SS Bataillon* Eberwein reported finally clearing the houses along the Utrechtseweg that had been a deadly bone of contention for several days and moving on the Hotel Hartenstein, making contact with *Kampfgruppen* Möller moving in from just a few hundred yards to the east in the process. *SS Junker* Rudolf Lindemann from *Unterführerschule* 'Arnheim' admitted after reaching the Hotel Hartenstein that 'it was not a real attack [because] the paras had gone already. We found only weapons and dead people.'[4]

To the north *Kampfgruppe* Bruhn and *SS Bataillon* Oelkers made similar progress through the territory previously held largely by the 7ᵗʰ KOSB, and made contact with the forces pressing in from the east and west at around midday; the Oosterbeek *Hexenkessel* was fully secured by 14:00.[5] *Hauptsturmführer* Hans Möller belatedly realised the significance of the pounding his *Kampfgruppe* had endured from 30 Corps' artillery, recalling that the 'Red Devils had withdrawn and disappeared during the night behind this curtain of dirt and destruction' although he was somewhat wary of the unnatural silence that fell over the battlefield thereafter; 'But then – it stopped all of a sudden – the silence appeared treacherous to all and almost "hurt". Was it all over? Would it start again?'[6] There was also reportedly a widespread sense of relief as the Germans had understandably assumed that their Airborne opponents would fight to the finish. 9 *SS Panzer Division's* chief-of-staff, *Hauptsturmführer* Wilfried Schwarz, observed that 'Morale was particularly good at the end. We had actually succeeded in forcing this elite British division to stop, and pushed the remnants over the Rhine!'[7] The German advance from the east was followed closely by Colonel Warrack and members of staff from the makeshift hospital he and Lieutenant-Colonel Herford had set up in the Dutch barracks in Apeldoorn, searching out and evacuating the abandoned wounded from the RAPs and other places across the now empty Airborne perimeter. They were assisted by the Germans who provided a fleet of thirty-six vehicles marked with the Red Cross to evacuate the casualties to Apeldoorn; Warrack commandeered a Jeep and personally scoured the eastern and western evacuation routes leading down to the Lower Rhine searching for casualties abandoned in the darkness and confusion of the withdrawal.[8]

The German occupation of the Oosterbeek pocket was not totally without incident, with isolated groups of sadly unsung Airborne soldiers fighting to the last through simple bloody-mindedness or because they received no word to join the evacuation and remained in place as ordered until overrun; Middlebrook refers to his contributors reporting two small groups from the 7th KOSB who were left standing by but never called to withdraw, two sentries from the 10th Parachute Battalion left behind on isolated sentry duty and men from the 2nd South Staffords and RA anti-tank-gunners similarly forsaken in the LONSDALE Force area.[9] Some missed the evacuation because they were simply unaware it was happening. Captain The Reverend Arnold Pare, Chaplain at No. 1 Wing GPR, had not been informed of the withdrawal for whatever reason and slept through the night in the Hotel Schoonoord in spite of the British bombardment and the German attack on the Poles on the Stationsweg–Utrechtseweg crossroads. He awoke to an unnatural quiet to be informed by an RAMC orderly that the rest of the Division had gone during the night and who begged him to inform the wounded still in the building as the orderly lacked the nerve to do so.[10] One of the larger groups was Lieutenant Alan Green and his nineteen survivors from D Company 1st Border on the Van Borsselenweg, who had to be persuaded that the withdrawal had taken place during the night by Sapper Stanley Holdsworth and several others left behind. The point was proven by the arrival of German troops in D Company's position who carried the seriously wounded away in a captured Jeep, marched the walking wounded away and set Lieutenant Green and the able-bodied survivors to gathering up the weapons and equipment strewn around the vicinity.[11]

Kampfgruppe Harder ran into resistance as it moved on the embarkation point while advancing from the east along the Benedendorpsweg as did *Bataillon* Worrowski, possibly accompanied by tanks from *Panzer Kompanie 224*, moving in from the west. Lance-Corporal Harry Smith from the 2nd South Staffords was among a group led into a hollow in the riverbank for cover by an unnamed lieutenant; the latter was then hit in the side by a 20mm round when he stood to wave a makeshift white flag. A former German national among the group was prevailed upon to shout 'Cease fire' in German as the enemy closed in; the ploy worked as there was no more firing and a single German soldier armed with a rifle and a large, white 'Kaiser Bill moustache' came over the bank alone and led the party away.[12] The number of prisoners taken in the immediate aftermath of the evacuation varies between accounts. *Kampfgruppe* Harder reportedly captured 170 men from the throng that had missed a place on the boats to the south bank for example, while in his typically vainglorious and self-serving fashion *Hauptsturmführer* Sepp Krafft reported that his *SS Panzergrenadier Ausbildungs und Ersatz Bataillon 16* had taken fifteen officers and 580 Other Ranks prisoner 'in a keen attack in the morning', which was likely news to the other German units pressing into the largely empty British perimeter.[13] The prisoners included Private Jan Szubert from the Polish 3rd Battalion HQ who discarded his Sten but held onto his Colt .45 pistol until twice ordered to discard it by an SS officer 'in a uniform cleaner than a whistle' wielding a Luger pistol and Lieutenant Albert Smaczny and some of his men from No. 8 Company. Smaczny had remained at the *Transvalia* house as instructed, vainly awaiting the promised runner with the order to withdraw. After waiting for several hours during which the stream of British troops passing the Poles' positions had dried up, Lieutenant Smaczny despatched Cadet Lance-Corporal Bielawski to the nearest British command post. When that proved to have been abandoned apart from two medical orderlies and some wounded, he led his men down to the river where he released them to make their own way if they preferred. When the shooting started Lieutenant Smaczny tried to lead his remaining men back into the woods but they were intercepted by two German tanks and obliged to surrender.[14]

Some men tried to evade capture. Three officers from the 1st Border, Captain Barry Ingram from HQ Company and Lieutenants Arthur Royall and Patrick Stott from B Company dumped all their kit apart from compasses, torches and pistols and set off at around first light in search of a house to hole up in until dark but became separated after coming under German machine-gun fire. Royall and Stott were captured shortly thereafter but Captain Ingram not only found a suitable house, but one that contained the body of a dead Royal Artillery Captain whose small pack contained emergency rations, a wash kit, a copy of the *Sunday Express* from 17 September and fifty cigarettes and, best of all, an undamaged bedroom complete with silk pyjamas. After a refreshing sleep followed by a shave and leisurely reading of the newspaper over the rations Ingram dressed in civilian clothes found in the house, padding them out as they were rather oversized, and boldly attempted to bluff his way through the considerable German activity on the surrounding streets. He was eventually stopped by a more observant patrol which searched him and discovered his issue torch, at which point Ingram admitted to being a British officer and was taken prisoner.[15] Many more men had better luck and over time the area around Arnhem and Oosterbeek became host to several hundred Airborne soldiers who had either evaded capture or escaped and avoided being transported to Germany, often with the assistance of the Dutch Resistance or courageous individuals.

The St Elizabeth Hospital and the temporary hospital in the Dutch barracks at Apeldoorn proved good locations for escapees. Brigadier Gerald Lathbury simply walked out of the former as soon as he was able and rapidly made contact with other Airborne evaders in the area, while Brigadier Hackett was smuggled out in a car in broad daylight once his wounds had healed sufficiently to allow him to be moved; he was lodged at Ede, ten miles west of Arnhem with the de Nooij family. A quartet of Dutch women looked after him until the Dutch Resistance arranged to get him to safety across the Lower Rhine in February 1945.[16] At Apeldoorn Colonel Graeme Warrack RAMC and Lieutenant-Colonel Martin Herford RAMC had given parole that they would not try and escape but decided that this no longer applied once the Germans began winding down the temporary hospital for closure on 26 October 1944, and arranged to make their exits along with some of the medical staff. Lieutenant-Colonel Herford escaped on 16 October and reached the safety of British lines after nearly a week, bringing with him a nominal roll of the 1,500 Airborne casualties in German hands; he was subsequently awarded the Distinguished Service Order for his work during MARKET GARDEN.[17] Colonel Warrack 'escaped' by hiding in the cupboard in his room for fourteen days before emerging and making his way out of the by then deserted Dutch barracks. After being given shelter by a courageous Dutch family he made contact with the Dutch Resistance who arranged for him to cross the Lower Rhine to safety in company with Brigadier Hackett in February 1945. For his courage and actions at Oosterbeek he too was subsequently awarded the Distinguished Service Order.[18] Not all escape attempts were successful and despite the overall exemplary German behaviour during the bitter fighting some Airborne soldiers were killed by their captors after surrender. According to Middlebrook three officers – one from the Royal Engineers and two from the GPR – and two paratroopers were shot very shortly after being taken prisoner. Four more were killed outright and two mortally wounded on 23 September when a guard panicked and fired indiscriminately into a truck carrying prisoners as it passed through Brummen, ten miles north-east of Arnhem, after Majors Anthony Hibbert and Dennis Munford jumped from the vehicle in an attempt to escape. The shooting also killed one of the German guards and one of the mortally wounded was Major Anthony Cotterell, a pre-war journalist working for the Army Bureau of Current Affairs attached to the 1st Parachute Brigade, who died two days later. Major Munford was recaptured but Major Hibbert got away and crossed the Lower Rhine to safety on the night of 22 October 1944.[19] Three other Airborne Officers died after escape and recapture. Captain John Keesey from 16 Parachute Field Ambulance died on 2 October 1944 after being shot and wounded trying to escape from a hospital train in Apeldoorn, likely during the closure of the temporary hospital in the Dutch barracks there.[20] Lieutenant Raymond Bussell from the 3rd Parachute Battalion and Lieutenant Michael Cambier from 156 Parachute Battalion escaped together from a hospital train on 25 September, having been slightly wounded in the arm and foot respectively. They were executed by *Untersturmführer* Ludwig Heinemann of the *Sicherheitsdienst (SD)* in Vorden on 10 October 1944 after being recaptured in civilian clothes eight days earlier; Heinemann was subsequently hanged for this and other crimes in Arnhem on 10 February 1947.[21]

Operation BERLIN marked the effective end of the 1st Airborne Division's involvement in Operation MARKET GARDEN and all the men who had fought in Oosterbeek and successfully escaped across the Lower Rhine were repatriated to the bases in the UK from which they had set forth up to nine days earlier with such high hopes by the end of the month. First away appears to have been No. 1 Wing GPR HQ which was moved entirely by air. The Glider Pilots were trucked from Nijmegen at 10:00 to the forward airfield at Grave where they were shuttled to Brussels at 14:25 and then on again just under two hours later, arriving at Harwell at 19:11 on Wednesday 27 September 1944.[22] They were trailed the following day by the 21st Independent Parachute Company which, after being driven from Nijmegen to Louvain where they remained overnight, embarked on US C-47s at Brussels airport for the flight to Saltby at 15:00 from where they were trucked to their billets in Newark.[23] The bulk of the Division's survivors were flown back to Britain on Friday 29 September, again involving a move by motor transport from Nijmegen to Louvain where many had an overnight stop including an evening's leave in some instances; at least some men were billeted in an abandoned monastery and others in a large barracks. They were then trucked the ten miles or so to Brussels airport from where they were lifted back to Britain in a shuttle of Dakotas from RAF No. 233 and RCAF No. 437 Squadrons, which appear to have been delivering supplies and equipment on the outbound leg.[24] The lift also seems to have involved C-47s from the US 61st and 314th Troop Carrier Groups, considering the airfields some of the survivors were delivered to and that at least one unit War Diary specifically refers to being lifted by US aircraft.[25] If the War Diary entries are any guide the US airfields also took the trouble to provide the returning Airborne soldiers with a warm welcome. 1st Airborne Division HQ and Royal Artillery HQ elements were back at Cottesmore at 19:00 and Barkston Heath at 18:00 respectively on 29 September for example, those arriving at Barkston Heath enjoying a 'very good meal, RAF band, and beer'.[26] The 1st Airborne Reconnaissance Squadron landed at Saltby and was also greeted with a hot meal, while the 1st Airlanding Light Regiment RA and 9th (Airborne) Field Company landed at Barkston Heath at 13:00 and 18:30 respectively; both also dining well, and the RA contingent mention an RAF band; perhaps the band was all played out by the time the 9th Field Company reached the mess.[27] The 2nd South Staffords left Louvain for Brussels at midday, emplaned at 14:00 and landed at Woodhall Spa and two other airfields at 17:00, possibly carried in Dakotas belonging to RAF No. 233 Squadron.[28] The 1st Parachute Battalion was possibly alone in being moved in two increments, the Battalion's advance party flying from Brussels on 29 September. The much-reduced main body of the Battalion flew from Brussels at 10:00 on Saturday 30 September and landed at Saltby at 12:15 to another 'wonderful welcome'; this may also have been the last of the 1st Airborne Division's air movements.[29]

The movements of the 1st Airborne Division's seaborne tail unsurprisingly proved to be a more complicated and drawn-out affair. The 1st Airlanding Brigade HQ seaborne echelon was divided into two components, the first of which had been unloaded at the JUNO landing area at 06:30 on 17 August and remained in Normandy until 2 September when it made its way across France, Belgium and up the Airborne Corridor to Nijmegen; it then retraced its route to Normandy for return shipment at some point after 30 September. The second increment does not appear to have disembarked at Arromanches after sailing from Tilbury Docks on 22 September aboard the MV *Samhern*, and sailed back to Tilbury on 29 September after seven days aboard ship, arriving safely the following day.[30] Returning the Division's seaborne echelon was a more protracted process, involving as it did moving a thousand vehicles by sea.[31] The Division HQ seaborne echelon was originally alerted for a three-day road march to Arromanches for embarkation via the MULBERRY harbour there, beginning on 1 October 1944.[32] This was cancelled in favour of returning via Ostend in Belgium, which both saved time and the protracted road march. Loading at Ostend began at 09:00 on 3 October, with the vehicles moving to the port in increments via a concentration area at De Haan, on the coast six miles east of Ostend. The first increment disembarked at Tilbury Docks on 4 October and vessels were then despatched daily until the final increment arrived at Tilbury on 8 October 1944.[33]

With the British Airborne end of the battle effectively over there remained the reckoning. On 17 September 1944 the 1st Airborne Division's strength stood at 8,969 All Ranks, although it is unclear if this figure included or excluded personnel assigned to the Division seaborne tail, which had been despatched to France by sea six weeks earlier.[34] In addition there were 1,338 men from the Glider Pilot Regiment and 1,625 men from the 1st Polish Independent Parachute Brigade, a total of 11,932.[35] By Tuesday 26 September 1944 between 1,485 and 1,543 were dead, and 6,525 were either prisoners of war or evading capture on the north bank of the Lower Rhine.[36] The ratio of Airborne killed to wounded and/or missing was the conventional approximation of one to two; the Glider Pilot Regiment suffered between 219 and 229 killed from a combined total of 730 killed, wounded or missing for example, while the 1st Polish Independent Parachute Brigade lost between ninety-two and ninety-seven killed from a casualty total of 342.[37] 30 Corps losses totalled 1,480 killed, wounded and missing between 17 and 26 September.[38] The air effort to deliver and supply the 1st Airborne Division was costly, the RAF transport formations losing a total of sixty-eight machines, forty-four Stirlings from No. 38 Group and twenty-four Dakotas from No. 46 Group; of these, twenty-five were brought down by anti-aircraft fire and the remaining eight were downed by German fighters. A total of 238 RAF and RCAF aircrew were lost with the aircraft, of which 157 were killed and 81 became prisoners of war, while another 152 avoided capture to become evaders. In addition, seventy-nine RASC despatchers working in the downed aircraft were killed and a further thirty-one were captured.[39] The USAAF lost eleven C-47s delivering elements of the 1st Airborne Division and the Polish Brigade, four from the 314th Troop Carrier Group and seven from the 315th Troop Carrier Group, along with twenty-three aircrew killed and three captured; a further twenty-three evaded capture and made their way back to Allied lines.[40] German losses are unclear due to incomplete records but estimates suggest the units fighting at Arnhem and Oosterbeek suffered between 2,565 and 5,175 casualties, and between 6,315 and 8,925 for MARKET GARDEN overall.[41] Nor was the cost restricted to the combatants. An estimated 453 Dutch civilians were killed across the MARKET GARDEN battlefield – but their ordeal did not end with the Driel evacuation. On 23 September 1944 the Germans ordered around 100,000 Dutch civilians out of a zone north of the Lower Rhine, which they then systematically plundered for materials for their new defences. Civilian rations in the Netherlands were significantly and deliberately reduced by the Germans, resulting in the death of 18,000 Dutch civilians in the 'Hunger Winter' of 1944-1945.[42] It is unsurprising that Prince Bernhard of the Netherland's responded to Montgomery's claim that MARKET GARDEN was ninety per cent successful with the observation that his country could ill afford another Montgomery success.[43]

Operation BERLIN did not mark the end of the fight for all the Allied Airborne formations involved in Operation MARKET. Although it is frequently overlooked, the two US Airborne Divisions remained embroiled in the fighting along the Airborne Corridor for several weeks after the British 1st Airborne Division had been repatriated to the UK to rest and refit. The 82nd Airborne Division was not withdrawn from Holland until 11 November 1944 after fifty-six days in continuous action, while the 101st Airborne Division remained in Holland until almost the end of November 1944; both formations were then back in action in the Ardennes by the middle of December. The scale of loss suffered by the two US Airborne Divisions during their longer time in Holland was of a similar magnitude to that of the 1st Airborne Division. The 82nd

Airborne Division suffered 215 killed, 790 wounded and 427 missing, a total of 1,432 men while the 101st Airborne Division lost a total of 2,118 men, 315 killed, 1,248 wounded and 547 missing; in addition, 122 US glider pilots were lost, twelve killed, thirty-six wounded and seventy-four missing.[44]

Two of the bridges around which MARKET GARDEN had focussed did not outlast the official end of the operation either. On the night of 28-29 September 1944 *Kriegsmarine* combat swimmers succeeded in dropping a complete span of the Nijmegen railway bridge and also damaged the adjacent road bridge, whilst it was being guarded by a Close Bridge Garrison commanded by 43rd Division CRE Lieutenant-Colonel Mark Henniker.[45] The Arnhem road bridge may have survived being the centre of several days' desperate fighting but did not survive the attentions of the USAAF's 344th Bombardment Group, which dropped the structure into the Lower Rhine just over a week after lieutenant-Colonel Frost and his men had been finally overwhelmed. The destruction of the road bridge trapped the bulk of the German force south of the Lower Rhine, and prompted *Generalleutnant* von Tettau to establish a bridgehead on the south bank of the Lower Rhine two kilometres downstream from the Heveadorp ferry on 1 October 1944. In a virtual mirror image of events in Oosterbeek just a week before, a force commanded by *Hauptsturmführer* Heinrich Oelkers crossed the river and held out for ten days under near constant artillery and mortar fire backed by ground attacks from the 5th Dorsets and then units from the 101st Airborne Division. The German bridgehead was finally evacuated on 10 October 1944 and Oelkers was the last man out on a riddled inflatable dinghy.[46]

There remained two pieces of unfinished business connected to Operation MARKET GARDEN. The first was the fate of those marooned on the north bank of the Lower Rhine, estimated to number between 200 and 400 men.[47] Some had been left at the embarkation point when the evacuation was called off, others had either evaded capture or been captured and escaped earlier in the battle. Lieutenant-Colonel David Dobie from the 1st Parachute Battalion had been wounded and captured in the brutal fighting on the Onderlangs on 19 September for example; he ran out of the civilian hospital where he was taken for treatment while the guard was distracted and was taken in and treated by a Dutch doctor in Arnhem before making contact with the Dutch Resistance. He was then moved to Ede where he was closely involved in locating and gathering the Airborne evaders along with other officers, notably Major Digby Tatham-Warter from the 2nd Parachute Battalion.[48] Dobie was smuggled across the Lower Rhine and River Waal by the Dutch Resistance on the nights of 16-17 and 17-18 October 1944 carrying intelligence for British 2nd Army HQ, which decided to evacuate the evaders.[49] Dobie then played a key role in Operation PEGASUS, a joint effort to evacuate a large number of evaders involving the Dutch Resistance, a Belgian SAS team, senior officers among the evaders and the 2nd Battalion 506th Parachute Infantry Regiment, which had maintained a frontage on the Lower Rhine opposite Wageningen from 3 October 1944.[50] Arrangements were made with Major Tatham-Warter via the still-functioning local civilian telephone system, which remained free from German monitoring, while a fighting patrol from the 506th Parachute Infantry Regiment's Easy Company was to bring the evaders across the river covered by a pre-arranged artillery box barrage and using twenty-three British-supplied assault boats.[51] According to one source the assault boats and crews were provided by the 43rd Division, although it is unclear if they were drawn from 204, 260 or 533 Field Companies RE or a combination thereof.[52]

The operation was brought forward twenty-four hours to take advantage of the road traffic created by a German village evacuation operation at nearby Bennekom, and thus went ahead on the night of 22-23 October 1944. The Germans remained oblivious to what was going on and matters proceeded without a hitch, apart from the evaders losing their bearings and initially missing the place where the boats were waiting alongside a 'rather annoyed' Lieutenant-Colonel Dobie.[53] They were all were safely inside the 506th Regiment's lines on the south bank by 02:00 on 23 October.[54] The precise number of men brought across the Lower Rhine is unknown but there were between 138 and 150, amongst them ten Dutch volunteers for Allied service, four USAAF personnel, two escaped Soviet prisoners of war and a solitary soldier from the US 82nd Airborne Division; all were brought across the Lower Rhine safely bar one of the Soviet prisoners, who disappeared at some point.[55] At least 120 were personnel from the 1st Airborne Division including Brigadier Gerald Lathbury, commander of the 1st Parachute Brigade, Major Tatham-Warter and Major Anthony Deane-Drummond from the 1st Airborne Divisional Signals.[56]

Major Deane-Drummond's prior activities had been quite an adventure. After spending three days cut off in a German-occupied house near the Arnhem road bridge with a small party of men from the 3rd Parachute Battalion, he swam the Lower Rhine only to be captured by a German patrol and incarcerated in a temporary holding centre in a large house at Velp to the east of Arnhem, where he hid in a cupboard from 23 September until 4 October, at which time the Germans abandoned the house. Deane-Drummond then made contact with the Dutch Resistance and played a leading role in gathering and co-ordinating the activities of the Airborne evaders.[57] Buoyed by the success of Operation PEGASUS, a second large-scale evacuation was planned for the night of 18-19 November, code-named, logically enough, Operation PEGASUS II. Led by Major Hugh Maguire, an Intelligence Officer from the 1st Airborne Division Staff, the second effort involved around 130 men including a larger proportion of Dutch civilians and non-Airborne personnel. Matters did not proceed as planned. The evaders ran into a German artillery position en route to the river and lost a number of men killed, wounded or recaptured, and a German patrol stumbled upon the evacuation in progress when it finally went ahead, possibly over two nights; two more evaders were killed, one of them Major John Coke from the 7th KOSB, and the remainder were obliged to scatter after only seven men had crossed the river to safety.[58] There were no more large-scale efforts thereafter and the Dutch Resistance smuggled the evaders out of German-held territory on an individual or small group basis, with preference given to doctors, Glider Pilots, soldiers and airmen in that order; as we have seen, they included Brigadier Hackett and Colonel Warrack.[59] According to Urquhart they were carried to safety via canoe, a means used with some success by the Dutch Resistance, with the Allied units on the south bank of the Lower Rhine being briefed to look out for the flimsy craft; Hackett was greeted on the riverbank by an officer from the 11th Hussars bearing a celebratory bottle of brandy.[60]

The second piece of unfinished business was the hanging out to dry of Major-General Stanislaw Sosabowski and, by extension, his men of the 1st Polish Independent Parachute Brigade. While the survivors of the 1st Airborne Division were being feted, fed and permitted to rest in the reception centre in Nijmegen and then repatriated to Britain, their equally battle-worn Polish counterparts had been assigned further duties in Holland. A Warning Order from Browning's Forward Airborne Corps HQ had been received by the Polish Brigade at 12:00 on Monday 25 September, ordering it to march to Nijmegen the following day for reassignment.[61] The Poles duly left Driel as ordered at 09:00 on Tuesday 26 September in numerical order by Battalion in pouring rain and under heavy German artillery and mortar fire that inflicted further casualties, before arriving at the Nijmegen bridges at 15:00.[62] Major-General Sosabowski had gone ahead to Browning's HQ to receive his orders in person, where he fell asleep after being left waiting. In the brief interview that eventually followed, Sosabowski gave Browning the losses his Brigade had suffered since arriving in Holland, which totalled 342 casualties, twenty-three per cent of the Brigade's Officers and twenty-two per cent of the Other Ranks; Browning responded by assuring the Polish commander that his formation would be withdrawn to Britain as soon as possible but that the gravity of the situation required their continued presence in Holland. He then handed Sosabowski over to a staff officer who informed the Polish commander that his unit was to be employed in guarding temporary airfields near Neerloon, ten miles west of Nijmegen, and providing lines-of-communication security; to add insult to injury, the Poles were to be subordinate to Brigadier J. D. Russell's 157 Brigade, the sea tail of the 52nd Lowland Division, which was originally to have been flown into Deelen airfield as a rapid reinforcement for the 1st Airborne Division. Transport was provided to carry the Poles out to their new home at 18:30, with Brigade HQ in Neerloon and the 1st, 2nd and 3rd Battalions billeted in the nearby villages of Herpen,

Ravenstein and Overlangel respectively.[63] There they remained until 7 October 1944 when they were trucked in the wake of their British counterparts to Louvain. Part of the Brigade was then flown back to Britain from Brussels airport in small groups when spare aircraft capacity could be found, until the Poles' air priority was rescinded on 10 October. The remainder of the Brigade then began moving by road to Ostend at 03:40, where they were reunited with the Brigade's sea tail and then shipped back in Battalion increments aboard four landing ships over the next few days. The final increment docked at Tilbury at 02:00 on 15 October 1944.[64]

Unsurprisingly, Major-General Sosabowski did not take his latest humiliation lying down and immediately on arriving at Neerloon he formally requested Browning in writing that he be released from subordination to command of 157 Brigade due to the organisation of his unit and 'seniority of rank'. Browning replied justifying the matter by pointing to Polish losses and alleged disorganisation, and the fact that 157 Brigade 'badly needed a reserve' in case of emergency but sweetened the pill by agreeing to the Polish Brigade reverting to British Airborne Corps command 'with effect from 08:00 hrs. 29th Sept'. The Poles were nonetheless to 'maintain present dispositions and tasks, working in very close liaison with 157 Inf. Bde'.[65] Sosabowski certainly viewed the episode as a deliberate slight, but appears to have been more concerned at the possibility of his formation losing its independence and being co-opted by the British for use as regular line infantry; he specifically raised this concern with the Polish liaison officer attached to 21st Army Group HQ when the latter visited Neerloon.[66] This episode was surely a continuation of the treatment meted out to Sosabowski at the Valburg Conference on 24 September, and subsequent events were to confirm that this was part of a deliberate strategy to shift the blame for the failure of MARKET GARDEN away from the British high command onto the hapless Poles, Sosabowski in particular.

On 7 October 1944 Montgomery criticised the Polish Brigade for being unwilling to take risks, complained that it had performed extremely poorly at Driel and demanded it be removed from his command in a letter to the Chief of the Imperial General Staff (CIGS), Field-Marshal Sir Alan Brooke.[67] On 18 November, Browning accepted the Order of *Polonia Restituta* at the Polish GHQ in the Hotel Reubens in London in recognition of his assistance in the establishment of the Polish Parachute Brigade, a process in which he played a marginal role at best. Two days later, he sent a letter to the Deputy Chief of the Imperial General Staff, Lieutenant-General Sir Ronald Weeks, claiming that Sosabowski had been incapable of grasping the urgency of the situation at Driel, that he had been needlessly argumentative and unwilling to obey orders, and cited Horrocks and Thomas as witnesses to these and other misdemeanours. It ended by recommending that Sosabowski be removed from command of the 1st Polish Independent Parachute Brigade because of his temperament and inability to co-operate.[68] A copy of the letter was forwarded to Montgomery and another to the Polish Chief-of-Staff in London, General Stanislaw Kopanski; Kopanski passed his copy to Sosabowski at a meeting on 2 December 1944 and asked him for suggestions for service away from the Parachute Brigade. Sosabowski responded by calling for an examination of his conduct as an officer and commander and for Kopanski's backing, and was granted an audience with Polish President-in-Exile Wladyslaw Raczkiewicz on 7 December 1944. The President assured Sosabowski that his conduct had been exemplary, but pointed out that he and General Kopanski could see no option but to comply with the British request for political reasons. Major-General Stanislaw Sosabowski was therefore relieved of command of the 1st Polish Independent Parachute Brigade on 9 December with effect from 27 December 1944. His soldiers, unaware of the political machinations behind the removal, were reportedly stunned and the 2nd Battalion and Engineer Company based at Wansford and the 3rd Battalion at Peterborough refused to enter their cook houses in protest; Sosabowski defused the situation by inviting them to eat with him and made his final address to the Brigade at Wansford on 27 December.[69]

The fact that the Polish Brigade lost a quarter of its strength including ninety-two dead clearly shows there was no substance to any of this. Furthermore, in an interview with

Cholewczynski forty-four years after the event, Major-General Urquhart roundly praised the Polish paratroopers in a manner that also gives the lie to the allegations: 'I could not fault them for co-operation. I never had any worries about that. Everything I asked was done, unless there was a very good reason.'[70] There was also the fact that Sosabowski had been deliberately lied to by British 1st Airborne Corps HQ on 21 September over possession of the north end of the Heveadorp ferry before he and the bulk of his men were dropped blind onto an unsurveyed and unsecured landing zone. That aside, as Montgomery did not visit Driel during the battle he had no first-hand knowledge on which to base his claims that the Poles had performed poorly and he must therefore have been informed second-hand by Horrocks and Browning; his motivation for involvement in the collective scapegoating of the Poles was presumably an attempt to deflect some of the blame for the failure of MARKET GARDEN. Similarly, the hostile treatment meted out to Sosabowski at Valburg by Horrocks and Thomas was also based on second-hand knowledge, and their motivation for scapegoating the Polish commander was to distract attention from the poor performance of 30 Corps and its constituent formations, which was the primary reason for the failure of the GARDEN ground force to relieve the MARKET Airborne force in a timely manner, and thus for the failure of the operation as a whole. Browning's motivation in the pillorying of Sosabowski was more personal and straightforward, and was primarily because the Polish commander had been a long-standing obstacle to Browning's ambitions. Sosabowski had repeatedly rebuffed Browning's attempts to absorb the Polish Parachute Brigade into his Airborne fief from as far back as September 1941.[71] More recently he had publicly and repeatedly pointed out the flaws in the plans for Operation COMET and Operation MARKET GARDEN, the means by which Browning intended to cement his increasingly shaky place in the Allied Airborne Pantheon; most unforgivably of all (to Browning), events proved Sosabowski to be right on the money. The scapegoating of Sosabowski and his men was a spiteful, unwarranted and unforgivable slur on a competent and conscientious commander whose only crime was to refuse to play Whitehall politics to Browning's satisfaction, and upon a courageous body of men whose only failing was an inability to walk on water. It is therefore difficult to disagree with Middlebrook's view that the episode was 'a shameful act by the British commanders'.[72]

The battle of Arnhem has been described as a tragedy of errors although it might be more accurate to describe it as a succession of needless errors, and any tragedy lay in failing to address the ones that mattered. However, while errors of whatever type undoubtedly played an important if not key role in the failure of MARKET GARDEN, they were not solely responsible. A host of coincidences and other factors were involved, many of which were benign or relatively trivial and thus easily overcome in isolation, some of which were unavoidable but few if any were fatal in themselves. The problem was their combination and interaction across the timeframe of the operation, during which they coalesced into a series of reasons and events that, in conjunction with errors, ultimately led to failure.

Although it is frequently overlooked because of the focus on the 1st Airborne Division's activities north of the Lower Rhine, the primary reason MARKET GARDEN did not meet its stated aim was simply the failure of 30 Corps to reach Arnhem on schedule, or indeed at all. To a degree this was due to events outwith the GARDEN force's control, specifically the German destruction of the bridge over the Wilhelmina Canal at Son on 17 September and their stubborn defence of the south end of the Nijmegen road bridge. However, the underlying problem, a collective failure to move with the urgency the situation warranted, was well within 30 Corps' control and disjointed the operational schedule from the very outset. The Guards Armoured Division did not move off until 14:35 on Sunday 17 September, after the MARKET force had been delivered and thereby squandered eight hours of precious daylight as 30 Corps HQ had banned movement during the hours of darkness. This was despite the fact they were scheduled to cover the fifteen miles or so to the 101st Airborne Division at Eindhoven by nightfall on 17 September, which occurred at around 19:00. The Guards Armoured did not reach Eindhoven until 18:30 on 18 September despite minimal German opposition. This was twenty-four hours behind a schedule that was supposed to see them forty miles further on at Nijmegen, or on the approach to Arnhem, and the additional time required to erect a Bailey bridge over the Wilhelmina Canal extended the schedule shortfall to thirty-six hours. The same lack of urgency was on display when the 2nd Battalion 505th Parachute was poised to carry the Nijmegen road bridge in the evening of 19 September and again when the Grenadier Guards finally pushed tanks across the bridge on the evening of 20 September, when the north end of the Arnhem road bridge was still in British hands and the intervening ten miles virtually undefended. In halting for the night after crossing the bridge the Grenadier Guards were once again following set routine, the only difference being the presence of the more vociferous Lieutenant-Colonel Reuben H. Tucker and his 504th Parachute Infantry Regiment drawing attention to the inappropriateness of the Guards' behaviour. The Nijmegen example was compounded by the Guards Armoured Division's idiosyncratic system of permanently pairing tank and infantry battalions by regimental affiliation, which constrained operational flexibility and in this specific instance militated against maintaining a reserve for rapid exploitation, a breach of basic military principles. The repeated failure of the Guards Armoured Division to press on after crossing the River Waal marks the point where MARKET GARDEN failed as originally envisaged.

Lack of urgency was not the sole preserve of the Guards Armoured Division. The 43rd Division's advance up the Airborne Corridor was leisurely even allowing for German pressure and traffic congestion. It was content to sit in place for almost three days after reaching the Lower Rhine and demonstrated much more alacrity in bringing forward elements of the bridging train after the decision to evacuate the Oosterbeek pocket had been taken than it had hitherto. To be fair, the tendency was less apparent at the Battalion and Brigade level and appears to have emanated more from the top of the Division, where Major-General Thomas revelled in his acerbic manner and ignorance of the realities of Airborne operations, as exemplified by his behaviour toward Sosabowski and his radio exchange with Urquhart on 24 September. Collectively speaking, neither Division performed particularly impressively after crossing the River Waal, even allowing for the constricted battlefield and stiff German resistance. The distinct impression created by both formations was that their job was done on crossing the River Waal, and the more so because the 1st Airborne Division had not fulfilled its end of the mission by holding a crossing over the Lower Rhine. Responsibility for this lay not with Adair or Thomas, but on the next rung of the ladder with Lieutenant-General Horrocks, who appears to have permitted his Division commanders sufficient leeway to consistently contradict his orders for haste with impunity. Admittedly this lack of grip may have been the result of illness stemming from Horrocks being seriously wounded in a German air attack in North Africa in June 1943 whilst commanding 10 Corps, which put him out of action for fourteen months, before using his leverage as a Montgomery protégé to secure command of 30 Corps from CIGS Sir Alan Brooke in August 1944. He was obliged to stand down from his command for several days at the end of that month; his unhealthy demeanour drew comment from onlookers during MARKET GARDEN and on 28 December Montgomery was obliged to send Horrocks home on sick leave as 'during the last ten days he has been nervy and difficult with his staff and has attempted to act foolishly with his corps'.[73] Illness would explain Horrocks' failure to properly control his wilful senior subordinates. It would also explain the contradictions in his GARDEN orders and intentions. Responsibility does not lie solely with him, but also with his superiors who placed an unfit man in a Corps-command position and, by extension, the patronage system which the upper echelons of the British Army used to allot senior command positions.

At the upper level of the Allied Airborne Command a number of factors that are frequently perceived as errors were simply unavoidable under the prevailing circumstances. Launching MARKET in a no-moon period ruled out a night landing for example, and lack of illumination was also a factor in restricting flight operations to one lift per day. Flying two lifts per day would have involved aircraft taking-off and forming up before dawn or returning after dark, for which the US 9th Troop Carrier Command providing the bulk of the airlift lacked sufficient navigators and training. The post-D-Day expansion of aircraft numbers had also created a shortage of groundcrew to service, refuel and repair the aircraft in the turnaround time available. Similarly, delivering the 1st Airborne Division in three lifts over three days was unavoidable as there were simply insufficient transport aircraft to move all three Airborne divisions simultaneously in their entirety, although the 1st Airborne Division could and should have mitigated this with some judicious prioritising and tailoring of loads, if only because it was naïve in the extreme for the RAF planners in charge of the British end of MARKET to assume that the Germans would sit passively by for three days while the 1st Airborne Division availed itself of the same landing areas. On the other hand, although the RAF planners have been criticised for selecting landing areas so far from the 1st Airborne Division's objectives, this too was unavoidable because there were simply no suitable areas for the purpose closer to Arnhem, as is clear from an examination of contemporary maps and the fact that several hundred Airborne soldiers were able to reach the north end of the Arnhem road bridge within six hours of landing shows the distance from the landing area was not the crucial obstacle it is sometimes portrayed as being.[74] It was feasible to put a parachute brigade down at the south end of the Arnhem road bridge but this would have meant separating the formation from its glider-borne heavy equipment and most crucially its anti-tank guns, as the information available to the planners at the time showed the terrain south of the bridge to be soft polder riven with ditches and thus unsuitable for glider landings, and Frost's battle at the north end of the Arnhem road bridge clearly showed the crucial importance of anti-tank guns in permitting the otherwise lightly armed Airborne troops to maintain an effective defence. Landing Horsas carrying Jeeps and 6-Pounder guns on the Arnhem–Nijmegen highway south of the road bridge might have been feasible as a way of overcoming this, possibly as part of a glider *coup-de-main* effort to secure the bridge as envisaged for Operation COMET, but that was edited out of the MARKET plan.

Dispensing with the latter was arguably an avoidable high-level error, although putting a large force on the Arnhem road bridge at the outset might have prompted a stronger and more determined German reaction; it can be argued that Frost's party at the Arnhem road bridge only lasted as long as it did because the Germans initially concentrated on keeping reinforcement from the west and south at bay, rather than recapturing the north end of the bridge. A larger British presence at the bridge at the beginning might well have provoked a reordering of German priorities. Despite his lack of Airborne experience, Urquhart certainly thought the *coup-de-main* a worthwhile idea, which he unsuccessfully attempted to have to reinstated with the support of the commander of the Glider Pilot Regiment, Colonel George Chatterton. He was rebuffed by the RAF planners – and Air Vice-Marshal Hollinghurst in particular – on the grounds of some rather unconvincing evidence topped with the claim that any revision would add additional complication to an already complex air plan, and Browning backed Hollinghurst's judgement when Chatterton subsequently approached him directly. There is no evidence that Browning actually approached Hollinghurst or the planners – probably because of the personal stake he had in MARKET GARDEN going ahead – but he did ask Major-General Richard Gale for a second opinion, which he then chose to keep to himself when Gale backed Urquhart's position. The episode provides an object lesson in the consequences of allowing the RAF planners total control of Airborne operations until the Army force was on the ground, with no requirement to heed Army requirements or systemic machinery for challenging planning decisions.

Regarding the failure to reinstate the Arnhem *coup-de-main* into the MARKET plan, Browning was essentially powerless owing to the total control the RAF exercised over the planning and delivery process, but he was connected to a number of errors and these were largely committed because of personal ambition. Whilst ethically distasteful, Browning's deliberate suppression of intelligence on the German forces in the vicinity of Arnhem proved to be relatively benign in the event, for despite popular assumptions based on deliberate misinformation in the British Official accounts, the 1st Airborne Division was not facing anything like a single *SS Panzer Division* on 17 September, never mind two, and the bulk of the German armoured, infantry and artillery units employed at Arnhem and Oosterbeek were drafted in from elsewhere. The same cannot be said of Browning's appropriation of thirty-two Horsa gliders from the first lift into Arnhem to carry his Advanced 1st Airborne Corps HQ into Holland, the means by which he intended to remedy his total lack of operational Airborne experience and shore up his position at the top of the Allied Airborne tree. This removed sufficient gliders to carry almost an entire Airlanding infantry Battalion, decreased the 1st Airlanding Brigade's infantry strength by almost a third at a stroke and this from a first lift that needed every rifleman it could muster. However, Browning's most serious interference was his prioritising securing the Groesbeek Heights in their entirety over seizing the Nijmegen bridges and his specific order binding Gavin to that flawed prioritisation. Browning's thinking here is unclear, but was presumably rooted in his total lack of operational Airborne experience because while the Groesbeek Heights were tactically important, they were strategically incidental to the MARKET GARDEN mission, while the Nijmegen bridges were absolutely key. Failing to secure the Nijmegen bridges as top priority at the outset condemned the Guards Armoured and 82nd Airborne Divisions to days of house-to-house fighting and a daylight assault river crossing with all that entailed, and more importantly provided the Germans with an extended opportunity to demolish the Waal bridges. *Feldmarschall* Model did not take that tack because he envisaged using the structures as a conduit for a counter-attack, but if he had ordered the bridges destroyed in the four day period between the initial landings and the Allied crossing of the River Waal, then Operation MARKET GARDEN would have ended in immediate and irrevocable failure.

Browning's presence in Holland contributed little if anything to the prosecution of MARKET GARDEN that could not have been achieved from his HQ at Moor Park, although that would not have aided his bid to maintain his position in the Airborne hierarchy. Radio problems prevented him communicating effectively from his Forward Airborne Corps HQ before 30 Corps reached Nijmegen, and he appears to have spent most of his time thereafter subordinating himself to Horrocks rather than applying himself in support of the Airborne soldiers he had played a major role in placing in harm's way; the spectacle of him sleeping in a comfortable bed while the 1st Airborne Division was fighting and dying on the way back across the Lower Rhine is an unedifying image. Browning was also responsible for saddling the 1st Airborne Division with a commander with no Airborne experience whatsoever over better-qualified candidates as a sycophantic sop to Montgomery, with serious consequences discussed below, and his role in setting up Major-General Sosabowski as the fall guy was as distasteful as his comfortable sleep on the night of 25-26 September. It is perhaps gratifying to note that Browning's Machiavellian scheming did not bear the expected fruit. He was replaced as Deputy Commander of the 1st Allied Airborne Army by the infinitely more qualified Gale in December 1944 and never held another operational command. He was instead despatched to Burma to serve as Chief-of-Staff to the Supreme Commander South-East Asia Command, Lord Louis Mountbatten – a far more appropriate employment of his undoubted political talents – before being further side-lined to the War Office in 1946 to serve as a Military Secretary. Two years later he was quietly removed from the active list and made Controller and Treasurer to Princess Elizabeth's Household, a position he held until retirement in 1952. Operation MARKET, rather than being the apogee of Browning's career (and guarantor of his place in the Airborne canon), effectively marked the end of it.

While 30 Corps' failure to reach Arnhem in time was the primary reason for the failure of MARKET GARDEN, the second most salient reason was the 1st Airborne Division's failure to secure a crossing over the Lower Rhine in sufficient strength to hold out until relieved by ground forces. The elements of the 1st Airborne Division's first lift tasked to secure the Arnhem bridges were noticeably slow in rallying and moving off from the landing area despite the accurate, timely and unopposed nature of the landing, and this may have been at least to a degree due to the overconfident attitude displayed by the 1st Parachute Brigade's constituent units, as noted by several officers in the period between January and September 1944. The 1st

Parachute Brigade was not on the move until just over an hour-and-a half after landing and the 1st Airborne Reconnaissance Squadron until two full hours had passed; the latter's tardiness was directly responsible for it running into the very northern end of *Bataillon* Krafft's blocking line east of the landing area, which had been set up just minutes before. The Reconnaissance Squadron then compounded its tardiness by remaining in place for almost three hours exchanging fire with *Bataillon* Krafft before quietly withdrawing to the landing area after the Squadron commander was summoned away, thereby abandoning its potentially vitally important mission following a skirmish that cost two Jeeps and nine men. To be fair, subsequent events show this seeming reticence to be very much the exception for the Reconnaissance Squadron and more importantly for the 1st Airborne Division's units as a whole, up to the Battalion level. These without exception fought with skill, fortitude and aggression over and above what might have been reasonably expected; the fighting on the Oosterbeek perimeter, at the Arnhem road bridge and in the vicinity of the Onderlangs provides numerous examples of units fighting virtually to the point of destruction while maintaining cohesion and focus upon their assigned missions. This shows that once battle was joined, there was very little, if anything, wrong with the 1st Airborne Division at the lower level despite the overconfidence and incidents of indiscipline that occurred in the run up to MARKET GARDEN – the problems lay higher up the chain-of-command.

This was not universally the case at the Brigade level. Despite coming from a cavalry background and therefore lacking operational airborne and indeed infantry experience, Brigadier Hackett made a passable job of commanding the 4th Parachute Brigade before being laid low by a German mortar bomb. Similarly, Brigadier Hicks, who had served with the 1st Airborne Division in North Africa and Sicily, did a very sound job of commanding the 1st Airlanding Brigade in particularly difficult circumstances, including successfully executing the withdrawal plan, although his tenure as Division commander in Urquhart's absence is best classified as passively competent rather than one of a commander-in-waiting. The problems were actually pretty much confined to Brigadier Lathbury at the 1st Parachute Brigade. Although he was the Division's senior Brigade commander, Lathbury lacked operational experience having spent his time in staff, training or administrative appointments until leading the 1st Parachute Brigade's operation to secure the Primasole Bridge in Sicily in July 1943. There, as a result of his own and a parallel lack of institutional experience, Lathbury's plan amounted to a manual of how not to perform an Airborne operation and these same errors were replicated in his plan at Arnhem. Despatching his Brigade along three separate and widely spaced routes en route to half a dozen equally widely dispersed objectives resembled a training exercise rather than a scheme for execution in a shooting war. It dispersed the formation's collective combat power, militated against effective co-ordination, effectively ruled out any prospect of mutual support and obliged each Battalion to fight its own battle in isolation and, in the event, without the benefit of guidance from above. Had events unfolded according to plan, Lathbury's force would have been spread wide and thin, with a third of the Brigade isolated on the high ground north of Arnhem, a third dispersed in company packets holding the pontoon bridge, the Arnhem rail bridge and the German HQ in the centre of Arnhem, and the remainder holding the Arnhem road bridge. The plan was therefore a recipe for the Brigade's sub-units to be isolated, overwhelmed and defeated in detail, although events took a hand in the matter before that point was reached.

All this was exacerbated by Lathbury's tendencies toward autocratic leadership and micromanagement. Lathbury was responsible for the delay in his Brigade leaving the landing area because he deliberately held it back while all the motorised support elements were gathered in, although to be fair this may have been a reaction to his experience in Sicily. Whether or not, from virtually the instant the Brigade moved off Lathbury busied himself motoring between his units harassing his subordinate commanders for greater haste. He virtually took control of the 3rd Parachute Battalion over the shoulder of its commander, peremptorily ordering a

Platoon attack that cost needless casualties and caused needless delay, and then brought the 3rd Parachute Battalion's advance to a halt for the night after Urquhart arrived at its location on the western outskirts of Oosterbeek, an action which his Brigade Major later pinpointed as the point where the Brigade's mission, and by extension that of the 1st Airborne Division, failed. Thereafter, Lathbury reverted to being a virtual observer to proceedings, passively accompanying his equally inert Division commander with the 3rd Parachute Battalion column until he was seriously wounded in an ill-conceived attempt to rejoin his Brigade in the late afternoon of Monday 18 September. It is perhaps instructive to note that the elements of the 1st Parachute Brigade that reached the Arnhem road bridge or made the most progress toward it did so without the benefit of Lathbury's direct involvement.

The bulk of the responsibility for what befell the 1st Airborne Division, however, lay at the top with Major-General Urquhart, largely owing to his total lack of operational Airborne experience. On the plus side, there is no evidence Urquhart sought the appointment. He made a good impression on his new command as well as identifying some of its flaws, and his ability to get to grips satisfactorily with his new role in the months between assuming command and MARKET GARDEN was severely constrained initially by the widely dispersed nature of his command, the bout of malaria that hospitalised him in April and May 1944, and then by being obliged to attend the constant round of planning meetings for the series of fifteen aborted operations the 1st Airborne Division was slated for in the run-up to MARKET. The evidence nonetheless shows that his grasp of the realities of Airborne operations in comparison to conventional ground operations was less than optimal, and he does not seem to have properly understood that Airborne operations were and are frequently affairs that require the force involved to be tailored to the specific mission, and do not automatically require the entire panoply of Division and support elements to be deployed as a matter of course; had he been more practised, Urquhart might have sought to restrict his first lift to infantry, anti-tank and possibly artillery elements, as did the more operationally experienced US Airborne Division commanders. This would in turn have reduced the need to remain in place to protect the landing area for subsequent lifts, although this would also almost certainly have provoked a likely unwinnable conflict with the RAF planners. That aside, the tenuousness of Urquhart's grasp was apparent in his acquiescing to Browning's appropriation of gliders to cut into the already stretched infantry component of the first lift when Divisional or HQ elements could have been trimmed instead, and in his failure to clarify the succession of Division command until virtually on the steps of his Horsa and ensure his wishes were disseminated and acknowledged by his senior commanders. The potentially serious repercussions of this on the ground in Holland were only offset by the diplomatic skills of his Operations Officer Lieutenant-Colonel Mackenzie and because Brigadiers Hackett and Hicks were willing to put aside the personal for the greater good.

While Urquhart's lack of experience and understanding are mitigating factors and go some way to explaining his behaviour, they do not absolve him of responsibility for the string of poor and potentially fatal decisions he made in the initial stages of Operation MARKET, beginning with his precipitate reactions to rumours about the non-arrival of the 1st Airborne Reconnaissance Squadron that he made no real effort to verify, apart from summoning the Reconnaissance Squadron commander to Division HQ to clarify the matter. This led to the abandonment of the Squadron's supposedly vital *coup-de-main* mission and also suggests that Urquhart was viewing the matters through the prism of his conventional operational experience, given that it potentially involved Major Gough motoring back and forth across miles of enemy-held territory. Urquhart then left his HQ on the landing area to inform Lathbury of the supposed non-arrival of the Reconnaissance Squadron in person, leaving no word of where he was going or how he could be reached, in the process severed his link to his HQ by having his signaller retune the Jeep-mounted radio; it can argued that at this point he effectively abdicated command of the 1st Airborne Division. On finding Lathbury with the 3rd Parachute Battalion column near Oosterbeek, Urquhart chose to remain there, prompting Lathbury to halt that unit for the night. He then accompanied the 3rd Battalion column – still out of contact with his HQ and by his own admission as little more than a passive observer – into the western outskirts of Arnhem, where an attempt to regain his HQ ended with him trapped in an attic with a German armoured vehicle parked outside the front door. There he remained for twelve hours before finally regaining Division HQ at 07:25 on Tuesday 19 September after a forty-hour absence, during which the 1st Airborne Division had been blocked from its primary mission and compelled to fight for its life. Simply put, Urquhart did not make a single correct decision in his first two days on the ground in Holland, and this only changed when the battle switched from an Airborne assault to a conventional defensive infantry battle, where he performed creditably, especially in drawing up and executing the withdrawal across the Lower Rhine. He was demonstrably out of his depth in the initial stages of Operation MARKET and his virtual abandonment of his men on reaching the south bank of the Lower Rhine in order to report to Browning casts additional doubt on his judgement. That aside, the fault for all this lay not solely with the hapless Urquhart but also with Montgomery and Browning, for placing patronage above experience and proven competence when making high-level command appointments.

It only remains to deliver a verdict on whether MARKET GARDEN was feasible and worth the potential cost in men and materiel. It has become received wisdom that the operation was a lost cause doomed from the outset and by extension a convenient stick with which to beat Montgomery; it is often overlooked that British and US Airborne Forces were established and configured precisely to carry out these kinds of missions and, perhaps more relevantly, that the Germans had successfully prosecuted something very similar to MARKET GARDEN in May 1940. More importantly, while it is doubtful whether success would have led to the grand strategic stroke Montgomery envisaged, if only because Eisenhower was unlikely to have been willing or indeed able to allot the necessary resources, the evidence does not really support this negative verdict. Rather, it can be convincingly argued that MARKET GARDEN could well have achieved all its objectives if only because – despite all the bad luck, coincidences and errors – it was such a close-run thing. Despite its leisurely advance and concomitant lack of urgency, 30 Corps and specifically the Guards Armoured Division still came within a few miles of the Arnhem road bridge while Frost's men were still holding out. Had the Guards Armoured moved with more despatch from the beginning and kept to the set timetable as ordered, and had Gavin been permitted to secure the Nijmegen bridges at the outset as he originally intended, then 30 Corps ought to have been able to reach the Arnhem road bridge by midnight on 20 September, even allowing for the destruction of the Son bridge over the Wilhelmina Canal. On the Lower Rhine, approximately 740 Airborne soldiers from a variety of units, accompanied by numerous vehicles and guns, covered the seven miles or so from the landing area to the north end of the Arnhem road bridge in under six hours, and then held onto their foothold for eighty hours before being overwhelmed. With a more workable plan, less interference and more haste the 1st Parachute Brigade in its entirety might well have reached the road bridge, and a force around three times larger than Frost's on the objective would have permitted a larger and thus more defensible perimeter. All success required was a very slight shift in fortune and a similarly slight change in the congruence of factors, because the margin between success and failure really was that narrow.

Notes

Introduction

1. Patrol member names cited in Stephen Ambrose, **Band of Brothers**, pp.160-161
2. Dobie's forename is missing and his surname is misspelled 'Dobey' in the 101st Airborne Division's semi-official history and the error is repeated in Ambrose's account; the latter also uniquely dubs him 'The Mad Colonel of Arnhem'; *see* Leonard Rapport and Arthur Northwood Jr., **Rendezvous with Destiny**, p.400; and Ambrose, p.160
3. For details *see* for example Martin Middlebrook, **Arnhem 1944: The Airborne Battle**, pp.190-199
4. Details from Rapport & Northwood, p.400
5. The precise number and makeup of the PEGASUS evaders varies between sources; *see* Middlebrook, p.438; Rapport & Northwood, p.401; and David Truesdale, **Brotherhood of the Cauldron**, p.161
6. *See* Truesdale, p.161
7. *See* Ambrose, pp.161-162
8. Ambrose and Truesdale refer to the operation beginning at or shortly after midnight, whereas Rapport & Northwood refer to 01:00; s*ee* Ambrose, p.161; Truesdale, p.161; and Rapport & Northwood, p.400
9. *See* Rapport and Northwood, p.400
10. *See* Middlebrook, p.438

Chapter 1

1. *See* David Derbyshire, Science Correspondent, **Briton Defies Doubters to Pilot Parachute Designed in 1485**, Daily Telegraph, 19 April 2001 at http://www.telegraph.co.uk/news/uknews/1345122/Briton-defies-doubters-to-pilot-parachute-designed-in-1485.html, accessed 26/09/2008
2. *See* Aislinn Simpson, **Leonardo da Vinci Parachute from 1485 Finally has Successful Landing**, Daily Telegraph, 28 April 2008 at http://www.telegraph.co.uk/news/1905000/Leonardo-da-Vinci-parachute-from-1485-finally-has-successful-landing.html, accessed 26/09/2008
3. Quoted in Michael Hickey, **Out of the Sky: A History of Airborne Warfare**, p.9
4. *See* John Terraine, **The Right of the Line**, p.669
5. *See* Gerard M. Devlin, **Paratrooper!**, pp.3-7
6. *See* Devlin, pp.8-14
7. *See* Lee Kennett, **The First Air War 1914-1918**, p.46
8. *See* John H. Morrow, **The Great War in the Air**, p.239
9. Sometimes rendered Heinicke
10. For a picture of the Henecke harness *see* Peter Kilduff, **Germany's First Air Force 1914-1918**, p.13

11. *See* Devlin, p.21
12. *See* Bruce Quarrie, **Airborne Assault: Parachute Forces in Action 1940-1991** pp.26-28
13. *See* Quarrie, p.28
14. *See* Roderick Grant & Christopher Cole, **But Not In Anger: The RAF in the Transport Role**, pp.16-17
15. *See* Sir Walter Raleigh and H. A. Jones, **The War in the Air**, Volume V, pp.278-280; and Grant & Cole, pp.7-14
16. *See* Grant & Cole, pp.14-16, 208
17. *See* Vernon Blunt, **The Use of Airpower**, pp.168-169
18. Quoted from Maurice Tugwell, **Airborne to Battle: A History of Airborne Warfare 1918-1971**, p.18
19. *See* Lt. Col. James A. Bassett, 'Past Airborne Employment', **Journal of Military History**, Volume 12, No. 4, Winter 1948, pp.206-207
20. *See* David M. Glantz, **The History of Soviet Airborne Forces**, pp.4-12
21. *See* for example F. O. Miksche, **Paratroops: The History, Organisation and Tactical Use of Airborne Formations**, p.22
22. *See* **AIR 5/1253** Operations: Iraq, Chapters 1 to 13, 1918-1924; and Grant & Cole, pp.54-66, 80-83
23. *See* David Omissi, **Air Power and Colonial Control: The Royal Air Force, 1919 – 1939**, p.72
24. *See* Captain R.G. Thorburn, 'The Operations in South Kurdistan, March-May 1923', **The Army Quarterly**, Volume 31 (October 1935-January 1936), p.270
25. *See* Grant & Cole, pp.80-83
26. *See* Grant & Cole, pp.91-94
27. *See* Thorburn, p.275
28. *See* Grant & Cole, pp.56, 71-80, 91-99
29. *See* for example **British Military Policy Between the Two World Wars**, pp.24-25, 33
30. *See* John Kennedy, **The Business of War: The War Narrative of Major-General Sir John Kennedy**, p.xv
31. For aircraft details *see* Owen Thetford, **Aircraft of the Royal Air Force Since 1918**, pp.28-33, 136-137, 289-291, 513-514, 519-520
32. For details *see* Devlin, pp.23-26
33. For a contemporary reference, *see* 'Notes of the Week', **The United Services Review**, (16 June 1938), p.3; and Lieutenant-Colonel T.B.H. Otway, **Airborne Forces**, pp.16-17
34. *Basmachi*: Russian slang term for a brigand or raider, the activities of which were and remain endemic in Central Asia
35. *See* A. Borisov, 'Desant onto the Sand in Aircraft', **Vestnik vozdushnovo flota** (January 1929) pp.11-13; for a less detailed contemporary account that may well be describing the same operation *see* A. N. Lapchinskiy 'Airborne Landings', **Voyna i Revolyutsiya** (1930) Book 6, as printed in A. B. Kadishev (Ed) **Voprosy Taktiki v Sovetskih Voyennykh Trudakh 1917-1940** (Moscow: Voyenizdat, 1970), pp.348-354: cited in H.F. Scott and W.F. Scott (Eds.), The **Soviet Art of War**, pp.64-65. I am indebted to Dr James Sterrett for locating and translating the Borisov article
36. *See* Colonel N. Ramanichev, 'The Development of the Theory and Practice of the Combat Use of Airlanding Forces in the Inter-War Period', **Military-Historical Journal**, No. 10 (October 1982), p.72 (Russian language publication); also cited in Glantz, p.4. I am indebted to the late Professor John Erickson for providing a copy of the Ramanichev article, and to Dr James Sterrett for translating it.
37. *See* Glantz, pp.4-9, 32; for details of the 1936 Field Service Regulations, *see* Richard Simpkin, **Deep Battle: The Brainchild of Marshal Tukhachevskii**, especially Chapters. 12-16.
38. *See* Glantz, pp.17-22
39. For details of the Khalkin Gol fighting *see* Alvin D. Coox, **Nomonnhan: Japan Against Russia, 1939**, Chapter 30; and Glantz, pp.38-39
40. *Komsomol*: Communist Union of Youth; *Osoaviakhim*: Society for the promotion of Defence and the Furthering of Aviation and of the Chemical Industry of the USSR

41. *See* for example Hickey, p.15; and Glantz, p.13

42. *See* Miksche, p.17

43. *See* Hickey, p.15; and 'Soviet Film of Kiev Manoeuvres', **The Army, Navy and Air Force Gazette**, Vol. LXXVII (12 March 1936), p.206

44. *See* 'Notes of the Week', **The United Services Review** Vol. LXXVII (10 December 1936), p.1; and Major-General H. Rowan Robinson, 'Air Infantry: How Can This Development Assist Great Britain?', in ibid., (17 December 1936), pp.5-6

45. *See* Miksche, p.19

46. LOPP: League for National Air Defence

47. *See* George F. Cholewczynski, **Poles Apart: The Polish Airborne at the Battle of Arnhem**, p.47.

48. Details from interview with Lieutenant-Colonel Jan Jozef Lorys (retired) during an interview conducted at the Polish Institute and Sikorski Museum, Prince's Gate, London, on 16 June 1998. Colonel Lorys participated in parachute training as an officer cadet in Poland before 1939, and later served with the 1st Polish Independent Parachute Brigade, including a liaison tour to observe airborne training in the United States. I an indebted to both Colonel Lorys and his wife, whose assistance proved invaluable in translating the present authors regional English accent, and also to Mr Andrzej Suchcitz, Keeper of Archives at The Polish Institute and Sikorski Museum, for both making the interview possible, and locating relevant files from his archive

49. *See* Cholewczynski, p.47

50. *See* Manfred Zeidler, **Reichswehr und Rote Armee 1920-1933** (Oldenbourg: Beitrage zur Militärgeschichte, 1994), p.215; I am indebted to Professor Hew Strachan for drawing my attention to this work, and for taking the time to translate the appropriate sections.

51. *See* Quarrie (airborne Assault), p.29

52. For details of Student's involvement, *see* Zeidler, pp.71, 107, 138-140, 161, 174, 272

53. *See* Callum MacDonald, **The Lost Battle: Crete 1941** (London: Papermac, 1995), p.15

54. For the Commandments in full, *see* Hickey, pp.21-22

55. *See* MacDonald, p.18

56. For a brief but compelling reappraisal of this ideological element *see* MacDonald, pp.304-306

57. *See* for example James Lucas, **Storming Eagles: German Airborne Forces in World War II** (London: Grafton, 1990), pp.370-371

58. Lucas (Storming Eagles), pp.33-34; MacDonald, **The Lost Battle,** p.17; and Cajus Bekker, **The Luftwaffe War Diaries** (New York: MacDonald, 1966), pp.124—125

59. Glantz, pp.41-43, especially the organisation details on p.43

60. *See* for example Richard Wiggan, **Operation Freshman: The Rjukan Heavy Water Raid 1942** (London: Kimber, 1986); and Kevin Shannon and Stephen Wright, **One Night in June: The Story of Operation Tonga, the Initial Phase of the Invasion of Normandy, 1944** (Shrewsbury: Airlife, 1994)

61. Lucas, **Storming Eagles**, p.33; and Bekker, p.118

62. *See* Bekker, pp.58-59; and Edmund L. Blandford, **Green Devils – Red Devils: Untold Tales of the Airborne in World War II** (London: Leo Cooper, 1993), pp.34-35

63. *See* MacDonald, **The Lost Battle**, pp.29-30

64. *See* Blandford, pp.35-36

65. *See* Bruce Quarrie, **German Airborne Troops 1939-45** (London: Osprey, 1983) pp.7-8; Blandford, pp.36-38; and MacDonald, **The Lost Battle**, p.30

66. Glider numbers and troop total cited in MacDonald, **The Lost Battle**, p.26, and Blandford, pp.47-48; the latter provides a group by group breakdown. Quarrie cites a figure of 438; the difference appears to arise from the latter including the glider pilots & co-pilots; *see* Quarrie (German Airborne Troops), p.8

67. for a detailed account *see* for example Bekker, pp.121-128; and Lucas, **Storming Eagles**, pp.36-46

68. for details of the scheme in its entirety, *see* **Militargeschichtliches** Volume II, pp.275-276; and Hickey, op cit., p.48

69. Bekker, p.132

70. *See* for example Bekker, pp.130-139; Lucas (Storming Eagles), pp.48-52

71. *See* for example MacDonald, **The Lost Battle**, p.34; and Blandford, pp.45-46

72. *See* Karl-Heinz Frieser, **The Blitzkrieg Legend: The 1940 Campaign in the West** (Annapolis: Naval Institute Press, 2005), pp.122-127

73. *See* Major L. F. Ellis **The War in France and Flanders 1939-1940** (London: HMSO, 1953) pp.244-246. 305

74. Figures calculated from statistics in Ellis (France and Flanders), pp.326-327

75. *See* Bekker, pp.149-150

76. *See* Blandford, p.46

77. MacDonald, **The Lost Battle**, p.37

Chapter 2

1. *See* Roman Jarymowycz, **Tank Tactics from Normandy to Lorraine**, p.201

2. Figures cited in Jarymowycz, p.198

3. Figures cited in Evan McGilvray, **The Black Devils' March: A Doomed Odyssey: The 1st Polish Armoured Division 1939-45**, p.54

4. Figures from United Kingdom National Archive (UKNA) File **WO 106/4348** Operational Research in North West Europe 1944 June-1945 July, Reports 17 and 79; cited in Militärgeschichliches Forschungsamt, Freiburg (Eds), **Germany and the Second World War, Volume VII: The Strategic Air War in Europe and the War in the West and East Asia 1943-1944/5**, p.613; the British official history quotes slightly different totals of 344, 2,447 and 252 respectively. The discrepancy may arise from differing definitions; *see* Major L. F Ellis, **Victory in the West, Volume I: The Battle of Normandy**, pp.447-448

5. Figure cited in James Lucas and James Barker, **Killing Ground: Battle of the Falaise Gap, August 1944**, p.160

6. Account quoted in Wilhelm Tieke, **In the Firestorm of the Last Years of the War: II SS Panzerkorps with the 9. and 10. SS-Divisions 'Hohenstaufen' and 'Frundsberg'**; cited in Michael Reynolds, **Sons of the Reich: The History of II SS Panzer Corps in Normandy, Arnhem, The Ardennes and on the Eastern Front**, p.93

7. The British official history refers to the weather clearing on 25 August, but Reynolds' more recent work drawing on German official records clearly states that inclement weather made it difficult for Allied aircraft to maintain the tempo of attack on the cross-Seine traffic. The latter also fits the chronology of 9 & 10 SS Panzer Divisions' movements; *see* Ellis, **Volume I: The Battle of Normandy**, p.455; and Reynolds, p.92

8. *See* Reynolds, p.94

9. *See* Ellis, **Victory in the West Volume I: The Battle of Normandy**, pp.454-455

10. Figures cited in Major-General G. L. Verney DSO MVO **The Guards Armoured Division: A Short History**, p.67

11. ENSA: Entertainments National Service Association. Set up in 1939, ENSA was intended to provide entertainment for British Armed Services personnel under the auspices of the Navy, Army and Air Force Institute, better known as the NAAFI. While ENSA employed stars like Gracie Fields and George Formby, the scale of its task also obliged it to use less accomplished acts, leading to a popular reworking of the acronym to 'Every Night Something Awful'; despite this, ENSA played a key and widely acknowledged role in maintaining the morale of British personnel across the North-West European campaign

12. *See* **WO 171/376** Guards Armoured Division War Diary, entries for 16, 20 & 23/08/1944

13. *See* B. D. Wilson, **The Ever Open Eye**, pp.57-58

14. *See* Verney, p.69

15. *See* Robert Boscawen, **Armoured Guardsman: A War Diary June 1944-April 1945**, entries for 12-28 August 1944, pp.93-101

16. **WO 171/376** Guards Armoured Division War Diary, entry for 27/08/1944

17. *See* Ellis, **Victory in the West Volume I: The Battle of Normandy**, pp.465-467

18. Reynolds, p.95

19. *See* Patrick Delaforce, **The Black Bull: From Normandy to the Baltic with the 11th Armoured Division**. P.114

20. *See* ibid., p.120

21. *See* **WO 171/376** Guards Armoured Division War Diary; Guards Armoured Division Intelligence Summary No. 58, 23:00 Hours, 06/09/1944, Appendix A, 'General Eberbach, Second Army Intelligence Summary No. 89'

22. *See* Reynolds, p.95; Ellis, **Victory in the West Volume I: The Battle of Normandy**, p.470; and Delaforce, pp.118-120

23. *See* Verney, p.78

24. *See* Reynolds, p.96

25. *See* **WO 171/1256** 2 Irish Guards (Armoured Battalion) War Diary Jan.-Dec., entry for 01/09/1944

26. *See* Reynolds, pp.96-97

27. *See* Martin Blumenson, **Breakout and Pursuit**, p.681

28. *See* Robert J. Kershaw, **It Never Snows in September**, pp.11-17

29. *See* Tieke, p.218; cited in Reynolds, p.97

30. *See* Kershaw, pp.19-20; and Blumenson, pp.682-683

31. *See* Reynolds, pp.97-98

32. *See* **WO 171/376** Guards Armoured Division War Diary, entry for 27/08/1944; and Wilson, p.59

33. **WO 171/376** Guards Armoured Division War Diary, entry for 31/08/1944

34. For an eyewitness account *see* Boscawen, pp.109-110

35. *See* **WO 171/1256** 2nd (Armoured) Battalion Irish Guards War Diary, entry for 01/09/1944; and Verney, pp.78-79. Lieutenant Swann is interred in Lille South Cemetery, Plot 5, Row A, Grave 5

36. *See* Verney, p.83

37. *See* ibid., p.82; and Wilson, pp.68-72

38. *See* **WO 171/376** Guards Armoured Division War Diary, entry for 04/09/1944

39. *See* Boscawen, p.117

40. According to the Guards Armoured Division War Diary, fuel stocks were as follows: 1 September = 80 miles, 2 September = 140 miles, 3 September = 110 miles, 4 & 5 September = no figs available, 6 September = 150 miles; *see* **WO 171/376** Guards Armoured Division War Diary, Summary of Events for September 1944, entries for 02 & 06/09/1944

41. *See* Verney, pp.73-74

42. *See* **WO 171/1256** 2 Irish Guards (Armoured Battalion) War Diary, entry for 04/09/1944

43. *See* Verney, p.89

44. 30 Corps was assigned two lines of advance, via Eindhoven-Grave-Nijmegen-Arnhem and Tilburg-Zaltbommel-Renkum; *see* Ellis, **Victory in the West Volume II: The Defeat of Germany**, p.7

45. *See* Verney, p.90

46. *See* Kershaw, pp.21-22

47. *See* Verney, p.53

48. *See* **WO 171/376** Guards Armoured Division War Diary, Appendix KKK, Narrative 1 – 30 September 1944, entry for 07/09/1944; and Ellis, **Victory in the West Volume II: The Defeat of Germany**, footnote 2, p.12

49. *See* Verney, pp.90-95; and Ellis, **Victory in the West Volume II: The Defeat of Germany**, p.12

50. Tank loss figures cited in **WO 171/376** Guards Armoured Division War Diary, Appendix KKK, 'Narrative 1 – 30 September 1944', entry for 07/09/1944

51. *See* Boscawen, p.120

52. *See* Verney, p.93

53. For full details of Sergeant Major Cowley's award citation *see* **WO 373/51** Combatant Gallantry Awards, 01/03/1945 (part)

54. ee Verney, pp.93-94; and **WO 171/376** Guards Armoured Division War Diary, Appendix KKK, 'Narrative 1 – 30 September 1944', entry for 9/09/1944

55. *See* Boscawen, p.119

56. *See* Verney, pp.91-94

57. for details of the kit bag and the Eureka/Rebecca equipment *See* Lieutenant-Colonel T.B.H. Otway DSO, **Airborne Forces**, Appendix 'D', pp.405-406, and Appendix 'E', pp.410-411

58. *See* **WO 171/594**, 4th Parachute Brigade War Diary, entries for 08–0 9/04/1944, and end of month notes April 1944, 'Exercise DOROTHY – Brigade Parachute Exercise with USAAF Aircraft'

59. *See* Clay Blair, **Ridgway's Paratroopers**, p.74

60. *See* James M. Gavin, **On to Berlin**, pp.82-83

61. *See* Blair, pp.34-35, 215-216

62. *See* Major-General R. E. Urquhart, CB, DSO, **Arnhem**, p.15

63. *See* for example William F. Buckingham, **Paras: The Birth of British Airborne Forces**, pp.191-192

64. for a detailed account of the thinking behind the establishment of the 1st Allied Airborne Army, *see* Otway, pp.201-206

65. *See* Lewis H. Brereton, **The Brereton Diaries**, pp.308-309; cited in Blair, p.299

66. *See* Blair, p.299

67. For the US perspective on the dispute, *see* Blair, pp.320-321; for the British, see Geoffrey Powell, **The Devil's Birthday**, p.39

68. For details, *see* Blair, pp.298-299

69. *See* Otway, pp.211-213

70. Withdrawal dates and casualty figures cited in Blair, pp.295-296; and Leonard Rapport & Arthur Norwood Jr., **Rendezvous with Destiny**, p.249

71. Sometimes rendered TRANSFIGURE

72. *See* **WO 171/1248**, 21st Independent Parachute Company War Diary, entries for 04, 06 & 10/08/1944; and **WO 171/1236**, 1st Parachute Battalion War Diary, entry for 10/08/1944

73. *See* **WO 171/1236** 1st Parachute Battalion War Diary, entry for 12/08/1944; and **WO 171/1237** 2nd Parachute Battalion War Diary, notes on sea-tail detachment in August 1944 section

74. *See* diary entries entitled 'Sergeant Kosimaki's Summer', in Rapport & Northwood, p.258

75. *See* Otway, p.211

76. *See* ibid., p.210

77. *See* **WO 171/1236** 1st Parachute Battalion War Diary, entries for 22, 24 & 26/08/1944

78. *See* **WO 171/1236** 1st Parachute Battalion War Diary, **WO 171/1237** 2nd Parachute Battalion War Diary and **WO 171/1248** 21st Independent Parachute Company War Diary, entries for August 1944

79. *See* diary entries entitled 'Sergeant Kosimaki's Summer', in Rapport & Northwood, p.259

80. *See* Blair, pp.318-319

81. *See* Omar N. Bradley, **A Soldier's Story** (New York: Holt, Rinehart & Winston, 1951), pp.401-403; cited in Blair, p.319

82. *See* **WO 171/1248** 21st Independent Parachute Company War Diary, entry for 29/08/1944

83. *See* **WO 171/1236** 1st Parachute Battalion War Diary, **WO 171/1237** 2nd Parachute Battalion War Diary, entries for 29/08/1944 & 31/08/1944 respectively; and diary entries entitled 'Sergeant Kosimaki's Summer', in Rapport & Northwood, p.259

84. *See* Powell, p.39

85. *See* Blair, p.320

86. *See* Stanislaw Sosabowski, **Freely I Served**, p.140; **WO 171/592**, 1st Parachute Brigade War Diary, entry for 05/09/1944; and **WO 171/1247**, 156 Parachute Battalion War Diary, entry for 07/09/1944

87. *See* **WO 171/1244**, 11th Parachute Battalion War Diary, entry for 01/09/1944

88. *See* **WO 171/1238**, 3rd Parachute Battalion War Diary, entries for 04 & 06/09/1944

89. *See* **WO 171/1236**, 1st Parachute Battalion War Diary, entry for 07/09/1944.

90. *See* **WO 171/1237** 2nd Parachute Battalion War Diary, 'Order for Operation Comet (Copy No. 18)' dated 07/09/1944

91. Hackett's comments are cited in Peter Harclerode, **Arnhem: A Tragedy of Errors**, p.54

92. *See* Urquhart, p.17; and Martin Middlebrook, **Arnhem 1944**, p.8

Chapter 3

1. *See* **WO 219/2506**, SHAEF Planning paper 'Post-Neptune Courses of Action After Capture of Lodgement Area'; cited in Carlo D'Este, **Decision In Normandy**, p.464
2. For details *see* for example Gordon A. Harrison, **Cross Channel Attack**, pp.78, 188, 438, 441
3. *See* Major L. F Ellis, **Victory in the West, Volume I: The Battle of Normandy**, pp.291-292
4. Id., **Victory in the West, Volume II: The Defeat of Germany**, pp.14-15
5. Figures cited in Martin Blumenson, **Breakout and Pursuit**, p.691
6. *See* Powell, **The Devil's Birthday**, p.24
7. *See* for example Ellis, **Victory in the West, Volume II: The Defeat of Germany**, pp.24-25
8. *See* George S. Patton, **War as I Knew It**, p.125; cited in Carlo d'Este, **Decision in Normandy**, p.468
9. *See* Blumenson, p.696
10. *See* ibid., pp.669-670
11. For a detailed account of the fight for Fort Driant, *see* Hugh M. Cole, **The Lorraine Campaign**, pp.264-275
12. *See* Blumenson, p.670
13. *See* Ellis, **Victory in the West, Volume II: The Defeat of Germany**, p.25
14. For Tedders's attendance *see* ibid., p.21
15. For establishment of SHAEF Forward HQ to Portsmouth from the main SHAEF HQ at Bushey Park near Hampton Court Palace in London in May 1944 see Ellis, **Victory in the West, Volume I: The Battle of Normandy**, pp.37, 139; for relocation of SHAEF Forward HQ to Granville *see* Stephen E. Ambrose, **Citizen Soldiers**, p.92
16. For the Leigh-Mallory telephone calls *see* D'Este, p.466; for the delay in despatching signals *see* Powell, p.24
17. *See* D'Este, p.466
18. Quote from Chester Wilmot, **The Struggle for Europe**, p.489; cited in Powell, p.24
19. Quoted from Bernard Law Montgomery, Viscount Montgomery of Alamein, **The Memoirs of Field Marshal the Viscount Montgomery of Alamein K.G.**, p.293; cited in Powell, p.26
20. Quotes from Tedder's communication to Portal cited in Ellis, **Victory in the West, Volume II: The Defeat of Germany**, pp.21-22
21. *See* extracts from telegrams from Montgomery to Eisenhower dated 11 September 1944 and from Eisenhower to Montgomery dated 13 September 1944 cited in ibid., pp.22-23
22. For a detailed discussion of events in this period, *see* D'Este, pp.467-475
23. *See* Ellis, **Victory in the West, Volume II: The Defeat of Germany**, p.22
24. *See* extract from undated telegram from Montgomery to the Vice Chief of Imperial General Staff reproduced in Ellis, **Victory in the West, Volume II: The Defeat of Germany**, pp.23-24
25. For details of Montgomery's M525 Directive to 2nd Army *see* A. D. Harvey, **Arnhem**, p.26
26. *See* Powell, p.26
27. *See* ibid., p.25
28. *See* for example the television documentary **Great Battles of World War II: Arnhem**, broadcast on UK Channel 5 on 23/08/2001
29. *See* for example Powell, p.25
30. *See* Christopher Hibbert, **Arnhem**, p.50
31. for a detailed account of this from the Dutch perspective, *see* Cornelius Ryan, **A Bridge Too Far**, pp.23-35
32. *See* for example ibid., p.93; Powell, p.29; and Middlebrook, p.11
33. *See* Ryan, pp.93-94
34. *See* Urquhart, **Arnhem**, p.4
35. *See* Baynes, **Urquhart of Arnhem**, p.87
36. *See* for example Powell, pp.29-30; and Baynes, p.87

37. *See* Baynes, p.85
38. *See* Ryan, p.94
39. *See* Harvey, p.7
40. *See* Baynes, p.87
41. *See* Powell, p.39; and Blair, **Ridgeway's Paratroopers**, p.320
42. According to Baynes the outline plan was drawn up by Dempsey, whereas Powell attributes it to Montgomery; *see* Baynes, p.87; and Powell, p.29
43. *See* Urquhart, pp.1-4
44. *See* Gavin, **On to Berlin**, p.144
45. *See* Baynes, p.87
46. Quote from **WO205/693** Operation Market Garden: Reports and Instructions; also quoted in Powell, p.30
47. For a graphic illustration of this scattering *see* Harrison, **Cross Channel Attack**, Map IX, '101st Airborne Division Drop Patterns, 6 June 1944'; and Map X, '82nd Airborne Division Drop Pattern, 6 June 1944', between pp.104-105
48. Peter Harclerode, **"Go to It!" The Illustrated History of the 6th Airborne Division**, p.71
49. *See* Shannon & Wright, **One Night in June**, pp.112-113
50. Quote from Gavin, **Airborne Warfare**, p.93; cited in Powell, p.77
51. Squadron figures cited in Otway, **Airborne Forces**, p.265; Otway erroneously refers to No. 38 Group providing ten rather than nine squadrons; for overall aircraft total *see* Powell, p.35
52. For details *see* Middlebrook, Appendix 3, 'Order of Battle, 38 and 46 Groups RAF and RASC Air Despatch Units', pp.462-463
53. For the 130 figure *See* Powell, p.33; for USAAF Group details *see* Middlebrook, Appendix 4 'Order of Battle, US Air Units Carrying British and Polish Parachute Troops on Operation "Market"', p.464
54. Aircraft figures from Powell, p.35; and Middlebrook, p.75
55. *See* **WO 219/319** Operation Market: Order of Battle and Plan; **AIR 37/260** No. 38 Group (38 Wing): Operation 'Market: Orders and Instructions; and Powell, p.34
56. *See* Blair, pp.199-200
57. *See* Baynes, p.92
58. *See* **AIR 37/418** 'No. 38 Group (38 Wing): Report of British Airborne Effort in Operation "Market" by Nos. 38 and 46 Groups'
59. *See* for example Middlebrook, p.443; Harvey, p.180; and Harclerode, **Arnhem: A Tragedy of Errors**, p.162-163
60. *See* for example Baynes, pp.91-92; and William F. Buckingham, **Arnhem 1944: A Reappraisal**, p.67; having reviewed the evidence, the present author has revised his opinion as laid out in the text
61. *See* Blair, pp.199, 220
62. *See* ibid., p.201
63. *See* Gavin, **On to Berlin**, pp.146-147
64. *See* Rapport & Northwood, **Rendezvous with Destiny**, pp.263-264
65. *See* Blair, pp.327-328, endnote referring to a private communication from Cutler
66. According to Powell, a copy of an alleged *flak* map showing the location of approximately a hundred gun positions was given to Major John Frost after the war, but its provenance and accuracy are open to doubt; *see* Powell, p.36
67. *See* **AIR 37/979** No. 38 GROUP (38 Wing): Operation Order No. 524: Operation 'Comet'; also cited in Powell. p.36
68. *See* Harclerode, **Arnhem: A Tragedy of Errors**. p.51; unfortunately there are no references in this work to indicate the source of information
69. *See* Kershaw, **It Never Snows in September**, p.73
70. *See* **WO 219/319** Operation Market: Order of Battle and Plan
71. *See* Urquhart, pp.6-7

72. *See* **AIR 2/7338**, paper from Air Ministry DMC Goddard to various AM recipients, 'Provision of Airborne Forces – Air Ministry Aspect', dated 23/12/1940
73. *See* for example Urquhart, p.7; and Powell, p.35
74. *See* Urquhart, pp.6-7; and Harclerode, **Tragedy of Errors**, p.54
75. *See* Harvey, p.45
76. Conversation between Browning and Chatterton cited in Harclerode, **Tragedy of Errors**, pp.51-52. Interestingly, Chatterton makes no mention of this in his combined memoir and history of the Glider Pilot Regiment, **The Wings of Pegasus**
77. According to Middlebrook, Gale confided this with the proviso that it was not to be revealed while any of those involved were alive. Norton passed the information to Middlebrook in March 1992; *see* Middlebrook, p.18, footnote 5
78. Major Urquhart was no relation the commander of 1ˢᵗ Airborne Division, Major-General Roy Urquhart
79. *See* Brian Urquhart, **A Life in Peace and War**, p.73; Middlebrook, pp.64-66; and Harvey, p.34
80. *See* for example **WO 171/393**, 1 Airborne Division War Diary, '1 Airborne Division Planning Intelligence Summary No.1'
81. Quoted from Otway, p.293
82. *See* Ellis, **Victory in the West, Volume II: The Defeat of Germany**, p.47
83. *See* Kershaw, p.28; and Reynolds, pp.102-103
84. *See* Powell, p.46
85. *See* Middlebrook, pp.66-67; and Powell, pp.46-47

Chapter 4

1. Twenty figure cited in Dugdale, **Panzer Divisions**, p.93; cited in Reynolds, **Sons of the Reich**, footnote 21, p.99
2. *See* Reynolds, pp.97-98
3. Figures cited in Kershaw, **It Never Snows in September**, p.38; and Reynolds, p.101; the former refers to this as the combined total for *II SS Panzerkorps*, whereas the latter infers it applied to each division. It is also unclear if this figure includes or excludes the personnel detached with *Kampfgruppe* Heinke
4. *See* Kershaw, p.104
5. *See* ibid., p.28; and Reynolds, pp.102-103;
6. *See* Kershaw, p.43
7. *See* ibid., p.40
8. *See* Ryan, **A Bridge Too Far**, pp.131-133
9. *See* Reynolds, p.102 and endnote 15, p.112; and Zwarts, **German Armoured Units at Arnhem**, p.16
10. in some accounts Gräbner's forename is given as Paul; vehicle types and numbers cited from TO&E charts in Zwarts, p.4
11. *See* Ryan, p.134
12. Figures cited in Kershaw, p.41
13. *See* ibid., p.104
14. Testimony from *Rottenführer* Paul Mueller, *SS Panzergrenadier Regiment 20*; cited in Kershaw, p.74
15. *See* ibid., p.41
16. *See* ibid., pp.41-42
17. Kershaw cites both strength figures in different places with no explanation for the disparity; *see* ibid., pp.36, 73
18. *See* Verney, **The Guards Armoured Division**, p.96; Lieutenant Frank is interred in Leopoldsburg Military Cemetery, Limburg, Belgium, Plot I, Row A, Grave 17
19. *See* **WO 171/1257**, 3rd Battalion Irish Guards War Diary, entry for 8 September 1944
20. *See* Wilson, **The Ever Open Eye**, pp.85-86

21. Casualty figures cited in **WO 171/1257**, 3rd Battalion Irish Guards War Diary, entries for 08 & 09/09/1944
22. Quoted from Wilson, p.87
23. *See* Verney, p.96; the bridge is variously rendered as Groot or Groote
24. *See* Wilson, pp.91-93
25. Figures cited in **WO 171/1257**, 3rd Battalion Irish Guards War Diary, entries for 11 & 12/09/1944; *see* also Verney, p.96
26. *See* **WO 171/1257**, 3rd Battalion Irish Guards War Diary, entry for 10/09/1944; Captain Edward Ernest Rawlence is interred in Leopoldsburg Military Cemetery, Limburg, Belgium, Plot 1, Row D, Grave 6
27. *See* Kershaw, pp.26-28
28. According to Kershaw the attack began on Friday 15 September, but the 3rd Battalion Irish Guards refer to an attack at the same time and location on 14 September, and to being relieved on 15 September. As Kershaw's dates are somewhat confused on occasion, the Irish Guards War Diary version is cited here; *see* Kershaw, p.29; and **WO 171/1257**, 3rd Battalion Irish Guards War Diary, entries for 14 & 15/09/1944
29. Quoted from Heinz Volz, 'Fallschirmjaeger Regiment von Hoffmann', *Der Deutsche Fallschirmjaeger* 2/55 (Donth); cited in Kershaw, p.29
30. *See* Verney, p.96; and Wilson, p.95
31. *See* **WO 171/1257**, 3rd Battalion Irish Guards War Diary, entry for 14/09/1944
32. *See* Kershaw, pp.29-30
33. *See* Wilson, p.96
34. Figures cited in **WO 171/1257**, 3rd Battalion Irish Guards War Diary, entry for 14/09/1944; Lieutenant Humphrey Oscar Coleridge Kennard is interred in Geel War Cemetery, Belgium, Plot II, Row D, Grave 2
35. *See* Wilson, pp.98-101
36. *See* **WO 171 /1257**, 3rd Battalion Irish Guards War Diary, entry for 15/09/1944
37. *See* Wilson, p.102
38. Figures cited in Verney, p.96
39. *See* **WO 171/1257**, 3rd Battalion Irish Guards War Diary, entries for 08/09/1944 and 16/09/1944
40. Quoted from Wilson. p.102
41. *See* Kershaw, p.43
42. Quoted from '*Die Kämpfe in Belgien und Süd Holland September 1944. Die Einsätze der Kampfgruppe Richter.*' November 1982; cited in ibid., p.43
43. *See* ibid., p.45
44. Quoted from Essame, **The 43rd Wessex Division at War**, p.116; cited in Powell, **The Devil's Birthday**, p.84
45. *See* **CAB 44/254** Part II: Operation MARKET GARDEN, Appendix C, RE Aspect of 'GARDEN'; and Harclerode, **Arnhem: A Tragedy of Errors**, pp.59-62
46. For the full details *see* for example **WO 205/192** Operation 'Market-Garden': outline plans and instructions; **WO 205/872** Operation 'Market' and 'Garden: Outline Plan and Organisation; and **WO 219/2887** Operation 'Market': Seizure of Maas, Rhine and Neder Rijn Bridge in Arnhem
47. *See* Urquhart, **Arnhem**, p.4; the term 'allegedly' is used because there does not appear to be any primary source or minutes for the meeting, at which Browning is also supposed to have made his famous but equally unsupported and fatuous assertion that MARKET GARDEN might be going 'a bridge too far'
48. *See* **CAB 44/254**, Part II: Operation MARKET GARDEN, Chapter IV, Section II, Part 12 'Comments by Narrator on the Ground Phase – Operation "MARKET GARDEN"', p.21
49. *See* Baynes, **Urquhart of Arnhem**, p.87
50. Quote from Horrocks, **Corps Commander**, p.99
51. *See* **WO 171/605** 5th Guards Armoured Brigade War Diary, Appendix D, dated 15/09/ 1944; and Appendix F, dated 16/09/1944
52. *See* Ryan, p.148

53. *See* Wilson, p.103
54. *See* Harvey, **Arnhem**, pp.35-36. The latter work cites the information as coming from **WO 371/341** XXX Corps' Operation Instruction No. 24 dated 15 September 1944, but that file designation does not appear to figure in the National Archive online database
55. *See* for example Ellis, **Victory in the West, Volume II: The Defeat of Germany**, pp.26-27
56. 20,000 vehicle figure cited in Powell, p.85
57. For details see for example Horrocks, **A Full Life**, p.175
58. Field Marshal Lord Alanbrooke, **War Diaries 1939-1945**, p.555
59. *See* Powell, pp.83, 183
60. *See* **WO 171/1236**, 1st Parachute Battalion War Diary, entries for 10-14/09/1944
61. *See* **WO 171/1238** 3rd Parachute Battalion War Diary, entries for 10-15/09/1944
62. *See* **WO 171/1244** 11th Parachute Battalion War Diary, entries for 10-13/09/1944; and **WO 171/1247** 156 Parachute Battalion War Diary, entry for 10/09/1944
63. *See* Diary of Sergeant George Kosimaki, cited in Rapport and Northwood, **Rendezvous with Destiny**, p.259
64. *See* Rapport and Northwood, p.284
65. The Molenhoek bridge is referred to as the Heumen bridge in some accounts
66. Quoted from MacDonald, **The Siegfried Line Campaign**, footnote 35, p.158
67. Quote from Gavin, **On to Berlin**, p.146
68. *See* ibid., p.149; and Powell, p.75
69. *See* Gavin, **On to Berlin**, p.147
70. *See* Powell, pp.75-77
71. *See* MacDonald, **The Siegfried Line Campaign**, pp.156-158
72. Quote from letter from Gavin, dated 25/07/1945; cited in MacDonald, **The Siegfried Line Campaign**, p.163
73. *See* Gavin, **On to Berlin**, pp.147-149, 151, 161-162
74. *See* Powell, pp.75-77
75. For full details of the 1st Airborne Division's lifts *See* Otway, **Airborne Forces**, pp.267-268
76. *See* ibid., p.265
77. Cited in unpublished memoir of Mr Jack Smith, formerly Trooper 881 Jack 'Red' Smith of the 44th Royal Tank Regiment, 4th Armoured Brigade. Mr Smith insisted that the plan involved a Polish parachute drop on the Zuider Zee, but the present author has thus far failed to locate any reference to this in the official documentation. I am indebted to Mr Smith for permission to cite his memoir.
78. *See* Urquhart, **Arnhem**, p.18
79. *See* Middlebrook, p.165
80. *See* ibid., p.76
81. *See* ibid., p.165
82. *See* Ryan, pp.173-174
83. Quote from Gavin, **On to Berlin**, p.150
84. Quote from ibid., p.150
85. Quoted from ibid., p.150
86. Quoted from Frost, **A Drop Too Many**, p.194
87. *See* for example Baynes, pp.72-73; Henniker, **An Image of War**, p.163; and Middlebrook, pp.21-22
88. Quoted from Sosabowski, **Freely I Served**, p.145
89. *See* Middlebrook, p.62
90. *See* comment by Urquhart in Hamilton, **Monty: The Field Marshal**, p.66; cited in Baynes, p.100
91. Quoted from Middlebrook, p.63
92. *See* ibid., p.64
93. Quoted from General Sir John Hackett, 'Operation Market Garden' in Foot, **Holland at War Against Hitler**, p.166; cited in Baynes, p.100
94. *See* Middlebrook, p.63

95. *See* Ryan. pp.160-161
96. *See* **WO 171/592**, 1st Parachute Brigade War Diary, entries for 13/09/1944 & 15/09/1944
97. PIAT: Projector, Infantry, Anti-Tank, a spring and recoil operated bomb thrower with hollow charge ammunition, the British equivalent to the US Bazooka and German *Panzerfaust*. PIAT ammunition were issued in carry cases containing three bombs; as the PIAT weighed 32 pounds and the bombs 3 pounds apiece, this was a not inconsiderable burden.
98. *See* Victor Miller, **Nothing is Impossible**, pp.83-85
99. *See* **WO 171/1236** 1st Parachute Battalion War Diary, entries for 14-16/09/1944; *see* also recollections from Lieutenant Eric Vere-Davies, cited in Middlebrook, p.64
100. *See* Middlebrook, p.64
101. *See* James Sims, **Arnhem Spearhead**, pp.28-30
102. *See* Ryan, pp.164-165
103. *See* **WO 171/1238** 3rd Parachute Battalion War Diary, entries for 15/09/1944 & 16/09/1944
104. *See* Sims, p.30
105. *See* Robert M. Bowen, **Fighting with the Screaming Eagles**, p.81
106. *See* Rapport and Northwood, p.256
107. *See* Gavin, **On to Berlin**, p.150
108. *See* Ryan, p.155
109. While the 50th Troop Carrier Wing's HQ was located at Exeter in Devon, the 439th, 440th and 441st Troop Carrier Groups were stationed in Nottinghamshire at Balderton, Langer and Fulbeck respectively. The 442nd Troop Carrier Group was despatched to Bonnetable in France, from where it carried out resupply sorties for MARKET
110. Quoted in Ryan, p.157
111. All quotes from ibid., pp.156-158
112. *See* Rapport and Northwood, pp.256-259
113. *See* Ryan, pp.154-155, 156; and Rapport and Northwood, p.257
114. *See* Ryan, pp.155-156
115. *See* Donald R. Burgett, **The Road to Arnhem**, p.16
116. Quoted from **The English Silver Summer**, an unpublished memoir by Mr Stone, kindly provided via private communication on 30 July 2000. I am indebted to Mr Stone for permission to quote his memoir
117. *See* Burgett, pp.16-17
118. *See* Miller, p.85
119. *See* Sims, p.30; and Ryan, p.163
120. *See* John Fairley, **Remember Arnhem**, pp.29-32
121. *See* Middlebrook, pp.73-74
122. *See* MacDonald, **The Siegfried Line Campaign**, pp.136-137; and Powell, p.51
123. *See* Gerard M. Devlin, **Silent Wings**, p.245

Chapter 5

1. 223 figure cited in Middlebrook, **Arnhem: The Airborne Battle**, p.74; 282 figure in Powell, **The Devil's Birthday**, p.51
2. *See* Ellis, **Victory in the West, Volume II: The Defeat of Germany**, p.31
3. *See* Middlebrook, p.74
4. *See* Devlin, **Silent Wings**, p.246; Powell cites a figure of 821 B-17s; *see* Powell, p.51
5. *See* Powell, p.51
6. *See* Miller, **Nothing Is Impossible**, pp.85-86
7. *See* Burgett, **The Road to Arnhem**, p.28
8. Figure cited in Powell, p.51
9. Figures cited in Middlebrook, Appendix 3: 'Order of Battle, 38 and 46 Groups RAF and RASC Air Despatch Units' and Appendix 4: 'Order of Battle, US Air Units Carrying British and Polish Parachute Troops on Operation "Market"', pp.462-464

10. Figure cited in Powell, p.51, but this total may only include British gliders and thus be significantly low. Although he cites a figure of 359 British gliders in the first lift including Browning's 38, figures compiled and listed by Middlebrook show the 1st Airborne Division took 442 Horsas and at least thirteen Hamilcars into Arnhem on the first day, giving a total of 455 machines, and adding the thirty-eight gliders Browning co-opted for his Forward Corps HQ lifts the total to 493, slightly more than Powell's figure. In addition, the 82nd Airborne Division took fifty Waco CG4 gliders into Nijmegen, and the 101st Airborne Division took an additional seventy Waco CG4s into Eindhoven. This raises the overall glider total to 613. For figures *see* Middlebrook, pp.75-76, 78 and Appendix 1: 'Order of Battle and Operational Details, 1st British Airborne Division and Attached Units', pp.455-460; and for example Devlin, **Silent Wings**, pp.242-243

11. Details from Otway, **Airborne Forces**, Appendix A Annexure: Glider Specifications, p.397

12. *See* Devlin, **Silent Wings**, pp.245-246

13. The 1st Airborne Division mounted out from eleven airfields, and the 101st Airborne Division from six. At the time of writing the author has been unable to locate a definitive list of airfields used by the 82nd Airborne Division. For locations *see* Middle brook, Map 2, 'The Air Armada', p.84; and Rapport & Northwood, pp.256-257

14. *See* Middlebrook, p.79

15. Figures cited in MacDonald, **The Siegfried Line Campaign**, p.137

16. *See* Powell, p.52

17. *See* **WO 171-1236** 1st Parachute Battalion War Diary, entry for 17/09/1944

18. *See* Sims, **Arnhem Spearhead**, p.31; and Alan T. Green, **1st Battalion the Border Regiment**, p.1

19. *See* Middlebrook, p.77

20. *See* **WO 171/1238** 3rd Parachute Battalion War Diary & **WO 171/1236** 1st Parachute Battalion War Diary, entries for 17/09/1944; and Green, p.1

21. *See* Steven J. Zaloga, **US Airborne Divisions in the ETO 1944-1945**, p.46

22. *See* Burgett, p.p.30-31; and Zaloga, p.46

23. *See* Burgett, p.32

24. *See* Gavin, **On to Berlin**, p.152

25. *See* Fairley, **Remember Arnhem**, pp.30-31

26. *See* Middlebrook, p.78

27. *See* Miller, p.86

28. *See* Fairley, pp.32-33

29. *See* Middlebrook, p.77

30. *See* Sims, p.31

31. Quoted from Chatterton, **The Wings of Pegasus**, pp.174-175; barathea is a soft woven fabric, in this instance probably worsted, and was smoother and of better quality than the serge issue item

32. *See* Urquhart, **Arnhem**, p.27

33. *See* ibid., pp.25-27; also cited in Ryan, **A Bridge Too Far**, pp.174-175; and Middlebrook, p.93

34. *See* Baynes, **Urquhart of Arnhem**, p.102. According to Ryan, Urquhart took Mackenzie aside as he prepared to depart and laid out the command succession; *See* Ryan, p.175. Interestingly, the exchange does not figure in Urquhart's account of the battle or in most others, although it is sometimes mentioned in connection with the quarrel it later prompted between Brigadiers Hackett and Hicks at 1st Airborne HQ in the late evening of Monday 18 September

35. *See* Urquhart, p.29

36. Interestingly Miller refers to taking off at 07:30, even though Ryan's research in air control and unit logs shows that take-offs did not commence until 09:45; *see* Miller, p.87; and Ryan, footnote p.170

37. Quoted from Miller, p.88

38. *See* Middlebrook, pp.78, 80

39. Testimony from Sergeant Wally Simpson, RAF No. 299 Squadron; cited in Middlebrook, pp.81-82

40. *See* Fairley, p.34

41. Testimony from Lance-Corporal Stan Livesey, 7th KOSB; cited in Middlebrook, p.85
42. *See* ibid., pp.79-80
43. *See* Green, pp.2-4
44. *See* Sims, pp.16-19
45. *See* **WO 171/1248**, 21st Independent Parachute Company War Diary, entry for 17/09/1944; and Ron Kent, **First In! Parachute Pathfinder Company**, p.95; US take-off time cited in Ryan, p.172
46. *See* Ryan, p.173
47. *See* Fairley, p.34; Gavin, **On to Berlin**, p.153; Sims, p.32; and Ryan, p.173
48. Figures cited in Ryan, p.173
49. *See* ibid., p.173; and Fairley, p.35
50. *See* Ryan, p.179
51. *See* Middlebrook, p.85
52. *See* Ryan, p.180
53. *See* Middlebrook, p.85
54. *See* Ryan, pp.178-179
55. *See* Middlebrook, p.86
56. *See* Ryan, pp.185-187; and Middlebrook, pp.92-94
57. *See* Middlebrook, pp.86-87
58. *See* William L. Brinson, **Airborne Troop Carrier**, p.140
59. *See* Ryan, pp.180-181
60. *See* Middlebrook, pp.87-89
61. *See* Ryan, p.190; and Middlebrook, p.97
62. *See* **WO 171/1248** 21st Independent Parachute Company War Diary, entry for 17/09/1944; Kent, pp.95-98; and Middlebrook, pp.96-97
63. Quoted from Miller, pp.92-94
64. *See* Middlebrook, p.100
65. *See* Green, pp.4-5
66. *See* Middlebrook, pp.103-104
67. *See* ibid., p.106
68. Quoted from ibid., p.106
69. *See* Fairley, p.36
70. *See* Middlebrook, p.102
71. Quote and figures from ibid., pp.104-105
72. *See* Sims, p.34
73. *See* ibid., pp.35-36
74. Testimony from Private Bob Elliott, 1st Battalion The Border Regiment; cited in Middlebrook, p.110
75. Testimony from Sapper Tam Hepburn, 1st Parachute Squadron RE; cited in ibid., p.109
76. Comment from Sapper Arthur Hendy, 1st Parachute Squadron RE; cited in ibid., p.111
77. Quoted from Sims, p.36
78. *See* **WO 171/1248** 21st Independent Company War Diary, entry for 17/09/1944; and Middlebrook, p.111
79. *See* Ryan, pp.190-191
80. Drop timing cited in **A Graphic History of the 82nd Airborne Division**, entry for 'D-Day, 17 September'. For numbers of men, guns and ammunition *see* Ryan, pp.220-221; and Blair, **Ridgway's Paratroopers**, p.330
81. *See* Gavin, **On to Berlin,** pp.153-155
82. Timing cited in **A Graphic History of the 82nd Airborne Division**, entry for 'D Day, 17 September'
83. Figures cited in Brinson, p.139
84. *See* T. Moffatt Burriss, **Strike and Hold**, p.106
85. *See* Brinson, p.140

86. *See* MacDonald, **The Siegfried Line Campaign**, p.160; and Ryan, p.218. The former claims Thompson's stick landed within 700 yards of the bridge, the latter 500-600

87. Timing cited in **A Graphic History of the 82nd Airborne Division**, entry for 'D Day, 17 September'

88. *See* Major Benjamin. F. Delamater, **The Actions of the 1st Battalion, 508th Parachute Infantry**, p.8

89. *See* MacDonald, **The Siegfried Line Campaign**, p.159

90. Cited in Delamater, p.8

91. Figures cited in MacDonald, **The Siegfried Line Campaign**, p.159

92. *See* Blair, pp.330-331; and MacDonald **The Siegfried Line Campaign**, p.159

93. *See* Ryan, p.222

94. *See* ibid., p.191

95. *See* Rapport and Northwood, **Rendezvous with Destiny**, p.279

96. *See* MacDonald, **The Siegfried Line Campaign**, p.145; and Rapport and Northwood, pp.268-279

97. *See* Rapport and Northwood, pp.269-271; and MacDonald, **The Siegfried Line Campaign**, p.147

Chapter 6

1. *See* **WO 171/605** 5 Guards Armoured Brigade War Diary, entries for 13-16/09/1944

2. *See* Wilson, **The Ever Open Eye**, p.104

3. OST: Ordinary Summer Time; sunrise and sunset timings quoted from **Field Order No. 11, 82nd Airborne Division**, Annex 1.a(1) to F.O. 11, Weather; Sun and Moon Tables, Para .2 "Sun and Moon Data", dated 11/09/1944

4. *See* Kershaw, **It Never Snows in September**, p.45

5. *See* for example Powell, **The Devil's Birthday**, p.82

6. Quoted from **WO 171/376** HQ Guards Armoured Division War Diary, 'Guards Armoured Division Operations Order No. 12, Operation Garden', Appendix JA, Paragraph 8 'Timings', dated 15/09/1944

7. *See* **WO 171/341**, 30 Corps September 1944, 30 Corps Battle Logs, September 1944, entry for 10:15, 17/09/1944; for MARKET take-off time *see* for example Otway, **Airborne Forces**, p.268

8. *See* **WO 171/1256** 2nd (Armoured) Battalion Irish Guards War Diary, entry for 12:00, 17/09/1944

9. *See* Wilson, p.103

10. *See* **WO 171/605** 5th Guards Armoured Brigade War Diary, Appendix D, dated 15/09/ 1944; and Appendix F, dated 16/09/1944

11. *See* **WO 171/1256** 2nd (Armoured) Battalion Irish Guards War Diary, entry for 13:15, 17/09/1944; and Wilson. p.104

12. 20,000 vehicle figure cited in Powell, p.85; 3,124 figure calculated from **WO 171/376** HQ Guards Armoured Division War Diary, January - September 1944, Appendix JA, 'Guards Armoured Division Operations Order No. 12, Operation Garden', Annexure to Appendix A, 'Order of March & Groupings', dated 15/09/1944

13. *See* **WO 171/376** HQ Guards Armoured Division War Diary, January - September 1944, Appendix JA, 'Guards Armoured Division Operations Order No. 12, Operation Garden', Appendix A - Grouping & Order of March, Para. 3, dated 15/09/1944

14. *See* John Sliz, **The Storm Boat Kings**, pp.30, 46

15. *See* **CAB 44/254** Part II: Operation MARKET GARDEN, Book III, Chapter VI, Appendix C, RE Aspect of 'GARDEN'; and Harclerode, **Arnhem: A Tragedy of Errors**, pp.59-62

16. *See* Verney, **The Guards Armoured Division**, pp.100-101

17. For the full details *see* foe example **WO 205/192** Operation 'Market-Garden': outline plans and instructions; **WO 205/872** Operation 'Market' and 'Garden: Outline Plan and Organisation; and **WO 219/2887** Operation 'Market': Seizure of Maas, Rhine and Neder Rijn Bridge in Arnhem

18. *See* **CAB 44/254** Part II: Operation MARKET GARDEN, Book III, Chapter VII, Section I

19. For development and employment details *see* Ian Gooderson, **Air Power at the Battlefront**, pp.22-29

20. *See* **WO 171/376** HQ Guards Armoured Division War Diary, January - September 1944, Appendix JA, 'Guards Armoured Division Operations Order No. 12, Operation Garden', Para. 9 'Air Support', dated 15/09/1944
21. *See* Verney, p.102
22. *See* **CAB 44/254** Part II: Operation MARKET GARDEN, Book III, Chapter VII, Appendix A, Section 1 'Movement Order for Phase I' & Section 3 'Gds Armd Div and forward units of 50 (N) Div - Narrative 17 Sep.'; and Wilson, p.104
23. *See* **WO 171/376** HQ Guards Armoured Division War Diary Jan-Sept 1944, Appendix JA 'Guards Armoured Division Operations Order No. 12 Operation Garden', Para 14 'Divisional Tasks'; Appendix A, 'Grouping and Order of March', Para 2; and Annexure I to Appendix A 'Order of March and Groupings', dated 15/09/1944
24. 19:30 nightfall timing cited in **CAB 44/254** Part II: Operation MARKET GARDEN, Book III, Chapter VII, Appendix A, Section 1 'Movement Order for Phase I' & Section 3 'Gds Armd Div and forward units of 50 (N) Div - Narrative 17 Sep.'
25. Kershaw, p.43
26. *See* ibid., p.30
27. *See* ibid., pp.30, 45-46, 79
28. Gun numbers cited in Kershaw, p.27; the latter also refers to the weapons being of 76mm calibre; *see* ibid., p.46
29. *See* ibid., p.46
30. *See* **CAB 44/254** Part II: Operation MARKET GARDEN, Book III, Chapter VII, Appendix A, Section 3 'Gds Armd Div and forward units of 50 (N) Div - Narrative 17 Sep.'; and Kershaw, p.79
31. *See* Verney, p.102
32. *See* Kershaw, p.79
33. For tank and crew losses *see* **WO 171/1256** 2 Irish Guards (Armoured Battalion) War Diary, entry for 14:35, 17/09/1944; for knocked-out armoured cars and tank crew PoWs, *see* Kershaw, p.81
34. *See* Wilson, pp.104-105
35. Eleven squadron figure cited in **WO 171/379** HQ Guards Armoured Division War Diary Jan-Sept 1944, Appendix JA 'Guards Armoured Division Operations Order No. 12 Operation Garden', Para. 12. 'Phases'; section (c,) 'Air'; the 15:12 start time, 116 sortie figure and target location distances cited in **CAB 44/254** Part II: Operation MARKET GARDEN, Book III, Chapter VII, Appendix A, Section 3 'Gds Armd Div and forward units of 50 (N) Div - Narrative 17 Sep.'
36. *See* Wilson, pp.105-106, 108; there is no reference to friendly fire casualties in the War Diaries of the units involved
37. *See* Kershaw, p.80
38. Quotes from Wilson, p.106
39. For German POW figure and 2nd Devons wood clearing *see* WO **171/1257** 3rd Battalion Irish Guards War Diary, entry for 17/09/1944; and **CAB 44/254** Part II: Operation MARKET GARDEN, Book III, Chapter VII, Appendix A, Section 3 'Gds Armd Div and forward units of 50 (N) Div - Narrative 17 Sep.'
40. *See* Kershaw. p.87
41. *See* **WO 171/1256** 2 Irish Guards (Armoured) Battalion War Diary, entry for 14:35, 17/09/1944
42. *See* **CAB 44/254** Part II: Operation MARKET GARDEN, Book III, Chapter VII, Appendix A, Section 3 'Gds Armd Div and forward units of 50 (N) Div - Narrative 17 Sep.'
43. Sometimes rendered Zon in US accounts
44. *See* Rapport & Northwood, **Rendezvous with Destiny**, p.274
45. *See* ibid., p.274
46. *See* MacDonald, **The Siegfried Line Campaign**, p.148
47. *See* Ambrose, **Band of Brothers**, p.125
48. *See* Rapport & Northwood, p.272; and Ambrose, p.125

49. For a vivid participant account of the 506th Regiment's assault on the flak guns at Son *see* Burgett, **The Road to Arnhem**, pp.35-43; *see* also Ambrose, p.126; and Rapport & Northwood, p.274

50. *See* Rapport & Northwood, pp.279-281; and MacDonald, **The Siegfried Line Campaign**, p.146

51. Sometimes rendered as Vechel in US accounts

52. *See* Rapport & Northwood, pp.275-277; and MacDonald, **The Siegfried Line Campaign**, p.145

53. *See* Kershaw, p.116

54. *See* Rapport & Northwood, pp.284-287; and MacDonald, **The Siegfried Line Campaign**, p.146

55. *See* Captain Carl W. Kappel, **The Operations of Company 'H', 504th Parachute Infantry**, pp.18-19

56. *See* Gavin, **On to Berlin**, p.156

57. *See* Ryan, **A Bridge Too Far**, p.220; and MacDonald, **The Siegfried Line Campaign**, p.160

58. Quote from T. Moffatt Burriss, **Strike and Hold**, p.106

59. *See* **A Graphic History of the 82nd Airborne Division**, entry for 'D Day, 17 September'; and Ryan, p.220

60. *See* **A Graphic History of the 82nd Airborne Division**, entry for 'D Day, 17 September'

61. *See* Burriss, p.107

62. Quoted from Charles B. MacDonald, **The Siegfried Line Campaign**, footnote 35, p.158

63. *See* Gavin, **On to Berlin**, pp.157-158; MacDonald, **The Siegfried Line Campaign**, p.161; timings cited in **A Graphic History of the 82nd Airborne Division**, entry for 'D Day, 17 September'

64. *See* MacDonald, **The Siegfried Line Campaign**, p.161

65. *See* Gavin, **On to Berlin**, p.147; and MacDonald, **The Siegfried Line Campaign**, p.162

66. *See* **A Graphic History of the 82nd Airborne Division**, entry for 'D Day, 17 September'; and MacDonald, **The Siegfried Line Campaign**, p.162

67. *See* **A Graphic History of the 82nd Airborne Division**, entry for 'D Day, 17 September'; Gavin, **On to Berlin**, p.160; and Ryan, p.221

68. *See* **A Graphic History of the 82nd Airborne Division**, entry for 'D Day, 17 September'

69. Quote from Gavin, **On to Berlin**, p.161

70. *See* MacDonald, **The Siegfried Line Campaign**, p.162

71. *See* Major Benjamin. F. Delamater, **The Actions of the 1st Battalion, 508th Parachute Infantry**, p.9; and ibid., 'Insertion to Monograph, **Extracts of Letter from Major J. E. Adams**, dated 07/04/1947, p.2

72. Quoted from letter from Gavin, n.d.; cited in MacDonald, **The Siegfried Line Campaign**, p.162

73. Quoted from letter from Lindquist dated 09/09/1955; cited in MacDonald, **The Siegfried Line Campaign**, p.163

74. *See* Gavin, **On to Berlin**, p.151; and MacDonald, **The Siegfried Line Campaign**, p.162.

75. This was not strictly accurate, for the bridges were protected a weak scratch force cobbled together from local units by an *Oberst* Henke from a nearby *Fallschirmjäger* training HQ until reinforced briefly at 19:00 by *Hauptsturmführer* Viktor Gräbner and elements of *SS Panzer Aufklärungs Abteilung 9*; *see* Kershaw, pp.99-100

76. Patrol details and departure time cited in Delamater, pp.9-10

77. Quoted from letter from Gavin, nd; cited in MacDonald, **The Siegfried Line Campaign**, p.163

78. *See* Delamater, p.9; and Adams, p.2

79. *See* Delamater, p.10

80. *See* Ryan, pp.223-224; interestingly Gavin makes no mention of this in his memoir

81. *See* Middlebrook, **Arnhem 1944**, p.165. Lieutenant Fuller Heath Gee in interred in Mook War Cemetery, Limburg, Holland, Plot I, Row E, Grave 17

82. Quote from **AIR 37/1214** Allied Expeditionary Air Force: Report on Operation 'Market' and 'Garden': Allied Airborne Operations in Holland, Para. 119; cited in Powell, p.118

83. *See* 'Army Air Forces Historical Study No.1: Development and Procurement of Gliders in the Army Air Forces 1941-1944', p.20; cited in Devlin, **Silent Wings**, p.73

84. *See* for example Rapport and Northwood, pp.19-20; and Devlin, **Paratrooper**, pp.118-120

85. Conversation between Browning and Chatterton cited in Harclerode, **Tragedy of Errors**, pp.51-52. Interestingly, Chatterton makes no mention of this in his combined memoir and history of the Glider Pilot Regiment
86. *See* **WO 171/1248** 21ˢᵗ Independent Parachute Company War Diary, entry for 17/09/1944; and Ron Kent, **First In!**, pp.98-99
87. *See* **WO 166/14933** 1ˢᵗ Airlanding Light Regiment RA War Diary, various entries 17/09/1944
88. *See* **WO 171/1513** 9ᵗʰ (Airborne) Field Company RE War Diary, entry for 19/09/1944
89. Lieutenant Roy Edward John Willetts Timmins, Corporal William Thomas Noel Takle and Sapper Peter Greig are interred in Arnhem Oosterbeek War Cemetery, Gelderland, Holland, in Plot 26, Row A, Grave 7, Plot 16, Row A, Grave 15 and Plot 16, Row A, Grave 16 respectively
90. *See* **WO 171/1513** 9ᵗʰ (Airborne) Field Company RE War Diary, various entries 17/09/1944
91. *See* Kershaw, p.72
92. Although the 2ⁿᵈ South Staffords War Diary does not mention it, the 1ˢᵗ Airlanding Brigade HQ War Diary explicitly refers to the South Staffords clearing Wolfheze before returning to the vicinity of Reijers-Camp Farm to dig in; *see* **WO 171/589** 1ˢᵗ Airlanding Brigade War Diary, entry for 17/09/1944; *see* also Middlebrook, pp.116-117
93. *See* **WO 171/1375** 2ⁿᵈ Battalion South Staffordshire Regiment War Diary, various entries 17/09/1944; and ibid., Appendix '2nd South Staffords at Arnhem 17-25 Sept. 44'. *Duitsekampweg* translates roughly to 'German War Way' in Dutch, and commemorated an internment camp for German detainees that stood nearby during the First World War; *see* Middlebrook, p.117
94. *See* **WO 166/15077**, 1ˢᵗ Battalion The Border Regiment War Diary, entry for Sunday 17/09/1944; and Green, **1ˢᵗ Battalion The Border Regiment**, pp.11-13, 16
95. CanLoan: codename for scheme by which Canadian officers could volunteer to serve with British Army units. By the latter half of 1943 the British Army was suffering from a shortage of junior officers while the Canadian Army had a surplus due in part to the disbanding of some Home Defence formations. A total of 673 Canadian officers served with British units under the CanLoan Scheme, the vast majority of them subalterns.
96. *See* **WO 171/1323**, 7ᵗʰ Battalion King's Own Scottish Borderers War Diary, entry for 19:00, 17/09/1944; and Middlebrook, p.163
97. *See* **WO 171/1323**, 7ᵗʰ Battalion King's Own Scottish Borderers War Diary, various entries 17/09/1944
98. *See* Middlebrook, pp.163-164
99. Depending on the source Helle's rank is given *Hauptsturmführer, Sturmbannführer* or *Obersturmbannführer*
100. *See* Kershaw, p.110
101. *See* **WO 171/592**, 1ˢᵗ Parachute Brigade War Diary, Appendix A 'Operation MARKET: Diary of Events, 1 Parachute Brigade HQ', entry for 14:10, 17/09/1944; and comment from Sapper Arthur Hendy, 1ˢᵗ Parachute Squadron RE; cited in Middlebrook, p.111
102. quote and timings from **WO 171/592**, 1ˢᵗ Parachute Brigade War Diary, Appendix A 'Operation MARKET: Diary of Events, 1 Parachute Brigade HQ', entries for 14:10, 14:20 & 14:25, 17/09/1944
103. *See* **WO 171/1236**, 1ˢᵗ Parachute Battalion War Diary, entry for 14:45, 17/09/1944; and **WO 171/592**, 1ˢᵗ Parachute Brigade War Diary, Appendix A 'Operation MARKET: Diary of Events, 1 Parachute Brigade HQ', entry for 14:45, 17/09/1944
104. *See* Middlebrook, p.150
105. *See* **WO 171/592**, 1ˢᵗ Parachute Brigade War Diary, Appendix A 'Operation MARKET: Diary of Events, 1 Parachute Brigade HQ', entry for 15:30, 17/09/1944
106. *See* **WO 171/592**, 1ˢᵗ Parachute Brigade War Diary, Appendix A 'Operation MARKET: Diary of Events, 1 Parachute Brigade HQ', entries for 15:10 & 15:30, 17/09/1944
107. *See* **WO 171/1236** 1ˢᵗ Parachute Battalion War Diary, entry for 15:40, 17/09/1944
108. *See* **WO 1/1/592**, 1ˢᵗ Parachute Brigade War Diary, Appendix A 'Operation MARKET: Diary of Events, 1 Parachute Brigade HQ', entries for 15:10, 15:30 & 15:45, dated 17/09/1944

109. The 1ˢᵗ Parachute Battalion was fully accounted for by 14:45 but was not ordered to move until 15:40; *see* **WO 171/1236** 1ˢᵗ Parachute Battalion War Diary, entries for 14:45 & 15:40, 17/09/1944; for Dobie's frustration *see* testimony from Lieutenant Vladimir Britneff, Intelligence Officer, 1ˢᵗ Parachute Battalion; cited in Middlebrook, pp.137-138

110. *See* Baynes, **Urquhart of Arnhem**, p.98

111. For details of the individual Battalion tasks and objectives *see* **Operation "MARKET": 1 Para Bde Operation Order No. 1**, dated 13/09/1944, Sept 1944, Paras. 6-8

112. *See* for example Otway, pp.293-294; and Powell, p.64

113. *See* **Operation "MARKET": 1 Para Bde Intelligence Summary No. 1** dated 13/09/1944, Paragraph 4: 'Enemy Forces'

114. For a potted overview of Lathbury's career *see* **World War II Unit Histories & Officers** (website), '1ˢᵗ British Airborne Division, Arnhem September 1944: Officers' at http://www.unithistories.com/officers/1AirbDiv_officersL.htm; accessed 17/09/2010

115. *See* **WO 171/592**, 1ˢᵗ Parachute Brigade War Diary, Appendix A 'Operation MARKET: Diary of Events, 1 Parachute Brigade HQ', entries for 15:30 & 13:45, 17/09/1944

116. *See* Middlebrook, p.127. There is no mention of such a message in the Brigade Diary of Events or Battalion War Diaries.

117. *See* Frost, p.210; and Middlebrook, p.144; again there is no record of this meeting in the Brigade Diary of Events

118. RV location cited in Fairley, **Remember Arnhem**, p.40

119. Although the Reconnaissance Squadron War Diary only refers to a single Horsa aborting from the first lift, Fairley refers to two, one carrying Lieutenant Graham Wadsworth and two Jeeps from HQ Troop, one of which belonged to the Squadron's second-in-command Captain David Allsop, and one carrying Lieutenant Douglas Galbraith and two Jeeps from A Troop. Both loads came in with the second lift on Monday 18 September; *see* **WO 171/406** 1ˢᵗ Airborne Reconnaissance Squadron War Diary, entry for 15:30, 17/09/1944; and Fairley, pp.34, 77

120. *See* **WO 171/406** 1ˢᵗ Airborne Reconnaissance Squadron War Diary, entries for 13:35, 15:00 & 15:15, 17/09/1944

121. For timings *see* **WO 171/406** 1ˢᵗ Airborne Reconnaissance Squadron War Diary, entries for 15:30 & 15:40, 17/09/1944

122. *See* Fairley, pp.40-41

123. For the establishment of the line *see* Kershaw, p.72

124. Lieutenant Peter Lacey Bucknall is interred in Arnhem Oosterbeek War Cemetery, Gelderland, Holland, Plot 16, Row B, Grave 5

125. Curiously Sergeant McGregor does not appear in the CWGC database

126. For a detailed account of the ambush and eyewitness testimony regarding the state of the bodies *see* Fairley, pp.45-47, 69-70

127. Timing cited in **WO 171/406** 1ˢᵗ Airborne Reconnaissance Squadron War Diary, entry for 16:00, 17/09/1944

128. Fairley refers to McNabb being a Captain, but the Squadron War Diary clearly refers to his rank as Lieutenant; *see* **WO 171/406** 1ˢᵗ Airborne Reconnaissance Squadron War Diary, entry for 16:45, 17/09/1944; and Fairley, p.47

129. The Squadron War Diary does not refer to a source for the order; *see* **WO 171/406** 1ˢᵗ Airborne Reconnaissance Squadron War Diary, entry for 18:30, 17/09/1944; and Fairley, p.51

130. *See* Fairley, pp.48-50

131. *See* Fairley, p.69. Lance-Sergeant William Clifford Stacey is interred in Arnhem Oosterbeek War Cemetery, Gelderland, Holland, Plot 15, Row A, Grave 4

132. *See* **AIR 20/2333**, 'Battle of Arnheim': German account, Sept. to Oct. 1944; also cited in Middlebrook, p.126

133. *See* Urquhart, **Arnhem**, p.36

134. *See* **WO 171/406** 1ˢᵗ Airborne Reconnaissance Squadron War Diary, entry for 15:40, 17/09/1944; and Fairley, p.41; the same point is made by Golden, **Echoes from Arnhem**, p.143

135. For a detailed account of the 1st Airborne Division's signal set up and its problems *see* Golden, pp.139-169. Then Major Golden served at Arnhem as Adjutant of the 1st Airborne Division Signal Section.

136. *See* Middlebrook, Appendix I, 'Order of Battle and Operational Details, 1st British Airborne Division and Attached Units', p.459; and Appendix 4, 'Order of Battle, US Air Units Carrying British and Polish Parachute Troops on Operation Market', p.464

137. *See* **WO 171/393** 1st Airborne Division HQ War Diary, entry for 16:30, 17/09/1944

138. *See* Golden, pp.150-151; the No. 68P Set was a manpack, speech radio with a range of three miles, powered by dry batteries and a power output of 0.25 watt; *see* ibid., p.140

139. *See* for example Baynes, p.106; Dover, **The Sky Generals**, p.135; and Middlebrook, p.128

140. *See* Urquhart, p.37; the No. 22 Set was a speech radio powered by rechargeable wet batteries with a power output of 1 watt and a range of five miles; *see* Golden, p.140

141. quoted from Middlebrook, p.128

142. *See II SS Panzerkorps* Warning Order, issued by telephone at 13:40 Hours on 17.9.44; reproduced in Kershaw., Appendix A, p.321

143. For timings *see* Kershaw, p.73

144. *See* Kershaw, pp.61, 74-75

145. Quoted from *II SS Panzerkorps* Order, issued by telephone at 16:30 Hours on 17.9.44; reproduced in Kershaw, Appendix A, p.321

146. *See* ibid., p.104

147. *See* Zwarts, p.8. Gräbner's action is confirmed, albeit circumstantially, by Kershaw who refers to SS *Panzer Aufklärungs Abteilung* 9 possessing forty vehicles but to Gräbner leading only thirty across the Arnhem road bridge toward Nijmegen; *see* Kershaw, pp.73, 96

148. *See* Kershaw, p.97; there is no mention of seeing the SS column in Middlebrook's participant based account or Frost's memoir

149. *See* ibid., pp.99-101; 750 figure cited in Reynolds, **Sons of the Reich**, p.121

150. *See* Ryan, pp.199-200

151. *See* Kershaw, pp.75-78; the portion of the 17:30 operation order dealing with the role to be played by 9 and 10 SS Panzer Divisions is reproduced in ibid., Appendix A, p.322; some sources give Brinkmann's rank as *Sturmbannführer* but Kershaw refers to him as an SS Captain (*Hauptsturmführer*); *see* ibid., p.97

152. *See* Kershaw interview with Harmel on 27 October 1987; quoted in ibid. p.41

153. *See* ibid., pp.125-126

153. Quoted from *II SS Panzerkorps* Order, issued by telephone at 17:30 Hours on 17.9.44; reproduced in ibid. Appendix A, p.322. However, there is a problem with part of this reproduction. The 'Co-ordinating Instructions' section at the end of the Order contains the following clause: 'SS Reconnaissance Battalion 10 now referred to as the Kampfgruppe Brinkmann is to attack and destroy the enemy parachute battalion occupying the northern ramp of the Arnhem bridge. This is in order to quickly fight a resupply route to the 10SS in Nijmegen.' The problem is that the final instruction is out of kilter with the remainder of the order and the well-established sequence of events. Gräbner and the bulk of *SS Panzer Aufklärungs Abteilung* 9 crossed the bridge without incident at c.18.00, the 2nd Parachute Battalion did not reach the north end of the Arnhem bridge until c.20:00, and *II SS Panzerkorps* only became aware of their presence after elements of *SS Panzer Aufklärungs Abteilung 10* found their passage blocked and reported back shortly thereafter. The final section of the 17:30 order is therefore reacting to an event some two-and-a-half hours before it occurred. As the majority of the 17:30 order fits with the established timeline, the final clause was presumably added in error from a later communication.

155. *See* ibid., pp.93-94, 96

156. *II SS Panzerkorps* Order, issued by telephone at 17:30 Hours on 17.9.44; *see* ibid., Appendix A, p.322

157. Quotes from *II SS Panzerkorps* Warning Order, issued by telephone at 13:40 Hours on 17.9.44; *see* ibid., Appendix A, p.321

158. *II SS Panzerkorps* Order, issued by telephone at 16:00 Hours on 17.9.44; *see* ibid., Appendix A, p.321

159. *See* interview with Harmel dated 27 October 1987; cited in ibid., p.99

160. Quotes from *II SS Panzerkorps* Warning Order, issued by telephone at 13:40 Hours on 17.9.44; reproduced in ibid., Appendix A, p.321

161. *See* Reynolds, p.121

162. *See* Kershaw, pp.60, 134

Chapter 7

1. *See* **WO 171/592** 1st Parachute Brigade War Diary, entry for 15:30, 17/09/1944; and **WO 171/1236** 1st Parachute Battalion War Diary, entry for 15:40, 17/09/1944

2. According to the 1st Parachute Battalion War Diary the meeting with Gough occurred at 16:00, but the Reconnaissance Squadron War Diary relates that the main body of the Squadron came under mortar fire in the vicinity of Wolfheze station at 16:00 and that Gough did not depart for Division HQ until 16:45; *see* **WO 171/1236** 1st Parachute Battalion War Diary, entry for 16:00, 17/09/1944; and **WO 171/406** 1st Airborne Reconnaissance Squadron War Diary, entries for 16:00 and 16:45, 17/09/1944

3. *See* **WO 171/1236** 1st Parachute Battalion War Diary, entry for 17:00, 17/09/1944

4. Testimony from Private John Hall, 1 Platoon, R Company, 1st Parachute Battalion; cited in Middlebrook, **Arnhem 1944**, p.139

5. *See* John Waddy, **A Tour of the Arnhem Battlefields**, p.57

6. Testimony from Lieutenant George Guyon, commander Mortar Platoon, 1st Parachute Battalion; *see* Middlebrook, pp.139-140

7. *See* **WO 171/1236** 1st Parachute Battalion War Diary, entry for 18:00, 17/09/1944

8. PIAT: Projector, Infantry, Anti-Tank. The British counterpart to the US Bazooka and the German *Panzerfaust* and *Panzerschreck*, the PIAT was a hand-held spring and recoil operated bomb thrower, which fired a hollow charge projectile weighing 2 ½ pounds, with a range of 115 yards

9. Testimony from Sergeant Frank Manser, 7 Platoon, S Company, 1st Parachute Battalion; cited in Middlebrook, pp.140-141

10. *See* **WO 171/1236** 1st Parachute Battalion War Diary, entry for 19:00, 17/09/1944

11. *SS Panzerjäger Abteilung 9* strength figures cited in Kershaw, **It Never Snows in September**, p.104

12. *See* **WO 171/1236** 1st Parachute Battalion War Diary, entries for 19:30, 20:00 & 22:00, 17/09/1944

13. Testimony from Major Christopher Perrin-Brown, OC T Company, 1st Parachute Battalion; cited in Middlebrook, p.142

14. For R Company casualties reaching the landing area *see* Middlebrook, p.142; Major Bune is interred in Arnhem Oosterbeek War Cemetery, Gelderland, Holland, Plot 27, Row B, Grave 6

15. Testimony from Lieutenant Vladimir Britneff, Intelligence Officer, 1st Parachute Battalion; cited in Middlebrook, p.142

16. Lieutenant MacFadden died on 10 October 1944; he is interred in Hanover War Cemetery, Niedersachsen, Germany, Plot 15, Row F, Grave 6

17. Figures cited in Middlebrook, p.142

18. Testimony from Major John Timothy, OC R Company, 1st Parachute Battalion; cited in Middlebrook, p.140

19. *See* Kershaw, pp.39, 47

20. *See* **WO 171/1236** 1st Parachute Battalion War Diary, entries for 04:30 & 05:30, 17/09/1944; Middlebrook, pp.175-177; and **WO 166/149033** 1st Airlanding Light Regiment RA War Diary, entries for 3 Battery Parachute Party 23:30, 17/09/1944 & 05:00, 18/09/1944

21. *See* **WO 171/592**, 1st Parachute Brigade War Diary, Appendix A 'Operation MARKET: Diary of Events, 1 Parachute Brigade HQ', entry for 15:10, 17/09/1944

22. *See* Frost, **A Drop Too Many**, p.210

23. Testimony from Major Digby Tatham-Warter, OC A Company, 2nd Parachute Battalion; cited in Middlebrook, p.145

24. Quoted from Frost, p.209; German POW & casualty figures cited in Saunders, **The Red Beret**, p.232; and Middlebrook, p.143

25. *See* Middlebrook, p.143

26. Testimony from Signalman Bill Jukes, 1st Airborne Division Signals attached to 2nd Parachute Battalion; cited in Middlebrook, p.144

27. *See* Frost, pp.209-210; and Middlebrook, p.144; for Lathbury's alleged 15:30 radio message *see* Middlebrook, p.127. There is no mention of such a message in the Brigade Diary of Events or Battalion War Diaries

28. *See* Frost, p.210

29. Quote from **WO 171/1237** 2nd Parachute Battalion War Diary, 'Account of the 2nd Battalion's Operations at Arnhem 17th December 1944' by Major J.A.D. Tatham-Warter

30. Testimony from Major Digby Tatham-Warter, OC A Company, 2nd Parachute Battalion; cited in Middlebrook, p.145

31. *See* Frost, p.210

32. Quotes from interviews with Captain A. M. Frank, 2 i/c A Company 2nd Parachute Battalion and Private S.C.E. Elliott, B Company 2nd Parachute Battalion; cited in Middlebrook, p.146

33. Quoted from James Sims, **Arnhem Spearhead**, p.40. Private George Davies died of his wounds the following day and is interred Arnhem Oosterbeek War Cemetery, Gelderland, Holland, Plot 18, Row A, Grave 8

34. Quoted from interview with Lieutenant Peter Barry, commanding 9 Platoon, A Company, 2nd Parachute Battalion; cited in Middlebrook, pp.147-148

35. *See* Middlebrook, p.148; and Kershaw, p.94

36. *See* Kershaw, p.93

37. Quoted from Middlebrook, p.128

38. *See* Urquhart, **Arnhem**, p.39

39. *See* Ryan, **A Bridge Too Far**, pp.245-246

40. Testimony from *Rottenführer* Wolfgang Dombrowski and *Hauptsturmführer* Hans Möller, cited in Kershaw, pp.74-75, 91-92. The timings provided by the participants should be treated with caution, given that they claim to have run headlong into advancing British paratroops in the outskirts of Arnhem at 16:30, at least an hour-and-a-half before any elements of the 1st Parachute Brigade reached that area

41. All four men are interred together in Plot 18, Row A in the Arnhem Oosterbeek War Cemetery, Gelderland, Holland, Lieutenant Peter Howard Cane in Joint Grave 13-14, Corporal Edgar Humphrey Rogers in Grave 16 and Thomas and Claude Gronert are interred in Graves 17 & 18 respectively

42. Quoted from interview with Corporal Robert Allen, A Company, 3rd Parachute Battalion; cited in Middlebrook, p.130

43. Lance-Corporal William Edwin Bamsey is interred in Arnhem Oosterbeek War Cemetery, Gelderland, Holland, Plot 19, Row C, Grave 1

44. Testimony from Lieutenant James Cleminson, commanding 5 Platoon, B Company, 3rd Parachute Battalion; cited in Middlebrook, p.131

45. *See* for example Kershaw, p.95

46. *See* **WO 171/1238** 3rd Parachute Battalion War Diary, entry for 17:00, 17/09/1944; and Middlebrook, pp.132-133. Corporal Benjamin Harry Cope is interred in Arnhem Oosterbeek War Cemetery, Gelderland, Holland, Plot 1, Row B, Grave 8' Gunner George Robson has no known grave and is commemorated on Panel 2, Groesbeek Memorial, Gelderland, Holland; the CWGC records give his date of death as 26/09/1944

47. Quoted from account by Lieutenant Leonard Wright, commanding 9 Platoon, B Company, 3rd Parachute Battalion; cited in Middlebrook, p.134

48. Testimony from Lieutenant Tony Baxter, commanding No. 3 Platoon, A Company, 3rd Parachute Battalion; cited in ibid., pp.134-135

49. *See* **WO 171/1238**, 3rd Parachute Battalion War Diary, Appendix D, 'Diary of Events - 3rd Parachute Battalion', entry for 18:30, 17/09/1944

50. Kershaw cites a withdrawal time of 18:00 but this was well before dark and the 21:30 timing cited by Middlebrook is likely more accurate; *see* Kershaw, pp.72-73; and Middlebrook, p.135

51. *See* '16th Waffen-SS Training and Replacement Battalion: Its First Day of Battle Against the British Airborne Troops near Arnhem, September 1944', in James Lucas and Matthew Cooper, **Panzer Grenadiers**, pp.104-113; and Middlebrook, p.135

52. *See* **WO 171/592**, 1st Parachute Brigade War Diary, Appendix A 'Operation MARKET: Diary of Events, 1 Parachute Brigade HQ', entry for 19:30, 17/09/1944; for Lathbury's justification for halting at 20:00 *see* audio recording of Major Hibbert's account of the incident at **Paradata Airborne Assault: The Living History of the Parachute Regiment and Airborne Forces** website, http://www.paradata.org.uk/media/519?mediaSection=Audio&mediaItem=1664; accessed 23/10/2010

53. Interview with Major Tony Hibbert, Brigade Major, 1st Parachute Brigade; *see* **Great Battles of World War II – Arnhem**, television documentary series episode broadcast on UK Channel 5 TV, 25/08/2001

54. *See* **WO 171/592**, 1st Parachute Brigade War Diary, Appendix A 'Operation MARKET: Diary of Events, 1 Parachute Brigade HQ', entry for 19:30, 17/09/1944

55. *See* Urquhart, pp.44-45

56. Quoted from ibid., p.45; also cited in Baynes, **Urquhart of Arnhem**, p.106

57. *See* for example Harclerode, **"Go to It!" The Illustrated History of the 6th Airborne Division**, p.64

58. *See* for example Baynes, pp.108-109

59. *See* **WO 171/1238**, 3rd Parachute Battalion War Diary, Appendix D, 'Diary of Events - 3rd Parachute Battalion', 'Account of C Company's Move to the Bridge by Sergeant Mason', entry for 17/9/1944

60. Testimony from Private W. Fred Moughton, Medium Machine Gun Platoon, HQ Company, 3rd Parachute Battalion; cited in Middlebrook, p.136-138. Middlebrook renders Private Moughton's name as 'Morton'

61. Testimony from Major Alan Bush, Battalion Second-in-Command, 3rd Parachute Battalion; cited in Middlebrook, p.137

62. *See* **WO 171/592**, 1st Parachute Brigade War Diary, Appendix A 'Operation MARKET: Diary of Events, 1 Parachute Brigade HQ', entry for 20:45, 17/09/1944

63. *See* **WO 171/592**, 1st Parachute Brigade War Diary, Appendix A 'Operation MARKET: Diary of Events, 1 Parachute Brigade HQ', entry for 20:45, 17/09/1944; for an audio recording of Major Hibbert's account of the incident, *see* **Paradata Airborne Assault: The Living History of the Parachute Regiment and Airborne Forces** website, http://www.paradata.org.uk/media/519?mediaSection=Audio&mediaItem=1664; accessed 23/10/2010

64. Quoted from audio recording of Major Hibbert's account at **Paradata Airborne Assault: The Living History of the Parachute Regiment and Airborne Forces** website, http://www.paradata.org.uk/media/519?mediaSection=Audio&mediaItem=1664; accessed 23/10/2010

65. Middlebrook, p.161

66. *See* Turnbull & Hamblett, **The Pegasus Patrol**, pp.69-71; and Robert Peatling, **No Surrender at Arnhem**, pp.18-19

67. Testimony from Lieutenant David Russell, commanding 7 Platoon, C Company, 2nd Parachute Battalion; cited in Middlebrook, p.160

68. Quoted from ibid., p.161

69. *See* David Truesdale, **Brotherhood of the Cauldron**, p.101

70. *See* Frost, pp.214-216

71. Testimony from Lieutenant Robin Vlasto, commanding 1 Platoon, A Company, 2nd Parachute Battalion; cited in Middlebrook, p.152

72. Testimony from Lance-Sergeant Bill Fulton, Section Commander, 3 Platoon, A Company, 2nd Parachute Battalion; cited in ibid., p.157

73. *See* Kershaw, p.101
74. Testimony from Signalman Bill Jukes, 1ˢᵗ Airborne Division Signals attached to 2ⁿᵈ Parachute Battalion; quoted from Middlebrook, p.158
75. *See* **WO 171/1509** 1ˢᵗ Parachute Squadron RE War Diary, entry for 22:00. 17/09/1944
76. *See* Frost, p.217; and Middlebrook, pp.157-158
77. Testimony from *Leutnant* Joseph Enthammer; cited in Kershaw, p.98
78. Testimony from Rottenführer Rudolf Trapp, 3 *Kompanie, Panzergrenadier Regiment 21, 10 SS Panzer Division*; cited in ibid., p.98
79. *See II SS Panzerkorps* Order, issued by telephone at 17:30 Hours on 17.9.44; *see* ibid., Appendix A, p.322; some sources give Brinkmann's rank as *Sturmbannführer* but Kershaw refers to him as an SS Captain (*Hauptsturmführer*); *see* ibid., p.97
80. *See* ibid., pp.96-97
81. Sergeant Thomas Edward Graham is listed as missing believed killed and has no known grave; he is commemorated on Panel 8, the Groesbeek Memorial, Gelderland, Holland
82. Lieutenant Peter Leslie Hibburt is listed as missing believed killed and has no known grave; he is commemorated on Panel 8, the Groesbeek Memorial, Gelderland, Holland
83. *See* **WO 171/1238**, 3ʳᵈ Parachute Battalion War Diary, 'Account of C Company Move to Arnhem Bridge by Sergeant Mason', Appendix D 'Diary of Events – 3rd Parachute Battalion', entry for 17/09/1944; and **The Pegasus Archive**, Battle of Arnhem Archive, Biographies Section 'Major R. Peter C. Lewis' at http://www.pegasusarchive.org/arnhem/pongo_lewis.htm, accessed 02/9/2011; and Middlebrook, p.159
84. *See* **WO 166/14933** 1ˢᵗ Airlanding Light Regiment RA War Diary, entry for 23:30, 17/09/1944; and Golden, **Echoes from Arnhem**, p.154
85. *See* for example Middlebrook, pp.161-162
86. Testimony from Leo Hall dated 2001 at **The Pegasus Archive**, Battle of Arnhem Archive, Biographies Section 'Bombardier J. Leo Hall', http://www.pegasusarchive.org/arnhem/Leo_Hall.htm, accessed 02/09/2011
87. *See* Fairley, **Remember Arnhem**, pp.73-74; and **WO 166/14933** 1ˢᵗ Airlanding Light Regiment RA War Diary, entry for 23:30, 17/09/1944 & 05:00, 18/09/1944
88. Testimony from Leo Hall dated 2001 at **The Pegasus Archive**, Biographies Section, 'Bombardier J. Leo Hall' at http://www.pegasusarchive.org/arnhem/Leo_Hall.htm; accessed 26/08/2011
89. *See* Fairley, pp.73-74
90. *See* **WO 171/1236** 1ˢᵗ Parachute Battalion War Diary, entry for 05:30, 18/09/1944
91. *See* **WO 166/14933**, 1ˢᵗ Airlanding Light Regiment RA War Diary, entry for 05:00, 18/09/1944
92. Quotes from **WO 171/1375**, 2ⁿᵈ Battalion South Staffordshire Regiment War Diary, Appendix '2nd South Staffords at Arnhem 17-25 Sept. 44' ; and **WO 171/1513**, 9ᵗʰ (Airborne) Field Company RE, comment at end of section for 17/09/1944
93. Testimony from Edward John Peters at http://thebritishairborneforcesclub.co.uk/pages/faces/peters.html, accessed 27/08/2011; *see* also Green, **1st Battalion The Border Regiment**, p.13
94. *See* Green, p.14
95. *See* testimony from Joseph Hardy, **The Pegasus Archive**, Biographies Section, 'Lieutenant Joseph Stephenson Davidson Hardy' at http://www.pegasusarchive.org/arnhem/joe_hardy.htm ; accessed 21/09/2011; *see* also Green, pp.14-15
96. *See* Kershaw, Appendix B, table 'Div Von Tettau 17-18 Sep 44', p.328
97. *See* Otway, **Airborne Forces**, p.266
98. *See* Kershaw, pp.108-111; and Map 2, 'The Formation of Kampfgruppe von Tettau', between pp.192-193
99. *See* **WO 171/1323**, 7ᵗʰ Battalion King's Own Scottish Borderers War Diary, initial untimed entry for 18/09/1944
100. *See* ibid., entry for 19.00 to 04:30, 18/09/1944;
101. *See* Kershaw, pp.108-111
102. *See* ibid., p.111 and Appendix B 'The German Order of Battle during Operation Market Garden 17-26 Sept', chart entitled 'Div Von Tettau 17-18 Sep 44', pp.328-329

103. For *Panzer Kompanie 224's* start location *see* Zwarts, **German Armoured Units at Arnhem**, p.65; for *Bataillon* Eberwein's estimated time of arrival *see* Kershaw, p.113

104. *See* Kershaw, p.113

105. For US map issue *see* Captain Carl W. Kappel, **The Operations of Company "H", 504th Parachute Infantry**, p.12

106. Kershaw, p.112

107. Quoted from ibid., p.120

108. Testimony from *General* Feldt; cited in ibid., p.121

109. *See* MacDonald, **The Siegfried Line Campaign**, p.160

110. *See* Gavin, **On to Berlin**, pp.160-161

111. *See* Captain Jack Tallerday, **The Operations of the 505ᵗʰ Parachute Infantry Regiment**, p.16

112. Quoted from letter from Gavin, nd; cited in MacDonald, **The Siegfried Line Campaign**, p.163

113. *See* Major Benjamin. F. Delamater, **The Actions of the 1st Battalion, 508th Parachute Infantry**, pp.9-10; and ibid., Major J. E. Adams, 'Insertion to Monograph, Extracts of Letter from Major J. E. Adams, Jr.', p.2; and MacDonald, **The Siegfried Line Campaign**, p.163

114. *See* Delamater, p.10

115. *See* Adams, p.3

116. *See* **WO 166/14933** 1ˢᵗ Airlanding Light Regiment RA War Diary, '3 Bty Parachute Party, 17th September 1944', entry for 17:00, 17/09/1944; the timing appears to be in error given that it was a further three hours before the lead elements of Frost's force actually reached the Arnhem road bridge

117. Kershaw, p.139; and Reynolds, p.133

118. Adams, p.3; *see also* Kershaw, p.101, especially footnote 16

119. *See* Delamater, pp.10-11; and MacDonald, **The Siegfried Line Campaign**, p.165

120. *See* Adams, p.3

121. *See* Kershaw, p.39; and Reynolds, p.133

122. *See* Adams, pp.3-4

123. Timings cited in Delamater, p.11; the latter cites a start time of 20:00 but that is unlikely to have been the case as Lieutenant-Colonel Warren did not give Captain Adams and Company A permission to move off from the rendezvous point on the outskirts of Nijmegen until that time, and it then took approximately two hours to reach the scene of the action

124. *See* Kershaw, pp.75-78; and Appendix A, p.322

125. Quoted from inserted comment by Delamater in Adams, p.2

126. Quoted from Rapport & Northwood, **Rendezvous with Destiny**, p.279

127. *See* for example ibid., p.279

128. Rendered Rafferty in some accounts

129. *See* Rapport & Northwood, pp.277-279

130. Quoted from Ryan, p.234

131. *See* ibid., p.234

132. *See* Kershaw, p.115

133. *See* Rapport & Northwood, pp.298-299

134. *See* ibid., pp.287-288

135. *See* **Headquarters Airborne Medical Company AOP 472** (US Army Medical Department, Office of Medical History), p.2 at http://history.amedd.army.mil/booksdocs/wwii/326thAirborneMedCo101stABDiv/326thABMedCo18Oct44.html, accessed 07/11/2011

136. *See* Kershaw, p.117

137. *See* Ambrose, **Band of Brothers**, p.126; and Rapport & Northwood, pp.274-275, 301

138. *See* Rapport & Northwood, pp.284-5, 287

139. *See* ibid., pp.284-7

140. *See* **CAB 44/254** Part II: Operation MARKET GARDEN, Book III, Chapter VII, Appendix A, Section 3 'Gds Armd Div and forward units of 50 (N) Div – Narrative 17 Sep.'

141. Quoted from Wilson, **The Ever Open Eye**, p.108

142. *See* **WO 171/1256** 2ⁿᵈ (Armoured) Battalion Irish Guards War Diary, entry for 20:30, 17/09/1944

143. *See* ibid., entry for 17:45, 17/09/1944; and Wilson, p.107

144. *See* Wilson, pp.106-109

145. Casualty figures cited in **CAB 44/254** Part II: Operation MARKET GARDEN, Book III, Chapter VII, Appendix A, Section 3 'Gds Armd Div and forward units of 50 (N) Div – Narrative 17 Sep.'; and WO **171/1257** 3rd Battalion Irish Guards War Diary, entry for 17/09/1944

146. Quoted from **CAB 44/254** Part II: Operation MARKET GARDEN, Book III, Chapter VII, Appendix A, Section 3 'Gds Armd Div and forward units of 50 (N) Div – Narrative 17 Sep.'

147. *See* **WO 171/1256** 2nd (Armoured) Battalion Irish Guards War Diary, entry for 22:00, 17/09/1944

148. *See* **WO 171/376** HQ Guards Armoured Division War Diary Jan-Sept 1944, Appendix JA 'Guards Armoured Division Operations Order No. 12 Operation Garden', Para. 14 'Divisional Tasks', dated 15/09/1944

149. *See* **CAB 44/254** Part II: Operation MARKET GARDEN, Book III, Chapter VII, Appendix A, Section 3 'Gds Armd Div and forward units of 50 (N) Div – Narrative 17 Sep.', Part ii. 'Supporting Units of 50 (N) Div.'

150. *See* Kershaw, p.87

151. *See* Wilson, p.112

152. *See* Horrocks, **Corps Commander**, p.99; cited in Powell, p.87

153. *See* **WO 171/1256** 2nd (Armoured) Battalion Irish Guards War Diary, entry for 12/09/1944; and Verney, **The Guards Armoured Division**, p.96

154. The same point is raised by Reynolds; *see* Reynolds, **Sons of the Reich**, p.125

155. Quoted from **WO 171/1341** HQ XXX Corps War Diary Sept 1944, Appendix 'O', 30 Corps Operational Instructions, '30 Corps Movement Instructions for Operation Garden (239/G1 15 Sept. 1944)'

156. *See* **WO 171/846**, 15th/19th King's Royal Hussars War Diary

157. *See* **WO 171/605** 5th Guards Armoured Brigade War Diary, Appendix D, dated 15/09/ 1944

158. *See* Wilson, pp.109-111

159. Quote from O'Connor's report on Operation COMPASS, cited in Pitt, p.162

160. *See* for example Ken Tout, **Tanks, Advance: Normandy to the Netherlands** (London: Robert Hale, 1987); and John Foley, **Mailed Fist**

161. *See* for example William. F. Buckingham, **D-Day: The First 72 Hours**, pp.263-264

162. For a detailed participant account of Operation TOTALIZE *see* Ken Tout, **Tank!**; for the advance from the Vernon bridgehead see for example Ellis, **Victory in the West Volume I: The Battle of Normandy**, p.470; and Delaforce, **The Black Bull**, pp.118-120

163. Quote from Horrocks, **Corps Commander**, p.99

Chapter 8

1. *See* Kershaw, **It Never Snows in September**, p.85. It is unclear what unit the attackers came from, given that Budel lay in the line of attack allocated to Lieutenant-General Sir Richard O'Connor's 8th Corps, and that formation did not move across the Meuse-Escaut Canal until the early hours of Tuesday 19 September 1944, twenty-four hours after the German account claims; *see* Powell, **The Devil's Birthday**, p.138. The discrepancy may be due to a dating error, or it may have been Richter and his men looking to justify their withdrawal in the same manner as Harzer at Cambrai on 2 September 1944

2. *See* Kershaw, p.88

3. *See* ibid., p.89; and Reynolds, **Sons of the Reich**, p.124

4. *See* Kershaw, pp.87-88

5. *See* ibid., p.89; and Reynolds, pp.134-136

6. *See* **WO 171/341** HQ GS File, 30 Corps, September 1944, entry for 18/09/1944

7. Wilson, **The Ever Open Eye**, pp.112-114

8. *See* Verney, **The Guards Armoured Division**, p.103

9. *See* **WO 171/1257** 3rd Battalion Irish Guards War Diary, entry for 18/09/1944; and Wilson, p.112

10. See **CAB 44/254** Part II: Operation MARKET GARDEN, Book III, Chapter VII, Appendix A, Section 6, '50 (N) Div - Narrative 18 Sep'; and **WO 171/1257** 3rd Battalion Irish Guards War Diary, entry for 17/09/1944

11. See **AIR 37/1249** 21st Army Group: Operation 'Market Garden', Part II, Section 8, Narrative 30 Corps and 1 Airborne Corps Execution of Operation 'MARKET GARDEN' period 17/26 September 1944, '30 Corps Operations 18 September 1944', Para 13, p.41

12. See **WO 171/1256** 2 (Armoured) Battalion Irish Guards War Diary, entry for 07:00, 18/09/1944

13. See **WO 171/376** Guards Armoured Division War Diary, Appendix KKK, Narrative 1 – 30 September 1944, entry for 9/09/1944; Verney, pp.93-94; and Boscawen, **Armoured Guardsman**, p.119

14. See **WO 171/1256** 2 (Armoured) Battalion Irish Guards War Diary, entry for 10:00, 18/09/1944; and Kershaw, p.89

15. See Wilson, pp.114-115

16. See **WO 171/1256** 2 (Armoured) Battalion Irish Guards War Diary, entries for 10:00 & 12:00, 18/09/1944

17. See Rapport & Northwood, **Rendezvous with Destiny**, pp.301, 306; and **CAB 44/254** Part II: Operation MARKET GARDEN, Book III, Chapter VII, Appendix A, Para. 4 'Gds Armd Div - Narrative 18 Sep'

18. See **CAB 44/254** Part II: Operation MARKET GARDEN, Book III, Chapter VII, Appendix A, Para. 4 'Gds Armd Div - Narrative 18 Sep'; and Verney, p.103

19. See **WO 171/341** HQ GS File, 30 Corps, Sept. 1944, entry for 18/09/1944

20. See **WO 171/1257** 3rd Battalion Irish Guards War Diary, entry for 18/09/1944

21. See **WO 171/1256** 2nd (Armoured) Battalion Irish Guards War Diary, entry for 18/09/1944; and **WO 171/376** Guards Armoured Division War Diary, entry for 18/09/1944

22. See Kershaw, p.89; and Rapport & Northwood, pp.301-302

23. For a detailed account see Rapport & Northwood, pp.302-305

24. See MacDonald, **The Siegfried Line Campaign**, p.149; and Rapport & Northwood, p.305

25. See Ambrose, **Band of Brothers**, p.127

26. See Kershaw, p.89

27. Quoted from MacDonald, **The Siegfried Line Campaign**, p.150

28. See Rapport & Northwood, pp.293-294; and Devlin, **Paratrooper!**, p.497

29. See Kershaw, pp.115-117

30. Unattributed participant quotes cited in Rapport & Northwood, pp.290, 291

31. Casualty figures cited in ibid., p.291

32. See ibid., pp.291-292

33. See *Heeresgruppe* B Situation Reports issued at 10:00, 15:30 & 20:00 17/09/1944; cited in MacDonald, **The Siegfried Line Campaign**, p.150; and Kershaw, pp.115-116

34. See Rapport & Northwood, pp.292-293

35. See ibid., pp.298-299

36. See 101st Airborne Division After Action Report – Summary of Operations 17-18 September 1944

37. See **Field Order No. 11, 82nd Airborne Division**, Annex No. 1. Intelligence, dated 13/09/1944

38. See Burriss, **Strike and Hold**, pp.107-108

39. See **A Graphic History of the 82nd Airborne Division**, entry for 'D Plus 1, 18 September'

40. See Guy LoFaro, **The Sword of St. Michael**, p.468

41. Early morning entries in 82nd Airborne Division G-2 Journal; cited in MacDonald, **The Siegfried Line Campaign**, footnote 59, p.166

42. Quoted from Gavin, **On to Berlin**, p.165

43. Quote from Gavin letter, nd; cited in MacDonald, **The Siegfried Line Campaign**, footnote 56, p.165

44. According to MacDonald's Official History, Company G was commanded by Captain Frank J. Novak, but Gavin and a more recent account refer to Captain Russell C. Wilde; see MacDonald, **The Siegfried Line Campaign**, p.165; Gavin, **On to Berlin**, p.163; and LoFaro, p.337

45. See Gavin, **On to Berlin**, p.163; and LoFaro, pp.336-337

46. *See* MacDonald, **The Siegfried Line Campaign**, p.165 & footnote 57, p.165
47. Departure time cited in LoFaro, p.337; and MacDonald, **The Siegfried Line Campaign**, p.65
48. *See* Phil Nordyke, **All American All the Way**, p.63
49. *See* Kershaw, pp.138-139
50. *See* Reynolds, pp.128-129; and Kershaw, p.139
51. *See* Kershaw, p.139; and Reynolds, p.133
52. *See* Nordyke, p.63
53. *See* LoFaro, p.337
54. *See* Kershaw, p.139
55. *See* Reynolds, p.133; and Kershaw, pp.139-140
56. *See* MacDonald, **The Siegfried Line Campaign**, p.165
57. *See* Kershaw, pp.120-122
58. *See* Gavin, **On to Berlin**, p.167
59. *See* LoFaro, p.339
60. *See* Captain Robert L. Sickler, **The Operations of Company "D", 2nd Battalion, 508th Parachute Infantry Regiment**, p.12
61. *See* Gavin, **On to Berlin**, p.167; and LoFaro, p.339
62. Quoted from Captain Kenneth L. Johnson, **Supply Operations of the 508th Parachute Infantry Regiment**, p.26
63. *See* Sickler, pp.12-13, 22. The SCR 356 was a hand-held set weighing 5.5 pounds with a range of up to a mile and a battery life of c.fifteen hours; the SCR 300 was a forty-channel backpack set weighing 38.23 pounds with a range of up to three miles and a battery life of 8-12 hours
64. *See* Sickler, pp.14-18
65. *See* Johnson, p.28
66. Quoted from Woodrow W. Millsaps, letter to Heather Chapman dated 27/07/1967, Cornelius Ryan Collection, Alden Library, Ohio University; cited in Nordyke, p.70
67. *See* Nordyke, p.58; the latter claims the action took place in the evening of 17 September, but this does not accord with participant testimony and other accounts. *See* for example Tallerday, **The Operations of the 505th Parachute Infantry Regiment**, p.17; and LoFaro, p.340
68. The *Möbelwagen* (furniture van) was a *Panzer* IV chassis mounting a 37mm *Flak 43* automatic cannon capable of firing 150 rounds per minute. The nickname came from the four large, rectangular armoured plates that enclosed the gun, which could be dropped to allow all-round traverse; doing this exposed the gun crew to enemy fire however, and it was common to leave the side and rear plates raised when engaging ground targets. In this instance the gun was unable to depress sufficiently to engage some US positions on the hillside.
69. *See* Nordyke, pp.50, 64-65
70. *See* Kershaw, pp.122-123; the 'Craoneer Heights' may have referred to Craonne on the Chemin des Dames ridge overlooking the River Aisne north of Reims, which was captured by the Germans in 1914 and was the scene of fierce fighting during the Nivelle Offensive of April 1917.
71. *See* LoFaro, pp.340-341
72. The Weertjesstraat appears as the Oranjewachtstraat on modern maps, presumably renamed in post-war redevelopment
73. *See* Sims, **Arnhem Spearhead**, pp.49-53
74. Figures and units cited in Middlebrook, **Arnhem 1944**, pp.287-288
75. Locations taken from Middlebrook, Map 11 'Arnhem Bridge', p.289; *see* also Sims, front endpaper; Zwaarts, **German Armoured Units at Arnhem**, maps on p.11; John Waddy, **A Tour of the Arnhem Battlefields**, 3D diagram and key on the rear of the enclosed 'Arnhem Battlefield Map'; and Kershaw, map/diagrams 'German Attempts to Recapture the Arnhem Bridge 17-20 September 1944', p.133
76. *See* **WO 171/1509** 1st Parachute Squadron RE War Diary, entries for 23:00. 23:15 & 23:45 17/09/1944
77. Account by Sapper George Needham, A Troop 1st Parachute Squadron RE; cited in Middlebrook, pp.289-290

78. *See* **The Pegasus Archive**, Battle of Arnhem Archive, Biographies Section 'Lance-Corporal Arthur S. Hendy' at http://www.pegasusarchive.org/arnhem/arthur_hendy.htm accessed 27/09/2012.

79. *See* **WO 171/1509** 1st Parachute Squadron RE War Diary, entries for 00:10 & 02:00-03:00, 18/09/1944

80. Fifteen figure cited with names in Niall Cherry, **With Nothing Bigger than a Bren Gun**, p.22

81. *See* for example Middlebrook, p.290; for the lack of mutual mention *see* **WO 171/1509** 1st Parachute Squadron RE War Diary, entries for 18-20/09/1944; and **WO 171/1238**, 3rd Parachute Battalion War Diary, 'Report on the Action by "C" Company, 3rd Battalion, The Parachute Regiment at Arnhem by Major R.P.C Lewis, "C" Company Commander'

82. *See* Kershaw, pp.125-126

83. *See* Sims, p.55

84. For 3 Battery relocation *see* **WO 166/14933**, 1st Airlanding Light Regiment RA War Diary, entry for 05:00, 18/09/1944; for target registration *see* for example Middlebrook, pp.290-291

85. *See* Zwarts, plate p.23

86. *See* Sims, pp.55-56; Frost, **A Drop Too Many**, p.219; and Middlebrook, p.291; vehicle locations from Zwarts, diagram 'Arnhem Bridge on 18-20 September 1944', p.11

87. *See* Reynolds, p.137; and Kershaw, p.134

88. *See* Zwarts, organisation chart, p.4 & p.23

89. Testimony from Lieutenant Arvian Llewellyn-Jones, Battery Captain 'A', 1st Airlanding Anti-tank Battery RA; cited in Middlebrook, p.291; *see* also Sims, pp.56-57. Interestingly only the dustbin lorry and two shot up trucks from SS *Panzer Aufklärungs Abteilung* 10 are visible on an oblique photograph taken by an RAF Spitfire reconnaissance aircraft later on 18 September; *see* for example Middlebrook, plate 10 between pp.118-119

90. for sunrise and sunset timings *see* **Field Order No. 11, 82nd Airborne Division**, Annex 1.a(1) to F.O. 11, Weather; Sun and Moon Tables, Para .2 "Sun and Moon Data", dated 11/09/1944

91. Quoted from Middlebrook, p.291

92. *See* Zwarts, p.11

93. Quote cited in Kershaw, p.128

94. Vehicle types and numbers taken from Zwarts, diagram 'Arnhem Bridge on 18-20 September 1944' and adjacent key, p.11

95. *See* Kershaw, p.129

96. Testimony from Major Dennis Munford, OC 3 Battery, 1st Airlanding Light Regiment RA; cited in Middlebrook, p.92. Interestingly there is no reference to this fire mission in other participant accounts or in the Light Regiment's War Diary, which does not refer to 3 Battery's guns being in action at Oosterbeek before 10:00; *see* for example Frost, p.219; testimony from Leo Hall dated 2001 at 'Bombardier J. Leo Hall', **The Pegasus Archive** website, http://www.pegasusarchive.org/arnhem/Leo_Hall.htm, accessed 02/09/2011; and **WO 166/14933** 1st Airlanding Light Regiment RA War Diary, entry for 10:00, 18/09/1944

97. For 08:00 time *see* **WO 171/592** 1 Parachute Brigade War Diary, entry for 08:00, 18/09/1944; for 08:30 timing *see* **WO 171/1509** 1st Parachute Squadron RE War Diary, entry for 08:30, 18/09/1944; for 09:00 *see* Kershaw, p.129; for 09:30 *see* Reynolds, p.128

98. *See* Frost, p.219

99. *See* Middlebrook, p.293

100. Vehicle types & locations taken from Zwarts, p.11

101. *See* **WO 171/592** 1 Parachute Brigade War Diary, entry for 08:00, 18/09/1944

102. *See* testimony from Signalman William Jukes, 2nd Parachute Battalion; cited in Middlebrook, p.294

103. *See* Cherry, pp.14-15; for Sapper Emery's Military Medal citation *see* **The Pegasus Archive**, Battle of Arnhem Archive, Biographies Section 'Sapper Ronald Thomas Emery' at http://www.pegasusarchive.org/arnhem/ronald_thomas_emery.htm accessed 27/09/2012.

104. For the adoption of the war cry *see* for example Frost, pp.110-111

105. *See* Sims, pp.58-59

106. *See* Middlebrook, p.298; and Cherry, p.16

107. *See* for example Middlebrook, pp.294-295; and Kershaw, pp.130-131; for vehicle numbers, types and locations *see* Zwarts, p.1

108. *See* **WO 171/1509** 1st Parachute Squadron RE War Diary, entries for 10:00 & 11:00, 18/09/1944

109. *See* Middlebrook, p.296; again, there is no mention of these fire missions in the 1st Airlanding Regiment's War Diary

110. *See* **WO 171/1509** 1st Parachute Squadron RE War Diary, entry for 13:00, 18/09/1944; for possibility of friendly fire *see* Cherry, p.15

111. *See* Middlebrook, pp.184-185; and Truesdale, **Brotherhood of the Cauldron**, pp.115-116

112. *See* **WO 171/1238** 3rd Parachute Battalion War Diary, entry for 08:30 [sic] 18/09/1944; and Middlebrook, pp.170-171

113. *See* **WO 171/1236** 1st Parachute Battalion War Diary, entries for 05:30 & 07:00, 17/09/1944; and Middlebrook, pp.177-178;

114. Testimony from Lieutenant James Cleminson, commanding 5 Platoon, B Company, 3rd Parachute Battalion; cited in Middlebrook, p.171

115. *See* Kershaw, p.165

116. *Kampfgruppe* Spindler unit strength figures cited in Reynolds, pp.118-119

117. *See* **WO 171/1238** 3rd Parachute Battalion War Diary, entries for 08:30 & 10:00-16:00, 18/09/1944. *Sturmgeschütze* III and *Sturmhaubitze* 42G vehicles from *Sturmgeschütze Brigade 280* operated in this area but did not arrive until the morning of Tuesday 19 September; *see* Zwarts, p.26

118. Middlebrook, pp.171-172; for radio contact *see* **WO 171/1238** 3rd Parachute Battalion War Diary, entry for 10:00-16:00, 18/09/1944

119. *See* **WO 166/14933** 1st Airlanding Light Regiment RA War Diary, entry for 10:00, 18/09/1944

120. *See* **WO 171/1236** 1st Parachute Battalion War Diary, entries for 07:00 & 08:00, 18/09/1944; and Middlebrook, p.178

121. Testimony from Lieutenant Jack Hellingoe, commanding 11 Platoon, T Company, 1st Parachute Battalion; cited in Middlebrook, pp.178-179

122. *See* **WO 171/1236** 1st Parachute Battalion War Diary, entry for 09:00, 18/09/1944; and Middlebrook, pp.178-179

123. Quote from Captain Geoffrey Costeloe, Adjutant, 1st Airborne Reconnaissance Squadron; cited in Fairley, **Remember Arnhem**, p.68

124. *See* **WO 171/406** 1st Airborne Reconnaissance Squadron War Diary, various time-stamped notes in entry for 18/09/1944; and Fairley, pp.63-81

125. *See* Middlebrook, p.186. Interestingly there is no mention of this in the Division HQ War Diary, although there are references to the ongoing failure to establish radio communications with Lathbury or Urquhart; *see* **WO 171/393**, 1st Airborne Division HQ War Diary, entries for 07:00 & 09:00, 18/09/1944

126. *See* **WO 171/393**, 1st Airborne Division HQ War Diary, entry for 09:15, 18/09/1944; and **WO 171/589** 1st Airlanding Brigade War Diary, entry for 11:00, 17/09/1944

127. For handover timing *see* **WO 171/589**, 1st Airlanding Brigade War Diary, entry for 11:00, 18/09/1944; and Middlebrook, p.187; for comparative strengths of British Airlanding and Parachute Battalions *see* for example ibid., Appendix 1, 'Order of Battle and Operational Details, 1st British Airborne Division and Attached Units', pp.455-457

128. The Battalion, Brigade and Division records all cite different departure times; *see* **WO 171/1375**, 2nd Battalion, South Staffordshire Regiment War Diary, entry for 09:30, 18/09/1944; ibid, Appendix A '2nd South Staffords at Arnhem 17-25 Sept. 1944' cites 10:30; **WO 171/393**, 1st Airborne Division HQ War Diary, entry for 09:45, 18/09/1944; and **WO 171/589**, 1st Airlanding Brigade War Diary, entry for 10:00, 18/09/1944

129. *See* **WO 171/1375** 2nd Battalion South Staffordshire Regiment War Diary, entries for 17 & 18/09/1944; and Middlebrook, pp.80, 88-89

130. *See* **WO 171/1232** 'B' Squadron, The Glider Pilot Regiment War Diary, entry for 18/09/1944; and Simon Haines, **The Holland Patch**, p.23

131. Lance-Sergeant Stanley William Charles Sears and Private Joseph Walker are interred in Arnhem Oosterbeek War Cemetery, Gelderland, Holland, in Plot 15, Row A, Grave 9 and Plot 15, Row A, Grave 7 respectively

132. *See* **WO 166/15077** 1st Battalion The Border Regiment War Diary, entry for 18/09/1944; and Green, **1st Battalion The Border Regiment**, pp.20-21

133. Rendered MacCartney in some accounts

134. *See* **WO 166/15077** 1st Battalion The Border Regiment War Diary, entry for 18/09/1944; and Green, pp.17-19

135. *See* **WO 166/15077** 1st Battalion The Border Regiment War Diary, entry for 18/09/1944; and Green, pp.21-22

136. *See* **WO 171/1323** 7th Battalion King's Own Scottish Borderers War Diary, entry for 06:00, 18/09/1944; and Middlebrook, p.221

137. *See* **WO 171/1248** 21st Independent Parachute Company War Diary, entry for 18/09/1944; and Kent, **First In**, pp.99-100

138. *See* Kent, p.100; and Middlebrook, pp.223, 233-234

139. *See* **WO 171/1323** 7th Battalion King's Own Scottish Borderers War Diary, entries for 07:00 and 09:000, 18/09/1944

140. *See* **WO 171/1323** 7th Battalion King's Own Scottish Borderers War Diary, entry for 10:00, 18/09/1944; and Middlebrook, pp.221-222. The former refers to 'at least six' vehicles being knocked out, but the latter cites testimony from the gun commander recalling only a single vehicle being knocked out with a single shot

141. *See* **WO 166/14933** 1st Airlanding Light Regiment RA War Diary, entry for 10:00; and Middlebrook, p.222

142. *See* Middlebrook, p.222

143. *See* ibid., p.222; Private Alexander McKay is interred in Ede General Cemetery, Gelderland, Holland, Row H, Joint Grave 19

144. *Planken Wambuis* was originally the location for cutting timber to make coffins, the term meaning 'wooden jacket' in Old Dutch; in English, when referring to a coffin, rendered as 'wooden overcoat'; *see* Middlebrook, Footnote 9, p.163

145. *See* **WO 171/1323** 7th Battalion King's Own Scottish Borderers War Diary, entry for 15:00, 18/09/1944

146. Quote from **171/1323** 7th Battalion King's Own Scottish Borderers War Diary, entry for 10:00, 18/09/1944

147. *See* Kershaw, pp.154-156

148. *See* **WO 166/14933** 1st Airlanding Light Regiment RA War Diary, entry for 10:00, 18/09/1944

Chapter 9

1. Aircraft figures and Hamilcar load details from Middlebrook, **Arnhem 1944**, pp.224, 245

2. *See* Albert Blockwell, **Diary of a Red Devil**, p.91

3. Middlebrook, p.224

4. *See* **WO 171/1511** 4th Parachute Squadron RE War Diary, entry for 17:30, 17/09/1944

5. Testimony from Major Æneas Perkins, Officer Commanding 4th Parachute Engineer Squadron; cited in Harry Faulkner-Brown, **A Sapper at Arnhem**, pp.33-36

6. *See* Alexander Morrison, **Silent Invader**, pp.52-53

7. *See* Blockwell, pp.90-91

8. *See* ibid., p.93

9. *See* **WO 171/1511** 4th Parachute Squadron RE War Diary, entry for 09:00, 18/09/1944; and **WO 171/1232** B Squadron Glider Pilot Regiment War Diary, entry for 09:00, 18/09/1944

10. *See* Morrison, p.55

11. *See* **AIR 27/473** No. 48 Squadron Operations Record Book, entry for 18/09/1944

12. *See* **WO 171/1231** A, D, G Squadron Glider Pilot War Diary, D Squadron entry for 11:26 & G Squadron entry for 11:30, 18/09/1944

13. It is unclear when the RAF Squadrons relocated but B Squadron moved to Manston on 5 & 6 September; *see* **WO 171/1232** B Squadron Glider Pilot Regiment War Diary, entries for 15:00, 5/091944, 10:30, 6/09/1944 and 12:15, 18/09/1944; and Middlebrook, Appendix 3 'Order of Battle, 38 and 46 Groups RAF and RASC Air Despatch Units', p.463

14. *See* **WO 171/1247** 156 Parachute Battalion War Diary, entry for 11:00, 18/09/1944; and **WO 171/1511** 4th Parachute Squadron RE War Diary, entries for 11:45 & 12:10, 18/09/1944

15. Figures cited in Middlebrook, p.225

16. *See* **WO 219/5137** Report on Operation Market: 1 Airborne Division; cited in Flint, **Airborne Armour**, p.137

17. *See* **WO 171/1232** B Squadron Glider Pilot Regiment War Diary, entry for 12:15, 18/09/1944

18. For reattachment *see* Middlebrook, p.225; and Maurice & John Davis, **The Allied Special Forces History: 299 Squadron – Special Operation Service – Arnhem De-briefs**, entry for 18/9/1944 at http://www.memorialgrove.org.uk/299squadronarnhemdebriefs.htm, accessed 11/04/2012; for Glider Pilot names and carry over to third lift *see* **WO 171/1231** A, D, G Squadron Glider Pilot War Diary, D Squadron entry for 11:26, 18/09/1944

19. Seven glider figure cited in **WO 171/1230** Headquarters, Commander Glider Pilots War Diary, Appendix 'Operation "Market" Air', entry for Second Lift

20. *See* Middlebrook, p.225

21. *See* **AIR 27/473** No. 48 Squadron Operations Record Book, separate entries for 18/09/1944

22. *See* Otway, **Airborne Forces**, p.269; and Middlebrook, pp.227-228

23. *See* **WO 171/1231** A, D, G Squadron Glider Pilot War Diary, D Squadron entry for 18/09/1944; Lieutenant Norman Vere Maxwell Adams is commemorated on the Groesbeek Memorial, Panel 8

24. *See* **WO 219/5137** Report on Operation Market: 1 Airborne Division; cited in Flint, p.137; and Middlebrook, p.226. Lieutenant Robert Leonard McLaren is commemorated at the Groesbeek Memorial, Panel 1

25. *See* Morrison, p.57

26. *See* **WO 171/1234** No.1 Wing Glider Pilot Regiment War Diary, entry for 15:00, 18/09/1944

27. *See* Brinson, **Airborne Troop Carrier**, p.141

28. *See* testimony from 2nd Lieutenant Glenn A. Ulrich, 310th Troop Carrier Squadron, 315th Troop Carrier Group; cited in Brinson, p.160

29. *See* Middlebrook, p.228

30. *See* ibid., p.229. Testimony from 1st Lieutenant Walter D. Nims, 50th Troop Carrier Squadron, 314th Troop Carrier Group; cited at **Fields of Honour Database**, http://www.adoptiegraven-database.nl accessed 13/04/2012

32. Middlebrook, pp.228-229. Captain Ottaway is interred in the American War Cemetery Ardennes, Plot A, Row 42, Grave 53; for crew details *see* **The Pegasus Archive**, Battle of Arnhem Archive: Roll of Honour – 314th Troop Carrier Group at http://www.pegasusarchive.org/arnhem/rollU314.htm accessed 13/04/2012. The remains of the eighteen paratroopers, which could not be individually identified, are interred and commemorated at the Jonkerbos War Cemetery, Gelderland, The Netherlands on Special Memorial 8, various panels

33. *See* Middlebrook, p.229. Crew details cited at **The Pegasus Archive**, Battle of Arnhem Archive: Roll of Honour – 314th Troop Carrier Group at http://www.pegasusarchive.org/arnhem/rollU314.htm accessed 13/04/2012; all three US casualties appear to have been repatriated to the US; Private John Arthur Barton is interred in Rhenen General Cemetery, Utrecht, The Netherlands, Plot 27, Row A, Grave 2

34. Testimony from Captain Frank King, OC Support Company, 11th Parachute Battalion; cited in Middlebrook, pp.229-230

35. *See* Stuart Mawson, **Arnhem Doctor**, pp.27-28

36. For details *see* George C. Merz, Lt Col. USAF (Ret) & Lewis E. Johnston, 1st Lt AUS (Ret), **Eyewitness to History: The Great Underground Escape from German Occupied Holland**, interview recorded at Dayton, Ohio, 12-14 October 2001; see Air Mobility Command Museum

website http://amcmuseum.org/history/wwii/underground_escape.php, accessed 15/04/2012; *see* also Middlebrook, pp.229-230

37. *See* Major R. Brammall, **The Tenth: A Record of Service of the 10th Battalion, The Parachute Regiment 1942-1945**, pp.51-52

38. *See* Brinson, p.140

39. Testimony from 1st Lieutenant Edward S. Fulmer, 43rd Troop Carrier Squadron, 315th Troop Carrier Group; cited at **Fields of Honour Database**, http://www.adoptiegraven-database.nl/index. php?option=com_content&view=article&id=7687:spurrier-james-h&catid=63:american-war-cemetery-margraten-s&Itemid=147, accessed 17/04/2012

40. Testimony from 2nd Lieutenant Clinton C. Denny, 43rd Troop Carrier Squadron, 315th Troop Carrier Group; cited at **Fields of Honour Database**, http://www.adoptiegraven-database.nl/ index.php?option=com_content&view=article&id=7688:hollis-william-t&catid=52:american-war-cemetery-margraten-h&Itemid=136, accessed 18/04/2012

41. *See* Brinson, p.141 and Appendix Five 'The Royalty of the 315th Troop Carrier Group', pp.288-297. Lieutenant James H. Spurrier and Corporal William T. Hollis are interred in the American War Cemetery Margraten, Plot K, Row 14, Grave 17 and Plot I, Row 7, Grave 9 respectively; Private Alfred William Penwill is interred in Arnhem Oosterbeek War Cemetery, Gelderland, Holland in Plot 9, Row B, Grave 4

42. Testimony from 1st Lieutenant William E. Bruce, 34th Troop Carrier Squadron, 315th Troop Carrier Wing; cited in Brinson, p.162

43. *See* Kershaw, **It Never Snows in September**, 156-160

44. *See* Middlebrook, p.234

45. *See* **WO 171/1323** 7th Battalion King's Own Scottish Borderers War Diary, entry for 10:00 to 14:00, 18/09/1944; **WO 166/14933** 1st Airlanding Light Regiment RA War Diary, entry for 10:00, 18/09/1944; and Middlebrook, p.234

46. Quotes from **WO 171/1323** 7th Battalion King's Own Scottish Borderers War Diary, entries for 10:00 to 14:00 & 15:00, 18/09/1944

47. *See* **WO 171/1247** 156 Parachute Battalion War Diary, entry for 14:00, 18/09/1944; **WO 171/1511** 4th Parachute Squadron RE War Diary, entry for 14:20, 18/09/1944; **WO 171/1244** 11th Parachute Battalion War Diary, entry for 18/09/1944; and **WO 171/594** 4th Parachute Brigade War Diary, Appendix C: 'Diary Kept by Brigadier J.W. Hackett, Commander 4th Parachute Brigade', entry for 18/09/1944

48. Drop figure and details cited in Middlebrook, p.234

49. Testimony from 1st Lieutenant Charles Vogelin, 43rd Troop Carrier Squadron, 315th Troop Carrier Group; cited in Brinson, p.158

50. Testimony from Corporal David Jones, 156 Parachute Battalion; cited in Middlebrook, p.240

51. Testimony from Captain Bernard Coggins, 43rd Troop Transport Squadron, 315th Troop Carrier Wing; cited in Brinson, p.161

52. Testimony from Private Jock Keenan, 156 Parachute Battalion and Signalman Arthur Winstanley, 4th Parachute Brigade Signals section; cited in Middlebrook, pp.235-236

53. *See* Ryan, **A Bridge Too Far**, pp.158, 316-317

54. Testimony from Corporal Frederick Jenkins, 10th Parachute Battalion; cited in Middlebrook, p.237

55. Quote from Ryan, p.317

56. *See* Brammall, **The Tenth**, p.53

57. Testimony from Private David Dagwell, 156 Parachute Battalion; cited in Middlebrook, pp.238-239

58. Testimony from Corporal David Jones, 156 Parachute Battalion; cited in ibid., pp.240-241

59. *See* Middlebrook, p.242; and **WO 171/1511** 4th Parachute Squadron RE War Diary, entry for 14:20, 18/09/1944. Captain Thomas' name is sometimes rendered Beaumont-Thomas

60. Figures cited in Middlebrook, pp.234, 242

61. *See* **WO 171/1323** 7th Battalion King's Own Scottish Borderers War Diary, entry for 15:00, 18/09/1944; and Middlebrook, p.234. Major Henry Ralph Hill is interred in the Arnhem Oosterbeek War Cemetery, Gelderland, Holland in Plot 23, Row A, Grave 1

62. *See* **WO 171/594** 4th Parachute Brigade War Diary, Appendix C: 'Diary Kept by Brigadier J.W. Hackett, Commander 4th Parachute Brigade'; and **WO 171/1247** 156 Parachute Battalion War Diary, entry for 14:30, 18/09/1944

63. Quote from **WO 171/594** 4th Parachute Brigade War Diary, Appendix C: 'Diary Kept by Brigadier J.W. Hackett, Commander 4th Parachute Brigade'; for details of pre-MARKET briefings *see* General Sir John Hackett, 'Operation Market Garden' in Foot (Ed.), **Holland at War Against Hitler**, p.166; and Middlebrook, p.63

64. *See* **WO 171/1231** A, D, G Squadron Glider Pilot War Diary, D Squadron entry for 11:26, 18/09/1944

65. *See* Middlebrook, pp.232-234

66. Testimony from Gunner Robert Christie, 1st Airlanding Light Regiment RA; cited in ibid., p.232

67. *See* **The Pegasus Archive**, Biographies Section, 'Squadron-Leader Trevor Southgate', at http://www.pegasusarchive.org/arnhem/trevor_southgate.htm accessed on 25/04/2012; and Alan W. Cooper, **The Air Battle for Arnhem**, Appendix 'RAF Losses at the Battle of Arnhem, September 1944', p.184. Curiously there is no mention of the loss in the 512 Squadron records, which reports Squadron Leader Southgate's Dakota landing at RAF Broadwell at 15:00; *see* **AIR 27/1972** No. 512 Squadron Operations Record Book, entry for 18/09/1944

68. *See* **AIR 27/2041** No. 570 Squadron Operations Record Book, entry for 18/09/1944; and Middlebrook, p.233; for crew details *see* Cooper, **The Air Battle for Arnhem**, Appendix 'RAF Losses at the Battle of Arnhem, September 1944', pp.170-171; and **The Pegasus Archive**, Roll of Honour Section, http://www.pegasusarchive.org/arnhem/rollR570.htm, accessed 25/04/2012. Pilot-Officer Charles William Culling RAFVR and his crew are interred in Heteren General Cemetery, Plot 2, Row A, Collective Grave 20-21

69. *See* Otway, p.269

70. *See* **WO 171/1231** A, D, G Squadron Glider Pilot War Diary, D Squadron entry for 11:26, 18/09/1944; and **AIR 27/473** No. 48 Squadron Operations Record Book, entry for 18/09/1944

71. *See* for example **WO 171/1231** A, D, G Squadron Glider Pilot War Diary, D Squadron entry for 11:26 with regard to Chalk No. 956, 18/09/1944

72. Quoted from Morrison, pp.56-57

73. Quoted from ibid., pp.57-58

74. *See* Middlebrook, p.242

75. Quoted from Morrison, pp.59-60

76. Testimony from Sergeant Patrick 'Paddy' Senier, E Squadron, No. 2 Wing, The Glider Pilot Regiment; cited in Middlebrook, pp.243-244; the Andy referred to was Staff-Sergeant Harold Andrews DFM & Bar, with whom Sergeant Senier flew into Normandy and Arnhem; for details *see* **The Pegasus Archive**, Biographies Section 'Staff-Sergeant Harold Norman' at http://www.pegasusarchive.org/normandy/harold_norman_andrews.htm, accessed 02/05/2012

77. *See* **WO 171/1375** 2nd Battalion South Staffordshire Regiment War Diary, section for 18/09/1944

78. For glider types and numbers *see* Otway, p.267; for Hamilcar details *see* **WO 219/5137** Report on Operation Market: 1 Airborne Division; cited in Flint, **Airborne Armour**, pp.137-138

79. *See* Green, **1st Battalion The Border Regiment**, p.24

80. *See* ibid., p.22; quote from Middlebrook, p.244

81. *See* Middlebrook, p.245

82. *See* ibid., p.245

83. Figures cited in ibid., p.246

84. *See* **WO 171/1248**, 21st Independent Parachute Company War Diary, entry for 18/09/1944; and Kent, **First In!**, pp.99-100

85. For details *see* **The Pegasus Archive**, Biographies Section, 'Flying Officer D. H. Balmer' at http://www.pegasusarchive.org/arnhem/d_h_balmer.htm, accessed 12/05/2012; Corporal

Alfred Ernest Barker is interred at Roosendaal-En-Nispen General Cemetery, Noord-Brabant, Holland in Row 3, Grave 1

86. *See* Otway, p.269; and Middlebrook, p.246

87. For casualty and aircraft loss figures *see* **The Pegasus Archive**, Roll of Honour Section, entries for 38 Group, 46 Group, 314th Troop Carrier Group and 315th Troop Carrier Group at http://www.pegasusarchive.org/arnhem/roll.htm, accessed 12/05/2012; and Middlebrook, p.246. The latter claims No. 570 Squadron lost three Stirlings on Monday 18 September 1944, although a fourth was lost in a take-off accident; *see* Cooper, Appendix 'RAF Losses at the Battle of Arnhem: September 1944' pp.170-171

88. Figures and units cited in Gavin, **On to Berlin**, p.168; Blair, **Ridgeway's Paratroopers**, p.336; LoFaro, **The Sword of St. Michael**, p.339,; and Nordyke, **All American All The Way**, p.67

89. *See* Lo Faro, p.342. According to Blair eleven gliders aborted or ditched; *see* Blair, p.336

90. Testimony from PFC John McKenzie, 456th Parachute Field Artillery Battalion and Corporal Lloyd Click, Battery B, 320th Glider Field Artillery Battalion; cited in Nordyke, p.68

91. Quoted from Captain Kenneth L. Johnson, **Supply Operations of the 508th Parachute Infantry Regiment**, p.28

92. Timing cited in MacDonald, **The Siegfried Line Campaign**, p.167

93. *See* Major Benjamin F. Delamater, **The Action of the 1st Battalion, 508th Parachute Infantry**, pp.12-13

94. *See* Captain Robert L. Sickler, **The Operations of Company D, 2nd Battalion, 508th Parachute Infantry Regiment**, pp.17-20

95. *See* Devlin, **Paratrooper!**, p.501

96. Figures and details from Delamater, pp.13-14; and Sickler, pp.20-21

97. *See* Captain Jack Tallerday, **The Operations of the 505th Parachute Infantry Regiment**, p.17

98. Testimony from Colonel William E. Ekman, commander 505th Parachute Infantry Regiment; cited in LoFaro, p.341

99. Quoted from Lieutenant Jack Tallerday, Executive Officer, Company C, 1st Battalion 505th Parachute Infantry Regiment; cited in Nordyke, p.76

100. *See* ibid., pp.76-77; and LoFaro, pp.341-342

101. Testimony from Private Arthur B. Schultz, Company C, 1st Battalion, 505th Parachute Infantry Regiment; cited in ibid., p.77

102. *See* ibid., pp.77-78

103. *See* Gavin, p.168; LoFaro, p.342; and Nordyke, p.76

104. *See* LoFaro, p.342

105. Figures cited in ibid., pp.342-343

106. Testimony from Captain Herman L. Alley, Commanding Battery A, 456th Parachute Field Artillery Battalion, 82nd Airborne Division; quotation cited in Nordyke, p.76; other details cited from Herman L. Alley, Personal Log at **The 505th Regimental Combat Team Website**, http://www.505rct.org/album2/alley_h.asp, accessed 23/05/2012

107. *See* Nordyke, p.75; and LoFaro, pp.342-343

108. Figures cited in Gavin, p.168

109. Figures cited in LoFaro, p.343

110. Quoted from *see* Captain Carl W. Kappel, **The Operations of Company "H", 504th Parachute Infantry**, p.22

111. *See* LoFaro, p.344; and Nordyke, p.78. For sixty per cent recovery figure *see* for example Johnson, **Supply Operations**, p.31; and Tallerday, **The Operations of the 505th Parachute Infantry Regiment**, p.18

112. US glider infantry regiments were originally formed with only two infantry battalions, but this was increased to three by splitting the 401st Glider Infantry Regiment and assigning its two battalions to the 82nd and 101st Airborne Division's glider infantry regiments before the Normandy invasion. Although it retained its independent status, Lieutenant-Colonel Allen's Battalion therefore functioned as the 327th Regiment's third Battalion; *see* MacDonald, **The Siegfried Line Campaign**, p.152, footnote 21

113. Units cited in Rapport and Northwood, **Rendezvous with Destiny**, p.299; pre landing figures cited in Devlin, **Silent Wings**, p.253
114. Timings and pilot details cited in Devlin, **Silent Wings**, p.254
115. *See ibid.*, pp.254-256
116. Numbers and timing cited in Rapport & Northwood, p.299
117. Quoted from Bowen, **Fighting with the Screaming Eagles**, p.86
118. *See* Devlin, **Silent Wings**, pp.253-254
119. Figures cited in MacDonald, p.152; Rapport & Northwood, p.299; and Devlin, **Silent Wings**, p.256
120. *See* Rapport & Northwood, p.299

Chapter 10

1. Testimony from Captain Bernard Coggins, 43rd Troop Transport Squadron, 315th Troop Carrier Wing; cited in Brinson, **Airborne Troop Carrier**, p.161
2. Quoted from Mawson, **Arnhem Doctor**, p.29
3. *See* Kershaw, **It Never Snows in September**, p.162
4. Testimony from Captain Brian Carr, HQ Company, 10th Parachute Battalion; cited in Brammall, **The Tenth**, p.52
5. *See* **WO 171/594** 4th Parachute Brigade War Diary, Appendix C: 'Diary Kept by Brigadier J.W. Hackett, Commander 4th Parachute Brigade', entry for 18/09/1944
6. Quoted from Brammall, p.54; *see* also the **Airborne Assault Para Data Website**, In Memoriam Section, at http://www.paradata.org.uk/media/5599?mediaSection=Biography+picture, accessed 24/04/2012. Lieutenant Patrick Wallace Alexander Mackey is interred in Ede General Cemetery, Row H, Grave 21; Sergeant Frank William Charles Bennett has no known grave and is commemorated on the Groesbeek Memorial, Panel 8
7. *See* Brammall, pp.53-54; Lieutenant Harold Cyril Joseph Roderick is interred in Arnhem Oosterbeek War Cemetery, Gelderland, Holland, Plot 5, Row B, Grave 9
8. *See* **WO 171/1244**, 11th Parachute Battalion War Diary, Appendix A: 'Account of Arnhem Battle, 11 Battalion The Parachute Regiment by Lt. J. E. Blackwood', entry for 18/09/1944; and **WO 171/1247** 156 Parachute Battalion War Diary, entries for 14:00 and 14:30, 18/09/1944
9. *See* **WO 171/594** 4th Parachute Brigade War Diary, Appendix C: 'Diary Kept by Brigadier J. W. Hackett, Commander 4th Parachute Brigade', entry for 18/09/1944; and **WO 171/1511** 4th Parachute Squadron RE War Diary, entry for 14:20, 18/09/1944
10. *See* Middlebrook, **Arnhem**, p.241
11. Timings and quote from **WO 171/594** 4th Parachute Brigade War Diary, Appendix C: 'Diary Kept by Brigadier J. W. Hackett, Commander 4th Parachute Brigade', entry for 18/09/1944
12. *See* **WO 166/15077** 1st Battalion The Border Regiment War Diary, entry for 8/09/1944; and Green, **1st Battalion The Border Regiment**, pp.19-20. Sergeant Hendry Burr is interred in Arnhem Oosterbeek War Cemetery, Gelderland, Holland, Plot 5, Row D, Grave 7
13. *See* Kershaw, p.163; the latter erroneously refers to this occurring on 19 rather than 18 September
14. *See* **WO 171/589** 1st Airlanding Brigade War Diary, entry for 15:15, 18/09/1944
15. *See* for example Otway, p.108
16. *See* **WO 171/393** 1st Airborne Division HQ War Diary, entry for 09:45, 18/09/1944; and **WO 171/1375** 2nd Battalion South Staffordshire Regiment War Diary, Month of September 1944
17. *See* **WO 171/393** 1st Airborne Division HQ War Diary, entries for 14:20 & 14:30, 18/09/1944
18. *See* Middlebrook, p.248
19. *See* **WO 171/594** 4th Parachute Brigade War Diary, Appendix C: 'Diary Kept by Brigadier J. W. Hackett, Commander 4th Parachute Brigade', entry for 18/09/1944. Interestingly the Divisional records refer to the 4th Parachute Brigade's drop taking place around an hour later than it occurred; *see* **WO 171/393** 1st Airborne Division HQ War Diary, entry for 15:15, 18/09/1944
20. *See* **WO 171/393**, 1st Airborne Division HQ War Diary, entry for 15:00, 18/09/1944
21. *See* **WO 171/594** 4th Parachute Brigade War Diary, Appendix C: 'Diary Kept by Brigadier J. W. Hackett, Commander 4th Parachute Brigade', entry for 18/09/1944

22. *See* for example Powell, **The Devil's Birthday**, p.110. Powell commanded C Company, 156 Parachute Battalion under Hackett at Arnhem

23. Quoted from **WO 171/594** 4th Parachute Brigade War Diary, Appendix C: 'Diary Kept by Brigadier J. W. Hackett, Commander 4th Parachute Brigade', entry for 18/09/1944

24. Quoted from **WO 171/393**, 1st Airborne Division HQ War Diary, entry for 15:00, 18/09/1944

25. *See* **WO 171/594** 4th Parachute Brigade War Diary, Appendix C: 'Diary Kept by Brigadier J. W. Hackett, Commander 4th Parachute Brigade', entry for 18/09/1944

26. *See* **WO 171/1511** 4th Parachute Squadron War Diary, entry for 17:00, 18/09/1944; 1 Troop strength cited in Faulkner-Brown, **A Sapper at Arnhem**, Appendix II, p.121

27. *See* Mawson, pp.31-34

28. *See* Middlebrook, pp.248-249

29. *See* **WO 171/1244** 11th Parachute Battalion War Diary, Appendix "A", entry for 18/09/1944

30. *See* **WO 171/589** 1st Airlanding Brigade War Diary, Appendix A '1 Air Landing Brigade: Operation "MARKET", 17th–26th September 1944', entry for 15:15, 18/09/1944

31. *See* **WO 171/1323** 7th Battalion King's Own Scottish Borderers War Diary, entry for 06:00, 19/09/1944

32. Rendered Waite in the 7th KOSB War Diary

33. Lieutenant Albert Edward Kipping is interred in Arnhem Oosterbeek War Cemetery, Gelderland, Holland, Plot 16, Row B, Grave 1

34. *See* **WO 171/1323** 7th Battalion King's Own Scottish Borderers War Diary, entries for 15:00, 17:00 to 10:00 and 19:00, 18/09/1944

35. *See* **WO 171/589** 1st Airlanding Brigade War Diary, entry for 17:00, 18/09/1944; and ibid., Appendix A, entries 09:05 & 15:15, 18/09/1944

36. *See* **WO 171/589** 1st Airlanding Brigade War Diary, entry for 19:00, 18/09/1944; and ibid., Appendix A, entry for 15:15, 18/09/1944

37. *See* Green, **1st Battalion The Border Regiment**, p.25; Green incorrectly renders Baillie as Bailey

38. *See* **WO 171/1323** 7th Battalion King's Own Scottish Borderers War Diary, entries for 01:00, 19/09/1944; **WO 166/15077** 1st Battalion The Border Regiment War Diary, entries for 19:00, 18/09/1944 & 05:15, 19/09/1944; and **WO 171/1235** No.2 Wing The Glider Pilot Regiment War Diary, entries for 19:00 & 20:00, 18/09/1944

39. *See* **WO 171/589** 1st Airlanding Brigade War Diary, Appendix A, entry for 20:00, 18/09/1944

40. *See* **WO 171/594** 4th Parachute Brigade War Diary, Appendix C: 'Diary Kept by Brigadier J. W. Hackett, Commander 4th Parachute Brigade', entry for 18/09/1944

41. *See* ibid., entry for 18/09/1944

42. *See* ibid., entries for 18 & 19/09/1944; and Brammall, p.54

43. *See* Brammall, p.54. Banwell identified the vehicle as a Tiger tank but this is unlikely; while the lead element of the first Tiger unit deployed to Arnhem, two Tiger Is from *schwere Panzer Kompanie* Hummel, arrived in the Arnhem area in the evening of 19 September after a fifty-mile road march from Bocholt, these vehicles were assigned to *Kampfgruppe* Brinkmann and went into action against the British troops holding the Arnhem road bridge at around 20:00; *see* Zwarts, **German Armoured Units at Arnhem**, p.56

44. Quoted from Brammall, p.54

45. *See* **WO 171/393** 1st Airborne Division HQ War Diary, entry for 17:00, 18/09/1944

46. Quoted from Mawson, p.40

47. Testimony from Major David Gilchrist, OC A Company, 11th Parachute Battalion; cited in Middlebrook, p.188

48. Quoted from **WO 171/1244** 11th Parachute Battalion War Diary, Appendix A: 'Account of Arnhem Battle 11th Battalion The Parachute Regiment by Lt. J. E. Blackwood', entry for 18/09/1944

49. *See* **WO 166/14933** 1st Airlanding Light Regiment RA War Diary, entry for 22:00, 18/09/1944; **WO 171/594** 4th Parachute Brigade War Diary, Appendix C: 'Diary Kept by Brigadier J. W. Hackett, Commander 4th Parachute Brigade', entry for 18/09/1944; and Middlebrook, p.188

50. *See* **WO 171/1247** 156 Parachute Battalion War Diary, entry for 20:00, 18/09/1944

51. *See* **WO 171/594** 4ᵗʰ Parachute Brigade War Diary, Appendix C: 'Diary Kept by Brigadier J. W. Hackett, Commander 4ᵗʰ Parachute Brigade', entry for 18/09/1944

52. For the identity of the ambushers *see* Kershaw, p.173; Private George Tansley is interred in Arnhem Oosterbeek War Cemetery, Gelderland, Holland, Plot 32, Row B, Grave 2

53. *See* **WO 171/1247** 156 Parachute Battalion War Diary, entries for 20:00 and 21:00, 18/09/1944; Middlebrook, p.252; and Powell, p.109

54. *See* **WO 171/594**, 4ᵗʰ Parachute Brigade War Diary, Appendix C: 'Diary Kept By Brigadier J. W. Hackett, Commander 4 Parachute Brigade', entries for 18 & 19/09/1944; and for example Middlebrook, pp.250-251. Interestingly there is no reference to Hackett's visit in the Division HQ War Diary

55. *See* **WO 171/1238** 3ʳᵈ Parachute Battalion War Diary, entry for 10:00-16:00, 18/09/1944; and Middlebrook, p.173

56. *See* **WO 171/1238** 3ʳᵈ Parachute Battalion War Diary, entry for 10:00-16:00, 18/09/1944

57. *See* **The Pegasus Archive**, Battle of Arnhem Archive, Biographies Section 'Lieutenant Leo Jack Heaps' at http://www.pegasusarchive.org/arnhem/leo_heaps.htm accessed 31/08/2012.

58. Testimony from Major Alan Bush, Second-in-Command 3ʳᵈ Parachute Battalion; cited in Middlebrook, p.172. Major Alexander Peter Harry Waddy and Company Sergeant Major Reginald Allen are interred in Arnhem Oosterbeek War Cemetery, Gelderland, Holland, in Plot 27, Row C, Grave 4 and Plot 22, Row B, Grave 11 respectively. CSM Allen's date of death is cited as 19/09/1944

59. Testimony from Lieutenant Edward Shaw, commander C Troop, 1ˢᵗ Airlanding Anti-tank Battery RA; cited in Middlebrook, p.173

60. *See* **WO 171/1238** 3ʳᵈ Parachute Battalion War Diary, entry for 16:00-dark, 18/09/1944

61. Quote from Urquhart, **Arnhem**, p.56

62. *See* **WO 171/1238** 3ʳᵈ Parachute Battalion War Diary, entry for 10:00-16:00, 18/09/1944

63. Quotes from personal communication between Sir James Cleminson and John Baynes, dated 18/01/1991; cited in Baynes, **Urquhart of Arnhem**, pp.109-111

64. Cleminson's account in Baynes clearly refers to an anti-tank gun, whereas Middlebrook refers to a self-propelled gun; *see* Baynes, p.110; and Middlebrook, p.174

65. Quote from personal communication between Sir James Cleminson and John Baynes, dated 18/01/1991; cited in Baynes, p.110

66. *See* Urquhart, p.66

67. Quote from personal communication between Sir James Cleminson and John Baynes, dated 18/01/1991; cited in Baynes, p.111

68. *See* **WO 171/1236** 1ˢᵗ Parachute Battalion War Diary, entries for 09:00 & 14:00, 18/09/1944; and Middlebrook, p.181

69. *See* Middlebrook, pp.179-181

70. *See* **WO 171/1236** 1ˢᵗ Parachute Battalion War Diary, entry for 14:00, 18/09/1944

71. *See* **WO 171/1238** 3ʳᵈ Parachute Battalion War Diary, entry for 10:00-16:00, 18/09/1944; and **The Pegasus Archive**, Battle of Arnhem Archive, Biographies Section 'Major Mervyn William Dennison' at http://www.pegasusarchive.org/arnhem/mervyn_dennison.htm accessed 31/08/2012.

72. *See* Middlebrook, pp.180-181; and **The Pegasus Archive**, Battle of Arnhem Archive, Biographies Section 'Lieutenant John Edward Hellingoe' at http://www.pegasusarchive.org/arnhem/jack_hellingoe.htm accessed 31/08/2012.

73. *See* **The Pegasus Archive**, Battle of Arnhem Archive, Biographies Section 'Sergeant John Thomas Richards' at http://www.pegasusarchive.org/arnhem/john_richards.htm accessed 01/09/2012

74. Testimony from Private Geoff Baker, 11 Platoon, T Company, 1ˢᵗ Parachute Battalion; cited at **The Pegasus Archive**, Battle of Arnhem Archive, Biographies Section 'Private Geoff Baker' at http://www.pegasusarchive.org/arnhem/geoff_baker.htm accessed 31/08/2012.

75. Testimony from Lieutenant Eric Davies, commanding 10 Platoon, T Company, 1ˢᵗ Parachute Battalion; cited in Middlebrook, pp.179-180

76. *See* **WO 171/1236** 1st Parachute Battalion War Diary, entry for 15:00, 18/09/1944
77. Testimony from Private Douglas Charlton, 1st Parachute Battalion; cited in Middlebrook, p.182
78. *See* **WO 171/1236** 1st Parachute Battalion War Diary, entry for 17:00, 18/09/1944
79. Testimony from Lance-Sergeant John Fryer, T Company, 1st Parachute Battalion; cited in David Truesdale, **Brotherhood of the Cauldron**, p.117
80. *See* ibid., p.118
81. *See* **WO 171/1236** 1st Parachute Battalion War Diary, entry for 18:30, 18/09/1944; and Middlebrook, p.297
82. *See* **WO 171/1375** 2nd Battalion South Staffordshire Regiment War Diary, entry for 18/09/1944 and Appendix; **WO 171/406** 1st Airborne Reconnaissance Squadron War Diary, A Troop War Diary, entry for 12:00, 18/09/1944; **WO 171/1232** B Squadron The Glider Pilot Regiment War Diary, entry for 18/09/1944; and Haines, **The Holland Patch**, p.26
83. *See* **WO 171/1375** 2nd Battalion South Staffordshire Regiment War Diary, entry for 18/09/1944 and Appendix; and **WO 171/1236** 1st Parachute Battalion War Diary, entry for 20:00, 18/09/1944
84. Testimony from Private Douglas Charlton, 1st Parachute Battalion; cited in Middlebrook, p.182
85. *See* **WO 171/1375** 2nd Battalion South Staffordshire Regiment War Diary, entry for 18/09/1944 and Appendix
86. *See* **WO 171/1375** 2nd Battalion South Staffordshire Regiment War Diary, entry for 18/09/1944 and Appendix
87. *See* **WO 171/393** 1st Airborne Division HQ War Diary, entry for 15:00, 18/09/1944
88. *See* **WO 171/1375** 2nd Battalion South Staffordshire Regiment War Diary and Appendix; and **WO 171/1247** 156 Parachute Battalion War Diary, entry for 21:00, 18/09/1944
89. Quoted from Kershaw, p.177
90. *See* **WO 171/393** 1st Airborne Division HQ War Diary, entry for 23:30, 18/09/1944
91. *See* **WO 171/1236** 1st Parachute Battalion War Diary, entries for 01:00 & 02:30, 19/09/1944
92. *See* **WO 171/393** 1st Airborne Division HQ War Diary, entry for 23:30, 18/09/1944
93. *See* Haines, p.36
94. *See* Middlebrook, p.183
95. *See* **WO 171/398** 1st Airborne Division Signals War Diary, entry for 07:30, 18/09/1944; and Golden, **Echoes From Arnhem**, pp.151-152
96. *See* **The Pegasus Archive**, Battle of Arnhem Archive, Biographies Section 'Major Anthony J. Deane-Drummond' at http://www.pegasusarchive.org/arnhem/deane_drummond.htm accessed 20/09/2012.
97. *See* Turnbull & Hamblett, **The Pegasus Patrol**, pp.71-78; Peatling, **No Surrender at Arnhem**, pp.19-21; and Truesdale, pp.118-119
98. *See* Sims, **Arnhem Spearhead**, pp.60-62.
99. *See* Frost, **A Drop too Many**, p.222
100. *See* Sims, p.63
101. *See* Middlebrook, p.297; and Frost, p.223
102. *See* Sims, pp.62-64
103. *See* Middlebrook, p.296
104. *See* **WO 171/1509** 1st Parachute Squadron RE War Diary, entries for 14:00, 18:00-19:30, 19:30, 20:00 & 21:00, 18/09/1944 and 23:59, 19/09/1944; and Cherry, **With Nothing Bigger Than a Bren Gun**, p.15
105. *See* Middlebrook, p.298
106. *See* Frost, pp.223-225; and **The Pegasus Archive**, Battle of Arnhem Archive, Biographies Section 'Major Charles Frederick Howard Gough' at http://www.pegasusarchive.org/arnhem/freddie_gough.htm accessed 27/09/2012.
107. Quoted from Sims, p.64
108. *See* Frost, p.225; and Middlebrook, p.298
109. *See* Middlebrook, pp.295-296, 298-299; and Cherry, p.16.

110. Major David William Wallis is interred in Arnhem Oosterbeek War Cemetery, Gelderland, Holland, Plot 18, Row C, Grave 10
111. *See* Middlebrook, p.299; and Frost, p.225. Interestingly Frost attributes Wallis' death to a German attack on A Company's sector rather than what would now be termed a friendly fire incident
112. *See* **CAB 44/254** Part II: Operation MARKET GARDEN, Book III, Chapter VII, Appendix A, Section I 'Operations South of Grave – 17/18 Sep', Para. 4 'Gds Armd Div – Narrative 18 Sep'
113. For timings *see* Powell, p.114; and MacDonald, **The Siegfried Line Campaign**, p.150
114. Quoted from Wilson, **The Ever Open Eye**, p.118
115. *See* ibid., pp.116-1190
116. *See* **CAB 44/254** Part II: Operation MARKET GARDEN, Book III, Chapter VII, Appendix A, Section I 'Operations South of Grave – 17/18 Sep', Para. 4 'Gds Armd Div - Narrative 18 Sep'
117. *See* Ambrose, **Band of Brothers**, pp.127-128
118. *See* Rapport & Northwood, **Rendezvous with Destiny**, pp.292-293
119. *See* ibid., p.296; and MacDonald, **The Siegfried Line Campaign**, p.151
120. *See* Rapport & Northwood, **Rendezvous with Destiny**, p.299
121. *See* Nordyke, **All American All The Way**, p.63
122. *See* Ryan, **A Bridge Too Far**, pp.222-223
123. *See* MacDonald, **The Siegfried Line Campaign**, p.168
124. Quoted from '82nd Airborne Division Chief of Staff Journal, entry for 07:00, 19 September 1944, reporting conference held at 15:30, 18 September 1944'; cited in MacDonald, **The Siegfried Line Campaign**, footnote 66, p.168
125. Quoted from Powell, p.119
126. *See* Gavin, **On to Berlin**, pp.81-83
127. Quoted from Willem Ridder, **Countdown to Freedom**, p.451

Chapter 11

1. For first light, sunrise and other timings *see* **Field Order No. 11 82 AB Div**, 'Annex 1A: Weather, Sun & Moon Tables, Para. 2 Sun and Moon Data', dated 11/09/1944
2. *See* **CAB 44/254** Part II: Operation MARKET GARDEN, Book III, Chapter VII, Appendix A, Section IV 'Operations South of Grave – 19/20 Sep', Para. 41 'Movement up the 30 Corps axis 19/20 Sep'
3. *See* **CAB 44/254** Part II: Operation MARKET GARDEN, Book III, Chapter VII, Appendix A, Section II 'Operations in the area Grave-Nijmegen – 17/20 Sep', Para. 16 'Gds Armd Div – Narrative 19 Sep.'; and id., Section IV 'Operations South of Grave – 19/20 Sep', Para. 41 'Movement up the 30 Corps axis 19/20 Sep'
4. *See* **CAB 44/254** Part II: Operation MARKET GARDEN, Book III, Chapter VII, Appendix A, Section IV 'Operations South of Grave – 19/20 Sep', Para. 41 'Movement up the 30 Corps axis 19/20 Sep'; and Ellis, **Victory in the West Volume II: The Defeat of Germany**, p.37, footnote 1
5. *See* Rapport & Northwood, **Rendezvous with Destiny**, p.320
6. Unloading date cited in Delaforce, **The Black Bull**, p.150
7. *See* Kershaw, **It Never Snows in September**, pp.118-119
8. *See* Ambrose, **Band of Brothers**, pp.128-131; the latter clearly states the action took place on 19 September, but the 101st Airborne Division's semi-official history refer to it occurring the following day; *see* Rapport & Northwood, pp.326-327
9. *See* Rapport & Northwood, p.311
10. *See* MacDonald, **The Siegfried Line Campaign**, p.151; and Rapport & Northwood, pp.296-298
11. *See* Rapport & Northwood, pp.310-312; and MacDonald, **The Siegfried Line Campaign**, p.152
12. *See* Rapport & Northwood, pp.308-310
13. *See* MacDonald, **The Siegfried Line Campaign**, pp.153-154; and Rapport & Northwood, pp.318-320
14. *See* Devlin, **Silent Wings**, pp.262-263, 267; and Rapport & Northwood, pp.312-313

15. Quoted from Rapport & Northwood, p.313
16. *See* Gavin, **On to Berlin**, pp.169-170; and LoFaro, **The Sword of St. Michael**, pp.345-346
17. *See* LoFaro, p.345
18. *See* MacDonald, **The Siegfried Line Campaign**, p.176
19. *See* **CAB 44/254** Part II: Operation MARKET GARDEN, Book III, Chapter VII, Appendix A, Section II 'Operations in the area Grave-Nijmegen – 17/20 Sep.', Para. 16 'Gds Armd Div - Narrative 19 Sep.'; Nordyke, **All American All The Way**, pp.83-84; and LoFaro, p.346
20. *See* **A Graphic History of the 82nd Airborne Division**, entry for D Plus 2, 19 September; and MacDonald, **The Siegfried Line Campaign**, p.176
21. *See* **WO 171/1509** 1st Parachute Squadron RE War Diary, entries for 19:30, 20:00 & 21:00, 18/09/1944; and Cherry, **With Nothing Bigger Than a Bren Gun**, p.15
22. Testimony from Lieutenant Leonard Wright, commander 9 Platoon, C Company, 3rd Parachute Battalion; cited in Middlebrook, **Arnhem 1944**, p.299
23. Testimony from Lance-Sergeant Norman Swift, A Troop, 1st Parachute Squadron RE; cited in Cherry, p.17
24. *See* **WO 171/1509** 1st Parachute Squadron RE War Diary, entries for 00:30, 02:00 & 03:00, 18/09/1944; Cherry, pp.16-17; and Middlebrook, pp.299-300
25. *See* Frost, **A Drop Too Many**, p.224; and Kershaw, p.135
26. *See* Frost, pp.226-227; Kershaw, pp.135-136; and Middlebrook, pp.302-303
27. *See* **The Pegasus Archive**, Battle of Arnhem Archive, Biographies Section 'Private Robert Alfred Lygo' at http://www.pegasusarchive.org/arnhem/robert_alfred_lygo.htm accessed 16/10/2012.
28. For text and photographs *see* Zwarts, **German Armoured Units at Arnhem**, pp.54-55
29. Testimony from Private Cecil Newell, 2nd Parachute Battalion; cited in Truesdale, **Brotherhood of the Cauldron**, p.114. The latter suggests the incident occurred on Monday 18 September in the aftermath of Gräbner's attempt to cross the bridge, but *Panzer Kompanie* Mielke's tanks did not reach Arnhem until the following day.
30. *See* **The Pegasus Archive**, Battle of Arnhem Archive, Biographies Section 'Private Len Hoare' at http://www.pegasusarchive.org/arnhem/len_hoare.htm, accessed 18/10/2012. This also suggests that the incident occurred on Tuesday 18 September rather than the following day.
31. *See* Middlebrook, p.301
32. *See* Sims, **Arnhem Spearhead**, pp.66-69
33. Testimony from Lieutenant Vladimir Britneff, Intelligence Officer, 1st Parachute Battalion; cited in Middlebrook, pp.190-191
34. *See* **WO 171/1236** 1st Parachute Battalion War Diary, entries for 01:00 & 02:30, 19/09/1944; and Middlebrook, p.191
35. *See* **WO 171/1238** 3rd Parachute Battalion War Diary, entry for 02:30-Dawn, 19/09/1944
36. *See* **WO 171/1236** 1st Parachute Battalion War Diary, entry for 04:00, 19/09/1944
37. *See* **WO 171/1236** 1st Parachute Battalion War Diary, entry for 04:00, 19/09/1944; for wording of Dobie-Dorrien-Smith exchange and Britneff's observation *See* Middlebrook, pp.191-193
38. **WO 171/1232** B Squadron The Glider Pilot Regiment War Diary, entry for 03:00, 19/09/1944
39. Quoted from Kershaw, p.168
40. Testimony from Private Bryan Willoughby, T Company, 1st Parachute Battalion; cited in Middlebrook, pp.195-196
41. *See* **WO 171/1375** 2nd Battalion South Staffordshire Regiment War Diary, entry for 18/09/1944 and Appendix: '2nd South Staffords at Arnhem 17-25 Sept 44'
42. Strength figure cited in Middlebrook, p.200
43. Testimony from Lieutenant David Russell, commanding 7 Platoon, C Company, 2nd Parachute Battalion; cited in ibid., p.200
44. Testimony from Sergeant Norman Howes, 10 Platoon, A Company, 2nd Battalion South Staffordshire Regiment; cited in ibid., p.200
45. Testimony from Corporal Stretton, 21 Platoon, D Company, 2nd Battalion South Staffordshire Regiment; cited in Haines, **The Holland Patch**, p.42. Lieutenant Ernest Roebuck is interred in Arnhem Oosterbeek War Cemetery, Gelderland, Holland, Plot 22, Row A, Grave 1

46. Testimony from Private Edwards, D Company, 2nd Battalion South Staffordshire Regiment; cited in Haines, p.42

47. *See* WO 171/1375 2nd Battalion South Staffordshire Regiment War Diary, Appendix: '2nd South Staffords at Arnhem 17-25 Sept 44'; and Middlebrook, pp.200-201. Captain Ernest Mariel Wyss is interred in Arnhem Oosterbeek War Cemetery, Gelderland, Holland, in Plot 15, Row C, Grave 10; his date of death is cited as 20/09/1944

48. *See* WO 171/1375 2nd Battalion South Staffordshire Regiment War Diary, Appendix: '2nd South Staffords at Arnhem 17-25 Sept 44'; Middlebrook, p.201; and Haines, pp.42-44

49. *See* **WO 171/1238** 3rd Parachute Battalion War Diary, entries for 02:30-Dawn & Dawn-10:00, 19/09/1944

50. *See* **WO 171/1236** 1st Parachute Battalion War Diary, entry for 02:00, 19/09/1944

51. Testimony from Lieutenant James Cleminson, commanding 5 Platoon, B Company, 3rd Parachute Battalion; cited in Baynes, **Urquhart of Arnhem**, pp.110-111

52. Mackenzie quote and Private Hancock details from Urquhart, **Arnhem**, p.84

53. Testimony from Sergeant Frank Manser, 7 Platoon, S Company, 1st Parachute Battalion; cited in Middlebrook, p.196

54. *See* **WO 171/1236** 1st Parachute Battalion War Diary, entry for 05:00, 19/09/1944; for details of Sergeant Barret's contribution *see* **The Pegasus Archive**, Battle of Arnhem Archive, Biographies Section 'Sergeant Dennis George Barrett' at www.pegasusarchive.org/arnhem/dennis_george_barrett.htm, accessed 01/11/2012

55. *See* **WO 171/1236** 1st Parachute Battalion War Diary, entry for 06:00, 19/09/1944

56. Figures cited in Middlebrook, p.195

57. *See* **WO 171/1236** 1st Parachute Battalion War Diary, entry for 06:30, 19/09/1944; and Middlebrook, pp.195-196; for Private Davies account *see* **The Pegasus Archive**, Battle of Arnhem Archive, Biographies Section 'Private Thomas Emyr Davies' at www.pegasusarchive.org/arnhem/tom_davies.htm, accessed 02/11/2012

58. *See* **WO 171/1236** 1st Parachute Battalion War Diary, entries for 06:30 & 07:30, 19/09/1944; and Middlebrook, pp.195-196

59. Testimony from Private Thomas Emyr Davies, Mortar Platoon, HQ & Support Company, 1st Parachute Battalion; cited at **The Pegasus Archive**, Battle of Arnhem Archive, Biographies Section 'Private Thomas Emyr Davies' at www.pegasusarchive.org/arnhem/tom_davies.htm, accessed 02/11/2012

60. Testimony from Private John Hall, 1 Platoon, R Company, 1st Parachute Battalion; cited in Middlebrook, pp.197-198

61. *See* **WO 171/1238** 3rd Parachute Battalion War Diary, entry for Dawn-10:00, 19/09/1944; and Middlebrook, p.199

62. Quoted from **WO 171/1238** 3rd Parachute Battalion War Diary, entry for Dawn-10:00, 19/09/1944

63. Testimony from Major Alan Bush, Second-in-Command, 3rd Parachute Battalion; cited in Middlebrook, pp.198-199

64. Testimony from Private George Marsh, Signals Platoon, HQ and Support Company, 1st Parachute Battalion; cited in ibid., p.199

65. Lieutenant-Colonel John Anthony Colson Fitch is interred in Arnhem Oosterbeek War Cemetery, Gelderland, Holland, in Plot 20, Row B, Grave 20

66. *See* **WO 171/1238** 3rd Parachute Battalion War Diary, entries for Dawn-10:00, 19/09/1944 & 15:30 21/09/1944

67. Figures cited in **WO 171/1236** 1st Parachute Battalion War Diary, entries for 18:30 & 20:00, 18/09/1944; **WO 171/1238** 3rd Parachute Battalion War Diary, entry for 16:00-Nightfall, 18/09/1944; and Middlebrook, Appendix I 'Order of Battle and Operational Details, 1st British Airborne Division and Attached Units', entries for 1st & 3rd Parachute Battalions, p.456

68. *See* **WO 171/1236** 1st Parachute Battalion War Diary, entries for 02:00, 09:00, 9:30 & 11:00, 19/09/1944

69. *See* Kershaw, pp.238-239; Major Kühme's name is rendered as Kuehne

70. For photographs *see* Zwarts, pp.26-27; for vehicle type breakdown *see* ibid, Figure 'Sturmgeschütze-Brigade 280', p.6; and **Defending Arnhem** website, German Order of Battle Section, 'Sturmgeschutzebrigade 280' at http://www.defendingarnhem.com/Sturmgeschutzbrigade280.htm, accessed 12/11/2012; for sunrise time *see* **Field Order No. 11, 82nd Airborne Division**, Annex 1.a(1) to F.O. 11, Weather; Sun and Moon Tables, Para .2 "Sun and Moon Data", dated 11/09/1944

71. *See* **WO 171/1375** 2nd Battalion South Staffordshire Regiment War Diary, Appendix: '2nd South Staffords at Arnhem 17-25 Sept 4"'; interestingly the War Diary gives Lieutenant Withers first initial a 'J'.

72. *See* Haines, pp.46-47

73. *See* **WO 171/1375** 2nd Battalion South Staffordshire Regiment War Diary, Appendix: '2nd South Staffords at Arnhem 17-25 Sept 44'

74. Quote from unpublished account by Major Robert Cain, OC B Company, 2nd Battalion South Staffordshire Regiment, Airborne Forces Museum File No. 54; cited in Haines, pp.47-48

75. *See* Baynes, pp.113-114

76. *See* Middlebrook, p.210; and Baynes, p.111

77. *See* **WO 171/589** 1st Airlanding Brigade War Diary, entries for 09:00 & 10:00, 19/09/1944; and ibid., 'Appendix A: 1 Airlanding Brigade: Operation 'MARKET', 17th-26th September 1944'. For some reason the timings cited in the Appendix are an hour or more earlier than those in the main Diary entries

78. Testimony from Captain John McCooke, second-in-command A Company, 2nd Battalion South Staffordshire Regiment; cited in Middlebrook, pp.210-211. Colonel Hilaro Nelson Barlow has no known grave and is commemorated on the Groesbeek Memorial, Panel 1; Lance-Corporal Raymond Singer is interred in Arnhem Oosterbeek War Cemetery, Gelderland, Holland, Plot 19, Row A, Grave 7

79. *See* **WO 171/1375** 2nd Battalion South Staffordshire Regiment War Diary, Appendix: '2nd South Staffords at Arnhem 17-25 Sept 44'.

80. *See* Middlebrook, pp.206-207. The rather sparse 11th Parachute Battalion War Diary makes no mention of the 09:00 order, although it does refer to A Company pushing forward to meet the 2nd South Staffords on 'non-receipt of orders'; *see* **WO 171/1244** 11th Parachute Battalion War Diary, Appendix A: 'Account of Arnhem Battle 11th Bn. The Parachute Regiment by Lieutenant J. E. Blackwood', entry for 19/09/1944. Company Sergeant-Major George Wilson Ashdown and Captain The Reverend Henry James Irwin are interred in Arnhem Oosterbeek War Cemetery, Gelderland, Holland, Plot 19, Row C, Grave 15 and Plot 26, Row A, Grave 2 respectively.

81. Testimony from Major Robert Cain, OC B Company, 2nd Battalion South Staffordshire Regiment; cited in Haines, p.48

82. *See* Zwarts, p.28

83. Testimony from Lieutenant David Russell, commanding 7 Platoon, C Company, 2nd Parachute Battalion; cited in Middlebrook, p.203

84. Testimony from a Private Edwards, D Company, 2nd Battalion South Staffordshire Regiment; cited in Haines, p.50

85. *See* Testimony from Lieutenant David Russell, commander 7 Platoon, C Company, 2nd Parachute Battalion; cited in Middlebrook, p.203; quote from **WO 171/1375** 2nd Battalion South Staffordshire Regiment War Diary, Appendix: '2nd South Staffords at Arnhem 17-25 Sept 44'

86. *See* Haines, p.50

87. Quoted from unpublished account by Major Robert Cain, OC B Company, 2nd Battalion South Staffordshire Regiment, Airborne Forces Museum File No. 54; cited in Middlebrook, p.202

88. *See* Haines, pp.51-52

89. *See* Zwarts, pp.41 & 48

90. *See* testimony from Major Robert Cain, OC B Company, 2nd Battalion South Staffordshire Regiment, Airborne Forces Museum File No. 54; cited in Middlebrook, p.202

91. *See* Haines, p.52

92. Testimony from Major Robert Cain, OC B Company, 2ⁿᵈ Battalion South Staffordshire Regiment; cited in Haines, p.53

93. Testimony from Corporal Perry, B Company, 2ⁿᵈ Battalion South Staffordshire Regiment; cited in ibid., p.56

94. Testimony from Major Robert Cain, OC B Company, 2ⁿᵈ Battalion South Staffordshire Regiment; cited in ibid., p.55

95. Rearguard details cited in Middlebrook, p.203; and Haines, p.53

96. 11:00 and 10:50 timings cited in **WO 171/1375** 2ⁿᵈ Battalion South Staffordshire Regiment War Diary, entry for 19/09/1944 and ibid., Appendix: '2ⁿᵈ South Staffords at Arnhem 17-25 Sept 44' respectively; 11:30 timing appears in testimony from Major Robert Cain, OC B Company, 2ⁿᵈ Battalion South Staffordshire Regiment, Airborne Forces Museum File No. 54; cited in Middlebrook, p.202

97. See **WO 171/589** 1ˢᵗ Airlanding Brigade War Diary, Appendix A: 1 Air Landing Brigade: Operation "MARKET" 17th-26th September 1944, entries for 05:00, 07:30, 08:00 & 09:00

98. See **WO 171/1235** No. 2 Wing The Glider Pilot Regiment War Diary, entries for 20:00, 18/09/1944 and 09:00, 09:30 & 11:00, 19/09/1944

99. See **WO 166/15077** 1ˢᵗ Battalion The Border Regiment War Diary, entry for 19/09/1944

100. See **166/15077** 1ˢᵗ Battalion The Border Regiment War Diary, entry for 19/09/1944; and Green, pp.28

101. See Green, p.28 Lance-Corporal King does not figure among the members of the 1ˢᵗ Border killed in Holland in Green's appended Roll of Honour or in the CWGC database

102. See **WO 171/406** 1ˢᵗ Airborne Reconnaissance Squadron War Diary, entries for 06:30 & 07:30, 19/09/1944

103. The Polsten gun was a lightened and simplified Polish version of the Swedish 20mm Oerlikon automatic cannon taken into general British and Commonwealth service in March 1944. The gun was seven feet long, weighed 126 pounds unloaded, had an effective range of just over 1,000 yards and fired 450 rounds per minute from thirty round box or sixty round drum magazines. The Airborne version was mounted on a lightweight two-wheel carriage intended to be towed by Jeep; the 1ˢᵗ Airborne Reconnaissance Squadron deployed two such weapons in a dedicated Polsten Section as part of Lieutenant John Christie's Support Troop; see for example Fairley, p.16

104. See **WO 171/406** 1ˢᵗ Airborne Reconnaissance Squadron War Diary, entries for 09:00 & 09:30, 10:00 & 11:00, 19/09/1944; and Fairley, pp.85-87

105. See Fairley, pp.88-89

106. **WO 171/594** 4ᵗʰ Parachute Brigade War Diary, Appendix C, entry for 19/09/1944

107. 04:00 timing cited in Middlebrook, p.254; Lieutenant Alexander Donald Milles Murray was actually killed during the action; he is interred in Arnhem Oosterbeek War Cemetery, Gelderland, Holland, Plot 16, Row C, Grave 18; the CWGC records give his date of death as 18/09/1944

108. See **WO 171/1323** 7ᵗʰ Battalion King's Own Scottish Borderers War Diary, entries for 01:00 and 06:00, 19/09/1944

109. For transfer time see **WO 171/589** 1ˢᵗ Airlanding Brigade War Diary, entry for 08:00, 19/09/1944; for Hackett visiting 7ᵗʰ KOSB HQ see **WO 171/1323** 7ᵗʰ Battalion King's Own Scottish Borderers War Diary, entry for 06:00, 19/09/1944, and **WO 171/594** 4ᵗʰ Parachute Brigade War Diary, Appendix C: 'Diary Kept by Brigadier J. W. Hackett, Commander 4ᵗʰ Parachute Brigade', entry for 19/09/1944

110. See **WO 171/1323** 7ᵗʰ Battalion King's Own Scottish Borderers War Diary, entries for 06:00 & 09:00 to 14:00, 19/09/1944; seven strafing casualties figure cited in **WO 171/594** 4ᵗʰ Parachute Brigade War Diary, Appendix C, entry for 19/09/1944

111. See **WO 171/1247** 156 Parachute Battalion War Diary, entries for 03:30 & 05:00, 19/09/1944

112. See **The Pegasus Archive**, Battle of Arnhem Archive, Biographies Section, 'Major John L. C. Waddy', at www.pegasusarchive.org/arnhem/john_waddy.htm, accessed 13/01/2013

113. *See* **The Pegasus Archive**, Battle of Arnhem Archive, Biographies Section, 'Major Robert Laslett John Pott', 'An Account of the Action of 'A' Company 156 Battalion The Parachute Regiment 18/19ᵗʰ Sep 44' at http//www.pegasusarchive.org/arnhem/john_pott.htm, accessed 09/01/2013

114. *See* **WO 171/1247** 156 Parachute Battalion War Diary, entry for 07:00, 19/09/1944; and Middlebrook, p.255

115. For warning *see* **WO 171/1247** 156 Parachute Battalion War Diary, entry for 20:00, 18/09/1944

116. *See* **WO 171/1247** 156 Parachute Battalion War Diary, entry for 08:30, 19/09/1944; and **The Pegasus Archive**, Battle of Arnhem Archive, Biographies Section, 'Major Robert Laslett John Pott', 'An Account of the Action of 'A' Company 156 Battalion The Parachute Regiment 18/19th Sep 44' at http//www.pegasusarchive.org/arnhem/john_pott.htm, accessed 09/01/2013

117. *See* Kershaw, pp.172-175; and Middlebrook, p.255

118. Testimony from Sergeant Andrew Thorburn, A Company, 156 Parachute Battalion; cited in Middlebrook, p.256

119. Lieutenants Lindsay David Delacour and Sydney Robertson Smith are interred in Arnhem Oosterbeek War Cemetery, Gelderland, Holland, Plot 25, Row A, Grave 13 and Plot 30, Row C, Grave 4 respectively

120. *See* **The Pegasus Archive**, Battle of Arnhem Archive, Biographies Section, 'Sergeant Louis Edmund Hagen' at http//www.pegasusarchive.org/arnhem/louis_hagen.htm, accessed 11/01/2013. (Louis Hagen is the author of *Arnhem Lift* and one other book, *Ein Volk, Ein Reich*, a series of interviews with Berliners immediately post-war, which, in the editor's opinion, will inform even the most diligent and well-read students of the war.)

121. Captain Terence Patrick Walter Rogers and Lieutenant Stanley Watling are interred in Arnhem Oosterbeek War Cemetery, Gelderland, Holland, Plot 6, Row B, Grave 16 and Plot 6, Row B, Grave 19 respectively

122. Private Alfred Dennis Trueman is interred in Arnhem Oosterbeek War Cemetery, Gelderland, Holland, Plot 30, Row C, Grave 10

123. *See* **The Pegasus Archive**, Battle of Arnhem Archive, Biographies Section, Major Robert Laslett John Pott', 'An Account of the Action of 'A' Company 156 Battalion The Parachute Regiment 18/19th Sep 44' at http//www.pegasusarchive.org/arnhem/john_pott.htm, accessed 11/01/2013

124. Testimony from *Sturmann* Alfred Ziegler, *SS Panzerjäger Abteilung 9*; cited in Kershaw, p.174

125. Testimony from Major John Waddy, OC B Company, 156 Parachute Battalion; cited in Middlebrook, p.258

126. Testimony from Private Ronald Atkinson, B Company, 156 Parachute Battalion; cited in ibid., p.259

127. Testimony from Private Edward Reynolds, B Company, 156 Parachute Battalion; cited in ibid., p.258; Private Desmond Ewart Ford has no known grave and is commemorated on the Groesbeek Memorial, Panel 9

128. *See* **The Pegasus Archive**, Battle of Arnhem Archive, Biographies Section, 'Sergeant Louis Edmund Hagen' at http//www.pegasusarchive.org/arnhem/louis_hagen.htm, accessed 16/01/2013

129. Testimony from Major John Waddy, OC B Company, 156 Parachute Battalion; cited in Middlebrook, p.260

130. Testimony from Private Ronald Atkinson, B Company, 156 Parachute Battalion; cited in ibid., p.259

131. *See* **WO 171/1247** 156 Parachute Battalion War Diary, entry for 09:30, 19/09/1944

132. For Major Waddy's account *see* for example Middlebrook, p.260; for the *Luftwaffe* strafing attack *see* for example **WO 171/1247** 156 Parachute Battalion War Diary, entry for 11:00, 19/09/1944; **WO 171/589** 1ˢᵗ Airlanding Brigade War Diary, entry for 10:00, 19/09/1944; and **WO 171/1511** 4ᵗʰ Parachute Squadron RE War Diary, entry for 11:00, 19/09/1944

133. *See* **Airborne Assault ParaData** website, Rollcall Section, 'Personal Account of Col. John Waddy's Time at Arnhem' at http://www.paradata.org.uk/article/2252/related/10078, accessed 20/01/2013; and Middlebrook, p.260

134. *See* **WO 171/1247** 156 Parachute Battalion War Diary, entry for 09:00, 19/09/1944

135. 03:00 time cited in Brammall, **The Tenth**, p.58; 04:30 time cited in Middlebrook, p.261

136. *See* Brammall, pp.55-56, 58

137. *See* Middlebrook, p.261; and **WO 171/594** 4th Parachute Brigade War Diary, Appendix C, entry for 19/09/1944

138. Testimony from Lieutenant John Procter, commanding 9 Platoon, D Company, 10th Parachute Battalion; cited in Middlebrook, p.264

139. Testimony from Captain Nicholas Hanmer, Adjutant, 10th Parachute Battalion; cited in ibid., p.263

140. Quoted from Brammall, p.58; *see also* Middlebrook, p.264

141. *See* Middlebrook, p.265

142. Testimony from Corporal Harry Dicken, Intelligence Section, HQ Company, 10th Parachute Battalion; cited in ibid., p.265

143. Testimony from Private George Taylor, 8 Platoon, B Company, 10th Parachute Battalion; cited in ibid., p.264. Private Albert Douglas Walter in interred in Arnhem Oosterbeek War Cemetery, Gelderland, Holland, Plot 25, Row A, Grave 16

144. *See* **WO 171/594** 4th Parachute Brigade War Diary, Appendix C, entry for 19/09/1944

145. *See* Brinson, **Airborne Troop Carrier**, p.140. Major Patrick Anchitel Richmond Anson was captured after being wounded at some point on or after landing on 18/09/1944 and died of wounds in *Stalag XI B* at Soltau in Germany eleven days later; he is interred in Becklingen War Cemetery, Niedersachsen, Germany, Plot 4, Row E, Grave 12

146. *See* Middlebrook, p.266

147. Testimony from Corporal Harry Dicken, Intelligence Section, HQ Company, 10th Parachute Battalion; cited in Middlebrook. P.265

148. *See* **WO 171/1511** 4th Parachute Squadron RE War Diary, entry for 08:00, 19/09/1944

149. *See* **WO 171/393** 1st Airborne Division HQ War Diary, entry for 08:45, 19/09/1944; and **WO 171/594** 4th Parachute Brigade War Diary, Appendix C, entry for 19/09/1944

150. Quoted from Middlebrook, p.267

151. *See* **WO 171/594** 4th Parachute Brigade War Diary, Appendix C, entry for 19/09/1944

152. *See* Faulkner-Brown, **A Sapper at Arnhem**, pp.39-40

153. **WO 171/1511** 4th Parachute Squadron RE War Diary, entry for 11:30, 19/09/1944

154. *See* Faulkner-Brown, p.40

Chapter 12

1. Testimony from Trooper Kenneth Hope, A Troop HQ Section, 1st Airborne Reconnaissance Squadron; cited in Fairley, **Remember Arnhem**, p.95

2. *See* **WO 171/406** 1st Airborne Reconnaissance Squadron War Diary, entry for 15:30, 19/09/1944

3. Testimony from Lance-Corporal Robert Thomson, D Troop, 1st Airborne Reconnaissance Squadron; cited in Fairley, p.96

4. Quoted from **WO 171/406** 1st Airborne Reconnaissance Squadron War Diary, entry for 13:50, 19/09/1944

5. *See* **WO 171/406** 1st Airborne Reconnaissance Squadron War Diary, entries for 12:30, 14:15 & 15:00, 19/09/1944; and **WO 171/393** 1st Airborne Division HQ War Diary, entry for 13:30, 19/09/1944

6. Testimony from Sergeant David Christie, 9 Section, C Troop, 1st Airborne Reconnaissance Squadron; cited in Fairley, p.97

7. Testimony from Trooper James Cooke, 9 Section, C Troop, 1st Airborne Reconnaissance Squadron: cited in ibid., p.100

8. Lance-Corporal Alan Coulthurst Baker and Trooper Frederick Brawn are interred in adjacent graves in Arnhem Oosterbeek War Cemetery, Gelderland, Holland, Plot 1, Row B, Graves 1 & 2 respectively

9. Trooper Raymond McSkimmings is interred in Arnhem Oosterbeek War Cemetery, Gelderland, Holland, Plot 1, Row B, Grave 17

10. *See* **WO 171/406** 1st Airborne Reconnaissance Squadron War Diary, entry for 16:20, 19/09/1944

11. Testimony from Lieutenant Tom Collier, Quartermaster, 1st Airborne Reconnaissance Squadron; cited in Fairley, p.102

12. *See* ibid., p.102; Trooper Stanley Tickle has no known grave and is commemorated on the Groesbeek Memorial, Panel 1; the CWGC records his date of death as between 25 and 26/09/1944

13. *See* **WO 171/406** 1st Airborne Reconnaissance Squadron War Diary, entry for 17:00, 19/09/1944; and Fairley, p.96

14. *See* **WO 171/406** 1st Airborne Reconnaissance Squadron War Diary, entries for 17:30, 18:00, 22:00 and 23:30, 19/09/1944; and Fairley, pp.106-107

15. *See* Green, 1st **Battalion The Border Regiment**, p.29

16. *See* ibid., p.29; the red parachutes denoted that the containers were loaded with ammunition

17. *See* **WO 166/15077** 1st Battalion The Border Regiment War Diary, entry for 19/09/1944

18. For timings, locations and vehicle details *see* Zwarts, **German Armoured Units at Arnhem**, pp.65-66

19. *See* Kershaw, **It Never Snows in September**, p.202

20. *See* **WO 166/15077** 1st Battalion The Border Regiment War Diary, entry for 19/09/1944; and Green, pp.29-31

21. *See* **WO 171/1236** 1st Parachute Battalion War Diary, entries for 11:00, 12:30 and 14:00, 19/09/1944; and **WO 171/1238** 3rd Parachute Battalion War Diary, entry for 19/09/1944

22. Quoted from Haines, **The Holland Patch**, p.53

23. *See* ibid., pp.55-56

24. *See* **WO 171/1375** 2nd Battalion South Staffordshire Regiment War Diary, Appendix: '2nd South Staffords at Arnhem 17-25 Sept 44'; for rearguard details *see* Middlebrook, **Arnhem 1944**, p.203; and Haines, p.53

25. Testimony from Sergeant Norman Howes, 10 Platoon, 2nd Battalion The South Staffordshire Regiment; cited in Middlebrook, p.204

26. Testimony from Lieutenant David Russell, commanding 7 Platoon, C Company, 2nd Parachute Battalion; cited in Middlebrook, p.203

27. *See* ibid., p.204

28. Quotes from Haines, pp.56-57

29. Testimony from Lieutenant David Russell, commanding 7 Platoon, C Company, 2nd Parachute Battalion; cited in Middlebrook, p.203

30. Quoted from **WO 171/1375** 2nd Battalion South Staffordshire Regiment War Diary, Appendix: '2nd South Staffords at Arnhem 17-25 Sept 44'

31. Quoted from **WO 171/1375** 2nd Battalion South Staffordshire Regiment War Diary, Appendix: '2nd South Staffords at Arnhem 17-25 Sept 44'

32. Testimony from Lieutenant-Colonel Derek McCardie, Commanding Officer, 2nd Battalion The South Staffordshire Regiment; cited in Middlebrook, p.205

33. Quoted from ibid., p.203

34. Testimony from Major Robert Cain, Officer Commanding B Company, 2nd Battalion South Staffordshire Regiment; cited in Haines, pp.57, 60-62

35. Testimony from Major David Gilchrist, Officer Commanding A Company, 11th Parachute Battalion; cited in Middlebrook, p.207

36. Testimony from Major David Gilchrist, Officer Commanding A Company, 11th Parachute Battalion; cited in ibid., p.207

37. *See* ibid., pp.207-208

38. Quoted from **WO 171/1244** 11th Parachute Battalion War Diary, Appendix A: 'Account of Arnhem Battle 11th Bn. The Parachute Regiment by Lieutenant J. E. Blackwood', entry for 19/09/1944

39. *See* Middlebrook, p.208; and **WO 171/1375** 2nd Battalion South Staffordshire Regiment War Diary, entry for 19/09/1944. Diependaal is sometimes rendered Diependal.

40. *See* **WO 171/1375** 2nd Battalion South Staffordshire Regiment War Diary, Appendix: '2nd South Staffords at Arnhem 17-25 Sept 44'; Major Philip Richard Thomas Wright is interred in Arnhem Oosterbeek War Cemetery, Gelderland, Holland, Plot 19, Row C, Grave 17

41. Quoted from Haines, p.62

42. *See* ibid., p.63

43. *See* **WO 171/1375** 2nd Battalion South Staffordshire Regiment War Diary, Appendix: '2nd South Staffords at Arnhem 17-25 Sept 44'; and Haines, pp.62-63

44. *See* **WO 171/1375** 2nd Battalion South Staffordshire Regiment War Diary, entry for 19/09/1944; and ibid., Appendix: '2nd South Staffords at Arnhem 17-25 Sept 44'

45. *See* **WO 171/1375** 2nd Battalion South Staffordshire Regiment War Diary, Appendix: '2nd South Staffords at Arnhem 17-25 Sept 44'

46. *See* **WO 171/1244** 11th Parachute Battalion War Diary, Appendix A: 'Account of Arnhem Battle 11th Battalion the Parachute Regiment by Lt. J. E. Blackwood'

47. Testimony from Sergeant James Drew, 2nd Battalion The South Staffordshire Regiment; cited in Middlebrook, p.205

48. Testimony from Gunner Eric Milner, C Troop, 1st Airlanding Anti-tank Battery; cited in ibid., pp.1-213

49. Testimony from Gunner 'Dickie' Bird, 1st Airlanding Light Regiment; cited in ibid., p.212

50. Testimony from Gunner Len Clarke, E Troop, 2nd Airlanding Anti-tank Battery; cited in ibid., p.212

51. *See* **WO 171/1375** 2nd Battalion South Staffordshire Regiment War Diary, entry for 19/09/1944; and **WO 171/1244** 11th Parachute Battalion War Diary, Appendix A, entry for 19/09/1944. The former refers to German tanks moving onto *Den Brink* at two separate points, and the latter refers explicitly to two tanks pursuing the Airborne withdrawal to Oosterbeek

52. *See* **WO 171/1244** 11th Parachute Battalion War Diary, Appendix A, entry for 19/09/1944

53. *See* **WO 166/14933** 1st Airlanding Light Regiment RA War Diary, entry 'Place: Arnhem, 10:00', 19/09/1944

54. *See* **WO 171/1244** 11th Parachute Battalion War Diary, Appendix A, entry for 19/09/1944

55. 150 figure cited in Middlebrook, p.209

56. *See* **WO 171/1375** 2nd Battalion South Staffordshire Regiment War Diary, entry for 19/09/1944; and ibid., Appendix: '2nd South Staffords at Arnhem 17-25 Sept 44'

57. Testimony from Major Robert Cain, Officer Commanding B Company, 2nd Battalion South Staffordshire Regiment; cited in Middlebrook, p.209

58. Figure cited in Haines, p.64

59. *See* Middlebrook, pp.325-326

60. *See* **WO 166/14933** 1st Airlanding Light Regiment RA War Diary, entry for 'Place: N.W. Arnhem', 14:00, 19/09/1944

61. *See* Middlebrook, p.326

62. *See* **WO 171/1375** 2nd Battalion South Staffordshire Regiment War Diary, Appendix: '2nd South Staffords at Arnhem 17-25 Sept 44'

63. *See* **WO 166/14933** 1st Airlanding Light Regiment RA War Diary, entry for 'Place: N.W. Arnhem', 14:00, 19/09/1944

64. Locations, occupation timing and Major Buchanan's command details cited in **WO 171/1375** 2nd Battalion South Staffordshire Regiment War Diary, Appendix: '2nd South Staffords at Arnhem 17-25 Sept 44'; *see* also **WO 171/1238** 3rd Parachute Battalion War Diary, entry for 16:00, 19/09/1944

65. *See* Middlebrook, p.327; Simonds is rendered Simmons

66. *See* **WO 171/1375** 2nd Battalion South Staffordshire Regiment War Diary, Appendix: '2nd South Staffords at Arnhem 17-25 Sept 44'

67. *See* Haines, p.67

68. Testimony from Gunner Len Clarke, E Troop, 2nd Airlanding Anti-tank Battery; cited in Middlebrook, p.328

69. *See* Middlebrook, pp.327-328; Zwarts, pp.48-49; and **The Pegasus Archive**, Battle of Arnhem Archive, Biographies Section, 'Major John L. C. Waddy', at www.pegasusarchive.org/arnhem/john_waddy.htm, accessed 03/05/2013

70. Testimony from Private Fred Morton, Medium Machine Gun Platoon, Support Company, 3rd Parachute Battalion; cited in Middlebrook, pp.213-214

71. Testimony from Corporal Arthur Hatcher, 16 Parachute Ambulance RAMC; cited in Middlebrook, p.215

72. Quoted from ibid., p.327

73. Testimony from Sergeant Norman Howes, 10 Platoon, A Company, 2nd Battalion, The South Staffordshire Regiment; cited in Haines, p.67

74. Numbers cited in **WO 171/393** 1st Airborne Division HQ War Diary, entry for 23:15, 19/09/1944; and Middlebrook, p.326

75. *See* **WO 166/14933** 1st Airlanding Light Regiment RA War Diary, entry for 'Place: N.W. Arnhem', 18:30, 19/09/1944; for South Staffords party move to Oosterbeek Old Church *see* Haines, p.66

76. *See* **WO 171/1375** 2nd Battalion South Staffordshire Regiment War Diary, Appendix: '2nd South Staffords at Arnhem 17-25 Sept 44'; and **WO 171/1244** 11th Parachute Battalion War Diary, entry for 19/09/1944

77. *See* Haines, p.66

78. *See* Middlebrook, p.257

79. *See* **The Pegasus Archive**, Battle of Arnhem Archive, Biographies Section, 'Major Robert Laslett John Pott', 'An Account of the Action of 'A' Company 156 Battalion The Parachute Regiment 18/19th Sep 44' at http//www.pegasusarchive.org/arnhem/john_pott.htm, accessed 05/05/2013; for details of the Dutch civilian rescuers *see* Middlebrook, pp.257-258

80. *See* **WO 171/594** 4th Parachute Brigade War Diary, Appendix C: 'Diary Kept by Brigadier J. W. Hackett, Commander 4th Parachute Brigade', entry for 19/09/1944; **WO 171/1247** 156 Parachute Battalion War Diary, entry for 14:00, 19/09/1944; and **WO 171/1511** 4th Parachute Squadron RE War Diary, entry for 15:00, 19/09/1944

81. *See* **WO 171/1247** 156 Parachute Battalion War Diary, entry for 14:00, 19/09/1944

82. *See* **WO 171/594** 4th Parachute Brigade War Diary, Appendix C, entry for 19/09/1944

83. For Reconnaissance Squadron involvement *see* **WO 171/406** 1st Airborne Reconnaissance Squadron War Diary, entry for 12:30, 19/09/1944; and Fairley, p.93. For Urquhart details & timings *see* **WO 171/393** 1st Airborne Division HQ War Diary, entry for 13:30, 19/09/1944; 14:20 timing cited in **WO 171/594** 4th Parachute Brigade War Diary, Appendix C, entry for 19/09/1944

84. *See* **WO 171/393** 1st Airborne Division HQ War Diary, entry for 13:30, 19/09/1944

85. *See* **WO 171/594** 4th Parachute Brigade War Diary, Appendix C, entry for 19/09/1944

86. *See* Middlebrook, p.268

87. *See* **WO 171/594** 4th Parachute Brigade War Diary, Appendix C, entry for 19/09/1944; and **WO 171/589** 1st Airlanding Brigade War Diary, Appendix A, entries for PM, 19/09/1944

88. *See* **WO 171/594** 4th Parachute Brigade War Diary, Appendix C, entry for 19/09/1944

89. Timing quote from **WO 171/594** 4th Parachute Brigade War Diary, Appendix C, entry for 19/09/1944

90. *See* **WO 171/1247** 156 Parachute Battalion War Diary, entry for 16:00, 19/09/1944; **WO 171/1323** 7th Battalion King's Own Scottish Borderers War Diary, entry for 15:00, 19/09/1944; and **WO 171/1511** 4th Parachute Squadron RE War Diary, entry for 16:00, 19/09/1944. The timing of events in the 7th KOSB Diary is consistently vague and are around one to two hour short of other cross referenced accounts

91. Exchange quoted in Brammall, **The Tenth**, p.60

92. *See* Middlebrook, pp.272-273; and Brammall, p.61

93. Testimony from Captain Nicholas Hanmer, Adjutant, 10th Parachute Battalion; cited in Middlebrook, p.274

94. Testimony from Company Sergeant Major Robert Grainger, D Company, 10th Parachute Battalion; cited in Brammall, p.62. *See* also **The Pegasus Archive**, Battle of Arnhem Archive, Biographies Section 'CSM Robert Edward Grainger' at http://www.pegasusarchive.org/arnhem/robert_edward_grainger.htm, accessed 22/05/2013. Lieutenant John Myles Henry is interred in Arnhem Oosterbeek War Cemetery, Gelderland, Holland, Plot 5, Row D, Grave 1

95. Flight-Sergeant Ray Ashley Hall has no known grave and is commemorated on the Runnymede Memorial, Panel 218

96. *See* Kershaw, pp.228-230

97. Pilot-Officer John Leonard Wilson is interred in Arnhem Oosterbeek War Cemetery, Gelderland, Holland, Plot 4, Row B, Grave 14

98. Testimony from Flying-Officer Stanley Lee, Wireless Operator, No. 512 Squadron, No. 38 Group; cited in Middlebrook, pp.389-390

99. Flight-Lieutenant David Samuel Anthony Lord VC is interred in Arnhem Oosterbeek War Cemetery, Gelderland, Holland, Plot 4, Row B, Grave 5

100. *See* Middlebrook, p.390

101. *See* George F. Cholewczynski, **Poles Apart**, pp.105-106

102. *See* Middlebrook, p.391; Air Mechanic Leonard Augustus Hooker and Squadron-Leader Cecil Aubrey Gerald Wingfield are interred in Arnhem Oosterbeek War Cemetery, Gelderland, Holland in Plot 4, Row B, Grave 5 & Plot 4, Row C, Grave 15 respectively

103. Quote from **WO 171/393** 1st Airborne Division HQ War Diary, entry for 16:30, 19/09/1944; for radio warning *see* Baynes, **Urquhart of Arnhem**, pp.113-114

104. *See* Kershaw, pp.231-232

105. Testimony from NCO Herbert Kessler, *Bataillon* 'Worrowski, *Ausbildungs und Ersatz Regiment* 'Hermann Göring'; cited in Kershaw, p.232

106. *See* **WO 171/1248**, 21st Independent Parachute Company War Diary, entry for 19/09/1944; and Kent, **First In!**, p.104

107. *See* Middlebrook, pp.400-401; Captain Desmond Thomas Kavanagh is interred in Arnhem Oosterbeek War Cemetery, Gelderland, Holland in Plot 6, Row B, Grave 1. Of the other four killed Corporal Albert Wiggins is also interred at Arnhem Oosterbeek Plot 6, Row B, Grave 12; Drivers Martin Field, James McKinnon and John Walford have no known grave and are commemorated on the Groesbeek Memorial, Panel 9

108. *See* Cholewczynski, p.102

109. For 06:00 departure *see* Cholewczynski, p.102; for 05:00 briefing *see* 43rd Troop Carrier Squadron Daily War Diary, 1 September to 31 September 1944; cited in Id., **Spanhoe's September**, p.22

110. Testimony from Lieutenant-Colonel Henry G. Hamby, Commander, 310th Troop Carrier Squadron, 315th Troop Carrier Group, 52nd Troop Carrier Wing; cited in Brinson, **Airborne Troop Carrier**, p.162

111. Testimony from 1st Lieutenant William E. Bruce, 34th Troop Carrier Squadron, 315th Troop Carrier Group, 52nd Troop Carrier Wing; cited in Brinson, p.163; for timings *see* Sikorski Institute **AV 20/31/27** 1st Polish Independent Parachute Brigade War Diary, entry for 10:00-15:00, 19/09/1944

112. For timing *see* **AV 20/31/27** 1st Polish Independent Parachute Brigade War Diary, entry for 17:00, 19/09/1944; for Kaczmarek details *see* Cholewczynski, **Poles Apart**, pp.111-113

113. For Down Ampney & Tarrant Rushton *see* **AV 20/31/27** 1st Polish Independent Parachute Brigade War Diary, entry for 12:00, 19/09/1944; for Keevil *see* **WO 171/1231** D Squadron, Glider Pilot Regiment War Diary, entry for 12:10, 19/09/1944; for take-off time *see* Cholewczynski, **Poles Apart**, p.102

114. *See* **WO 171/1231** D Squadron, Glider Pilot Regiment War Diary, entry for 12:10, 19/09/1944; and Cholewczynski, **Poles Apart**, pp.106-107

115. *See* Middlebrook, p.270

116. Quoted from Cholewczynski, **Poles Apart**, p.108

117. Figures cited in Middlebrook, p.270

118. Testimony from Sjoert Schwitters, resident of Oosterbeek; cited in ibid., p.271
119. Testimony from Marek Swiecicki, Correspondent, Polish Ministry of Information; cited in Cholewczynski, **Poles Apart**, pp.107-109
120. Testimony from Sergeant Ronald Driver, A Squadron, No. 1 Wing, The Glider Pilot Regiment; cited in Middlebrook, pp.271-272; *see* also Cholewczynski, **Poles Apart**, p.108. Staff-Sergeant John West and Sergeant James Bonham are interred in Arnhem Oosterbeek War Cemetery, Gelderland, Holland in Plot 3, Row D, Graves 19 & 20 respectively; Staff-Sergeant West's rank is recorded as Sergeant in the CWGC records
121. *See* **The Pegasus Archive**, Battle of Arnhem Archive, Biographies Section 'Staff-Sergeant Ralph Gordon Bishop' at www.pegasusarchive.org/arnhem/ralph_gordon_bishop.htm, accessed 16/05/2013
122. *See* Cholewczynski, **Poles Apart**, pp.109-110
123. *See* Middlebrook, p.272
124. Testimony from Captain Nicholas Hanmer, Adjutant, 10th Parachute Battalion; cited in ibid., p.274
125. *See* **WO 171/1323** 7th Battalion King's Own Scottish Borderers War Diary, entry for 14:00, 19/09/1944
126. *See* Kershaw, p.204; and Brammall, p.66
127. Testimony from Captain Nicholas Hanmer, Adjutant, 10th Parachute Battalion; cited in Middlebrook, p.274
128. *See* **WO 171/1248**, 21st Independent Parachute Company War Diary, entry for 19/09/1944; and Kent, p.102
129. Quoted from Kent, p.105
130. *See* Brammall, p.62; and Cholewczynski, **Poles Apart**, pp.110-111. CSM Lashmore does not seem to appear in the CWGC database
131. *See* Cholewczynski, **Poles Apart**, footnote, p.110
132. *See* Brammall, p.63; Lieutenant Herbert Charles Noel Radcliff is interred in Arnhem Oosterbeek War Cemetery, Gelderland, Holland in Plot 6, Row D, Grave 1
133. *See* **WO 171/594** 4th Parachute Brigade War Diary, Appendix C, entry for 19/09/1944
134. *See* **WO 171/1323** 7th Battalion King's Own Scottish Borderers War Diary, entry for 15:00, 19/09/1944; and Middlebrook, p.275
135. Quote from Kent, p.105
136. *See* **WO 171/1248**, 21st Independent Parachute Company War Diary, entry for 19/09/1944; and Kent, pp.105-107
137. Quotes cited in Kershaw, pp.205-207
138. *See* for example Cholewczynski, Poles Apart, p.111; and Middlebrook, p.272
139. Quoted from **WO 171/594** 4th Parachute Brigade War Diary, Appendix C, entry for 19/09/1944
140. Quoted from **WO 171/594** 4th Parachute Brigade War Diary, Appendix C, entry for 19/09/1944
141. Quotes from **WO 171/594** 4th Parachute Brigade War Diary, Appendix C, entry for 19/09/1944
142. Quote from **WO 171/1323** 7th Battalion King's Own Scottish Borderers War Diary, entry for 15:00, 19/09/1944
143. Quote and other points from **WO 171/594** 4th Parachute Brigade War Diary, Appendix C, entry for 19/09/1944
144. *See* **WO 171/1247** 156 Parachute Battalion War Diary, entry for 16:00, 19/09/1944
145. Quoted from Urquhart, **Arnhem**, p.91
146. *See* Brammall, p.68; and **WO 171/1247** 156 Parachute Battalion War Diary, entry for 16:00, 19/09/1944
147. *See* Middlebrook, pp.275-276
148. Quoted from **WO 171/1323** 7th Battalion King's Own Scottish Borderers War Diary, entry for 15:00, 19/09/1944
149. Testimony from Colour-Sergeant Tony Thomas, 156 Parachute Battalion, 4th Parachute Brigade; cited in Middlebrook, p.277
150. *See* **WO 171/594** 4th Parachute Brigade War Diary, Appendix C, entry for 19/09/1944

151. Quoted from Urquhart, p.88

152. *See* Kershaw, p.206; and **WO 171/1323** 7th Battalion King's Own Scottish Borderers War Diary, entry for 15:00, 19/09/1944

153. *See* **WO 171/1511** 4th Parachute Squadron RE War Diary, entries for 16:00 & 17:00, 19/09/1944; Faulkner-Brown, **A Sapper at Arnhem**, pp.43-45; and Middlebrook, p.277

154. *See* **WO 171/1323** 7th Battalion King's Own Scottish Borderers War Diary, entry for 15:00, 19/09/1944

155. Testimony from Lance-Corporal O'Neill Berry, 7 Platoon, B Company, 7th Battalion The King's Own Scottish Borderers: cited in Middlebrook, p.279

156. *See* Faulkner-Brown, p.48

157. Quoted from **WO 171/594** 4th Parachute Brigade War Diary, Appendix C, entry for 19/09/1944

158. For details and the VC citation *see* Brammall, pp.66-67; *see* also Middlebrook, pp.279-280. Captain Lionel Ernest Queripel VC is interred in Arnhem Oosterbeek War Cemetery, Gelderland, Holland in Plot 5, Row D, Grave 8

159. Quoted from Kershaw, p.207; for Krafft's report in full *see* **AIR 20/2333**, 'Battle of Arnheim': German account, Sept. to Oct. 1944

160. *See* **WO 171/594** 4th Parachute Brigade War Diary, Appendix C, entry for 19/09/1944

161. *See* **WO 166/14937** 2 Airlanding Anti-tank Battery RA War Diary, entry for OPERATION 'MARKET'; and Middlebrook, p.279

162. *See* **WO 171/594** 4th Parachute Brigade War Diary, Appendix C, entry for 19/09/1944; Brammall, p.68; and Middlebrook, p.280

163. *See* **WO 171/1247** 156 Parachute Battalion War Diary, entries for 16:00 & 19:00, 19/09/1944; **WO 171/594** 4th Parachute Brigade War Diary, Appendix C, entry for 19/09/1944; and Middlebrook, pp.276-277

164. *See* **WO 171/1323** 7th Battalion King's Own Scottish Borderers War Diary, entries for 15:00 & 17:30, 19/09/1944

165. *See* **WO 171/594** 4th Parachute Brigade War Diary, Appendix C, entry for 19/09/1944

166. Quoted from Urquhart, p.101

167. *See* **WO 171/398** 1st Airborne Division Signals War Diary, entries for 09:47 & 20:55, 19/09/1944

168. *See* **WO 171/393** 1st Airborne Division HQ War Diary, entries for 19:00 & 23:30, 19/09/1944

169. *See* **WO 171/1247** 156 Parachute Battalion War Diary, entry for 19:00, 19/09/1944; and Brammall, p.68

170. *See* **WO 171/1511** 4th Parachute Squadron RE War Diary, entries for 18:00 & Night, 19/09/1944; ibid, 'Appendix I by Captain J. J. Cormie', entries for 18:00 and 19:00, 19/09/1944; and Faulkner-Brown, pp.45-48

171. *See* testimony from Lieutenant Kenneth Evans, Troop Officer, No. 1 Troop, 4th Parachute Squadron RE; cited in Middlebrook, p.330; and Faulkner Brown, pp.48-49

172. *See* Cholewczynski, **Poles Apart**, pp.111-113; and Faulkner-Brown, p.49

173. *See* Turnbull & Hamblett, **The Pegasus Patrol**, pp.80-82; and Peatling, **No Surrender at Arnhem**, especially pp.22-24. Sergeant Henry Louis Callaway is interred in Arnhem Oosterbeek War Cemetery, Gelderland, Holland in Plot 30 Row A, Grave 2

174. *See* **WO 171/398** 1 Airborne Division Signals War Diary, entry for 18:02, 19/09/1944

175. Quoted from Sims, **Arnhem Spearhead**, pp.69-70

176. Testimony from Signalman George Lawson, 1st Airborne Division Signals; cited in Middlebrook, p.306

177. *See* **WO 171/1509** 1st Parachute Squadron RE War Diary, entries for 07:00-10:00, 10:00, 10:30-12:00 & 12:00, 19/09/1944

178. Testimony from Captain Antony Frank, Second-in-Command and subsequently Officer Commanding A Company, 2nd Parachute Battalion; cited in Middlebrook, pp.301-302. Lieutenant Andrew Johnston McDermont is interred in Arnhem Oosterbeek War Cemetery, Gelderland, Holland Plot 6, Row D, Grave 7

179. *See* **WO 171/1509** 1st Parachute Squadron RE War Diary, entries for 12:30-15:00, 19/09/1944

180. *See* Frost, **A Drop Too Many**, p.223

181. *See* **WO 171/1509** 1ˢᵗ Parachute Squadron RE War Diary, entries for 16:15 & 17:00, 19/09/1944

182. *See* Kershaw, p.228

183. *See* Zwarts, p.56; Knaack is sometimes rendered Knack

184. *See* **WO 171/1509** 1ˢᵗ Parachute Squadron RE War Diary, entry for 19:00, 19/09/1944

185. Testimony from Sapper George Needham, B Troop, 1ˢᵗ Parachute Squadron RE; cited in Middlebrook, p.304

186. Quoted from Sims, p.73

187. Thirty minute period cited in **WO 171/1509** 1ˢᵗ Parachute Squadron RE War Diary, entry for 19:30, 19/09/1944

188. Testimony from Private Kevin Heaney, Ordnance Field Parks RAOC, 1ˢᵗ Airborne Division; cited in Middlebrook, p.305

189. *See* Sims, pp.73-74

190. Testimony from Corporal Horace Goodrich, Defence Platoon, 1ˢᵗ Parachute Brigade HQ; cited in Middlebrook, pp.303-304

191. *See* Frost, p.227

192. *See* Sims, pp.75-76; Lieutenant Woods was wounded rather than killed, but died of his wounds in captivity on 14 October 1944; Lieutenant Reginald Bryan Woods is interred in Becklingen War Cemetery, Niedersachsen, Germany, Plot 8, Row C, Grave 3

193. *See* Frost, p.227

194. *See* Cherry, **With Nothing Bigger Than a Bren Gun**, Appendix E, p.33

195. *See* Zwarts, p.56

196. *See* **WO 171/1509** 1ˢᵗ Parachute Squadron RE War Diary, entries for 21:00 & 23:59, 19/09/1944

197. *See* Middlebrook, p.305

198. Testimony from Sapper Thomas Carpenter, No. 2 Platoon, 9ᵗʰ (Airborne) Field Company RE; cited in ibid., p.307

199. *See* ibid., p.307

200. *See* **CAB 44/254** Part II: Operation MARKET GARDEN, Book III, Chapter VII, Appendix A, Section II 'Operations in the area Grave-Nijmegen – 17/20 Sep.', Para. 16 'Gds Armd Div - Narrative 19 Sep.'; Nordyke, **All American All The Way**, pp.83-84; and LoFaro, **The Sword of St. Michael**, p.346 LoFaro

201. *See* Nordyke, p.84; and LoFaro, p.346

202. *See* Nordyke, pp.82-83

203. *See* **CAB 44/254** Part II: Operation MARKET GARDEN, Book III, Chapter VII, Appendix A, Section II 'Operations in the area Grave-Nijmegen – 17/20 Sep.', Para. 16 'Gds Armd Div - Narrative 19 Sep.'

204. *See* **CAB 44/254** Part II: Operation MARKET GARDEN, Book III, Chapter VII, Appendix A, Section II 'Operations in the area Grave-Nijmegen – 17/20 Sep.', Para. 16 'Gds Armd Div - Narrative 19 Sep.'; and LoFaro, p.347

205. 16:00 start time cited in **CAB 44/254** Part II: Operation MARKET GARDEN, Book III, Chapter VII, Appendix A, Section II 'Operations in the area Grave-Nijmegen – 17/20 Sep.', Para. 16 'Gds Armd Div - Narrative 19 Sep.'; and LoFaro, p.346. Nordyke refers to the attack commencing at 13:45 but this contradicts the 30 Corps and 1ˢᵗ & 2ⁿᵈ Battalions Grenadier Guards War Diaries and the 82ⁿᵈ Airborne Division's G2 Report for 19 September 1944, all of which cite times between 15:00 and 16:45; *see* **CAB 44/254** Part II: Operation MARKET GARDEN, Book III, Chapter VII, Appendix A, Section II 'Operations in the area Grave-Nijmegen – 17/20 Sep.', Para. 16 'Gds Armd Div - Narrative 19 Sep.', Author's Comment; MacDonald, **The Siegfried Line Campaign**, p.175 and Footnote 2, p.176; and Nordyke, p.84

206. *See* LoFaro, pp.346-347

207. *See* ibid., pp.348, 368; and Verney, **The Guards Armoured Division**, p.105. The *Keizer Lodewijkplein* roundabout is referred to as the *Keizer Maria Plein* in some accounts.

208. For details *see* LoFaro, p.347; and Nordyke, pp.88-91

209. Quoted from ibid., p.349

210. *See* **CAB 44/254** Part II: Operation MARKET GARDEN, Book III, Chapter VII, Appendix A, Section II 'Operations in the area Grave-Nijmegen – 17/20 Sep.', Para. 16 'Gds Armd Div – Narrative 19 Sep.'; and LoFaro, p.350. Corporal Boling is referred to as a Private and Private First Class elsewhere in this work and by Nordyke
211. *See* Verney, p.105. Lieutenant John Alan Moller is interred in Jonkerbos War Cemetery, Gelderland, Holland Plot 22, Row F, Grave 1
212. *See* Nordyke, p.99
213. *See* LoFaro, p.369
214. *See* **WO 171/1253** 1 (Motorised) Battalion Grenadier Guards War Diary, entry for 19/09/1944; and Forbes, **The Grenadier Guards in the War of 1939-45**, p.134; both cited in Reynolds, **Sons of the Reich**, p.143
215. *See* Nordyke, pp.98-99; and LoFaro, p.350
216. *See* Horrocks, **Corps Commander**, pp.109-110; cited in LoFaro, p.350
217. *See* Gavin, **On to Berlin**, pp.170-171
218. Quotes from ibid., p.172
219. *See* Kershaw, pp.144-145; for six Panther figure *see* Rapport & Northwood, **Rendezvous with Destiny**, p.317
220. *See* Kershaw, p.145
221. *See* **CAB 44/254** Part II: Operation MARKET GARDEN, Book III, Chapter VII, Appendix A, Section IV 'Operations south of Grave – 19/20 Sep.', Para. 41 'Movement up the 30 Corps axis 19/20 Sep'; and Rapport & Northwood, pp.315-317
222. *See* Rapport & Northwood, p.317; and Kershaw, pp.146-147
223. Quoted from Rapport & Northwood, p.317

Chapter 13

1. *See* for example **The Pegasus Archive**, Battle of Arnhem Archive, Biographies Section 'Lance-Sergeant Harold Padfield' at www.pegasusarchive.org/arnhem/harold_padfield.htm, accessed 16/06/2013
2. *See* Frost, **A Drop Too Many**, pp.223, 229
3. *See* **The Pegasus Archive**, Battle of Arnhem Archive, Biographies Section 'Lance-Sergeant Harold Padfield' at www.pegasusarchive.org/arnhem/harold_padfield.htm, accessed 16/06/2013
4. *See* Frost, pp.228-229
5. For details *see* Otway, **Airborne Forces**, pp.47-48
6. Quoted from Sims, **Arnhem Spearhead**, pp.77-78
7. Testimony from Driver James Wild, 3 Platoon, 250 (Airborne) Light Composite Company RASC; cited in Middlebrook, **Arnhem 1944**, p.309
8. *See* Middlebrook, p.308; and **The Pegasus Archive**, Battle of Arnhem Archive, Biographies Section 'Lieutenant John Patrick Barnet' at http://www.pegasusarchive.org/arnhem/pat_barnett.htm, accessed 18/06/2013
9. Testimony from *Sturmann* Horst Weber, possibly from SS *Panzergrenadier* Regiment 21; cited in Kershaw, **It Never Snows in September**, p.178
10. *See* testimony from Leo Hall dated 2001 at **The Pegasus Archive** website, Biographies Section, 'Bombardier J. Leo Hall at http://www.pegasusarchive.org/arnhem/Leo_Hall.htm, accessed 24/07/2013; and **WO 171/398** 1 Airborne Division Signals War Diary, entry for 08:40, 20/09/1944
11. *See* **WO 171/393** 1st Airborne Division HQ War Diary, entry for 08:20, 20/09/1944; quotes from Urquhart, **Arnhem**, p.104
12. *See* **WO 171/393** 1st Airborne Division HQ War Diary, entry for 09:25, 20/09/1944
13. *See* Frost, p.228
14. *See* **WO 171/1509** 1st Parachute Squadron RE War Diary, entries for 07:00-09:00 & 09:15, 20/09/1944
15. *See* **WO 166/14933** 1st Airlanding Light Regiment RA War Diary, entry for 07:00, 20/09/1944
16. *See* Urquhart, pp.99-100

17. Testimony from *Rottenführer* Rudolf Trapp, 3 *Kompanie*, SS *Panzergrenadier* Regiment 21; cited in Kershaw, p.177

18. Testimony from *Rottenführer* Rudolf Trapp, 3 *Kompanie*, SS *Panzergrenadier* Regiment 21; cited in ibid., pp.177-178

19. *See* Middlebrook, p.310

20. Timing cited in **WO 171/1509** 1st Parachute Squadron RE War Diary, entry for 09:40, 20/09/1944

21. *See* for example Powell, **The Devil's Birthday**, pp.131-132; and Nordyke, **All American All The Way**, pp.82-100

22. *See* Urquhart, p.100

23. Testimony from Lieutenant Donald Hindley, OC HQ Troop and Intelligence Officer, 1st Parachute Squadron RE; cited in Middlebrook, p.311; timings and strength cited in **WO 171/1509** 1st Parachute Squadron RE War Diary, entry for 10:00, 20/09/1944

24. Timings and strength cited in **WO 171/1509** 1st Parachute Squadron RE War Diary, entries for 10:20, 11:00 & 11:30, 20/09/1944; for Lieutenant Hindley's wounds *see* Middlebrook, p.311. For details of Lieutenant Grayburn's VC citation and the recovery of his body *see* **The Pegasus Archive**, Battle of Arnhem Archive, Biographies Section 'Lieutenant John Hollington Grayburn' at www.pegasusarchive.org/arnhem/jack_grayburn.htm, accessed 31/07/2013. Lieutenant John Hollington Grayburn VC is interred in Arnhem Oosterbeek War Cemetery, Gelderland, Holland, Plot 13, Row C, Grave 11

25. *See* **WO 171/589** 1st Airlanding Brigade HQ War Diary, entries for 02:30 and 04:45, 20/09/1944; and **WO 171/398** 1 Airborne Division Signals War Diary, entries for 02:00 and 04:40, 20/09/1944

26. *See* **WO 171/393** 1st Airborne Division HQ War Diary, entry for 01:40, 19/09/1944

27. *See* Ryan, **A Bridge Too Far**, pp.285-287; Middlebrook, p.233; and **WO 171/1513** 9th (Airborne) Field Company RE War Diary, entry for 19/09/1944

28. *See* **WO 166/15077** 1st Battalion The Border Regiment War Diary, entry for 19/09/1944; and Green, **1st Battalion The Border Regiment**, p.33

29. For details of Browning's campaign to secure control of the 1st Polish Independent Parachute Brigade *see* for example William F. Buckingham, **Arnhem 1944: A Reappraisal**, pp.43-48

30. *See* Sikorski Institute **AV 20/31/27** 1st Polish Independent Parachute Brigade War Diary, entries for 08:45, 09:15 & 10:00, 20/09/1944; quote from Cholewczynski, **Poles Apart**, p.115

31. For details of *Festung MG Bataillon* 37 *see* the **Defending Arnhem** website, German Order of Battle, Battle for the Betuwe Section, 'Fest. MG Btl 37' at http://www.defendingarnhem.com/Fest-MG-Btl-37.html; accessed 23/08/2013

32. *See* Kershaw, pp.228-233

33. Quoted from Urquhart, p.103

34. For the conference call *see* **WO 171/393** 1st Airborne Division HQ War Diary, entry for 06:00, 20/09/1944; for attendees *see* **WO 171/1234** 1 Wing Glider Pilot Regiment War Diary, entry for 08:10, 20/09/1944; and **WO 171/406** 1st Airborne Reconnaissance Squadron War Diary, entry for 09:00, 20/09/1944

35. *See* **WO 166/14933** 1st Airlanding Light Regiment RA War Diary, 'Report by Lieutenant-Colonel R.F.K. Thompson', entry for 20/09/1944; and Middlebrook, p.327

36. For Dutch Resistance involvement in bringing the existence of the Heveadorp ferry to Urquhart's attention *see* Ryan, pp.334-335; for Major Winchester's survey *see* **WO 171/1513** 9th (Airborne) Field Company RE War Diary, entry for 19/09/1944

37. *See* **WO 171/589** 1st Airlanding Brigade War Diary, Appendix A, entry for 08:30, 20/09/1944; Captains Edward Alfred Moy-Thomas and William Raymond Burns and Lieutenant Anthony Robert Thomas are interred in Arnhem Oosterbeek War Cemetery, Gelderland, Holland in Plot 16, Row B, Grave 15, Plot 1, Row A, Grave 16 and Plot 1, Row A, Grave 11 respectively. Captain Stuart Leslie Blatch has no known grave and is commemorated on the Groesbeek Memorial, Panel 2

38. *See* **WO 171/406** 1st Airborne Reconnaissance Squadron War Diary, entry for 08:00, 20/09/1944

39. Quoted from **WO 171/1238** 3rd Parachute Battalion War Diary, entry for night 19th/20th, 19/09/1944

40. *See* **WO 171/1244** 11th Parachute Battalion War Diary, entry for 20/09/1944

41. *See* **WO 171/1244** 11th Parachute Battalion War Diary, Appendix A, entry for 20/09/1944

42. For timings, vehicle numbers and destruction of the lead assault gun *see* **WO 171/1236** 1st Parachute Battalion War Diary, entry for 08:00, 20/09/1944; **WO 171/1238** 3rd Parachute Battalion War Diary, entry for 08:00, 20/09/1944; for damage to the lead *StuG see* Zwarts, **German Armoured Units at Arnhem**, p.48

43. Testimony from Private James Gardner, 1st Parachute Battalion; cited in Middlebrook, p.332

44. *See* ibid., p.333; for the destruction of the half-track from SS *FlaK Abteilung* 9 *see* Zwarts, p.17

45. *See* **WO 171/1236** 1st Parachute Battalion War Diary, entry for 11:00, 20/09/1944

46. *See* **WO 171/589** 1st Airlanding Brigade War Diary, entry for 11:00, 20/09/1944; and **WO 171/1375** 2nd Battalion South Staffordshire Regiment War Diary, entry for 20/09/1944; and ibid., Appendix: '2nd South Staffords at Arnhem 17-25 Sept 1944'

47. *See* **WO 166/14933** 1st Airlanding Light Regiment RA War Diary, entries for 07:00 & 11:00, 20/09/1944

48. *See* **WO 171/1244** 11th Parachute Battalion War Diary, entry for 20/09/1944; **WO 171/1238** 3rd Parachute Battalion War Diary, entry for 12:30, 20/09/1944; and **WO 171/1236** 1st Parachute Battalion War Diary, entry for 14:00, 20/09/1944

49. *See* **WO 171/1248** 21st Independent Parachute Company War Diary, entry for 19/09/1944

50. *See* **WO 171/1511** 4th Parachute Squadron RE War Diary, entry for 'Night', 19/09/1944; and ibid., Appendix I, entries for 18:00 & 19:00, 19/09/1944

51. *See* **WO 171/1235** 2 Wing Glider Pilot Regiment War Diary, entry for 20:30, 19/09/1944; and **WO 171/1248** 21st Independent Parachute Company War Diary, entry for 19/09/1944

52. *See* **WO 171/1323** 7th Battalion King's Own Scottish Borderers War Diary, entry for 19:00, 19/09/1944; and **WO 171/589** 1st Airlanding Brigade War Diary, Appendix A, entries for 19:30 & 24:00, 19/09/1944

53. *See* **WO 171/1323** 7th Battalion King's Own Scottish Borderers War Diary, entries for 01:00, 04:30 & 04:30-09:00, 20/09/1944

54. *See* Faulkner-Brown, **A Sapper at Arnhem**, p.51

55. *See* **WO 171/1511** 4th Parachute Squadron RE War Diary, Appendix I, entry for 08:00, 20/09/1944; and Faulkner-Brown, pp.51-52. The latter refers to the man killed by the sniper being Lance-Corporal Cyril Brown, but Lance-Corporal Brown is listed later in the work as being evacuated across the Lower Rhine at the end of the battle; *see* ibid., Appendix IV '4th Parachute Squadron, Royal Engineers No. 3 Troop', pp.124-125. Neither does Lance-Corporal Brown appear anywhere in the CWGC database

56. *See* Faulkner-Brown, p.53

57. *See* **WO 171/1511** 4th Parachute Squadron RE War Diary, Appendix I, entry for 10:00, 20/09/1944; and Faulkner-Brown, pp.53-54. The War Diary entry refers to Captain Thomas being killed outright and to Captain Brown seeing him dead, but Faulkner-Brown's account explicitly refers to him visiting Thomas in the RAP and to him dying shortly afterward. Captain Nigel Beaumont Thomas is interred in Arnhem Oosterbeek War Cemetery, Gelderland, Holland in Plot 17, Row A, Grave 11; the CWGC renders his surname Beaumont-Thomas

58. *See* **WO 171/1323** 7th Battalion King's Own Scottish Borderers War Diary, entry for 09:00 to 13:00, 20/09/1944. Lieutenant Alexander Kirk Crighton is interred in Arnhem Oosterbeek War Cemetery, Gelderland, Holland in Plot 17, Row A, Grave; his name is rendered Creighton in the War Diary

59. *See* plate and caption in Faulkner-Brown, p.52

60. *See* **WO 171/1323** 7th Battalion King's Own Scottish Borderers War Diary, entry for 09:00 to 13:00, 20/09/1944

61. *See* Green, 1st **Battalion The Border Regiment**, p.42

62. *See* ibid., pp.40-41; the latter renders Lieutenant Bainbridge's forename as John

63. Sergeant John Hunter is interred in Arnhem Oosterbeek War Cemetery, Gelderland, Holland in Plot 28, Row A, Grave 3

64. Testimony from Corporal Walter Collings, 10 Platoon, A Company, 1ˢᵗ Battalion The Border Regiment; cited at **The Pegasus Archive**, Battle of Arnhem Archive, Biographies Section 'Corporal Walter Collings' at www.pegasusarchive.org/arnhem/walter_collings.htm; accessed 16/10/2013

65. Testimony from Lieutenant Edmund Scrivener, OC 10 Platoon, A Company, 1ˢᵗ Battalion The Border Regiment; cited at **The Pegasus Archive**, Battle of Arnhem Archive, Biographies Section 'Lieutenant Edmund Filford Scrivener' at www.pegasusarchive.org/arnhem/edmund_scrivener. htm; accessed 16/10/2013

66. *See* Testimony from Corporal Walter Collings, 10 Platoon, A Company, 1ˢᵗ Battalion The Border Regiment; cited at **The Pegasus Archive**, Battle of Arnhem Archive, Biographies Section 'Corporal Walter Collings' at www.pegasusarchive.org/arnhem/walter_collings.htm; accessed 16/10/2013; and Green, pp.38-39

67. *See* Green, p.39. Corporal Thomas Edgar has no known grave and is commemorated on the Groesbeek Memorial, Panel 4; the CWGC gives his date of death as 24/09/1944

68. *See* **WO 171/1513** 9ᵗʰ (Airborne) Field Company RE War Diary, entry for 11:00, 20/09/1944

69. *See* Green, pp.38-40. Private James Wells is interred in Arnhem Oosterbeek War Cemetery, Gelderland, Holland in Plot 17, Row A, Grave 14

70. For timings *see* **WO 171/594** 4ᵗʰ Parachute Brigade War Diary, Appendix C, entry for 20/09/1944; and **WO 171/1247** 156 Parachute Battalion War Diary, entry for 07:00, 20/09/1944

71. *See* Middlebrook, p.282; for details of route, strengths etc., *see* **WO 171/594** 4ᵗʰ Parachute Brigade War Diary, Appendix C, entry for 20/09/1944; and **WO 171/1247** 156 Parachute Battalion War Diary, entry for 07:00, 20/09/1944

72. *See* **WO 171/594** 4ᵗʰ Parachute Brigade War Diary, Appendix C, entry for 20/09/1944

73. 07:17 timing cited in **WO 171/594** 4ᵗʰ Parachute Brigade War Diary, Appendix C, entry for 20/09/1944; 08:00 timing cited in **WO 171/1247** 156 Parachute Battalion War Diary, entry for 08:00, 20/09/1944. The former refers to the 07:15 timestamp 'fairly precisely' but timings in this account are generally vague and several of the six-figure map grid references cited are also rendered incorrectly. As 156 Parachute Battalion timings are generally correct throughout, the latter timestamp is likely the more accurate

74. *See* **WO 171/1247** 156 Parachute Battalion War Diary, entries for 08:00 and 10:00, 20/09/1944; and **The Pegasus Archive**, Battle of Arnhem Archive, Biographies Section 'Major Geoffrey Stewart Powell' at www.pegasusarchive.org/arnhem/geoffrey_powell.htm, accessed 31/10/2013. Lieutenant William Stewart Donaldson is interred in Arnhem Oosterbeek War Cemetery, Gelderland, Holland in Plot 21, Row B, Grave 10

75. Quoted from **WO 171/594** 4ᵗʰ Parachute Brigade War Diary, Appendix C, entry for 20/09/1944

76. Hackett's War Diary account refers to the summons arriving at 07:40, but the Division HQ War Diary records the contact at 08:22; *see* **WO 171/594** 4ᵗʰ Parachute Brigade War Diary, Appendix C, entry for 20/09/1944; and **WO 171/393** 1ˢᵗ Airborne Division HQ War Diary, entry for 08:22, 20/09/1944

77. Figures cited in **WO 171/1247** 156 Parachute Battalion War Diary, entry for 10:00, 20/09/1944

78. Quoted from **WO 171/1247** 156 Parachute Battalion War Diary, entry for 12:00, 20/09/1944

79. Quoted from **The Pegasus Archive**, Battle of Arnhem Archive, Biographies Section 'Lieutenant Joseph Winston Glover' at www.pegasusarchive.org/arnhem/pat_glover.htm, accessed 30/10/2013

80. Quotes from **WO 171/594** 4ᵗʰ Parachute Brigade War Diary, Appendix C, entry for 20/09/1944

81. *See* Brammall, **The Tenth**, p.72

82. *See* Middlebrook, p.282; Captain Cedric Michael Horsfall has no known grave and is commemorated on the Groesbeek Memorial, Panel 8

83. 13:10 timing cited in **WO 171/393** 1ˢᵗ Airborne Division HQ War Diary, entry for 13:10; quote from Urquhart, p.108

84. *See* Rapport & Northwood, **Rendezvous with Destiny**, p.318; and **CAB 44/254** Part II: Operation MARKET GARDEN, Book III, Chapter VII, Appendix A, Section IV 'Operations south of Grave – 19/20 Sep', Para. 39, '30 Corps action in area Eindhoven-St. Oedenrode 19/20 Sep'
85. *See* Kershaw, p.147
86. *See* Rapport & Northwood, pp.323-325
87. *See* Kershaw, p.147
88. *See* Rapport & Northwood, pp.325-326
89. For a detailed account *see* ibid., pp.329-337
90. *See* **CAB 44/254** Part II: Operation MARKET GARDEN, Book III, Chapter VII, Appendix A, Section II 'Operations in the area Grave-Nijmegen – 17/20 Sep', Para. 17 'The capture of the Nijmegen bridges – 20th Sep'; and LoFaro, **The Sword of St. Michael**, pp.351-352
91. *See* ibid., p.368
92. *See* Nordyke, **All American All The Way**, pp.105-106
93. *See* LoFaro, p.368
94. *See* Nordyke, p.105
95. *See* LoFaro, pp.368-370
96. *See* **CAB 44/254** Part II: Operation MARKET GARDEN, Book III, Chapter VII, Appendix A, Section II 'Operations in the area Grave-Nijmegen – 17/20 Sep', Para. 17 'The capture of the Nijmegen bridges – 20th Sep'; and LoFaro, 369
97. *See* ibid., p.370
98. *See* Nordyke, pp.106-107
99. *See* MacDonald, **The Siegfried Line Campaign**, p.177
100. *See* Kershaw, pp.189-190; and Nordyke, pp.104-105
101. *See* MacDonald, **The Siegfried Line Campaign**, pp.177-178; and Nordyke, p.111
102. Quotes from LoFaro, p.353
103. *See* ibid., pp.353-354; timings cited in Gavin, **On to Berlin**, p.172

Chapter 14

1. Sometimes referred to as the Hof van Holland in US accounts; *see* for example MacDonald, **The Siegfried Line Campaign**, p.181
2. *See* MacDonald, **The Siegfried Line Campaign**, p.181; cited in Nordyke, **All American All The Way**, p.145
3. *See* LoFaro, **The Sword of St. Michael**, p.354; and Burriss, **Strike and Hold**, p.110
4. Testimony from Captain Carl W. Kappel, commanding Company H, 3rd Battalion 504th Parachute Infantry Regiment; cited in LoFaro, **The Sword of St. Michael**, p.354
5. *See* Gavin, **On to Berlin**, p.175
6. *See* Ryan, **A Bridge Too Far**, p.379; also cited in Nordyke, pp.103-104.
7. *See* Nordyke, p.125
8. *See* Captain Carl W. Kappel, **The operations of Company "H", 504th Parachute Infantry**, pp.26-27; and LoFaro, p.355
9. *See* Nordyke, p.125
10. *See* ibid., p.124; and LoFaro, pp.355-356
11. *See* LoFaro, p.356; and Nordyke, p.125
12. 14:40 timing cited in LoFaro, p.356; 14:50 timing attributed to Captain Keep in Nordyke, p.126
13. *See* Nordyke, p.126
14. *See* Burriss, p.112; and LoFaro, pp.356-357
15. *See* LoFaro, p.356
16. *See* Nordyke, pp.126-128
17. *See* LoFaro, p.359
18. Quoted from ibid., p.359
19. *See* Burriss, pp.1143-114; and Nordyke, p.129
20. *See* Kappel, **The operations of Company "H", 504th Parachute Infantry**, p.29

21. *See* LoFaro, pp.359 -360

22. *See* MacDonald, **The Siegfried Line Campaign**, p.180

23. Quoted from LoFaro, p.362

24. *See* Kappel, **The operations of Company "H", 504**th **Parachute Infantry**, pp.363-364

25. *See* Nordyke, pp.109-111

26. *See* **CAB 44/254** Part II: Operation MARKET GARDEN, Book III, Chapter VII, Appendix A, Section II 'Operations in the area Grave-Nijmegen – 17/20 Sep.', Para. 17 'The capture of the Nijmegen bridges – 20th Sep.'; and LoFaro, pp.369-370

27. *See* Verney, **The Guards Armoured Division**, p.106. Captain The Honourable Vicary Paul Gibbs is interred in Jonkerbos War Cemetery, Gelderland, Holland Plot 22, Row G, Grave 4

28. *See* **CAB 44/254** Part II: Operation MARKET GARDEN, Book III, Chapter VII, Appendix A, Section II 'Operations in the area Grave-Nijmegen – 17/20 Sep.', Para. 17 'The capture of the Nijmegen bridges – 20th Sep.'; Verney, p.106; and LoFaro, p.371

29. *See* Nordyke, pp.120-122

30. The 16:20 start time is cited in MacDonald, **The Siegfried Line Campaign**, p.181

31. *See* for example Nordyke, pp.122-124

32. *See* **CAB 44/254** Part II: Operation MARKET GARDEN, Book III, Chapter VII, Appendix A, Section II 'Operations in the area Grave-Nijmegen – 17/20 Sep.', Para. 17 'The capture of the Nijmegen bridges – 20th Sep.'

33. *See* LoFaro, p.371; and Kershaw, **It Never Snows in September**, p.213

34. *See* Nordyke, p.144; and LoFaro, p.364

35. *See* Burriss, pp.121-123

36. *See* **CAB 44/254** Part II: Operation MARKET GARDEN, Book III, Chapter VII, Appendix A, Section II 'Operations in the area Grave-Nijmegen – 17/20 Sep.', Para. 17 'The capture of the Nijmegen bridges – 20th Sep.'; and LoFaro, p.366-367

37. Quoted from LoFaro, p.366

38. *See* ibid., p.366; and Ryan, p.416

39. *See* **CAB 44/254** Part II: Operation MARKET GARDEN, Book III, Chapter VII, Appendix A, Section II 'Operations in the area Grave-Nijmegen – 17/20 Sep.', Para. 17 'The capture of the Nijmegen bridges – 20th Sep.'; for a detailed account *see* Ryan, pp.416, 418-419

40. *See* LoFaro, pp.373-374

41. *See* Ryan, pp.417-418; and LoFaro, p.372

42. *See* **CAB 44/254** Part II: Operation MARKET GARDEN, Book III, Chapter VII, Appendix A, Section II 'Operations in the area Grave-Nijmegen – 17/20 Sep.', Para. 17 'The capture of the Nijmegen bridges – 20th Sep.'; and Wilson, **The Ever Open Eye**, pp.129-130

43. *See* Kershaw, pp.198, 212- 214

44. Figures cited in Nordyke, p.149

45. *See* Ryan, pp.421-422; and Burriss, pp.123-124

46. *See* Gavin, **On to Berlin**, pp.181-182

47. Quoted from Wilson, p.133

48. *See* Ryan, p.423

49. *See* Powell, **The Devil's Birthday**, p.163

50. *See* LoFaro, pp.387-388

51. *See* Gavin, **On to Berlin**, pp.175-176

52. *See* MacDonald, **The Siegfried Line Campaign**, p.178; and LoFaro, pp.381-382

53. *See* Nordyke, **All American All The Way**, p.109; and LoFaro, **The Sword of St. Michael**, pp.382-384

54. *See* Gavin, **On to Berlin**, pp.176-177; MacDonald, **The Siegfried Line Campaign**, p.178; LoFaro, pp.384-386; and Nordyke, p.150

55. *See* Major B. F. Delamater, **The Action of the 1**st **Battalion, 508**th **Parachute Infantry**, pp.17-20; and Nordyke, pp.108-109, 117-118, 149-150

56. Testimony from Major Michael Forman, OC B Company, 7th Battalion The King's Own Scottish Borderers; cited in Middlebrook, **Arnhem 1944**, p.284

57. Testimony from Lieutenant Dennis Kayne, commanding 8 Platoon, B Company, 156 Parachute Battalion; cited in ibid., p.285

58. Testimony from Lieutenant Dennis Noble, commander Medium Machine Gun Platoon, Support Company, 156 Parachute Battalion; cited in ibid.. p.285

59. For withdrawal timing *see* **WO 171/1247** 156 Parachute Battalion War Diary, entry for 13:00, 20/09/1944; for 'troop stonk' details *see* **WO 171/594** 4th Parachute Brigade War Diary, Appendix C, 'Diary Kept by Brigadier J.W. Hackett, Commander 4th Parachute Brigade', entry for 20/09/1944

60. *See* **WO 171/594** 4th Parachute Brigade War Diary, Appendix C, entry for 20/09/1944; and Middlebrook, pp.72, 283

61. Major Charles Neville Bruce Dawson and Captain George Minto Blundell are interred in Arnhem Oosterbeek War Cemetery, Gelderland, Holland in Plot 6, Row C, Grave 11 and Plot 27, Row B, Grave 7 respectively. Captain Gibbs was captured during the fight while Captain Wainright was cut off; he evaded capture and was instrumental in organising the evacuation of other evaders across the Lower Rhine via Operation PEGASUS on the night of 22-23 October 1944

62. Quoted from **WO 171/594** 4th Parachute Brigade War Diary, Appendix C, entry for 20/09/1944

63. *See* **WO 171/1247** 156 Parachute Battalion War Diary, entry for 13:00, 20/09/1944; and **The Pegasus Archive**, Battle of Arnhem Archive, Biographies Section Major Geoffrey Stewart Powell' at www.pegasusarchive.org/arnhem/geoffrey_powell.htm, accessed 31/10/2013

64. Testimony from Sergeant Andrew Thorburn, A Company, 156 Parachute Battalion; cited in Middlebrook, p.283. Lieutenant –Colonel Sir William Richard de Bacquencourt Des Vœux is interred in Arnhem Oosterbeek War Cemetery, Gelderland, Holland Plot 6, Row C, Grave 10

65. *See* **WO 171/1247** 156 Parachute Battalion War Diary, entry for 13:00, 20/09/1944

66. *See* **WO 171/594** 4th Parachute Brigade War Diary, Appendix C, entry for 20/09/1944

67. *See* Urquhart, **Arnhem**, p.109

68. Major Michael Stuart Page is interred in Arnhem Oosterbeek War Cemetery, Gelderland, Holland in Plot 28, Row B, Grave 7

69. Figures cited in **WO 171/1247** 156 Parachute Battalion War Diary, entry for 17:00, 20/09/1944

70. *See* **WO 171/594** 4th Parachute Brigade War Diary, Appendix C, entry for 20/09/1944

71. *See* for example Middlebrook, p.286

72. *See* **WO 171/1247** 156 Parachute Battalion War Diary, entry for 18:30, 20/09/1944

73. *See* **WO 171/393** 1st Airborne Division HQ War Diary, entry for 18:50, 20/09/1944; Urquhart, p.110; and **WO 171/594** 4th Parachute Brigade War Diary, Appendix C, entry for 20/09/1944;

74. *See* Green, 1st **Battalion The Border Regiment**, p.40

75. *See* ibid., p.42

76. For details & plates *see* Zwarts, **German Armoured Units at Arnhem**, pp.66, 69

77. *See* for example **The Pegasus Archive**, Battle of Arnhem Archive, Biographies Section Lieutenant-Colonel Robert Guy Loder-Symonds at www.pegasusarchive.org/arnhem/robert_loder_symonds.htm, accessed 02/12/2013. The above account erroneously refers to the *Flammpanzer B2 (f)* approaching from the direction of Arnhem to the east, whereas it was moving along the *Utrechtseweg* from the west

78. Quoted from **WO 166/15077** 1st Battalion The Border Regiment War Diary, entry for 20/09/1944

79. *See* Green, pp.41-42

80. *See* **WO 171/1513** 9th (Airborne) Field Company RE War Diary, entry for 20/09/1944

81. *See* **WO 171/589** 1st Airlanding Brigade War Diary, Appendix A, entry for 18:30, 20/09/1944

82. For timings *see* **WO 171/397** HQ Royal Engineers War Diary, entries for 17:40 & 19:55, 20/09/1944; for Mackenzie's presence *see* **WO 171/393** 1st Airborne Division HQ War Diary, entry for 18:00, 20/09/1944

83. *See* **The Pegasus Archive**, Battle of Arnhem Archive, Biographies Section 'Captain Michael Douglas Green' at www.pegasusarchive.org/arnhem/michael_douglas_green.htm, accessed 07/12/2013.

84. Quoted from **WO 171/397** HQ Royal Engineers War Diary, entry for 21:10, 20/09/1944

85. *See* **The Pegasus Archive**, Battle of Arnhem Archive, Biographies Section 'Captain Michael Douglas Green' at www.pegasusarchive.org/arnhem/michael_douglas_green.htm, accessed 07/12/2013.
86. *See* **WO 171/1511** 4ᵗʰ Parachute Squadron RE War Diary, Appendix I, entries for 10:00 & 18:00, 20/09/1944; and Faulkner-Brown, **A Sapper at Arnhem**, p.55
87. Quoted from Urquhart, p.111
88. Quoted from Faulkner-Brown, p.56
89. *See* Urquhart, pp.111-112
90. *See* **WO 171/398** 1 Airborne Division Signals War Diary, entry for 12:00, 20/09/1944
91. For timings *see* **WO 171/1511** 4ᵗʰ Parachute Squadron RE War Diary, entries for 11:10 & 15:15, 20/09/1944
92. *See* Faulkner-Brown, p.56
93. *See* **WO 171/1511** 4ᵗʰ Parachute Squadron RE War Diary, entry for 19:00, 20/09/1944
94. *See* **WO 171/1248** 21ˢᵗ Independent Parachute Company War Diary, entry for 20/09/1944; and Kent, **First In!**, pp.109-110
95. *See* **WO 171/1323** 7ᵗʰ Battalion King's Own Scottish Borderers War Diary, entries for 13:00-19:00 & 19:00-24:00, 20/09/1944
96. *See* **WO 171/1244** 11ᵗʰ Parachute Battalion War Diary, Appendix A, entry for 20/09/1944
97. Testimony from Captain Frank King, OC Support Company, 11ᵗʰ Parachute Battalion; cited in Middlebrook, pp.333-334
98. *See* **WO 171/1244** 11ᵗʰ Parachute Battalion War Diary, Appendix A, entry for 20/09/1944
99. Lieutenant Leslie Arthur Curtis has no known grave and is commemorated on the Groesbeek Memorial, Panel 8
100. For Lance-Sergeant Baskeyfield's VC citation *see* for example **The Pegasus Archive**, Battle of Arnhem Archive, Biographies Section 'Lance-Sergeant John Daniel Baskeyfield' at www.pegasusarchive.org/arnhem/john_baskeyfield.htm, accessed 18/12/2013; Lance-Sergeant John Daniel Baskeyfield has no known grave and is commemorated on the Groesbeek Memorial, Panel 5
101. *See* **WO 171/1236** 1ˢᵗ Parachute Battalion War Diary, entries for 15:00, 16:30 & 19:00, 20/09/1944; and **WO 171/1238** 3ʳᵈ Parachute Battalion War Diary, entries for 16:00, 18:00 & 18:30, 20/09/1944
102. *See* **WO 171/393** 1ˢᵗ Airborne Division HQ War Diary, entry for 18:15, 20/09/1944; and **WO 171/589** 1ˢᵗ Airlanding Brigade War Diary, Appendix A, entries for 15:00 & 19:20, 20/09/1944
103. *See* **WO 171/1236** 1ˢᵗ Parachute Battalion War Diary, entries for 19:00 & 20:30, 20/09/1944; **WO 171/1238** 3ʳᵈ Parachute Battalion War Diary, entry for 18:45, 20/09/1944; and **WO 171/1244** 11ᵗʰ Parachute Battalion War Diary, entry for 20/09/1944
104. *See* **WO 171/1236** 1ˢᵗ Parachute Battalion War Diary, entry for 20:30, 20/09/1944; and **WO 171/1238** 3ʳᵈ Parachute Battalion War Diary, entry for Night Sept 20/21', 20/09/1944
105. *See* **WO 171/1244** 11ᵗʰ Parachute Battalion War Diary, entry for 20/09/1944; **WO 171/589** 1ˢᵗ Airlanding Brigade War Diary, Appendix A, entry for 19:20, 20/09/1944; and Middlebrook, p.336
106. For Lonsdale comment *see* **WO 171/1238** 3ʳᵈ Parachute Battalion War Diary, entry for 12:30, 20/09/1944
107. *See* 'Report on Operation 'MARKET'' by Major S.M. Frazer, RAMC 181 Air Landing Field Ambulance', entry for 19/09/1944; cited at **The Pegasus Archive**, Battle of Arnhem Archive, Biographies Section 'Major S. M. Frazer' at www.pegasusarchive.org/arnhem/sm_frazer.htm, accessed 21/11/2013; *see* also Mawson, **Arnhem Doctor**, p.72
108. *See* Mawson, pp.86-87; and Middlebrook, pp.336-337
109. Quoted from Mawson, p.87. Captain The Reverend Bernard Joseph Benson died on 27/09/1944; he is interred in Arnhem Oosterbeek War Cemetery, Gelderland, Holland Plot 4, Row B, Grave 10
110. *See* 'Report on Operation 'MARKET'' by Major S. M. Frazer, RAMC 181 Air Landing Field Ambulance', entry for 20/09/1944; cited at **The Pegasus Archive**, Battle of Arnhem Archive, Biographies Section 'Major S. M. Frazer' at www.pegasusarchive.org/arnhem/sm_frazer.htm, accessed 21/11/2013; ibid., Battle of Arnhem Archive, Biographies Section 'Lieutenant-Colonel

Arthur Trevor Marrable' at www.pegasusarchive.org/arnhem/arthur_marrable.htm, accessed 23/11/2013; and Mawson, pp.87-91

111. Quoted from Mawson, p.91

112. For 12:00 timing *see* 'Report on Operation 'MARKET'' by Major S. M. Frazer, RAMC 181 Air Landing Field Ambulance', entry for 20/09/1944; cited at **The Pegasus Archive**, Battle of Arnhem Archive, Biographies Section 'Major S.M. Frazer' at www.pegasusarchive.org/arnhem/ sm_frazer.htm, accessed 21/11/2013; for 11:00 and 13:30 timing *see* **WO 171/393** 1ˢᵗ Airborne Division HQ War Diary, entry for 13:30, 20/09/1944

113. For Lieutenant Macduff-Duncan's involvement *see* **The Pegasus Archive**, Battle of Arnhem Archive, Biographies Section 'Lieutenant Colin Edmund Macduff-Duncan' at www. pegasusarchive.org/arnhem/colin_macduff_duncan.htm, accessed 21/02/2014

114. For Colonel Marrable's reporting in person *see* **WO 171/589** 1ˢᵗ Airlanding Brigade War Diary, Appendix A, entry for 14:45, 20/09/1944

115. *See* Brammall, **The Tenth**, p.72; and **The Pegasus Archive**, Battle of Arnhem Archive, Biographies Section 'Lieutenant Joseph Winston Glover' at www.pegasusarchive.org/arnhem/ pat_glover.htm, accessed 27/11/2013

116. *See* Brammall, pp.72-73; and **The Pegasus Archive**, Battle of Arnhem Archive, Biographies Section 'Major Peter E. Warr' at www.pegasusarchive.org/arnhem/peter_warr.htm, accessed 27/11/2013

117. *See* **The Pegasus Archive**, Battle of Arnhem Archive, Biographies Section 'Lieutenant Joseph Winston Glover' at www.pegasusarchive.org/arnhem/pat_glover.htm, accessed 27/11/2013

118. Testimony from Private McEwan, 18 Platoon, D Company, 10ᵗʰ Parachute Battalion; cited in Brammall, p.79; Major Charles Frederick Ashcroft is interred in Arnhem Oosterbeek War Cemetery, Gelderland, Holland, Plot 5, Row D, Grave 11

119. *See* ibid., p.79

120. *See* ibid., pp.72-73

121. *See* **WO 171/1247** 156 Parachute Battalion War Diary, entries for 18:30 & 19:30, 20/09/1944

122. *See* Cholewczynski, **Poles Apart**, pp.116-119; and **WO 166/14933** 1ˢᵗ Airlanding Light Regiment RA War Diary, entry for 11:00, 20/09/1944

123. For 13:55 cancellation *see* Sikorski Institute **AV 20/31/27** 1ˢᵗ Polish Independent Parachute Brigade War Diary, entry for 13:55; for engine start time and cloud ceiling *see* Cholewczynski, **Poles Apart**, pp.119-120

124. Testimony from 2ⁿᵈ Lieutenant Robert L. Cloer, 34ᵗʰ Troop Carrier Squadron, 315ᵗʰ Troop Carrier Group, 52nd Troop Carrier Wing; cited in Brinson, **Airborne Troop Carrier**, p.162

125. *See* Brinson, p.163; and Cholewczynski, **Poles Apart**, p.120; return timing cited in Sikorski Institute **AV 20/31/27** 1ˢᵗ Polish Independent Parachute Brigade War Diary, entry for 17:00

126. *See* Cholewczynski, **Poles Apart**, p.122

127. *See* ibid., p.122

128. *See* Middlebrook, pp.391-392; for contacts with Moor Park *see* **WO 171/393** 1ˢᵗ Airborne Division HQ War Diary, entry for 01:40, 19/09/1944; and **WO 171/398** 1 Airborne Division Signals War Diary, entry for 07:20, 20/09/1944

129. *See* **AIR 27/473** No. 48 Squadron Operations Record Book, entry for 20/09/1944

130. For take-off timings and aircraft numbers *see* **WO 171/2177** HQ Air Despatch Group RASC War Diary, entries for 13:00 and 15:55, 20/09/1944

131. *See* Middlebrook, p.391; and **The Pegasus Archive**, Battle of Arnhem Archive, Unit Histories Section '196 Squadron' at www.pegasusarchive.org/arnhem/batt_196.htm, accessed 18/12/2013

132. Testimony from Warrant Officer Joseph Corless, RAF No. 299 Squadron; cited in Middlebrook, p.392

133. Testimony from Warrant Officer Bernard Harvey, RAF No. 299 Squadron; cited in ibid., p.293

134. *See* ibid., p.393; Pilot-Officer Karl Benjamin Ketcheson RCAF is interred in Brookwood Military Cemetery, Surrey, UK in Plot 55, Row C, Grave 8

135. *See* **WO 171/2177** HQ Air Despatch Group RASC War Diary, entry for 21:15, 20/09/1944

136. *See* **The Pegasus Archive**, Battle of Arnhem Archive, Unit Histories Section '295 Squadron' at www.pegasusarchive.org/arnhem/batt_295.htm, accessed 19/12/2013; Pilot-Officer Neil Banks Couper RNZAF in interred in Druten (Puiflijk) Roman Catholic Churchyard, Gelderland, Holland, Grave 1

137. *See* **The Pegasus Archive**, Battle of Arnhem Archive, Unit Histories Section '570 Squadron', at www.pegasusarchive.org/arnhem/batt_570.htm, accessed 19/12/2013

138. Quoted from **WO 171/393** 1ˢᵗ Airborne Division HQ War Diary, entry for 14:06, 20/09/1944

139. *See* **WO 171/2177** HQ Air Despatch Group RASC War Diary, entry for 18:05, 20/09/1944

140. *See* **WO 171/2177** HQ Air Despatch Group RASC War Diary, entry for 15:55, 20/09/1944

141. Testimony from Warrant Officer Arthur Batten, RAF No. 190 Squadron; cited in Middlebrook, p.392

142. For container and pannier figures see **The Pegasus Archive**, Battle of Arnhem Archive, Unit Histories Section '620 Squadron' at www.pegasusarchive.org/arnhem/batt_620.htm, accessed 19/12/2013

143. *See* **AIR 27/473** No. 48 Squadron Operations Record Book, entry for 20/09/1944

144. Quotes from **WO 171/393** 1ˢᵗ Airborne Division HQ War Diary, entry for 17:00, 19/09/1944; and **WO 171/400** 1 Airborne Division RASC Airborne Element War Diary, entry for 15:00 [sic], 20/09/1944

145. Timings and aircraft numbers cited in **WO 171/2177** HQ Air Despatch Group RASC War Diary, entry for 23:59, 20/09/1944

146. *See* Frost, **A Drop Too Many**, pp.229-230; and **The Pegasus Archive**, Battle of Arnhem Archive, Biographies Section 'Major Douglas Edward Crawley' at www.pegasusarchive.org/arnhem/doug_crawley.htm, accessed 21/12/2013

147. *See* Middlebrook, p.311

148. *See* **WO 171/393** 1ˢᵗ Airborne Division HQ War Diary, entries for 14:40 & 15:45, 20/09/1944; and **WO 171/398** 1 Airborne Division Signals War Diary, entry for 14:00, 20/09/1944

149. *See* Zwarts, p.56

150. For details of Major Lewis' wounds *see* Cherry, **With Nothing Bigger Than A Bren Gun**, p.21

151. *See* **WO 171/1509** 1ˢᵗ Parachute Squadron RE War Diary, entries for 14:00, 14:10 & 14:30, 20/09/1944; and Middlebrook, p.312

152. Testimony from Lance-Sergeant Norman Swift, 1ˢᵗ Parachute Squadron RE; cited in Cherry, p.18

153. **WO 171/1509** 1ˢᵗ Parachute Squadron RE War Diary, entry for 14:30, 20/09/1944

154. *See* Middlebrook, pp.312-313; **WO 171/1509** 1st Parachute Squadron RE War Diary, entries for 14:45 & 14:55, 20/09/1944; and Cherry, p.20

155. Testimony from anonymous member of 1ˢᵗ Parachute Squadron RE; cited in Middlebrook, pp.313-314

156. For 15:10 timing *see* **WO 171/1509** 1ˢᵗ Parachute Squadron RE War Diary, entry for 15:10, 20/09/1944; for other details *see* Middlebrook, p.314

157. *See* **WO 171/1509** 1st Parachute Squadron RE War Diary, entry for 20:00, 20/09/1944

158. Testimony from Lance-Corporal Arthur Hendy, B Troop, 1ˢᵗ Parachute Squadron RE; cited in Cherry, p.20

159. For timings *see* **WO 171/1509** 1ˢᵗ Parachute Squadron RE War Diary, entries for 15:15 and 15:45, 20/09/1944; *see* also Ryan, pp.424-425; and **The Pegasus Archive**, Battle of Arnhem Archive, Biographies Section 'Captain Eric Maclachan Mackay' at www.pegasusarchive.org/arnhem/eric_mackay.htm, accessed 24/12/2013

160. Testimony from Signalman George Lawson, 1ˢᵗ Airborne Division Signals; cited in Middlebrook, pp.314-315. Private George MacDougall Waterston is interred in Arnhem Oosterbeek War Cemetery, Gelderland, Holland Plot 20, Row B, Grave 17; the CWGC database cites his date of death as 18/09/1944

161. Testimony from Private Kevin Heaney, Ordnance Field Parks RAOC, 1st Airborne Division; cited in Middlebrook, pp.315-316

162. *See* ibid., p.316

163. *See* **WO 171/393** 1ˢᵗ Airborne Division HQ War Diary, entries for 15:45, 17:10 & 18:25, 20/09/1944

164. *See* Kershaw, p.217; and Zwarts, pp.23, 56-57. For Munford's final transmission *see* Golden, **Echoes From Arnhem**, p.154; the source is cited as the 1ˢᵗ Airlanding Light Regiment RA War Diary, but there is no record of the signal in the copy of the War Diary seen by the present author

165. *See* **The Pegasus Archive**, Battle of Arnhem Archive, Biographies Section 'Bombardier J. Leo Hall', at http://www.pegasusarchive.org/arnhem/Leo_Hall.htm, accessed 31/12/2013

166. *See* Golden, pp.154-155; and **The Pegasus Archive**, Battle of Arnhem Archive, Biographies Section 'Major James Anthony Hibbert' at www.pegasusarchive.org/arnhem/tony_hibbert.htm, accessed 01/01/2014; the former refers to the contact with 30 Corps occurring in the morning of Tuesday 19 September, but Major Hibbert's account strongly suggests it took place a day later. For the unidentified set *see* Sims, **Arnhem Spearhead**, pp.82-83

167. *See* Kershaw, p.215

168. *See* Sims, p.85

169. Quoted from **The Pegasus Archive**, Battle of Arnhem Archive, Biographies Section 'Major James Anthony Hibbert' at www.pegasusarchive.org/arnhem/tony_hibbert.htm, accessed 01/01/2014

170. Testimony from Gunner Dennis Bowles, HQ Group, 3 Airlanding Light Battery, 1ˢᵗ Airlanding Light Regiment RA; cited in Middlebrook, p.316

171. *See* extracts from Major Hibbert's personal diary cited at **The Pegasus Archive**, Battle of Arnhem Archive, Biographies Section 'Major James Anthony Hibbert' at www.pegasusarchive. org/arnhem/tony_hibbert.htm, accessed 01/01/201

172. Transmission quoted in Golden, p.154; *see* also caveat regarding cited source above

173. Quoted from **The Pegasus Archive**, Battle of Arnhem Archive, Biographies Section 'Bombardier J. Leo Hall', at http://www.pegasusarchive.org/arnhem/Leo_Hall.htm, accessed 01/01/2014

174. *See* Middlebrook, p.317

175. *See* Sims, pp.83-84

176. *See* Frost, p.230; and Ryan, p.427; for 20:00 timing *see* at **The Pegasus Archive**, Battle of Arnhem Archive, Biographies Section 'Major James Anthony Hibbert' at www.pegasusarchive. org/arnhem/tony_hibbert.htm, accessed 02/01/2014

177. Quoted from Sims, pp.84-85

178. *See* Frost, p.231

179. Quoted from Sims, p.85

180. Quoted from ibid., p.85

181. *See* Frost, pp.231-233

182. *See* Kershaw, pp.217-218

183. *See* **The Pegasus Archive**, Battle of Arnhem Archive, Biographies Section 'Major Charles Frederick Howard Gough' at www.pegasusarchive.org/arnhem/freddie_gough.htm, accessed 04/01/2014

184. *See* Frost, p.231

185. *See* Sims, p.86; and **The Pegasus Archive**, Battle of Arnhem Archive, Biographies Section 'Major James Anthony Hibbert' at www.pegasusarchive.org/arnhem/tony_hibbert.htm, accessed 05/01/2014

186. *See* Sims, p.86

187. *See* Kershaw, p.216

188. Testimony from Captain Francis Hoyer-Millar, Second-in-Command, B Company, 2ⁿᵈ Parachute Battalion; cited in Middlebrook, pp.318-319

189. Quoted from **The Pegasus Archive**, Battle of Arnhem Archive, Biographies Section 'Major James Anthony Hibbert' at www.pegasusarchive.org/arnhem/tony_hibbert.htm, accessed 05/01/2014

190. *See* Frost, p.230

191. *See* **The Pegasus Archive**, Battle of Arnhem Archive, Biographies Section 'Major James Anthony Hibbert' at www.pegasusarchive.org/arnhem/tony_hibbert.htm, accessed 06/01/2014

192. Testimony from Corporal Dennis Freebury, 1ˢᵗ Parachute Brigade HQ; cited in Middlebrook, p.318

193. *See* Frost, pp.231, 233; and Sims, pp.86-87

194. Testimony from Captain Francis Hoyer-Millar, Second-in-Command, B Company, 2ⁿᵈ Parachute Battalion; cited in Middlebrook, pp.319-32

195. *See* Ryan, pp.429-430

196. *See* Middlebrook, p.320; and Ryan, p.429

197. Testimony from Lieutenant Thomas Ainslie, Administration Officer, HQ Company, 2ⁿᵈ Parachute Battalion; cited in Middlebrook, pp.320-321. Major Francis Raymond Tate is interred in Arnhem Oosterbeek War Cemetery, Gelderland, Holland, Plot 20, Row C, Grave 13

198. Quoted from Ryan, p.430

199. *See* Middlebrook, p.319; and **The Pegasus Archive**, Battle of Arnhem Archive, Biographies Section 'Major James Anthony Hibbert' at www.pegasusarchive.org/arnhem/tony_hibbert.htm, accessed 09/01/2014

200. Figures cited in Middlebrook, pp.287-288, 321

201. *See* Sims, pp.88-89

202. *See* Kershaw, p.221

203. *See* Frost, p.233; and Ryan, p.430

204. Quoted from **WO 171/1237** 2ⁿᵈ Parachute Battalion War Diary, 'Account of the 2ⁿᵈ Battalion's Operations at Arnhem 17ᵗʰ September 1944 by Major Tatham Warter, Officer Commanding 2ⁿᵈ Parachute Regiment [sic]'

Chapter 15

1. *See* **WO 171/1235** 2 Wing Glider Pilot Regiment War Diary, entry for 03:30, 21/09/1944

2. *See* **WO 171/1236** 1ˢᵗ Parachute Battalion War Diary, entry for 20:30, 20/09/1944; and **WO 171/1238** 3ʳᵈ Parachute Battalion War Diary, entry for 'Night Sept 20/21', 20/09/1944

3. *See* Urquhart, **Arnhem**, p.114

4. *See* **WO 171/1513** 9ᵗʰ (Airborne) Field Company RE War Diary, entry for 'Approximately 09:00', 21/09/1944; Sapper Gilbert Robert James Gwilliam is interred in Arnhem Oosterbeek War Cemetery, Gelderland, Holland, Plot 18, Row B, Grave 19

5. *See* **The Pegasus Archive**, Battle of Arnhem Archive, Biographies Section 'Lieutenant Leo Jack Heaps' at http://www.pegasusarchive.org/arnhem/leo_heaps.htm accessed 16/01/2014; **WO 171/393** 1ˢᵗ Airborne Division HQ War Diary, entry for 03:40, 21/09/1944; and **WO 171/589** 1ˢᵗ Airlanding Brigade War Diary, Appendix A, entry for 03:50, 21/09/1944

6. *See* **WO 171/589** 1ˢᵗ Airlanding Brigade War Diary, Appendix A, entry for 05:45, 21/09/1944; there is no reference to the order or to any patrols being despatched in the 11ᵗʰ Parachute Battalion War Diary

7. *See* **WO 171/1511** 4ᵗʰ Parachute Squadron RE War Diary, Appendix I, entry for 23:30, 20/09/1944

8. *See* **WO 171/1323** 7ᵗʰ Battalion King's Own Scottish Borderers War Diary, entries for 00:01 to 04:30 & 04:30, 21/09/1944

9. *See* Kershaw, **It Never Snows in September**, p.238

10. Testimony from *Hauptsturmführer* Hans Möller, commander *SS Panzer Pionier Abteilung 9, 9 SS Panzer Division*; cited in ibid., pp.237-238

11. For details of the *Möbelwagen* deployments *see* Zwarts, **German Armoured Units at Arnhem**, p.15

12. *See* Kershaw, pp.235, 238; there may also have been other German units and vehicles involved, but those cited are verifiable from the sources available.

13. Worrowski is sometimes rendered Wossowski

14. *See* Kershaw, pp.233-235

15. *See* **WO 166/15077** 1ˢᵗ Battalion The Border Regiment War Diary, entry for 21/09/1944; and Green, **1st Battalion The Border Regiment**, p.45

16. *See* **WO 171/1513** 9ᵗʰ (Airborne) Field Company RE War Diary, entry for 06:00, 21/09/1944; and **WO 166/14933** 1ˢᵗ Airlanding Light Regiment RA War Diary, entry for 06:00, 21/09/1944

17. *See* **WO 171/393** 1st Airborne Division HQ War Diary, entry for 06:50, 21/09/1944; **WO 171/397** 1 Airborne Division HQ Royal Engineers War Diary, entry for 06:50, 21/09/1944

18. *See* **WO 171/400** 1 Airborne Division RASC Airborne Element War Diary, entry for 07:00, 21/09/1944; and **WO 171/1232** B Squadron Glider Pilot Regiment War Diary, entry for 21/09/1944. Sergeants Dennis Andrews and Denis Bernard Frank Raggett are interred in Arnhem Oosterbeek War Cemetery, Gelderland, Holland in Plot 31, Row A, Grave 10 and Plot 31, Row A, Grave 9 respectively

19. *See* **WO 171/1247** 156 Parachute Battalion War Diary, entry for 07:00, 21/09/1944; and **WO 171/1236** 1st Parachute Battalion War Diary, entry for 07:30, 21/09/1944

20. *See* **WO 171/589** 1st Airlanding Brigade War Diary, Appendix A, entry for 10:00, 21/09/1944; and **WO 171/393** 1st Airborne Division HQ War Diary, entry for 10:05, 21/09/1944

21. *See* **WO 171/393** 1st Airborne Division HQ War Diary, entry for 09:00, 21/09/1944; Urquhart, pp.120-121; and **WO 171/589** 1st Airlanding Brigade War Diary, Appendix A, entry for 07:30, 21/09/1944

22. *See* **WO 171/1234** 1 Wing Glider Pilot Regiment War Diary, entry for 08:00, 21/09/1944

23. For *Hexenkessel* label *see* Kershaw, p.239; figures cited in Middlebrook, **Arnhem**, p.339; Urquhart also refers to the perimeter containing 'some three thousand men'; see Urquhart, p.121

24. Quoted from Otway, **Airborne Forces**, p.262

25. For contacts with Moor Park *see* **WO 171/393** 1st Airborne Division HQ War Diary, entry for 15:05, 20/09/1944; for criticism of Urquhart *see* for example Middlebrook, p.340; and Christopher Hibbert, **Arnhem**, p.140

26. For presence of Lt. Edwards' 17 Platoon *see* **WO 171/589** 1st Airlanding Brigade HQ War Diary, entry for 09:00, 21/09/1944

27. *See* **WO 171/1232** B Squadron Glider Pilot Regiment War Diary, entry for 20/09/1944; and Urquhart, p.121

28. *See* **WO 171/393** 1st Airborne Division HQ War Diary, entry for 09:00, 21/09/1944

29. Numbers cited with caveat regarding accuracy in **WO 171/594** 4th Parachute Brigade War Diary, Appendix C, entry for 21/09/1944

30. *See* **WO 171/393** 1st Airborne Division HQ War Diary, entry for 09:00, 21/09/1944; **WO 171/594** 4th Parachute Brigade War Diary, Appendix C, entry for 21/09/1944; and **WO 166/14933** 1st Airlanding Light Regiment RA War Diary, entry for 16:00, 21/09/1944. Major David John Madden is interred in Arnhem Oosterbeek War Cemetery, Gelderland, Holland in Plot 2, Row B, Grave 14

31. *See* **WO 171/1066** 84 Medium Regiment RA War Diary, entry for 00:15, 21/09/1944; there does not appear to be any record of contact in this regard in the 1st Airborne Division records

32. *See* **WO 171/396** 1 Airborne Division HQ Royal Artillery War Diary, entry for 09:00, 21/09/1944; and **WO 171/398** 1 Airborne Division Signals War Diary, entry for 09:00, 21/09/1944

33. According to Urquhart, MacMillen was operating from 1 Battery's Command Post, but another source refers to him being located in the 1st Airlanding Brigade's HQ; interestingly the Airlanding Brigade War Diary refers to Urquhart bringing news of MacMillen's contact. *See* Urquhart, p.121; **The Pegasus Archive**, Battle of Arnhem Archive, Biographies Section 'Captain Christopher John Salter MacMillen' at www.pegasusarchive.org/arnhem/christopher_john_salter_macmillen.htm, accessed 02/02/2014; and **WO 171/589** 1st Airlanding Brigade War Diary, Appendix A, entry for 10:30, 21/09/1944

34. *See* **WO 171/1059** 64 Medium Regiment RA War Diary, entries for 09:35, 10:35 & 11:00, 21/09/1944

35. *See* **WO 171/393** 1st Airborne Division HQ War Diary, entry for 09:45, 21/09/1944; and **WO 171/589** 1st Airlanding Brigade War Diary, Appendix A, entry for 10:30, 21/09/1944

36. *See* Urquhart, pp.121-122

37. *See* **WO 171/1059** 64 Medium Regiment RA War Diary, entry for 11:30, 21/09/1944

38. Quoted from Urquhart, p.122

39. *See* **WO 171/1059** 64 Medium Regiment RA War Diary, various entries between 13:00 and 16:00, 21/09/1944; and **Royal Artillery Units Netherlands 1944-1945** website,

'Account by 64 Medium Regiment of their support for 1 Airborne Division' at http://www.royalartilleryunitsnetherlands1944-1945.com/support-1st-airborne.html, accessed 02/02/2014

40. *See* **WO 166/15077** 1ˢᵗ Battalion The Border Regiment War Diary, entry for 21/09/1944; and **WO 171/589** 1ˢᵗ Airlanding Brigade War Diary, Appendix A, entry for 06:00, 21/09/1944

41. Worrowski is sometimes rendered Wossowski

42. Testimony from Herbert Kessler, *Bataillon* Worrowski, *Ausbildungs und Ersatz Regiment* 'Hermann Göring'; cited in Kershaw, pp.235-236

43. Testimony from Lance-Corporal Albert Wilson, 11 Platoon, B Company, 1ˢᵗ Battalion The Border Regiment; cited in Middlebrook, p.342. Private Henry Bragg has no known grave and is commemorated on the Groesbeek Memorial, Panel 4; the CWGC database gives his date of death as 20/09/1944

44. Lieutenant John Arthur Wellbelove and Sergeant Thomas Watson are interred in Arnhem Oosterbeek War Cemetery, Gelderland, Holland in Plot 30, Row C, Grave 2 and Plot 18, Row B, Grave 13 respectively. Private Francis Edward Jarvis has no known grave and is commemorated on the Groesbeek Memorial, Panel 4; the CWGC database gives his date of death as 24/09/1944

45. Testimony from Herbert Kessler, *Bataillon* Worrowski, *Ausbildungs und Ersatz Regiment* 'Hermann Göring'; cited in Kershaw, p.236

46. *See* Green, pp.45-46; and Middlebrook, p.342.

47. Company Sergeant-Major Alfred McGladdery is interred in Utrecht (Soestbergen) General Cemetery, Utrecht, Netherlands, Plot 12D, Row 1, Grave 9; the CWGC database gives his date of death as 22/09/1944

48. *See* Green, pp.48-49; and **WO 171/589** 1ˢᵗ Airlanding Brigade War Diary, Appendix A, entry for 09:00, 21/09/1944

49. *See* Green, p.33

50. *See* ibid., pp.48-49

51. *See* **WO 166/15077** 1ˢᵗ Battalion The Border Regiment War Diary, entry for 21/09/1944; and Green, p.50

52. *See* Green, p.50. Lieutenant Joseph Tate is interred in Arnhem Oosterbeek War Cemetery, Gelderland, Holland in Plot 29, Row A, Grave 8

53. *See* ibid., pp.49-51. According to the Battalion War Diary Lieutenant Barnes withdrew to the *Hemelsche Berg*, an area of high ground near D Company's position east of the *Van Borsselenweg*; *see* **WO 166/15077** 1ˢᵗ Battalion The Border Regiment War Diary, entry for 21/09/1944

54. Testimony from *Oberst* Fritz Wilhelm Hermann Fullriede, commander, *Ausbildungs und Ersatz Regiment* 'Hermann Göring'; cited in Kershaw, pp.236-237

55. Lieutenant Philip Summer Holt is interred in Arnhem Oosterbeek War Cemetery, Gelderland, Holland in Plot 22, Row C, Grave 18

56. *See* **WO 171/400** 1 Airborne Division RASC Airborne Element War Diary, entry for 15:00, 20/09/1944; and Green, p.51

57. Lieutenant George Eric Tiplady Brown has no known grave and is commemorated on the Groesbeek Memorial, Panel 4; the CWGC database gives his date of death as 23/09/1944

58. *See* Green, pp.51-53; Corporal Thomas Langhorn is interred in Arnhem Oosterbeek War Cemetery, Gelderland, Holland in Plot 21, Row A, Grave 4; the CWGC database gives his date of death as 22/09/1944

59. *See* **WO 171/1511** 4ᵗʰ Parachute Squadron RE War Diary, entry for 11:00, 20/09/1944; and **WO 171/1235** 2 Wing Glider Pilot Regiment War Diary, entry for 03:30, 19/09/1944

60. *See* **WO 171/1511** 4ᵗʰ Parachute Squadron RE War Diary, Appendix I, entry for 08:00, 21/09/1944; quote from Faulkner-Brown, **A Sapper at Arnhem**, p.57

61. *See* **WO 171/1511** 4ᵗʰ Parachute Squadron RE War Diary, Appendix I, entry for 09:00, 21/09/1944; and ibid., entries for 07:30 & 09:15, 21/09/1944; and Faulkner-Brown, p.59

62. *See* **WO 171/1511** 4ᵗʰ Parachute Squadron RE War Diary, entry for 15:30, 21/09/1944; and Faulkner Brown, pp.59-60. Lieutenant Michael Charles Eden is interred in Arnhem Oosterbeek War Cemetery, Gelderland, Holland in Plot 20, Row C, Grave 10

63. *See* **WO 171/1323** 7th Battalion King's Own Scottish Borderers War Diary, entry for 09:00, 21/09/1944; for Sergeant Keyes' Military Medal citation *see* **The Pegasus Archive**, Battle of Arnhem Archive, Biographies Section 'Sergeant Dennis William Keyes' at www.pegasusarchive. org/arnhem/dennis_keyes.htm, accessed 18/02/2014

64. *See* **WO 171/589** 1st Airlanding Brigade War Diary, entry for 16:00, 21/09/1944

65. *See* **WO 171/1323** 7th Battalion King's Own Scottish Borderers War Diary, entries for 09:00 & 12:00 to 16:30, 21/09/1944; Lieutenant Joseph MacLean Hunter is interred in Arnhem Oosterbeek War Cemetery, Gelderland, Holland in Plot 21, Row B, Grave 3

66. *See* **WO 171/1323** 7th Battalion King's Own Scottish Borderers War Diary, entry for 16:30, 21/09/1944

67. *See* Faulkner-Brown, pp.60-61

68. Testimony from Sergeant George Barton, Anti-Tank Group, Support Company, 7th Battalion King's Own Scottish Borderers; cited in Middlebrook, p.347

69. Testimony from Captain James Livingstone, Second-in-Command, C Company, 7th Battalion King's Own Scottish Borderers; cited in Middlebrook, p.347

70. *See* **The Pegasus Archive**, Battle of Arnhem Archive, Biographies Section 'Lieutenant Colin Edmund Macduff-Duncan' at www.pegasusarchive.org/arnhem/colin_macduff_duncan.htm, accessed 21/02/2014

71. Quoted from **WO 171/1323** 7th Battalion King's Own Scottish Borderers War Diary, entry for 16:30, 21/09/1944

72. Testimony from Private Henry McClusky, likely C Company, 7th Battalion King's Own Scottish Borderers; cited in Middlebrook, p.348

73. *See* **WO 171/1323** 7th Battalion King's Own Scottish Borderers War Diary, entry for 16:30, 21/09/1944; and Middlebrook, p.347. Major Alexander Verner Cochran and Sergeant Andrew Graham are interred in Arnhem Oosterbeek War Cemetery, Gelderland, Holland in Plot 20, Row C, Grave 7 & Plot 17, Row A, Grave 8 respectively; the CWGC database gives Major Cochran's date of death as 22/09/1944

74. *See* **WO 171/1323** 7th Battalion King's Own Scottish Borderers War Diary, entry for 16:30, 21/09/1944

75. Testimony from Private Alan Dawson, 21st Independent Parachute Company; cited in Middlebrook, p.348. Lieutenant Arthur Derek Lind Sharples is interred in Arnhem Oosterbeek War Cemetery, Gelderland, Holland in Plot 5, Row D, Grave 20

76. *See* **WO 171/1323** 7th Battalion King's Own Scottish Borderers War Diary, entry for 16:30, 21/09/1944

77. For sixty figure *see* **WO 171/594** 4th Parachute Brigade War Diary, Appendix C, entry for 21/09/1944. According to Middlebrook Major Powell was placed in command of the 1st Reconnaissance Squadron in its entirety, but Fairley's semi-official history only refers to his taking command of A & D Troops; *see* Middlebrook, p.337; and Fairley, **Remember Arnhem**, p.129

78. *See* **WO 171/1247** 156 Parachute Battalion War Diary, entry for 07:00, 21/09/1944

79. testimony from Trooper Alfred Webb, 1 Section, A Troop, 1st Airborne Reconnaissance Squadron; cited in Fairley, p.130

80. *See* **WO 171/406** A Troop 1st Airborne Reconnaissance Squadron War Diary, entries for 07:00, 10:00 & 11:00, 21/09/1944

81. *See* **WO 171/406** D Troop 1st Airborne Reconnaissance Squadron War Diary, entries for 09:00 & 11:00, 21/09/1944

82. *See* Fairley, p.133

83. *See* **WO 171/406** A Troop 1st Airborne Reconnaissance Squadron War Diary, entries for 12:00, 13:00, 13:30 & 14:30, 21/09/1944; for a detailed account *see* Fairley, pp.131-136

84. *See* **WO 171/406** D Troop 1st Airborne Reconnaissance Squadron War Diary, entries for 12:00, 13:00 & 16:30, 21/09/1944; and Fairley, pp.136-137

85. *See* **WO 171/1247** 156 Parachute Battalion War Diary, entry for 14:00, 21/09/1944

86. *See* **The Pegasus Archive**, Battle of Arnhem Archive, Biographies Section 'Lieutenant Joseph Winston Glover' at www.pegasusarchive.org/arnhem/pat_glover.htm, accessed 01/03/2014

87. *See* **WO 171/594** 4th Parachute Brigade War Diary, Appendix C, entry for 21/09/1944

88. *See* Middlebrook, p.344

89. *See* Mawson, **Arnhem Doctor**, p.95

90. *See* Kershaw, pp.235, 238

91. *See* Brammall, **The Tenth**, p.83

92. Testimony from *Rottenführer* Wolfgang Dombrowski, *SS Panzer Pionier Abteilung 9, 9 SS Panzer Division*; cited in Kershaw, p.239

93. *See* Middlebrook, p.344; Kershaw, p.239; and **The Pegasus Archive**, Battle of Arnhem Archive, Biographies Section 'Lieutenant Joseph Winston Glover' at www.pegasusarchive.org/arnhem/pat_glover.htm, accessed 02/03/2014

94. *See* **WO 171/393** 1st Airborne Division HQ War Diary, entry for 18:40, 21/09/1944

95. Testimony from Lance-Corporal George Wyllie, 10th Parachute Battalion; cited in Brammall, p.84

96. Testimony from Major Francis Lindley, OC Support Company, 10th Parachute Battalion; cited in ibid., p.84. Lieutenant Peter Argent Saunders is interred in Arnhem Oosterbeek War Cemetery, Gelderland, Holland in Plot 27, Row A, Grave 6

97. *See* account by Mrs Bertje Voskuil; cited in Middlebrook, pp.345-346. Lieutenant-Colonel Kenneth Bowes Inman Smyth and Private Albert Willingham are interred in Arnhem Oosterbeek War Cemetery, Gelderland, Holland in Plot 18, Row B, Grave 8 and Plot 27, Row A, Grave 10 respectively

98. *See* Testimony from QM Lieutenant Joseph Winston Glover, HQ Company, 10th Parachute Battalion; cited in Brammall, pp.83-84. *See* also **The Pegasus Archive**, Battle of Arnhem Archive, Biographies Section 'Lieutenant Joseph Winston Glover' at www.pegasusarchive.org/arnhem/pat_glover.htm, accessed 02/03/2014

99. *See* **WO 171/594** 4th Parachute Brigade War Diary, Appendix C, entry for 21/09/1944; **WO 171/393** 1st Airborne Division HQ War Diary, entries for 19:05 & 20:10, 21/09/1944; Urquhart, p.129; and **WO 171/1059** 64 Medium Regiment RA War Diary, entries for 19:45 & 19:58, 21/09/1944

100. *See* **WO 171/594** 4th Parachute Brigade War Diary, Appendix C, entries for 21/09/1944 & 22/09/1944

101. *See* **WO 171/1236** 1st Parachute Battalion War Diary, entries for 09:00 & 11:30-13:00, 21/09/1944. Lieutenant Alastair Duncan Clarkson is interred in Arnhem Oosterbeek War Cemetery, Gelderland, Holland in Plot 6, Row A, Grave 11; the CWGC database cites his date of death as 22/09/1944

102. *See* **WO 166/14933** 1st Airlanding Light Regiment RA War Diary, entries for 11:00 & 12:00, 21/09/1944; and Middlebrook, p.343. Lieutenant Keith Creighton Halliday is interred in Arnhem Oosterbeek War Cemetery, Gelderland, Holland in Plot 2, Row B, Grave 8; the CWGC database cites his date of death as 23/09/1944

103. *See* **WO 171/1375** 2nd Battalion South Staffordshire Regiment War Diary, Appendix: '2nd South Staffords at Arnhem 17-25 Sept 1944'

104. Testimony from Major Robert Cain, OC B Company, 2nd Battalion The South Staffordshire Regiment; cited in Middlebrook, p.344

105. *See* **The Pegasus Archive**, Battle of Arnhem Archive, Biographies Section 'Major Robert Henry Cain' at www.pegasusarchive.org/arnhem/robert_cain.htm, accessed 05/03/2014; and Middlebrook, pp.343-344

106. *See* **WO 166/14933** 1st Airlanding Light Regiment RA War Diary, entries for 11:00, 15:00 & 16:00, 21/09/1944

Chapter 16

1. *See* **WO 171/1236** 1st Parachute Battalion War Diary, entry for 11:00, 21/09/1944; and **WO 171/393** 1st Airborne Division HQ War Diary, entry for 12:44, 21/09/1944

2. *See* Middlebrook, p.393; and **WO 171/2177** HQ Air Despatch Group RASC War Diary, entries for 10:25 and 11:30, 21/09/1944

3. For take-off timings and aircraft numbers *see* **WO 171/2177** HQ Air Despatch Group RASC War Diary, entry for 14:30, 21/09/1944

4. *See* Middlebrook, p.393; and **AIR 27/473** No. 48 Squadron Operations Record Book, entry for 21/09/1944

5. *See* **AIR 27/473** No. 48 Squadron Operations Record Book, entry for 21/09/1944

6. *See* Middlebrook, p.394; for details of US 8th Air Force bombing raids *see* **Combat Chronology of the US Army Air Force, September 1944**, entry for Thursday 21 September, European Theatre of Operations (ETO), at http://paul.rutgers.edu/~mcgrew/wwii/usaf/html/Sep.44.html, accessed 11/03/2014

7. Quoted from **AIR 27/473** No. 48 Squadron Operations Record Book, entry for 21/09/1944

8. RCAF Warrant-Officer David Arthur Webb and his co-pilot Flight-Sergeant Dennis Hardy Ralph Plear are interred in Zeeland Roman Catholic Churchyard, Nord Brabant, Netherlands in Joint Grave 1; Warrant-Officer Gordon Birlison in interred in Uden War Cemetery, Nord Brabant, Netherlands in Plot 1, Row I, Grave 13. The fourth member of the crew, Pilot-Officer R. C. Clarke, does not appear in the CWGC database

9. *See* Middlebrook, p.395; **AIR 27/473** No. 48 Squadron Operations Record Book, entry for 21/09/1944; **AIR 27/1574** No. 271 Squadron Operations Record Book, entry for 21/09/1944; and **WO 171/589** 1st Airlanding Brigade War Diary, Appendix A, entry for 14:45, 21/09/1944.

10. For Edwards details *see* Middlebrook, p.395; and **Royal Air Force Commands**, Hugh A. Halliday, 'Arnhem and '"Jimmy" Edwards' at http://www.rafcommands.com/archive/20086.php, accessed 11/03/2014; for No. 48 Squadron details *see* **AIR 27/473** No. 48 Squadron Operations Record Book, entry for 21/09/1944

11. *See* **WO 171/2177** HQ Air Despatch Group RASC War Diary, entry for 18:15 to 20:15, 21/09/1944

12. *See* Urquhart, **Arnhem**, p.127

13. *See* Sikorski Institute **AV 20/31/27** 1st Polish Independent Parachute Brigade War Diary, entry for 09:00, 21/09/1944; and Sosabowski, **Freely I Served**, pp.156-158. According to Middlebrook, a copy of the signal is held in the Polish Institute and Sikorski Museum, London: *see* Middlebrook, pp.402-403

14. *See* **WO 171/393** 1st Airborne Division HQ War Diary, entries for 15:05, 20/09/1944 and 04:15, 05:45 & 06:45, 21/09/1944

15. *See* **WO 171/398** 1 Airborne Division Signals War Diary, entry for 03:45, 21/09/1944

16. *See* Middlebrook, p.403; and Brinson, **Airborne Troop Carrier**, p.142

17. *See* Cholewczynski, **Poles Apart**, p.127; for visibility and cloud ceiling *see* Brinson, p.141

18. Testimony from 2nd Lieutenant Robert L. Cloer, 34th Troop Carrier Squadron, 315th Troop Carrier Group; cited in Brinson, p.164; *see* also ibid., p.142

19. Testimony from Flight-Officer Robert O. Cook, 43rd Troop Carrier Squadron, 315th Troop Carrier Group; cited in Brinson, p.166

20. Testimony from 2nd Lieutenant Charles Voegelin, 43rd Troop Carrier Squadron, 315th Troop Carrier Wing; cited in ibid., p.165; and Middlebrook, p.403

21. *See* ibid., pp.164, 165

22. Figures cited in Cholewczynski, **Poles Apart**, p.132

23. *See* **Combat Chronology of the US Army Air Force, September 1944**, entry for Thursday 21 September, European Theatre of Operations (ETO), at http://paul.rutgers.edu/~mcgrew/wwii/usaf/html/Sep.44.html, accessed 17/03/2014

24. *See* Middlebrook, p.403

25. For 957 figure *see* Sikorski Institute **AV 20/31/27** 1st Polish Independent Parachute Brigade War Diary, entry for 17:18, 21/09/1944; for timing *see* Cholewczynski, **Poles Apart**, p.139

26. Quotes from 1ˢᵗ Lieutenant Oliver J. Smith and 2ⁿᵈ Lieutenant James R. Wilson, 310ᵗʰ Troop Carrier Squadron, 315ᵗʰ Troop Carrier Group; cited in Brinson, pp.168, 176-177

27. Quotes from Lieutenant-Colonel Henry G. Hamby and 1ˢᵗ Lieutenant Monroe Zartman, 310ᵗʰ Troop Carrier Squadron, 315ᵗʰ Troop Carrier Group; cited in Brinson, pp.173-174

28. *See* testimony from 1ˢᵗ Lieutenant Oliver J. Smith, 310ᵗʰ Troop Carrier Squadron, 315ᵗʰ Troop Carrier Group; cited in ibid., p.168

29. *See* ibid., p.142

30. *See* ibid., pp.142-144

31. *See* testimony from 1ˢᵗ Lieutenant Oliver J. Smith and 2ⁿᵈ Lieutenant Richard T. Ford, 310ᵗʰ Troop Carrier Squadron, 315ᵗʰ Troop Carrier Group; cited in ibid., pp.168-172

32. Testimony from Lieutenant-Colonel Henry G. Hamby, Commanding Officer, 310ᵗʰ Troop Carrier Squadron, 315ᵗʰ Troop Carrier Group; cited in ibid., p.173

33. Testimony from Flight-Officer Robert O. Cook, 43ʳᵈ Troop Carrier Squadron, 315ᵗʰ Troop Carrier Group; cited in ibid., pp.167-168

34. *See* Cholewczynski, pp.137, 139

35. Quote from Ryan, **A Bridge Too Far**, p.446; and Cholewczynski, **Poles Apart**, p.138

36. Quoted from Sosabowski, p.161

37. Testimony from Lance-Corporal Bazyli Borowik, Medical Company, 1ˢᵗ Independent Polish Parachute Brigade; cited in Middlebrook, p.404

38. *See* Sosabowski, p.162; also cited in Ryan, pp.447-448

39. *See* Kershaw, **It Never Snows in September**, pp.246-247

40. *See* Cholewczynski, **Poles Apart**, pp.139-140

41. The 1ˢᵗ Battalion went into Operation MARKET with 354 men, the 2ⁿᵈ Battalion with 351 and the 3ʳᵈ Battalion with 374; figures cited in Middlebrook, Appendix 2: 'Order of Battle, Polish Independent Parachute Brigade Group', p.461

42. *See* Cholewczynski, **Poles Apart**, pp.143-144

43. *See* Sikorski Institute **AV 20/31/27** 1ˢᵗ Polish Independent Parachute Brigade War Diary, entry for 17:18, 21/09/1944; *see* also Cholewczynski, **Poles Apart**, footnote, p.142; and Middlebrook, p.405

44. *See* Cholewczynski, **Poles Apart**, pp.140-141; Middlebrook, pp.405-406; and Truesdale, **Brotherhood of the Cauldron**, p.119

45. Testimony from Lieutenant Stefan Kaczmarek, Brigade Quartermaster, 1ˢᵗ Polish Independent Parachute Brigade; cited in Middlebrook, p.406

46. *See* Sikorski Institute **AV 20/31/27** 1ˢᵗ Polish Independent Parachute Brigade War Diary, entry for 21:00, 21/09/1944

47. *See* **WO 171/398** 1 Airborne Division Signals War Diary, entry for 17:15, 20/09/1944; and Cholewczynski, **Poles Apart**, pp.146-147

48. *See* **WO 166/14933** 1ˢᵗ Airlanding Light Regiment RA War Diary, entry for 22:00, 21/09/1944; Sikorski Institute **AV 20/31/27** 1ˢᵗ Polish Independent Parachute Brigade War Diary, entries for 22:30 & 24:00, 21/09/1944; Middlebrook, p.407; and Cholewczynski, **Poles Apart**, p.148

49. *See* Reynolds, **Sons of the Reich**, p.133; and Kershaw, Appendix B 'The German Order of Battle During Operation Market Garden 17-26 Sep', Table 'Build Up of Kampfgruppe 10SS For Defence of Nijmegen and Betuwe "'The Island" S. Of Arnhem 18-21 Sep 44', pp.331-332

50. *See* Zwarts, **German Armoured Units at Arnhem**, p.18

51. *See* Cholewczynski, **Poles Apart**, p.158

52. *See* Kershaw, p.244; and Reynolds, pp.156-158

53. *See* **CAB 44/254** Part II: Operation MARKET GARDEN, Book III, Chapter VII, 'Section V – Operations on the Island 21 to 26 September', Para. 44 '30 Corps orders for 21 Sep'

54. *See* **CAB 44/254** Part II: Operation MARKET GARDEN, Book III, Chapter VII, 'Section V – Operations on the Island 21 to 26 September', Para. 45 'Gds Armd Div fails to break through 21 Sep'

55. *See* Ryan, p.431

56. *See* LoFaro, **The Sword of St. Michael**, p.391; and **Royal Artillery Units Netherlands 1944-1945** website, '153rd (Leicestershire Yeomanry) Field Regiment' web page entry for 21/09/1944 at http://www.royalartilleryunitsnetherlands1944-1945.com/153-field-regiment.html, accessed 08/10/2016

57. *See* Verney, **The Guards Armoured Division**, p.104

58. *See* Wilson, **The Ever Open Eye**, pp.130-131

59. For 504th Parachute Infantry Regiment perimeter *see* LoFaro, p.389; unsuitability quote from Lieutenant-Colonel Giles Vandeleur, commanding the 2nd (Armoured) Battalion Irish Guards; cited in Ryan, p.431; *see* also ibid., p.423

60. *See* **CAB 44/254** Part II: Operation MARKET GARDEN, Book III, Chapter VII, 'Section V – Operations on the Island 21 to 26 September', Para. 45 'Gds Armd Div fails to break through 21 Sep'; and Roden Orde, **The Household Cavalry at War** website, '14 Days in September' web page at http://daimler-fighting-vehicles.co.uk/14%20Days%20in%20September.pdf, accessed 10/10/2016

61. *See* Kershaw, pp.214-215

62. Quote from *Brigadeführer* Heinz Harmel cited in Kershaw, p.215

63. For timings *see* Kershaw, Appendix B 'The German Order of Battle During Operation Market Garden 17-26 Sep', Table 'Build Up of Kampfgruppe 10SS For Defence of Nijmegen and Betuwe '"The Island" S. Of Arnhem 18-21 Sep 44', pp.331-332; for vehicle strength of *II Bataillon SS Panzer Regiment 10 see* Zwarts, Table '10.SS-Panzer-Division "Frundsberg"', p.4

64. Quoted from Wilson, p.133

65. *See* **CAB 44/254** Part II: Operation MARKET GARDEN, Book III, Chapter VII, 'Section V – Operations on the Island 21 to 26 September', Para. 45 'Gds Armd Div fails to break through 21 Sep'

66. Ressen is given as Bessen in the Guards Armoured Division history.

67. Quote cited in Ryan, p.433

68. *See* LoFaro, p.391; and **CAB 44/254** Part II: Operation MARKET GARDEN, Book III, Chapter VII, 'Section V – Operations on the Island 21 to 26 September', Para. 45 'Gds Armd Div fails to break through 21 Sep'; for artillery ammunition shortage *see* Para. 48 '43 Div breaks through – 22 Sep'

69. *See* **CAB 44/254** Part II: Operation MARKET GARDEN, Book III, Chapter VII, 'Section V – Operations on the Island 21 to 26 September', Para. 45 'Gds Armd Div fails to break through 21 Sep'; and Ryan, p.434

70. *See* for example Verney, pp.109-110; and Ryan, pp.432-435

71. *See* **CAB 44/254** Part II: Operation MARKET GARDEN, Book III, Chapter VII, 'Section V – Operations on the Island 21 to 26 September', Para. 45 'Gds Armd Div fails to break through 21 Sep'

72. Quoted from Ryan, p.434

73. Quoted from Verney, p.110

74. Quote from Reynolds, p.158

75. The Guards Armoured Division semi-official history only mentions a single company, commanded by Major J.S.O. Haslewood, being involved in an attempted right-flanking movement; *see* Verney, pp.109-110

76. *See* Zwarts, p.53

77. *See* Ryan, pp.423, 435

78. *See* Wilson, p.182

79. Testimony from Lieutenant John Reginald Gorman MC, 2nd (Armoured) Battalion Irish Guards; quoted in Ryan, p.435

80. For withdrawal order *see* **WO 171/589** 1st Airlanding Brigade War Diary, entry for 16:00, 21/09/1944; for 7th KOSB strength *see* **WO 171/393** 1st Airborne Division HQ War Diary, entry for 18:05, 21/09/1944

81. *See* **WO 171/1323** 7th Battalion King's Own Scottish Borderers War Diary, entry for 16:30, 21/09/1944 **WO 171/1248** 21st Independent Parachute Company War Diary, entry for 21/09/1944; and **WO 171/1511** 4th Parachute Squadron RE War Diary, Appendix I, entry for 18:30, 21/09/1944

82. *See* **WO 171/393** 1st Airborne Division HQ War Diary, Appendix: Report of Operation 'Market'; Part 1 Outline of Operations, entry for 22 Sep – 24 Sep; Urquhart, pp.131-132; and **WO 171/594** 4th Parachute Brigade War Diary, Appendix C, entry for 21/09/1944. There is no specific mention of the conference in the Division HQ War Diary

83. *See* **WO 171/1248** 21st Independent Parachute Company War Diary, entry for 21/09/1944; according to the 1st Airlanding Brigade records the order was issued at 21:52 and the contraction was ordered at 22:00, but these timings appear to be in error given that the 7th KOSB began moving to its new location at 21:30; *see* **WO 171/589** 1st Airlanding Brigade War Diary, Appendix A, entries for 21:52 & 22:00, 21/09/1944

84. *See* **WO 171/1323** 7th Battalion King's Own Scottish Borderers War Diary, entries for 18:00 to 21:30 and 21:30, 21/09/1944

85. *See* **WO 171/393** 1st Airborne Division HQ War Diary, entries for 18:40 & 20:10, 21/09/1944; **WO 171/594** 4th Parachute Brigade War Diary, Appendix C, entries for 21/09/1944 and 22/09/1944; and Urquhart, p.129

86. *See* **WO 171/1238** 3rd Parachute Battalion War Diary, entry for 15:30, 21/09/1944; and **WO 171/1236** 1st Parachute Battalion War Diary, entry for 16:00, 21/09/1944

87. For reference to the artillery barrage *see* **WO 171/1236** 1st Parachute Battalion War Diary, entry for 16:00, 21/09/1944; for Airlanding Light Regiment involvement *see* **WO 171/589** 1st Airlanding Brigade War Diary, Appendix A, entry for 15:15, 20/09/1944; for possible 64th Medium Regiment *see* **WO 171/1059** 64 Medium Regiment RA War Diary, entry for 15:15, 21/09/1944

88. Quoted from **The Pegasus Archive**, Battle of Arnhem Archive, Biographies Section 'Major Richard Thomas Henry Lonsdale' at www.pegasusarchive.org/arnhem/dickie_lonsdale.htm, accessed 30/03/2014. Major Lonsdale reprised his performance in the 1945 film of the battle **Theirs is the Glory**, and the door he pencilled the speech onto as a crib was displayed in the Airborne Museum 'Hartenstein' in Oosterbeek

89. Quoted from Middlebrook, p.336

90. *See* **WO 171/1236** 1st Parachute Battalion War Diary, entries for 16:00 & 21:00, 21/09/1944; and **WO 171/1238** 3rd Parachute Battalion War Diary, entry for 15:30 onward, 21/09/1944. Captain Geoffrey Richard Dorrien-Smith is interred in Arnhem Oosterbeek War Cemetery, Gelderland, Holland, Plot 6, Row A, Grave 10

91. Testimony from *Sturmann* Alfred Ziegler, SS *Panzerjäger Abteilung* 9; cited in Kershaw, pp.240-241

92. *See* Kershaw, p.228

Chapter 17

1. *See* Sikorski Institute **AV 20/31/27** 1st Polish Independent Parachute Brigade War Diary, entry for 01:00, 22/09/1944; and **WO 171/1513** 9th (Airborne) Field Company RE War Diary, entry for 20:00, 21/09/1944

2. *See* Sikorski Institute **AV 20/31/27** 1st Polish Independent Parachute Brigade War Diary, entries for 02:00, 03:00 & 05:30, 22/09/1944; and Cholewczynski, **Poles Apart**, pp.150-151

3. Quoted from Urquhart, **Arnhem**, p.133; for timings *see* **WO 171/393** 1st Airborne Division HQ War Diary, entry for 05:15, 22/09/1944; *see* also Cholewczynski, **Poles Apart**, p.150

4. *See* **WO 171/393** 1st Airborne Division HQ War Diary, entries for 06:17 & 07:40, 22/09/1944

5. *See* Urquhart, p.134

6. *See* Cholewczynski, **Poles Apart**, pp.153, 155; the Polish Brigade War Diary makes no mention of any pre-dawn departure but does refer to an officer-led reconnaissance patrol being despatched toward Elst at 10:00, around two hours after the British vehicles reached Driel. The disparity is presumably due to the War Diary being typed up at some point after the event; *see* Sikorski

Institute **AV 20/31/27** 1st Polish Independent Parachute Brigade War Diary, entry for 10:00, 22/09/1944

7. Attack timing cited in **WO 171/393** 1st Airborne Division HQ War Diary, entry for 11:20, 22/09/1944

8. *See* Sikorski Institute **AV 20/31/27** 1st Polish Independent Parachute Brigade War Diary, entry for 10:00, 22/09/1944. There is no mention of the encounter with the Polish patrol in Captain Wrottesley's account of the journey to Driel; *see* Ryan, **A Bridge Too Far**, pp.460-461

9. For 08:00 timing *see* Ryan, p.461; for 08:45 timing *see* Sikorski Institute **AV 20/31/27** 1st Polish Independent Parachute Brigade War Diary, entry for 08:45, 22/09/1944; for 08:50 timing *see* Cholewczynski, **Poles Apart**, p.155

10. *See* Sikorski Institute **AV 20/31/27** 1st Polish Independent Parachute Brigade War Diary, entry for 08:45, 22/09/1944; Cholewczynski, pp.153-156; Ryan, pp.460-461; and Verney, **The Guards Armoured Division**, p.110

11. *See* **WO 171/398** 1 Airborne Division Signals War Diary, entry for 09:05, 22/09/1944; and **WO 171/393** 1st Airborne Division HQ War Diary, entry for 11:20, 22/09/1944; *see* also Urquhart, p.134

12. *See* Cholewczynski, **Poles Apart**, p.155; and Ryan, p.461

13. *See* Zwarts, **German Armoured Units at Arnhem**, p.53; and Verney, p.109

14. *See* Cholewczynski, **Poles Apart**, pp.155-156

15. *See* Major-General Hubert Essame, **The 43rd Wessex Division**, p.124

16. *See* **CAB 44/254** Part II: Operation MARKET GARDEN, Book III, Chapter VII, 'Section V – Operations on the Island 21 to 26 September', Para. 48 '43 Div Breaks Through – 22 Sep'; and Ryan, pp.461-462. Trooper Harold George Patrick Read of the Life Guards is interred in Jonkerbos War Cemetery, Gelderland, Holland, Plot 18, Row C, Grave 4

17. *See* Sikorski Institute **AV 20/31/27** 1st Polish Independent Parachute Brigade War Diary, entry for 09:00, 22/09/1944; and Cholewczynski, **Poles Apart**, pp.150, 154, 156-157

18. *See* Kershaw, **It Never Snows in September**, p.244; Reynolds, **Sons of the Reich**, pp.156-158; and Cholewczynski, p.158

19. Testimony from *Feldwebel* Erich Hensel, *Nachrichten Kompanie*, unknown Division; cited in Kershaw, p.247

20. *See* Sikorski Institute **AV 20/31/27** 1st Polish Independent Parachute Brigade War Diary, entry for 10:00, 22/09/1944

21. *See* Cholewczynski, **Poles Apart**, pp.158-164. 2nd Lieutenant Richard Kresge Tice is interred in Arnhem Oosterbeek War Cemetery, Gelderland, Holland, Plot 34, Row A, Grave 13

22. *See* Cholewczynski, **Poles Apart**, p.163

23. *See* Sikorski Institute **AV 20/31/27** 1st Polish Independent Parachute Brigade War Diary, entries for 10:00, 11:00 & 11:30, 22/09/1944; and Cholewczynski, **Poles Apart**, pp.158, 166

24. *See* interview with former *Obersturmbannführer* Walther Harzer; cited in Kershaw, p.263

25. *See* ibid., pp.263-265

26. *See* ibid., p.230

27. Quoted from Kershaw, p.265

28. *See* **WO 171/393** 1st Airborne Division HQ War Diary, Appendix: Report of Operation 'Market'; Part 1 Outline of Operations, entry for 22 Sep – 24 Sep; and Urquhart, pp.131-132

29. *See* **WO 171/1248** 21st Independent Parachute Company War Diary, entries for 02:30 & 05:00, 22/09/1944; **WO 171/393** 1st Airborne Division HQ War Diary, entry for 02:00, 22/09/1944; **WO 171/594** 4th Parachute Brigade War Diary, Appendix C, entry for 22/09/1944; and Kent, **First In!**, p.116. Private Maurice Langton May is interred in Arnhem Oosterbeek War Cemetery, Gelderland, Holland, Plot 28, Row C, Grave 8; the CWGC database cites his date of death as 21/09/1944

30. *See* **WO 171/1511** 4th Parachute Squadron RE War Diary, Appendix I, entry for 01:30, 22/09/1944; strength cited in Faulkner-Brown, **A Sapper at Arnhem**, p.63

31. *See* **WO 171/1511** 4th Parachute Squadron RE War Diary, Appendix I, entry for 04:00, 22/09/1944; and Faulkner-Brown, pp.61-63

32. *See* **WO 171/1323** 7th Battalion King's Own Scottish Borderers War Diary, entries for 01:00, 04:30 to 06:30 & 06:30 to 19:00, 22/09/1944

33. *See* **WO 171/1323** 7th Battalion King's Own Scottish Borderers War Diary, entries for 06:30 to 19:00 & 19:00 to 24:00, 22/09/1944

34. *See* **WO 171/589** 1st Airlanding Brigade War Diary, Appendix F, entries for 07:30 & 09:00, 22/09/1944

35. For testimony on the incident from CSM Fielding *see* Middlebrook, Arnhem 1944, p.355

36. *See* **WO 166/15077** 1st Battalion The Border Regiment War Diary, entry for 22/09/1944; and Green, **1st Battalion The Border Regiment**, p.58. Warrant Officer 1st Class Albert Pope is interred in Arnhem Oosterbeek War Cemetery, Gelderland, Holland, Plot 22, Row B, Grave 13

37. *See* **WO 171/1375** 2nd Battalion South Staffordshire Regiment War Diary, entry for 22-25/09/1944; and ibid., Appendix: '2nd South Staffords at Arnhem 17-25 Sept 1944'

38. *See* **WO 166/15077** 1st Battalion The Border Regiment War Diary, entry for 22/09/1944; and Green, pp.58-59

39. *See* **WO 171/1244** 11th Parachute Battalion War Diary, entry for 22/09/1944.; the War Diary refers to the new position being south of the 'OOSTERBEEK WEG' but no road of that name or similar was within the 1st Airborne Division's perimeter by 22 September; for cancellation of the effort to retake the Heveadorp ferry terminal *see* **WO 171/393** 1 Airborne Division HQ War Diary, entry for 21:45, 22/09/1944; and **Wo 171/590** 1st Airlanding Brigade HQ War Diary, Appendix F, entry for 21:45, 22/09/1944

40. *See* Cholewczynski, **Poles Apart**, p.173

41. *See* **WO 166/15077** 1st Battalion The Border Regiment War Diary, Appendix A, entry for 22/09/1944; **WO 171/589** 1st Airlanding Brigade War Diary, Appendix, entry for 16:00, 22/09/1944; and Green, p.59

42. *See* Green, p.60; the problem was not highlighted in the unit War Diary until the following day; *see* **WO 166/15077** 1st Battalion The Border Regiment War Diary, Appendix A, entry for 23/09/1944

43. For aircraft numbers and cancellation *see* **WO 171/2177** HQ Air Despatch Group RASC War Diary, entries for 07:20, 12:00 & 12:15, 22/09/1944

44. *See* Middlebrook, **Arnhem 1944**, pp.396-398

45. *See* Green, pp.61-62

46. *See* **WO 171/1235** 2 Wing Glider Pilot Regiment War Diary, entry for 22/09/1944

47. Quoted from Henk Capelle, **My Airborne Experience**, unpublished memoir kindly provided by Mr Capelle via personal communication on 2 July 2016. I am indebted to Mr Capelle for permission to include his account in this work

48. The French Somua S35 was designated *Panzerkampfwagen 35S (f)* in German service. One account suggests that the vehicle involved was a Renault R35 but *Panzer Kompanie 224* exchanged its holding of such vehicles for *Char* Bs in March 1944; *see* Zwarts, p.65. For reference to the Renault vehicles and Sapper Coulsting's involvement *see* the **4th Parachute Squadron Royal Engineers** website, Arnhem Section, 'September 22' at http://myweb.tiscali.co.uk/4parasqnre/ arnhem%20page%205.htm, accessed 05/05/2014

49. Details and timings cited in **WO 171/1511** 4th Parachute Squadron RE War Diary, entries for 09:10, 11:15, 11:36 & 16:10, 22/09/1944

50. Testimony from Lance-Corporal Maurice Weymouth, Sapper Arthur Ayers and Sapper Eric Richards, HQ and No. 3 Troop, 4th Parachute Squadron RE; cited at **4th Parachute Squadron Royal Engineers** website, Arnhem Section, 'September 22' at http://myweb.tiscali. co.uk/4parasqnre/arnhem%20page%205.htm, accessed 05/05/2014

51. *See* Faulkner-Brown, pp.71-72. For Sapper Hyatt's citation for the Military Medal *see* **The Pegasus Archive**, Battle of Arnhem Archive, Biographies Section 'Sapper Philip Andrew Hyatt' at www.pegasusarchive.org/arnhem/philip_hyatt.htm, accessed 06/05/2014

52. Testimony from *Standartenführer* Michael Lippert; cited in Kershaw, p.264

53. *See* ibid., p.264

54. *See* **WO 171/1236** 1st Parachute Battalion War Diary, entries for 06:30 & 09:00, 22/09/1944; and **WO 171/1238** 3rd Parachute Battalion War Diary, entries for 07:00 & 11:00, 22/09/1944. For Sergeant Whittingham's contribution *see* **The Pegasus Archive**, Battle of Arnhem Archive, Biographies Section 'Sergeant Harold Whittingham' at www.pegasusarchive.org/arnhem/harold_whittingham.htm, accessed 19/05/2014; Whittingham is rendered 'Wittingham" in the 3rd Battalion War Diary

55. *See* **WO 171/1244** 11th Parachute Battalion War Diary, entry for 22/09/1944; there is no record of the redeployment in the 1st Airlanding Brigade HQ War Diary

56. *See* **WO 171/1375** 2nd Battalion South Staffordshire Regiment War Diary, entry for 22-25/09/1944; ibid., Appendix: J.1. '2nd South Staffords at Arnhem 17-25 Sept 1944'; and **WO 166/15077** 1st Battalion The Border Regiment War Diary, Appendix 'A', entry for 22/09/1944

57. *See* **WO 171/1375** 2nd Battalion South Staffordshire Regiment War Diary, entry for 22-25/09/1944; and ibid., Appendix: J.1. '2nd South Staffords at Arnhem 17-25 Sept 1944'

58. *See* **WO 166/14933** 1st Airlanding Light Regiment RA War Diary, entry for 22/09/1944; **WO 171/589** 1st Airlanding Brigade War Diary, entry for 17:00, 22/09/1944; and ibid., Appendix, entry for 17:00, 22/09/1944. Major Arthur Fairfax Norman-Walker has no known grave and is commemorated on the Groesbeek Memorial, Panel 1

59. *See* Kent, **First In!**, p.118; the original group photograph and subsequent frames showing the group scattering due to German fire were on display at the Airborne Museum at the Hotel Hartenstein; *see* also Middlebrook, Plate 17, between pp.246-247

60. *See* **WO 171/1248** 21st Independent Parachute Company War Diary, entry for 05:00, 22/09/1944; **WO 171/594** 4th Parachute Brigade War Diary, Appendix C, entry for 22/09/1944; and Kent, pp.116-117

61. *See* **WO 171/400** 1 Airborne Division RASC Airborne Element War Diary, entry for 05:00-06:00, 22/09/1944; and **WO 171/594** 4th Parachute Brigade War Diary, Appendix C, entry for 22/09/1944

62. *See* **WO 171/1247** 156 Parachute Battalion War Diary, entry for 22/09/1944

63. *See* **WO 171/1248** 21st Independent Parachute Company War Diary, entry for 05:00, 22/09/1944; and Kent, p.117

64. *See* **WO 171/594** 4th Parachute Brigade War Diary, Appendix C, entry for 22/09/1944; and **WO 171/1247** 156 Parachute Battalion War Diary, entry for 22/09/1944

65. *See* **WO 171/1248** 21st Independent Parachute Company War Diary, entry for 16:00, 22/09/1944; and Kent, p.118. Private James Vincent Fiely is interred in Arnhem Oosterbeek War Cemetery, Gelderland, Holland, Plot 30, Row A, Grave 4. There is no reference to ordering the patrols or extending the Independent Company's frontage eastward in Hackett's Brigade HQ account

66. *See* **WO 171/1248** 21st Independent Parachute Company War Diary, entry for 03:00, 23/09/1944; and **WO 171/594** 4th Parachute Brigade War Diary, Appendix C, entry for 22/09/1944

67. *See* **WO 171/594** 4th Parachute Brigade War Diary, Appendix C, entry for 22/09/1944. Curiously, there is no reference to the ultimatum or subsequent discussion in the Division HQ War Diary, Urquhart's account or Captain Stuart Mawson's account of events in the MDS, although both Hackett and Urquhart's accounts refer to German demands for an evacuation the following day; *see* ibid., entry for 23/09/1944; and Urquhart, p.147

68. *See* Mawson, **Arnhem Doctor**, pp.125-127

69. Quoted from Urquhart, p.136

70. *See* **The Pegasus Archive**, Battle of Arnhem Archive, Biographies Section 'Lieutenant-Colonel Charles Baillie Mackenzie' at www.pegasusarchive.org/arnhem/charles_mackenzie.htm, accessed 25/07/2016.

71. For departure timing *see* **WO 171/393** 1st Airborne Division HQ War Diary, entry for 12:10, 22/09/1944; and **WO 171/397** 1 Airborne Division HQ Royal Engineers War Diary, entry for 12:10, 22/09/1944; for other details *see* Urquhart, pp.135-136

72. *See* **WO 171/393** 1st Airborne Division HQ War Diary, entry for 13:50, 22/09/1944; **WO 171/397** 1 Airborne Division HQ Royal Engineers War Diary, entry for 12:10, 22/09/1944; and

Cholewczynski, **Poles Apart,** p.167. Interestingly there is no reference to Mackenzie and Myers' arrival or presence at Driel in the Polish Parachute Brigade War Diary

73. Quoted from Cholewczynski, **Poles Apart,** p.167

74. *See* Cholewczynski, pp.**Poles Apart,** 167-168

75. Quoted from Urquhart, p.137

76. *See* **The Pegasus Archive**, Battle of Arnhem Archive, Biographies Section 'Lieutenant-Colonel Edmund Charles Wolf Myers' at www.pegasusarchive.org/arnhem/eddie_myers.htm, accessed 26/07/2016.

77. *See* Cholewczynski, **Poles Apart,** pp.168-169, 171

78. *See* Middlebrook, pp.407-408. Lieutenant Stanislaw Antoni Slesicki, 2nd Lieutenant Richard Tice and Sergeant Antoni Salwuk are interred in Arnhem Oosterbeek War Cemetery, Gelderland, Holland, Plot XXXIV, Row A, Graves 15, 13 & 16 respectively

79. *See* **WO 171/393** 1st Airborne Division HQ War Diary, entry for 15:50, 22/09/1944; and **WO 171/398** 1 Airborne Division Signals War Diary, entry for 09:05, 22/09/1944

80. *See* Cholewczynski, **Poles Apart**, pp.169-170

81. The Polish Brigade War Diary refers to the 8th Company moving up to the crossing point at 22:00, but Cholewczynski refers to Lieutenant Smaczny being in place for almost two hours before the crossing commenced; *see* Sikorski Institute **AV 20/31/27** 1st Polish Independent Parachute Brigade War Diary, entry for 22:00, 22/09/1944; and Cholewczynski, **Poles Apart,** p.174

82. *See* **WO 171/398** 1 Airborne Division Signals War Diary, entry for 03:20, 22/09/1944

83. *See* **WO 171/393** 1st Airborne Division HQ War Diary, entries for 06:17 & 07:40, 22/09/1944

84. *See* **WO 171/393** 1st Airborne Division HQ War Diary, entry for 11:20, 22/09/1944

85. Locations and timings cited in **CAB 44/254** Part II: Operation MARKET GARDEN, Book III, Chapter VII, Appendix G, Tables 'Movements up 30 Corps Axis from 19 to 22 Sept 1944, Recce and Harbour Parties Excluded'

86. *See* **CAB 44/254** Part II: Operation MARKET GARDEN, Book III, Chapter VII, 'Section IV – Operations South of Grave – 19/20 Sept', Para. 40 '30 Corps Action in Area of Veghel-Uden, 19/20 Sep'; and ibid., Para. 41 'Movement Up the 30 Corps Axis 19/20 Sep'

87. *See* **CAB 44/254** Part II: Operation MARKET GARDEN, Book III, Chapter VII, 'Section IV – Operations South of Grave – 19/20 Sep: Movement up the 30 Corps Axis 19/20 Sept'; and ibid., Appendix G, Tables 'Movements up 30 Corps Axis from 19 to 22 Sept 1944, Recce and Harbour Parties Excluded'

88. Quoted from Chester Wilmot, **The Struggle for Europe**, p.518; cited in Powell, **The Devil's Birthday**, p.183

89. *See* Powell, pp.182-183

90. *See* **CAB 44/254** Part II: Operation MARKET GARDEN, Book III, Chapter VII, Appendix G, Tables 'Movements up 30 Corps Axis from 19 to 22 Sept 1944, Recce and Harbour Parties Excluded'

91. *See* **CAB 44/254** Part II: Operation MARKET GARDEN, Book III, Chapter VII, 'Section V – Operations on the Island 21 to 26 Sep', Para. 47 '30 Corps orders for 22 Sep'

92. *See* **CAB 44/254** Part II: Operation MARKET GARDEN, Book III, Chapter VII, 'Section V – Operations on the Island 21 to 26 Sep', Para. 48 '43 Div breaks through – 22 Sep'

93. *See* **CAB 44/254** Part II: Operation MARKET GARDEN, Book III, Chapter VII, Appendix G, Tables 'Movements up 30 Corps Axis from 19 to 22 Sept 1944, Recce and Harbour Parties Excluded'

94. *See* **CAB 44/254** Part II: Operation MARKET GARDEN, Book III, Chapter VII, 'Section V – Operations on the Island 21 to 26 Sep', Para. 48 '43 Div breaks through – 22 Sep'; and Essame, **The 43rd Division at War,** p.127

95. For timings *see* **CAB 44/254** Part II: Operation MARKET GARDEN, Book III, Chapter VII, Appendix G, Tables 'Movements up 30 Corps Axis from 19 to 22 Sept 1944, Recce and Harbour Parties Excluded'

96. *See* **CAB 44/254** Part II: Operation MARKET GARDEN, Book III, Chapter VII, 'Section V – Operations on the Island 21 to 26 Sep', Para. 46 '43 Div action on 21 Sep'

97. Quote cited in Ryan, p.462; timings and other details cited in **CAB 44/254** Part II: Operation MARKET GARDEN, Book III, Chapter VII, 'Section V – Operations on the Island 21 to 26 Sep, Para. 45 'Gds Armd Div fails to break through 21 Sep'; Para. 46 '43 Div action on 21 Sep'; and Para. 48 '43 Div breaks through – 22 Sep'

98. Details cited in **CAB 44/254** Part II: Operation MARKET GARDEN, Book III, Chapter VII, 'Section V – Operations on the Island 21 to 26 Sep', Para. 48 '43 Div breaks through – 22 Sep'; and Essame, pp.124-125. Major Sidney Charles Wayman Young is interred in Jonkerbos War Cemetery, Gelderland, Holland, Plot 1, Row F, Grave 2

99. DUKW: acronym for **D**esign (year 1942) **U**tility (amphibious) **K** (all-wheel drive) **W** (dual rear axles). Colloquially known as the Duck, the DUKW was a standard US Army 2.5-ton GMC truck, factory-modified with a boxy watertight hull, a propeller and a specially manufactured reinforced-windscreen. With a payload of 2.5 short tons and a top speed of fifty miles per hour on roads and just over six miles per hour on water, over 21,000 examples were produced in the US by General Motors; 2,000 of these were supplied to Britain under the Lend Lease programme

100. *See* Ryan, pp.463-464

101. *See* **CAB 44/254** Part II: Operation MARKET GARDEN, Book III, Chapter VII, 'Section V – Operations on the Island 21 to 26 Sep', Para. 48 '43 Div breaks through – 22 Sep'; for column details *see* Essame, p.125

102. *See* Ryan, p.478

103. Polish official records cite 20:00, their British counterpart 20:15, although this may refer to the time Lieutenant-Colonel Taylor arrived at Major-General Sosabowski's command post; the Polish War Diary also mistakenly refers to the 5th DCLI being part of 130 Brigade rather than 214 Brigade. For some reason Ryan's timings are two hours earlier than other accounts, possibly due to mixing up the Allied and German times. *See* Sikorski Institute **AV 20/31/27** 1st Polish Independent Parachute Brigade War Diary, entry for 20:00, 22/09/1944; **CAB 44/254** Part II: Operation MARKET GARDEN, Book III, Chapter VII, 'Section V – Operations on the Island 21 to 26 Sep', Para. 48 '43 Div breaks through – 22 Sep'; and Ryan, p.478

104. The 5th DCLI's feat is commemorated today by a plaque affixed to the Roman Catholic church in Driel by the Regimental Old Comrades Association; *see* **Paul Reed's Battlefields of WW2** website, '5th DCLI Memorial, Driel' Page at www.http://battlefieldsww2.50megs.com/5th_dcli_memorial_driel.htm, accessed 06/09/2016

105. *See* Cholewczynski, **Poles Apart**, pp.171-172

106. Trooper Reginald Alfred Holmes of the Life Guards is interred in Jonkerbos War Cemetery, Gelderland, Holland, Plot 12, Row A, Grave 2

107. *See* **CAB 44/254** Part II: Operation MARKET GARDEN, Book III, Chapter VII, 'Section V – Operations on the Island 21 to 26 Sep', Para. 48 '43 Div breaks through – 22 Sep'; Cholewczynski, **Poles Apart**, p.172; and **On Active Service – Household Cavalry 1939-1945: The Daimler Fighting Vehicles Project Website**, 'The 2nd Armoured Cavalry Regiment (Guards Armoured)' Section, pp.14, 24 & 28 at www.http://daimler-fighting-vehicles.co.uk/DFV-File%20Part%20D001a-Houshold%20Cavalry%201939-1945.pdf, accessed 08/09/2016

108. *See* **CAB 44/254** Part II: Operation MARKET GARDEN, Book III, Chapter VII, 'Section V – Operations on the Island 21 to 26 Sep', Para. 48 '43 Div breaks through – 22 Sep'; and Zwarts, pp.19, 57

109. *See* **CAB 44/254** Part II: Operation MARKET GARDEN, Book III, Chapter VII, Appendix D '5 DCLI Advance from Nijmegen to Driel on 22 Sep 1944', Section 'Account by C.S.M. Philip [sic], DCM'

110. For details and photographs of the knocked-out tanks *see* Zwarts, pp.19, 57

111. *See* **CAB 44/254** Part II: Operation MARKET GARDEN, Book III, Chapter VII, Appendix D '5 DCLI Advance from Nijmegen to Driel on 22 Sep 1944', Section 'Ambush on the Tigers: Major Parker's Story'; and Essame, pp.126-127

112. Company Sergeant Major Reg Philp DCM passed away on 17 February 2012 aged 92; for his obituary *see* **The Telegraph**, Obituaries Section, 28 March 2012 at http://www.telegraph.co.uk/news/obituaries/9172080/Reg-Philp.html, accessed 11/09/2016

Chapter 18

1. The Polish Brigade War Diary refers to the 8th Company moving up to the crossing point at 22:00, but Cholewczynski refers to Lieutenant Smaczny being in place for almost two hours before the crossing commenced; *see* Sikorski Institute **AV 20/31/27** 1st Polish Independent Parachute Brigade War Diary, entry for 22:00, 22/09/1944; and Cholewczynski, **Poles Apart**, pp.173-174
2. *See* Faulkner-Brown, **A Sapper at Arnhem**, pp.66-67
3. Captain Brown's account refers to selecting twelve men, Middlebrook cites fifteen while the official records refer to twenty-four; *see* Faulkner-Brown, p.68; Middlebrook, **Arnhem 1944**, p.410; and **WO 171/1511** 4th Parachute Squadron RE War Diary, Appendix I, entry for 19:45, 22/09/1944
4. Quoted from Faulkner-Brown, p.69
5. *See* Faulkner-Brown, p.69; and Cholewczynski, **Poles Apart**, p.174. For Lieutenant Bottomley's involvement *see* Middlebrook, p.410. The No. 1 Wing War Diary makes no mention of Lieutenant Bottomley or any other personnel being detached to act as guides although he was reported as accompanying No. 1 Wing's commander, Lieutenant-Colonel Iain Murray, visiting the Wing's positions in the early morning of Saturday 23 September. However the 1st Airlanding Brigade HQ War Diary explicitly refers to Glider Pilots being deployed in this role; *see* **WO 171/1234** 1 Wing Glider Pilot Regiment War Diary, entry for 05:50, 23/09/1944; and **WO 171/589** & **WO 171/590** 1st Airlanding Brigade War Diary, Appendix F, entry for 17:25, 22/09/1944
6. 23:00 start time and Polish order of crossing cited in Sikorski Institute **AV 20/31/27** 1st Polish Independent Parachute Brigade War Diary, entries for 22:00 & 23:00, 22/09/1944
7. *See* **Wo 171/590** 1st Airlanding Brigade HQ War Diary, Appendix 'F', entry for 23:45, 22/09/1944; and **WO 171/393** 1 Airborne Division HQ War Diary, entry for 23:45, 22/09/1944; interestingly, there is no mention of the Poles' arrival in the 1st Airlanding Light Regiment War Diary
8. *See* **Wo 171/590** 1st Airlanding Brigade HQ War Diary, entry for 23:00, 22/09/1944; and ibid., Appendix 'F', entry for 23:45, 22/09/1944
9. *See* Cholewczynski, **Poles Apart**, pp.174-176; and Sosabowski, **Freely I Served**, p.175
10. *See* Kershaw, **It Never Snows in September**, p.265
11. Quoted from Faulkner-Brown, p.70
12. *See* Faulkner-Brown, pp.69-71; and Cholewczynski, **Poles Apart**, p.175
13. *See* Essame, **The 43rd Wessex Division at War**, p.126
14. *See* Essame, p.127; and Sosabowski, p.174
15. *See* Sikorski Institute **AV 20/31/27** 1st Polish Independent Parachute Brigade War Diary, entries for 03:00 & 04:00, 23/09/1944
16. *See* Faulkner-Brown, p.71
17. Fifty-two cited in Sikorski Institute **AV 20/31/27** 1st Polish Independent Parachute Brigade War Diary, entry for 03:00, 23/09/1944; for thirty-six *see* Cholewczynski, **Poles Apart**, p.178
18. *See* Sikorski Institute **AV 20/31/27** 1st Polish Independent Parachute Brigade War Diary, hand-written footnote to entry for 03:00, 23/09/1944
19. For reference to rain *see* for example **WO 171/1234** 1 Wing Glider Pilot Regiment War Diary, entry for 07:00, 23/09/1944
20. *See* **WO 166/15077** 1st Battalion The Border Regiment War Diary, entry for 23/09/1944; and **WO 171/1236** 1st Parachute Battalion War Diary, entry for 07:00, 23/09/1944
21. *See* **WO 171/393** 1 Airborne Division HQ War Diary, entry for 07:35, 23/09/1944; **Wo 171/590** 1st Airlanding Brigade HQ War Diary, Appendix 'F', entry for 07:30, 23/09/1944; and **WO 171/1323** 7th Battalion King's Own Scottish Borderers War Diary, entry for 06:30 to 13:00, 23/09/1944

22. *See* **WO 171/393** 1 Airborne Division HQ War Diary, entry for 08:40, 23/09/1944

23. *See* **WO 171/1248** 21ˢᵗ Independent Parachute Company War Diary, entry for 03:00, 23/09/1944; Kent, **First In!**, p.119; and **WO 171/594** 4ᵗʰ Parachute Brigade War Diary, Appendix C, entry for 22/09/1944

24. Quoted from Brammall, **The Tenth**, p.93

25. According to Middlebrook the party was under the command of Captain Ignacy Gazurek, temporary commander of the Polish Brigade's 3ʳᵈ Battalion, and a Polish source also states that Captain Gazurek crossed the Lower Rhine at the same time as Lieutenant Smaczny, on the night of 22-23 September; *see* Middlebrook, p.410; and Krzysztof Komorowski, **Chronicle of the Polish Army 2005**, p.225. However, Cholewczynski's participant account-heavy work clearly shows that Captain Gazurek did not cross the Lower Rhine until the night of 23-24 September, and Lieutenant Smaczny was thus the ranking officer commanding the first increment of Polish paratroopers to cross the river

26. *See* Brammall, p.93; Cholewczynski, **Poles Apart**, p.178; **WO 171/594** 4ᵗʰ Parachute Brigade War Diary, Appendix C, entries for 22/09/1944 & 23/09/1944; and **WO 171/393** 1 Airborne Division HQ War Diary, entry for 07:35, 23/09/1944

27. *See* Kent, **First In!**, p.120; Sergeant Dennis Basil Martin is interred in Arnhem Oosterbeek War Cemetery, Gelderland, Holland, Plot 20, Row C, Grave 5; the CWGC records give Sergeant Martin's date of death as 20/09/1944

28. *See* **WO 171/1248** 21ˢᵗ Independent Parachute Company War Diary, entry for 07:15, 23/09/1944; and Kent, **First In!**, p.119. Private Francis Joseph Hillier is interred in the Reichswald Forest War Cemetery, Nordrhein-Westfalen, Germany, Plot 36, Row A, Grave 1; the CWGC records give Private Hillier's date of death as 20/09/1944

29. *See* **WO 171/393** 1 Airborne Division HQ War Diary, entry for 08:40, 23/09/1944

30. Quotes from **WO 171/1236** 1ˢᵗ Parachute Battalion War Diary, entry for 07:00, 23/09/1944; and **WO 171/1238** 3ʳᵈ Parachute Battalion War Diary, composite entry for 22/09/1944

31. *See* **WO 171/1244** 11ᵗʰ Parachute Battalion War Diary, entry for Saturday 23ⁿᵈ September 1944 ; and **WO 171/1236** 1ˢᵗ Parachute Battalion War Diary, entry for 20:00, 23/09/1944

32. *See* **WO 166/14933** 1ˢᵗ Airlanding Light Regiment RA War Diary, entry for 23/09/1944

33. *See* **WO 171/1244** 11ᵗʰ Parachute Battalion War Diary, entry for Saturday 23ⁿᵈ September 1944

34. For barrage timing *see* **WO 171/1236** 1ˢᵗ Parachute Battalion War Diary, entry for 18:00, 23/09/1944

35. *See* **WO 171/1238** 3ʳᵈ Parachute Battalion War Diary, composite entry for 22-25/09/1944. Lieutenant James Arnold Stacey Cleminson passed into German captivity and was incarcerated in *Oflag IX A/Z* at Rotenberg an der Fulda in central Germany

36. For regular German fire on the Oosterbeek church *see* for example **WO 166/14933** 1ˢᵗ Airlanding Light Regiment RA War Diary, entry for 17:00, 22/09/1944; for Major Blacklidge's death *see* **WO 171/1244** 11ᵗʰ Parachute Battalion War Diary, entry for 23/09/1944. Major Guy Lechmere Blacklidge has no known grave and is commemorated on the Groesbeek Memorial, Gelderland, Holland, Panel 8

37. *See* **WO 171/1375** 2ⁿᵈ Battalion South Staffordshire Regiment War Diary, entry for 23/09/1944; for details of Major Simonds wounding on 19 September 1944 *see* **Winchester College**, 2016, 'Simonds, John Mellor' at http://www.winchestercollegeatwar.com/archive/simonds-john-mellor/, [accessed 14/11/2016]. Major John Mellor Simonds has no known grave and is commemorated on the Groesbeek Memorial, Gelderland, Holland, Panel 5

38. *See* Kent, **First In!**, p.120. Private John Paul Avallone and Sergeant Benjamin Clayton Swallow are interred in Arnhem Oosterbeek War Cemetery, Gelderland, Holland, Plot 5, Row A, Grave 4 and Plot 18, Row C, Grave 16 respectively; Sergeant Swallow's date of death is given as 13/12/1944

39. *See* Kent, **First In!**, p.118 and testimony from Sanders Kremer, cited in Middlebrook, p.368. Kent gives the impression that Corporal Rosenfeld might have been killed on Friday 22 September but the CWGC database clearly states his date of death as 23/09/1944. Corporal Hans Rosenfeld

alias John Peter Rodley is interred in Arnhem Oosterbeek War Cemetery, Gelderland, Holland, Plot 23, Row A, Grave 11

40. For fifteen casualty figure *see* **WO 171/1248** 21ˢᵗ Independent Parachute Company War Diary, entry for 07:15, 23/09/1944; Sergeant Ernest Victor Thompson has no known grave and is commemorated on the Groesbeek Memorial, Gelderland, Holland, Panel 8

41. *See* **WO 171/1248** 21ˢᵗ Independent Parachute Company War Diary, entry for 07:15, 23/09/1944; and Kent, **First In!**, p.120. The cook may have been a Private Dixon who carried out a similar feat against German tanks the following day, although on that occasion he was reported to be a member of No. 3 Platoon; *see* **WO 171/1248** 21ˢᵗ Independent Parachute Company War Diary, entry for 15:00, 24/09/1944

42. The *StuH* 42 was a *Sturmgeschütze* III adapted for close infantry support by replacing the vehicle's dual-purpose 75mm gun with a 105mm howitzer. The ten-vehicle detachment from *Sturmgeschütze* Brigade 280 despatched to Arnhem included three *StuH* 42 organised into a single *Zug* (platoon); *see* Zwarts, **German Armoured Units At Arnhem**, Table 'Sturmgeschütze-Brigade 280', p.6

43. *See* Fairley, **Remember Arnhem**, pp.164-166

44. *See* **WO 171/406** 1ˢᵗ Airborne Reconnaissance Squadron War Diary, entry for 09:00, 23/09/1944; and **WO 171/594** 4ᵗʰ Parachute Brigade War Diary, Appendix C, entry for 23/09/1944

45. *See* **WO 171/406** D Squadron, 1ˢᵗ Airborne Reconnaissance Squadron War Diary, entry for 10:00, 23/09/1944. Only two Tiger units participated in the fighting at Arnhem. The Tiger I equipped *schwere Panzer Kompanie Hummel* was at this time deployed in the area of Elst on the south bank of the Lower Rhine. The other, two companies drawn from *schwere Panzer Abteilung 506* equipped with Tiger II *Königstiger* tanks, did not arrive in the Arnhem area until the night of 23-24 September, and the *Kompanie* assigned to the fighting at Oosterbeek did not go into action until Monday 25 September; *see* for example Zwarts, pp.59-60

46. *See* Fairley, p.167

47. *See* ibid., pp.167-168; for timing *see* **WO 171/406** D Squadron 1ˢᵗ Airborne Reconnaissance Squadron War Diary, entries for 10:00 & 11:00, 23/09/1944

48. For Sergeant Pyper's citation for the Military Medal *see* **The Pegasus Archive**, Battle of Arnhem Archive, Biographies Section 'Sergeant James Pyper' at www.pegasusarchive.org/arnhem/james_pyper.htm [accessed 06/12/2016]

49. *See* **WO 171/406** 1ˢᵗ Airborne Reconnaissance Squadron War Diary, entry for 14:30, 23/09/1944; and Fairley, p.168

50. *See* **WO 171/406** D Squadron, 1ˢᵗ Airborne Reconnaissance Squadron War Diary, numerous entries from 15:00 to 22:00, 23/09/1944

51. *See* Fairley, p.169

52. *See* **WO 171/406** A Squadron 1ˢᵗ Airborne Reconnaissance Squadron War Diary, entry for 12:00; and Fairley, p.178

53. *See* **WO 171/406** A Squadron 1ˢᵗ Airborne Reconnaissance Squadron War Diary, entries for 12:00 & 14:00; and Fairley, pp.169-170

54. *See* **WO 171/1247** 156 Parachute Battalion War Diary, entry for 12:00, 23/09/1944; the attackers may have been reinforced with elements of *Ausbildungs und Ersatz Regiment* 'Hermann Göring' deployed on the western side of the Oosterbeek perimeter, which reportedly included two *Panzer* V Panther tanks; *see* Reynolds, **Sons of the Reich**, p.169; and Kershaw, p.301. There do not appear to be any photographs of these vehicles deployed at Oosterbeek

55. *See* **WO 171/1247** 156 Parachute Battalion War Diary, entries for 14:00 & 15:00, 23/09/1944

56. *See* Fairley, pp.169-170. Captain Raymond Harold Stevens is interred in Arnhem Oosterbeek War Cemetery, Gelderland, Holland, Plot 29, Row A, Grave 2

57. *See* **WO 171/1247** 156 Parachute Battalion War Diary, entry for 15:00, 23/09/1944

58. *See* Ryan, **A Bridge Too Far**, pp.494-495

59. Quoted from Mawson, **Arnhem Doctor**, p.133

60. *See* ibid., pp.134-135

61. *See* Kershaw, p.271
62. See Mawson, p.136
63. *See* ibid., pp.136, 139-140
64. *See* ibid., p.140
65. The precise identity of the Polish group is unclear, for while Lieutenant Smaczny and his thirty-six-strong party from No. 8 Company moved to the vicinity of the Utrechtseweg crossroads at 06:30 they were despatched to reinforce the 1ˢᵗ Border on the Benedendorpsweg near the municipal gasworks at 08:00, although the number of Poles varies between sources; *see* **WO 166/15077** 1ˢᵗ Battalion The Border Regiment War Diary, entry for 23/09/1944; **WO 171/393** 1ˢᵗ Airborne Division HQ War Diary, entry for 11:47, 23/09/1944; and Cholewczynski, **Poles Apart**, pp.178-180 However, the 1ˢᵗ Airlanding Brigade War Diary refers to approximately 100 Poles being despatched to reinforce the 4ᵗʰ Parachute Brigade, Mawson's account specifically refers to Lieutenant-Colonel Marrable visiting Poles near the MDS in the evening of Saturday 23 September, and German accounts also refer to fighting Poles in the vicinity of the crossroads at that time; *see* **Wo 171/590** 1ˢᵗ Airlanding Brigade HQ War Diary, entry for 23/09/1944; ibid, Appendix 'F', entry for 23:45, 22/09/1944; Mawson, p.149; and Kershaw, pp.270-271
66. *See* Mawson, pp.141-142
67. *See* **WO 171/393** 1ˢᵗ Airborne Division HQ War Diary, entry for 13:00, 23/09/1944; and Urquhart, **Arnhem**, p.147. There is no reference to this or subsequent discussion at Division HQ in Hackett's account in the 4ᵗʰ Parachute Brigade HQ War Diary
68. Exchange quoted from Urquhart, pp.147-148
69. Quoted from Baynes, **Urquhart of Arnhem**, p.138
70. *See* **WO 171/594** 4ᵗʰ Parachute Brigade War Diary, Appendix C, entry for 23/09/1944; 600 casualty figure cited in Mawson, p.146
71. *See* **WO 171/594** 4ᵗʰ Parachute Brigade War Diary, Appendix C, entry for 23/09/1944; and Urquhart, p.149
72. *See* **WO 171/393** 1ˢᵗ Airborne Division HQ War Diary, entry for 15:27, 24/09/1944
73. *See* Mawson, pp.144-149
74. *See* **WO 171/1323** 7ᵗʰ Battalion King's Own Scottish Borderers War Diary, entry for 04:30 to 06:30, 23/09/1944
75. *See* **WO 171/1323** 7ᵗʰ Battalion King's Own Scottish Borderers War Diary, entry for 06:30 to 13:00, 23/09/1944
76. *See* **WO 171/1323** 7ᵗʰ Battalion King's Own Scottish Borderers War Diary, entry for 06:30 to 13:00, 23/09/1944
77. *See* **Wo 171/590** 1ˢᵗ Airlanding Brigade HQ War Diary, Appendix 'F', entry for 14:52, 23/09/1944; and **WO 171/1059** 64 Medium Regiment RA War Diary, entry for 15:20, 23/09/1944
78. Drum-Major Tait's surname is sometimes rendered Tate: *see* Middlebrook, p.275
79. *See* **WO 171/1323** 7ᵗʰ Battalion King's Own Scottish Borderers War Diary, entries for 06:30 to 13:00 & 13:00 to 19:00, 23/09/1944
80. *See* **WO 171/1511** 4ᵗʰ Parachute Squadron RE War Diary, entry for 13:15, 23/09/1944
81. Quoted from the 4ᵗʰ **Parachute Squadron Royal Engineers** website, Arnhem Section, 'September 23' at http://myweb.tiscali.co.uk/4parasqnre/arnhem%20page%206.htm, accessed 28/05/2017
82. *See* the 4ᵗʰ **Parachute Squadron Royal Engineers** website, Arnhem Section, 'September 23' at http://myweb.tiscali.co.uk/4parasqnre/arnhem%20page%206.htm, accessed 28/05/2017
83. *See* Faulkner-Brown, pp.74-75
84. For four wounded and five dead figure *see* **WO 171/1511** 4ᵗʰ Parachute Squadron RE War Diary, entry for 07:10, 23/09/1944; for eight wounded figure *see* **WO 171/1511** 4ᵗʰ Parachute Squadron RE War Diary, Appendix I, entry for 07:30, 23/09/1944
85. Sapper Bernard Higgins and Sapper Leonard Dennis Rawlings are interred in Arnhem Oosterbeek War Cemetery, Gelderland, Holland, Plot 16, Row C, Graves 1 and 4 respectively

86. *See* **WO166/15077** 1ˢᵗ Battalion The Border Regiment War Diary, Appendix A, entry for 23/09/1944

87. For barrage commencement time *see* **WO166/15077** 1ˢᵗ Battalion The Border Regiment War Diary, Appendix A, entry for 23/09/1944

88. *See* Green, **1ˢᵗ Battalion The Border Regiment**, p.67. Lieutenant Robert Hugh Coulston is interred in Arnhem Oosterbeek War Cemetery, Gelderland, Holland, Plot 26, Row A, Graves 15

89. *See* ibid., p.67. Corporal Thomas Edgar is interred in Arnhem Oosterbeek War Cemetery, Gelderland, Holland, Plot 2, Row A, Graves 17. The CWGC database gives his date of death as 24/09/1944

90. *See* **WO166/15077** 1ˢᵗ Battalion The Border Regiment War Diary, Appendix A, entry for 23/09/1944; and Green, p.67

91. For 17:30 timing and Major Neill's DSO citation *see* **The Pegasus Archive**, Battle of Arnhem Archive, Biographies Section 'Major William Neill' at www.pegasusarchive.org/arnhem/william_neill.htm, accessed 05/06/2017; for 19:20 timing *see* **WO166/15077** 1ˢᵗ Battalion The Border Regiment War Diary, Appendix A, entry for 23/09/1944; and Green, p.69

92. *See* **W0 171/590** 1ˢᵗ Airlanding Brigade HQ War Diary, Appendix F, entries for 09:30 & 12:00, 23/09/1944; and **WO166/15077** 1ˢᵗ Battalion The Border Regiment War Diary, Appendix A, entry for 23/09/1944

93. Quoted from Green, p.63

94. *See* ibid., pp.63-64

95. *See* ibid., pp.64-66

96. *See* ibid., pp.66-67

97. There is no reference to the redeployment in the 1ˢᵗ Airlanding Brigade HQ War Diary.

98. *See* Cholewczynski, **Poles Apart**, pp.179-180, 183

99. *See* **W0 171/590** 1ˢᵗ Airlanding Brigade HQ War Diary, Appendix F, entry for 23:45, 22/09/1944; and Green, p.67

100. *See* Cholewczynski, **Poles Apart**, pp.183, 189, 192

101. *See* ibid., pp.185-186, 191

102. *See* ibid. pp.189, 192-193, 201

103. *Panzer Kompanie 224* began the battle with seventeen vehicles; one Somua S35 serving as a command tank, two *Panzer B2 (f)* gun tanks and fourteen *Flammpanzer B2 (f)*; *see* Zwarts, p.6

104. *See* Kershaw, pp.274-275

105. For pre-loaded aircraft *see* **WO 171/2177** HQ Air Despatch Group RASC War Diary, entry for 12:15, 22/09/1944 and after entry for 14:10, 23/09/1944. Middlebrook refers to the drop involving seventy-three Stirlings from No. 38 Group and fifty Dakotas from No. 46 Group, which tallies with the entries in the various Squadron Operational Record Books; *see* Middlebrook, p.396 and various Squadron Operational Record Books. The figures cited in the HQ Air Despatch Group RASC War Diary total fifty-five Dakotas, but do not tally fully with the various Squadron Operational Record Book totals

106. *See* **AIR 27/2046** No. 575 Squadron Operations Record Book Summary of Events, entry for 23/09/1944; and **AIR 27/1972** No. 512 Squadron Operations Record Book, entry for 23/09/1944; for Air Commodore Darvall's plan *see* Middlebrook, pp.397-398

107. *See* **AIR 27/1433** No. 233 Squadron Operations Record Book, entry for 23/09/1944; **AIR 27/1876** No. 437 Squadron RCAF Operations Record Book, entry for 23/09/1944; **AIR 27/473** No. 48 Squadron Operations Record Book, entry for 23/09/1944; and **AIR 27/1574** No. 271 Squadron Operations Record Book, entry for 23/09/1944

108. *See* **AIR 27/1167** No. 196 Squadron Operations Record Book, entry for 23/09/1944; **AIR 27/1654** No. 299 Squadron Operations Record Book, entry for 23/09/1944; **AIR 27/2134** No. 620 Squadron Operations Record Book, entry for 23/09/1944; **AIR 27/1154** No. 190 Squadron Operations Record Book, entry for 23/09/1944; and **AIR 27/2041** No. 570 Squadron Operations Record Book, entry for 23/09/1944

109. *See* **AIR 27/1433** No. 233 Squadron Operations Record Book, entry for 23/09/1944

110. **WO 171/589** 1ˢᵗ Airlanding Brigade War Diary, Appendix F, entry for 16:00, 23/09/1944; and **WO 171/1234** 1 Wing Glider Pilot Regiment War Diary, entry for 16:15, 23/09/1944

111. *See* **Combat Chronology of the US Army Air Force, September 1944**, entry for Saturday 23 September, European Theatre of Operations (ETO), at http://paul.rutgers.edu/~mcgrew/wwii/usaf/html/Sep.44.html, accessed 25/06/2017

112. *See* **AIR 27/473** No. 48 Squadron Operations Record Book, entry for 23/09/1944; **AIR 27/1433** No. 233 Squadron Operations Record Book, entry for 23/09/1944; **AIR 27/1876** No. 437 Squadron RCAF Operations Record Book, entry for 23/09/1944; and **AIR 27/2041** No. 570 Squadron Operations Record Book, entry for 23/09/1944

113. *See* Middlebrook, p.397; and **AIR 27/1433** No. 233 Squadron Operations Record Book, entry for 23/09/1944

114. *See* **AIR 27/1574** No. 271 Squadron Operations Record Book, entry for 23/09/1944

115. *See* **AIR 27/1876** No. 437 Squadron RCAF Operations Record Book, entry for 23/09/1944; and Alan W. Cooper, **The Air Battle for Arnhem**, Appendix 'RAF Losses at the Battle of Arnhem, September 1944', p.184. Flying Officer William Richard Paget RCAF is interred in Arnhem Oosterbeek War Cemetery, Gelderland, Holland, Plot 4, Row B, Grave 8; his crew, Flying Officer Donald Lawrence Jack, Warrant Officer First Class Ray Irving Pinner and Flight-Sergeant Denis Joseph O'Sullivan are also interred in Arnhem Oosterbeek War Cemetery in Plot 4, Row B, Grave 20, Plot 4, Row B, Grave 19 and Plot 4, Row B, Grave 18 respectively. The four despatchers from 223 Company RASC (Air Despatch), Corporal Thomas Henry Baxter, Corporal Leslie John Clark, Driver Frederick Walter Beardsley and Driver Paul Williams are also interred in the Arnhem Oosterbeek War Cemetery, in Plot 17, Row C, Graves 6, 4, 5 and 7 respectively

116. Testimony from Flight-Sergeant Derek Gleave, No. 48 Squadron RAF; cited in Middlebrook, pp.396-397

117. *See* Middlebrook, p.397. Pilot Officer Walton Ralph Pring has no known grave and is commemorated on the Runnymede Memorial, Surrey, UK, Panel 212. Warrant Officer James Leroy Springsteele RCAF and Sergeant Henry Everest Colman RCAF are interred in Arnhem Oosterbeek War Cemetery, Gelderland, Holland in Plot 4, Row B, Grave 3 and Plot 26, Row B, Grave 3 respectively. The CWGC database lists both men as Pilot Officers but the above ranks are taken from the 48 Squadron records; *see* **AIR 27/473** No. 48 Squadron Operational Record Book, entry for 23/09/1944

118. *See* **AIR 27/1154** No. 190 Squadron Operations Record Book, entry for 23/09/1944; and **AIR 27/1167** No. 196 Squadron Operations Record Book, entry for 23/09/1944

119. *See* Cooper, Appendix: 'RAF Losses at the Battle of Arnhem, September 1944', p.169

120. *See* **AIR 27/1654** No. 299 Squadron Operations Record Book, entry for 23/09/1944

121. For gun figures *see* Kershaw, Appendix 'Operations to Reduce the "Cauldron" Oosterbeek Sep 20-26 1944', TO&E Table '*FlaK* Brigade "Svoboda"', p.337; for German change of tactics *see* Middlebrook, p.396

122. *See* **AIR 27/2134** No. 620 Squadron Opérations Record Book, entry for 23/09/1944; and Cooper, Appendix: 'RAF Losses at the Battle of Arnhem, September 1944', p.175

123. *See* **AIR 27/2041** No. 570 Squadron Operations Record Book, entry for 23/09/1944; and Cooper, Appendix: 'RAF Losses at the Battle of Arnhem, September 1944', p.172. Pilot Officer William Kirkham is interred in Arnhem Oosterbeek War Cemetery, Gelderland, Holland in Plot 4, Row A, Grave 17. Flying Officer David Henry Atkinson, Flying Officer Morris Hand and Sergeant Harrold Ashton are interred in the same Plot & Row in Graves 15, 16 & 14 respectively; Pilot Officer Ernest Charles Brown and Lance-Corporal Gerard Reardon are interred in Plot 21, Row C, Grave 11 and Plot 16, Row A, Grave 3 respectively

124. *See* **AIR 27/2041** No. 570 Squadron Operations Record Book, entry for 23/09/1944; and Cooper, Appendix: 'RAF Losses at the Battle of Arnhem, September 1944', pp.173-174. Flying Officer William Baker RCAF is interred in Arnhem Oosterbeek War Cemetery, Gelderland, Holland in Plot 31, Row A, Collective Grave 2-7 along with Flying Officer John Dickson DFC, Flying Officer Robert Carter Booth, Warrant Officer Francis George Totterdell, Flight Sergeant Dennis James Blencowe and Flight Sergeant Richard Bert Bond; Driver Robert William Hayton RASC and

Driver Reginald Shore RASC are interred in Plot 15, Row A, Grave 5 and Plot 31, Row A, Grave 1 respectively. The CWGC database lists Dickson as a Flight Lieutenant, Totterdell as Pilot Officer and Bond as Sergeant, ranks cited are taken from No. 570 Squadron Operations Record Book; Cooper renders Blencowe as Blencoe

125. *See* **AIR 27/2041** No. 570 Squadron Operations Record Book, entry for 23/09/1944; and Cooper, **The Air Battle for Arnhem**, Appendix: 'RAF Losses at the Battle of Arnhem, September 1944', p.173. Flying Officer Beck's crew are interred in Heteren General Cemetery, Gelderland, Holland, Plot 2, Row A as follows: Driver Cyril William Lightwood and Flight Sergeant Harold James Stell in Grave 13A and 13B, Flight Sergeant John McGarrie in Grave 14, Flight Sergeant Erle Mayne Milks RCAF and Flight Sergeant Pierre Cormiere RCAF in Graves 15A and 15B respectively

126. Quoted from **AIR 27/2041** No. 570 Squadron Operations Record Book, entry for 23/09/1944

127. *See* **AIR 27/1654** No. 299 Squadron Operations Record Book, entry for 23/09/1944; and **AIR 27/1876** No. 437 Squadron RCAF Operations Record Book, entry for 23/09/1944

128. *See* **AIR 27/473** No. 48 Squadron Operations Record Book and **AIR 27/1574** No. 271 Squadron Operations Record Book, entries for 23/09/1944

129. *See* **Wo 171/590** 1st Airlanding Brigade HQ War Diary, Appendix F, entry for 16:00, 23/09/1944

130. *See* **WO 171/400** 1 Airborne Division RASC Airborne Element War Diary, entry for 05:00-06:00, 22/09/1944; and **WO 171/594** 4th Parachute Brigade War Diary, Appendix C, entry for 22/09/1944

131. *See* **WO 171/393** 1 Airborne Division HQ War Diary, entry for 16:05, 23/09/1944

132. *See* **Wo 171/590** 1st Airlanding Brigade HQ War Diary, Appendix F, entry for 20:00, 23/09/1944

133. *See* Middlebrook, p.403

134. *See* Cholewczynski, **Poles Apart**, pp.170-171

135. For numbers of men/parapacks *see* Brinson, **Airborne Troop Carrier**, p.145; for take-off time *see* Cholewczynski, **Poles Apart**, p.186

136. For 16:43 timing *see* Brinson, p.145; for 16:47 timing *see* Cholewczynski, **Poles Apart**, p.190

137. The Polish Brigade War Diary notes the arrival of the 1st Battalion and part of the 3rd Battalion at 16:00 but also states that Brigade HQ was not informed of the fact and continued to list the units as missing; *see* Sikorski Institute **AV 20/31/27** 1st Polish Independent Parachute Brigade War Diary, entry for 16:00, 23/09/1944

138. *See* Cholewczynski, **Poles Apart**, pp.190-192, 196-197

139. *See* **CAB 44/254** Part II: Operation MARKET GARDEN, Book III, Chapter VII, 'Section V – Operations on the Island 21 to 26 Sep', Para. 49 '30 Corps Orders for 23 Sep'

140. *See* Ellis, **Victory in the West, Volume II: The Defeat of Germany**, p.42; Essame, **The 43rd Division at War**, p.128; and **CAB 44/254** Part II: Operation MARKET GARDEN, Book III, Chapter VII, 'Section V – Operations on the Island 21 to 26 Sep', Para. 51 '30 Corps Operation Instructions No. 25 of 23 Sep'

141. For twelve figure *see* Cholewczynski, **Poles Apart**, p.197; for fourteen figure *see* John Sliz, **The Storm Boat Kings**, p.53; sixteen figure cited in Essame, p.131

142. *See* Essame, p.131; and **WO 171/1586** 204 Field Company RE War Diary, entry for 21:00, 23/09/1944

143. *See* **CAB 44/254** Part II: Operation MARKET GARDEN, Book III, Chapter VII, 'Section V – Operations on the Island 21 to 26 Sep', Para. 50 'Narrative 23 Sep'; and Essame, p.129

144. *See* **CAB 44/254** Part II: Operation MARKET GARDEN, Book III, Chapter VII, 'Section V – Operations on the Island 21 to 26 Sep', Para. 50 'Narrative 23 Sep'; and Essame, p.129

146. Quoted from Essame, p.130

147. *See* **CAB 44/254** Part II: Operation MARKET GARDEN, Book III, Chapter VII, 'Section V – Operations on the Island 21 to 26 Sep', Para. 50 'Narrative 23 Sep'; and Essame, pp.129-131

148. *See* Sikorski Institute **AV 20/31/27** 1st Polish Independent Parachute Brigade War Diary, entry for 09:00, 23/09/1944; Sosabowski, p.177; and Cholewczynski, **Poles Apart**, p.180

149. *See* Sosabowski, **Freely I Served**, p.177

150. *See* Cholewczynski, **Poles Apart**, pp.189-190; for Grave drop timing *see* Brinson, **Airborne Troop Carrier**, p.145

151. *See* Middlebrook, p.412

152. *See* **The Pegasus Archive**, Battle of Arnhem Archive, Biographies Section 'Lieutenant-Colonel Charles Baillie Mackenzie' at www.pegasusarchive.org/arnhem/charles_mackenzie.htm, accessed 16/07/2017; and Ryan, p.481; for Forward Corps HQ location *see* Middlebrook, p.412

153. Quoted from **The Pegasus Archive**, Battle of Arnhem Archive, Biographies Section 'Lieutenant-Colonel Charles Baillie Mackenzie' at www.pegasusarchive.org/arnhem/charles_mackenzie.htm, accessed 16/07/2017

154. Quote from Ryan, p.482

155. *See* ibid., pp.482-483

156. *See* **The Pegasus Archive**, Battle of Arnhem Archive, Biographies Section 'Lieutenant-Colonel Charles Baillie Mackenzie' at www.pegasusarchive.org/arnhem/charles_mackenzie.htm, accessed 16/07/2017; and Ryan, p.483

157. *See* Middlebrook, pp.412-413; and Ryan, p.482

158. Pre-19:00 timing based on Polish representatives returning to Driel at that time; *see* Sikorski Institute **AV 20/31/27** 1st Polish Independent Parachute Brigade War Diary, entry for 19:00, 23/09/1944. For Mackenzie's disquiet over the perceived lack of urgency, *see* Powell, **The Devil's Birthday**, p.203

159. *See* Cholewczynski, **Poles Apart**, pp.178-179

160. *See* ibid., p.185

161. *See* ibid., pp.180-181, 184

162. Quoted from Sosabowski, p.178; *see* also Cholewczynski, **Poles Apart**, p.186

163. *See* Sikorski Institute **AV 20/31/27** 1st Polish Independent Parachute Brigade War Diary, entry for 16:30, 23/09/1944; and Cholewczynski, **Poles Apart**, p.188

164. Quoted from Sosabowski, p.178

165. *See* Cholewczynski, **Poles Apart**, p.180. There is no mention of the unnamed Brigadier in the Polish Brigade War Diary or Sosabowski's account

166. *See* Cholewczynski, **Poles Apart**, p.182

167. Quotes from ibid., p.182

168. Cholewczynski's initial mention refers to eighteen vessels capable of carrying twenty-four passengers but subsequently refers to eighteen passengers; *see* Cholewczynski, **Poles Apart**, pp.182, 194 & 197; for the sixteen capacity *see* Middlebrook, p.411. The precise model of assault boat is unclear; *see* for example James Ladd, **Commandos and Rangers of World War II**, Appendix 4 'Landing Ships, Craft, Amphibians and Other Vehicles', p.247

169. *See* **CAB 44/254** Part II: Operation MARKET GARDEN, Book III, Chapter VII, 'Section V – Operations on the Island 21 to 26 Sep', Para. 52 'Narrative – night 23/24 Sep'; **WO 171/1586** 204 Field Company RE War Diary, entry for 21:00, 23/09/1944; Essame, p.131; and Cholewczynski, **Poles Apart**, p.182

170. *See* Sikorski Institute **AV 20/31/27** 1st Polish Independent Parachute Brigade War Diary, entry for 19:00; and Sosabowski, p.177

171. *See* Cholewczynski, **Poles Apart**, p.194; and Sikorski Institute **AV 20/31/27** 1st Polish Independent Parachute Brigade War Diary, entry for 23:00, 23/09/1944

172. *See* Sikorski Institute **AV 20/31/27** 1st Polish Independent Parachute Brigade War Diary, entry for 19:00, 23/09/1944; and Cholewczynski, **Poles Apart**, p.194

173. *See* Sikorski Institute **AV 20/31/27** 1st Polish Independent Parachute Brigade War Diary, entry for 21:30, 23/09/1944; and Cholewczynski, **Poles Apart**, p.194

174. Quoted from Cholewczynski, **Poles Apart**, p.194

175. *See* ibid., pp.194-195

176. *See* **WO171/397** 1 Airborne Division HQ Royal Engineers War Diary, entry for 19:15, 23/09/1944

177. *See* **WO 171/393** 1st Airborne Division HQ War Diary, entry for 23:45, 23/09/1944; for Mackenzie's decision to keep his reservations to himself see Ryan, p.483; Urquhart, p.152; and **The Pegasus**

Archive, Battle of Arnhem Archive, Biographies Section 'Lieutenant-Colonel Charles Baillie Mackenzie' at www.pegasusarchive.org/arnhem/charles_mackenzie.htm, accessed 17/07/2017

178. *See* Cholewczynski, p.195
179. *See* Sikorski Institute **AV 20/31/27** 1ˢᵗ Polish Independent Parachute Brigade War Diary, entry for 23:00, 23/09/1944
180. The US D-Ration chocolate bar, officially known as the 'Field Ration, Type D' was introduced in the late 1930s as a vitamin-enhanced emergency ration. Produced by the Hershey Chocolate Corporation, the D-Ration was usually issued in a waxed cardboard box containing three bars, each of which weighed four ounces and contained 600 calories; the three bars in total provided the 1,800 calories considered necessary for a day's intake. Pemmican was a concentrated mixture of dried and ground lean meat mixed with fat and sometimes augmented with fruit berries, which could be stored for years with no detrimental effects. Invented by Canadian native Indian tribes, pemmican was used by fur trappers, Arctic and Antarctic explorers, and was issued to British Army units serving in the 2ⁿᵈ Boer War as part of their emergency 'iron' ration.
181. *See* Cholewczynski, **Poles Apart**, p.196
182. For 22:30 timing *see* Cholewczynski, **Poles Apart**, p.196; for 23:00 timing *see* Sikorski Institute **AV 20/31/27** 1ˢᵗ Polish Independent Parachute Brigade War Diary, entry for 23:00, 23/09/1944

Chapter 19

1. *See* Cholewczynski, **Poles Apart**, p.197
2. *See* Sosabowski, **Freely I Served**, p.179
3. For Myers' involvement *see* Middlebrook, **Arnhem 1944**, p.411; and Faulkner-Brown, **A Sapper at Arnhem**, p.76. For 1ˢᵗ Airlanding Brigade Defence Platoon acting as guides *see* **WO 171/589** & **WO 171/590** 1ˢᵗ Airlanding Brigade HQ War Diary, Appendix F, entry for 23:55, 23/09/1944
4. *See* Cholewczynski, **Poles Apart**, p.194
5. *See* **WO171/1513** 9ᵗʰ (Airborne) Field Company RE War Diary, entry for 19:30, 23/09/1944. However, Lieutenant Brown's memoir clearly states that he spent the night of 23-24 September near the 4ᵗʰ Parachute Brigade HQ alternating guard duty with Captain James Smith from 1 Troop; *see* Faulkner-Brown, p.76. As the timing and wording in the 9ᵗʰ Field Company War Diary entry is almost identical to an entry the previous day in the 4ᵗʰ Parachute Squadron War Diary the former might simply have been entered in error under the wrong date; *see* **WO 171/1511** 4ᵗʰ Parachute Squadron RE War Diary, Appendix I, entry for 19:45, 22/09/1944
6. *See* Cholewczynski, **Poles Apart**, p.198
7. *See* Sikorski Institute **AV 20/31/27** 1ˢᵗ Polish Independent Parachute Brigade War Diary, entry for 00:20-00:30, 24/09/1944; Cholewczynski cites a precise time of 00:23; *see* Cholewczynski, **Poles Apart**, p.197; for 4ᵗʰ Dorsets reference *see* Essame, **The 43ʳᵈ Division at War**, p.131
8. *See* **WO171/1586** 204 Field Company RE War Diary, entry for 21:00, 23/09/1944
9. For Polish mortars and 43ʳᵈ Division artillery *see* Sikorski Institute **AV 20/31/27** 1ˢᵗ Polish Independent Parachute Brigade War Diary, entry for 03:00, 24/09/1944; and Cholewczynski, **Poles Apart**, p.198
10. Timing cited in Sikorski Institute **AV 20/31/27** 1ˢᵗ Polish Independent Parachute Brigade War Diary, entry for 03:00
11. *See* Cholewczynski, **Poles Apart**, pp.198-199
12. Quoted from ibid., p.199
13. For gas main *see* ibid., p.198; *see* also Sosabowski, p.179
14. *See* Sosabowski, p.179; and Cholewczynski, **Poles Apart**, p.199
15. *See* Cholewczynski, **Poles Apart**, p.199
16. *See* ibid., **Poles Apart**, p.200
17. *See* Sosabowski, p.180
18. *See* for example Cholewczynski, **Poles Apart**, p.204. All three officers involved in controlling the crossing points on the south bank received awards for their actions. Lieutenant Grünbaum was awarded the Silver Cross Order of Military Virtue Fifth Class, whilst Lieutenants Dawidowicz

and Skulski received second awards of the Cross of Valour; *see* **The Pegasus Archive** website, Battle of Arnhem Archive, Awards Section, Polish Awards Pages, www.pegasusarchive.org/arnhem/awards.htm, accessed 21/09/2017

19. *See* Cholewczynski, **Poles Apart**, p.203. 2nd Lieutenant Waclaw J Jaworski is interred in Arnhem Oosterbeek War Cemetery, Gelderland, Holland, Plot 25, Row B, Grave 20; his date of death is given as 26/09/1944. Lance-Sergeant Tomasz Lepalczyk has no known grave and does not appear in the CWGC database. According to Cholewczynski he was buried in a shallow grave on the polder close to the north bank of the river shortly after the crossing ceased; *see* Cholewczynski, **Poles Apart**, p.207

20. *See* Cholewczynski, **Poles Apart**, pp.200-201; for reported firefight *see* Middlebrook, p.412

21. *See* Cholewczynski, **Poles Apart**, pp.201-202

22. Quoted from *see* **Wo 171/590** 1st Airlanding Brigade HQ War Diary, Appendix 'F', entry for 01:45, 24/09/1944

23. *See* Cholewczynski, **Poles Apart**, p.199

24. *See* ibid., p.201

25. For 05:00 arrival time *see* ibid., p.204

26. *See* Sosabowski, p.180; and Cholewczynski, **Poles Apart**, pp.204-205

27. *See* Sikorski Institute **AV 20/31/27** 1st Polish Independent Parachute Brigade War Diary, entry for 05:05, 24/09/1944; and Cholewczynski, **Poles Apart**, pp.205-206, 208

28. *See* for example Middlebrook, p.411

29. 153 figure cited in Sikorski Institute **AV 20/31/27** 1st Polish Independent Parachute Brigade War Diary, entry for 05:05, 24/09/1944; *see* also handwritten reference at bottom of page reading 'These numbers do not include those casualties suffered on boats and after debarking who were immediately brought back to the southern bank of the river.'

30. *See* **WO171/1586** 204 Field Company RE War Diary, entry for 21:00, 23/09/1944

31. *See* Sosabowski, p.180; and **CAB 44/254** Part II: Operation MARKET GARDEN, Book III, Chapter VII, 'Section V – Operations on the Island 21 to 26 Sep', Para. 52 'Narrative – night 23/24 Sep'. For forty casualties arriving at the Driel MDS *see* Cholewczynski, **Poles Apart**, p.216. 163 Field Ambulance RAMC was attached to 30 Corps for MARKET GARDEN; for escorting Polish seaborne medical echelon *see* **WO 177/359** Assistant Director Medical Services 1 Airborne Division War Diary, entry for 22:00, 23/09/1944

32. *See* **WO 171/589** & **WO 171/590** 1st Airlanding Brigade HQ War Diary, Appendix F, entry for 01:45, 24/09/1944

33. Figures quoted from Sikorski Institute **AV 20/31/27** 1st Polish Independent Parachute Brigade War Diary, entry for 05:05, 24/09/1944

34. *See* Cholewczynski, **Poles Apart**, p.207-208; for British reference to the ponds *see* for example *see* **WO 171/589** & **WO 171/590** 1st Airlanding Brigade HQ War Diary, Appendix F, entry for 23:55, 23/09/1944

35. *See* Cholewczynski, **Poles Apart**, pp.208-209

36. Quote from **WO 171/589** & **WO 171/590** 1st Airlanding Brigade War Diary, Appendix F, entry for 01:45, 24/09/1944

37. *See* Cholewczynski, **Poles Apart**, pp.209-210, 211

38. *See* ibid., pp.208, 210

39. For barrage commencement timing *see* for example **WO 171/1234** 1 Wing Glider Pilot Regiment War Diary, entry for 07:00, 24/09/1944; Lieutenant Jan W. Kutrzeba is interred in Arnhem Oosterbeek War Cemetery, Gelderland, Holland, Plot 25, Row B, Grave 6

40. *See* Cholewczynski, **Poles Apart**, p.209

41. *See* **WO 171/589** & **WO 171/590** 1st Airlanding Brigade HQ War Diary, Appendix F, entry for 09:00, 24/09/1944; and Cholewczynski, **Poles Apart**, pp.209, 213

42. *See* **WO 171/393** 1 Airborne Division HQ War Diary, entry for 01:20, 24/09/1944; and **WO171/397** 1 Airborne Division HQ Royal Engineers War Diary, entries for 01:20 and 07:29, 24/09/1944

43. *See* **WO 171/396** 1 Airborne Division HQ Royal Artillery War Diary, entry for 24/09/1944; and **WO 171/398** 1 Airborne Division Signals War Diary, Index C, '1 Airborne Div Signals: Operation MARKET: Diary of Events at Div HQ', Paragraph 9 for D+7

44. *See* **WO 171/393** 1 Airborne Division HQ War Diary, entry for 05:35, 23/09/1944. Interestingly the Division Signals section log reports Phantom contact established with 2ⁿᵈ Army and 30 Corps twenty-five minutes later; *see* **WO 171/398** 1 Airborne Division Signals War Diary, entry for 06:00, 24/09/1944

45. There is no mention of the exchange in the Division HQ War Diary but the Division Signals War Diary refers to being connected to 130 Brigade from 08:00 and to the Phantom net being operative again from just after midday after damage to the aerial approximately two hours earlier; *see* **WO 171/398** 1 Airborne Division Signals War Diary, entries for 08:00, 09:55 & 12:30, 24/09/1944

46. Quoted from Urquhart, **Arnhem**, p.154

47. Quoted from ibid., p.154

48. Quoted from **CAB 44/254** Part II: Operation MARKET GARDEN, Book III, Chapter VII, 'Section V – Operations on the Island 21 to 26 Sep', Para. 53 '30 Corps plan – 24 Sep'

49. Private Mieczyslaw Krzeczkowski is interred in Mook War Cemetery, Limburg, Holland, Plot 4, Row C, Grave 11

50. *See* Cholewczynski, **Poles Apart**, pp.212-213, 231-232

51. *See* ibid., p.232; and Green, **1ˢᵗ Battalion The Border Regiment**, p.71

52. For move to Brussels *see* **AIR 27/2046** No. 575 Squadron Operations Record Book, entry for 23/09/1944; for details of alleged drop at Oosterbeek *see* Cooper, **The Air Battle for Arnhem**, p.124

53. *See* **AIR 27/2046** No. 575 Squadron Operations Record Book, entry for 24/09/1944

54. *See* **AIR 27/2134** No. 620 Squadron Operations Record Book, entry for 24/09/1944

55. *See* Cholewczynski, **Poles Apart**, pp.233-234, 243

56. For 19:35 timing *see* Green, p.72; for German infiltration on BREESE Force's right flank *see* **WO 171/590** 1ˢᵗ Airlanding Brigade HQ War Diary, Appendix 'F', entry for 12:00, 24/09/1944

57. *See* Green, p.71; for Sergeant Clark's DCM citation *see* **The Pegasus Archive** website, Battle of Arnhem Archive, Biographies Section 'Sergeant Stanley Clark' at www.pegasusarchive.org/arnhem/sidney_clark.htm, accessed 09/10/2017

58. *See* **WO 171/590** 1ˢᵗ Airlanding Brigade HQ War Diary, Appendix 'F', entry for 19:00, 22/09/1944

59. Lieutenant George Norman Austin and Warrant Officer Class II Leslie Morgan are interred in Arnhem Oosterbeek War Cemetery, Gelderland, Holland, in Plot 20, Row C, Grave 18 and Plot 26, Row B, Grave 4 respectively

60. *See* **WO 171/590** 1ˢᵗ Airlanding Brigade HQ War Diary, Appendix 'F', entry for 12:00, 24/09/1944

61. *See* **WO 171/1059** 64 Medium Regiment RA War Diary, entries for 18:46 and 18:57, 24/09/1944; quote from **WO 171/590** 1ˢᵗ Airlanding Brigade HQ War Diary, Appendix 'F', entry for 19:30, 24/09/1944

62. *See* Green, p.72

63. For 19:05 timing *see* **WO 166/15077** 1ˢᵗ Battalion The Border Regiment War Diary, Appendix A, entry for 24/09/1944

64. *See* Green, p.72; and **WO 171/590** 1ˢᵗ Airlanding Brigade HQ War Diary, Appendix 'F', entry for 19:35, 24/09/1944

65. *See* **WO 166/15077** 1ˢᵗ Battalion The Border Regiment War Diary, Appendix A, entry for 24/09/1944; and Green, pp.71-72

66. *See* **WO 171/590** 1ˢᵗ Airlanding Brigade HQ War Diary, Appendix 'F', entry for 09:00, 24/09/1944; and Cholewczynski, **Poles Apart**, pp.213-214

67. *See* **WO 171/1511** 4ᵗʰ Parachute Squadron RE War Diary, Appendix I, entry for 24/09/1944; and **WO 171/1609** 261 (Airborne) Field Park Company RE War Diary, Appendix H, entry for 24/09/1944

68. Quoted from the 4th **Parachute Squadron Royal Engineers** website, Arnhem Section, 'September 24' at http://myweb.tiscali.co.uk/4parasqnre/arnhem%20page%207.htm, accessed 15/10/2017

69. *See* 4th **Parachute Squadron Royal Engineers** website, Arnhem Section, 'September 24' at http://myweb.tiscali.co.uk/4parasqnre/arnhem%20page%207.htm, accessed 15/10/2017; and **WO 171/1513** 9th Field Company RE War Diary, entry for 24/09/1944. Sapper Thomas Cunningham is interred in Arnhem Oosterbeek War Cemetery, Gelderland, Holland, Special Memorial Plot 1, Row A, Grave 5; Captain Roger Basil Binyon RE has no known grave and is commemorated on the Groesbeek Memorial, Gelderland, Holland, Panel 2

70. *See* **WO 171/957** 1st Airlanding Anti-Tank Battery War Diary, Appendix 'Operation Market HQRA'

71. *See* **WO 171/590** 1st Airlanding Brigade HQ War Diary, Appendix 'F', entry for 12:30, 24/09/1944; and **WO 171/1323** 7th Battalion King's Own Scottish Borderers War Diary, entry for 13:00 to 19:00, 24/09/1944

72. *See* **WO 171/1235** 2 Wing Glider Pilot Regiment War Diary, entry for 24/09/1944; and **WO 171/590** 1st Airlanding Brigade HQ War Diary, Appendix 'F', entries for 14:07 & 17:00, 24/09/1944. The 7th KOSB War Diary gives the time of the Glider Pilot's withdrawal as being 'short after midnight, although this may be a misspelling of midday given the entry timing; *see* **WO 171/1323** 7th Battalion King's Own Scottish Borderers War Diary, entry for 13:00 to 19:00, 24/09/1944

73. *See* **WO 171/1609** 261 (Airborne) Field Park Company RE War Diary, Appendix H, entry for 24/09/1944; and **WO 171/1511** 4th Parachute Squadron RE War Diary, Appendix I, entry for 16:00, 24/09/1944

74. *See* **WO 171/1323** 7th Battalion King's Own Scottish Borderers War Diary, entries for 00:01 to 04:30, 06:30 to 13:00 & 13:00 to 19:00, 24/09/1944

75. Quote and figures from **WO 171/1323** 7th Battalion King's Own Scottish Borderers War Diary, entry for 13:00 to 19:00, 24/09/1944

76. *See* **WO 171/1016** 1st Airlanding Light Regiment RA War Diary, entry for 24/09/1944

77. *See* **WO 171/1059** 64 Medium Regiment RA War Diary, entries for 18:11 and 18:20, 24/09/1944

78. Quoted from **WO 171/1323** 7th Battalion King's Own Scottish Borderers War Diary, entry for 13:00 to 19:00, 24/09/1944; *see* also **WO 171/590** 1st Airlanding Brigade HQ War Diary, Appendix 'F', entry for 19:15, 24/09/1944

79. Quoted from **WO 171/406** 1st Airborne Reconnaissance Squadron War Diary, entry for 06:30, 24/09/1944

80. *See* **WO 171/594** 4th Parachute Brigade War Diary, Appendix C, entry for 24/09/1944; for timing *see* **WO 171/393** 1st Airborne Division HQ War Diary, entry for 07:40, 24/09/1944. There is no reference to Hackett's visit in the Reconnaissance Squadron War Diary, although his visit at 09:00 the previous morning is noted

81. *See* **WO 171/594** 4th Parachute Brigade War Diary, Appendix C, entry for 24/09/1944; and **WO 171/393** 1st Airborne Division HQ War Diary, entry for 07:40, 24/09/1944. For No. 1 Wing timings *see* **WO 171/1234**, 1 Wing Glider Pilot Regiment War Diary, entries for 08:30 & 09:55, 25/09/1944; for some reason the No. 1 Wing Diary cites events that took place on 24 September under the following day's heading; and Urquhart, p.154

82. Quoted from **WO 171/406** 1st Airborne Reconnaissance Squadron War Diary, entries for 09:30 & 10:15, 24/09/1944

83. For timing *see* **WO 171/406** 1st Airborne Reconnaissance Squadron War Diary, entry for 14:15, 24/09/1944; for sortie details *see* Powell, **The Devil's Birthday**, p.209; and Ian Gooderson, **Air Power at the Battlefront**, p.97

84. *See* **WO 171/406** 1st Airborne Reconnaissance Squadron War Diary, entries for 10:15, 15:30; 15:35 & 19:30, 24/09/1944; and Fairley, **Remember Arnhem**, p.183. Trooper Alfred Herbert Odd is interred in Arnhem Oosterbeek War Cemetery, Gelderland, Holland in Plot 22, Row A, Grave 17; at age 19 Trooper Odd was the youngest member of the Reconnaissance Squadron to be killed at Arnhem

85. *See* **WO 171/406** D Troop 1ˢᵗ Airborne Reconnaissance Squadron War Diary, entry for 07:00; and Fairley, p.179

86. *See* **WO 171/406** D Troop 1ˢᵗ Airborne Reconnaissance Squadron War Diary, entries for 10:00 & 11:30; and Fairley, p.182. Captain John Reginald Charles Robert Park, Lieutenant Alan Frank Pascal and Trooper Thomas Alfred Williamson Walker are interred in Arnhem Oosterbeek War Cemetery, Gelderland, Holland in Plot 21, Row A, Grave 13, Plot 3, Row D, grave 1 and Plot 21, Row A, Grave 10 respectively

87. *See* Fairley, p.180

88. *See* **WO 171/406** D Troop 1ˢᵗ Airborne Reconnaissance Squadron War Diary, entry for 13:00; and Fairley, pp.185-187; the Squadron War Diary makes no mention of the Reconnaissance party's capture and escape, stating that they remained hidden near D Troop's location until the following night

89. *See* **WO 171/406** A Troop 1ˢᵗ Airborne Reconnaissance Squadron War Diary, entry for 01:00, 24/09/1944; and Fairley, p.178

90. *See* Fairley, pp.178-181

91. *See* ibid., pp.181-182, 184

92. *See* **WO 171/1248** 21ˢᵗ Independent Parachute Company War Diary, entry for 24/09/1944

93. *See* **WO 171/1248** 21ˢᵗ Independent Parachute Company War Diary, entry for 24/09/1944; and Cholewczynski, **Poles Apart**, pp.222-223

94. *See* Kent, **First In!**, p.122

95. *See* Middlebrook, p.410; and Cholewczynski, **Poles Apart**, p.222

96. *See* Cholewczynski, **Poles Apart**, p.223-224; Private Mikolaj Bzowy is interred in Arnhem Oosterbeek War Cemetery, Gelderland, Holland in Plot 25, Row B, Grave 3; the CWGC records give Private Bzowy's date of death as 23/09/1944

97. For 156 Parachute Battalion withdrawal *see* **WO 171/1247** 156 Parachute Battalion War Diary, entries for 14:00 & 15:00, 23/09/1944; for details of Captain Gazurek's ill-fated move up the *Stationsweg* back gardens *see* Cholewczynski, **Poles Apart**, p.224-225. Captain Ignacy Gazurek is interred in Arnhem Oosterbeek War Cemetery, Gelderland, Holland in Plot 25, Row B, Grave 5

98. Testimony from Sander Kremer; cited in Middlebrook, pp.410-411. Mr Kremer refers to the incident as occurring on Saturday 23 September rather than the following day

99. *See* Cholewczynski, **Poles Apart**, pp.225-226

100. *See* **WO 171/1248** 21ˢᵗ Independent Parachute Company War Diary, entry for 24/09/1944; and Kent, **First In!**, pp.122-123

101. Lance-Corporal Konstanty Wesolowicz and Private Emil Mentlik are interred in Arnhem Oosterbeek War Cemetery, Gelderland, Holland in Plot 25, Row B, Graves 1 and 16 respectively

102. *See* Cholewczynski, **Poles Apart**, pp.229, 231

103. Dispositions cited in Kent, **First In!**, pp.116-117

104. *See* **WO 171/594** 4ᵗʰ Parachute Brigade War Diary, Appendix D, entry for 24/09/1944

105. *See* **WO 171/1248** 21ˢᵗ Independent Parachute Company War Diary, entry for 24/09/1944; and Kent, **First In!**, pp.122-123

106. *See* Ryan, pp.495-496

107. Quoted from Colonel G. Warrack, **Arnhem Diary** (unpublished memoir); cited in Baynes, **Urquhart of Arnhem**, pp.140-141

108. Quoted from Ryan, p.496

109. *See* ibid., p.496

110. *See* Kershaw, **It Never Snows in September**, p.271

111. *See* Ryan, pp.496-500

112. *See* **WO 171/393** 1ˢᵗ Airborne Division HQ War Diary, entry for 16:52, 24/09/1944; according to Captain Mawson the evacuation was well underway by midday; *see* Mawson, **Arnhem Doctor**, p.158

113. Quoted from Mawson, **Arnhem Doctor**, p.154

114. *See* Cholewczynski, **Poles Apart**, p.230

115. *See* **WO 171/393** 1st Airborne Division HQ War Diary, entry for 07:10, 24/09/1944; for details of the press team *see* Ryan, **A Bridge Too Far**, footnote p.484; for Byam and Maxsted *see* for example Vincent Dowd, 2015, **WW2: Guy Byam, The BBC's Lost Reporter** at http://www.bbc. co.uk/news/magazine-34144792, [accessed 18/12/2017]

116. *See* Cholewczynski, **Poles Apart**, p.230

117. *See* **WO 171/393** 1st Airborne Division HQ War Diary, entry for 15:27, 24/09/1944

118. *See* **WO 171/1248** 21st Independent Parachute Company War Diary, entry for 15:00, 24/09/1944

119. *See* **WO 171/393** 1st Airborne Division HQ War Diary, entry for 19:00, 24/09/1944. There is no mention of this incident in the 21st Independent Parachute Company War Diary however, and it is possible it is a slightly altered reference to the incident with the two Panzer IVs recorded in the Pathfinder War Diary *see* **WO 171/1248** 21st Independent Parachute Company War Diary, entry for 15:00, 24/09/1944

120. Quotes from Mawson, pp.154-155

121. *See* Julian Thompson, **Ready for Anything**, pp.196-197

122. *See* **WO 171/594** 4th Parachute Brigade War Diary, Appendix D, entry for 24/09/1944; The **Pegasus Archive** website, Battle of Arnhem Archive, Biographies Section 'Brigadier John Winthrop Hackett' at www.pegasusarchive.org/arnhem/john_hackett.htm, accessed 23/12/2017; and ibid., Battle of Arnhem Archive, Biographies Section 'Captain Alexander Lippmann-Kessel' at www.pegasusarchive.org/arnhem/alexander_lipmann_kessel.htm, accessed 23/12/2017

123. Quoted from Mawson, p.158

124. *See* ibid., pp.155-169; for Mawson's service at *Stalag IV G see* **The Pegasus Archive** website, Prisoner of War Archive, Camps History Section 'STALAG IVG: Red Cross Report 11th-16th March 1945' at www.pegasusarchive.org/pow/cSt_4G_report1.htm [accessed 28/12/2017]

125. *See* **WO 171/1236** 1st Parachute Battalion War Diary, entry for 24/09/1944

126. *See* **WO 171/1244** 11th Parachute Battalion War Diary, entry for 24/09/1944; and **WO 171/1375** 2nd Battalion South Staffordshire Regiment War Diary, Appendix J1 '2nd South Staffords at Arnhem 17-25 Sept 1944'

127. *See* **WO 171/1236** 1st Parachute Battalion War Diary, entry for 24/09/1944; and **WO 171/1238** 3rd Parachute Battalion War Diary, composite entry for 22/09/1944 to 25/09/1944. Lieutenant Philip Brandon Evans passed into German captivity and was incarcerated in *Oflag IX A/H* at Spangenberg in central Germany

128. *See* **WO 166/14933** 1st Airlanding Light Regiment RA War Diary, entry for 24/09/1944

129. *See* **WO 171/393** 1st Airborne Division HQ War Diary, entry for 19:00, 24/09/1944; **WO 166/15077** 1st Battalion The Border Regiment War Diary, Appendix A, entry for 24/09/1944; and Green, pp.71-72

130. Quoted from **WO 166/14933** 1st Airlanding Light Regiment RA War Diary, entry for 24/09/1944; and **WO 171/1375** 2nd Battalion South Staffordshire Regiment War Diary, Appendix J1 '2nd South Staffords at Arnhem 17-25 Sept 1944'

131. *See* Victor Miller, **Nothing is Impossible**, p.168

132. *See* **WO 171/396** 1 Airborne Division HQ Royal Artillery War Diary, entry for 24/09/1944

133. *See* Fairley, p.179

134. Quoted from **WO 171/1248** 21st Independent Parachute Company War Diary, entry for 24/09/1944

135. *See* **WO 171/1323** 7th Battalion King's Own Scottish Borderers War Diary, entry for 06:30 to 13:00, 24/09/1944; for details of Sergeant Tilley's involvement and his DCM citation *see* The **Pegasus Archive**, Battle of Arnhem Archive, Biographies Section, 'Sergeant Russell Frederick Tilley' at www.pegasusarchive.org/arnhem/russell_tilley.htm, accessed 19/01/2018

136. *See* **CAB 44/254** Part II: Operation MARKET GARDEN, Book III, Chapter VII, 'Section V – Operations on the Island 21 to 26 Sep', Para. 54 'Narrative 24 Sep'

137. Quoted from Essame, **The 43rd Division at War**, p.135

138. Major Mowbray Morris Souper is interred in Arnhem Oosterbeek War Cemetery, Gelderland, Holland, Plot 10, Row B, Grave 7. According to Essame the 1st Worcesters also lost a Major Gibbons killed on 24 September, but the Commonwealth War Graves Commission has no record of an officer of that rank or name; *see* Essame, p.135

139. *See* **CAB 44/254** Part II: Operation MARKET GARDEN, Book III, Chapter VII, 'Section V – Operations on the Island 21 to 26 Sep', Para. 54 'Narrative 24 Sep'; and Essame, p.135

140. Quoted from **CAB 44/254** Part II: Operation MARKET GARDEN, Book III, Chapter VII, 'Section V – Operations on the Island 21 to 26 Sep', Para. 53 '30 Corps plan – 24 Sep'

141. Quoted from **CAB 44/254** Part II: Operation MARKET GARDEN, Book III, Chapter VII, 'Section V – Operations on the Island 21 to 26 Sep', Para. 53 '30 Corps plan – 24 Sep'

142. *See* Sir Brian Horrocks, **Corps Commander**, pp.122-123; cited in Powell, p.213; and **CAB 44/254** Part II: Operation MARKET GARDEN, Book III, Chapter VII, 'Section V – Operations on the Island 21 to 26 Sep', Para. 53 '30 Corps plan – 24 Sep'

143. *See* **CAB 44/254** Part II: Operation MARKET GARDEN, Book III, Chapter VII, 'Section V – Operations on the Island 21 to 26 Sep', Para. 53 '30 Corps plan – 24 Sep'; and **WO 171/393** 1 Airborne Division HQ War Diary, entry for 05:35, 23/09/1944.

144. Quoted from Essame, p.132

145. *See* **WO 285/10-15** Dempsey Papers: Personal War Diary, entry for 24/09/1944; cited in Powell, p.218

146. *See* Ellis, **Victory in the West, Volume II: The Defeat of Germany**, p.43; quote taken from Alanbrooke Papers, 14/32; cited in Powell, p.218

147. Quote from Essame, p.131

148. *See* ibid., pp.132-133

149. *See* for example William F. Buckingham, **Arnhem 1944: A Reappraisal**, pp.46-47

150. *See* Sikorski Institute **AV 20/31/27** 1st Polish Independent Parachute Brigade War Diary, entry for 10:00, 24/09/1944

151. *See* Sosabowski, p.182

152. *See* Cholewczynski, **Poles Apart**, pp.214-215

153. *See* Sosabowski, p.182

154. *See* Cholewczynski, **Poles Apart**, p.217; for departure time *see* Sikorski Institute **AV 20/31/27** 1st Polish Independent Parachute Brigade War Diary, entry for 11:30, 24/09/194

155. *See* Sosabowski, pp.182-183

156. *See* Essame, pp.132-133

157. *See* Middlebrook, p.415

158. For Lieutenant Dyrda's account and quotations *see* Cholewczynski, **Poles Apart**, pp.217-221

159. *See* ibid., p.220

160. *See* ibid., p.183

161. *See* **CAB 44/254** Part II: Operation MARKET GARDEN, Book III, Chapter VII, 'Section V – Operations on the Island 21 to 26 Sep', Para. 53 '30 Corps plan – 24 Sep'; and Ellis, **Victory in the West, Volume II: The Defeat of Germany**, p.43

162. Quotes from Sosabowski, pp.183-184

163. *See* **CAB 44/254** Part II: Operation MARKET GARDEN, Book III, Chapter VI, 'Preparations for Operation 'MARKET GARDEN', Appendix C – 'RE Aspect of Operation "GARDEN"'; and Sliz, **The Storm Boat Kings**, pp.40-41

164. *See* **WO 171/1586** 204 Field Company RE War Diary, entries for 16:45, 20/09/1944 and 11:00, 21/09/1944

165. *See* **WO 171/1586** 204 Field Company RE War Diary, entries for 18:00 & 22:30, 21/09/1944 and 06:00, 22/09/1944

166. *See* **WO 171/1586** 204 Field Company RE War Diary, entries for 15:15, 22/09/1944 & 21:00, 23/09/1944

167. *See* **WO 171/1608** 260 Field Company RE War Diary, entries for 18:00, 20/09/1944; 10:00, 21/09/1944; and entries for 22, 23 & 24/09/1944

168. *See* Sliz, **The Storm Boat Kings**, pp.41-42

169. *See* **WO 179/3129** 20th Field Company RCE War Diary, entries for 07:30 & 19:30, 16/09/1944 and 06:30 & 17:00, 17/09/1944; Eksel is rendered Exsel in the War Diary

170. *See* **WO 179/3129** 20th Field Company RCE War Diary, entries for 10:30, 12:30, 16:00 & 22:00, 21/09/1944

171. *See* **WO 179/3129** 20th Field Company RCE War Diary, entries for 12:00 & 14:00, 22/09/1944 and 06:30, 23/09/1944

172. *See* **WO 179/3129** 20th Field Company RCE War Diary, entries for 11:00, 12:00 & 13:30, 24/09/1944

173. *See* **WO 179/3130** 23rd Field Company RCE War Diary, entries for 16/09/1944 and 17/09/1944

174. *See* **WO 179/3130** 23rd Field Company RCE War Diary, entries for 21, 22, 23 & 24/09/1944

175. *See* Cholewczynski, **Poles Apart**, p.228

176. *See* Sosabowski, pp.197-198

177. *See* **WO 171/1286** 4th Battalion The Dorsetshire Regiment War Diary, entry for 16:45, 23/09/1944; Essame's account renders the 4th Dorsets' commander's surname as Tilley

178. *See* **WO 171/1286** 4th Battalion The Dorsetshire Regiment War Diary, entries for 12:00, 14:00 & 16:00, 24/09/1944; for use of Driel church tower and 16:30 Brigade O Group *see* Essame, p.133

179. Essame cites the involvement of Major Rooke and four vehicles but later refers to six vehicles; *see* Essame, pp.133, 134

180. *See* **WO 177/359** Assistant Director Medical Services 1 Airborne Division War Diary, entries for 10:00 & 10:30, 24/09/1944; and Essame, pp.133, 135; the latter cites four DUKWs on the former page but six on the latter; for Lieutenant Tiernan and 181 Airlanding Field Ambulance *see* Middlebrook, p.420; Middlebrook cites Tiernan's forename as Jimmy and gives his rank as Captain

181. *See* **WO171/1586** 204 Field Company RE War Diary, entry for 11:00, 24/09/1944

182. *See* **WO 171/1286** 4th Battalion The Dorsetshire Regiment War Diary, entry for 18:00, 24/09/1944; and Essame, p.133

183. Testimony from Major Philip Roper, OC C Company, 4th Battalion The Dorsetshire Regiment; cited in Middlebrook, p.419

184. *See* **WO 171/1286** 4th Battalion The Dorsetshire Regiment War Diary, entry for 19:30, 24/09/1944; and Essame, p.133

185. *See* **WO171/1586** 204 Field Company RE War Diary, entry for 24/09/1944

186. *See* **WO 177/359** Assistant Director Medical Services 1 Airborne Division War Diary, entries for 08:00, 10:00, 10:30 & 14:00, 24/09/1944; **The Pegasus Archive** website, Battle of Arnhem Archive, Biographies Section 'Lieutenant-Colonel Martin Edward Meakin Herford MBE, MC' at www.pegasusarchive.org/arnhem/martin_herford.htm [accessed 20/03/2018]; and Middlebrook, pp.418-419, 437. Captain Percy Louis has no known grave and is commemorated on the Groesbeek Memorial, Gelderland, Holland, Panel 9

187. For 17:00 briefing *see* Cholewczynski, **Poles Apart**, p.233; for 22:00 timing *see* Sikorski Institute **AV 20/31/27** 1st Polish Independent Parachute Brigade War Diary, entry for 11:30, 24/09/1944; there is no mention of the 17:00 briefing in the War Diary

188. For crossing order *see* Sikorski Institute **AV 20/31/27** 1st Polish Independent Parachute Brigade War Diary, entry for 11:30, 24/09/1944; for varying numbers *see* ibid. and Cholewczynski, **Poles Apart**, p.233 respectively; for transport details & timing *see* Cholewczynski, **Poles Apart**, p.232

189. *See* Cholewczynski, **Poles Apart**, pp.233, 234, 237-238; for arrival timing *see* Sikorski Institute **AV 20/31/27** 1st Polish Independent Parachute Brigade War Diary, entry for 19:30, 24/09/1944. Cholewczynski cites an arrival time of 23:00, but this is contradicted by the Polish Brigade War Diary and Sosabowski's account, which refers to the 1st Battalion arriving 'early in the evening'; *see* Cholewczynski, **Poles Apart**, p.237; and Sosabowski, p.184

190. For departure time *see* Sikorski Institute **AV 20/31/27** 1st Polish Independent Parachute Brigade War Diary, entry for 21:00, 24/09/1944; for Engineer Company *see* Cholewczynski, **Poles Apart**, p.238

191. *See* Essame, p.133; and Cholewczynski, **Poles Apart**, p.237
192. *See* **WO 171/1286** 4ᵗʰ Battalion The Dorsetshire Regiment War Diary, entry for 21:45, 24/09/1944; Sikorski Institute **AV 20/31/27** 1ˢᵗ Polish Independent Parachute Brigade War Diary, entry for 21:45, 24/09/1944; and Sosabowski, p.185
193. Quoted from Essame, p.134
194. Quoted from Sosabowski, p.185
195. *See* Cholewczynski, **Poles Apart**, p.238; and Essame, p.134
196. *See* Cholewczynski, **Poles Apart**, pp.238-239
197. For cancellation timing *see* Sikorski Institute **AV 20/31/27** 1ˢᵗ Polish Independent Parachute Brigade War Diary, entry for 22:45, 24/09/1944

Chapter 20

1. *See* Middlebrook, **Arnhem 1944**, p.419; and **WO 171/1586** 204 Field Company RE War Diary, entry for 11:00, 24/09/1944. According to the former some vessels were manned by personnel from 533 Field Company RE
2. *See* Mark Henniker, **An Image of War**, p.188; for examples of the tactic being employed in Normandy and Germany *see* Essame, **The 43ʳᵈ Division at War**, pp.83-84 and 167-168
3. For departure time *see* **WO 171/1286** 4ᵗʰ Battalion The Dorsetshire Regiment War Diary, entry for 01:00, 25/09/1944; for 112 Field Regiment RA Forward Observer teams *see* Middlebrook, p.420
4. *See* **WO 171/393** 1ˢᵗ Airborne Division HQ War Diary, entry for 06:05, 25/09/1944
5. *See* Middlebrook, p.419; and Kershaw, **It Never Snows in September**, p.288; the latter gives the unit title as 'Schiffsturmabteilung'
6. *See* Essame, p.134
7. For Major Crocker details *see* Middlebrook, p.419; for Captain Hall details *see* **The Pegasus Archive**, Battle of Arnhem Archive, Biographies Section 'Captain Ronald Francis Hall' at www.pegasusarchive.org/arnhem/ronald_francis_hall.htm, accessed 10/04/2018
8. *See* Green, **1ˢᵗ Battalion The Border Regiment**, pp.72-73
9. *See* Middlebrook, p.420
10. *See* **WO 171/1016** 1ˢᵗ Airlanding Light Regiment RA War Diary, entry for 06:00, 25/09/1944; and Middlebrook, pp.420-421; for arrival of the Dorsets liaison officer at the Hotel Hartenstein *see* **WO 171/393** 1ˢᵗ Airborne Division HQ War Diary, entry for 08:40, 25/09/1944
11. *See* Middlebrook, p.421; Captain Thomas Douglas Rose is interred in Arnhem Oosterbeek War Cemetery, Gelderland, Holland in Plot 24, Row B, Grave 16
12. *See* Essame, p.134
13. *See* Ryan, **A Bridge Too Far**, p.513
14. *See* Green, pp.73-74
15. *See* **WO 171/1286** 4ᵗʰ Battalion The Dorsetshire Regiment War Diary, entry for 02:15, 25/09/1944
16. *See* Essame, pp.134-135; and Middlebrook, p.420
17. *See* **WO 171/393** 1ˢᵗ Airborne Division HQ War Diary, entries for 06:05 and 09:40, 25/09/1944
18. *See* Middlebrook, pp.421-422. Private Harold Wyer has no known grave and is commemorated on the Groesbeek Memorial, Gelderland, Holland, Panel 5
19. *See* Essame, p.134; and Middlebrook, p.421
20. Testimony from Private Aubrey Steirn, C Company, 4ᵗʰ Battalion The Dorsetshire Regiment; cited in Middlebrook, p.421
21. *See* Kershaw, p.288
21. *See* Green, pp.74-75
23. *See* Kershaw, p.288
24. For figures *see* **WO 171/1286** 4ᵗʰ Battalion The Dorsetshire Regiment War Diary, entry for 02:15, 25/09/1944; Middlebrook, Arnhem 1944, p.422; and **WO 171/1586** 204 Field Company RE War Diary, entry for 11:00, 24/09/1944
25. *See* Essame, p.134-135; and **WO 171/1586** 204 Field Company RE War Diary, entry for 11:00, 24/09/1944

26. *See* Middlebrook, p.422

27. *See* **CAB 44/254** Part II: Operation MARKET GARDEN, Book III, Chapter VII, 'Section V – Operations on the Island 21 to 26 Sep', Para. 51 '30 Corps Operation Instruction No. 25 of 23 Sep'; and ibid., Para. 53 '30 Corps Plan – 24 Sep'

28. *See* **CAB 44/254** Part II: Operation MARKET GARDEN, Book III, Chapter VII, 'Section V – Operations on the Island 21 to 26 Sep', Para. 56 '30 Corps plan – 25 Sep'

29. *See* **CAB 44/254** Part II: Operation MARKET GARDEN, Book III, Chapter VII, 'Section V – Operations on the Island 21 to 26 Sep', Para. 55 'Narrative 130 Bde night 24/25 Sep'

30. *See* Urquhart, **Arnhem**, pp.163-165; interestingly, Browning's rather less than useful missive is reproduced in full, whereas the communication from Thomas is merely paraphrased in three sentences

31. *See* Urquhart, p.165; and **WO 171/393** 1ˢᵗ Airborne Division HQ War Diary, entry for 06:05, 25/09/1944

32. *See* Essame, p.135

33. *See* Middlebrook, p.423

34. *See* **WO 171/393** 1ˢᵗ Airborne Division HQ War Diary, entries for 08:08 and 10:30, 25/09/1944; and Urquhart, **Arnhem**, pp.165-168

35. *See* Kershaw, p.291

36. *See* ibid., p.293

37. *See* ibid., p.291

38. *See* ibid., p.228

39. *See* **WO 171/1234**, 1 Wing Glider Pilot Regiment War Diary, entries for 06:15, 25/09/1944

40. *See* for example **WO 166/15077** 1ˢᵗ Battalion The Border Regiment War Diary, Appendix A, entry for 25/09/1944; **WO 171/1016** 1ˢᵗ Airlanding Light Regiment RA War Diary, entry for 25/09/1944; and **WO 171/1234**, 1 Wing Glider Pilot Regiment War Diary, entries for 05:30, 25/09/1944

41. *See* **WO 171/1323** 7ᵗʰ Battalion King's Own Scottish Borderers War Diary, entry for 06:30 to 13:00, 25/09/1944

42. *See* **WO 171/589** & **WO 171/590** 1ˢᵗ Airlanding Brigade HQ War Diary, Appendix F, entry for 10:00, 25/09/1944

43. *See* Green, p.78

44. Captain William Kitching Hodgson is interred in Arnhem Oosterbeek War Cemetery, Gelderland, Holland, Plot 1, Row C, Grave 2

45. Corporal Lawrence Cowin is interred in Arnhem Oosterbeek War Cemetery, Gelderland, Holland, Plot 19, Row C, Grave 1; his name is rendered Cowan in Green's Battalion history

46. *See* **WO 171/589** & **WO 171/590** 1ˢᵗ Airlanding Brigade HQ War Diary, Appendix F, entry for 14:30, 25/09/1944

47. *See* **WO 171/589** & **WO 171/590** 1ˢᵗ Airlanding Brigade HQ War Diary, Appendix F, entry for 14:30, 25/09/1944; for 15:30 & 16:00 timings *see* **WO 166/15077** 1ˢᵗ Battalion The Border Regiment War Diary, Appendix A, entry for 25/09/1944

48. *See* Green, p.77

49. *See* for example **WO 166/15077** 1ˢᵗ Battalion The Border Regiment War Diary, Appendix A, entry for 25/09/1944; **WO 171/1511** 4ᵗʰ Parachute Squadron RE War Diary, entry for 25/09/1944; ibid., Appendix I, entry for 25/09/1944; and **WO 171/1513** 9ᵗʰ (Airborne) Field Company RE War Diary, entry for 25/09/1944

50. *See* **WO 171/1323** 7ᵗʰ Battalion King's Own Scottish Borderers War Diary, entries for 04:30 to 06:30 & 06:30 to 13:00, 25/09/1944

51. *See* **WO 171/1059** 64 Medium Regiment RA War Diary, entries for 11:47, 12:45 & 13:45, 25/09/1944

52. Testimony from Private Alfred Robin Holburn, Mortar Group, Support Company, 7ᵗʰ (Galloway) Battalion The King's Own Scottish Borderers; cited in Middlebrook, pp.426-427

53. *See* John Fairley, **Remember Arnhem**, pp.188-189

54. *See* **WO 171/1247** 156 Parachute Battalion War Diary, Appendix C: 156 Bn Parachute Regiment Arnhem, entry for 14:00, 25/09/1944

55. *See* Cholewczynski, **Poles Apart**, pp.234-235

56. *See* ibid., pp.237, 240

57. *See* ibid., pp.241, 247

58. *See* **WO 171/1248** 21st Independent Parachute Company War Diary, entry for 25/09/1944

59. *See* Kent, **First In!**, p.127

60. *See* **WO 171/594** 4th Parachute Brigade War Diary, Appendix D, entry for 25/09/1944; and **WO 171/1248** 21st Independent Parachute Company War Diary, entry for 25/09/1944

61. *See* for example Zwarts, **German Armoured Units at Arnhem**, p.59; for commander's names *see* the **Defending Arnhem** website, Eastern Sector Order of Battle Section, 'Schwere Panzer Abteilung 506' page at www.defendingarnhem.com/schpzabt506.htm, accessed 01/05/2018

62. *See* **WO 171/1016** 1st Airlanding Light Regiment RA War Diary, entry for 25/09/1944; and **WO 171/590** 1st Airlanding Brigade HQ War Diary, Appendix 'F', entry for 10:00, 25/09/1944

63. For 10:00 timing *see* **WO 171/1016** 1st Airlanding Light Regiment RA War Diary, entries for 10:00, 25/09/1944 and **WO 171/589 & 590** 1st Airlanding Brigade HQ War Diary, Appendix 'F', entry for 10:00, 25/09/1944; for 11:00 timing *see* **WO 171/1238** 3 Parachute Battalion War Diary, composite entry for 22/09/1944 & after; for early afternoon timing *see* **WO 171/1375** 2nd Battalion South Staffordshire Regiment War Diary, Appendix J1 '2nd South Staffords at Arnhem 17-25 Sept 1944'

64. Quoted from **WO 171/1236** 1Parachute Battalion War Diary, entry for 25/09/1944

65. *See* **WO 171/589 & 590** 1st Airlanding Brigade HQ War Diary, Appendix 'F', entry for 09:00, 19/09/1944

66. *See* **WO 171/589 & 590** 1st Airlanding Brigade HQ War Diary, Appendix 'F', entry for 10:00, 25/09/1944

67. For dispositions *see* **WO 171/1016** 1st Airlanding Light Regiment RA War Diary, 'Appendix', sketch map appended to end

68. *See* **WO 171/1016** 1st Airlanding Light Regiment RA War Diary, entry for 10:00, 25/09/1944

69. *See* **WO 171/589 & 590** 1st Airlanding Brigade HQ War Diary, Appendix 'F', entry for 10:51, 25/09/1944

70. *See* **WO 171/1016** 1st Airlanding Light Regiment RA War Diary, entry for 10:00, 25/09/1944

71. Testimony from Gunner Robert Christie, 2 Battery, 1st Airlanding Light Regiment RA; cited in Middlebrook, p.424. Middlebrook gives Christie's rank as Gunner but another member of 2 Battery refers to him being a Lance-Bombardier; *see* **The Pegasus Archive** website, Battle of Arnhem Archive, Biographies Section 'Lance-Bombardier Percy Parkes' at www.pegasusarchive.org/arnhem/percy_parkes.htm, accessed 04/06/2018

72. *See* **The Pegasus Archive** website, Battle of Arnhem Archive, Biographies Section 'Lance-Bombardier Percy Parkes' at www.pegasusarchive.org/arnhem/percy_parkes.htm; 'Lieutenant Adrian Donaldson' at www.pegasusarchive.org/arnhem/adrian_donaldson.htm; and 'Lance-Bombardier James Henderson Dickson' at www.pegasusarchive.org/arnhem/james_dickson.htm, both accessed 04/06/2018

73. *See* **WO 171/1016** 1st Airlanding Light Regiment RA War Diary, entry for 10:00, 25/09/1944

74. Quoted from **WO 171/1244** 11th Parachute Battalion War Diary, entry for 25/09/1944

75. Quoted from **WO 171/1375** 2nd Battalion South Staffordshire Regiment War Diary, Appendix J1 '2nd South Staffords at Arnhem 17-25 Sept 1944'

76. *See* **WO 171/1059** 64 Medium Regiment RA War Diary, entries for 13:135 and 15:56, 25/09/1944; and Baynes, **Urquhart of Arnhem**, p.147

77. For timings and quotes *see* **WO 171/1059** 64 Medium Regiment RA War Diary, entries for 13:35, 13:45, 14:50, 15:25, 15:40, 15:56, 16:55, 17:11, 17:34, 18:35 and 19:30, 25/09/1944

78. Quoted from **WO 171/1238** 3 Parachute Battalion War Diary, composite entry for 22/09/1944 to 25/09/1944

79. Quoted from **WO 171/1236** 1Parachute Battalion War Diary, entry for 25/09/1944

80. Quoted from **WO 171/1375** 2nd Battalion South Staffordshire Regiment War Diary, Appendix J1 '2nd South Staffords at Arnhem 17-25 Sept 1944'

81. *See* **WO 171/1375** 2nd Battalion South Staffordshire Regiment War Diary, Appendix J1 '2nd South Staffords at Arnhem 17-25 Sept 1944'; and Middlebrook, pp.425-426. Major John Mellor

Simonds has no known grave and is commemorated on the Groesbeek Memorial, Gelderland, Holland, Panel 5

82. For a list of German units that fought at Oosterbeek and in some instances their date of arrival *see* the **Defending Arnhem** website, 'Order of Battle' page at www.defendingarnhem.com/OoB. html, accessed 07/06/2018

83. *See* **WO 171/589 & 590** 1st Airlanding Brigade HQ War Diary, composite entry for 23 and 24/09/1944

84. *See* **CAB 44/254** Part II: Operation MARKET GARDEN, Book III, Chapter VII, 'Section V – Operations on the Island 21 to 26 Sep', Para. 56 '30 Corps plan – 25 Sep'

85. *See* **CAB 44/254** Part II: Operation MARKET GARDEN, Book III, Chapter VII, 'Section V – Operations on the Island 21 to 26 Sep', Para. 57 'Narrative 25 September'

86. *See* Essame, pp.135-136

87. *See* **CAB 44/254** Part II: Operation MARKET GARDEN, Book III, Chapter VII, 'Section V – Operations on the Island 21 to 26 Sep', Para. 57 'Narrative 25 September'

88. *See* Essame, p.136

89. *See* Sikorski Institute **AV 20/31/27** 1st Polish Independent Parachute Brigade War Diary, entries for 04:00 & 05:00, 25/09/1944; and Cholewczynski, **Poles Apart**, p.243

90. *See* Sikorski Institute **AV 20/31/27** 1st Polish Independent Parachute Brigade War Diary, entries for 12:00, 17:30, 18:00 and 19:00, 25/09/1944; for Sosabowski's shock *see* Cholewczynski, **Poles Apart**, p.249

91. *See* Cholewczynski, **Poles Apart**, pp.254-255; for heavy casualties quote *see* Sikorski Institute **AV 20/31/27** 1st Polish Independent Parachute Brigade War Diary, entry for 19:00, 25/09/1944

92. *See* **WO 171/1286** 4th Battalion The Dorsetshire Regiment War Diary, various entries, 25/09/1944

93. *See* **CAB 44/254** Part II: Operation MARKET GARDEN, Book III, Chapter VII, 'Section V – Operations on the Island 21 to 26 Sep', Para. 57 'Narrative 25 September'; and Essame, p.136. For 43 Reconnaissance Regiment involvement *see* John Sliz, **The Storm Boat Kings**, p.74

94. *See* **CAB 44/254** Part II: Operation MARKET GARDEN, Book III, Chapter VII, 'Section V – Operations on the Island 21 to 26 Sep', Para. 57 'Narrative 25 September'; and Essame, p.136

95. Quoted from Essame, p.136

96. For 1,000 vehicle figure *see* **WO 171/393** 1 Airborne Division HQ War Diary, Appendix: 'Report on Operation "Market": Part II – The Administrative Aspects of the Operation: Seaborne Tail', Para. 218

97. For transit area location grid reference *see* **WO 177/359** ADMS 1 Airborne Division War Diary, entry for 16:00, 25/09/1944

98. *See* **WO 171/394** 1 Airborne Division HQ Seaborne Element War Diary, entry for 09:00, 25/09/1944

99. *See* **WO 171/394** 1 Airborne Division HQ Seaborne Element War Diary, entry for 15:00, 25/09/1944; and **WO 171/590** 1st Airlanding Brigade HQ Seaborne Element War Diary, entry for 25/09/1944; the Airlanding Brigade Diary has the evacuation taking place on 26 and 27 September, rather than 25 and 26 September

100. *See* **WO 177/359** ADMS 1 Airborne Division War Diary, entry for 16:00, 25/09/1944

101. *See* **WO 171/394** 1 Airborne Division HQ Seaborne Element War Diary, entries for 15:00 & 22:00, 25/09/1944

102. For a detailed map of the crossing sites *see* fig. 'Operation Berlin' in Sliz, pp.58-59

103. *See* **WO 179/3129** 20th Field Company RCE War Diary, entry for 12:00, 25/09/1944; and **WO171/1586** 204 Field Company RE War Diary, entry for 06:00, 25/09/1944

104. *See* **CAB 44/254** Part II: Operation MARKET GARDEN, Book III, Chapter VII, 'Section V – Operations on the Island 21 to 26 Sep', Para. 58 'The Evacuation – night 25/26 September'; Essame, p.136; and Sliz, pp.55, 61, 75-80; the citation on p.61 is referenced to the 43rd Division War Diary

105. Quoted from Mark Henniker, **An Image of War**, p.189

106. *See* ibid., pp.189-190

107. For storm boat details *see* Sliz, pp.13, 32-35; for cutaway diagrams of vessel and Evinrude outboard motor *see* ibid., figs 'Storm Boat Mk.1' and 'Evinrude Model #8008', pp.36-37

108. *See* Essame, p.136

109. *See* **CAB 44/254** Part II: Operation MARKET GARDEN, Book III, Chapter VII, 'Section V – Operations on the Island 21 to 26 Sep', Para. 58 'The Evacuation – night 25/26 September'; Sliz, pp.62, 65; and **WO 171/1608** 260 Field Company RE War Diary, entry for 25/09/1944

110. *See* for example Sliz, p.62; for Henniker's own explanation and a brief account of his service in the 1st Airborne Division under Urquhart *see* Henniker, pp.162-166

111. Quoted from Sliz, **The Storm Boat Kings**, p.57; for the 551st General Transport Company RASC *see* ibid., pp.41, 84

112. *See* **WO 179/3130** 23rd Field Company RCE War Diary, Appendix 'Report on the Evacuation of Survivors of 1st Airborne Tps from their bridgehead at Arnhem and the River Neder Rijn at Arnhem'; for the trades breakdown of the 10th Field Park Company RCE maintenance party *see* Sliz, p.63. Sliz also refers to the maintenance party travelling with the 20th Field Company, but the 23rd Field Company War Diary clearly states that it moved up to Valburg with the 23rd Company's column and was reassigned there

113. *See* **WO 179/3130** 23rd Field Company RCE War Diary, Appendix: 'Report on the Evacuation of Survivors of 1st Airborne Tps from their bridgehead at Arnhem and the River Neder Rijn at Arnhem'

114. *See* **WO 179/3129** 20th Field Company RCE War Diary, entries for 12:00 & 14:30, 25/09/1944; and ibid., Appendix VI

115. *See* **WO 179/3130** 23rd Field Company RCE War Diary, Appendix: 'Report on the Evacuation of Survivors of 1st Airborne Tps from their bridgehead at Arnhem and the River Neder Rijn at Arnhem'

116. *See* **WO 179/3129** 20th Field Company RCE War Diary, Appendix VI; and **WO 179/3130** 23rd Field Company RCE War Diary, Appendix: 'Report on the Evacuation of Survivors of 1st Airborne Tps from their bridgehead at Arnhem and the River Neder Rijn at Arnhem'

117. *See* **CAB 44/254** Part II: Operation MARKET GARDEN, Book III, Chapter VII, 'Section V – Operations on the Island 21 to 26 Sep', Para. 58 'The Evacuation – night 25/26 September'; and **WO 179/3130** 23rd Field Company RCE War Diary, Appendix: 'Report on the Evacuation of Survivors of 1st Airborne Tps from their bridgehead at Arnhem and the River Neder Rijn at Arnhem'

118. For O Group termination time *see* **WO 179/3130** 23rd Field Company RCE War Diary, Appendix: 'Report on the Evacuation of Survivors of 1st Airborne Tps from their bridgehead at Arnhem and the River Neder Rijn at Arnhem'

Chapter 21

1. For the few moments quiet *see* Baynes, **Urquhart of Arnhem**, p.146; for 08:08 message *see* **WO 171/393** 1st Airborne Division HQ War Diary, entry for 08:08, 25/09/1944; for Phantom message *see* Ryan, **A Bridge Too Far**, p.515. There is no reference to the Phantom message to Browning in the 1st Airborne Division HQ War Diary or in Urquhart's biography, but it does appear to have been noted in the Signals War Diary; *see* **WO 171/398** 1 Airborne Division Signals War Diary, entry for 10:31, 25/09/1944.

2. For the commander's conference summons *see* **WO 171/393** 1st Airborne Division HQ War Diary, entry for 10:30, 25/09/1944; **WO 171/594** 4th Parachute Brigade War Diary, Appendix D, entry for 25/09/1944; and **WO 171/589** 1st Airlanding Brigade HQ War Diary, Appendix 'F', entry for 10:30, 25/09/1944

3. *See* Urquhart, p.167; for details of Gallipoli withdrawal *see* for example Nigel Steel and Peter Hart, **Defeat at Gallipoli**, p.388

4. First quote from Major-General Roy Urquhart, extract from personal recollection notes entitled 'Still More Random Reflections', cited in Baynes, p.147; second quote testimony from Urquhart cited in Ryan, p.516

5. Quoted from **WO 171/396** 1 Airborne Division HQ Royal Artillery War Diary, entry for 25/09/1944

6. Testimony from Major Philip Tower, Brigade Major Royal Artillery, 1st Airborne Division; cited in Middlebrook, **Arnhem 1944**, pp.423-424. Slidex was a paper-based encryption system that used a series of word cards in conjunction with code strips placed vertically and horizontally along the top and edge of the word cards; the latter were placed in a folding case with cursors to create word cells for the encryption/decryption.

7. *See* Urquhart, p.168

8. *See* **WO 171/397** 1 Airborne Division HQ Royal Engineers War Diary, Appendix B, 'Operation "MARKET": Report of Activities 9 Field Company RE', entry for 25/09/1944; and **WO 171/1513** 9th (Airborne) Field Company RE War Diary, entry for 'Approx 11:00', 25/09/1944

9. *See* Urquhart, pp.168-169; and Ryan, p.518

10. Testimony from Colonel Graeme Warrack, Assistant Director Medical Services, 1st Airborne Division; cited in Ryan, pp.517-518

11. Quote from Urquhart, p.169

12. *See* **WO 171/393** 1st Airborne Division HQ War Diary, Appendix 'Report on Operation Market', Part I: General Outline of Operations, Section 9 'Operations from 0001 hrs, 21 Sep to 2000 hrs, 25 Sep', Paras. 185-188

13. Quoted from Urquhart, pp.169-170

14. *See* **WO 171/1513** 9th (Airborne) Field Company RE War Diary, entry for 13:00, 25/09/1944

15. For 13:30 timing *see* **WO 171/589** 1st Airlanding Brigade HQ War Diary, Appendix 'F'; and **WO 166/15077** 1st Battalion The Border Regiment War Diary, Appendix A; for 13:00 *see* **WO 171/1323** 7th Battalion King's Own Scottish Borderers War Diary; for 14:00 *see* **WO 171/1235** 2 Wing Glider Pilot Regiment War Diary; and for 15:00 timing *see* **WO 171/1511** 4th Parachute Squadron RE War Diary, Appendix I

16. *See* **WO 171/1323** 7th Battalion King's Own Scottish Borderers War Diary, entry for 13:00, 25/09/1944; **WO 171/1235** 2 Wing Glider Pilot Regiment War Diary, entry for 14:00, 25/09/1944; **WO 166/15077** 1st Battalion The Border Regiment War Diary, Appendix A, entry for 25/09/1944; and Green, **1st Battalion The Border Regiment**, p.76

17. *See* **WO 171/1511** 4th Parachute Squadron RE War Diary, entry for 14:00, 25/09/1944; ibid., Appendix I, entry for 15:00, 25/09/1944; and Faulkner Brown, **A Sapper at Arnhem**, pp.79-80

18. For BREESE Force role *see* **WO 166/15077** 1st Battalion The Border Regiment War Diary, Appendix A, entry for 25/09/1944; for route marking *see* **WO 171/1513** 9th (Airborne) Field Company RE War Diary, entry for 19:45, 25/09/1944

19. For 7th KOSB withdrawal timing *see* **WO 171/1323** 7th Battalion King's Own Scottish Borderers War Diary, entry for 13:00, 25/09/1944; for loss of contact with D Company 1st Border *see* **WO 166/15077** 1st Battalion The Border Regiment War Diary, Appendix A, entry for 25/09/1944; **WO 171/589** 1st Airlanding Brigade HQ War Diary, Appendix F, entry for 14:30, 25/09/1944; and Green, pp.76-77

20. *See* **WO 171/589** 1st Airlanding Brigade HQ War Diary, Appendix F, entry for 13:30, 25/09/1944; **WO 166/15077** 1st Battalion The Border Regiment War Diary, Appendix A, entry for 25/09/1944; and **WO 171/1235** 2 Wing Glider Pilot Regiment War Diary, entry for 21:00, 25/09/1944

21. *See* **WO 171/1323** 7th Battalion King's Own Scottish Borderers War Diary, entry for 13:00, 25/09/1944

22. *See* **WO 171/594** 4th Parachute Brigade War Diary, Appendix D, entry for 10:30, 25/09/1944; and Faulkner Brown, pp.79-80

23. *See* **WO 171/594** 4th Parachute Brigade War Diary, Appendix D, entry for 25/09/1944

24. **WO 171/1248** 21st Independent Parachute Company War Diary, entry for 16:00, 25/09/1944

25. *See* **WO 171/592** 1st Parachute Brigade War Diary, Appendix 'D': Diary of Events – 3rd Parachute BN, entry for 16:00 in composite entry for 22/09/1944

26. *See* **WO 171/1247** 156 Parachute Battalion War Diary, Appendix C, entries for 13:00 & 14:00, 25/09/1944; for quote *see* testimony from Major Geoffrey Powell, Officer Commanding C Company, 156 Parachute Battalion; cited in Ryan, pp.518-519

27. *See* **WO 171/592** 1ˢᵗ Parachute Brigade War Diary, Appendix 'D': Diary of Events – 3ʳᵈ Parachute BN, entry for 22:30 in composite entry for 22/09/1944

28. *See* **WO 171/1236** 1ˢᵗ Parachute Battalion War Diary, entries for 17.00 & 20:00, 25/09/1944; **WO 171/1244** 11ᵗʰ Parachute Battalion War Diary, entry for18:00, 25/09/1944; **WO 171/406** 1ˢᵗ Airborne Reconnaissance Squadron HQ War Diary, entries for 19:30 & 20:00, 25/09/1944; and **WO 171/406** A Troop 1ˢᵗ Airborne Reconnaissance Squadron War Diary, entry for 16:00, 25/09/1944

29. *See* **WO 171/406** A Troop 1ˢᵗ Airborne Reconnaissance Squadron War Diary, entries for 15:00, 15:30, 16:00, 17:30 & 19:00, 25/09/1944; **WO 171/1247** 156 Parachute Battalion War Diary, Appendix C: '156 Bn Parachute Regiment Arnhem', entry for 14:00, 25/09/1944; and Fairley, **Remember Arnhem**, p.190

30. *See* Cholewczynski, **Poles Apart**, p.255 *see* ibid., p.255

32. Members of the Kremer family recalled Major Ogilvie wearing his kilt and frequently visiting No. 8 Stationsweg; *see* testimony from Sander & Ans Kremer, cited in Middlebrook, pp.368-369. For a photograph of Captain Ogilvie so attired *see* for example Urquhart, plate captioned 'A jeep party about to set off into Arnhem' between pp.96-97

33. *See* Cholewczynski, **Poles Apart**, p.253

34. *See* Baynes, p.148

35. *See* for example Kent, **First In!**, p.128; Victor Miller, **Nothing is Impossible**, p.179; and Middlebrook, p.428; for Celanese panels *see* Cholewczynski, **Poles Apart**, p.257

36. For Downing & Toler recollections *see* Ryan, p.519

37. *See* **WO 171/406** 1ˢᵗ Airborne Reconnaissance Squadron HQ War Diary, entry for 20:30, 25/09/1944

38. *See* **WO 171/1513** 9ᵗʰ (Airborne) Field Company RE War Diary, entry for 19:45, 25/09/1944; and Middlebrook, p.428

39. *See* **WO 171/1232** B Squadron Glider Pilot Regiment War Diary, entry for 25/09/1944; Fuller is rendered Futter in the entry, but no officer of that surname appears to have served with the 1ˢᵗ Airborne Division at Arnhem

40. *See* Miller, p.179-182; and **WO 171/393** 1ˢᵗ Airborne Division HQ War Diary, Appendix 'Report on Operation Market', Part I: General Outline of Operations, Section 9 'Operations from 0001 hrs, 21 Sep to 2000 hrs, 25 Sep.', Para. 187

41. *See* **WO 171/398** 1 Airborne Division Signals War Diary, entries for 19:00 & 20:00, 25/09/1944; for Signalman Cockrill's account *see* Ryan, pp.520-521

42. *See* **WO 171/406** A Troop 1ˢᵗ Airborne Reconnaissance Squadron War Diary, entry for 20:00, 25/09/1944; and Fairley, p.191

43. *See* **WO 171/1247** 156 Parachute Battalion War Diary, Appendix C: '156 Bn Parachute Regiment Arnhem', entry for 20:15, 25/09/1944; and Harry Bankhead, **Salute to the Steadfast**, pp.161-162

44. The 21:15 evacuation timing would appear to be in error, given that the RCE and RE units that carried out the evacuation at the eastern site reported putting first boat into the water at 21:30 and reaching the north bank ten minutes later; *see* **WO 171/1608** 260 Field Company RE War Diary, entry for 25/09/1944; and **WO 179/3130** 23ʳᵈ Field Company RCE War Diary, Appendix: 'Report on the Evacuation of Survivors of 1ˢᵗ Airborne Tps from their bridgehead at Arnhem and the River Neder Rijn at Arnhem'

45. *See* **WO 171/397** HQ Royal Engineers War Diary, entries for 20:30, 20:40 & 21:15, 25/09/1944; for Captain Green details *see* **The Pegasus Archive**, Battle of Arnhem Archive, Biographies Section 'Captain Michael Douglas Green' at www.pegasusarchive.org/arnhem/michael_douglas_green. htm, accessed 05/07/2018.

46. *See* **WO 171/1234**, 1 Wing Glider Pilot Regiment War Diary, entries for 20:30, 21:00, 21:20, 21:35 & 22:05, 25/09/1944

47. *See* **WO 171/406** 1ˢᵗ Airborne Reconnaissance Squadron HQ War Diary, entry for 20:50, 25/09/1944; and Fairley, pp.191-192. Squadron Quartermaster George Ellis Holderness has no known grave and is commemorated on the Groesbeek Memorial, Gelderland, Holland, Panel 1

48. *See* **WO 171/406** D Troop 1st Airborne Reconnaissance Squadron War Diary, entries for 20:00 & 21:30, 25/09/1944 and 02:00, 26/09/1944; and Fairley, pp.190-191
49. *See* **WO 179/3130** 23rd Field Company RCE War Diary, Appendix: 'Report on the Evacuation of Survivors of 1st Airborne Tps from their bridgehead at Arnhem and the River Neder Rijn at Arnhem'; and Sliz, **The Storm Boat Kings**, p.64
50. *See* **WO 179/3129** 20th Field Company RCE War Diary, entry for 18:30, 25/09/1944
51. *See* **WO 179/3130** 23rd Field Company RCE War Diary, Appendix: 'Report on the Evacuation of Survivors of 1st Airborne Tps from their bridgehead at Arnhem and the River Neder Rijn at Arnhem'
52. *See* Sliz, p.65
53. *See* **WO 179/3130** 23rd Field Company RCE War Diary, Appendix: 'Report on the Evacuation of Survivors of 1st Airborne Tps from their bridgehead at Arnhem and the River Neder Rijn at Arnhem'
54. *See* **WO 179/3130** 23rd Field Company RCE War Diary, Appendix: 'Report on the Evacuation of Survivors of 1st Airborne Tps from their bridgehead at Arnhem and the River Neder Rijn at Arnhem'; and Sliz, p.64
55. *See* Sliz, pp.65-67
56. *See* **WO 179/3129** 20th Field Company RCE War Diary, Appendix VI
57. Testimony from Lieutenant W. W. Gemmell, 20th Field Company RCE; cited in Sliz, p.75
58. *See* ibid., p.77; Sapper Thicke's name is rendered Thickie. For Sapper Thicke's Military Medal citation *see* **The Pegasus Archive** website, Battle of Arnhem Archive, Awards Section, 'Sapper Dacker H. Thicke' at www.pegasusarchive.org/arnhem/harry_dacker_thicke.htm, accessed 07/07/2018; the forenames are transposed and use a different spelling in the citation
59. Testimony from Sapper Donald Somerville, 23rd Field Company RCE; cited in Sliz, p.65
60. *See* ibid., p.67
61. Testimony from Lieutenant John Cronyn, 23rd Field Company RCE; cited in ibid., p.67
62. *See* **WO 179/3130** 23rd Field Company RCE War Diary, Appendix: 'Report on the Evacuation of Survivors of 1st Airborne Tps from their bridgehead at Arnhem and the River Neder Rijn at Arnhem'; and Sliz, pp.68-70
63. For storm boat and outboard motor weight and numbers required for unloading *see* Sliz, pp.35, 67
64. Quoted from **WO 179/3130** 23rd Field Company RCE War Diary, Appendix: 'Report on the Evacuation of Survivors of 1st Airborne Tps from their bridgehead at Arnhem and the River Neder Rijn at Arnhem'
65. Testimony from Lieutenant Russell Kennedy, 23rd Field Company RCE; cited in Sliz, p.71
66. Testimony from Sapper Donald Somerville, 23rd Field Company RCE; cited in ibid., p.71
67. *See* ibid., pp.73, 67; for reassignment of the Maintenance Section from the 10th Field Park Company RCE *see* **WO 179/3130** 23rd Field Company RCE War Diary, Appendix: 'Report on the Evacuation of Survivors of 1st Airborne Tps from their bridgehead at Arnhem and the River Neder Rijn at Arnhem'
68. *See* **WO 179/3130** 23rd Field Company RCE War Diary, Appendix: 'Report on the Evacuation of Survivors of 1st Airborne Tps from their bridgehead at Arnhem and the River Neder Rijn at Arnhem'; and **WO 171/1608** 260 Field Company RE War Diary, entry for 25/09/1944
69. For 21:00 timing *see* for example **CAB 44/254** Part II: Operation MARKET GARDEN, Book III, Chapter VII, 'Section V – Operations on the Island 21 to 26 Sep', Para. 58 'The Evacuation – night 25/26 September'; **WO 179/3129** 20th Field Company RCE War Diary, Appendix VI, Para. 3; and **WO 171/1248** 21st Independent Parachute Company War Diary, entry for 18:00, 25/09/1944. For the 20:50 timing *see* **WO 171/406** 1st Airborne Reconnaissance Squadron HQ War Diary, entry for 20:50, 25/09/1944; and Middlebrook, p.427. For 21:15 timing *see* **WO 171/1248** 21st Independent Parachute Company War Diary, entry for 18:00, 25/09/1944. Interestingly there are very few references to commencement of the covering artillery fire plan or the bombardment itself in the 1st Airborne Division unit War Diaries

70. *See* **CAB 44/254** Part II: Operation MARKET GARDEN, Book III, Chapter VII, 'Section V – Operations on the Island 21 to 26 Sep', Para. 56 '30 Corps Plan 25 Sep'

71. *See* **WO 171/1066** 84 Medium Regiment RA War Diary, entry for 21:00, 25/09/1944; and **WO 171/1059** 64 Medium Regiment RA War Diary, entries for 21:00, 21:04, 21:10, 21:25, 21:40, 22:10, 22:22 & 22:58, 25/09/1944

72. Quoted from Middlebrook, p.431

73. *See* Miller, p.182

74. *See* Kent, **First In!**, p.129; also cited in Ryan, p.520

74. Quoted from **WO 171/1248** 21st Independent Parachute Company War Diary, entry for 18:00, 25/09/1944

76. *See* Kent, p.129

77. *See* **WO 171/1248** 21st Independent Parachute Company War Diary, entries for 19:25 & 22:00, 25/09/1944; and Kent, pp.129-130

78. *See* Kent, p.130; Private Kenneth Roberts is interred in Jonkerbos War Cemetery, Gelderland, Holland in Plot 15, Row B, Grave 3

79. *See* **WO 171/1248** 21st Independent Parachute Company War Diary, entry for 22:00, 25/09/1944; and Kent, p.130. According to the latter Lieutenant Horsley was killed outright but the CWGC records give his date of death as 27/09/1944; Lieutenant John Horsley is interred in Arnhem Oosterbeek War Cemetery, Gelderland, Holland in Plot 18, Row C, Grave 6

80. *See* **WO 171/1323** 7th Battalion King's Own Scottish Borderers War Diary, entries for 13:00 to 21:15 & 21:15, 25/09/1944

81. Quoted from **WO 171/1323** 7th Battalion King's Own Scottish Borderers War Diary, entry 21:15, 25/09/1944; *see* also **WO 171/589** 1st Airlanding Brigade HQ War Diary, Appendix F, entry for 23:00, 25/09/1944

82. For HQ move off time *see* **WO 171/589** 1st Airlanding Brigade HQ War Diary, Appendix F, entry for 23:00, 25/09/1944

83. *See* **WO 171/1323** 7th Battalion King's Own Scottish Borderers War Diary, entries for 21:15 and 22:15 to 02:00, 25/09/1944

84. *See* **WO 171/1511** 4th Parachute Squadron RE War Diary, entries for 21:15 & 21:20, 25/09/1944; and **WO 171/1513** 9th (Airborne) Field Company RE War Diary, entry for 21:15, 25/09/194

85. *See* **WO 171/1511** 4th Parachute Squadron RE War Diary, entries for 22:15 and 22:30, 25/09/1944

86. *See* **WO 171/1513** 9th (Airborne) Field Company RE War Diary, entries for 21:27 and 22:30, 25/09/1944

87. *See* **WO 171/1609** 261 (Airborne) Field Park Company RE War Diary, Appendix H, entry for 25/09/1944. Sapper Lennox Tod Anderson is interred in Amerongen (Holleweg) General Cemetery, Utrecht, Holland, Grave 7. Sapper Clarke is listed by the CWGC as belonging to the 9th (Airborne) Field Company RE but the name Clarke does not appear in that unit's casualty roll, although a Sapper Clarke is listed and noted as failing to reach the 261 Field Park Company RV on the south bank of the Lower Rhine whilst attached to the 9th Field Company; *see* **WO 171/1609** 261 (Airborne) Field Park Company RE War Diary, Appendix H, Para. '17 Sep Transit Camps UK' and entry for 25/09/1944; and **WO 171/1513** 9th (Airborne) Field Company RE War Diary, 'Appendix "B": List of Casualties on Operation "Market"'. Sapper Kenneth Clarke is interred in Arnhem Oosterbeek War Cemetery, Gelderland, Holland in Plot 18, Row B, Grave 15

88. *See* **WO 166/15077** 1st Battalion The Border Regiment War Diary, Appendix A, entry for 25/09/1944; and Green, pp.78-79

89. Quoted from **WO 171/589** 1st Airlanding Brigade HQ War Diary, entry for 23:00, 25/09/1944; *see* also ibid., Appendix F, entry for 23:00, 25/09/1944

90. *See* Green, pp.79-80

91. *See* **WO 166/15077** 1st Battalion The Border Regiment War Diary, Appendix A, entry for 25/09/1944; and Green, p.80

92. *See* Cholewczynski, **Poles Apart**, pp.260-261

93. *See* **WO 171/589** 1st Airlanding Brigade HQ War Diary, entry for 23:00, 25/09/1944; and Green, p.80

94. *See* **WO 179/3129** 20th Field Company RCE War Diary, Appendix VI; and Sliz, pp.77-78

95. Quoted from **WO 179/3129** 20th Field Company RCE War Diary, Appendix VI

96. *See* Sliz, p.79-80

97. For Sergeant Petrie's MM citation *see* **The Pegasus Archive** website, Battle of Arnhem Archive, Biographies Section 'Sergeant Frederick John Petrie' at www.pegasusarchive.org/arnhem/frederick_john_petrie.htm, accessed 21/07/2018

98. *See* **WO 179/3129** 20th Field Company RCE War Diary, Appendix VI

99. *See* **WO 179/3129** 20th Field Company RCE War Diary, Appendix VI

100. Quoted from Henniker, **An Image of War**, pp.191-192

101. *See* ibid., p.191

102. *See* ibid., pp.189-190; and Sliz, p.81

103. *See* Ryan, p.522; and Middlebrook, p.430

104. *See* Sliz, p.81

105. *See* Ryan, p.530

106. Quoted from ibid., p.524; *see* also Bankhead, p.162

107. For Sergeant Hilton and Sapper Denmark's Military Medal citations see **The Pegasus Archive** website, Battle of Arnhem Archive, Awards Section, 'Sergeant Fred Lord Hilton' at www.pegasusarchive.org/arnhem/fred_lord_hilton.htm and 'Sapper Arthur Ernest Denmark' at www.pegasusarchive.org/arnhem/arthur_ernest_denmark.htm, accessed 20/07/2018

108. *See* **WO 179/3130** 23rd Field Company RCE War Diary, Appendix: 'Report on the Evacuation of Survivors of 1st Airborne Tps from their bridgehead at Arnhem and the River Neder Rijn at Arnhem'; and Sliz, p.82. Lieutenant James Russell Martin in interred in Holten Canadian War Cemetery, Overijssel, Holland in Plot 11, Row G, Grave 3; Lance-Corporal Daniel W. Ryan is interred in Rhenen General Cemetery, Utrecht, Holland in in Plot 27, Row B, Grave 2; Sapper Harold Magnusson is interred in Gorinchem General Cemetery, Zuid-Holland, Holland in Plot L, Row 7, Grave 3 with a date of death of 14/11/1944; Sapper Leslie Joseph Roherty has no known grave and is commemorated on the Groesbeek Memorial, Gelderland, Holland, Panel 10

109. *See* **WO 179/3130** 23rd Field Company RCE War Diary, Appendix: 'Report on the Evacuation of Survivors of 1st Airborne Tps from their bridgehead at Arnhem and the River Neder Rijn at Arnhem'; and Sliz, **The Storm Boat Kings**, pp.83, 87. Sapper David L. G. Hope interred in Rhenen General Cemetery, Utrecht, Holland in in Plot 27, Row B, Grave 7; Sapper Neil A. Thompson is interred in Groesbeek Canadian War Cemetery, Gelderland, Holland in Plot 29, Row A, Grave 8

110. *See* Sliz, p.83

111. Testimony from Lieutenant-Colonel Henry Preston, Assistant Adjutant and Quartermaster General 1st Airborne Division quoted in Christopher Hibbert, **Arnhem**, p.178; cited in Sliz, p.84

112. Testimony from Lieutenant John Cronyn and Sergeant Sandy Morris, 23rd Field Company RCE; cited in Sliz, pp.83-84

113. *See* Cholewczynski, **Poles Apart**, pp.257-259, 263-265

114. *See* **WO 171/396** 1 Airborne Division HQ Royal Artillery War Diary, entry for 22:00, 25/09/1944

115. *See* **WO 171/393** 1st Airborne Division HQ War Diary, entry for 22:30, 25/09/1944

116. *See* Urquhart, p.174; for Private Hancock becoming Urquhart's batman *see* Baynes, p.31

117. *See* Urquhart, p.172; and Baynes, p.148

118. *See* Urquhart, pp.174-175; for a photograph of Urquhart standing next to the lance and pennant *see* for example Baynes, Plate 18 between pp.82-83

119. *See* Urquhart, pp.174-175

120. *See* Middlebrook, p.430

121. *See* for example Steel & Hart, pp.413-414

122. For Brigadier Hicks *see* Middlebrook, p.430; for Major Lonsdale *see* for example **The Pegasus Archive**, Battle of Arnhem Archive, Biographies Section 'Major Richard Thomas Henry Lonsdale' at www.pegasusarchive.org/arnhem/dickie_lonsdale.htm, accessed 16/07/2018

123. *See* Kershaw, pp.316-320

124. For lack of reverse gear *see* Sliz, p.82

125. Quoted from Urquhart, pp.176-177

126. *See* **WO 171/396** 1 Airborne Division HQ Royal Artillery War Diary, entry for 22:00, 25/09/1944

127. *See* **WO 171/1016** 1st Airlanding Light Regiment RA War Diary, entry for 22:00, 25/09/1944 & 05:00, 26/09/1944; for firing off ammunition and removing breech blocks *see* Ryan, p.526

128. *See* Cholewczynski, **Poles Apart**, pp.256, 259, 262-263

129. *See* **WO 171/1236** 1st Parachute Battalion War Diary, entries for 23:00, 25/09/1944 and 04:00, 26/09/1944

130. *See* **WO 171/1238** 3rd Parachute Battalion War Diary, composite entry for 23:30, 25/09/1944

131. *See* **WO 171/1244** 11th Parachute Battalion War Diary, entry for 23:30, 25/09/1944 and 26/09/1944; and Middlebrook, Appendix 1 'Order of Battle and Operational Details, 1st British Airborne Division and Attached Units', entry for 11th Parachute Battalion, p.457

132. Quoted from **WO 171/1375** 2nd Battalion South Staffordshire Regiment War Diary, Appendix J1 '2nd South Staffords at Arnhem 17-25 Sept 1944'

133. *See* **WO 171/1375** 2 South Staffordshire Regiment War Diary, Appendix J1 '2nd South Staffords at Arnhem 17-25 Sept 1944'; and Haines, **The Holland Patch**, pp.105-107

134. 139 figure cited in **WO 171/1375** 2nd Battalion South Staffordshire Regiment War Diary, Appendix J1 '2nd South Staffords at Arnhem 17-25 Sept 1944', broken down to six Officers and 133 Other Ranks; 124 figure cited in Middlebrook, Appendix 1 'Order of Battle and Operational Details, 1st British Airborne Division and Attached Units', entry for 2nd South Staffords, p.457

135. *See* **WO 179/3130** 23rd Field Company RCE War Diary, Appendix: 'Report on the Evacuation of Survivors of 1st Airborne Tps from their bridgehead at Arnhem and the River Neder Rijn at Arnhem'

136. Quoted from **WO 179/3130** 23rd Field Company RCE War Diary, Appendix: 'Report on the Evacuation of Survivors of 1st Airborne Tps from their bridgehead at Arnhem and the River Neder Rijn at Arnhem'

137. *See* **WO 179/3130** 23rd Field Company RCE War Diary, Appendix: 'Report on the Evacuation of Survivors of 1st Airborne Tps from their bridgehead at Arnhem and the River Neder Rijn at Arnhem'; for additional discussion of the point *see* Sliz, p.87

138. *See* **WO 177/359** Assistant Director Medical Services 1 Airborne Division War Diary, entries for 07:00, 12:30 and 16:00, 25/09/1944

139. *See* **WO 177/359** Assistant Director Medical Services 1 Airborne Division War Diary, entries for 23:30, 25/09/1944 and 01:00, 26/09/1944; and **WO 179/3130** 23rd Field Company RCE War Diary, Appendix: 'Report on the Evacuation of Survivors of 1st Airborne Tps from their bridgehead at Arnhem and the River Neder Rijn at Arnhem'

140. *See* Sliz, p.84

141. *See* Essame, **The 43rd Wessex Division at War**, p.137

142. *See* **WO 177/359** Assistant Director Medical Services 1 Airborne Division War Diary, entries for 01:00 & 04:30, 26/09/1944; for details of the Reception Centre *see* **WO 171/394** 1 Airborne Division HQ Seaborne Element War Diary, entries for 09:00 and 15:00, 25/09/1944

143. *See* **WO 177/359** Assistant Director Medical Services 1 Airborne Division War Diary, entry for 05:00, 26/09/1944; and Essame, p.137

144. Testimony from Lance-Sergeant George King, 23rd Field Company RCE; cited in Sliz, p.89

145. *See* **WO 179/3130** 23rd Field Company RCE War Diary, entry for 26/09/1944; and Sliz, **The Storm Boat Kings**, p.94 and Appendix 4: The Casualties, p.118. Sapper Ronald Tracy McKee is interred in Arnhem Oosterbeek War Cemetery, Gelderland, Holland in Plot 9, Row C, Grave 1

146. *See* **WO 166/15077** 1st Battalion The Border Regiment War Diary, Appendix A, entry for 25/09/1944; and Cholewczynski, **Poles Apart**, p.262

147. Testimony from Lieutenant-Colonel Henry Preston, Assistant Adjutant and Quartermaster General 1st Airborne Division, quoted in Hibbert, p.178; cited in Sliz, p.84

148. Quoted from Fairley, p.194

149. Quotes from **WO 171/1608** 260 Field Company RE War Diary, entry for 25/09/1944; and **WO 179/3130** 23rd Field Company RCE War Diary, Appendix: 'Report on the Evacuation of Survivors of 1st Airborne Tps from their bridgehead at Arnhem and the River Neder Rijn at Arnhem'

150. *See* **WO 171/1608** 260 Field Company RE War Diary, entry for 25/09/1944

151. Testimony from Private D. J. Charlton, R Company 1st Parachute Battalion and Lieutenant John Cronyn, 23rd Field Company RCE; cited in Sliz, pp.85-86, 87

152. *See* ibid., pp.87-89

153. *See* ibid., p.89

154. For details *see* ibid., p.35 and figs 'Instruction Plate Detail' & 'Evinrude Model #8008' diagram, p.37

155. *See* ibid., pp.89-90

156. *See* Fairley, p.194

157. Testimony from Private John Crosson, No. 6 Platoon, B Company, 7th KOSB; cited in Sliz, p.92

158. *See* ibid., p.90

159. Testimony from Major Alan Bush, Second-n-Command, 3rd Parachute Battalion; cited in Middlebrook, p.430

160. Testimony from Lieutenant John Stevenson, OC 1 Section, A Troop, 1st Airborne Reconnaissance Squadron; cited in Fairley, p.194

161. For 150 figure and quote *see* **WO 179/3130** 23rd Field Company RCE War Diary, Appendix: 'Report on the Evacuation of Survivors of 1st Airborne Tps from their bridgehead at Arnhem and the River Neder Rijn at Arnhem'

162. *See* Ryan, pp.525-526, 527

163. *See* Fairley, p.195. Captain James Graeme Ogilvy's body was recovered from the Lower Rhine by Dutch Resistance members the following day fifteen miles downstream near Rhenen; he is interred in Rhenen General Cemetery, Utrecht, Holland in in Plot 27, Row C, Grave 12

164. *See* **WO 179/3130** 23rd Field Company RCE War Diary, Appendix: 'Report on the Evacuation of Survivors of 1st Airborne Tps from their bridgehead at Arnhem and the River Neder Rijn at Arnhem'; and Sliz, p.94

165. *See* **WO 179/3130** 23rd Field Company RCE War Diary, Appendix: 'Report on the Evacuation of Survivors of 1st Airborne Tps from their bridgehead at Arnhem and the River Neder Rijn at Arnhem'; and Sliz, p.92; for Sapper LeBouthillier's Military Medal citation at **The Pegasus Archive** website, Battle of Arnhem Archive, Awards Section, 'Sapper Raymond LeBouthillier ' at www.pegasusarchive.org/arnhem/raymond_lebouthillier.htm, accessed 20/07/2018

166. *See* **WO 179/3130** 23rd Field Company RCE War Diary, Appendix: 'Report on the Evacuation of Survivors of 1st Airborne Tps from their bridgehead at Arnhem and the River Neder Rijn at Arnhem'; Ellis, **Victory in the West, Volume II: The Defeat of Germany**, p.55; and Middlebrook, p.435

167. *See* **WO 171/394** 1 Airborne Division HQ Seaborne Element War Diary, entry for 06:00, 26/09/1944

168. *See* Urquhart, pp.181-182; Brammall, p.97; Fairley, p.198; and Middlebrook, p.435

169. *See* Middlebrook, p.435. Interestingly there is no mention of the prisoner in the 21st Independent Company War Diary of semi-official account

170. Quoted from **WO 171/1323** 7th Battalion King's Own Scottish Borderers War Diary, entry for 02:00 to 06:00, 26/09/1944

171. *See* Fairley, pp.195-196

172. *See* **WO 177/359** ADMS 1 Airborne Division War Diary, entry for 22:30, 25/09/1944

173. *See* **WO 171/406**, 1st Airborne Reconnaissance Squadron War Diary, appended account in entry for 25/09/1944

174. *See* **WO 166/15077** 1 Border Regiment War Diary, Appendix 'A', entry for 26/09/1944; and WO **171/1375** 2 South Staffordshire Regiment War Diary, entry for 26/09/1944; and ibid., Appendix J1 '2ⁿᵈ South Staffords at Arnhem 17-25 Sept 1944'

175. Testimony from Trooper Stanley Collishaw, HQ Troop, 1ˢᵗ Airborne Reconnaissance Squadron; cited in Fairley, p.195

176. *See* **CAB 44/254** Part II: Operation MARKET GARDEN, Book III, Chapter VII, 'Section V – Operations on the Island 21 to 26 Sep', Para. 58 'The Evacuation – night 25/26 September'; and Essame, p.137

177. Quotes from **WO 171/1236** 1 Parachute Battalion War Diary, entry for 04:00, 26/09/1944; and **WO 171/1323** 7ᵗʰ Battalion King's Own Scottish Borderers War Diary, entry for 02:00 to 06:00, 26/09/1944

178. *See* Faulkner-Brown, pp.84-85

179. *See* **WO 177/359** ADMS 1 Airborne Division War Diary, entry for 05:00, 26/09/1944; for Stevenson quote *see* Fairley, p.196

180. *See* **WO 171/1236** 1 Parachute Battalion War Diary, entry for 04:00, 26/09/1944; **WO 171/1234** 1 Wing Glider Pilot Regiment War Diary, entry for 01:30, 26/09/1944; **WO 166/15077** 1 Border Regiment War Diary, Appendix "A", entry for 26/09/1944; **WO 171/1323** 7ᵗʰ Battalion King's Own Scottish Borderers War Diary, entry for 02:00 to 06:00, 26/09/1944; and **WO 171/1375** 2ⁿᵈ Battalion South Staffordshire Regiment War Diary, Appendix J1 '2ⁿᵈ South Staffords at Arnhem 17-25 Sept 1944'

181. *See* Ryan, p.532

182. *See* Fairley, p.195

183. *See* **WO 177/359** ADMS 1 Airborne Division War Diary, entry for 08:30, 26/09/1944

184. *See* **WO 171/394** 1 Airborne Division Seaborne Element War Diary, entry for 23:30, 25/09/1944; and **WO 171/590** 1 Airlanding Brigade HQ Seaborne Element War Diary, entry for 26/09/1944

185. Quoted from **WO 171/1323** 7ᵗʰ Battalion King's Own Scottish Borderers War Diary, entry for 02:00 to 06:00, 26/09/1944

186. *See* Kent, p.131

187. *See* Ryan, p.530; and HMSO, **By Air to Battle**, p.130

188. *See* **WO 171/394** 1 Airborne Division Seaborne Element War Diary, entry for 06:00, 26/09/1944

189. *See* **WO 171/590** 1 Airlanding Brigade HQ Seaborne Element War Diary, entry for 26/09/1944

190. *See* Arnhem, p.178; and Henniker, p.192

191. *See* Urquhart, p.179

192. *See* **WO 171/393** 1 Airborne Division HQ War Diary, entry for 14:30, 26/09/1944; and ibid. Appendix 'Report on Operation Market', Part I: General Outline of Operations, Section 10 'The Return from Nijmegen to UK', Para. 198; for dinner party *see* Urquhart, p.184

193. *See* Urquhart, p.183

194. Quoted from ibid., p.179

195. *See* ibid., pp.179-180

196. *See* Baynes, p.151

197. *See* Urquhart, p.180

198. *See* Sliz, p.96

199. *See* **CAB 44/254** Part II: Operation MARKET GARDEN, Book III, Chapter VII, 'Section V – Operations on the Island 21 to 26 Sep', Para. 58 'The Evacuation – night 25/26 September'; and Henniker, p.192

200. For 04:00 timing *see* **WO 179/3129** 20ᵗʰ Field Company RCE War Diary, Appendix VI

201. *See* Henniker, p.192

202. *See* ibid., p.192

203. *See* **WO 179/3129** 20ᵗʰ Field Company RCE War Diary, Appendix VI; **WO 179/3130** 23ʳᵈ Field Company RCE War Diary, Appendix: 'Report on the Evacuation of Survivors of 1ˢᵗ Airborne Tps from their bridgehead at Arnhem and the River Neder Rijn at Arnhem'; and **WO 171/1608** 260 Field Company RE War Diary, entry for 25/09/1944

204. *See* Sliz, p.95

205. Testimony from 2nd Lieutenant Szczesny Relidzinski, Brigade HQ Section, Signals Company, 1st Polish Independent Parachute Brigade; cited in ibid., pp.95-96. For Major Vinycomb's presence *see* Essame, p.138; and Henniker, p.192

206. *See* Sliz, p.96

207. *See* ibid., p.96

208. Testimony from Private John Ranger, 20 Platoon, D Company, 1st Battalion The Border Regiment; cited in ibid., p.97

209. *See* ibid., p.98

210. Testimony from Lieutenant Russell Kennedy, 23rd Field Company RCE; cited in ibid., p.98

211. For the Lieutenant Kennedy's Military Cross and Sapper McCready's Military Medal citations *see* **The Pegasus Archive** website, Battle of Arnhem Archive, Biographies Section 'Lieutenant Russell Jordan Kennedy' at www.pegasusarchive.org/arnhem/russell_jordan_kennedy.htm; and 'Sapper David John McCready' at www.pegasusarchive.org/arnhem/david_john_mccready. htm, accessed 25/07/2018

Chapter 22

1. *See* **WO 171/393** 1st Airborne Division HQ War Diary, Appendix 'Report on Operation Market', Part I: General Outline of Operations, Section 10 'The Withdrawal to Nijmegen', Para. 195; **WO 171/1608** 260 Field Company RE War Diary, entry for 25/09/1944; and testimony from Private John Ranger, 20 Platoon, D Company, 1st Battalion The Border Regiment; cited in Sliz, **The Storm Boat Kings**, p.97

2. Quoted from Henniker, **An Image of War**, p.19

3. *See* Kershaw, **It Never Snows in September**, p.299; for clashes *see* for example **WO 171/1236** 1 Parachute Battalion War Diary, entry for 23:00, 25/09/1944; and **WO 171/1248** 21st Independent Parachute Company War Diary, entry for 22:00, 25/09/1944

4. Quoted from Kershaw, p.299

5. *See* ibid., pp.299-301

6. Testimony from *Hauptsturmführer* Hans Möller, commander *SS Panzer Pionier Abteilung 9*; cited in ibid., p.301

7. Quoted from ibid., p.301

8. *See* Urquhart, **Arnhem**, pp.180-181

9. *See* Middlebrook, **Arnhem 1944**, p.432

10. *See* Ryan, **A Bridge Too Far**, p.534

11. *See* Green, 1st **Battalion The Border Regiment**, p.85

12. *See* Middlebrook, pp.433-434

13. For 170 figure *see* Kershaw, p.299; Krafft quote from **AIR 20/2333** 'Battle of Arnheim: German account, Sept. to Oct. 1944; cited in Middlebrook, p.435

14. *See* Cholewczynski, **Poles Apart**, pp.261, 264, 267-268

15. *See* Green, pp.84-85

16. For details *see* for example Waddy, **A Tour of the Arnhem Battlefields**, p.181; and **The Pegasus Archive**, Battle of Arnhem Archive, Biographies Section 'Brigadier Gerald William Lathbury' at www.pegasusarchive.org/arnhem/gerald_lathbury.htm, accessed 27/07/2018; and ibid., 'Brigadier John Winthrop Hackett' at www.pegasusarchive.org/arnhem/john_hackett. htm, accessed 27/07/2018 .

17. For details and Lieutenant-Colonel Herford's DSO citation *see* **The Pegasus Archive**, Battle of Arnhem Archive, Biographies Section 'Lieutenant-Colonel Martin Edward Meakin Herford MBE, DSO, MC & Bar' at www.pegasusarchive.org/arnhem/martin_herford.htm, accessed 27/07/2018

18. For details and Colonel Warrack's Distinguished Service Order Citation *see* **The Pegasus Archive**, Battle of Arnhem Archive, Biographies Section 'Colonel Graeme Matthew Warrack' at www.pegasusarchive.org/arnhem/graeme_warrack.htm, accessed 27/07/2018

19. *See* Middlebrook, p.437; and **The Pegasus Archive**, Battle of Arnhem Archive, Biographies Section 'Major J. Anthony Cotterell' at www.pegasusarchive.org/arnhem/anthony_cotterell.htm, accessed 28/07/2018. Major John Anthony Cotterell is interred in Enschede Eastern General Cemetery, Overijssel, Netherlands in Joint Grave 200-201

20. *See* Middlebrook, pp.436-437. Captain John Howard Keesey is interred in Becklingen War Cemetery, Niedersachsen, Germany in Plot 8, Row C, Grave 1

21. *See* Middlebrook, p.437; and **The Pegasus Archive**, Battle of Arnhem Archive, Biographies Section 'Lieutenant H. Michael A. Cambier' at www.pegasusarchive.org/arnhem/michael_cambier.htm, accessed 28/07/2018. Lieutenant Raymond Meyrick Bussell and Lieutenant Harry Michael Ashbrooke Cambier are interred in Vorden General Cemetery, Gelderland, Netherlands in Graves 16 & 17 respectively

22. *See* **WO 171/1234**, 1 Wing Glider Pilot Regiment War Diary, entries for 10:00, 14:25, 15:05, 16:10 & 19:11, 27/09/1944

23. *See* **WO 171/1248** 21st Independent Parachute Company War Diary, entry for 15:00, 28/09/1944

24. *See* **AIR 27/1433** No. 233 Squadron Operations Record Book, entries for 29/09/1944; and **AIR 27/1876** No. 437 Squadron RCAF Operations Record Book, entries for 29/09/1944.

25. The USAAF units cited were based at Barkston Heath and Saltby; for reference to being lifted by US aircraft *see* **WO 171/1248** 21st Independent Parachute Company War Diary, entry for 15:00, 28/09/1944

26. *See* **WO 171/393** 1st Airborne Division HQ War Diary, entries for 17:00 & 19:00, 29/09/1944; and **WO 171/396** 1 Airborne Division HQ Royal Artillery War Diary, entries for 11:00, 15:30 & 18:00, 29/09/1944

27. *See* **WO 171/406** 1st Airborne Reconnaissance Squadron War Diary, entry for 29/09/1944; **WO 171/1016** 1st Airlanding Light Regiment RA War Diary, entry for 13:00, 29/09/1944; and **WO 171/1513** 9th Airborne Field Company RE War Diary, entries for 14:30, 'Approx' 15:45 & 'Approx' 18:30

28. *See* **WO 171/1375** 2nd South Staffordshire Regiment War Diary, entry for 29/09/1944; and **AIR 27/1433** No. 233 Squadron Operations Record Book, entries for 29/09/1944

29. *See* **WO 171/1236** 1st Parachute Battalion War Diary, entries for 10:00 & 12:15, 30/09/1944

30. *See* **WO 171/590** 1st Airlanding Brigade HQ Seaborne Element War Diary, entry for 28 to 29/09/1944; and ibid., Appendix '2nd Seaborne Element', entries for 22/09/1944, 23/09/1944 & 23 to 30/09/1944

31. For a full breakdown of vehicle types & numbers by unit *see* **WO 171/393** 1st Airborne Division HQ War Diary, 'Appendix "G" to Part II: Seaborne Transport'

32. *See* **WO 171/394** 1 Airborne Division HQ Seaborne Element War Diary, entry for 29 and 30/09/1944

33. *See* **WO 171/394** 1 Airborne Division HQ Seaborne Element War Diary, entries for 09:00, 03 /10/1944, 04/10/1944, 5,6 and 7/10/1944 and 08/10/1944

34. Figure cited in HMSO, **By Air to Battle**, p.98 which matches Middlebrook; *see* Middlebrook, Table 1, p.439. For despatch of Division seaborne tail six weeks in advance of Operation MARKET *see* **WO 171/393** 1 Airborne Division HQ War Diary, Appendix: 'Report on Operation "Market": Part II – The Administrative Aspects of the Operation: Seaborne Tail', Para. 218

35. For 1,338 Glider Pilot figure *see* **WO 171/1230** HQ Cmd. Glider Pilots War Diary, Appendix 'OPERATION "MARKET" GROUND', Section headed 'CASUALTIES'; for Polish Brigade total of 1,625 *see* Sikorski Institute **AV 20/31/27** 1st Polish Independent Parachute Brigade War Diary, entry for 09:00, 26/09/1944 . The Glider Pilot HQ War Diary figure is higher than that cited in **By Air to Battle** (1,126) and Middlebrook (1,262), while the Polish War Diary figure is lower than that cited by Middlebrook (1,689); using the figures from the latter two sources the overall figures are 11,784 or 11,920. *See* HMSO, **By Air to Battle**, p.98; and Middlebrook, Table 1, p.439. As the precise source of the figures cited in the secondary works is unclear, the primary source figures are given preference.

36. 1,485 figure cited in Middlebrook, Table 1, p.439; for 1,543 figure *see* John A. Hey, **Roll of Honour Battle of Arnhem, September 1944**; cited in Reynolds, **Sons of the Reich**, p.173. The

6,525 overall figure is cited in Hey and Middlebrook while the HMSO official account refers to a total of 7,605 killed, wounded and missing; the higher total may reflect early accounting before the number of prisoners and evaders became clear; *see* HMSO, **By Air to Battle**, p.130

37. 219 and 229 figures cited in Middlebrook, Table 1, p.439 and Reynolds, p.173 respectively; 730 figure quoted from **WO 171/1230** HQ Cmd. Glider Pilots War Diary, Appendix 'OPERATION "MARKET" GROUND', Section headed 'CASUALTIES'. Polish killed figure of ninety-two cited in Middlebrook, Table 1, ninety-seven from Reynolds, p.173; overall Polish casualty figure of 342 quoted from Sikorski Institute **AV 20/31/27** 1st Polish Independent Parachute Brigade War Diary, entry for 09:00, 26/09/1944

38. Figure cited in Reynolds, p.173

39. Figures cited in Cooper, **The Air Battle for Arnhem**, Table 'RAF Losses at Arnhem', pp.158-159

40. Figures quoted from Middlebrook, Appendix 4: Order of Battle, US Air Units Carrying British and Polish Parachute Troops on Operation 'Market', p.464

41. *See* Kershaw, pp.339-340; and Ryan, p.539

42. *See* Powell, **The Devil's Birthday**, p.229

43. Cited in Ryan, p.537

44. Figures quoted from MacDonald, **The Siegfried Line Campaign**, p.199

45. For details Henniker, **An Image of War**, pp.195-201

46. *See* Kershaw, pp.316-320

47. 200 figure cited in Powell, p.226; for 300 estimate *see* Middlebrook, **Arnhem 1944**, p.439; the British Official Airborne history cites a figure of between 300-400; *see* Otway, **Airborne Forces**, p.283

48. *See* for example **The Pegasus Archive**, Battle of Arnhem Archive, Biographies Section 'Lieutenant-Colonel David Theodore Dobie' at www.pegasusarchive.org/arnhem/david_dobie. htm, accessed 12/08/2018.

49. For details of Lieutenant-Colonel Dobie's activities in this regard *see* **The Pegasus Archive**, Battle of Arnhem Archive, Reports Section 'Evasion Report: 21st September – 23rd October by Major A. D. Tatham-Warter, 2nd Parachute Bn., Annexure 1 to Appendix 'F', "Report on Operation to Liberate Personnel from Northern Holland by Lt. Col. D. T. Dobie DSO'" at www. pegasusarchive.org/arnhem/RepPegasus.htm, accessed 12/08/2018

50. A Belgian SAS team was parachuted into the area north-west of Arnhem to gather information on German troop movements around Utrecht two days before Operation MARKET commenced; *see* Powell, p.100; for Belgian SAS involvement in Operation PEGASUS *see* ibid., p.227; and Middlebrook, p.438; for the 506th Parachute Infantry Regiment's arrival on the Lower Rhine *see* Rapport and Northwood, **Rendezvous with Destiny**, p.379

51. for details of the overall scheme *see* **The Pegasus Archive**, Battle of Arnhem Archive, Reports Section 'Evasion Report: 21st September – 23rd October by Major A. D. Tatham-Warter, 2nd Parachute Bn., Annexure 1 to Appendix 'F', "Report on Operation to Liberate Personnel from Northern Holland by Lt. Col. D. T. Dobie DSO", Para. 'Plan' at www.pegasusarchive.org/ arnhem/RepPegasus.htm, accessed 12/08/2018; for the US account *see* Rapport and Northwood, pp.400-401

52. *See* Waddy, p.182

53. for detailed accounts of the execution of the Operation *see* Waddy, pp.181-188; and **The Pegasus Archive**, Battle of Arnhem Archive, Reports Section 'Evasion Report: 21st September – 23rd October by Major A. D. Tatham-Warter, 2nd Parachute Bn., Para. "The Crossing'" at www. pegasusarchive.org/arnhem/RepPegasus.htm, accessed 12/08/2018

54. Ambrose and Truesdale refer to the operation beginning at or shortly after midnight, whereas Rapport & Northwood refer to 01:00; *see* Ambrose, **Band of Brothers**, p.161; Truesdale, **Brotherhood of the Cauldron**, p.161; and Rapport and Northwood, p.400

55. *See* Waddy, p.187

56. The precise number and makeup of the PEGASUS evaders varies between sources; *see* Middlebrook, p.438; Rapport & Northwood, p.401; and Truesdale, p.161

57. *See* HMSO, **By Air to Battle**, pp.131-132; and **The Pegasus Archive**, Battle of Arnhem Archive, Biographies Section 'Major Anthony J. Deane Drummond' at www.pegasusarchive.org/arnhem/deane_drummond.htm, accessed 12/08/2018.

58. Major John Secheverell A'Deane Coke is interred in Arnhem Oosterbeek War Cemetery, Gelderland, Holland in Plot 23, Row B, Grave 17

59. *See* Waddy, pp.188-189; Powell, p.228; and Middlebrook, p.438

60. *See* Urquhart, pp.195-196

61. *See* Sikorski Institute **AV 20/31/27** 1st Polish Independent Parachute Brigade War Diary, entry for 12:00, 25/09/1944

62. *See* Sikorski Institute **AV 20/31/27** 1st Polish Independent Parachute Brigade War Diary, entry for 09:00, 26/09/1944; and Cholewczynski, **Poles Apart**, pp.272-273

63. *See* Cholewczynski, **Poles Apart**, p.273

64. *See* ibid., pp.280-281; and Sosabowski, **Freely I Served**, pp.190-191

65. Sosabowski's letter and Browning's reply are reproduced in Sosabowski, p.189

66. *See* ibid., p.190

67. *See* Richard Lamb, **Montgomery in Europe**, p.251; cited in Cholewczynski, **Poles Apart**, p.286

68. The report is reproduced in full in ibid., pp.312-313

69. *See* ibid., pp.285-287

70. Quoted from ibid., footnote, p.286

71. For details *see* William F. Buckingham, **Arnhem 1944: A Reappraisal**, pp.43-48; for a more detailed analysis of the Polish input into the development of British Airborne Forces *see* Id. **Paras: The Birth of British Airborne Forces**, pp.179-193

72. Quoted from Middlebrook, p.448

73. Quoted from Alanbrooke Papers 14/36; cited in Powell, p.183

74. The present author originally considered the distance between the landing area and objectives to be a salient factor in the failure of the Arnhem portion of Operation MARKET but modified his view as a result of further research

Bibliography

UK National Archives Files

AIR 5/1253 Operations: Iraq Chapters 1-13

AIR 20/2333 16th SS Panzer Grenadier & Reserve Battalion Report

AIR 27/473 No. 48 Squadron Operations Record Book

AIR 27/1154 No. 190 Squadron Operations Record Book

AIR 27/1167 No. 196 Squadron Operations Record Book

AIR 27/1433 No. 233 Squadron Operations Record Book

AIR 27/1574 No. 271 Squadron Operations Record Book

AIR 27/1654 No. 299 Squadron Operations Record Book

AIR 27/1876 No 437 Squadron RCAF Operations Record Book

AIR 27/1972 No. 512 Squadron Operations Record Book

AIR 27/2041 No. 570 Squadron Operations Record Book

AIR 27/2046 No. 575 Squadron Operations Record Book

AIR 27/2134 No. 620 Squadron Operations Record Book

AIR 37/418 'Report on the British Airborne Effort in Operation MARKET by 38 & 46 Groups RAF'

AIR 37/775 1944: Subsidiary Airborne operations to Further Operation OVERLORD

AIR 37/776 1944: 1st Allied Airborne Army: Formation and Employment

AIR 37/1214 1944: Report on Operation MARKET GARDEN: Allied Airborne Operations in Holland

AIR 37/1249 1944: Operation MARKET GARDEN

AV 20/31/27 Sikorski Institute, 1st Polish Independent Parachute Brigade War Diary

CAB 44/252 The Advance to the Siegfried Line and the Battle for Arnhem, 29 August to 30 September 1944 Part I

CAB 44/252 The Advance to the Siegfried Line and the Battle for Arnhem, 29 August to 30 September 1944 Part II: Operation MARKET GARDEN

WO 166/15077 1 Border Regiment War Diary

WO 171/341 30 Corps HQ War Diary

WO 171/376 Guards Armoured Division HQ War Diary

WO 171/393 1 Airborne Division HQ War Diary

WO 171/394 1 Airborne Division HQ Seaborne Element War Diary

WO 171/396 1Airborne Division HQ Royal Artillery War Diary

WO 171/397 1 Airborne Division HQ Royal Engineers War Diary

WO171/398 1 Airborne Division Signals War Diary

WO 171/400 1 Airborne Division RASC Airborne Element War Diary

WO 171/406 1st Airborne Reconnaissance Squadron War Diary (includes separate Diaries for A, C & D Troops)

WO 171/589 1 Airlanding Brigade HQ War Diary

WO 171/590 1 Airlanding Brigade HQ Seaborne Element War Diary

WO 171/592 1st Parachute Brigade War Diary

WO 171/594 4th Parachute Brigade War Diary

WO 171/605 5 Guards Armoured Brigade War Diary
WO 171/638 32 Guards Brigade War Diary
WO 171/957 1st Airlanding Anti-Tank Battery RA War Diary
WO 171/958 2nd (Oban) Airlanding Anti-Tank Battery RA War Diary
WO 171/1016 1st Airlanding Light Regiment RA War Diary
WO 171/1059 64 Medium Regiment RA War Diary
WO 171/1066 84 Medium Regiment RA War Diary
WO 171/1230 HQ Cmd. Glider Pilots War Diary
WO 171/1231 A, D, G Squadrons Glider Pilot Regiment War Diary
WO 171/1232 B Squadron Glider Pilot Regiment War Diary
WO 171/1234 1Wing Glider Pilot Regiment War Diary
WO 171/1235 2 Wing Glider Pilot Regiment War Diary
WO 171/1236 1 Parachute Battalion War Diary
WO 171/1237 2 Parachute Battalion War Diary
WO 171/1238 3 Parachute Battalion War Diary
WO 171/1243 10th Parachute Battalion War Diary
WO 171/1244 11th Parachute Battalion War Diary
WO 171/1247 156 Parachute Battalion War Diary
WO 171/1248 21st Independent Parachute Company War Diary
WO 171/1253 1 Grenadier Guards (Motorised Battalion) War Diary
WO 171/1256 2 Irish Guards (Armoured Battalion) War Diary
WO 171/1257 3 Irish Guards (Motorised Battalion) War Diary
WO 171/1286 4th Battalion The Dorsetshire Regiment War Diary
WO 171/1323 7th Battalion King's Own Scottish Borderers War Diary
WO 171/1375 2 South Staffordshire Regiment War Diary
WO 171/1509 1st Parachute Squadron RE War Diary
WO 171/1511 4th Parachute Squadron RE War Diary
WO 171/1513 9th (Airborne) Field Company RE War Diary
WO 171/1586 204 Field Company RE War Diary
WO 171/1608 260 Field Company RE War Diary
WO 171/1609 261 (Airborne) Field Park Company RE War Diary
WO 171/2177 HQ Air Despatch Group RASC War Diary
WO177/359 ADMS 1 Airborne Division War Diary
WO 179/3129 20th Field Company RCE War Diary
WO 179/3130 23rd Field Company RCE War Diary
WO 205/313 Operation MARKET GARDEN Part 1
WO 205/693 Operation MARKET GARDEN: Reports and Instructions
WO 361/629 1st Parachute Battalion War Diary
WO 361/642 2nd Parachute Battalion War Diary

Unpublished Sources

A Graphic History of the 82nd Airborne Division, Operation "Market", Holland, 1944 (82nd Airborne Division, 1946)

Capelle, Henk, **My Airborne Experience**, unpublished memoir. As a small boy Mr Capelle lived at No. 35 Nassaulaan in Oosterbeek and was present during the Battle of Arnhem. I am indebted to Mr Capelle for permission to include his account in this work

Delamater, Major Benjamin F., **The Action of the 1st Battalion, 508th Parachute Infantry (82nd Airborne Division) in the Holland Invasion, 15-24 September 1944 (Personal Experience of the Battalion Executive Officer** (Advanced Officer's Course 1946-1947: The Infantry School General Section, Military History Committee, Fort Benning, Georgia, n.d.)

Field Order No. 11, 82nd Airborne Division

Johnson, Captain Kenneth L., **Supply Operations of the 508th Parachute Infantry Regiment (82nd Airborne Division) in the Invasion of Holland, Arnheim [sic] Operation 15 - 19 September 1944 (Rhineland Campaign) (Experiences of the Assistant Regimental S-4)**, (Advanced Officer's Course 1948-1949, The Infantry School General Section, Military History Committee, Fort Benning Georgia, n.d.)

Kappel, Captain Carl W., **The Operations of Company "H", 504th Parachute Infantry (82nd Airborne Division) in the Invasion of Holland 17 - 21 September 1944 (Rhineland Campaign) (Personal Experience of a Rifle Company Commander)**, (Advanced Officer's Course 1948-1949, The Infantry School General Section, Military History Committee, Fort Benning Georgia, n.d.)

Sickler, Captain Robert L., **The Operations of Company "D", 2nd Battalion, 508th Parachute Infantry Regiment (82nd Airborne Division) at Nijmegen, Holland, 17-18 September 1944 (Rhineland Campaign, European Theatre of Operations), (Personal Experience of as Platoon Leader)**, (Advanced Officer's Course 1948-1949, The Infantry School General Section, Military History Committee, Fort Benning Georgia, n.d.)

Stone, William J. **The English Silver Summer**. Unpublished personal account. Mr Stone served in Holland with Battery B, 321st Glider Field Artillery Battalion 101st Airborne Division. I am indebted to Mr Stone for permission to include his account in this work

Tallerday, Captain Jack, **The Operations of the 505th Parachute Infantry Regiment (82nd Airborne Division) in the Airborne Landing and Battle of Groesbeek and Nijmegen, Holland 17 - 23 September 1944 (Rhineland Campaign), (Personal Experiences of the Battalion Executive Officer)**, (Advanced Officer's Course 1948-1949, The Infantry School General Section, Military History Committee, Fort Benning Georgia n.d.)

Operation "MARKET": 1 Para Bde Operation Order No. 1, dated 13/09/1944

Published Sources

Alanbrooke, Field Marshal Lord, edited by Alex Danchev and Daniel Todman, **War Diaries 1939-1945** (London: Weidenfeld & Nicolson, 2001)

Ambrose, Stephen E., **Band of Brothers: E Company, 506th Regiment, 101st Airborne Division from Normandy to Hitler's Eagle's Nest** (New York: Touchstone, 1993)

Idem, **Citizen Soldiers: The US Army from the Normandy Beaches to the Bulge to the Surrender of Germany, June 7, 1944 - May 7, 1945** (New York: Simon and Schuster, 1997)

Bankhead, Harry, **Salute to the Steadfast: From Delhi to Arnhem with 151/156 Parachute Battalion** (Eastbourne, Sussex: Ramsay Press, 2002)

Baynes, John, **Urquhart of Arnhem: The Life of Major-General R. E. Urquhart, CB, DSO** (London: Brassey's, 1993)

Bekker, Cajus, **The Luftwaffe War Diaries** (New York: MacDonald, 1966)

Blair, Clay, **Ridgeway's Paratroopers: The American Airborne in World War II** (New York: The Dial Press, 1985)

Blandford, Edmund L., **Green Devils – Red Devils: Untold Tales of the Airborne in World War II** (London: Leo Cooper, 1993)

Blockwell, Albert & Maggie Clifton (Ed.), **Diary of a Red Devil: By Glider to Arnhem with the 7th King's Own Scottish Borderers** (Solihull: Helion, 2005)

Blumenson, Martin, **Breakout and Pursuit** (Washington DC: Office of the Chief of Military History, Department of the Army, 1961)

Blunt, Vernon, **The Use of Airpower** (London: Thorson's, 1942)

Boscawen, Robert, **Armoured Guardsman: A War Diary June 1944-April 1945** (Barnsley: Pen and Sword, 2001)

Bowen, Robert M., **Fighting with the Screaming Eagles: With the 101st Airborne from Normandy to Bastogne** (London: Greenhill Books, 2001)

Bradley, Omar N., **A Soldier's Story** (New York: Holt, Rinehart & Winston, 1951),

Brammall, Major R., MBE, TD, **The Tenth: A Record of Service of the 10th Battalion, The Parachute Regiment 1942-1945 and The 10th Battalion, The Parachute Regiment (T.A.) (City of London) 1947-1965** (London: Eastgate Publications Ltd., 1965)

Brereton, Lewis H., **The Brereton Diaries: The War in the Air in the Pacific, Middle East and Europe, 3 October 1941 – 8 May 1945** (New York: William Morrow & Co., 1946)

Brinson, William L., **Airborne Troop Carrier: Three-One-Five Group** (New Orleans: Walka Books, 2003)

Buckingham, William F., **Arnhem 1944: A Reappraisal** (Stroud, Glos.: Tempus Publishing, 2002)

Id., **D-Day: The First 72 Hours** (Stroud, Glos.: Tempus Publishing, 2004)

Id, **Paras: The Birth of British Airborne Forces from Churchill's Raiders to 1st Parachute Brigade** (Stroud, Glos.: Tempus Publishing, 2005)

Burgett, Donald R., **The Road to Arnhem: A Screaming Eagle in Holland** (Novato [California]: Presidio Press, 1999)

Burriss, T. Moffatt, **Strike and Hold: A Memoir of the 82nd Airborne in World War II** (Washington: Brassey's Inc., 2000)

Chatterton, Brigadier George, DSO OBE **The Wings of Pegasus: The Story of the Glider Pilot Regiment** (Nashville: The Battery Press, 1982)

Cherry, Niall, **With Nothing Bigger Than a Bren Gun: The Story of the Defence of the Schoolhouse at the Arnhem Road Bridge September 1944** (Warton, Lancs: Brendon Publishing, 2007)

Cholewczynski, George F., **Poles Apart: The Polish Airborne at the Battle of Arnhem** (London: Greenhill Books, 1993)

Id, **Spanhoe's September: An English Airfield During Operation MARKET-GARDEN** (New Orleans: Walka Books, 2008)

Cole, Hugh M., **The Lorraine Campaign** (Washington: Historical Division, Department of the Army, 1950)

Cooper, Alan W., **Air Battle for Arnhem** (Barnsley: Pen & Sword, 2012)

Coox, Alvin D., **Nomonhan: Japan Against Russia, 1939** (Stanford: California University Press)

Curtis, Reg, **Churchill's Volunteer: A Parachute Corporal's Story** (London: Avon Books, 1994)

Delaforce, Patrick, **The Black Bull: From Normandy to the Baltic with the 11th Armoured Division** (London: Chancellor Press, 2000)

D'Este, Carlo, **Decision In Normandy: The Unwritten Story of Montgomery and the Allied Campaign** (London: Collins, 1983)

Devlin, Gerard M., **Paratrooper! The Saga of US Army and Marine Parachute and Glider Combat Troops During World War II** (New York: St. Martin's Press, 1979)

Idem, **Silent Wings: The Story of the Glider Pilots of World War II** (London: W.H. allen, 1985)

Dover, Major Victor MC, **The Sky Generals** (London: Cassell, 1981)

Dugdale, J., **Panzer Divisions - Panzer Grenadier Divisions - Panzer Brigades of the Army and the Waffen SS in the West, Volume I** (Milton Keynes: Military Press, 2000)

Ellis, John, **The Sharp End: The Fighting Man in World War II** (London: Pimlico, 1993)

Ellis, Major L. F., **The War in France and Flanders 1939-1940** (London: HMSO, 1953)

Idem, **Victory in the West, Volume I: The Battle of Normandy** (London: HMSO, 1962),

Idem, **Victory in the West, Volume II: The Defeat of Germany** (London: HMSO, 1968)

Essame, Major-General Hubert, **The 43rd Wessex Division at War 1939-1945** (London: William Clowes & Sons Ltd., 1952)

Fairley, John, **Remember Arnhem: The Story of the 1st Airborne Reconnaissance Squadron at Arnhem** (Bearsden: Peaton Press, 1978)

Farrar-Hockley, Brigadier Anthony, **Airborne Carpet: Operation Market Garden** (London: Macdonald, 1969)

Faulkner-Brown, Harry, **A Sapper at Arnhem: The Memoirs of Harry Faulkner-Brown** (Renkum: R. N. Sigmund Publishing, 2006)

Flint, Keith, **Airborne Armour**: Tetrarch, Locust Hamilcar and the 6th Airborne Armoured Reconnaissance Regiment 1938-50 (Solihull: Helion & Company, 2004)

Foley, John, **Mailed Fist** (London: Panther Books, 1957)

Foot, M.R.D., (Ed.), **Holland at War against Hitler: Anglo-Dutch Relations 1940-1945** (London: Cass, 1990)

Forbes, Patrick, **The Grenadier Guards in the War of 1939-45** (London: Gale & Polden, 1949)

Frieser, Karl-Heinz, **The Blitzkrieg Legend: The 1940 Campaign in the West** (Annapolis: Naval Institute Press, 2005),

Frost, Major-General John, CB, DSO, MC **A Drop Too Many** (London: Sphere, 1983)

Garlinski, Jozef, **Poland, SOE and the Allies** (London: Allen & Unwin, 1969)

Gavin, James M., **Airborne Warfare** (Washington DC: Infantry Press Journal, 1947)

Idem, **On to Berlin: Battles of an Airborne Commander, 1943-1946** (London: Leo Cooper, 1979)

Glantz, David M., **The History of Soviet Airborne Forces** (Essex: frank Cass, 1994)

Golden, Lewis OBE, **Echoes From Arnhem** (London: Kimber, 1984)

Gooderson, Ian, **Air Power at the Battlefront: Allied Close Air Support in Europe, 1943-45** (London: Frank Cass, 1998)

Grant, Roderick & Christopher Cole, **But Not In Anger: The RAF in the Transport Role** (London: Ian Allan, 1979)

Green, Alan T., **1st Battalion The Border Regiment: Arnhem, 17th September-26th September 1944** (Carlisle: The Museum of The Border Regiment and The King's Own Royal Border Regiment, 1991)

Hagen, Louis, **Arnhem Lift: A Fighting Glider Remembers** (Barnsley: Pen & Sword, 1993)

Haines, Simon, **The Holland Patch: The 2nd Battalion of the South Staffordshire Regiment at Arnhem** (Manchester: Patch Publications, 2003)

Hamilton, Nigel, **Monty: The Field Marshal 1944-76** (London: Hamish Hamilton, 1986)

Harclerode, Peter, **"Go To It!" The Illustrated History of the 6th Airborne Division** (London: Caxton Editions, 1990),

Idem, **Arnhem: A Tragedy of Errors** (London: Caxton, 2000)

Harrison, Gordon A., **Cross Channel Attack** (Old Saybrook, Connecticut: Konecky & Konecky, 1950)

Harvey, A. D., **Arnhem** (London: Cassell, 2001)

Hey, John A., **Roll of Honour Battle of Arnhem, September 1944** (Oosterbeek: Society of Friends of the Airborne Museum, 1986)

Henniker, Mark, **An Image of War** (London: Leo Cooper, 1987)

Hibbert, Christopher, **Arnhem** (Moreton-in-Marsh [Glos.]: Windrush Press, 1998)

Hickey, Michael, **Out of the Sky: A History of Airborne Warfare**

HMSO, **By Air to Battle: The Official Account of the British First and Sixth Airborne Divisions** (London: HMSO, 1945)

Horrocks, Sir Brian, **A Full Life** (London: Collins, 1962)

Idem, **Corps Commander** (London: Sidgewick & Jackson, 1977)

Jarymowycz, Roman, **Tank Tactics from Normandy to Lorraine** (Boulder, Colorado: Lynne Rienner, 2001),

Kennedy, John, **The Business of War: The War Narrative of Major-General Sir John Kennedy** (London: Hutchinson, 1957)

Kennett, Lee, **The First Air War 1914-1918** (New York: The Free Press, 1991)

Kent, Ron, **First In! Parachute Pathfinder Company: A History of the 21st Independent** (London: Batsford, 1979)

Kershaw, Robert J., **It Never Snows in September: The German View of MARKET-GARDEN and The Battle of Arnhem, September 1944** (Marlborough: The Crowood Press, 1990)

Kilduff, Peter, **Germany's First Air Force 1914-1918** (London: Arms & Armour Press, 1991)

Komorowski, Krzysztof, **Chronicle of the Polish Army 2005** (Warsaw: Polonia Militaris Foundation, 2006)

Ladd, James **Commandos and Rangers of World War II** (London: Book Club Associates by arrangement with McDonald & Jane's Limited, 1978)

Lamb, Richard, **Montgomery in Europe 1943-1945: Success or Failure?** (London: Buchan & Enright, 1983)

LoFaro, Guy, **The Sword of St. Michael: The 82nd Airborne Division in World War II** (Cambridge Mass.: Da Capo Press, 2011)

Lucas, James and Matthew Cooper, **Panzer Grenadiers** (London: Macdonald and Jane's, 1977)

Id. and James Barker, **Killing Ground: Battle of the Falaise Gap, August 1944** (London: Batsford, 1978)

Idem, **Storming Eagles: German Airborne Forces in World War II** (London: Grafton, 1990)

MacDonald, Charles B., **The Siegfried Line Campaign** (Washington DC: Office of the Chief of Military History, Department of the Army, 1993)

MacDonald, Callum, **The Lost Battle: Crete 1941** (London: Papermac, 1995)

McGilvray, Evan, **The Black Devils' March: A Doomed Odyssey: The 1st Polish Armoured Division 1939-45** (Solihull: Helion & Company, 2005)

Margry, Karel (Ed.), **Operation Market-Garden: Then and Now**, Vol. 2 (London: Battle of Britain International, 2002)

Marsh, Elizabeth (Kennedy) & Russell Kennedy, **Boats, Bridges & Valour: The 23rd Field Company, Royal Canadian Engineers in WWII** (Ottawa: Doculink International, 2008)

Mawson, Stuart, **Arnhem Doctor** (Staplehurst: Spellmount, 2000)

Middlebrook, Martin, **Arnhem 1944: The Airborne Battle** (London: Viking, 1994)

Millar, George, **The Bruneval Raid: Flashpoint of the Radar War** (London: The Bodley Head, 1974)

Miller, Victor, **Nothing is Impossible: A Glider Pilot's Story of Sicily, Arnhem and the Rhine Crossing** (Staplehurst: Spellmount, 1994)

Meredith, Captain J.L.J., **The Story of The Seventh Battalion The Somerset Light Infantry (Prince Albert's)** (Private Publication, n.d.)

Miksche, F. O., **Paratroops: The History, Organisation and Tactical Use of Airborne Formations** (London: Faber, 1943)

Militärgeschichtliches Forschungsamt, Freiburg (Eds) (Research Institute for Military History), **Germany and the Second World War, Volume II: Germany's Initial Conquests in Europe** (Oxford: Clarendon Press, 1991)

Idem, **Germany and the Second World War, Volume VII: The Strategic Air War in Europe and the War in the West and East Asia 1943-1944/5** (Oxford: Clarendon Press, 2006)

Montgomery, Bernard Law, Viscount Montgomery of Alamein, **The Memoirs of Field Marshal The Viscount Montgomery of Alamein K.G.** (London: Collins, 1958)

Morris, Eric, **Circles of Hell: The War in Italy 1943-1945** (London: Hutchinson, 1993)

Morrison, Alexander, **Silent Invader: A Glider Pilot's story of the Invasion of Europe in World War II** (Shrewsbury: Airlife Publishing, 1999),

Morrow, John H., **The Great War in the Air** (London: Smithsonian Institute Press, 1993)

Nordyke, Phil, **All American All The Way: From Market Garden to Berlin: A Combat History of the 82nd Airborne Division in World War II** (Minneapolis MN: Zenith Books, 2010)

North, John, **North-West Europe 1944-5: The Achievements of 21st Army Group** (London: HMSO, 1953)

Omissi, David, **Air Power and Colonial Control: The Royal Air Force, 1919-1939** (Manchester: Manchester University Press, 1990)

Orde, Roden, **The Household Cavalry at War: Second Household Cavalry Regiment** (London: Gale & Polden, 1953)

Otway, Lieutenant-Colonel T. B. H., DSO, **Airborne Forces** (London: Imperial War Museum, 1990)

Packe, Michael, **Winged Stallion: Fighting and Training with the First Airborne** (London: Secker & Warburg, 1948)

Patton, George S., **War As I Knew It** (Boston: Houghton Mifflin Co., 1947)

Peatling, Robert, **No Surrender at Arnhem** (Wimborne Minster: Robert Peatling, 2004)

Pitt, Barrie, **The Crucible of War, Volume I: Wavell's Command** (London: Cassell & Co., 2001)

Powell, Geoffrey, **The Devil's Birthday: The Bridges to Arnhem, 1944** (London: Leo Cooper, 1992)

Quarrie, Bruce, **German Airborne Troops 1939-45** (London: Osprey, 1983)

Idem, **Airborne Assault: Parachute Forces in Action 1940-1991** (Sparkford: Patrick Stephens, 1991))

Raleigh, Sir Walter and H. A. Jones, **The War in the Air**, Volume V (Oxford: Clarendon Press, 1935))

Rapport, Leonard and Arthur Northwood Jr., **Rendezvous with Destiny: A History of the 101st Airborne Division** (Fort Campbell Kentucky: 101st Airborne Division Association, 1948

Reynolds, Michael, **Sons of the Reich: The History of II SS Panzer Corps in Normandy, Arnhem, The Ardennes and on The Eastern Front** (Staplehurst, Kent: Spellmount Publishing, 2002)

Ridder, Willem, **Countdown to Freedom: Nazi Occupied Holland, May 10 1940 – May 5 1945** (Bloomington, Indiana: AuthorHouse, 2007)

Rottman, Gordon, **US Army Airborne 1940-90** (London: Osprey, 1990)

Ryan, Cornelius, **A Bridge Too Far** (London: Hodder & Stoughton, 1977)

Saunders, Hilary St. George, **The Red Beret: The Story of the Parachute Regiment at War 1940-1945** (London: Michael Joseph, 1950)

Scott, H.F. and W.F. Scott (Eds.), **The Soviet Art of War** (Boulder: Westview Press, 1982)

Shannon, Kevin and Stephen Wright, **One Night in June: The Story of Operation Tonga, the Initial Phase of the Invasion of Normandy, 1944** (Shrewsbury: Airlife, 1994)

Sims, James, **Arnhem Spearhead: A Private Soldier's Story** (London: Imperial War Museum, 1978)

Simpkin, Richard, **Deep Battle: The Brainchild of Marshal Tukhachevskii** (London: Brassey's, 1987)

Stainforth, Peter, **Wings of the Wind** (London: Grafton Books, 1988)

Sliz, John, **The Storm Boat Kings: The 23rd RCE at Arnhem 1944** (St. Catherine's, Ontario: Vanwell Publishing Limited, 2009)

Sosabowski, Major-General Stanislaw, **Freely I Served: The Memoir of the Commander - 1st Polish Independent Parachute Brigade 1941 -1944** (Barnsley: Pen & Sword, 2013)

Steel, Nigel & Peter Hart, **Defeat at Gallipoli** (London: Papermac, 1995)

Terraine, John, **Right of the Line: The Royal Air Force in the European War 1939-1945** (London: Sceptre, 1988)

Thetford, Owen, **Aircraft of the Royal Air Force Since 1918** ()

Tieke, Wilhelm, **In the Firestorm of the Last Years of the War: II SS Panzerkorps with the 9. and 10. SS-Divisions 'Hohenstaufen' and 'Frundsberg'** (Winnipeg: J. J. Fedorowicz, 1999)

Thompson, Julian, **Ready for Anything: The Parachute Regiment at War 1940-1982** (London: Weidenfeld & Nicolson, 1989)

Tout, Ken, **Tank! 40 Hours of Battle, August 1944** (London: Sphere, 1986)

Idem, **Tanks, Advance: Normandy to the Netherlands** (London: Robert Hale, 1987)

Truesdale, David, **Brotherhood of the Cauldron: Irishmen in the 1st Airborne Division from North Africa to Arnhem** (Newtonard, Co. Down: Redcoat Publishing, 2002)

Tugwell, Maurice, **Airborne to Battle: A History of Airborne Warfare 1918-1971** ()

Turnbull, Jack & John Hamblett, **The Pegasus Patrol** (Marple, Cheshire: 1994)

Urquhart, Brian, **A Life in Peace and War** (London: Weidenfeld & Nicolson, 1987)

Urquhart, Major-General R. E., CB DSO **Arnhem** (London: Cassell, 1958)

Verney, Major-General G. L., DSO MVO, **The Guards Armoured Division: A Short History** (London: Hutchinson, 1955)

Waddy, John, **A Tour of the Arnhem Battlefields** (London: Leo Cooper, 1999)

Wiggan, Richard, **Operation Freshman: The Rjukan Heavy Water Raid 1942** (London: Kimber, 1986)

Wilmot, Chester, **The Struggle for Europe** (London: Collins, 1952)

Wilson, B. D., **The Ever Open Eye** (Durham: The Pentland Press Ltd, 1998)

Wright, Lawrence, **The Wooden Sword: The Untold Story of the Gliders in World War II** (London: Elek, 1967)

Zaloga, Steven J., **US Airborne Divisions in the ETO 1944-1945** (Oxford: Osprey, 2007)

Zeidler, Manfred, **Reichswehr und Rote Armee 1920-1933** (Oldenbourg: Beitrage zur Militärgeschichte, 1994)

Zwarts, Marcel, **German Armoured Units at Arnhem, September 1944** (Hong Kong: Concord Publications, 2001)

Journal Articles

Captain R.G. Thorburn, 'The Operations in South Kurdistan, March-May 1923', **The Army Quarterly**, Volume 31 (October 1935-January 1936), p. 270

Colonel N. Ramanichev, 'The Development of the Theory and Practice of the Combat Use of Airlanding Forces in the Inter-War Period', **Military-Historical Journal**, No. 10 (October 1982), p. 72 (Russian language publication)

Lt. Col. James A. Bassett, 'Past Airborne Employment', **Journal of Military History**, Volume 12, No. 4, Winter 1948, pp. 206-207

Major-General H. Rowan Robinson, 'Air Infantry: How Can This Development Assist Great Britain?', **The United Services Review** Vol. LXXVII (17 December 1936), pp. 5-6
'Notes of the Week', Idem, (10 December 1936), p. 1
'Notes of the Week', Idem, (16 June 1938)
Quarterly Army List – January 1940
'Soviet Film of Kiev Manoeuvres', **The Army, Navy and Air Force Gazette**, Vol. LXXVII (12 March 1936), p. 206

Television Sources
Great Battles of World War II – Arnhem, documentary series episode broadcast on UK Channel 5 TV, 25/08/2001

Internet Sources
Air Mobility Command Museum website, 'Eyewitness to History: The Great Underground Escape from German Occupied Holland', interview recorded at Dayton, Ohio, 12-14 October 2001 at http://amcmuseum.org/history/wwii/underground_escape.php, [accessed 15/04/2012]
Combat Chronology of the US Army Air Force Website, September 1944 Section at http://paul.rutgers.edu/~mcgrew/wwii/usaf/html/Sep.44.htmlWebsite [accessed 17/09/2018]
Commonwealth War Graves Commission Website at https://www.cwgc.org/, [accessed 17/09/2018]
Defending Arnhem Website, Various Sections at http://www.defendingarnhem.com/ [accessed 17/09/2018]
Derbyshire, David, Science Correspondent, 'Briton Defies Doubters to Pilot Parachute Designed in 1485', Daily Telegraph, 19 April 2001 at http://www.telegraph.co.uk/news/uknews/1345122/Briton-defies-doubters-to-pilot-parachute-designed-in-1485.html, [accessed 26/09/2008]
Dowd, Vincent, 2015, 'WW2: Guy Byam, The BBC's Lost Reporter' at http://www.bbc.co.uk/news/magazine-34144792, [accessed 18/12/2017]
Fields of Honour Database, http://www.adoptiegraven-database.nl [accessed 13/04/2012]
1st British Airborne Division Arnhem September 1944: Officers website at http://www.unithistories.com/officers/1airbdiv_officersa.htm, [accessed 17/09/2018]
The 505th Regimental Combat Team Website, 'Herman L. Alley Personal Log' at http://www.505rct.org/album2/alley_h.asp, [accessed 17/09/2018]
The Daimler Fighting Vehicles Project website, 'Index of Regiments that used Daimler Fighting Vehicles' Section at http://www.daimler-fighting-vehicles.co.uk/hcr%20regiment.html [accessed 17/09/2018]
Paul Reed's Battlefields of WW2 website, 'Arnhem Battlefields Section' at http://battlefieldsww2.50megs.com/arnhem_battlefields.htm [accessed 17/09/2018]
The Pegasus Archive Website, 'Battle of Arnhem Archive' at http://www.pegasusarchive.org/arnhem/ [accessed 17/09/2018]
Royal Air Force Commands website, at http://www.rafcommands.com/tags/halliday/, [accessed 17/09/2018]
Royal Artillery Units Netherlands 1944-1945 website, at http://www.royalartilleryunitsnetherlands1944-1945.com/index.html, [accessed 17/09/2018]
Simpson, Aislinn, 'Leonardo da Vinci Parachute from 1485 Finally has Successful Landing', Daily Telegraph, 28 April 2008 at http://www.telegraph.co.uk/news/1905000/Leonardo-da-Vinci-parachute-from-1485-finally-has-successful-landing.html, [accessed 26/09/2008]
Philp, Reginald, The Telegraph, Obituaries Section, 28 March 2012 at http://www.telegraph.co.uk/news/obituaries/9172080/Reg-Philp.html, [accessed 11/09/2016]
Winchester College website, 'Simonds, John Mellor' at http://www.winchestercollegeatwar.com/archive/simonds-john-mellor/, [accessed 14/11/2016]

Index

THOMPSON Force 287, 338, 339
Glider Pilot Regiment:
No. 1 Wing 75, 171, 175, 287, 289,
337, 338, 385, 399, 419, 421, 457,
458, 460, 461, 477, 482, 484
- A Squadron 176, 263
- B Squadron 171, 176, 206, 225,
263, 337, 338, 419, 458, 460
- D Squadron 175, 176, 177, 178,
183, 239, 263, 322, 338, 362, 374,
389, 421, 446, 458, 459, 475
- G Squadron 255, 338, 374, 426,
427, 449, 460
No. 2 Wing 176, 177, 198, 235, 289,
334, 338, 372, 395, 458
- C Squadron 176, 235, 256, 263,
289, 417, 448, 458
- E Squadron 184, 263, 264, 289,
334, 343, 361, 372, 394, 395, 418,
428, 445
- F Squadron 177, 235, 334, 343,
361, 372, 395, 418, 445, 470
1st (Airborne) Divisional Field
Park RAOC 161, 274, 284
1st (Airborne) Division Provost
Company 75, 125, 161, 272
1st Airborne Reconnaissance
Squadron 64, 65, 66, 70, 74,
76, 78, 83, 84, 104, 105, 106, 107,
108, 109, 111, 115, 118, 123, 125,
161, 170, 198, 230, 236, 237, 246,
249, 264, 287, 322, 328, 334, 338,
346, 361, 374, 389, 390, 418, 419,
427, 446, 459, 460, 461, 473,
474, 476, 477, 484, 493, 494
1st Airlanding Anti-Tank Battery
RA 34, 64, 65, 68, 70, 80, 105,
117, 121, 161, 167, 175, 201, 250,
275, 362
1st Airlanding Light Regiment RA
64, 66, 73, 80, 121, 167, 169, 171,
173, 174, 181, 183, 185, 186, 195,
199, 207, 236, 246, 254, 255, 284,
287, 288, 289, 313, 314, 318, 323,
328, 329, 336, 338, 339, 342, 346,
349, 354, 356, 361, 374, 385, 388,
410, 412, 413, 417, 418, 426, 427,
440, 443, 444, 445, 448, 449,
451, 457, 465, 471, 475, 478, 484
- 1 Battery 171, 173, 236, 257, 289,
339, 349, 374, 417, 427, 448, 449,
450, 471
- 2 Battery 200, 236, 254, 257, 348,
374, 448, 449, 450, 471
- 3 Battery 117, 125, 129, 161, 163,
164, 166, 169, 199, 204, 205, 255,
284, 289, 323, 328, 329, 374, 388,
417, 448, 449, 450, 451, 471
1st Parachute Squadron RE 64, 68,
84, 85, 105, 121, 125, 127, 129, 161,

162, 163, 166, 200, 201, 211, 221,
222, 227, 229, 250, 273, 274, 276,
285, 325, 326, 338, 460
No. 1 Forward Observation Unit
RA 339, 349, 374, 391
2nd (Oban) Airlanding Anti-Tank
Battery RA, 176, 178, 183, 185,
195, 199, 239, 255, 256, 269, 314,
315, 348, 387, 418
4th Parachute Squadron RE 175,
176, 181, 182, 194, 195, 197, 199,
238, 244, 258, 259, 268, 269,
271, 272, 289, 290, 315, 316, 317,
335, 338, 343, 344, 361, 369, 372,
373, 386, 395, 397, 410, 417, 418,
445, 458, 465, 477
9th (Airborne) Field Company RE
64, 76, 102, 103, 108, 119, 123,
128, 130, 161, 198, 207, 213, 286,
287, 292, 316, 323, 334, 336, 337,
338, 351, 364, 370, 377, 384, 395,
408, 410, 417, 445, 457, 458, 459,
460, 465, 484
14th Field Squadron RE
(sometimes rendered
Company) 91, 94, 307
16 Parachute Field Ambulance
RAMC 64, 84, 121, 125, 126, 167,
257, 283, 320, 423, 424, 425, 483
21st Anti-Tank Regiment RA
280, 358
21st Independent Parachute
Company 31, 32, 34, 70, 77, 78,
81, 82, 101, 173, 186, 248, 262,
265, 271, 286, 289, 308, 316, 317,
334, 338, 343, 344, 345, 361, 369,
374, 375, 387, 389, 391, 392, 393,
420, 422, 424, 426, 427, 447,
448, 458, 464, 476, 481, 484
43 Reconnaissance Regiment 378,
404, 405, 452, 453
64th Medium Regiment RA 339,
341, 348, 361, 374, 417, 418, 440,
443, 445, 450, 456, 464, 478
84th Medium Regiment RA 339,
464
112 Field Regiment RA 439, 440,
464
130 Field Ambulance 453, 472, 476
133 Parachute Field Ambulance
RAMC 182, 183, 194, 197, 198,
244, 256, 320, 436, 437
153 Field Regiment RA 296, 358,
359
163 Field Ambulance RAMC 413,
436, 437, 472
181 Airlanding Field Ambulance
RAMC 64, 103, 130, 198, 242,
244, 256, 320, 391, 392, 425, 436

204 Field Company RE 404, 408,
411, 413, 433, 435, 436, 437, 439,
442, 453, 486
250 Light Composite Company
RASC 84, 105, 125, 161, 210,
262, 283, 374, 402, 422, 426
260 (Wessex) Field Company
RE 434, 453, 454, 463, 468, 473,
474, 479, 481, 486
261 (Airborne) Field Park
Company RE 395, 417, 418,
445, 465
551st General Transport Company
RASC 454, 462, 473
553 Field Company RE 453, 462,
467, 486

Britneff, Lt. Vladimir 224, 225
Broadwell, RAF 31, 32, 73, 77, 177,
325, 350, 399
Brooke, Field Marshal Sir Alan
39, 61, 429, 488, 490
Brown, Capt. Henry 'Harry'
RE (sometimes rendered
Faulkner-Brown) 244, 245,
268, 269, 270, 271, 290, 316, 317,
343, 344, 361, 369, 384, 385, 386,
387, 410, 458, 477
Brown, Lt. George 291, 342
Browning, Lt. Gen. Frederick 28,
29, 30, 31, 33, 34, 40, 41, 42, 43,
47, 49, 50, 51, 60, 61, 62, 63, 64,
65, 66, 70, 75, 78, 80, 87, 100,
101, 103, 137, 139, 141, 215, 220,
279, 280, 301, 310, 351, 376, 403,
405, 406, 408, 428, 430, 432,
433, 434, 435, 436, 442, 443,
456, 478, 487, 488, 489, 491,
492, 494, 495
Bruhn, *Hauptmann* Hans 239,
240, 242, 269
Brummen 54, 111, 121, 483
Brussels 24, 25, 26, 37, 43, 58, 145,
177, 351, 354, 372, 399, 416, 434,
484, 488
Buchanan, Maj. John 171, 173,
234, 254, 255, 257, 287, 472
Buchanan, Maj. Robert 104, 132,
197, 237, 267
Buchanan, Capt. The Reverend
Alan, RACD 226, 250, 251
Buck, Capt. John RAMC 345, 395
Budziszewski, Capt. Piotr 355,
366, 376, 377, 384, 386, 408,
409, 410, 411, 412, 438
Bune, Maj. John 116, 117
Burriss, Capt. T. Moffatt 86, 97,
153, 154, 301,302, 303, 304, 307,
308, 309